GW01339632

THE STAR-LADEN SKY

THE STAR-LADEN SKY

Mariah Hourihan, Editor
Christel Brown de Colstoun, Assistant Editor
Valerie Grosman, Assistant Editor

THE INTERNATIONAL LIBRARY OF POETRY

The Star-Laden Sky

Copyright © 1997 by The International Library of Poetry
as a compilation.

Rights to individual poems reside with the artists themselves.
This collection of poetry contains works submitted to the Publisher by individual authors who confirm that the work is their original creation. Based upon the authors' confirmations and to the Publisher's actual knowledge, these poems were written by the listed poets. The International Library of Poetry does not guarantee or assume responsibility for verifying the authorship of each work. Address all inquiries to Jeffrey Franz, Publisher, Poets House, Cremers Road, Dolphin Park, Sittingbourne, Kent ME10 3HB.

The views expressed within certain poems contained in this anthology
do not necessarily reflect the views of the editors or staff
of The International Library of Poetry.

All rights reserved under International and Pan-American copyright conventions. No part of this book may be reproduced, stored in a retrieval system or transmitted in any form, electronic, mechanical, or by other means, without written permission of the publisher.

ISBN 1-57553-414-2

Printing and Binding by
BPC Wheatons Ltd, Exeter, UK

FOREWORD

Throughout life, we store information collected from experiences and try in some way to make sense of it. When we are not able to fully understand the things which occur in our lives, we often externalize the information. By doing this, we are afforded a different perspective, thus allowing us to think more clearly about difficult or perplexing events and emotions. Art is one of the ways in which people choose to externalize their thoughts.

Within the arts, modes of expression differ, but poetry is a very powerful tool by which people can share sometimes confusing, sometimes perfectly clear concepts and feelings with others. Intentions can run the gamut as well: the artists may simply want to share something that has touched their lives in some way, or they may want to get help to allay anxiety or uncertainty. The poetry within *The Star-Laden Sky* is from every point on the spectrum: every topic, every intention, every event or emotion imaginable. Some poems will speak to certain readers more than others, but it is always important to keep in mind that each verse is the voice of a poet, of a mind which needs to make sense of this world, of a heart which feels the effects of every moment in this life, and perhaps of a memory which is striving to surface. Nonetheless, recalling our yesterdays gives birth to our many forms of expression.

Melisa S. Mitchell
Editor

Editor's Note

> "I think Poetry should surprise by a fine excess and not by
> Singularity—it should strike the Reader as a wording of his
> own highest thoughts, and appear almost a Remembrance . . .
> Its touches of Beauty should never be half way ther[e]by
> making the reader breathless instead of content: the rise, the
> progress, the setting of imagery should like the Sun come
> natural . . . to him—shine over him and set soberly although
> in magnificence leaving him in the Luxury of twilight—but it
> is easier to think what Poetry should be than to write it . . . "
> —John Keats
> *from a letter to John Taylor (27 February 1818)*

Perhaps one of the most well-known Romantic poets, John Keats is also one of the most beloved. His influence cannot be questioned, although his literary reputation often has been. Poetry in Keats' time was an occupation of the upper class, for those blessed with education and refined sensibilities. Keats was not born into this elite group and had to work diligently to make up for the perceived inadequacies resulting from his "low" birth. From his letters, one can see that he laboured, humbly and enthusiastically, to become a great poet. It is partially for this reason that many find Keats' poetry so accessible and engaging. Anyone who has attempted to write a poem knows that shaping experiences into words can be a difficult task. Many a poet has developed his own axioms for good poetry and, like Keats, has found it is easier to comment than to create. The poets whose work is contained in this anthology share with Keats in this labour of love. *The Star-Laden Sky* showcases the fine fruits of their efforts.

Keats' influence on one particular poet included in *The Star-Laden Sky*, Alfred Behrmann, is certainly undeniable. Behrmann has skillfully crafted a tribute to the life and death of the poet in his work, "Keats" (p. 283). The poem takes place at the Piazza di Spagna in February of 1821—the setting for Keats' untimely death at the young age of twenty-six. Keats had been battling consumption for some time—a painful disease for which the only treatment at the time was to dull one's mind with laudanum. On the advice of his doctor, who thought Keats could not survive another English winter, he left for Rome where he continued to write his now-famous letters and poetry. But he would not survive the Italian winter either, dying peacefully in his room on the Piazza di Spagna, in the arms of his good friend, Joseph Severn. Keats referred to these last months in Italy as his "posthumous existence". Behrmann uses these biographical details like building blocks, to construct a final resting place for Keats, in words and in water:

> The fountain's voice, outside,
> When the square falls asleep:
> ……………………………………
> Sabrina, nymph of the Severn,
> Lost now, abandoned, —ah,
> A posthumous life. The laudanum
> Has been removed. No prayers.
> His mail unopened. Joseph, sent out . . .

The reference to "Severn" in this poem serves several functions. Severn is, of course, the surname of Joseph Severn, the friend who was with Keats at his death. It is also the river said to be named after the nymph, Sabrina, who, according to myth, was forcibly robbed of her innocence and murdered along its banks. Like Keats, she was struck down with the dew of youth still upon her.

As he lay dying, Keats wrote his own epitaph. Convinced until the end that he had had no great influence on the world and would be quickly forgotten, he requested the following be engraved on his tombstone: "Here lies One Whose Name was writ in Water". Water, unlike stone, is transient, mutable, undetermined. In his personal memorial to Keats, Behrmann uses a clever twist of language to both indulge Keats' last self-effacing wish and to repudiate it. The central image, symbolising Keats in the poem, is the fountain at the Piazza di Spagna, where he died. He is in the fountain waters. The persona hears him, the "fountain's voice", as the "square falls asleep". Night and day, the "water echoes", resounding with permanence. The fountain waters move and shift, but their movement is an essential thread in the timeless fabric of Rome, just as Keats is in English literature.

James McNalty discusses a token of timelessness in his poem, "The Souvenir" (p.1). In the wake of a broken love relationship, the persona finds himself alone with only a forgotten jacket by which to remember his departed lover. Having discovered the persona's hidden desire for another, "her peer", his lover leaves him in anger:

> She knew I dreamt about her peer
> She smelt it on me—wished me death
> ……………………………………
> Ah, but an autumn sunset soldier!
> Whose pursed lips are soft and twee.
> She slowly throws the hands that hold her
> The woman simply walks from me—

The persona, however, is accepting of his fate. He "wonders at the running gone", but does not pursue her. He is content to have just this memento of her: "I'm glad you see, and curl upon / The still-warm flesh of clothing". He is glad to have this physical, warm remembrance of her, but it is insubstantial. Although he clings to the jacket now, he is eager for the tide to come in and wash it free, and to wash him free of her:

> She's left her jacket with me
> The tide will soon be coming in
> To stroke it out, to wash it free
> Of rocks remaining in soiled skin.

The soiled skin is the persona's. He has entertained the unfaithful thoughts, whether or not he has acted upon them. Once the jacket and his relationship are erased by the tide, so shall be his offense.

In "Covering Up (For My Mother, Mina)" (p. 281), Donna Wilson also explores human relationship—a relationship between mother and daughter. The child gazes into the mirror as her mother lies ill on the bed behind her. She paints herself with her mother's make-up: "I stood looking in the mirror wanting to see your reflection / And when it did not appear I painted it on." Knowing that her mother is dying, she tries to restore and preserve on her own face the image of the woman she has known and loved; but there is nothing in the make-up to help her do this. Her mother wakes to see her daughter painted as herself:

> But as in a mirror image you saw exactly what I do
>   when I look closely
> My attempt to cover up was as feeble as yours
>   had once been.
> Nothing can be hidden.

The daughter will always be what she is, despite her pretending. She realizes that underneath the cosmetic, the superficial, she will never be far from her mother. In the last stanza it becomes apparent that her mother did indeed die. Despite her mother's passing, the persona realizes she will always have her mother's blood coursing through her own veins:

> In the time that followed my tears washed away the blue
> But that blood red kiss of reassurance was a lie—
> ....
> It remained even after it had long faded
>   but the colour was not needed.
> How could it be when your blood quickens
>   constantly through me,
> For just as you are me—I am you.

There is an enormous number of poems that merit careful reading in this anthology. Be captured by the creative language of an "Urban Creaturescape" by Kleanthis Paraskevopoulos (p.131). Take a different look at ageing through Dale Churchill's eyes in "On Starting the Menopause" (p.107) or through Gerardine Meany's intense imagery in "Black on Grey" (p.186). Search for "Proof" with John McDermott (p. 254). Gaze at Marilyn Holliday's haunting portrait of a lost man and his "Distant Dreams" (p. 113).

Once again, I would like to thank all of you for your many submissions and to congratulate you on helping to create this fine anthology. I hope you enjoy reading the many excellent works in *The Star-Laden Sky*. I wish you all the best of luck in your creative pursuits.

The publication of *The Star-Laden Sky* is the culmination of the efforts of many individuals. Judges, editors, assistant editors, customer service representatives, graphic artists, layout artists, office administrators, and data entry personnel have all brought their respective talents to bear on this project. The editors are grateful for the contributions of these fine people.

Mariah Hourihan
Editor

Cover art: Steve Kimball

Winners of the International Open Amateur Poetry Contest

Grand Prize Winner

James McNulty / Ayrshire

Second Prize Winners

Alfred Behrmann / Berlin
Dale Churchill / Derbyshire
Deirdre Curley / Dublin
Marilyn Holliday / Newcastle-Upon-Tyne
John McDermott / Glasgow
Gerardine Meany / London
Charles Muller / Jedburgh
Kleanthis Paraskevopoulos / Nicosia
Nadine Risso / Bristol
Donna Wilson / Co. Antrim

Third Prize Winners

Rowland Ablett / Devon
Ruvina De-Alwis / London
Pat Aphra / Middlesex
Abena Poku-Awuah / London
J. Bentley / Lancashire
Jo Bicanic / Western Australia
Susan Biggin / Venezia
Kitsy Brady / Sligo
Edward Carlton / Hampshire
Mariella Cassar / Island of Gozo
Bruce Collocott / Surrey
Ruth Counihan / Co. Clare
Mark Cowley / Derbyshire
Donna Crawford / Hampshire
Bruce Downie / Bialystok
R. H. Dymond / East Sussex
M. Stephenson-Ellams / Warwickshire
Isabel Ellis / Cornwall
Naomi Faulkner / Herefordshire
Kitty Fox / Surrey
Alan Garvey / South Yorkshire
Wendy Gaynair / London
S. M. Gonsalves / Hertfordshire
Kathryn Gray / Cornwall
A. Grundy / Lancashire
Flo-Louise Hart / Manchester
David Hendtlass / London
Robert Holding / Gloucestershire
Stuart Holmes / Staffordshire
Georgina Howell / West Midlands
Carol Humby / Hampshire
Mehita Iqani / Germiston
Karmjeet Kaur / West Yorkshire
R. Kazmi / West Yorkshire
Paul Kester / Suffolk
Henry King / London
Mia McKay / Aberdeenshire
Anne Micklethwaite / North Yorkshire
Jonathan Millican / Bevere
W. Moore / West Lothian
Gail Neville / Lincolnshire
Michaela Philp / Lincolnshire
James Reid / Clydebank
G. Phillip G. Robinson / Hampshire
Angela Rogerson / Wigtownshire
David Russell / London
Louise Shelton / Northamptonshire
Mary Simpson / West Midlands
Tony Skidmore / Hertfordshire
Tracy Smith / Dublin
Kathryn Stevens / Glasgow
Elizabeth Stevenson / Nottinghamshire
Anna Szeremeta / Nottinghamshire
J. C. Thompson / Perth
Corinna Leigh-Turner / Somerset
C. Watkins / Oxfordshire
Elizabeth Wilson / Cheshire
Audrey Young / Tyne & Wear
Gary Young / Worcestershire

Congratulations also to all semi-finalists.

Grand Prize Winner

The Souvenir

Rolling betwixt, I catch a tear
And drink to taste its tiny breath
She knew I dreamt about her peer
She smelt it on me—wished me death.

Ah, but an autumn sunset soldier!
Whose pursed lips are soft and twee.
She slowly throws the hands that hold her
The woman simply walks from me—

(!a dream of red reamed cord!
to fray, the morning after yesterday)

She's left her jacket with me
The tide will soon be coming in
To stroke it out, to wash it free
Of rocks remaining in soiled skin.

I'm glad, you see, and curl upon
The still-warm flesh of clothing
And wonder at the running gone
And vow I smell

  Of nothing.
      James McNulty

The Gift of Light

The twinkle of Starlight cannot discriminate between the eyes of a Blind Man or the eyes of one who can see.
The effect is the same, both reflect the Light that is freely given and pass it on unwittingly to whomever they are facing at the time.

It is the same with Candlelight. No matter how small the flicker, it is instantly shared. You may be facing someone who has blotted their copy book as far as you are concerned, but the outcome is identical, regardless of hurt feelings.

Now just imagine what happens when you add a smile to the ingredients, a smile that starts in your Heart and by the time it reaches your eyes, Wow!! what a priceless gift you have given and it hasn't cost a penny, but the value is immeasurable.

May all your lives be filled with Light. Keep your eyes open and share with all, your Light from within. Always remember that where there is Light, there is Love and where there is Love there is You and where You are so is God.

Dolly Little

Tomorrow's Sunrise

Slowly the darkness gives way to light,
And moon and stars retreat as a new day dawns.
Day breaks once more and all living creatures are astir.
One cock's crow is swiftly answered by another,
And, like an echo their calls resound,
Shattering the stillness of the crisp, cool morn.

Rising, slowly and majestically in the east,
The sun's orange dome emerges over the distant horizon,
Gradually spreading brilliant light where darkness once prevailed.
Intricate spider webs and leaves bedecked with morning dew,
Glisten like jewels as its rays penetrate the heavy mist.

Soon a medley of sounds will herald the start of work and play.
All who awaken to see the light prayerfully give thanks for yet another day.
Morning quickly runs into afternoon and evening greets the setting sun.
Soon the night will come and there will be one tomorrow followed by another,
Each with its sunrise.

Rema A. Green

Parish of Angels

Death makes life unable to find
For nonbelievers of the eternal mind.
Life makes death a question to be
Stars in the night sky, you cannot see.

Death's parish of angels rides swiftly in the breeze
Picking up souls who have been granted to be free.
The ones left behind the dark shadows shall devour
The wind gets up, but the shadow is a flower.

Paul Scott Taylor

Sunrise Serpent

Daylight crept upon its belly,
Silently slithering beneath the drapes.
Cautiously coiled, poised above unknowing slumbering victims,
To strike like lightning between tightly shut eyes.
Eyes pop open to the sting of sunshine while
Bright light plays upon the retina.
Hypnotized, the covers would not be pulled,
For daylight beckons and the sleeper
Has fallen captive to its beauty once again.
Held by the magic of its changing hues
The benevolent serpent summons as it sways.
Every morn the playful hunt commences.
Shutters shut and curtains closed
Duvet draped around a reposing head.
Serpent slips, slides through a keyhole,
Through the cracks in every wall.
Sunrise serpent strikes with speed.
Rising reptile wins each morn.

Mariella Cassar

A Thought for Today—and Tomorrow!

Because of you and what you are,
Our guiding light and shining star.
When all around is bleak and cold,
Your Christmas story will be told.

It matters not religion or race,
For no-one yet has seen your face.
Your master plan long ago devised,
We try to follow throughout our lives.

Is peace on earth a reach too far
For that guiding light and shining star?
Within us all the power of love,
A gift bestowed from one above.

Not enough do we extend its arm,
To help someone or keep from harm.
How long must we take to achieve your aim,
For we are the players in a life-long game.

So let's join together with people afar,
And keep all our eyes on that bright, bright star.

D. C. Kershaw

Buoys Mark the Hidden Rocks

Buoys mark the hidden rocks in society,
But I, like most of us, haven't got a chart.
Old people may give advice about propriety,
But when we're young, how few of us take it to heart!

We learn by experience, lucky if we avoid
The breakers, or a hole below waterline,
Gossip, or friendship unknowingly betrayed,
Or unexpressed cold rage, like the floating mine.

In old age most of us have a short sea mile
A channel where we are pilot and know the way.
Yet we forget, when at others' errors we smile,
We too would be equally lost, if we dared to stray.

Diana Richardson

Life Goes On

Life goes on.
When the sun shines life goes on
When the rain falls life goes on
When the sun shines or the rain falls
Life goes on

When you're happy life goes on
When you're sad life goes on
When you're happy or you're sad
If you're good or if you're bad life goes on

When you're laughing life goes on
When you're crying life goes on
If you're laughing or you're crying
If you're living or you're dying life goes on

Elizabeth Quinn

Granddad

He sits in silent huddled pose,
Gnarled hand upon a cane.
His face reflects the years he's spent in sun and
Wind and rain.
His thinning hair of steely grey, bedecks his furrowed brow.
His eyes once keen as a kitchen blade are failing
Him right now,
But behind these mirrors of his soul, there lies
a twinkling smile.
A wise old man, whose frail old bones, his strength
does now beguile.
He's lived a million moments, and survived them all.
Despite his tiny stature, he towers strong and tall.
He's loved, and well respected. He may be old and grey,
But he cheers my soul, and warms my heart,
I love him more each day
I know he cannot stay forever, too soon we have to part
I know he'll never really leave, he lies within my heart.

Joan Jarvis

Everybody Thinks You're Wonderful

Everybody thinks you're wonderful.
They don't know you like I do.
Last year you took me for a fool,
But they don't know you like I do.

I was happy, used to sing all day,
Then you came along my way.
I was oh! So thrilled, fell in love;
Thought you were sent from heaven above.

But you hurt me, told me you were free.
Should have known you then and seen
You had me hanging on a string.
I couldn't concentrate, couldn't sing.

Everybody thinks you're wonderful.
They don't know you like I do.
Michael Charles Philp

Tess the Kitten

I came in to this family, from the RSPCA,
Collected by two people, one January day,
When they asked my Pedigree, I hung my head in shame,
For I did not have a Pedigree, nor did I have a name.

Anyway, enough of that, for that is in the past,
For luckily, they brought me here, I had a home at last.
I still need lots of nursing, 'cause I am really frail,
Kirsty and her mum do that, and I know they'll not fail.

By the way, they call me Tess, and I think that is fine,
For now you see, I have a name, and that is always mine.
When I go to the bathroom, they put me in a tray,
But when they turn their back to me, I try to run away.

The problem when I run, is, that I'm not very tall,
But usually I beat them, when running down the hall,
And lie there by the fireside, on Mr. Pouncer's mat,
I call him Mr. Pouncer 'cause, he's a great big cat.

Pouncer's always patting me, with his big heavy paw,
One day soon, when I get big, I'll chase him through the door,
Until then, I'll just rely, on Kirsty and her mum,
To keep those big paws off me, and HIM under their thumb.
T. M. Devaney

Invisible Influence

It swishes in the tree tops.
It moans in the chimney can.
  It gently swirls the dust on a journey,
  or causes a havoc along the dale.
Its power can fill the yachtsman's sails.
Its calm does bring a peace.
The clouds all flurry past a-peace,
As they travel onwards to some distant space.

Skies are often streaky.
Sailors look aghast.
They expect these signs to be followed,
  by a thunder clap, or maybe a blast.

Dawn heralds itself with sunshine rays,
Sunset glows red in the west.
As these brilliant 'pictures' miraculously unfold,
one's memory forgets the history of wind that's blown past.
These wonders of creation are monitored by God's hand,
from the beginning of life, to the final post in time.
A. R. Harcus

Christmas

As we read the familiar pages
Passed down to us through the ages,
We learn from those faithful shepherds of old
How their wondrous story did unfold.
With joy they were able to recall
How they were led to that lowly stall.
let us pause a moment midst the joy and mirth,
To offer prayers of thanks for Christ's wondrous birth.
Joyce Boast

Navy Days—Chatham—1941

Where are they now?
Those jolly "Jacks" and Captains few,
The C.P.O.'s and "Killicks" too.
The duty W.R.N.S. and N.A.A.F.I. girls.
Where are they now?

Many are gone beyond recall,
But some are left to carry on.
Age takes its toll with one and all;
Its travels done and homeward bound.
No more "Wakey-Wakey"—"Rise and shine,"
To rouse us at the break of dawn.
"At the double"—"Get fell in";
"Stand easy"—"Out pipes"—
"Clear up for rounds" and "Darken ship."

These are echoes long since past,
For fading memory comes at last!
O. A. Tighe

The Great Divide

We all live under one sun,
whether we are red, yellow, black or white.
We all live on one planet
and share both day and night.
We voyage over the same oceans.
We fly across the same sky.
We journey to our destination.
We are born; we live; we die.

Under our skins
we are all the same,
with hearts, brains,
livers and lungs,
with muscles and bones
and flexible tongues.
Why then do we
shun each other?
Who invented the terms
'sister' and 'brother'?
Susan Margaret Palmer

Nowhere Else to Go

Oh, my dearest where have you gone?
  Why leave me so distraught, how will
I manage without you? You did all for me.
  Have to answer knocks with doors opening.
Onto until streets, never had to before.
  Sit dreaming of happy events, all good thoughts
As ne'er bad happened between us
  If only I showed how much you meant to me,
Arise each morning, do my chores, but for what purpose?
  Everything I did for you, how could you desert me?
Life has come to an end, just dreams to look forward to.
  You are in them all, I wait patiently for the end of all
My dreams so we can be together again.
  Then dearest, you will never leave me again
As there will be nowhere else to go.
I. K. Skinner

Autumn

The holiday crowds have left the shore,
Summer has ended—the sun no more
Tempts the bathers—picnickers gone,
Missing the warmth of the summer sun.

On the path by the river
The conkers lie, shiny and bright
Nature's jewels, prizes of eager smallfry,
Hardened and polished, ready for fight.

Gold leaves turning brown as they fall from the trees,
Warm coats and boots donned for walks to the Leas,
Curtains are drawn, crumpets for tea,
Cheeks are aglow from our walk by the sea.
Marjorie Mellor

Rhoda

A persistent perfume pervades the air
From a solitary rose so fragrant and fair.
Petalled profuseity in delicate pink
High in the hedge, in the remotest chink
Out of reach, unblemished, unique
This Grecian rose, so charming and chic
In woody surrounds, is beyond compare.
Edward Carlton

Ending

Window to the world, window in my head.
When the glass mists over, then I'll know I'm dead.
Once the picture fades, once the light has gone,
Then I'll know for sure, my soul has just moved on.
Till then my life will move, from here to there and back.
My moods will change from day to day, from clearest white to black.

Window to the world, why does it fade so fast?
It only happened now, it's already in the past.
What does the future hold? We'll have to wait and see.
I hope your future's better than the one I see for me.
Till then my life will move, from here to there and back.
My moods will change from day to day, from clearest white to black.

Window to the world, picture fading fast,
I think my life is over, the end is here at last.
Gently now I'm sliding, down a tunnel long and bright,
Suddenly I'm there in the lovely soothing light.
No more will my life move, but rest once more in peace.
Finally I'm home, at last, and all my pain has ceased.
L. Cotton

Moving On

The humble home lies empty now
Its walls are stripped and bare.
Yet, shadowy images
Reflect pictures once hung there.
Behind the crumbling paper,
Like strands of hydrated peel
Are the sounds of aged old voices
With their gaiety and zeal.
From the cob-webbed corners
Captured memories abound.
The eras of generated lifetimes,
Halt and listen to the sound.
The trudge of the weary soldier
As he returns from futile war.
The spontaneity of the children
Playing games upon the floor.
The agony and the ecstasy of mother giving birth
And the wonderment of Christmas past, lisle stockings hanging bare.
The endless firefly summers, glorious songs of harvest home.
Step around. Turn the key. Lock it there.
Glenys Fishburn

Tender—Moments

The lightest brush of a kiss,
The finest whisper, barely audible to the ear,
   The soft rustling of clothes
     Another time, another place.

Woman of the Universe
   Woman of my world,
     Encircle my body, my being,
Let your gossamer fine touch
   Bring me back to life.

Let me taste your love,
   Eyes closed,
     to let emotions enter,
       shut out all,
         everything,
But—
   The tender—moments we have alone.
Peter Keogh

Judgement

Farewell dear friend,
I cannot hold you now;
too high for me to reach
from lowly depths;
aware I never could attain the heights so far above.

I wondered often, what you found in me
potentially of use or interest,
but now I know.
I never could provide the thing you sought.
You know it, too.
I see it in your coldness now
which was not there before.

I do not feel at fault;
I just am me.
The blame, if any, then, is there in you,
misjudging of my powers.

Now you have judged again
and I am left,
bereft.
Geraldine Squires

The Deep Blue Sea

My love for you is like the deep blue sea.
As the tide flows in onto the sand,
I kneel and touch the deep blue sea
And make believe I'm touching your hand.
When the tide flows out,
I stand and watch.
The waves get stronger as they flow away
It's like my love for you.
When you're far away
I think I've lost a little of my heart
To the deep blue sea.
I'll wait again till the tide flows in.
To touch the sea.
Then I'll think of all you mean to me.
D. Brown

Cheeky

Do cats go to Heaven? I surely hope they do.
Fluffy little cheeky cat, let's hope they care for you.
Homeless, but head held high, you waltzed straight through
Bit of dinner, kip by the fire, that's what suited you.
Pretty little pink nose, squeaky little voice,
You decided to live here—we just had no choice!
Ever the playful little soul, perhaps a bit too much,
Evermore the baby, fluffy to the touch.
I guess we'll just never know exactly what happened that night
You'd gone off to play and were well out of sight.
It was a sad discovery, on details I won't dwell.
A life of energy and mischief, with no story left to tell.
Hopefully causing chaos from your place above,
At least your last few weeks of life were ones filled with love.
We're all gonna miss you, why did you have to die?
Best wishes little buddy—go in peace, goodbye.
Tim Challis

Who Knows

Are you laughing at me for loving you so?
Do you think "what a fool that I am?"
Do you smile when I jump at the sound of your name?

Do you love me or don't give a damn
When the telephone rings and my heart skips a beat
And I freeze at a knock on the door
And the back of a head or a face in the crowd
Makes me miss you a little bit more

I keep telling myself what a fool that I've been
To let you get under my skin
I'll just laugh and pretend that I don't really care
Who knows maybe one day I'll win?
Joan Hartland

Mother

I want to thank the Lord above,
For giving me my mother's love,
Search the world: but you'll never find
A lady half as sweet or kind,
She has a nature full of grace,
And such a beautiful and kindly face,
So thank you God, my thanks sincere
For giving me this lady dear,
I'll keep her safe from any strife,
And cherish her—all my life.
Ralph L. Harris

Unrequited

How many times have I heard those words
'Just good friends!'
If I keep hearing them again and again, I'm sure I'll go 'round the bend.

Why can't he face the fact that I love him,
That my feelings are here to stay?
I'll always be there if he needs me
Waiting for that special day
When he tells me he really likes me,
And has done for some time
If only he'd told me sooner,
Days ago he could have been mine.

But I know he doesn't love me,
"Just get over him", they say
How hard this is when the passion will burn forever and a day.

Life goes on, or at least it should
But he means so much to me
And "Just good friends" is more appealing than being his enemy.

I guess I have to live with it and find other things to do
Hoping his words will change someday
To a different three: "I Love You!"
Lucinda Highley

The Bullfighter

Cheering crowds, the Arena's full
And Matador awaits the Bull
Blood red is the sand from victims before
As they enter the ring you hear the crowds roar.

The Bull trots around with its horns in the air
Pawing the ground with frustration, despair
Suddenly tension mounting no one utters a sound
As the Matador drags his cloak on the ground

Snorting wildly the Bull takes to the bait
Charges his foe not knowing his fate
The Matador's sticks are plunged deep with great skill
In the back of the Bull who now bends to his will

Then with sword in hand and arm held high
Now the animal knows he's going to die
With a flash the sword strikes the final blow
What purpose this slaughter we'll never know.
Beryl Willetts

Vision

It's the small things in life that make our day
And lift our hearts in a gentle way.
It's the busy people who take the time
To 'phone or help when we are past our prime.
As we grow older and time rushes on
It seems like a dream to look back upon
If we could hold Time in our cupped hands,
Just the lovely parts, you understand?
We would fill our minds with peace and love
And concentrate on the things above.
We would blend with others who feel the same
Then form a legion and stake our claim
For a better life for all who care,
Who have love, vision and trust to declare.
Kathleen Croall

The Journey

Waterfall, waterfall, so powerful, yet beautiful
From a trickle to a torrent
On your journey to the sea,
With the past far behind you
The future still to be.

As you ripple over stoney beds
Reflecting silhouettes dance overhead,
As you flow alongside river banks,
Spraying wild flowers who nod with grateful thanks.

Bubbling, churning, you are never still,
As you travel through green valleys
With their mystic, shadowy hills,
Your journey is ending, your final destiny
Into the arms of the open sea.
Wendy L. Patrick

A Promise to Flo

One thing there is that I can justly take,
Not purposing aught in return to give,
As long as on this Earth I still can live
And such one-sided seeming bargain makes:

   There underneath your soft eye whence it came
   I find it on your cheek, soft also, lying.
   Though dignity subdues your silent crying,
   That single tear is waiting just the same.

It waits for me, before it disappears,
To bend—and with my lips now make it mine.
This taking without giving is the sign
That you will have no cause, through me, for tears . . .
Peter S. A. Cooper

Ethiopia

Miles and miles of drought ridden land
Hungry children hold out their hand
Bewildered faces, not knowing why
Even so young, they may have to die.

Brown tiny faces with huge haunted eyes
Tears flow sadly, infested with flies
Human suffering, far too much to bear
Do you see it God, do You really care?

Brown spindly legs on shoeless feet
Their greatest wish is just to eat
Pot bellied children unable to stand
Doomed to live in this dry barren land.

We say we are starving when missing a meal
How can we possibly know how they feel
Some food is sent, usually grain
They'd grow their own if it would rain.

Many assist try hard to contend
Bringing dreadful torment to an end
With a problem so huge, an area so vast
Can they deal with success this enormous task.
A. Richardson

Grand Entrance, September 25th Ninety-Six

I have been cooped up for nine months,
Punching, kicking in my sleep;
Floating helplessly in my own little universe,
of strange sounds and multi-coloured lights;
Now the day has arrived,
with joy, I leap!
For others retire,
that I may be born;
Time so slow, road's so long,
Eventually I push that last inch,
My head squeezes out,
I scream with delight and terrible fright,
For I am starting my flight,
to new Millennium ways,
And to my parents, scary days!
Paul Gallagher

The Sky

The sky is the sea, upside down,
Clouds are the waves in billowing abound.

Reflections in cloud waves, of differing colour hue,
Are the suns rays not quite getting through
That sea of cloud, rolling past,
Making shapes to imagine;
"There's a ship with a mast".

That thunder is the waves, crashing against rocks,
That murmur of wind is seabirds flying in flocks.

As daylight ends and darkness draws nigh,
That is sea mist, forming up in the sky.

That bright star, now and again seen,
Is a lighthouse, must watch its beam.

The moon appearing is a port town,
The sky is the sea, upside down.

P. J. T. Porter

Sunrise, in December

Transcendent colours, in the morning sky,
Glimmer through night-black trees, in red and gold.
Mounted in settled earth, the tall trees stand
Erect upon the grass which, flat and plain,
Spreads out in dull, uncomplicated green.
As the light strengthens, and the naked trees
Lay their bare branches over trailing gold,
The bright hues fade; the solid-seeming sun
Creeps, scarlet, past Earth's rim, to bring the day;
Colours diminish; light blue filters in,
To fill the passive sky; the daylight grows,
Uncompromising, sharp; and darkened trees
Reveal bright branches. Pastel sunlight glows.

Noele Mackness

Mystique

Majestic and proud the castle stands
regal its surveyance o'er the land,
what secrets within its aged walls,
what feet still tread the cold dank halls.

The turrets like the years do fall
strewn waste in the valley below,
like the clash of swords, the battle cry
that died so long ago.

Dark shadows stroke the crumbling
shell as clouds the moon doth pass,
like sighs the wind to pays its call
and gently moves the grass.

Lie proud yon laird of long ago
whose mighty arm helped vanquish foe,
at ease in death your sword arm still,
in tranquil slumber lie until the skylarks
trill doth break the peaceful melancholy.

Olga Johnson

The Question

What do we say when we ask oneself,
What things do we treasure on earth?

Is it the trees at the first breath of Spring?
The soft velvet of the pussy willow?
The brightness of the blackbirds eye?
The still grace of the bluebell?

Purple heather on the mountains?
The crystal of a stream?
Countless things of beauty
The magic of a dream

All these things of mystery of wonder and delight
These are treasures, like caskets of gold
To store in your heart for all time
With love and the hope and the joy just for living
It's here and it's yours and it's mine

Iris Payne

Ode to the Millennium

The Millennium is coming so what shall we do?
  Just check our calendars and see if it's true
Time and tide will wait for no man
  It's been like that since time began
Do we pray more or less every day
  In faith and hope to share anyway
Will there be more wars in Africa or strife
  those poor refugees struggling for life
And how do we feed them on charity alone
  let's make these warlords surely atone
Send no more arms in their will to fight
  but help all the victims that is their right"
Then three years from now only time will tell
  of their quest for freedom and no road to hell
Citizens of each Country awake to their needs
  let us ensure of peace and very good deeds
Now we must plan a definite rally from all
  to sow the best seeds and answer the call
Time is on our side therefore make it the best
  we shall not fail them when put to the test.

J. Kops

It's Only a Matter of Time

Pick a bit here, pick a bit there
forget about the pain
no-one else seems to care

Be friendly, be helpful, be understanding, be polite
don't cry all through the day, pick a bit here
don't cry all through the night

Keep things to yourself, best not let them get out
ignore the things you're going through, pick a bit there
that's what life's about

Don't get bad tempered, try not to be scared
don't dwell on the times, pick a bit here
when it seemed that they cared

Just keep acting this way things will get better you'll see
just stay calm, pick a bit there
for the moment this is how it has to be

Things will get so bad that your world will fall apart
but then and only then will the time come
for you to mend your broken heart

Lisa Robertson

A Whimsical

I could not let this occasion go by,
Without reference to comet on high.
This time round it has been named "Hale-Bopp",
But who is to know it hasn't been given a swap!

Brighter it gets as it approaches the sun,
The tail vaporizes for its outward run.
It passes the earth by millions of miles,
This gives the populace a chance for smiles.

The comet's tail takes up much of the sky,
And is easily visible to the naked eye.
The nucleus is thought to be 25 miles across,
But this could be a scholar's gloss!

The "Yanks" are sending rockets high,
To measure composition as it passes by.
I suppose the politicians will claim the jest,
And pretend it gives them divine right of blest!

Graham Smith

Lady of the Sand

Silently the tide sifts the sand,
Burying my heart on a coral sea shore,
Along with those who have lived their lives in times past,
And for those to find in futures to come.

But for now, I am the Lady of the Sand,
No more than a grain—to my Greek Romeo.

Rachel Smith

The Blackbird's Song

His song breaks through the cold grey dawn
   In ecstasy:
Its rich tones entrance the new morn
   With their beauty.

From roof-top his largesse is thrown
   Prodigally,
The golden music pouring down
   Unceasingly.

While hurrying commuters stay,
   By melody
Entrapp'd, and briefly thrust away
   Reality.

And housewives in their daily round
   Pause wistfully,
Enchanted by that lovely sound
   To sweet memory.

Gay songster, may you ever sing
   So joyously,
For to man's restlessness you bring
   Serenity.
   R. M. Shallard

Spring

Up through the cold dark earth
A gleam of life breaks through,
Telling us it's time to awake
And bring new life to you.

First we see the snow drop
Then the crocus follow on,
And all at once that beauty
The daffodil follows with song.

It's time that Winter left us
With its snow, sleet and rain,
And Spring says I am coming
To welcome you again.

How sweet the world with all its glory,
All its seasons one by one,
However hard we find the winter
We know that Spring will come.
   Mary Campbell-Bridgman

Soft Silent Statues

All the whispers and snide remarks slowly started to take shape
The sarcasms and lies which she had learnt to live
with, like a newborn, had taken its first breath
Jupiter had given this monster life, and now the
legless lizard was slivering towards its victim
The snake woman looked deep into the eyes of her prey
Medusa's cold gaze had turned another soul to stone
And now, whilst the "anima" was trapped in the temple
of the forgotten Gods, another lifeless shell walked
the silent Earth.
   Alexandra Frattali

Confusion

Where must we look for a solution
To all this worldwide confusion
When really we are faced with delusion
meted out to us in profusion?
   Gullible to the state of extinction,
   can we not make a distinction
     to avoid what could become an addiction
     to things creating a dangerous infliction?
Is there not even one inhibition
Which would create a happy condition?
Thoughts, expressed in words, on a mission
Requesting, for the sins of the world, a remission?
   Is this playing with words an affection?
   Sometimes fun, and no more than fiction,
   With a message there within my diction.
   Claude A. Knight

The Firework Display

A waft of warmth fills the cool night air.
Bonfire and lanterns flicker and flare.
The look of wonder in a small child's eye,
As a cascade of snowfire lights up the sky.

The crowd looks on in sheer delight,
As rockets ascend, out of sight.
Like dancing stars in a moon kissed sky
Sprinkling, sparkling way up high,
bang crickle crack!
Up and away like a jumping jack.

Children with their sparklers hold,
"do be careful" they are told
Like magic wands a wondrous sight,
Twinkling twirling in the night,
"A bowl of soup wouldn't go amiss"
"Jacket Potatoes mm delish!"

The bonfire slowly burns away
"Yes we've had a lovely day".
Everyone says their last goodbyes
As the last of the Guy Fawkes, withers and dies.
   Wendy Watkin

"Return to Cyprus"

Dear Cyprus, my Cyprus, I have come here to stay,
and I'm yours till the end of my dying day.
I'll fortune, you see, yet took me once more,
and again I am with you, for it's you I adore.

So protect me, my love, from age and decay,
till my spirit leaves me with sorrow one day.
How blessed I will be to see blossom so sweet,
to breathe roses in bloom with petals so neat.

Your friendship, my life, brings me hope from despair,
and I'm walking and dancing once more in the air.
The perfume, your jasmine, your sea O! So blue,
your beauty, your breezes, your hills kissed with dew!

My hungry eyes feast on your grace and your charm,
your valleys, your mountains, your fir trees so calm!!
Your sapphire sea eases my poor aching bones,
your evenings, your music, to dance to its tones.

I have suffered much pain and torture you see,
so my life and my heart I offer to thee.
To dear God I will give my soul, if I may,
to enfold in His arms forever and aye.
   Hebe Georgiades-Mitchell

A Friend

Though my treasures are but few,
No price could ever buy them.
Not even the man with the richest purse,
Though I'll speak of them to you gladly.

If you like me, have a trusted friend,
You possess a treasure rare.
For a friend in need is a friend indeed,
When you're down and in despair.

They'll stand by you through thick and thin,
They'll never let you down.
How can you state the price of a friend?
Who's worth more than a million pounds!

A friend is there when you need them,
A friend will share in your pain.
A friend is someone steadfast and true,
What a treasure I have, what a gain!

So for silver and gold, and money untold,
A wasted life you may spend.
But of the treasures I speak, I ask you to seek,
They are deep in the heart of a "Friend".
   Joyce T. Newman

Justice

Have you ever thought whether justice is served
To the people who should get what they deserve.
Shouldn't the people who've been a victim of a crime
Have a say to how long the criminal serves time.
It doesn't seem fair to the families of their loved one,
Whose murderer gets off free for what they have done.
It doesn't seem fair that victims who report an assault
Are dismissed or blamed for being the sort.
The sort of person who goes out looking for a fight
At all times of day being morning or night.
The ones who are arrested and convicted
Are the type that are always predicted
From birth will be trouble and strife,
Who will fight and probably carry a knife.
Why is it that when people finally decide to co-operate,
It is usually five months after the crime's date?
And it is usually too late
For anything to be done because of the long wait.
Where is the justice?
That's all I ask.

Kelly Etridge

Lesley's Garden

You whisper in the gentle breeze,
You nestle, quiet, among the trees.
It was your garden, where once you strolled,
Kissed by the sun, dreaming your dreams untold.
Now you're gone, your earthly life is done;
So young you were, a mere three tens and one.
But still your sweet soul stays and watches o'er
The precious, innocent child you bore,
As she plays in your garden happily,
Where now you rest so peacefully.

Pamela Flavin

Memories

Memories of childhood days,
portraying thoughts of happier days.
Life was full and care-free then,
without a worry to contend.
Youth's innocence shines
through a young child's eyes.
Life was full of happiness and surprise.

But life in reality is full of ups and downs.
With trials and tribulations and experiences to confound.
Courage and strength can falter at times.
It takes faith and determination to ease our troubled minds.

As time passes by and we start to grow old.
Memories of times gone by start to unfold.
We yearn for that inner peace, contentment of our soul.
Only then will we realize, we have reached our goal.

Poet Sutton

Portrait of an Unknown Girl

Around me the murmur of a viewing public,
And echoing footsteps on a polished floor,
The rustle of papers in gesticulating hands,
The intermittent swish of an opened door.
But this picture of a golden girl before me,
Displayed on walls of meaner hue,
Lures me away from this inconstant company,
Transforms my space into a hallowed pew.
Delightful glints from clouds of auburn hair,
And soulful eyes that break the heart.
I am transfixed; I can hardly breathe,
Bewitched, benumbed by the painter's art.
This form and beauty created by a hand,
Has in my soul created stifling discontent.
If only I were painted there beside her,
That would relieve my aching heart's torment.

John Young Simms

Untitled

The father sits at the head of the table
Sharing all . . . and what he's able.
For with this family he does share
The positive love will always be there!
This family holds the strongest bond
Together they know, they belong!
Through all obstacles of life
They fought as man and wife!
They hold the trophy to succeed
They push out all their needs!
As a family together!
This they want forever!
Honesty comes before they lie,
They don't want the family to die!
They all know, the world so wrong
Because the family knows where they belong!

Suzan Gumush

An Ode to a Rose from Alberta; A Young Canadian Flower

Erin what words can I say
you radiate warmth and love in a natural way
you're a rose from Alberta, a breath of fresh air
your laugh is affectionate and full of fun.
In all of Scotland I've never seen, a lassie
display grace in such a true, pure innocent way.
Erin what you have is rare, a loving spirit
quite divine, it effects all who are around
you, which only you can do.
You're a joy, the apple of your mother's eye,
she's a young girl again in your company.
I've seen her eyes twinkle when she looks at
you, which speaks volumes of her love
pouring out to you.
What a unique special affection has touched
our hearts. I miss these cheeky eyes,
now only memories, and I shall always
remember the visit of a Rose from Alberta a
young Canadian flower.

Peter Laird

You in Mind

How beat my heart, at a lonely pace,
As I live this life, in time and place
To look and see, into your eyes, is good
For me and good, for I, I love you well,
I love you true, nothing will part us two
O, how I long for time and fun and
Will live this life, for you.
  Just one.

George Henry Fish

The Search (Part Two)

A blue shadow still chasing after me
I would never look back again
It's hard to see a way, that I have gone on
But the shadow always be everywhere I am
Just because, it is the reflection of myself
I'm still searching for love
In the darkness of the jungle in your heart
When those rocks hit my feet
I won't call your name anymore
Because you have gone in a mountain of fear
That is in your soul
Still the tears running down my face
I'm trying to give you my sweetest smile
When I see you, when I want you
I'd like to catch you and I swear
If I do, I won't let you go away again
This search will never end
Till I can touch you with my fingers
Till our breathes run together
And your love would leave me never, forever . . .

Agatha Setiawan

It's Not Just a Flash in the Pan! . . .

"Gotten hold of any heart;
So we never love to part;
Gently do smile up your way,
Then the angels never stray;
Sky-high records we do seek;
Then we feel the finest heat;
Gotten hold of you alone, then I can sit you on any throne;
Sky-line always plays a game;
For there is no better way;
Let the fortunes play their realm;
Then there is no better balm;
For it is something that is nice;
Nothing ever comes amiss; kiss me Cherie and be a hit;
Forever friends we love to be, then we can play in harmony;
See things always in God's light, then we can always shine alright;
Nothing ever does go wrong for we are so very strong;
Kiss me Cherie and feel so free, then angels always will be near;
Most of all there are no stormy seas;
We can chase each other when there is the need;
Feel much loved we are a bond, then we are forever strong;

Emma Sperring

Answer to a Prayer

In the long awaited dawning,
Quite without fair warning,
Came the screaming, diving carrion birds attacking from on high;
I attempted to defend her with my gun and all our shot,
But I fought a losing battle, and my gun got smoking hot.
But our neighbours came a-riding, having sought us through the night
And the carrion birds had told them of our presence, and our plight.
So then carefully they took her to the place she loved the best,
To the quiet chapel garden of "Our Lady of the West."
Where carefully and prayerfully they laid her down to rest.
And the mason made a gravestone, with letters deep impressed
Saying "Et in hora mortis nostrae", her whispered last request.
And when I come to visit I will say, with bated breath,
Her Latin words just read to me "At the hour of our Death."

Charles Charnock

Now and on Dear Ones

Love is blind also, sees us to the safety of the womb,
When the war is gone Away,
And in other lands raging,
And their love angels,=
Needs to do the haven on their day
And flaming rest! stage in
Life is a stage=equals yen. And each stage by stage=self reassured towards=and encouraged to arrive, and enjoyed then. Fans and swells. No deprive!

A. Garton

Reflections

A river-trip in Sunshine's ray'
Was planned to mark an 'end of stay';
Alas; the morn brought sullen skies,
Ignoring soul-despairing sighs! . . .
But dark clouds cannot weep forever;
Translucent light embalms the river;
Increasing to a soft perfection;
Basking in its own reflection.
Mystic waters, flowing deep;
Many river secrets keep.
　Still as a statue carved from stone,
　A cautious Heron guards his home.
　Perchance his neighbour's habitat
　Belongs to Mole, and Water-Rat;
　There, just beneath the feathered Willow
　Rustling in the soft wind's billow!
　Ducks are a-dabbling; from afar
　Comes a toot . . . Toad's Motor-car?? . . .
The river gleams; her spell is spun!
And no-one thinks to mourn the Sun!.

Patricia Woodley

Lest We Forget Eleventh Hour, Eleventh Day, Eleventh Month

Should we forget the anguish we felt so long ago?
Youth destroyed in battle against a mighty foe.
Those who remember, oft, a silent tear will fall,
Trickle down the cheek as sadness is recalled.

There was no safety zone as bombs shattered peace,
They fell amidst the helpless, disturbing nightly sleep.
Loved ones of fighters away on battle-fields,
Joined the fight to conquer, helping those in need.

Huge mounds of rubble, once, family homes,
Folk buried deep beneath, blitzed, no longer free to roam.
So where indeed was the battle zone in World War II?
It was everywhere, the vital key to truth.

So oft one hears. "Forget war it's living in the past"
Not for those who lived it, poignant memories last.
To fully understand, courage must have passed that test;
Those who remember say. "Lest We forget".

And wear a poppy with pride.

Penny Beddard

Hill Rise

Why is it on this hill stand I, as daylight breaks the dawn?
When down below ten thousand souls sleep on unconcerned.
Unafraid of loneliness, such places food for thought.
Before a sun could rise, I'll be nature wizened-wise.

Two foxes crossed a meadow, from farm to finney wood.
Had from the path they veered. A rabbit would be gone.
A hare's still in the ploughing, crouching furrow down.
That blackbird's startled note, will have exercised the wings.

Tempered not the breeze, I prefer a howling wind.
A mind more activated, more score for sentiment.
It's seen at daybreak too, not all of those below.
Would rise this day, to climb this way, leaving graves behind.

David Pooley

The Empty House

The trees stand silent in the fading light,
With branches bare and stark against the sky.
The birds on hastening wings have taken flight,
And left the old grey house is solitude to lie.
Past times, the sound of laughter rent the air,
And hurrying feet danced o'er the waving grass.
But now the shuttered windows sightless stare,
And see no more the children as they pass.
No smoke trails rise from fluted chimneys tall,
The present inmates, ghosts from former years.
The creaking of the door—a haunting call,
And raindrops fall on cobweb's lace like tears.
But weep no more, put saddened thoughts away,
For time will bring new life, new dawn, new day.

Edith N. Kellow

The Coming of the Dawn

The darkness long, so black and deep,
　In dreamless time, the mind inert.
Beneath the lashes, slowly creeps,
　A glimmer shines, the night reverts.
Slowly, darkness slips away,
　as pinkish hues invade the shade.
Patterns on the wall display.
　Rays of sunbeams now parade.
The "cheeping" sound of early bird,
　alone at first it makes its call,
Then other sleepy sounds are heard,
　from hedge and bush, and garden wall.
Arising, stretching, peering through the glass,
　the rainbow sky that heralds dawn.
The emerald droplets on the grass,
　the myriad pastel shades of morn.

Terry F. Ward

One of the Best

A legend in the Nineties was Red Rum,
All he liked to do was jump and run,
The Grand National was his very own,
Three times a winner he scampered home.

Horse and trainer were in high esteem,
As he proudly ran, anyone's dream.
Opening fetes he loved to make friends,
As well as racing these were the trends.

He had a long good life that is true,
As years passed by he did things anew.
Sadly the day came when he had to rest,
The remains of him were at the racecourse
Where he had done his best.
Evelyn M. Harding

Windows

From my bedroom window I can see—
many children playing happily,
there's green grass and leafy tree,
song birds singing merrily,
but should these lovely things depart
I'll treasure still the windows in my heart.

Safely stored are memories that last,
Little bits and pieces from the past
I oft recall when days are dark and drear,
although alone, my loved ones are so near.

The windows of my mind are shining bright,
prayer helps me when they're far away—out of sight,
and as the years go by I'll recall—
babies, toddlers, teenagers, strong and tall;
what a mighty mansion of windows now I hold,
wealth of family and friends are worth more than gold.
Lavinia Brown

Sweet Dreams

Oh Santa I'm so lucky to be sitting on you knee,
You hold me just like daddy, when he cuddles me,
I went to bed real early because it's Christmas eve,
But suddenly I saw you; you were about to leave.

Oh Santa you are lovely, just how I thought you'd be,
So very kind and gentle, the same as daddy is to me,
My mummy she is also kind, she tucks me up each night,
kisses me and says "God bless"; then puts out my light.

Oh Santa how I love you, your beard is soft and warm,
Just like my little pillow, it makes me want to yawn,
Tomorrow I will see my toys, knowing you have been,
But Santa I won't tell a soul; they'd say it was a dream.
R. A. Wenn

An Abrupt End to Forty-Eight Years of Marriage

I shan't be long, I'll get the veg.
She looked at him
with love she said don't smoke
and stop to drink,
I'll stay here and wait upon the bed.

I promise I'll be quick old dear.
Come kiss me then
for then you cannot lie,
you never could
hurry back, I'm scared when you're not here.

Of course he kissed his love, poor man
and went out.
He kept his word and came
right back again
but she was gone
and he was left,
the veg just slipping from his hand.

He knew it then, how long he had.
I shan't be long
He said, with love and lit a fag.
Laszlo Clements

B.S.E.

B.S.E. a tragedy,
owing to one man you see,
feeding cows with raw meat,
Which made them all fall off their feet.

People dying from B.S.E.
what a terrible tragedy.

Now a cull has been called,
and all our cows are doomed to fall,
because of B.S.E. a tragedy.

Even worse the fumes of death,
polluting air, but do we care,
poor cows grazing without knowing,
that tomorrow they will be going,
to their death.

Please God let the Scientist see, that all
creatures are like you and me, they want to
live happily free from B.S.E. a tragedy.
Rita Rea

Beach Encounters (On Parting, May 1995)

The tide has washed away both dog and bull
Foot-drawings in the ever changing sand
Left stranded winkles in a small rock pool
And thrown forgotten debris on the strand

Is love a sea that carries all with hope
Only to cast them broken on the shore
And do rejected lovers learn to cope
By dreaming of the sea's embrace once more

Ebbing and flowing
Rising and falling
This is the rhythm
Of living and longing
Alex Valentine Jr.

Soul Mates

Amongst, all the odds, no matter how much I tried.
There is something there, my heart, will not hide.
God knows, I tried and tried.
There is something there, God will not hide.

Through my soul,
There is something, in you . . . God desires.
Through my soul,
Desires, desires, desires.

The pains, of being apart.
Ache, ache, ache, within, my heart.
The pains, of uncertainties,
Ache, ache, ache, beyond, all of me.

It is, in my soul, it will not go.
God speaks, to me, my soul knows.
Bonded together, in God's unity.
In both, our souls, for eternity.
Jenifer Ellen Austin

As Grace through Time

As grace through time,
Your movement is divine,
Your body is one of beauty.
As a person you live, walk, talk, and breathe
And as through nature you do things like sneeze.
But you have a grace, a spirit, and a loving soul,
As fragile life you survive very well.
A perfect female being,
One of grace and a capability to swear,
An act of freedom without a care.
But a knowledge that you must pay your way,
To survive day after day,
Which you do very well,
As everyone around you can tell,
As your movement is divine,
As grace through time.
Paul Waldock

Birth

Chlorophyllic needles bursting from the skin,
From carpets of humus to blighted wastes,
Escaping the midnight prison of cloying tarmac
Reaching for the brass-eyed sun.
Tendrils lift anorexic arms in leafy prayer,
While whiplash branches clutch the sky with gnarled digits
And rag-tagged roots suckle at Mother's breast:
Offspring of sun and water;
Energy in Pimpernel guises,
chained in cyclic bondage.

The ridge-backed saurian in deadly repose,
The furtive panther with dappled hide;
And the soaring condor sailing on thermal waves:
Brothers in biorhythm;
Seeds of an ill-formed infant with tortured lungs
That crawled from the amino swamp
To explore a world buckled from violent birth,
Belching fiery plasma from its living cauldron,
The humblest yet the mightiest of pioneers.
Don Cousins

Farewell Visit

She lay on the bed, frail, eyes closed as in deep sleep
I stroked the white head unsure if she knew I was there
Mixed emotions flooded through me, love, sorrow,
Remorse for things done and things left as yet undone.
Slowly she slid sideways on the pillow till her shoulders
Touched my arm, as if in recognition of my need of comfort
And her capacity to understand.
A stillness seemed to envelope the room, yet elsewhere
The daily business of the Nursing Home went on as usual,
Sounds of a television set came from further down the hall
And the clatter of cutlery upon china indicated that
Tea would be served up soon.
I kissed her on the forehead before I took my leave
And felt her stir slightly against my sleeve,
Outside, the cold fresh air stung my eyes already full
Of unshed tears, only my heart cried out in pain in remembrance
Of close ties soon to be broken and of someone
I would not see alive again.
Elizabeth N. S. Gray

In the Dark

I know I am kept in liquid dark
No sun-kissed beams alight on my being.
Yet within this foul miasma, a thought
My mind is still constantly far seeing.

I am fed with a substance named manure,
The stench fills my nostrils yet sustains
Kind words and truth they cannot be fewer
Yet I still flourish in the growth of pain.

Oh if I could be replanted in a bed,
Amongst sumptuous delicate coloured flower
Not just a mundane mushroom to be fed,
Kept in the dark, a morsel for a palate to savour.
Jay Baker

On Looking at a Bust of Beethoven

When I look on thee, Beethoven, I see
A latent and magnetic might imbued
Within thy pregnant mould. Thy fix ed eye
Rolls and flashes with a divine passion.
Thy mouth, muted as clouds whose strange calm perturbs,
Bursts forth in an eloquence that echoes the eddying ocean
In grievous vehemence. Thy graven, whelming brow
Defies creation, thou elemental god!

Beethoven, thy name is full of the roaring wind
And the subdued sweetness after storm, for thou
Didst grapple with revolting thunder while lightning
Hurtling lashed the sky. E'en so thy music,
Like some eternal cataract rings in mine ears,
Ever lifting the spirit to sublime empyrean.
Harold Kopel

Burgh-by-Sands Church

The Romans came,
With armour shining in the mid-day sun;
With muscles rippling as they heaved the stones
To build a fortress.
Down the coast
They raised an altar to a pagan god.
But they fell.

In later times
The stones were shaped into a house of prayer
That dwelt in soft rain and in watchful skies.
A tower of love
To live through long years,
Gently blessing those who lie
For ever safe in warm earth,
Under stones, reflecting sunlight
And the gift of peace.

Swords into ploughshares,
Rest after battle,
Through eternity.
Eunice Barnett

The Bully

He is tall, strong, big and a bully,
Bad tempered, cruel, daft and silly.

His brain is little and his body is big.
Tough, heartless and as stubborn as a pig.

He continues to bully whoever his eyes catch.
He makes sure they're weak and not his match.

He hits, kicks and punches in the face.
He doesn't care if you're bad or ace.

For him, the school is a boxing ring.
He's the boxer, referee and the king.

The lessons are not important nor are the books.
What matters for him is to keep his angry looks.

No respect for a parent, colleague or a teacher,
No respect for religion, norm or a preacher.

But time will run very fast,
And as he continues to be daft,

He will find himself left alone,
And with a bad fame will be known.

Nobody will like him or respect.
No future or job, only prison to expect.
M. A. Adlan

Manhattan

God surely toiled with man
to build Manhattan, a living pattern,
fashioned out of concrete,
these homes, these dwelling places
for the races the world over to see,
that on one soil, people of all nations can toil
and live and laugh and love and die under one sky.

This dream, this glorious city, tremendous majesty
cast as in a mould, with bridges
strong, graceful, lovely to behold,
spanning deep and softly flowing rivers
people and concrete caught in time, 1979.

This splendid city, this melting pot
leading the world into light?
Moving forward in God's sight?
Her statue of liberty, her flags unfurled a dream,
a hope for all the world and people black, white and yellow
a part to play, something to say, on God's side.

He looks down on this city with infinite love and pity.
Manhattan, blocks of living stone high rise,
Manhattan reaching for the skies.
Joyce Adlington

The Dark One

I ascend from the depths of Hell,
Through labyrinth tunnels along the way.
I struggle to reach the deepest well,
Just to see the light of day.

Seeing the light through the depths of water,
My personality begins to wonder,
Why, on Earth, did I bother?
This place is worse than that other,
The Hell through which I used to wonder.

And the blackness covers me again,
As I descend, back to the depths below.
To the place where I am home again,
My Kingdom. My Hell.

With memories of the world above,
And of the people that call me the Devil,
With a deep seated knowledge and understanding,
That I am not the one who's Evil.

The darkest dark and deepest hour,
The greatest fear and sharpest skewer,
Your friend, The Devil's Keeper.

S. Savage

Sentimental Value . . . How Can It Be Measured?

Small blue glass cup, given long before she could remember,
sat upon each shelf as family moved from place to place;
from prairies wide, way out to the coast they went.

Small blue glass cup, still there through teenage years;
watched as sweetheart came to call; hope chest filled;
then happy faces circled on her wedding day.

Small blue glass cup, packed again and unpacked, then perched
on yet another shelf. Words of war heard from young husband
in navy blue; tall and slender, with son to make a family now;
two daughters more. Such happiness . . . and sometimes tears.

Small blue glass cup crystal clear; grandchildren to say,
"Hi grandma, hi grandpa too, we've come to play".
Time passed too quickly . . . precious words left silently unsaid.

Small blue glass cup, origin unknown, watched mute;
beloved husband, father, friend . . . tall and slender still
slipped away a higher life to live amongst the stars.

Small blue glass cup, tenderly packed once more, moved
to another home, in the sunlight, closer to her children
up the valley. One day, perhaps, great-grandchildren to say,
"Hi grandma, we've come to play" . . . and seal it with a hug.

Moyra Teresa Burnett

The Bottom Drawer

A treasured chest graced great grandma's home,
Charmingly carved, a beauty to own,
Majestically clothed, this wood once stood
Far in the forest of old Robin Hood,
Sweethearts signed two hearts entwined.

Loving hands created this chest,
Great grandma said it was the best,
Photos placed in pride of place,
Nooks and crannies, drawers all bar one
Held everything she depended upon.

The bottom drawer, her memories lay
Slowly, secretly storing for her wedding day
Little gifts, lovely things, treasures only true love brings,
One by one the drawer did fill,
Finally with love she said, I will.

This bottom drawer cradled each new born
Safe from cold, cosily warm,
Tiny babies free from harm,

Some day her feather bed to share
Lots of love in great grandma's care.

Anne Oddie

The Wanderer

I came from a town, dust and smoke
I wandered among the country folk,
Lifted my eyes to the leaves of a tree
How pure the earth, how free.
I wandered on, as if in a dream
Until I came to an old mill stream.
It bubbled, and sparkled as it ran
Far away, from the sight of man.
As I stood on the crest of the hill,
I felt its peace, stood perfectly still,
For God was there,
Near that old, old mill.

Joan Gentle

My Son Billy

God gave to me a gift of a son.
To have and to hold, till a mother's job's done,
The joy that you give me no-one can share,
To be without you, I just could not bare,
You laugh and you smile at the silliest thing
Oh, what happiness a baby can bring,
Your eyes so big they shine so bright
They have the look of a mystic delight,
Your little fingers and tiny toes
Not forgetting your button nose,
Your tiny body so neat and compact,
We all love you and that is a fact,
You have no worries of life or of crime
I thank the Lord that He made you mine,
You probably think I am mad and silly
To write this poem of you, my son Billy.

Shirley Sackett

The Child

He comes unmoving through the feathered trees
Through shades of light entrapped by the dawn
Where incense hides her glory from the morn
And silence breaks the humming of the bees

In bliss the offsprings of the sun bow low
Before the splendour of his majesty
And from all sides there comes a harmony
That fires the waters of the earth below

In soft seclusion on a sapphire lake
Yielding her petals to the rising glow
A peerless lily sees her royal foe
And from her drops of crimson dew does shake

He steps beside her close retreat and on
Her flaming cheeks does glance, before he stoops,
And swift as eagle birds of gold do swoop
Upon their prey, he plucks, and he is gone.

Matthew T. Calderwood

Two Summer Days

Clouds scurry across the threatening sky.
The rain comes intermittently and fast.
The sun, now sulking, plays at hide and seek.
Trees toss their heavy branches endlessly.
Flowers, roughly blown about, are in distress.
Children explode into noisy laughter
At the wind's caprice; and wildly race around.
Cats and dogs so intently chase their tails.
The ice-cream vendor soon packs up his wares.

Clouds carefully keep their appointed place,
Fearful of intruding in the azure sky.
The sun, unchallenged, blazing, stands his ground.
Trees are erect, tall, motionless and straight.
Flowers turn up their bright faces to the sun.
Children splash about in clear, fresh water:
To keep cool is their priority today.
Cats and dogs lazily seek out the shade.
The ice-cream vendor toils, while others rest.

Eileen Reilly

The Mysterious Girl

The dead leaves danced under the moonlight,
Empty souls walked into the night.
A girl dressed in white stepped out,
My lips trembled as I tried to shout.
Her eyes were empty, her face was pale,
She drifted along, leaving no trail.
I was shaking nervously, out of control,
Was she the shadow of a young girl's soul?
I watched as a motionless tear fell down her pale cheek,
She had no future to seek.
I reached out to touch her, to tell her she was alright,
But as I did, she vanished deep into the night.
I could feel the wind getting stronger
As the eerie night grew longer.
I couldn't stay awaiting for her return
As she made my empty stomach churn.
She was back where she belonged,
And with her fellow ghosts she could bond.

Sarah Kind

Hope

"Go to hell" said the girl to the world inside,
"If I go" said the earth "I'll take the best of your mind".
"Take it, I need it as little as you" she replied.
So the Earth took it and the girl sadly died.

"Go to hell" said the girl to the world inside
"If I go" said the Earth "I'll take the best of your mind"
"I need my mind, it keeps me sane".
So the Earth went home and the girl dreamed again.

"Go to hell" said the girl to the world inside
"Not you again, I thought you kept your mind".
"My mind hurts, I want to die", she said
"Your soul's gone, you're already dead".

Liz Fisher

Life Begins at Forty

Life begins at forty, or so I'm often told;
I already have some wrinkles, will they get worse as I grow old?
I cover up my crows feet with new and expensive creams;
Oh! How I yearn to be younger as I was in all my dreams,
I used to wear a ponytail and always looked quite sporty;
But this is not acceptable, when one is reaching forty.
I used to be a blonde you know but now I'm going grey,
I have to use That treatment that washes it away;
I am size 10 I always say, clothes fit with the use of a pin,
The sizes here are small today, says the assistant with a grin;
What a lovely pair of trousers and they are just my size,
I try them in the changing room but they're covering someone
    else's thighs.
I will take them anyway, a good diet's what I'll try,
Knowing deep down inside, that pigs don't really fly;
My husband doesn't understand me, he thinks that I'm just right,
He doesn't know why I'm so depressed with the constant flab
    I have to fight,
I weigh myself each morning and he says that with every pound,
I shouldn't really fret too much as there's more of me to go round,
I sit and read the diet books and I look for inspiration,
I'll have that chocolate biscuit, just for consolation!

Carol Ridgley

The Wedding

The dress she wore upon her day
So stunningly bright, what could I say
Her blonde hair glistening in the sun
The glittering smile, she's having fun

The flowers cradled in her arms
The stems caressed upon her palms
The dress is flowing so clear and bright
Oh, how she looks toward the night

Reception time they're out to dance
They sure look sweet upon a glance
They cut the cake and pieces passed
Let's hope this lovely marriage lasts

Stephen J. Craddock

Cat

Cat,
Inscrutable,
Proud and tall,
Sat at the window
Looking out over all.
Disdainfully turned an enquiring head
As her dish with delicious food was spread.
Then, gracefully swooped with effortless bound,
Flicked tail and minced languidly over the ground.
After delicate sniff and tentative taste, consumed the meal at
leisurely pace

From deep in a murky, malodorous bin could be heard a
scrabbling,
clanking din.
A gaunt, scrawny animal, ill-nourished and wild
Frantically scavenged food—rotten, defiled—
Putrid fish heads, worm-ridden tripe,
Decaying sausages, fruit over-ripe.
When to deposit rubbish
A man raised the lid
It hissed and spat,
And out sprang
Cat!

J. Harding

My Old Friend (Ria)

Each season brought new joy for you
The spring with crisp sunshine
You rolled in grass, the frost still wet
New smells were yours to find

The summer heat, it warmed your coat
Under our tree for shade
Cuddles on the sun bed
I wish you could have stayed

In autumn, leaves are falling
Darker nights, walks in the rain
Muddy paws and footprints
I want to clean them up again

The winter's cold with falling snow
More fun, the snowball fights
The Christmas tree and presents
Are there for your delight

We talked, I laughed, you were my friend
The best one in the world
Now season's stop, there is no spring
without you, my old girl.

Carolyn R. Cunningham

Those Who Die Tomorrow

How it hurt to say goodbye to a friend I truly loved,
To see his lifelight fade before my eyes,
But I couldn't do a thing,
Only watch him suffering,
To comfort him I had to tell him lies.

As I heard his dying breath yet another link was lost,
Another link was lost from life's gold chain,
My hurt was beyond measure,
His memory I treasure,
How many times can one man take the pain?

Each of us must suffer until we can rest in peace,
We watch each other suffering in hell,
But it still goes on and on,
And he's not the only one,
There are other lifelights going out as well.

As much as we pretend, love won't conquer all my friend,
And life will always go on as before,
We will feel the sorrow,
For all those who die tomorrow
And our tears will flow again for many more.

Alan Charles West

Ode to Rossall

In eighteen-forty-four a fine school was founded.
May her ethos remain
In a defiant domain,
Though by recession's waves pounded.

Let this stately seat of learning
Still prosper and flourish,
Her pupils to nourish,
To satisfy academic yearning

Inside her proud portals
Are the archway, the square and gazebo by shore,
Giving a graceful gloria,
Making many mighty mortals,
Like those who have passed before
To continue singing "Floreat Rossallia".

Christopher Richards

Jane

The nursery was silent for once,
In the first cot slept baby Brown
Plump and pink and beautiful
Her mother was young and pretty
And did not want her daughter.
Algernon was in the next cot
Fat as Michelin man
And adored by his parents
Then came the twins with legs like sticks
And wrinkled old men's faces.
Jane put on a gown and mask
to go in the next unit
Test Tube babies tiny and frail

With watching parents
"You don't know what it's like"
Jane gave a rueful smile
And thought of all she'd gone through
And breathed a silent prayer
"Please God give me a baby of my own"

Marjorie Hedley

A Lonely World

Loneliness is standing in a big empty space,
With no voices to hear, no friendly face
When you run around the deserted hall,
No kind hand picks you up when you fall

You can live in a world where only you can go,
But whatever you do there, who will ever know?
There, when you do good, you're not congratulated,
And that world can never stop your feeling hated

With loneliness, you never know which way to turn,
With no one to guide you, how can you learn?
It's the barrier only you can break,
However long it takes you, that effort you must make.

Elaine Ede

Tranquillity

There's a world that you enter when
Your own world is grey, where the past
Becomes the present, merging with
Tomorrow's distant day.

And in that realm of wonder, no pain,
No tears transgress the reality of
Tranquility of your enduring happiness.

There's a Shadow in that crystal land
Who guides your secret way, the guardian
Of your presence there, in that
World far away.

And I'll befriend the Shadow and he'll
Relate the secret that is you, in that
World of silent mystery,
That private Xanadu.

Jim Glen

God's Creations

Tarns once covered by snow and ice still
Steadfastly withhold the mysteries of life
Wherein God's creations of splendour
Oh! Untouched by mortal hand the
Ebbing waters flow only
To become enraged when the wintry gales let fly
Ah! It be the devil's work so to destroy
God's fragrant blossoms amidst
A wondrous countryside wherein
Two loving hearts are bound
Together beside a homely fireside
Ah! Shrouded by a hazy mist so I gazed upon
Grandeur mountains betwixt earth and sky
So I stood and solitude was mine upon
God's creation of mystic splendour
Amidst the sweeping downs and fells
And vastly wooded mountainsides
So angelic chimes of steeple bells
Come from afar carried by gentle
Summer breezes amidst a brilliant even tide

Margaret Howens

Dreams

Find me an angel, an angel of dreams
that I can examine his wares
and chose for myself, a dream of delight
to chase away, all my worldly cares.

Bring me an angel, an angel of song
all light and carefree and gay,
So I can abandon these chores of mine,
and listen, at least for a day.

Bring me an angel, an angel of joy
More precious than diamonds by far.
The joy that is spring,
The joy that is summer.
And light from the evening stars.

Lilian S. Seton

The Monarch!

At the edge of a wood, majestically he stands
The red deer, in splendid array,
Red glossy coat, magnificent antlers spread wide
Ready to keep all intruders at bay.
   Silhouetted against a pale, white moon
He views his domain with pride,
For he is monarch of the forest
Which no other creature may over-ride.
   Head held high, his nostrils quivering
To sense the approaching foe
Large liquid eyes searching for movement
Gives him the signal, "go"!,
   Then down comes the massive head
And with antlers bent low, he soon scares the enemy away,
And when it is over, the red deer is still
Monarch of all he'll survey!

Margaret McHugh

Mystical Magic

Heavenly wonders in the sky.
Forever changing clouds
Revealing shadowed graves.

Whispering woods, skeleton trees
Casting a spell with its witch-like branches.
Ghostly silence is among the air.
Mysteries still yet to be discovered.

Lonely creeks, lost lands
Lie within the hidden doom of lust.
Isolated, solitary
Sky scraping mountains reach the sky.

Contrasting colours—black, green and blue
Give the fragile feel of darkness.

Kerry Elsworthy

God's Garden

As I sit in God's wonderful garden
The world so still and at peace
Then I hope that our sins He will pardon
And the rows and the bickering will cease
The flowers in all of their splendour
And the birds on the wing upon high
To these things Mother Nature will lend a
Helping hand as she passes by
Man does not know what he's doing
When he destroys the fields and the trees
He's taking away all our nature
And God gave us all of these
So stop what you are doing
Before it becomes the end
For while you're playing with fire
You will never have any friends
God grant us some of His wisdom
For all of us to see
And let peace reign once again
Upon this earth for you and me

R. Guy

Firebird

The deep river flowed beneath the weeping bowers,
Reflecting all the tragedy and charred, damp towers.
A lone swan gazed through the choked black reek,
And quietly mourned the moment, but couldn't speak.
He drifted from a waking dream and craned his neck,
While hoses rained their tears on the grey-black wreck.
No mortal understood all his sadness of goodbyes,
Or saw the welling tears in the swan's dark eyes.
Still woeful, he recalled the how his dear love died,
And wailing sirens echoes as the lone swan cried.
Steadily he swam, though his head was bowed in sorrow,
Without his love he couldn't face his loneliness tomorrow.
He waved his mighty wings and softly whispered a goodbye,
As flames consumed the firebird in the blood-red sky.

Diane L. Brown

Pathways

To go forward, keep going
but always wondering what if.
If I turned back what would happen?
If I took the right instead of the left.
To ignore the signs, trust my instincts.
To follow my heart over my head.
To take the risk, dare to be different,
To take the right, when others flock to left.
Pathways are like choices, choices like pathways.
The right ones lead you out of the woods.

Sarah Walsh

The Rugged Cross

Jesus, as we see you hanging
Upon that rugged cross
We will never know the pain
You suffered,
But we know it was for us.

How will we know how much
You suffered,
Will we ever know your pain?
Please help us to draw near you
As we ask for forgiveness again and again.

Jesus, as we kneel before you
And look upon your face,
We ask for your mercy and for
Your wonderful grace.
Help us to draw close to you, each
And every day, so that we can become
More like you. In your name
    Only I pray!

Jacqueline Green

Dawn

I saw the sky this morning
As dawn began to break,
And watched in awe some wonder:
The miracle of light.

Fingers of gold spread o'er the sky
To push the night away.
And vapour-trails like banners
Climbed up into the sky.

Night creatures scurried to their lairs,
And birds awoke to sing,
And people stirred from slumber
To welcome in the light.

As the sun rose higher
And daylight ruled our world,
Still I stood and marvelled
At the miracle of light.

Emma Hunt

Untitled

More precious than silver, more precious than gold
And very much more so, precious to hold
Is a love that goes deep, and tender, and true
And not just a surface of soft rosy hue.

Nothing so passionate as like a young love
But steady and quiet, a feeling above
That look in your eyes, not a word need be said
A sense of well being, content, peace, is read.

Just to sit by your side with a feeling secure
And let the twilight of evening mature
the happiness that does lie on your face
Will stay there for ever with God's good grace.

And when we grow old it will still be there
That love of ours so deep and rare
And then on the day we're taken away
That love is preserved and here to stay.

Joan Vincent

Dipper

A dipper glints along the rainless stream,
skimming moss-dark stones.
Abruptly he alights,
surveys the shadowed Bodnant calm;
then off he whirrs again,
patrolling territorial waters,
performing nonchalant aquatic feats,
dipping, diving, swimming, daring,
running underneath the surface,
defying his specific gravity
in search of lurking water snails.

Clive Craigmile

A Word to the Wise

Listen to your intuition, it's guiding you still.
A word to the wise, hear if you will.

A fool learns nothing from the mistakes of the past.
Walks blindly into the known,
with scathing disregard.

Dumping the debris of his folly on those who care.
Waving away their concern with an arrogant air.

Then the tide turns and the effects hit home,
will you want to hear? I told you so.

Travel life's long road, experiences abound.
Look deep into your soul, the answers are there to be found.
Open your eyes the truth will astound.
If only you will see what is there to be seen.

Listen to your intuition, it's guiding you still.
A word to the wise, hear if you will.

A. Holness

Untitled

The earth's rotation is once in twenty four hours
Its revolution once in three sixty five days
Yet it appears it never minds its earthlings

The great may die, yet the earth never stops, It moves on
The lowly may depart, it continues its movement unhindered.

Even, when a loved one passes on
It will be as if the night will never fall
But it will and even neglect the mourning and turns morning.

Hun!
Many pass unsung by it.
But the earth only doffs its cap for those
Who in their lifetime had
Caused a revolution in its rotation
And a rotation in its revolution.
Wole Joshua

Little Ladies' Linen

The woodland snowdrops hang their heads,
each pure white dainty dangling
atop its stem erect,
all swaying in the warming breath of spring,
for all the world resembling
the faerie's petticoats from far and near
hung on the breeze to dry.

In all your dreams you'd not suspect
that this is faeries washing day
as petals flutter gently in the air.
So pluck them not, nor take a one away
to fade and wither as you reach your home.
'Twere wrong to steal the laundry of a little fairy Fay
or to crush it 'neath your footsteps as you roam.
For when the woods are bathed in silver moonlight
and you are sleeping cosy in your bed,
the faerie's petticoats are prancing, dancing in the night
and swinging on the moonbeams overhead.
Diane Bennett

Winter Time

I often think of winter days
And cold blue nights
With snowflakes, cascading down to Mother Earth
To cover all in white
Then tomorrow brings
Such crisp Air and frozen Trees
That crackle in the Winter breeze
Snow drops popping through the snow
White waxen petals, so delicate to touch
Yet strangely, they penetrate this frozen waste
Such hope they give to all of Us.
Joan Ester Maryan née Cooper

Libra

Today I am tired, sunk in some cold and wintry hibernating self,
Battling with the Autumn garden, a broken fence,
The soft wet leaves, the smell of vegetation intense.
It seems a thousand years of bindweed growth
Has attached its strangling fingers everywhere,
Challenging, mocking me to win this old campaign
Before the first frost, the icy blast
Skeletonises plant forms, each leaf a ghost face from the past.
A half tame blackbird follows my spade's way,
Bolder still a robin seeks grubs in the cut clay.
Yearly I swear no more to tame this patch,
Let it to Nature happily return,
And the wild poppies blow at will over my Avalon.
Here unseen hands broadcast the weed's seed,
Coaxes dark moss to smother the garden path,
Scatters untidily in gusting winds leaf patterns,
Symbols, cryptic messages over the wet grass.
Today I am tired, yet aware among fallen red haws
Are drops of my blood, a premature return to earth, form to spirit,
For this I am glad, nor would change it if I could.
Frances M. Searle

The Land

The land around me is so desolate,
 no-one out here has any emotions;
No feelings towards the men they have killed,
 the families they have destroyed.

The land is covered, carpeted with bodies;
 after this carpet, a lake of crimson blood;
Dead lifeless bodies, all crumpled up, with no-one to care.

The land cries out in piteous pain and anguish,
 she wonders what she has done to
  have this inflicted upon her;
Her life had been one of joy and happiness,
 now she is a lifeless void.

The land, will it ever be the same again,
 with children running free alongside the animals?
The life we had once known, snatched away,
 without a second thought.
Zahra Dhamani

Roseville

No welcome sign upon this door,
No-one lives here any more.
An air of sadness all around,
Windows closed against all sound.
Weeds are growing very past.
In gardens tended in the past.
What happened many years ago,
Is something no-one seems to know.
Why didn't the owner come to dwell,
With boxes and cupboards and cases as well?
Things all wrapped neatly for their protection.
Still in the boxes, quite a collection!
This is a mystery I'd like to see solved,
But folk around here just won't get involved.
Nobody is willing, some questions to ask,
So now I live here it's become my own task.
I'm not being nosey or anything like that,
I take pride in this road and when visitors chat,
They ask me about this house in decay,
I tell them I'll find the answer one day!
D. E. Miller

Fantasy

It is you, is it not that the shadows have caught
With the mood of the night in your eyes?
You are the one that my spirit has sought
Since the dawn settled there in the skies.
It was you in the Cloudland before we were born
Who laughed at me over the moon—
I did not know then that the smile you had worn
Would be greeting me here quite so soon!
But the shadowy souls of the Great Beyond
Are joined by a silken chain,
And, sooner or later that timeless bond
Is continued on Earth again.
E. M. Dickson

The Dead

The rumble of guns as they roar out their hate,
The screaming of shells at an incessant rate;
The shrieks of the wounded, a horrible fate,
All mingle with nightmarish dread.
In the midst of this hell lay the dead.
The dead! What a dignified name for the scraps that remain,
The flesh, torn and mangled, the mess that was brain,
But all this was manhood, the blood spent in vain!
They were blasted to shreds. But the dead cannot fear,
They no longer see; they no longer hear.
The fortunate dead! No more horrors of war,
With its mud, and its filth, and the sickening gore,
With destruction that no man can ever restore;
For the dead all this chaos must cease.
Their dying achievement is Peace.
Henry Caplin

My Way to Freedom

My Car, to you, just a small Gold coloured Volvo,
To me, it's very special,
I keep it clean and shiny too,
My Friend from the Garage keeps it up to Par.
Years gone past, during the War,
My Ambulance was my Pride and Joy
As an A.T.S. Driver.
Years have gone by, and many cars too,
Now there's just the children, my Home, and the Car.
To me she spells Freedom,
I can go here, there, in fact almost everywhere,
even share her with my friends and children too.
God willing, there is not one charge on my licence,
through the years,
I want to keep her till I die,
Because she means Freedom, and the World to me.

Joan Ester Maryan née Cooper

A Poet's Choice

I cannot write, for you are on my mind;
The theme I find but sadly not the word.
Oh 'tis absurd, for surely love inspires
And fires a poet to recite his rhyme
In words sublime, with lyrics to assuage
The inner rage of he who can't possess
The gift of happiness. But I am mute!
Must I refute the joy of love, o'erthrow it,
To be a poet? Rather the reverse!—
Perchance a verse I'll write if we must part,
Not from the heart; a sorry song instead,
Its spirit dead, and you still on my mind.

Elizabeth A. Dewey

A Cry in the Wilderness

I hear a cry in the wilderness,
A cry I have heard before.
Children crying from lack of food,
And babies in mothers' arms!
I hear a voice in the wilderness,
A voice we know and love.
"Fear not my children, I hear your cries!"
"I will not abandon you."
For I am with you all the while,
And beside you I will always be,
Walking down that road of life,
Helping you every step of the way!
Fear not, dear children, I will provide,
And make you strong again
To walk down that road of life,
Until the journey's end.

Florence M. Wells

Untitled

Oh Man of Past and Future Generations
With helping hands for soft and brutal Creation
You hold your pain as if it were a lesson
To show this world that life is but a sphere
We travel and we stumble for a reason
We question and we kill and yet remain
We live, we love, we learn how to be tender
And every time we do a mask we gain
While trees grow and seasons change
Our silence shouts
Our words melt
Our eyes cry
Our bodies die
Only our souls remain.

Look upwards
Eyes are dying
Be outwards
Hearts are sighing
Be gentle
Someone's crying—somewhere

Lynn Allen

King Neptune

Lying low beneath the tumultuous waves,
King Neptune in his palatial caves,
Amongst his courtiers ruling supreme,
Along with his regal, beautiful queen

Bedecked with jewels from sunken wrecks,
His daughters cavort along the decks,
Joyously playing hide and seek,
Daring to venture in the creek.

Oysters gladly giving up their pearls,
With a quick spin and a few twirls,
At the feet of their omnipotent king,
Whilst in the distance ship's bells ring.

Swimming maidens, sparkling diamonds in their hair,
Enticing the unwary to their lair,
Serenading with harps of gold,
Sweet music to the brave and bold.

He is the master of all he surveys,
From vast, mighty oceans and waterways,
Sometimes raging, sometimes benign,
He raises his tridents and roars, "the power is mine."

Irene Greenall

The Visit

I traveled miles to see you, to have a glance
again. But when I reached those prison gates
all I had was pain

When I saw the boys outside, I think it hurt me then,
that inside that cold building,
held a very dear friend.

As I slowly walked, I felt guilty as sin
and tried my hardest to keep my
tears within.

I lost my speech and could not think.
I needed a very strong drink

The hardest part was saying goodbye I really needed to cry
to leave you in that place alone, it didn't feel right
you lusted for home.

One last glance, before I left, just to make sure
you were o.k. and tried to convince myself
I will see you again, some day.

Until then, all you have is memories and dreams,
until reality makes its way through
the smoke scream.

Diane Thomson

Make Time to Pray

A time of prayer with God each day
Is absolutely vital;
How easy otherwise to go astray;
But don't make your prayers a "recital."

Speak to the Lord as you would to a friend,
For that is what He'll always be.
No better, more faithful a friend can one have:
Remember He gave up His life just to save
Sinners like you and like me.

Give Him the thanks, the praise and the glory
That are His in His very own right.
His love for you is unending—
He'll never lose you from His sight.

His arm's always there to uphold you,
To take you through trials thick and thin.
When you do something wrong, quietly tell Him,
He'll always be quick to forgive you
When you repent and confess your sin.

So don't let a day pass without coming in prayer
To our Father in Heaven who is always there.

Peggy C.

My Husband—A Love Poem

He seems to hold the secret of eternal youth
To me, in a world of lies he is the only truth.
He has never claimed his rightful due
For he has an utter contempt for all but an elitist few.
His life was bestrewn with hardships and potential disaster
But he overcame them all and proved himself the master.
There has been much strife in his life,
When confronted with an unjust will he fought and
Won his case and purged a foul disgrace.
When confronted by a bullying yob he fought and
Left him concussed in a pool of blood.
I wish that scum's skull had not mended and that
His life had been ended for he too was a foul disgrace.
I have won my lovely one's love for which I give
Eternal thanks to the Lord my God above.
I was most unhappy and many times ill till I met my darling,
But to me, he is gentle and kind.
He has healed a hidden hurt and the sickness of my mind.
Vivienne Hemmant

Nothing but Love

We'll never be famous it's just not meant to be
We'll always be poor, but rich in love you see.
We came into this world with
But skin on our bones.
And the only thing were rich in, is love love love.
We work and we strive to make ends meet
Chase a rainbow down the street
Hold out a hand to greet a friend
A few kind words at the end.
We watch the years pass us by
Hoping that one day we won't be poor
But we will always be rich in love.
Patricia M. R. Fall

The Dove of Peace

O bird of snow!
If we could pluck the green leaves from your
tender bill,
And watch aglow,
The setting sun behind you when the air is still;

If we could hear
Your sweet song echoing o'er us through the
gathering storm,
What should we fear,
While sheltered by the haven of your wings till
dawn?

O may we know
The peace that passeth all things 'neath your
spreading tree
Until we go
To that calm land where birds and beasts and
men are free.
Anna Seifert

Untitled

They come, baying, baying,
Across the ravaged land
Those rabid dogs of war,
And from foetid lungs and putrid gland
oozes death, and, from out of every pore,
the stench of putrefaction
on the heavy, humid air,
and they ready themselves for action
amidst the corpses rotting there.
And they howl their hatred at a pallid moon
And snarl their rage at an unquiet sea
Scream their anguish then, at a blood-red sun
then whimper in puzzled misery.
For all their world lies barren
the rivers run sluggish, blooded, red.
No longer may they follow the Gods of war
for all that lived lies—dead!
Jean Baines

The Pack of Life

Life deals us yet another card,
When at last you feel you can smile again
Lie back and relax again
Up it pops,
Another bad card from the pack of life.

Dull at least it's not,
Exciting, well not a lot.
More like a bolt of electricity!
More's the pity.

However when one reflects back on life
Isn't it the bad cards
That can sometimes make us laugh
Even though it sounds really daft.
Pauline Conway

Forever Friends

Sarah and I were born,
Only a few short months apart,
So we had a very special bond, that bound us heart to heart.

We had a very special friendship,
That no-one came close to sharing,
We did everything together, and shared everything we had,
Even down to the clothes we were wearing.

I remember the day so clearly,
The day they told me that you'd gone,
I thought they must be joking or playing some cruel trick,
Because I never thought you'd leave me, by myself and all alone.

They said you'd been hit by a car,
It had all happened very quick,
"She didn't suffer" I heard that's a comfort at least,
But the thought of you lying all alone makes me sick.

Not a day has gone by I don't thick of you Sarah,
Still no-one's come close to ever taking your place,
Were still forever friends and that will never change,
Until the day when we meet again, the two of us face to face,

Sleep tight Sarah, never forgotten.
Lisa Marie McKell

Spring

Silently amid the mellow fields of Autumn,
creeps Winter
With the shroud of death gently caressing
each retreating growth.
Escaping back to the bowels of mother
earth, awaiting rebirth, when, the
gentle spirit of Spring will skip with silent feet.
blowing the breath of life and growth
back into every atom, rejuvenating every
cell of being.
Debbie Wander

Parliament

In parliament our peers meet,
Each other they are pleased to greet,
Or so it seems, before they're seated,
But once installed the talk is heated.

They can't agree, they moan and groan,
Wishing they'd all stayed at home,
Three days each week, too much to work,
Though of their duties they won't shirk.

They work from half past nine 'till ten,
As ink runs dry from tired pen,
A holiday is what they need,
As taxpayers to their wishes heed.

So jetting off our peers go,
Our hard earned cash will freely flow,
They'll greet the sun, the sand and sea,
As from old England they quickly flee.
Philippa C. Benacs

Winter

It's Winter again and the trees are all bare
The North wind is blowing he hasn't a care
Each brilliant white snowflake that falls to the ground
Flutters and dances until a safe place is found
The ponds are all frozen and only the sea
Bustles on daily at its destiny to be
From the sheep in the fields with their warm winter coats
To the sea with its harbour's and its ships and its boats
All caught in the grip of winter's cold chill
Until it gets weary and whilst it is still
The Spring and the flowers are beginning to bloom
And Winter is melted with a flowery perfume

J. G. Wileman

Echo

First day. Tears, fears and uncertainty.
Last day. Just fear and uncertainty.
I walked your long passages again today.
My last time as a pupil.
I heard the echo of the thousands before me,
the clammer of the bell, the rush of voices,
and the race begins.
I won't run the race anymore. Silence.
Echo, remain there, you are my only proof.
And the furniture didn't even notice.
It's only a building, it's only a school.
An empty locker, and some old books.
A named carved on the oak tree
and an echo in the corridor.

Jacqueline A. Maguire

Wall of Life

On the artist's wall for all to see
Lies a world of true reality,
Faces filled with pain, the scenes of war,
The anguish pictured here before.
A sombre mood, a sea of rage
Denotes the anger there—portrayed.

Then the settings change to tranquility,
Of peace and perfect harmony . . .
A summer's day, a clear blue sky,
Still waters trickling quietly by,
Cattle grazing lazily in the fields,
A pond with ducks amongst the reeds.
A mother with baby on her knee,
Eyes smiling down so tenderly.
Children running, barefoot, through the sand
Are captured 'neath the artist's hand.

The love . . . the hate . . . the pain . . . the strife
Relived . . . upon the "wall of life".

Christine E. Smith

Selling Yourself to the End, My Dear Friend . . .

I walk down this street, almost once every day,
The pavements are littered, but some people are gay.
There are lights all around, from the sex shops come sound,
Of music in beat, on that dirty street.

Some looking for love, some looking for dope,
Some, looking for someone to give them some hope.
Some, they are rich, just having a fling,
Not knowing the hitch those young people are in.

Behind that stoned look, behind that deep well,
Those people I see, in their private hell.
I feel them you see, and I'm glad it's not me,
But I've sorrow inside, for their loss of pride.

I go through this street, and my heart, like it, beats
Out a prayer every day, "Not to see you again,
Selling yourself, to the end, my dear friend,
Not to see you again, selling yourself to the end, my dear friend."

1983—Denmark

Barbara Byron-Rasmussen

Spiritual Moma

Moma is love she's like a dove
Moma is love
I feel her around me she's cool about me
Moma is love
But I don't mind I love her near
Moma is love
As she was a dear
Moma is love
She cares for me even when she's above
Moma is love
She flies around like a dove
Moma is love
In the spiritual world is she
Moma is love
In the world above with flowers all around her
Moma is love
And the sweet smell of perfume around her
Moma is love
She flies like a dove
Moma is love

Barbara Ann Linney

To My Husband

I love you with all my heart
I also know we will never part
I thank you dearly for all you do
because I cannot fully look after you.

You're there for all my wants and needs
And you fulfil these everythings at such
an ease.

And so my love I've wrote these words,
to say my thanks, which I can do
at such an ease because they've come
straight from my heart.

Yvonne P. Dyson

Paula MacAskill

Paula MacAskill is Scotland's number one,
If you go to her concerts you'll have lots of fun,
She's got a lot of C.D.'s and cassettes,
You'll probably like them all I bet,
She sings so nice on stage under all the lights,
They're all so colourful and so bright,
She was nominated with the best album of the year,
And her husband packs up all the gear,
She has a beautiful and clear voice,
If you want a good night out, she'd have to be first choice,
She's great at playing the keyboards,
And was voted most promising newcomer to country music at
the 1996 Awards.

Ashley Wells

An Escaping Figure

High up on the long hill
Where everything was still,
Her eyes dazzled by the rising sun,
It seemed like the time had finally come.

The sea melted below a primrose horizon.
A breeze drew the hot air out to sea
Rising and piling, whitely as far as the eye could see.
And a distant figure outlined by the golden sun.

Flocks of gulls lazily rose,
As a young, white girl approached the emptying coves,
Her pace slowed,
As she showed,
Her heavy, dark brown hair
Falling in despair.

The sea yawned and went up to her mouth,
Then creamed and died.
Oh, what in God's name was it all about?
But, only her body came back with the incoming tide.

Beverley J. Wright

Cannon Fodder

Like cattle to the slaughter,
Or a fish out of water.
The end result, is just the same.
We can be wounded, killed or maimed.

They called us heroes, I wonder why?
They just sent us here to die.
All night long we sleep in mud,
But in the morning, there's a deafening thud.

Cannon shells falling all around,
Wounded and dying, lay all around.
In my foxhole I start to tremble,
For I see my enemy as they assemble.

Across no man's land, they start to advance,
My gaze fixed on them, as if in a trance.
"Fire, fire!" the command gets louder,
Down come the shells,
Were they just cannon fodder?

Russell David Gill

Mysterious Beauty

   She floats around in gold and silver
Musical bells upon her fingers
Like wind chimes in the breeze
She does just as she pleases,

   I hear her whispering through the trees
And calling over seas
Like an echo from a mountain top
She always puts my soul at ease,

   Her silhouette hides in the shadows
Does she ever go to heaven?
Bewitching siren from a bygone age
Leaves me spellbound with fascination,

   She lives in the past and the present
Like a haze through a maze
Her fragrance still lingers on
Tormenting me from dusk till dawn,

   She radiates with such a glow
A flicker a flame ignites me so
She's shot an arrow through my heart
Mysterious beauty don't depart.

Sandra Boosey

Death

Death, Death, Death,
Why is it that we are afraid of death,
When there is no reason why we should,
because death is the key to eternal life.

Stuart Hart

Hawk's Tally-Ho

Robins sparrows starlings and larks
Mingling around in gardens and parks
Looking for food in the winter snow
Flying high and searching low
Blue tits thrushes and all sorts of finches
A crust of bread the blackbird pinches
From a table of peanuts and stale old crumbs
The big ones frighten the little ones

Some migrate and some stay behind
Hanging around to see what they can find
Will they survive the ice and frost
Die of the cold or perhaps get lost
Seagulls zooming in all directions
Erasing the yellow hammer's tiny reflections

A couple of crows looking bold and proud
Squawking and appearing very loud
Looking for something under a tree
Until a hawk comes along and they all flee
The garden is left empty and bare
While they look for something tasty and rare

Ann Copland

Raindrops

Raindrops begin to fall from the sky,
As peacefully on my bed I lie,
They splash upon the window pane,
And drop to the ground in welcoming rain.

The sound of the rain as I fall asleep,
Comforts me and I curl up in a heap,
But the distant thunder awakens me,
Now the room grows dark, I can hardly see.

The rain falls fiercely down,
And dances on the pavement all around,
People shelter in shop doorways for a time,
Hoping it will soon turn out to be fine.

Puddles are now large after the rain,
Children splash as they run down the lane,
Oh! This wonderful water so refreshing to taste,
Vital and precious we cannot waste.

Joan Jasiek

Age on the Beach

Sea shells on the seashore,
He picked them one by one,
From early dawn to rise of sun,
And yet his task was on.

Full eighty years he seemed to me
As frail he trod the strand;
His voice a childish treble was,
His hand held light the brand.

With fragile net he dared the waves
To snatch from them his ware;
The little things that make life gay
For these poor souls of care.

The shells he'll burn for his white lime
To take his betel chew.
And in the evening by his fire
Perhaps dream dreams anew.

For sea and man appeared to be
In perfect harmony!
The one his long life's secrets kept
The other its awful symphony.

Nalini Elapata

Loneliness

Is hearing a noise when no-one's there,
watching the mirror with its stranger with a fixed stare.
Walking an echoing rainy street,
The samba of footsteps you'll never meet.
You're lured down a corridor searching for a door.
The wrong choice, just a cold gust of
the ocean roar.
The wind carries the curse of a Norse fisherman
The sigh of an Icelandic night-watchman.
You find the last door, you hear the noise,
It's a harlequin party no-one to recognize,
A tide of robotic figurines rocking about.
Empty laughter at the futility of the act
they are playing out.

Frank Hall

Return to the Womb

Being is a state of decay,
It is a state in which you cannot be happy,
So you know what you must do to protect yourself from harm,
Step in the footsteps of our eastern brothers,
And follow the Lama's charms.
To a place and plane where you can be content,
Relax,
Search back,
Separate yourself from this existence of pain,
And return to the womb,
The calmness from whence you came.

Stefan Seddon

Life Sentence

Restricted, constricted, confined, chained,
Caught in a trap, an animal maimed.
Nowhere to run yet nowhere to hide
Except in my heart deep down inside.
Want to escape, want to break free,
yet sentenced to life by society.
Obey the law's one thing but having to conform
to the abnormal norm
'cos in the age of society
difference is so ugly.
Things I want, to do and to say
but I'm losing myself along the way
of Hope in the forest of life
stuck in a hedge, full of knives.
I don't want to go and sell my soul
'cos I'm a diamond among a heap of coals.

Pravin Jeyaraj

Forever

We watched the years go rushing past
We knew our love was made to last.
Not for us '"Til death do part"
Our love was deep within the heart.

We lived our life, the good, the bad,
Mostly happy, rarely sad.
Our love was deep when well or ill
And though you've gone, I love you still.

That love endured from ages past
It will live on forever.
Until we meet again at last,
Our love will leave us never.

I could not wish you back with me,
To suffer all that pain
But love still binds us very close
Until we meet again.

Mary Jones

The Lord's Way

When a new dawn breaks each day
Give thanks to the Lord and pray
Ask the Lord to stay by your side
Pray for His love and you to guide
Along life's paths we all must tread
Some paths will be very hard and long
But our dear Lord will keep us strong
With the Lord beside us all the way
We should not fear each new day
Just walk along in faith and pray
Our dear Lord keeps us safe from harm
Just put your trust in his safe hands
The Lord's guiding light will show our way
Helping us all through another day
Each night send the Lord your love
To thank Him for everything sent from above

Joan Baguley

The Pottery Class

My husband goes to pottery class, every Tuesday morn,
He's going to make a coil pot, the patio to adorn,
He starts to roll the clay, ready for the base,
Then he makes the coils, and puts them into place,
It takes a bit of doing, this shaping by hand,
Now it's nearly finished, it's looking rather grand,
It's time to have a coffee break, and a little chat,
To praise each other's work of art, they talk of this and that,
Then it's back to his creation, he gives his pot a pat,
It's ready now to be fired, he brings it home to view.
Then some bright spark says, is it my eye or is it a bit askew,
He says he'll try the wheel next time, but I'm not so sure,
The last time he tried it, it ended on the floor,
So he'll stick to making coil pots, when all is said and done,
They all will be his masterpiece, every single one.

Dulcie Beatrice Gillman

I Remember Peggy

I remember Peggy
Walking on the banks of the Humber river
Where the lambs play and the mayflower give a
Scent to the air and the rabbits live a
Life of contented ease.

I remember Peggy
Head up in the air and pigtails aflyin'
Struttin' her way to the shop to buy in
Christmas presents 'coz her dad was lying
In a watery grave that year.

I remember Peggy
Her dad was the captain of a battered old "oiler"
Flogging back and forth to Hispaniola
Dodging the U-boats like a game of Tombola
'Til a Stuka got him one night!

I remember Peggy
Stepping down the aisle through a happy gathering
Of friends who'd known her in her years of suffering
Knowing that her daddy would still be watching
As she married the boy next door.

Chris Hudson

Kisses

I had no idea a simple kiss
Could bring delight of such perfect bliss.

My feelings suddenly come alive
And soon I go into overdrive.

Without warning my body's on heat,
Watching you my heart misses a beat.

Your lips meet mine, delicious kisses
Far better than savoury dishes.

I drink deep of that sweet honey dew,
Of the warm magic I know is you

The urgent need far too insistent
For me to be at all resistant.

Your touch so compelling and tender
That I cannot fail to surrender.

My senses stirred, fast flowing in spate
Melt down in your impassioned embrace.

Flaming desire fuses in one
Two who were just enjoying the sun.

Laura Edwards

The Autumn Leaves' Narration

In the autumn sunshine I pass by a big chestnut tree,
While I come back from the college on my way.
The dry, yellow leaves under my feet crack,
And they seem to me to murmur and narrate.

In spring we come out as buds on each branch,
And try our best to grow as fast as we can.
We get water and nutriment from the thick trunk
Which carries them from the roots to our hands.

Summer sees our glory and highlight:
We crown the tree in the lovely green sight
With the help of branches, we open the big shade umbrella,
And often hear people under us burst out into laughter.

Autumn's winds dry us yellow and drop us to the ground,
But nobody under the tree can be found.
Some sunshines roll and crack us,
While cold rains soften and shatter us.

Winter sometimes has us covered with white snow,
And where we are nobody does know.
We've been melting into the food to the roots
To help the chestnut tree next year faster grow.

Wang Zhi-Jun

Which Way

Why do people change direction
From the wrong path to the right
What makes them really feel
That at last, they've seen the light?

When their life is in a turmoil
Backwards forwards to and fro
And their life is so confusing
Knowing not which way to go

They can, then, turn to our Saviour
Knowing he will understand
Asking him for his forgiveness
To receive his helping hand

In their hearts, there's much less sorrow
For their lives now feel complete
Standing in his house of worship
Gladly kneeling at his feet

It's a never ending story
One that should be boldly told
Spreading the word of Jesus Christ
Amongst the lost, the young and old

Dennis N. Davies

Aftermath

Broken now. All gone away, all lost.
I reached out to touch. I failed and fell. The cost
Was all I was and a deeper loneliness than before.
They closed the exit on me and locked the door.

Out here it is cold and white, but darkly alone.
I am guilty of caring and I know not how to atone.
I should not now, after all this, still want to care,
But I do. Even though I know, for me, no one is there.

I stand alone, bathed in the cold light of accusatory dark.
Inside me, I am broken, shattered. It has left its mark.
I want to walk away, let it go, but I keep going back.
It filled my life. Now it is gone. I am held by that lack.

I may find others to help me. Or I may remain like this.
How I regret that burning passion lit by that first kiss.
Now I have none left. I am not a woman anymore.
I am less now. Lesser than I thought I was before.

Who will ever wake this in me, this doused flame?
Do I want it rekindled, knowing that I fell by that game?
If only I could let it go, move on, find the hidden ways.
I search for myself and that time, all my remaining days.

Jackie Lowy

The Mermaid

As I look out of my bedroom window,
At the sea and sand outside,
Everything seems so perfect,
By the calm and beautiful tide.

Then I see the mermaid,
A truly wonderful sight,
Her hair was as gold as the morning sun,
Her eyes were shiny and bright.

She looked so perfect there,
Sitting on the rocks,
I could see her faint smile,
As she looked at the nearby docks.

Then suddenly she dived into the water,
And she was gone in a flash,
she left many pretty ripples,
In the great and mighty splash!

I miss the beautiful mermaid,
I wish I could see her again,
So I looked out of my window,
But all I saw was rain.

Racheal Timbers

Aftermath

The wind's blowing cold
across this bare and barren land
where there should be trees of burnished gold
blackened skeletons stand and hold
a few broken boughs
to the surrendering sky

The bird song has long since died away
and dark carrion in listless circles
wheel and cry
Words like "hope" and "glory" are buried
in an unknown grave
and no-one's left to count the brave
or take the blame or count the cost
since all the meaning has been lost.

Sarah Randall

The Passion Flower

The passion flower can speak to us
Of the time when Christ passed on the cross,
From His life on Earth to the realms of glory,
The following is the flower's story:
His tormentors' hands are seen in the leaves
Tendrils to persecute twine around these;
The five petals and sepals might mean to you
The ten apostles, for two were not true,
For Judas betrayed and Peter denied
And so they left our Brother's side;
The stigmas three could mean to us
The nails which held Him to the cross;
Five stamens show his wounds so red
Which shows the blood for us He shed;
Then in the centre the corona is seen
Like a crown of thorns, this could also mean
It became on His passing His Halo of Glory
This my friends is the flower's story . . .

D. M. Williamson

Human Race

We all come in different shapes and sizes, different colours too,
It really doesn't bother me, nor should it bother you,
You shouldn't judge a person by the colour of their skin,
Instead you should consider what the person's like within,
If people had this attitude, the world could be a better place,
Instead of judging people, by the colour of their face,
In time the problem will get worse, it will escalate,
If parents teach their children how to judge and how to hate,
So put a stop to racism, that's not what children need,
They shouldn't learn to judge another, because of race or creed,
Whether you're tall or thin or small or just a little fatter,
Whether you're yellow, black, white or red it really doesn't matter,
Accept that we're all equal, and put your prejudice aside,
Learn to love your neighbour, because we're all the same inside.

Bettina Shergold

A Past Friend

Many years ago I met a bonnie lass
Her name was Norma Jean
Who came from Aberdeen
She would walk barefoot in the grass
She was such a happy lass
With eyes so blue her long curly hair
The colour of honey with a freckle here and there
On such a lovely face scrubbed clean
She would share her thoughts and give you a
Helping hand, but never her money
She was a canny lass from Aberdeen
I really envied her that day
So carefree in every way
The smile she gave me as I went on my journey far away
I will always remember that bonnie lass
And wonder where she is today
Still walking barefoot in the grass
Along side another mountain pass.

Jean Goliger

Laura

You came into the world one night,
To give us joy and pure delight,
So lovely but so very small,
Two pounds three ounces I recall,
Problems came, and problems went,
You fought them all with great intent,
As weeks passed by you proved us right,
And showed the world you have great fight,
Your smile beams out and brings great cheer,
To all you meet, you are so dear,
Cherished moments are here to stay,
With you dear Laura everyday,
To us you are a pure treasure,
Cradled with love and total pleasure,
Our lives were changed on that first night,
Now the future looks so bright,
To have a grandchild such as you,
Makes us proud and that is true.

Trevor Reeve

The Peacemakers

The darkness crept silently in like an old friend visiting.
Her welcoming smile licked and curled across the
face of compassion, muffling the ears of an uncaring
world. Sleek and smooth as black ice, she sculpted
the frozen heart of power; blinding its eyes, and
filling its mouth with the songs of war.

Below her feather soft blanket of reason, children
were born, their sweet melody of innocence unheard
above the orchestrated lullaby of scorching guns.
Still smiling she twisted and shattered the jungles
of concrete, whilst men sipped champagne beneath her
parasol of cease-fires, ultimatums and neutrality.

Yet in the crushing darkness over all the world,
someone heard. Gentle hands soothed fears and suffering,
caring hearts acknowledged pain; and in a circle lit
by loving, angel voices quietly offered the wonderful
gift of peace. As tender and healing as tears still to fall.

Chris Senior

Bracken Moor

Winter sunlight reflects across the bracken moor.
Filled with a stillness of days long ago
A stone cottage. Who did live there in the past?
  We will never know
Is that someone at the door? A lady smiles at me
  as we walk the bracken moor.
I turn to wave, but there is no one at the door.
It is but a shadow of days gone by.
The winter sunlight playing games of seek and hide
Or did I see a lady on the lonely moor?

Barbara Deutsch

Our News

No period came, the second since trying
  Andy, I'm pregnant, no I'm not lying
A grin on his face, me in his arms
  I'm glad he's mine with all of his charms
Now let's make plans, what first should we buy?
  It's a lot of money, he says with a sigh
Never mind that now, a boy or a girl
  I say with excitement, my head in a whirl
Those sleepless nights, mugs of black coffee
  He says to me now, is he getting stroppy!
See past the pound signs, its not about money
  To see a babe's face can be ever so funny
A button nose, a cheeky grin
  A baby contest to possibly win
These are the good things that outweigh the bad
  Instead of happiness I'm now feeling sad
I'm only joking, he's says with a smile
  Just wait for the sickness that comes in a while
He gives me a kiss, says "I love you" out loud
  Money doesn't matter, I'm happy and proud

Deborah Bearman

The Day We Said Goodbye

Written for my Dean Crowley

I've reached a big decision,
But one that made me cry,
To let us go our separate ways,
And for us both to say "Goodbye."

The pain, I feel, increases,
As everyday goes by,
And from time to time, I know I will
Keep asking myself why?

You see you meant the world to me,
And now we are no more,
And occasionally have wondered how
I survived, alone, before.

Please know this that I could never
Forget the times we shared,
And the thing inside that keeps me going
Is the fact that you had cared.

So without each other we will go on,
Many times I'll break down and cry,
When I sit alone and remember well,
The day we said "Goodbye."

Maria Cracknell

Wilt Thou . . . ?

Wilt thou as by thy fireside warm
Remember those so cold in wind and storm

Wilt thou as in thy bed all soft and deep
Spare thought for those on concrete hard that sleep

Wilt thou with shoes and clothes so grand
Share glove with someone cool of hand

Wilt thou so full and satisfied with wine
Invite some poor and lonely wretch to dine

Wilt thou with mansion, servants, wealth
Greet the poor and drink to their health

Wilt thou with greatest strength and might
Assist the frail and weak in plight

Wilt thou with happy mind, contentment, blessed
Comfort those with heart and soul distressed

Wilt thou the adolescents face
And raise them free from all disgrace

Wilt thou with conscience face thy faults
Be fair with all and share their thoughts

Wilt thou who know there is no end
With others fruitful life ascend

Nicholas Bryans

An Ancient Atmosphere

However long we halt between two opinions
there is a curious kind of truce to find,
a suspension of hostilities
to relax the mind from its automatic
pendular swing between two poles,
ticking out its ever inconclusive time
as senseless as the seagulls unavailing
yelling at each other over the sea,
where you might hear the rustle of leaves
swaying softly in a warm wind,
or mayhap even a harvest-mouse munching
on a sun-warmed ear of wheat;

and the mind deepens within itself
into a calm, a stillness where you find
that being alone is not a loneliness
but a harmony with a strange presence,
a continuity with an indefinable truth,
an immemorial acceptance—
a soft secret surviving Sunday
and the ancient atmosphere in church.

Douglas Dunker

Four Seasons

A tiny bud unfolds;
A newborn babe in the Spring of life
Clenches her fists and yells,
Impatient to get on with living,
Not knowing what the future holds.

The wife and mother strives
For all that is best in the Summer of life.
She guards her family well,
And always puts their welfare first,
In order to better their lives.

The well dressed woman smiles.
Calm and assured in the Autumn of life,
Her children having flown;
She learns to live and love again,
And uses all her latent wiles.

The aged one in her chair,
Sad and alone in the Winter of life,
Ponders her past, and dwells
On all the things that 'might have been',
For life, she found, had not been fair.

Phyllis M. Spooner

Compassion

Dear Friend,
My life, my future lies in this wheelchair,
So please do not stop and stand and stare.
I am here through no fault of my own,
But by God's will, His seed has sown.
Speak to me, I have a voice,
My legs are gone but not by choice.
Remember friend, I have a soul,
I am a being though not whole.
My world is black, I cannot see
Its beauty hovering over me.
But I am normal, I am sane,
So do not treat me as if I have no brain.
Just let me take your gentle hand
and lead me to your wondrous land,
That's filled with warmth and tender love
Given to you from God above.

Jennifer Polledri

Oh! To Be a Mother

It's fun to be a mother
Giving children all your love
We kiss and cuddle and play with them
Then we feel it is time for a hug

As children start to walk
They get into everything
They empty cupboards and ransack the place
And life can get very bored

When the children go to school
They start a brand new life
Mum is up and down to school with them
To learn to read and write

As children grow older
They change in their ways
They think they are clever
And want longer days

The next step they are married
And have children of their own
So parents stop longing after your children
And let them look after their own.

Irene Ring

People on Ships

When I sailed on a ship this was my revelation,
Every soul on that ship whatever
their station,
Whatever their colour, religion or nation,
Still they sail the same ship to the same destination.

Abigail Osborne

Beautiful Is . . .

Beautiful is the sea, a person maybe me,
Beautiful is a dream, a rainbow or sunbeam,
Beautiful is a song, a poem, short or long,
Beautiful is a stream, or emeralds that gleam,
Beautiful is the sky, a blackbird flying high,
Beautiful are the trees, rustling in the breeze,
Beautiful are the deers, beside a river running clear,
Beautiful are the clouds, lightning thunder that's loud,
Beautiful are the mountains, or pigeons around the fountains,
Beautiful is emotion, love and sweet devotion,
Beautiful are the hilltops, fields of corn and wheat crops,
Beautiful is a flower, a second, a minute, an hour,
But ugly is the bomb, the beauty is all gone!

Heiderose Wong

Winter

When Summer's hold is loosened
as Winter entices life away,
it's the sweet earth damp smell that beckons,
life gives way to decay.
Soon the hispid holly will bear berries rubicent and round
and in the rustic backwood roric webs will hang abound.
As the hoarfrost cometh,
sheet stiff frosted fingers stand ready to the chill,
while fearful foxes fossick about the coppiced hill.
A distant crow caw calls with all its pagan power
in splendid celebration of Winter's solstice hour!

Philippa Trump

They Remember

During the cool of the summer night,
The peace of the country is a delight,
Plants are refreshed by overnight dew,
The rising sun kisses the darkness adieu.

Wriggling worms found in the ground,
The blackbird collects, to his nest he's bound,
Where hungry babes with open beaks
Noisily await some food to eat.

Alarm clocks awaken the sleepy heads
Who yawn and totter from their beds.
Reluctant children amble to school,
While girls with boyfriends play the fool.

The arthritic elderly shuffle in pain,
They know their life is on the wane.
The wisdom of their twilight years
Enhances the memories they endear.

They remember the summer nights,
Being with loved ones in the moonlight,
They remember red poppies in fields,
The peace of mind when Church bells pealed.

Janet Boulton

The Wind in the Willows

The wind in willows, was swaying this way and that,
On the banks the grasses,
Were bowing their heads, and whistling in the wind,
To, and fro they would go,
But no one notice or even heard, the
Wind which was whistling in the grass stems,
The wind in the willows,
Was very strong and cold,
But on a windy day,
You could hear children and laughter and see,
Kites flying in the sky,
Up, up, and away they would go.
As the wind in the willows, was very strong,
Like the grass, on the banks,
Bowing their heads,
The kites, in the sky,
Pulling on their strings and bow ties,
But not as free as the wind in the willows.

June Bloomfield

My Darling My Dear

On my way home from work one night, wondering what was
in store for me, and there she was on the door step.
My darling my dear, waiting for me, after a cuppa,
and did my usual, a shower and shave and all that
had my tea, then watched T.V. And I enjoyed all that,
after a while, I looked across the room, and there
she was, my darling my dear, on her favourite
chair, I stroked her hair, and gave her a hug
and everything seemed to be alright, later that night
my darling my dear, went out, not for long, then
she was back, soaking wet, so I dried her off
that was alright, then we both sat in front of the fire,
for the rest of the night.
   You know who I am talking about don't you.
  No, not the wife, the cat
   Colin Baker

Song of the Sprites Child of May

"May child of tears bright, our song will take plight away;
rainbows flitter bright, like butterflies flight,today;
we fashion buds white, with hare bells frail slight, nosegay;
catch dew crystallite, make necklace? We might . . . and—yea!
a gift from us sprites, for you, smiling bright, we say;
and daisy crown light, with may blossoms white, rose spray;
clouds cover sunlight, fairies flee from sight, dismay!
dissolved in mist white, and for sun-kissed light, they pray;
but on the grass bright, gold daisies chain slight, there lay;
now child with face light, our song was so right, sweet May."
   Teresa J. Smith

Water for Life

As children in the countryside, we knew water should not be wasted.
It was drawn up from a well. Hard work, but how good it tasted.
When rain fell on the roof into a water butt it would drain.
How soft it made our hair in the days before acid rain.

We learned how to conserve it, wait for the next big shower.
And we learned how to share it with every plant and flower.
Now we are using more and more, take it so much for granted
We have water on tap and use it whenever we want it.

Cracks in our reservoirs let this precious liquid drain.
With changes in our climate we are not getting so much rain.
Every day we use washing machines, wash the car, water the lawn
Use water indiscriminately, on us it does not dawn

That with pollution in the air, pollution in the sea,
This gift of abundant water could some day cease to be.
If we are not careful, we are heading for strife.
For when we are wasting water, we are wasting life.
   Elizabeth Wren

Prayers at Midnight

I miss you, how I miss you, pure words just can't convey,
The longing and the sheer despair I feel from day to day,
When you were taken from me I couldn't quite believe,
How deep the chasm of emptiness which nothing could relieve.

The world had stopped a turning, no day transcended night,
The bees forsook the honey, the flowers put to plight,
Whate'er befell the dawn chorus, the birds forgot to sing,
The church bells calling the faithful alas they didn't ring.

No twinkling stars to study along the milky way,
No moon to brighten up the night for lovers at their play,
The tides had turned to static, there was no ebb and flow,
Cupid misplaced his arrow, wherever did it go.

The roses wept without the dew to replenish them each morn,
No frisking of the newborn lambs as time approached the dawn,
The sun withdrew her fellowship, no warmth in which to play,
No butterflies of splendour pirouetted in display.

I miss you, how I miss you, pure words just can't convey,
The sadness that is manifest within my heart each day,
When time approacheth midnight I lay my head to rest,
Praying that in dreams you'll come to ease me sore oppressed.
   Anne Williamson

Madame Anxious

Life is too short for chess, was it Byron or is it me?
Too little time to spend on idle folly,
Long cold are our bones, dark are our graves,
Why do we worry and weep to become Convention's slaves?

Life is a cavern full of chambers and passages,
The directions we take are the narrow linkages,
If we stumble why cry and moan?
Was it not our choice to be shown?

The frost at midnight grows so clear,
Oh beautiful and uniform rust!
The wind blows from year to year,
But in whom do they place their trust?

Be skittish with youth, oh joyous existence,
Listen to Lawrence and smile,
Hare, dweller of the mountains, we're his abhorrence,
For his freedom they would hunt a mile.

Too many eyes are fixed upon the dial,
Too many ears listen avidly to the bell,
Father Time recoils, to him we are vile!
Why cannot we live, and live it well?
   Alethea Andrews

Be Thankful for Music

The sculptor shapes and the painter paints,
Artists in their own right, so then they are saints.
And the maker of music, be it secular or sacred,
Brings pleasure to everyone, hath he no hatred.

To have a life without music is to be in solitude,
A life complete of misery, no family, friends nor food.
Of wisdom and sincerity in the young and in the aged,
Is music life's epitome, its light is never faded.

Golden burns the eternal flame,
In our hearts and minds it will remain.
The truest word to the soul uplifts,
To hear such music is God's ever gift.

The troubles the world has seen year after year,
The wars and strifes we have witnessed with tears.
Let music be our unity, to the world bring it peace,
It's the universal language, that will our chains release.

Jubilant are we of the pleasure it lends,
With instruments and voices, let us sing to the end.
Thankful are we to child, father and mother,
With music we will celebrate the love for one another.
   Christopher Wilson

Henry My Bassett

I often think of my beautiful bassett hound
He was large warm cuddly and a rascal I'll be bound
When left on his own he slept in fact a little Angel
On my return home what mischief he would cause I could not tell
He loved the phone to ring and thought that's my cue
Mums engaged so I'll grab anything does not matter whether
it's old or new
Once he stole a large piece of raw beef which was ready for
the oven
He bolted outside as the door was left open
On one occasion he stole a string of pork sausages
Dragged them upstairs to devour with me to clear up the mess
Everyone knew Henry and he loved to be admired
After going for his walk he would come home tired
At last some peace but not until he was sprawled on my lap
He loved to cuddle up close and tight for his evening nap
Sometimes during the day I could hypnotize him to sleep
I would say, Henry, you are tired, stroke
him, and suddenly not a peep
We all miss that lovable bounder and
have many funny fond memories
of him I can tell my grandchildren
endless, laughable stories
   Dorothy Stevens

It Doesn't Cost a Fortune

The trouble with the world today
It's full of greed and strife
Too many people have forgot
Why Jesus gave His life

Upon the cross at Calvary
He suffered for our sin
So that goodness and mercy would survive
In this world that we live in.

There's no need to be a martyr
Like Jesus on that day
Just be kind and helpful
To make the world more gay

It doesn't cost a fortune
To be charitable and kind
A thoughtful word of comfort
Can give others peace of mind

You don't even have to go to church
To pray or sing out loud
Just do a good deed every day
That will make the Good Lord proud
Douglas Parley

Marathon Man

A burst of excitement fills the air.
And the joy that we feel,
Is quite beyond compare.

As you cross the winning post.
We will raise a glass,
And drink a toast.

You have struggled so hard
To reach this goal,
You have put in your very heart and soul.

As you jog the streets each day,
With sheer determination,
That cannot be taken away.

You crossed that bridge,
You made that mile,
And you did it in your own inimitable style.

Congratulations, and well done
Sit back, relax.
Until the next marathon
You run.
Gillian Grainger

Comrades in Arms

Walking the fields of France one hot summer's day
I came across a frail old man along the way
he was on his knees with pain etched upon his face
let it all end, he whispered as he stared into space

He spoke in a strange and eerie way
can't forget the slaughter, he sobbed thousands every day
the noise, the mud, the stink and death always so near
I agreed, and the men and boys grovelling with fear

He glared at me as if I were directly to blame
yes I'm German, I said, in Russia it was the same
with his head in his hands he rocked to and fro
I was in a dilemma, should I stay or do I go

I stayed as he fought the demons within his mind
to be tormented, for years, it's an insanity of a kind
but I could understand his personal plight
the world wars were over, his returned every night

A year to the day he was lowered into his grave
an old soldier, a dear friend, so proud yet so brave
his demons are finally gone, they had lasted for eighty years
alas, I still have mine, those dreadful nightly fears.
R. J. Baird

Snowflakes

Snowflakes are falling gently from the sky,
as I look up to see one falls gently in my eye.
O' God what a beautiful white winter's day,
Snowflakes are falling from the sky I wonder why,
Maybe it's to remind me that when I die I will
float gently to Heaven like a snowflake falling
from the sky.
Edward Travers

Editor's Choice

The best is yet to come,
Oh yes, the best is yet to be.
Ink flowing like a fountain
Form words into poetry
Creating pictures—maybe a song—
Now what could go wrong?
A misspelt word—a misplaced comma or two—
And none of this would make sense to you.
My grammar is sad, it's always been poor
And punctuation never entered my mental door.
The dunce's corner was my playground
There intelligence never came around.
Gray was the world I once knew,
Bright horizons were never in view.
Many are the stars which shine above,
Sweet is the healing hand of God's love.
Flowing ink—its running stream—
Brought fulfillment of a childhood dream
That I would one day rejoice
When a poem of mine became editor's choice.
Audrey Luckhurst

Forgive My Intrusion

Forgive my intrusion, I thought I was invited!
I thought that my arrival
Would have found you quite delighted,
But all I find are teardrops upon a saddened face;
I feel that I am not welcome,
To share your time, your space.
You know I can't control it, what will be, will be.
Please forgive my intrusion,
But you invited me.

Forgive my intrusion, do not treat me with contempt,
I would not have come, could not have come,
If no invitation had been sent.
But sent it was, and now I'm here, in mind, in body, in soul
Now the choice is yours, you are in command,
You are in control!
My mother? Or my murderer? You hold my destiny!
Please forgive my intrusion,
But You Invited Me!!
R. S. Strong

Remember Me

I have children, four in all, three daughters and a son,
But time has flown, and they have grown,
And left me, one by one.
I hardly see them anymore, they seldom write or ring,
And I'm just left, to ask myself,
How could they do this thing?
I recall, when they were small, how close we used to be,
When I meant everything to them
As they still do to me.
We all must go and live our lives, but when it's time to part,
Don't make the break a final one,
And leave a broken heart.
Mum's not just there for when you're small,
Her love goes on and on,
Don't shut her out of your new life
Because her job is done.
Remember that her love and care,
Helped make you who you are,
Don't let the way back home be lost,
It's never very far.
Florence Baldwin

Quiet Walks

I am the bluebell,
  My fresh-blown blossoms are thine,
    For you to behold,
      When awakened spring is mine,

Set fair by the wayside,
  Or to the walks of a wild wood green,
    My trailing mazarine carpet,
      Gathers sunbeams to gleam.

Let me abide here awhile,
  Let hand not idly deface,
    All that which by right,
      Is mine own state of grace,

Lightly tread where your footsteps
  Would lead you to stray,
    That others may pause,
      To share my smile the day,

For my ephemeral mantle,
  Is fleeting sent to ever cast,
    Sweet recollections,
      To memorably last!

   Jacqueline A. Andrews

Faith

A lonely shadow with nowhere to go
But to follow the wind and the rain and the snow
Until you find one of music and intentions true
Who'll curl at your side and gather against you
And will stay there forever, regardless of state
Or the blows that are dealt by the hands of fate
To enter one mind and imagine a nest
Where pain cannot visit nor invite for unrest
Who needs you as I do, to create and inspire
To feed off your beauty and long for desire
And ever be faithful in thought and in deed
Will walk with you always your shadow is freed
Then the oceans may turn and the clouds may part
For love will have found you with faith in your heart

   David Newton

The Lonely Echoes

There, whispering through the full leaved trees
Soft stirred by summers gentle sigh,
Hear the lonely echoes come
Through time's dim mists, the faintest cry,
Like whispered words by lovers said
Or music that to tears can move
And footsteps soft, to meetings dear;
All through the day and empty night
The lonely echoes still I hear.

   Robert Holding

The Sufferings

Lost to a future the victims fall,
Taking the talented of them all.
AIDS in abundance and cancer too,
Ecoli, arthritis, heart failure and flu.
All cause slow suffering, while death lures,
Although we've tried, there are still no cures.
The pain's so bad some ask to die,
A decision of their's, should we ask why?
So many taking drugs for a happier life,
Characteristic changes, life's cut by a knife.
For all that can be cured in this world,
Still the sufferings go on.

Ecstasy, heroin, aspirins and coke,
Drugs taken for pleasure, just a big joke.
Smoking and drinking, all seem such fun,
Spending pounds and pounds, a nice tidy sum.
Powerful poisons in the body's system,
Because of the nation's refusal to listen.
For all that can be cured in this world,
Still the sufferings go on.

   Angela Henderson

The Flower

Little wild flower growing all alone
How did you get there beneath the stone?
Shall I pick you for a moment's pleasure
To hold in my hand like some small treasure?
A gift of nature you have grown
From a seed the wayward wind has blown.
Oh no! I could not be so cruel
As to rob this stone of such a jewel.
One splash of colour on the drab grey ground
A drop of beauty I have found.
Shy little flower so velvety blue
I am glad to have spent this moment with you.

   G. M. Shiels

The Ghost of Jan Palach

Jan Palach, your ghost lives today,
Though the flames, took your flesh away.
But your fire still burns, everywhere.
It blazed again, in Tiananmen Square.

It smoulders, in the oppressive hell,
Of every tyrant's torture cell.
Jan Palach, your ghost cannot die,
For from your ashes, the bird will fly!

   Michael Walsh

All Over by Christmas?

Eagerly, he'd volunteered
Then marched away—well wishers cheered.
He's barely trained to maim and kill
The faceless troops of Kaiser Bill,
Then he's sent out there.

Flares, shells, shouting, bullets rain.
Ear shattering chaos, sudden pain.
Falls—still now—struggling to explain
Paralysis, the spreading stain.
Now . . . all's quiet out there.

Sharp gasps, gulps air, heart races, slows.
Calm now, reflecting how life goes.
As life's flame flickers fitfully
Thoughts turn to this year's christmas tree,
And it's cold out there.

At home, all festive. Celebrations.
Christmas coming—decorations.
Can they know? Will they remember
'John died, twenty-fourth December'?
As life ends . . . out there.

   Gary Bingley

Bring Back the Smiles

The time has come for everyone to stop
and think out loud, and try
and make the powers that be take notice of the crowd,
a crowd of unemployed, a crowd who have no
home, a crowd of down and outs, who have to live alone.
No one deserves to live this way, barely existing from
day to day, society must take all the blame,
for all these people, being put to shame.
The shame of living on the street, of having to beg
from people they'd meet.
Imagine, not even having a bed on which to rest their weary head.
People need more jobs to do, and live a life, like me and you.
They need a home in which to live
and prove they have something to give,
like showing their neighbours how to care,
and all things they have they want to share.
People should not have to beg or steal in order to get a decent meal
give them back their dignity, and let's all live in harmony.
Teach children how to show respect,
and everything they'd do would be correct.
Now, wouldn't that just bring back the smiles, for miles,
and miles, and miles, and miles.

   Annie Pollington

The Call

Ah, tempter, dost thou speak to me
In sweetest accents of a friend
Or of a dear one, all unknowingly
Pleading with voice of love to dissuade
 me from that vision pure?

Such reason thou dost give in words most clear
That would persuade me from God's way:
My loved ones—thou dost speak through them,
Enjoining me to stay tethered to home and
 earthly success.

Nay, not so—get thee behind me, Satan—
I will not fall and worship thee.
I follow Christ, my Lord and King
Whose call has come with vision clear,
To which, with eagerness and joy of youth,
 I rise to follow.

Mildred Florencia Long

Keep Going

You must keep going! No, no why?
You must keep going, I'll tell you why:
The people who love you, family and friends,
The flowers the trees, the warming sun.
The birds that sings, the baby who cries
The child who laughs, the child who dies.
You must live for her, you must sing for her.
You loved her, she loved you.
Never let go whatever you do.
I'll try to keep going, it's not easy you see.
Where there's only two there should be three.

Audrey Savage

A Child's Encounter

I heard Your footsteps by me
Soft hair blew in the wind
A rustle in the twigs
Tresses brushing ear and skin
Pale mantle enfolding me within
How could I resist? I knew I could not win—
When I was a child.

Aspen leaf all shaken
Joy and exultation!
Trembling at the Presence
A voice spoke deep within—
How can you evade Me
Child of every whim? Do you know I made thee
Died to ransom you from sin?

I rose again to set thee free
To share with Me eternity
In Love's triumphant ecstasy!

Jeannie Hay

Tory Poll Tax

The tax payers know it's not fair
Nearly all MPs end up millionaires
The last PM let down and ditch
Wrote a book that made her rich
We old UNS would like to see
the MP's live on money like the OAP
I dare say one MP would try?
All the bills and food to buy?
Give up your lifestyle for just a year
live in a council flat without a beer
Don't forget the poll-tax did fail
and put a few innocent people in jail
OAP's a quality of life
Just ask a few of Britain's housewives
Saying it could be made better
Honest truth as I write right this letter,
They don't get much that is free
Licence in Australia on TV you see
British people will not let it rest
All the sell off (will save NHS)

T. Blaney

Blood from a Stone

I found a stone bleeding on the street,
It was someone I knew very well indeed,

A brother I could remember, solid as a rock
To life's bitter streak, was parked on the pavement
Asking for help, but nobody stopped except for me,

As I picked it up this stone had cracked, being thrown
In misery, telling he'd been disowned finding
Life tough to beat.

Since a friend explaining the end took his girl from
Right under his feet,

I didn't believe you could get blood from a stone,
But he'd been cut internally.

Oh I found a stone washed up and beached,
He was smouldering like an ember after the fire,
All burnt out and weak,

A brother I could remember, as hard as nails
Cool as could be, who I thought would never
Crumble under the heat.

Paul Maton

Night Time

As the day draws to a close and all about is still
the silence being broken by a lonely midnight owl
a silent breeze caresses me and helps to wash away
the rigours and the trials of a long and arduous day

The day was filled with chaos and rushing to and fro
the sights and sounds assail us no matter where we go
it starts to rain, but lightly, a soft and distant sound
to ease away the bustle of the noisy trading town

Now darkness draws in closer, the day is at an end
sleep finally overcomes us with its gentle, loving hand
and although my body is at rest, my mind, it is at play
recalling and reviving, the events that shaped the day

The incidents that happened are delicately changed
and altered advantageously, until our dreams are made
in our fairy dreamland, we're the best that we can be
the strongest and the quickest in our flights of fantasy

But dreams can turn to nightmares, as sometimes is the way
and frighten the unwary, the courageous and the brave
awakened by such nightmares, where is it that I'm turned
my fears are strangely banished by your soft and gentle hand

Dave Skeaping

Sweet Sixteen

There goes our song, it's a haunting refrain,
Down through the years it echoes again,
My eyes fill with tears as I recall the pain,
We sang it in springtime, long, long ago,
When I was sixteen, and you were my beau.

The melody sweet reminds me of the time,
When you knelt at my feet and my world was sublime
My joy was complete, I was bathed in a glow,
The universe was mine, for you were my beau.

We sat beneath the shade of an old apple tree,
I in love with you, as you said you were with me,
I was held in your arms, bewitched by your charms,
Blind to all alarms, for I loved you so.

Then everything changed and you said you must go,
Like a ship in a storm I was tossed to and fro,
After you'd gone I was left all alone,
The tears fell like rain, and my heart turned to stone.

Years have gone by but the hurts still remain,
I try not to cry when I hear our refrain,
Could I forget you—the answer is "no",
On you my heart was set long, long ago.

Mary G. Kane

Food for Thought

I'm a dinner lady and I'm sure you'll agree,
How much my green overall and hat suit me.
I take pride in my cooking, the veggies I peel
To serve those dear children a gourmet meal
And when they all rush through the canteen door
I know I'll serve something that they will adore.
I've learnt how to duck when the bread rolls are thrown
And I don't even bother when they start to moan
About the lumps in the gravy . . .
A little disaster!
The darlings just flick it and it all becomes plastered
On the walls and the ceiling, but I don't really worry
For tomorrow I'll cook a delicious hot curry
I'll just scrape it all off, place it back in the pan.
Well, I was told to make cutbacks
Wherever I can.

Josephine Burnett

Secret Love

Every once in a while, I see your smile,
The rest of the time I live a lie.
Our secret love that no one knows.
When I see you and we are alone
there are a million things I want to say on my own.
We are so near but sometimes I feel so far.
I don't know what you think about
I don't know what you really are.
How can I believe everything you say?
How do I know you soon will not go away?
I am not what you think I am, very strong.
I am scared of things, they might go wrong.
I don't want my hopes really high
because if this time they drop
I will not be able to get over it, I'll just die.
Our secret love that no one knows.
It does not matter nothing lasts forever
We will end one day, don't you say never.

Satveer Sandhu

Lonely but Never Alone

We can have physical contact with people
　around us, but we are still lonely.
What we need is a meaningful relationship, then
　lonely we will never be.
We need to have a close relationship with God
　our Heavenly Father.
He has a cure for everything, he is our
　greatest Healer.

　To be alone with God is Heaven sent,
　God's present to us is his presence.

People are lonely because they turn away from
　God and do their own thing,
Instead of having a relationship with God and
　walking next to Him.
You will never walk alone when you walk with
　God, you are in the best company,
Even though you cannot see or feel Him next to you
　at your side He will always be.

Linda Roberts

Paul

Love is not a fiery star hitting out of the blue
No, love is fate that sneaks then strikes true
Fireworks did not crackle and bang in the sky
But they would not last fade and die
Things are very different for now you warm my heart
And life is very golden now since you've been a part

Love is truly beautiful and like you so very rare
To find someone this amazing with a soul to share
I hold your hand. Never want to lose its feel
For this feeling named love feels fantastically unreal
I thank God or chance or whomever it maybe
For bringing my soul mate so completely to me

Gill Williams

To My Daughter

My daughter's born, a great delight,
　To love and hold so very tight,
To watch her grow and feel so proud,
　Protect forever is what I vowed.
She loved and laughed and sometimes cried
　I understood and how I tried
To be a good mum and her friend,
　Our closeness, it would never end.
But now my days are long and grey
　She's made her life and moved away,
Not in hours and not in miles
　But in her hugs and lovely smiles.
My memories will always be
　The love she used to have for me,
The happy days, a friendship shared.
　I hope and pray you really cared.
No one can take from me those years
　I should be grateful, not shed tears.

Nadine Cope

At the Front

What hope have we as mortal men
To rouse a spirit long since spent
Uniforms that boasted braid of gold
Now torn and streaked with blood and soil
In our self-made grave we lie
Waiting for nothing but to die
The sky so black, like the death
Draws from the earth its final breath
Sounds of war call us free
A challenge to meet our destiny
Driven blind by the bugler's air
Our time is now, it waits out there

I. S. Caddie

. . . Of Decision

And those years cannot fly back
Those months never can resurrect from the grave again
Those valuable days remain interred
And those records remain closed,
Closed on the pages of unturned leaves of opportunities
But the memories fly across vividly of those golden moments
And of the unsung hours sunk over the years.
Now that to the grave I come soonest,
Those seconds down the drain never can come back useful again
Neither those well carved out dreams realized.
Then as I close my eyes in death
After spending thousands of hours on earth and never did utilise any
It dawned on me that time is one out of many
Of the greatest gifts God has given man
Yet the most perishable and unused
And many a one shall stand guilty before His throne
Come the day of Decision

Wole Joshua

The Passing

Let this be my last goodbye,
A passing smile 'twixt you and I,
The memories of time's gone by.
Let this be our last farewell,
You loved me and I alone could tell,
Heaven's precious moments, nought 'would'st I sell.

Come tis' but a moment's passing,
May I not hear you once more laughing,
The time we had was just a chancing.
Let me now this Earth forsake,
Er'e the end will not long take
As I succumb to death's quiet lake.

Do not be sad at my departing,
I give up the ghost for new life starting.
Dos't not thou heed thy breaking heart,
For tis' mine that yearns and feels to break,
I go for thine and mine own's sake . . .

Christina M. Clarke

I Gaze upon These Castle Walls

They came from days of tyranny
Of Norman lord and Saxon serf
When furrows marked man's destiny
And humble peasants tilled the earth

The nobles feasted in the halls
Reduced to ruins by today
I gaze upon these castle walls
They stand majestic in decay

From morning mist when daylight dawns
To brightness when the sun is high
Then casting shadows on the lawns
When sunset fills the western sky

I wish I'd seen the things they've seen
The ancient battle on a hill
Surrounding town when fields of green
Before the urban overspill

Mark Sampson

On Reflection

She sits apart and contemplates
Of life, lost loves and of her mistakes;
Good intentions and a selfish mind,
Gave her a foolish heart and made her blind

She has it all, yet it's not enough,
She's always searching for the better stuff
With a selfish mind and a foolish heart,
She fights to tear her life apart

And when she's done and stained with blood,
Surrounded by casualties face down in the mud,
The pain's still with her, it's just the same
And she only has herself to blame

But she is a fighter, not a quitter,
And she'll fight until the day it hits her,
That love's the only cause that's worth the fight;
And then she'll no longer be alone in her plight

Annabelle Charbit

To My Darling Husband

I wake up each morning with you by my side,
And I reach out to touch you with pride.
You move sleeplessly to my touch and look my way,
And the look you give me moves me and tells me much
more than words can say.
They tell me what I'm thinking that our love is true.
That you love me, just as much as I love you!
It's a special day for us today once more,
It's just as special as this time last year and all the years before.
Because today's our Wedding Anniversary number twenty-nine,
And because today I'm still yours and you're still mine,
The years have made our love stronger than anything I know,
I love you just as much and more as I did when we became
one all those years ago.
So Happy Anniversary darling, I'm so glad you're mine.
For being the most loving husband and making my life so divine.

Vera Margaret Collins

Old Age

Oh, woe is me, who once was young and bright,
caring for others, greeting every day
with rapture! Now I dread the morning light
That once I viewed with hope as strength and stay
Upholding me; now hope gives way to dread,
So much to miss, so much for ever lost,
So many once familiar, sick or dead,
The morning sun replaced by fog and frost;
Yet a warm glow remains, a heartfelt glow
as in my very weakness, I can see
Heaven draw nearer, as fades life below,
Heaven grows brighter, "Nearer my God to Thee"

Mary Stanley-Smith

Anne

Many years we have spent together
  If only it could last forever
Like the endless waves that sweep
  Towards the shore.
Our love to each has lasted,
The summers have since passed by
Flowers bloom, then fade and die,
The hours, the days, and the years,
We do not remember too well,
But our love to each has lasted.
Anne, my wife, my sweetheart, my love
I love you, God only knows from above.
Your smile, your kindness have kept me near,
Our love to each has lasted,
Darling put aside all the fear
And think of happiness in future years.

E. F. Smith

The Universe

The moon so bright and stars that shine
As into space my eyes did climb
In wonder as to things beyond
If I could wave my magic wand
To satisfy a curious appetite so strong
And enter into Heaven and Earth's such secret throng

The Architect with Company sublime
All moulding, shaping, guiding planets throughout time
Great wisdom so deliriously imparted
To multitudes who labour since life started

The experiment, achievement so precise
All fashioned by so many men and mice
Who knows the true extremity and purpose
Of this grand universe about us

Nicholas Bryans

Peace

What is Peace,
Peace is when a crying baby goes at last to sleep.
When a Calf is born to a bellowing cow,
When a man storms out to go to the pub,
After a family row.
Peace is the calm one finds in a Park
or a garden, the scent of flowers after dark.
Peace is the joy at the end of a war
When lights go on, and there's food in a store;
A missing piece from a jigsaw puzzle
or the warmth of a dog, when it gives you a nuzzle.
Peace is the calm at the end of the day
When toils of life are put away,
To lay one's head on a soft clean bed
And dream of the place where loved ones meet.
Sure the greatest peace for man was given
by the Lord himself of a place in Heaven
a Peace for the world in our prayers are asked
each night as we fall asleep at last.

Margaret Vinall-Burnett

The Forgotten Mothers

It wasn't my fault I had to give you away
as soon as you had seen the break of day.
They call it circumstances,
but that was an excuse
because problems built up
with this tiny sprite,
so they came to collect him
one night.
This tiny morsel, that grown inside,
was disappearing from my side.
It wasn't my fault I had to part
with a little bit of my body, and my heart.
Everyone was worried about this baby
and what his life would be,
but no one thought about me.

Iris Tennent

The Beast Within

I'd love to ride across the moors
Or sail the oceans through the storms
To fly above an angry sky
And watch the passing world go by

What is this beast within my soul
That makes me want to be so bold
To feel the wind whip through my hair
And make me feel without a care

The beast it lives through night and day
It does not work it does not play
It rages deep within my being
Never looking, only seeing

And when the storms and seas are calm
Then still the beast it rages on
What turn in life made me this way?
I do not know, I cannot say

For once I liked such simple things
Like summers past and mountain springs
But now I feel to live again, I must succumb and feel the pain
I must allow the pain to flow, for only then, the beast will go

Suzanne P. Lynch

Where Peace Abides

Among the hills in nature's realms
As I oft in wonder gaze,
It seems a heavenly peace abides
Where sheep and cattle graze.

As the dawn breaks through and the birds awake
To trill their songs on high,
The sunlight flickers through the trees
And the clouds float softly by.

The little lambs begin to play
Neath their mother's caring eyes
And with bleating chorus join the birds
In their praises to the skies.

Far away from the pace of life
Where men battle to survive,
The oak stands firm and rocklike
In beauty there to thrive.

Yes! Here among the pastures green
As on gently flowing tides,
Serenity itself is born
And Heavenly Peace abides.

John Osborne

The Eclipse of Summer

And thus the winter shall take its bow
And fire an arrow into all our woe
Twist the blade of its tempered sword
Into the heart of summer and its worshipping hordes

The invasion is imminent taking a sabbatical path
Carrying the cold independence of its fury and wrath
Ambushing the people enrolled in its class
While the petrified trees all surrender en masse

The council of winter is woven and spun
Answerable only to nature and the migrating sun
The law of survival is law of belief
Permission is granted to suppress the last leaf

Plans have fermented the vows are all sealed
The assassin strikes has the victim kneels
Its dark manic shadows shall multiply and thieve
And steal the land as the summer bleeds

Thus winter will claim its political seat
Has heir to the moment the victory is sweet
Celebrations are waiting as the territories extend
The eclipse of summer is the final revenge

David Bridgewater

That Pub Down Memory Lane

Cloth capped workmen playing dominoes,
Their silver tankards brimming with ale,
Burning woodbines and piped tobacco,
Laughing jokingly at a dirty tale.

A brief relaxation from their working toil,
A welcome interlude from their rigorous life,
For the men who farm the sea or soil,
To earn a wage to butter their knife.

Still they play their 'Knock Knock' game,
Still they laugh and tell dirty jokes,
But now they all seem rather tame,
Cloth capped heroes, now elderly folks.

Around them suited businessmen pace,
Drinking wine from a sparkling glass,
Modern day executives with fairer face,
A different generation, A different class.

I sit within these walls once again,
And look around, but I don't know,
Is this that pub down Memory Lane?
No, that disappeared a long time ago.

Kevin Langwith

Little One

Did I do right, my precious little one,
To bring you into this world?
Conceived in love,
And nurtured in my womb these many months,
So tiny in my arms you lie,
Trusting in my love.

What will life offer you in years to come?
What will it bring you, this world?
How can we know?

My heart aches with love, my precious little one,
My tears flow
As you, curled in my arms slumber on.

How shall I guide you, now that you're here?
What shall I tell you, to quiet your fear?
When should I stand back, and when be so near,
To be there when you need me?

Did I do wrong my precious little one
To bring you into this world?
I believed in love!
Now you are that love.

Isabel Abbott

The Secrets of the Deep

The sea is so magnificent
When angry, her waves do tower
She dominates everything around her
With all her strength and power

Crashing into the craggy rocks
Relentlessly she does pound
But they are mighty in their right
And defiantly stand their ground

Next she's serene, so peaceful
Breathtaking views can be seen all around
Gentle waves keep giving a sigh
Tiny ripples are the only sound

People delve into her waters
New places they want to explore
Give her respect that she deserves
She'll see you safely to shore

But men that have tried to conquer her
Met a watery grave in the deep
For in the bowels of the seabed
Some secrets she wants to keep.

Judith Clements

A Scarlet Dream

Stirring for e'er stirring, through the trees,
Where midnight flowers shine
Where the heart is o'er whelmed in time,
So timeless, an awesome magic, has been found

Where a Mighty Woman walks, so profound,
So beautiful and proud, so very delicate
Rich and classical, O wondrous female,
Articulate, venerating a myriad of words

Ardent addiction, almost enticed, the affair,
The torch, the beauty of your hair, shining ringlets
Rosy white your skin, so dignified, so colourful,
O the galaxy of far away stars in sheer wonder

A passion of the night, a scarlet dream
Only where lovers go, so intimate, so tender
Flaming like a golden-lit candlestick,
Where the old moon shows her smile

Feu de joie, the wedding hour, where Venus watches,
Where red Rubies are picked, where a quiet kiss is received
Where romance is enacted between a man and a woman,
The essence of nature unites in splendour.

James Stephen Cameron

Regrets

Your love was solid as a rock,
Protecting me from life's every knock.
You showed that love in so many ways,
Bringing sunshine to all my days.

You'd look at me and my heart would melt,
But why couldn't I tell you how I felt?
You never stopped saying how much you cared,
But I took for granted all that we shared.

You never ceased to bring me pleasure,
Trying to provide life's every treasure.
Your gentle smile I'll never forget,
But now I must live with my regret.

Why can't I turn back the hands of time?
Back to the days when you were mine.
Back to the days when our love was new,
I could tell you then how I loved you.

For now you've gone and I'm alone,
No-one left to call my own.
I should have shown what I felt for you,
But now you're gone and you never knew.

M. Muirhead

Oh Lonely Me

As I walk this path of life,
once knowing friends with husband and wife,
Now through the lonely path of night
All alone with my dreams of fright.

No one seems to notice me,
No open arms will hear my plea,
How quiet when living with a dream,
Of things that could or might have been.

People help or so it seems,
but when they are gone it's back to dreams,
As I walk this lonely road,
Bearing this burden of a heavy load.

Loneliness, it can be shared,
If only to find someone who cared,
With a friend who knows the lonely road,
who will help to share the once heavy load.

Now close your eyes, and dream,
Things are not quite what they seem,
You'll find there are times, the sun shines through,
So don't give up, it will happen to you.

F. H. Hounsell

Fools

It's not fair to laugh at them
because they're different from you
you wouldn't be quite so smug
If it was them that were laughing at you

You think you're smart and clever
but really, you're just a fool
they have feelings too, you know.
So less of the ridicule

Their colour or their shape
doesn't really matter
It's what's inside that really counts
so stop this foolish patter

If you knew the harm you cause
would you still be laughing then
can't you see the person inside
and the misery you're causing them

It takes all kinds to make a world
of that there is no doubt
but there's already enough sadness and hurt
so your kind, we could all do without.

Nicola Laidlaw

For Men on Benches

Four men on a bench. White and flaky.
Staring out to sea, it's raining.
Talks of times, long gone astray
By a sandy shore, they watch the children play.
Sad eyes for Autumn, fond memories fading.

The sun it's gone now. Dim light with twilight eyes.
A winter's scorn is pending, a season of rain
Tear sending, old men sighing. The night air is chilling
As a pale moon dips and the ghost frost is rising.

Some men on a bench, staring. Still failing.
The thoughts, they talk, are seldom dry. A damp
Spring is ebbing, one cries, another dies.
Time is passing, a pause by a bench.
The grey sea watching, old breath signing.
Friends go in passing. Memories lost in dying.

Spring showers, rain-tears are mocking.
These are sobbing days as little children play.
A bench by the sea, never moving. Sad old lips praying.

Four men on a bench. Fresh green and flaky.
Staring out to sea. It's still raining.

Gerard K. Sweeney

Our Homeless

I often think when snow and ice or frost lies on the ground,
of people in a cardboard box, no home for them is found,
on city streets they sleep at night, in bags to keep them warm,
in wet and windy weather they lie in huddled form.

A doorway or an alleyway is very often best,
they give them some protection and let them get some rest,
but as the dawn breaks overhead, their bed they fold away
and mingle with the city crowds to start another day

Their breakfast is a mug of tea, perhaps a piece of bread,
a soup kitchen, or hostel meal, at lunch time may be fed,
but scrounging in the back streets bins is often seen to be,
the only source of daily food these people ever see

In summer time it's not too bad, the nights stay longer light,
but still these homeless people stay on the streets at night.
They vary in their age groups, some are in their teens,
whilst others are the elderly without support or means.

So when the nights get darker and the autumn winds do blow,
and we are in our lighted homes with fires all aglow,
our thoughts must be for the homeless, so cold upon the streets
as we snuggle in our soft warm beds beneath the clean bed sheets.

S. Brooke

Tableau of Beauty

Dramatic situations I find myself in.
Among a group of people be silent.
Motionless I hope I win.
I'll compose a song of lament.

Such beauty God has given me
I'll carry on the hard labour.
And if the scene as chosen me.
To kill I would with a sabre.

Look fourth with such pale beauty
A sickening waste of life.
And if boldness is quietly.
It's been worth the hard toil and strife.
   Stephen Gambles

Dreams beneath Our Souls

We awake from our dreams,
Mine so bitterly unkind,
Yours so loving, so vastly different than mine.
We are together, but as one, an individual,
The waves come closer,
Whistle of the wind, pulling me into the sea, with such loud roars,
Overlooking you, you look upon a bay,
Looking down to the water, blue skies, a sun ray.
Falling down to the pebbles beneath my feet,
Many surround me, whispering deceit.
Deceit around circles, around my mind,
You're my love, yet you seem to have the sun,
Mesmerised in your eyes,
Sights of love, for you have no cries,
Fallen into the shadows, trapped,
There's no way out from thy dream,
Yours has a light out,
But mine has not, (it seems).
   Helen Devlin

Crying for Help

A child is crying tonight.
Crying out for help.
But no one hears their shouts.
For their mothers and fathers are lying.

A child is crying tonight.
Hoping that someone will come.
But the child is left alone
Afraid and left in the dark.

A person is crying tonight.
Thinking of the child that once cried in the night.
No one heard and no one came.
The child inside still waiting for help.

Childhood memories that haunt me at night.
Hearing my shouts, and tasting my tears
Thinking of my childhood years.
   Claire Morgan

The Powerhouse

Emotion is free . . . so use it,
Find the best, leave the rest,
Don't abuse it.

Smiles are beginnings of giggles inside,
When laughter is born,
and misery denied.

Love so vital, encompassing and heady,
feeds the wonder of caring
with a grin at the ready.

The brain is your powerhouse, keep it mellow and clear,
Ease off the worries,
Down shift woe's gear.

There's no rehearsal, your life is but once,
So keep it mellow,
Give laughter a chance,
   E. Mugford

The Old Children

The two old children have finally left
home both feeling like a retiring drone.
Their children came round this morning to help, more like to help
themselves, has they started collecting their parents' shelves.

Mum you won't need this where you're going
so I will take this off your hands you understand.
The 2 old children both looking up
towards their daughter with a touch of confusion with the hope
that they would soon wake-up from their shared delusion.

Do we have to go to the old people's house
she said quietly and reluctantly as a mouse.
Mummy I am sorry, but you have to go she said greedily,
has she slowly went through the old shiny cutlery.

Were these the same children that we taught to care
and most of all to share, for it is surely certain,
we would never be able to draw our own curtain, in their eyes.
The two old children would talk quietly,
one to another like mischievous children.
'Do you think we should' as the two children
started to enter into their second childhood.
   William Clarke

Drought

Oh, sky above, why must you smile,
Why must your sun still glare?
Our lands is parched, our crops are dry,
don't you really care?

I know we now can boast a tan,
but novelty is over,
we long to see green fields again
with cattle 'midst the clover.

Are you so pleased no cloak of green
hides our naked earth?
Your smile was pleasant for awhile
but now it's only mirth.

Where are the clouds to dampen your brow,
will you ever weep
And let your tears smooth out the cracks
that now are wide and deep?

The earth cries out for change of heart.
Cry for just a while,
And when the earth brings forth young shoots
'Tis then oh, Sky — you smile.
   Mary A. T. Keeley

Countryside Musings

Did you ever smell the flowers
amidst the cobwebs of the dawn—
Or have you seen a dewdrop
on a brand new harvest morn?

Have you ever glimpsed the beauty
of both sunrise and sundown—
Were you ever in the country,
yet on the edge of town?

Have you ever felt the wing-beats
of a fragile butterfly?
Or felt and smelled that new Spring grass,
and pondered . . . as time goes by;

'Tis nice to bask and doze a-while,
beneath a spreading bough;
And seek to move to where the breeze
does move the leaves . . . and how!

From early light to near midnight,
one hears and leaves bird song;
Drifting in and out from tree and hedge—
and this lasts all day long.
   Kevin McCann

Club Night

Lightly creeping through the bushes,
softly down the garden path,
keeping closely to the shadows
fresh from dozing by the hearth.

In two's and three's the Members gather,
seated round the goldfish pond,
calling soft their feline greetings,
Masonic paw shakes seal the bond.

Chairman calls them all to order,
sober Gent in black and white,
four white spats and suede-look collar,
silky coat all sleek and tight.

Secretary reads the Minutes,
clad in ginger, faintly striped;
giant Tabby collects Subscriptions
fish heads from the kitchen swiped.

Discussion getting rather heated,
yowls and Cat-calls fill the air.
Neighbour tips a shower of water,
suddenly there's no one there.

Peggy Netcott

Legacy

When first on Runnymede's broken turf strode forth
The mellow corruption of a poxed land's redress;
From the gallows of splintered myth swung sweet prophecy
Tempered by an indolent rage to cruel respite forfeit.

Rescued from a prison whose window expelled the light,
In grim repose, dwelled regal countenance forsook.
Who stole a province to force-feed a fiery lust
And paid amorous false ransom for symmetry to behold.

Shadowing the battlements of a winter's spent remorse,
With eyes baleful and thirst slaked by a continent of wisdom,
Advised only by ridicule tugging her tattered dress
Seared eyes, half-open for an invitation to craft despair.

From towering dominion rampant to servitude unreconciled,
The past swallows the future curse to vomit.
And a cradled dribbling infant begs question unfulfilled:
For whose present is life's treasure rendered fool's gold?

She turned and faced him with blossomed gaze eternal
That trembling in an empty scabbard spilled mortality;
When acquisition was deformed to miserable spoliation
The donor beseeched leave to bewail its blindness.

David A. Russell

The Sea

I'm watching the sea as the waves gently flow
Today all is quiet—they just come and go.
It has the effect of keeping you calm
How can such sea ever do harm?

On a day bright and sunny when all is still
I'm sat on the coast—my own Selsey Bill.
Folks walk the dogs—the children are there.
There is no place like it—that I can compare.

I've walked on that coast when skies were black,
With rumblings at sea and I've hurried back.
I've watched lightening and heard thunders roar
Watched stones being thrown by the sea to the floor.

I've gone to the beach, very early, when no one is there.
I've shouted out loud—had the wind in my hair.
I've let go of tension—and cried bitter tears,
Told the sea and the stones of my sadness and fears.

One day—not too far—I'll live by this sea
The days then to follow will be happy for me.
Listening in bed to the sea and its sound
When that day arrives—my joy will abound.

Pamela Duley

Caravanning

Him and me would you believe
Go caravanning and the whole world to see
But do we agree? No—not him and me
He thinks he knows it all—you see

The destination he has chosen for our visit
Discusses it with me? No, he doesn't
You see, he says that he knows best
He's the driver I follow best

A one and a half hour journey takes us three
He thought I would like the scenery you see
Stop in a lay by for tea and a snack
For him a quick look at that map

Ah, he says that's where I should have turned off
I missed it because you were yapping your head off
Never mind, we won't now bother
Get sleeping bags out, we'll keep here 'till tomorrow

Campsite found, the facilities twelve showers in a line
A gigantic bath, it holds about nine
One night here, Dave, and then we're off.
It doesn't matter if there's a water storage or not.

Mary K. Clark

Springtime

I'm sure that spring is here
When the daffodils start to appear
With their colours of golden honey
Enticed by days warm and sunny

Yellow trumpets with a silent sound
Encourage others from the ground
Soon the dainty primrose heeds the call
Her pretty flowers displayed to enthral

In the dappled copse the air is clear
The bluebells tinkle, imagine you can hear
Anemones their petals white as the departed snow
Announce that summer's coming don't you know

The birds contrive to build their nest
Hurrying, far to busy to stop for rest
Gathering twigs, grass and bits of straw
Humble sparrows, robins even the rare jackdaw

The wonder Mother Nature has supplied
Man could never match, even if he tried
Surely we should all try our very best
To appreciate and keep these with which we're blessed

R. B. Fellingham

"Seek Out the Harbour of Your Dreams"

To cast a magic spell with a kiss
We escape this earth by metamorphosis
And skyways climb the stairway to heaven
Your footsteps soon will not be leaden
Follow the paths of the sun and moonbeams
Seek out the harbour of your dreams
And place them in the vaults of heaven

There in God's great creation
A journey of discovery and experience you cannot miss
Let begin your own special Genesis
Spirits soar in what direction you may
With the sun to rule the day
And the moon to govern the night
The starry firmament's a wonderful sight
Touch clouds of Cumulous, Nimbus and Cirrus
Form them into pillows for those like us
Rest your weary head and dream
Earthly problems are not what they seem
Within this perfect celestial constellation
Find your own personal consolation

Granville Angell, Lord of Cannock

Heaven Is Missing an Angel

They say heaven is missing an angel. Of that I'm certain you see,
For I left my wings with St. Peter; said I had somewhere more important to be,
I had a soul to save, a life to give,
But I signed a heavenly contract, sealed with a silvery star,
Not to fall in love with the one I help, to stay distant, aloof and afar.

Now St. Peter is calling, I have done my work,
Saved that soul,
I've given him life, I've given him love, I've given not half but the whole,
Do I call it a day and retrieve my wings, or do I stay and hope for better things, the light it beckons, the gates are opening, only your decision can be my making.

St. Peter's hand is now offered to take me away from here,
He will lead me to my redemption, to a life with no worries, no fears,
My heart says stay, my mind says go, my body is aching as only you would know, leaving you is the hardest thing I have done in all my years, but St. Peter is there with the softest of clouds to wipe away my tears.

As I take one last look back, in your eyes I see the pain,
Are you hurting as I am deep inside? You know I can remain,
Your decision can be my making, just say the words and you will see, St. Peter will see the love,
That is everlasting between you and me.

Joan Abrahamson

The Train

The train was going somewhere as out of the dark it came,
The girl had come from nowhere, I remember her just the same,
The window created a picture frame for the girl in velvet brown
As she sat watching the raindrops fall, in a hat with a fringe hanging down.

Where was she going that Friday, who was she going to see,
Why didn't she look over my way, why didn't she notice me?
Was she going to meet her lover, her Svengali with eyes of green
Was she already enslaved by him or was she his beautiful queen?

As the whistle blew, the guard waved his flag, the train moved on once again,
I started to move but my feet seemed to drag
And she stared at me through the rain.
Looking through the window watching the rain.

I saw a boy in a mackintosh, he was staring at the train.

He seemed to be staring closely at the carriage where I sat
His eyes were black and rather intense, he seemed to look at my hat.
Although we stopped for a moment it registered in my mind
That he wanted to travel with me, then we moved, he was left behind.

As long as I live I'll remember the boy at the railway track
With eyes intense and tender, trying to call me back.

K. W. Liepins

My Kind of World

If I could start the world afresh, I'd replenish it with endless joy.
A world of peace and happiness, where love and peace can never cloy.
A world where birds soar freely, through the cloudless sky.
Swiftly and gently, way up high.
A world that's like a turtle dove, so divine and perfectly pure,
Where there's no such thing as poverty, discrimination, and war.
A world without hunger rivalry, and greed,
Without racial prejudice, regardless of country, colour, or creed.
A commodious world without selfishness, like chimneys belching smoke,
And oil polluted seas where birds and fish are liable to choke,
The atmosphere is unpolluted, the sky a serene blue,
A world of bliss and happiness, where all desires come true.
A world where animals roam free, and nature fills the sky,
There is no such thing as animal testing for cosmetics for you and I.
There is no such thing as cruelty, violence, and crime,
But just an Earthly Paradise, that's full of beauty divine.

Emma Jayne Thackway

The Passing of a Day

I wake in the early hours, the night-time slipping by,
I peer through the darkened window
and see the clouds hanging in the sky.
Another day is dawning, the minutes ticking past
I'm chasing around to get ready and having to move fast.
At last I'm out and on my way,
the rabbits and hedgehogs keep well at bay.
Trees and hedges go flashing by
but the clouds still hang there in the sky.
The day is long and strenuous, no windows to look outside.
Everything is happening out there, but we are having to hide.
I've done my day, I'm as free as a bird.
The day has gone, this is absurd.
I'm now driving home slowly, to understand why,
the same clouds are still hanging there in the sky.
The day is done, the day has gone.
This is just classed as another one.

T. J. McOwen

City Blues

In the shimmering chaos of city sites,
   amongst the flashing neon lights
You stand so very alone, with nowhere you can call home.
Drinking in a back street bar, you know that you'll never go far.
If you reminisce about days of old, castrate the past, be bold.

Step out of the shadows of darkness, your life's not such a mess.
I hold out my hand to you, a friend who'll stop you feeling blue.
Once you blossomed like a flower, with a personality of great power.
Have the strength to carry on, I hate to see you so put upon.

Pick up the pieces of your heart,
   I know you thought she'd never part.
Become one, like the sunshine, something that's truly divine.
Walk through those walls of pain, you're the one with most to gain.
See the future as bright and true and I'll be there to help you through.

Daniel J. Parish

So Sad

It is so sad to see all the things happening around me,
I wake to find another change, another goal, a new range,
So sad is it I could start to cry, but such is life we do try,
I have very little to call my own, I live in with my boyfriend in his home,
My job is so bad it makes me sigh, sometimes I feel the end is nigh,
With every day a new trouble begins,
I think somehow I'm full of sins.
Life seems full of toil and woe, and I still have so far to go,
There is a little to learn, little to see, why do only bad things happen to me?
The saying is "there's light at the end of the tunnel,"
Not if you're me looking through a closed funnel,
I work so hard I try so much, but seem to ruin everything I touch,
All in all I wished I could be someone else and happy . . .

S. Elliott

Peace

God of hope
We pray for the people of this world.
God bless the leaders and negotiators,
Help them respond in action and love
Without fear or judgement.

Let us all pray together
For peace and harmony
In this wonderful world of ours.
Put an end to this avalanche
Of fighting, killing, looting,
Descended on the poor
And displaced people of this world.

Please God and people
Don't turn a blind eye
To our suffering neighbours!
Positive peace be everywhere
God bless and long live peace and harmony.

Katie Kent

Farewell Lancelot

That gallant knight of old, or so it was foretold
Pursued his lady fair, and doughty deeds would dare
Superior was he, as master he would be.
His lady called him "Sire", and wooed him with her lyre,
So chaste, and oh so pure! And infinitely demure,
She dare not raise her eyes, in case of some surprise.
Some food she brought her Lord, not heard of bed and board
A "taster" hovered by, the poisoned bits to try

The gauntlet threw he down, in front of all the town
To fight right to the death, my lady holding breath.
He conquered like as not, victorious on the spot.
His lady cheered and smiled, was just a mite beguiled
And what's the tune to-day? What is the state of play?
My lady rules the roost, and has her knight seduced,
She nags him right and left, he's henpecked and bereft
And where is he, the ninny? In the kitchen in a pinny!
Doris Holland

The Dream of Love

The other night I had a dream.
I dreamed I was walking down a long winding corridor,
Every so often there was a door.
As I looked through each door I noticed that the door lead to different parts of my life.
Looking back I realized that each door lead to the mistakes that I had made during my life.
Looking through the last door I saw how different I was.
I noticed a glow around me.
This glow was not with me when I looked through the other doors.
I then realized that it was the glow of happiness and love.
I was happy because I was with you.
You have touched my heart in such a way,
Nobody makes me feel like you do.
I know that I do not want to leave the last door.
Waking up I realized that I had made many mistakes.
But the biggest mistake I ever made was not entering the last door sooner.
Louise Robertson

The Belle of the Ball

How she came to be invited, I shall never know!
But when she makes her entrance, you sense the general flow
Of conversation slacks, as all eyes turn her way
And appreciative males in competitive display,
Each in their own peculiar manner attempt to gain her attention
As she bestows her favours with queenly condescension.
The dress she wears so daring, with the skirt slit to the thigh
And how enchantingly she smiles as she brushes by,
Reducing all the female guests to a frustrated angry feeling.
Light as softest thistle down, she floats into eager arms,
The belle of the ball, this dark eyed beauty with her seductive charms
The cause of many heartaches and matrimonial strife.
How do I know so much about her? She used to be my wife!
Irene Huswait

Breath of Life

Beached upon the pebbles with the sea crashing around, lies my life.
Battered by driftwood and entangled with seaweed, entwined with rope.
Shellfish cling to me as I am smothered and lie underneath.
Through the debris I can see out—and feel the sunshine.
I feel my heart beat, and if I really strain I can gulp some air.
Life giving air.
Raindrops quench my thirst, the seaweed drops away from my side.
Along with the shellfish, no longer using me for their life by feeding off me.
As I grow stronger I can break out—out of the rope.
I can leave behind the restrictions from the past. And the pain.
I have sunshine, I have rain, I have air.
And life will be my food.
And for love?
I will learn to love myself.
Tracey Wilkes

Scaefell (The Mountain)

West-South-West, the compass read, as I walked amongst the mist,
Two Flares, One Map, No Whistle "Damn," I didn't check my list.

I pitched the tent and made my bed, the dog began to bark,
"Visitors on Scaefell" surely nothing, not this close to dark.

It was an eagle, to my delight, off he flew and began to soar,
Two dives, One Shimmy, he danced, come on eagle show me more.

"The Camera," "Where's the blasted camera," I cried; I withdrew it from its case,
The eagle roared and dived once more, and disappeared without a trace.

The cold was upon us now, I made a lemsip to fend off flu and colds,
Let's go to sleep my Furry Friend,
and dream of what tomorrow holds.

We rose at dawn, for our descent, the ice began to thaw,
We dropped down to 2000 feet, and I was amazed at what I saw.

There were thirty streams at first count,
they funnelled down to four,
And I'll be back in Lakeland next spring, to climb Scaefell once more.
Glyn Sinkinson

Obsolescent Optimism

How furious you were as you saw my regret. As my foolishness flurried from my eyes as I could no longer hide nor deny my feelings. Your concern was not noticed as my skin became terrifyingly white, as the very life in me drained away.

I long to find some means, any means, of reversing the passage of time, and undoing the deed that has cost me so dearly. The increasing swelling of my heart, aching, stretching with pain to try to fill my lame body with meaning to continue. Hunger for love rumbles from deep within and confusion crowds my head with sour thoughts and restless regrets.

Tense, stiff air is all that lies between us. Unflavoured language leaves our lips as we snap and scream during what should be precious moments. Suspicion fills my head as I tiptoe back to enchanting days of friendly words and try to forget these days that have inspired my hatred for you.

I think deeply, trying to destroy destiny's desires for me with feeble hope. But all I can remember is my hope being shattered by you. Once again my mortal discomfort is preserved and the sinister silence makes me impatient. But I shall not retreat to cowardly revenge, for that truly would be a sin.
Kate Hobbs

Humanity Who Are You and What Are You:
To You Whoever You Are

Leopards, hyenas, lions, elephants, hippos, rivers, sand,
Trees, crocodiles, doves, grass, know why don't you know?

Who are you? Who are you? What are you?
Do you really know?
Pain, hunger, thirst, hurting, murder, loving, caring, and more.
What does matter to you? More than one million years have passed and all of us have ancestors to prove the indisputable reality of the fact that we exist.

Who are you? Who are you? What are you? Do you know?
Sometime you might find out; only don't leave it too late.
Time for you, time for me is not forever.
The choice is yours, but don't expand ideas of false consciousness and that people will always be waiting for you, just for you.
If you have taken the time to think about yourself, what do you think about me? If you will know, only if you rap back and really listen.
The snakes will also tell you. The baobab tree will also tell you.
The value of knowledge and understanding is yours only if you will listen. If you don't listen and pay attention, apana, go on tell your lies, carry on cheating, enjoy your lies and stupidity, I will enjoy my honesty and my truthfulness; signed off. Just Me.
Norman Rass

The Crimson Lake

Please Lord forgive them for they know not what they do!
A message of forgiveness from the heart of one so true.
Those words spoken long ago, but what difference did they make?
As tears of grief and sorrow help form the Crimson Lake.

And as the news that yet another, is taken from life's stream,
how can those tears of grief be stopped? The answer to a dream.
A country decimated by religion that leaves terror in its wake,
and tears spilled for a loved one add to the Crimson Lake.

He turns; his task is over, then a loud bang resounds,
and another mere statistic lies face down on the ground.
But what of those he leaves behind, when will their news break?
Their tears, and his blood replenish the Crimson Lake.

Why can't their eyes be opened by the suffering that they cause?
God's beautiful creations destroyed by all these wars.
In the name of God they murder, but they aren't for God's sake,
just merely to satiate themselves and flood the Crimson Lake.

How can we prevent these killings and the heartaches that
they cause?
Do we have the power to put an end to all these wars?
Love thy neighbour was the message, and if in this we all partake,
we can help in our small way to dry up the Crimson Lake.

Kevin Foreman

Fantasy and Dreams

Your manlike images rend my mind,
And I remember love's not kind,
I sit and think how it could have been,
And now the problems came unforeseen.

For you, I'd travel to the ends of the earth,
I'd give you everything I'm worth.
Why is it that love is so unfair?
We could have been the perfect pair.

By yonder moon your face does beam,
Reflecting beauty more than it seems,
Let's share in love's triumphant glory,
You'll be the main character in my story.

By the open fires on harmonious ground,
Not a whisper, not a sound, we are alone, once more I feel
This time our love must be for real.

A time for playing, fantasy and dreams,
We'll show love for all that it means,
Every night, we'll laugh and joke, until your heart I do provoke.

But I shall wait until the day,
When we're together and there we'll stay,
this is where this poem ends
Are you sure you just want to be friends?

Kerry McKay

In the Beginning

One day, when the Earth was still young
And there was only one, family.
Brothers and the sisters had a meeting to decide
To leave the family and find, the end of the world.
The family agreed that if the sisters and the brothers
Found a better life afar, they would share the Earth's riches,
All the plants, beasts and fishes, keep the family as one, for evermore.
It meant teaching the children from whence they had come,
That all peoples were equal, all brothers and sisters,
One family, under the sun.
But it wasn't long before, the travelling peoples saw
Life could be easy and they could consume more and more.
The family they'd left behind, no longer entered their minds
And the promise that they'd made to share, became a myth,
  for they no longer cared.
And even though there was enough for all, they decided
To get rich and let the poor learn to crawl.
It went on for a thousand years and a day
Then the sisters and brothers found they'd lost their way.
But instead of embracing the whole family
They destroy what they have, to sustain their greed.

Nyx Darke

The House

The large old house looked desolate,
As it stood 'neath the pale moonlight;
And no sound could be heard from within its walls,
Nor from its windows a gleam of light.

The house, it was a shambles,
Weeds choked its garden wall;
And not one friendly puff of smoke,
Came forth from its chimneys tall.

Then suddenly the scene did change,
The house was filled with light;
And a by-gone lover's serenade,
Broke the silence of the night.

The garden then became alive,
The musk of rose perfumed the air;
And from within the house emerged
A young girl so slim and fair.

As she ran into the minstrel's arms,
So fervently they kissed;
And their spirits fused together,
To disappear into a mist.

Edith Garcia

Heart, Body and Soul

I want you Sean, I need you so much,
Since the night that we danced
You felt warm to the touch,
You had your arms round me,
I felt safe and secure.
Now I'm yearning for you
With a love that's so pure.

You started to talk.
But no response did I speak,
Instead I just went back and sat on my seat.
I should have told you how I felt,
I should have let you know
Of the burning hot passion deep down within,
Making me fret, with so much guilty and sin.

Now I'm approached by so many
But I just have to say 'No'.
You're the one I desire,
The one that makes my heart glow,
I'll wait for you always,
  Heart, body and soul.

Susan Elisabeth Senior

Gems and Miracles

The myriad of sparkling diamonds twinkling way up high
Set in random upon black velvet of the night sky,
The gleaming moon, its crystal crescent showing face,
The Milky Way, its opal streamer stretching out and into space.

Creeping slowly, the ruby sun as if its fire has just begun
Changes the black velvet sky into an ocean of red set to run,
And change into a sheet of deep blue sapphire fluffy cotton,
The dawn has broken, a new day's begun,
  a sight never to be forgotten.

The sun changes to golden amber, attracting flowers like bees
  to nectar,
The opening buds stand upright reaching, hungry for warmth
  and filling nurture,
The pearlescent dew drops fade away under the sun's warm gaze,
No cooling breeze, just shimmering heat and a warming haze.

Across the ocean of shimmering sapphire, from nowhere did appear
Clouds of cotton wool dappled with grey from the atmosphere,
Change, a chill in the air, and distant looming angry thunder,
Interwoven with brilliant lightning, earlier gems gone asunder.

Life giving globules pounce and dance upon the earth,
The drink of life with emeralds lapping for all their worth,
How glad to be part of the miracle of life's colourful world,
The kaleidoscope of gems before our eyes unfurled.

Valda Teasdale

Storm!

The peaceful night is shattered by a loud crack,
Lightning slices through the sky like a whip on some
poor animals back.

The wind howls around the sturdy walls that protect me,
Its angry fists pounding on my window pane,
It's fighting to get in, but fortunately for me, its fight is in vain.

Like rocks, the raindrops pound down onto my roof,
Thank goodness that my roof is waterproof.

The frightful thunder growls with all its might,
Like a pack of savage dogs ready for a fight.
But in spite of all this beastly war, I remain unharmed,
In front of a blazing fire, in my house's loving arms.
Stephanie Bannon

To My Boys

I love them so, though there were times I wished them far away
The first so gentle I felt pure joy, the moment would not stay.
Then came another, too soon I thought the anguish and the pain
The love I gave the first was gone, but no it was the same.

We struggled through, love, jealousy and life went on and on
Emotions pulled right out of me, through them and then were gone.
But love comes back, renews itself, denies anguish, time and worry
They grow away, have secret lives, they long for life to hurry.

I long to reach out, touch and hold, but stand back, swallow tears.
They laugh and joke about mistakes to hide their secret fears.
The future lies ahead for them—you pray, you watch, you care.
The boring, mundane, uncool things which they pretend
aren't there!

But . . . You have to let them go and find life, they alone can choose.
And you stand back, with love and know that you are going to lose.
Mary Smith

The Haunting

On a dark dank night under the stillwood trees
Beckons danger of new omens
The dead are angry
As the gravestones shift on sifting soil
Marking delay and neglect
Their souls are alive and watching
Earnest for respect from a new generation
The town clock tinkles the sound
Of chimes denoting midnight
But as the dawn beckons
Spirits are to be seen
In the hapless hopeless undergrowth
Gravestones denoting the Crimean war
Are fragmenting in a crackle of indifference
As the flagrant dawn approaches
The sun rises on Rochester cemetery
And the danger has passed for another day
Finnan Boyle

Earthly Rights?

Perceive the bird in daily flight.
Watch its daily work, perforce.
Its voice held forth in pure delight.
Unsullied by the world's crude course.

All creatures roaming on this earth,
Emoted by survival's needs.
Innocent remain from birth,
Not tainted, stained, by worldly deeds.

Look at the fish that swim around.
Creatures living in and on the ground.
All creatures given wings to fly.
Then ask the question, why Oh! Why
Is earth so plagued by man?

Evil ways, evil deeds, evil thoughts, evil needs.
Murder, pillage, lies, deceit, rape, torture, indiscreet,
Hurtful, loathsome, brutal, wild.
What rights to earth, has human's child?
Terry Elloway

Our Andrew's Fifty

Back in '47 our Andrew's life began,
Filled with loads of problems—the youngest of our clan.
Not much was known of 'Mongols' then, the Doctor shook his head,
"Just leave him here, forget him Mum, pretend that he is dead!"

But Mum and Dad insisted he'd have his chance in life,
They took him home and nurtured him midst worry, pain and strife!
His progress, it was very slow and sometimes it would stop,
But everyone encouraged him with love and laughs nonstop.

At first he didn't go to school but Mum, she did her best,
He learnt to scribble, cut things up and even get undressed.
We struggled through and at fourteen he finally went to school,
The Elms in Preston took him on and soon found him—no fool!

His next step was to go to 'work', at Deepdale Adult Centre,
Making coat hangers each day with mates and happy banter.
He carried on till '87 when our Mum and Dad were taken,
He came to live in Kirkham with his family links unbroken.

Andrew has reached his 50th, his family are delighted!
Working hard at Sunnybank and following 'Leeds United'.
His life is great, he's full of fun and nearly always happy.
Though times have changed, we always knew, he'd be a
special chappie.
Pauline Holford

A Payment in Kind

From all the corners of the earth, they flew by day and night
Through rain and storm, hail and sleet, and even by moonlight.
Exhausted, tired, with heavy hearts, at last there came in view
The one that they'd been searching for, a friend so good and true.

No more to feed and care for them, no more to heal their hurt,
For naked, beat and slain, she laid there in the dirt.
They formed a ring around her, kept everyone at bay
Like sentinels on duty, they guarded where she lay

They covered her with rushes, with grass and sticks and moss;
And so they made a shroud for her, they could not contain their loss.
Then all at once, the sky grew black, and with mighty roar
They found what they were searching for, behind the chapel door.

They screeched and screamed, and pecked at him,
    until they heard him cry
"I didn't mean to kill her, I didn't mean for her to die."
And then a miracle occurred, they talk about it to this day.
They gathered up her body, and flew so far away.

And when the nights are quiet, some folks are heard to say
Her singing with her little friends, beyond the milky way.
For love it knows no boundaries, and I think that you will find
The birds repaid her precious love, with a payment in kind.
Sarah Shovlin

Loneliness

Loneliness . . . what is it?
Loneliness . . . how do you feel?
Loneliness . . . whose fault is it?
Is happiness really up to you?
Or is that untrue?

Loneliness . . . how can that be?
Surely God is listening to me?
Don't ever forget . . .
That life is whatever you want it to be . . .
So when loneliness comes . . .
Yearning to invade you soul . . .
Fight, with all your might because solitude should never be
your goal
It should be an enemy with no control

So come on . . .
Bombard your life with joy and passion . . .
Enjoy every second God provides . . .
Benefit from the gift of life . . .

And remember strive to deprive,
Cry of happiness not of pain because then you'll see
. . . How life will never be the same
Dina Benzaquen

Morning Thoughts

Early sunshine, cobwebbed dew, thoughts of me, thoughts of you,
Misty hillsides keeping us apart, why can't you be here close to my heart?
Why can't we share this sunrise, this beauty that's all around?
Why can't you be here beside me and live together on the same ground.

If you were here beside me, everything would look brand new,
As we shared life's little moments, that's how good it would be with you!
Everyday things would have new meanings if you were by my side,
Sharing together unexpected pleasures like waves coming in with the tide.

Moonlight on mountains sharing magical mysteries, times together in the sun
On rocky beaches, white capped water explored by hearts that beat as one.
Through eyes that have love shining in them, life's meaning looks different it seems;
While others struggle through their lives we seem to be actually living our dreams.

Precious moments like these rarely happen; we must treasure them and keep them alive,
shared together as we work to make our love survive!

Janet Muchmore

Before Nelson

From opposite ends of the earth I came to meet my white stepbrother, his home due north where blacks and whites live together with one another.
But for me it's always different, I'm all alone in this place,
abused, mistreated and beaten because of my colour and race.
I'm black! What's the difference? I can't see it can you?
Inside I'm still a person, though many don't know who.
So here he comes towards me in his clean white shirt and jeans, here's me, in my linen shorts with their patches and splitting seams I tell him about the racism, the soldiers, apartheid. He turns to say "don't worry" and I needn't join the fight. He asks me to move in with them, he tells me I can stay but what about my family? I just cannot move away.
Here, it's not like Cape Town, people here have fun.
South Africa is different, the white man holds the gun.
The black man is the slave, the servant and the cook.
Never taught to write or count, or even read a book
he thinks of his wife and family living far away.
No I must return to Africa, as we will have our day.
So I walk the thirteen miles home in the burning sun.
With hopes and dreams of miracles, one day he will come.

Selena Ledgerton

The Cry of a Beautiful Oak Tree

The smoke is choking, dark acid fumes.
It's getting closer, the leaves are crinkling, crackling, shrivelling,
The animals are running, running,
It's getting closer, this heat is too much, burning, crackling howling noises.
It's getting too close, go, go away, my friends, run, run it's sad but you must go, there is nothing you can do.
They are stronger, mightier with money and matches, they hurt, they burn, they destroy.
That red strong heat is almost here.
I am so sad, so sorry, these bright young trees, how I weep for you, the scar they charred.
It is here I can feel it now, closer and closer, the twigs are crackling, branches falling.
Now I cannot see, cannot hear, they have destroyed us, everyone of us, a whole generation.
They are laughing, laughing, ha! Ha! Watching.
The pain is too much.
I have served here for ninety (90) years or more, they have destroyed us in five (5) minutes.
They are destroying this land, our land, their land, yet they cannot see, so blind by their lust and greed.

Sally Mowlah

The White Rose

The wee little York, alone he stood, outside the battle raged.
He hoped and prayed his loved ones could this day the red rose cage.
In his dark room he lay, with thoughts of that proud day.
When he would be of age.

He waited patiently for the hearing of his brother's victory, the king!
All around him the crowd stood cheering for King Edward's grand welcoming.
On his mighty war-horse he came, looking anything but tame
With the pride and power of any high king.

The news came of the dying king, his brother. As soon as he heard he rushed to his side.
Richard's heart filled with sorrow, for like this great man there could be no other.
He knew what was killing Edward was pride.
But even such a strong warrior would never be sorrier
To leave all behind: his mother, his brother, and his beautiful bride.

He was now king, his job: to enforce. He remembered his beloved brother strong and well
And again his heart filled with remorse.
His first battle as king, he might win, forget not, Lancaster fell.
He fought with all the might in his heart and to say the least, he did his part.
But because of treason he went down with these last words,
"My kingdom for a horse."

Shanon Knedlik

Another Place

How many times I wonder, do we really look and see
The wealth of creature comforts that surround both you and me.
We tend to take for granted the food upon our plates
And never know a winter without fire in our grates.
If we'd to dig for water to survive another day
We'd find it just as hard as seeking needles in the hay.
Yet there are those who do this and have nothing of their own
The water's bad, no electric there, and squalor is their home.
These people are a proud race, and all they ask of we
Is the means to cultivate their soil, to feed their family.
They never ask for riches, just water, clean and pure
And schooling for their children, and good health
and not much more.
The third world man just wants to work, not ask for charity
And we can help him find his way through his own ability.
If we that have a lot, compared to those that have so few
Gave a little more each year to help our brothers through
Then we would sleep more soundly in our warm and comfy bed
Knowing that we'd lent a hand, and not turned away instead.
For if you think about it, and do give it a try
You'll see, there, but for the grace of God, go I.

Christine Stubbs

The Button

When my cousin turned eighteen, to Australia she went,
Married a fine gentleman and there, her life spent.
Her aged parents' heart she broke that sad day
As they loved her dearly and begged her to stay.
Her Mother pined to hear the voices of loved ones,
So my cousin placed a recorder in her home, just for fun.
Those tapes recorded the happiest goings-on
Of a bright cheery homestead, but of their tears, there were none.
She amassed a collection of different circumstance
Then sent them to her Mum, so she could listen at every chance.

Her Mum would arise early to push the button on those tapes,
Listening to her daughter seeing to the kids, off to school late.
When they were bathing, her grandchildren would shout
"Gran, we're off to bed now, don't forget to turn the lights out!"
But Grandma was grieving and dying for sure,
Realising full well she'd see them no more.
And on her death-bed, with eyes seeing no one,
Her finger reached out to push that button.
Her daughter's loving voice she heard whispering, tenderly,
"Mum, I love you loads, try to sleep now, peacefully."

Amy Greenfield-Goodman

War!

Boys, who are now men,
Shake each time the shells come whistling overhead,
Waiting for the one that will drop on them,
Drained of strength,
Unable to show emotion as their comrades die,
Only praying for the end.

Boys, who joined the throng of men, willing to defend their country,
Not knowing how they would spend their time,
Waiting for the orders to move,
Out of their foxholes and into the field of fire,
Hoping they will survive the sortie,
Looking forward to going home, some day.

Boys, who no longer worry about death,
They have seen it all,
Hoping when it comes, it's quick and painless,
War has destroyed their feelings for their fellow men,
Now they live day to day, with no feelings for tomorrow,
Only praying for the end.
Bruce M. Long

Dillusional Regret

And I don't know, but I'm afraid these tears won't stop falling.
What's happening today? I don't know if this is my end.
Can't stop thinking over the past, all the things I left unsaid.
I've never felt this sad before. I can see all the people once more,
All the people I've loved and lost, and I can bring them back somehow.

I'm circling over my funeral, I can hear a million thoughts "she wasn't a bad sort, pity to have died so young, bit on the melancholy side, she didn't take her chances, she let them pass right by."
But it's yours for sure I know. "her love for me she couldn't show, in limbo she will always be I know, but she was the part of me that was pure, and who am I now that she's gone?"

It's judgement day in my head today. I can see the past, I can see them pass my way. If I went back what would I change, what would I rearrange? I wouldn't have let them slip out of my hands so easily, I would fight, I wouldn't have wept so easily.

Maybe it's not the end, but it's the end of my third life, and I'm facing my fourth life, even though I'm only sixteen. And I'm crying for all that was familiar and is lost forever even though it hurts me so. Maybe it'll be good, my fourth life. And I'm not afraid, I'm looking forward to what I'm about to see and all that I'll be.
Patricia Luby

Jack Frost Tears

You stand against the wind sniffing the breath from smoky skies.
Above the city beneath the moon solitary creature your fate is doomed.
Why fight all beasts and men? With energy best spent on love.
Bloodstained tears simmer gently, cold bitter caskets overflow in pain.

Why does your pride lie between us? Feasting upon the guts and gore.
That once grazed between sweet crisp life now wedged against my heart and yours.
I will climb your ragged mountain ledge, tormenting your soul with spiky toes.
Each step twisting into your well done flesh until remorse weakens the defending bricks.

Huddled inside your deep thick fleece you curl away from my icy touch.
Determined to win you shut me out rejecting the chill from our tainted love.

You stand against the wind the breath of air that once sustained you.

Freezing my spirit with Jack Frost tears, my heart stops beating immortalized by stone.
Janette Crawford

Chains, Sin Then Love

I was once bound by chains, chains of sin, past hurts and pains.
But now by the blood Jesus shed for me and the grace God sends,
Those chains are broken, soon all will see; as the Lord's constant love heals and mends.

That new different chains now bind this body of mine,
I have found a new identity given by my Lord divine.
Another chance He gives as He tells me I am His, now and for all eternity.

Chains of rubies, red as His blood, bind body, mind and soul,
As through tears of repentance, God makes me whole.
Now chains of diamonds encase my body, soul and mind,
Showing the great love the Father has for me, and my love for Him
A new love I have found, not marred by sin.
As chains of silver entwine me around, to ensure my obedience is wholesome and sound.

To say, "Yes I am yours, Lord, do with me as you will", as I sit at His feet, listening quiet and still.
Chains of righteousness made of pure gold, declare I AM SAVED; not rejected or cold.
No self-condemnation can I utter a word, for to call God a liar would be absurd.
I like this new me I have found, as in the beginning I was tossed around.

But with His love He did unlock those chains of sin that kept me earthbound.
Now the chains of His love will keep me whole, in my mind, body and soul, binding me to my Saviour, "Jesus the Rock".
Maureen Rawlings

Ode to George

My husband George has passed away, he is in no more pain.
The funeral has taken place all in the wind and rain.
The flowers left upon the ground will wither there and die,
As I ponder where I stand, I think. There but for the grace of God.

Now I am left with memories, and all the tears are shed,
And I recall those happy times that George and I have led.
Our holidays and travels, our days so filled with love,
I know now that he's happy in the paradise above.

I know one day I'll meet him there, never more to part,
And somehow, now without him, here the rest of my life must start.
I know it won't be easy without the one I love,
But one day he will guide me to his paradise above.

Then we shall be together, such happiness there will be,
With George and I united for all eternity.
And I shall leave this earthly life for a far more peaceful place.
So meanwhile I will bide my time, when at last I'll see his dear face.
Ellen J. Hunt

Ode to Megan Louise

There's a space in our house where you used to be and an ache in my heart that I carry with me
There's no furry face to meet me at the door and the tail that always wagged doesn't do it anymore
Your big brown eyes no longer see, you ask no more for walks with me
The sound of your bark is no longer here and I don't comb each silky ear
So many things about you that I miss, no tummy to tickle, no black button to kiss
No begging for morsels to fall to the floor—and who's to tell me when someone's at door?
Megan Louise is your name, life without you won't ever be the same
You brought us joy the day you came to stay and broke our hearts when you went away.
But—way up there where special doggies go—someone will love you,
this I know and when we see the brightest star
Then we will know—just where you are.
But, there's a space in our house where you used to be, and an ache in my heart that travels with me
There's no furry face to greet me at the door and the tail that always wagged
Doesn't do it, anymore . . .
M. Kennedy

First Flight

Ambition steps nervously into the breeze,
The briefest flutter of feathers, a faltering cry
Before life takes this frail creature and begins its interminable shaking.
A few heavy gasps, a frenzied thrashing of wings.
A desperate struggle to stay afloat,
Until the pitiful brown bundle hurtles, with a flurry of dust
To the ground below.
The frail body lies limp in the dirt, while the elements continue their assault.
Only the faintest heartbeat emanates from deep within the soiled feathers.

And yet, within moments, gentleness bends and scoops with open palm.
A warm caress, the soothing satin tones of loving encouragement effect a vague awareness.
In little time all wounds are healed
And the battered creature is lifted as if in holy reverence, to the skies.
A timid look, cautious movements
Before he dives gracefully into a delicate stream of air.
Wavering, hesitant at first, but buoyed by his new discovery he weaves a bold trail across the sunset.
The heavens become his playground
And from this magnificent height, he knows the world is his.

Louise Shelton

The Nightingale's Song

The sweet, sweet song of the nightingale,
  as she sings to this heart of mine,
Of the wonderful night, when you held me tight, the music so divine,
The sweet, sweet colours of the nightingale,
  perfectly feathered to fly,
Soaring above on the crest of the wind, so free so high in the sky,
But the sweet, sweet remedy, for the love I have,
  is to bring you close to me,
For to hold you in these arms of mine, I would never set you free,
Well the sad, sad truth of it all is just, that I cannot hold you near,
Like the sweetness of the nightingale, 'tis the path you take so dear,
Freedom has its price to pay, when you have love to share,
Because the soul of man, if it only can, belongs to those who care,
So, loving you is not the thing to do, if freedom costs so much,
All the wonders of the magical bird, cannot compare to touch,
Belonging is the magical note, for the song of love to heal,
Heartwarming sensations on every path, is the only way to feel,
So I say goodbye, on the wings of a cry, to you my angel sweet,
For once we met, but we now regret,
  the nightingale's song of defeat . . .

Carol Roberts

Wetatonmi Speaks: Indian Summer, September 1877

It was lonesome, the leaving, all the husbands dead.
Smoke whispered up like a prayer from the ashes of teepees.

The child is heavy across my back, but I could not leave him there
Where his vanquished father and my infant lay, where the earth bled.

My breasts ripen with milk.

We struggle, mile by mile, the women, without sound.
If there are trees we will find them. I will ease my firstborn
From my shoulders, weave a bed of branches on which to place him.
Before many moons have passed, the snow will cover
My loves, like a blanket of frozen tears.
My eyes have no tears to flow.

The great wheel of the sun has turned beyond the hills
In that barren place where we, the women, beggared by pale strangers go.
Oh husband and infant, who have come away full from my body;
Oh my son. What will my hands do now that lie stiff
And numb with longing on my knees?

My sisters slowly gather firewood.
The old women dribble and moan; they will not sleep.
My eyes are dry.
Only my breasts, ignorant, ache for the hungering mouth and weep.

Donna Devine

Our Precious Prem Daughter of One Pound One and a Quarter

Our little Nikki is very poorly with us and God there's a small chance surely,
I cuddled her for hours on the trot, with a big thick jumper I became very hot.
Her father and I are smoking again, "well" we needed something to keep us both sane.
It's very hard at a time like this, when you can't even give her a big hug or kiss.
Tears stream down my face and drop to the floor, I often said 'I can't take much more'.
But Colin keeps me very strong, to give up he thinks would be very wrong.
It's hard to believe it's happening to us, but we try and stay calm, and not cause too much fuss.
Nikki's got an abscess on the brain, a needle was inserted, we hope not again. At the moment she's stable, but not very good, the Doctors are trying we've understood. On the 17th a phone call to rush us away, she looked puffy, ill and yellowish, I would say.
Now she's a nice colour but still very ill, only people who's been through this would know how I feel.
You have to think God's watching over her day and night, just keep praying and keep fingers crossed tight.
A miracle might happen soon we hope, that's the only way we can cope.
Keep going Nikki we're all behind you, even though your chances are very few. God keep watching over her every day, I know You'll look after her that's all I can say.

Susan Biggs

The Long Road Back

"It's not too far away" he said,
  As we wound our way around
The french mountain road.
  His hair still blonde
And eyes so blue.
  "Another mile will see us through".

Many years have passed,
  Water under the bridge they say.
A long time—since love came to stay.

"A few more miles, we'll be there soon".
"There will be dancing
  Under the stars and the moon.
We'll eat and we'll drink
  And laugh like before.
And who knows—maybe
  We'll find ourselves
In love once more".

L. Shorrocks

Eagles

Standing on tall white peaks,
Viewing your kingdom from on high,
Watching your borders shrinking by man's greed
for your valleys and your plains
Seeing him rule forward in chariots
Dragging his pollution behind:
Leaving barren fields in his wake,
Ignoring your graceful flight,
Not seeing your warning shadow that he treads on as he passes by.

Oh, mighty hunter, as you fight the elements with muscular frame, Tearing at stormy wet skies and hurricane winds with strong pointed talons,
Using swiftness of flight to dispatch unguarded prey
To feed future young, so your species can survive.

As you glide on warm currents
Blowing in from Mediterranean seas
Soaking up sun rays as it brings forth life below.
Making tapestries for your keen eye
As you see its green carpets for your pleasure,
As it should be for a king's flight.

Patrick Donnelly

My Fair Lady

Oh! What a beauty,
The likes of which I have never seen.
Radiating like the early morning sun,
She casts a brilliance all around and glows with an intensity
As amazing, to the eyes of men
As it's unprecedented, on the sands of time.

Oh! What a dear, the rarest of gems, a priceless diadem
With neither contemporary nor foe, all are confounded in her presence
Possessing a desirable physique
A sonorous golden voice and queenly disposition to match

Oh! What an angel, she does not bicker or batter
Neither bites nor barks at anyone but with celestial wisdom and love
Lives and interacts with all and sundry
So that all have same things in common
Love, respect and understanding, for her

Oh! What a marvel
Which surpasses human knowledge, how does one appraise the most perfect
Or fault at all, the dearly flawless
An epitome of the creator's artwork
And the delight of every man's heart.

Ikenna Apakama

What Have I Done?

I walk along the street, I see the people turn away.
They don't stop to talk, can't think of anything to say.
I think "What have I done?", but I know the reason why.
I find it difficult myself, since my daughter Margaret died.

I feel I have been to Hell, but time will bring me back.
It helps to sit and remember, all the good times that we had.
The Dog Shows we went to, they would cheer us up a lot.
Meeting friends we made throughout the years, then discussing who they
   had brought.

We had such a love for dogs, we never had enough.
Each litter that we bred, we had to keep a pup.
We'd look at each other and say "No, not again!".
How on earth will we ever explain it to the men?

But they'll just have to understand, with us we couldn't stop.
Well, that is until we get to the top.
The C.C.s we aim for, always seem out of reach.
But I'll go on trying, there's always next week.

Well my lovely daughter, I will not let you down.
If there's any chance at all, I'll trail from town to town.
You can be sure I'll do my best, and from God's heavenly home.
I'm sure you're watching over me, I do not walk alone.

Agnes Bell

Diane

The thing I regret more than any other
is the fact I never had a brother,
Someone to protect me all my life
until he found himself a wife.
This of course was not the plan
and I had a sister called Diane.
Family life was not too bad,
the two of us, with Mum and Dad.
Most of the time went very well,
though sometimes I made her poor life hell.
But since we've gone our separate ways
I often think of those far away days
and how lucky I am that I have known
a lovely sister of my own.
Diane is special in many ways,
she works very hard and spends her days
thinking of others, and to show she's there
she makes me gifts with tender care.
She's very generous and loving too,
Dear Diane, I think the world of you.

Christine Goodchild

Horse

The sun creeps to the grey horizon's open mouth, while the descending pink blankets the cool pale sun, glowing in hues of pink, peach and mauve. A black figure brilliantly silhouettes this breath-taking cascade of colours. Seemingly on the summit of the sleeping sun it stands. Head aloft, gallant as a knight, a mane as wild as a stormy sea—and eyes as bright as a glittering sun. Snorting, it leaps from its pedestal of glory, and with eyes bright, legs agile and stealthy, it cuts through the air like a knife. Mane and tail flying and a whinny so haunting it pierces the deafening silence. With an urge of ecstasy, I push myself on its smooth silky back and hold on to its thick ragged mane. Never before have I been captivated with such beauty—the horse—enveloped in a blanket of amazing colour. She gathers speed, and the breeze cuts my ears, blinds my eyes, unravels my hair and takes my breath away. With thud of light hooves she gracefully hits the spitting spray of the lapping shore.

Arms round the beautifully arched neck, she floats on the foam—silver in the deepening dusk—cast by the rays of the wakening moon. Wave by wave she carries me closer to the sun's place of rest. Soaking my feet, my legs, my arms and my hair. Holding my breath I wait in breathless anticipation for the magical leap to the peaceful heaven beyond. I feel myself rising, I let go of my beautiful horse's mane. . .
and then . . . I wake up.

Davina Sands

Ibbar . . . Rabbi (My Brother)

O, world teachers of divinity to life,
How come one must live and strife,
Breaking bread, for brothers to live, oh yes
Our life giver, Jehovah God, is Jesus still. And bless,
Why divide, close off, reject others so
If your teaching is God, direct, open the door,
All brothers are sons, have mothers too
Must live to fulfill from Adam's rule . . .

We would adore your teaching, open your door,
Every name church for Jesus, and God lures,
Never a published tract nor book of Rabbi, why.
Millions pass on could not tell us try

Since Jesus is direct your brother too,
He feeds the multitude, raises the dead, justice He does,
To the river, to the sea all and friendship
He dying on Calvary cross for Rabbi and me.

Open King James, Christianity, reading, and bless
All hearts, life, and soul is one's digest,
When life is no more, it's Jesus calling, be
Has Rabbi teaches the world tranquility?
Why hide and divide all your mysteries, our Lord God in Heaven,
Life and love, is eternity . . . Bless one and all, His trinity.
Amen . . .

Dudley H. Callender

Life's Purpose

Life must have a purpose, for why else are we here,
If we knew the answer, the reason would be more clear,
But the fault of most humanity, is their only thought is self,
And the prime aim of our role in life, is accumulating wealth,
The more we have, the more we want, with no other thought in mind,
Selfish thoughts, are all we have, few of the loving kind,
Our arrival in this lovely world, with nothing but our health,
Was the greatest gift we ever had, that truly was our wealth,
On the day we leave it, we will take nothing out,
So it's how we live it in between, what it's all about,
Let us make the target, at which we all should aim,
One to be more proud of, not one to cause us shame,
When you've got, all you can get, what is it, you've got?
If you analyze its worth, it isn't worth a jot,
Treat this world you live in, as a fortune you should share,
With those who live it with you, as ones for whom you care,
Colours and religions wouldn't mean a thing,
We would just be one big family, with only God the King.

J. R. Robinson

Dreaming

You've put me under your spell with your words,
Your magic touch sends shivers up and down my spine,
My heart misses a beat when we touch,
Your smile I long to see, your body I long to hold,
I tremble at the sound of your voice, should I be so bold?

Teardrops roll down my face as I try to forget these feelings so strong
Maybe I'm foolish or even crazy, could I really turn you on?
What's on your mind, in your head? Are you smiling or frowning?
You fill me with wonder and ecstasy and heighten my desires.
Are you teasing and deceiving, are you sincere? Or is it just fantasy?

Every day I feel it, I'll feel it all my life.
How much can I take or give?
Is it worth the trouble and strife for this secret life?
We're in two different worlds; sometimes I wish I'd never met you;
but now I have, you may never come again, what do I do?
Take my hand, take a minute, an hour, or even just a moment.

You see I melted into your arms, floated on your kisses,
drowned in your laughter and for the closeness of your body I long,
Is it right or is it wrong? But then I wake up and you're gone.
   Jo-Anne Stoker Holmes

Light and Shade

Darkness loses out, splinters of light penetrate the rafters of the sky.
The sun peeps, hesitant, through a gap in the clouds; dawn is
but a trick away.
The rain that was, winks on the myriad shafts of a rainbow.
The moon has slithered away, giving way to two-tone
balloons of cloud.
The first reveille of the cock breaks the night's stranglehold.
Distant gulls rehearse for the trawlers.
In the fathomless waters, the fish glides lazily; unaware that
death is but a trick away, as the early angler baits his deadly trap.
Silence on the seashore; bearable yelps and bleats from the farmyard.
Breakfast noises for early risers, cups drop; bacon sizzles;
alarms disturb the peace; acquitted by the already ready.
The city wakes to the clang of the first tram; taxis bleat, cars horn;
bicycles ring on cobbled streets.
The ghosts have had their chance and are even now scampering
back to their eternal graves.
Creation has survived for another day's toil; eyes cast to the ground,
heads never upward, wondering.
Oh perfect sight; all that's holy lies in the heavens; all that's
bad repeats itself, without a thought of boredom.
Look up, you fools; you, invalids of death; a man that sees
God is immortal, with death the penitent's reward.
   The sky's beauty is God's . . .
   K. W. Staley

A Life Span

From a modest beginning it swelled and grew. A vision, yet
novel idea, came true.
The success of the venture brought good fortune to many,
with no class;
Distinction, soon acclaimed, was uncanny.

But much is the case and many a time the entrepreneur's skills
fail to filter the line.
Only when it's too late does instruction begin for the wealthy
but ill-prepared Kith and Kin.

Competition advanced far ahead, in the field, switching
volumes and discounts to meet subtler demand. The moment
was missed to update with the rest therefore how could one
hope to reside next to the best?

The spirit was strong and while battle ensued employees were
pressed to catch up and succeed. Pressure alone could not
counter the problem innovation was needed to consort with
the chosen.

When the founder passed over the shareholders knew their lack of
experience would cause them to feud. Those seniors tried to save the
empire while the siblings felt obliged to conspire.

Seven decades have passed since the humble outset now
rumours abound that the plan is to split. So sad for the founder but
surely he knew without his delegation there could be no crew.
   Clair C. Snee

October Hills

We climbed together in our youth,
Never once asked the truth,
Discoverers of life,
In pale shadows and bright sunlight,
Passions strayed, at love we played,
On October hills.

In sunbeams' daze upon those silent hills we lazed,
The raindrop tears held no fears,
Grey clouds we swept away,
Our bodies danced together,
We weathered the thrills,
On October hills

Long stormy paths we climbed,
Your tapered fingers enclosing mine,
We lay in pastures aged in time,
Autumn passed, winter too,
And changed the time I spent with you,
On October hills.
   Joan McAvoy

A Spider's Tale

Along the floor above the ground,
Small and silent my kind all around.
A need to survive so I patiently wait,
My web a trap for others their fate
This woven net translucent and fine,
Entangles my victims so I can dine.
It could be a fly or maybe a moth,
Quickly I strike before they fly off.
I know it's cruel, but try to forgive,
It's our way of life, it's the way that we live.
   Trevor Codd

The Path to Peace

God gives to men the strength to see
   that all wars fought are infamy
Grants them courage so they will seek
   to promote peace by what they speak.

For wars have never been a winner
   it is a chosen path for every sinner,
So let's take each comrade by the hand
   and show to them God's promised land.

It's the only chance for the Human Race
   to beat the Nuclear War they face,
In Nuclear War we won't survive
   peace is the only way that we will thrive.

So let's make every one a friend
   that every war comes to an end,
Remember God's words of peace to all
   let this be our rallying call.
   Lachlan Taylor

Little Crocus

Oh where, oh where has she gone?
She is nowhere to be found.
Is she sleeping and resting underground?
All Summer it is sad not to see her having fun
When every other blossoms are happy under the sun.
But at the first signs of Spring she lifts up her head
When we thought she was dead.
There is still snow on the ground,
But when we look around
We will find her under a tree
In all her beauty to see.
She indicates that it is Spring.
If she were a bell she would ring.
She nods and peeps.
She's not asleep;
She tries to stand tall,
Oh little Crocus
You are loved by all.
   Doris Hogan

The Turn of the Orchard

The roar of the wind
whistles through the trees,
the spider returns to his web,
the blossom scatters the floor of the orchard,
the apples roll around in turn,
they hit the fence and . . .
the wind direction changes.
The flowers of the orchard,
so cheerful, no bright, even
uproot as the wind turns to a gale.
The orchard then becomes scary place,
the trees creak, moan.
But all of a sudden the gale
turns into a breeze, slowly.
The sun shines through the
clouds, the trees.
The birds sing softly,
the spider crawls out,
for that was the "turn of the orchard."

Victoria Woods

Silence for War

I wasn't born for bloody wars,
Yet to the Anzacs I will say,
Thanks for all who fought and died,
For the giants at Gallipoli and the ghosts on Suvla Bay,
Thanks to all canucks, who died at Vimy Ridge,
Thanks to Denny Bretheridge and the lads on the Pegasus Bridge,
Thank you all the blooded lion who for my freedom died,
Thanks to all the soldiers dead, that war has crucified,
Silence is not enough for the price in full you paid,
Silence is not enough for the ghost of bravery laid,
For my father's fathers and for my son's own sons,
I believe the debt be paid forever, so lower the bloody guns,
Play back the sounds of glory, may that barrage never cease,
But give the brave, for what they fought and carved in granite,
Peace.

Alan Ryder

The Waves of the Sea

Waves can be so calm lapping the sand,
like a tight fitting coat,
or moderately rolling in,
with soft white horses on the crest of the waves.

The high tides bring huge roller coasters,
dashing the rocks and sea walls,
often wild like a cape swirling over your head
when the wind has lifted it over your shoulders.

Whatever the size of the waves,
they make beautiful scenes of nature,
sometimes cruel,
the waves of the sea

D. M. E. Harrison

In My Heart

There's an ache in my heart that is sometimes a pain,
It won't go away, 'til I'm with you again.
There's a love in my heart that is trusting and true,
Protected by faith, and kept only for you.

There's a song in my heart, with its own melody—
No one else hears it—just you and me.
There's a key to my heart that is made of pure gold,
Just you and I know how its secrets unfold.

There's pride in my heart, when I think of you,
So clever, so strong, and so handsome, too!
There's peace in my heart, for a dream come true,
Your love for me, and mine for you.

There are thanks in my heart—the reason you know—
For you made me your wife, just a year ago.
There's joy in my heart, as I write this to you,
For a new little heart, is now beating there, too.

Pearl Williams

Through My Eyes

Oh, mother why was I born this way?
Why can't I run out and play.
When people stand and smile at me,
I wish they would bend and talk, you see.
I may not understand all that you say,
But oh, how it would brighten my day.
I am a person in my own right you see,
So next time you see someone like me.
Bend and speak and happy I will be . . .

Isabella Muir-Ward

The Bitter Ending of a Relationship

Anger ever raging
Replaces everlasting love;
Waves rise and fall,
Vengeance with increasing rage,
Volcanoes burst with untempered fury.

Hate everlasting,
The fountain rages,
Then becoming empty,
You walk through life alone.
The hollow rock lies desolate, and unloved.

The great weight of sorrow,
Brings consuming emptiness,
Everlasting peace, lost,
Pride prevails over remorse,
The darkness descends with the unconscious hope of light.

Stephanie Brown

The Deadly Element

There's a deadly element on this earth, that's known to us as man.
These poisonous vipers we have tried to tame, but no-one ever can.
We feed them, clothe them and treat them well, we care for them each day.
We stand by them and cover their butts, whatever comes their way.
They come to us from out the blue, in many shades or form.
I'm sure they did not look this bad, the day that they were born.
What really do we see in them, these creatures great and small?
If I could only have my way, I would gladly shoot them all.
The good, the bad and the ugly, whichever one we see,
The small, the medium, the oh! My God! It doesn't bother me
Whether you are young or old, on one unsuspecting night
The poisonous venom he will release, with one soft but deadly bite.
Then you will be trapped in his grip, never to be freed,
But very soon you will find out, the snake is full of greed.
So be warned, my friends, and take my word, now this message I have sent.
Beware! Of this thing what's known as man "The Deadly Element".

Sheila Reeves

Is It Only a Dream?

A swirling mist covers a scene almost like a shroud,
The rocks, though barely visible, appear as a crowd,
Up there somewhere is the sun.
Was it like this when time had begun
Or is it only a dream?
A glimmer of sunlight exposes a scene, was it like this
Or what might have been?
The waves lap gently too and fro, sea life hovering,
Some will go back to the ocean with the flow,
Some will stay, shells will appear, discarded homes,
Some in disarray.
To those of us who stroll the shore, content to wander
and explore, hear the gulls come screeching, never still.
Crabs come scuttling down the hill, back to the rocks,
to the deep beyond, the mist lifts slowly, showing
not a pond, but an ocean so strong.
Now, the sunlight filters through the hue, allowing
blue skies to reflect the view.
Is this how it's always been
Or is it only a dream?

Helen Phillips

Russell James—My Little Brother

I would croon you lullabies, you would close your drowsy eyes
Then as I softly crept away you'd wake and have your rowdy say.

I was ten and you were 'nought', when this wily fight was fought.
You had me dancing on a string, and you demanded everything.

When I grew to be fifteen, you were my devoted slave,
You were five and would fetch and carry anything I'd crave.

When I was twenty you were ten,
And I spoilt you now and then.
I bought you little shoes in tiny boxes,
And matched them up with little soxes.
Sometimes I'd take you to a Matinee,
And endure two noisy hours of kids at play.

Then when David used to come around,
you would hover somewhere near the ground.
Then we married and moved to Lower Hutt,
And each August you came to visit us.

August the 23rd 1964 . . . It doesn't rhyme anymore!
You were fifteen!
You were drowned!
Your picture's in a frame . . .
Noeline Cutts

Child Embrace

The magician's way is to mask with tricks
the ignorant, like a pile of building bricks.
He plays with his babies, brings so quick
while they focus on his magic stick.

The dancer dances in spirals and weaves
his patterns of skill for those to believe
with his mastery of ?? And mind,
it can choose to enmesh or unbind.

We all weave a merry dance and yet
some of us just can't forget
the pinky winter mid-sun glow,
the after-life; before-life; and how we grow.

And if but half my talks were told, I'm sure
for those who know of understanding pure,
untainted with the patriarchal gauze,
would find abide by universal laws.

Now—my little son, so cherub-faced
sings and dances—and laughs in my place.
And the pinky-ins mid-sun glow
rest in his cheeks, and spirit-flow.
Kai A. Langford

Snowdrop Valley

Snowdrop valley is the place to be. Panoramic views, all for free.
Seas of white all around.
Over the years many pictures taken of this beautiful ground,
In amongst the sea of white and blue,
The green of the grass blends in too.
A beauty such as this you simply cannot miss.
The time of year is right, for you to take flight
And head for this unforgettable sight.
It is to be true, an awesome view
The green, the white, and the blue.
Snowdrop valley once was unknown.
Now it is televised, written about and we are all shown
The destination of this once unspoiled place, as its popularity
    has grown.
Down a narrow road into the valley.
So much traffic used to flow, you'd have thought it was a rally.
The latest idea is 'park and ride,' which comes complete with
    its own guide.
The guide is not needed, the place is so small
Its beauty hits you like a 'brick wall.'
You will have to stop and stare as there simply is nothing to compare
With its splendid rustic charm, which in time will need all our care.
Rosalind Mary Robinson

The Real Me

Sometimes I wish I wasn't me.
With a different soul and a different face.
I feel alone yet am in a crowd
I wonder if this is my destiny.
This feeling of emptiness won't go away,
For a part of me feels trapped
Yet unwilling to stay
One day I hope I can break away,
At last feel free to be the real me.
Julie Higgins

Questions and Answer

Where am I going? Where have I been?
What am I doing? What have I seen?
So many questions when life's span is nearly done
who will remember me when I'm gone?
My family of course will remember my name
but I haven't done any great deeds of fame
I haven't climbed mountains or yet tramped the earth
just package holidays for what that is worth
I know what I'll do, I will write me a rhyme
perhaps get it published in 'A Passage in Time'
A beautiful book for my grandchildren's room
and maybe one day a family heirloom.
E. Fisher

"Heaven on Earth"

At "Southchurch Hall Gardens", a welcome awaits you.
Ducks come to greet you, they always do,
To see the tempting morsels you've brought them to eat.
They waddle towards you, quacking at your feet,
As they line up in single file.
They always raise from me a smile,
'Tis a treat, pure Heaven on Earth to see,
There's no other place, that I'd rather be.
Their performance has ended, on the water they glide,
With a smug satisfaction that is difficult to hide.
Peace and tranquility have covered the pond
As if a magician had just tapped his wand.
A magical healing of spirit is felt,
A joyous feeling that makes my heart melt.
My troubled thoughts all disappear,
And, at once, all seems very clear.
The beauty of the gardens, with the freshness of greenery
And "Heavenly Scents", from the floral scenery,
Uplift my spirit to another plane
Until next time, when it does wane.
Joyce Susan Harvey

What Kind of a God?

God speaks through water.
What kind of a God made water?
It has no shape, no colour, no smell,
but it can sustain life, it can take life,
God speaks through water.

God speaks through colours.
What kind of a God made colours?
Look at the blue of the sky, the rainbow,
the reds, golds and browns of autumn,
so breathtaking it reels your senses,
God speaks through colours.

God speaks through love.
What kind of a God made love?
Love is a mother cuddling her baby, a new bride,
sixty years of marriage,
people embracing each other in The True Faith.
God is love.
God speaks through love.
What kind of a God made these things?

A living, loving God.
Denise Cameron

People

People are like the deep and wondrous ocean
So great the contents hidden in their depths.
Thoughts, like a shoal of fishes dart around,
Many to never see the light of day.
Like an unopened oyster often a pearl enclosed
White, black, or pink, within their secret folds.
Far in dark caverns, endless hopes encased,
And, like gold strands of seaweed, interlaced
With love and joy, or disillusionment untold
Lying, like sea anemones in shadowed cold.
Which ope' and shut some things to be resealed
Only to be cut up, and then revealed.
Like sudden storm at sea destroying much
But when the sun beats down and waves release their clutch.
On oceans' bed, plans may be smoothed and tranquil till men's heads,
Spirits with warmth, renew themselves once more.
In calmest waters, beauty and best inventions breed it's sure
And courage like the tides return to ebb of flow once more.

Ann Cubitt

The Coming of Eternity

Eternity is life, it is hope,
It gives strength to those who are weak.
Eternity is a light to the world,
It's like a tunnel, symbolised as a birth canal,
As a passageway or a positive root,
From one phase of life to another.

The coming of eternity brings peace to my heart,
Like a never ending river flowing over me,
Knowing as the water of life,
It gives me strength through bad times,
It gives me hope to live each day as it comes and goes.

Many people need something in their lives,
To give them hope, eternity will give hope,
Eternity is deep, full of life and everlasting,
The hope I have is the coming of eternity!!

Joanne Wright

Sunset

The Sun rises once again
Another day is born.
Lent to all from thee
'Almighty One'
Thus given, it is not our right!
Let us all make the most of it . . .
When the Sun sets in 'blaze of colour'
Our labours will have ceased.
Good an' bad alike
The Sun sets over both.
Who is to know if we get a second chance?
Do you . . .!

James J. Connolly

Life's Journey

Innocence creates faith,
A blank page
Where nothing has been written,
Wonder, awe, faith and love
Open to all of these,
Looking out from the eyes of my soul,
A flower, a tree,
A river, a butterfly,
Absorbing the miracle of creation,
Such a beautiful childlike place
Conditions have not yet been learnt,
I believe because I have no reason not too,
Until, this innocence slips away
I thought it would last forever,
My being longs for its return
Searching everywhere,
Lost, separated from me,
I will go back
This is my journey, home.

Brenda McAuley

Siren of Oblivion

You were my Sister:
My antithesis, nemesis and friend.
My unimaginable self.

Hidden thoughts
Burned behind your swollen eyelids.
Entranced by inner tumult
You tumbled on.
You drove unheeding through our lives
Foot on floor
Locked to self-destruct.

I would have helped,
Shown my need to care;
But anguish passed unnoticed.

Was I to know I would be disregarded for playing favourites with oblivion?
What events forged your sparkling indifference?
Polished to a shine.
You never heard me shout.

I showed you all my love:
You turned the other way.

Caroline Le Jeune

Ever Near

Dedicated to my late brother, Geoffrey Wells

Dear brother, how my life has changed
Since you have passed away.
I didn't see you very much
But miss you more each day.

We had our spate of arguments
We joked, we laughed and cried
And shared a mutual agony
The night our Father died.

Who would have guessed that you'd be next
So active and so strong.
The envy of many, cut down in your prime;
Taken from where you belong.

What I'd give to hear your voice,
To see you smile again.
To end my feelings of emptiness,
Of grieving and of pain.

If there's a God and I'm sure there is
Then you're with us still, it's true.
And you will know within your soul
The depth of my love for you.

Christine Ash-Smith

Bosnia (The Blue Berets)

Bosnian heroes with berets of blue
Doing their best to see a job through
The fight is not theirs, but there they must be
To try and bring peace to this war torn country.

The children follow food lorries for miles
Hopeful faces, with tears and smiles,
The tears are plenty, the smiles are few,
The men in blue berets, they sometimes cry too.

Children in rags, with hands out to greet
The blue beret hero, who comes with a treat,
this country, once proud, decided to die.
People went crazy, we'll never know why.

Round tables, square tables, the powers that be,
Sit around squabbling, for the right to be free.
Leaders of men, and politicians
Representing all the United Nations.

Nations United? It doesn't seem right,
That neighbours, once friendly, suddenly fight,
And through all this, working night, working day,
Are the heroes that wear the blue beret.

A. E. Midwinter

The Emigrant

The seventeen year old girl walked away from her mother
and home with a tangle of sadness, fear, hope and excitement
all knitted up into a ball inside her.
Her mother stood and watched her go, tears welled up in the grey eyes.
Hope burned in her breast that the girl could cope with being an outsider.
The girl arrived with two pairs of everything, a coat and a hat.
But material possessions meant little to her,
and she was grateful for that.
The girl got through a training that was gruelling, but fair and fulfilling,
She married and bore children who became her joy and her purpose for living.
But the girl never forgot where she came from, her mother, her home.
Nostalgia was an emotion that often caused her sadness and an ache in each bone.
The immigrant here, the emigrant there, and sometimes life didn't
Seem altogether fair to that seventeen year old girl with the very dark hair.

Tara Barnard

Just One of Those Days

Do you ever have "Just one of those days"
When nothing goes right and everything wrong?
Even by lunch you're still in a daze
Wondering why the day is so long!

On "one of those days" you should stay in bed,
But you don't know it is one until you are up,
When you speedily find how up you are fed
And how sorrowfully full to the brim is your cup!

This I'm afraid has been "one of those days"!
I'll spare you the details and hope day is done.
Perhaps now it's dark fate has mended her ways
And we can relax for an evening of fun!

Patrick Davies

Colours of the Day

Dawn breaks against the dark blue velvet night,
The unseen artist adds the welcome light.
He paints a landscape, wondrous to behold,
Blue fades to purples, pinks then palest gold.
The patchwork blanket, made from greens and browns,
Cloak hills and fields, till they reach the concrete towns.
Where shades of grey now take their place with pride,
Amongst their brighter brethren, they abide.
The demure blush of the roses catch the eye,
See crimson berries, bright against the sky.
White daisies nod their heads as breezes blow,
Bronze leaves dance to the ground before the snow.
The silver rivers meander to the shore,
Just as they did in the years that went before.
The rainbow coloured fish now dart and hide
From rainbow-coloured birds that swoop and dive.
Too soon, the day is drawing to its end,
And once again the artist's colours blend.
Pale gold to pinks, then purples turn dark blue,
And night now hides the colours from our view.

Maggie Moore

Land of Dreams

I liken my life to a barren land
    Where dreams and ambitions drift in the sand
Where fantasy floats in a ratified clime
    Then wither and wilt with the passing of time

From the shadowy sidelines of like I look in
    To the realm of reality, great achievements therein
As to fortune and fame, I can hardly lay claim
    I wallow in reverie futile and tame

Delusions of grandeur I think is the phrase
    For one who lives life in euphoric haze
Yet had I the power these dreams I'd erase
And wake up to real adulation and praise

John Nicholson

Speak for Love

If I were mute and couldn't speak
What bloom would give me voice,
To shout those perfect thoughts I seek
Which make my heart rejoice.

Not just mere words like, "I love you!"
How can these express the whole,
Translating express the whole,
Translating all that's good and true
Essence of the heart and soul.

For talk abounds like summer tares
That spring forth will little thought,
But fail to lay the spirit bare
And unearth the passions sought.

Yet stemming from the living clay
The roots of my emotion,
Blossom in language that can say
All my love and devotion.

For personified in flower
Alone it has the power.
My feelings grown entwined above,
The rose it speaks for love.

John Bernard Elford

Life Is Bleeding

Life is Bleeding into the Hand you Stretched Out
to the Bleeding Sunset—I am in the Bleeding Sunset
into the Bleeding Life—my Eye is Crying with
into the Eye of the Bleeding Sunset
into the Bleeding Flame of the Fire
into the Bleeding Sunset
into the Dark Dusk of the Night of Summer
my Life is Bleeding with—into the Bleeding Sunset
into the Darkness of the Night of Summer
you came to—as a Shadow in the Dark
with your Hand Stretched Out
to the Bleeding Sunset
into the Begged Life you are Begging with
your Life of Dog
into the Bark of Death of the Dog
you Came with to Die into my Bleeding Eye
into the Bleeding Sunset—into the Bleeding Life
my Soul is Bleeding with
into the Life of Dog—you are Giving to me with
your Life—into the Bark of Death of the Dog

Greatwood Gabriela

Blood in Her Eyes

Child . . . where are you?
Where are your dreams, where is your laughter?
How come you've always been here,
but now, when I need you the most, you've faded somewhere else?

Child . . . I wish you could know my sorrow.
I wish you'd know your sister's tears.
Yes . . . I am your sister.
I am your lonely sister on earth.

Hey child . . . Are you there?
Tell me . . . Does God ever listen to my prayers?
Do you even care for what I say?
Could you tell me how it feels to be the innocent one in heaven?

You know . . . I really hoped He'd see what you've done.
I hoped He'd realize you're not the one I thought you'd be.
But even He is too blind to know your sins.
And now you've joined His army.
You are one of His angels . . .

Well . . . I hope you drown in the clouds . . .
I hope, your eyes are bleeding . . .
I hope you see the dirt in your heart . . .

Margareta Ferek

Alone to the Grave

One day I'd like a wife and a family and all those sort of things
The joys, disappointments, smiles and teas a family brings
Suppose I grew old and never settled down, I'd be alone
Sure I'd have my friends but I'd still be on my own
I'd have no one to love me, no one to show my love to
No one to wake up next to, no one to tell "I love you"

What a terrible thought, it's enough to make you depressed
And what about when you die and you're laid to rest?
Alone to the grave, another pauper's funeral unattended
Being carried in my coffin by strangers, stone cold dead

Put a bit by, just enough to be buried
No one there paying their last respects, not a tear shed
No wreaths, no flowers, no messages from any loved ones
I regret not getting married, no daughters and no sons

So there I am six foot under, the sun and the wind above the ground
No one visits my grave, lost friends are buried miles around
Friends and relatives visit headstones on special occasions like father's day
No one visits me, my grave's been left untouched, today was my birthday
My grave's plain, but if I'm lucky some kind lady might take pity
She might pull one flower from her bunch and kindly place it above me

Brian Stoneman

Rapture of Spring

Over the village the meadow larks sing, to welcome the sun and the coming of spring. Each fluttering flower, each moderate breeze, heralds the gift of new life to the trees.

Daffodils dance, swaying golden and green, bank upon bank of them, where snow has been. Mother and child pass along, hand in hand, walking enraptured through wakening land.

Over the churchyard pink blossoms have grown, foaming above, ever restless, wind-blown. White, like the breakers that rush to the shore, spread in profusion round trellis and door.

Trees which lay dormant through winter's dark night, raise happy arms now, to welcome the light. Row upon row of them border the lawn, verdant and green now that spring has been born.

Murmuring soft, like a child at its rest, grass is returning to land that is blessed, all-coloured flowers in gaudy array, grow in profusion now, close by the way.

Streams which stood frozen where icicles hung, laugh through the village where bells are now rung, there in the church precious souls gladly sing, thanking their Lord for the rapture of spring.

Richard Langford

Schiehallion

Snow peppered pinnacle pointing to the sky;
Looks like a recumbent brassiered breast
Fondled by passing nympho' nimbus—they're not shy!
Wish I'd climbed that erotic crest!

Obtusely pitched declivities surrender to cloud ditched snow;
Sunlight conquers hoar cumulus and beams down on an argent glow.
The flocculent woolpack clouds cast shifting adumbrations:
One moment dusky hues; the next, etiolations.

Oh, conical eminence towering like a lofty sentry bold,
Keeping watch over the centuries, what secrets do you hold?
What memories lie beneath your brackened slopes:
The chronicler of Perthshire, of its dreams, its hopes?

General Wade and his troops, bridging the Tummel, did you spy on
When they marched over the brae from Rannoch to Glen Lyon?
When Queen Victoria halted by the Tummel shore to rest
Did you block The Queen's View with your prominent crest?

Like a mighty laird commanding mirador views atop the brae,
Surveying your domain from Rannoch Moor to Loch Tay;
Every burn and loch, Lyon to Garry—and each names a glen,
Mysterious, esoteric mountain what do you ken?

Jeffrey Campbell

Roast Lamb

Oh little lamb, why were you born,
On a very cold, and frosty morn,
God gives you life, but for how long,
Man kills you to eat, and that is wrong,
You are just a baby, not long born,
You will never reach, being old and worn,
You are really cute, and cuddly too,
But that doesn't stop them, killing you,
You will never grow, to a ewe or a ram,
And all because man, likes to eat roast lamb.

Florence J. Gillanders

Untitled

A sunset, intense yet placid as I sit to watch; the
colours; profound; evoke memories
that never quite leave my attention, unwavering
with every passing day; or
night; when I look to the stars, and maybe even
wave; at the man in the moon. Thinking of;
times gone past, days gone by. Discovering
new emotions. And recalling those that tell
tales of sorrow, and tales of
joy; and with those tales come the aroma of;
A perfume; a man; a last kiss. What was that smell?
Never known; but always remembered like;
Yesterday or today, as the autumn leaves fall; the
colours; profound; flame, gold; evoke memories
that never quite leave my attention, unwavering
with every passing day; or
night; as I stroll along the beach, listening;
to the crash of the waves against the
shore. Cut out to show the beauty of;
Organised Mayhem.

Claire Edwards

Night

An endless stretch of velvet black,
a mystery to us still,
dotted with eternal stars,
observing at your will.

From dusk till dawn you spread once more,
across our many skies,
the closing of the day has come,
the sun once more shall die.

So many things not said or done,
questions still remain,
for it is time to close our eyes,
now you have come again.

Stacey Blackman

Papers Lives

I was a paper from the tree of life.
Cut, ground and processed into clean,
snow white and first class quality.
I was separated from the womb of my happy kingdom,
transferred from place to place, position to position,
from palm to another.
For good?
You have painted my face dirt of different colours.
Blown by the wind, to the farm, to the drainage,
on the streets, and everywhere.
Spat and spewed by the sky, laughed by the scorcher sun,
mucked by subduing wind, goggled by the moon,
stamped by you feet and rolled over by your boastful wheels.
Still, the process moves on,
carried by the wind everywhere.
What will happen to me?
Will there be heads to stoop and hands to pick me up
to recycle my life even just to light up the garbage mountain?
Will my life end up rotting and wasting away on the streets and canals?
Master, why?

Harry Ventura Relator

Rivington Moor Is a Special Place

I go there to escape.
The peace and stillness and beauty
of scenes are just like being in a dream.

I can drift all day from
dawn till dusk.
I never tire of the beautiful day,
raining, hail, sun I stay,
time to rest and think awhile,
let my memories wonder.
I've been up here with Dad a lot
he's given this to me,
a love of life, of space
and air; it's free to breathe
and laugh and stare,
I just don't give a care,
it lifts me up and sets me free,
the wind blowing so silent,
let's go home now Dad,
we are happy again and not sad.

A. A. O'Malley

The U.F.O.

Looking up in the sky on a dull late night
Suddenly appeared a large bright light
Seems to be so clear and white
As I looked again the colour was not right

All it done was fly round and round
Leaving in the air this humming sound
Could it be a homeward bound
Or will it even come to ground

Why does it not land I ask
Could there be a spaceman wearing a mask
Or are they here, on their own task
Now I'll never know who to ask

J. S. Foster

Our Blessings

If only we would realize how wealthy we all are.
A golden sun that shines by day a silver moon shines from afar.
The twinkling stars are crystals our jewels to behold.
Showers of blessings our Lord sends as in the days of old.
The roaming fields of cattle. The fields of waving corn.
And in the sunny springtime the little lambs are born
No money from the Lottery we never could compare.
With all the treasures that are there if only we would share
With all our brothers far and wide and peacefully abide.
In the rainbow of life's way, the promise from our Lord.
True health and wealth and happiness. We never could afford.

Kathleen Heyden Dale

Wonderland

Dreams drift away to fade and die,
As drowsily in bed I lie,
I turn to see the light of day,
And catch a wonderland at play,
With fairy ferns and dreamlike trees,
All bending in a gentle breeze,
With ne'er a bird or insect there,
Or animal to cause me fear.
But life I see, the trees have grown,
I wander crystal paths alone,
And gaze in awe at all I see,
With sunlight dancing in each tree,
Each branch and twig of crystal made,
The sun shines through, there is no shade,
The crystal grass and lovely fern,
Fill me with wonder each in turn,
The sun beats down the warmer air,
Makes tree and fern all disappear,
But I know I'll see them again,
The frost trees on my window pane.

Charlie Boy Smith

Brain in a Bottle

Sweet irony, that it should be preserved
in the very substance that caused it now
to be gazed upon with sense of mystery
by a stranger.
He knew perhaps less than we who come
to bear witness to his testimony.
All matter of your life revealed; much that
became concealed from all but your creator.
Machine shut down intelligence supreme.
Closed doors cloaked you in the solitude
of death.
The final search for ultimate truth is yours.
For you have found that which he has not.
Left alone he doth avert his gaze from
the incision.
Whilst I weep to erase this shocking
vision . . .

A. Lucas

Trouble on the Roads

Before cars were invented, more people walked,
Now with all the traffic and hold ups,
So much time is wasted so people have to talk,
It means more petrol is used and work time cut.
Children years ago walked to schools and home,
Now it is mostly by buses or cars taken to the schools,
They nearly all went home for their midday meal,
Now mostly the dinners are brought to the schools.
Years ago working people had their jobs near to home,
Now most have to travel miles to their work,
So it means having their evening meal at home,
It costs most a great deal to go to and from work.
Rural railways, some were closed down, making more on roads
The rivers, mostly are not used for passenger service or trades,
Most of the money is spent on the big main roads,
To the neglect of the country by-roads and the peoples' trades,
Would it not have been better if more thought had been given
To the harm some cuts in services could do,
When lots of inventions in the workshops happen,
It can cause lots more people on the dole.

J. E. Storton

Coming of the Spring

It's a lovely time of year.
When everything comes to life
The flower's coming into bloom.
The birds also busy building their nests
And singing their hearts out.
And also the sun shines above.
Makes everyone feel alive and kicking
The gardens too make one know
That spring is on its way.
With all fresh growth and scents.
That the gardens give out.
It makes one think of the new life
That spring does bring with it.

A. F. Hiscocks

Seasons' Delights

Lammikin, lammikin, fill up your pannikin,
  Gather the briar
  To build up the fire.
See how the water so merrily bubbles.
  Put tea in the pan.
  It's all ready, Gran.
Oh, a picnic in summers, the greatest of feasts.

Lammikin, lammikin, nights have grown dark again.
  Winter is here
  With frost cold and clear.
Draw close the curtains—all snug and warm.
  Marshmallow toasts,
  Tales about ghosts
And pictures in fire flames—oh, winter's such fun!

Margaret M. Osoba

The Land and the Sky...

Give me the land and the clear sky above,
A winding river and towering trees;
Fitting together like hand in a glove,
All in the creation for God to please.

Keep it in your mind and keep in your head,
For your life's time will roll on like the sea;
Or the thoughts in your mind will all be dead,
And fall away like the leaves from a tree.

What makes you breathe and what makes you to think?
But we shall never know that for to say;
We journey on and we eat and we drink,
But the gift of life is taken away.

So live on the land with sunshine and hay,
A winding river and towering trees,
Today is yours and tomorrow your day,
Till our life and our thoughts all fade away.

Dennis Parkes

The Year

Spring is here and the primrose is showing
Down in the wood where the windflowers are blowing
The buds on the trees are turning to green
And the earth's re-awakening all around can be seen

Now here comes summer—spring must give way
The flowers all bloom in their finest array
Long lingering twilights to close each day
And the farmers are busy making the hay

Russet and Gold tell us Autumn is here
The days grow shorter now I fear
But the beauty of autumn is there to behold
Try not to think that the year's growing old

Icy fingers grip the earth
Cold winds blow for all they're worth
Mankind shivers now Winter is here
But spring will come—as it does each year.

E. Fisher

Friends

Someone to laugh with,
there through the good and the bad.
For me to lean on,
me for them to lean on.
To help each other out when in need,
to have long gossips with.
To draw each other away from the bad things,
guide to the good.
Help each other to make something positive out
of our lives.
That's what a good friend is for.

Natalie Cave

Lost in the Wind

Never again will I believe such trust
So delicate and fragile it breaks like a crust
Will good will alone see me through
Only distant images remain of you
Lost in the wind the promises made
The betrayal in my heart will never fade
Alone I stood and you walked away
How this still haunts me day after day
I believed you and all that you said
Dreams so vivid, dreams I dread
Like the eternal fire that doesn't go out
A longing for water from the long drought
No one can bring back what is past
Oh regret, regret will not be the last
Nothing can stop the march of time
Nor can man erase his crime
Time is not kind to fools in its way
Lost in the wind forever they stay

Nicholas Fletcher

Where You Are, There I Am

I found your loving message,
That you had written me,
The joy in finding it was sheer ecstasy,
For I know how much love and concern you had for me,
I found it in our favorite book,
I knew it had to be
Something very special that you had given me,
It read, "Where you are there I am."
Now whenever I am low and long to be with you,
I think of what you wrote to me,
With so much love and thought,
Which gives me joy and comfort,
And restores my energy.

Dagmar W. Meyer

Love

If you should die and leave me
What would I see
A room so bare with no one to care
Or you sitting in a chair
If you should die and leave me
How would I feel
Empty and sad
For all the things we should have had
If you should die and leave me
How would I cope
Some days very well
But mostly not at all
With no one there with a cup of tea
Or a touch or a smile
When things are sad and you need a helping hand
If you should die and leave me
My heart will be just empty as can be
For you see you are to me
My whole world my dreams and you are me.

Gillian G. Cox

Ode to the Third Kingdom

Mysterious cavern of restless beauty,
Earth and musk and mist and fire,
As sunlight dawns on this fashioned world
Which awaits sad darkness to declare an entry.

Black shadows cast long, mourn the
Sparkling heart of summer; lazy trees
Stand naked, swaying and singing to themselves:
"How you enter this kingdom of diversity!"

Multitude of wist and fear powered by sensation,
Amber, red, gold, olive—all caught against the frost.
Ancient wood smoke and crisping hue of cold;
This celebration of a dusky, healthy dream.

Early morning sparsity creates frustrated trance
As the overpowering aura resigns to my senses,
And I am suddenly overwhelmed by it all,
By this orgiastic terror of time.

Katarina Lindroth

The Green Grass of Home

Life is full of struggles, it has its
ups and downs, you live each day
of your life, but do you ever look around?
Around at the beauty, the beauty you ignore, that brings
a smile to your face when you open your front door.

Nature's beauty is a precious thing that lives through
every day, it changes with the seasons and blooms
mostly in April and May.
Now, nature likes to take care of herself but something
else she likes to do, is to try and bring a smile to the
faces of me and you.

For if we feel tired and weary or we feel lost and alone,
we all can take great comfort when we see the green
grass of home.

Sarah L. Gilhooly

My Home Town

The morning mist has risen,
Another new day born,
I thank the Lord he's given me,
Another day to carry on.

The peace and sheer tranquillity,
That a country scene can bring,
To me is now a reality,
And I treasure everything.

Before I moved to the country,
The town life was all I knew,
There were no beautiful birds and trees,
Only people and long bus queues.

The noise of the rushing traffic,
The fumes from their exhaust,
Is not the place that I would pick
For me, if I were lost.

Yes, for me there's nothing like it,
It's the only place to go,
To walk, to dream, or even sit,
In my country home Brisco.

Ann Hunt

Long Black Hall

It's cold at night in my lonely bed,
I've got the ice-cold sheets over my head,
cause I'm afraid of the dark.
Moon is shining through the window,
the shadows are dancing on the wall.
I hear footsteps in the hall, is it you?
It could not be you, cause you
died last fall.
I hear you calling me, so I look
out in the hall.
But there's nothing there but
a long black hall.
Maybe it's just me, I could be
insane, I could be dead and I just
don't know.
It's cold at night in my ice-cold bed,
I've got the sheets over my head,
I'm afraid of the dark.

I'm afraid of what might be
out there beyond the door,
The door to the long black hall,

Tracy Lee Smith

Joyce Goodchild, 1911-1994

I first met you, dear Joyce, a long time ago.
When from girlfriend, to girlfriend moved to and fro.
At the time I fancied your dear Jacqueline,
As striking a lady as I'd ever seen.
It was clear from the start you were on my side,
And when you sensed I wanted her as my bride
You said "just adopt a more positive stance,
I happen to know you are in with a chance."
Encouraged, I asked her, Jackie smiled and said "Yes"
(Later thinking, why did I get into this mess;
I was given the chance to travel Down Under,
Why did I blow it, I shall always wonder!)
Three children were born, Deborah, David and Lizzie,
Throughout you were there, ever helpful and busy.
When I was ill, your help was immense,
There for the family in every sense.
Towards the end of your life you lived in our house,
A most welcome guest, there was never a grouse.
So God Bless, and farewell, I salute you, dear Joyce,
As a mother-in-law, you quite the best choice.

Michael Carter

The Unfamiliar Song

The first chord on the guitar
And my heart leaps up for more.
The tune seems so familiar,
Though I've never heard this song before.

His voice like heavy whispers,
Every word breathes in my head,
Unaware of what I'm hearing
As no words are being said.

And now the song is hurting
The pain screams through the tune,
Imprisoned by these four walls,
I cannot escape this room.

The whispers become shouting,
The guitar begins to roar.
And I swear I hear laughter,
As I collapse to the floor.

My body explodes in flames,
As this song ends in my head.
The guitar plays his final chord.
All alone . . . I lie dead.

Carrie Bevins

The Drifting Clouds

I look up to the pale blue sky,
and watch the clouds go drifting by,
the white ones move with precise little ease.
The grey ones dance but show little romance.

Then upon the horizon
the black clouds form,
we are then aware
of a pending storm.

The winds do blow,
the gales will howl,
as they bring the rain
along with the hail.

There's a flash of light
in distant skies
and a crash of thunder
goes rattling by.

So quick of rise
and likewise fall,
the storm has passed
and peace will prevail.

P. Little

Love, Passion and Pain

I have felt the heartache and pain
I have seen my miseries through the rain
I know what it means to have a broken heart
I know how it feels when your world falls apart
I had it all the good and the bad
Yeah, love and tears was all I had

But suddenly I see fire in your eyes
Suddenly I feel loving in a big size
What makes this night, oh so complete?
Then the fire and passion, the kisses and the heat
We got it all after years of struggling and pain
Deep in our soul and up in our veins

And I keep on feeling how our hearts beat together
I keep on seeing this love staying forever
Cause, I know what it means to be with you each night
Mm, I know how it feels when you hold me so tight
We got it all now to never let it go again
Cause, now I'm your woman
But baby, you are my man

Tonia Deliens

Summer Swallows

It's April and it's funny,
How the swallows seem to know,
The season with the summer rain,
To start the roundabout again,
Winds blow, oh so gently, help them on their way,
Don't tire, or delay them, on an April sunny day.

A weathered creaky old barn,
Cobwebbed rafters stretching far,
Kept warm and dry for you, summer swallows you are due,
To start to build your nests once more
With downy feathers, mud and straw
You weave and make them safe and warm,
Your babies soon will form.

Summer swallows perched on rafters high,
You teach your babies how to fly,
For with the swallow, comes a part of life
That will never die.
Nature starts its tune again, timing things just right,
The many miles that you do comb,
Summer swallows flying home.

Barbara Flamson

Why Did You Do It?

A fisherman lies on the seas cold floor,
grieving for loved ones, he left on the shore.
Cast down to infinity's empty cartel,
he reasons—unheard, from the depth of his well.

"I fought with you, from dawn till dusk.
Fishing for fish, was my daily must.
I foolishly challenged your superior might,
thinking you'd honour, our unequaled fight.

There were days when you teased, without any rest,
releasing a little, while keeping the best.
And the times when you threatened, with fearsome delight,
retaining the catch—to further my plight.

You watched, and waited, in silent resent,
until one day you left me, tired, and spent.
You choose that moment to wash down the deck!
In your watery tongue, I was less than a speck.

Now, here I lie, struck down by your hate,
your awesome intentions, I found out too late.
My life is minuscule, in all that you own—
Oh!, why did you do it?",—the answers unknown.

Anna Junor

The Surgeon

Wearily they enter the village hall; Multi-national strangers.
A stranded train—a blocked track—dark, distant dangers.
A white-faced lonely figure, so thin his bones to see:
Something special about him, no ordinary man was he.
Unsteady was the cup he held, for his hand did shake.
On his arm a tattooed number of a prison camp inmate.
A coloured boy on father's knee—a sick child held by mother
Sparked image of another boy; a friend he called a brother.

Two little boys, hands held together, solemnly did agree
A future entwined in work for mankind—surgeons they would be.
Years of promise for Eli and Sam, sharing family affection.
Both hungry for knowledge, inspired by dreams of perfection.

Hell came without warning—The screams! The blows to the head!
Bullets flying, good people dying and Sam, my Sammy was dead.
Why did you murder those people—In what way inferior to you?
And father, greatest of surgeons, cruelly struck down too.

Oh Sam, I've seen many dying. Must I see this child die too?
He felt Sam's presence—"Have courage! It's now all up to you."
He stood at the makeshift table; steady his hand on a knife.
Electric silence around him—The surgeon was saving a life.

Toby S. Endlar

Lament for a Lost Love

Our meeting was wonderful, too brief
Now come the parting and the grief
For love, re-kindled, burns you see
Though you cannot belong to me.

My mind's a whirl at my heart's plight
For it's soaring like a kite
I thought that love was all in the past,
Too late now, the die is cast.

It was all my fault, I must confess,
To hold you close, cuddle and caress
My lips on yours, I was to blame
I felt you respond, to my shame.

Do feelings of love when we were young
Last so long, have they suspended hung?
Deep inside I fear that's true
I kept that old photograph of you.

Be happy, my love, may the years bring you pleasure,
Those few stolen moments I'll forever treasure,
But should you look into my eyes again
Just see me, my love, don't see the pain.

Gordon Jack Crisp

My Garden

Like a gay kaleidoscope every year
my flowers in order of the month appear.
Daffodils an forsythia soft spring days proclaim.
Rockery bursting into colour, flowers too numerous to name.
Snow-in-summer tumbling in profusion over wall.
Mixing with blue of aubrieta as it falls.
The gentle pinks, for a short while, perfume the air.
Sweet smell of stocks and new cut grass everywhere.
Honeysuckle tapping windows in the breeze
Fills the house with perfume and the drone of bees.
Roses in profusion, velvet petals scattered over paving stones.
There, perhaps the season to me most dear,
Balmy, golden days of autumn are here.
Michaelmas daisies, starry flowers bright against the fence,
Targy chrysanthemums, gold and bronze, in clumps so dense,
Hiding barks of apple trees, their fruit rosy against the sky
Waiting to be picked and stored in garrets high.
Then come cold winds and frost which make the last flowers die.
The garden is still beautiful in winter, I can see
Golden laurel, con fires, against the snow bright holly tree.

F. Ramsden

It Happened in Westgate

It was early in the morning
when I came to greet the sea,
the beach was still deserted,
and oh, what did I see?
The sun smiling at the sea!

There was none to disturb them,
and sure, she looked her best:
So young and fair and newborn,
so untouched and so blest.

But there was more to it than meets the eye,
that pureness! —Oh that purity
that hovered between sea and sky!

Salt! —I thought for a moment
and thoughts came to my mind,
how pure was all that God had made
and how He loved mankind!

What a wonderful experience!
And it was on Westgate's shore
that God took pride in His creation
as I'd never felt before.

Ida Potter

My Favourite Time of Year

In nature's scented halls filled with sage and finest thyme.
Glorious fruit baskets with ripe lemons and green lime.
A dome of fine aromas, so dear and all so sweet.
Here is where ripe blackberries and elderberries meet.

As humbly, I set foot among grand arches of late flowers,
with awe beholding autumn, winds, cascading petal showers.
On chandeliers of rosy apples, dew-drop-cobweb-lace.
I lift my eyes towards heaven in amazement of God's grace.

Melancholy, autumn queen, you dance with shades of fall.
Your jewels are drops of rain and mist,
by winter's king you're softly kissed.
Blushed, red, you leave the ball.

Soon a sparkling veil of snow and diamond ice will cover
ground; and all around behold the winds endlessly hover.
And therefore "autumn" I will hold in fondest memory.
A time for eyes and mouth to dine—more beauty I shan't see!

Beate Monk

The Unwilling Pupil

Now Yvonne is this young girl's name,
Her looks could fill any picture frame.
Very early she rises on most mornings,
Then sits by the fire for some warming.

But when it's time to go to school,
She acts about just like a frozen fool.
Spirit is numb and movement dead slow,
Deep into coat pockets her hands do go.

Schoolwork is not her favourite topic,
If she could she would quickly hop-it.
Oh' but alas, teacher is aware of this,
So it's aggro for our poor little miss.

The daytime passes with miserable strain,
With due attention forced upon her brain.
School bell rings when lessons are done,
Now it's homeward bound at a very fast run.

That school homework is her next big hurt,
So she'll seek some help from brother Bert.
But oh! That could prove a very sad mistake,
As his exam results have been bad of late.

Her dad's due home from work about eight,
She'll go to meet him at their front gate.
For reluctant pupil this young girl may be,
She knows when he arrives it's time for tea.

A. E. J. Selfe

Survival

The cock crows at dusk, farms are being deserted,
Hoes are slung over shoulders,
The narrow roads are quickly filled.

They chatter and greet while heading down to the village,
But one stays behind, burdened by his troubles.

He sits on a stone and stares into space,
The silence of a graveyard,
Is the only thing to comfort him.

He ponders and worries for his little farmland,
It is unyielding and infertile, not a plant will grow.

To go home now to his nagging wife and hungry children,
Is a prospect too painful to contemplate.

Every day she scolds, every night she nags,
The same question she asks, over and over again.

What shall we eat, how shall we live?
What shall we do, how shall we survive?!

He broods and prays for an answer to come,
He falls down and cries out to his "chi,"
He's only prayer now is for survival.

Kechi Uche Ogbuagu

Tears of Sadness

In this life I lived the pain you set me free
you came to touch my hand it felt so good
to me in this life I lived the grace at hand
I lived for you support you when I can in
this life I lived I did my best the love you
showed in return don't picture or blame yourself
smile and think of me let your tears be full
of grace smile and be happy for in this life
I lived in pain, suffering and torment is now
at an end for me as I say in this life
picture the grace the beauty of the world
in grace and harmony don't picture or blame
yourself your love you felt for me when you
touched my hand a part of my life came back
to you be happy in your life smile and think
of me this pain I had in life you lived
to set me free so let your tears of
sadness be the last goodbye so in this life
I say God bless and keep you safe always
And let your tears of sadness be your last goodbye for me

M. Jackson

One Last Kiss

The winds of time have blown this way and that
The hands of fate have chimed a thousand times
Then came the day destiny called
and beckoned you to its door.

To move to another dimension,
To sore with the angels
To light the stars and eclipse with the moon

You drifted from my arms
I had so much to say
But you had gone to soon

The memories linger onwards
and you will be dearly missed
but on your loving and your leaving
your lips I did tenderly kiss.

Sandra Dyer

Black Friars—December 24th

A life's in peril on the bridge
whilst moonlight strafes across its ridge,
because standing lonely in the dim
he thinks this world is not for him.

Far down below the darkness thickens
on muddied water as it slickens,
where whirlpool, eddies, twist about
to show that they lack little doubt.

Chill winds also take a toll
when hands lose grip in stiffening cold,
on girders meant to withstand time
though bear as witness to his crime

The tide of life just flowed too strong
and played for him a saddening song.
His body's floating, bloated, blue
a sad unknown that no one knew.

Martin Victor Emmins

My Declaration

As I sit here, alone, by the fire dear,
  My darling, I'm dreaming of you.
I've been trying to write you a poem,
  With words, that I mean, and are true.
But somehow, the words, they elude me,
  I just cannot, get them to rhyme.
It seems, they've been used, all before dear,
  By wordsworth, and old father time.
But somehow, I know, I'll keep trying,
  In the meantime, the best I can do.
Is to tell you, quite honestly, darling.
  That there's nothing, I love, more than you.

John M. Thomas

Silence

We hear the lark, as he soars and sings
But not the blade of grass from whence He springs
We hear the noise of trains as they pass by
But hear not the silent flit of a fire fly
We hear the drums, as they do roll
But near, a whisper from a person's soul!
We can hear aeroplanes, way on high
But nothing from the clouds as they scurry by,
We hear the noise and chatter of people at work or play
But not one sound of the silent passing of a day.
We hear not the moments that make up time
But we tick them off with a metallic chime
Our thoughts, our feelings, they come and go
And we still hear not the gently fall of snow!
Our eternal soul you cannot see or hear!
And a lifetime of silence holds no fear
Noises cease! Time stand still
And let our souls with this silence fill!

James Barnes

Survival

Owls a hooting
cats a screaming
You wonder if you're awake or dreaming;
But when it's dark
The night is still
All the creatures come out for the kill.
And screams you hear
Can fill you with fear;
Some have to fight, nowhere to hide
Some are scared
And run for their lives,
It's a fight for survival in the night
Until it's light.
Big ones, small ones
Trying to stay alive
Some are lucky to have survived,
But they can rest when it is light
From morning again, until it's night.

R. Maskill

Escape

To walk carelessly, over the fields
   Of the leafy countryside.
To linger on the river bank,
   Or to sail out on the morning tide.
To remove the shackles of despair
   And fly off to some distant land.
To free one's mind, of doubt and fear,
   Then turn again, when homeward bound.
For if you dream eternally,
   Your dreams become reality.

P. A. Bennett

The Local

The pub on the hill is the place to meet
after a hard day's work it's a welcome retreat
"I'll have a beer" said Bill to Ben
"It's my turn is it, I'll get 'em in then"
"Shall we play darts it's double or top
when I've drunk enough beer I'll have to stop"
They picked up some cues and went to play pool
but the ball shot off the table the knocked Fred off his stool
they propped up the bar and Bill had a smoke
Ben had more beer but Bill only a Coke
"How's ya missus was it the flu"
"I" said Bill "Is yours still with you"
She is at the minute still moanin' and groanin'
she'll never change, still does her roamin'
They took out the cards and started to deal
when Ben's wife burst through the door dog at her heel
"Come on Ben you've about had enough"
"It's work in the mornin' even though you'll feel rough"
So he bid his farewell and slumped to the floor
But his mates knew he'd be back tomorrow for more.

P. Pease

A Prayer

One step at a time, Lord,
That is all I ask.
To put my best foot forward
As I endeavour to do thy task.
Keep me in the light, Lord,
In the steadfast way.
As I walk with thee, Lord,
Throughout this perfect day.
O Lord you are my Master,
My Friend and Divine Love.
Give me peace this day, Lord,
Until I am with thee in glorious Heaven above.
For I have seen your light Lord,
Keep me free from sin.
Until I am with the angels
And the seraphim.
All that lives is Holy
In my earnest fight.
Help me Lord as always
Do only what is right.

Lena Maureen Raine

Greetings

Inside most cards for Greetings
To the text I am averse,
The sentiments expressed are bleatings
In banal, trite, or perverse verse.

But let's be cordial in our cards,
Just send our friends the Best of Cheer,
Without employing unctuous bards,
To those whose friendship we hold dear!

Donald Burt

Autumn

See . . . crisp cornflake leaves whirled in earth's bowl
   by autumn's blasts which scour the soul.
   A glorious top they seem to be . . .
   whipped by icy energy!
No silence now, no stealth can creep
upon a victim half asleep,
for sound rebounds, Snap! . . . Crackle! . . .Plop!
We hear each move, each tiptoed hop.
Frost sprinkled trees have shed their dress
and flowers prepare for winter's rest.
Now fruits drop in abundant shower
to fall in nature's harvest bower,
and rest there . . .undisturbed, to grow
replenishing earth's cyclic flow.

Then . . . Savour Autumn's crystal air.
   Protect its purity . . .with care.

Margaret R. O'Brien

My Beloved Les

There was a man who stood out in a crowd
A man who wore his clothes oh so proud
A man who moved with even grace
A man with a very handsome face
A man who greeted life with hope
Who wouldn't sit around and mope
A man proud to be called brother
A man not like any other
He was too friendly without a doubt
Always helping others out

No one would doubt his merit
His was such a very willing spirit
Until that fateful day
When thieves took everything away
Gone is all his happy feeling
Life has lost all of its meaning
Now there is doubt where once was trust
He drags his feet and lets things rust
The one he loves and spent his life
He distrusts everyone except his wife

Elizabeth White

Lament

I could have played with children of my age,
And made from them some lovely friends for life.
I could have grown up strong and unafraid
Amid a world's obscene tempestuous strife.

I could have painted canvas; or carved stone:
Or written poems to outlive my span;
Maybe begotten children of my own:
Just think of it, I could have been a man.

I could have helped the weak to battle through,
So they, themselves, could help some kindred souls.
I could have found so many things to do;
Encouraged others to achieve their goals.

My children could have gone to greater heights
With talents to outstrip my own small scope,
Enjoyed so many manifold delights,
And filled their world with love and joy and hope.

But all my aspiration have been thwarted.
A surgeon came; and I was just aborted.
Ken Waite

Man of the House

Up in the morning, quiet and tame,
Running water, and a gasp of pain,
As he shaves, blood mingles with suds on his face.
Silence reigns, it's early dawn,
Then gurgle and splutter, silence is torn.
Groping blindly for towel misplaced,
Sounds of muttering as it's replaced,
Scuffle of slippers in the small parlour,
Clock ticking seconds of the small hour,
Accompanying singing of kettle's refrain
Clinking of china, tinkle of rain, to and fro setting a tray
After using, putting away, things he no longer requires,
Carries the tray to the wife he admires,
Who proudly lies in bed there waiting,
In her arms, the cause of the catering.
For the man of the house his new baby was waking.
Dee Nelder

Loneliness

Loneliness—do you know what it means?
Believe me, it isn't all that it seems.
The observe on the anger which once more a ring.
A mother knowing she'll no longer hear her child sing
The elderly and infirm, sitting neglected, waiting for their turn.
The absence of a shoulder to cry on, no ears to listen
when everything goes wrong.
No comforting arms, or tender embrace.
A distinct lack of phone calls, letters . . . what a waste!
Remember the lonely in the time of need.
They won't ask you for favours, beg, borrow or plead.
Don't let a neighbour's life go astray.
As one day, you may find yourself heading
the same way.
Lucy Rickhuss

A Company Cat

I've got a cat, a company cat.
A company cat, now what is that?
Just listen awhile and I'll tell you what!
I'll tell you exactly what he is not!!
He's not a cat to roam very far . . .
And he likes to be wherever I 'are' . . .
He sometimes accompanies me to the post . . .
And I'm often afraid that he might get lost . . .
But no, he always comes back again . . .
And he doesn't like to be out in the rain . . .
He chases the mice and let's them go free . . .
Catches them again and eats them for tea . . .
He sleeps on my bed, then wakens me up . . .
When he wants to play like a frolicsome pup . . .
He's adorable, handsome, a company cat . . .
His name is Timmy and that is that!!!
Helen Reid

Arthur's Reawakening

"Merlin, tell me how it will be?"
"Much as it was. You will grow
Under a ruler whose country is divided.
They will lose their way.
You, Arthur, are what a King should be,
You feel the pain of the people,
You do not want for yourself.
You remember the earth and what it gives.
The people will call you King.
They will say, 'He is Arthur Pendragon reborn.'
Even though the name you bear may be different
You will bring them to the Trinity.
One summer solstice eve, you will feel a power
Drawing you to the circle of the Druids,
There you will kneel and remember all.
When you reclaim Excalibur,
Everyone within the realm will be full of joy.
This is your destiny."
Pat Russell

Daybreak

Awake ye now from slumber, for a new day now is born.
Perceive the Curtain of Night being slowly withdrawn.
Slowly the approaching Sun now sets the Sky aglow
So resplendent in Glory, above the clouds below.
A Panorama, unsurpassed, reveals to all the Birth
Reflected in full detail, to those mortals on Earth.
Slowly, more and more wonders are still to unfold
From the glorious Sunrise of colour and gold.
Softly breaks the Dawn, fleeting clouds speed on their way
As if on a special mission to forestall the light of day.
Mother Nature now awakens to prepare the daily chore
And rouses her proteges from their slumber the night before.
From the blade of the dewy grass to the nest on the highest tree
And the hedgerows, festooned with cobwebs, gleaming for all to see.
From the lowing in the meadow, where the lambs so softly bleat
To the rancour and the hub-hub heard on the narrow street.
Birds reclining in their nests, with little or no surprise
Reluctantly take to their wings, and decorate the skies.
Mother Nature in her glory, has no surely proved her worth,
With a curtain embossed with colour, draping Mother Earth.
Frederick William Westley

World Peace

Let's reach out across the seas,
And say hello brother
Let's show the hand of friendship
Towards one another
Let's have no more wars, trouble or strife,
No more loss of precious life,
Let's start the world turning with peace and love,
By setting free a white turtle dove.

And only then when we all disarm
Will there be a lasting calm.
E. V. Helman

My Party Piece

I have to do my party piece,
I have to get up and do a speech,
I've got to stand in front of you,
To sing or dance, oh what could I do,
I thought I'd tell a joke or two,
But then I thought that you'd all boo,
Maybe a song or a dance would do,
And then a thought it came to me,
As I felt sad for a little donkey.
The road it walked so long ago,
I know that we would praise it so,
And so my party piece tonight,
Is for all of you to keep in sight,
The story of Jesus, the shepherds' delight,
At a little donkey
  What a joyful sight
Iris McFarland

Till We Meet Again

Bright eyes beheld your every rise,
The world a panorama of golden corn,
How fragile the beauty of earth's disguise,
As moist eyes now perceive each morn.

Heavy drapes the curtain over departed joys,
Shielding the lights and happiness of by-gone years,
The darkness cannot sink the love that buoys,
Even through the incessant torrent of tears.

Through the sadness shines a glowing beacon,
Signal of love and life that is not lost,
A flare lighting my way to her welcome,
But the parting of loves—is such a cost!

Bearing this hope and tender emotion,
Bearing the struggle of dark days of pain,
Bearing this climb through earth's commotion,
Our love will be the greater as we meet again.
Geoff Powell

A Mountain Tear Drop

It starts as a trickle on the top
Then flows, in abundance from that spot,
Winding down the shivering mountain.
Snowflakes fall, as if from Heaven,
Gushing! As the cold air blows,
Then twisting faster as it goes
Passing by the rocky edges,
Heading for the distant ledges,
Swooshing by the nearby trees
Then settling safely, in the seas.
William D. Watt

The House in the Wood

The windows are bare, there's a creek on the stairs,
The chimney's pot tumbling down.
Through the broken down door blows a wind rough and wild,
A place of excitement to any small child.
That old rustic house, in the midst of the wood,
Which once very grand and majestically stood.

On the floor of the hall there's a carpet of leaves,
Blown from a tree that's near by.
Autumn's rich colours, brown, orange, and red.
A soft springy carpet, a warm cosy bed.
For the little field mouse, whom her family would keep,
Save from all danger as soundly they sleep.

In those days long ago when it stood very new,
Each window and door very sound,
I wonder who lived there, who built it with care,
Of laughter and love, did it have its full share,
That old rustic house, in the midst of the wood,
which once very grand and majestically stood
Constance Joyce Cooke

Yester-Years

Come—sweet memories of the past
Come haunt my reverie while I am alone,
Scenes of yester-years parade before me
In this quiet evening's fire-glow.
This burning longing in my heart
Recalls each dear beloved face,
They smile again and speak with me
The past is mine the present holds no place.
I see my dear mother once again
I feel her tender loving care
And father fondly smiles on me
My world secure because they are there.
I hear my sister's running feet
She calls my name I see her laughing eyes
And feel her hand in mine again.
Those far off days are gone—I know
But never past recall,
They always live with in my heart
Whatever may befall.
Marjorie Dawson

The Namid

The beauty of symmetrical shape
pyramidal in form
displays a strange but
fascinating world of sand.
It is as if God's hand
created a new environment
suspended in time.
With daytime heat and
night time cold
the harsh realities set there
suggest this place allows no life
to live in this extreme
climate.
Yet if one looks, there grows some grass
or bush or other plant
and in its borders snake, beetle
and lizard all survive;
life in a hostile environment;
there are creatures who are alive.
David J. Fairweather

Abstinence

The juice of love has many different tastes;
some bitter, some sweet and some halfway between.
Take my hand and I in yours,
for tomorrow will be different and final.
The sadness of loss is ours, but which ever
way we turn the experience did enrich our lives.
Every breath you take and every night
when the stars shine, a girl and boy discover
what it is to have loved and ultimately lost.
So let me touch your skin and hold
your soul one last time.
Rachel Shuckburgh

Feelings!

We all express our feelings,
In completely different ways.
People may be mistaken,
By what you mean to say.

Sometimes people seem happy,
When they're really sad.
And as no-one realizes,
They're doing something mad.

We all express ourselves
In love—anger, behaviour and madness.
To everyone you may seem happy,
When in fact you're feeling sadness.

Your feelings towards someone,
Will reflect their feelings towards you.
So if you feel love and anger,
It will reflect in the things you do!
Giovanna Violo

A Heart of Innocence

Innocence from birth
born into a family of love
A special boy who has eternal affection.

A boy who could find nothing wrong with the world.
This boy grew up in the hearts of his family.
This special boy went to a special school, where there
were kids like him.
He grew up with these kids and graduated with them.

He is not a boy anymore. He is all grown up. Where did
the time go.
Through the years he has never lost his innocence or
charm. This boy is my brother.
He will always be a boy to me.
It doesn't matter how old he gets.
He will always be my lovable, affectionate and adorable
brother. The love lingers on.
Laura Jayne O'Keeffe

The Salvationist

As she came to address the meeting
Songs that were sung were known to all.
Gently and slowly she led them along
Along the path of a well loved song.

What can this mean?
A song and a tale of the Salvationist's life
And the way of it all.
Hardly to be understood by the ladies who sat there
Nodding and wondering about "the call".

Suddenly she gathered strength
Made an appeal to the religious sense.
So much joy, such a faith so strong
The hymns she sang carried all along.

A new emotion held many there
The effect on them of someone so rare.
She gave a glimpse of a perfect way
The path the Salvationist took every day.

Gladys Eileen Brunell

Free as a Bird

Ready to go, ready to fly,
The young bird soars high into the sky.
His parents watch, his siblings too,
As he takes flight, it's a dream come true.
Away from the nest, time to go it alone,
He leaves one place to make another his home.
It's time to show what he can do
To the next generation, when their time comes too.

Amelia Weller

Very Same Day

I miss my Grandad ever such a lot
in my heart he shall never be forgotten.
He was so kind to me,
My pain inside—I knew he could see
I knew he was always there,
he used to lecture me, but I knew it
was out of care.
I never said 'I love you',
I just hope that even though I didn't say
that deep down he knew anyway.
when I was told he was ill, I tried to fight the tears
and push aside my burning fears.
Then I could not fight it anymore,
and the tears kept coming like never before.
Then my family saw him lying in that
hospital bed,
it's just not Grandad is what they said
I realized that in this world he could not stay,
and sadly he died on that very same day.

Naomi Pelling

Fear

I am hurting deep inside,
This awful secret I must hide,
Is it fair what you have done to me?
Who can I tell? Please set me free.

I'm afraid I will lose my friends,
If I tell what happened then.

I was just a girl of eight
When the abuse started. I'm filled with hate,
I feel so dirty deep inside,
My thoughts are spinning. Where can I hide?

People, they all look at me,
I feel so guilty. Can they see?

Don't you know it's not my fault?
I screamed and cried and begged 'let go.'

But I was just a child you see,
He wouldn't stop and set me free.

Jean Ross

Everything Which Was Still Is!

Mist sweeps in covering o'er the land
The trees turn sinister fears set in
Where once I thought nothing of to stand
Around my ankles there's a carpet of mist
All movements become expressive
As round and round my body it twists
"Night Owl" oh wise owl looking down from upon high
Why? With your distinctive call do you
discourage me from drawing nigh
your sounds, my silent sounds, echoing in this place
be they real, be they not, you would, I would
laugh ole friend to see such telling on my face
dawn creeps in like a thief stealing the night
everything which was, still is
But has now new meaning in the daylight

Mark Farley

News at Ten

In the holy land they see the Christ weeping
It's a miracle they say.
No one heeds the warning He's been keeping
Until this our Judgement Day.

Suddenly, water has been found on the moon
In readiness for His people's arrival
For all the good will be there soon
As God repeats the Bible.

We've used all the wood, so we cannot use Noah
Rockets will fly us to where we will live
Our resources on earth are getting lower and lower
It's easy to take, but what did we give?

Gay Jones

Thoughts

As the birds above me sing in the sky,
I tread through this jungle of war and I don't really know why.
With death and destruction on my mind,
I think of the men who lie dead behind.
Just what it is like to hear a human cry out in pain,
and the hell to see another human die as they lie face down in the rain.
Are these really the acts of war,
and what do people kill and fight for?
Is it for some unknown cause,
or do we just like causing wars?
The men who fought and the men who died,
these are the faces I keep inside.
All the enemy wants is to fight for their land,
all I want to do is shake their hand.
As I am sure our differences we can mend,
please shake my hand as I come as a friend.
I found that war is hell and war is bloody,
it's a waste of time and war is a waste of money.
Now the war is over as I stand on this land,
as we fought and we died for the cause (Vietnam).

Philip Wilkinson

Somewhere

Somewhere in the shadows
of yesterday, she left us
and went on her way.
We know not just where
she is resting, she is lost
and we are lost without her sweetness,
but what can we do? When death takes
the hand of one we adore and leaves
us in darkness, we see her no more.
Her life was on loan, her years quickly
sped and her words and her smile and her
bright golden head, all are gone and we
wonder why and mourn and cry and know we must
follow and heave a sigh for life's so
uncertain and death so sure.
We pray Lord we'll be ready
to meet her once more.

Louise Millson

Untitled

My dearest love,
  Although I've had to leave you, we are not
so far apart. I can still put my arms around you
and hold you close to my heart. I've proved you were
right my darling, we certainly do live on. We just
pass through an open door and the pain is gone
I know of your little problems, of your daily needs I'm
aware. I'm oft by your side at eventide, there's never
a vacant chair, it's a beautiful world I've entered,
the sky is always blue, there are lovely flowers and
song birds, and old friends I've met anew. They were
waiting there to greet me, to guide me on the way,
into the everlasting life where it's eternal day,
to keep praying for me darling, you have helped
to bring me light, until we meet again on this
heavenly plane, God bless my love goodnight
Elsie Barker

Rotating Aircraft

Rotating aircraft how you glide through the sky
to stop suddenly, to hover and crackle above my
sight no one see or hear you coming through
the stars at night in the speed of light.
No Air force across the World would greet you with respect.
No nation welcomes you with open arms amongst its people.
Not all Scientists believe in you, some will speak
or whisper your name amongst themselves in
secrecy, for they know you are here to stay for
years to come, to seek and research in the land of mankind.
Rotating Aircraft in the name of our Father, return
home safely to speak the peace of life in the
land of your own.
Daniel Enticknapp

Famous Lady

Grace Darling was her name
When she came to fame
A brave lass was she
saving passengers from the sea.

She had a heart of gold
so I am told,
Farne Islands was isolated
lonely and cold
And she was so bold

She died young and saved others to live on.
Through wind, rain, and storm
She saved all alarum.

The lighthouse daughter
and father saved many a life
Queen Victoria heard
and gave word,
That Grace and her father
should have a reward.
Valerie Ryan

Pleasures of the Flesh

The beauty of it
Oh! The exquisite excellence
The sensitive thrill of light caresses
The magic delight of warm moist kisses
Her soft evening sighs fill your mind
Thoughts of giving in your soul
Yes, pleasures of the flesh?
No! Pleasures of unselfish love

The loveliness of it
Oh! The wonderful exuberance
The tender touch of loving tongues
The down-like feel of fawny hair
The mood sparkles in the mirrors of her eyes
Thoughts of giving in your soul
Yes, pleasures of the flesh?
No! Pleasures of caring love.
S. P. Kennedy

The Boaster

Through the cloud of dust strode the bellicose crowd,
The Boaster had spat out his words too loud,
You could feel furnace heat from both of the fighters,
The cut-glass sharpness of their words to press writers.

As the contest progressed, rules were transgressed,
It was becoming a brawl as you will have guessed.
Then the 'old-one-two' hit The Boaster's chin,
People were wondering whether he was in.

Odin's Valkyries he saw from within,
At this moment in time they were not pointing at him.
Then he slid on a caster of sweat in the ring,
The Ref' started counting, no bell did ring.

Then he sprang to his feet and tore into his foe,
With the courage that only a true Boaster could show.
He won the contest, fighting many more rounds
A peculiar way to earn a few pounds.

But he'd always boasted he'd beat any man
Whether he was strong or a fancy dan.
The Gods knew he would fight for zero-nought-all
Money did not rule The Boaster at all.
Thomas Anthony Liddell

Going for a Walk in My Head

Memory Lane, most daunting of places
where I go for a walk in my head,
re-treading the paths of yesterday with excitement—some-
times dread.
Maybe along the road of past delights and frights
I'll meet, with gladness or with fear, some old familiar faces.
Up the hills and down the dales
with cross-roads marking each decision
that led to a meadow, or hidden bog,
and praises, or derision.
Fallen trees that blocked the way caused detours
for better or worse,
to a picnic in a leafy grove, or following a hearse.
I climb a misty hill with shrouded spire,
it might have been a fairy castle there
or a dragon breathing fire.
This walk I take inside my head,
sometimes strolling, sometimes racing,
Both happy and sad to get back safely home,
but a journey worth re-tracing.
J. Bentley

Seasons

Alas! Another year has passed,
As winter slips away beneath its cloak of frost,
Though, still, the evil deeds of men hold sway,
Defiant in the mould of Nature's way.
When with her once again, have come and gone
Events imbibed in life's cocoon,
A trail of births and lives and deaths forlorn,
Is hitherto enacted . . . to be forgotten soon.

To weave a cycle into history's schemes,
That so reflects the nuance of perpetual dreams,
Of latent life that beckons resurrection from the deep,
Disturbed again by echoes from compelling sleep
That so incites the active equinox of Spring,
With all its force and wetness, crops to bring
To bear on hungry mouths the substances of toil,
Infused with human sweat on Summer's soil.

When, by its rape, the fruits of husbandry is wrest,
To bare the seeds of Nature's future boon, lest
They chant survival's issue and recite its worth,
And so excite to riot Autumn's will
For struggle, in the guise of constant birth,
Persists, while evils that beset Man linger still.
Errol C. McKenzie

Hearts Left in Darkness

Here all alone in darkness, I lie unknown.
Away from the world of hell with hearts of stone.
Tears keep on falling, like mountain streams,
As my broken heart lies moaning with silent screams.
The clouds show their anger with thundering cries,
As lightening and rain shatter the skies.
Flowers close their petals as rivers cry at last;
Rain washes my tears away like time has wiped the past;
Sand lies on lonely beaches, waiting for the sea to wake from rest.
Still loving someone special, my hearts put to the test.
Daylight breaks with morning sun as seagulls fly above,
Awakened suddenly all wet and cold with eyes still crying for love.
The fish still swim the oceans to flee the sharks they fear.
Still lying lost and lonely, only the sun to dry each tear.
Like an alien left deserted, no friends to help or care,
Hearts search for love and affection as minds walk past and stare.
I walk past my friends unnoticed as if I don't exist.
Only tears left in darkness, a broken hearts last kiss.

Amanda Woodcock

My Father's Land

One day foreign soldiers took my father,
the priest and others from the town.

Fear and confusion all around.
One day my father came back with all the men,
Protected by the Red Cross.
Bruised and weak, taken of the lorries of
peace, on land not my father's.

Now 22 years on, my father's land has hotels
built on it, Tourists travel from all across
Europe to this peaceful, beautiful land.

They try to forget that the land is torn.

My Grandfather's grave is no more,
The church is no more,
The religion is no more,
The school is no more.
Famous people build big beautiful houses
on my father's land.
Who will remember the truth of my father's land?

Chris Antoniou

The Journey

Passing long grass and neatly cut lawn,
Driving between the dark and dawn,
Everything is quiet, there is not a sound,
But on the motorway the noise is found,
The clouds of dirt horrible and thick,
Under the wheel, a breaking stick.

The car shakes as a lorry passes,
The wind blowing through the long grasses,
Looking for sign posts to where we are going,
Passing a cyclist, reflectors glowing,
Time we were home, it's getting late,
Stuck in a traffic jam we have to wait.

Melanie Royles

The Way Forward

Meeting each other, their destiny and fate
Arranging that first very special date
Romantic dinners, chocolates and flowers
Ringing each other, talking for hours!
In time, engagement leading the way
As prelude to their wedding day
Groom and bride, sharing love in life
Exchanging vows, to be man and wife!
Devoted they were on their wedding day
Ideal for each other in every way
Vows then broken, promises unkept
Over the years, many tears wept
Resigned to separation, living apart
Court intervention, proceeding to start
Ending by decree—again single and free!

Mary Wood

A Woodland Walk

Savouring the wonder of a woodland walk,
Feet and mind meandering,
Now weary from the many winding paths,
I rest in a glade,
In the sanctuary of the shade,
In the balm of a breeze,
The tranquillity of the trees,
And watch the lilting leaves aloft,
Silhouetted against the noonday sun,
Dancing kaleidoscopes on a carpet of clover,
The ever-moving pattern of minuscule lights and shadows
Flickering before my eyes like playful will-o'-the-wisps.

A copious cloud covers the celestial spotlight,
The curtain falls on the dappled dance of nature,
And the matinee performance of creation's cabaret concludes.
I linger wistfully awhile
To contemplate the ineffable beauty of simple things,
Until, restored in body and spirit,
I am fit to embrace the forest path anew.

Ken O'Sullivan

Dreaming

What's his name . . .
Whatever he wants it to be,
Where's he going,
Somewhere sandman he's never been,
So, shade off that daylight
And be gone time begone,
And ease your tired mind
in slumber's foolhardy thoughts,
In dreams so strange engaged for that purpose,
To emerge you a victor,
Replenish your image,
Sleep soundly sweet soul and gather your strength,
And deliver your value,
When you wake from that trance,

Hugh Jackson

Cast a Cold Eye (—Gaunt and Ill)

Anorexic Yeats — gaunt and ill,
With his back to the greasy till,
Without the aid of a monocle,
Forced to look at the spectacle
Of the beating down of the wise,
And Barton Smith's beaten down.
Moon washed gables
Etching a drunken silhouette
Against the cold artistry of a leaden sky.
No sound to break the silence,
Only a sigh of a sea-water,
Sucking despondently
On the broken shells of an empty bay.
Yeats ponders, tense and lonely,
And he wonders why
The silence of the night
Accentuates the turmoil in his mind,
Or why he has to linger
In this vast nothingness,
Of sea and sky and calm indifference.

Kitsy Brady

Memories

April—our special month has gone my son.
And you—who brought me joy and love
Have left this world—too suddenly.
No time for sad goodbyes, no time
To watch your children grow, or me grow old.
Only the yearning in my heart
When Spring flowers die, and earth is cold.
The flowers will rest and bloom again next year,
But you will never walk with me around the garden paths.
And yet—when soft winds blow, and Summer raindrops fall-
I'll hear a whisper in my dreams
And know you're still close by.

Patricia Elizabeth Walker

Lost Love

A centurion awaits upon a wall
dreaming dreams for night to fall
and in his dream a lady calls.
To fall in love with a soldier's dreams
they fall in love for eternity,
until he wakes to find her gone
to search his life for years to come,
for that lovely maiden of so long ago
only in his dreams does she show,
until you came along so many years
had passed,
to be reawakened a love that was thought
to be lost,
our life begun upon a wall so many
many years before.

C. A. Arthur

My Dad

He was a Peter Pan, a child till he died,
Children loved him and to them he was an equal.
But alas he died after a long dreadful illness
That robbed him of his mind,
And no one recognized the child that was still there;
No one wanted to see him in that state,
No one went to see him in that place.
And yet at odd moments lucidity returned
In fleeting words and phrases, and then was lost again.
Clouded expressionless eyes once more endless repetitive useless
movements took over once again and father was lost to us.
How many deaths do we have to suffer?
How many times do we have to grieve?
Most people die once, dad died several times in that year.
Every time he recovered his memory and lost it
That was to us another death. Until finally he really died
Our tears by then were of relief not grief,
But we will never forget that terrible year,
I sometimes find it hard to remember how he was before
And that hurts even more.

Joan Smith

Sonnet

I blame myself that I have failed in life,
that I ne'er tasted of deserved success,
for I was but a citadel of strife
wherein the waters of unhappiness
slashed forth in one atomic driven wave,
and I, a part of that almighty main,
was to the tidal moon a passion slave,
a holocaust half living, yet half slain.

But through the mists of doubt and fear I saw
a garden stretched upon yon floating cloud,
and I would fain have reached that distant shore
if it had anchored and dispersed its shroud . . .
can I dare hope of Jacob's ladder now,
or must I perish in the winter snow?

Suzanne Low Steenson

Would I Be Missed

Would 'I' be missed if 'I' were gone? I really could not tell.
In all I did, I did my best, I thought I did it well,
But then I wonder what I did, that I did that was so bad
For whatever I thought, or spoke, or did, I seemed to make
them mad.

They were my life, my only world, without where would I be?
But then it seemed within their world, there was no place for me.
Just remember my beloved children, I will always love you so,
Never in your path I'd stand if 'you' should want to go.

If ever you wished to return, to the house that was your home,
If you felt lost and weary and no longer wanted to roam,
The door would always be open, a shelter from all harm
And I'd be waiting there to welcome you, with loving open arms.

Mary Leight

Just War

What is the meaning of War,
I only know of death that is on par.
Men went to war because of the slave age,
To free all human beings from bondage.
Men went to war because of women,
For Cleopatra was desirable to all men.
Men went to war because of land,
And yet there is so much on hand.
Men went to war for the sake of religion
Yet the same God is worshipped by a nation.
Men went to war because of man's colour,
Yet we are men with so much valour.
Men went to war for the sake of freedom
For man wants to move freely in his kingdom.

John Naidoo

Landmines

The war has been over for many years now
   Or so they say!
Time to forgive and forget,
   Time to put behind us old bitterness,
Time to forget the horror—the mess—
   All the killing and the strife;
   All the horrific loss of life.

But yesterday, my grandfather went out to work,
   His duty he would not shirk.
In spite of the dangers lurking there,
He dug the soil with the utmost care.
   Last night they carried him home again;
      Suffering—crying out in pain.

Today—I must go out—
   My husband—my children;
Always—every day—we wonder when—
   When is it our turn
   To be blown limb from limb?
Will men never—ever—learn
   To love?

Margery J. Patrick

Will Somebody

Will somebody ever love me
I mean really love me
The times when I need a shoulder to cry on
A kiss, a hug that special cuddle
Someone to really love me!
Will somebody ever know me
I mean really know me
The times when I'm really sad
And I put on an act
Will somebody ever see through that!
   I wonder "Will Somebody"

Jennifer Hoffman

Untitled

The old cat, dreaming by the fire
Of hunts and fights—all things that tire—
No longer does such active plays
Arouse in him great zest or joys
By fire he curls to warm his back.
For this he has got quite a knack.
He snoozes there most of the day.
"Poor Old Bill" laughingly they say.
He has few teeth—he cannot chew,
So many things he cannot do.
But when mum taps spoon on a cup,
Slowly he rises and gets up;
He totters on unsteady feet
Towards the kitchen for his treat.
For old Bill now has but one wish:
To eat, with care, his well-cooked fish.
One day the old cat did not awake.
So sad! We thought our hearts would break.
There never was so dear a "Puss" . . .
Friends said "Poor Bill"—we say "Poor us"! . . .

Sophie Tetlow

Wisdom Begins

A man born of woman is put here to share
The joy and the laughter, the sadness and despair.
Whatever is needed to help us to grow
Life's journey will teach us and then we shall know.

So let's welcome the bad for we're told this is right,
From troubles we learn and gain Godly insight.
Our journey is long with its twists and turns,
But wisdom only comes if within us it burns.

So study with care the things you now say,
For the words of your mouth put your soul on display.
To consider the peace that lies deep in the heart
Will make you unique and set you apart.

At the end of your journey to say with real pride,
I travelled my road, yes, I took every stride.
With courage and strength I suffered it all,
And in the darkest of times with God's help I stood tall.

At the end of your days when your wisdom is great,
To the young and the sad you may wish to relate.
A lifetime of knowledge shared with others with love
Is the greatest wisdom there is and must come from above.

Roger D. Higgs

And Not Weep

How can I think of you, and not weep?
You invade my waking thoughts, my sleep.
The affinity we shared, you and I,
was bound to tightly to untie.

So kindred spirit, lover, friend,
although our time has had to end,
memories we shared, are mine to keep.
But, how can I think of you, and not weep?

Susan Barlow

Life

This place, although strange is securing,
but another place is luring,
it's a strong surge, overpowering and tempting me,
and wanting to become my destiny.

I curl in a ball, hiding my fear,
but within the walls of my home another pain does sear,
I see in the distance a welcoming light,
I make my way towards it, not knowing my plight.

I've left my security, my safety, my womb,
will this place I'm going, be my home or my tomb?
I'm gasping for air, crying and scared,
has this journey I've endeavoured ever been shared?

I've now lost my home in the womb I once curled,
and must fight for life in this new home called "world"
will I face hunger, sadness and pain,
or will there be love and achievement to gain?

Tracy Ann Morgan

The Red Trees of Vermont

I had a dream when I was small
One day I'd see Vermont in Fall.
The story of a child like me
Who told me she'd seen a red tree,
Made me say, when I was grown
I'd make that journey my own.
Now I am here and it's all true
Although, I'm now full sixty-two,
It's all come true, just like they said,
And many trees are brilliant red!
They alone go through every shade
Golds and green and reds and jade
Some dreams don't turn out as you'd believe
But the Fall in Vermont as I leave
Has fulfilled for the child, now old,
The sight of red trees as was told

Grown tall in Autumn in Vermont.

R. C. Christian

The Crow and the Magpies

The crow's unerring flight is said to be
the measure of a distance straight and true,
once in a time he's known to swerve ogee,
he swooped upon a nest built almost new.

Magpie designers of this dome-shaped pile
resent the crow's intrusion on their rig,
dive-bomb the dark invader in good style;
and so begins a mid-air aerial jig.

The crow retaliates with all his might
as feathers fly in time to raucous tune;
protagonists concede unequal fight;
defeated crow retreats but none too soon.

Instinct declares it never pays to claim
what seems is yours is so in all but name.

Struan Yule

Untitled

"Youth's a stuff will not endure",
Of this indeed you can be sure,
For Shakespeare got it right
When he wrote it in Twelfth Night.
He had it sung by a clown
To raise a smile, not a frown;
His message was quite plain to see:
To seize each chance for jollity.

So, when you sit upon a bench
And at your side's a comely wench,
'Twould be a crime, if you should miss
The chance to steal a merry kiss
Or let your heart beat on a pace
And hold her in a warm embrace;
Since later, when you're past your prime,
If you do that, 'twill be a crime!

George R. Emmett

New Life

Springtime comes in blooming glory,
bouquets of blossoms fill the land.
Leaflets and shoots peep out from hiding,
exploring new life only God could have planned.
A warm and gentle touch of air,
plays through the fields no longer bare,
raising life up from the earth.
With awe! Comes forth, the season of birth.

Colette Shires

The Futility of War

Fields of white stone fingers, each pointing heavenward,
Mark a million souls sleeping, beneath the sward;
There are no real victors whatever, in warfare,
Only death, destruction, distress, despair.

Many wars have plagued mankind, o'er countless years,
With annihilation, anguish, ruin and fears;
"Will countries ever learn, of war's sheer folly?"
Not unless world blessed, with hagiocracy!

Man has assembled the most frightful weaponry,
For launching attacks from land, air and sea;
And should a mad world, let atom bombs, again fall,
This Armageddon, would be an end for all.

Civil war is a conflict, all countries would dread,
Where harassed, pass slaughtered, on roads stained red;
And as these victims of vengeance, rush and stumble,
Some clutch their sole possessions in a bundle.

"Ye shall hear of wars and rumours of wars!" Christ said,
Since then, rivers of blood and tears, have been shed;
Yet mankind prays that amity, will again reign,
And war is no more—with death, grief and pain!

H. W. F. Collard

Country Side

Listen to the Wonderful sound of the countryside
The sheep bleating and grazing side by side.
The Birds in all their Wondrous song sing out in rapture
in a blaze of song.
Trees bending in the Breeze, the Beautiful Buzzing of the
honey Bees.
I sit and look all around and admire the lovely sight and the
lovely sound.
Running Rivers, Brooks and Streams, these are things of our Dreams.
These are soon to be a thing of the past because the people of
this planet are ruining them fast.
People of this planet, I say "leave the earth a pleasant way.
Please leave the Earth and Land alone, make it a health and
Beauty zone."
Of this planet we must look after for the next generation and
the one after.

Wayne Lloyd

Frustration

People stare and talk, as if I, wasn't there.
They should remember, I can see,
My feelings, they should spare.
I know every word they mention,
To speak, would be my intention.
I know exactly, what I'd like to say;
I just can't get it out, their way.

I am a human being,
My heart beats like theirs
The only difference I have
Is, a damaged motor nerve.
Now, if "I" were "you"
You, would be me!
How different it would be,
Alas, "you" are you—"I" am me.

Maisie Roberts

Guilt

Why did I do it? I know you can't know,
As I'm asking inside of my head.
And you must feel me staring, you turn to me smiling
To a face that holds no smiles, just blankness instead.

You ask me what's wrong, I can see your concern,
Again here is a chance to come clean,
But how could you see that you mean the world to me
When hearing the words that will destroy our dream.

So I'll live with my secret, as hard as it is,
I'll live with the guilt and the lies,
But how long can I go on, wanting answers where there's none
When it's breaking my heart to look into your eyes.

Life without you seems just unthinkable
And I know what I've done is so bad,
So it might all turn good, as I know this is love
If before that this guilt hasn't driven me mad!

Sarah Barrow

Nancy's Trip

Nancy—so sorry to hear that
While watering the dirt
You tripped on the hose
And ended up hurt.
Watering the garden
While the veggies were cooking,
You went down the steps
Without properly looking.
Irrigating and cooking without demur,
And the thanks that you get is a broken femur.
Not really unheeding,
Busy, writing and reading,
And unaware of your fall
When he heard you call,
David says he now feels repentance,
For saying when called "When I've finished my sentence."

Pam Brown

Gail...

There are lots and lots of reasons...
Why I chose you for a friend,
The main one is I know you will
Be with me till the end.
You're married with a family...
I'm living on my own,
But you're always there when needed
And I've always got the phone.
It seems a long long time...
From the days when we were young,
Whoever could have known
That life would be such fun?
We have also shared some bad times...
And we've had our ups and downs,
But we're together when it matters
And that's what really counts.
So when I'm old and grey...
And telling everyone a tale,
I'll tell them to treasure their dearest friends
   ...Just like I treasure Gail!

Sylvia Pigg

Ash Wednesday

Sin builds up in people's hearts,
Blackening them in barren layers of ash,
Lent is a time to spring clean your heart,
Do it joyfully, in a dash.
God shall break the ashes black crust,
Like rust in a metal that's soaken.
We shall hold God's words in our hearts and mind,
Wherever there's love God and Jesus we'll find.
We'll celebrate Lent for ever and ever,
Holding God's love, gentle as a feather.

Jan Rozycki

The Tree of Life

   Blessed are the thorns that hide the forbidden fruit
The prize that was Eden's curse
   Seek but do not eat your heart,
The ear will open the eye.
   At the tree of life,
There we separate the source
   And the offsprings of thought.
Illusion in a mist,
   The eye that seeks thee is lost
Go!
   And make glad the heart you eat.
The head is the tree of life
   And the harvest is in the eye.
Obsession is a question
   It is no place of rest—
It is a journey
   The trap of self is in a wandering mind.

C. George Abangwu

Spring

It awakens,
Life,
Suddenly it jumps out at you,
Bringing love,
Blinding you, the sun reaches its zenith,
Standing there, proudly, watching the darkness,
Keeping at bay.
The daffodil is the sun, warming the frozen grass,
It shivers and sheds its silvery coat of ice
   showing its luscious green,
It overwhelms all that meekly peer out,
They slowly crawl,
   the creatures of spring,
Hardly daring to reveal themselves,
   but they must
For the true beauty of spring draws them out
as it draws us.
Life is here once more.

Kiri Dinnal-Allen

Nature's Way

A tree stands tall, its branches
laced against the sky. A pair of
magpies nesting there way up
high. The grey squirrel innocent
of their fate, have many young,
prey to the magpies, who devour
them one by one.

Walking in the park, one day
I was compelled to look up,
I saw what seemed to me,
a drama unexpectedly, nature's way.
A squirrel escaped death,
when his predators were too near.
A cat climbed the tree,
and sensed the squirrel's fear.

The cat stalked the magpies,
until they moved back,
quickly—the squirrel jumped from tree to tree,
agile to the sway—this time still free

Rosalyn C. Ellis

Winter

Skeleton trees adorned with sparkling lace,
Icy garlands hang in every space,
Icicles glitter like rainbows in the sun,
Footprints in the snow where children run.
A curtain of snowflakes falling from on high.
Wild white horses fly across the sky.
Hailstone tapping on the window pane,
Tell you winter's here again.

Jean Peck

A Nova Star

Into each life journey comes that one person
We call our 'best friend', but our most 'special friend'
Is the one we've known from childhood.
Such a deep friendship is forged through the years,
So steadfast, mysterious, and ever constant—
Like a nova star growing in brilliance.
Obscured at times by storm clouds,
Only to reappear as each storm passes,
Glowing with reliable dependency.
Such was my special friend. We romped through life together
Sharing good times and bad for some fifty years.
We laughed. We cried. We shared our secret dreams.
Ours was a friendship like that nova star—
Burning with incandescent warmth, reaching out to all.
But now, like a candle flame flickering in the darkness—
Consumed in its own aura, that star
Glows with radiance. My special friend
Has ascended to eternal glory. I stand alone
Wrapped in my memories of an intangible friendship,
To treasure—until we meet again.

Rhonda Byrne

My Home

A gate in the hedge, a path to the door
With hanging baskets and flowers galore
A joy to the heart, a delight to the eye
For all the people passing by.

Come into the sitting room where you'll find
Treasured trinkets of every kind
Given over the years with deepest love
By those who now dwell up above.

The silver teapot has pride of place
Won by Father in sword practice
How Mother would polish it in days of old
And handle it like rarest gold.

Peace and tranquillity here you'll find
A balm for troubled heart and mind
Put a City man here and what would he say?
"I wonder what Wall Street is doing today?"

Megan Harris

Can Somebody Tell Me

Can somebody tell me, without being a bore
What is the reason and what we're here for
Is life so important or not, as may seem
Is it truly quite real or maybe a dream

Is there really a plan, for all human life
And is this the real reason why some have such strife
and suffer and fret through wars and its pain
But have to come back to repeat it again

Is there a reason why some that are born
Have got built-in defects that make some people scorn
Why some are born black and some are quite fair
Some being yellow with really jet hair

Please also tell me that why is it so
That babies are born to a life they'll not know
For just a few hours what do they derive
It does seem a shame such a short time they're alive

There must be an answer can somebody say
You're here for an instant and then whisked away
It's not really an instant it's a lifetime in fact
Before your life ends and once more you're pulled back

E. M. Budge

Seek Peace and Pursue it!

Come on, you catholics and protestants, break with
Entrenched traditions, give peace a chance and
Cultivate love and forgiveness for one another,
　Give peace a chance.

The son of God came to earth to break with man's
Traditions. He showed the way of peace but you
Have to pursue it, remember it may cost you something;
　it cost him his life!

The Bible has the answer, love your enemies
Bless them that curse you, return evil to no
one. So seek peace and pursue it, remember it was
Jesus, who said "you will know my followers by
Their fruits and intense love for one another."

The priests of his day killed him because of
Their traditions. They made God's word invalid because
Of them. So put away your traditions and start to
Live again. Follow in Jesus' footsteps

Turn your back on violence, turn your back on
Guns, remember the sermon on the mount. Read it!
Pursue it and have God's blessings
　If you don't, you don't stand a chance!

J. Ramsden

Captured

Green-eyed Leopard, lithe and strong,
far from the place where you belong,
far from the forest, and the plain,
where you roamed at will,
thinking of the chase, and urge to kill.
Green eyes smouldering in frustration and anger,
growling and pawing, sensing danger,
seeking freedom, pacing and turning
back and forth in a cage.
Noises of wheels turning, turning, Leopard crouched in fear,
when into the light, he reared, ready to flee,
all senses alert, muscles straining against the bars,
tough as steel.
They let him free in a small enclosure,
snarling he looked around,
his sense of smell led him to the meat,
they had thrown upon the ground;
he had to learn, no more the chase;
he was captured by the human race.

Olive A. Powles

The Forest Art Form

The scented dew from a fallen petal
Caressed by the goodly forest ground
With earth' awakening transition
may your health and happiness abound.

To the scenic nature's picture
I bequeath my painted trust
Then to you my pasliged darling
Through goodly years and prayers diseased.

Now I know life's time existence allowed
on transfer of thought of goodly deeds
tumultuary worlds will disappear
and once again our lives be free

The thought of wars and wanton destruction
with needless horror abound
Return to the summer forest darling
To God given inherent ground

To this my friend reckoning
Drawn curtains shut out the brilliant light
In each lettered verse of true thought a soft voice pleading
Return to innocence as when life began

Walter Legender

Heavy Rain, Heavy Heart

What can I do? What can I say
To take away your aching pain?
All I can do is offer my hand,
Hold on to it tight, I do understand.
Cling to each other, be strong in your grief,
Because your baby is safe now
In God's arms he does sleep.
For somewhere up there God has other plans
I know it's so cruel you do not understand.
Your hopes of your future, they are not all gone,
They're just on hold for your next little one.
Today your tears rain down heavy from the sky
You scream in your heart "Oh why God why?"
But when your tears stop,
A new morning will dawn,
There is another baby just waiting to be born
So be strong for each other,
Dry your eyes once you've grieved
And together, hand in hand
A new baby you will soon receive.

Alaina Deans

Here Today Gone Tomorrow!

That walk in the towering trees of prolific life
Like faces in a crowd very distinctive and full of spice
Those cones bearing softwoods tower endless before your eyes
Streams of colourful light cutting a presence in the skies

Hemlock, Balsam and Pine, climbing it seems forever
Breathing, feeling and seeing the stillness how inspiring!
Each one a little different from its neighbour
Freedom to grow and strive towards their creator

Touching the deep blue sky the peace of their presence
Creating a stillness from their very essence
300 Feet up of manufacturing importance
Satisfying our hearts with their very magnificence

The birds and bees of natural living beauty
Building and lodging in their strength and density
Using the raw materials of this majestic creation
Not wasting or abusing like human intervention

Mill hands and managers thriving on their yield
Road builders and road users won't stop until they've felled
Another day, another tree to satisfy the consumer
Here today gone tomorrow, extinct or rumer!

Dean F. Meazza

Carve Her Name with Pride

Second World War . . . France occupied
By Germans from East-to-West,
Men and women die, with many already dead
Trying to free the world from a Nazi Beast.
A woman from our beautiful land,
(Mother of her little girl),
Was sent to harass, on her errand,
Enemy, regardless Peril.
And, like many before her, she died,
Leaving her name in our breasts;
And George Cross to her little child
Was given in a memory of her mother's rest.
The story ended without tears,
But in a deep grief Nation not forgot
To honour true and fearless
And to discern the heart of a Patriot . . .

Stanislaw Paul Dabrowski-Oakland

My World
To Matthew

In a world of darkness, you are my only light,
In a world of blackness, you are my only white.
In a world of terror, you're all I do not fear,
In a world so far away, you are all that's near.
In a world of emptiness, you're all that fits in place,
In a world of chaos, you are my only space.
In a world of loneliness, you are my only friend,
In a world that finishes, you're all that doesn't end.
In a world of ambition, you're all I need to succeed,
In a world of kindness, you are my thought and deed.
In a world of everything, you're all that I desire,
In a world of determination, you're all that I admire.
In a world of lowness, you're all that is above,
In my world it's you and me, in our world of love.

Beth Amanda Harris

Beauteous Bewdley, 1996

Music, mosaic, poetry and print,
Binge, fringe, ballet, cabaret scarcely hint
Of fond memories that go back with goods
To the River Severn in all its moods.

Stand on Bewdley bridge for frightening flood,
On those few occasions, you truly could
Have walked across, scarce wet child, without fear
And claimed a sand bank as your castle's den.

How I danced and pranced, glee paddled and preened,
Whilst a distraught mother bade me keep cleaned.
Little did she know, neither then nor now
That Bewdley had me in unending tow.

Mildred Bateman

An Evening Stroll

Clear crystal pools amidst dark lagoons,
The starry skies and the waxing moons,
The damp night air so fresh and cool,
A solitary deer drinking by the pool,
Rustling trees in the gentle breeze,
My favorite moments are times like these.

Forest streams trickle silently past,
To the swollen river that runs so fast,
The timid field mouse the elk's untamed fear
Life's precious moments so calm and clear,
As I roam through these shady trees,
How wonderful the hours of tranquil peace.

The bracken that hides the lonely shrew,
With narrow paths were people walk through,
Children play in the meadow beyond,
Fishermen sit patiently by the pond,
I wander home with my soul renewed,
It was such a peaceful interlude

Adrian Martin

One Special Lady

A lady of pure distinction
With a soul that really cares,
A kindness I've never felt before
In a person that always shares.

A heart so warm and tender
With a smile so gentle and sweet,
A courage that can conquer any storm
Which sweeps me off my feet.

If it ever gets all too much
For your spirit and soul to bear,
Give me a call, I won't let you fall,
Because for you I will be there.

Sometimes when the going is really tough
You think that you can't pull through,
I don't know why you have such doubts
As I have so much faith in you.

You're a lady with an open heart
A character better than all the rest,
I hope that you never ever change,
You are just, simply the best.
  Gregory Button

Jack Jones

Why oh why can I not be two,
To be a pair and go right through?
Married life together to laugh and trust,
It would be so good, wouldn't it just!
Spending life together, getting in a fizz,
Just like a pair, hers and his;
Mr. and Mrs., a child makes three,
How long must I wait, to start a family tree?
Born of a woman, am now a young man,
One wonders how long to discover God's plan.

Two swans together who never part,
A mate for life, that one true heart;
Together forever will always be,
Personalities gel, too blind to see.

There's nothing like a woman's true love,
Nurtured when ill under the wings of your dove;
So fragile yet strong with hair all curled,
Let's face it mate, it's a woman's world!
Seen only through that one true light,
Is that magical beauty of a woman so right!
  Graham Peter Childs

I'm There with You

Don't weep for me I did not die
   I'm there with you every time you sigh
I know right now you are feeling pain
   but it will pass like falling rain

When you're sitting lonely in your chair
   feeling nothing but despair
Remember the happy times we had
   and smile a little don't be sad.

Life must go on and you must live
   for you have so much love to give,
I'll be there to help you through it all
   and hold you up so you don't fall.

When you feel the wind in your hair
   then you will know that I am there
When the sun is warm on your skin
   that's me hugging you from within

And when the nights are cold and dark
   look up and you will see a spark
of light shining through
   then you will know I'm there with you
  Evelyn Howard

As Usual, Never Late

Mid-morning, I boarded a haunted
bus, jolting its way through countryside,
frog-fashion, through tree and shrub.
Grub-like, my fingers held to the seat
in front, drilling backwards the cold
feel of chromium rest into my heart.
Misty mirroring-glass pane away
the winter grass from narrowed,
spectral, passenger-eyes, hunting.
Thrice somebody rang the bell,
thrice the brakes screeched, thrice
the frogging creep did start again.
Forenoon and we did wade
suburban plain, with ghostly
towers beckoning through lashing rain.
Then the race with a demented
train, galloping over a bridge; and the
feel of horrors at the station's
gate. You, my man, under an
umbrella. As usual, never late.
  Theresa Vella

Great Expectations

They look in amazement at everything they see.
Everything that is, from an ant to a huge great tree.
Their eyes light up; they clap their hands with glee,
There's lots of things in this great wide world to see.
Life is so uncomplicated, at this very young age.
This small child is at a wonderful stage
Growing in strength every day and night
That every small child I love, with all my might.
  Marion A. Lee

Winter Lament

It's a long time till Spring,
A long time till Winter's dreary cloak is lifted from the ground.
Birds once again will sing,
And the countryside will come alive with joyous sound.

It's a long time till Spring,
A long time to wait for green shoots to appear again;
Dazzling flowers they will bring,
Which open in the sunlight and close up in the rain.

It's a long time till Spring,
When swallows make their long and arduous trip
And blue-bells softly ring
Attracting insects to their flowers to sip.

It's a long time till Spring,
But I will not despair—it will arrive,
And then I myself will sing
For Spring makes everybody come alive!
  B. P. D. Thorne

Inner Thoughts

There I was lying still,
   dozing in my bed,
When all at once a tidal wave
   came rushing in my head.
From where it came I do not know,
   I guess from deep within.
Is this a precious gift for life
   or just a passing whim?
They come when least expected
   In restaurants, rain, through sleep
To me the canvas is wondrous
   for others it's just a peep
At times the ink flows quick with ease,
   with words I've not yet said.
There are other times I taunt and tease
   The words to leave my head.
Yet, in the end I know I'll find
   Stored somewhere deep, within my mind
The phrase that fits, the word that rhymes
   The ending to writings for mankind
  Sharon Russell

Death Bed Soliloquy
Dedicated, in memory, to "Jim"

Was with her when the death rattle came
in the stillness of the hospital night.

When conscious, did say to her—
"You have been good mother-in-law to me."
Slowly, she shook her head containing no teeth
with which to challenge me.

Her husband was elsewhere, the daughter at home.
Out of harm's reach—the pair.

Owed it to her to stay until the end.
She would not be alone—am glad I did.

Those, the last words did we exchange—
A reply too ill to voice—
A flicker of the eye-lids did tell me so.

Dawn came—I watched her die.
She slipped away not knowing where she was.

Now, she knows where she is gone—
And waits for me?

My turn will come, probably alone.
A new day dawns.
Let us not waste a single day.
Howard Trevor Gaunt

Gulag Dream

I met you in my dreams last night
With outstretched arms you beckoned me,
The mist it swirled and curled about,
A minute seemed eternity.
Two hands reached out across the void,
In vain the quivering fingers stretched for love.
Almost afraid to touch they were
Lest the vision depart like a frightened dove.
They touched and feelings warm with care flowed out,
No cry, no shout, just a smile, and a look from those eyes said all.
Then time he took his toll at last,
He'd come to pay his call.
It was then that I awoke and reality walked in,
Only the bright and single bulb with the damp grey walls around,
Told me the truth of where I was as I lay upon the ground.
No warmth, no feeling of you felt
Nor the scent of your soft brown hair,
Just the smell of this dank and deathly room
And those who died in there.
I'll wait for you my own till the mists of time have gone,
But my love, my joy, my spirit will always linger on.
D. N. Paxton

Communication

Isn't it great to communicate.
We talk on the phone.
We talk at home.
Speech is what we use.
If that is what we choose.
Radio and T.V. too.
Help communicate to you.

Writing communicates just the same.
It even helps you to know my name.
Write a letter send it on.
Answers back, to and from.
Computers, fax, newspapers too.
Help communicate to you.

Deaf people cannot hear words.
They cannot hear the chirp of birds.
But they can learn what's going on.
Sign language, lip reading, other codes too.
Help communicate to you.
Isn't it great to communicate?
Nicola Oliver

November

Amazing quiet descended on the countryside.
The harsh wind rushed over the waste,
touching lonely, barren boughs that stretched their arms to the sky,
choked and twisted, black against the clouds.

The light dimmed, and with it came an irreparable chill.
Then, the sky's silent squalor evolved into drops of rain,
the grey drizzle streamed down the pane
like the hot, angry tears that burned down my cheeks.

That night rolled in like a summer storm,
the clouds scudding over the glassy surface of the sky.
Outside, the chill stealthily crept up from the fields
into the hearts of those hungry for the warmth and light.

The rain's comfort calmed my tears,
Its subliminal euphony soothing my mind.
And here, our hearts were drawn into slumber,
the near night creeping through the persistent rain.

But here, wrapped in warmth where nothing matters,
sharing the closeness that we radiate,
the night cannot swallow us,
the chill cannot wrap its icy fingers around our hearts.
Caroline Boyce

Rapport

Do you dance up there, as we danced when you were alive
In tune, in unison, our single shadow outlined on the floor?
Yes, we dance here too, though we dance as if on air
Our feet alert to every vibrant beat

Do you sing up there, the way we used to sing
The lyrics so much less than the meaning in our eyes?
Yes, we sing here too, in a way that's hard to describe
The joyous notes soaring through our very being

Can you feel things there, as I used to feel your touch
Your warm embrace, the comfort of your arms?
Yes, we feel things here, as we felt them in my life before
Yet feel them with more clarity than you can know

And do you weep there, as I weep every day
Persistently, since you took your leave and went away?
No, we weep not here, how could we with such joy
To be through the mist, ascending the golden thread?

And do you yearn up there for those that you have lost
As I yearn here for you, my heart gripped in a vice?
No, no, my love, we do not grieve, nor could we in this state
Which is true reality, where life was but a dream
Dudley Paget-Brown

Canteen Blues

As I sit here in the canteen gazing all around
And watch some happy face as a piece of meat she's found;
It was actually hidden, underneath a small baked bean
Feeling so ashamed, not wanting to be seen.
I've never heard of peas, or carrots with a curry
But guess that's all there was, when made in a hurry.
We even get peas with spaghetti bolognese
And often with the fish there is a kind of maize.
And as we stand there waiting for our piece of small gateau
Someone's shouting "Where's the Cherry?", as if she didn't know
They're going to the board room, where the big nobs hang around
For when it comes to us, there's not a cherry to be found.
And if you should forget to put your name upon the sheet,
You have to sit there at the table, without a thing to eat.
It really doesn't matter, if you're starved and looking thin
There's nothing you can do, to make any one give in.
May be, if you're lucky, you will get an extra share
But it's only someone else's which they couldn't bear.
So, while I sit here gazing, watching everybody eat,
Someone's lifted up my bean, and pinched my blooming meat.
Joy Parnwell

My Man

I watched him running down the street,
He hadn't any money,
His body bent, his face was plain,
I thought him rather funny,
Some folk said he wasn't right,
Some said he was quite mad,
But when he smiled his smile at me,
He really made me glad,
I'd met no-one like him before,
I really was surprised,
When he said "Will you marry me?",
I looked into his eyes,
And there I saw an honest man,
Perhaps a little strange,
So I said yes and promised him,
A wedding I'd arrange,
Now we've been married twenty years, I've really come alive,
He's taking me to Paradise, when we reach twenty-five,
A second honeymoon he says, one thing I know is true,
He loves me very much, and I love him too.

Eileen Southey

My Daughter Thomasina

My daughter's life was so full of care
She loved to dance, and sing and do most everything.
Then one night while she was asleep she heard the angels sing.
They came and took her away.
She has been with them right up till today.

3 years have passed; my love still grows for her ever now.
The love she gave me while she was by my side
Was true and strong,
Will last me throughout my life or even a while longer.

I sit sometimes and think of her,
The way she laughed and the way she moved.
She was really beautiful to watch,
Like nothing I have ever seen.

Christine Friery

To You Who Gave Life Meaning

If I remember rightly, for it was some time ago,
I mused that with the passing years, the tears would cease to flow.
Kind friends advised me gently "in time you will forget"
But today is here, and on my mind, your memory lingers yet.

The days continue to unfold, I do what is required,
The tasks that once gave joy to do, I now do uninspired.
With you, I could do anything, no challenge too great or small,
With you to love I could overcome whatever might befall.

When twilight falls I still recall the warmth of your caress,
The nights when I would fall asleep, my head upon your breast.
These arms still ache with longing, these eyes have yet to see,
Another, who would mean as much, as you still do to me.

Pat Brace

Spring

Today I heard a bird sing,
And snowdrops pierce the grass.
A soft little breeze then blew through the trees
And ruffled my hair as it passed.

It's the yearly awakening
Of our cold wintery earth.
Green shoots will appear, for spring's almost here.
A magical time—a rebirth.

Flowers hold up their bright heads
For the sun's tender embrace.
Trees awake from their rest, birds build their nests.
There's new hope for the human race.

Nothing can ever compare
With this pulsating event.
Blue skies are so bright, clouds, fluffy and white.
This season must be heaven sent.

Carol Liddle

Below the Wing

Below the soaring gliding feathery wing,
The sun tips its rays on an endless flight
Of beaches, coves and battered weathered cliffs.
Where nesting boxes suckle precocious young,
And the wind screams like a demon through
Ever widening crevices, where the sea's creative hand
Has ravaged and shaped the rock into new dimensions
Of eerie night lights and spectacular sunrises
When the mist nestles beneath the morning tide,
The fairytale cliffs are launched seaward.

Pat Sani

A Friend like Sam

I don't know when she came here,
To me she has always been,
When I was down,
She would make me feel
Like a flower that could sing.

I knew she couldn't talk to me,
But she was a comfort so warm
She was more than words could say,
The love that she gave to me,
You couldn't do or say.

I thought that she would stay forever,
Then came that day in March,
When her life that she shared with me,
Just cried right from my heart.

I couldn't imagine life without her,
But now it is so clear,
When she passed away from me, my world just disappeared.

But how my mind is now at rest, she was led by a peaceful hand,
with grass so green, and sun so bright,
she can run and play, my Sam.

Dawn Sheppard

Memories, A True Tale

When I was born, I wished it was warm
As the place I had just come from hence
Then my Mothers arms made me forget my yearns
With the warmth of her love round me fenced.

I played ev'ry day as all babies may
Till walking I started to roam
A black cock'rel did fly, his spur cut near my eye
All I saw was his great scarlet comb.

My Mother got mad at that cockerel so bad,
She chased him around with an axe
But the owner came then, pleaded "Don't kill my hen
In the future I won't be so lax".

Now as time went on, seems he had done more harm
'Cause outside I refused to go.
Of his basilisk stare and his spurs I was scared
So they made him a barred coop, of oak!

That cockerel still lived and some pleasure did give
He was handsome in an evil way
Yet some good came of it, though 'war effort' was hit
For our breakfast his hens did all lay.

Eileen Ashworth

Onwards or Not

Spiritual doors awaken for me
Is it a long journey for I cannot see?

Separation, departure, disunite
Beneath the world of roots and ashes

Is it the end or just the beginning?
Destinations begun to continue

Fertilization, gestation, birth, death and decay
What of my soul where does it lie?

R. Watts

Temperature Changes

We are now gradually learning, but only by degrees,
That changing over to Centigrade can be quite a tease!
And though one hundred means boiling, and zero, a freeze,
I'd sooner have old Fahrenheit's way, much better, if you please.
Before entering Europe, it was our happy lot,
With thirty-two for freezing, but should you want it hot,
Applying two hundred and twelve degrees would truly boil the pot,
And, in a room at seventy, how nicely warm you got!
There must be many 'old sweats' like me,
Who, with this innovation, do strongly disagree.
And, if you are a chap of my own heart,
Mathematically, for sure, you can play your part.
For temperatures given in the Centigrade range,
It's fairy easy to make the desired change,
Just double the number, and from this take
One tenth away, and with this make,
By adding an extra thirty-two,
Your Fahrenheit scale—as good as new!
Then you'll feel warmer—more cosy too!!

H. Preston

Scotland

Scotland, the place of Lochs and Bens,
Cold mountain streams running down the Glens.
Of different seasons that can change so fast,
The land where hope and freedom last.
Longing for people far away,
And think of Scotland every day.
Never to be forgotten friends of old,
Dreams that hearts and minds enfold.
  Scotland my home!!!

Isabella Muir-Ward

A Ghostly Call

Black eerie shadows, hovering the ground . . .
I listened, I listened, not a sound! . . .
It was just a legend we've heard, that's all.
Listen now! . . . What a ghostly call.
Black eerie shadows all around . . .
My heart's beating faster, my head begins to pound!

Running, walking, no time to turn,
"Why me?" I ask this ghostly call.
Black eerie shadows now all around . . .
My legs and body weary with fright
I ran, I ran with all my might . . .
Alas, my body now bedraggled fell to the ground
Black eerie shadows hover all around.
A hand on my shoulder, my body still,
Clinging, grasping tightly to a vine,
Oh!! Peace, now, at last my mind begins to
Unwind. In the distance I could see a light.
"A light", "A light", I recall . . . now . . .
I'm content in mind, happy to have joined
This ghostly call! . . .

C. L. Rayers

How Lovely

We stroll along it's late at night
The moon is out, the stars are bright
And you are with me here tonight:
How lovely you look to me under the stars;
I love to feel you in my arms
close to me with all your charms.
How lovely you look to me in my arms:
As morning comes I wake with you,
The morning sun shines on you.
How lovely you look to me under the morning sun:
We stroll along the sky so bright
We hug, we kiss and hold hands tight
We smile we laugh we sometimes cry
But we both know that our love won't die!
How lovely it is to be in love with you.

Jennifer Hoffman

Day-Dreamer

I walked along thinking of things,
Of beautiful houses and diamond rings.
I thought of the sun that lights my day,
What would we do if it was taken away?

I had ideas of posh silk shirts,
Of no more pain and nothing that hurts.
My ideal book and a blazing fire,
Total honesty and no more liars.

No more crime and no more jail,
Always a success and never a fail.
Thinking of joy and happiness,
No more desolate wilderness.

I think of healing the sick and dying,
Endless blue skies and people flying.
I imagine bringing an end to war;
Have You dreamed this dream before?

Clare Welsh

Oh Son of Mine!

Break not this heart, oh son of mine,
Share your thoughts, when you have time,
For when you travel far and wide,
My heart, my son, travels by your side.

Break not this heart, oh son of mine,
What did I do that was such a crime?
I try to think, and begin to cry,
Torn apart, and I don't know why.

Break not this heart, oh son of mine,
Perhaps one day in the passage of time,
I will understand what I did to you,
That makes you feel the way you do.

Break not this heart, oh son of mine,
A love so precious and divine,
No matter how you think of me,
This heart, my son, belongs to thee.

Dianne Womack

My Motto

My motto, my motto is to go
forward, and let the people and the
developments talk of me, and for once I
know the truth is there I shall never, never,
never, never worry.
  And also if you give a man a fish
He will only have a single meal
but if you teach him how to fish
He will always eat his life up to death.

Emmanuel Kwabla Dzanado

Time Spirit

I feel the beauty and grace
that runs across your face,
I see you sitting in thought,
careful consideration and love
always there by your side.

The innocent touch that fills your heart,
all warm, with something unknown to words,
that spoken breath of feeling,
one changing form in beauty made.

Your soul tells of enchanting,
everlasting, evergiving love,
spoken in the poetry of your special wisdom,
loves passion left behind, and the essence captured.

Time spirit, spirit of the age,
yours is to last forever.

The spirit of an age,
long ago past, brings forth
a special kind of poet,
and his will last forever.

Deborah Jayne Berry

Our Teacher's Driving Lessons

Her instructor said "Try to do an emergency halt,"
But she seemed to think he said "Let's somersault,"
   That happened the next minute
   With the two of them in it
She pressed the wrong pedal — it was never her fault!

At crossroads she decided she would go straight ahead
Ignoring the traffic lights when the colour was at red,
   She said "Why all the fuss
   Just for missing a bus,"
He said "Fuss? Very soon, miss, you'll have everyone dead."

At a roundabout her instructor said "Take exit three,"
But she drove to the right, and was met by a P.C.,
   She said "I've come out tonight
   And done everything right
So why are you stopping to put questions to me?"

She took ten movements to maneuver a three point turn
Reversed into a garden gate and advanced into a burn,
   He said "Please miss, let me out"
   She said "There's no need to shout"
He said "Just stop now, and please miss, do not return!"

   Betty Hay

Irish Princess

So scared of what she feels,
but, the Irish princess, she hides in her dreams.
Alone in a field of tears,
where, the Irish princess relives it again.
For the rest of her life, pain and regret,
for an Irish princess,
 forever regret.

   Richard Westwood

She Watched the Candle Burn

At the casement she sat, gazing over the sea, and watched the candle burn,
She had promised this, her vigil, until he should return,
He said farewell, to sail away to some far distant shore,
But every time he waved goodbye, would he return once more?

Before he left to go away he didn't seem the same,
The cheeky smile less happy, the excuses seemed more lame,
He'd never know the heartache, the waiting and the fears,
Though her love had never wavered through the lonely years.

She always kept her faith in him, that he wouldn't let her down,
For hadn't he said he loved her and this little coastal town,
Grey streaks now running through her hair, wrinkles on her face,
And her tender smile hid all the tears in her handkerchief of lace,

She sees at last him coming, showing years of weathered burn,
No questions, no reminders, no more watch the candle burn.

   KatieHill

My Dad

My Dad was a funny old guy,
Laughing and joking, the odd white lie,
The life and soul of any party,
He would joke and laugh whole heartily,
A real character in our village,
To know him was a privilege,
He enjoyed a pint on a Friday night,
When it came to money, never tight,
He had so many friends
The list never ends.
He loved his family from the bottom of his heart,
One day he would drive me to get wed, in a horse and cart,
But sadly that day never arrived,
As his life didn't continue to thrive,
At fifty two his life was tragically taken,
Sadly in hospital he did not waken,
We all take our Families for granted,
My dad was the best dad someone ever had wanted,
I miss my poor old Dad,
Now it makes me so very very sad, I love you dear Dad.

   Francine Cracknell

Thank You God

Gone once again is Winter's dull care, and here
once again, renewed hope in the air.
The promise of Springtime is with us once more.
New life all around as God opens the door.

No more do the trees bend their backs
to the sighs of the wind
as it scurries dark clouds o'er the skies.
The blankets of snow have rolled back to reveal
the wonders of God that none can conceal.

The field mouse has stirred in his snug little bed.
Stretching and listening to birds overhead.
Sing their hearts to the skies, greet the new Sun, and each
promise of Spring, now cruel Winter is done.

Jack Frost has been banished from Milldams and streams, the
hedgerows are budding, and man has his dreams. Of dear ones he
loves, of his hopes and his fears, for peace in the world, for
goodwill and no tears.

   Gordon Hoare

Supper for One

Down behind the railings, either end a figured stone,
'Neath' Victorian stairwell, a lady dines alone,
Each and every lunch time as I pass by the house,
The table in the window, set for one, there is no spouse.
Her cloth of cleanest, brightest checks,
Pressed neat, no puckers there,
And all the condiments for one, stand each, upon a square,
Her nets are laundered every month, they hang as white as snow,
To cheat the nosy passerby as on their way they go.
The room is lit by one large lamp, her colour shades of green,
And matched by cultured careful eye, her ornaments are seen,
Cushions sewn by clever hand, with love in every stitch.
Her planned and ordered lonely life, goes daily without hitch.
Then one fine day, the strangest thing, disorder is espied,
Unruly objects scattered round, and ribbons all untied?,
The answer is supplied, as my daily walk reveals,
The lady, wreathed in smiles, walks out, a puppy at her heels.

   Jenny Langridge

Thanks 4 No. 1

Thank you both for the beauty you conceived.
With my heart, body and soul D.D. I received,
I have loved her so deeply right from the start
So a place for you both I keep in my heart.

You accepted me with open arms
With no quips or quibbles or any qualms,
I have saved some love to give to you both
And will treasure our No.1, you have my oath.

I love her so much it hurts real bad
And with her love for me I will never be sad,
So it's thanks from the heart to her dad and mum
For this beauty of ours who's my No. 1

   T. C.

The Spider and the Fly

How I can fly said the spider to the fly,
Buzz-ah you fly with your sticky bed,
You glide on your thread, one I am not going to tread,
I shall fly about and laugh instead.

Ah but can you catch me like I you?
Says the spider to the fly with a wink in his eye,
I shall spin a web to catch your rival remarks,
says the Spider and eat your wings for dinner.

Buzz-ah you are for sure bizarre,
You're the one who sat down beside her,
Indeed I am the spider said,
sat in the middle of his bed.

Half a day goes by and still you fly,
quietly sneers the spider of the fly,
as yet buzzes about his sticky net.

   Deborah Jayne Berry

Moonlit Proposal

The water glistened with the light of the moon,
As my lover and I walked arm in arm,
Since the day we had met, I had known no gloom
And life had become one romantic calm.

Each day, and each minute, together we shared;
Our obvious love would last us for life,
But never was I in the slightest prepared
For his asking me to become his wife.

When, out of the blue, he went down on one knee
And took my hand on that beautiful night,
Everything went silent, even the sea;
It's obvious my decision was right.

The commitment we decided we would make
Is forever and it always applies.
The wedding vows we made, we will never break,
As we can see our love in our child's eyes.

Helen Lovell

Waiting for the Letter

Waiting for the letter that never comes,
Waiting each morning for the Postman.
Waiting to find he has passed us by,
You know it is coming, but when?

Maybe it's the exam results, maybe news from the family,
Maybe the job interview, maybe——?
Whatever news that the letter will give,
We'll carry on waiting, we have to, you see,
We are waiting to live.

Valerie Jennings

Precious Life

For each and every one of us
    There is a precious life
If we only took the time to pause
    As each day passes slowly by.

For every new born baby,
    A parent's love, and guiding hands.

The trees bear leaves and branches
    Berries and their fruits,
Feeding and protecting
    Our birds of many species.

The countryside has open spaces,
    And the fields, their grass of green.
The sky above, its clouds of white,
    And the oceans, . . . Their treasures of the deep.

The sun and rain, to purify and feed
    The wondrous earth.
To give to everyone of us
    The gift of "Precious Life"

Jim Carlin

Easter

Jesus said "I do not forget the
sorrow of my Mother Mary who
gave me everything, she suffered
all sorrows, I give her joy.

I suffered myself, slander, hatred.
I suffered Peter's lie, Judas' betrayal
Who sold me, feigning love. I suffered
the passions of man and Calvary

I suffered knowing, centuries on earth
Some still prefer death to eternal life.
My sacrifice." "What did we do Lord?
What we do yet, Be our vision Lord
Help us forget

Sorrows of the spirit Lord
Turn us right around,
Show us new dimensions Lord
Here, on the ground.

Anne Llewellyn

Beethoven's Ninth Symphony

Majestic, unsoiled,
Full of blithe Celtic wit,
That is what the great symphony is.

Warm in its pulsations, full of blithe melancholy,
Swelling on the tide of loving-kindness,
Eternal symphony surpassing time's misconstructions:

Generous work, tiding over the great hollow
In the mind of man, mysterious masterpiece
Untarnished by the years,
I would love you
As I have proved to myself that I am able to do,
Praising your blithe places, adoring your hushed silences,
Making merry over your vigourous outpourings,
Silent in face of your great awe,
Chilled by your majestic fullness,
Light in heart at the thought of your leaping gladness,
Great symphony to outlast time's brutal sway!

Iver Eaglesham

Footsteps

Going back into the past
Retracing footsteps from long ago,
Memories pouring oh! so fast,
The years so quickly go!

The sky above, the same paths below,
Feeling young at heart reliving, rekindling
What we once treasured an still do,
Our lost loved ones, so vividly brought nearer

Old friendships renewed, such happy times remembered,
People don't change, just mature and progress.
Raising children, families increasing,
Exchanging our news broadening horizons,
Still caring for our fellow men, God helps us preserve this

Rita Violet Holder

The Rat

Every sewer you go to I'll be there,
Spreading my dreadful disease here and there.
The smell the dirty air is what temps me,
I couldn't leave it, I've loved it since childhood you see.
My sagging skin all freckled and grey,
Gets dirtier and dirtier everyday.
My shape is oval, but rigged and fat,
With bulging creases all tit for tat.
My friends and I roll around in the waste,
But we don't eat it, we hate the taste.
I love being a rat, proud of it too,
But I hate my killing disease, harming people one and two.

Kiran Lyall

Turn the Page

Don't judge a book by its cover
Is an adage old and true
To go beyond the exterior
Could be a surprise for you.

That quiet person with no obvious charm or clout
Can have thoughts and wisdom
Waiting to be brought out.

The world has many lonely folk
Who hide behind a facade
They want to belong to the chatty crowd
But find it much too hard.

So hold out the hand of friendship
Say hello and smile
Try to open this closed book
As you chat awhile

A good story you could overlook
By keeping closed a good book
Go on, turn the page and begin
To find the story hidden within.

W. Slym

Coming of Age

Today's the day you come of age,
Son now you have to earn a wage,
So go into the big wide world,
And fight to keep what you can hold.

You're on your own for ever more,
You'll have the key for your front door.
To live the life you want to live,
But, make sure your heart has love to give.

To be alone is bad enough
No one to love is very tough,
Your heart will ache or maybe break,
Get someone to love for your own sake.

At sixteen years the world is yours,
Your charm and smile must open doors
To get the best out of this life,
You do not want a life of strife.

Today's the day you come of age,
Now your life must turn a page,
Put away your childish things
And let yourself take on new wings.

David H. Rogers

Ode to a Rhododendron Flower

You gaze upon this lovely flower,
midst its green and leafy bower.
The colours in mad profusion,
senses stirred in wild confusion.
lovely is the Rhododendron Flower.

The mystic waxen petals of this flower,
form exotic fantasies that overpower
the senses. Colours of every hue,
white to pink, mauve to blue,
their fragrance fills the leafy bower.

Hold forever in sheer rapture, pure,
flowers with exotic, mystic allure.
Hold this wonder within the eye,
pray this beauty will never die,
our hearts desire this wonder to endure.

The rain must fall, winds blow cold,
Touch the flowers, furies untold.
petals marred, tossed to the ground,
broken blossoms lie around.
Adieu, my sweet Rhododendron Flower.

Kay Aukett

A Highland Tour

Among the hills and bens at early dawn
A mist hangs over, then is gone.
A beautiful picture comes into view
Those hills and bens have changed to blue.

The dark blue lochs and silvery streams
Are awakened by the sunlight beams,
The winding road where shadows fall
Of trees, so stately and so tall.

The tourists amble on their way
With scenery changing every day,
And as the sun sets in the west
The weary traveller goes to rest.

No hurry or bustle, tomorrow will do
Like a boat on the water without any crew.
This is the life of the people up there
In the heart of the highlands, no place can compare.

The holiday's over and making back home
With beautiful memories I won't feel alone;
I'll picture those scenes and remember always
The highlands and islands with colour ablaze.

Jessie Williamson

The Voice of Silence

I saw you there
And loved you
In silence.

For long, long have I waited,
To hear a word,
A tender word,
A word that would awaken
This bud, I hold, to see it
Burst into bloom,
But all is silence.

Sometimes the smile you gave
Warmed me through,
Would set my heart a leaping,
But all is silence

I must leave now, for
I cannot bear this calm your silence brings
I will regret our parting
But tell me,
Is your name silence?

Gertrude Holloway

Peace on Earth

Many years ago, a child was born one day.
For the sins of the world, this child would pay.
He came from heaven, to teach his father's word.
He came to us, he showed the world he cared.

Throughout his days on earth, he gave love.
Each night he would pray, to his father above.
A special person was he, for all to see.
In his father's kingdom, everyone is free.

He performed miracles, he cured the lame.
Life on earth, would never be the same.
Love and peace, were his to give.
In heaven above, love again will live.

Troubled times, will always come and go.
The love from the father, the son will show.
Peace on earth, to all those who pray.
Heaven's doors will open, to all on judgement day.

He made the world, for us all to live.
He died for us all, his life for us to give.
God the father, God the son, Creator of all you see.
A world of love and peace, awaits for you and me.

Kevin P. Collins

Celebration

Dancing in the moonlight, beneath a starlit sky.
Leaping over moonbeams, to please the heavenly eye.
The faeries they are dancing, the panpipes play the tune
With elves in chorus singing as they dance beneath the moon.

Wraiths appear from o'er the mound,
In wheel like pattern they dance around.
Like burning candles they light the night,
Enhancing the glow of the pale moonlight.
The faeries join the spiraling dance,
Whilst nightly creatures watch entranced
By the myriad of patterns that shine so bright,
On such a beautiful and rareness night.

From orange glow to silvery white,
Their colours changed throughout the night,
And as they danced, their lights grew stronger
Until the stars were seen no longer.

As the haunting tune spreads through the night
And all is veiled from mortal sight,
In unison they dance and sing,
To celebrate the Rites of Spring.

Joseph Michaels

The Big White Deer

Looking over ane of the stoney bouts,
There I did see a mickle white deer
What looked as if it wore wet clouts.
Duddie was its coat—as if pulled from a mote.

A strange glower it gave with its deep dark eyes
Its mouth stayed shut as if surprised.
Springing to all fours it started to ryke
For an opening in the bout,
A cutty jink to the right and it shot out.

At first it hesitates in which direction to go
But it soon skelps up the brae with lightning speed,
To see the deer disappear at the top into the snow
Was a braw sight indeed.

A ghaist of a colour that much I did see
Not the usual reddish-brown,
Forever in my memory
I'll remember a mickle white deer
With an unforgettable frown.

Alexander Bryce

Sunset

In the autumn when the sun sets low
and the distant mountains seem to glow,
The Heavenly Artist way on high
begins his paintings in the sky.

His colours come from great green trees
mixed with sun, sand, and seas.
The shades of orange, reds and blues
give us heavens natural hues.

His sky-filled paintings, never rushed
with help from nature gently brushed.
His canvas is the clouds above
his sketches filled with colours of love.

The end of day clouds come and go
gently flowing to and fro
And with the dying of the sun
another painting has begun

Thus our sun in golden shrouds
creates a canvas in the clouds.
Its magic done, it leaves the sky
and gives the painting chance to dry.

Peter Pursey

Destiny

A word, a feeling, a time of jolting reality;
"We did all we could, I'm sorry ma'am, he confessed.
To dust, as from dust we all came,
here lies our destiny.
Destiny?
Of what fate are you to me,
understanding you I believe is my only Ignorance.
I wonder why you twist and get me twisted too,
your dose of fate escapes no one,
not even a babe in a womb.
What are dreams for, with your curious presence,
countering, changing, crushing our most
sought sort after hopes,
dishing out on both good and bad
with you mighty hand
Our tomorrows and today.
Mingling sorrows, happiness, confusion in your great cauldron,
Preparing this stage called life,
For all your depending victims.
Landing us in this vicious cycle.

Anne Ekong

Sue's Tarzanagram

"Oh No", said Sue in a shock and a maze,
I could see very clearly she was in a daze,
It was so unlike her, this state—almost screaming,
Perhaps then I thought she'd got behind with her cleaning.
"Calm down Sue, and tell me", I said over coffee,
And offered her a biscuit with chocolate and toffee,
"On the 15th", she told me, "It'll happen that night,
Something that will make my face turn chalky-white.
"Well tell me", I pleaded, just dying to know,
What on earth it could be that made Sue's face look like snow,
"Oh listen to me, Nicky, I'm not being a prude,
But strippers and chips, well it seems a bit rude . . .
"Is That All?!!!" I blurted, "You're just being silly,
As far as I'm concerned, I can't wait to see his . . . Performance!!!
Really though, Sue, you are a good sport,
And know that with Tarzan if you'd really been caught,
You would have laughed and gone along with the joke,
And even offered our jungle friend a drink of iced coke
And then looked around at your so called good friends,
And in your '97 Diary plotted Your Great Revenge!!!

Nicky Berezai

Deadly Harvest

Lying on a cold, white slab
A drug-filled marble effigy
Red eyed observers, mute and numb
Their inner torment, Ecstasy.

They spill out from the Public Inns
Aggression etched in youthful lines
Watched by a silent adult group
Who scurry, muttering, to their homes.

The gym-slip mums pushing their prams
Their school books heavy on their backs
Ignoring whispers behind hands
Of glass house dwelling hypocrites.

Our children fed a constant meal
Of violence and sex and drugs
From images on TV screens
Viewed from cosy hearthside rugs.

What have we done to our children?
Where did their childhood go?
We plant poison seeds, ignoring their needs
And they reap the harvest we sow.

Ethel Wilson

What Will My Children See

How many years can I be
What will my children see?
Pathways of velvet, cranberry sand,
Waving of a mystical, magical hand,
Orange pathways built in line,
Yellow, blue and indigo signs,
Magical skyways, planes of gold,
Will this be there when I am old?
Carry me imagination, make me free!
My children ask "What is a tree?"
Will they smell the breeze, clean and fresh
Or will their trees be encased in mesh?
How many years can I be
What will my children see?

We must all try and make our world bright,
We want our children to see the light,
The things we took for granted,
The seeds new shall now be planted
How many years can I be
What will my children see?

Susan Graves

This Nature

When comes the hour to yield this nature
No reason for regret;
During life the poacher's trap bit tight
If only otherwise . . .
Different sentiments might beget.

This nature was imposed without consent
No feel of wrong from right;
Helpless, in a maze of twists and turns,
Life evaporated
In the loathsome depths of filthy night.

So on the arrogant judgement day
From lofty-minded bench,
Will trial by ordeal be commanded
As life before was spent,
Or on this nature will tears of pity drench?

W. M. Tolley

Autumn

In what some people call 'The Fall'
Americans do—but that seems all—
Here we refer to it as Autumn
And sweep up leaves—'ere winds have caught 'em!
'Tho these are signs of cooler weather
Abloom in gardens there's still Heather
There are varieties young and old
And most withstand both ice and cold,
Available at Garden Shops with ease
The flowers, long lasting, always please.
Not even spoilt by ice and snow
They take it in their stride—and grow!
Don't overlook these plants long bloom
You'll not regret you found them room!

Joy Winskill

The Flying Scotsman—Bonny Scotland

Through mauve heathered glens and over mountain
  moors the railway winds
bearing to all Highland parts passengers and cargoes
  of all kinds.
Past closed carriage windows glide green pines
  and silent mountain lochs
amid forest and burns that come tumbling down moss-covered rocks.
The flying Scotsman with steam power from coal
roared up the line towards the Northern Pole.
Two deer from out their Argyle forest haunts appear
and then bound away from machines and men they fear.

Seated, homeward bound, a Scottish lad and kilted
lass gaze at each other, then at a distant mountain mass
Through beautiful scenery for miles and miles
goes the bonny railroad for the Western Isles.
High above, on the wings, in the blue sky, a golden
  eagle soars and flies.
The ever-changing scenery feasts and delights our
  wondering eyes.

Simon Clarke

The Sea of Life

The sea of life is strewn with rocks,
And many ships have I lost there;
I mourned their passing for a while,
For they were all a part of me.
But time and tide swept them away,
And I survived to sail again.

You're my new ship, my precious love,
More valuable than crates of gold;
We will sail the sea of life,
Together we will ride the storms.
But if the rocks should take their toll,
And you are lost beneath the waves,
I'd mourn you till eternity.
No other ship could take your place;
I'd never put to sea again.

Tim Stevens

Sulking

Sulk on your self-imposed exile island
Walk along unsmiling lanes of loneliness
Where friendly faces have turned to the wall.
Reach up for comfort,
Touch dull cumulus clouds
That condense to darken the windows of the soul,
Closing out the tempting light of reconciliation.

Let self-pity seep through tired tissues,
Its sweet juices soothing the ache of injured pride.
Sip, at will, the inner sobs of unused sorrow
Distilling from delayed sympathies,
Then emerge from under your dark cloud
A better person, brighter for the dullness.

Raise your eyes again to wispy cirrus clouds of hope
And, adding determination to the sound of sighing,
Make no stick with which to beat yourself,
But making further wishes, tie them to the shaft of resolution
To make a brush to sweep clean the heart,
And a magic broom to escape from lonely-exile-island
To the main-land of communicating love.

W. Haisley Moore

With Flag Unfurled

They march down the street, with heads held high.
Their colours displayed, aloft to the sky.
Their feet in step to the beat of the drum.
Its message loud and clear.
For the people to come.

Their instruments shining, to greet the dawn.
Happy expressions match this glorious morn.
It's the day, when Jesus arose from the dead.
Bringing to pass, all His Father, had said.

Crowds gather round, from far and near.
Little children included, without any fear
For they know, these are people, of whom the soon learn
Are an army to trust, and to whom they can turn.

Margaretta Rosewell

Months of Spring

March, April and May,
Dawn awakens each day,
On pastures in woodland's dew,
Cowslips yellow, bells blue.

Strolling peacefully along country lane,
Fragrant May flowers bloom again.
Tree shed its blossom, awaiting to bear
God's fruit so all can share.

May flies hover over water reeds,
Bulrushes sparkle of pearly white beads;
Where swifts and swallows soar;
These months of Spring I adore.

John David Copper

Sun Rise Sun Set

As I woke from my darkness dream
to see the sun rise to comfort me
another day have come to me
The air I breath will let me flee,
from the morning breeze I must be free
Another day have come to me, as I push
my wheelchair free from the garden path I must
speed to speak to the birds who will sing to me.
Another thought came over me
let the flowers grow with joy day by day
for you and me
Another day have come to me
Children come to play and laugh with me
Sun Set on a tiring day for me.
The air I breath has slowly past away from me.
Sun Rise for the birds to sing
Sadly not for one cheerful child to see.

Daniel Enticknapp

Portrait of a Mother

Beneath the portrait of a mother.
　Stood a lonely lost child,
A child who has lost a mother,
A mother whose life was taken by another,
　a child with no mother,
long gone is the father from this world,
　now there is no other,
Only the portrait of a mother.

Beneath the portrait on the wall,
a lonely child called 'Oh Lord hear my prayer!
Mine is the life that was given by a mother.
A mother whose hands once cradled her child tenderly
whose arms once rocked her crying child gently,
hands that comforted a fallen child,

Lost is the mother that sang sweet Lullabies,
Gone is the voice that scolded a naughty child,
Gone is the mother that taught a child a prayer,
Gone are those eyes that watched her daily,
Now, mine are the eyes that looked on that
　portrait of a mother.
　　Veda Estien

Sleepless

Sleep has not been my friend since you have been.
The night has caught me restless and weak,
The thought of your face, eyes so blue and gentle,
Fill my being with ecstasy.
My new acquaintance is a small pill,
Who takes me by the hand to darkness and solitude.
But your face still haunts,
Voice still echoes around my mind.
Sleep may never be my friend again.
　　Robina Hafiz-Alam

Hours of the Day

By the morning hours
When the sun awakes,
And the nursing mother calls to her day's work,
And when noise, laughter and roaring of cars echo out loud,
When man goes in search of his sweat,
When the owl returns to his sleep,
and all children go to school,
A tender feeling of joy runs inside me
Leaving me full of life and happiness.
And by the evening hours, when it is still and dark,
And all the stars and the moon come out from their hiding places,
When man returns home from his daily chores,
When the sighing mother puts her children to sleep,
When all shadows whisper in the dark,
When the owl awakes to search for its prey,
And when all evil plotters put their plans to sound,
After my prayers have been said,
I feel relieved of a burden; I see not nor hear of.

Hours of the day, hours of the night,
All nearly coming to an end in a twinkle of an eye.
　　Aisha Isa Ahmed

Lost and Found

You filled my emptiness with love
gently kindly like the dove
each peck warmed my heart sincerely
with feelings to last eternally

You taught me how to proudly fly
above emotions which made me cry
my confidence you restored to blossom
in our romance with feelings awesome

You lifted me high up to the skies
we shared our dreams and sometimes sighs
stay my friend I need you now
our future, will be great somehow.

Like fresh spring breeze waving daffodil
you massage my mind and heart fulfil
　　Jack O'Neill

The Tramp

The tramp he wonders up
And down the streets lots
of strange looks but he
stares back at them why not what have they got?
He keeps trundling along
Yes and even sometimes
Breaks out into song why not?
He turns up a side street
And pats a dog he meets
Along the way that dog might be like
Me he thought just another stray
Making its way to where
if it's like me it won't know or care
I am just trying to pass the day
Nighttime will come and
I will lay my head down somewhere
But I won't pray for another day even though
I am used to living now this way.
I close my eyes and in my dreams.
Yes I am having a better life now.
　　Kenneth Gillion

With Open Eyes

I tremble as I touch the rose,
aware of my certain fate
to contemplate a life of hope
and carry no more weight.

The restless hour struggles
as it breaks free from the night.
The darkness now is gathered up
replaced by golden light.

Flowing through me an energy of triumph,
leads me on to the path I took
when I was sure of its destination,
did not hesitate to look.

I learned to look and now look to learn
at beauty from above,
admiring all without criticism
just simply with love.
　　Sarah Burness

Dreams of Childhood

Church bells resound from a distant hamlet,
Tolling for a future not yet born.
Daffodils sway in the gentle breeze,
Heralding a time of renewal.
Dewdrops sparkle like a myriad of diamonds,
Truly a treasure of the dawn.
Trees proudly display a new apparel
And birds nest in the mantle of green,
Greeting each day with a melody of joy.
A child looks with wonder at the carpet of gold,
A treasure of primroses, a promise of spring.
Springtime memories of yesteryear, so clear, so pristine.
Memories of loving arms reaching out to embrace.
Voices long since stilled speak words of love
And souls unite with a childlike trust.
Truly a precious moment suspended in time.
Let all rejoice and be filled with wonder,
At God's precious gift of remembrance.
　　Wilma Hogg

The Face at the Window

The face at the window,
I always see, just waves his hand,
And smiles back at me.
If, I could hear his words,
I think they'd say.
No need to complain,
For that is that,
I'm doomed to live in this high rise flat.
　　S. A. Jenkins

Sea Gull's Heaven

This Sea Gull's life just fascinates me . . .
whether living on Land, in Air, on Sea.
Going wheresoever I choose . . .
in this life I have nothing to lose.

'Round the Ecrehous, Minquiers and Channel Isles . . .
is where I spend my 'waking hours'.
Occasionally I catch fishes in the Sea . . .
but usually those silly people—they feed me.

Technically I could live on the likes of raw fish . . .
but I prefer it Deep-Fried, in Batter, with Chips.
With salt and vinegar—it goes down quite well . . .
and happily those humans—they think so as well.

The Channel Isles in Summer are the best . . .
with those tourists I barely need leave my nest.
The logic in their sharing I can see . . .
one chip for them, a Dozen for Me!

In the Channel Isles in Summer I do 'Right-Well' . . .
in the Winter . . . —that's a different tale to tell.
The tourists have gone and the pickings are rare . . .
but never mind—they'll be back next year.
Vincent Cooper

Doors

Behind closed doors we meet and stand
We cannot even touch a hand.
Behind closed doors a beautiful face
We cannot touch or embrace.

Behind closed doors we've laughed and cried
We cannot say 'come home' for hands are tied.
Behind closed doors there is a sight of light
We cannot keep it, as it vanishes from sight.

We cannot understand life beyond the other side
Just knowing all the smiles and tears that hide.
We cannot keep the tears, often silently cried
Just as the doors shut behind parting life outside.

We cannot speak the way we freely know
Just seeing makes this world aglow.
We cannot understand why? It seems so unfair
Just love and hope, but never, ever despair.

Behind closed doors we ask why so long
We cannot account for months that have gone.
Behind closed doors a happy voice and song
We cannot fade in a world we all belong.
Susan Martin

The Time   2 p.m. Sunday 21st May, 1995
The Place   Wellington Barracks (The Square)

<u>Overheard</u>: en passant!

Are you marching today? Don't think so old son
Rheumatics are chronic, I'm far from A1.
But soon they all form up and set off in style
How the h— do they do it, when a yard seems a mile.
The "young 'uns" who joined in the march, so I'm told
Tongue in cheek, took some stick, from the 'old and the bold."

We know we must honour in thanks and in praise
The lads whose "tomorrows" gave us our "todays."
But how can a day such as this be called "Black"
When faces and names and events tumble back.
And the handshakes and "bevvies" and shouting and fun
Come alongside the sadness of friends who have gone.

Remembrance Day's over once more for this year
But more get-togethers are happily near.
The coaches arrive and we all climb aboard
Joe's counting and cussing his own wayward crowd.
"All the Best" we yell out as we start on our way
See you again on "Grenadier Day."
Sylvia Crowe

Untitled

Thirty years on if you are lucky,
you may read with a certain dismay
many things that were told as they happened,
didn't really happen that way.

In the passing of time will it matter?
as you fall fast asleep in your chair,
you may noisily dream of what might have been
had you taken the trouble to care.

Don't believe everything that is told you,
don't follow the crowd in its dust,
find time for thoughtful expression.
Then explode into print if you must.

Probe deeply the things that concern you
give political pundits no rest,
then people may say at your graveside
"well at least the old boy did his best".
Colin L. Larmer

Mother Earth Is Dead

I can see how it will be in some far flung galaxy
Where the sky is light and the sea is deep
There it will be read and said from head to head
"Mankind is no longer, Mother Earth is dead"

As the story is told and the facts unfold
There they will declare that it wasn't fair
Computer error was the cause of terror
Night and day just blown away
'Cause one single missile went astray

But they will learn from our tale of woe
"Nuclear weapons we must forgo"
Garry Mark Yates

January 9th

I have heard the sound of death, and the silence of the tomb.
Heard it in the darkness of the slowly swaying room
While high above, life seemed to stand looking out at death,
Waiting, waiting patiently for the slow exhaling breath.

There we lay upon the floor in darkest privacy,
Little specs of breathing life on the edge of eternity.
And then the light came on again, and we all said a prayer,
Thankful death had passed us by a threat upon the air.

Two houses just across the field were flattened to the ground,
All those living there were killed, because death looked around.
Who they were, I do not know? Their names were never read,
We were unaware of this as we went back to bed.

We were twelve feet away or maybe even less?
The school was shaken to the core;
The yard was just a mess.
Had they built the shelter
There, as well they might have done?
I would have been a memory of 1941.
Harry James Jeanes

Exmoor Enchantment

The harsh winds blew as snowflakes fell,
and I came under winter's spell,
all night the snowflakes floated down,
as exmoor lost its coat of brown,
as morning broke, there lay a view,
a fresh white blanket ever new,
vast frosty landscapes all could see,
dwarfed by magic Dunkery,
great moody badgers shuffle by,
while windswept saplings gently sigh,
they watch me with their eyes so grim,
and beckon with each twisted limb,
forget the crowds and fume-filled day,
replaced by nature's fine display,
so many cannot know just yet,
the beauty that is Somerset.
John Fuller

The Teign River

Rustling, gushing, splashing along,
Sometimes silent, sometimes noisy,
Going under bridges
Sometimes fast, sometimes slow.

Wiggling, meandering along, blues and greens,
People walking along the river bank,
Listening to the river's song, singing along.

Ducks swimming, quacking, sleeping in their nests,
When they wake feathers get left,
Suddenly there's a water wheel and an old mill,
They are not in use anymore but still a pretty sight.

Then we see the estuary, very wide it is,
We see boats bobbing up and down,
Trying to get away from the ropes that hold them.

Then we come to the quay,
Pollution lies around making the water look not very nice,
More boats bobbing up and down,
Cargo coming in making it very noisy.

Then we come to the mouth, going out to sea,
Now the river has come to its end, now out to sea.
Kirsty Tidball

I Will Not

I will not think of you tonight,
As I go to bed, put out the light.
I will not dream in the early hours,
Of you standing there, with magnetic powers.
I will not wake with you in mind,
for knowing that I would only find
You have gone away to a place that I,
Cannot go—And it makes me cry.
Eve Henderson

Sonnet My Love

My love has grown stronger throughout this week,
For the one that burns a hole in my heart.
His face, his smell, he's the one that I seek,
With dark green eyes that pierce me like a dart.
He has a slim, tanned and muscular frame;
With a smile like the crescent of the moon.
Taking my heart, he has won, like a game,
When we kiss the next is never too soon.
To me he's the world and all that I need;
A knight in shining armour in my dream.
If food is love, then let him be my seed,
Together we would be a perfect team.
Purely that, I love him and he loves me;
For I am a lock and he is the key.
Hayley Vargeson

War

A helpless scream in a pointless war,
A bloody cage without a door,
Death and famine and despair,
And disease laid thick upon the air.

A year from now what's been achieved?
Thousands of people left to grieve.
An orphan cries — a heartbroken waif —
In a place controlled by the privileged safe.

Bombs, blood and tragic loss,
Anger seething in the frost,
Love had gone but hate is left,
Children kill with toys of death . . .

They see fellow man spasm, hear close friends scream,
True hope existed in yesterday's dream,
Before men were called to fight and die,
Before wives hated fate and questioned why.

Each pawn fights for perceived perfection,
In a callous quest with no reflection,
That the value of life may soon be gone . . .
And still the killing cries on.
Gail Leanne Neville

Gargoyle

A laugh of mocking laugh,
"You cannot enter here."
For all the land around us,
this wall is where your peer
Stood bold, stood strong,
Impermeable to impish sneer.
You come in many forms,
but I can match your leer.

Downwards I cast my defiant glare.
So malevolently you dance,
the ground begins to flare.
Once fallen you claim your plight again.
Clambering eagerly, your piercing face meets mine
Of lecherous nature and diabolical aim.
Constant battle through ravages of time.
Your raging fires begin their game.
But only I can douse your flame.
Adele Draper

Love

Love your neighbour all the year through,
Love them and they will love you,
Love sometimes can bring a tear,
Love is my Bobbie here,
Love can also bring sometimes sorrow,
Love is now and tomorrow,
Love is something that you can't buy,
Love is here till the day you die,
Love is what you call a friend,
Love is something that you cannot bend,
Love is now, and to the end,
Love is like an opening and closing door,
Love can be strong and also poor,
Love can reach in some ways,
Love goes on from day to day,
But to love is something we all need,
To give your best yes indeed.
Ronald J. Warman

Yesterday's News

Blood on an empty page.
Is like ink on a carpet.
It tells a story

Of life flowing on,
Of life dripping past.
Soaking up an empty page,
Writing a story.

Scream at death.
See release written in blood
A drying stain on an empty page
Is painting a story

For all to interpret in their way.

In the final bloody moments of death,
See yesterday's news captured on a blank page.
Louise Harland

When I Went to Pray for Africa Twice I Saw

A continent of beauty with such hate,
Full of nature so rich: yet so poor,
Rains of tears, fear and death,
"I want to live," but power is the name of the game.
Can you feel my pain—God please hear—
Answer Africa—"Apple of my eye."

"Africans," another Ultimate, masterpiece of God in creation
Forest so thick and vast; is the splendour of the wild.

Rich soil in minerals, Yes! Food we can grow.
It is not ours too keep, it is time to turn, to look, to mend to:
Cherish our children, the coming generation
"Africans"—
The greatest of these is:
Power—Greed—Creed—Race—Hate?   "Love."
Jennifer W. K. Uzele

Departing Soul

For that young face smiling
As it did across the table.
It was, you thought the face of
A young man happy and stable

But that face was a lie.
Another exertion of cover.
Instead it masked a mind riddled with dark thoughts.
Never reaching in this world
The great heights sought.

Behind the mask lay a mind
Handicapped with a stream of thought
Flowing like hot lava of torment.
Burning into the mind, soul and body
Of this young living person.

A mind simmering, slowly, hourly, and nightly alone.
A mind so black with disillusionment
That it found death more acceptable
Than the fruits of this earth and a long life
A mind contemplating his own departure
And with the new dawn the end came.

Michael Machale

After Storm

Above the quiet fields
the grey and ragged clouds
are mirrored in the flood-waters
spread below.
No wind disturbs the broken branches
of the fallen trees,
or breathes a sigh
among the hedgerows'
shattered lines.
The only movement in this serenity—
the sweeping glide of sea-birds wings—
the only sound, a curlew's haunting cry . . . .
I love this quiet after storm;
the brooding air, which holds the earth suspended
in sweet tranquillity.
The Master Artist's hand has brushed the clouds
with fiery pen, and blazed a trail of glory
toward the ebbing sun;
Whilst, all around, the sleeping hills
reflect the splendour of the after-glow,
their shapes, like shielding wings, embracing land and sea.

D. Williams

The Photograph

I found a photograph last night,
Edges curling in a dusty drawer.
And I remembered her
And how she looked that September afternoon,
Black velvet hair, dark, faraway eyes
Standing slight and strong
With me so close but she, already gone

Sunglasses across her head
A vizor to protect
As she adventured

I thought it was hello,
But it was goodbye
As she viewed the future
With me already in the past,
Standing close behind

The picture taken by a stranger
A passerby and chronicler
Of that brief encounter's final moments
Now only the photograph remains
Together with her name, resting once more in that dusty drawer

Jonathan Millican

Shame

With downcast eyes and head held low
She shuffles past — nowhere to go
She pulls her tattered coat round tight
A clear blue moon — there's frost tonight

Not for her a cozy bed
Or feather pillow to lay her head
Her home has doors without locks
Home for her is a cardboard box

Her bed is hard, her pillow cold
She's in her teens, but looking old
Each day's a battle just to live
Relying on those who sometimes give

Some shake their head and turn away
No time for her in their busy day
Perhaps it's not that no-one cares
Perhaps they know her shame is theirs

Shame on those who will not see
"But for the Grace of God goes me"
Shame each time they turn their head
For shame IS theirs when she is dead.

Georgina Howell

Wild Spirits

As I walk down to the fields afar
Calling their names, I hear not a stir and I see no face,
I see only the mist embracing the ground
It's so enchanting,
Perchance it's been sent to hide them.

If but one person should dare enter,
I shall be lost forever.
Instead I tempted with exotic tones,
All of a spur there came an explosion;
Its din was like someone thrashing the ground,
It was impending.

Out of the cloud appeared not one but a party of faces,
With their manes swinging they beheld fair and graceful,
So bewitching, bold and full of spirit.

Yet they still advanced,
Paralysed with their sorcery
They befell upon me.
A shiver descended down my spine,
I looked but they had departed, like an illusion.
So had the mist that cloaked my vision.

Jane Elizabeth McCann

Waiting

Waiting By the Phone,
Eager for the friendly tone,
I sit alone waiting, waiting by the phone.

A noise! I rush to the door,
Looking at the letter box. Is it empty no more?
I sit alone waiting, waiting by the door.

I go out to shops I know,
Find a warm place, friendly face,
To converse with people who are not terse,
I sit alone waiting, waiting, I then go home.

I cook my food wishing a neighbour will intrude,
Sharing my food, if I think it's not too rude,
I sit alone waiting, waiting in my chair,
My food no one will share.

May as well be dead, I go to bed,
To dream of things unseen,
To hear a voice that may have been.
I lay alone waiting, waiting, my dreams dissipating,
My life I'm hating.

Layne Woodway

Why

Why do people drink beer?
Why do people drink lager?
It only makes things unclear
Besides, the cost is very dear.

Why get high on drugs?
When you hallucinate, bugs —
They're a danger to your health
Which slowly diminishes your wealth.

Why the objection of wearing protection
To save virginal maids from getting AIDS?

Why are people prejudicial?
Why are people detrimental?
Their excuses are always lame,
Although we're all born the same

Why do some have understanding?
Which I think is worth mentioning
And others don't seem to care
Which I think is totally unfair

I've come to the end of this little ode
Why! Not try to amend the ethical code.

P. A. Hunter

Lights Out

The lights are out,
The room is dark,
And everything is silent.

Floorboards ache as someone silently creeps,
I hear a tap dripping with a leak,
Mutter from down the corridor,
A groan, a whisper, a giggle,
Stuffy rooms, heavy breathing.

The window sways open,
The curtains fly back.
The cool air wafts in from the dark night,
A chill goes down my spine, hot water
Bottle burns my feet.

The window slams,
The door bangs,
A torch blinds my eyes but quickly
Switches off, and on, and off.

Cats wail on the lawn, a pillow falls,
Silence once more.
The lights have gone out.

Kitty Fox

Starless Sky

So many things I wanted said,
From in my heart and within my head,
Forgive me I was not close by,
As you slipped away into the night,
I can't describe the sadness,
That cuts me up inside,
And I can't describe the emptiness,
Except a starless sky,
I can't describe the aching,
That goes through me so hard,
Except an unfit runner,
That's pushed himself too far,
Brave yet weak you fought it all,
Head held high and standing tall,
Memories cherished for eternity,
And a love outdoing infinity,
You feel so near yet so far away,
Like holding the string of the highest kite,
I'll miss you more each passing day,
Dear Grandad hear my whispered goodbyes.

S. Docker

The Somme

I never thought the world would be
So full of the horrors that I've seen.
It's a new experience, just a game.
A chance of adventure and of fame.
"Join up", they said, "have some fun.
You'll be hero when we've won."
So like sheep we followed the orders,
Got sent away to the German borders.
I remember the sounds, the tastes and the smells,
The rotting of flesh and the screech of shells,
The dry taste of fear and the deadly barbed wire,
The tanks and the shrapnel, the signal to fire.
And who can forget those blood-sucking lice,
The boils and the ulcers, the flies and the mice.
And now I look back on that trauma and hell
To think of those dead and to think I did well
For because of that war I can no longer walk,
I'm hard of hearing and find it difficult to talk.
But I was lucky, or so they tell me,
As I fought for my Lord, my king and country.

Katherine Elsey

When Present Meets Past in Assisi

Down cobbled streets we made our way
On a dark Assisi night:
Medieval students caroused in the bars
While their horses whinnied with fright.

In brown-black cowls, the friars emerged
From out of the dim-lit church.
Deep in prayer, their heads were bowed;
For God they were in search.

The pilgrims moved to the beckoning shrines,
And great was their relief
That the stigmata were there, and the lacrimae Christi,
To strengthen their belief.

Refreshed in spirit, they slept at the inns
Where men had rested before
The dawn of the age of a loving king
Who all the future saw.

The bells all tolled so loud and clear
On that dark Assisi night,
When present met past in the lengthening year
Of God's eternal sight.

Eve Edmonds

Granny

Granny I love you
and will never forget
how you softened my heart
with your tender touch.

God never gave me
a chance to say
how much I love you
in every possible way

Why did you go
and leave me behind
without your love
and faith combined

Sometimes I wonder why you not me
We were a team now there's just me.

I'm all alone with no-one left
Soon my turn will come and we can be together.

You left me with a question "Why"
Why did you go why did you die

Janice Doonan

Stupid

Hide behind that word of an excuse,
Sit there looking pathetic.
Everybody knows you're gazing deeply into self pity.

Avoid eye contact,
Afraid of what you might hear?
Afraid I may whisper another crack, afraid of me?

You look nice today, casual,
If only you'd feel that way too.
If only you'd use that key, open the door and race through.

If only you'd wake up to yourself and realize,
Life hurts, as we do but for different reasons.
You push me away because you love her, so I hurt because I love you.

Konce Ramadan

My Parents' Son

It's only now I realize
how much they mean to me,
and what a shallow person
without them I would be.
Always pleased to see me
no matter what I've done,
So I am eternally grateful to be my parents' son.
Always there to pick me
up and slow me down when needed,
Good advice always given
but sometimes never needed because mistakes are
made and often I do wrong.
But if there is bad feeling it's never there for long,
so as I sit I ponder I thank the Lord above,
that I have been the recipient of such
a flexible kind of love; it's why I feel so lucky
when all is said and done,
Because I've had the pleasure
to be my parents' Son.

Joe Vernon

Sonnet
Composed after Reading and Hearing
The Prince's Choice

From Shakespeare's mighty panoply of people you choose
To assemble this living gallery of humanity.
On virtue and vanity with sympathy you gently muse
And marvel at mankind's infinite variety.
For Falstaff rejected you display compassion.
And Jacques echoes for you life's brief span;
You identify Cleopatra's despairing passion,
And how Iago's cunning like poison ran.
Amidst kings and commoners you foretaste your future part,
And reflect, as does Hamlet, on the soul's dark night.
The wayward course of England's history you chart
Whilst hearing the Chorus that pleads the soldiers' plight.
  Your choice of Shakespeare's insights from high and low
  Reveals that aloneness which only a monarch may know.

J. H. Higginson

Is Life a Dream

When I lie on my pillow my body asleep
Will my eyes remain dry if I start to weep.
Are the thoughts in my dreams the same when awake
Am I the same person or am I a fake.
Do I live through the day or live when I rest
It's all so confusing, I'm doing my best.
If I bleed in the night and think I might die
Why then no wound when morning is nigh.
The pain that I felt is forgotten at dawn
But my mind is still puzzled as to why I was born.
The faces of people they seem so unreal
Are the thoughts they are voicing the ones that they feel.
Are they dreaming of beaches when out in the cold
Do they dream of tomorrow when days just unfold.
Will I dream when I die is the question I ask
That the answer to this be known at last.

Lynn Warren

A Lull in the Battle

And at the end of the sixth day,
On the cooling of the heat of the struggle
She took up her pen
And wrote such words as she knew she would never speak:

"If then, My Lord, we have now touched souls
And felt the shock and joy of recognition,
Let us also gather up the poor, frail covering of our deeper selves
And coil them, carefully, one about the other.
And in half slumber, head to head and heart to heart and all to all
Search gently on for each other's sadness.
In the searing pains of desperation shared
We shall find, each time, a little birth."

Within suffering there is joy, for those who can see,
And in ecstasy there is sorrow, the fear of loss.
Lady and Brave Warrior, only keep the faith!
Believe in the brightness of the little births
Until it is time to be again
Alone, but serene in the cool breath of timelessness
And endless light . . .

Patricia Evelyn Grounds

I Know

How awkward you are.
How strange with your shaky lip
And uncertain hand.
How comfortable I am with you
When everywhere I look you are,
But how guilty I am.
When you throw those large eyes at me
And I can see the love to the back of your head.
How odd that you should sit there and I here
And not one word should pass between us.
How old we are now,
So few words and touches
Joined by the truth of so many days.
How simple we are,
With our books and our poems,
And our bread and our cheese.
How peaceful we are as we sit and we lie
And talk about dull matters.

Tania Waghorn

Saved

It's like a land of ice; vastly everlasting
a passion that slowly, so slowly melts:
Each drop to the ocean, like a voice to the wind
and inside, to the warm touch, a fire begins.

How I love the light that burns in her eyes
dancing sweetly over seas and skies.
The feeling within melting to the grace,
Of the beauty that shines from her face.

So hold me in your essence, and I'll fly so free
in the coloured sky of your soul.
I'll dance in the power, the energy and light
and fear no more, my dark, dark nights.

Sarah J. White

My Regrets

When I was born I didn't know the type of life to live,
I didn't know the time, or energy I had to give.
I know the joy I have, remembering the past,
I realize the sadness of the joy that did not last.
The time and energy I gave to my children and my wife.
Now only a memory I have for all my life.
But as we know, as time goes on, our memories don't last.
They disappear, melt into shadows, dark corners in the past.
My past is something, something gone, I would not try to change
The tears and joy, the happiness, and leased of all the pain.
Are memories to me, and yet, these things I remember,
The things that I regret.

Brian H. Aindow

The Awakening

Quietly, child-like—sleeping you lie.
Under the cold gleaming stars and the man in the hay,
Malta, famed island that we have known,
In times of high courage, and of hope almost flown.
Sleeping now with all secrets laid bare,
To the watchful observer on Sea, Land, and in the air.
Till suddenly, the Blue Blackness of the Eastern sky,
Gleams, mutely, delight as if passing by.
Someone had drown from a window curtain tight
The curtain for the moment let in the light.
Stars sounds of night are dimming, fading away
Only patiently the moon, is lingering to welcome the day.
Sounds, new sounds are rising, thrusting forming a band,
Linking together stretching out a hand,
Welcome the new day.
Refreshed, renewed, Malta goes on her way,
Sublime, unconquered, still equal to the fray.

Reg Baxter

Vocal Cascade

What sense?
What meaning?
Whose voice creates the feeling?
Unbind me, set me free
Unfettered, a voice, my voice.

Listen to my voice, your choice
Unchain me, follow the wind, be free
Acknowledge your insignificance, acceptance
Know relief.

Swallow my voice, taste the meaning
It's more than you know, it's nothing
Feel what I say, let me in
Sense my singing.

What voice?
You have a choice.

Suzy Shanley

Homeless

I wonder why people runaway,
And on the streets they lay.
Sometimes they're all alone,
Away from family and home.
All I'd like to say nobody's rejecting you,
Just bear in mind there's nobody out there
Protecting you.

Why did I runaway
From all that play?
I should have stood there,
And would have understood.
Maybe I was worried,
Or maybe I was wrong.
Facing the consequences.
However scared I was.

Shabana Kousar & Rehana Kousar

Hope

If you hold on long enough
To keep your courage high
You are sure to see a rainbow
Somewhere in the cloudy sky.
If your prayer is strong enough
So that it reaches heaven's heights
Things will change somehow sometime,
Then start to turn out right
If you keep on moving forward,
Though the light seems to have gone
With nothing but your faith and hope
To guide and spur you on.
In a way you cannot explain,
You reach a point where life begins again.
There, suddenly the sun breaks through
Upon a place where dreams come true.

V. B. Howard

Learning to Die

Resignation walks the streets,
Frail legs supported by a walking stick,
Grey head raised, watery eyes, wide open.
Nothing missed.
Stop to chat to an old friend, a quiet joke in passing.
How many years have we shared?
Wonder once more, at the green of the trees,
The warmth of the sun,
Learning to die.
Strong men grown gentle,
Bold girls tamed with serenity,
Acceptance for all but the foolish,
We are all learning to die.

Linda Stemp

The Silent Sea

Laps at my feet as warning
Runs away from the searching fingers, long and wide
That seize to push me under
Escapes before the waves crash
Covers me with the dark shroud

Heavy anchor pulls me deeper
Smooth murky walls surround and swallow
Saltwater rushes down
Panic grips now; the fingers tight around my being
Dragging the pain through my chest
Hurts until I'm numb

The calm after the storm
Looking at myself,
Lying on a distant dry land
My lifebelt sits next to me
Safe and secure

Until high tide.

Sarah J.

Roumania

Sad eyes staring through cot bars
What has Man done to cause these awful scars
To little souls, whose life had just begun,
Whose laughter cannot reach the morning sun?
Why should we make these little children suffer?
Why should they be the cruel world's buffer
For man's inhumanity to man?
These children pay the price before their lives began

O Man! Learn from these cruel lessons well,
Before your own dark soul will burn in hell.

A. M. G. Lewis

Dementia

I sit in a chair, too big for my frame,
I hear the nurse calling, but I've forgotten,
My name, the minutes, turn into hours,
Which seem like days, I sit, and stare,
In a constant gaze.

I have a family, visit me, they are so very
Kind, their faces, seem familiar, but their names,
Don't spring to mind, one minute, I am aware,
Then my memory goes, oh why am I so much trouble,
God only knows.

I am so confused, in a world of my own,
I am sitting here, when I should be going home,
You wash, and bathe me, and comb my hair, your
Tolerance, and devotion, your loving care,

My memory's a blur, my mind not so clear, excuse,
If I shout, it's because I can't hear, I look around,
And what do I see, people sitting, the same as me,
A burden, I never wanted to be, God, has given you,
Patience and understanding, to look after me.

June Cameron

Cultivated Work of the Blanc Poet
(Life Experience 23)

From a distant nobody
To a more plausible excuse for a person,
He strode the sky, singing as he went,
And we smiled with diseased awe coming from nowhere
    perpendicular.

Not because he was bad but because I needed to be even,
Making my dangerous hands defy the intensity barrier
Or only on a positive high where my hair is better or greener
    or something
Whilst sound waves skive across the void that could be my
    birthday cake

And you smiled, allegedly, as you blew out the candles
Whilst melting the images that came before
the man changing to the boy.
And the flickering fetish that awakened my soul claimed my
    heart and furry arteries.

Whilst saying good night in French, yet not dismissing Latin
as we might have done back then in our blighted futures,
Because deviation was not an option used willingly or sparingly
As man fell hitting the grandeurs of his own major
And we left then knowing we had broken the rues and had
    hesitantly as well as momentarily
escaped the monotony of our four lined stanzas and saw a
    land where trees are red.
And that's that.
Kathryn Gray

The Road to Paradise

Aged fifteen years in 1948,
The War at last all over,
I found that I could hardly wait,
To board that boat at Dover!

Despite the gales which greeted us,
That dark cold winter night,
The sea so rough—but we made no fuss,
Eagerly awaiting the light!

Then the excitement as we made
First steps on foreign soil,
Dunkirk and all it meant must fade,
At this moment—right and royal!

As we drove on that day through France,
It was a sorry sight,
Downtrodden villages and towns to glance,
Potholes left and right.

But then we came to such a land,
Of beauty, sun and snow,
La Suisse did take us by the hand,
And had us all aglow!
Jill M. Ronald

A Lonely Room

I am a very old room,
Who's been left to my doom
Nobody knows or cares for me.
I've got cobwebbed nooks
And chewn down books,
It's a feast for the rats, you see.

I'm nothing but an icy cold floor,
Four cement walls and one great door.
I'm not the least bit grand to you.
Teddy bears everywhere,
The smell of dampness in the air,
Oh! Come enter me, please do!

Spiders crawl about,
Clay dolls anywhere but out!
I'm forgotten by everyone, poor me.
I'm a sight nobody can bear,
With pieces of junk everywhere,
And an ignored part of the house, spare me please.
Iresha Udayamalee

Falling Shadows

Neath skies of grey and falling shadow,
The reddened bodies in the meadow,
Guns in turrets stood up high,
A man below, his deathly cry.
Whistling bullets past my ear,
And pain — is this the end so near?

Death to me I do not know,
But things I see in hazy glow,
A man beside me wrapped in white,
A bandaged figure in the light,
Turns to me and moans and stares,
Sadness in his eyes he bares.
As I stare back into eyes which have ceased to wonder,
All gone the rage which once was thunder

Victims are we of the war,
Where lives are lost and hurt once more,
In a blazing rage of cold, cold steel,
A killing field of furied zeal,
Where anger takes the moral soul,
And the finer things defer, as pain becomes the leading role.
Alan Garvey

We Walk Together

As we walk down the path together
At the dawn of the rising sun
Our hands clasped together and holding
Our spirits entwined as one
Your company will always be with me
To give me courage, peace and good cheer
To deal with the problems of life
The price is sometimes so dear
But with you Lord beside me forever
A companion who's steadfast and true
You give me the strength to help others
The strength that's always from you
So I thank you dear Lord forever
For the day you came and found me
For now I walk down a path that's new
Holding hands with Thee.
Jill Munday

Remembering

I remember the day when we walked through the park,
Our words flew like doves, the weather was fine.
I remember the day when we held on to hope,
Embracing denial, a hug on the bench.

I remember the day when the boundaries broke,
A poison seed seeped through and the wilting began.
I remember the day when a darkness returned,
Enveloping you in its ominous cape.

I remember the day when you willingly left,
Seduced by the past and an arrogant man.
I remember the day when I walked through the park,
Our bench stark and empty,
The weather was fine.
John Dale Shelabarger

Please

Please can you tell me why it had to die
This silent bird should be in the sky.

Please can you tell me on this chill morn
This once proud rhino lies without his horn.

Please can you tell me why on this trader's stall
A tiger skin hangs that once walked tall.

Please can you tell me what's that eerie call
Must be the monkey as it starts to free fall

Please can you tell me what's that sorry sight
And why the hunter is putting the ducks to flight

Please can you tell it puzzles me so
Why man has pulled the curtain on nature's show.
Pauline Thompson

An Ode to Stephen

When you looked at me, what did you see?
All the things you wanted to be all those years of confrontations.
Trying to meet your expectations,
I was your puppet, you pulled my strings,
Always striving for better things.
Now you're gone, how do I cope? You're my inspiration and hope.
How will I manage now I'm finally free,
To be the person I wanted to be?
It's true I hated but I've loved much more,
So I swallowed the impulse to settle the score.

I tried to give you your satisfaction,
To be your star, your main attraction.
The glamour calls, the people cheer and
No one cares if I cry in my beer.
I turn on the charm that belies your years.
And the laughter that hides a million tears.
Time to show I can stand on my feet.
I don't regret the things I have done,
At the end of the day I had so much fun.
But I need to be liked, I need to be loved.
As I start to single there's one thing I asked
Please judge by the person and not by the Mask!

Natasha Girasole

Christmas Is Gone

The innocence of Christmas is gone,
The childhood excitement extinguished.
Just as sure as New Year's Eve condemns the year,
The mystique is passed Over.

The fun, the presents, the magic of youth,
The belief, the wonder, the joy, the love,
Mummy and Santa are no more.

The highlight of my life,
Once every year, always, for ever
Has passed into before, beyond, and lost,
But with God, so not forgotten.

Nothing can match your festive cheer, none will fill the void,
We shall never replace the noise, the energy, excitement and life,
Of one lost so quickly — and for so long.

So to you, my Mum, now resting in peace,
I say five words to aid your release,
From the pain of this life, to one everlasting,
To a better place where you will light the candles, lay the table,
Smile, as ever, and wait for us

I say, my Mum Happy Christmas, we love you.

Mark A. Thomas

My Childhood

As a child I played in the fields and splashed in the stream.
I would look for the fairies and sit and dream.
I picked the buttercups and daisies few.
I wouldn't go home unless I really had to.
I loved to wander over the hills and up to the farm.
To watch as Mary milked the cow with great ease and charm.
I loved to go and watch the blacksmith who was over the road.
I wasn't allowed to cross on my own,
or else I would get squashed like the big old toad.
The horses were special for me even then,
inside the forge lived a big black hen.
She winked one eye and then jumped to the ground,
She pecked at the floor without making a sound,
Then out of the blue she'd fly at you, she wasn't a nice hen.
She made me frightened until I was ten.
Sometimes my friends would come and play.
We would go on adventures and stay out all day.
It was lovely until we had to go in for tea.
I was the youngest and my big sister picked on me.
The next day I was up with the lark my mum said I couldn't go
out because it was still dark.
I waited and waited until it was time.
Just to be told the field was covered with lime.

Susie Pickles

A Ship Called Friend

Far out to sea where the seagulls fly
With no land within their sight
Round each ship you hear their cry
Until darkness comes with night
Inside we feel these lonely hours
What our life span should it be?
Each day we look upon the powers
That separate land from sea
Now sometimes in life, we do ignore
For our life like a ship will sway
Down-hearted we struggle to some distant shore
For some help, we forgot to pray
Such faith then comes like a fraying rope
By our own will we make our way
Heart and soul we loose all hope
Like sheep who have gone astray
It should be now that the shepherd's rod
That would guide us to such an end
Prayers of thanks we give to God
By His grace we have found a friend.

James Caldwell

Spirit of the Earth

It glides across the land like a bird in the hand,
it sweeps through the seas like the wind through the trees,
It fills our hearts with love and compassion,
Helping us to love one another, with hearts full of passion.
It knows what we're thinking,
It knows what we do,
It knows how to gently knock some sense into you.
What is the thing that does all of this?
What is it that gives us this feeling of bliss?
It's a spirit descending upon us like a dove,
Poured out from the Heavens, and filling us with love.
The spirit of the earth is a mysterious thing,
And of its power, we will sing.

Claire Smith

My Fight

I hate all men, you have made sure of that.
You left me feeling like a no good doormat.
You took away my pride and my self respect.
When mixing with society I am a complete defect.
I hope that you suffer and you are never set free.
I never can forgive you for what you did to me.
The outcome of your actions has destroyed my life.
I cannot meet a man, settle down and be his wife.
The cuts and bruises, they have gone away.
But the damage to my mind looks like it's here to stay.
I've replaced my clothes, the ones you ripped apart.
But it does not make up for this broken heart.
My body belongs to me, you do not have the right
To rag me and to take me and turn out my light.
I just don't see a future, you've taken away my hope.
I cannot be myself again, in life I cannot cope.
Believe me when I say, on this I do not dwell.
I am trying so hard to escape this living hell.
And push out you, my nightmare, forget the past.
And start to communicate, just be myself at last.

Imelda Bigley

My Underworld

I walk to the ocean and jump into the sea,
I discover a new world, it comforts me.
It's peaceful down here, there's no fighting or war.
It opens my eyes to what I never acknowledged before.
I swim with the fish, I feel one of them now,
They all stay together, no separations or rows.
I will take my last breath here, It will be refreshingly clean,
Unlike the polluted air in the rush hours main stream.
Nature can grow wild, and no-one can spoil it.
I fade as the sun shines, my underworld is lit.

Sharon Jennings

Lost Beauty

I saw a flower enclosed within a velvet frame;
"If only this flower was for me!" the moisture cried
The moisture seemed to be finer than finest dust
Collected from all the far reaches of the body
Where the very soul dictated that its presence be felt.
Gathering its harvest from these far away places
With never a question of "may I?" from its maker
Disregarding the vain attempts to stop the harvest.
The very soul pulled as if for ever against the will.
There the will failed with a sudden long sigh,
This accumulation gathered of those far reaches,
Rolled from the eyes with complete abandon
Only to be brushed aside as if caused by chill winds.

I. T. Howard

Sally's Crows Holding a Photograph

World had no boundaries. Instinct and
common sense come in different quantities.
Sally's crows held a photograph two little
girls 25 years gone, time to watch them
fly. Never knowing why.
Oranges are not the only fruit. Sally let her
crows fly, it feels like November. Running
to see Sally's crows.

Loved to watch them dive
and soar. Never saw those
birds again.
There is also a flower it
buds, but can't remember
when. Close my eyes and
Sally's crow's fly.

Miss Helen O'Neil

Wood Eye, The Trees

From where you are standing, say, what you can see?
Not counting shrubs or hedges. Can you really see a tree?
A British Oak, majestic Beech, a Chestnut, wide and high,
It's getting so that all these kings, now evade the eye,
A new road has to go here, or a new housing estate,
What e're the reason or excuse, me think they leave it late,
We shouldn't need a Monarch to come to claim his throne,
To justify the planting of one tree, all alone,
Go back to planting Avenues, or fields of forestation,
Like Savernake, or Sherwood, or a dozen like plantations,
Where trees like these will stand a guard, surrounded by their brothers,
The Elm or Ash or Birch, and many many others,
No more the stately galleons, with solid warmth of feel,
Any ships produced today, are cladded out in steel,
You may observe, there's not the need to plant them just from duty,
Them plant them sir, I beg you, that we may see their beauty.

R. A. Curtis

Granddaughter

I saw you there looking at me,
wondering what your eyes could see.
A tiny babe, with eyes of blue,
a cute little nose, and mouth where petals
of a summer rose had fallen in repose.

You looked at me, with eyes so wide,
and a little smile on your face doth slide.
You've entered a world of wonder and hope.
Be strong and forward thinking, I thought.
You have a beauty beyond compare.
One of nature's wonders there, as you lay content
in your mother's arms, blessed by her beauty,
and her charms.

You will succeed, do not have doubt.
Though you may wonder what it's all about,
you are perfect, an image for whom
God would be pleased.
You are my own granddaughter
Kelly Louise.

Margaret Haswell

The Zeebrugge Disaster

I think of this terrible disaster
Which happened at dark, deep in the water,
People battling with their lives,
Men rescuing children and wives.

Children on adults' backs
Struggling on rescue ropes like rags,
Some trying to swim to a boat
Even though they don't know how to float.

Bless the man who made a human bridge
Letting people pass from the devastated fridge,
I would love to meet this kind fellow
And say how brave he was below.

Relatives are anxiously waiting for news,
Reporters are seeking the survivors' views,
God helps those who are still suffering everyday,
Please take their fears of nightmare away.

Bina Masand

Night's Company

The squinting man
hardly tall, and ragged master plan
dragging from his
reeling pockets
the flimsy sticky figure
and the misused characters in
his novel-shaped head
the spring rain hawks its wares
the mare scans the human race
and finds the
wind to have no face
the hum of a smoking typewriter
rattles out the lead light window
seven forty-five
and the harbour is engulfed by
a company of night's cornucopian soldiers

Craig Youden

Conscious

Black liquid thoughts linger languidly,
oozing their way through the tunnels of my brain.
Slowly and painfully, forever there in my consciousness:
Like long fingernails on the hands of death
Grasping a hold, digging in; not ever letting go.

The relentlessness, the pressure
A silent scream building to a crescendo.
The crashing and banging: The screeching mind
longs for release.
But never finding, forever searching
for something that is not there.

Mischelle Ball

Seville 88

I walk through sleepy streets
Where citrus glow in green velvet darkness,
And the cicada sings his lonely song,
Under a brooding crescent moon,
And a murmurous quiet surrounds.

From my balcony I see the lemon tree
Just flowering in the patio below
While water whispers in the fountain
Dropping slow down the greened stones
To the limpid pool, unquestioning, eternal.

High in a purple velvet sky,
Glides a translucent moon,
Through the slow water's ripple.
I listen, as I dream, to the world's breath,
Longing for morning and the fresh mimosa breeze.
But where is love that still, and still, awaits?

I do not know. For all I know is now.
The cicada's song still saddens me,
While orange bloom enchants.

Linda Shepherd

His . . .

His touch sends shivers up your spine,
His hand makes you feel warm inside,
His arms around you make you feel
safe and secure,
His voice brings a smile to your face,
The sound of the telephone makes your
heart jump up and down,
The tenderness of his body next to yours,
makes you feel tingly all over.
His body and mind are perfect in
everyway.

Gemma Gardner

You or Me

I see the weather oh so cold
I think about the infirm and old;
All alone they just peep out.
It's very cold, no one peeps about.

Spare a thought and nip next door
Have a chat and chat some more;
Put on the kettle, make some tea,
Keep them warm, it's nice to see.

A caring neighbour can be such a friend.
It will come to us all in the end.
If there's no family round and about.
When dinners ready give them a shout,
See their faces light up with glee.

Please remember it could be you or me.

Ellen McLaughlin

My Love

My love for you burns like a flame,
my dreams are you, I whisper your name.
I call to you yet there's no reply,
for morning is day and day is night.

You leave at night unable to stay,
I think about you on my bed as I lay.
If only I could hold you through the night,
I'd love and care and hold you tight.

I say a pray and close my eyes,
I dream of you that's no surprise.
I see your face, it seems so near,
I reach out to touch you and you disappear.

You seem so close, yet you're so far away,
It's like a game but I can't play.
There are no instructions, rules or clues,
Whatever I do I always lose.

My dreams last forever,
My love for you too.
How long is forever?
For as long as there's you.

Emma Jayne Kazer

Mauritius, My Home-Island

The wind blows gently in the Casuarian trees
I sat, nonchalant, admiring the vast Indian Ocean.
Deep valleys, grassy mountains,
Green fields, rushing fountains,
Golden beaches, rocky coats,
These are the things I miss most.
Morning: First I watch the clouds
   forming shapes before my eyes,
   sometimes horses, sometimes crowds
   of silver shadows in the skies.
Night: The stars, they dance and play
   until the dawn breaks for the day;
   they form patterns of delight
   as they shine with radiance bright.
The wind blows gently in the Casuarina trees
I sat, nonchalant, admiring the vast Indian ocean.

Rene Seren-Dat

The Flower

A seed is born it starts to grow
within the confines dark below
wrapped up within the earth it stays
while nature helps it on its way.

As seasons change it carries on
developing well and feeling strong
for soon this spritely little thing
when sunshine comes its heart will sing.

Its effort has rewarding merits
that journey through the dark inherits
all the joy that new life brings
into this world a little plant springs.

The world seemed large which it had found
with hosts of colours all around
this new plant grew among its peers
and flowered there for many years.

Morag Sutherland

Personal Importance

The closing of the door when my loved one comes home
Weekends together with freedom to roam
The chatter of birds, and the scent of a flower
Children playing for hour upon hour

The warmth of the sun, and sand on my feet
Listening to the waves as they pound on the beach
The sound of the wind blowing, outside, at night
And a hug from friend when things are not right

To watch the sun going at the end of a day
Laughing with friends, and having plenty to say
Strolling at midnight, studying the stars up above
But most of all, the feeling of love

S. J. Long

Guilty

Emptiness fills my body
Where life lives no more
The large white walls consume my screams
While wanting consumes me
Loneliness and fear.

Wondering where my protector is
but she can not reach my pain
Confusion is all I really understand
Can love cancel all my sins
Selfishness and guilt.

Forgetting would be too easy
Images come back to haunt me
No one can really sympathize
I don't even deserve your pity
Death has murdered my soul!

C. Moore

The Wonders of the Wind

An invisible force we cannot control,
It takes down trees as it goes,
It roams around like it has no soul,
It's like nothing natural.

It flies through villages and through towns,
The people know it's getting close,
Because of its awful whining sounds,
They dare not leave their homes.

The first house to go was old man Finn's,
It took it away and left him alone,
The next house it hit was widow Quinn's,
It took her up and blew her away.

Now the wind has come to rest,
The town is sad and wrecked,
The people are mourning and in distress,
Old widow Quinn is Dead.

Jonathan Bell

Clock Island

Through days and nights that blend into one
And the stars in the sky just follow the Sun
Because nothing determines what's first or last
What it holds for the future it's history and past
Not too many people will know what this means
To this bustling world only fruitless dreams
By thinking the same day after day
This life that I long for in some simple way
I hope this would suit me and never turn sour
And no ticking of clocks that would strike on the hour
No limits on meters or be late clocking in
No 7 o'clock shadows appear on my chin
No mints to eat 'cause it's just after eight
Or unlucky thirteen to determine your fate
These might seem like numbers
On the surface just fine
But my island you see no clocks no time
Thomas Mitchell

Times

I often thank the Lord above
I was born into a family with lots of love
Little money, wholesome food,
Mindful of others in every mood
Hardworking, fun loving always caring
In times of plenty often sharing
A close-knit family in every way
Where are such families today?

We live in a Welfare State
Often neighbours don't relate
Television has taken over
People want to live in 'Clover'
Avoiding work by sheer endeavour
Just want 'Dosh' and lives of leisure
Others try for jobs—in vain
Oh when will good times come again?
Myrtle Wright

Feelings and Thoughts

My thoughts have taken me on a journey.
I have served my purpose, now it is time to go.
I feel happy because I have achieved,
I too feel sad because I have to let go.
I do not want to weaken and become selfish.
I then ask myself, once again, am I being too nice?

I tried to ease your pain and take away your
worry, but I hurt, and you were sad.
Let's live our lives and achieve our goals,
Our time together has had its day.

Whenever you feel lonely and sad,
close your eyes and think of me.
I will feel your emotions touching me,
. . . I will be there for you.
Deborah Mawer

The Stone-Waller

Alone he worked upon a windswept hill,
Shaping each chosen piece of stone until
He put it in his wall, to be held there
By other stones which he had placed with care:
No need then for mortar to retain it,
Only his skill in handling millstone grit.
Rarely he saw a human passing by,
Content he was to hear the curlews cry;
Yet if, by chance, a walker came his way
He would, still chipping, pass the time of day.
No builder he of architectural fame,
But his rude, calloused hands could all the same
Provide a structure that would hold the eye,
Stretching, stretching beneath a Pennine sky;
And he could look upon his walls with pride
And by his ancient craft be satisfied.
R. A. Randall

Winter

Winter morning is cold and droopy
The snow is like crispy silk
It shines like silver
And is bright like the sun

Winter morning is so cold and freezing
The snow falls down on your bare hands
It melts on your gloves
In the morning of the cold breezy air

Winter morning you have some fun when the snow is down
Winter morning you have some tea
You boil the kettle
And your mouth is warm and nice

Winter morning you find the flowers are not there
The snow is white and the ground is white
Your feet are numb
And your hands are gone

Winter morning the snow falls down
Just like a bird falling
The wind pushes the snow
So it looks like it's flying through the air.
Adam James Lee

Blue

She gazed upwards and looked into the sky,
For she could see more than the average eye.
"How Blue", she thought; but how saddened she became.
She would stay there all day, until night came.

What she saw, nobody knew,
When she was questioned, she gave no clue.
This lady would stand like a statue. Cold.
So frightened; so helpless; so old.

And as she stared so harshly above,
She reminisced about. . . her love?
Oh, what pray does she seek?
Of what can this woman not speak?

But fear and despair was all I saw,
I see no place; no open door.
I see anger, hatred and despair.
For this is on ordinary 'air'.

You may see some clouds and gladness true,
However, my dear, all I see is blue.
Fleur Andrews

My Three Cornered Field

Along the lane I slowly walk,
Approaching my three cornered field,
Where sky larks sing and lambs do spring,
In my three cornered field.

Grass so fresh green and mellow,
Primroses make a tinge of yellow,
Rabbit families scurry by and to their burrows hurry,
How can I explain to them from me they have no worry,
In my three cornered field.

The stream is flowing sparkling free,
Happy sparrows bathing, feathers preening, smoothing.
Dragonflies do hover by,
Tadpoles softly glowing,
In my three cornered field.

I take a rest just for a while,
My mind so full of happy smiles,
My birds that sing my rippling stream,
My grass ashine with yellow,
I love this place, my own sweet place,
Yes, my three cornered field.
Jennifer Burton

Sweet Dreams

Beloved! Object of my desire.
Am I your naiad of the night, the one to quench your fire?
You, who are so powerful, are yet powerless to prevent
The wild fantasia of my mind, the scenario I invent.
You star nightly in the moving pictures of my dreams,
And though you may protest,
I write the script, I set the scenes;
You cannot change a single line,
I'm your romantic lead, and you are mine.

Perhaps you see me in your sleep,
That unknown face that haunts your dreams,
But though you toss and turn away,
I'm still the author of the play,
And you must act the scene I set,
Be Romeo to my Juliet.

Perhaps, eventually, when we meet
I'll maybe tell you of my schemes,
To show you tender love so sweet,
As in the drama of my dreams.

Vera Meister

The Seagull

Recognizing its solitary view,
A lone seagull gave a desolate mew,
Sought and rode an unexpected thermal
Above bobbing masts lined up so formal.
Then wheeled and winged slowly down the river
To the open sea which stretched forever.
Barques, hugging the coast, turned leeward tacking.
The wind soughing and keening—then slacking.
The waves, white-capped, like horses sporting
Under the master's whip, pranced cavorting.
The tall ships heaved in the waves together,
Making fine game for the fickle weather.
Lowly barges, seeking a safe harbour,
Groaned and creaked with the stress of harsh labour.
The seagull dipped and wheeled hard to starboard,
Then veering inland once more to larboard.
Following the route that the river carved,
The seagull mewed in a fashion half-starved,
Searching for some tasty morsel to steal
From some unsuspecting fisherman's creel . . .

Gwen Douglas

A Waltz with Death

Death clasped him in her foul embrace.
A withered hag, with bony, ugly face.
He tried to plead, to reason with his death,
Her sentence, harsh, spat out with tainted breath.
"Grant one more day to comfort those I left,
Of husband and of father now bereft."
The crone retained her grasp of captive's hand.
"Change partners!" cried a voice in stern command.
The gloating hag, reluctant to obey,
Like snow upon the desert, melts away.
In place, a graceful girl, with smiling face,
Awaits, with outstretched arms, the man's embrace.
"Your wish is granted. So, too, is your life.
Go hence from here to comfort grieving wife."
The man awoke. His wife slept by his side.
In grateful tones and gratitude, he cried,
"Oh, spirit fair, and bringer of delight,
Forever grace this ballroom of the night.
Where, by your touch, is goodness born again,
To wipe away life's heartache and the pain."

Emanuel Herwald

People

My garden is my Paradise, it's not very big but it's
very nice. I grow a few plants with a shrub in between
and then comes a tree which is nice to be seen; and
it looks quite divine 'cause it's mine. It gives a great
pleasure to people, you see, as they pass and say "hello,
How are you today?" "I am O.K.—are you?" Some people
are helpful—some people are not and sometimes
you have to contend with the underhanded and
deceitful lot. But it's not all bad. People have
different and peculiar ways—they only live for themselves,
days after days.
They don't stop to think of the wrong they are doing
and think it will go on and they won't be noticed
hanging around, bullying and causing mischief
to people who are wise to their trick and treat disguise.
They think we have stars in our eyes,
We know they are cheats, deliberately it's done; but I
will not say that for everyone. Most people are happy,
few do not understand. They try to run
other people's lives; but people will not let them be in command.

Annette Brotherton

If Only

The first time we met, you talked
I listened, I fell for you
Looking deep in to your eyes
Your eyes, so black, so appealing
Falling further and further into a trap
If only I'd opened my eyes
If only . . . if only . . .

You knew, knew all along
That my love for you was for real
But you lied, over and over again
Tearing me apart with each word you spoke
If only I'd opened my eyes
Listened to them and not to you
If only . . . If only . . .

You left me in darkness, in a solitary place
Darker and deeper than the colour of your eyes
A place where I had no say
I was heart broken, hurt and lost forever
If only I'd open my eyes
To see that you were a liar and not a lover if only . . . if only . . .

Sadia Hussain

Mr. Tuesday

In the night, I saw a man,
Who in his thoughts, remembered his dreams,
As he sat in a cafe in London Town,
When the rain came pouring down.
Though not an old man,
His life was not as it should be,
Drugs, alcohol, and cigarettes,
Lost loves and silhouettes,
That faded and cloaked everything he wanted to see.
But all he was left with was a memory,
Of his childhood, running free.

And as he stirred his cup of tea,
I thought I saw pools in his eyes,
As tears began to form,
And sorrow began to rise.
Distance began to occur, as he moved himself away,
To that World belonging to yesterday,
Where he was safe, problems at bay,
So long, Mr. Tuesday . . .

Emma Nyman

My Vision of Spring

Harshness of Winter has left without shout.
Citrus colours of Spring are around and about,
Defying hard frost to penetrate earth.
This born again season, so full of mirth.

For this is the time when earth stands revealed.
No longer will coldness keep its treasures sealed.
With ice chains unbound, then nature is free.
When Spring gives the order, winter will flee.

All stand to attention and turn to the Sun.
The lambs in the meadow so full of fun.
Each daffodil standing erect in the field,
definitely saying, "We will not yield."

Powerful forces are raring to go.
Instructing all young things, "Be ready to grow!"
Flowers in bud suddenly bursting with glee.
This is the season that reflects all I see.

Wendie Rosemary Johns

The Forgotten Soldier

Nothing knew he at Hide and Seek when child
Of distant jungle hot and wild
Where perforce to play again the game
Under a new sinister name
No healthy scamper with ecstatic squeal
But a stealthy alert crawl
Through a reluctant slimy green wall
And constant threat of mortal steel

Griff

Untitled

There's a pathway so narrow
and a roadway so wide
The choice is before us
each one must decide.
The wide road is crowded
and pleasures abound
How loud is the laughter
How empty the sound.
But where does it lead to
when death rings the bell?
We are told in God's word
It is to Satan's hell.
The pathway so narrow
is the highway to Life
With many a hardship to bear,
But Jesus before us
left footprints to guide
as all of His people walk there,
with dogged assurance that this is the Way
If His Truth and His Life we would share.

Wesley

Jack Frost

Shut the windows. Shut the doors
Jack frost is about. He is so clever
As he freezes everything in sight,
he makes us feel so cold, snow lies
like a white sheet. Birds looking for
Somewhere to hide out of the cold.
Robins hopping about in the snow
trying to find scraps of bits that have been
thrown out so they can have something to eat.
Wishing it was spring again. Winter is now
here. We shall be glad when winter
has gone, we don't like those cold and
frosty mornings.

But never fear spring will soon be here.
No more jack frost for another year.
Time to put away our winter woollies,
hats, gloves and scarfs, and get out that
summer's gear, lovely sunshine that
makes us feel happy and cheerful.

Doris Osborn

A Prayer to Dunblane

You were so young,
You weren't old.
You were bonny,
You were bold.
Now you're ageless,
Now you're timeless
And now you sleep
Amidst the world's kindness.

You were loving,
You were true.
You were gentleness through and through.
You stood out amongst the crowd
And your laughter rang
out so loud.
But the Lord alone knows
Why that mighty river has to flow.
Why the wind whips a whirl.
Why fleeting shadows curl.
So until we see you all again,
You're the mighty legend of Dunblane.

David Ashley Reddish

Life

Life is the greatest gift in our lives,
with so much to say and so little time.
Most peoples lives are so full of anger
pain and joy.

In life it is hard to forgive and forget
and yet we all still live with regret,
so make the most of your life
with love and happiness but no strife,
so try to enjoy your happy life.

C. A. Thomas

The Ultimate Summons: Paradise

Walking now at a slower pace,
Keeping clear of the competitive race.
Going forward without a backward glance,
Not worried about any dire consequence.
He thinks where he is going is the best place to be,
Watching over you and me.
I can see the look of relief on his face,
Will I follow his trail or return to base?
Momentarily, I closed my eyes,
When I opened them, I saw him rise.
Crying out, he would not hear me,
He can see things now, invisible to me.
Abandoned, I tower alone,
Bitterness and disillusionment,
Becoming acceptance and survival.
Thinking life is getting better,
Each day is a new beginning.
He has reached his paradise, mine is being reborn.

Evelyn B. Hubbard

His Challenging Life

I sit here with no life ahead of me
Nothing to do because I can't do anything for myself
Who will help me if my parents die before me?
Who will look after me then, dress me, feed me things like that.
I can't do anything myself
I wish to be like others who can do everything
I'd do or give anything to be like them, I see
them running and playing about they're normal not like me.
Sat in this "thing" all day long I can't even move it myself!
I wish I had friends to go out with, have a laugh,
I can't even do that easily!
Everyone looks and stares at me, I can't help the way I am.
I can't control my feelings or my actions
I can't even control my brain.
I'm slowly going, going!
One day I'll be gone, hopefully that day will be soon—
Goodbye.

Adam Steer

She Hugs Herself to Sleep

Mother's at work
he's drunk again, up the stairs he creeps
She closes her eyes, with her back to the door
pretends that she's asleep
She hears him stumble and a slamming door
that makes her small heart leap
With a plea to God, a cry for help
she wants to be asleep
He shouts her name, only to receive silence,
but around her door he peeps
She sees the light through the lids of her eyes
will he think that she's asleep
The door closes as he goes back outside
as the frail child starts to weep
In the middle of the bed in a tiny ball
she hugs herself to sleep
  D. H. Howe

Rose

Rose you have done me proud this year,
  while I have treated you like a bear.

One year, I loved and mollycoddled you,
  the next year I clean forgot you.

Oh! What a life you've have with me,
  thousands of blood-red petals you gladly gave me.

In return you heard my joys and woes,
  oh! My silent Red Rose.
  M. E. Dziecielewski

A Frightening

I harkened to the eerie sound of silence,
Unease was definitely in the air,
I felt a disquiet all around.
No birds or sound of human voice,
As darkening skies lumbered overhead.
'Twas like night this afternoon,
As if not long to wait a thundering,
And tremoring all about.
With flickering lightning searing close,
A deafening roar amidst the traffic lights
An opening of the heaven's spite,
Rain fast, tumbling, fell
And quaking of a lonesome soul or two
Praying hard as if their doom was near.
Thoughts of mind opening wide
Clear as clear.
Heavens above protect our lives
We'll promise to behave.
A sudden fright like this
Makes them think a while,
How precious is their gift of life.
  Jack Allerston

Tears of a Child

When you have a lovely child
There are lots of bridges to build
Because over the years
There will be tears and tears
At first it's all the bumps and falls
Then when we are over those pitfalls
It's over to harry the hamster, budgie, fish and cat
Some live longer than others
But that does not stop the tears as they fall
And your child as they call
Why oh why did he die!
Then you try and make them understand
But as the years roll by and by
No matter how old they come to be
You will still hear them cry
But you'll be there
To wipe away the tears as they fall
Like you did when they were small
  Loraine Elizabeth Hannaford

The Beautiful Arctic

Landscapes of pure white snow
In the sunset what a glistening glow
Icebergs tower from the frozen sea
Standing there so majestically

Polar bear cubs with little black snouts
Penguins jostling, slip-sliding about
Snowy white owl swooping down
Looking for prey on the ground

The arctic fox is on the prowl
In the distance we hear them howl
The echo sound all around
Apart from this so still, no sound

Eskimos roam on this baron land
Dog and sled working hand in hand
Hunting fishing before the storm
Another day another dawn
  C. H. Beck

The Storm

The rain slapped my face
Like freezing cold hands
Sending shivers up my spine

The thunder rolled above my head,
Like the sound of elephants,
Trumpeting to one another

Lightning flashed before my eyes,
Like millions and millions of cats' eyes,
Glowing luminously together in a massive clump in the sky.

The sky was a mass of colours,
Like an artist's paint palette
Being thrown up in the air.
  Lucie Agolini

Wolf in Sheep's Clothing

Lapping lamb like around the shores of Cornish seas
hippy king, leading the children; sheep like we followed.
Splish splashing my sins in waters dirtied by tears
as lion-proud you confessed your own perfection.
Yet never worked, only smirked as I alone provided
your cars and homes, and never once took me out.
"My friends won't think you're good enough for me"
was your ode, after my body you'd rode.
Were you blind, out of your mind? They said I should model
and the men wished I were free . . .
It was only you who couldn't see.
Long greasy hair, scruffy clothes, slip slopping along
in a world of your own. I was house bound;
your conscience pebble bound, lost at sea. But when
you needed a bed you knew the rules of kindness then
mother hen, bumble bee buzzing around my sickbed.
A liar, the fire of the Holy Spirit never burnt you as chaos
licked about your feet with the incoming tides of deceit.
Lapping lamb like around the shores of cornish seas
leaving me to bleed . . . leading away my child.
  Elaine Pomm

In the Darkness of Winter

In the darkness of winter, when the chill winds blow stark,
the light from his love is like a candle in the dark.

When there's snow on the ground, but no leaf on the tree,
the warmth of his love glows brightly for me.

A long time ago, winter winds blew to chill, alone like
a stranger, my heart it stood still.

Then along came this man, like the fresh breath of spring,
bringing love to a heart, that felt useless and dim.

So now, when those chill winds blow, till the tall trees
are bare, I know that his love like the sun will be there.
  Sheila Walker

A Memoriam to Dunkirk

There was a time in the history of this land,
When our defeated army stood on foreign sand.
Nine months before they had been so sure
That they would win this curséd war.
This gestation period would only bare
A child of failure and despair.
In spite of this, no man, his duty would he shirk
On those summer days at Dunkirk.
The sand was there, and so was Death
With watching eye and waiting hand.
The wind was soft and low as breath
Conflict for this gallant band.
Soon flotillas of boats both large and small
Would draw near to snatch them all;
Three hundred thousand souls from off this beach,
And get them back to England, out of the enemy's reach.
The memorial for this tremendous feat
When victory crept its way through stark defeat.
We must remember those who suffered, and the men who fell.
Freedom was kept for us. By their valour on this beach of Hell.

Harry Ruhrmund

A Vodka for the Comrades
(A Russian Remembrance Day)

More than the flag-waving crowds
More than the martial music
More than the clanking rumbling tanks
More than the high-stepping troops
More than the salvo of artillery blanks.

The sad memories are elsewhere
Brought to life
On a hill-top battle site
Where four old soldiers pass round and share
A bottle of vodka, as in the old times,
Leaving a cupful at the bottle's end
To gently pour upon the earth,
In memory of young comrades
Who were killed so many years ago.

For the old men, the pageantry
Is more than the tear ducts can stand,
So they have their own quiet ceremony
To pour out a vodka for old friends,
And remember.

Brian Reck

Loneliness

Loneliness is a state of mind
Fairly shared by all mankind.
When wandering on the pathway, lost,
With loneliness we pay the cost.

If, when these thoughts of isolation
Come to haunt our meditation,
Could we just feel the power untold,
 for every soul to hold.

Not one on path alone are we,
But of a throng, in eternity,
They've gone before, they come again,
At one with love and trust to reign.

Tis we are blind and lost alone
And cannot find our own way home,
Hope's the key to peace of mind,
Its lack, the greatest scourge, you'll find.

Friends and help are all around,
Some seen, some not, some lost, some found..
If we just give a thought to others,
Then all mankind can live as brothers.

Teresa Wright

Mountain High

She sits in her room at the top of the stairs
gazing up at the Mountains high. She puts pencil to paper,
looking up now and again.
She moves the paper back and forth as fast as she can.

When all is done she gives a big sigh
If only I could climb that mountain high

When a voice in her head seem to say, you can
go any where you want, if only you did but try.

How can I, she weeps, when my legs are so weak I can't
even walk to the end of the street.

Can't you see, said the voice in her head, you can go
any where with your psychic eye.

Before she has time to blink she's all ready to the top
of the mountains high.

With the sun on her face the cool breath of air
blowing through her hair.

Yes, yes she cries, I can even go up to the heavens above
with my psychic eye

G. M. Baxter

Cloning Is Suspiciously Incestuous

Emotional verbal attack based on ignorance,
is as good as breaking wind in public.
A trivial and irritating pursuit!

Insults hurled at me truly don't hurt,
for I'm as armour insulated as the tortoise.
Blunt spears can't penetrate the rhinoceros' hide.
I'm as tough as the hippopotamus, I remain unscathed.

Surely like anybody else, I would like to be listened to;
Hopefully to be widely read, understood, and be questioned.
But I've been insulted and accused of serious crimes of thought
Of being a pedlar of philosophical rot,
morally debased and on the brink of madness,
a proponent of violence and anarchy
of being cynical, suicidal and anti-establishment.

But let it be said that; the boat should be rocked,
its strength against angry waves be tested,
long before the turbulent journey.
Let it be known that difference is strength,
so my fellow beloved, I beg to differ,
cloning for me sounds suspiciously incestuous.

B. P. Gabokgatlhe

The Unsuccessful War

Ten soldiers marching through the mud,
Wounded, with hardly any life ahead of them,
Fighting for the country others live in,
Some may never see the country they fight for,
Some don't have the strength to live another day,
As they come to a river bank,
A sudden bomb is heard near them,
Men fled for the bushes,
But it was too late,
Bodies lay on the ground,
No movement no sound,
Blood everywhere,
A soldier lay shivering,
Burns on his face,
His dull green clothes now red,
His eyes blood shot,
As his eyes closed the silence was broken,
As the French soldiers laughed,
For they had won the war.

Natalie Stanton

Hope

What hope to the future we hold in our hands
For the next generation to follow in our land
Gone will the industries to the future lies rust
Why oh why must every thing die
No more will the next generation see
That is passing us by

For everything now is beginning to die
We must now correct our fault
And draw to a halt
This future we risk for we will cease to exist

The forests grow small and buildings grow tall
The animals that were once vast
Are now a thing of the past
The fish in the sea were a plenty
But now almost empty

To wonder if it is too late
To start to amend and stop and correct
Our future to end
Mary Bradford

And the Dog Lies Chained in the Yard

The family next door—they chat all day long,
The children are happy—I hear them in song;
The Mother is out—hanging washing on the line—
It will dry by tomorrow—the weather's so fine,
But The Dog Lies Chained In The Yard.

The Dad goes to work with his horse and his cart,
Up at six in the morning for an early start;
The kids go to school to read and do sums;
The Mother sits gossiping with the other Mums,
But The Dog Lies Chained In The Yard.

They feed him and water him—that's all they'll do;
He'll not know comfort like the rest of us do.
No play and no cuddles—no lovely long runs;
His life is pure boredom—while they have the fun,
As He Lies Chained In The Back Yard.

My dream is that one day the tables will turn,
And that type of human a lesson will learn.
Let the dog seize control and take over their home
And feed them on scraps and the odd bit of bone,
And Chain Them All In The Back Yard!
Anne P. Giles

Flying

I wonder what it must be like to fly,
To soar and to swoop way up in the sky,
You could fly for miles without making a sound,
You could fly for miles without touching the ground.

You could go anywhere you pleased,
You'd take off, fly away,
And you'd do it with ease.
You could fly for hours at a time,
On a warm current of air,
Into the clouds you would climb.

To wash and to preen, would be a daily routine,
And to hunt and to hill, would be part of the drill.
And you wouldn't have a care in the world.

Man has always been jealous of the birds' ability to fly
And has tried for years to get himself into the sky.
The best he has managed is in a plane.
The efforts he's used it's a wonder he's still sane,
Now man knows he will never fly under his own steam,
For flight has eluded us,
And for man it will only ever be a dream . . .
S. Lewis

Tomorrow

A surprise awaits at the Hall—
The wooden hut used by the school—
Reality will soon unfold
Its dreadful truth—the story's told:

On Sunday, playing in the drive
Behind the houses you were hid;
Those yellow locks in health did thrive;
Those perfect teeth, you blue-eyed kid!

Monday is school—it starts again,
And dinner-time, there'll be no treat
As when the Sandwich-People come—
That empty space will be your seat.

Crushed by a car the day before
A girl-child's life is there no more:
No longer chattering as we eat,
No more your looks, so gentle, sweet!

Tomorrow always comes again
For me,—I'll see you with this pen:
For every time this poem's read
You'll float to me as in a dream!
Roger Frederic De Boer

To My Son

I often sit alone and gaze at the sky,
Watching the clouds go drifting by.
Or walk on the sands along the seashore,
As the waves ebb and flow forevermore.
My thoughts turning to years gone by,
When I was young and my hopes were high.
I think of the plans I made, things I meant to do.
They somehow never materialised,
    most were pipe dreams,
    I realised, as older I grew.
Yet one of my greatest wishes came true,
The day God graciously gave me you.
So although I often sit alone
    with my thoughts of days gone by,
Your presence will always be in my home,
However far away you are, like the sun shining bright,
    and the stars at night, so near and yet so far.
I cannot reach out and touch you,
Yet in my heart you will always remain.
I pray God will always bless you until we meet again.
Doris Brown

The Raging Bull

The sea is a raging bull
Dark and silent
Until he spots his prey
Running with the waves to catch the victim

The prey is not to be caught easily
Lowering and surrounding the victim
He is not to be fooled
Easily he catches it with his raging horns

Crushing its victim's bones
Against the rocks
Thrashing its body
The bull is calm
The prey is dead
The waves carry its body
Far to the distance

The sea is calm again
Until another innocent victim
Dares
To trouble the bull
Amanda Ross Quinn

The Blot

Oh! The pureness of Heart
As a new baby is born into the World
The faces lit with joy to behold this image
Sometimes a cloud shroud the minds of others.

As the tender limbs begin to grow strong
so the spirit begins to feel the thrust around
A warm welcome may liven the pathway
sometimes a disgruntle growl will the light dim

As awareness and understanding increase
The path of destiny begins to unfold its shell
laughter and chivalry are highlighted in some
Inhibition and worthlessness on others abide

Some are said to come out with a golden spoon
Others to eat from the sweat of their brow
But the Lord Jesus hath all created
Only God can wipe away all the tears from their eyes.

Humphrey A. Epie

B, A, H

Hear I lay alone on the coach
 I'm nothing to her I'm just her shout
But in the morning you wait and see
 The first thing she'll look for
  that I'll be me
And once again she'll drain away
 The contents with in me in the
  first of the day
I can't resist I cannot let go
 When her lips surround me
  I perfectly glow
Again and again she puckers up
 he lips around me she can't get enough.

Denise Anderson

Untitled

I really would love to see
other places, and races
Big ones, tall, black, white and all.
I really would love to see them all.

We must remember we
Are all God's beings
Never mind the colour.
God loves us to be, seeing us.
Bless us all.

I would love to see other
races, black, white, tall,
I really love to see them all.

The world is a vast place.
We would like to wander,
But then, we all like
To think, we are safe
Not to squander.
But then, we see other places, which make us think
We should realize, we are better off at home.

S. I. Bullingham

Silent Whispers . . .

The ominous fog looms—
Morality prevails, Immorality exhales
Voices creep, Reality? Reality? mind won't sleep.
'Tis time, this time . . . No . . .

Darkness, beating, pulse "Quickens" . . .
Heartbeat r.a..c . . . e . . . .s . . . ., focus focus
Childhood memories r.u..s . . . h.in,
Childhood sounds original sin, original sin.

Re-evaluate old fears, re-capture old joys.
Be gone doubt, anguish disappear
Feelings disarmed, vulnerability here.
Remember, Rem . . . .Forget, forgotten . . .

Donna McTaggart

Three Words

Taking me a length to declare three words.
I'm not coy, just afraid for us instead.
I hold reasons. You must guarantee me . . .
. . . .I won't be absurd, you won't run away.
Knock and kill nerves, fear and insane questions.
Longing for me to whisper, but I don't.
It's neither selfish nor deliberate.
Your patience merits more before it thins.
Aware I want to drift asleep with you . . .
. . . endlessly sensing your warm arms and eyes.
My heart observes I do and sense applauds.
Your pledge, kiss and truth aren't wasted on me . . .
. . . I love you.

Ruth Counihan

Frightening Lightning

Your powerful searchlight sweeps the sky,
 Your strong beam strikes trees black.
  In the most startling way.

Your golden colour makes an impressive show of bright light,
 Scorching through the black clouds.
  In the most alarming way.

Your silent spikes knife through the clouds
 With jagged jumps, forking down to the ground
  In the most intimidating way.

Your weird form waits in the dark sky,
 Lurking in the clouds,
  Stabbing your victims
   In the most unnerving way.

Your thundery home is the clouds.
 Your bolt zig-zags through the clouds,
  You strike terror in people's hearts.
Searing down to earth
In the most shocking way.

Colin Wood

Dedicated to My Nan Who Passed Away on the 7/2/97

Our nan was a lady through and through,
Nothing would she miss, she always knew,
Such a strong willed person with a great deal of pride,
Knew what she wanted didn't have to decide,

Her mind so sharp, her thoughts made clear,
Wherever there is dust you know she'll be near,
I'll always remember her at the kitchen sink,
Scrubbing and washing and taking time to think,

Wherever you are Nan, you'll always be in our hearts,
We knew you couldn't wait any longer, you had to depart,
We'll love you forever, your place with us will stay,
Reunited with Grandad, for you both we'd like to pray.

Victoria Logan

Unfolding Dreams—Deja Vu

Squashed between worlds,
the sublime, the mundane,
providence tightens the cords
the pendulum swings;
from pain to pleasure
and in-between, I can't bear the pressure.
I will myself to balance,
like the clichéd phoenix, I rise from the ashes
I glance askance, then I see your face,
in spite of the passage of time; ages, eons,
it means nothing to minds that have
throbbed, stormed and boggled
there's a rhyme.
Do you see the effortless familiarity?
Of the lines and dents of the face? of hearts, souls?
Deja vu.
The shroud is unravelled, so arcane;
yet so new.
Listen, the pendulum swings still . . .

Lara Ewuosho

On the Death of a Friend
Dedicated to Warrick Alcock

Everybody knows life
  Does not stand still.
Everybody knows time
  Must march on.
Everybody knows change
  Is inevitable.
Everybody knows you
  Have to be strong.
But
  I don't know how to deal with it.
  I don't know how to let go.
  I don't know how to stay in orbit.
  I don't know how to rise from this low.
  Donna-May Range

Untitled

Trust in Jesus our Lord and Saviour,
He's done us all a great big favour,
One we cannot e'er repay;
He died that we might live alway.
The difference in our lives will be,
A change so great for all to see,
If we believe in Christ our Lord,
Following the holy word.
Our lives will be the more fulfilling,
And we will find we're much more willing,
To do the things we know we should,
But never thought we ever could.
He'll be with us to the end,
Jesus ; Counsellor, Saviour, Friend.
  R. J. Ogunnaike

Past and Present

Loud whistles blow as it approaches
Pulling the magnificent cream and brown coaches.
The massive dark engine looms into sight
With plumes of smoke, light-grey and white.
Brass plates on the engine and regal doors gleam
Is this really happening — or is it a dream!

We abandon our chores and let out a cry
"Quick it's the Orient Express going by!"
A leisurely trip on a quiet Sunday morning
Always heralded by the bright whistle warning!
Again in the evening it trundles on by
With white smoke billowing in the dark night sky.
There is something quite magical about this sight
As the pullman coaches disappear in the night.

But, whilst still lost in memories past
Another long streak has just flashed passed
A sleek pointed engine in yellow and grey
Has just jolted us back to the present day.
A contrast in transport to countries afar
The old 'Golden Arrow' and the new 'Eurostar'!
  J. M. Preston

The New-Traditionist

  Poems he loved—by Chaucer, Shakespeare, Keats,
    Byron and Hopkins, Hardy—after these,
Music of Mozart, Beethoven and, (best),
Tchaikovsky's passionate intensities.
Paintings by Poussin, Turner, Dali caught
His eye, (after great Michaelangelo,
Whose statues seemed to him pre-eminent),
And the pre-Raphaelites' rich, sensual glow.
  Under the influence of such as these
He sought his own distinctive voice to speak
  The message of experience
Half-deaf, half-blind to their profound critique.
  Unheralded, unnoticed, all his arts he gave
    To transcend fashion's shrouds; defy life's senseless grave.
  J. A. Bosworth

Photos

How stiff and starchy Grandma's pose,
As all the family waits for the flash.
With stiffened smiles and Sunday clothes
They stare at me from distant past.
Our snaps are tiny, dark and dim;
Our wedding photo formal, still
It never graced the mantel shelf!
And parent's photos, scarce and poor,
Tell us so little of their lives.
But now, our albums full of snaps,
Our family videos and films,
And thousand wedding photos fill
Albums and cupboards to the brim.
Yet valued as these records are,
Will they bring back sad memories
Of vows forgotten, of broken homes?
Perhaps the pictures from the poor
Record a life more secure and safe
Than this expensive grand array of colour photos, large and small.
That will our present times recall.
  Mary Yates

Me and My Zimmer

Now that I possess a zimmer
My fear of falling is much slimmer,
It's true I still cannot walk quick,
But it's safer than a walking stick,
From here to there is very slow,
It's determination that makes me go.
The days are long-gone since I rode a bike
And used to go for a nice long hike,
It's very painful to look back
At all the energy that I now lack,
Never mind you must agree
There are lots of folk worse off than me.
  Phyllis Richardson

Me and My Dog

I had a dog, I named him blue.
He'd do almost and anything I asked him to
He'd fetch me my slippers and sometimes my pipe
Then stand there and look with his head on one side

I'd go for a walk with him by my side
He'd never wander far out of my sight
He'd roll in the grass then jump in the air
The children they loved him without any fear

We'd sit down and talk till late in the night
His tail would be wagging his eyes were so bright
Then up I'd get and off to bed.
Then blue boy would go to his own little bed

I got up next morning with some sort of fear
No blue boy to meet me at the foot of the stairs
I went to his basket and called out his name
"Come on blue boy, this is no game."

I knelt down beside him
With tears in my eyes
Blue boy had left me
For the wide open skies
  Eric Winfield

Children

I watch the children run around my feet
And I watch them as they grow
I want to look inside their heads
And find out what they know.
Their powers of speech are limited
But I know what they're trying to say
No matter what it is they want
They tell you in their own way.
But it's the thoughts that race through their heads
I wonder what they can be
I wonder how they look at life
And what they make of what they see.
  D. Griffiths

Why

My best friend laid dying at my feet.
He laid on the floor calling out to me.
"Jimmy . . . Jimmy . . . James, please come, please hurry."
We had survived two whole years together,
Flown planes together, formed attacks, killed people.
Killed people, we had killed people and now someone was killing us.
I held my friend,
My Charlie, my dear Charlie.
I hugged him close and tried to keep him warm.
The smell of alcohol wafted past our noses,
I tried to make him drink but he wouldn't take it.
He was dead.
I held him close while watching him breathe his last breath.
"Why..? Why..? Why him, why not me?" I cried.
But nobody could hear me, nobody listened.
And with the sound of bombs falling to the ground,
Planes roaring in the sky
And men praying on their knees.
I cried for him and for me.

Jennifer Cooke

Ode to My First Love

The years were many the days were long
I turned around and you were gone
Then one Friday in November
In you came made me remember
Gold locks gone freckles faded
Didn't care just glad you made it
Finally said hello and kissed
Forgotten what I had really missed
Didn't mind . . . better late than never
Could it be we'll get together?
Nice to hear your voice each day
Didn't think I'd feel this way
You always remember your first love
Thank you to that man above
The longer it goes the closer we'll be
This time you won't get away from me.

Robert Bowers

My Children

My children, so special to me,
Came from the Lord as a present you see.

First, bundles of joy so little and weak,
Into children with mischief and plenty of cheek.

But more than the mischief and cheek that I see,
Is the pleasure they give me and the love that will be.

You see, the Lord thought me special when he made me a mum,
So I praise him and thank him for all that's to come.

For my children are the future in which the Lord has his plan,
To love them and shape them, I pray that I can.

Jacquline Hartwell

Love Fulfilled

My love has mellowed with the years,
Like purple grapes upon the vine,
With joy and laughter, smiles and tears,
It ripens like a vintage wine.
With happiness it fills my cup,
Intoxicating to my soul,
And of its sweetness let me sup,
And in its essence play my role.

Though I have witnessed stormy strife,
In deepening shades of sorrow's gloom,
When raindrops fell upon my life,
To test the vows of bride and groom,
Yet like the vine, my love will climb,
And strengthen in the falling rain,
To turn the water into wine,
And raindrops into sun again.

June Vanhoven

The Jagged Heart

The sharp edged spiked perimeter that is
left around the lost souled heart.
Each one a part of pain carved in.
Love of a man, that never was,
too vain, too proud, too selfish to care,
care of a woman that never was,
each one together for a time that never was
did it happen or did it not?
Seven years that never was.
Alone now you have gone, gone for good,
I cannot look back, to see the space.
The space of a lost love that never was.
Abandoned love, now ready to be filled
by what, a word called love, that never was
no, do not look back! And see the love that
never was, look forward and see the love yet
to come, it's warm, it's soft, it's like the sun.
It heals the spike that never was.

N. Hemming

Reflections through the Glass

Don't shut me away from God's fresh air
To the sun, to the sky, allow my face to bare.
Let me walk in the fields, along a country lane,
Don't let me stare out through a cold windowpane.
To feel the rain lash down upon my hair
All nature's seasons let my senses share.
At night when the stars shine in a velvet sky,
Give me wings like a bird, let me fly
Through the beauty that belongs to you and me.
So much to feel, to experience, to see.

Let me lie on a beach, hear the waves crashing down,
See the surf like a frothing bejewelled crown.
See a fish slithering amongst the water so green,
So many sights and sounds to be heard and seen.
The beauty of a sunset can it ever be compared
Beauty enhanced when with a loved one it is shared.
Don't shut me away, please hear my prayer,
Let me be free and with my love let me share
A flower, a raindrop, a distant sound in the night,
Take my eyes, let me see every beauty, every glorious sight.

Pamela Menday

Sonnet II

When naked Nature's shyly waiting for
Her dress of fragile green and rosy white
To meet her golden groom as blushing bride
And go on honeymoon to distant shore,
While leaving us, as precious souvenir,
Her transient veil of yellow, red and brown,
All overwept with tears of joy, come down
Like vintage wine with musky fragrance dear;
As even boisterous nights then softly bring
A downy cover to protect the fruit
That grows in her, providing it with food,
And hold their breaths to hear the snowdrop's ting,
   My sweet, remember then, through bliss and pain:
   A bond of Love is never linked in vain.

Mike Roysons

Middle Class Blues

The house is always tidy,
Everything you lost is tidied away.
(Like the pub crawl, the terrace,
Alcohol abuse and spending nights away.)
Nine o'clock, early night,
Too tired to think of making love.
Kids are playing up again!
You want to give your life a shove.
Next door are off to Egypt,
So you're saving for a worldwide cruise.
Where is all the fun you had?
Lost amongst those middle class blues.

Kaye Axon

The Best Thing Ever

Love is the best thing ever,
   For love you don't have to be cool, pretty
Or clever.

Everyone needs a little love now and then,
   They can't just hold their breath
And count to ten.

No one can survive without love,
   It's the softest feeling
Just like a dove.

Jennifer Megson

Untitled

I tell you, whatever man does,
He cannot remove the curse.
Because the world belongs to man.
And like man it must grow, fragile and innocent at birth,
Nothing but hail on earth,
But look! The older it gets,
The more the curse bears down on it.
Why can't good proceed good?
Why must a bad act be repeated . . . constantly?
Science!
Silence! What is science?
Is the greedy search for immortality the solution?
Do not embrace science because like rain building into a storm,
So shall a discovery become a misery,
Then a mystery and finally, irreversible,
I tell you, the world is the world
And science . . . is the world.

Elsie O'Freddie

Finding the Light

I've sailed the dark in lonely boats
I've donned some colourful happy coats
I've ne'er gone inside to find the light
I've always assumed I'd have to fight

I've looked for love in many places
Studied sadness and happy faces
Concluded; existence is all there is
And life went downward into Abyss

Into the darkness I fell unwanting
Existence in life I found most daunting
And then, by chance, I found the light
Amazed, I had found it without a fight
Surrounded by light, I'd also found
That love was there, both in and around

Love overflowing the river of life
No more sadness and no more strife
Love is my helper, love conquers fear
Love won't desert me, it's always right here
I use it, abuse it, there's always enough
I never will empty the great well of love.

Catherine Janet Meldrum

A Mother's Pain

They say that you have, a very rare syndrome,
And you're trapped in a lonely, cruel world, of your own
Unable to talk and unable to see.
In just a few years, you'll be taken from me.
You scream and you shout, you lash out in vain,
You don't understand, mummy too feels your pain.
I try to get close, as I whisper your name,
But you push me away, and I feel I'm to blame.
Although nearly three, you still cannot walk,
You can't sit alone and you never will talk
Powdered milk is the only food, you will know,
But despite what you drink, you never will grow.
Baby's body and mind are just washing away,
And each day that you wake, for your comfort I pray.
Mummy will always love you, but soon is the day,
When I cuddle you gently, as you slip away.

Kathryn Shaughnessy

Sweet Dreams

Sweet dreams my darling, let sleep help you grow
Your cute little dimples, when you smile do show
A little giggle here and a little gurgle there
Glittering blue eyes and short spiky hair
Your dribble gets everywhere on your chin and your clothes
Perhaps you'll have teeth soon for us to show
You in your romper suits, all clean and pristine
The toys on the floor, with cushions to lean
Your balance isn't there yet, for you are to small
You can't crawl or walk yet, when you sit you fall
Your time will come soon now when these you can do
My cute little man boy, this one is for you.

Ann Saunders

Snowtime Pleasure

The snow fell silently from the sky
the ground was frosty so it would lie
it was very windy so it would drift
but it gave the children such a lift
Toboggans were found in the school shed
no thought at all of going to bed
to the top of the hill the children went
and such an exciting time was spent
gliding down from the top of the hill
the wind was bitter but gave a thrill
the moon shone brightly in the sky
casting shadows where deep drifts lie.

Joyce Strong

To My Baby

I wanted to be together
Just us from the very start
When you were taken from me
Self hate poured from my heart

Please find it in your heart to forgive me
My love for you goes deep
I need to know that you love me too
And that you are mine for keeps

Families always change things
They have a funny way
Of making you feel guilty
When you need to have your say

Only next time I shall know
That what's in my heart is true
I just need one more chance
Then I could prove it to you

So it's goodbye for now and ever
Remember my love will never cease
To me you mean the world, so
Please God, let her rest in peace

Donna-Marie. Fowler

An-X

A rose in a glass isolation.
I see you in the clarity of my eye.
A liquid crystal representation, to be
Forever untouched by the passage of time
I dare not breathe on you,
For my faintest breath shall
Irreversibly shatter your fragile petals.
The very breath that gives me life shall
Bestow upon thee the wrath of apocalypse.
I wonder how something so simplistic
Has painted me so.
I long to smell, taste and touch your every secret.
There you stand in the brilliance
Of your aura, so appealing.
I would not mind your thorny stem
Piercing my skin to draw blood.
As in every sense it is real.
Does the rose look at me the same?
Or does it grow in obliviousness to me?

R. Kazmi

Shadows

I saw a secret something
in the shadows of last night.
I turned to kiss my lover
expectant of the joy of him,
the anytime, all the time, happiness of him,
the arms and smell and smile of him.
But the room was small, and brick.
So I rolled out the other side
and fumbled through to our son.
In the night light gloom, with bears afloat,
and unicorns,
I couldn't catch the dream
and ask whether it was you,
or was it me,
that dreamed of play
in a safe garden.

Chirene Hughes

The Shadow of Greatness

I am uncapable of crying
I cannot breathe
I have feelings
That I cannot perceive.
Outside, it is cold.
In the shadow of greatness
Stood my wishes, wishing.
I searched for just one bright star
To tell me you're there, I saw none.
I searched the sky, for one dull star,
One, just one.
My imagination saw glimpses
Everywhere, but I saw none.
I imagined I saw the sky open,
You pour through, surge within me . . .
Yet I knew, it was sheer coldness
Numbing my soul, making me dream
Ignoring the calls; thoughts of comforts
Thoughts of grief, being incomplete
You were my piece.

Helen Payne

Waiting for Spring

The weather is cold, not very bright,
waiting for springtime. Just long for the sight
of snowdrops and crocus, awake soon from sleep,
little heads peep from soil, their seasons to keep.
As evenings get lighter, our gardens we tend,
feeling quite tired at the day's end.
Full of contentment as results can be seen,
lifting the weeds—leaving lawn smooth and green.
It's not just the warm sunshine; add soft gentle rain
bringing God's nature into play once again.
As each of the seasons brings beauty to see;
a clear running stream by an old willow tree.
At the end of each day we should all say a prayer
thanking God for our lives, and all we hold dear.

J. Martin

The Ones We Love

The ones we love won't be here forever.
But we mustn't forget them, no not ever.

Please, try to think of all the good times
And all the things that make you laugh.

Yes we must think of childhood memories,
The fun times when our loved ones would act daft.

Don't worry we must never forget them.
My love lost will always be in my heart.

But then my heart will always be broken,
Quiet simply because there's a missing part.

The ones we love won't be here forever,
But you and I mustn't forget them no, not ever

Christina Peters

Angel-Eyes

You need a man,
who will treat you like the woman you are,
these little boys are just playing around with your heart,
what are you going to do now you are on your own again,
he was not man enough to hold on to you,
he just tried to rule you and use you as a slave,
but just like Cinderella,
You will go to the ball, he will regret losing you,
his day will come when he will look back and remember what he lost,
but he won't be able to get you back no matter the cost,

You need a man, who will treat you like the woman you are.

I look into your eyes and they make me start to shiver
I kiss you on the lips and they make me start to melt.
You touch me with your fingers, and my body juices flow,
You start to make love to me, and then I really know,
I want you more each minute.
Every second of the day,
I think of you more than a clock ticks in the day,
I go to bed and dream of you
My hands caress my body
and all the time darling I wish that it was you,
Bear.

Elainea Arter

Are We Ready

When Jesus comes, what will he find?
Earth's pleasures only on the mind.
So many plans, so much to get through,
Not thought for him, we've too much to do,

When Jesus comes, what will he hear?
Words so unkind, they may cause a tear.
Some need our help, do we pass by,
Say we haven't time, so turn a blind eye?

When Jesus comes, what will he see?
Lying and cheating, stealing maybe,
If someone gets hurt by our actions each day.
They're only people, who cares anyway!

When He comes for you, will He say "Well done,
You told others of me, and souls were won,
You showed my love, you tried your best,
My Father says, come, take your rest."

When Jesus comes at the end of time.
To gather His own from every clime,
He'll come to reign as King of all Kings
What will it matter then of worldly things?

Doris Sparrow

The Death of a Stag

He stands with his head raised high,
Silhouetted against the early morning sky,
The undisputed monarch of the glen,
Surveying his vast domain.

Superb antlers—his golden crown,
The morning sunbeams glisten his coat of reddish-brown,
He is truly a magnificent beast.
It took myriads of time to produce this masterpiece!

Alas, a hunter chances upon the scene,
He cannot see nor sense the beauty,
he can only see his friends' envy,
When he shows them his latest, splendid trophy.

He raises his gun and carefully aims.

Oh, the hunter's empty, arrogant pride,
as he proudly looks at what he has destroyed,
That he impoverishes the world
by his murderous act. . . he cares not.

The only thing that matters to him
is—to be
The toast of the stag-hunters's annual dinner party.

Brynne Shaill

Wrong Man, Wrong Choice, Wrong Ending

Last time you fell in love
Though you pretended being tough
I apprehended he was not serious
And I definitely knew it wasn't righteous
You made the wrong decision
But you didn't want to see my vision
I said open your blinded eyes
For you can see all the lies
I can't hold back my tears
Can't push'em away, my fears
Trying to make the best out of it
Like you always did
But don't you tell me you wouldn't care
Cause you know exactly it's not fair
This time I'm gonna wipe the tear away
Even though I know you're not gonna stay
Now I want to go
My heart beats slow
First darkness, then a glary light
I don't care anymore whether it's day or night

Melanie Kiener

Memories by the Sea

How I remember the sea, foamy, bright gentle and blue,
with a beautiful horizon for all to view.
Constant like the stars in the sky, a quiet calm,
oblivious I sigh.

The smell of salt air, on my face tongue and hair,
the occasional blast of sea sand, that gets everywhere.
People push past to find their own place, I choose the
dunes as my own private space. Past and future
go by so fast, I wonder why it never lasts.

Curly waves crashing on the shore, people starting to
brave the waters a little afraid and unsure. Stumblers,
divers, creepers, you'd see different types of people
with different ways of meeting the sea.

Ours is a course we cannot change, but memories
even good can haunt this old face. Older and wiser
yes I maybe but give me them happy days of
youth, sun and sea.

Jessica Maher

Hurt

When someone close to you has gone,
Life is dead, there is no sun.
You'll never again see them, they have left,
But it doesn't seem fair, it's like a theft.
Life's not worth living, it's all too much,
You miss their smile, their tender touch.
Why couldn't they just live in peace?
Instead of having to go, decease.
Will they be looked after by God?,
Does God exist? Is He a fraud?
Yes I know they had a good life,
But now I have to live in strife.

Charlene Stanley

Raindrops

I sit alone and as I look out of the window I watch the rain
I notice that the window looks like it is crying
Each tear represents an emotion and as the tears trickle
They join together I realize that as my tears flow my emotions join

With sorrow there is happiness with pain there is joy
And with each emotion there is a new strength
So when all our weaknesses join a new strength begins
We learn to cope with what we have and learn our own limits
And as we develop our strengths those limits decrease

After each day and every year you learn that
A part of love is hate and a part of life is death
As the rain dries from the window so the tears dry
We forget that they were ever there until the next rainfall.

Caroline Perkins

That Special Hook

The old chair stands where she used to work,
and her hands were busy all the while,
I would sit by her side and we would talk,
she was always ready to listen, with her knowing smile.
Her hook was old, but oh, so fine,
she didn't even need glasses to see.
Those intricate patterns she could easily combine,
with silks and pretty colours, all to please me.
I tried to learn her wonderful art,
but crocheting for me was not so good
although she tried with a willing heart,
I couldn't do it, but she understood.
I wish she was here today, just to see that smile
to watch her use that hook and sit for a while.
There are memories of her everywhere, mats and nic-nacs too,
mended teddies and covers for the roll in the loo
There's one in the shape of a cross, I use it to mark my book,
All these happy memories of a very special crocheting hook.

Margaret Meadows

Together . . .

I listen, I try, please don't say goodbye,
A card, a call, a nod, a wink
Sometimes maybe a little drink,
From the heart we surely speak.
Let's always stay strong, never weak.
Is a touch, a kiss really wrong, or for these
moments do we long?
Two hearts together beating as one,
In Heaven and earth thy will be done.
The Lord our God does He care, or
does He give us our cross to bear.
So close your eyes and think in mind,
One day the man himself will be kind,
Let's not ask for riches and gold,
Only your hand in mine to hold.

Christopher Robinson

Loved Up

Here I lay all alone
   Wondering if I should pick up the phone
Lots of memories on my mind
   Blocking out, that you have no time.
My friends keep saying, I could do better
   All I keep thinking is, should I write you a letter
To express how I feel
   To you I know, is no big deal
So I'll stay loved up
   For I do not hold the winning cup
Love is like an addictive drug
   And this situation is beginning to bug
I can't continue holding on
   But I do still feel, that we will always belong
At night in the distance I hear your voice
   Reminding me you're my only choice
So the way that it stands
   Is that you're out of my hands
When dawn comes and awakes me
   I pray that you'll come and take me

Bal Dhillon

The Wooden Lord

One evening strolling I stopped to notice
A Wooden Lord, sitting proud,
On a height that cannot be found,
In secret silence, lit twilight blue by tired out stars.
A hint of warmth and friendly glow arrayed
Soft and subtle, from fiery sun's foe
Whilst shadows scour the picturesque scene.
This tree that stood one thousand years
Scorns on my presence,
And feeling the unwanted chill
I regressed to my home upon a chestnut hill.

Niamh Healy-Moore

Sweet Spring

How I long for the Spring on a day like this
   when its howling and whistling outside
And the trees are bent down by the force of the wind
   And the sea by the roaring tide.

It seems to have been a long winter this year:
   Some snow, much frost and grey skies.
Yes, skies that seem endlessly threatening and black
   Which have curtained the sun from our eyes.

But to day in the garden there are snowdrops a nodding
   The forsythia is nearly a-glow.
And the blackbird, full throated, proclaims his dominion
   While squirrels crack nuts down below.

My footsteps feel lighter, my spirits are cheered
   At the thought that its nearly spring,
That wonderful season of magic awakening
   When life all around seems to sing.
Barbara Winifred Tattersall

Patience

Across the opening porous;
Emissions of guilt
Infusions of light.
The underdogs of the unblemished hand
Follow you to the depths of your despair.
Everything now is accomplished;
Duty goes on its way
And the spirited, hasty departure of
Your confusions live on.
Allow them to shed light
On your dreams of reprisal.
The overture opens: Decision time again,
You owe me this and yet you
Know not what it means.
Lynda Martin

Sunlight at 7 AM

It's 7 am and very bright
it shines through my curtains
it's no longer night

The day has broken
and I'm awake
I think I'll take a swim down by the lake

The sun glistens brightly across the lake
it seems so bright
I now know I'm awake

The sun it shines all through the day
it's lovely to see
I watch the time just fade away

It's nice and romantic down by the lake
I listen to the birds and the breeze
I'm so glad to be awake

And the flowers they're so bright
but time presses on
and now it's turned night
the day now has gone
Steven Hinds

Devon—January

The storm winds have raped the fretted leaves
From their pithless stems in the emeried earth.
Hollow husks and shallow shells
Of peppered grasses tip and whistle.
Like skated glass the frost-shot puddles shine
And the hoary air hangs . . .
The crouching jewel-eyed hare
Unseen, sees all.
Beneath a clay-grey horizon
Clings a stony knot of sheep
As a thread of geese on hushened wings
Steals waterward . . .
Corinna Leigh-Turner

Love's Requiem

The wasted time is etched on my face
You tasted and soured youth's precious bloom,
This deep wound can never heal at this pace,
The Fates weave, the Furies enter in the gloom
With screams and howls they race to hound a fool.
The seasons pass without you by my side
How could someone so gentle be so cruel
Letting me hope for so much while you lied
Alone I will soon return to the dust
The swift sands of time have almost run out
All is lost for one man's lust
Solely bequeathed is my lack of doubt.
   Running to the future from the bleak past
   Many things may die, but memories last.
Ruth Penfold

Just a Whisper

My heart is so heavy, I feel the pain
Just knowing I'll never touch you again.
To talk with you Mom, to hear you laugh
Those precious moments belong to the past.
Tears, they come and sting my eyes,
Sometimes impossible to disguise.
Our love, Mom, is so strong and true
Teach me to cope each day without you.
I said my prayer, then I heard you say
Don't worry, I'm only a whisper away.
Jean Parker

Your Loving Presence

Your loving presence is always near,
releasing our worries and fear,
your righteous word will spread throughout,
you died, rose again; of that there's no doubt.

Strength is given to fight the fight,
all that's wrong is soon made right,
your love unconditional and oh so strong,
kept safe in your arms where we belong.

Because you endured so much pain,
we learn to live and love again,
when the day comes, all will see,
paradise will be ours for eternity.

You are everything to me Lord,
my all, my destiny,
you died to set us free Lord,
I will love you eternally.
Karen Ovington

Who Said Friends Are Forever?

We, once, were a group of friends, united by fate
Been through love and war, eventually learned to relate
But by accepting it all, and each other, we learned
There will always be tears and pain, where friendship is concerned.

Then the intruders came from another group and
Wormed their way into our lives.
Their sweetness only fooled half of us
casting shadows over their eyes.

So, then our group was split in two.
Jealousy of the intruders knocked us off our feet,
As our friendships slipped into the dark,
dank crevices of the street.

Since then, all the loyalty and trust
Is evident only in the past.
Each day, it is further away
And the memory of them, disappearing fast.

Now it would just be a waste of time
To search for love between the lines.
Have we been fooling ourselves all along
holding onto friendships, that are dead and gone?
Aoife Connors

Night Journey

Eye socket in shadow, dark oval
Floats over the blurred jaw line.
Tooth gleams, hanging in the unskulled
Gape — pearl in a rotten bed.
Lurid city lights snicker beyond
Dark slacks and patches of river.
Shifted lights print a blind white code
On flaccid river top, oily, glutinous.
Livid falls of willow flop, float
Winged aside by the push of a
Pale rippled corpse, floating in the river, long—
Turning, rolling in a random current
Down, pursued by snaking halo of
Its own dead hair.
Water untucks the skin
From its bone. The damaged face
Swims through floods, and slides away
Flake by flake.

Michaela Philp

Untitled

Storm,
Dancing passionate over my hills,
Claiming sky with frightening grace.
Storm,
Power shatters as anger spills,
Laughing and screaming, she raises her face.
Storm,
Calmer now, she's thundered by,
Flashing past like a God alight.
Calm,
Beauty unclothes violet sky
As Storm shrieks wildly into night.

Abi Hamer

May I

May I share your troubles
May I wipe away your tears
May I shelter you from harm
May I worry for you.

May I buy you gifts
May I give you flowers
May I hold you tight
May I look after you.

To all these questions should you say yes
Then happy I shall be.

May I be with you
May I look into your eyes
May I hold your hand
May I touch you.

May I pull you close
May I fall into your arms
May I kiss your lips
May I love you.

To all these questions should you say yes
Then happy I shall be.

James E. Potticary

Beach Walk—Mudeford, Dorset

The sea is calm, but deep within stirring tides
  From oceans far, and from those depths
Along the shore, patterns form in sands
  once more and in those sands a tale
Is cast from seas far beyond bringing form
  to colour still, the sands of time and tides.

Winter seas pound the shore line, spray and sands
  thrown high with flotsam of the seas to ground
For birds of prey to feed and search

The seas recede, to EBB and flow, for seasons yet
  to come, the hint of spring with golden glints
To summer song once more.

P. M. Lyons

Didn't You Know?

Like the fist of Hercules in the pit of your stomach
Like your head is full of helium and about to burst
Like the room is spinning and the others are mute
And the fact they are mute makes it worse.

When you claw back through memories looking for signs
When you curse your oblivion and misplaced trust
When you alternately attack and defend your actions
And the image you cannot shake is their lust.

And you hate them with a venom that would make Satan blush
And you hate yourself much much more
And you fantasize revenge and you picture their deaths
And you search your plan for flaws.

But you sleep on it, and sleep on it, and you sleep yet more
And you weep and you sob and you roar.
And you're glad that you had, though you knew it was bad,
That encounter with Adonis next door.

Claire Francine Drake

Colours

Once there was a graffiti artist,
Red, Yellow, Pink and Blue.
He loved painting, you would always see,
Red, Yellow, Pink and Blue.
Some people would say "What a mess".
Some other people would say "Cool".
That's very good, that's the thing about,
Red, Yellow, Pink and Blue.

William J. Clark

If I Were a Cloud

If I were a cloud
I could drift across the sky,
Destroying hate
Creating happiness.

If I were a cloud
I could float through the sky,
Destroying poor
Creating wealth.

If I were a cloud
I could sweep through the sky,
Destroying cruelty
Creating love

If I were a cloud
I could wander the sky,
Destroying war
Creating peace.

If I were a cloud
I would have the sky's power to do this.

Amanda Elphick

A Garland

Make me a garland of flowers,
Of primroses, violets, or May;
Slip it around my neck, Darling,
Just as the light fades away.

Now let us look at each flower,
Enjoying their colour, and think
How daintily hued is each petal—
Soft yellow, bright purple, or pink.

The work is so wondrously fashioned,
Like words woven into a ring,
Each echoing emotions or feelings
Flowing colorfully from our heart's string!

The result is a garland of poems—
A garland without any end:
For poetry goes onward for ever,
Around and around you, dear friend.

Eileen K. Atkinson

Memories

Memories, happy thoughts
The good times you can relive forever
Things you want to forget
Or maybe never went to
A song, smell or a place
Which bring back secret memories,
Locked deep inside your mind
your first love, and first kiss
Things you can remember,
when the smile's gone from your face
Memories which make you sad to remember
saying farewell to those you love
Old wounds which don't heal as easily as you hope
Memories, to take you back through your life.

Rhonda Dehavilland

Lifeboat

Silver Orb that drags the tide to shore,
That builds the crashing waves,
Where men wait with bated breath and awe,
Where seagulls screech, and whirl and cry,
The wind whipped storm fate driven steamers ride,
The running tide to doom,
While men wait with bated breath and awe,
The call that fellow men are doomed,
That breaches politic, race or creed,
To snatch from nature's foulest mood,
In Lifeboats ride the bravest breed.

E. H. Buchanan

What Changing Times?

As the Twentieth century to an end draws near,
With its many a sorrowful or happy year
History we are writing each day of our life
Reporting stories of diseases, famine and strife.

Since the days of Cain and Abel it's been much the same.
Jealousy and hatred, finding someone to blame
The child in the cradle learns from what he has seen
From the dawn of the ages that's the way it's been.

In the next century parental models will rarely be found
With telly, camera, video and computers around.
Our offspring will be brainwashed and by a number be known
And all business transactions take place on a new type of phone.

Will parents be more tolerant, thoughtful and kind
Rearing their offspring with love, peace and justice in mind?
This pattern of life we have been trying to better
It's impossible to change: just like locked in a fetter.

Education seems, to all problems the answer
So we teach our children about sex, drugs and cancer,
The Holy Bible no longer encouraged to be taught
But history of battles and where they were fought.

V. H. Walsh

The Wind Effect

Oh ye wynter wynde, how fiercely cold dost thou blow,
Cometh thee from far, far away lands
And continents covered o'er with snow,
To make us mortals thee respect, and freeze our hands.

Thine icy breath is country wide and long,
Oft so omnipotent and unceasing to havoc wreak
The populace amongst, weak and strong,
Doth make us hide, and for shelter seek.

When thou'rt truly angry, and thine icy blast
From nor'east doth come, can'st thy frenzy
The whiteness into chaos whip, first and last,
Travellers disrupt, the country halt, and then some.

Ah, but how fickle are we when summer doth arrive,
When swelter we all, and a ransom gladly would give
For a cooling breeze to make us feel more alive
And more comfortable our lives to live.

Manley L. Lucas

Remembrance

Do you remember the golden days,
When love was new and shining bright
When each day brought us fresh delight
Do you remember?
Do you remember the darkest days,
When love seemed lost, and all was night,
When nothing in the world was right,
Do you remember?
And will you remember these marvellous days
Now love has survived and won the fight,
And given us back ours hearts delight,
Will you remember?

D. Bennett

September

Full circle, it's that time of year again
Glossy dark leaves quiver
Buds of ivy, pinballs scattered skywards
Russet berries thrust from cover.
Sunlight filters through open window
illuminating words and ink and polished oak
Black ball stretches lazily, yawns
and returns to sleep.
Peace is warm, is light, is silent.

Mary Garrard

Emigrant's Return Ship Journey to Cobh

Fermoy, an area dancing on map.
Those lines of Ireland, those counties they save
The emigrant's soul on a wet-wild day,
From New York harbour, the blue-hills of waves

Act like a barricade of foam-form blocks.
Those days of childhood; rounders, howling play!
A team; team-spirit in the sport of luck.
Lucky, we were, finding freedom in play.

Fermoy hills, up corrin.
No skyscrapers to point at me: "Go to school!"
No subways with crowds tense, in crammed speed car.
"Go carry school books!" I was elastic fool.

Strangers in a strangeford, foreign essay;
At school, I'm stranger in New York class'. Fear
Acting as stalk — hawk trembles to me
Tears on eyes, swell up, high school no fun. Free

Race to quay, dock that I stood on prime new
scholar. I write essay sketch: ship to cobh; cost,
at twelve, wallet of fun, employ of dreams.
In Geography class, a rap in norch, it screams.

Pauline O'Kelly

Untitled

Misty moods and misty minds,
Words of love and words unkind,
Actions great and noble and bad,
Things that make you happy and sad,

Work to be done and work to undo,
Thoughts of me and thoughts of you,
All are part and all together,
Provide love and life forever,

Sometimes hard sometimes strong
Some in a kiss, some in a song,
Sometimes weak, sometimes easy,
Sometimes still, sometimes breezy,

It's all there to see, but nothing to look at,
It's all mills and it's all flat,
It's all here, and it's all there,
It's all about and that's why I care,

It's all me and it's all you,
It's all old and it's all new.
So eat the bread and drink the wine,
And we'll learn to love 'cause we're part of mankind.

Phil Ironside

And It Goes On . . .

And it goes on, still,
as autumn sweeps in the close of the year,
and absences not yet forgotten,
linger in the grey horizon.
Harsh breezes whip up,
and the biting edge of day closes
in around us, frightening and familiar.

I fear the hungry, lost eyes
of the roads and trees;
The traipsing back and forth of daily life.
And it goes on, still, forever
unending and we, enduring the cold,
the loneliness. And you go on, without me;
I see you in the mind's eye,
wrapped up in a breeze on my grey road home,
you and the leaves,
spinning, unending,
ever on.

Anne-Marie O'Callaghan

War

The letter looked official is what they had said,
The message it brought her was your son is dead,
The words kept on sounding out loud in her ears,
The words that fulfilled all of her greatest fears.
Her tears warm and salty rolled down her tired face.
Remembering the boy she once used to chase.
She covers her face and asks why, tell me why,
Why did my beautiful son have to die?
The young boy that used to sit on her knee,
Those laughing eyes she would no longer see.
My son, my son I will always remember,
That terrible day, the 5th of September.

Louise Kankaanpaa

Silence

Peaceful silence in a quiet place,
   The happiness on a pleasant face.
Silence in the early morn,
   Waking at a quiet dawn.

Silence between friends,
   No need to talk or pretend.
Understanding both each other,
   Like a baby, with its mother.

Splendid silent sun, with all its beams full bright,
   And the moon, which shines in the deep velvet of night.
In spring, when the grass is green and new,
   And up above, the lovely sky of blue.

In the woods, beneath the trees,
   No breeze rustling through the leaves
What beautiful tranquility here is found.
   With fragrant flowers all around.

One could feel lost in silence as in a desert vast,
   Or think back in time, to things that are past.
When far away and alone
   In our hearts, we think of home.

Gladys Mary Brown

Untitled

Noo, noo, is a very fine cat.
Noo, noo, is Miranda's cat.
Noo, noo, would not harm a fly,
But watch him chase a butterfly.
Noo, noo, chases leaves as well, as any
other cat.
Noo, noo, is Miranda's cat,
Noo, noo, is a very fine chap.
A true romantic Noo, noo, is, and a very
Affectionate cat.
Noo, noo, is Miranda's cat, and that's that.
Noo, Noo, Miranda's Cat.

Iain P. Milne

The Life of Jesus

In the hall where we sat in
'twas ever so inspiring
to see the scenes of long ago
where Jesus walked the earth below.

Our hearts and minds just warmed to him
who endured such anguish
to cleanse us from sin.

Preaching and healing wherever he went
because he was divinely sent
to have compassion on those in need
and with wisdom rebuke hearts filled with greed.

How cheering it was to see Zaccheus
sitting up the tree
his heart just filled with glee
when Jesus said, I'm coming to your house for tea

What a changed man he became
giving back four fold
the money he gained.
So may each one of us respond to
such a wondrous love.

A. Robinson

If

If I held out my hand,
would you take it?

If I smiled at you,
would it warm your day?

If I touched your hand,
would it make you stay?

If I held you close and you saw my soul,
would you run away?

If I told you my deepest pain,
would you love me even harder?

If you held out your hand,
I would take it and never let go.

If you smiled at me,
it would warm my life.

If you touched my hand,
I would surrender to you.

If you showed me your soul,
I would cradle you.

If you told me your deepest pain,
I would love you beyond reason.

If I told you I love you,
would you love me too?

Tania Black

Battersea Power Station (Kent 1996)

Four towers pointing to the sky
This relic of an age gone by stands
Like a monument to our ever
Growing need, of power.
This empty husk with shattered shell
Stood in the dust, a tale could tell of
Heated homes and source of light, to
Brighten up the darkest night.
Now the life force gone from the
Cabled veins, and only the girded
Corpse remains of the four silent
Sentinels which still stand, and guard
The past as if sculptured by an unskilled hand.
Now no longer of a use to man, as their
Wherewithal it holds no plan in the
Human scheme, for as coal mines
Close and our use of steam is long since
Gone, it was just another sacrificed to
Man's move on.

Ben Herbert Brumel

Who Is Me

Who is me what am I,
Why was I born under this sky,
Where am I going, what ambition have I,
Why did I let life pass me by,
Where did I go the real me,
Why do I live in fantasy,
This is just make believe,
This isn't me; where is the person I used to be,
I agree for agreeing sake,
No point of view give I,
But I am not you, my own man am I,
I've lived quite a while in this rut you see,
But today, today I have found me,
I've captured a moment here in mid air,
Felt it, touched it, became aware,
That I am exclusive, I'm not a clone,
I am my own, I am my own.

Margaret Tew

Faith

Faith is—yearning to do your will,
Faith is—learning, just, to keep still,
Faith is—that you, do, understand,
Faith is—that all is planned.
Faith is that, as we pray in faith,
That you are with us, to help us face
The work you are giving us each day
Will be guided and blessed all the way.
The people we meet, and, how we greet,
The inner joy of all those whom we seek
Faith will give us the power of speech.
Faith O Lord, comes from you, complete.

Antonia Burgess

Goodbye, Farewell, Why?

Brown eyes full of woe,
Like windows of a house with bad memories.
A glint of red and dash of gold,
Flickers of silver near the temple.
Dangerous minds seek dangerous lives,
She wanted mercy and love.
She wasn't a beggar and yet she couldn't choose,
A heart that kept on beating hard.
Calling for the key to open the door of love,
Her hot breath against my face.
Trying to warm the cold hearts of failures,
To show that she cannot be ready to leave.
She smelt of winters and other seasons,
Days of emotion and of love.
A time when our hearts had the key to the door of love,
Then we lost it through our foolishness.
Another door opened to cold reality,
Beckoning the way to the answer.
As her emotions flew away,
My dog fell asleep in the vet's arms.

Kelly Charles

India '95

In a foreign country, on foreign land,
a different culture with rupees in hand,
had no inhibitions to sit and stare,
or prolong a fortunate glance.
We were white, we were rich, I thought so supreme.
Our clean cut clothes, and curly crimped hair,
our prominence there.

I edged across the concrete floor, away from staring eyes,
was confronted by a boy on wheels, for which I could have cried.
Perched upon redundant legs, folded away and out of sight.
His puny hand raised up to me, and eyes opened wide,
the agony on his strained face,
I know I could have cried.
With a wan smile, and a weary eye,
I realised then there, I was richer
but only than, the little boy perched there.

Patricia Bullen

Untitled

Demonstrators in the street.
Families struggling to make ends meet.
So many thousand "on the dole",
They've closed all the pits.
So now there's no coal.
Elderly people afraid to come out,
In case callous thugs should knock them about.
We have men who fought in two world wars
While the women at home helped each other with chores.
Life can't have been easy, it was worse than today,
With little food, and not much pay,
There were no microwave ovens, or washing machines,
And the most some of us had was a bowl of baked beans.
It may have been tough in those days gone by,
But at least we felt safer, you and I.

We could walk down the streets in the dark,
Our children could play in the park,
We could step outside, leaving the door ajar,
There was no need to be vigilant, watching the car.
What we owned was ours, and ours to keep,
And at night we were able to just go to sleep.

Jean McDonald

Ypres

I visit Ypres every year,
a special trip that I hold dear.
'Twas Christmas time in thirty nine
that Dad went out 'to hold the line'.

I was a child, one of four,
who slept in a shelter, 'cause this was war'.
I lost my dad, it's sad to say.
Thought of him on many a day.

As I went into adult life,
work, wages, I became a wife.
The loss of my dad just grew and grew
where he was buried I never knew.
"Write to war graves", I was told.
They sent 'details', so my story unfolds.

On Armistice Day I proudly stand
at a military headstone, poppy in hand.
Rank, Name and Number is what I can see
but no words can say what it means to me.

Iris Casson

In His Mind's Eye

Look deep in his eyes
What do you see?
Do you see hatred or glory to be?
The deeper you look the deeper you go,
the more you learn the less you know.
There is no use in calling out, no point in a cry
because no one can hear you and no one knows why
As his mind goes, keeps going
around and around
Where he is going, you can't touch the ground
Deep in his mind you can see all his dreams
With great blue butterflies and fast running streams
And as you leave, just drift away
You return to reality and face another day
Is it safer out here? . . . or is it in there?
Would you rather be back
drifting in air?

Michelle Bannister

The Voice

Jose Carreras is music to my ears
Erasing all my negative thoughts and fears,
When I am feeling down and blue
This beautiful voice will help me through,
To find purity, peace, and tranquillity all around
Relaxing in the beauty of its sound.

Valerie Daniels

Final Moments

Here I stand awaiting my fate,
The gas chamber cell will be my final date.
Staring down the long last mile,
I have my pride, I try to smile.

They open the cell and tell me to walk,
I'm feeling nervous as I try to talk.
My boyish smile has become a frown,
This is the end I'm going down.

I don't know why, but I try to scream,
Perhaps I'm hanging on to a final dream.
It's true your life flashes before your eyes,
Remembering yesterdays, those final good byes.

The nightmare is over, I'm at the gas chamber cell,
A few more minutes and I'll be at the gates of hell.
For the crimes I've committed, will they let me in,
Will Satan ever forgive me for my moment of sin?

I face the people I so longed to be,
I hope that none of them ever end up like me,
Sentenced to death for the killing of my wife.
The gas pellets drop, here endeth my life.

Spencer Cole

My Love for You

If my love for you was a home, it would be a castle
lived in by five hundred people.
On a monopoly board, a hotel in Mayfair.

A time of year would be Christmas
with friends and family around the tree,
or summer's song—full of laughter, light and joy.

If my love for you was a vision,
it would be lambs leaping
under the first rainbow of spring.
And, in nights of darkness,
a shooting star seeking out its sun.

If my love for you was a feeling,
... an exploratory touch of virgin white snow.
Or beneath a heated sky, swimming in a pool under fall.

If my love for you was ambition,
it would take me around the world—
But no matter where I venture
or things that I could do

I could not find the words to match
the love I feel for you.

Graeme Asquith

And the Whiteroom Glistened

They sat wrapped up in their selves,
and the tap water dripped, dripped, dripped.
No-one listened.
For the first time they opened their mind
and the whiteroom glistened.

She washed the bloodstains from his clothes,
He sealed her with a bedspring kiss —
The white man came with the "Happy Juice"
to hit the vein and quench the thirst I never miss.

She watched him leave with muted steps
I liked my lips—my mouth was wet,
the sickness came out from my nose,
he closed the door and some life goes.

Left thirsty from the injected calm
a battle of brains inside my head.
I am no longer my own person—
I'm all of them instead.

Won after by the power personalities,
I'm left alone again,
Nameless, isolated and empty, labelled only—Insane

Mia Jo McKay

Why Do Children Cry?

They cry when they can't go outside to play,
Or when they want their best friend to stay,
They cry when they're tired,
They cry when they're hurt,
They cry when their teddy falls down in the dirt,
They cry when they don't want to go to bed,
Or when their brother hits them on the head,
They cry when they can't get their own way,
And when Mummy says 'You're not being nice today',
They cry when they have to clean up their room,
They cry when the party ends too soon.
They cry at the loss of a much loved pet
And when they see their Mummy's upset.
This child cries cause the Daddy she loves,
Isn't there anymore to give her a hug,
Or to say 'Well done, Good try'
Or just simply to say.
 "Hey Shush,
Don't cry!"

Rebecca Duncan

Sky Delight

The sky a heavenly mass of delight.
The darkest sky opens to pure blue light,
Its heavenly blue is relaxed like a
Tropical summer's day, a sea on a
palm fell beach, just melts away.
White flakes of snow fall to make
the earth look heavenly and pure.
Whatever the day just look deep
into the sky a stressless wonder
of delight.

Shirley Ann Parker

Lust

Twilight dims the light,
Patched velvet screens the night,
The last lullaby sung sweet—
In dark and hush, she sleeps . . .
To Moon's gaze through chinks, she stirs,
Chiffon layers contour curves
Secrets and promises hiding,
Glimpsed peaks tantalizing
In sensuous, expectant state—
Restless, she waits.
Sequined velvet stretches her gaze
And in drowsy awareness she lays
Aside the covers, seductive, sighing,
To eager caresses abandoned lying
In silvered haze; hills and hollows tender
She surrenders.
Secrets and promises shared night-long
Till passion gone.
In swirling chiffon, on glimpsed peaks—
Satiated, she sleeps.

Patricia Maubec

The Fall

Revelation has stolen Eden
In the wake of your embrace;
The anthems of life resolve into shades of melody
Which summon the gods of my temple to ashes.
I grieve innocence at the eve of its awareness.

The promise in your mystery beckons without direction;
Without condition; without redemption.
Lingeringly, the sentence of being is absolved
By the apocalypse of life.

Deliver me love, from my misguided demons
And lead me to your own.
We can recover each other's divinity
Before the rose withers,
Before the flame consumes itself
And its light dissolves into darkness again.

Nadine Pilar Risso

The Song of the Nightingale

The long day has gone, the sun grows weak and pale.
All is still but for the song of the nightingale.
Echoing, beckoning for someone to hear, like the chime
of a grandfather clock his song is crystal clear.
"Sweet little nightingale I hear your cry, sing for me
once more before it's time to say goodbye."

I sit in the garden and feel the soft, cool breeze,
relaxing to the sound of the rustling trees.
Of all the birds there are none so rare, nothing as
sweet that you could compare.
Why does his song seem to haunt me so, holding
me fast, never letting me go.
He holds my attention and plucks at my heart,
when all the other birds are sleeping his song will
suddenly start.
Of all the birds I love the best it is him without fail,
I love my little feathered friend and the song of
the nightingale.

Sheila O'Donovan

To My Virgin Widow Bride

Dear Joan, when I behold thee in thy room
Which thou regard'st as but a prison cage,
Racked by the surgeon's knife, and by old age,
Thinking that life holds nought but pain and gloom,

Reflect upon the joys of days well-tried
Thou widow of a friend killed in Hong Kong,
And yet thou cam'st to me a virgin bride,
In marriage destined to be sweet and long.

Two splendid daughters blessed our happy life;
Many's the hour we worked, and played, and smiled;
For fifty years with thee I was beguiled,
Thou wast the perfect and fulfilling wife.

Recall the good times, happy once again
To join me in a stroll down mem'ry lane.

Rodney Barnett

Bucket and Spade

My bucket and spade is always to me
the best thing ever to take to the sea.
I love to play making a sand castle,
far away from the rush and hassle.
But leaving it on a deserted beach,
The tide comes in taking it out of reach.
I always take them on holiday with me
looking forward to hours of fun and glee;
they are a wonderful toy,
Suitable for a girl or boy.
Roll on to the warm summer time,
When I can get away from the city grime.

D. Snow

Despairing Soul

A sense of belonging, a sense of worth,
That's what I am searching for on this earth.
I have no direction, my mind is a mess,
I need someone to love tonight, of that I can confess.

Screaming voices in my head,
Just leave me alone is all I said.
They follow me still, even to my bed,
Sometimes I wish that I were dead.

This screwed-up world where all hope is lost
Can't be bought back no matter the cost.
The system is running, the wheels are in motion,
No one gives a damn about my emotion.

Politics and power that's what it's all about
Me I am just another bum on his way out.
They don't care about me not if I live or die
Just as long as I do it quietly and out of the public eye.

Richard Tippett

God's Love

Silence steals o'er the land,
As snow blankets the earth,
Such a silence, as can be felt
Within each small abode.

And as the sun rises,
A bird begins to chirp,
Doors are flung open and out children pour,
Their laughter filling the air.

God must never grow weary of such a sight,
It must gladden his heart to see,
That his creation is being enjoyed
By his children here on earth.

We are made in the image of God,
We are capable of great things,
And loving one another is the greatest of these,
Caring for those in need.

B. Kerfoot

Sweet Return

'Tis at that time when first I see,
Lent—lilies bright come bursting through,
I raise my eyes to the promising skies,
And rejoice at spring anew!

Now soon to fade away in the warm morning sun,
Mists like thistledown softly rise with the dawn,
While cuckoo calls and crow cautious struts,
Along the by-ways of new-grown vernal corn.

And what of he my fine gentleman friend,
Dressed in his swallow-tailed coat so smart,
Will he again return with his lady fair,
The one true love of his doting heart?

For 'tis when I make welcome that much-travelled pair,
On first hearing their song full of cheer,
I turn my eyes with gladdened heart to the skies,
Overjoyed both they and Summer are here!

Jacqueline A. Andrews

A Winter's Sunday

I wake quite early—the wife's first cuppa,
Yes after ablutions I'll get another.
Then 'tis the wafting odour of toast
And drooling thoughts of the Sunday roast.

Then hats and coats on for the PM walk,
The inevitable chatter, the friendly talk.
When nearly home we think of a brew,
The tea I'll make for just us two.
We're inside now in our sheltered bliss
Coats on pegs—give TV a miss,
Get out the scrabble, that wholesome game
Without which nothing appears the same
'Tis six o'clock looking forward to tea
And to watch a modicum of TV.
Our eyes get sleepy. 'Tis nearly eleven,
Soon to be tucked up in upstair's heaven.
Another Sunday's over another night's here
Then 'tis Monday again so very clear,
A day so stark, like a flag unfurled,
As outside we go to face the real world.

Nigel Membury

The Silent Scream

Quietly waiting for peace to descend,
Alone, as I silently scream for a friend.
Buried inside me, a wonderful dream,
Locked up inside, as I silently scream.
Waiting in patience, I yearn for another,
Silently screaming my need for a lover,
Solitude taunts me and when it is through,
I sit here in silence, screaming for you.

A. Wilson

Illusion

Silence fills the room as we bond
Illumination, but a feeble old beast
Calm is our friend, the still giant we grow fond
The forest hum sits near, of whom we love the least

Impatient is the morn, for it calls as we lay
Motion doth appear a distant thing
I must get on, it seems to say
Be off with you, twin hearts at rest slowly singing

The room grows cold and dark once more
O heavens, what evil trickery courted my day
For while I skipped and danced in love's faint allure
Life's clock mocked me silly and took me away

Kenneth Oboh

The Pirate

As the pirate sat in his favourite chair,
only laughter could be heard
from the small child sitting on his knee,
stroking his black beard.

He told her wondrous stories,
kept her shrieking with delight.
His dark eyes danced with mischief
and smile, always, shone so bright.

Misunderstanding helped years come and go
and families were torn apart,
often the girl thought of the big man,
whose spirit touched her heart.

But sadly, time, too soon, ran out
and when his health did fail,
he brought up his golden anchor
and with the angels he set sail.

I'll always remember his gentleness
and a pirate he will always be.
His laughter locked within the heart
of the woman, once the small child on his knee.

Gill Harvey

Live for the World

The world will live for centuries more
Regardless of our lives and how we lead them
But the only way the world serves its function
Is if we serve the world.
Nothing matters if you live for yourself
For without love you leave nothing behind
When you depart.
Life is only what you give it
Those who give it everything live to prosper
But those who only take from the world
Live to die.

Charley Kemble

Dearest Pauleen

T'was many years ago today,
That we both took our vows
The love I had for you then,
Just grows and grows and grows.

When I look in your eyes,
That flame still grows bright
As it did on the first day,
I had you in sight.

The warmth in your heart,
Your tender embrace
That loving look shines,
All over your face.

The hopes the dreams the prayers we share,
No matter what happens, I know that you're there
Darling you're few and far between,
My one and only, Dearest Pauleen.

J. T. Castle

Untitled

Every day he drove that way.
Leaving before the sun rose
Returning as it set.

Leaving his wife pregnant,
Then his children in the pram.
He left his son's first step
And his daughter's first word.

He returned to eat his dinner
Alone with the evening paper,
Before going to bed

Then one day a patch of ice
On that familiar corner
"Somebody died in that crash last night"
The man in the paper shop said
But he didn't know his name when I asked.

Paul Barber

Helplessness

I see pictures of helplessness
Of babes without a hope,
Of ever becoming fit and strong
Or given the ability to cope,
I see the helplessness of teenagers
Ravaged by drink or smack
Having fallen into a living hell
With no hope of climbing back
The world seems full of helpless ones
With eyes reflecting pain
"Won't someone reach out and touch me
That I may live again"
But the helplessness I fear the most is right within my heart
My helplessness to do anything, how can I play my part?
I give the little that I can, to causes that touch my soul.
But I want to reach out loving arms, to suffering as a whole
So I put pen to paper, and to my readers everyone
I say together we are not helpless, together we can get things done.

I. Spencer

Passage of Time

The years have gone so quickly by
where did they go, why did they fly?
to live the life that used to be
when you were young and needed me

You still need me, oh that I know
but how cruel is time, how fast you grow
from babies in your mother's womb
to adult life it comes too soon

You are married now with children too
I love them dearly as I love you
you love and cradle them, just as I
cradled you in days gone by

So treasure every day the joys
the tears and laughter of your boys
one day you will look then look again
To see not boys but full grown men

Brenda Honess

To Mick

I say your name, and people smile—
Yes, they know you
My heart gets warm, I feel a strange glow
Yet again, I long to meet you
But you're way up there on the wings of fame
The highest flier—the man with the golden name—Jagger

Everyone smiles and remembers
The 1960's, rhythm 'n blues and rock 'n roll
I wish I could have known you then
Out there on your cloud
I would say your name again
And watch the gathering crowd.

Deborah Trikomitis

Please Stay

How do I explain?
How do I start?
When all that I'm feeling is pain in my heart
I act all casual pretend I don't care
but after your visits it's obviously there
your daughter she loves you and she's only three
she gives you a cuddle as she sits on your knee
and when you are leaving she says daddy please stay
you then tell her you'll be back another day
The tears fill my eyes
and I'm wanting to cry
for the sake of my daughter
I smile say good-bye
we stand at the steps
As you wave your good-byes
it's only when I close the door
That I break down and cry.
Sharron Wise

The Loneliness

Have no fear, I am the loneliness,
Only I have time for you.
I creep into your life but everybody fears me.
Treat me with respect, don't send me away.
I want to tell you something!
Don't be upset with me, I mean no harm to you.
I give you the peace you deserve.
I help you to think, so that you will not forget.
I play with your thoughts, do my duties.
I protect you, that you do no harm.
You have time and you feel fine.
Some long for me, the ones who live in stress,
believe me!
You can be happy with me, don't be upset.
You can do anything you want with me around
and finally rest from life.
I don't cost you a penny, I come to you because
I feel happy with you.
No one disturbs your peace,
  you should love me!
Elizabeth Nowak

My Window Poem

The car drove down the lane
As slow as a snail
While I watched there, looking

The trees blowing
The wind howling like mad,
The flowers bursting open into bloom,
While I watched there, looking,

The poor bird finding twigs for a nest,
The man walking his dog,
While I watched there, looking.
Anna Clarke

Baba Baba

Baba baba you're so sweet
You've really swept us off our feet
Our precious cherub in your bed
Slumber to your heart's content.

Your dada is at work today
And labours on for not much pay
There's always hope it'll be steady
If not then we'll be ready.

We'll scrimp and scheme to save the day
and protect you come what may
If things get tough you'll be fine
Because we love you—you're divine.

May angels guard you as you sleep
We're trying hard not to weep
For we'll move on one lucky day
Where it's safe for you to play.
Lydia Tweed

Life and Cricket

Life is like a game of cricket,
Full of "Bye-laws" to obey,
The "Ins and outs" of daily living,
Simply will not go away.

There are always "Catches" somewhere,
In the things we have to do,
Often we "Run out" of ideas,
And try to think of something new.

Worries often "Crease" our foreheads,
Oh, to wield a perfect bat!
When we are "Stumped" for good solutions,
In cricket, they would shout "Howzat?"

In life, we sometimes meet the "Wide Boys"
Those who "Spin" a tale for money,
A "Wide" in cricket helps the batsman,
The bowler does not think that funny!

So when we say that "It is cricket"
Everything will be well done,
We hope to play a perfect "Innings",
And maybe, even reach a "Ton"!
Joan Letts

Reflections of the Past

I look in the mirror and what do I see?
A vision of my sister looking back at me.
With tears in my eyes,
I begin to smile.
I will always remember her lovely smile.
She suffered like others,
A pain you can't see or feel
You only know, it's so awful and real.
It has taken her smile, no more to see,
Only to remember,
And be passed on by me.
Lilian Collins

From My Window

As I look through my window from the comfort of my room,
I see the pansies in the flower tubs lying down in gloom.
A pair of squirrels play on the crisp and frosty lawn,
While bluetits fly from bush to bush to keep themselves warm.

The heron makes his daily tour and lands upon the fence,
He gazes in the pond for his breakfast with intent.
Could he be the one who dives with delight
At the oncoming motorway traffic in full daylight?

By noon the sun is shining and the frost has disappeared,
Snowdrops bravely open up and the blackbird sings for all to hear.
The Magpies and the pigeons are busy preening in the trees,
While pansies lift their heads and wave in the breeze.

The sun has gone now and dusk is fast approaching,
A fox, alert, sniffs around for something worth poaching,
The snowdrops have closed up tight for the night,
A Jay takes flight, all is calm, until another day is light.
Hazel Mary Paton

The Little Old Lady Next Door

The little old lady that lives next door
A gas leak, with a smell
The man that came to sort it out, too dangerous Love.
The old lady left in the cold, no one to talk or laugh with.
Wrapping her coat around her, hot water battle and a cup of tea,
Trying to keep warm as the temperature drops.
She feels so alone.
Then she remembers the Yuletide to celebrate
Baby Jesus was born in a stable.
I wonder if he was so cold.
This used to be a time for family to sing carols by the fire.
I wonder will things get better soon.
Maybe someone will remember the little old lady
Who lives next door
This Christmas time.
Kathleen Ambrose

The Lovers

Night's black tresses are lightning now
With a warm and rosy hue.
And all but one, the stars bright points
Have bidden him adieu.
Somewhere beyond my casement
A blackbird sings his lay
As night takes off his velvet cloak
And wakes his bride, the day.
She, in all her beauty glows
As crowned with golden sun,
With smiles and tears, the hours
She steers until her work is done.
Then, quiet she grows, serene and warm,
Exquisite in her charms.
To fall asleep in sweet content
Within her Lord's dark arms.

Mary Evelyn Slatter

Pure Gold

The Word conserved its Beauty in its Silence
All garbled chatter agony to hear!
Why waste energy in that which doesn't matter?
What is there in silence you need fear?

For Silence is the soil of fertile thought,
The prerequisite of all acts of the Creation
The mystic's land, a haven he has sought
For purging of all wasteful aberration.

This Silence that I speak of is pure gold
Hard won through alchemy and burning fire
As step by step, the steps themselves unfold
The ascent from the abyss of desire.

And with each step the noise below diminishes
'Til finally it seems a single note.
The Music of the Spheres in Silence finishes
That Overture Celestial Beings wrote.

Ken Alexander

Three-Score and Ten at the Millennium

Now on New Year's Eve of 1999
We hear the word of Celebrations Fine;
Romance and Excitement of Bygone Eras
Captured forever by the World's Carers.

Throughout years making Four-Score and Ten
We remember and tell of how life was then;
Our Elders told memories 'At The Helm'
It's then our turn to defend the Realm.

Discoveries and inventions were of the Best;
The World has put them to the Test;
No longer have we Pounds and Pence;
Going Metric, now cash in Tens is spent.

Now all Generations on Continental Holidays go.
Remember! We say 'Thank God' that is so—
So, Celebrating Go! Go! Go!

Dorothy M. Street

The Eagle

An eagle glides through the sky,
With a fierce look in his eye,
He soars round and round,
Whilst on the ground,
A field mouse scarred,
To and fro,
Always in a terrible scamper,
For it is a food hamper he seeks,
to take back to his nest,
To eat before he lies down for his nightly rest.

Still above the eagle so high,
Spotting the mouse who is always in a scurry,
Swoops down to fill his hunger pains,
The poor little mouse fills his hamper no more,
As he is locked inside the eagle's stomach door.

Sue Francis

Awakening

Although he was swimming upwards
he was still drowning
he knew it and the
rest of the world (had they cared to acknowledge it) knew it too

He had been struggling for most of his quite short life
his mind analysed this
even as he continued his fruitless struggle towards the light

Glimpses of his past
fought to be dominant within his conscious
alongside the more pressing desire to inhale huge lungfuls
of life giving air

Since being a young boy
he'd had idiosyncrasies that had
marked him out as being, well odd really

But that didn't matter now
self-preservation (which he'd often cursed)
finally lent a hand and he kicked for all his worth
and as he opened his mouth to accept the fate of drowning
he drank in nothing but sweet cool air
and his first thought? . . . Thank goodness I left her when I did

John Vickers

The Four Seasons

Spring is the time for blossoms and flowers,
Lambs on the hills, March winds, April showers,
Trees grow their leaves, birds lay eggs in their nests,
Farmers plant seeds to grow crops, not for pests.

Summer is the time for sunshine and play,
Crops turn to golden for making the hay,
Holidays, travel, swimming and sports,
Sailing and cricket and tennis in courts.

Autumn is the time to harvest the crops,
Leaves turn bright colours, food's cheap in the shops,
First Harvest Festival, then Halloween,
Apples and bonfires and fireworks are seen.

Winter is the time for frost, sleet and snow,
Fogs, mists and cold, days short, nights long and slow,
At Christmas families meet together,
New Year is greeted in every weather.

All year round the seasons follow each other,
Spring and summer, then autumn and winter,
The laws of Nature say what course to run,
As year by year the Earth moves round the Sun.

Susan Mary Robertson

On Starting the Menopause

Is this how it starts?
mumbling round the supermarket singing louder than you should
snarling at the hordes
Is this how it starts?

I saw you in Central Park pulling your trolley of life
bits of the city gleaned as you moved across the edges.

Bag lady Sad lady
Angry and glad
The fragments of your life spilling out for all to see.

How does it start
this drift towards insanity—or it is perfect clarity?

The giving up of conventions
The drink too much
The head on over drive

Does it start with a whispered hush or a screaming shout?

How are you different from I?
What marks the line — what makes you transgress?

How does it start?
Is this how it starts?

Dale Churchill

Horrendous H2O

Waves smashing, bashing, crashing against the
mystical, marvelous, magnificent rocks.

Rain falling pit-a, pat-a, pit-a
on the green, grassy, glazed, far, far fields.

When water freezes it turns into snow,
and starts to glow, but when the sun rises . . .
 . . . .It starts to go!

Waterfalls going, flowing, knowing
that it's got to get ready, steady for a . . . .

 . . . ..Smash! Crash! Bash!
Stephen Howsam

The Time Watcher

In the twisted echoes of this cry
Deep engraved thoughts am I.
Lost within my song of life
I swallow my words with ice.

Forever watching the birds fly high
Far away in the blue surrounding sky.
In my time lock I watch them go
Into crystal winter snow and then the
Blazing summer cries,
That do sweat from my eyes.

Here among my people's town
In this place of sight and sound.
Do these flies buzz too fast or too slow
On trains home.
Where I watch and sit all lost
In my box at times sold cost.

Once again to fall observing
This human world of life's full yearning.
An I inside this picture scene
Or a passer by in my own dream.
Ninder Sembhi

Run Off My Feet

I feel snowed under, I feel closed in,
I cannot cope with the rush and the din.
The children are shouting, the washer is on,
My life's more complex with each "mod con".
The microwave rings, then up pops the toast.
A peaceful solace is what I need most.
Mopping the floor, whilst feeding the cat,
Husband is shouting "The car battery is flat."
The baby is looking for his misplaced Teddy,
As I explain, "We must get ready."
Up to the school at last we all run,
I kiss the boys "bye", and tell them "Have fun."
Do a quick shop, then home for a break,
Just get a cup, a spoon and a cake.
Feet up with a coffee, I gather resources
Running a family, "why don't they run courses?!!"
Pauline K. Thomas

Growing

I was born so small,
5 lbs 0 oz at all,
But soon I shall have grown,
Out of my doll's clothes,
Into babes and then young girl's clothes,
For soon I shall have grown,
Into a young lady,
And hopefully one day
A mum I shall be,
For shall it be a boy or girl
I am not bothered at all,
Shall it be big or small,
I am not bothered at all,
Just as long as it is healthy,
Boy or girl.
Della B. Burwell

Untitled

Beginning to end is a well known road
Travelled by all by many a mode
Some ride a carpet edged with gold
Others they walk it and shiver with cold

Beginning to end is a well known road
Travelled by all by many a mode
There you will meet the strong and the weak
Forgetting not the mild, the meek

Beginning to end is a well known road
Travelled by all by many a mode
Others are good, some misunderstood
Have you really done all you could?

Beginning to end is a well known road
Travelled by all by many a mode
As for the sad and those in despair
Remember always of those who care

Beginning to end is a well known road
Travelled by all by many a mode
It's the love that's important while we're here
That cradles us softly when the end is near.
Vivien Nineham

God's Little People

Hello Mum, I am here because of your and Dad's desire,
A gift from God in a beautiful romantic fire.
But as you see by way of this very magic eye,
I am so different, darling Mum, but please don't cry!

My loving Queen, go home and consult your King,
I am sorry of the sadness that I bring.
Unite together and visit God's little people who are like me,
We have no hate but care and love, we are almost he-av-en-ly.

Combine your heart with mine, let us form a bond of love,
I promise you, my precious, I will be as gracious as a dove.
You see, I am special, my mind, my heart is true,
I'll see you on the outside, thanks Mum I do love you.

As I grow at first, I shall very little talk,
I will be slow in learning and also slow to walk.
Dad and Mum, please mould me into the way you think is best,
Also please remember, I am to stay, I will never leave your nest.

As I develop, I shall them begin to boast,
Yes I will be your butler, yes I will be your host
Yes I will entertain you in acts that are theatrical
Because I told you Mum, I know that I am special
Lewis Jones

A Poem of Love

I sit and write this poem of love,
as I look up at the stars above.
Wondering if you can see them too,
I whisper softly "I love you."

For though we are many miles apart,
you're always with me inside my heart.
It's like a cup, full to overflowing,
my love for you I'm not good at showing.

Fancy cards, chocolates and flowers
may satisfy you for a couple of hours.
But one thing that I really miss
is the perfume I smell, as we stand and kiss.

Until the day we're reunited,
My love for you I'll keep ignited.
In dreams, of passionate love we'll make,
and exotic holidays we'll take.

Making love underneath the stars,
on sandy beaches for hours and hours.
I wonder if you dream them too,
and again I whisper "I love you."
P. A. W. Tattersall

A Love for All Seasons

I loved you
with the fervour that youth brings in spring,
in all its innocence.
I loved you
from the very depth of my soul,
through loves timeless age.

I love you still
though the innocence of youth is no longer mine,
I love you
and our love will flourish
as a summer rose.

I will love you
tomorrow, when the autumn of our lives
is within our grasp
and winter's darkness
is our eternal future.

Susan J. Roberts

Daydreams

Lost in a daydream
I'm wandering through
A garden so lovely
Too good to be true.
Pansies, Petunias, in that garden grow
With Pinks, Polyanthus and sweet peas,
Hollyhocks, Heliotrope, Freesias and Phlox,
Lad's Love, and Lavender Blue,
Scented Stocks, Jasmine, Japonica,
All crimson and white.
Peonies, Primulas, for what a sight,
Candytuft, Narcissi, in delicate shades,
Larkspur and Lilies with heavenly perfume.
Poppies for remembrance and London pride,
Roses, Lilac, our favourites of all,
With swaying trees full of singing birds
The cascade of water, trickles in gleam
Make this my garden, too beautiful for words.

M. Gannon

How Do You Feel?

When we walk, how do you feel?
Are we on a even keel,
Do you feel how I feel
That all our feeling merge?

Did you say that you would never stray?
Did you say that you would not go away?
Did you ever tell a lie?
Could I ever learn to fly?
No.

Could we be free like the sea
Or a buzzing bee?
Just live in pure ecstasy
With places to go, places to see,
Places where no one else has been.

So, do you feel how I feel,
Do you see what I see
When I am looking in your big blue eyes
That look like the open sea?

Natalie Humphries

The Unsolicited Gift

Of course I know it is not sense
To make house room for the gift
You neither asked for nor required.
It has to be disposed of.

There was room in no-one's life
For your life.
So why do I regret so much your passing?
You never lived.
A few divided cells.
The only lack of sense is mine.

Christine Fretin

My Boy

Blonde, Blue eyed, just three feet tall
Oh! What a naughty boy!
Spills the flowers in the hall, breaks up every toy,
Always hates to go to bed, splashes in the bath,
Makes a mess each time he's fed, and loves to raise a laugh.
Such a dirty little face, ragged trousers too,
One shoe on without a lace, favour, tries to woo.
What can I do? I love 'my boy', he rules my whole life through
He looks at me with eyes so coy, the bluest of the blue.
I try to frown, I try to scold, his manners to improve
One look, and love he can unfold, heartaches he can soothe
I lay him in his cot to sleep, I look at him and pray
'Please God' this naughty boy keep safe
To wake another day.

Rita Downs

Grandpa

Did you know that I'd miss you, even now to this day?
Did you know all the words that I wanted to say?
Did you know how I wished I was there and I'd stayed
By the hospital bed where your body was laid.

And I knew how you hated that inhuman cell
The shuffling, the banging, the madness, the smell.
Sane minds can't survive where insanity dwells,
Feasting on souls to leave only a shell.

And I knew from the look in your eyes when I went
That I'd turned your heart leaden and your soul
had been spent.
And I knew when you asked who I was what you meant,
And that bitterness reigned in the message you sent.

Did you know how I wept when they told me you'd gone?
Inconsolable bleakness where happiness shone.
Did you know that your memory still makes me cry?
Do you know that I still want to tell you
Goodbye.

Alison J. Hunter

Hurting Deep Down

Why do I hate myself so,
my life is so confusing I don't no which way to go.
I feel so hurt inside,
all I want to do is run and hide.
I end up cutting myself to cause myself pain,
when all I want to do is pick up and start again.
I mark my body until it bleeds,
why can't I find someone that will understand my needs.
I'm in so much pain.
and I'm not sure if I'll do it again.
because the hurt inside won't go away,
It will come back again one day.
I've shed my tears and my fear,
I hope someone will soon hear.
Please help me I pray,
oh God, please help me to stay.

Michelle Taylor

Untitled

Dread not the coming of the unborn day,
Nor fear, as evening falls, the night too long.
Strengthen your soul, to keep despair at bay.
Assuage your spirit's sadness with a song.
Each day the gentle heart is grieved anew,
On every side man wields his blood-stained sword,
And they who'd stay his way are pierced through,
And they who plead for mercy are ignored.
The homeless seek for shelter from the cold,
The hungry beg for bread, and slowly die.
The dying cling to life, but lose their hold,
And in the darkness, little children cry.
Yet keep your faith, and in the gloom of night,
Have confidence in Christ. Pursue the Light.

G. Phillips

Life after Life

Dear reader you may at times agree
Our song at the end will cease.
But what if the tune will also serve
As a gentle and rhythmic release?

A release from the stress of mortal pain
When the body no longer responds
And the spirit will call for lighter garb
In another creative domain?

But even in violent death perhaps
A sleep of a healing kind
May calm the shock to those frightened souls
As they awake to the power of the mind.

The power which shapes the shade of thought
No matter how dark or light
To fashion a home of personal style
With the choice to enhance or blight?

World within worlds—what searching thought
May harbour a Grand Design
To bring us within a natural Law
For progress in measureless time?

Lillian G. Hart

Wishes

Oh could the world be a better place
Where children play with a smile upon their face
No longer would we need to fear the gun
Nor dread that war has once again begun
At last we will gaze into a cloudless sky
Where the lark with glorious voice proclaims "All's well!"
There will be Peace and Happiness in every eye
For finally there would be no more Hell.

There is no reason why this cannot be
For man alone can make the world a better place
Let Peace create the Joy that we would see
And fill our lives with a very special Grace.

Sally-Anne Hardie

The Feelings I Experience When Phoning Him

I hear the clock ticking away,
Like a small metallic sound in the background.
I look at the clock, 7:00 o'clock then 8:00 o'clock
Why does he always take his time to phone?
I guess it's true what they say,
Good things do come for those who wait.
But I could not wait, so,
I pick up the phone, my hands dripping with sweat.
I dial the number and wait.
As I hear a masculine voice at the other end,
My heart experiences the sound of drums drumming away.
We talk for a good length of time,
The sweat from my hands gradually evaporating.
As he acquaints me with one of his ludicrous jokes,
I laugh out loud, hoping no one heard.
What an amusing guy I think to myself,
He makes me laugh, sometimes he even makes me want to scream.
But what can I say, who can ask for someone more suitable than him.
The phone clicks at the other end.
I position myself in my bed, close my eyes, and slowly fall asleep.

Priti Patel

Spring

Birds are singing flowers are popping
Snails are moving frogs are hoping
Grass is green daffodils are out
All the flowers are starting to sprout
The air is filled with laughter and love
Nights are light the sky is blue above
Sitting in the garden listening
To the birds sing
Yes! Winter's over at last it's spring.

Linda Coulston

Fury

You've taken the legs from under me
And left me with no vanity.
Clipped my wings in reality.
No word of praise has ever crossed your lips.
Critical, cynical, stupid small town meanness.
When my cup overflows you scrape the dregs
And strip achievement to the bone
To bring me down a peg.
I note the applause but hear only your silence.
Won't you listen when I tell you
Nothing's achieved in condemnation,
But bitterness all round.

Katherine O Riordan

Silver Wedding

"Happy Anniversary my Darling,
Twenty-five years of married bliss.
Oh, how on earth can I ever forget,
The first time that we both kissed.
I longed to tell you for ages,
It was you who I dreamed of at night.
But I thought you'd say I was joking,
And we'd only end up having a fight.
Many a sleepless night did I spend,
Alone in my room late at night.
Just praying that you'd say you loved me,
And make my eyes fill up with delight.
That day you walked up the aisle,
You were the best bride there could ever be.
You looked as stunning as ever,
And you were walking there just for me.
I love you my darling just as much as that day,
And I know that you love me too.
Happy Anniversary my lovely,
I'm so glad I married you."

Debbie Morgan

Precious Thoughts

My most precious thought of all,
Is to hold you once again,
To kiss you ever so slowly
Over your gentle, loving face.

My most precious thought of all,
Is to know you once again,
At a steady, breathtaking pace.

My most precious thought of all,
Is to hear your voice once again,
Whispering sweet nothings, face to face.

So as each day passes,
It brings you closer, nearer to me . . .

My most precious thought of all.

J. T. Read

Soulmate

People often ask you how it is you feel today,
For the sake of courteous comment you say that you're okay.
But behind the smiles hides sadness.
Like the trees your moods do sway.
In the winds of discontentment, you wipe your tears away.
For the passing of a soulmate, you often dream away.
And think of times much happier when you'd play the days away.
You wake up in the morning, and their clothes you start to lay.
And then in tears of thunder, you start another day.
Why are the Gods so wicked, you ask them everyday.
For what was the reason they took your love away.
You will never find the answer, the pain you learn to bear,
And the anger deep inside you is the thing that does repair.
You'll always feel the sadness, the memories are still there,
But you shared their life completely, they always knew you cared.
At the time of life passing, when the angels came to bear.
They came to take the soul away, but in the heart they found
  you there.

Mark Pearce

Dream Free

A black highland horse I'd love to be
But my owner will not let me be,
I'm a black highland with my tail to the floor,
I'm battered and bruised like never before,
They say they love me,
But that's only when they want to ride me,
And then they will kick and hit and whip me,
And tell me that I am bad and that makes me sad,
Exercise I need but it impossible,
Without a good feed,
No hay have I had or oat and bran have I eaten,
And now my field is bare,
I dream of been stole or even just taken away,
For if some would really love me and care for me,
A real black highland horse I could be.

M. D. Cooper

The Clouds Are in the Street

"Daddy, come quick, the sky's fallin' down.
The clouds are in the street!"
The tiny girl looked on the town
Beneath its vast white sheet.

The snow had fallen all around.
At dawn a warmer air,
Condensing on the frozen ground,
Had formed mist everywhere.

How wondrous the wonder a child reveals:
So much to see and know!
But wonder the wise man ever feels,
For it is ever so.

Could all Man's knowledge my one mind fill,
Childlike would I repeat:
"My Father, so much eludes me still.
The clouds are in the street!"

Jim MacDonald

Big Trouble!!!

Hearts are beating
Time is racing
Pens are scribbling
The teacher's pacing
Up and down the classroom, like a stalking lion
With his bullying glare
"stop talking Brian", "But I didn't speak!"
"You're speaking now" (Under my breath) "moaning old cow"
"What did you say!", "Me! I haven't spoke"
"I'm not laughing Brian, it's not a joke",
"I didn't say it was"
"Don't answer me back" The class was all laughing
"Stand up Jack!" Jack my best mate, had tears in his eyes
He couldn't stop giggling "Everyone rise!"
The headmaster stepped in, he said nothing, just glared,
The whole class was silent, the whole class was scared
"Brian come here, and you Jack"
He slammed down his cane with a nasty crack!
He stood silent, tapping the cane that he held
Until he bellowed out "You're both expelled!"

Rachael Hunter

The Unknown

I'm scared of letting go, unprepared
of what I don't know
What will happen who can tell
But all the time trouble it seems to spell.

Trouble I can do without
So I'll have a good scream, and a good shout
This will relieve my frustration
It may even remove my temptation

The temptation I swear it is so deep
It makes my blood boil and my bones creep
This I tell you is all so true
So if you were me what would you do.

T. C. Weaver

Stop Fighting in 1996

There's so much fighting in this world of ours,
That just wasn't meant to be,
It doesn't matter who is right,
Because soon there will be no-one left to fight.
No trees, no grass, no flowers, no plants,
People have forgotten,
The greatest gift there is, is life,
No-one has the right to take that from you.
People are born everyday,
People die everyday,
Is it fair that some people are never given a chance?
It takes a lifetime to love someone,
A split second to take someone's life.

A. Lander

A True Experience

My favorite historical character is St. Francis of Assisi,
A Friar who taught humility and chose a life of poverty.
Being of gentle temperament, birds quick to understand,
When surplus grain he offered, took it from his hand.

With household shopping laden, one chill December morn,
I glanced behind, only to find, pigeons tagging along.
Perhaps God knows I'm trying a better life to lead,
More appreciative of wildlife, ever mindful of each deed.

I couldn't understand it, a saint I'd never be,
So why were all God's pigeons intent on following me?
Then I realized the truth, boxed cereal had burst,
This was a pigeon 'free-for-all' each eager for a taste.

How they savored flakes of wheat, sliced pecan and banana,
A honey coated breakfast treat with raisin and sultana.
St. Francis sprang to mind, of course, food he shared with many,
And there, upon the pavement gleamed a golden good luck penny.

Adela Graham

Untitled

A great man; my father—lover of all
He once stood proud and oh, so tall!
But gripped by a disease which tormented his mind
He took himself off, lay down, and died

My last words to him—"Don't leave me here on my own"
I said unaware he had to do it alone
So I searched 'til I thought my heart would break
Not knowing he'd gone for dignity's sake

He found his own peace
But how do I find mine?
Do I trust in the Lord
Will he send me a sign?

And the years go by, and my memories still haunt me
And newspapers give false hope to those who, like me,
Wonder if they'll be jolly 'old timers'
Or will they succumb to the living death; Alzheimer.

Pam Hoult

Vigil

This day, I stand vigil to you my love
On this, the day of your passing.

A key of love unlocks the mind
The sun, the moon, more happier times.

With my soul's eye I can see
Through your eyes I see.

It grows such an amber,
No sorrow, nor anger, just dreams of happier times.

A heart bleeds, a tear shed
Trickling down her cheeks.

No cares to earthly fire
The extinguish of a fading desire

So, this day I stand vigil to you, my love
On this, the day of your passing.

Robert Winter

In Sutherland

The breeze has muscle today,
   When the buzzard, motionless,
   Sits, sits, sits on a shelf of wind
   A cliff height above the headland;

When ravens ride all day,
   Wings half closed,
   Down the long wind-slides,
   Or helter-skelter down
   Twirling spirals of air.

This is a day for lifting heart and voice,
   For shouting in jubilation
   Of air and of freedom and of blood
   In sheer exultation at simply being alive.

Mark Walker

And Still I Dream

When I dream of people—I dream of you.
When I dream I'm happy—I dream of you.
Touch me where it matters,
But reach not for my heart
For when I dream of people,
We are always apart.
Touch me in the morning
Hold me, when I fear
My only hope is people
Because that's when you are near.
When I feel I'm hoping,
And thinking with my heart
When I feel I'm winning,
I've lost you from the start.
So, when I dream of people—I dream of you.
And when I dream I'm happy—I dream of you.

Jacqui Allan

Words from the Heart

I've tried to be a Mother, also a very good friend,
But neither of these! you can comprehend,
No matter what I say or even what I do,
These things! are not good enough for you,
I've tried so hard for all of us, in everything I do.
Even then! it's not good enough for all of you,
A thousand words would never do,
To explain that what I do! I do for all of you,
Put you on the right road, oh! How I've tried,
Because you all ignore me, a million tears I've cried,
I'm left with a broken heart, and some happy memories too,
Some of those memories sons! they are of you,
If that is all I can have of you,
Then sons! that will have to do,
With these memories, I shall never part,
Because sons! they are every part of my heart,
I never fail to think of you, I never cease to care,
If only you could understand me,
   would be the answer to my prayer.

Vie Jones

The Astronaut

I shall remember this day,
Here, in the green woodland;
The small stream purling along
On its way to the distant river.
I shall remember the sunshine
Casting dappled shadows through the leaves.

The spring flowers,
And sweet bird-song
Which steals across my aching heart today.

Yes, I shall remember
This sweet day in this quiet
Woodland glade, for tomorrow
I shall be in OUTER SPACE,
Perhaps never to return.

Cicely M. Hart King

My Childhood Friend

Our tree stands tall,
Its branches outstretched,
Its naked body,
Shivering in the cold,
Its branches bent like people crippled with arthritis,
Struggling to stand up straight,
Remembering its former beauty,
Filled with lots of berries and leaves,
Where we used to climb and swing with ease,
And the rustling of leaves in the summer breeze,
Our favourite tree.

Lynn Rivett

The Willow

Down by the river a willow tree hung,
Woefully restful, its anguish unsung,
Martyr to silence; a tragedy wrung
From the tears of the weeping willow.

Standing alone as the young couples passed,
Secretly rippling a tender trespass,
Feelings encapsul'd and gratefully grasped
By the tears of the weeping willow.

Deeper reflections the long stems imbibed,
Clutching the hopes that had long drifted by.
Watery comfort of memories revived
For the tears of the weeping willow.

Mellowed with moonlight and jewel bedewed,
Springing from sorrow the branches ensued.
Rustling the old expectations renewed
With the tears of the weeping willow.

Long leafy tendrils the water caressed,
Hiding the years in their shady recess.
All of the sadness of beauty expressed
In the tears of the weeping willow.

Julie Rayner

Who Made My Enemy?

Warlike thoughts, the evil thoughts of mankind
The killing, the killing the suffering all of a kind
How I wish my mind to peaceful thoughts
Could be,

That there never was an enemy
Why in my head this awful thought of victory
I who was schooled so thoroughly?
Who made my enemy?

These thoughts in my head so firmly
What made me see someone differently?
Who closed my heart from pity?
Can I be blamed for my family
Who made my enemy?

Martin O'Dwyer

Why

Why do I love you, can anyone say why?
There's magic and beauty like a rainbow in the sky.

Why does a river flow down the stream?
Why does our heart makes wishes when we dream?

Why do birds fly south when the weather turns cold?
Why are our tears so clear and our love so bold?

Why in the summer does the sun shine above?
Why when I'm near you is my heart filled with love?

Why do the waves crash against the shore?
Why can't this feeling last forevermore?

Why does the moon's glow shine on me in the night?
Why is my head so very heavy and my heart so very light?

Why do I love you? I will tell you why,
Why I know without you I will surely die.

Lisa Anne Archer

Distant Dreams

His bed is an unfamiliar territory
His territory is non-existent
A distant dream hovering on a falling star
Half expecting a caring hard to catch it.

His food, a dustbin delicacy
His thirst washed down with stagnant water
Visions of his dreams fall like droplets
From a bitter air of silence

His warmth, a memory half forgotten
Shadowed by the unconcerning chill
Surrounding his diminishing body
Causing his limbs to harden like stone

His language, an absence of words
That no-one hears or answers
An ignorance of today's mankind
Oblivious of innocence beneath a tarnished mask

His lost soul roves aimlessly within
He searches for his dreams of freedom
A home he can call his own
A distant dream hovering on a falling star.

Marilyn Holliday

Progress?

As we approach the 21st century
Let us look back at what we have achieved.
More advanced technology,
Remote controlled T.V's.

Computers to store information for us
To ensure that we never forget.
We have microwaves and compact discs
And now we have Internet.

Car phones, fax and processors
Brilliant! Cool! Neat!
Making life easier for all concerned
Yet we dare not walk down our streets.

Rape, murder and burglary,
Crime increases and our prisons grow,
Hospitals become short of beds and staff
And our schools need funds you know.

When we can walk down the streets, safe at night.
When people no longer covet or greed,
Assist not attack, love not hate
Only then, can human beings succeed.

Rose Anne Hush

The Fate of Eternity

Rising on the winds of change
I'm still, on high in thought and mood
The steam of power my view obscures
When through a space of air I move

With focused thoughts and feathers trim, I drop
My body close formation makes, I slip
Between the layers of air, I go
Forces tightly trimming my form, increasing speed and weight

My vision jumping left and right
With time and distance running out, I focus
I close on fate, with empty talons bristling sharp
To feed their need of fateful use

With speed and force I strike, my emptiness now filled
With weights increased, the banks below my destiny seeks
The need to rest now fills my being
I gather strength and look around, content

This form beneath my weight I view, its inner-self breaks free
To soon it rises on untroubled airs
With downward looks its spangled form it took
And saw the fate of life its stillness form now makes.

Keith G. Massey

Marion

Marion my friend was a lovely person
So kind and helpful to all.
She laughed with me and cheered the day.
And bad days flew away
But now my heart is heavy.
And tears now fill my eyes.
No longer can I see my friend
or see her lovely smile.
But in my heart she will remain
forever and a day
For now my loss is heavens gain
My friend has passed away.

Joan Muirhead

Untitled

I tried to write a poem, I didn't know where to start.
I figured I would cheat
but then I didn't have the heart.

"Plagiarize! Go on, give it a try!"
Said the devil on my shoulder
as I caught his beady eye.

"Don't be ridiculous, I wouldn't dare",
I replied as he gave me an evil stare.

"They've all done it, you know"
He encouraged me still.
My resistance waned and I lost my will.

"Alright", I relented, "throw me a line"
To which he replied,
"I simply don't have the time".

"There are plenty more devilish things to be done
than to steal others' poetry in the name of fun".

Karen Johnson

What Is Bliss?

When the weather is kind on the bride's big day
The farmer enjoying a pint, after labouring in the hay
A good night's rest, after weeks of pain
A comfortable seat, on the morning train
Asked to voice an opinion, and wonder if you should
The expression of a child, when told to be good
Exam results, that make you proud
Chance of solitude, away from the crowd
Achieving success, after trying for years
Told the 'lump' is benign, dispelling fears
Time to meditate, soaking in the bath
Relief when your straying pet, walks up the path
Finding the right place, from given the wrong address
Bliss is the release, of tension and stress.

Mabel Wall

Loneliness

I rot in the sea, sinking, drowning,
fearing that I will never be free
of the suffering that impales my heart.

For the life that I've led,
the uselessness that I feel
for the want of a life to live I shed the pain
grieving, like a hunger gnawing away at my soul.

Life has become an explosion of solemn decay,
I feel so alone, invisible in a downpour of a
heavy depression,
overshadowed by the emptiness,
the bleakness of a thousand days,
an eternal struggle from which I cannot see.

For the want of a life
I cannot live, I cannot feel
I cannot give,
causes an endless way
a life of shattering dreams
of my spirit and mind

Alan Moore

A Summer Day's Dawn

How I love this time of year.
With warm sunny days,
And blue Jamaican skies.
Rising early for tea on the lawn,
Watching and listening,
As birds sing a new dawn.
Then with a jolt the world comes alive.
Windows are opened, milk and post arrive.
Children near and far start to whirl again,
Drinking in the freedom,
As they run along the lane.
Soaking up their laughter,
Like a sponge in life's fresh bath,
Loving each and every day,
And wanting each to last.

Angela Edwards

I Wonder

I wonder if there's life on Mars
tall buildings even motor cars
I wonder if there's poverty and pain
and lots of snow and lots of rain
I wonder if they have rock concerts there
with "Guns n' Roses" even "Slayer"
to ease the pain
I wonder if they snort cocaine.

I wonder if the babies cry
when hunger makes them want to die
I wonder if their animals are extinct
it would really make you think
I wonder if there's road rage on Mars
when they crash into the stars
I wonder if there's mad cow disease
or anything like frozen peas.

I guess we'll all know soon enough
and Mars airways
will be all booked up

A. Spain

Desert Night

The wind whispers through the date palms
Whose blades rattle gently in reply.
Sand bleached white in the moonlight,
In the distance a fox's cry.
The sky above like thick, black velvet
Studded with crystal stars.
On the horizon the glow from a distant town,
Faint sounds from passing cars
Whose headlights sweep through centre stage
of the magical desert night
Visitor from another age and time
silhouetted in black and white.

Karina Al Muls

The Stable

May we come inside the stable, may we see this wondrous place
May we touch His tiny fingers and gaze upon His face;
May we greet His mother, Mary, and share her heartfelt joy
The one whom God has chosen to love this holy boy?
For we would come to greet Him and make here a fresh new start
For the Lord of all the nations is the Saviour of each heart.
May we talk to faithful Joseph, the guardian of the two
So lovingly supportive in all he's asked to do;
May we look around the stable amidst the hay and corn
Where ox and ass were waiting at the time when He was born?
They were quite the first to see Him upon this sacred night
They looked into their manger, and saw the Lord of Light;
May we come inside the stable, leaving doubts all far behind
To witness here the wonder—God's gift for all mankind.
Let us kneel beside our Master, and gaze upon His face
This is the wondrous message—that God is in this place;
Let us go forth to serve Him for He's in your heart and mine
This tiny babe of Mary, so human—yet divine.

Joyce Watt

The Graveyard

Walking through the graveyard
It feels quite cold
Recent coffins with flowers and a card
Gravestones that are young and old
A few people buried together
And some on their own
Some wanting to live forever
When others just wanted to be alone
A few probably committed suicide
A few in a crash
People who wanted to be cut off from the world and hide
But all their lives ended up in a flash
Some of them with their life ahead
Now it's been taken away
And now they're dead
Hoping they'll come back one day

Some of their lives were rotten
But by family and friends they're gone but, not forgotten

Helen Tolly

Seasons

When Winter's here the garden looks damp and dead,
then Spring comes and raises its head,
every bulb, bush, flower and tree, all alive, a new
world to see, colours of every hue, birds singing songs
anew, all by some miraculous hand everything right
across the land, all take on a different look like
turning the pages of an old familiar book,
Oh how can it be all God's Creation here to see, Summer,
Autumn, follow too, but Spring is the season of everything new.

M. Andrews

Covent Garden

A certain orange-girl once took her stand,
Enchanting Good King Charles in Drury Lane,
For commerce and the arts go hand-in-hand
In those bright haunts of fragrance and refrain.

A certain G.B. Shaw envisaged there
A Cockney flower-girl in her native setting,
For he could snatch a romance from that air
So rich in tortured vowels and plaintive fretting.

A certain echo of past glory lingers
About the Opera House—O Mozart! Britten!
For these and all the others, first-rate singers
Still honour with impeccable rendition.

The lettuce-heart of London, begging your pardon,
Must surely be the festive Covent Garden.

Mary Pratt

Love and Hate

How can I love you this much?
And how can I hate you?
I look into your eyes and see
All that you are
I then look harder and see your darker side

I want to love you but . . .
You hurt me so badly
When you look at someone else
I'm so full of rage
Then you tell me you care
And I'm confused all over again

How long can we do this?
Go on hurting each other
You know I want to be close to you
So stop pushing me away

Why do we play these games?
All they cause is grief
Love and hate is all that it is
And we have to stop it right now.

Jolene Garriock

The Long, Long Night

An urgent call roused me from my sleep
The rain outside coming down in sheets
Your Mum had phoned, you were on your way
So in my bed I could no longer stay

It was a long, long night waiting for you
Every hour thinking you were due
Your Mum very calm, so happy with herself
Awaiting the moment of this special birth

It is now nine hours since that call last night
At last you have decided the time is right
In no time at all you are safely born
And all of us gaze at your tiny form

Your Mum and Dad's faces alight with joy
So pleased they have a perfect little boy
Your sister, Maria, told she now has a brother
The two of you always to be there for each other

When I left you were sleeping in the arms of your Mum
And I thanked the Lord for a lovely Grandson
The sky is now blue, the sun shining bright
And all of the world is now put to right

Dian Clark

A Child's Mother

A woman who holds an everlasting bond
Of love with her child from birth.
A woman who protects her child if her
instincts predict.
A woman who advises her child on a daily
basis, morning, noon, and night
Teaches worthy from worthlessness.
A woman who demonstrates love and affection
and comforts her child at the appropriate times.
A woman who smiles and praises, encourages
her child's confidence to rise.
A woman who accepts all her child's weaknesses and
strengths.
A woman who knows her child better than any
other and wants all that is best for her child from
birth to adulthood, morning, noon and night.
A mother is a woman who is wise, lovable,
and good, assists her child to advance out
into the world and meet others in the social world.
The world respects mothers who hand down their
Qualities to their children
who in turn will also stand out in the world.

A. Aduwa-Ero

Little Miss Mary

A little girl called Mary
She knew there were fairies
She was told "There are no fairies on this earth"
By her rotten Grandma Berk

Mary didn't believe her "It's true", she says.
"I've seen them dancing by the pond with their
wings and magic wands. I spoke to them and they
tell me that they will grant my wish at 2 o'clock
and turn you into a cat."

Grandma Berk laughed at her
Her voice croaked, would never purr
At 2 o'clock Grandma Berk vanished
And was never seen again
Outside her house, a terrible wailing
meowing sound from an ugly old cat that
Mary had seen

The moral of the story is
Some things do come true
And don't believe by any means
It'll never happen to you.

Estelle Brightwell

A Walk on the Wild Side

A walk on the wild side amongst bracken and trees, overgrown grass, sharp stones. I am reminded of the wildness of life and the risks we take.

Running too fast in the fast lane out of breath, no time to think. Driving yourself too hard in a cool limousine. Will it meet the test it brings to heart and soul.

Oh to stand still amongst the quietness of water and trees to reach out and touch the calm.

What is life all about! Another gray hair and decline of being. Take time to see all that creation is saying with every change. Each season brings its own beauty. Do we take note of its perfection in time?

Jennifer Miers

Destiny Beckons

We travel far through life's maze,
While the serpent licks the bones of weary men,
Trying to find its secrets through ash and haze,
Some travel back where they have been before,
Knocking on the same old door,
Others go to fight in life's troubled wars,
Only to find heart ache, pain and gore,
Through it all love spins its web,
While matching, making, and breaking men.
Like a well in the desert where we quench our thirst.
And snow on the mountains as cold as the mind,
Destiny takes us to her bosom to make us all equal
Like when first conceived.

Sidney Jackson

Winter Days

Frost twinkling and glistening on tall
woodland trees.
Even the shivering school boy covers his knees
Hedgerow birds look for berries hard,
It looks so much like a Christmas card.

Crunching, noisy footsteps on the forest trail
The deer scatter hurriedly in the sunlight pale,
Wood pigeons, pheasants, blackbirds too.
Join in the chaos and hullaballoo!

Quiet again, the grey squirrel dashes this way,
and that, panicking rabbits o'er countryside flat,
Old tawny owl shifts restlessly on
His chestnut perch
For his nightly supper he soon must search.

Gently, drifting snowflakes fall to the ground
The earth is silent, no longer a sound.
Mother Nature sleeps quietly, the beck does not run.
Yet,—all will awake in the warmth of the sun.

Dorothy Ann Cundall

Blazing Colour

Rising sun of scarlet red,
Changes to gold and clears.
Shining down on mountains high
Stirring everything awake

Purple heather, lilac and white
Shimmers under sunshine and heat.
Nature cannot but enjoy a scene of scent and colour.
Birds and bees, hares and badgers
Enjoy this God given gift.

Cooling breezes gently blowing
Scatter clouds of white and purple glow.
Sweeping gently across the horizon,
Purple hue to heaven flowing.

Setting sun turns gold then red,
Causing mountains to seem ablaze.
Red and gold, purple and brown
Amazing colours seem ablaze.

Evelyn Coyle

Between Two Cities

It started with a letter, that dropped through the door.
With an overseas postage stamp, you wonder what message is in store.
It's from that beautiful country, that special town.
Where that special person showed you around.
With each letter comes the memories of past
You hope each letter would not be the last.
Each one you receive, you read between the lines
Mostly good, rarely bad, but always good signs.
Could these words, be letters of love?
Flown across the waters by a snow white dove!
What a beautiful way for a friendship to begin
Expressing one's thoughts, and feelings, with words from within.
Love between two cities over 600 miles apart.
It began with a letter, romantic from the start.

Alexandra Campbell

Innocence

On the beach the children play,
Dream their dreams and while the time away,
Build castles in the sand, run hand in hand,
Theirs is such a happy land.

In their world of make believe.
Shining eyes that do not see
The strife and struggle of this age.
Only history writes the page.

Make the most of childhood years, they quickly fly.
Laugh and run, have fun beneath an azure sky.
When young—daydreams—woven in the mind we find.
When grown, filter through our hands like sand.

Only children stay
In all their innocence.
For the lost tender years
We remember through our tears.

Hazel June Hooper

The King

There was not a single thing wrong.
Days come and centuries have gone.
I was sitting in my antique chair,
Thinking to myself, everything was fair.

I was wearing the Imperial King's ring.
I wonder, am I Ruler, am I King?
The truth, angel, devil and other thing?

When I kicked myself, I was not there.
Mysterious voices told me "you need mental care"
If I am not there, nothing else could be fair.

Even the day, night and devil are fair,
I will never sit again in the time killing chair.

Who is going to rule the world? I don't care,
I don't want to be the King, Kingship is not there.

T. Kaplan

Restless Waves

We've now come to meet with restless waves,
    dancing gently forever sustain.

Farewell O demanding rocks of shore,
    your silence chilled joyful hearts and more,

Oceans and oceans for us to trot,
    no hills or borders for us to stop.

The promising breeze sings for us to dazzle,
    the waves carry us far from trouble.

The sun will reveal its secrets suddenly,
    as the seagulls complete their act in harmony.

No leaving today for this show is to stay,
    and I am now part of this beautiful play.

Hanan Abussaud

The Dance of a Seahorse

Tucked into a wall supporting creepers of green
An arched dark oak dusty carved door is seen.
Groups of leaves, scrolls and fruit boldly stand out
Leaving niches and backdrops to catch thistledown.
In a web across part of this picturesque gem
Reigns a spider displaying its historical emblem.
One quivering strand is attached to the nose
Of a "Could do with a role" lion iron knocker.
Leaves lift off the ground in swirls of fringed tiers
Conkers appear round the step flaunting shiny veneers,
Strand to nose gives an angle for one leaf to tangle
So "Could do with a role" now acts as a stage.
That spider darts near to peer from the wings
As the leaf into metamorphose swings.
No booking was made, no money was paid
To watch "The Dance of a Seahorse" by Swirl and Fringe.
Standing room only does not matter at all
At this fine performance discreetly tucked into a wall.

Yvonne I. Wawman

Time

Born of eternity's vast dark womb
And slumbered long on glaciers still,
Was fostered by the barren moon
Time, quickened life the earth to fill,
The stars and seasons formed the plan
For calendars, sundials and clocks,
All fashioned by the hand of man.
Yet he breaks not, time's prison locks,
Balancing mystic suspense from shore to shore
And kindling illusion where men tread.
Time, life's stealer will keep the score
While fate swings on her pendant thread,
This span that lasts beyond our dreams
Of past, present or what future brings,
Changing, shaping and compelling, still
Redeems what has been ravaged by its wings.

Rosson Gaskin

A Mother's Love

People often say "you have two fine sons",
But in my heart I have three.
Two bright sons so fit and well
Though you'll always be special to me.
Two lovely sons who are my pride and joy
When just a fleeting glance of you
Had to do, my darling boy.
Two great sons who have brought me laughter
Who I couldn't ask 'would you look after?'
When I'm gone . . . .
My mental and physically handicapped one.
Two good sons with their own lives to live,
So my third one back to God I give
And ask Him to keep you in His care
Till I can come and be with you there.

Sheila Margaret Parker

In the Beginning

Of all the seasons of the year,
To me there is none so dear
As Springtime.
For all things new begin to grow,
And you know the feeling
Of senses reeling with the beauty of it all.
It is the promise of fresh start, new life, new loves,
All of these, but wait — that apart,
You will see nature spreads, it's all to show
The early flowers, the budding trees,
The Lambs in the field,
What beauty it will yield — that brown earth,
And you know it's all been worth while,
To live through Winter with a smile.
For very soon Spring will appear,
In all its gentle glory,
For each year, it is always the same, sweet story.

Freda Tester-Ellis

Trees

The oak tree proud and strong it stands
On many a Duke's and Monarchs' land
The Elm is regal proud and straight
With slippery bark, and berries late
The Sycamore, with flowers then keys
Swish and Sigh, in the breeze

The chestnut bears the nutty fruit
Children scramble for its foot.
The ash tree seems the lonely one
Mostly standing on its own
The birch whose bark is silver grey
Makes witches besoms so they say

The oak, the ash, or any tree
Is such a wondrous sight to see
There's always flowers, fruit, or leaves,
Until the winter months bereaves
Through the winter the yews and firs
Will the needles, and cones bear
Then there's always the prickly holly
With beautiful red berries, as their crowning glory.

Ivy Barton

Diana the Queen of Compassion

A princess both noble and brave so fit to queen this fair realm.
Made great through Royals and through statesmen of vision
and noble deeds. Was ever crusader more daring than she,
who walked the wine ress of grief, sorrow and suffering or
trod the Ruorta mine fields!
While statesmen in session debating the gun, their sports life
in balance, she, with courage, dons a Flak jacket and through
those minefields she hurries.
She touches the wounds of the scarred ones, her love
reaching out to them all. The blind, the maimed, the limbless,
the orphans, e'en babes in their mother's arms. Her heart
filled with anger against power-seeking, greed and ambition,
the drive to such suffering, pain and destruction.
In heart-rending words, eyes filled with grief, she throws out a
challenge—ban the guns, the knives, the bomb and the mines,
let peace reign over all. With little time left of this century
filled with wars, disasters and grief, let our thoughts breed
deeds of compassion and love for our fellow-beings.
Let's touch the hard hearts of our statesmen, helping them see
the less favoured, let's strive to see God in humanity and man
in the glory of God. Hence the call of this Queen of Compassion will not have been made in vain, and the year 2000 will
host in an era when justice and peace will reign.

Elizabeth G. O'Mahony

Dying Soldier

As that soldier lies wounded
He uses his last breath.
To plead to God almighty
To save him from death.

To greet his wife with joy,
To watch his young son grow,
To live to tell his stories
To receive medals he could show.

But not long after,
He had begged to live
Death had snatched away his youth
Taken all he had to give.

His death was solitary,
His body left to rot,
There were no church bells, only screams
And bullets which were shot.

No one came to his funeral
To pay their last respects,
But many others joined him in death
As in a War, only one can expect.

Marlena Ong

The Wind

The wind you can't hold it, but you know it is there,
Caressing your skin, gently ruffling your hair.
High on a cliff, with salt spray in your face,
Held suspended in time, lost somewhere in space.

Imagine the ghosts of loved ones passed on
The memories of faces, and a haunting sad song.
In the warm salty breeze, you know in your heart,
Death isn't the end, it's merely the start.

So don't ever be sad when remembering lost friends
Heaven awaits when life on earth ends.

Barbara King

Shift Worker in Winter

Frost sparkles on the pavements
Thin snow smothers green of lawn
As I shamble, shabby, tired to death
Towards the raw-edged silhouette
Of the factory at dawn.

A bitter wind cuts through me and chills me to the bone
But still I choke on my regret that I have lit a cigarette
As though the belching factory smoke
Was not already in my throat
And in my lungs and heart and soul.

There are others now about me, skeletal figures in the gloom
Mute shufflers passing through the gates
With no desire to contemplate
The sprawling mesh of steel and wires
That will hold us caged for the next 12 hours

Life now hangs suspended like my coat on the rest-room door
I'm an automaton in greasy overalls.
Interred within four leaden walls
And no tinted safety glasses could soften the infernal scene
As the acrid haze of acid fumes meet the fog of scalding steam

Tony Skidmore

The Cairngorms

High are these rugged mountains the Scottish Cairngorms
Covered by snow in winter and lashed by raging storms
Hidden in dense mist are deep curries and wild glens
So resplendent in the summer when the sun shines once again

The Cairngorms they stretch for miles and border Aviemore
They stand supreme in mist and cloud above Loch Morlich's shore
With slopes so dense in forest of the mighty Scottish pine
Majestic are these mountains of this Highland home of mine

I love to roam their forests and listen to the sounds
Of the bird singing in the trees and see the wildlife that abounds
Then as I walk on my way home as the day draws to an end
I know one day I will return to these lovely mountains once again

Anthony V. Carlin

Cries of Hunger

Dragons stones and which moans
deep and dark with weeping tones
that float around the midnight clouds.

Roaring hounds search the grounds
but food just can not be found
it does not just lay around for
those screaming hounds that scream
cries of hunger

Then comes the thunder and the
lightning that crashes to the ground
to dim the sounds of those hungry hounds.

It comes around and around
until the moment when you can't
even hear your own cries
As you lay upon the ground,
then there is now more sound

Zoe Maltby-Baker

There's No Place Called Home

Summer fades, winter's there, leaving all the trees hung bare,

Fruit has gone, leaves are dust, nature wills as nature must

Dark comes and the fears of cold
discomfort as winter nears

Heat exists in confined spaces but
not for those in other places

Winter's cruel on the street,
numbed bodies allow no deceit.

People busy going home, leaving others outside alone

No thought as we soak up heat of those
existing on the street,

No balance between our lives and
the quiet despair outside

No understanding of the fear inspired by winter moving near

Protection bought with sturdy locks is not available in a box.

Unseen by passers by who avert their
eyes to a place nearby

Some live well beyond their needs others
only fight and bleed

Whose referendum will enshrine the human spirit is not confined.
Evelyn Thorn

My Life Just Feels So Empty

My life just feels so empty
My smile is long and sad
I have a wonderful man in my life
So why do I feel so bad?
I've got friends there all around me
But when I need them they disappear,
My brain is mixed and muddled
What the hell am I doing here?
I had a special friend called Jim
He was funny, gentle and kind
Life got too much for him in his head
Now he's gone and left us behind.
Amanda is my only child
And makes me smile when I'm feeling down
She sees my mood swings come and go
But I didn't think this time she can.
I feel I'm just existing
I'm just stood here like a clown
I know that people do love me
But yet, I still feel on my own.
Julie Baggott

Late Night Movie

I blunted the edges of grief with life in the fast lane,
Making new friends and travelling the world.
I built up my life again, brick upon brick,
Carefully plastering over the cracks.
I walled up the past.

At last my daylight world stands firm and strong again
And, if I think of you at all, I smile and say
That what is past is dead and gone.
Now I am free.

But when the dark has come and I close my eyes to sleep,
Then starts again my late-night movie show.
Flickering, moving pictures of the past.
The well-remembered scenes and those grown dim.
The full-supporting cast, the minor roles.
And you, at the centre, glittering star,
Stealing the show.
Making me laugh and making me cry,
Crumbling my world into dust.

Now I am free of you.
Who am I kidding?
Heather Goddin

Apple Blossom

Loveliest flower, within thy chalice hold
The glowing apple, born of English rain
And busy buzzing bees of black and gold
Until the luscious fruit to press is ta'en
And treated with historic art and skill
In Wye's great vat. The big brown bottles fill
With cool, crisp tang of cider, to revive
The thirsty worker, breaking from his toil
Or at his English dinner of roast beef
Or after work, where he would seek relief
With merry jest with friends. Release the foil
Of witty Puck within the sparkling foam
And let us drink to industries of home.
In winter's frost or summers steaming heat,
The dew within thy cup is hard to beat.
M. Stephenson-Ellams

Things I Wanted

There's a doll I never had, and really wanted
but the one I got I loved so very much
cuddled her with glee
because you must agree
The other was to look at not to touch

Then the party dress that I had set my heart on
it was beautiful, and put me in a trance
But I knew if I could wear it I'd be so afraid to tear it
That I never would have had a single dance

Then the man I never had, and thought I wanted
I am thankful, and so glad that fate knew best
For I love, and know I'm loved
And I know the world can see
That true love always stands up to the test.
Annie L. Price

A Country Churchyard

The old grey church and its graves have seen
    Thousands of seasons come and pass.
A high-sky sun is beating down,
    As a heat haze hovers over the grass
Wandering weeds tumble and trail
    In joyous abandon amongst the stones,
Beneath which lie those cast off bones.

Age, weather and moss now all combine
    To obliterate many a name a date.
But on many of them the word 'beloved'
    Has survived the ravages of time;
As if this word can outlive fate.

Under a yew tree there's a seat,
    Battered and old, not now complete;
But still it offers a cool retreat
    Away from the blistering, shimmering heat,
And a chance to rest one's aching feet;
    And sit . . . and dream . . . and sleep.
Mary Coles

Who Ever Said Humans Should Rule

Who ever said humans should rule?
I never heard God say so,
Who said humans are better than animals?
Who said this I do not know,

If I meet them I'll tell them a thing or two,
Something I think they should know,
That dogs or monkeys or lizards or cats,
Could do better at ruling our world.

For they do not riot with guns and arms
And fight for their countries so called rights
They eat, drink, play and all sleep happily at night

I think we should learn a lesson from these beautiful
creatures of God.
And together let's protect our needy world.
Shyrell Kelly

Sky Gazing

Sky gazing forever, all so amazing,
Clouds drift along punctuated, by blue sky,
No untruths, no more lies, always looking to the skies,
Tree tops blowing in the wind,
Must be nice to be a tree, to live a life so free!
Are they free? Tied to the ground for life,
Only chance to move in the breeze.
They're not free, neither are we.
Grateful I'm not a tree, stuck in one place,
So turn my face to the sky,
Forever gazing at the sky,
Sky gazing forever.

Michaela Shaw

Seasons

Spring emerges miraculously from the depths
of winter's tightened grip.
Abundant shades of green toned hues reclaim
the once bare landscape.
Delicate blooms dance freely on warming
winds, anticipating summer's distant call.

Bursting forth with a profusion of magical
colour, summer takes the stage.
Life abounds in every direction.
Vivid shades greet widened eye.
Pungent aromas float gently on life's course.

Autumnal tones of yellow, brown and red,
begin to capture summer's heady rule.
Chill winds between the trees pick up the
copper carpet of leaves, and claim their hold,
as pollen no longer drifts upon the breeze.

Then winter turns its icy tourniquet,
as once young life is squeezed from hedgerow, tree and meadow.
Though lying dormant beneath the frozen earth,
is next seasons' life-force waiting for its birth.

Ian James Tovell

The Arrival of Death

Listen for the Crow,
The time has come to go,
The blood, it will now pour,
On shattered glass and door,
Innocence lies sleeping,
Death comes on tip-toes; peeping,

Listen for the Owl,
Before the cannibals growl,
Death lies on powdered snow,
In the dark where light won't show,
Innocence wakes in fright,
As Death comes round to steal the night,

Reena Mistry

Flight of Fancy

There are those who won't believe me
And others who say I am right
But I saw an UFO today a most remarkable sight.
I drew the curtains to look at the sky,
And there before my eyes
An object hung suspended
Against the pink sunrise.
I gaze in wonder, deep in thought.
Was it from outer space
Or an optical illusion,
My thoughts ran on apace.
If there are intelligent beings in space
A theory that is rife
What will they think of us here on earth
With our endless wars and strife?
Will they come to teach us "Peace on Earth"
Or leave us to our bombs and wars
And endless loss of life?

Iris M. Rutherford

Lost Love

The minutes slip by into hours, and I think of you,
The hours drift by into days, and I long for you,
The days are lost by the night,
And my dreams are filled with your presence,
As the time passes by with a sorrowful yearning,
My love for you ebbs like the sands of time
With the pain from a heart that is burning.

Kim Allen

The Changing World

Once upon a time fairy tales were told
Soft lullaby songs and nursery rhymes
To sleepy heads nestled in their beds
Dreams of wander and happy times.
As morning dawns to the games they played
Hopscotch and marbles then skipping rope games
Cigarette card flings and the pals they made
Hide and seek and rally vo fames
The chalk on the wall was always rubbed off,
The bouncing ball, hop skip and a jump
These games all forgotten, gone down with a bump.
Ribbon bows in your hair you were a little toff.
Now the roads are full of petrol fumes,
The play streets have all gone
The parks are all broken, where the band never plays
The language of children and bullying is fun.
Maybe times will change once again
The one parent families will grow up once more,
To bedtime stories and happy games
To fun and true laughter and an open door.

Blanche Naughton

Passionately

Take a deep breath,
Do you feel it?
It is burning within, hot and red with pulses of purple,
leading you towards your inner desires.
If you are free you will run,
and with your fiery wings you will fly.
It is passion and passion is personal truth.

Anthea Nicolaou

Bluer Gold

If you're not the praying sort, or pray with some restraint.
Remember we're all human we can't all be a saint.
But if you reach out a hand to help a fellow man,
Or even give a friendly smile as often as you can,
Then you'll be doing the very work God put us here to do.
To do good unto others as you'd have them do for you.
A nod and smile cost nothing but mean an awful lot.
For the love we give to others
Is the most precious gift we've got.
And while we're philosophizing shall we just take a look around,
And wonder at the treasures with which our lives abound.
Let's gaze up at the ever changing sight,
Of the sky, lit by the sun by day, the moon and stars by night
And closer to home the living things
The birds, the flowers, the trees.
Surely no Aladdin's cave e're hid such jewels as these.
Then thank Almighty God for this land which gave us birth,
And when you say your prayers tonight say one for Mother Earth.

Ted Baxter

The Idea

Floyd Lloyd and the brothers Boyd
Ingested some small geometric shapes
Wondering, the three of them toyed,
With an idea involving capes.
Capes made for the intake, and made his presence known,
On the lake, with a fake dinosaur bone.

Andy Brighty

The Reprieve

From the bonds of closing shadows freed,
Run, swift with flashing wings of life
Unfettered in the sunlight; speed
Across verdant nature's vibrant fief,
Where the wild free spirit of the wind acclaims,
And friendly fronds and flowers wave welcomes.
Chase the clouds to catch the sunbeams lancing;
Thrill to the rolling thunder of the sea,
Throw glistening showers with light feet dancing
Where white swirled wavelets share my glee.

Now, in this new wrought temple of the sun,
Pause—and tiptoe down the path of close affinity,
To find her, wrapped in mists of anxious melancholy,
Watching, waiting distant news with sad serenity.
Gently smile away the veil. Then ecstatic
Kiss, and swirl her dancing, laughing, singing,
Through all the harmonies of joy laid bare,
Till ardour rests upon the rainbows rime.
Thence gaze across a future gained, to where
New dawns call beyond the curves of time.

G. Phillip G. Robinson

Untitled

I drift on a sea of loneliness,
Arrogance and intolerance my boat,
The distant shore my friends.

I drift away and away
Because I cannot overlook
The pebbles of their faults.

Overhead the grey clouds
Is formed my self-pity,
The stormy sea is full of my selfishness.

Hazel Hands

Life and Times of a Latter-Day Hermaphrodite

Embryo - birth - baby - child,
life - living - love:
Marriage - commitment - responsibility,
resentment - loss of individuality;
acquisition - pain - immortality:
Debutantes metamorphic leap - cloaked in metachrosis garb,
impact - refracting - visual acuity;
chic - cliquism - antipathy:
Claws drawn - innocently plunged,
deep - into - virgin flesh;
hurting - bleeding - pain - dying - death:
He - she, me - we;
I one!

Paul T. Fensom

He's No . . . Tramp!

He holds back and doesn't know
what to do or where to go,
He cries for help, don't mean to beg
but has no home, has no bed.

As people pass they may look down
But, only to shake their heads and frown,
They see all that's being shown
A dirty huddle, a beard that's grown.

But deep inside under the dirt
they cannot see the man that's hurt,
He had a job, he had a wife
and all the good things that make a life.

One knock down he lost it all
And now leaned up against a wall,
He has pride, but has no choice
and as people ignore his worn-out voice,
he sits there ready to rot away
to him just another empty day.

Sarah Louise Winch

My Borrowed Life

I've never looked comely,
I live a life of dolour,
Having no leg to stand on,
In a ghetto, I was born and bred,
I feel naked at borrowings, of my borrowed life.

Borrowed means of living,
Add more dreams, to my life of dreams,
As I patch my garment.

On the breadline, My parents have long been.
For a dear son, they had to borrow a coin,
For fee, to've me educated.
It's now an old, bad debt.

Calamities 've come in plenty,
I've got a neighbour's daughter into trouble.
And poverty makes me hum, an aria of my bane,
As the neighbour demands, I borrow the title,
To acquire In-laws, ere his ire renders me doom.

Left or right, where do I go,
To avoid borrowing anymore,
And I was born to a life of troubles?

Kamau Wa Njuguna

If Only

If only—I could love you If only—you were here
If only—I would hug you If only—you were near.

If only—I could make you happy
If only—instead of sad If only—I could love you
If only—life wouldn't be so bad.

If only—I could kiss you If only—I could touch
If only—I would love you If only—it wouldn't hurt so much.

If only—I had read your mind
If only—I had known your heart
If only I had seen the signs
If only—we would never part.

If only—we had never met
If only—but it's fate
If only—I'd have learnt
If only—to love and not to hate.

If only—I would love you
If only—you could see
If only—I could love you
If only—you would love me . . .

If only!

Jenny Pearcey

Storm

The first light of dawn unleashed the storm.
Raving its wet bitter kiss on the waterfront.
Lapping the awaking morn with its reckless form.
Scorning the receding night, amiss, like an utter truant.

Over the moor it raged a resounding laughter.
Dribbling of chaos, stirring with its fiendish dance.
Everything it touched, it ravaged, and spurned further
Like a bogus trapping, squirting from troubled lungs.

Into town it heaved with a heart—full of wrath,
And a mind screaming from pain and misguided intention.
Its roving eyes beamed with lustful writhe,
Seeking understanding, whilst it rained its decision.

The swift taste of panic erupted in the violent breath,
Heightening the sense of terror which gripped the town,
And the confused scenic beauty distorted in the stormy path.
The local's cry filled the hour, their grief watered down.

Time glanced at the storm, questioning its motives,
Daring it to do its worst. It peered at its handiwork
Panting, too exhausted to strum again the fears of the natives.
It turned slowly west, and disappeared into a speck.

Jacob Asare Brobbey

But That's Life

I sit there and watch them
dying.
They're so helpless, all the young children
crying.
They feel a million miles away
dying.
All I can do is sit there watching them
crying.
"Why Mummy, why are there people in Africa
dying?"
"I don't know darling, look at them still
crying".
"It's life" says Daddy.
"It's not" I replied.
"It's ignorance."

Samantha Bourton

Twilight Goodbye

One night as I lay dreaming, all tucked up in my bed,
I dreamt I saw an angel, who gently stroked my head.
She looked at me and softly spoke; she said, "You are my child,"
Her face was kind and gentle and I recognized her smile.
She wiped the sadness from my heart and teardrops from my eye,
She said, "There wasn't time before to say our last goodbye."
She was the image of someone who died not long ago,
She kissed me on the forehead and said, "I have to go."
She looked just like a princess in soft embroidered lace,
My hand reached out to touch her, but she faded without trace.
Did I really dream it, or was she really there,
Are there really angels who come back to show they care?
I travel on life's journey never knowing what it means,
Do you believe in angels who visit in your dreams?

Christine Hanlon

Untitled

I wake, I listen, all is quiet, not a
sound can I hear.
But something woke me;
I look out the window, not a soul do
I see, only the trees lightly swaying
in the breeze.

Then I found what woke me.
It was a stray cat, who comes every night.
He sits in a branch of the tree next door,
and looks longingly at the window.
For sitting at the window is the most
beautiful cat he has ever seen.
But all he can do, is look and dream.
She knows he is there, for she preens and prances,
and looks about her to see if her mistress
spots him in the tree.
She knows she will be cross and shoo
him away but also knows he'll be back
another day.

V. K. Dilloway

Silence

They say that silence is golden
But where can it be found
For everywhere I seem to go
There is so much noise around

The whine of a vacuum cleaner
The noise of a pneumatic drill
The sound of children playing
With their voices oh so shrill

The roar of rush hour traffic
The chattering on the train
When will this dreadful noise stop
And I find peace again

At work the printers clatter
The telephones persistently ring
Back home I go to bed and sleep
But all too soon the birds start to sing

Mary E. Penney

Us

Two lovers strolling arm in arm
along the golden sands
we were in the forces then and
could not know what would happen next,
or what or where or when
but in this sublime moment in time,
blissfully happy all else forgotten.
The months rolled by and then came,
that happy demob day
mixed blessings of joy and sorrow!
I could not let you go
I loved you then as I love you now!
Some fifty years ago.
Then you said you would be mine,
so we tied the knot and wed!
and raised a family,
four boys in all, as happy as can be!
Now they come to visit us with their families!
Life's bonus! In grandchildren
just for you and me.

E. W. Middlebrook

Mankind

The soul starts to burn as God drifts away
The devil walks the earth on this summer's day,
Man found intelligence or intelligence found man.
Evil did fester and deceit formed a plan:
One up on your brother, one down on mankind,
Tear out your soul, see what you find.

But who will save us, who gives a damn,
Though heaven is waiting what's the master plan?
Walk on willing not wanting the old
Or hold on grimly and to hell with the bold.
A ripe old death at the hand of our greed
Still grasping at the money, that which our heart pleads.

Geoff Richards

Children

We never asked to come, you brought us here,
We left another world to come to you.
Although our memory of that place is like a dream,
We look around us here and think what might have been,
We are merely copies of yourselves, the way you were,
Your planted seed, with all your failings and your grace.
Beat us if you must, what can we do?
But suffer at your hands, ah yes, it's true.
Starve us and abuse us, it's not unknown,
You are strong, but we are weak and so alone.
When the years have passed and we have grown,
We stand before you, 'the finished product' as they say.
Do not blame us for mistakes, they are your own,
You were the 'clever sculptors', we the clay.
We try to do our best, but if we fail,
Remember, perfect blooms from imperfect seeds, cannot be grown.
You are us, and we are you, it must be known,
Our good points and our bad points,
Are your own.

Linda May Gubbins

Your Sacred Peace

Behold. This green and peaceful land,
Outspread and gently undulating.
Fields formed like a patchwork quilt,
Laced with hedgerows, circulating.
Enchanted are the secret places here
Few have ever trod.
Amongst the cedars, their protective branches
Bowing to the earth is where you'll find God.

Behold. The Sylvan lands and their imposing solemnity.
Hush! A dawn age susurrus: The numinous charm.
Presiding the numen, you feel no alarm.
Yet across the space a new age takes place.
You hear voices and strange laughter.
What will become of your world hereafter?

Alan Brett Smith

Why?

Why,
As we age from child to grandparent we witness new physical creation and sights that would make our inner souls cry out in utmost anger?

Why
Is love what it is?
Why does it rip us apart?
We think we rule it but it rules us,
A roll of the dice we have no call.

Why do we battle our souls never die?
We are only postponing what must be
Until the tasks are done,
Until we become one.

Why were we banished to this small desolate place?
In a way beautiful but only as the ignorant ones amongst us remember.

Is beauty really what it is or is beauty ugly for what it could be?

We bury our dead alive, they're with us always,
Watching us, haunting us.

God didn't make us we made God.

James Wood

My Love Has Gone, Where Memories Enshrine

My love has gone where memories enshrine,
The girl that knew no love but mine,
But torrents of tears will not assuage,
In terms of time, difficult to gauge.

Eyes of cornflowers blue, hair of spun gold,
These things I remember, none that I am old,
But time will not dim my love for her,
It stays strong as ever, after all these years.

In days gone by, when she was mine,
Living by the river Tyne,
Oh! For those halcyon days of yore,
When we were young, but not any more.

Bravely and lovingly, she raised our two sons alone,
Missing my support, and no one to atone,
For my absence, and strength, she needed me about,
Faith in each other, was never in doubt.

Come to me darling on fleeting wings,
Come, while a triumphant chorus sings,
Of a love that triumphs over all,
While the cheerless years that separate us, one by one fall.

Fred O. James

A Song of Love

From beneath last Autumn's golden floor,
Snowdrops raise their tiny heads,
Dresses, white with purity, to adore.
Spring is here, to show us God's Love,
If only we will look and listen.

Across the moors, once cold and bleak,
A rich blanket now unfolds,
Purple heather shimmers in the heat.
Summer is here to show us God's love,
If only we will look and listen.

Over the hill tops and through the dale,
As if caressing each tiny flower,
The mist hangs so gently, like a veil.
Autumn is here to show us God's Love,
If only we will look and listen.

Above an eiderdown, soft and white,
Summer's last rose hangs its head,
As if nature had forgotten its plight.
Winter is here to show us God's Love.
O Father, help us look and listen.

Christine Campbell-Sturgess

How Long Is a Piece of String

How long is a piece of string?
A meter long, a titchy thing
To tie your little brother up tight,
To make him scream and make him fight

How long is a piece of string,
From here down to the garden wall
From flower bed to ten feet tall,
Past the bushes or round the pond
Across to the shed and far beyond.

How long is a piece of string
A reef knot far from the sea
Whose tied was always meant to be,
The puzzle in this verse is knot
Quite what it was supposed to be.

How long is a piece of string
Is someone pulling it, I don't know
From nappy pin to graveyard hymn
Long enough for a highland fling
Because life's too short for a piece of string.

Stuart M. Holmes

God's Gift of Flowers

There are roses in our garden
and daffodils there too.
Honeysuckle there of course
and violets of blue.
Pansies of colour bright
and scented stock in the night
Droopy heads of blue bells.
Crocus and snowdrops, coronations too
Forget-me-nots and dahlias pushing their way through
Blue and white loballia, a bordering part they play
Wallflower and sweetwilliam, colour bright and gay
and all the other lovely flowers that brighten up our day
Let us all remember God's hand is in it all
He planted all the little seeds
However great or small
He sends us lovely sunshine
He also sends us rain
Thank God for all the little flowers that spring up after rain

R. J. McFarland

Always Aware

Stop a minute, breathe in the air
Life is seldom without a care,
But notice the view—whether green or stone
It does not matter—you are not alone,
All that is given for us to share
Be truly thankful and always aware.

Olive Jones

First Fall of Snow

Cold November Morning,
It fell without warning.
Icy snowflakes, delicate lace,
Fluttered on lashes, hair and face.
Descending flurries, heavy now,
Pile so high on every bough.
Feathered foliage frozen white.
Conifers cuddle close, so tight.
A last blushing rose, has turned so pale.
Her frosted head, she looks so frail.
The lawn, now a carpet looks so pure.
Not yet a footstep has it endured,
The birdhouse with its brand new thatch
That served all spring the newly hatched.
All the shrubs, now scarcely seen.
Except berries of orange red and green.
Glowing like lanterns they burn so bright,
To feed the birds, with no supper last night,
The garden is sleeping, a slumber so deep.
Concealed in a blanket, so silent — asleep.

Linda Clark

Day at the Camp

Shivering in a corner,
Tearful and afraid,
Each melancholy soul
In silence and adversity, prayed.
The evil officers' daunting shadows
Flicked across pools of light,
Trickling down the damp, dark wall,
And sliding off into the night.
The screams of poor, innocent souls
Echoed all around,
The impassive officers' eyes bored into their minds,
As they whimpered on the cold, hard ground.
Then he came; the man they feared would come.
Who was next? They did not know,
But the news was here;
Some of them had to go.
A list of names was read,
Someone let out a despairing, fearful cry,
"That is me, it is the end,
It is my time to die."

Amy Barnes

Chilli and Pepper, The Sauce Boys

Two little kittens, with no inhibitions
Were looking for something to do.
Said one to the other, "Let's go and ask mother
Please can we go to the zoo?"
With a lot of conferring, demurring and purring,
She wearily said "Okay."
With numerous warnings and licking and yawnings,
Then finally, "have a nice day."
But when they got there, the cages were bare,
The keepers had gone on Safari
So home they did come
With faces so glum
And spent the night drinking Campari

M. Denyer

Hardly Known (The Cruel Man)

I smell your stink through the open door,
Your footsteps echo on the concrete floor.
Your breath lingers with an odious smell
I hear your voice as you begin to speak.
Hard, callous and cruel utterances through rotten teeth,
An unpopular man, loved by none
For the unkindnesses you have done.
What quality of life you must have!
Material gain, but no love, warmth or joy
To liven your soul.
Hardly known by anyone,
The inner you.
On life's journey going,
To heaven or is it hell?

David J. Bennett

Emptiness

He was everything to me,
Without him I just cannot see
Past this stage of cold emptiness,
To a time of warmth and happiness.

I shall never again feel his happy glow,
Enjoy his soft and seductive woe,
I shall never again have him by my side,
Be utterly grateful and filled with pride.

I won't ever see him laugh, sing or joke,
Or watch him curl up in his chair and have a smoke,
I won't ever see him desperate or mad,
Or do that frown that used to remind me of a little lad.

I have to realize I've lost him for good,
But right now I don't think I could,
So I'll just enjoy remembering the past,
And hope the memories will always last.

Liz Moody

The Seasons

Winter, Spring, Summer and Autumn, they all follow
one another. Like a mother and father with their
two children following behind laughing and playing.
   Winter would represent father,
rugged sometimes cold and hard but fun to
have around. Spring and summer would
represent the children. The younger one being
spring, lively and alert. Just like the daffodils
and tulips popping out of the ground looking for
adventure. Summer for the older child.
Lupins, foxgloves and roses all sturdy looking
over the smaller plants.
   Autumn would represent mother. Leaves
falling from the trees, making a safe and warm
protective carpet over the ground ready for the
winter months to come.
   The seasons will always remind me of families.

Timothy Quigley

The Orphanage

We watched from the window, my sister and I
Seeing the cars and people going by.
We prayed each time they would call our name,
Hoping we'd been chosen, when the visitors came.

But slowly the children dwindled down to a few
Till the final day came, when there were only us two.
We thought we were doomed to live there for life.
When this handsome man came with his beautiful wife

They looked at us and then at each other
Our lovely new dad and our beautiful mother.
We know God was watching when he chose both of you
To take on the job to care for us two.

'Tis many years on now but we love you so much
For sharing a wonderful life that had God's tender touch.

E. F. Ellner

Determination

If you have a goal, that's nothing, unless
you're willing to achieve it.

If you want something badly, that's nothing
unless you are willing to pursue it.

If you want to be accepted, that's nothing
unless you are willing to do the right things.

It's not enough to learn the truth unless
you also learn to live it.

It's not enough to know the right thing unless
you are strong enough to do it.

It's not enough to reach for love unless you give it.

Q. Do you have Determination?

Savita Barrowes

Snow and Ice

Snow in winter, crisp and clean.
Stomping, making footprints.
Snow ball fighting, being mean,
Cold and crunchy crisp and clean.

Snow white, soft and smooth,
Crispy layers, frost on top,
Sheets of ice, sleek and smooth,
Ducks slipping about, on the move.

A white soft sheet,
Of clean crunchy snow,
Sometimes cold on the feet,
You've always got friends in the snow to meet.

Speeding, sledging down the hill,
Through the slush and the snow.
Once you're done and had your fun,
You must climb back up the hill.

Jennifer Reilly

Memories

Sometimes I often sit and stare,
And wonder why you are not there,
It is hard to believe that you are gone,
But my memories of you will linger on.
Your charming ways, your smiling face,
Will always leave an empty place,
You had a smile for everyone,
And also a heart of gold.
But now your smile is gone forever,
With just a memory to hold.
You have gone to leave us for a while,
Out of this restless and weary world.
Where there will be no partings, troubles or pain,
And thanks to God's wonderful promise.
One day Dad, I will meet you again.

Isobel Lyons

Weather

The storm is raging from the sea,
the rain, like spikes of glass and needles,
ricochets from wall and street.
His mind churns round in useless riddles.

The palm trunks bend: You'd think they'd snap;
the harbour boats wrench, bump and grind;
the sunshades tear from out their bases,
and fly—or flatten soaked on sand.
But greater far is storm of mind.

Storm and wind cease both together,
and sunlight glints on sea and ground;
it gleams on water-coated leaves;
and rainbow drops run down the frond;
But nothing calms the inner storm
of typhoon strength within his mind.

David Hanson

Partnerships

I turned around and you weren't there
I really wished I didn't care
I tried to imagine my life without you
But all I could see was a darkness so blue
I tried to remember the good times we had
All I could do was cry—it's so sad
Our life wasn't perfect
But truly I'm glad
Because really it wasn't that bad
I fought back the tears as soon as I saw
It really was you walking back through the door
I laughed through the tears
As I recalled the years
But all I could see were visions of you
And of a love born to be true.

C. Mountney

My Sit Up and Beg

To me it meant freedom on two wheels
My 'Sit-up and Beg,'
I'd fly down our hill with all the speed I could egg,
Defying the "what-ifs" and a fall.

The war took us both by rail to our duty
From our airfield to digs across flat
   Lincolnshire beauty.
One day she had a puncture as a young man past by
Who stopped to solve my needless fears, and
Stayed to mend whate'er for fifty years.

Freedom won, we're home again
My 'Sit-up and Beg' and I
To ride once more down hill and lane
But oh! What cars—what a pain!
My shopping dangled o'er front and back,
But 'twixt us both in skill we nothing lack.
My joy of Life had surely come
When four young voices in Chorus ask
What you brought us, Mum!?

Rachel Booth

My Epitaph

When it's time for me to die,
remember me with just a sigh,
I need not sorrow nor a cry
only . . . lay me down to lie.

I have many times cried my own tears
and now must face unknown fears.
Tho' when my time to finally depart nears
I can proudly hold my head high with my peers.

During my long life, so it must be told,
I've courted much risk and have been bold,
on some things done I deserve a scold
but never a friend have I sold.

When the life-light leaves my face
I hope to go with dignity and grace.
Of all the people who have known me,
"remember our best times" is my plea.

Weep not when I'm laid to rest,
kindly fold my hands across my breast.
Just the final kiss . . . before I expire,
. . . from my wife, is all I desire.

J. Fred Jackson

In Penpol Creek

Just downstream from the water plummeting
Out of the tunnel under the tube-fenced road
Into the awful depth of the petrifying pool—
Where the bustling stream divides and is friendlier,
Graciously slowing to shed firm sediment such that a man
Might not sink (though surrounded by brooding banks of mud).

This is where the children built their Dam.

Scarce-breakfasted on this fantastical August Friday,
They hurried there from Point and Feock too,
To realize what had been whispered for days.
Pausing only for drink and harsh words, they slogged
Cunningly, hemmed the unsuspecting water in,
Attacked the centre last. Four times failure, then a
Founding plank threw the water back.

Wide-eyed they watched the progress of the lake,
The metamorphosis of the creek, the pool swallowed whole.
Homeward replete, though they knew that night
The Dam would lie drowned and shattered under the tide's
embrace . . .
It did not matter, was not important.

We had had our Day.

A. L. Colman

The Winning Ticket

As do all, I dream of winning,
  of my life, make a new beginning,
would it change me, not at all,
  or would it be? My eventual downfall.

Each week the same special numbers I choose,
  apart from some tenners, I always lose,
yet, while I'm still playing, there is hope,
  if I did ever win the lottery, could I cope?

As I sit in front of the box each week,
  the balls are drawn, I feel my adrenalin peak,
one, that's two, yes I've got number three!
  three more to go and I'll live my life free.

Why is it that balls, four, five and six,
  never seen to be the numbers I pick?
Still a "tenner" is better than nothing at all,
  but why does picking the last three seems too tall.

Oh well, only another week to go,
  the pounds I spend, like seeds I sow,
one day I know my numbers will come up,
  then the champagne will over filleth my cup.

A. J. V. Welch

At One

I can see his eyes in every flickering flame of fire,
And I know that within, his powerful soul towers ever higher,
It does not matter how many suns and moons pass,
His voice is in the wind that will forever last.

And yet he is a land apart from me,
And the flowers bow with native melancholy,
He is not within the driving snow tonight,
Nor will he be in the morning light.

But at Reculver, I know that he is there,
You can feel his breath in the salty sea air,
He is in the power of the waves,
In the violent water in which the chalk bathes,
He is there destroying relics of forgotten times,
Within the stone walls whispering seductive rhymes.

He who was once human, has become a spirit of the sea,
Watching over all the others raining sorrow onto me,
He is in the swash that submerges the beach,
I can feel and touch his hand but it is far out of reach,
When the air is silent where do you go?
Do you sleep within an old shell that lived long ago?

Alethea Andrews

The Nativity Play

The thespians gathered, lines well rehearsed,
Adorned in their costumes so grand,
Their outfits so splendid, the likes rarely seen,
This side of the Holy Land.

"Mary, where's Joseph?" the teacher called out,
"I told you to keep hold of him."
"He went to the toilet Miss" she replied,
"And now he's locked out of the gym."

"They're sent to try us" the teacher sighed,
"But, I'll win in the end, never fear
The parents all love the Nativity play,
It's such a success every year."

"Angels and Kings go up to the back,
Pigs cattle and sheep in the front,
Innkeeper and wife go stand at the door,
And who told that pig he could grunt?"

Words are mixed up, people move out of turn,
Mary's smile turns into a sneer,
The audience applaud, such a wonderful show,
But then Nativity is a success every year.

Jean Dinning

The Flame

The rasping prayer ends in a gasp of wonder
As the flame is born
Flaring instantly then with a sigh drawing back
It becomes a single perfect leaf
That does a slender matchstick branch adorn

A magic wand with its brilliantly blazing star
Which waves away the gloom
Like a comet diving through the hush of night
To brush the ivory waxwork tower
Igniting a fragile glow that illuminates the room

For a few seconds both flames softly flicker
But soon the elder dies
And a lake created by the candle's melting heart
Spills silently its first tear
As the pale and lonely figure wistfully cries

The pure white thread dressed in funeral black
Curls up as if in pain
Amid constant weeping the memory burns bright
Until finally the fire goes out
And the sad reddened eyes are closed once again

S. M. Gonsalves

The Birth of a Poet

Well, wouldn't you just know it?
As a fellow would-be poet
that in moments there's a doubt,
as to what to write about!

So, you take your pen to paper,
and two hours roughly later
you've exhausted every view
as to what on earth you do!

And what of the times we have heard,
Some of which were quite absurd!
Why not now when needed most
the words won't gather round their host?

So at this point I'd like to say
the word is "mightier" for today!
But the verse is mine by early morn
and that is how a poet is born!

Lisa M. Sheffield

Stones (Thoughts While Gardening)

Uncovered from the cold dark peat,
Large stones appear, they seem to speak
In tongues I understand.
Stones that have lain for many an age,
Turn the leaves of history page by page.
Their voices whisper of the days
When dinosaurs ruled the world uncaged,
And more of mountains towering high,
Their peaks up—pointing to the sky.
They tell of how the world was hushed,
And where the mighty waters rushed
Untamed, down to an ocean wide
To where no creatures had to hide.
They speak of ferns, majestic, tall,
When no man walked the earth at all.

Barbara Dyer

Friends

There won't be absolutely no fun,
Unless of course there's more than one.
Yes they're the ones to rely on,
The ones you can cry on.
Friends are there,
For the pain to bear.
With real friends there won't be a catch,
So you won't be dispatched.
Friends are to play,
Today and everyday.
When you're in a fight,
They'll stand by tight.
You can share
With groups with pairs.
No curves with friends,
No bends no ends.

Sarafat Ibn Momen

Jack Frost

When the time arrives, it's clear to see,
Leaves hav'en fallen from above.
Flowers, now so few in number,
Fight the icy winds of the north
With the evening now near,
A winter's sunset gives us a golden-sky.
Still a 'leaking' sun—but—without its hat on!
All the ground now covered with snow,
A child's playing field.
Wrapped up they help move the white
Fashioned in balls,
Only to be replaced with the fallin' snow,
Local bells chime the hour,
A mother's call can be heard.
Dusk is nigh—silence all around.
'Jack Frost' makes his nightly appearance
A yearly visit—without any invitation.

James J. Connolly

The Twilight

They sit in the evening twilight
Watching the day go by
The hustle and bustle of daylight
Is lost in the evening sky
The birds are quiet and peaceful
The flowers have gone to sleep
The trees are gently blowing
And the world is all at peace

But soon the sun will be shining
And the world will come back to life
The birds will be singing softly
And the flowers will be shining bright
The mother feeds the children the husband kisses his wife
They are feeling very happy the baby has slept through the night
They are such a happy family they live for the children alone
Hubby goes off to work longing to be coming back home

Another day is over he's back in this own little home
The children are all in bed so they have some time on their own
So they go and sit in the twilight thankful for what they have got
They sit in the peace and quiet and thank God for their little lot

Sandra Hughes Douglas, Isle of Man

A Sentence of Death, No Apologies Please

The ocean waves, to the sands of Time, this world of ours, not yours,
not mine. New Horizons, beyond mountains high or fading
dreams, in the beckoning sky? Valleys of moonshine, where
deep rivers run, to buttercup meadows, of rich golden sun.
Sweet, fragrant roses, tease summers cool breeze, mysteries of
the earth, entwined in the trees.
Mother natures beauty, a delicate flower. The seasons of life,
awesome power. Freedom to live, where wild eagles fly,
yet, crimes we commit, destined to Die.
All the magic and wonder, in children's eyes,
pure, innocent believers, of false promises and lies.
Their visions, their dreams, painfully stolen away,
in their dying world, cursed with decay,
what is your answer, to the child that asks WHY?
Do you expect any pity, when you breakdown and cry.
The truth is, as always, too difficult to bear.
The ultimate question, did we really CARE,
for our suffering world, through mankind's abuse, When
accused of our crimes, we have no excuse. All too apparent,
A Sentence of Death, worthless apologies,
No beginning please.

Our world that needs justice, what kind of criminals are we.

Michelle O'Flaherty

S-O-S

Aggression is the scourge that has society in its grip.
A disease that's spread throughout the world. There's no
escape from it.
With a countenance that's ugly, this Godforsaken breed
Spits out from each contorted mouth the slime of evil seed.

Safely well embedded, richly nurtured all the way
The seeds of poison flourish with encouragement each day.
No beauty can emerge, nor all that beauty can impart.
There's nothing but the thumping beat of venom in the heart.

Right from wrong. The difference? Too well they know the score.
Fostering evil intent firmly bolts the conscience door.
Imagine each new villain—once the miracle in a cot
Destined to become a rogue. Sans fear! Sans love! Sans God!

Existence is their privilege, but they've yet to get it right.
Murderers, rapists, thieving perverts mock the gift of life.
Ambassadors of Christ can't save them. Words are just a bore.
Dear God in your wisdom, help them free the conscience door.

Their next potential victim is a constant worry—WHO?
This ever present nightmare could be me. It could be you.
The world's become a breeding ground of hatred and ill will.
The power of thought is mighty—A CONSCIENCE mightier still!

Sylvia M. Linney

Home Land of Shepherds

Merrily do we tour our land daily
Its air so serene stores sweet scent.
The soil sits silent, never soils
Seasons so varied, some even boil
Yet it never sheds its sheen.

From floods forth are swarded fields
Upon which descend the flock, carpeting
Intently reading the ground to select of future wield
For in loyalty to the day is the sun, parting
And to a deserving shepherd delivers, the utmost yield.

Day after day together shepherd's child and lambs grow
Not only on the same field
But nourished by same milk offered raw.
Baa cries the lamb, baa-ba cries the child
Then retires each soundly snoring, dreaming, as draws in morrow.

Pastoralists in prayer offer praises
In rituals do we host God
Who in return sends us rains
The water serves our thirst and blooms our land.
Though exist no estates, the taste of our state is sweet, its lifebland.

Hamad Ilkul JB

Time Is Not a Barrier

Time is not a barrier for love so true
Though we have parted your presence is felt near
Memories of us both are so crystal clear
Forever I shall continue loving you

Time is not a barrier for love so pure
Surely sharing love with you was destined fate
Memories of us together simply great
Our hearts romantically entwined for sure

Time is not a barrier for love so strong
Precious were the moments spent with you my dear
Memories of your sweet whispers in my ear
My heart now yearns for you whom it does belong

Time is not a barrier for love so real
Sensational feelings that made my heart race
Memories of your unforgettable face
Nothing could possibly change the way I feel

Time is not a barrier for love so right
The strength of my love shall keep away all fear
Memories of you once immortally here
The love we shared shall glow like stars in the night

Ladee Bassett

In a Big Empty House

To live alone in a big empty house,
the floor boards are gone
no room for a mouse.
Each room it is dark and
the windows are broken,
the wires are bare, no longer in action.
The people are gone
and I'm on my way,
My light's at the top
and there's warmth, anyway.

I hope I move soon
'cause it's folks I like most,
not wide empty rooms,
broken, dusty, and lost.
Those rooms once held people
whom I held dear,
Each room I could go in
without any fear,
as they were my neighbours
now—they are not here.

B. D. Byron-Rasmussen

The Man Who Shadowed Death

Did he serve with Lee or Sherman, in the Travis County War?
Ride at night with Quantrill's raiders meting out their brand of law?
Fine-chased pistols, pearl—carved handles,
   menace like the desert breath;
Heart chilled like a winter ghost town was the man
   who shadowed death.

It was whispered in Missouri, in a youthful distant life,
Outlaws murdered in Laredo his twin daughters and a wife;
Lovelier than a nameless vision was this half-breed Texan bloom.
Bowed, he buried them in silence warm tears on an earthen tomb.

Then he trailed the River Pecos, legend traced on every page,
Witchita, then through the Badlands,
   and the path of Deadwood's stage.
So he rode his chestnut sorrel, like a phantom without rest,
For Death's grasp was cold upon him,
   and he had not solved his quest.

On a spring day in Salinas, he heard four men in the street;
Careless, coarsely name his loved ones—Hell lay open at their feet!
He had ridden with the Devil, but he prayed to God for power,
Grant my wife eternal peace, as I face my curtain'd hour.

Triple flame burst from his paired guns, and like them he met his fate,
For a while his soul then hovered, trembled by that darkened gate.
Then his face seemed changed and younger,
   only love was in his eyes,
In my dreams I think his daughters, drew him gently to the skies.

Christopher Rothery

The World Round

The mountain dew of whirlwinds,
The encompassing forceps of enterprise,
The untouched atmosphere of fresh spring waters.
The naturalistic love of each embodied species,
The acknowledgement of the deepest earths, found,
All are evaporated of human touch or sight,
Utilised by the Sun's morning kiss, and weapon
Of reflection, untouched by rejection.
Sobriety of the keepers kept quiet yet so still,
The thirsting points of atmosphere,
In the wandering tree of the human eye.
Daring the rose buds to shudder or sigh
To meet the eclipse of day and night.
Enveloping the skies to their perfumed right.
As literature flies the hemisphere,
With kisses wist of tomorrows good-byes,
Glistening star dust enlightens the world
Of yesteryear by (off) tone and compassion.
In line without connection,.
Masquerades take their toll in high opinions ball.

Marie Bruce Collins

The Child Has Learnt to Speak

Imagination running wild, as if the mind of witless child,
Who lives by love alone, but free, as in its own adversity,
Dispatched to lands of fantasy, to land on feelings, fancy free,
Travelling to what parts they reach, planting ideas to beseech,
So they will grow in nature's quest, maturing only where they rest,
Nurtured, cultured, filled with zest, built-in time which can infest,
But when invested, knows no bounds, frightening ideas
which astound,
Leaving marks, as if a seed, planted only to be freed,
However, likely to succeed, when sought with selfishness and greed,
As when a child has grown in stature, mature in knowledge,
slow but sure,
Whose mind which once would dwindle carelessly and now
runs wild, down time, to see
what lies at ends of rainbows spectrum, better still, where
rainbows come from,
Out of blue, where raindrops shine, immortal spines hung in a mind,
To grow, as if with sunshine warmed, nurtured ideas gently swarm,
To make imagination peak, formed, the child has learnt to speak.

Mark Abrahams

Mi' Pension, an' T'old Lass

I wer' walking across t' city; mi' pockets full o' brass.
I'd just drawn mi' pension; pension fo' mi' and t' old Lass.
As I walked thro' one o' them subways, two 'Yobboes I
'appened to meet
I 'eard one say to 'tother; lets gi' t' old man a freight.

Thi' said; come on old man; and or' thi' brass!
I replied; that kidding, this is for mi' and t' old lass.
Come on they said! Nobody will 'ear thi' even if tha' tries to shout.
So just 'and o'er thi' money, or both on us will gi' thi' a clout.

I said to one o' Yobboes; the one wi' greasy hair
Just gi' mi' two secs' to teck' off mi' specs,
An' I'll fight thi' right fair and square.

Wi' sparred around for two minutes, and I went down wi' a clout.
They wer' on mi' back in a minute. Mi' wallet they, d'tecken it out.
They laughed wi' glee as they opened it; then dropped it an
ran for their lives.
There wer' no money; in mi' wallet; just a picture, I'd tecken'
o' wife.
Now, I walk around the city; no worries and full o' life,
'cos I 'ave a picture, in mi' lapel; the one I'd tecken' o' wife.

Lade Henderson

Reality

How would you feel, out in the field
trench foot, mortar bombs
always on the alert, soaking, dripping wet
sleep an impossible dream
hearing, seeing, feeling every scream
gunpowder smoke, gunpowder smells
metal fragmentations whizzing by
hearing, seeing, feeling buddies cry
razor barbed wire, blood seeping
your eardrums blasting, pounding sore
knowing long ago you could take no more
flames exploding, bodies exploding
stomach churning, filled with fear, incendiary bombs dropping near
red guts spilled, red limbs hanging
eyes stinging, scraping lids, every finger there if God forbids
shouting, bawling, belly crawling
red, red mud, growing pools of warming blood
just an arm
a human face in your gunsights, knowing to pull the trigger
isn't right and all for glory . . .end of story

James Reid

Down Memory Lane

When I look back on the days gone by,
My eyes fill up and I start to cry;
A family of seven, who loved each other,
We had a good father and a wonderful mother.

There was Phil, Fred, and Don and Glenys,
and not forgetting our Dennis the Menace;
We had no toys and seldom had a treat,
We were so happy just playing in the street.

Not like the children of today;
If they can't spend money, they don't know how to play.
There was very little we could afford,
So we'd go to chapel at the end of the road;
There would always be a welcome there,
and whatever they had, they would always share.

I can picture Mom, making cake, she worked all day,
never had a break,
Never went out, had little pleasure,
But to us, she was our biggest treasure.

The good 'old days', I don't agree,
they were not very good to me,
They were difficult years, not very kind,
I'm glad we've left them all behind.

Morfydd Shepherd

Stripping

I have layers built
   from fear; fantasy;
from years of construction,
the heart is such a tedious friend
and I have broken more backs in
   its maintenance
than with the effort it takes to
   move mountains
   create flowers,
we build nothing, we find
nothing of ourselves in these concrete layers,
these flimsy walls of excuse,
I will undress in moonlight,
   in sunlight, in starlight
I will remove the garments of myself
and leave a trail of silken longing
in the meadows, by the river,
I will float like an Ophelia now living,
stripped of the myth I have created
   reborn in nakedness.

Angela Pearse

On the Tragic Death of My Son Gordon—Aged 31 Years

Words! Used to convey meaning; used by writers for effect,
But poetic artifice shall not steal sincerity from my words.
They must speak grief, violent screaming terror in my being
Masked by an outer self assumed to help others exist around me.
So! Let words serve their dreadful purpose.

Friday the 19th of April 1996, began a normal Friday,
Ended with shredded strips of mind dangling in false normality.
Normality? The wrong word now, I can never be normal again!
But normal was the right word when I left you on Thursday,
No hint of fearsome pain ahead, our precious closeness intact.
I carry that within my soul now you are gone.
Memory bequeaths exquisite pain of how we were my son.

Your final hours were spent apart from me—you died alone.
How that distresses me!

The police used official words to explain your passing,
'Sorry . . . ruptured spleen . . . the result of a severe beating.'
Inquest Verdict: Open: My mental wounds left gaping.
Open, a word dislodged as truth slips thro' murderous silence.
May guilt and fear canker the worthless souls of your assassins.

The cemetery is quiet. I still keep our faith my bonny brave boy.

Ilona Rowena MacPhee

White Paper Doves

An ancient isle where saints' desires,
Bequeathed their grace and tallest spires,
God's own sweet nature there did bestow,
And laid his emerald cloak below.

Eastern skies where dawn's first rays,
Awakens dreams enlightened ways,
Western hills with sunset kiss,
Radiates a depth of bliss.

Clear sweet sound of silver streams,
Hints of hazy mystic dreams,
Pure crystal notes reap golden strings,
Majestic harps melodious rings.

The land's true heart of simple ways,
In silence bore the troubled days,
With mingled prayer and multi praise,
The spirit of the land to raise.

White paper doves calm troubled air,
Speak of peace and soothe despair,
The people's voice with God's is one,
With prejudice and war have none.

Audrey Ducharme

Yesterday's Disregard Is Now Today's Sorrow!

Alang Arbirlot road I yest tae walk,
Crossing many a stoory and muddy track,
At ane with the world, jist me and mi dog,
We'd count an abundance oh hairy caterpillars, lizards and frogs.

These days I look but kin fund neen.
The road stretches oot fir miles. Bare! Empty!. And clean!

Oor kin must be squirming in their grave!
As they watch fit we've done and the way we behave,
Neglecting oor wildlife, their environment's a paved,
All in the name of progress, and luxuries we crave!

The Geordie wids is a sitting bare!
'Twis grand shelter for many a mole, fox, rebbit and hare!

And far's a the hedgerow? Oh I loved it so!
Watching the holly and berries in the winter's snow glow,
With the birds, caterpillars and bugs that jumped to and through.
Alas, they pair cratures hive nay hames left to go!
Noo they scurry and scrip in furrowed fields doon-a-low!

Barbed wire replaces the hedgerow, ensuring land owners profits flow!
In these fertilized, insecticide washed wastelands, only embolden seeds grow.
The disregard of yesterday now fills mi heart with heavy sorrow!

W. Graham-Gordon

The Leaf

A sigh was in the air—a chill of sadness with no flair—
As the dying leaf broke from the tree
To float, like a silent thief, no longer held by sap,
But free to gloat, and show its age, as life wains
With thin vascular whorls, that wrap, dried within the veins
Whose span is spread across its shrunken skin
Of deathly grey, chrome yellow and faded sage—
Its mortilized, serrated fingers—transparent, thin—
Now lie upon the loam of autumn's earth—
Its life is gone—yet still it lingers,
Surplus—of no concern or worth except to mould
And wrest, in obscure shapes, a withered fold
Of shrivelled gauze—too fine, too nebulous to hold,
Yet—confusingly—a familiar part of me . . .

If only Time would pause! Let Eros have the key!—
Give us another Life!—But no: torn and knurled,
Distorted by cruel vagaries and strife,
It is as if, now unshackled, the year at last is free
From the unforgiving land

But this leaf portrays the end for me: its twin is my left hand!

Dorothea R. Payn Le Sueur

We Ask Ourselves from What Do We All Dread

The insurance man is becoming a great dread
when he refuses the money when you are dead.
I was struck by lightning which caused me dread
as they refused to pay out when I assured them of my dread
Hill House Hammond Insurance are a great dread
as they refused to pay out my house insurance dread
I changed my DR from whom I always dreaded.
My next was no different from whom I dread.
He nearly had me very for a while very dead.
At forty thousand pounds they are something to dread.
I had to call upon a quack with my shear dread
who stated I had an absecc upon the pendix dread.
She cured my absecc within two weeks of dread.
How is that for a good cause ending two weeks of dread
my DR put me on no alcohol tablets which I have to dread.
I had my windows all double glazed so I would have no dread.
I got them to change my door so I would have no dread,
but it has been nothing but fear and for to end my dread
as he has fitted my door with no letter box causing me dread.
The postman is now in a great way about no letter box to dread.

F. Scott

Infinite Seclusion

On this Granite rock I gaze out to sea and ships,
Sand and shale merge in to rocky pools, and footprints
lead on to secret coves.
Overshadowed are the Cornish Hills of clay and protrusions
of stack and stone.
The earth vibrates in forgotten scars, reverently ruptured
by industrious hands.
Small white dwellings reflect the early mornings brilliance,
and sheep and cattle pattern the quartered lands of slate
and stone divisions.
Verdant hills of this peaceful haven compose my mind's
frustration merging into a world of peaceful serenity, tuned
into the rhythm of the people, who are the very soil of grass
and tilled crustation.
Have I loved once in distant dreams? I feel your depth of
tolerance and splendid courage, portrayed in local scenes, of
man with net and reel, of sea soiled hands in boat and hooks
and fish revealed.
"How long will infinite seclusion stay? Cornishmen, make fast
the bowline years ahead, secure your land; 'tis yours alone,
each man his loved and cherished plot, each man his path that
leads his home."

Maurice J. Saunders

A Promise Within

What goes on behind the closed doors in a street
Of houses that all look the same?
Maybe there is laughter, perhaps a few tears,
Or occasionally a dull ache or pain.
Do the people that live there have a good moan
As they rush around at the start of a new day?
Is it always so important to be first in that queue,
Never minding whom they hurt on the way?
Do other people's troubles fall upon deaf ears,
Have they neither sympathy or time they can spare?
Oh what a different life they could lead,
If everyone, their problems could share.
Can the people that live there rejoice in a God
That gave them the flowers and the trees?
Do they ever stop and listen to the birds in song
And ask themselves what treasures are these?
How much richer and fuller their lives could be
If they started each day with a smile.
If they listened and cared, and promised themselves.
To be last, in that queue, for a while.

D. V. Bryan

Just a Boy!

Curly headed little five-year old, nestling close by Mummy's knee.
Saying his evening prayers, as good as good can be,
Please God! Make me a good boy!
And please! I didn't mean to be bad,
When I tell off the garden shed and made my Mummy sad,
And please God! Bless my Mummy and my Daddy, too!
Oh! And don't forget to bless me and make me good
'Cause dear Lord! I needs it so, cause I knows I do!
My Daddy says there never was another boy like me,
For finding out the naughty things and doing them, you see!
Oh! If I peep 'tween my fingers just like this
I kin see my doggy wriggling, Ha! He'll give me a kiss!
Oh! I nearly forgot—bless baby Jim and make him grow up fast,
Then perhaps he'll be able to play some games with me at last!
Please! I'm very sorry I tied Granny to her chair,
But she looked sort of awful wobbly sitting there!
Wasn't it fun in my bath tonight!
And didn't I laugh when I splashed and gave Mummy a fright!
Oh! Please bless all the poor girls and boys,
Who haven't a home and lots of nice toys,
And please God! Keep me safe all the night through,
'Cos I got lots of nice things tomorrow to do!!!

Dorothy Ventris

The Passing of Time

The western sky ablaze with light,
A lovely sight to view,
As sunset heralds in the night
We bid daylight adieu.

The twittering of the birds has ceased,
They settle in the trees,
They know that soon up from the East
The sun will rise with ease

As daylight dawns the world awakes
To start a busy day.
The rooster crows, the noise he makes
Resounds across the way.

And so the time clock ticks away.
Days, weeks and years just fly.
We must attempt to fill each day
With love, and help the lonely passer-by

Doreen Cruickslanks

The Morning of the Tears

I looked across the Highland hills lashed with snow and cloud
I felt the chill that blew so cruel until I nearly cried aloud
I gazed upon that poor burnt croft that had stood forlorn for years
And in my heart I still recall the morning of the tears
As a hundred troopers with bayonets bright stood ready to
    suppress men's right
The factor's men with hearts of stone dragged the crofters
    from their home
And when this deed was done they fired the roof and
    smashed the walls
As red coated officers drank their Lord's health with Highland alcohol
Then marched away with jaunty step as poor men's cries rent the air
Their children's wails pierced their hearts and they bowed
    their heads in despair
The factor's men on bended knee reported to Lord Sutherland
    with glee
The croft was gone the crops laid waste the land ready for
    sheep not men
The wretched tenants no where to go on where to rest set sail
    by ship to the west
And now I'm old my eyes are dim and I see haloes round the stars
I still recall with aching heart the morning of the tears
As children's cries rent the air like the screeching of the gulls.
And I wonder if my land is held in thrall by a new breed of red-
    coated men
Who twist the law and speak the words that mean not what they say
For the law is there in black and white still used to suppress
    men'sright
To this very day

John A. Steedman

Un-Real (Maybe!)

As the frothy water tumbles on the rocks,
A sensational rainbow forms over the falls.
The birds chirp in their trees,
Their beautiful sound, filling the falls with joy.
As the sun descends,
The lights reflect over the tumbling giant,
Projecting radiant colours of crimson and silver.
The moon smiles down,
Proudly showing off his whitish shimmer.
The scene behind the falls is un-real,
Orangy glows glisten on the water below.
The stars twinkle in their sockets,
Sparkling in the dusky pink sky.
The flow of water never ends,
Like a permanent billowing wind.
People gaze in awe at this natural feature,
Taken a back by the power of the water.
It never sleeps—just eternal.
The next day, the sun rises high in the sky,
It is an end and a beginning combined.

Helen Roberts

Bruce

Bruce my dear friend you have gone out of my life.
Fate was kind and granted you a quick release.
For almost two decades you were my devoted
companion and friend.
Without you my declining years are lonely
and empty.
None other can take your place.
I do not think of you as in the clay near the
laburnum tree.
You are walking with me along the river bank . . .
Through the woods so full of the song of birds.
Emerging joyfully from the river after the swim
you enjoyed so much;
The grass your bathing towel.
You are cosy by the fire with me as the dreary
winter winds howl and rain splashes
the window.
Your head on my lap gazing with affection into my eyes.
You dispelled all loneliness and fear, we were contented and
at peace.
You were a wonderful dog, Bruce, man's best friend.

Nora Cotter

Ower afore It Begun

Shi' wiz foster't as a baby, 'cos 'er mither coodna' cope,
'Ere wiz nae faither figger, so 'er wiz nae ither hope,
Mony 'ears gid passin' by, 'n' 'er young life wiz fu' o' pain,
'N' th' wumman' at gied birth tae 'er, wiz niver seen again.

Shi' wiz abuse't, 'n' rape't, 'n' batter't, thro' a' 'er tender 'ears,
Shi'd naebuddy o' 'er ain tae tell, 'n' spint ilky nicht in tears,
Shi' ran awa' a puckle times, bit aye shi' wiz brocht back,
Tho' shi'd get awa anither time, fin security wiz a bittie slack.

Afore 'er fourteenth birthday, shi' wiz roughin't in a park,
Tire't 'n' weak, 'n' hungry, 'n' scare't witless o' thi' dark,
Next day shi' met a mannie, 'n' 'e offer't 'er a job,
'E said 'e wid keep 'er hidden, 'n' shi'd earn a gweed few bob.

Shi' thocht 'er life wiz changin' fin 'e showed 'er a bonny room,
Little at ess pint did shi' ken, shi'd almost met 'er doom,
Th' pimp hid 'er sellin' drugs a' day, 'n' sellin 'ersel'ilky nicht,
It wizna ony better'n bein' in care, God, wid naethin, ever ging
  richt.

So shi' thocht shi'd try a peel 'ersel', tae help block oot'er past,
Syn shi' slip't inta a coma, 'n' seen shi' breathe't 'er last,
Shi' wiz born bit niver wintit, 'er life wiz sae afa sad,
Lovin' wiz a' shi' needit, bit it's a thing 'at shi' niver had.

Irene A. R. Smith

Autumn Embers

When the summer sun has lowered, when our light begins to wane;
When our fragile bodies bear the price of past life's strain;
When we grow too old and weary to hardly want to tread the way;
When our eyes and ears betray us, too frail to make sense
  of the day;
Still we'll feel the passion surging when our thoughts
  recall with pride
How we needed one another, a love which could not be denied.

I can remember the ache when time was master and, poor me, a
  simple pawn,
Longing to see that certain smile, I waited for proof with every morn,
To re-assure my anxious mind that promises we'd made in haste
Still meant the same to you and be renewed when we embraced.
A gentle word, a soft caress could soothe a love-sick pain,
Our passion had to be subdued to ease away the strain.

No longer am I insecure, I've learned to trust you dear
And realise it was only love that made me suffer fear.
Time no longer is the master, it races past as we stand still
And my fear no longer a disaster, as I've gained a stronger will.
Even now, though, I search your eyes, which once held a
  carefree twinkle,
And wonder why, through all the years, our love grew with
each new wrinkle.

Jean Taylor

Symphony of Wonder

From far beyond horizons, comes the timbrel sound of drums,
As clouds appear and hover, and wind it gently hums,
The wind like mellow violins, in the tranquility of our mind,
Plays music in the distance, for what follows on behind.

The light goes out as the dark clouds rise, and before us now is set,
A symphony of wonder, that we never will forget,
The rumbling and the drumbeats, in the distance rise in tone,
Then the flash and clash of cymbals, reverberate through
every home.

As we listen in hushed silence, as the clouds go rolling by,
For the lightning, wind and thunder, to crescendo in the sky,
With the peak of the orchestration, as the thunder fades away,
The emotion felt as the sky it clears, is applause in its own way.

Marjory Davidson

Poetic Mind Games

Once again I start to write,
Poetry based on my life,
The world's just recognized my daily routine,
And tries to cut through it like a knife.

It's blanked my mind of all knowledge,
I have nothing to write but what is,
I have no past, no future,
It dissolved with a plop and a fizz,

Nothing is all I remember,
Amnesia is all I'll obtain for the night,
Tomorrow all will come flooding back,
When I haven't the urge to write,

So for now I'll put pen to paper,
I'll pretend to be a bard,
For tomorrow I'll know what has been and what will,
And writing it down will be hard.

Claire Piwowarski

Bare Threads

The fine line is swinging between silent love and silent hate,
And a man called "Power" with a verbal scissored tongue
Makes clean cuts with piercing sounds;
The coffee percolator silenced by "a chance of heart,"
The "neighbour" breathes her last "why?"
Dying, she stretches to grip the life of the crop she shared with you.
Someone's "grandmother," unanchored and going nowhere,
Sinks to her death drowning beneath a sea of stones.
A "young woman" balancing the weights of life pensively
Finds the weights are hollow and has no choices
But one: she climbs a tree and hangs alone;
She is wearing a red cardigan, no one knows her name.
The man called "Power" is trying to tie knots with fine lines;
He leaves only a pile of throwaway tangles.
So the man called "Power" is now playing Chinese skipping,
Trying to make nice patterns, it's too late:
The land is crying with pain.

Anna Szeremeta

Missing You

This is just a verse to say how much I love you on your birthday,
I only wish that you were here, I only wish that you were near,
I only wish you could hear me, I only wish you could see,
How I'm sat here all unhappy and my insides are torn in three,
I always think of you everyday
And how much I miss you in every way,
I miss your face, I miss your smile,
I'd run anywhere for it even a mile,
Part of me is missing and, Craig, that part is you,
Why you had to go away I only wish I knew,
I loved you then, I love you still, and you can be sure I always will,
I hope you are with Lindsey and both of you are at rest,
God knows what He's doing because He only takes the best,
No-one will ever take your place there could never be another,
Because you are and always will be a very special brother.

Alison Taylor

The Scarecrow

The scarecrow is out in all kinds of weather he makes all the birds fly away in displeasure. The crows come to take all the corn and maize but the scarecrow gives them an icy gaze.

The birds come back at the end of the day but the scarecrow will not go away. He guards the field like a sentinel but he really wishes everyone well. The farmer is pleased to see the birds go as they pinch all of the seeds at one go. It will soon be autumn and the trees will be green the sun will be out to make the birds beam. The farmer soon dismantles the scarecrow he is very sad but when the birds see it they are very glad soon it will be Christmas and the snow will be bad. The birds fly away to warmer climes but will be back next year to much better times. Goodbye said the scarecrow. It is very sad to go but perhaps one day I will come back to the fields and help the farmer to make lots of yields.

Peter Morgan

Our Environment

Self-inflicted are the ills and worries of mankind
As we use our hurried span of life
In the daily, greedy grind:
Giving very little thought to the vast production,
The invention of, and distribution of
Materials of dire destruction.
We do not have the right to destroy
Nature in all her gladness
By polluting this planet, and all of life
In our race of commercial madness:
How better can we employ it?
Than to spare some of our precious time
To deter those who might destroy it.
Purity of air, sparkling waters, clean beaches
Are gifts from nature's store
Together, we should protect this heritage
And keep it safe forevermore.

Peggy G. Newell

Urban Creaturescape

Us,
we nest in the spleen of the city,
tossing at times our insatiable tongues
to confirm that it's
us,
the blurred images we aim at,
in the mirror to be called
our private cloud.

Us,
decent trolls of departure,
hammer our nocturnes
with castanet yells.
By daylight
we coil up like embryos in smoke-rings
and rush to our icicle cradles concealed.

Kleanthis Paraskevopoulos

Lady Jenny

There she sat, my little cat gazing at the fire,
Those bright green eyes were mesmerized by flames
that licked from side to side.
How straight she sat, her head held high, staring in disdain
at our poor dog who tried to hog a place where she could gain
a little space to sleep and dream in comfort by that fire.

A pretty cat, a dainty cat, a lady through and through.
When she was young, to bask in sun would be her dream come true.
She'd stretch and reach those ticklish feet as far as they would go.
She'd dab and play, chase her tail and scratch upon the fence.
Her claws grew sharp but never once were used in her defence.

A gentle cat, a purring cat loved by all mankind,
as she grew old her heart grew sick, her eyes grew dim and blind.
I held her gently in my arms to die in painless peace, and sent her to that heavenly place,
Where she could take the sun all day and rest her tired mind.

Sheron Cenizo

The Old Mystic

He sits upon a withered stool, bent of back and twisted
With eyes of ice to chill your soul, whilst all your thoughts are sifted.
Ageless 'neath this wizened shell, a deathless heart resounds
which burns with fire both fey and fell and knows no mortal bounds.
Beware the sidelong, shifting glance—evade the reaching fingers
And pray he calls you not to dance in the realm where half light lingers. For he is the piper, the keeper of keys,
The master of wise men and all such as these—
A catcher of dreams, a betrayer of lies who takes life to the edge and then over it, flies! Divine and accursed, feared and reviled,
His powers are coveted by fools who are blind.
Hunted by princes, courted by queens—only lovers of truth understand what he means. Unfound down the ages, so dark and so dread, he has left us behind, for we would not be led.
Yet sooner or later, he knows all men shall follow to thence dwell in the light and welcome the 'morrow.
But for now he remains an enigma—a shadow—who must walk upon grounds considered unhallowed and endure the fear of men.

Behold the Shaman!

Cathryn Saveker

As If I Ever Could

How I wish a butterfly would settle on the palm of my hand
Such a beautiful timid creature could anything be so grand
Slowly give it confidence I wouldn't harm it any single way
Make it know it would be a welcome visitor each and every day

I would impart to it secrets I've kept hidden deep within my heart
Giving it my complete and utter trust from the very start
Tell it of my childhood fears my hopes and youthful dreams
Learning in my adolescence everything isn't all that it seems

Tell it of moments filled with happiness others which were sad
I recall smiles outweighed the tears I should be really glad
Tell it of some anxious years when outwardly I appeared quite shy
Until a special someone said hello to my timidity I said goodbye

How I looked forward to the daily visit of my oh so fragile friend
Listening intently to what I said proving humanity and nature can blend
I'm really up to date now I've hardly any more stories to tell
I've enjoyed your company hope you've enjoyed mine as well

Yesterday both of us knew instinctively we were going to say goodbye
Momentarily you brushed my lips then soared up to the sky
My fragile friend all I've told you I'm sure you understood
You have my solemn promise I won't forget you as if I ever could.

David Robert Screen

In the Crook of Daddy's Arms

In the crook of daddy's arms, a world of safety away from harm
The bad times he kept at bay, ever watchful night or day
With his babe he paced the floor, letting mother sleep some more
While he tried his best to earn a better wage to feed his bairn.

In the crook of daddy's arms, with his toddler lifted high
Piggy-back upon his neck, when little legs became too worn
Sleepless nights of care and worry, as childhood ailments struck him down
And playing games to deter boredom, urging his tot to start to learn.

In the crook of daddy's arms, a young son sat on his lap
Two strong arms full of protection, read out stories and fairy-tales
Later on helped with his homework, taught his boy the manly games
And the most important lesson, the things that make a good man.

Then the time came when this young lad, a teenager had become
The rebellious years of youth digging deep into his soul
But when black clouds of doubts arose, his mentor was by his side
To keep him on the straight and narrow and not lose sight of his goal.

Under the guidance of dad's wisdom, the lad grew and fell in love
Now he understands what father taught him as he looks down on his own son
Sleeping soundly, in trusting safety, against his strongly beating heart
Just as he'd done so long ago, in the crook of his father's arms.

M. J. Ellerton

Why Only Now...?

Why only now do I feel the wind that whipped my cheeks on
   carefree days?
Why only now do I feel the free and reckless love that held no stays?
Why only now when age hold chains and limbs are weary,
   weak and slow
Do I enthrall at far gone thrills of dance and spills, and daring-do?

Did I not on those windswept moors feel the same joys my
   memories bring?
Was that first kiss the burning flame that brings my searching
   heart such bliss?
Were the stern words 'to keep my head' spoke by my mother
   stern, if fair
A brake on the glorious tastes that life laid in my path, my
   youth to share?

   Frances Alder

Mind's Eye

Far away in the depths of the world,
Lies the Golden Land.
But although it is hidden,
It is filled with the whistling of the birds sailing in the breeze,
And the rustle of the wind breathing gently through the trees,
And the rushing of the river gliding swiftly on its way.
It is surrounded by an aura of happiness and peace,
For nobody enters the Golden Land.

If I gaze into the furthest corners of my mind,
I can see that magical world,
But already its sharp edges are blurring, its features are
indistinct.
Man has forgotten how to wish, to hope, to dream,
He has more important things to do,
He has bombs to throw, and innocent people to kill,
And as he continues his war against himself,
The Golden Land fades.

   Abena Poku-Awuah

Woman Ways

Scratch, scratch, beneath the floorboards, pitter patter
   through the house.
Scratch, scratch, moving upwards,
   quick hide the cheese we've got a mouse.
Up the stairs, the youngest daughter, on a chair inside her flat.
Begging, screaming, near hysterics, fiance runs to fetch the cat.
Brings in pussy, sets her hunting, tail and whiskers all atwitch,
along the skirting creeping, jumping, prey is caught without a hitch.
"Stop him! darling. He will kill it. Look how it trembles, Oh!
   Poor thing".
"Oh! You horrid wicked pussy." "As for you sir—Keep your ring."
In the pub—his brain awhirling, orders quick, a large Guinness.
Just can't grasp the female logic that has left him loverless.
So take heed Sir If you're courting, don't set deposit on a house.
Till you are absolutely certain, she's not frightened of a mouse.
Make doubly sure your understanding of the devious female brain,
covers all events and happenings, then sir, stop, and think again.

   J. Holloway

The Vagabond

In the stillness of the fall I gaze far and beyond into the dark
forest, where strange and elusive lights are twinkling in the distance.
As I look upwards at the deep blue sky I see the wandering birds
flying over towards the misty mountains and into the warm south.
For a while I listened to the myriad sounds of the forest. I
could hear the soft ripple of meandering streams in the
mysterious valleys of echo. In harmony with the songs and
cries of unseen creatures of the forest in a haunting melody.
It made me think of my boyhood, when I often listened to
these ever changing musical rhapsodies. I thought
of my mother who helped me in everything I tried to do. My
father who was a good soldier and I hardly ever knew.
All of a sudden my thoughts were brought back to the
present, when I noticed how quickly the shadows of the night
were coming down. Bringing with them an icy cold and the
early signs of winter. First the lone little robin then the silent
fall of lingering snow.

   John Burns Murphy

In Memory of Beau

Our big, beautiful Beau—how we loved him so much.
Who could have delivered such an evil touch?
We called him constantly throughout the day
But he did not return in his usual way.
And then someone found him tied up, close to death,
With string bound tightly around his neck;
Our poor little Beau—his face now twice the size,
His claws cut and bleeding and also blood from his eyes.

Days passed, he had treatment—he's alive, thank the Lord!
His little mind, though, still tormented and trusting few who he saw.
But then one day he went out again and never returned;
To see him again—oh how we prayed, how we yearned.
Alas it was not to be for him to come home again
And life here without Beau would not be the same.
No more would we see him walk through our door,
Hear his loving response with that wonderful purr.

But we know he's at peace now in Heaven above
Where he's constantly surrounded by our Lord's perfect love.
And one day we will seem him there and know that pussycat touch
Of our big, beautiful Beau—how we loved him so much.

   Martine L. Shelton

Troubles with My Car!

I once had a motor car, but now I haven't any,
You see, my troubles used to be little ones, but now they are many.
Oh yes, I have a couple of Kids, but indeed they are my pride,
The thing that causes my heartache is, I taught my wife to drive!

It used to be, "take me here and there" or, "over to my mother's"
And, "run the children to the school", or "let's go and see my
   brothers?"
I only thought I'd been pestered then, in those days gone by,
But having lost my lovely car, makes me somehow cry.

I could of course get another car, one to suit me you see,
But I fear what happened to a friend of mine,
   could also happen to me?
He bought himself a lovely big car, after his wife took the old,
And if you saw this poor man today,
   it would make your blood run cold!

He drives around in the smaller car, while his wife, she has
   claimed the new,
She says she needs the larger one, as the Kids need lots of room?
She passes him along the road, her driving causes heads to turn,
And everyone knows her as the lady, that can make the
rubber burn!

I have now decided what I'll do, I have given this lots of thought,
For what I've seen in the past, is a lesson I'm well taught!
So from now on, when you see me, hang your heads not in despair,
As all my travelling from now on, shall be done on "Shank's Mare".

   Edmund Rogan

The Solemn Night

Like a valley with no breeze to whisper
A cold chill, as though the dead of winter
Like a buzzard, falls the darkness upon the earth
Desolate as though a desert in a waste land
The flowers close to hide from the cold dark night
But the trees cannot hide
They blow in the wind, as if the devil possessed them.

The windswept leaves scatter around the gutters
Like a blanket of smoke
The clouds slowly cover the moon, as if to hide its face
The town is silent
Only the cats prowl around the dull, dark alleys
The street lights barely show the way
No one knows who's in the next dark place

A creaking door disturbs the tranquillity of the night
Whilst humans sleep, the wild cunning predators come out to
seek food
But soon it will be morning
The streets alive once more
And the darkness will slowly depart
From the midst of the night

   Paul David Gough

Attitude

Whatever I say, seems to be the wrong thing . . .?
Deliberate or not—controversy I bring!
Wherever I go; appointment, friends . . ."Polite I am being" . . .??
Guaranteed there'll be a verbal exchange,
Some pen-pusher's face, I'll want to re-arrange.
Nosey know-it-all's really get me down,
Sitting there frowning non-believing . . . "clown" . . .!

Systems that treat individuals as if they are "dim" . . .
Shouldn't know one's rights . . ."
not as knowledgeable as her or him" . . .?
They patronize and lie and get taken quite aback,
It's unbearable, and I have to voice—"integrity—they lack"!
Do people get trained to treat persons this way?
. . ."Never help the enquiring" . . .or, "we'll deduct one's pay" . . .?

The voice on a phone. Always arrogant—"the worst kind" . . .
Never resolve any problem. You vow; "One day you'll find" . . .!
These persons I speak of, would say the same about me . . .
Some state . . . "extremely abusive" . . .! To them I'd say . . .
"Not half as much as I'd like to be" . . .!

Andrea Garvey

Halo

That night! I shall never forget!
We were married then: Husband and wife
And oh, I did so love you—my good and gentle man.

What made me arise, I wonder, in the dark, before the dawn?
Yes, I went "walkabout" and you still sleeping.
I tiptoed not to wake you.

But when I returned from nocturnal walking,
Musings—I saw you differently.
Still sleeping, on your side, your face
So calm, so peaceful,l eyes closed . . .

And yet—so different: Something new about you..
About your head a halo and from your eyes shone pure, pure light:
A giant halo of silver-gold!

That light of strange translucence
Shone from your eyes like headlamps from a car,
Outlining the window curtains on the far side of the room
And I, in awe and wonder, witnessed this strange, unique,
phenomenon.

Months later you died, my strong-souled, loving hero.
I mourn alone. How can I live without you?
But if I am good, as Christ and you were good,
Maybe I'll earn the same distinction; find Heaven a second home!

Connie L. Francis

Sad People of Rwanda

They trudge along the open roads with no safe place to go.
The sad poor people of Rwanda are pulled too and fro.
A weak mother with a little child cradled on her knee.
A face that tells it all, will some one listen to her plea?

When aid gets through it starts again she'll fight for what she can.
With arms outstretched and fighting, she has to be the man.
A lone boy lost as parents flea, and strive to get back home.
He stands alone on the road of gloom, a small boy left to roam.

Men women and children lie injured and dead all around.
Some hugged together in little groups blocking out the mad sounds.
Others wonder about in tears and wonder when will it end.
Some giving up and just laying around, without even a friend.

No mother deserves seeing her children wiped out, and pain
she goes through.
 But she must see why among the hail of bullets there's
nothing she can do.
The aid workers risk their own lives, when helping these
people in need.
It makes me feel so sad, as a lot of it is caused by greed.

It's been like this since time began, with tribe fighting tribe.
With people running hungry and scared, with no were to hide.
Why has this to happen, you may wonder how it can.
For revenge, greed, and power, that is all caused by man.

Shirley Ann Quinn

Graveyard

Where else is there land tranquil as this
Or any place else bereft of bliss?
For graves are tombs which are made of stone,
Beneath is many a resting bone:
Some were lazy, a disgrace to all,
Others worked hard, had no rest at all.
Some were healthy, gay, others were sick,
But all are buried here, take your pick,
For only a few can read the name,
The rain washed and chipped, most look the same.
Who can tell if they were king or queen
Or if the bones a beggar had been?
For they are to all, the same to me,
They remain as bones for all to see.
No matter how good we are in life,
Or how bad we be during our strife,
The bones remain as to all in death
The same as the rest, there is no breath.

Norman E. Grimes

Decland

The rain lashed against the window pain, reminiscence of tears
tumbling onto rosy porcelain cheeks.
A painted smile would fool not one being!
Rhythms that rock one's stormy emotions—from a torrid
metamorphosis of teardrops to waterfalls of white foam.
But the face remains unchanged, as if hidden by a solitary
mark captured by the stimulus of the moment.
Though the dancing rain appears to be laughing through
a mysterious cloak draped, as for a king over the shoulders
of a cloud, and yet an orange hue lights the faded sky,
to uncover the secrets of the fire bird passing this way.

She sees nothing!

Surrounded by an exhibition of all that is nature and calm,
but for the presence of a silver spaceship with a knight in
shining armour in its charge, a statue which hastens to
approach! But disappears again along with the rain.

Escapism is such a beautiful notion for her.

Jean Jones

Tartarus

In the beginning of life, there was love, there was life, no strife
only life. Good that the great God gave us, I only hope that I
don't go to Tartarus.

If you are bad and don't repent your ways, you will never see
better days. The great God knows our ways, so do what you
know is right, and with a ray, a beam of light, look at the stars,
you know what's right. Strength and duty is the call, or you
will fall, and that means Tartarus that you will befall.

Tartarus who wants that? Better to be kind and never look back.
Who wants to go where there is no love or peace? Please God keep
Me contented and guide Me through this life, give Me
strength and wisdom to get things right. Tartarus I will say
good-night.

Peace and love will win through, forgiving what others do to you.
I pray that others in the human race, will find grace, understanding,
that we all are born in sin, but some-how I know we can win.
If you do what the great God has to say, you will then keep
Tartarus at bay.

David Campbell Stuart

Little Boy Lost

Little boy lost where are you, little angel with eyes of blue,
you are here but you are not, trapped in your autistic world
from where there is no escape. We can't get in you can't get
out. You laugh at us all day, your smile brightens up our lives
in a very special way. We love you son and that's no lie, a
love that will never die, on that you can depend and never
worry. We'll try to make everything all right
and make your world forever bright.

Andrew & Renee McAlpine

The Angry Cloud 04-12-96

The black and grey cloud hung over the pleasant little town
The Sunny Dunny is the vernacular used by all and sundry around
From my viewpoint high above where birds tame the air
My thoughts turn to that dark cloud full of dismay and despair

The lightning forks they thrashed and tore at trees and
  buildings alike
Most stood up to that force thrown down with incredible might
To be fair the majority came out of it without so much as a care
Then there are others left with nothing, and are still running scared.

Some buildings lost roof tiles, damaged ridge tiles and runes
Walls were collapsing, throwing up dust clouds with audible moans
A story that was related to me gave me quite a great scare
The total loss of your roof sounds like a living nightmare

The perch I had chosen on that cold November day
Is a landmark of Fife with some controversy I heresy
An Indian or Chieftain Warrior in slumber I was told
Just like the Fife miners Dick says, they were true and were bold

The snow lay deep and in drifts on that beautiful hill
And I assure you that the Chieftan lay incredibly still
Perhaps from past experience he knew just what to do
Just lie and be quiet and hope that the cloud does not kill

Peter Sandford

The Isonzo River

From high up in the Triglav mass descends a river-ribbon blue,
the Slovene mountains watch her pass
and gurgle with the joy of youth.
Long pathways chisels in the Karst,
and scours out limestone caverns dark
that never see Sun's glinting tricks—
condemned, like waters of the Styx.

But, look, her art has outside led:
she sparkles through Gorizian vines,
but youth's long caution makes her bed the Italian-Slovene
  borderline.
Now forced to skirt a jutting hill,
abandoning her Patria, spills
her waters onto blood-stained ground, and battlefields curves
her sinews round.

Isonzo, did the war-time howls
come haunt you, that your home should leave?
Did fear or passion drive you down towards the Adriatic Sea?
An ancient call to meet your fate and mix your waters infinite?
I know that shoreline, all these years,
still moistened by your heartache's tears.

Susan Biggin

Today's People

If you go to the town or shopping centre today
You will see the economy flourishing away.
There's plenty of money everywhere: money to spend or
throw away.
People driving expensive cars and dressed like royalty,
Everything is above standard and no sign of poverty.
People speak of high standard and the economy is strong.
People have plenty of everything—proof of nothing is wrong.
But if you care to look a bit further, you are in for a big shock,
Some people have a low income or have no income at all.
For those people, the poverty is all around the clock.
What else can make them begging, steeling,
and sleeping in a cardbox?
Many people suffer unnecessarily and crime is very high
Especially with old people who are scared of being victims of crime,
And some people, they have no place to live or they haven't
got a dime.
There are some sick and invalid who are suffering too long
Because the hospitalization and treatment are out of control.
No beds are available and the hospitals staff cannot cope
And the sick and invalid remain suffering and hope.

Stephanos Pallicaros

The Changing

A bright crisp autumn morning, light frost competing with
summer's last attempt to linger, and winning.
Nature's fullness bowing to the season's pressure,
leaves brown and branches thinning.
This stark reminder to us all that change is always racing
and we must meet with it head on, embracing.

If life is likened to the year, time marked by the changes
and the phases like the seasons.
Then child and youth will sprout and grow to maturity
where he will understand the reasons.
When winter days so dark and cold begin to point the finger,
it is but that sad season's time reminding,
The purpose is fulfilled and cannot linger.

The autumn phase marks time to reap what has been sown
with knowing and reflecting.
Relating the experience, resigning and respecting.
Life and time, await no one, as part of heaven's plan
the world will keep revolving
As surely as the seasons change our kind will keep evolving.

Frances Morgan

First Flight

I rose from bed with time enough to get things done before I leave,
first flight nerves and I'm feeling rough, butterflies you would
not believe!
Can't change my mind, the taxi is here, driver waiting to take the case,
leaving the street without a tear, wishing now for a faster pace
to start the journey up to town, another cab 'cross the city,
catch the Airbus, glad to sit down, looking forward, no self pity.
Terminal two, enormous place, check in the case and book my seat,
time to put a smile on my face, look for a drink, something to eat.
Everyone out while search is made 'til unknown object found
and clear, now all the flights have been delayed, sit on the
plane, take-off is near.
Gathering speed we leave the ground climbing through grey
sky and the cloud,
brilliant sunlight circling us round, now I relax and feel quite proud.
Another world where time stands still, the earth below so far away,
thought of the height gives quite a thrill, forgotten fear at start of day.
Time for descent has just begun, chew a sweet to help clear the ears,
the change of pressure not much fun, ready to land as ground
appears.
Never a bump, we hurtle on down the runway, starting to slow,
stopping at last, the flight is done, the first of many, this I know.

Ann Odger

Untitled

It was almost noon
And it couldn't come a moment too soon
I'm a Data Entry clerk
And on my Lunch I would embark.

The afternoon went smoothly for a while
But on my supervisor's face was this soppy smile
She called me over—"A word I'd like
You're not up to standards dear—so on your bike . . ."

I packed my bags and made my home before 4.00
I'd be more positive in the future and that was for sure . . .
I'd visit my daughter—that would cheer me up
I asked her "Would you pour me tea in a china cup"

She was in a foul mood—there was no doubting that
Lisa seemed an almost hideous monstrous brat
"Make it yourself, I'm watching my favorite programme now
And don't be so lazy—it's something I don't abide or allow . . ."

How dare my daughter talk to me like that
I'd be more assertive in the future—my meekness I would
have to combat!
I have now learnt to be more bold as this poem will unfold.

Carole Hyer

The Toy Soldier

One day when my mother was cleaning,
she asked me to clean out her cupboard.

Apart from some packets of garden seed,
I threw out all the things she did not need.

Some old shoes she did not want, a half tin of paint that had gone
hard, a picture frame, an old Christmas card.

As I swept the dust from the bottom of the cupboard a spider
scuttled away, then to my surprise in the corner of the
cupboard a little toy soldier lay.

I put down the brush and picked him up and sat on a chair nearby,
as I rolled him between my finger and thumb,
I thought how good he still looked in his helmet and gun.

With a little smile I stood him up,
remembering long ago when he was me and I was him,
and we won all the battles we were in.

But sadly as the years went by
to him and my childhood—it was Good Bye.

Thomas Bell

Life Here!

What makes man have faith in the ephemeral human
relations is an enigma unsolved.
Perhaps it is the debt of the past or a prologue to the future.

Being born an accident or design we do not know
With parents we did not choose.
Or even augur so a design? We do not know.

Our todays and tomorrows seconds, minutes, hours,
Days, week, months and years.
Shared, joyous, lamented and laid bare, emotions.

Gained, lost, given or taken correctly, robbed or cheated
Moments of despair.
Struggled, succeeded failed and prospered but what?

Everything seen enjoyed and collected in abundance
Treasures more dear.
Then left the world departed with nothing I declare.

Still we live, share, trust, yearn, relate with friends and
family but why care?
When we do not know what makes man have faith in
ephemeral human relations . . . ?!

H. S. Bhogal

Nightmare

Again the boom of the drums drums of doom
as past and present meet and mingle on the windy up land
path the path of the tomb and the leaves rise and swirl and
swirl in eddies across the path of dreams as the dead lie sleeping
and the sleeping are dying

Then I see him eternal itinerant with shambling gait
face sere like a leaf and crisscrossed with grief
never ending anguish beyond relief
staggering from doss house to doss house with the stink of
gaol upon him casting the blackened stumps of yellowed teeth
upon communal garbage dumps with his hair full of the blood
of ticks and sores like ponds upon him the incubation of all
human misery the incarnation of debased humanity

Tremble at self's future vision and pray when the prison and
the madhouse open wide their jaws to engulf forever behind
barred windows and locked doors when sinister shadows
assemble in tenebral darkness and gone forever is endymion
then in mercy let the soul fly to fields elysian or enter naked
into the wind along the road, and the void enigma open to
oblivion

Maurice Hemmant

Plod

There is a man who walks our streets, who stands out from the crowd
He wears a dark blue uniform, of which he's fiercely proud.
He's known by all around the place, for years this beat he's trod
Some call him by his proper name; by most he's known as Plod.
He likes the title "Constable", though some folk think it formal.
To those he knows, who've been inside, it strikes them as quite
normal to pay respect to Mister Smith who, oft times had them lifted.
He'd watched them all as they grew up and into crime had drifted.
He'll tackle all that's on his plate and, always, with a smile.
He only needs to meet you once. He doesn't need a file.
With names and faces he's a whizz, his memories superb.
He spoke with you five years ago, for parking on the kerb!
Something you'd forgotten, but not so PC Smith.
It's all there in his memory-bank and comes in useful if
a crime has been committed and leads are hard to find.
Just speak to PC three-two-two and he will turn his mind
to solving yet another complex case of "Who did what"
He is so omnicompetent, he really has the lot!
He talks to children in their class. He makes his lessons fun.
To them he is top of the cops, he's always number one!

John Eden

Soup of Security

Ingredients:
  1 jar of happy tears
  1/2 a jar of sad tears
  2 bowls of hugs and kisses
  a spoonful of respect
  a pinch of doubts
  2 portions of trust and faith
  1/2 a spoon of chopped fights and quarrels
  a cup of understanding and tolerance

Method:

Stir fry a spoonful of respect with 1/2 a spoonful of chopped
fights and quarrels. Leave it till it gives an aroma of tranquillity and serenity. Then pour 1 jar of happy tears and 1/2 a jar
of sad tears. Mix them well by stirring with much smiles. Add
in 2 portions of trust and faith, a cup of hugs and kisses, a
bowl of understanding and tolerance. Stir the mixture with
abundance of joy and patience with a magical ladle of affection. Make sure that the soup is boiled under the hot and
passionate fire of desire. Don't forget to add a pinch of
doubts then sprinkle with eternal love. Now pour the soup of
security into 2 bowls of heavenly love and it's ready to be
served in each and every day.

Suie Yim Boey

The Daffodil

I have been underground for a long time,
all curled up asleep.
My golden shine in darkness and grime,
underneath the ground so deep.
I have worked my way up to the new sky,
but the wind is strong and rushes by.
I slowly start to open my eyes,
and take in all that is new.
Surrounding me are all my friends,
the sky is a heavenly blue.
I slowly start to open,
with encouragement from the crisp sun.
As I start to feel the air,
Spring has surely begun.
I am now with my friends and just see how I shine!
Although I know I have to go in just a little time.
Just for now I shall stand proud and use my bright call
to shout out loud, spring is here! Yes it has come! Let everyone
know down below, to bring their colours and come!
For that is my will, as the dancing daffodil, to let everyone
know spring has sprung!

Fiona Martin

Dear Mother Earth

Dear Mother Earth we love so well, what of the future can you foretell?
Will the mountains always reach down to the sea?
Our children!, will they always cherish thee?
Will the stars, twinkling bright! Glisten and light our way at night?

Will music forever be the food of love?
May lovers in such times of bliss, reach for heaven! Yet sometimes miss,
Will changing seasons year by year, engender on trees some fruit to bear?
The scent of flowers which make us swoon!
Our gardens! Will there be sufficient room?

As you get smaller day by day, while concrete jungles have their sway
Do we have enough to say, to save you from the throning mass
The cars and lorries which crowd our land,
This modern age which we believe? Revolves for all around T.V.
Can we save us from ourselves?
Go back to when we used to shop, for sherbert dabs and lollipops

Eric Jeffrey Johnson

The Morning After

Blue sky's shadow on a fresh green earth awakens the dream of a night.
Sunbeams flicker and cobwebs glitter and wood smoke climbs to a height
while a thrush sings to its audience the world.
Bacon crackles and coffee brews, a new day's problems present.
And after the storms and thunder roll the sun fingers its way to this earth and gathers the tears she cried.

Maria Mulholland

Togetherness

As the days of Autumn lengthen into Winter
The ecstasy of our encounter will fade
As is the state of man
Eve she came, enchantress, Lover
To find her Adam, Wholesome and Sound

Headlong from Paradise
We may be slung
But not like Lucifer
Chained to the burning stake
So
As the light fades
Let us remake our Souls
Together
On our earthly journey
A whole
Formed out of two halves.

John E. Paul

The Enchanted River

As I stand by the riverside and gaze in wonder at the beauty of the Swans gracefully drifting by,
I see reflected in the waters deep down a bright blue sky

Beneath the river gently lapping at my feet I catch sight
of fish of great variety, endlessly searching for visitor's treats.
For the mirrors of the World are rivers, sparkling as diamonds in the golden sunlight;
Cascading down natural waterfalls the river, joyously flows along,
silver fish leaping, joining in the fun, a rare and beautiful sight.

I follow the river through fields of yellow ripening corn, and there, in the meadows, cattle contentedly grazing and along side of them their newborn;

Surrounding these wonders of Nature, a mass of red poppies swaying in the gentle breeze, all reflected in the restless rive, as rubies glistening enhanced by the Sun.

For mirrors of the World are rivers reflecting all things near and far, God's gift to mankind from above
To be nurtured and cared for, with our love.

Dorothy F. White

Ode to Bengad Woodrush

Unable to strike out, unwilling to rear,
Unable to manage a small running tear,
Not once in his lonely, sad, little life
Did he ever deserve such trouble and strife.
Life was hard, when torn off the moors,
Mankind is viscous, brutal and course.
Poor and unhealthy, sick, skin and bone,
What had he done? How to atone?
So badly beaten, a back full of sores
A man did this! To settle old scores?
I found him, nursed him, brought him back home
Fed him and groomed him, made him my own
Then one lonely morning after five years
My cup runneth over, my heart filled with tears
A mishap in the stable, he was taken away,
His neck badly broken at the dawn of the day
Now Pony Heaven looks after my Ben
Where he will stay till we meet again.

Dawn Cunningham

Heritage

Listen, can you hear it, the silence all around,
the stillness and the beauty, it's so peaceful
I have found.
The mountains so majestic, but so dangerous as well
all this beauty takes my breath away
craggy peak, to mossy fell.

This wonder all around me, so abundant and so real
I let it just surround me, all that energy I feel,
it's so seldom that we see it, we're so busy, day to day
we take it all for granted, we just treat it, by the way.

All that nature has to offer, we never stop to think,
how we use it, and abuse it, we push it to the brink.
We should nourish it and keep it, with tender loving care,
to ensure our children's children
can enjoy that stillness there.

Freida Murray

The Last Roses of Summer

The last of the roses are finished this season,
the gardens look bare, there is a reason.
They've to face a hard winter, snow, winds and rain
they will still be lovely when they flower again
the leaves on the trees now are copper and gold
but trees lose their beauty as the weather turns cold.
The berries are left as food for the birds,
there is beauty around us we can't put into words
now take a look round you and what do you see
killings and road rage with no harmony.
Innocent children their lives just beginning.
There will always be killings while guns are around,
there will always be blood shed were there's knives to be found.

E. Ward

Lili-Mae

This little baby we have made,
Her skin so soft it feels like suede,
Her beautiful body held within me,
Waking and sleeping, as warm as can be.

Her eyes that twinkle, glow and shine,
Lips so perfect, like her body and mind,
So sweet and innocent as can be,
That's why we're so proud, her Daddy and Me.

Her hair is golden like the sun,
She has tiny feet waiting to run,
We hold her close when she cries,
Sharing a love that never dies.

Waiting for a voice that will say to me,
I love my Mummy and Daddy
As much as they'll always love me.

Rachel A. Hyland

Untitled

As I wander through the land of dreams,
My thoughts fly past me.
Bells of my wedding ring around me.
I am now trapped.
I am a bird trapped in a cage.
Someone please open a door
To this tedious and unhappy life of mine.
Let me run through the dark woods.
Hurt and confused is me.
Wake me up.
Please wake me up from myself.

Suzanne Harrison

Looking for Love

Cometh one day I shall find
That in which I seek so much,
To give my heart to one so kind.
Even if you feel the Love to touch,
From within me you will find
A lonely soul for you to touch.
So tread carefully within my heart
As it is broken from within.
Each day I hope to feel
That love in which I never have found.
Is it too much to dream, as I lay upon my bed?
The morning brings hope as the birds make their sounds.
Today life shall bring forth some hope.
Love is all I ask, how can I cope?
Who knows what life will bring today.
Come let it bring the best of things
Until my heart is filled with joy.
I shall sit each day and pray
For someone to reach out and touch my heart.

Micheal Byrne

Lost in a Bottle

I have lived in a bottle and it doesn't work
It helps at the time but only leaves hurt.
I've lost loved ones, more than a few
But the bottom of a bottle doesn't help you.

It helps for a while and eases the pain
But when you're sober it hits you again.
What you need is someone there for you
To tell you the best thing that you can do.

Family or friends who have been there before
Can help you through it and to live life once more.
Not feeling like this will be totally bliss,
They couldn't want you to feel like this.

Life goes on whatever the future holds
what happens tomorrow no one knows,
So live life the best you can for now
Just don't hit the bottle and throw in the towel.

Barry Taylor

The Pier

As I walk along the pier I see my reflection in the water,
The reflection has no worries, no fears and nothing to do,
And for a moment I see myself as a small child,
Happy, carefree and nothing in the world can bother me,
Now those memories are washed away by a sea of
hatred, guilt, problems, worries and many more things.
What has gone wrong, when did I go this way?
I am gone, the real person inside is dead,
I am just a body with no spirit,
My spirit's dead and gone.
The pier looks dark and grey and I will not see it bright again,
The way I will remember the world is dark,
Now it is over, time is up, the sun will never rise again for me,
The pier dark and grey, a light shines on top of me and I see
Another reflection happy, cheerful, telling me what I can be like,
The face is smiling.
A smile I will remember always,
Now I think of what beauties the world will bring to me tomorrow.

Karen Cunningham

Dedicated to Mike . . .

My life was so empty,
Until you came along,
You put a smile back on my face,
And made me feel real strong.

Forever there, forever wanted,
My lover and trusted friend,
My guide and mentor,
Until the very end.

Morning, noon and night,
Spending every minute together,
Walking, laughing,
Braving all kinds of weather.

Trial and error will conquer all,
We've both had heartaches in the past,
So let's bury them deep,
And make this relationship last,

Loving you is easy,
That's all I'm trying to show,
And to tell you how much I love you,
More than you'll ever know.

Nadine Jacobs

Season Fairies

Spring does arise! Little are we aware
That the previous night the delicate fairies were there,
They roused the ground with the kiss of the sun,
Then shed a tear on the tip of each blade of grass,
Fluttering 'round the daffodils, they dressed each one in gold.

Spring transforming to Summer, the fairies lend a helpful hand,
They chase the yellow sun until it gets fiery red and angry,
They encourage the flower buds to open,
Like a sergeant waking his tired troops for battle,
Then they positioned cotton-wool clouds in the sapphire sky.

They make a brew of Autumn colours; copper, fire and clementine,
They pour it on the leaves; a kaleidoscope in the trees,
Oh! Whisper to the thistledown, hum to the dandelion seed!
They dance and sing in the trees, each leaf falls to the floor,
Dancing over, they weave together the clouds now diamonds fall.

In Winter their wands cast a glacial spell,
The leaves grow grey and wrinkled and lay to die in the soil,
The fairies hurl through the sky, riding tiny white horses,
They pound on the waters wearing heavy snow boots,
The poor water, weary from the weight, stands still.

Sarah Page

My Wish of Love

You are not here, you have gone away,
Out of our lives, our lives to stay.

We said goodbye in the dead of night.
You had to go, his time for you was right.

He needed you to help him, this we know is true,
For the love you gave everyone, he could only have chosen you.

You are now with family, friends and all,
But if it's possible, you will hear my call.

I'm sure you see me and hear me talk,
When I'm alone, alone I do not walk.

You are my father, my one and only,
Sometimes I wish I wasn't so lonely.

I couldn't tell you I loved you, it wasn't what we did,
I cared for you and helped you through, but this guilt I cannot rid.

If only I could turn back time, I would tell you so,
To tell you I love you, I know the pain would surely go.

So now I wish upon a star, number 3 from the left of the moon,
I now tell you "I Love You" and will surely see you soon.

Linda Conboy

Alone

When life begins you're on your own, fighting one's own war,
As you get older, you may think you've been before,
Through all life's struggles, hopes and fears,
Many times you will shed some tears,
But through all this you must sometimes smile,
As you pass over another of life's turnstiles.

Along with age the body becomes weak,
Bones and muscles grind and creak,
Wrinkles show on hands and face,
Simply because of life's big race;
A race with time: One cannot win,
Only pass it on to next of kin.

Then as the final breath draws near,
All the senses, they disappear,
Alas, the fight with time is lost,
Only a life can pay the cost.
Alone at birth. Alone at the end.
It's sad, you have to die to meet a friend.

John Hampson

What I Miss Now That I Am Blind

I miss the birds,
I miss people although I can hear their words,
I miss the colour of autumn trees,
I miss the ripples on the water from the breeze,
I miss watching the squirrels nut fall,
I miss the spider climbing the wall,
I miss the sight of my father and mother,
I miss my brother,
I miss watching my granny knit.
But most of all I wish the darkness could be lit.

Tara Chapple

Time

As a child awaiting Christmas it took so long to come
And the summers seemed to last forever and were filled with
   so much fun
Rushing over breakfast to be first down on the sand
Sundays lying in bed serenaded by the Salvation Army band
Time was something that passed slowly with learning all the way
So why it is when we're older time rushes by each day?
From being a child yourself you become a busy mum
A little older, yes, but still relatively young
The children become adults and leave on adventures of their own
Suddenly it's quiet with just the two of you at home
Then you realize how precious is this time that you have free
Before the family return to put grandchildren at your knee
You can't believe it's happened but time has passed for you
Time isn't just something that passes for the select few
Memories we gathers as we move along with time
Something to keep hold of—I wouldn't be without mine.
As long as time gives some meaning then it really was worthwhile
To have participated willingly in times uncharted mile

Shirley P. Rowntree

One Desperate Thought . . .

I wish a freedom from unnecessary burdens,
The heavy load I can no longer bear,
Slacken the weight strapped across my shoulders,
Strains my back, forces muscle to tear;
Please loosen the vice that tightens so around my skull,
As pressure is building up inside my head.
I will surrender, admit myself the weaker one,
For if life returned as it was once,
I'd have the energy to carry on.

Perhaps I have been a fool,
A slave to a world I helped create,
Now at its beckon call,
Nurturing an existence only to suffer so alone through it all,
Sacrificing every single moment,
everyday until the day I die,
Without chances to challenge the reasons,
as my own life passes by . . .

Lisamaria Miller

Sonnet

When there appears no purpose to the pain;
When nobody is near enough to see
The deep dark melancholic strain
Coursing through and devastating me;
When it seems I've squandered much of life,
Talents and trials in Time's tempestuous haste
And thoughts like these are thrusting like a knife,
Wounding awareness with that sense of waste;
Endure, endure is all that I can do,
In turmoil yet refusing to be hurled
To where grows only rosemary and rue
Along this lonely clifftop of the world.
   I am victorious in only this: to keep
      From trespassing on others when I weep.

Zoë Lee

Waiting for Tomorrow

Each day I wait for the postman to arrive
Just a few short lines will do to let
me know you're still alive
I never for a moment stop thinking of you
Waiting for you to get in touch and say
you love me too
But each day comes round, and with a
tear in my eye
I know before he gets here, he'll walk
straight by
But I must go on hoping, for without
hope one is lost
And life has to go on at any cost
Perhaps tomorrow, or the day after that
I'll see that long awaited letter lying
there on the mat
Then I'll open it up and see
"Hello Mum"
Oh, dear Lord, if only tomorrow would come.

Jaime Betts

If Only!

Seven score years and ten,
Widowed, alone, family grown,
Time to wonder if and when,
Would I have changed, had I know then.
The things one learns as one grows old?
How different life would then have been
If into the future I could have seen
To make use of the things I had been told,
Instead of waiting 'till I grew old.

Barbara J. Carr

The Swan

The Swan sent her letter to Pinetree Road.
Was it the beginning, or an end to her new abode?
Please God, let him reply,
that much he surely could not deny.

Their letters began to flow between
telling of all those years and shattered dreams.
For Boxing Day a date was set,
such a long time since they had met.

So much to say in such a short time
but with all nerves forgotten they got along just fine.
They arranged to meet next day
for a walk, and lots more to say.

Then off they went to Birmingham
to a Gala Dinner for the Swan and her man.
A perfect night with her perfect friend,
it was truly a shame it ever had to end.

Though end it did and home she came
to hope and dream for more of the same.
Now for her future the stage is set
she must follow her heart for it's not over yet.

Sally Drummond

Evacuation

I feel so alive,
Away from the hideous war,
that will lose many lives and ruin yards of land.

I was delighted at the sight of the shimmering eggs.
Laid by the pondering hen,
who stood silently in the stony yard,
pecking at the tiny corn.

Terrified at the sight of a strange earthly machine,
that broke up the dirty soil with a peculiar pattern.
I roared like thunder as it scored the parched field,
leaving dust clouds and scattering birds in its path.

Bursting with energy I grew excited.
Climbing over a wooden fence into a grassy field,
as I stared with joy at a herd of cows.
Astounded as they grazed peacefully in the golden sunlight.

The sun shone heavenly upon the farm,
catching the blossoming trees.
The beautiful fragrance of the land,
spoiled only by the misery of war.

Claire M. Martin

Me

What happened to that young girl I once knew?
What happened to that body I had?
I look in the mirror and see what is there
And say that isn't the girl I once knew.
The hair isn't golden it's grey now,
The waistline is thicker these days,
My left leg is wonky and makes me all cronky;
It's changed my lifestyle and my ways.
Things don't look good I say again and again.
What ever is happening to my little brain?
The memory is going. Oh what a shame!
When I can't remember, I say What's His Name

Jacqueline Bormond

The Priceless Gift of Good Health

How many healthy people truly see
　The plight of those denied such luck ?
How many understand the daily battle
　They fight with such defiant pluck ?

Can any of us picture what it means,
　To lose one's sight and thus be blind ?
Can any visualize the black distress,
　Which goes with illness of the mind ?

Can any comprehend the endless silence,
　When the doors of hearing close ?
Can anyone conceive the searing pain
　Severe arthritis can impose ?

How many have a realistic concept
　Of what a wasting illness means ?
How many gauge the guilt the sick one feels
　Towards the one on whom he leans ?

It's sad so many seem to be so helpless
　T'wards those who try so hard to cope !
Too many healthy folk are just 'too busy' . . .
　To give their hapless brethren hope !

Stuart Morrison

Bon-Fire Night

It's bon-fire night, it's bon-fire night
Thousands of faces full of delight
Catherine wheels swirling around and around
Dazzling rockets fall to the ground
Flying saucers fly in the air
Lots of people come to stare
All different colours red, blue and green
Huge bright sights have been seen
What a wonderful night we all have had
When it comes next year, oh, I will be glad.

Sara Blackhall

Alone

Sitting alone amongst silence,
The world a mere background set,
Watching a distant cast perform,
Whilst re-writing the script.
For now I am alone!

Ourselves in solitude,
So unlike the selves that prying minds do see,
Motionless, silent, content,
Judged only by the inner being,
Watched only by the mind's eye.
Scene by scene the play goes on!

Willing the hero to defeat the growing crowd,
Spurring on his blade,
The faded lines of act one now lost.

Alone is still.
Alone is sacred.
Alone is true.

The curtains fall,
The world awaits!

Sarah Cooksley

The Drowned Pup

It is very very wet, and cold outside,
I saved the life of a nearly half drowned pup,
Which filled my heart with a lot of pride,
But my hands were so cold I dropped a cup.

It smashed into pieces all over the floor,
I had to bend down but my knees were sore,
I found it quite hard to get myself up,
I tried to make it to the front door,
But realized the pup I saved had just died.

I took it outside and buried him under a tree,
And said a little prayer now your spirit can roam free,
That's what happened to me on a cold winter's day
And now that's all I have to say.

All of a sudden, I felt a nice warm glow,
And a little voice said it's time to go,
You have to spread the chosen word,
Because now your voice has to be heard.

H. Clark

Untitled

Tell the children "sorry for throwing their futures away
For the planet we are killing each and every day
For the hunger, pain and suffering we have caused on the way"
Tell the children "sorry that the ozone layer is fading away,
and the scientists are running out of things to say
For bringing them into a world of trouble and decay
A world where the strong get stronger and the weak fade away".
Tell the children "sorry that we threw it all away".

Tony Wild

Poppies

Guns, shooting, firing, killing, that's the way we remember the war.
People, running, screaming, dying, now the people suffer no more.
Another way to remember the brave
Is to wear a special flower on a special day.
Poppies as red as blood to show we feel,
We know the war that caused pain was real.
So wear your poppy with sadness but pride,
To remember the people who fought in the war and died.
Families lose members, they'll never feel the same.
It could have just finished as a silly game.
But it went on leaving a trace,
Killing men, changing the world, to a sad instead of happy face.
First it was ten, then grew to more.
Soon people needed to dig huge holes in the floor,
Acting as graves for those millions who died.
Ringing in our ears, crying people whose loved ones have died.
So wear your poppy with sadness but pride,
To remember the people who fought in the war, and died.

Katherine Steadman

Evil

The evil that surrounds us
has victory for its own
as long as we do nothing
it's free to roam and roam.

Picking on the weak
it's not a caring thing
waging war upon its victims
with pain and suffering.

Lost within a world
where pain is all we know
what chance is there for hope
and happiness to grow?

Helen Thompson

Tilted Trilby

Soothed, a morn of summer's balm
to calm her mood in arbour shade
with lemonade at fingertips
sweet the taste upon her lips
she glimpsed the lawn of dappled green
this the scene of first her glance
upon his tilted trilby stance
a yesterday to ne'er forget
nor let the moment slip away
the memory shall always stay
and be her own forever
ne'er to fade, yet there to find
at will, in her mosaic mind
tender thoughts when days like this
teased her mood in total bliss
then, a game of true romance
to dance upon the balmy air
now, a game of solitaire
pining for his absent charm
yet soothed, a morn of summer's balm.

Elizabeth Wilson

Ode to an Eagle

O bird of prey with mighty wings
Unlike the nightingale who sings
Her songs at night.
For you I have no love to give,
While on the smaller birds you live
And soar to any height.
I have no pity in my heart
For you. So now depart!
But as you raise your cruel wing
Listen! And hear that small bird sing.

Frances Heckler

Futility

A young soldier went to war,
Though much against his will,
He didn't want to fight,
Nor did he want to kill.

A young soldier went to war,
He turned to wave goodbye,
He felt it was the last time,
We saw him give a sigh.

A young soldier went to war,
They gave to him a gun,
They said he had to fight,
Until the war was won.

A young soldier went to war,
He never asked them why,
He didn't want to fight,
Nor did he want to die.

A young soldier went to war,
To face the battle's strife,
Why did he have to fight,
Why did he give his life.

James T. Wray

Dignity Departed

All her worldly chattels
Crammed in a single case
Lying crumpled in a corner
She's going no special place

Home is someone's doorway
Food scavenged from a bin
Cigarettes and whisky
And lager from a tin

Dignity's a by-gone day
Pride scattered round her feet
A dismal, wretched consequence
Of living on the street

She drinks until oblivion
Has dulled her every sense
No longer must she think about
The system she resents

Eyes that hold such sorrow
Pain has touched her heart
It hurts so much remembering
She forgets the painful parts

Gwen Dingwall

The Poppy

The brightness of a poppy
Of petals strong and bold,
Reminds us of those who
Gave their lives in such a way,
For they gave their todays
For our tomorrows,
Tears shed for loved ones
The white headstones
Line upon line, row after row
Little wooden crosses
Standing in the cold with
Bright red poppies for a heart.
Brave men and women
We remember in prayer,
Who sadly gave their yesterdays
For our today.

Maureen Alderson

Canine Cruelty

Dog breeders straight from hell
Degrade your name, mine as well
May everyone expose your cover
You are not a real dog lover

Who cannot cringe at the sight
Of an emaciated animals plight?
The only interest can be gain
Oblivion to a creature's pain

Innocent suffer from what you do
Caring people yet whip lashed to
May you never be thanked for the harm
That lies within a puppy farm

Bridget Eyre

Indoors and Out

Your love for me
is like the wind in the trees,
the warmth of the sun,
like all the birds singing:
and you hold between your hands
the bird that is my secret soul.

My love for you is as strong
as the four walls of a house,
shielding all within:
warm as the glow from its windows,
watching, waiting,
an opening of the door,
a welcoming.

Rosanne Gomez

Colours

I look out of the window
And see great sights
Sometimes dark, sometimes light
The last leaf of Autumn
The suns' dying rays
The colours of roofs
The blues and the greys
The street lights are amber
As light quickly fades
The sky turning dark
The clouds tinged with Jade
The window I look through
Will soon be oblique
As I pull across the curtains
And shut off the street.

Dorothy Gray Chatterton

Gentle Tide

Shore withstood waves' force
Erosion didn't change cliff face
Ammonites stayed bedded
In centuries of sleep;

Old graves withheld bones
From sea's white broth;
Church will go down
Tide's roar muffled ancient bells
Currents washed altar clean
Of wine and clinging prayers;

Today's tides seemed gentle,
Deceptive as a cat
Playing with shadows,
Cliff edge still clung
To leaning fence.

Anne Micklethwaite

A Happy New Year to Be

Here's to you
I've only had one or two,
One more for the road
And my leave I will take.
Another for his sake
Another for hers,
Where's the dark stranger
To cross my threshold.
I drink to my daughter
In bed though she lies,
I wish for good fortune
To keep bad at bay.
We'll sip to our friendships
We'll sip to our loves
But don't forget me,
My health with the above.

Sally Craddock

Rejection

When the snow lays on the ground
When the springtime comes around
And in summer it is found
    My deepest love for you.

When the Autumn winds blow cold
When the leaves have turned to gold
Even, when we are very old
    I'll still be loving you

When you put me from your side
When there's no place left to hide
And all is gone, except my pride
    There'll be my love for you

When this world stops turning round
When there is no sight or sound
And there's nothing to be found
    Except my love for you.

Sylvia Woodrow

Flowers of Heaven

Love is never ever gone,
It's an everlasting flower.
Growing in its beauty,
In our Heavenly Father's bower.
Many are the blossoms
Beauteous to the sight.
Showerings of blessings
In the land of Heavenly tight.
Names like truth, and peace and love
Are only but a few.
Created by Our Father
To give to me and you.
In such a blessed garden
Good health and hope abound.
Alongside joy and laughter
Great happiness is found.
Ones like faith and kindness,
Growing gloriously,
But the greatest flower of Heaven
Is the one called charity.

Enid Rathbone

The Fear

Someone wise once told me
"That Earth belongs to man
It was given to us to make us feel
As important as we can".
But something in his theory,
Seems a little wrong to me
That's not the way it could, or should
or ever ought to be.
Man's been on this planet
For a small amount of years,
But in his short time on earth
He's introduced "The Fears".
The fears that keep our world
Free from future damage
For finally man's realised
The harm that he can manage.
If all supposed wise men
Would heed the things they hear
The importance that they crave so much
Wouldn't cost them half as dear.

Wayne M. Clark

My Friend

My friend,
Is as bright as the sun,
Is as gentle as the moon
As wonderful as the stars,
And as perfect,
As perfect can be.

Alan Harrison

Out-Reach

Come hither
said his eyes
and his smile
in disguise
magnet drawing metal
pins . . . bouncing
a time bomb
simmering, on the boil
waiting, to explode
crocodile eyes
half submerged
under the water
we can dance
by the whirlpool into oblivion
among the sea-horses and mermaids.
left
shaken together
entangled by seaweed
in a bottomless tomb
he scrambled away.

Pat Jones

Santa Claus

Santa Claus, Santa Claus
you are on your way
To bring joy to girls and boys
On this Christmas Day.

Down the chimney sliding neatly
You will crown our tree completely
Good old Santa Claus.

Fill the reindeers up with power.
See they rise across the towers
With your sleigh crammed full of toys
All the kinds they will enjoy.

Down the chimney sliding neatly
You will crown our tree completely
Good old Santa Claus.

Dolls and trains and aeroplanes
Footballs, soldiers, trucks and cranes
Fill all stockings up to top
Hey, presto, what a Christmas Crop.
Good old Santa Claus.

Nancie J. Abrey

Unhappiness

My love is fading
As each day goes by.
What was once a happy time
Now brings unhappiness more and
more.

As each day dawns,
I awake and wonder
What is going to happen now.
Nothing seems to go right.

Whatever I do
Kindness and love I show
are shunned.
Nothing is returned
Except anger and scorn.

When will it end,
and my life can return
To a happy one once again.
I hope it's soon.

Margaret Wood

Snow

Snow fell softly through the night
Covered everything in sight
Laid upon each bush and tree
A gown of white purity
Give to every nearby roof
A sweet while icing look
And to every boy and girl
Lots of sledging sliding joy
But softly softly as it came
It softly went away again.

Mary Elizabeth Sandover

Sadness

Sadness is like a wall of
love and hate,
blocking out the rest of the world.
It brings us down,
drags us underground.
Sadness is like the ocean . . .
deep and cold.
Sadness is melancholy
and is far from happiness.
Sadness is like a long
life of misery.
It is mournful and
regretful . . .
Sadness.

Nadine Sargent

Quietus

How gently did the river flow
Around your tortured mind,
As slowly, sinking down below,
You left this world behind.

How softly did the branches sway
Upon your final scene,
As if to rock you on your way
And make your death serene.

How calmly had you planned that day,
Within your family life
And did you really mean to lay
That burden on your wife.

How quietly did your children weep,
Beside your simple grave,
As if the pain would be too deep,
If they could not be brave.

How fondly did they speak your name,
With tenderness and pride,
Or did they lead a life of shame,
Long after you had died.

Rossline O'Gara

A Cry for Help

To my Grandma, Margaret Ward, for holding her head up throughout her illness and for her loving and giving to all who loved her.

I've wanted to cry
And haven't known why,
Maybe life would be easier
Without all the tears!

As days go by
The hurt inside soon disappears
Amongst the rest is
Just hurtful years.

The pain is the same,
Playing in my mind.
To you it might seem
Just a childish game!

The tears from my eyes
Are no longer there,
The world would be happier
Without all the despair.

Emma Long

Remember the Rainbow

When your promise has gone
And the long night is done
When your luck has run out
And your life's full of doubt
Just pause for a while
And try hard to smile
Then brush off the blues
Shake the dust from your shoes
Remember the rainbow
That promise remains so
A promise so strong
Where nothing is wrong
Take comfort in that
And have a good chat
With that then in mind
Leave worry behind
Look forward in trust
As indeed you must
With light heart give way
To a fresh bright new day.

Norma Anne Macarthur

Memory Lane

Memory Lane is the longest lane
That ever your feet will tread,
And as you travel back again
It slowly unfolds ahead.

It's like a beautiful patchwork quilt
Spread out under your feet.
The only place where you will find
Your past and your present meet.

Each footstep is a memory dear
Sometimes dark, but often bright.
A lesson that you will have learned
As dawn follows the darkest night.

So come along with me my friend
And let us travel together.
We'll share our memories on the way
In every kind of weather.

Soon all our memories will be past
When we've reached those gates of gold
To find that we are young again
And have never really grown old.

Vicki Marshall

Class Act

The worker's rights are very few
And worse they will become,
Until compassion changes hearts,
The system's built for some.

But let's examine, this mighty Master,
Who rules by fear and rage,
And treats employees with scant regard,
As they pocket the highest wage.

What care they, about what's right,
Can the workers check on them,
When mistakes are made and money lost,
And covered up by pen.

Power is their sword, and shield,
Where justice has no place,
And exploitation, sneers its grin,
On the weakest of the race.

What price it costs a nation,
When greed sends forth its lure,
And loving one another,
Means sacrifice the poor.

Duncan M. MacNicol

Snowflakes

Swirling and whirling
Like swansdown they fall.
Gently and quietly
Surprising us all.

Disguising the bleakness
With softness and light
Creating new landscapes
A sheer, sparkling delight.

Forming, lacy white fringes,
A cloak for the bareness
Of dark, winter hedgerows,
Bending down low.

Cushioning the snowdrops,
Waiting for spring,
Protecting the tenderness,
which lies within.

Those tiny, white snowflakes,
So cool and so fragile.
Change the grim starkness,
To something quite magical.

Hilda Mason

Untitled

Sit alone amongst short green
grass, sitting there beside
that lump of stone.

Talk, and into the air your
words go.
And wish that someone
was listening.

Bare your heart and wish
someone would talk to you
And wish and wish
someone would say Hello!

No doubt they've heard,
but cannot speak.

But, whilst you're sitting
by that gravestone, they're
listening to you.

Philip Trenor Williams

Conceit

"I am a clever chap" he said
And then he smiled and shook his head
"It is a pity, I can see
That others aren't as bright as me."

"I'm very good at Maths, you know
And I can knit and I can sew";
And with a smirk upon his face
He said he'd won the Steeplechase.

"I'm also pretty good at gym"
(We looked in disbelief at him)
"I climb the ropes and jump the horse—
I am the very best, of course."

"And writing, that's my special thing
And I can dance, and I can sing
And though I'm not a man to boast
I cook a superb Sunday roast!"

We'd hoped that we would never meet
Someone so bold with such conceit,
Then, as he strutted down the lane
He fell into a manhole drain!

Janet Jones

Alive

I woke up this morning
Thank God I am alive
I've no wife
Or a job
I don't smoke
Nor do I drink
Thank God I am alive

William Corbett

Precious Hours

In life's golden moments.
If we had but the power
To make those moments timeless
And keep that precious hour

Looking back on happy memories
That we've had in the past
Wouldn't it be wonderful
If it could only last?

Taking each day as it comes
No yesterday or tomorrow,
Sparing thoughts and minds and souls
Much heartache and sorrow.

We're always looking forward.
Wasting moments anyhow.
Little do we realize.
The precious hour are how.

Moira Laing

My Work

I started work when I left school,
And I've kept it up since then,
But now I'm quite content,
To be putting down my pen.

The job I got was office work,
From nine till five each day,
And when I first commenced it,
I got one pound per week of pay.

They gave me shorthand notebooks,
A manual typewriter too,
Pass-books, Day-books, and Ledgers,
For the task I had to do.

The work was quite rewarding,
I enjoyed many happy years,
But when they brought computers in,
I was reduced to tears.

To grasp all the technology
Almost caused me to expire.
I've completed forty years now,
And to-morrow I retire.

Mary Brady

The Tortoise

Today is the first day of spring
What a wondrous, glorious thing
The tortoise from his sleep awakes
To find a new day breaks

There he goes in search of food
Of whatever takes his mood
With lettuce and tomatoes to eat
And even strawberries as a treat

Now the days are getting longer
He's more mobile and stronger
Nothing seams to hold him back
Even in a corner, he gets stuck

On several times of getting out
He has given us cause to doubt
With luck he wasn't very far
He just decided to follow a car

Now his chances are very slim
He has truly been penned in
Now he can freely roam
For this now is his home.

Maureen Hyam

One Little Snowdrop

One little snowdrop
drooped its head.
"Where are the others?"
was all it said.

They are all still buried
beneath the ground.
Not a leaf could be seen
in that little mound.

"I'm so lonely,"
the snowdrop said,
"I think I might
as well be dead."

Suddenly the sun came out
and the little snowdrop gave a shout.
Little shoots began to appear
and the little snowdrop shed a tear.

"I now have friends
and I'm glad I'm alive,"
the little snowdrop said
and counted five.

Violetta J. Ferguson

Gardens of England

Flowers and trees, birds and bees,
Fresh cut lawns, frogs that spawn,
Wind and rain, again and again,
Winter white and Spring delight,

Summer abundance, harvest delight,
autumn fall, with colour change,
All the plants to rearrange,
Back to winter, feed the birds.

When their water turns to ice,
only you can make things nice,
Fill their bath, give them food,
Life in the garden is so good.

Pauline Clay

Wealth

City of structures,
all financed;
just shapes of art,
'are we entranced?'

True wealth we find,
is more than things;
in spiritual lofty realm, we find,
love rises up with wings.

World of comfort,
free from stress;
but greatest gifts,
the poor possess.

Will war destroy
the things we praise;
or peace evolve,
'till sights we raise?'

All creation,
it is ours;
words and deeds,
our truest powers.

Roland Hiller

Spring

Someone is talking,
Who? That I don't know
Someone is walking,
Who?—That I can't see.
To the world of snow,
Over the roaring sea,
Someone that I don't know,
Coming nearer towards me,
Whispering in a sweetest tone,
That the time is turning,
As the robe of a season,
Is now worn out and torn.

Tokiko Iwamoto

Mr. Solo

You have faced reality.
You are now no longer a day dreamer.
So say good bye to the past.
Dream of something that you can make.
Think of something that you can take
Say hello to a new beginning.
Say hello to a new challenge.
Love the job which you do.
Love the place where you live.
There is a wild world outside.
There are bad people outside.
They are all looking for a new name.
They are all waiting for a new game.
In a wild world
You can have a place at the top.
Among bad people
You can be a real hero,
If only you can become Mr. Solo.

G. G. Gench

Godly Poem

God is beautiful
God is delightful
God is powerful
God is wonderful
God is brilliant
God is elegant
God is radiant
God is jubilant
God is magnificent
God is benevolent
God is intelligent
God is marvellous
God is ubiquitous
God is judicious
God is gracious
God is inspirational
God is phenomenal
God is exceptional
God is sensational

Amarjit Singh

Oh! Dawn

You are my dawn
You are my joy
The words are drawn
Out of my coy
To get your picture
To get your clan
I look towards you
With heart so sawn
You appear on horizon
So serene and yawn
Spectrum of the universe
With beauty you pawn
With your short stay
The earth you adorn
Planquim of your seat
Is one of sultan
Sunrays come to glow
Over my gardens lawn
Feelings fly and flow
After you are gone oh! "Dawn"

Sarwan S. Deol

A Thought

As early shadows fall long,
haunting, is the lone bird's song.
For in chorus, not many do sing
when cold dark Winter creeps in.
Most have gone on a swirl of wing
to a softer clime, forever Spring.
Those not gone take mantle to wear
puffed up feathers, layered with air.
With a garland, a wreath of mist
and all, with rain spangles kissed.

Dorothea Green

Painting a Miracle

When making your impression
On times waiting canvass
Sit a while and dream.
Observe each moment
Dip your brush into the future
And paint what you have seen.

Think not of the glass
That contains the murky water
Where you rinsed your brushes past,

But paint your wishes
as you wished them
Into the portrait of your dreams
And let them form
As you have asked.

David Allen

Claire Marie

I am so lucky to have a friend
As kind and supportive as Claire,
And when I am faced with problems,
I know she is always there.

I have many happy memories
Of Claire and I together.
We would go out and have fun,
No matter what the weather.

Claire has always been close to me,
I have known her for many years,
The thought of breaking up with her,
Is one of my worst fears.

She is definitely one in a million,
Just being with her gives me pride,
She gave me her deepest sympathy,
when my brave Grandad died.

Racheal Timbers

Loneliness

Crowds of people everywhere,
But I can only stand and stare.
Each going their own way,
Life's game to play.

Will someone talk to me?
Or is it they do not see?
They always rush past.
Perhaps someone will stop at last.

But no, they never do,
Every day through and through.
So, I hurry back home,
Again to be alone.

Perhaps one day a friend I will meet.
It would be such a treat.
But as the years go by,
My only companion is the sky.

The clouds look down on me.
Do they really see
How lonely it can be
For someone like me?

J. V. Ford

Mum

A Mum is a Mum, all the time.
The love she has for us will never end,
It shows in all her ways,
It is there for us each day,
And a Mum is
Our only one true friend!

Roochi Khullar

A Bowl of Fruit

We have a bowl of fruit
Upon our table top,
The fruits not very happy
They prefer it in the shop,
They're wondering who's the next
To be eaten, from here
They are all so very nervous
They're wondering in fear.
They think, why do people eat us?
What gives them the right?
It's not very nice
For us fruits; it's a horrid sight.
But they start to get hot
And begin to go brown
They're not very happy
And they all start to frown.
"The bin's the next place"
The apple says; "for us few,
Then they'll be getting
A bowl full of new."

Sally Elizabeth Burton

Beauty Revealed

The Beauty that was Yesterday
is seen the same To-day,
But there is a difference
seen in just another way.

It takes awhile to realize
there's more to it not known.
It isn't only just 'Skin-deep'
and perhaps not always shown.

It isn't only outwardly
that God creates a life,
A Deeper Beauty of a soul
that shows in deepest strife

It is when hardship shows its hand
that God shows what He has done,
deep within that lovely life
a secret strength for one.

So Beauty shows that precious gift
and comes to Pastures Green,
revealing what was hidden there
but now so clearly seen.

H. Herring

Jazz

Jazz the Ritz
  And the glamour,
The razzmatazz.
    The sounds that one hears
     Takes you to another realm,
      The tones
       The bass, trumpet and drums
        Each has a sound
         Very much to one's
          Ear to please.
           Pleasure of Jazz
            Razzmatazz
             Jazz Jazz Jazz.

Sally Davis

Castle

Florentine castle in mid-air,
Turn the latch,
As you climb the stair,
Open the door,
For there's no one there,
Gone are they,
On steeds of grey
Off to fight in the crusades,
With scimitars for steely blades,
In my mind's eye,
I hear their war cry,
"To do or die"
When they come back,
They'll launch a fresh attack,
And marry Spanish maids.

Alan Pow

Him

I think about him all the time,
My head is filled with constant song.
The joyous thoughts that fill my mind
And occupy me all day long.
He is my morning, night and noon,
I hum an ancient unknown tune,
Known only to the persons whom
Have truly been in love.
Each step I take is oh so light.
The clock stops ticking just for me.
My dreams of him fill up each night.
His love exceeds infinity.
And as he holds me in his arms,
And I am smothered by his charms,
I know we can come to no harm
For this came from above.

Naomi Turner Rankin

Lifeboat

The rolling seas, the stormy winds,
The heavy lashing rain,
But off you go, no ifs or buts
The lifeboat's out again.

You are a special breed of man
You go against the grain,
Maroons are set, the crew is met
The lifeboat's out again

And wherever would we be
Without these fine brave men
Who put to sea, to save you and me
The lifeboat's out again.

The rescue is the object
Although the seas may roar
No thought in mind, but seek and find
The lifeboat's out once more.

Adrianne Bird

Untitled

Is birth the beginning of everything?
Or the end of feeling secure?
Is being born like waking up?
Not remembering what was before?

Is birth the start of all feeling?
Or the end of a different pain?
Is being born the start of death?
Or do we come back again?

Is death the end of everything?
Or the start of something new?
Is dying like drifting of to sleep?
Or a nightmare you can't get through?

Is death the end of all feeling?
Or the start of a new kind of pain?
Is dying the start of rebirth?
Or don't we come back again?

Jackie Whittaker

The One-Eyed Monster

Sitting in a corner of the room,
Its single eye lights up the gloom,
Children sit there mesmerized,
At changing scenes before their eyes,
Taking them to far-off places,
Watch the reactions on their faces,
Never changing their position,
Totally engrossed, by television.

E. I. Lowrie

Those Are of No End

Useful moments.
The kinds that soothe
the sorts that help,
the ones which benefit
those are of no end.

Conversations that wander,
make them so boring
keeping to no point,
going on about one's story
those are of no end.

A sight of behold,
saw that very vision
have seen with my eyes
the focus of your lies,
those are of no end.

You are the centre,
the middle of the core
you expect us to adjust,
directing to your way of thought
those are of no end.

Saira Khan

Fata Morgana

Be quiet, heart, it is not real,
The eyes behold a dream.
It's an illusion, what you feel,
These lands aren't what they seem.
Just a mirage, a Fata Morgana.

Be still, my heart, there is no peace
In our world today;
For never have I seen a place
That looks like this in any way
Like a mirage, a Fata Morgana.

Take care, my heart, or you believe
The wonder of this land;
Take care, for what the eyes perceive
I can't hold in my hand,
Only a mirage, a Fata Morgana.

And yet, dear heart, it is no lie.
These are the thoughts of God.
Peace, joy and beauty, by and by,
Created by His word.
My Highlands—no Fata Morgana.

Helga I. Dharmpaul

Silver Wedding Anniversary

Happiness taken for granted
Promises easily made
Twenty-five long punishing years
Since the ludicrous wedding charade

Anguishing eyes—wearied
Desperately craving love
Transfixing the veil of hopelessness
Passing moments wove

Years bereft of tenderness
Laboured to destroy
Two souls ensnared in dreams of love
When living offered joy

Distrust—despair—frustration
Fruits of bitter years
Grew heavier still as life dragged on
Yielding endless fears

Too late the quest for answers
Or even for regret
Perhaps the path of destiny
Was paved before they'd met

Anna MacDonald

Stoneware, Earthernware, Raku and Glaze

I don't think I'll make a potter.
I could be a potter's mate
Mashing clay and water
Into a working state!

I'd watch your wheel a'turning.
And I'd cut off pots with wire,
And see the kiln was burning
With red or white-hot fire!

I could learn to paint and decorate
The pots and jugs you throw,
I'd sell them in the marketplace
And watch the coffers grow!

I don't think I'll make a potter,
Don't think I have the skill
I could help you when you need me,
You know I always will.

I'll pack the kiln and bank the fire
And when the day is done,
We'll rest awhile from potting,
Relax—and have some fun!

Mary C. Thomas

The Unknown Child

I am the child you do not know
I am the child you will never know

In to your womb was I thrust
Either by mistake or by lust

No joy to you did I bring
I was just that unwanted thing

Not for me was it to be blest
To rest my head against your breast

Not for me the love in a mother's eyes
In answer to a baby's cries

Torn from your womb whilst I slept
That day in heaven the angel wept

I will never know the reason why
I was conceived just to die

But the love you did not give to me
I have now with my Father in Eternity

Kenneth Benoy

Pencil Drawing: Eve

The lines move simply—
delicate, discovering the skin;
curving, strong, unhesitant
about the flesh; good and
taut over bones.
Sensuous lines, fine draughtsmanship,
exploring in detached delight.

You could just imagine how it was
there in the studio:
he impatient at first,
then engrossed in his work, oblivious;
she, lying in her pose,
complaining of the cold until
finally,
grown tired of watching him,
she fell asleep
to dream of apples.

Piffa Schroder

Sister Jean

No one could ever replace you
If I lived one thousand decades through
So sweet gentle kind and true.
I also died that morning too,
When came the final sad adieu
Now with God above the skies so blue
I hope to meet up there with you,
Death the bond between us cannot sever
Dearly loved, within my heart forever.

Helen Maxwell

I Am

I am the wind as it rustles,
Whispering through the leaves;
I am the tear of a small child
Whose pain cringes in a corner
To escape failing hands;
Hear me as my words kiss your ears
Feel me as I sing to you,
Because I am the song of the haunted,
The lonely and the lost;
My words will find a path
And exorcise the ghosts
Shadows will be swept away
In my arms.
So trust me, little boy, little girl;
I will mend the fractures.
I will breathe mother and hold you
As that distant woman cannot,
Because I am the song of home
And I will save you.

Emma Wilson

Inner Sanctum

There's a place where I go
When I need some peace
It's kind of inside me
A place to sleep
No-one there knows me
Or the things I've done
It's quiet safe
If you want to come
The clocks stop ticking
The world disappears
There are no regrets
And certainly no fears
No-one can take it
Away from me
My place of peace
And tranquillity.

Melissa Gardner

Noches

In this terrible land
  black night is flame.
  Searing
  the shell. Whitening
into a powdered dream
  the flesh within.

In this terrible land
  fear burns my skin.
  At night
  I creep, deformed,
  into a harsh cocoon
  of desperate sleep.

In this terrible land
  night flails the day.
  Whipping
  the cool pink dust
  into a monstrous mist
  with taunting eyes.

Margot Collingbourn-Beevers

Spring Flowers

Weary, nerves a-wrack,
  I solace found me.
In God's own country,
  And of His bounty free.

Crocuses and daffodils,
  Beneath trees tall and still,
I paused and hesitated,
  then drank my fill.

In golden sunshine,
  on gently sloping banks,
Waved their lovely heads,
  in silent serried ranks.

Mauve, white and yellow,
  between a sea of green,
What wonder I gave thee thanks,
  for the beauty I had seen.

Dorothy Ventris

Christopher

Christopher's my son,
He's truly unique,
He suffers from autism.
He can be difficult to reach.
There is no cure.
There's no one to blame.
But it doesn't stop the hurting.
All the same.
The tears often fall.
The anger sometimes comes.
But, I love him just the same,
After all, I'm his Mum.

Mandy Hilton

My Vision

An image came before me
As I went within my mind
Dressed in white, He walked towards me
With a mist not far behind.
He was holding out His arms
And He was reaching out to me.
He was showing me Himself
I understood what I could see.
With a smile upon His face
He stood quite still and on His own
And I now know in this life
No matter what, I'm not alone.
And His warmth and friendly face
was showing me that He was pleased.
And I know our special Moment
Was His way of telling me.

Maureen Barber

Year 2000

Dead and buried,
that's where I hope to be,
when the earth gets
swallowed up by the sea.
If I were alive,
I think I'd pray
for a nice place
for eternity to stay.
Heaven is in the sky,
hell is in the ground,
which will you pray for,
when you pay your last pound?
Is this what it will be
like in the year 2000?
or will there be partying
all around us?

Lynsey Watkins

In Loving Memory

  I remember Spring so clearly
now that Spring is here once more.
We'd run through dew-soaked meadows
and laugh at lamb's galore.
  You held my hand and I held yours
as we jumped across clear streams.
We'd gather growing buttercups
and share each others' dreams.
  I loved you in your uniform,
it used to make you say,
"One day when this is over
I won't need to go away."
  But you did, my lovely soldier,
you went to far off lands,
to fight for King and Country
with a rifle in your hands.
  And now the War is over,
yourself you could not bring.
Instead, a single Telegram
and the prospects of Spring.

Helen Long

The Hat

Wear it with glamour,
Wear it with style.
Show it off at a wedding,
Or just admire for a while.
The people around you will smile
When they see—
How it sets off your outfit so
Beautifully.
A day at the races,
Or down by the sea,
Wear it with pleasure
And think of me.

Ann Christine Blair

John Patrick

Little angel watching over all,
Safe in heaven forevermore,
So young yet you answered God's call,
Cradled now in the arms of loved ones,
Who have journeyed on before,
No words can express the sorrow,
The sudden emptiness and pain,
We live knowing you will always be,
In our hearts tomorrow,
For our love will never wane.

Eamonn James McGrath

Thinking of You

Looking at your photograph
And staring into space
Not a single tear not a single laugh
Just an empty face

Your blue eyes shining brightly
Your soft and tender smile
My loyal heart is breaking dear
I'll stay for just a while

I am always thinking of you
All day and all night
I will always be there for you
Between the darkness and the light

Close your eyes and dream of me
I'll be there looking for you
Because I love you, I think of you
I always will my whole life through

Suzanne McCormack

The Distant Shores

Not knowing where
These cross-roads lead
As I reach this wayside inn
A lonely traveller
in the blue of the night

Not knowing who
Sent you this midnight
With a dimly-lit candle
Yet seeing his kindness
In this infinite emptiness

Not knowing how
To express my gratitude
Moments merge
Into lengthy silence

Here, in a rented room
This sleepless night
Staring at the walls where
Shadows play charades, I realise:
The shores of wisdom lie
How far away!

M. K. Bhasi

The Coming of Mr. X

Tall, dark and handsome;
Blonde, short and weak,
Academically brilliant,
At home with a shovel and
Pick; a ladies' man, with
A feminine voice, can drive
A Porsche, or a Chieftain tank;
Built like an athlete but
Hopeless at sport, a wonderful
Son to his motherless father;
On a crowded street he appears
Mr. Average, but beneath
His hair an indelible
Number—hell and damnation,
His gift to mankind.

David Mobberley

First Love

I gazed into the mirror,
The face looked back at me,
A few old lines, some bits of grey,
But these I did not see.

The face I saw was young and clear
Joy of life and love was there,
For all the world to see.

First love it is a wondrous thing,
It colours all you do.
Cherish it, protect it,
Be grateful every day,
That you have loved
Been loved in turn,
No matter come what may.

E. R. Dudgeon

My Summer in Slovenia

The day comes to a close.
The sun decides to wrest
Upon a cloud,
Toward the west.

The sky turns dark,
And parties start,
As the stars alight;
This place wins my heart.

The morning arrives
With birds singing sweet,
Idrija wakes up
To morning heat.

The choice I had
Here or Australia,
Oh, what a fantastic
Summer in Slovenia.

Christopher Wright

Untitled

Our God is good and loves us all,
Life and death are in His hands,
He plans our lives and helps us through
All by his holy commands.
Sometimes disappointments come,
But we just trust and pray,
He helps us through in good or bad days
Holding our hands all the way.

Mabel Gess

Unknown Love

Just a kiss to say goodbye
that was how it started
a love to last forevermore
began when we parted

You went away to foreign parts
leaving me all alone
not realizing how I felt
my love for you unknown

I was not free to fall in love
but how to tell my heart
a love like ours could never be
I knew right from the start

On your return a welcome kiss
a hug to say I missed you
the love that grew from day to day
was there when I kissed you.

Our lives are many worlds apart
we would not make it together
but let us save it in our hearts
a love to last forever.

G. Wilson

The Lonely Old Man

He had no friends
he had no looks,
His only pleasure were his books.
They lined the walls and
covered the floors, and
some were propped against the doors.
They gave him joy these
dusty things, when he
never heard no door or
phone bell rings.
This man will die at some
time soon, and they will
come and clear his rooms,
I wonder what they will
think or say, when his
collection is cleared that day.

R. H. G. Francis

For My Dad—Malcolm Semark

No-one understands me
half as much as you,
and no-one could love you
half as much as I do.
Thanks for being my dad,
Thanks for all you've done,
You are my Idol dad,
My friend, my number one.
I love you more
with each passing day,
Your rosy cheeks and all,
Your twinkling eyes,
Your cheeky smile,
I think that says it all.

Donna Semark

Legendary Pool

Mystical mere
fathomless watery grave
A city interred
by storm, sand and tidal wave

Nestling in dunes
and the putrid quagmire
Forever guardian
to the city and its fabled church spire

Drowning whirlpool
with choking weeds
Retribution and vengeance
fulfilling satanic needs

Fetid of breath
ere the storm
Three chimneys smoking
until break of dawn

At the limpid pool,
it is said, in calmer times
One can see the spire
and hear the bell's chimes

W. Graham Price

Bonfire

The smoke is rising
from the bonfire.
Red and yellow flames
The sticks are burning
into dust and
leaves are turning grey.

The twigs and sticks
Are burning fast
The sky is turning grey
The children are gathered
Around the bonfire
The smoke has covered
the sky.

Saoirse Barrett

Our Wend

Every snowflake is different,
Not one being the same,
So in this world of conveyor belts,
Don't play man's game.
Stand apart and be different,
Think how important you are,
Just stand up and be counted,
You're brighter than any star.

Joan Guignard

To Be a Friend

To be a friend
You must be kind
And always keep
An open mind.

To be a friend,
You must listen well
And always know
When not to tell.

To be a friend,
You must take care
And always learn
How to share.

To be a friend,
You must take heed
And always remain
A friend indeed.

Ruth J. Davison

Sunlight

As night retreats through misty skies,
Sunlight begins to glow,
Soon to shine its radiance,
Onto the Earth below.

Streaks of light shine brightly,
Move traces of the night,
The welcomed sun has risen,
And earth is bathed in light.

Along the river's winding way,
In lakes, o'er seas and streams,
Reflected in the water,
The brilliant sunlight gleams.

Warm rays stream down on houses,
People, busy on their way,
On streets, fields, animals,
And children at their play,

At close of day, the setting sun,
More beauty still unfolds,
Lighting the sky in glowing shades of
Crimson, pink, and gold.

Pauline R. Markham

Enigma

Out of nowhere it came
And lit up the sky;
How did this happen?
I'll never know why.

To nowhere it goes
And I know what I saw
Was no shooting star
That filled me with awe.

This explosion of light
That woke up my soul
Took me up and away
And made me feel whole.

A flight through the heavens
Mere man could not stop;
What else can compare
With the comet Hale-Bop.

Ann Marie Page

Sunshine Days

May your days be full of sunshine
with friends and family there.
Much laughter, joy and happiness,
sparkling eyes with love to share.

Waken to the dawn's fine chorus
bringing cheer to a new day.
All those colours of a rainbow
maybe rain is on the way.

Those delicate crystal droplets
glisten beauty to delight.
Precious showers full of goodness
hidden jewels then brought to sight.

Always smile unto your neighbour
greeting with a word or two,
finding such peace within your heart
and those treasures all year through.

Margaret Jackson

Where the Heather Hills Adorn

Where the heather hills adorn,
Yearning for you, lost, forlorn.
Sweeping down from sky to sea,
Purple haze you beckon me.
Brushed by clouds borne on my sighs,
Exile's dreams light dimming eyes.
Reaching out could I but touch
Tartan snagged in bracken's clutch.
Wrenched from out the sodden soil,
Your roots, my heart, how you toil!
When the torrent's run its course,
Lay me down in bed of gorse.
Softer still than distant dune.
Breathless piper; timeless tune,
Swirling o'er dank, wooded glen,
Reeling wild with folk I ken.
Skerry bleak adrift no more,
Sound embraced by kindred shore.
Love betrothed when I was born
Where the heather hills adorn.

Brian J. Davison

Tracey—
Granddaughter Two Years Old

This little one with cherub smile
And eyes so dark and bright
Her silken hair and clinging arms
Fill me with sheer delight
Her chattering words and baby talk
Are only just a few
The nicest of them simply say
"Nana, I love you"

Beryl Clark

Life

There're times in life
When we're not prepared
for things that lie ahead.
It's best that way not to know,
We'd worry more instead.
We wake each day and feel just fine
And carry on the same
We take it all for granted
And sometimes even complain.
But life's a precious gift to us
Taken a day at a time
There's no guarantees at all
Everything seems just fine.
We worry about such trivial things
That really aren't that bad
But at the time there's nothing else
That really makes us sad.

It's Life.

Margaret Prouse

Reflections

Television and Video's
Monitors and Stereo's
Disc records and personal telephones
Star wars and astronauts
Rockets and laser beams
UFO's and green men
The world will never be the same
Thunder and lightning
Heat waves and tornados
Hurricane and devastation
Surely will destroy the nation
If this world is to survive
We must all stay alive
Motor cars and deadly fumes
Sun rays and cathode ray tubes
They say there is life on Mars
Soon we will be fighting wars
With men from outer space
That then will be the end
Of us—(the human race)

Eileen Griffiths

Halloween

Witches on broomsticks
Fly through the air,
Ghosts appear from everywhere.
Groans and wailing all around,
Spirits rising from the ground.
It's Halloween
A night of scares
I'm afraid to go upstairs.
"H-a-a-a-a-a-a-g",
Something's crawling on my neck,
Gosh, I'm becoming a nervous wreck.
I won't get any sleep tonight.
I'm not switching off the light.
I'll pray the dawn's not far away,
I can't wait for a brand-new day.
I'll try to forget
This night of horror.
While I sit here trembling
Till to-morrow.

Nora Kathleen Cooper

Untitled

Without reason
I love him.
He loves me.
 Still
I must be free.
His jealous rage
a storm at sea.
The waves crashing
against the shore,
The banging of the door.

Bernadette O'Reilly

Amber

Your eye was cut
Your ribs stuck out
You'd been abused you see.
We brought you home
You sniffed the air
It's lovely here. You'll see.
We gave you food
We gave you love
We put the T.V. on.
You heard the tune
You sang and song
You felt at home you see.
Your eyes grew bright
Your coat grew too
Your hurt was gone
It's trust you see.

Eunice M. Birch

Dignity

He pokes at the ash
With a stick in his hand
Hoping to spark a fire
Hidden in the grey
His life so lonely
His clothes so frayed

Stammering around town
By night or by day
Time does not matter
It has slipped away
Such a life he leads
What a passionless day

If you see him today
Will you turn your eyes away
Will you feel any pity
As he hobbles away
You have taken nothing
But his dignity away

Gary Murray

Searching

I climb the mountain,
To my destination.
All alone.
Cold.
Weak.
Tired.
Hungry.
Why should I go on?
I have so many feelings.
But I want one more.
There's a feeling I have not got.
A feeling I want bad.
Greedy I may seem.
But it's for love,
For love I go on.

Donna Jones

Crazy

I must be going crazy
It's Sue Mullen's fault you know.
She dragged me down to Rylands Rec.
And said "Now have a go".

American and Western Line dancing
"It's all the craze" she said
I've never sweated so much you know,
I think I must be dead.

I went along and caught the bug
We walked through each dance at first
But when the music's played at speed
I feel like I'm going to burst.

The ones who know the dances
Help out the ones who don't
And if I want to sit one out
They make sure I won't.

But after just a couple of weeks
I certainly feel a lot better
I still sweat like a pig you know
But I must be getting fitter

Colin Bowden

The Fruit of Life

You surrender to love
Love conquers any human
heart.
For love is the fruit of life.
The joy of being well
The sensation that brings joy
And makes a lonely heart
rejoice.
A reason to feel alive.

Alice Field

Sand Dunes

As in some far off distant land
We two as one life joys command
See floating clouds on painted hills
Light soft our feet sand silver spills
To where on grass dunes inland shore
A sleep more perfect than before
Will keep safe vigil through the night
In paradise chaste black demon flight
So wake beneath dawn's drowsy head
To greet the morn from silken bed
A kiss yonder yester's kiss beget
Lips kissed under the moon she set
Love's faith all as lovers we pursue
Tomorrow's kiss shares bliss so true

Patricia Thompson

Through the Eyes of a Child

Give me time to understand,
Give me time to hold your hand,
Give me time to walk down stairs,
Give me time to say my prayers,
Give me love and hold me tight,
Kiss me when you say good-night,
Treat me right and treat me good,
Treat me like all mothers should,
Maybe if I'm good for you,
You'll treat me as you ought to do,
After all I'm only three
And still sit upon your knee.

G. Ecclestone

Reflections

All the way to wonderland,
 To lead one by the hand.
Through fear of flying packs of cards,
To the shelter of looking glass.

Where hoping you and I together,
 can act in my defence.
Without indeed my aged man
Who said don't touch my fence.

I did not need my aged man,
When police knocked at my door,
Pushed my door and grabbed me
Not telling me what for.
But I did send court the detail
Of why I could not appear.
Hold without hand bag and glasses
Over matters never made clear

So be very, very careful
About admitting to one's friend.
For fear of what might happen
If called in your defence.

Ann Townsend

I Don't Want to Be Alone

I've lived for certain years
And I've shed so many tears
And still I don't know
where my life is going to

I've been in and out of love
And flown so high above
And still my life means
little to me

Find me somebody who can care
With who my life could share
And save me from the fate
I seem headed to.

The yellow daffodils in spring
And all those lovely things
To me, would look so much
better with you.

Sarah Marquis

Reflections

Sitting by my bed at sunset
To the Lord my soul to keep
Quietly till the light at sunbreak
Another morning! Another week!

When will this chalice pass me?
(From the bible, so to speak)
With this deep dark descending
Lovers laying soft and sweet.

Then it comes, the light transcending
Is this the hope I waited for?
What love what hope ne'er ending
Peeping round the bedroom door

But to see my hope awakening
Counting sounds and counting sheep
Finding grace and blessings plenty
Feeding soul and spirit deep.

So to this tale the ending,
If an ending so there be,
Will you listen to my story?
Here's to God and liberty!!

Pauline N. Mullan

Path to Heaven

As I make my path to heaven
To love that is freely given
Who I meet on the way
Is for God not for me to say
Of all the people that I meet
We join together we all pray
We do our best to help each other
Through the trials of life
Down in the valley up in the mountain
Be it sunshine or be it rain
We do our best to maintain
The life that God has given us
For our God he does reign

Elizabeth Docherty

What is a Grandma?

Someone who loves you dearly,
as she did your mum all her life,
from the day you were born,
until the end of her days,
she followed your steps,
filled with pride and joy.

Prayed for you every night,
hoped you would come through,
all life's tests alright,
also all your bad times,
you were ever in my mind,
all the days of your life,
wished you to hold on tight.

You will soon be like your mum,
ready to face life and strife,
Grandma hopes you will win that fight.
also that life treats you right,
then I can sit back and enjoy,
with pride the rest of my life
"My lovely grandchild"

V. M. Moore

Because

Because of you the day is gold
The sweetest story ever told
Of love, the magic that it brings
Your laughter and the sweetest things
My spirit flies on angel's wings
Soon we hear angelic voices sing
Oh what a wondrous world we see
When thoughts recall my love and me

Ada Forrest Jones

Silence

Silence! As it speaks
  To silence,
Disturbed by one
  Who strolled along

Observing the scene
  Of willow trees
Overhanging gracefully
  In the slight warm breeze.

Reflections in a stream
  Natures photography.
Clear, sharp, clean,
  A sheer delight to see.

Even the colours, thus,
  Deeply viewed
Willow green, lime, yellow musk
  Such a distinction of hue's.

Quiet silence! Speaks
  To silence, mystically
God's very own
  Artistry

Mabel Layland

Dreaming

When I fall asleep to dream
I dream about what might have been.
Like walking through meadows.
Watching cows graze.
Oh those wonderful lazy days.
Then I stopped for a bite, to eat
like cakes and chocolates that are
so sweet.
Then I walked through grassy hills
between the crowds of daffodils.
Then I sat for a while and looked
at the sky
and watched the clouds as they
passed by.
Then I watched the children play
as I went walking on my way.

Stephen Blundell

Christmas Time

Christmas is so festive
Christmas is exciting
and Religious with
Children singing and
The pleasure of a
Christmas holiday
time.
Dining and wining
snow and ice at
winter time
at Christmas time.

B. A. Linney

Craig

I've walked on the road which
leads nowhere
In a world that doesn't care
People have hurt me without knowing
my name
They took me by the hand and led
me to pain
I've listened to my heart weep
in the night
Afraid to trust, I gave up the fight
Then you were thrown into my life
by fate
Is love strong enough for me to
forget the hate?
I offer you a love sweeter than lies
And pray this time it's not my
heart that cries.

Samantha Lee

Christian Science, As It Was

Heal the sick,
Cleanse the lepers
Cast out demons
Then it was, why not now?

For the many, they were healed
Some were sick, some had demons.
One sick woman touched his garment
Then it was, why not now?

For a while, lost was the way,
Still to come, another day.
Never was said, his work I do
Then it was, why not now?

Christian Science shows the way
The way was lost, never the day.
For a Science, to show how,
Then it was, why not now?

Kenneth Roy Munns

Love

The splendour of love
To have and to hold
To give and to take
It's something to share.
Love when it's real
Means and awful lot more
A life time together
That's love
No less but much more.

Michael Major Atkinson

Sweet Bliss

It was a split second in time,
When your cheek touched mine.
A moment of sweet bliss,
That my heart almost missed.

How I've longed for that moment,
And now it has gone,
To live in my memory,
For my heart to call upon.

I never thought it could happen,
For you're out of my reach.
Belonging to another,
Who's as sweet as a peach.

Through my tears I re-live,
That sweet moment of bliss.
For your touch was as gentle,
As a butterfly kiss.

Lara

Maybe Tomorrow

"Why not do it today?"
Then I would always say
"Maybe Tomorrow"

Longing to see,
Someone so precious to me
"Maybe Tomorrow"

"I love him so much"
I will get in touch
"Maybe Tomorrow"

The hurt never goes away,
I could end it today,
"Maybe Tomorrow"

I would no longer hide,
If I could regain some pride,
"Maybe Tomorrow"

Will I ever see him again
I wonder when,
"Maybe Tomorrow"

J. R. Marsh, the Red Rose

Retirement Years

The working years come to an end
One dreams of this so many times
  No regrets
The time was good
Many laughs, a few tears
And everlasting friendships made
  A new era starts
Will I be bored, some people ask
  No never
So much to do, a slower pace maybe
Get up at nine instead of seven
That alone is such a treat
Stop and choose, what will I do
Gardening, shopping, reading
Or whatever I may fancy
  Oh Retirement Days
  They hold so much
  A dream come true

Margaret Munro

A Rose

What can a rose do
To ease your sorrow and pain?
It is a memory for the children
A sign of our sorrow and love,
A message to show that we care
and think about those that we lost,
Sending our deepest regrets
To you from all of us.
It is just a small offering,
A memory to hold forever
Remaining as a simple rose
To remind us day after day,
That they will live for eternity
In our hearts they stay.

Natalie Olley

Regret

I loved you
So much
So much
My tears are crying down my face
I cannot believe
What you have done
I cannot believe
I am so upset
So upset
I feel I want to die
But I won't
No way will I
I will survive
Through God's love
I feel like dying
Today dying
When love was living yesterday

Cynthia Osborne

Winter Beauty

Winter has arrived
The snow is falling fast.
It's so lovely to see
I hope it will last.
As I wrap-up warm,
out into the garden I go.
I like to walk, in the new fallen
snow.
I scatter some food, for the birds
to eat.
They're all so hungry, they hop
up close to my feet.
I see icicles that glitter, like
diamonds on a tree.
There's beauty all around,
for me to see.

Christina Russell

Source

I prick my finger
on the moving pin
and see the bright blood start;
I know it's nothing, really,
yet it's everything,
it's from my heart.
Such is my love for you,
it is so deep,
yet hardly shows at all,
above the surface
of life's moving circle;
only a certain glance,
a touch, when you are near,
a single tear, a sigh
when we're apart;
I know it's nothing, really,
yet it's everything,
it's from my heart.

Robert Lindsay

Awakening Love

I wake it's early dawn,
 I hold out my hand
  but you are gone.

"Were you here,
 or was it a dream?"...
For a Beautiful moment,
 How real it did seem.
I remember it all so
 Perfectly well,
Like sleeping beauty
 in the fairy tale
The prince who gave that
 "One magical kiss,"
  "Awakening love."
or "Robert,"
 "did I only
  dream of this?..."

J. R. Marsh, the Red Rose

Being Good

I didn't want to play with you
but mummy said I should,
'cos you're my little sister
and I do want to be good;

I wish that I could loose you
you will only spoil my game,
why don't you find your own friends
it would almost be the same;

Your legs are just too short you see
so you can't run very fast;
and if we played at racing
you would only come in last;

I'll play with you tomorrow
or, when my friends aren't here;
'cos you're my little sister
you'll be bigger by next year!!

Marilyn Lacy

Atmosphere

There's a strange mist upon us
Its fragile lustre shows
Beyond man's recognition
Who sees, who cares, who knows?
We'll move along awhile
Before any major effect
Are we ozone friendly?
Do we have any respect?
Is nature closing in on us?
We don't know the reason why,
We must have recognition,
Or kiss the Earth goodbye.

Hazel Forrest

A Friend in Need

There was a flower that I saw once
I never knew its name.
But the sound of a bee as it hunts
Made me turn to watch the game.

The bee found the flower alone
In the bracken, that each day I past.
Alone was I then, and with a groan
I went on my own, at last.

The bloom grew old and faded.
And when the seed bud ripened,
Our love grown cold and jaded,
I was alone and frightened.

I took the bud and grew the flower
Again and again.
And though our love grown sour
Means you'll not come in sun or rain.

But should by chance you pass my way
In late April or early May,
Please stay and meet my friend.

Peter Sowter

Our Little Secret

I've got a little secret
That I'm going to share with you
You're not allowed to tell no one
It's just for us two
I keep it in my pocket
And it goes wherever I go
It's something that you gave to me
Not so long ago
It has to be kept quiet now
So hush don't say a word
A one inch troll, my good luck charm
Worth more than all earth's gold
I'd like to tell somebody else
Someday I might do that
But if I do then they will know
What's really in my heart
I know another secret
That I'm going to share with you
Tell any-one tell every-one
I really do love you.

David M. Took

Untitled

Life's not what I thought
It would be distractions
Of a man I wanted to be
All these places all I can
Do is dream thinking of
Times that have never been
When my life's over what will
They say a lonely person
Who had nothing to say.

Richard Kenneth Lyon

Contentment

When you're around, all is right,
Even through the dead of night.
Your lamp is bright with steady flame,
To light me down each narrow lane
Of doubt, despair or woe.
It always shows me, at the end,
A glorious sun that is your soul.
To share with you another year
Of happiness sublime, makes me
Heady with the purity of your wine.
May your days be filled as well
With strength from an inner spring
That wells in me for your use.

Ron Stuart

Forest of Dreams

Wandering aimlessly
Deep in thought
Remembering and wandering
So many dreams you sought.

And was it all worth it
Going through the pain?
'Of course it was' you tell yourself
How else would you gain?

It happened for a reason
Is all you need to know
We each live and learn
Let your heart tell you so.

As you continue through the forest
Looking back to your past
A smile appears upon your face
For no dream is ever the last.

Tamzin Hardy

How Do You Know?

How do you know
If your dreams will come true
And what if they don't
What will you do?

Nobody knows
What life has in store
Everyone dreams
That's what we're here for

Some of us make it
For reasons unknown
For others the thought of failure
Turns our hearts to stone

So how do you know
What will become
Of the fame that you crave
It only happens to some

The rest of us live
With different hopes inside
But all of us strive
To maintain some pride.

Tamzin Hardy

No Peace

Alone in the night,
 and feeling so much fright.
Everything seems so quiet,
 no sign of a riot.
Then all of a sudden "Bang",
 My heart goes like a rang-a-tang.
It's no longer quiet,
 and now starts yet "another" riot.

Charlene Whelan

Dream Maker

Hello there
Little dream maker
Whose dreams
Are you making today?
What hopes
And joys
Have you given
To those
Who have lost their way?
What hope
Do you give
For the future,
What place
For the lonely to stay?
Oh do tell
Little dream maker!
Whose dreams
Are you making today?

A. J. Marshall

The Coming of a Woman's World

I suppose the time has come
Progressing to the world of man
Those steps of power to be won
The coming of a woman's world

With motives sharp, so very clear
Seats in the house they now fill
Boardroom ships they help to steer
The coming of a woman's world

Decisions made, their perceptions find
Skirt the dangers, dress the wounds
Creating wealth, with peace in mind
The coming of a woman's world

As world leaders they will excel
Their fragrance on the highest stage
With expertise and guidance to foretell
The coming of a woman's world.

Kenneth C. Burditt

A White November Day

The snow is falling around the
  bungalows and o'er all
  the street,
Time for hot woolies and boots
  upon our feet,
Thick coats whoever you intend
  to meet,
scarf, hat and gloves, thick socks
  too, makes our
  clothes quite complete,
For the hail, snow and sleet.

Lynne Charlton

The Coming of Spring

Daffodils appearing on the scene
Dotted among the evergreens.
Crocuses spreading beneath the trees
In cloaks of purple yellow and white.
Making such a wondrous sight
Bluebells primroses everywhere
As their perfume fills the air
Trees in every shade of green.
As Mother Nature paints the scene
And the river running fast through
Fields where cattle chew new grass
As the spring is here at last
Soon buttercups and clover peep
As meadows grow beneath our feet
And everything in live feels sweet
As birds singing fills the air
They spread their message everywhere
As they Herald in the spring

Margaret Watson

Life!

Life is a game,
and we all are playing.
Hoping to gain,
just like we were saying

Never make mistakes
for we must pay.
Hoping for a new something
to help us on our way.

Life is a game
Like daggers and knives.
Some can't take the pressures
and others thrive.

Life is good,
Life is bad,
make someone happy,
but never sad.

Nicola Gabrielle Wilkinson

Honour Bound

Of finest steel they fashioned me
Burnished to their pride
A scabbard then was finely made
To place me there inside
Unsheathe me not without honour
Tarnish not nor blunt my edge
For I am that moment of truth
To this I shall in valour serve
Let not dishonour break me
Nor lay me to the ground
Till we both lie in silence
Forever honour bound
And when at last our story
To others will unfold
The truth that was our glory
made us brave and bold

Edward J. Costello

Autumn

The music flutters,
Unsure of its next tone
The dancer is left in anticipation.
Will the next note be stronger
Will it finally fade away
The dancer is unsure what the
Next step will be
Will it lift her through the clouds
Will it leave her stranded on the floor
What dictates the tone.

Okolo Bonaventura

Sharing and Caring

Less of I
And more of we,
More of us,
And less of me.

Would make this world
A better place,
For the young and old,
Of every race.

Enjoy all things,
Ignore all greed,
Share and care
For those in need.

I and me,
You'll be amused,
Are two selfish words
Most often used

More of giving,
And less taking,
This world would be,
Of excellent making.

Kathleen Blanchfield

The Fawn

In the beautiful still air the sun
Rising at dawn
The river runs with cold water
And there it appear a
young fawn
His mother looks with awareness
And love
And as the sun rises and shines
from above
The young deer falters a little
But feels safe and sound
Drinks the cold water and
Returns to the bracken the
Safe ground.

Paul J. C. Hunter

What Music Means to Me

Music is my salvation
in relation to health.
Music gives me pleasure
and leisure
to express
my moods
from the roots
of depression
which is pure
and cures
my emotions.
Without music
I cannot survive.
I must give
So that music
Continues to live.
Long live music!

Vivian Paulette Aston

Some New Pictures

I see
you
but
I don't see
myself

in the reflection
of
your eyes
it seems
as
my love
ain't
enough
anymore

Josipa Supan

Defenseless Love

The men all adore her
As she walks,
Does not rush,
But with sweetness
Of wild, invisible springs.
With her footsteps she will crush
The seasons of life;
But with tender feeling
She walks on the hearts
Of scattered roses
As she walks by.
In defenseless passion
Of my first love,
She walks on my heart
That bleeds in the clouds of her dust.

Lee Hayward

Thee Do

How could it matter to you or I.
we can't take it any further,
for we'd hurt each others lives.
too much confusion, misery and pain,
for your love, is driving me, insane.
we try not, for this feeling.
but heaven is coming around again.
how do I keep on falling,
for a love, so in vain.
How could I want you,
when all we do is care.
oh how we have a friendship,
one that will always be there.
oh how can I honestly see you,
when I'm not completely true.
for all I really want,
is just to honestly have, you.

Helen Devlin

Cars

There are to many cars in England
To many cars by far
And folks do not want to walk
They go everywhere by car
But little do they realize
As they go riding round
That they do need the exercise
To keep them safe and sound
The exhaust that's in the atmosphere
Is bad for all the rest
There are people with bad asthma
And pains up in the chest
So please try to give a thought
And take a bus or train instead
Then perhaps some of these people
Won't spend so much time in bed
The air will be much cleaner
And pollution almost free
Perhaps it will be a happier place
For all like you and me

Ada Lane

Happiness

The sound of laughter or a giggle,
The sight of smiling or a grin,
A warm contentment, felt deep within,
No time for sorrow or a tear,
Just a feeling of joy;
Which brings great cheer!

Karen Faulkner

Both of Us

Light and dark,
Sun and moon.
Oppositely wondering,
What each other thinks,
Is thinking.
Are we the same,
Do we agree.
No, nothing.
Complete opposition.
Perhaps,
Or is it in my head,
Do we fit,
Pieces of a puzzle.
Watertight,
No escape.
Do we wish to.
Together,
In separate lives.
One thought,
Occasionally.

Keith Bainbridge

The Lonely Head

I'm sitting in this cafe
Wanting to call
or just hoping
You'll walk through the door.
I can't help thinking
What I said did you wrong.
But as time goes by
I still want to belong,
To hold you in my arms
Till my heart burns out.
If I don't get you soon
I'll start to scream and shout.
Pour a cup of coffee.
There's something to say to you
I don't care if you don't listen.
"Will our love pull us through?"
Every sip of coffee
Stronger than I recall.
I think you'll find
I've never loved you more.

Samantha Hicks

Mitzi

It was a cold December.
When you first came to stay.
You were wet, cold, and hungry,
I thought you were astray.

You hissed when I approached you.
But your coat was matted so;
And your little ears were bleeding,
I could not just let you go.

I look you to the fireside,
Gave you food, and warm milk.
Dried your little body,
With its fur as soft as silk.

I fed you, and I groomed you,
And very soon you see;
You learned how to purr again,
To be proud; and to be happy.

You did not have to stay,
You were always free to go:
But I was pleased that you stayed.
Because I loved you so.

Patricia E. Price

Confronted to You
What Shall Your Soul

Because the beauty of your soul
The world becomes brighter
The flowers open their lives
The ocean gets clear and calm
The birds sing aloud
The mountains get green
Because the beauty of your soul
A child can smile
A song can be heard
Good things for the world could happen
Because the beauty of your soul
You can share happiness
You can share peace
You can share love
Because the beauty of your soul
You can teach others to love
You can teach others to share
You can teach others to feel
Don't ever lose the beauty of your soul
That is the only thing you can never
Lose and transplant into others . . .

Lorraine Diana Fraser

Christmas Time

Christmas time
a sad time
a lonely time.
Memories
of loved ones
of joy and peace
intensify the grief.

Memories of
childhood.
A carefree time
a trusting time
when others bore the brunt
of reality.

The New Year brings
a glimmer of hope.
Will the future bring
true happiness?
A sense of peace?
Or am I suffering
from over-optimism?

Helen K. Reece

Time Passing

Do you stand and look
At the setting Sun
Then think back
To the wonderful things
That you could have done
To lay your heart bare
Then travel the past
Knowing your dreams really don't last
Thinking of people that you have known
Their simple kindness
The love they have shown
Places to wander
Fields—Beaches—Ocean's Edge
Gentle water lapping your legs
Time to oneself that's a desperate need
The Sun slips away darkness falls
Bringing the hush of night's own call
Days turn into weeks
Weeks into years
   Life's Passing

Monica Drury

The Passing

Creative and artistic in every way,
And never wasting her time,
But using her abilities every day.

She taught me about life to discover
That, she was my very best friend,
And a wonderful caring mother.

So now she's sitting in the sun,
Looking fit and very young,
In a garden full of flowers.

Time she has galore.
When starting to paint and draw,
Sitting at the easel all those hours.

Very artistic in her leisure,
And taking a very great pleasure,
Of anything that may catch her eye.

She loved the beauty of trees,
Animals, birds, and the bees,
But now she has her studio in the sky.

Barbara Webb

Death

Like a black velvet blanket,
closing slowly over my empty shell,
Falling perfectly without a crease,
erasing me from existence.

Like a deep dark void of nothing,
drifting in space,
nowhere to go,
nothing to see.

Like a weightless object,
suspended in air,
motionless,
drained of all existing energy.

The depth of a never ending hole
emptiness engulfs me.

Emma Hines

Desire

What I really want but I can't have,
   The desire of my emotion,
A dream that never will come true,
   Like the uneasiness of oceans.

It's like a dream, but more of a wish,
   Like thin air, I cannot touch.
I tend to dream, I'm not a liar.
   I'll tell the truth for my desire.

Shah Abdul Karim Ali

Unfulfiled

A sadden heart filled with emptiness
Silently cries for love and joyfulness
Nobody listens, nobody knows

One that is tearfulness
Brought down by loneliness
Nobody knows, nobody cares

For one that is needfulness
Help me find you happiness
Nobody hears, nobody knows

Only fulfilled in dreaminess
Needs one of realness
Nobody knows, nobody sees

All but of one and that is thee
So why won't he answer me

Ruth Watts

My Prayer

I have prayed, God give us guidance.
  Please cleanse us of all sin.
I have prayed for health and happiness
  for all my kith and kin.
Dear Lord, please in thy wisdom
  protect us one and all
From all earthly vice and wickedness
  until we hear thy call.

Frank McArthur

The Clown

Roll up, roll up, come see the clown,
Applaud the foolish smile.
Come in and watch the funny act,
Pray, please do stay awhile.
It's good to see the people laugh,
Enthraled by wonderland,
But don't look closely at the clown,
You might not understand.
Beneath the painted funny face
The clown is in despair,
And must not disappoint the crowd
By showing all his care.
The show goes on, it always does,
Despite his broken heart,
He tumbles on, and cries within,
But always plays his part.
Roll up, roll up, come see the clown,
Applaud the foolish smile.
Come in and watch the funny act,
Pray, please do stay awhile.

Sue Fishwick

Miss December

I used to watch the snowflakes
Painting colours in her hair,
Sapphire and cerise and
Vermilion, they were there,
And I'd watch our breaths
Swirling together in the winter air.

We would walk beside
Fish-filled frozen streams,
And I would tell her
About my wild schemes,
And her eyes would light up,
As if they were sunbeams.

Many rivers have flowed
Under bridges we had chosen,
Still my memories about her
Remain December-frozen,
It was some time ago,
But I still remember her,
I miss her,
I miss my Miss December.

Peter Vaughan Williams

Abortion

Mummy, can you hear me
mummy, can you see,
I hope you're out there, mummy,
listening to me.

My eyes as blue as day, mummy,
my skin as soft as snow,
please don't leave me, mummy,
please don't let me go.

What's the world like, mummy?
Is everyone like you?
I want to come out now, mummy,
so I can be with you.

It's time for me to go, mummy,
they're pulling me apart,
it's time for me to go, mummy,
they've reached my tiny heart.

A. Anthony

You Think Too Much

You think too much
But can you?
Think about it.
But not too much.

Would you credit it?
I'm doing it again.
What a hopeless case.

Inside is no anger.
No vengeance
Only sorrow.

Do they deserve it?
Of course not.
But some do.
Which some though?

Confusion . . . maybe
Lost . . . certainly
Without aim . . . Yes.
Perhaps.

Paul Davis

Mother's Prayer

No place to sleep,
No place to eat,
Nowhere to go,
Except the streets.
She trudges around,
A small bundle she holds.
She fears for their lives,
If only she'd been told.
Sleeping in doorways,
Begging for food,
She dreams of a life,
A life with some good.
As they fall asleep,
Blue with the cold,
She prays that her child,
Will live to grow old.

Theresa Terris

Why

Why does man have to create wars,
and tear our world asunder?
Why is man so full of hate,
Why does he pillage and plunder?
Why does man have to set his bombs
So that they injure and maim?
And why can't man admit he was wrong,
Why can't he accept the blame?
All over the world, there is suffering
Of one kind or another,
So why can't man live in peace
and harmony, like brother to brother?

E. V. Helman

The Fear That Lies Within

Is of love that is lost and never found
Is of battles you cannot win
Is of tears that just won't flow
Is of speaking and not hearing a word

The fear that lies within
Is of loving and never being loved
Is of trying to make a new start
Is of leaving and not being followed
Is of pain from a broken heart

The fear that lies within
Is of all these things and more
Is of losing you my friend
Is of watching you walk out the door
Is of knowing this could be the end

Emma Burton

Night Wind

There was a night wind and silence,
Shadows on the lawn, then fade.
A whisper in the wind and nothing,
Lightning in the sky, then shade.

There was a sweet life, then death,
A memory of youth, then age,
A seeking for truth, then lies,
A hope for life, then rage.

There was a night wind and silence
as man turned to God and sighed
There was a prayer, redemption
And then a world that died.

Jacki Larcombe

Time Has a Limit

A world you have come through
with no understanding.
It's the future that you are faced
with which you are now seeing.
From the time you were born,
till the day that you will die.
The hidden secrets which have
now opened your eyes.
To a door that you are doubtful
to gaze.
Will you be shocked?
Or will you be amazed?
It's the question that you
must ask yourself.
Do I want to be here?
Or do I want to be somewhere else?
It's hard to predict what lies ahead.
It's best to set out to do what
you had said.
Others will depend on fate.
Is that the answer?
Or for them will it
be too late?

Tricia Wynter

That's Love

In the wonders of the prairie
comes my true love to me,
hand in hand we go along
sing an ancient, native song.

Love and magic is all round,
like a bell is every sound,
the sun is smiling in the sky,
the wind is dancing all the way.

That's love, truly love my heart,
we will never, ever go apart,
we see the world in a silvershine,
we love the earth, we drink the wine

C. J. Chamberlain

Out of a Clear Blue Sky

Heart stoppingly, startlingly,
Out of a clear blue sky,
A sudden thrill of sound
And eye-defying flight;
A soaring lift and swoop and glide,
A flash from sight
Before the mind has thought.

What this? What this?

Perhaps young men, airbourne,
Glorying in their strength
And new-found skills;
Testing nerve and sinew
In reckless gay abandon
And Douglas Badering their youth
In frenetic aerial dance.

Is this then this?
Not so; not so.

Just Kamikaze blackbirds
Over the lanes of England.

Joy Playford Ward

Dying Breed

Gestures
disturbing my eyes—an indication
I imagine myself as one of the others
a dying
a dying flame
embracing the thoughts and acts of
those
those who know—those who are
a dying breed

Help me and help yourself
I can not
I am just one of those
those
who do not know
those who can not
help
help themselves

Henrik Rivera Hansen

Intrusion

I am a shadow,
Catch me if you can,
I, so cunningly,
Enter into your thoughts.
I sneak into your mind
When you least expect me.
I tiptoe into your memory,
I embed myself deep.
I penetrate your dreams,
Whilst you lay asleep.
Can you hear me weep?
I know that you regret
Having met me,
But I cannot let you,
Forget me.

Elizabeth Ann Condron

All about Her!

She was kind,
She was old. She was never ever cold,
In her beautiful house all alone.
  She was lonely, but happy,
everyone respected her,
everyone was kind to her,
She planted flowers all around,
in her house and in the ground,
she was the best, the best of the rest.
Where has she gone?

Denise L. Tucker

Emerging Souls

All alone. I lie here,
Engulfed by society's eyes,
Poverty has overcome me,
It is now a part of our lives.

I cry. Searching for food,
People look in disgrace,
Can't they see the person
That belongs to the human race?

Help. The pressure is intense,
I cannot bear the strain,
The begging and the hunger,
It causes all the pain!

Life. I look with hateful eyes,
Upon my parents, and love.
Can I escape this nightmare,
I pray to God above.

Birth. The coldness overtakes me,
I really want to die,
The cruelness and the hurt,
All I ask is why?

Clare Saggers

The Dark of Night

Sitting silent in a tree
The dark of night
But the owl it can see
Its eyes shut quick
Like a camera lens too
But the owl captures
A film in its glare twit tawoo
The little mouse upon the ground
Is unaware the owl makes no sound
But in one swift swoop
The mouse is dead
It's the chain of nature
The owl has to be fed
Daylight comes and with it sound
Nature is with us all around
A bird of prey can take to flight
A pleasing art to the human sight
Thankful for nature we should be
It's a chain reaction do you see

Stephanie Brown

Verses to a Baby Boy on His Christening

On this your dedication day
Sweet baby undefiled
Upon your birth and early life
The Lord has surely smiled

For you are blessed with parents kind
And joy attends each day
Family love is yours to share
Godparents for you pray

But babyhood will pass too soon
As you become a lad
Then years will roll on steadily
With good times and with bad

For the good times thank your Maker
In the bad times seek his aid
And you will find that life somehow
Gets better when you've prayed

Remember his Commandments too
No better guide you'll find
To help you live your life at peace
With God and all Mankind

W. A. N. Ferguson

The World with Crime

The smell of the breeze
As it waves through the air
The smell of the flowers
Even though they're not there.

The whistling of the wind
As it passes each day
The crying of the children
That can't go out and play.

The sound of the trees
As they brush to and fro
The howling of the buds
That have no strength to grow.

What have we done
To the world today
All of this crime
Someday we will pay.

Bernadette Pinnock

The Beast

There once was a being,
With fearsome rage,
Who ate all his enemies,
And didn't like his friends.

He hunted like a shark,
Smooth and yet quite sharp,
And ate like an Emperor,
While drinking like a fish.

He never combed his fur,
and acted like a slob,
He liked to eat and sleep a lot,
But that was about all.

He lived in the city,
Strolling 'round the streets,
He blended in so perfectly,
You'd never ever find him.

Then suddenly he disappeared,
Leaving not a trace,
No one's ever seen him since,
But maybe he's still out there.

Mark Frost

Oh . . .

Oh, for a world,
That's free from war.
Where, starving people,
Will be no more.
Where we each would be,
In a snug warm home.
Living in a world that's free.

A. S. Moore

To My Children

All through the laughter
The smiles and the tears
I thank you my children
For these golden years

Remember what I said
"Don't grow up too fast"
And cherish every moment
Whilst the childhood lasts

You all ooze innocence and beauty
From those lovely big eyes
From the time you all awake
Till it's time for bye-byes.

And if you all love each other
As much as I love you
Then life should be just wonderful
The whole way through.

Julie Maguire

A Tribute to Sixteen Angels and Their Guardian Angel (Mrs. Mayor)

God loves to walk in his garden
As the day draws to its close
He lingers long and lovingly
As he gently caresses 'The Rose'
So tall and yet so graceful
With a perfume beyond belief
He smiles at the rose's perfection
This was surely his Masterpiece

But wait . . . his eyes have grown misty
In silence the teardrops start
For there at the feet of 'The Master'
Sixteen rosebuds form a golden heart

Pauline E. Beer

A Teddy Bear

A teddy bear is a cuddly toy,
Loved by every girl and boy.
They were a really bonny golden shade,
But now in almost any colour made.

They are a very special friend,
Taken places without end,
Cuddled close in bed or cot,
Such a comfort to every tot.

They are carried round by leg or arm,
In the house or on the farm,
Help to cure a bump or fall,
Certainly the best pal of all.

Wrapped in a shawl he'll go to sleep,
He does not need to count sheep,
Staying there until time for tea,
And loves to sit upon a knee.

Comfort to many a child they bring,
And some are really made to sing,
From Heaven they bring such pleasure,
With happy memories to treasure.

E. R. Shepherd

Sadness

Sadness is a sorrow,
Full of pain,
But if you can forget your sadness,
You'll regain control again.

Susan Kirkwood

Foolish Things

Let's talk of things,
Like dragons on gossamer wings,
Magic cloaks, mysterious rings,
That do bad and beautiful things,
Why do we do these foolish things?

The power one finds,
In imaginative minds,
Then strange things unwind,
Virtual things of one kind.

Vampire bats and flying mats,
Spell-casting in funny hats,
Talking to half-tame black cats,
Who sit ignoring all the rats.

Let's talk of things,
To see what good luck it brings,
To hide from the real things,
Or rewards working hard can bring,
Why do we do these foolish things.

Let's, let's talk of things.

K. R. Hirons

High Hopes

My racing mind just never stops
If only it would give in—
And pause a while and settle down—
Then maybe I would win.

Like a seesaw up and down
Little wonder I wear a frown
A chink of hope and up it goes
Expectations, higher hopes.

A fleeting moment, not a care
My head is clear, as light as air.
A surge of joy comes over me
A taste of how it used to be.

Could it be I'm coming out?
Now that would be something
    to shout about.

Rita Snaith

Dreaming

Dreaming of a better place,
Dreaming of a happier tune,
Waiting for a different race,
Waiting for the bells to chime.

Looking for a better chance,
Looking for a happier way,
Hoping for a different dance,
Hoping for a clearer day.

Searching, hoping it will work,
Searching for a better deal,
Wanting prose, some thanks, a perk,
Looking for some prod to steal.

Jealous of the glowing faces,
wondering why life does not rhyme,
wanting better times and places,
Dreaming of a happier tune.

Daniel Moore

On the Plain

Looking around,
From East to West and North to South,
You see the Land
Stretch far and wide and all about;

Watching closely,
At every tree or plant there is,
You see a shrub,
Its leaves a mass of green foliage;

Looking afar,
From top to down and side to side,
You behold a hill,
Towering above with a broad base;

Pondering quietly,
You ask yourself again and again,
Is all this real,
Or just something imaginary?

James Ansah-Eshon

Crimson Kiss

In the high mountain waters,
Where the wild cats bathe,
Lies the island of the sun.
Though its body is twisted by cold
And its yellow skin wrinkled
By the poor scrapings of peasants,
Still the sun promises
Each evening with crimson kiss
To return to his lover's shores.
And still, though centuries
Have long since chilled
The heat of their last embrace,
Still the island waits.

Bruce Collocott

Leaving the Past

Leaving this house,
with memories past,
the haunting reminders,
a history cast
aside and buried, but!
Never to be forgotten.

We will start anew,
to begin again.
What was before
brought great pain,
forward we go, but!
Never to be forgotten.

Objects are kept,
precious and dear,
never to be lost,
our biggest fear,
holding the past, but!
Never to be forgotten.

A. Henderson

The Storm

The stormy night,
The fear and fright,
The thunder roars,
Rain trickles and pours,
The ominous cloud,
The storm so loud,
The lightning lashes,
The tree then crashes,
You snuggle up tight,
On that stormy night.

Jennifer Craig

The Cloth

See the cloth as it unfolds
What are the secrets that it holds?
Old and yellowed by the years
As it fills the world with fears.
Oh! what a test of faith it hands
As whispers go throughout the lands.
Were we meant to love and pray?
Or will we know the truth someday?
And in a voice that feels no pain
Will we still our faith proclaim?
As like the cloth the truth unfolds
And bares the secrets that it holds.
Can we free this world from doubt
And know the truth of the Turin Shroud?

Sheila E. McMillan

Lost Love

Lost in the mist of time,
when our hearts were young
and you were mine.
We wander hand in hand,
seeking, seeking,
a first love, mine and thine.

Far distant shores, moonlight
dancing on golden sands,
we wander hand in hand,
seeking, seeking.
A paradise once we knew,
now cast forever in a lonely
land for me and you.

Fading shadows greet the dawn,
hoping for a brave new moon,
we wander hand in hand,
seeking, seeking
a new love is God's keeping,
love is fleeting, fleeting, fleeting.

Ruby De Gruchy

Loneliness—Sparrow-Style

From an avian plethora,
A single sparrow hoppited out.
It perched itself on a nearby window,
with keenest of eyes, peered inside.
Then with a leap into the air
and with a flap of its wings,
away it went to affront
a hanging mirror inside.
It pecked at its image in the glass.
It pecked and pecked and pecked,
to coax its mate in the mirror
to step out and end its quest,
or invite it in like Alice
into a wonder-escape.

Shehnaz Somjee

Untitled

The life you lead is not for me,
the life you lead should not be.
You live your life on the street,
being kicked by careless feet.
Spare a penny I hear you call,
like the stumble before a fall.
It's for a cup of tea,
please you beg someone help me.
You sleep in a door,
do you have a friend with a floor?
Somewhere nice, somewhere warm,
where you'd never feel the storm.
All your friends have moved on.
A job, money then they've gone.
You have been left behind.
Who said life was kind?

T. Mevor

Locked

To talk he'll try but cannot talk,
His tongue gets all a' twisted.
His twisted tongue then ties the tongue
To tangle the talk attempted.

The heart is
LOCKED.
No trace of a key.
The cold door
BLOCKS
A caring, sharing relationship.

The silence ushers tears
Down the yearning lover's face.

His mouth opens.
Facts tumble;
Dense empty statements
DRAINING
The warmth from her cheeks.

His cynical speech
STILLS
The ice sculpture's stare.

Louise Wray

Life

They've stolen dreams,
They've killed imagination.
They've destroyed our faith
And denied our salvation.
They've taken language,
They've wasted passion,
They murdered sex
And gave us fashion.
They gave us cliche
That's why I can't say
What I feel for you
Because I think
They took that too.

Shani A. Lewis

So Near Death

I had no signs of worry or pain,
I did not realize that night,
Those awful pains I suffered,
Were in fact a heart attack,
It was a fight for life in fact,
I could only pray so hard for oblivion.

In those twilight hours ahead,
Unknown to me I was put to sleep.
Not knowing my fight for life
    "To survive or die"
But God I do believe was near
As I went through that black tunnel
    "So near death"

God took my hand in his, I know.
Gave me another chance
To survive in fact for life
Along that weary road of pain
    "To carry on"
I often wonder why really,
"As I was seventy nine"

V. M. Moore Suffolk

Alcoholic

Are you really there
Can you hear me talk
Or is my voice explosive
Like the popping of a cork?

Do you understand
What I'm trying to say
Or should I spare my breath
And try another day?

You are not the same
As I knew before,
I don't know how to reach you
Or what I'm trying for.

Where is your strength of will?
Please come back to me.
So we can again communicate
And set your spirit free

To talk of common things
And share a smile or tear
And be a normal happy pair
Throughout a normal year.

Jennifer Young

Cariad—(Sweetheart)

I left my Wales to emigrate,
and I packed up my dreams
    By the garden gate,
I've had it all,
    The glitz and the glamour,
The partying times
    and the men who clamour
Then I heard my grandmother
    quietly say,
    "Come Home Cariad
    before it's too late
and we'll both
    weave your Dreams
By The Garden Gate"

Margaretta Phillips

The Turf Cutters

They've heeled through time and tossed
    A thousand thousand years
With just a glance,
    To set a hearth
To feed and warm a day, a night
    And a dance.

Laurence M. O'Reilly

Imagination

Imagine taking a walk with me
On a beautiful spring like day,
The birds are singing in the trees
And the lambs are all at play.

Imagine now we are in the park
Oh listen to the dim,
The boys are playing football
And the goalie has just let one in.

Imagine now the flower beds
The perfume fills the air,
The daffodils dancing in the breeze
While people stop and stare.

Le'ts move along to the water's edge
And watch the river go flowing by,
The ducks and swans go paddling on
Quick, look! There goes a dragonfly.

Now our journey is over
And we are safely home again,
Next time I take you for a walk
I think we'll go to Spain.

May Kay

The Dalmatian and the Labrador

The cape was sold with great delight
The hood was neat all smart and bright
It seems that spots are in Vogue
When one comes tripping along the road

It must be chosen with great care
So that people stand and stare
For this spotty is very special,
I hope it's not a little devil.

By now you have guessed whom it's from
Good health, luck, and happiness
in years to come

Now I know they will stand and stare
When they see the little pair
One all sleeky long and black
The other white with spots on her back
May their joyous barks and squeaks
Bring the roses to your cheeks

Mae Winterburn

Moon Clow

  I saw a moon
in the sky and it looked
very shy so I decided to
fly up into the sky like a fly.
And give the moon a tie
and the moon was not shy.
So I said I will fly away.

Gemma Baker

Winter

Wiping the condensation away
from the eyes of the house,
The window reveals
the frost and the snow
in a frozen quartz forest garden
fragmentedly feline
by a pattern of paws across the lawn

The gales from Scandinavia
cut harshly over the land,
White petals twirl in a frenzy,
in a swirling hostile dance

The Sun so readily surrenders
early to the night
The wind rustles through the laurels
into the cobalt coloured sky.

John Kirkham

Seasons and Sadness

I am the Sun, the Rain
   and Snow,
The icy Lake, the Autumn blow,
The clear blue Sky—
   the Flowers that grow.
But I still feel sorrow
   for the World
With pollution and corruption
   and Evil on this Earth

I wish for Peace and Happiness
   for all
And not for Death and Sadness
   or disease—
At all!

Steven Allen

Memories

His smiling face,
Was there once more,
The face of the man,
That I adore,
His eyes shone
As they met mine,
Yes our love
Was so divine.
Our lips met,
In a lasting kiss
Did every young couple
Love like this?
It is so good
While it lasts
For now it's a memory
Of the past
As I sit here
Old and grey
And live for my memories
Of yesterday

Yvonne Smith

On Learning to Walk

Up till then, the journey small
From hand and knee to chair.
Those faltering footsteps put to risk
All that love did care.
When suddenly before our sight
Our darling was foot-borne.
Those sparking eyes, I've got it now
I'll show you what I mean.
And all the journeys of this world
On one small face did gleam.

Philip P. Murphy

The Winter Bathe

The bathing belle was pink and well
And everyone did say
"How brave you are to take a swim
This chilly winter's day"
She sallied forth upon the rocks
The sea was grey and grim
Not fit for such a pretty sight
And icy cold within.
She tottered in the murky depths
A fierce wave rushed in fast
And whirling round her dragged her down
That cold bathe was her last.
Her friends ran screaming up and down
And flung their arms about!
But naught could save the drowning girl
Nor hope to pull her out.
And in the surf her bathing cap
No longer on her head.
Just fluttered like a butterfly
While she, poor soul, was dead.

Leonora Simpson

The Thwarted Tiger

The tiger creeps on stealthily
His ears are pricked, his senses keen
He moves along so quietly
Ahead he sees the river's gleam

Steadily through the long grass
On silent paws he pads along
His quarry is quite unaware
He makes no noise as he creeps on

Suddenly the silence is broken
By the warning of bird song
Enraged the tiger then does leap
But too late! His prey has gone

Elizabeth Anderson

The African Violet

Rich purple petals, peeping
out of me.
Golden centered stamens
There for all to see.
Where did you get your
colour, and you velvet rue?
Why are you not white, and
not this purple hue?
Is it not the same for people,
in this world of ours?
Some have dark skins, with
their velvet sheen.
Others have white skins,
Of which some may preen
All however, have a heart
Each feeling love, pain
Some the suffering caused
by human powers.

Diana Radford

Life

Life is like a flower
It blossoms and grows
Then all of a sudden
the blossoms go.

Life is like a tiny bud
each day it grows a little more
Then all of a sudden
it becomes a full grown bloom.

Life is like an ocean deep,
each time it flows
Then all of a sudden,
it changes and grows.

Life is like an endless tide,
moving in fast, moving out slow,
Then all of a sudden,
that life has gone, and died.

Christine Rands

Dreams

I love to wander fancy free
Into a world of dreams
Where fantasy overcomes me
And things aren't as they seem

Flooding my mind a mirage of things
Feelings of contentment sweet
As relaxed—my dream begins

Happy, safe and warm I feel
Harm cannot come to me
Hideous monsters—are they real?
I turn my back and flee!

Gently now I rouse from sleep
As night transforms to day
Elusive dream—I cannot keep

It now seems far away.

Sandra Budd

Heaven on Earth

I have a perfect sanctuary
whenever I'm perplexed
where heart and soul will reunite
and my body is refreshed

I know it may be selfish not to
share this place with you,
but I treasure this time alone
my spirit to renew

Sometimes my back is aching
my mind is in a whirl
but know in peaceful contemplation
all answers will unfurl.

Such warmth I find around me
in my most treasured space
Two hands to help and guide me
with tasks I cannot face

You may have found this sanctuary
or perhaps you'll only laugh,
for my loving blissful heaven on earth
you've guessed— it is my bath!

Olive Bedford

Too Young to Be Out

On the tip, the very edge
Of horizon, I glimpsed the moon,
Striving to cling to moving clouds.
Untrustworthy, unstable clouds
Offer no protection,
The moons too young to mistrust
Their instability.
So very new, the buffeting winds
Continue, caring nothing for his youth.

Night's blackness will bring ease
So that the moon may grow,
Grow in size but not in sense.
He will repeat his mistake,
Go out when too young
To be battered again,
He will not learn.
And surely he is old enough,
And should know better!

Elizabeth Wooliscroft

My True Love

His touch is warm, his eyes are
filled with love for me, his strong
arms draw me into his warm
and longing body, his lips gently,
then passionately caress my lips,
my neck, my closed eyes, I'm
lost and absorbed totally into
his being, our souls meet
and we are one.

Ruth Lea

Peace of Mind

To all of us there comes a time
   when we must take a look
Deep inside—to read our thoughts—
   for life is like a book.
With characters where everyone
   is different from the rest,
But each will see that he or she
   with many things—is blessed.

Some are troubled—others tired.
   there are those with fears,
Hunger, heartache—spirits low—
   courage, laughter, tears.
All this is one small part of life,
   much more we've still to find
As we scan the pages of our book,
   in search for 'Peace of Mind'.

Sidney A. Kerrison

Ever-Changing Goals

Inwards,
Upwards,
Outwards.

Inner development taking years and
many lifetimes.

Up towards the moon and stars reaching
for ever changing goals.

Out,
Way out to some,
But to others who see
Out, up and within.

You,
Me,
Only those who see,
Know.

Pat Aphra

Twenty-Two Forever

Babies are born they grow up
They grow old
Hot Summer nights
Then the Winter and cold
Beauty is something
That comes then it goes
As we grow older
As everyone knows
We're born and we grow
We live and we die
And no-one on earth yet
Can tell us just Why
But you my Dear child
Will know nothing of this
No marriage no children
All this you will miss
But you'll still be Beautiful
Till life is through
Forever and ever
You'll stay Twenty-Two

Millie Whitney-Holmes

Dreams

Dreams fall from your eyes
Beads of rest
Like tiny pearls
Cultured, strung together haphazardly.
Guitar strings lull the adult's mind
Lullaby, the child's.

Irene Patricia Kelly

Fly-High, Fly-Free (continued)

On Christmas morn, I held you close
And silence filled the air
I loved you both so tenderly
We did not have a care.

But fate stepped in, one tragic day
And with it broke my heart,
For three days from that Christmas morn
My world was torn apart.

For in the nest, tucked well away
His little head held high,
Was "Baby" Pan my little man
And he had said "Goodbye".

Now left alone, just us two
Amid winter's long cold days
Di and I will see it through
Closer in our ways.

Three weeks later from that day
Di was also gone from me,
They are both together now,
Flying high and flying free.

Wendy Osborne

Tell Him

This message is for anyone,
With a Dad as great as mine,
Tell him that you love him,
While you still have the time.

No need to write a story
Three simple words will do,
Now slip your arms around him
And whisper "I love you"

A father is a special gift
Bestowed on us at birth,
So just remind him how you feel
Tell him what he's worth.

I tell mine very often,
In fact, I tell him all the time,
I simply say "I love you—
I'm proud that you are mine."

So if you want to tell him
You really must not wait,
Don't leave it till tomorrow
It might just be too late.

Geraldine Griffiths

Somewhere

The night is calm and clear
The new moon shining bright
Stars are twinkling in the sky
Lighting up the night.

Somewhere far above us
A million miles or more
Far beyond the moon and stars
There lies another door.

They say it's for the future
These things we should find out
They will all keep searching
But still there will be doubts.

Who knows what will happen
In one hundred years or less
None of us will be around
To see this future place.

Something somewhere tells us
In space our future lies
The moon and stars will still be there
Lighting up our skies.

Elaine Marie Wilson

The Postman

Please think and post a letter
To a lady with white hair
She sits and waits and watches
Does anyone really care?

Sometimes we are busy
Yes this is an excuse
For really we can find the time
Just for things we want to do.

Sit down and write a letter
To a friend alone and sad
Then tomorrow morning
A dear old lady will be glad

Give your life to others
To the lonely and the sad
Sit down and write a letter
For money do not grab.

Then the postman will be calling
Not passing the house by
Remember in the morning
An old lady will not cry.

Enid Wilcox

Viva Septuagenaria

The veins are clearer now
To be seen
On the surface of those hands
That once were marble smooth
One Church ring morning.
Hands holding for us on that day
A posy of celebrate flower
That you turned
Into a garland host
Of all our tomorrows.
Hands that shared with mine
The moving hour
Of unrelenting rhythm
That brought us
In the keep of time
To this autumnal awhile.
Hands that I
Times lift upward to my face
And caress the constancy
Of their enduring grace.

Elwyn Johnson

Inspiring Autumn

Mellow autumn on her way
What a lot she has to say
Leaves falling fast upon the ground
Pathways no longer to be found

Colours and hues a beautiful sight
Soon will be covered in glorious white
Sun lies low in heavenly sky
Do you ever stop to ask why

Birds are preparing a vacation
Taking up another station
Bulbs and shrubs for spring are grown
Peeping where the leaves have blown

Come dear autumn pay your call
Raise up your head strong and tall
We'll welcome you with open arms
A lifelong friend who'll do no harm

S. M. Bradshaw

Delights of Spring

Oh! To hear the singing of
the lark. To herald the
forthcoming of the spring
and all the delights, it will
bring. The warm sun. The
pretty flowers. What a
delight to the eye.
To see the birds
flying across the sky.

Eileen Scaplehorn

Untitled

Sword versus sword
Pike versus lance
The start of aggression I fear
Bows and arrows
And crossbows too
The reasons were not so clear
Then gunpowder—what a mistake
Hand-guns and big guns remember drake?
Next bombs from the sky
From zeppelin and plane
So thick and fast
As heavy as rain
To reach zenith the hydrogen bomb
What will we have in the millennium
Let's pray for peace
Sport and leisure
All over the world
Creating pleasure

Edward Jellicoe Pickett

Moments of Serenity

I wander down my favorite walk
the avenue of trees.
My mind shuts out the world of stress
and strain, and gazes at all the
beauty that comes to us for free.

Why must we live in fear of war.
Praying all the time for peace.
People starving, people dying.
Is there any need for this

As my walk comes to an end,
and my mind drifts back to reality.
I thank God for my moments of serenity.

June Ritchie

This Is Your Life Denise

Oh Denise
How you'll sneeze,
When you bite on
A lump of cheese.
And then your legs
Will feel like lead,
When you have a bite,
Of mother's pride bread,
Then later on, your
Dad with pride,
Will walk you up the aisle,
And you, a blushing bride,
Oh how happy you will be,
A lovely grown up,
Busy busy, D.

Hilda Gibbons

Certainty

I don't need the way broken
for to tread unbroken roads;
I don't need the words spoken
to hear the unspoken words.
I don't need the impression
of your body on my bed
to decipher love's confession
and to know what is unsaid.

John W. Sexton

Father's Path

Up till now led a merry dance
Through winding roads and searching
chants
Captivity held this man in pain
From eagerness to past insane
Where to now soul searching done
His time for fun has now begun

Suzelle Longman

Mum

The angels said, "Darling,
It's time so let's go,
Come with us and we will show
All of the good things you wanted
To know."
They say there's life in heaven,
And that is surely true,
Especially for a treasured one
Especially one like you.
You'll only meet the good up here,
We only take the best,
For down below's the place to go
If you're among the rest.
He only takes the very best and
That is surely true,
Because, Mum, we lost the very best
The day that we lost you.

June Clear

The Cottage

Deep in the woods
in a far-away place.

Stands an old cottage
with such style, such grace.
It's been there awhile
How long no one knows!

If the cottage could talk
what would it say?

About the people who lived there
The children who played.

The memories it holds in the
walls that are grey.

They will be there forever
they won't go away.

When we are all gone
to that far away land.

The cottage will stand
in such style, such grace
Deep in the woods.
What a beautiful place!

Ginny Shand

I Miss You

I miss you every single day
In every single little way
The whispering in bed at night
The kissing in the morning light
I miss the smile that's always there
The smell of perfume in your hair
The shining eyes that show the love
That sparkles like the stars above
The perfect lips that taste divine
The heart that beats in time with mine
I miss you every single day
In every single little way

Stephen Hislop

The Swing

Flowers, overgrown
in a garden of my childhood
and I can see myself
moving towards the place
where I know I can be
alone, a slow moving swing.
The movement a comfort, for
realising, even in my childish
innocence, these feelings
are to be endured,
contemplated, as they are
part of me.

All this from then,
stored, waiting within.
Forever returning
to my mind, my dreams.
A vision
of myself as I was.

Marco Farina

Life Behind Bars

A bird in a cage lives to a
reasonable age,
four or even five,
But he will never take to the
deep blue skies.
He looks up to the rest,
wishing he could travel west.
The cage has little space,
now do you think the bird's
life is waste.

Leanne Watson

Our Lives

Our lives are like a tapestry,
Each day we weave a part.
Sometimes we don't always show
the feelings in our heart.
We hide away the sad thoughts
thinking friends won't want to know.
We feel that joy and happiness
is all that we should show.
It isn't always possible
to realize our plans.
The future doesn't rest with us,
It's entirely in God's hands.
So we can only hope and pray
our lives will turn out right one day.

Betty Yates

The Enigma

A cloud of gas afloat in space
A cataclysmic bang
No deity to plan the race
Was this how it began

No guiding force to touch the fuse
The universe to form
Or with intelligence infuse
The matter newly born

From gas to sludge to solid state
Was there no design
Did accident our world create
And not a love divine

Will grapes produce a vintage wine
With no guiding hand
Or the iron ore a plough or tine
Without the help of man

Ere we have run our earthly race
And our day is done
May the pieces all fall into place
So we with God are one

T. D. M. Smith

Ship in a Bottle

Standing on the deck
Watching people pass
Don't know what's happening
I'm just looking through glass.

Nothing much to do
Sitting around all day
The rope near the lifeboat
Has nearly torn away.

Dust is starting to gather
Closing in on me
I wish I was a bigger boat
Out on the open sea.

Katherine O'Gorman

Be Mine

*To Mark my perfect love,
and our unborn child*

You pick me up, you put me down
My head is spinning round and round
My heart keeps beating like a drum
My life is like a spinning top
I'm terrified, when will it stop
I love the way you comb your hair
The way your laughter fills the air
The bitter sweetness of your smile
You make my life seem so worthwhile
The sadness in my heart I'll keep
It hurts so much it's very deep
Until the day you can be mine
My life, my love holds no sunshine

April Rowe

Forgotten Children

Forgotten children of the world
Who stare from tearless eyes
Your faces show the sorrow
That you feel and try to hide
If you could speak to someone
Who would understand your fears
It then would make the life you have
Much easier to bear
Whose fault is it you wonder
Why this world is so unkind
There is no answer we can give
To you, the innocent child
Another day you've yet to face
Where guns and bombs are common place
When will it ever be the same
Where happy children play their games
Running, playing in the fields
You remember in the past
When will it all return again
And there is peace at last?

Maureen O'Leary

To My Love

To see you in so much pain
breaks my heart in two,
I'm so sorry that it happened,
Sorry for what you're going through.

You did nothing wrong that night
it was just a quirk of fate.
It was pure misfortune
that he crossed and did not wait.

We're so sorry that he had to die
that it happened, why? Oh why?
But I'm grateful that we're together
the girls and you and I.

Life is cruel—of that we're sure—
and when I think I could have lost you
it just makes me love you more.

Julie Worthington

Injection of Obscurity

A ribbon of memory enhanced
A revision of totality
Prior to substance abuse.
Clerical dignity
Attaches itself to such
Indefensible clockwork.
Innovative hourglass
Of hostilities, Maniacal denials
Representative of children.
Evidence summarized as airships
Butchered against struggles;
Where the bruising of the clouds
Suffices
as a Prelude to Assistance.

Michelle Brown

Summer Serpent

Round, green mouth ready
To breathe aqua vita
Instead of flame.
Coiled in the Sun,
Its emerald body
Awaits the evening
When it will uncurl—
Long, ribbed and shining,
To twist and leap
Along its length
Away from the patient knight
Who endures this twilight vigil,
This challenge of the serpent
Which is his garden hose.

Beatrice Mary Ewart

Galilee

The thrill to walk by Galilee
Where Jesus walked before
The thrill to stop the boat and pause
Where Jesus stilled the storm.
What a wonder to be where
His pierced body lay
And visit church and chapel
The manger filled with hay
The Arab guards the Muslim doors
The dome that hides the clay
The Jewish zealots once who fled
To mountain top away.
A lift will carry to the top
The visitor today
Or down below Ein Gedi calls
To bathe your pains away.
The hill that once did house the cross
The garden where He prayed
"Lord not my will but Yours be done."
All Heaven out of doors.

Lesley Marr

Across the Atlantic

Across the Atlantic so vast
You will find my family
Grandchildren, growing up so fast
My daughter, husband so dear to me

On this side of the Atlantic,
My son, his wife and four grandchildren
Who, sometimes drive me frantic
Hopefully, in the summer
Whatever the weather,
Across the Atlantic
We will all be together.

Inez Felix

Seasons of Love

Spring was when our love began
Instant, total
Woman and man.

Summer time our life was sweet
Vibrant, healthy
Longing to meet.

Autumn came, I hid the tears
Watched you fading
Filled with fears.

Winter time you left my side
Black despair
I could not hide.

Now you live inside my soul
Always with me
Half of my whole.

Glenys Buckle

Why!

Why do we always waste our time
hoping that maybe one day
"That boy will soon be mine"
"friends is enough" is what they say
when you think you're close
they always push you away
why do we always waste our time
wishing we could be
sending us through all the heartaches
but they never seem to see
hurting us deep, without even knowing
and when they are told
they couldn't see it showing
so why do we always waste our time
wishing he was ours
I really do think that love
should be kept behind bars.

Ella-Dee Selvester

Magical

The sun shines through my windowpane.
Spring is here it's back again.
I know I'm happy the winter's gone.
I have you to keep me warm.

Children playing in the street.
Birds are singing oh! So! Sweet.
A silent wonder in itself you know.
I'm over come a special warmth, that
magic glow.

Natural beauty is a wonderful thing.
Joy to all hearts it could bring.
Stop for a while look around, at this
Magical world I have found.

Linda Chrystal

My Kilt

My kilt is my delight they say
It keeps the tongues go'n anyway
From Glasgow to the Isle of Wight
They say they ne'er saw such a sight

I wear my kilt with so much pride
I love the tartan-red
My boyfriend cannot match my stride
He'd rather stay in bed

I'm looking for a husband
With tastes the same as mine
Like porridge, haggis and pease brose
And lots of ginger wine

I want to be a blushing bride
With bridesmaids two or three
A lovely man would make my day
'Cause I can't wait—you see

For girls are few who say "I do"
In the church that "Mungo" built
And fewer still—who say "I will"
In a bonny tartan kilt

A. Henderson

Jack Frost of the Jungle

The lakes are iced over
With memories of you
And traced upon the window
Are patterns that we grew
Jack Frost is painting jungles
Of creepers, flowers and vines
He remembers his other life
The happy warmer times
It was there he swung from tree to tree
And shouted Tarzan is my name
"I'm the king of all the jungle and
Never have known shame"
Then Jane she came upon her Tarzan
And offered him the forbidden fruit
And when he bit upon it
his heart was severed at its root
He lost his Eden forever
And was sent to colder lands
Where he sits away from fires
And never warms his hands

Steven Baker

My Friend

We humble people can't pretend
To know the ways of God,
But must find comfort in the knowledge
That we tread the path he trod.
The good, the bad, the rich, the poor,
Must all reach their journey's end,
As so tragically it seems to us,
You came to yours, My friend.

C. Robinson

Thirst

In the dark night she roams,
walking carefully and steadily,
"Will I secure anything today?"
growls her sixth sense.
For she needs to quench her thirst.

The site, full of people,
with fat pockets,
to smear their one month's sweat
is only a golden chance.
For she needs to quench her thirst.

As happy as ever.
Ready to display her old tricks.
The remedy for fire is fire.
Money is for all.
For she needs to quench her thirst.

She acts expatriately,
to draw his attention.
Who in return will quench her thirst,
by quenching his thirst.
For they need to quench their thirst.

Clive Mwenesi

Mr. Fox

A sly silent animal
with a home underground
who creeps into gardens
and steals without sound.

His territory is large of
gardens and wood land
and he hunts stealthily alone
and not in a band.

He will eat almost anything
that you care to leave out,
But is skittish enough to run
if you dare to shout.

We do him an injustice
this master of cunning
we steal his home to build houses
and send him running.

But clever Mr. Fox
with a family to feed
has made our home his
to satisfy his every need.

Sarah Richardson

Valentine Love Poem

In Spring you are my flower
Smelling like roses in bloom
In Summer you are my sun
Warm like in a Mother's womb
In Autumn you are my tree
Shredding your leaves with such grace
In Winter you are my warmth
Keeping the cold off my face

As every new day dawns
I see your face aglow
It gives a feeling of Happiness
Especially when I'm low
TO me you're someone special
A friend as well as lover
If I could be like this to you
We would not need no other

For better or worse
Till death do us part
I will always love you
With all of my heart

Steven Rolls

Two Souls

I feel you close,
The black all around,
You sit and quiver
Without any sound.
We're floating high,
Above the ground and floor,
My peace of mind,
I have no more.
I can feel the sky
With the sunny blue.
It's all around
And I feel you.
We walk above
The earthen floor
Holding hands
Together once more.
It's all in me
And it's all in you
The rays of light
Just shining through.

Claire Denning

Untitled

An owl hooting
A moonlight sky
A shooting star
Make a wish
 A wish

To wake up to the dawn, chorus
A cuckoo singing his
first song of spring
The red gold sun-rise
The start to a perfect day

A wish come true
 Perhaps
To even better days
 yes I wonder

C. Cowell

He's Helpless

The sunshine cools over
on a cold windy day.
The fox watches over
as the prey walks away;
with the strength of his paw
out reaching for more
Nothing is found.

His legs are stained
by the trap that was made.
By a farmer who's property
was being blamed.

As his bottle green eyes
Shut down with a sigh.
As a crackle was heard
from a blue titted bird
The earth pushed in
by the cruelty within.

Lucy Brown

Untitled

Despair pulls me down
My heart is heavy
My thoughts are sad.

How to dispel this feeling
Think light thoughts.
Let the sun warm my heart.

Alas I cannot fight
This darkness, but
I must reach the pit,
before I can rise and overcome.
My despair

Pauline B. Bevins

Monsters

I can only quiver,
Seeing in the night
Intruding shapes that haunt my dreams,
Spirits taking flight.
Faceless stare,
Floating monster head,
Watching 'till I try to move,
Frozen in my bed.
I hate it when the stillness comes
Creeping up around,
Adrenalin betrays the taste of grass,
And feeds off every sound.
Sleep is far away now,
I am not alone,
The presence of the underworld
Chills me to the bone.
Nights are all oppressive,
Air is thick with eyes,
Hear the whispering of ghosts
Torture me with sighs.

Stuart Grant

Autumn

Trees gently arching
in a purr of leaves,
a leisurely
undressing
to bask in loving warmth,
unchanging rituals
in golden cloisters
offering sanctuary
and spreading contentment
under our soles.

Elizabeth Stevenson

Ballad for Lost Lovers

Disdain is dead!
Burning curses the restrained
Refrains of a high requiem,
Will they here
Sweetly sing soft songs?

Thrushes trilled on the
Opening buds, butterflies
Blended to the stirring waltz;
They did not whisper
The mouth-watering melody.

When the sun slept longer
To the moon's lullaby
O, the despondent slide
Of their tepid tango.
Death, will you
Inspire a divine duet?

Michele Glazer

Wonderful, Wonderful Spices

O Sale Marino
Purificato e grosso
I need you for my dishes
with you I fulfil my wishes

Dear pepper green and pepper red
without you, life I do dread
They spice up my food
and keep me in a good mood

Lovely curry delicious
never are you malicious
And garlic dear
you always provoke a tear

All this spice
It's just too nice
Life without you
C'est vivre sans vous

Leonard Davis

Grandmother

I miss her,
miss her so much.
Miss her holding me,
Miss her caring touch.

Her thin, old face.
Her sparkling warm eyes
The engraved wrinkles,
showing me how wise.

I remember her stories,
Her animated tales.
I recall them fondly,
When all else fails.

I took her for granted,
I couldn't really see.
Now the silver moon rises,
Like hope before me.

Karmjeet Kaur

Spring Time

It's spring time
Back again,
It's time for the leaves to grow
With the sun and rain.

It's over for the coldness
And for hibernation,
It's time to make way
For the next generation.

Spring weather moves about
That's why it gets its name,
And all the pollen's just come back
And the routine's just the same

Tony Stansfield

Human Destroyers

These are our rain forests,
But we keep cutting them down.

These are our oceans,
But we keep polluting them with junk.

These animals are rare,
But we keep trying to wipe them out.

These are our children,
But we cause their misery with war.

This is our ozone layer,
But we keep spraying it away.

These are our people,
But we keep causing hatred between us.

This is our world,
But we keep trying to destroy it
Why?

Amanda Elphick

Myself

You have sent me on this journey
Exploring; then to find
Down the dark and twisted tunnels
Of a once enlightened mind.
I am reeling, sinking deeper
The illusion draws me in
To see my soul reflected
In hell's dungeons lit so dim
Several winding passageways
A door that's drawn and locked
Oh how I think upon that door
That I should not have knocked,
For inside lay my torment
In a satin sheet of grace
And in the coffin by the hearth
Lays the body with my face.

Louis J. A. Horne

Reflections

In the shop window I see jewellery
    which costs a lot of money.
I want it but can't have it,
    that's the way it is, honey!

Besides me, a man looks in the window
    dressed in a nice suit.
In his pockets are credit cards
    he has plenty loot.

He can buy anything he wants
    for himself, his kids, his wife.
He's not on the poverty line,
    he has got a life.

I look at him, he looks away.
    is it pity that I see
In the reflection on the window
    as he makes his choice today?

Pat Harrison

In Quiet Reflection

Alone in quiet reflection I am wishing
For all the impossible things.
Alone in quiet reflection I am dreaming
All the impossible dreams.
If only I could live in a better world.
If only all that was good and true
could triumph.

Alone I am left to the emptiness that
is myself.
Alone I know the horrors of time.
If only darkness then no hope.
If only despair then no light.

Then something stirs my soul.
Grace? I am saved once more.

And life is still a gift to me
When I think of all that I have known.

The light shines brighter for those
who know what the shadows are.

V. L. Burns

The Wind

I am the wind in darkness
    caressing dusty window panes,
Howling thro' the chimney tops
    and whistling down the drains,
I carry rain before me
    it falls on tree tops high
Then drips upon the soil
    like a giant crying eye
Remember me for I'll be back
    like vengeance I do roam
I wave the lofty willows
    and swirl the grass like foam

K. D. Rhodes

Awaken Dreams

Voices of a dream,
Shadows of the unknown,
Nothing to identify,
Sounds of beating hearts,
In darkness of a dream.

Sounds not yet known to man.

Inexplicable movements and motions.

Uneasy feelings,
Unidentified objects in way of
soundless sleep.

Mist from your disturbed breath,
A heavy haunting inexistence,
Oceans of trapped darkness,
Rapid eye movement.

Leah Couzens

My Dog Samson

I have a dog
His name is Samson
He follows me wherever I go
He is a Welsh Border Collie
Lovely and faithful,
He fills my need.

Long walks we take together
Each day,
Whatever the weather
His favourite game is fetching a stick
Shaking his paw his special trick.

His coat is smooth
Black and white
His eyes are brown
Shining bright
At night, he curls up on his bed
He snores
He grunts
His day complete.

Elaine Day

Night Time

When daytime is finally at an end,
The night time now begins;
It comes alive with movement,
And all sorts of living things.
The Moon shines with a silver glow,
A candle in the night;
The creatures of the darkness
Are grateful for her light.
A vixen visits the farmer's hens,
And kills, with one fast bite;
She takes it home to hungry cubs,
To them, a welcome sight.
Barn owls hunt misty meadows,
Mice creep in soft green grass,
Hoping the owls won't see them,
And they will quickly pass.
A nightingale, in the coppice,
To his mate he sweetly sings,
As dawn is quietly breaking,
So another day begins.

Anna Broom

Why?

Why do people suffer?
Why? There is no answer.
Why is its own poem

Corina Beal

Celebration of Life

The day begins pale, rosy haze;
The fiery orb o'er mountain top
Peeps first, then mounts—
A blood-red prize!
Thin streaks appear to east and west
Of deeper crimson hue. The skies
Are royal dressed in bright array.
What majesty! What cosmic pride
Adorns the day.

The ermine clouds are under-tinged,
As higher still a brightness sharp
The eyes do shade—
But, calm, serene,
Ascending yet, the form is lost
As liquid gold ribbons the scene
From centred sphere. In mute accord
I sit and gaze-in silent awe,
As on the sea as path of gold meets
with my soul.
This day the Lord's.

Lynden

Tilly

I used to be a naughty girl
My head was always in a whirl
 I took the risks
Without a care.
 I didn't think, that life was fair.

But now, I have a reason to live
And I have a lot of love to give
My baby daughter melts my heart
She's given me, a brand new start

I've learnt to live
life's simple things,
My heart has found
what true love brings

The crazy nights,
and mornings after
just don't compare
to love and laughter.

Sara Kennedy

Untitled

My friend, you are my friend
And all I own means nought to me
And all I've seen there is to see
Portraits always meant to be
The landscapes mingle with the sea
For you and I like colours blend
To be as one please stay my friend.

P. A. Burnham

You Are . . .

You are a nurse
 who mends my ills.
To keep my heart beating,
 so my life fulfills.

You are the Samaritan
 who comforts my fears.
Holds me close,
 and wipes my tears.

You are my guardian angel
 who watches over me,
Guides me down the path
 to a safe destiny.

You are the heartbeat
 I hear pounding away.
It gives me energy,
 each and every day.

So who are you
 that gives me life?
Loving and caring,
 you are my wife.

Alan Wallace

War Child

A weeping child sits all alone
With tear strains on his cheek
His mother, father all have gone
This child sits lonely weak.

The bodies lie all around
Blood and rubble what a mess
All is quiet, not a sound
but war goes on no less.

The innocent who did no harm
Women, children, men
While others sit so very calm
and people die again.

And we are civilized they say
intelligence so high
will we ever see the day
when children never cry.

Heather Turner

One of These Days . . .

One of these days
There'll be the two of us together,
Talking about
The way life used to be.
Sharing all those happy memories,
Grieving over all the bad things;
But still—there'll be the two of us.

One of these days
We'll make the future seem bright.
Just us,
Talking about our lives;
Wanting to hold each others hands
Wanting to live each others lives.
But still—we'll be the two of us.

Katherine Ruth Openshaw

Behind Doors

Knock knock
Who's there?
A child screaming loud,
Silence, now tears.

Neighbours hear, but don't,
The pets turn a blind eye,
The bed calls her selfish,
The sheet very muddled.

Mother is out again,
But in he will surely stay.
Dare not say stop, don't
The stick will have revenge.

Tell her mother, tell her walls,
But they are both made of bricks,
The structure is too solid,
The light is blocked out of the tunnel.

Ruth Shankland

Emmanuel Church

Emmanuel is the church we love
Many worship there
Many more we'd like to see
And tell them of God's care
No one else can love like him
Utterly loyal and true
Eternal life he promises
Lasting peace for you

Come and worship, praise and pray
Happiness you will find
Unless you turn to him today
Regret could fill your mind
Christ for our sins, the debt has paid
Has, on himself, our burdens laid.

Jean Dawson

Farewell

Beautiful tree
A friend to me
Where I played my childhood games
From your branches high
I touched the sky
And sheltered from summer rain
The moon above
I wooed my love
Beneath your spreading leaves
Secluded there
Our secrets shared
Of love and hope and dreams
I climbed up high
And touched the sky
With you until the end
I heard you cry
Shudder and die
As they cut you down old friend

Christine Payne

Someone

Someone who loves me,
 someone who cares.
Someone to need me,
 and always be there.
Someone who shares
 the everyday things.
Someone to see the joy
 that it brings.
Someone to share the
 laughter and tears.
Someone to share the
 hopes and fears.
Someone who's honest,
 loving and kind.
Someone who's taken a
 lifetime to find.

C. Hammond

Twenty-Five Years of Violence

Twenty-five years of violence,
I've never known peace,
Why can't anyone tell them,
When will this fighting cease?

Twenty-five years of fighting,
Sadness, sorrow, pain.
When they seem to stop,
They always start again.

Twenty-five years of killing,
Many victims pay the price,
Someone has to help us,
Stop this sacrifice.

Twenty-five years of shooting,
It has to stop soon,
All this fighting,
Deepening the wound.

Twenty-five years of hatred,
Build up walls inside,
How can I stop it,
Has all hope died?

Louise Hamill

In Your Glory

As I look out of the bedroom window
I see the sun rising in the East
The ground is shimmering with frost
And the trees are cloaked in mist
I feed the touch of your fingers
As you pull me close
And though my face is wet with tears
I look up at you
To be planted with a gentle kiss
And like the ground and trees outside
My sadness disappears
As like the sun
The warmth of your love
Brightens up the day.

Deborah Carter

The Widow (Grief)

Oblivion for a few hours
In the brief solace of sleep,
Then the awakening
And the sharp pain
As with swift clarity
Memory floods the mind.
If I could only creep
Back to the comforting dream
But I must wash
Put on my clothes again
Drink my tea
Then live another day—without him.

Mary Pym

A Get-Well Card for an Extremely Sick World

My shopping done—I lingered.
I knew that she was ill;
But I knew not where to send it,
For a place in space she filled.

Amongst her sister planets,
Whom she is desperate to contact,
No medicine is forthcoming,
That would gently lead her back.

In the past, our doctors, bravely,
Scientific preaches they have been.
One of whom in recorded history,
Was hung upon a cross.

They preached the right ingredients,
Of truth, purity and love;
But it never seems to dawn on us,
That there is: "Someone else above"

Our lives are so engrossed you know;
And in the silence of the night,
We hear those haunting words abound:
"Ye who repent at the last hour".

Cyril C. Evans

My Friend

I think I'm going to kill my friend,
She's driving me insane.
I think I'm going to kill her,
Then I'd better change my name.

That way no-one will ever know,
That it was me that killed her dead.
I'll give my name to someone else,
And they'll get blamed instead.

A gun, a rope, a dagger,
Which method should I use?
Perhaps I'll buy some dynamite,
That should blow her fuse.

I'll drown her in the bath tub,
I'll stick her in cement.
I'll do something really horrid,
Like sending her to kent!

I think I'm going to kill her,
She really drives me crazy.
To stay in touch is not a sin,
But she's just too damn lazy!

Leiann Webster

We Need a Friend

We need a friend to call upon
When we're happy or just sad
To listen to our troubles
And help us to feel glad.

To lighten all our burdens
To brush away the tears
What it is to have a friend
To drive away our fears

To have a chat and gossip
With a cake and pot of tea.
We laugh about the trials of life
Or just a memory

They are there whenever needed
To lend a helping hand
What would we do without them
They really are just grand

But when our life has ended
To be sure they will be there
To help us on our journey
Say goodbye with a silent prayer

Dorothy Winkley

Unknown

A whirling image, twisted in my mind,
pale and blur, elusive to the touch.

Fractured dreams and nebulous desires;
voices in the ethereal, shadows in the
dark: guardians of my conscience.

Snow white, blazing luminosity;
wraithlike figures clowning in the
glow, my love is lost.

Emerald heat: diamond sharp:
blind fury, burning lust, screaming
pain: Reality Bites.

Trembling heartbeats, and sizzling
kisses, muscle contractions,
amniotic fluid spurting into the
darkened void; peaceful slumber
and restful solitude, twined in a
marriage of frenzied emotions.

Destiny beckons, an uncertain
future, unthreaded territory
yearning to be mapped, I scream
in fear of the unknown.

John Singh

Grandpa

As I sit upon your knee
  Speaking of your love for me
Lots of stories you have told
  Grandpa, why are you old?

You sit at my right hand
  Pouring out your love
Guiding me down life's path
  Grandpa, come hold me,

My children never held you tight
  Your tales I have told them
They listen when I speak of you
  Grandpa, now I'm old

Never have you failed me
  When I'm sad you hold my hand
You, gave me the gift of love
  Grandpa, come save me.

A grandson now upon my knee
  I sow the seeds you gave me
He's the love I dreamt about
  Your love, he now gives me.

June Diggory

Missing You

Sitting here, beside the sea
I wonder, do you think of me?
All I know, so far away is
I am missing you.

I miss you each time I awake
I miss the "eyes" you often make.
All I knew so far away is
I am missing you.

I miss you all throughout the day
I miss you all along the way.
All I know so far away is
I am missing you.

I miss you in the evening time
I miss your hand in mine.
All I know so far away is
I am missing you.

I miss you in the dark of night
I miss your glow so bright.
All I know so far away is
I am missed by you.

Roy Townsend

Chemistry

You arrived   I was there
You looked   I looked
Eyes met
Room empty   Chatter gone
Together
Alone
We met   The world went away
Time stood still
Parted
People   Lights   Laughter
No regret   Can't forget
I look   You look
We look
Same me   Same you
Never again the same

Joan E. Stone

Untitled

I hold in my hand
the pencil you chewed.
Little is left
of the eraser end.
It consumed
many lifeless thoughts.
Rubbings like ashes
scattered in the sea
of papers;
fingerprints of a mood,
allowed to exist
outside of my head.
A dried tear of ink
near the end, almost
fools me whenever
I go to place my finger on the figure,
the blood stain of executed letters.
And shooting out
at the very tip
Lead.

Soraya El Arabi

Listen to Me . . .

Listen to me.
Can't you see
The red in my eyes
From the tears that I cry.
I'm scared and I'm angry
And no-one can save me.
You don't understand
How much death is on this land.
You don't hear the screams
That end all our dreams.
How would you cope
When all you have is hope.
Well, what when that's gone,
It will be the end of our song.
Listen to me.
Help us please.

Susan Edwards

Kylemore Pass—August 1964

I saw the little people
I tell you 'tis no lie,
For the mountain bent to touch me
As I went softly by.
I saw the little people as I walked
through Kylemore Pass,
I heard the heather rustle as I
passed them in the grass.
They were swinging in the rushes,
And floating by in seeds.
They had plumes of mist for helmets,
They had purple mountain coats,
And each a shining dewdrop
To fasten at his throat.

Rhoda Dawtry

Soul Erosion

Grains of sin
Weathered rocks
fragmenting
  break
      ing
off and falling
clattering
rumbling
in a landslide of passion

Flaccid rains
drizzle down cheekplains
burning furrows that
cannot be erased by
  gentle breeze
    or howling gales
Eroded spirit
Wasted self

Weathered emotions in a
  tender rock face
  remain.

Mehita Iqani

Leaving St. Helena a Child at Sea

The ship so large
I lost my way.
It's getting dark.
I've got to stay
Up or Deck,
I see the sky,
The Hills the boats
Are small like flies.
The ship is pulling out
Once more
I wish I had not left our shore,
The tears they flow.
And will not stop,
I left my heart on that little rock.
But why weep now
When I am free,
To do God's work,
Over the sea.

Maglan Noden

Temple of Perception

Midnight reaches inside me
Digging for gold but finding sorrow.
Again, his foolish beautiful death
Sings out to the soft creature decaying
In the swollen ocean of deceit.
Wishes fall like rain around the years
Silence can be danced upon
And jealousy caressed.

Judy Horne

Passing of a Life

Inexorably the days went by,
Inexorably the years,
Where did all the loving go,
Where went all the years?

All the hours of love and care,
All the years of fun,
Children, family and friends
How lovely to belong.

I feel as if I am becalmed
Upon a shapeless sea,
I know not yet who to become
Not yet whom I should be.

Love is a blessing from the Gods
Which does not always last,
How sad something so beautiful
Sadly has to pass.

Nancie Crowther

Without You

So alone—so sad,
Darkness fills inside me,
Empty—cold,
No longing arms around me,
No noise!
Only the sound of a ticking clock,
Watching anxiously,
Awaiting your face, your voice,
Nowhere to turn, nowhere to run.
Can't find my way—so lost.
I think shall I give up—forget,
But how!
My heart won't let go!
With each passing day, the pain,
The agony, the wanting,
My darling!
I am not complete without you!
My love
Listen to your
heart!

Sue Longyear

A Thought

If tears could build a stairway
and heartaches make a lane.
I would walk right up to heaven
and bring you down again.
I know it's all in vain but
because I believe in resurrection,
I will see you again

V. I. Plume

A Song of Praise

To You, O Lord,
Almighty Eledumare,
I give thanks, honour and glory,
For Your love and mercy,
Your care, concern and attention,
And Your remembrance of me,
By answering my prayers,
After over a tortuous decade
of almost hoping against hope.

Then you show Thyself;
That You are that You are;
An unchanging God,
The one who answers Prayers,
And grants Requests,
Using a method and style,
That is unique and different
From people expectation
And a time that is Best.

Igbaroola Samuel Oluseye

A Blossom of Life

The Earth sees herself
through our eyes
dances our senses
to each new day's surprise.
The rainbow of existence
says stay
stay you
stay delicately conscious,
mindfully awake
for life is
life is like she is,
never empty never full
but never too much
never too much beauty
never too much love
never too much life

to discover . . .

Aze

Remembering

She's not really dead;
How can she be?
I think of her all the time:

The spring blossom comes
How she loved it!
The promise of warmer days.

The summer garden blooms,
And there she is,
On the sun-soaked garden bench.

A tiny child grows;
He smiles like her
Small actions bring her to mind.

A friend's loved one dies
And it returns:
The sharpness of my own grief.

But I know so well
She's in my heart,
And nothing will take that away.

Rachel Molloy

Mental Indiscretion

The initial exchange,
a mere fleeting glance;
not a whisper of suspicion aroused.
The next lingers longer,
with the hint of a smile.
So to the next stage,
moving in closer.
The gentle brush of clothing
against clothing.
The electric tingle of desire.
Shameless.
Actual conversation follows.
He compliments her,
she smiles, flattered.
Mutual attraction.
Hearts flutter, pulses race.
both married to someone else.
Put it out of the mind
just a mental indiscretion.

Kim Louise Turner

Danny

Graceful feline creature,
Your soft black velvet fur
Covering lithe supple frame,
As on my lap you lie and purr,
"Danny", I softly whisper your name,
Half-closed eyes gaze dreamily,
Black cat you mean a lot to me.

Patricia A. Davies

The Awakening of Mr. Mystic

Arising at the dawn of mystery,
Floating through a silent melting sky,
Seeking new music's wave of ecstasy,
Mr. Mystic's martyred cry.

Oh, master musician
We are tuned for eternal life again,
Breaking through the last curtain,
To greet the heart, the mind the life.
This is the cure of all worldly strife.

Born as nature's children all,
Searching the signal to awake,
The music to create the heart call,
The echo to kill the modern fire.

Although the victory now is hollow
From the earth new clouds shall rise,
And through the sad cries of sorrow,
New music shall anoint the eyes.

T. Henry Baird

His Prisoner

I am a prisoner
   And I can't surrender
I am a prisoner
   For he was a pretender

I am lost in my memories
   And I am drowning in tears
I am lost in my memories
   For I am surrounded by fears

He thrust me in a web of deceit
   And I gave him all my trust and care
He thrust me in a web of deceit
   For who said love is fair?

In my anguish he feasted
   And I alone stand
In my anguish he feasted
   For I am waiting for this man

   For he alone can heal my heart
   That he has torn apart

Reham Abul-Wafa

Goodnight Nan

Goodnight, my darling
Now it's time to sleep,
Still so many things I want to say
But now they'll have to keep

Goodnight, my darling,
Now it's time to dream
Of precious memories
Tears and laughter, places we have been

Goodnight, my darling
I will miss you so much
Miss your wisdom, clip round the ear
Miss your smell and your touch.

Goodnight, my darling
Time to close your eyes
A big kiss from the children
Please understand their cries

These are the last words I have to say
That's why they took so long to write
Nan I love and adore you in every way
Goodnight my darling, sleep tight.

Samantha Jayne Webb

Nothing Is Forever

Nothing is forever,
forever is a dream,
what we have, it may
not last, all's not
what it seems.
But, I will try to
make
all our dreams
come true.
So forever is
within our reach
because
the one I love
is you . . .

Jade Watkins

1997

In this year of ninety seven
Is it going to be hell or heaven?
If I turn around will I see
The end of all this hostility?
When all the world is crying Peace,
Will all the troubles cease?
Just think no more fuss or bother
Where men can call each other brother.

Pamela Stebbings

Eternal Darkness

Down and lonely, bitter and hard,
Sorrow cuts in like a knife.
Nothing will ever heal the wounds
Of rejection throughout a bad life.

Evil thoughts and wicked deeds
Trap the soul too tight.
Demons dance and mourn the loss
Of the heart and mind to fight.

Never will the heart be light,
Of innocence be free.
Their time has gone and all that's left
Is pain and misery.

E. J. Connelly

The Little Furry Squirrel

Give you a lot of fun
just watch the little creature
and see how fast he can run
doing tricks an escapologist
could not achieve
and the amount of nuts stored for
his winter feed you could not believe
He swings from branch to branch
taking care not to fall
he's very aware if anyone calls
A furry little creature very funny
watching them you never want to hurry
So if you see them don't tut, tut.
Just throw them a handful of nuts.

M. Wood

Ruined Castles

Ruined castles of our nation,
Symbols of a by-gone age,
Each a fort and habitation,
Each a line from History's page.

Firm they stood in times of danger,
Keeping trouble from the land;
Now the goal of many a stranger,
Silent, ruined, still they stand.

Past and faded are their glories
Of the distant long ago,
And their once exciting stories
Few there be who want to know.

Some there be who understand
Ancient walls severe and grey,
Who, when touring this fair land
See beauty even in decay.

I, like them, have travelled far
And many ruined castles seen;
I do not see them as they are,
But rather as they must have been.

John H. E. Rendall

Beauty

Questioning, trusting gaze,
   from wide-spread eyes.
Parted ready lips.
The slight inclination of the head,
   held away in calm tension,
From the narrow, relaxed shoulders.

The pale, drawn face,
   with its well-defined cheekbones,
And the edged cuffs,
   slightly drawn back,
From slender wrists, tapering down,
To the tiny hands laid delicately,
   within the folding material.

Pettr Manson-Herrod

My Garden

My garden is an awful shambles,
full of grass with weeds and brambles.
Oh, wondrous joy I will have fun
in making plans, to get it done.
To dig it first that's for sure,
but by now it seems a chore!
I've made a sketch, so I can see
just how pretty it will be.
Choosing plants and sowing seeds.
A mass of colour, instead of weeds.
Trees and bushes, for the birds.
to flavour meals, a choice of herbs.
Climbing roses, growing tall,
Honeysuckle on the wall.
A nice green lawn, with edges neat.
A gravel path and wooden seat,
Where I can sit to pass the hours
And watch the bees amongst my flowers.

Nita Horrobin

You Were the Best

All of a sudden
A dream came true
It must have been luck
That I met you

The first kiss was the best,
In a special place,
The twinkle in your eyes,
The way you touched my face.

Even though you broke my heart,
I still think of you,
And fall apart.

Charlene Potter

The Homecoming

She waited in fear
for his homecoming.
While he drank his beer
he thought nothing of her.
The doorbell rang with impatience.
Startled she jumped up in terror,
slowly the chain was unlatched
and there he stood, anger in his eyes.
Walking backwards into one kitchen,
tears flowing from her eyes,
he followed removing his thick black
leather belt.
He lashed out at her, with joy;
she dared not scream;
the children were upstairs;
too late feet pattered along the floor.
She had seen their lonely faraway look,
the terror in their eyes.
Slowly they left.
Knowing what was happening.

Gemma Saunders

A Piece of Blue

This piece of jigsaw is all blue.
It could be sea, sky or wallpaper
but whichever it turns out to be
accept it for what it is.

Other pieces have contained places,
people and activities which
make up into whole lives,
But that is in the past.

Concentrate now on the piece of blue,
find out all about it,
how it links with the rest,
then enjoy the continuity.

Godfrey Dodds

Inner Spirit

Borne as on the wings of Eagles
seen not with mortal vision
grown from the seeds of truth

Founded on a faithful belief
not of this worlds folly
spent in the cause of virtue

Not of military might
weak in the eyes of some
judged not by its outer garment

possessed not of all men
healer of the poorest spirit
cleanser of the soul

A secret sometimes never learnt
discovered by a few

A. R. Purnell

For Want of Love

Too late, too late, my love
for excuses, apologies or regrets
they'll do no good now
after all this time
this long, lonely time
without a single word or any sign
that you remember me
my heart has suffered long
for want of your love
and now I am gone
perished, pined away.
Too late, too late now
for you to say to me
I've changed my mind
I do love you, too.
I'm sorry for I am gone now
and there's no return.

Janis Wolfenden

Did the Earth Move for You, Darling?

On a noon constitutional
Strolling along Paphos prom,
The ground turns to jelly
And wobbles malevolently,
Cocking a snoot
At man. Or woman.
"Beware, tiny creatures",
It laughs through the thunder,
"I can rid myself of you with a shiver.
It is just that, for the moment,
I choose not to."

Linda Blesi

From Dusk till Dawn at the Beach

I was watching the stars fade,
As dawn came to bay,
I was watching the sunset,
And decided to stay.

The sand was so soft,
The sky was so blue,
The sun was shining down,
As the wind softly blew.

Later that day,
The rain started to fall,
The sky got rough and grey,
As the waves became so tall.

A man came along,
And swept me off my feet,
And said oh darling, oh darling,
I'm so glad we meet.

Katherine Sandie

Time to Let Go

I am sorry to say
That I must go
Even though it hurts
I want you to know,
That life goes on
No matter how sad
Everyday is new
And for that be glad.
Start again afresh
Forget what we never had
Lay the foundations today
To build on tomorrow.

Sahara Begum

A Single Tear

A single tear in my eye,
Grows larger as each day goes by;
And every moment we're apart
Slowly breaks my tender heart.
Sweet memories I can't forget
Of when your lips and mine first met.
I long to be in your arms again
And your love will soothe away my pain.

Alison Clydesdale

Deborah

Beauty has no agent,
No place to call its own
No calling card to leave
Behind its self,
A land of which none is known,
Beauty blooms in the strangest
of places,
It closes mind to fear,
And eyes open to love,
I can feel your presence near.

Tom Malone

Terminal Velocity

She released me,
I'm falling, free falling,
Flailing feet feeling
For firmness that escapes me,
Dancing like a marionette
Trying to fly, yet
Inextricably tried to life,
I won't miss her anymore,
I won't feel anyone,
After love there is nothing,
She leaves me cold,
She leaves me
Swinging in the wind.

David Atkinson

Black Coffee

Cannot sleep worrying,
I go to the doctor,
"Do you drink coffee?"
  "Yes," I replied,
"I do not like tea."
"Well then," said the doctor,
"Do not drink black coffee."
  I told him that it
Does not make sense as
I only drink 3 black coffees a day,
  reply,
"Come back next week."
What a waste of time that was.
Cannot wait to get back home,
  I'm going to have
  A big mug of
"Black coffee"

Rosemarie Doherty

From My Kitchen Window

From the kitchen window
Of my small abode,
I cherish great joys
And recite a few odes.

From my kitchen window
I see nature grow:
Birds busy nesting,
Mating on the bough.

The gentle quadruples
My roses they munch,
As my mackerel kitten
Climbs to a branch.

Butterflies and bees,
Lady birds and moths;
The cute field mice
Following nature's course.

Life fully evolves
Season after season;
A truly Eden Garden
By my kitchen window.

Virginia Verity

God's Bounty

Oh why am I so contented
With the minute things of life?
Content to walk in a circle
A little area of strife.

Oh why do I scan the pavements
For pleasures so transient?
When God is waiting to show me
Horizons of true content.

Oh why do I take so little
From the table God prepared?
When plenty would still be over
After all the world had shared.

Oh why are my thoughts so puny
Ranking in value just nought?
When the word is full of wisdom
Gained by all who sought.

Oh why do I dwell in twilight
Contented with things so dim?
When oh, He's mine for the asking
The light of the world, 'tis Him.

A. C. Heritage

The Call of Duty

My soul is dark and brooding,
It suffocates in night,
It feels the burden of the lost,
It needs to bathe in light.

My mind is swamped in tired despair,
It feeds on desolation,
It shifts and struggles to control
Its own sad damnation.

My body droops, but carries on,
It bears a heavy load,
It tries to obey my mind's commands,
It walks a narrow road.

My very psyche and emotions cry,
They shriek in silent pain,
They are rubbed raw with life's needs,
When called upon again.

Alas; we have to pay the piper,
We cannot call the tune,
We are swamped by tides of duty,
To our eternal doom.

Avril C. Deall

My Garden of Eden
For Evelyn

When I look at you
I think of summer
Buttercup meadows
And sweet cherry blossom.
When I'm next to you
I think of a starlit night
The gentle breeze
Warm firelight.
I sit all day and think of you
Dreams of flowers
The sky so blue.
The calmest oceans
And rainbows high
While I watch the clouds
Float slowly by.
All this beauty is so true
In my garden of Eden
I share with you.

Stephen Lee

Black Thorn

You've tried to hurtle me barbed,
through my own soft roses
only, I never fell,
I just crumbled
weeping ash-dust petals for you.

Your river that made me smile
slowly dried its silence across my will
and left me dull, thirsting.

While you smothered my heart
with utter insincerities
I changed colour
and black like a picket fence
I turned,
waiting,
for you to hang yourself.

So and foolish now,
you haunt the social corridors,
or listening for me
like sun-soft flesh,
caught on my spines.

Wendy Sanderson-Smith

Damsel Flies

Electric blue filaments,
Like airborne seahorses
As they comb the air,
And mate in tandem;

So next year we will
See their antics and say,
Ah, damsel flies again!

Hazel Weight

The Mirror

Look into my light
with your eyes
reach into my soul
and touch with your hand
see with my shine
your gentle touch
hear your laughter
for it's my joy
your scent is
my feeling
kiss away my tears
for it's your sorrow
live within love
and peel complete,
For when you love me
it is love for
yourself.

Mal West

Lost Children

Where did she go that day
To town to shop she said
Can we come too
No not today
Go out with friends and play

She hasn't come back
What will we do
Where will we go
No-one answers our questions
There's three of us you know

He said she's left us
Never loved you or cared
We can't believe it
Just stand and stare
Tears and emptiness within

Pack her bags, now, straight away
Be sure you leave no trace
One daughter, two sons
Remain without a mother
Not knowing the loneliness we will face

Sue Lord

The Book of Life

A chapter draws to a close
And a new is begun
With tragedy or triumph
The story carries on.

A book of endless chapters
A tale of endless tales
Of happy lives and sad ones
And that love alone ne'er fails.

'Tis the simplest little story
That thrills the heart to read
Of human hopes and follies
And whither they do lead.

Yet no tale is ended completely
For the story still unfolds
And what lies beyond earth's telling
Alone The Author holds.

R. J. Matheson

The Flowers of Heaven

You were so sweetly gentle when
You left
Adorned in nature's loveliest,
And all the sunshine of my days
Was in your smile.
Its warmth enfolded me the while.
As you passed—the flowers of heaven
Perfumed the air.
And mirrored in your lovely eyes
Unspoken was the promise,
Awaiting me in paradise!

Jeannine Anderson Hall

Untitled

I am a tired and weary carer
And me feet are really sore
Me head it is a throbbing
And me poor old hands are raw
If you mention the word hoover
Or even worse the name of shop
I swear I'll take a swing at you
And bash you with me mop
Cause you know I'm only fifty four
Which isn't very old
But days when I can take no more
Come more often I am told
I long to put me feet up
In front of a fire with a cup a tea
Oh yes I've made me mind up
That's just the life for me.

J. M. Tovell

Getting to Know You

We cannot help our feelings
As each moment tells us why.
Emotions way out of control
When there's something more to love
Maybe yet it's not ours
Only in times that we share
Is everything we hold dear.
We see the faces
Hearing each other's voices
Yet when we wake
Only softness of pillows
Comforts our lonely faces

Sharon Evans

Balm for a Sore Heart

Tiny flecks of moonlight
Filched when moon is new
Drops of dew at dawn-light
Just a trembling few
Snippets from the rainbow
Borrowed from the sky
Tiny peals of laughter
From a child's supply.

Mix the magic potion
In a leaf of gold
Adding gaily tenderness
From a love that's old.
Then drink this blessed nectar
The while you yield to joy
And sorrow which had crowded in
Will fade and pass you by.

Charles Nono

Proclamation of the Raw

Depth of the drunk,
Hides within.
Heat of passion,
Bull of red.

Ride along.
Alone.
Mountains of chaste,
Crawl.

Cry.
Divide.
Blue over green.
ph 7.

Break floral cave of 7.

Cry.
Divide.
Part.

Sonia Reilly

A Memory of Mother's Day

Eyes so blue
A smile warm and loving
Nice to see you
No card needed
We can say it all
Happy Mother's day
The love that surrounds me
Like the warm summer sun
Set in a golden haze
of stillness and peace
A kiss says it all
I love you
Awaken to remember
Mother's day alone
Memories are forever
Throughout my life
Happy Mother's day.

Margaret Ponder

The Flowers of Winter

The barren fields refuse to sway,
they slumber, cold and bare.
The trees contort into visions of hell,
bleak, and filled with despair.
Blanket skies grow heavy and dense.
Cotton white clouds grow dark.
The flowers of winter softly fall,
Covering earth and bark.
Icicles hang, like glistening teeth.
The glass lake mirrors the sight,
of silver blooms drifting down,
transforming a bleak winter's night.
Often I float back to that hour,
the enchanting aura behold.
The glory of a snow-clad world
is worth its weight in gold
My memory of that vision sweet,
for the earth, I wouldn't part.
As the joy I felt on that winter's morn
ignites my frozen heart.

Melanie Parker

Madonna

Once there shone a beam of light,
A halo, round, it sparkled bright.
And with this image a face of beauty
Heavenly sent for God's own duty.
Her rosy complexion,
both rare and fair.
A beauty of long, golden, locked hair.
Eyes of ocean coloured glare.
Mouth of perfumed, scented air.
Hands of comfort eased the pain
a longing for her to visit again.
A person of grace,
and unique splendour.
A caring nature, pure and tender.
Each night as I lay in bed
From the Heavens above.
Please! Watch over me, I beg.

Sharon Gallery

Weather

The sun shines,
The rain falls,
Weather weather
Comes and goes.
The wind blows,
The frost bites,
Weather weather
Comes and goes.
The snow falls,
The thunder roars,
Weather weather
Comes and goes . . .

Jack Smith

Unleashed

Dark clouds move across the sky
in the ever fading light. Unleashed
is Mother Nature on this awful
winter's night.
Her tears freeze on
icy breath, as they turn from
rain to hail. A metal monster of
mankind laying helpless off its rail.
Water rises up at the touch
of her great hand. Sending man's
great cities beneath the silt and sand.
Struck down, man's toy planes
in the blinking of an eye. Yet
man will breathe again as her temper
starts to die.

Keszeg C. Michael

To the Rev'rent Bloom

Once, your petals held my gaze
When I saw fit to stop and laze,
I pondered still on far gone years
And drenched you with my flowing tears.

Now fragrant meadows fill my heart
And clouded skies have drawn apart,
Letting sunlight through at last
To rid me of the solemn past.

Sweet music sounds, melodic sighs
And vapours dance as morning dries
Its dew decked diamonds from the earth
In readiness for this day's birth.

The seasons have all gone their way
And now I come to you this day,
Because your beauty gladdens me
Beneath this wooded canopy.

A sapphire bluebell on the ground
Which broke the spell of sadness found,
To me remains a priceless gift
In lifetimes that diminish swift.

K. J. Tourle

Spring Not Quite

The rain.
The hail
The snow
The wind
This is March and all it brings,
The sun that glistens.
Raindrops on the branch.
Is spring here.
Not a chance.
I feed the birds and
Watch them scurry.
In and out
off the next snow flurry.
The rain.
The hail.
The snow.
The wind.
Is spring here
Not a chance.

D. H. Holohan

I'll Be There

I'll be there when you need me
In the good and the bad.
I'll be there when you're happy.
I'll be there when you're sad.
I'll be there to support you.
In every way.
I'll be there for you.
Night and day.

Angela Barley

Madness

Them—
 Mother is a man
 Father is her silhouette
 living our their Nazi plan
 Not with passion or regret.

Me—
 I got butterflies in my stomach
 Snakes and bubbles in my head
 Birds in my return
 and my genitals are dead

You—
 Your intention is to treat me
 to control me and defeat me
 Why change my hand to fit my glove?
 and do it in the name of love!

Bill Campbell

The Morning Bird

Sometimes bursting with colour
There is light breaking through,
Where the shadows kiss sunshine
Close your eyes and see blue.

Always touched by a whisper
When a chill leaves the air,
For a moment it has gone
Brush your cheek it is there.

Often peeking from cover
So shy and unsure,
Falling gently to life
Take a breath and feel pure.

Never dazed by another
Darkness swallows each breath,
Search your heart for tomorrow
As this day dies its death.

Natasha Maria Murrell

Tribute

As he hung up on the cross so high
No one heard his muted cries
The blood flowed freely from his wounds
Intensifying all the gloom

Why should this man bear all this pain
Our wicked ways should take the blame
He was prepared to suffer much
To guide us with his healing touch

We are so blind we cannot see
The suffering was for you and me
To wipe away our sinful shame
And know that heaven is our gain

While here on earth to do our best
Lord Jesus gives us perfect rest

Mary Tickle

Retrospect

Were I to live my life again
Free from every fetter
I wonder would it be the same
Or would I live it better
Would the chances I have lost
Be mine again to take them
Would I unheeding pass them by
For want of faith forsake them.
Too the words that I have said
Were better left unspoken
Would I now say more kindly ones
Speak love for ones own token.
'Tis hard to think how we would act
If our lives began anew
Perhaps we'd live a better one
Perhaps we'd mar that too.

Maureen Mahony

Your Blessings

Your blessings Lord
I now receive
no longer here
To be deceived
I'm learning of
your character now
the addictions
we all carry around
no longer need
to have us bound
discern your program
and turn it around
a brand new life
will then be found.

Noeleen Delamore

The Promise of Dawn

Over the rugged hills,
Flow the golden rays
Of the rising sun
Slowly heralding the dawn.

Spreading gently, insidiously,
Across the waves and inlets of the sea,
Tinted with reds and blues,
Turning the dark clouds away.

Another day has begun.
A day of promise for some,
Toil and sorrow for others,
Still a golden dawn.

To the glowing sun,
Man is an ant on the Earth's face.
And tonight the sun will set
On all the deeds of man.

Yet another day will dawn,
And fill our minds with light.
To laugh and cry or play,
With the promise of: "A new day!"

Elizabeth Robertson

Music

The flow of songs came drifting through
the trees forlorn and bare,
music soft it blew
amidst the silent air.

Notes came tumbling down
and settled on the lawn,
while some sprang up with merry sound
as though they'd just been born.

Crochets, quavers, minims too
rustled and quivered along the stave,
some in bunches, all too few,
some alone not afraid.

This tranquil sound pervades my ears
and floats inside my breast,
as from my eyes come flowing tears
upon my lap to rest.

So music ripples along the score
up and down it wends,
producing rhythm and more
our souls to cleanse.

Marion de Souza

My Brother

Daddy takes a car to try
From the garage down the road.
And when he's very happy
The garage man says Sold.

Now this new baby brother
Who sleeps in my old cot.
Always wets his nappies
And cries an awful lot.

I don't know why they keep him
He's second-hand for sure.
His head is marked all over
And he's got two spots or more.

He's certainly not pretty,
He's got no hair at all
But Mummy says he's lovely
And she's going to call him Paul.

I 'spose Jesus had a rush on
And forgot about his hair.
We really ought to send him back
And get one with less wear.

C. Nicholson

The Dancer

As the curtain is rising,
For the opening night
It is hardly surprising,
She has some stage fright.

Then the music starts,
Everyone will agree,
She brings joy to the hearts
Of people like me.

As pirouetting, she spins
Around and around,
She turns and she grins,
With a leap and a bound.

Gliding through the air
With style and grace,
No fears now she's up there,
Just a smile on her face.

She's made her big break,
All that's left is the decision
For the dancer to take
Up her final position.

Tracey-Jane Marchant

Killed in Action Age 21

My brother twin
Age twenty-one
Was killed in action
By enemy gun

Deep in the jungle
Out in Korea
Against the communists
Who were politically feared

While on patrol
He marched through hell
And gave his life
For the freedom world

Now rest in peace
In a foreign land
Having served his country
He's a forgotten man

A. Sumner

Untitled

That warm glow of serenity
of peace and contentment
Of total love
You give to me so freely
Unconditional in its offering
I am bemused but smiling
Standing in this blessed pool of light
My spirits are uplifted
And I am free

Jessica Tyson

Sleep Little Baby

Sleep little baby
Without fright,
God's arms are around you
At dead of night,
When you awaken
In early down,
Showered with gold
The way angels are born.
Peace be upon you
All your innocent life,
In the heart of your family
Free from strife,
No evil shall fall upon you,
But love everlasting.
The rest of your years.
God shall be with you.

Alexander Turnbill

My Sister

This will be the year
Where all our troubles disappear
One by one, our dreams will come true
And that my Sister, will include you
When you feel so tired and so low
There is only one way your life can go
  There are 3 kinds of people
    of this I am sure
  The group who have found
    what they are looking for
  The group who no longer search
    for what they desire
  And the group who are still free
    to burn life's fire
So my dear Sister
  However life may seem
A woman so special
  Must, one day, find her dream.

Mark T. Martin

Derek and Jenny

Once upon a time not too long ago
Two bundles of joy came into this
World along with all of its
uncertainties.
I never knew what life had in store
for you both
As time passed with things going
wrong all around
I dug in deep and held on tight.
I would not let go of the love
that I had for you.
And at this time of my life it is
stronger now than it has ever been.
And though we cannot be together
we will never be apart.

Nothing in the world will ever
separate us you are both always in
my heart. I love you
Daddy.

D. A. Parker

Mother

I was only five when you,
Dear mother, died,
My sisters were fourteen
And they cried and cried.
No one had told me that you
Had not survived,
Everyone was sad and I
Did not know why.
My heart still aches with
Sadness when I think of you,
The secret tears will always flow,
Why did you have to die, mother?
No one will ever know.

Gemma Sykes

Twenty Golden Daffodils

Twenty golden daffodils,
Appeared from underground,
They promptly got their trumpets out,
And sounded all around.
Playing tunes of innocence,
And melodies of romance,
All took partners in the breeze,
And performed a graceful dance.
But soon the music faded,
Into a graceful sigh,
As twenty golden daffodils,
Curled up, Content to die.

Katie Reevell

Friendship

Somewhere I slipped
Upon the way
And hurt someone
In a thoughtless way.

Forgive me my friend
For an impulsive act
I shall always remember
Our treasured hours
Of the past

K. J. Cooper

The Loss of a Child Kym

We cannot see our Daughter,
We cannot touch her hand,
The Lord came down and took Her,
To what He calls the Promised Land.
The pain, the hurt, the heartache,
For those that are left behind,
We do not think the Lord, to us,
Has been so very kind.
What is Life to us without Her,
Only memories for us to share,
They tell us that the pain will go,
But please Lord tell us where.
Lord we try to be forgiving,
For knowing that You're there,
But you took our Daughter, Kym,
from us and left us in despair.
We cannot Pray at this sad time,
We don't think that it's fair,
The only peace that we shall have,
Is when we meet Kym there.

Aubrey Abram

Ode to Planet Earth

Planet Earth, as seen from space
Looks to be a wondrous place.
A spinning orb of blue and white
Shadowed by its satellite.

A rainbow arcs across the sky
A colour spectrum seen on high
The strobing of the Northern Lights
The wonder of all natural sights.

Across Earth's surface can be seen
Tracts of browns and swathes of green
Polar regions white with snow
Watery wastes where wild winds blow.

Life abounds upon this sphere
Seasons changing through the year
Winter grey to autumn gold
Spring and summer hues unfold.

Insects, birds and fish abound
Plants and trees spring from the ground
Myriad kinds of creatures birth
We salute you, Planet Earth.

P. Walsh

Then the Moment's Gone

When the years go by so quickly
And some had many tears
the nights were oh so lonely
I forget then to count the years
when I walk in the darkness
the hills they seem to glow
when the moon shines on the valley
deep and crisp with snow
those days with you I remember
and counted one by one
now as I grow older
I thank God for everyone

Doris Moore

The Hill

As you climb the hill beyond
Through heather wet with dew
With nature you will bond
With a silence, just for you

There is a peace beyond this hill
Where I sit in solitude
There is a bliss beyond this hill
Where no one can intrude

At one with nature
May sound trite
But for me, the loner,
It sounds, just right.

Andrew Shaw

Shooting Star

Shooting star burning bright
in the middle of the night
Zooming through the galaxy
on the way to me

I'll wish a wish before I'll die
And tumble down to the starry sky
that once again one magic night
I might see you burning bright

Laura Ann Ripley

Untitled

Why do I sit alone, walk alone,
Talk alone?
Why can't I see the sky,
Or touch the trees?
Why do I not smell the flowers
Or your perfume in the breeze?
Why can't I touch you again,
Or hold you again?
Why do you cry my dear,
Why that silent tear?
Do you not understand I am gone,
And can no longer hear?

Do not be sad my love,
Do not grieve my love,
We have shared our love,
Enjoyed our love,
Be happy for me, be good for me,
Be proud of me.
But most of all my love,
Do not hurry to be with me.

D. W. Dickinson

To a Darling Child Who Is Now in Heaven

To heaven there is no rail
No road—no telephone
No daily mail

So darling on your grave
These lovely flowers we lay
With this tiny verse
Just simply to say
We'll love and think of you
Even more today
Because my darling
It's your birthday
On your birthday
And all the year through
I pray that God
Will grant to you
The blessings you are so
Deserving of
His peace His guidance
His care His love

G. Woodward

Spring

The wings of my heart
led me through tears
like mist of the sea
onto a forlorn shore

No melody of old
could release the strings
which kept me enslaved
and unfold the pain
to come and hold

And yet—in spring
my restless soul
sings of love
of buds on a tree
and my aching heart
beguiles my own
destiny

Paula Wandscher

Untitled

Miles of sea may part us
The world seems so cruel
With miles of peak topped mountains
My tears in a pool

My heart so full of love
Through endless fields so green
The memories so clear
Never to be seen

My tiny hand in yours
The trees so brown and still
The smell of morning rain
Life serves a bitter pill

Miles of sea may part us
The skies seem so blue
But my love for you is near
I'll always be thinking of you

Lisa Wyatt

Untitled

I love to watch a little brook,
winding through a leafy nook.
I listen as it ripples on,
resembling laughter or a song,
so free from care it journeys on
The sights I see, the sounds I hear,
are pleasant to my eyes and ears,
I think of those less blest than me,
who hear no sound, nor beauty see.

Mary Findlay

Little Old Lady

Children liked this little old lady,
We often knocked on her door,
She used to make us straw whistles,
We always went back for more.
She taught us in the Sunday School,
Her bonnet was flowered and gay,
Around her shoulders she had a cape,
Which she wore on a rainy day.
When she walked on a rainy morning
She clutched at her trailing skirt,
Her care-worn fingers held it up,
Cut of the puddles and dirt.
I remember counting the colours,
As we knelt in the chapel at prayer,
In her lovely flowered bonnet,
Ribboned under her hair.
Others no doubt have their memories,
Though it's many years ago,
We loved this little old lady.
I'll never forget her I know.

Pearl Burch

Oil Painting

If only . . .within limits
Philosophy of light,
Chiaroscuro mouldings
The weathering of plight.

But only . . .within rhythmics,
Melodious of night,
Charismic effervasions,
The nearing of insight.

If only . . . .within limits
Philosophy of light,
Perpetual recreation,
Producing pure delight!

T. R. Jones

Life's Enigma

Everyone who's been born must die,
Like everyone, I wonder why.
Are workers needed on this earth
Is that why there is this birth?
Some believe they're born again
They know not how or where or when.
Some believe God calls them home
Never more to grieve or mourn
Where love and happiness abound
And only joy and peace are found.
Others think there is a hell
Where the very wicked dwell.
Some believe this is the end
No more of you and me, my friend.
I do not know, I cannot tell
Which I think is just as well.
The answer we must wait to find
When we leave this world behind.

Gladys E. Yates

Insight

The Blind can see a light
Better than those who see
For this is no Sun Beam
But comes from inside me.

Many search to see it
And use their eyes to find
It doesn't come from the sky
But from inside the mind.

They search the World to see it
Under rock stone and mound
For only in the soul
Will it be surely found.

It comes in many disguises
And called different names
Hope Faith and Love
It holds a thousand claims.

Call out and it will find you
Close your eyes and you will see
The light is inside us all
Your Heart holds the key.

Stephanie White

To the Citizens of the World

How long
Can you abuse a friend?
How long
Before you lose a friend?
How long
Can your money-making last
Before you realize
The golden age has passed?
The things you think you own
Are only yours on loan,
Today you throw a loaded dice,
Will you be around to pay the price?

Thomas C. Ryemarsh

The Hunt

The misty atmosphere clung,
As the hair on my back rose
The impending doom heightened
With the passing night.

Then I heard it
That hateful horn
Catching at my feet,
As I run to hide.

Is that pounding my heart?
And that howling the wind?
The drops on my flanks
Is that rain?

I feel their breath
Hot on my flanks
I run like the wind
But they close every second.

Donna Heath

Something for Everyone

All alone? You're not alone,
Just think of what's around you!

From trees that move
When winds do blow;
To birds in flight,
How can you feel so low?

Tiny lambs skip and ooze
With life's powerful might,
Flowers grow and cruise
Towards the sunlight.

The lakes, the rivers, the seas,
What else?
Many things, lovely things
and then, there's you!

Barbara Hopson

Paul

Your candle burns no longer
Your laughter has now ceased
And all that is now left of you
Are memories and grief

Happy thoughts and photos
And single cheerful tears
As we chat and laugh about
Those blessed nineteen years

But even though we sometimes cry
And always ask the question why
I'll always get some peace of mind
To know you're finally somewhere kind

Jennifer Nicholls

Love Is

Love is always being there for someone
    when they need you
If I get upset I can cry on you
    and you can cry on me too

Love is listening to each other
    when they are down
I will be here for you so
    don't you ever frown

Love is being near to someone
    that you love
Darling, I will be your turtle dove

Love is telling your partner
    that you love them.
Because our love will be forever
    our love is so special
I don't want our love to end
    never.

Paula Stewart

The Vumba

In a world of so much trouble,
So much conflict, pain and strife,
When we dread the coming morrow,
In this so uncertain life.
Let us leave this world of thraldom
And in our fancies flights,
Let us wander in the dreamland
In the Vumba Heights.
Let us wander up this pathway
Dazzling gold the sunlight gleams,
As we climb from vales of sorrows
To the summits of our dreams.
For the mists down in the valley
Of myriad shades of hue,
Are the mists of human longings
For the lovely and the true,
But now my heart is singing
And my whole world bathed in light,
For I've had a glimpse of heaven
In the Vumba Heights.

Viola Wylson

Moonlight on Snow

A world so still and white,
Reflecting light
from frosty skies.
Each tree, a silhouette,
and yet,
where moonbeams
reach in silver streams,
phantom outlines mystify
and satisfy imagination.
In hollows formed of breeze blown snow,
no light will go.
What lurks below deep shadow?
All the mysteries of the night,
captured in bright starlight.
Void of sound, the hidden ground
lies dormant . . .Resting . . .
Then like dreams, all moonbeams
fade and die, and from the far Horizon,
Another snowy morn is gently born,
and night bids a soft Goodbye . . .

Carol King

Shalom

Early morn.
Rays of light
Slowly fissure
Through the branches
Of tall trees,
Which vibrate
With recent rain.

Diverse
Rays of splendour
Awaken,
Through the trees
Surrender
To presence,
At dawn.

Margaret Irving

Young, Single and Free

We were not meant to be
together,
forever to eternity.
I understand,
you chose her, not me;
Because,
she is young, single and
free,
unlike me . . .

Lucy Catley

The Storm

Pitter, patter, pitter, patter on
the window pane.
Pitter, patter, pitter, patter
here comes the rain.
Thud, thud goes the thunder,
wind swooshes over and under.
Crash, bang here's the lightning,
babies scream because it's
frightening.
Sleet slapping on the ground,
like little stones small and round.

Mechelle Moody

After Life

At first nothing but darkness,
Black as night,
Not a shadow stirred,
Or an atmosphere change.

Then cries and wails,
Of long since dead sinners,
Shout out their tortured pain,
And scream to confess their sins.

A light appears,
Like a beacon of life,
You drift like an angel,
It becomes blinding to the eye.

It splits in two,
One dark and evil,
The other joyful and happy,
You float from side to side.

A terror strikes at the heart,
As you slowly cruise towards death,
Your skin starts to burn,
As you enter your worst nightmare.

Bobby Dickins

Flight of Fancy

Look to where the Ospreys fly
O'er strath and beneath highland sky
Look to where the Ospreys fly
And you too may learn we never die.

Hark the curlew loud and shrill
O'er shap fell and arten gill
Watch them wheel and soar above
And you could find another love.

When you're alone and want to cry
Just look to where the Ospreys fly.

K. W. Fordham

Untitled

You lie lost to us, beneath sea's blue.
Your demise it is a mystery.
Great minds have tried to find you.
Throughout your silent history.
Elegant ladies, sun-bronzed men.
They went with you in fear.
Never to be seen again.
Their loved ones cradled near.
Some say they know your whereabouts.
Boasts mad men make so bold.
All they want is not your beauty.
But your wealth untold.
So great wonder of this world.
For now you must stay lost.
Because immoral men out there.
Would rape you to our cost.
I talk not of a sunken ship.
But of something built of stone.
A city called Atlantis.
Who some once called their home.

R. Meadows

Untitled

Like the morning sun
Alighting on a solid oak,
Enveloping its solemn greatness
With ethereal majesty,
So we two embrace each other.
And which is the sun,
And which the oak
Is Life's ever-changing mystery.

Keir Howeld

Home

Home is the humblest place on earth,
It's the folks that count within,
The feeling of just togetherness
when all the family's in.

The comfort of love, within its walls,
It's the knowing you're wanted there,
A glow of a fire, that's snug and warm,
And the lull of a rocking chair.

It's the laughter of happy children
echoing through the hall,
Tearing up the stairway,
Drawing pictures on the wall.

My thoughts will often wander
to where I'd love to roam,
But there would be no peace on earth,
If I couldn't come back home.

So weary body, take a rest,
Go to the place the heart knows best,
Though hill and valley you may roam,
There is no place on earth like home.

Kathleen Moore

Untitled

Love grew between them
So slowly it seemed,
Like a flower unfolding
Then likened to a thunderclap.
Jealousy showed itself,
Suspicion, doubt, mistrust
Then excitement, let down
He had to leave
Without goodbye.
Each blamed the other
For mistakes that were made.
A year passed by
With fleeting glimpses,
Seen through railings and trees.
Recrimination after recrimination
She senses his return
He knows she's near
Love is more intense
They each seem more dear.

J. Leadbetter

On Top of the World

I'm in heaven up here,
on top of the mountain,
I cannot believe my eyes,
The view so spectacular,
my heart is so light,
beating rapid with my sighs,
It is so beautiful up here
The excitement is ecstatic!
I feel as if!
I am on top of the world,
I want everyone to share it,
I want everyone to love it,
As I do!
My mountain,
My world.

Barbara Anne Scrivener

Confusion

Confusion has taken
Over my mind
It has even made me
Feel rather blind
My feelings are mixed up
I'm in quite a mess
But I always try to look my best
I try to cover
The way I feel
But I must admit
I feel rather ill
It hurts so much
I know not
What to do
If only I could say
How I truly feel
But no one cares
Or even can see
That I'm not as happy
As I make out to be.

Lena Godding

2000 Human

Man Evolved, Mated, Multiplied
Man mature, hungered
Man explored, conquered, destroyed.
Man discontented
Man educated, man loved.
Man possessive, Man creative,
Man conceited, Man hate.
Man alienate,
Man segregate.
Man unfulfilled.
Mankind discover a universal face,
Man without race, without gender,
Man without hate
Man become human.

Marie Brandon

Shadows on the Nile

Black on black, night watching
'neath the silver, shadowed moon,
the cat turned witch's eyes
to an unseen star;
with throaty purring, called to
the throne of Bast:
Neglected now; long crumbled into dust.
Razed by desire; turned
to ashes in the wind.

Trudy Pickering

Untitled

Eyes as wide as their extended bellies
Hands held out in despair
Is anyone out there?
Does anyone care?

How can this plight return,
Again, and again, and again?
The help they are given each time
Disintegrates down the line.

Cries of anguish, hunger and terror
Replace nature's balance
Unknown to them the sounds of birds
The fall of leaves and bending trees.

Will there ever be a childish giggle
A hug to show we care
The running of feet on earth in play
Or will this devastation forever stay?

As one who lives this side of earth
I've seen the photos, heard their cries
Without a doubt I know I care
How many of you do out there?

Lesley-Anne McGuinness

Cinnamon

Her miaow was fading out
lying on the garden's grass
the yellowish-brown fur
splashed with her blood
her look of grief a question mark
for the crime of someone
claiming the title of human.
I hold her in my arms
calling her Cinnamon
trying to comfort her
asking her forgiveness
for my fellow men.
If her eyes would close
they would stop my heart.
We both survived
she is now a mother
and in moments of rest
we communicate in silence
wishing for this world
to find its lost paradise.
Alexander Tomaras

Mend Me

My heart has been broken
My tears have fallen
My pain inside
is a wall of emotions
I loved him once
I still do
but life goes on
and so must you!
Sharon White

Dreams

Lost in dream;
light, floaty, hear the scream.
Was it me, the voice within
or the dream that I'm in . . .

In my dream
did I see, the white dove
fly with me?

The knight in shining armour;
was it you?
The dream I want it to be;
awake and then I see; reality . . .

Snuggle close and dream again,
fly the clouds and then;
peace, rest and calm within,
meet the day;
refreshed, anew,
go forward; free with you . . .
Helen Connolly

Effacing (Earth)

New, pragmatic forest
of the Andes,
defunct and spiritless,
scarcely abundant
with your former resplendence.

Gone is your bountiful luxury
of fruits, colours, essence,
gone are your teeming rivers sparkling,
your invigorating citrus,
your tropical incense.

Here are the deformed, hideous
and despondent,
hazed in smog buildings,
their drab turrets marring
the now sombre sky.

Here is man, as usual,
obliterating his very own earth.
Alison Cowdell

Dear Olive

I can't believe that you're gone
to that very special place,
where once again we
have to wait to see your face.

Smiling laughing with friends
brothers and sister oh how
we all miss you.

Mother, will be having a chat
the weather is sunny you can't
beat that!

Eden was waiting for another bloom

A rose a sunflower you will be a boon,
to God's big garden in the sky
I will just say goodbye.
A. M. Finlay

To Dear Kathy

A special poem for Dear Kathy;
I see you sitting in the park
In the old English Garden,
Full of beauty like you.
The smell of the dew on the flowers.
Gives you many happy hours.
You have a gift of love
You share with others.
As you are sitting in a dream,
Tony appears before you.
When you are together you
Dream forever.
Molly Buckingham

Out of the Blue

Floating, drifting, without a care
Moving, changing, light as air
First a ball, then a train
Turn around to find a crane.
Laugh as an elephant becomes a fish
Smile, then make a wish.

Not day nor night can quell the might
Of life with no substance and white.
All earthly pleasures can be outdone.
Reflecting colours of the sun
Moving with freedom of the wind
Pure nature is not a sin.

Lost in imagination.
Never stagnation.
Swirling around the globe
No borders can control
This life so quiet and yet so loud
I would love to be a cloud.
Sarah Thorp

Solace

Will you walk beside me
As I stumble on my way,
Touch my hand and guide me
To help me face each day?

When I am in my lonely bed
And tears fill my sleepless eyes;
I feel your presence near me,
And sweet dreams invade my mind.

As I live my life without you
The pain of loss still there
I take courage from your presence,
Just feeling you are there.

As my sight grows dimmer
And my faltering footsteps slide,
I know you will be waiting
Across that great divide.
Emma Hunt

Arrivals

Here he comes, Mr. Very Important
Designer suit, nose in air
Cursory nod to liveried chauffeur
Not a pleasantry to spare.

Here he comes, Mr. Not So Important
Catalogue briefcase, ill at ease
Wary smile for foreign colleagues
Hand out held for sweaty squeeze.

Here he comes, Mr. Unimportant
Back pack, grin from ear to ear
Smacking kiss for waiting girlfriend
Relaxed and happy to be here.
Dawn Stafford

Have No Fear

Water me and watch me grow.
Talk to me and let me show
You how unselfish I can be.

Feed me with your food of love.
Need me now and from above
I'll have the strength to carry on.

Have no fear then I will live.
And from my soil I'll try to give you
All you need and win a smile.

Show your faith to ease my pain.
And each new day I'll see a gain
Of one more inch towards the Sun.
Jacqueline Evans

The Walk at Dawn

With the sun rising
Over the misty hills,
The day is dawning
As we walk at will.

It was but six o'clock
With a cold morning chill,
  care not did she,
  But rain with glee
  in the heather so free.

The gloom is breaking
With a hazy chill,
A skylark sings
To shatter the still.

The morning blues
Fade away with the dew,
As the warmth of the rising sun,
Spills across the land.
  Care not did she,
  But barked at me
  As we walked so free.
Matthew Lee Smith

Playground of My Childhood

Walking through a wood,
Childhood dreams of the past,
but where I ran and played,
was never going to last,
The trees have been felled,
the birds have all gone,
I wanted to shout,
Where's it gone? Where's it gone?
I suppose the farmer sold it,
for the thought of cash in hand,
I only wish he'd left me,
my little piece of land.
Nothing stays the same,
or so that's what they say,
but no one spared a thought,
for the place I used to play.
J. M. Wallace

Adult Education

Flooded by bureaucracy,
loaded with paper work
deafened by computer,
telephone and fax
we no longer stand to gossip
with teachers and with staff.
Money's the aim,
funding councils the god.
Stick certificates on every course
and money will pour in.

Our students want a skill, a friend,
a stimulus or two;
not confinement to the syllabus,
but freedom to confer.

Let's get back to pen and paper.
Spare our eyes from nasty screens,
offer students warm welcome
and share their joy
in bold endeavour.

Jenny Hamilton-Sneath

Waterfall

Once a bird
Sings a lonely song
'Rain in Spain'
Weather's strong.

A land of matadors
A land of crowds
I got a tree
To sit under
And wonder about.

I stare at the sky
I stare at the people
A ticket to bullfight
Has got 'no use'

I look for waterfall.

Saleha Chowdhury

Ginger

Ginger was a lovely cat
he loved to lay upon the mat

He was a pest when it came to night
he loved to play and loved to fight

He went out one fine day
and hasn't come back to this day

We loved that stupid ginger cat
and wonder were the hell he's at

We hope and pray that he's okay
and would love to see him another day.

Mandy Lee

Untitled

Drips fall into the steamy bath,
The level rises slightly.
Ripples form, ever expanding,
to disappear in the vastness.

Her body lies motionless,
The level keeps on rising.
Drips grow louder,
filling the silence of the room.

Near to overflowing,
Yet she can not stop it.
The knife edge glistens,
sunk deep in her chest.

Blood red water spills on the floor.
Stained drops fall into the bath.
Her bubble-filled sanctuary,
so cruelly stolen.

Kirsty Stansbie

See You Soon, My Love

I cannot see, the flood
of my tears leaves me
sightless. What was it
she said "A bientot, Cheri"

See you soon my love,
cries my heart. The
anguish, in at the kill
tearing me apart.

The future looks bleak,
My love lies desolate.
A lonely island amidst
an ocean of grief.

The flowers, fading now
with the passage of time,
bow their weary heads
in sadness. My heart aches

As I kneel here by her grave
in sorrow I whisper
"Au revoir, a bientot.
A bientot, ma Cherie".

John Vernon

How I Loved

I loved the sparkle in your eyes
when I came into view

I loved the dimples in your cheeks
when laughter came to you

I loved to see the rays of sun
gleam upon your hair

I loved the way you hugged me
when you'd had a little scare

I loved the way your gentle hands
slipped trusting, into mine

I loved you then and always will
until the end of time

I loved you so my little girls
and often have I cried

For little girls I loved and lost
but time cannot divide

For you are little women now
with children of your own

I wonder, will you feel this way
when they are fully grown.

Brenda J. Grainger

One-Way Mirror

In the middle of the night
I wait for your coming to
make a call.

I saw you passing, the
white of your trousers,
in the front hall.

Your gentle touch and
your voice in my ear.
You have not gone far
you are ever-so near.

The smell of strawberries
in the air,
I reach out and long to
touch your beauty ever so fair.

The one-way mirror of
life's transition,
proves life still goes
on and you are on a mission.

Sheila Shaw

The Beam

I looked up to the sky one night
And saw the stars all shining bright,
One sent a beam straight down to me
And lifted me up
And I was in flight,
I looked down
And I could see myself
Looking up into the night.

V. I. Powell

Our Street

A robin sings
a cat to pounce
a dog to bark
stoned by a boy
for father to trounce
home and slam the gate
the sun's stark
rays bleach.
Tethered sheep wait
and bleat.
There are many of each
on our street.
Tripoli, late afternoon,
a life cycle complete
and fairly quiet
on our street.

John Ashley

Haunted

Haunted by a deed he didn't do
The pain and the anguish the TV drew
Hoping against hope he won't be caught
His soul the devil has not yet bought.
Mind moving on a separate plain
Thinking of those he hadn't slain
Lying beneath an empty stone
Flesh still rotting upon the bone.
Haunted by a deed he didn't do.
He didn't do it—nor did you.

Leoni Brynin

Untitled

A star so far
away from every day
out of reach
for you to teach
yourself. Not from a book
to get a better look.
So join that nasty race
which is always taking place
and at the end
you will find that friend
who is meant to stay
and will show the way
to inner peace of mind.

Harriet Sheldon

The Witch's Spell

The whisk of a mouse's tail
The sneeze of a frog
The gleam of a star
The roar of a bear
The tear of a dog
The snore of a pussy cat
The quack of a duck
All mixed together in the witch's pot
She stirred and stirred and stirred
until the pot shivered and brr . . .ed
and she made a
Spell

Josephine Turner

Despair

The gloom that overwhelms me,
the total and utter despair,
The tears that flow unyielding,
'What hope' I ask is there?

Life has been so cruel,
So much I've had to bear.
Are there any answers?
Is love not anywhere?

My mind just seems so empty,
Reason has all but gone.
Pain is deep not obvious,
I feel so weak—not strong.

I just want to turn away,
Forget the world outside.
Curl up in a corner,
Run away and hide.

Everything has just collapsed,
Thoughts are all awry.
My life is just a total mess,
And all I do is cry.

Julie Barnes

Jack Frost (26-05-1995)

Softly, silently, slowly,
He moves across the grass,
And before anyone knows it
He's left his mark and passed.

From the tip of the tall trees
To the water in the pool,
Everything's felt his influence
And is very, very, cool.

I saw him early this morning
As I drove along the way,
He looked so very beautiful
I wished that he could stay.

The green grass in the paddock
Gleamed like icing on a cake,
The tall trees looked like polar bears
Standing by the gate.

But Jack Frost has a rival
And before very long,
Old Mr. Sun came out to say,
"Jack Frost, you must be gone."

Betty Jeffrey

With Fewer Senses

What is that scent?
What can I feel?
What was that sound
my ear did heed?

You who walk with me
tell me where I am.
Tell me my surroundings
—the colourful charm.

Help me link the fragrance
to what there is to see.
Help me see the colours
that are all around me.

Describe the little anthill,
describe the flowers too.
I need your wordy portrait
of what we're passing through.

I know it's often arduous
to have to tell me all,
but it brings vivid splendour
of all my nose does call.

Helena Bjornsdottir

For Maggie

Oh miggety moggety maggiety madge,
oh miggety maggiety moo,
with pony tail and sticky-up fringe
and dangly earrings too.

With polka dots on mini skirt
and tights all woolly and knitted,
for collegey days, and on the town
she's totally out-fitted.

With girly giggles and childy chuckles
and jokes and fun and burbles.
with bovver boots and denim black,
and baby sizéd gurgles,
sits a life and soul of jollity
on collegiate corridor floor.
With coffee black and butties brown,
and crisps and fags galore.

Oh miggety dear, oh maggiety dear,
oh goodness gracious you!
Oh miggety moggety maggiety madge,
well tickety tackety boo!

B. Morgan

Belfast Lough

My ship sailed by an Irish lough
Just as the sunset glowed:
The hills around burned cherry-red;
The lough—a Golden Road,

And up above it all I saw,
Or so to me it seems,
The glory indescribable—
Fair goal of all my dreams.

James M. Adams

22nd April

As they cut the twisted cord
The vicious world took over
The job that was for months
Only mine.

You can go anywhere now
Anyone can be your 'Mother'.
A small white clip
Showed me there was a division
Between your life and mine.

All that waiting time
We were only one.
Now we're definitely separate,
A cold sad loss,
I feel you leaving me already.

You must do
Whatever you are destined to
And I will always be here.
I've kept that small white clip
Emotionally we will be joined
Forever.

Alison Crawford-Ward

Lonely in a Crowd

A sea of faces swim by each day
As people pass along the way
Among them I could scream out loud
About being lonely in a crowd.

The outside shows the bravest face
Emotions safely in their place
But inside is not quite so proud
Of being lonely in a crowd.

No one for me to confess
About a life that's such a mess
So silently, the pain I shroud
And stay so lonely in a crowd.

Tricia Adam

The Mask

It's not there in the morning
When I am all alone
It's not there late at night
When I am all alone
But it's with me when in company
Fixed on really tight
An invisible great barrier
A shield to deflect the fright
It keeps all people at arm's length
Forbidden to enter the zone
I wonder what it would be like
To leave my mask at home.

Nik Wardle

Second Chance

This world in which we live
Only comes to us but once,
We are so easily parted
So we must take a chance.

My eyes have been opened
By everyday things,
A new day beginning
And the joy that it brings.

I'm glad it was you that I met
You've shown me my life's not over yet,
It's time to start our life anew
Because you love me
And I love you.

J. Fortune

The Dump

My dear old Dad has a hobby
That keeps him occupied
It involves visiting the local dump
Then searching far and wide
For he can find such treasures
Others never seem to want
A toothless comb, a bottomless jug
An orange plastic font
A sandal for your left foot
A welly for your right
A table with nearly all its legs
A torch without a light.
And if the dump should close
He'll prey on local skips
Whilst others sneak their rubbish in
Her rummages and dips
Till he finds more tempting things
To take home with his other treasures
And would my poor Mum change him?
I fear the answer's never!

Bernadette Peters

Sea of Sky

I saw the pale silver moon,
Sailing, in the sea of sky.
The clouds just seemed to disappear.
I stared and stared,
Until all was clear.
I was just going to blink,
But something,
Something had caught my eye.
The moon, it seemed to jolt,
and tremble.
In the place that it was sitting,
right up there.
In the sea of sky.
The clouds seemed like waves now.
Gushing against the rocks in the sea.
And after all, it would be like this,
seeing as it is,
a very wet night.
But still, I stared up there,
in the sea of sky.

Kalsi Rupinder

Words

When wind is howling in the night,
And long before dawn's early light,
I'm lying here, propped up in bed,
And words are tumbling round my head.
So many things they want to say,
I wish they'd wait till break of day.
Words, so impatient to come out,
To tell their tales of fear and doubt,
Adventure, fame and fantasy,
Of intrigue and great mystery,
Lovers who have loved in vain,
Shattered dreams, deep hurt and pain.
These words that will not let me be,
Are crying out to be set free,
To let them go, one thing is sure,
If I should open up the door,
To all these words, I'm bound to say,
Perhaps I'll write a book one day,
And when they're out I think I'll find,
That I have gained my peace of mind.
Margaret Ashman

Tea for Two

You are worth a mint to me,
so I come to make the tea.
I put a tea bag in a cup,
and then I fill the kettle up.
I put the boiling water in a mug,
while I do this I hear it "glug".
Then I let the sweeteners fizz,
to make a little laughing whizz.
Now I serve the tea for two,
and I do all this just for you!
Anja Sharpe

The Ladies on the Patio

Deep in conversation,
Smiling here and there,
Dappled sunlight through the trellis
Playing in their hair.
The ladies are lunching;
Sharing their time,
When a wasp joins their table
And Laura almost spills her wine.
The wasp avoids their swatting
And goes on to pollinate;
The ladies go on plotting,
No worry of being late.
Their time's their own,
Their children grown,
Their middle years await,
As the ladies on the patio
Enjoy a luncheon date.
Sandra Margaret Shram

It Begins with a Seed

My eyes have seen the glory,
    In a yellow daffodil.
My ears have heard the glory,
    In the early morning trill.
My heart has felt the glory,
    In the love surrounding all.
My soul waits for the glory
    Of our Loving Saviour's call.
Though dust I am, and certainly.
    I will return to dust.
Our Lord's a skillful gardener,
    In Him, I put my trust.
That as I lie unnoticed
    He will come with love and power.
Then take the bit that's left of me
    And make this weed a flower!
Each one of us, a seedling,
    A blossom that is stored.
Oh, to be a lovely flower,
    In the garden of Our Lord!
Phyllis Frankish

A Dream Shared

He once had a dream
a dream that must come true
never do to others
what you don't like done to you
forget about religion
and the divisions within it
turn to peace and love
then the candle will be lit
He once had a dream
a dream that must come true
to try to show the world
that righteousness is due
it doesn't really matter
if you're black or if you're white
judge a person for themselves
and try to see the light
He once had a dream
a dream that must come true
a dream to show to others
what they have to do
Jacqueline Yuill

A Question of Love

Does this mean you've time to spare
Time to show someone you care
Time to walk across the sand
Time to stroll on some strange land
Far away from work and folks
Time to share some silly jokes
Time to cuddle and caress
Time for things less serious
Time with you is such a pleasure
Répondez-vous, at your leisure.
Linda Cawley

Peaceful Echoes

The echoes of my heart
Pound with tense ripples,
Like the corrugated sands
On a white desert dune;
Hot, dry, and full of destitution,
yet hoping with each
freshly blown cascade of pulses
for the shower of love from
An open heaven spray.

A refreshing moisture of peace
And calm within my world
of chaos everywhere, without, within,
thinking back on the valleys
of Eminence and the Elation of hope,
wishing for the oasis of tomorrow,
and the eternity it brings.

Thoughts like these, such thoughts
are persistent, perpetual, succeeding
an eventual continuum between
Myself and my ultimate destination.
Helen E. Sutcliffe

I Am Because You Are

My mate
    my crazy pulse rate
my date of a dish
    my 'oo' to 'a-tish'

My wish of a bone
    my strawberry cone
my zone of the 'o'
    my green light to go

My beau of the ball
    my treasure-trove haul
my call to the wild
    by you, I'm beguiled . . .
Anne Campbell-Ashwell

Living

I live in a nightmare
world
where only ghosts
goblins
and ghouls
prevail,
there is no
light, only
darkness,
in
creepy corners
where no sun can
slip
I survive
among evil-smelling
shadows that
loom and retreat
twisted in agony,
amid the recess
of my mind.
Margaret Martin

Colours

Blue is the colour of water
That sparkles in your eyes.
Red is the colour of slaughter,
Because you cry when someone dies.

Green is the colour of nature,
Green is the colour of stems,
I don't like animals in danger,
It just does not make sense!
Danielle Roman

The Coming of Dawn

Awake, oh Milton
Enough sleep and rest
You enjoyed centuries over:
Look: Britain is booming
Leave the grave, come quick,
Wipe off your tearful eyes,
Rejoice—smile and dance
Your cherished dream
Britain's Paradise flashing
Lead us all, youth and old
With a message of Universal Peace
Burying forever 'Power-Supremacy'
Be it monarchy or Democracy,
Be it Republic or Marxist:
Universal Peace Proclaiming
All the world over
Burying Power Supremacy dead and gone
Our 'Lost-Paradise' regaining
Britain is booming.
Anjali Bhattacharji

Silent Proposal

On a still November evening
With a clear and cloudless sky
A myriad of stars were gleaming
To match the sparkle in your eyes
A chill was in the air
The ground a glistening white
The fragrance of your hair
Shining golden in the night

And somewhere in the night sky
A full moon shining bright
A different sparkle in your eyes
Reflects what has come to light
The chill no longer in the air
But not the memory of this place
For I knew the answer then and there
Clearly written on your face
Andrew Murray

Father to Son

He is to me
What I am to you
From father to son
A love that flows free

Like the sun in the summer
That shines so bright
Summer shall turn to winter
And darkness will cloak the light

Sometimes I'll stop to wonder
About happy times passed by
Even now the bond grows stronger
As the tears swell in my eyes

It was your time to leave
As one day it shall be mine
Go board that peaceful train
For one day we'll meet again

So now I am to you
What he was to me
From father to son
A love that can never die.

Duncan Hamilton

Grief

Seeing her on the
Cold grey stone
Just lying there
Lifeless
And covered in
Cold grey shadows
And looking lonely, still
And cold
You glance at her
Cold grey body
And feel the
Nausea rising in your throat
You break down
Start to cry
And run from the room
Smelling of Death.

Kerry Lewis

A Drowning Mood

Cry I can't,
Water has no feeling.
Its motions so provocative,
Yet stagnant because I need it so.
I wish I could harness its strength,
Ride its wildness,
Escape.

Strange no matter how I try,
Still not a ripple,
Not even a crest.
Trapped inside,
A current drawn deep below,
By the cage of its mercifulness tide.

Jayne E. Russell

Mum

My love for you
will never die,
the memories will never fade.
To say goodbye I could not do
to say I love you I will do
to have you by my side
Is very hard to do,
but when I'm feeling down
and need you by my side
all I have to do, is just close my eyes
and I see your smile.
To see your smile is all I need
to cheer me up.
And dry my tears away.

Margaret Proud

Water Men

I close my eyes and see the sea.
Its infinity is amazing.
Its beauty is beyond compare.
And its power is awesome.
I close them tighter.
I am underwater.
Dolphin song echoes in my ears.
I see your smooth grey skins.
And your friendly broad grins.
That small black eye shining
Just like a precious stone.
You dominate the sea.
Just like the earth we.
We are both intelligent mammals.
But I often wonder which are animals.

Damian McGuinness

Ireland

*To my firstborn son, Patrick-Joseph,
who died at birth, 10th June 1992*

Age old trees
Fields of golden corn
Dew drenched hedges
Of blossoming white-thorn

Daisies sway in the breeze
While the stream trickles on
Rabbits fidget as they feed
Birds crying their song

Bees humming as they fly
From flower to flower
Fading sun low in the sky
What a magical twilight hour.

Maree O. Gorman

Quiet Nature

Snowdrops worship,
Their heads subdued,
Purple crocuses prosper,
On slabs of rock,
The robin dances,
Quick, furtive glances,
Stone to stone,
Insects nestle in words,
Carved in granite,
Marble glistens,
Cloaked in dew,
Cold stone, warm words,
Hushed and gentle,
Mourners weep,
The Earth breathes,
Nature lives,
Silent world,
Amongst death,
Life lives anew,

Lesley Williams

My Love

Thank you my love
for yesterday.
With all its happy memories.

Thank you my love
for today.
And the ability to enjoy it.

Thank you my love
for tomorrow.
And the things to look
forward to.

Thank you my love
for all the joy you give me.
And the good time we
have together.

Ann Addison

Untitled

Though sometimes I'm still down
and sometimes I may fight you
never doubt my sincerity
or question where my heart lies.

My vivacity may be far away
but my heart and soul
lie by your side
and shadow in your footsteps.

My spirit is where you are,
you may hold my dreams
close to your heart
resting softly in your hands.

Never doubt me,
my heart is not fickle—
it lies with you
but please don't let it slip.

Susan Westmore

Seasons

Can you picture the rainbow
All the colours so bright,
We planned our life together
But someone pulled out the light.

We reached for the stars
But they were miles away,
You tried to steal one for me
But that's where they're meant to stay.

We tried to chase the sunset
It hid behind the mountainside,
And then you too disappeared
Oh how my heart cried.

My tears dropped like the rain
And turned into a river,
I will always love you
Though now my heart is bitter.

Kerry Finch

The Weightlifters

Push, pull, strain,
The weightlifters train,
Sweat, muscle, stretch,
The weightlifters flex,
Pump, iron, willed,
The weightlifters build,
Pose, shape, stance,
The weightlifters dance,
Hands clasped, belt buckled,
Chalk dusted, bare knuckled,
Yes gain, yes pain,
The weightlifters' fame.

David Hawes

Dreams before Death

How far would I have to go
'til I touched the sky?
How high would I have to jump
'til I reached the top,
and ran my fingers through the clouds?
Some days it seems so far away,
and others just a stone's throw away.
If I could fly
I would touch that sky
watch the tiny world from up high.
Hear nothing, see all,
jaywalk along a cloud
and fall
plummet to Earth, sting my face,
blind my eyes,
then I die
but I had touched the sky.

Jessica Owers

Beyond

Illusive fields
Of vision's light,
Where rest my dreams
Through darkest night.
There sings my soul
In spheres unknown.
Distanced, coloured, copious tones.
Then gently through the greyer zones,
As life creeps in one's creaking bones,
The disconnecting scenes and time
Soon vanish from my daytime mind.

Margaret Herbert

Reflections

In the park the children played
As the gums so gently swayed
See those magpies overhead
And the children playing dead?

Can you hear the birds twittering?
And can you hear their cries?
Can you see those children playing
Running and chasing butterflies?

Can you see the children forts
And horse swings scattered round?
Can you see the gum nuts
Lying on the ground?

Can you see the children pant
As they play dead ants?
Can you see the gum trees
Swaying in the breeze?

In the park the kites flew high
Then the sun began to die
Where have all the children gone?
Now I'm here alone

Anne Laird

Little Death

Silent scream when mouths are straining
throat is tight life is failing
Eyes are open seeing space
Shadows on face like delicate lace
Fingers holding tearing life
The stress the sins of bodies strife
Are we living loving or dying?
Only the breaths of each are sighing.

Beverley Kalantzis

Dusk

The heavens were ablaze,
I gazed in wonder
Through the shimmering haze
To such ardent splendour.

It glowed in its glory,
Casting shadow and light,
Who knows of its story,
With its stupendous might.

Watching and sighing,
As the horizon it neared,
As if it were dying,
It slowly disappeared.

In its heavenly bliss,
As the darkness descended,
The hills it did kiss,
For the day had now ended.

The breeze brushed my face
As I went on my way,
What natural grace,
For the end of a day.

F. G. Hulme

Saga

Mountains to climb
Paths are walked
People to meet.

Waters of life
Sun unfolds
Puzzle piece.

Treasure attained
Wisdom euphoria
Home but a way.

Intervened
By machine
As it screams.
Saaagaa!

Edward Lee Crosby

Mississippi Swans

And now swim into view
two swans, serenity afloat,
drawing the circle of their world,
swimming a waltz,
at evening's fall
to strange silent music,
and homing to rest,
ritual complete,
in perfect stillness
beside their gentle—
ever so gentle
undulating boat

Denis O'Neill

Life

Life is an adventure
And if lived to the full
Our hearts will muster
All kinds of fun.
There are mountains
To be climbed,
And there are treasures
To be found.
And you know what else
Is there?
I'll tell you
You see, the list
Is endless
So get out there
And find what is yours.

Carolie Pemberton

Ma

I'm up in the morning
At half past seven
To lie in bed
Would just be heaven

Get the kids ready
And get them fed
Oh how I wish
I could go back to bed

Make the beds
And clean the rooms
Emptying the Hoover
Found my missing spoons

Sort the washing
Hang it out
Quick dust and polish
One last look about

Cook the dinner
Make the tea
Everything done now
I can watch TV

Cindy McDonald

Times Gone By

Gone are the days
Of laughter and happiness
When life was lived
Like a cool dawn breeze.

Walking in the forest
Listening to nature
Feeling the warm rain
On a dry barren earth.

Sitting on the river bank
Watching the hippos
Yawning and basking
In the hot summer sun.

Climbing to the top of the hill
To watch the sun come up
Or go down in the sky.
And dreaming of my life.

Where is this wonder?
Why it must be Africa!
My land and my home
In my heart forever.

Frances Bowen

The Despoilers

Does the lion defy God's laws
When it feeds upon its prey?
No, only man could give Him cause
To ever rue the day.
He made the sun, the stars, the moon
He gave us fields of grain.
How could He know, that all too soon,
We'd contribute acid rain
He gave us trees, and flowers too,
The change from warmth to snow.
How could He know what we would do,
And just how far, we'd go?
The poisoning of His sweet good earth
Accomplished with such haste
How could He know, around its girth,
We'd bury nuclear waste.
This legacy we leave our young,
The blame cannot be shelved.
Of course He knows, we are the ones
The despoilers are—ourselves!

Audrey Knight

Untitled

I never kissed your sleeping head,
I never said goodbye,
You didn't say you were leaving,
I always wondered why,
I never felt you slip away,
Though I knew the time was near.
You tried so hard to carry on,
I never saw a tear.
Won't you please watch over me,
Stay close to me this way.
And I will keep on loving you,
Till we meet again, some day

Joan Aldridge

Summer Sun

Summer sun summer sun
Today we'll have lots of fun
We'll have a picnic in the park
run around and hear dogs bark
Hear the children loud and
clear screaming louder
hear them cheer
now we'll go fishing
and catch some fish
get the plate ready
we'll make a dish.

Samantha Thompson

War's Punishment

Marching to their graves
The men of glory and ambition
The majestic confrontation of death
The end is celebrated
Faces of stone and eyes of ice
Theirs souls are punished forever
There are no winners of war
Only the distinguished few survive
Who lived as the disabled
And died a lonely life

Katie Sheila Scott

Lost but Found Again

It's been nine months
since I saw you last,
You left without a trace,
No note, no phone call,
You just went away.

One day there was a
knock at the door,
I couldn't believe my eyes
when I saw you standing there,
A child in one arm
a man in the other.

Our friendship was lost,
When you went away
and found again,
When you returned that day.

At least you came home,
Alive not dead,
You were lost but
found again.

Pamela Moloney

Feeling

You are special
I just wanted you to know
How you make me feel
And that I love you so
Today I felt your touch
Saw the love in your face
That I have craved so much
I fell into your embrace
As my fingers kissed your skin
You drew all my love out
That was so deep within
I had to show you how I felt
You say you are under my spell
And that I am beautiful
I feel that way about you as well
Darling you are wonderful
I know our love is deep because
When our fingers touch and entwine
You know that I am yours
And my love you are mine

Julie Morgan

The Oak

It stands bare and isolated
in the grim winter's evening.
Naked brown branches stretch
across the lifeless countryside.
The tree itself bears no
life. Fruitless.
The thought of it
bearing lush green leaves
in the summer seems
miraculous. But the great
Oak shall stand proud
as a lion. It shall give
life and shade to all
creators great and small.

Siobhan O'Regan

The Story Begins

From the darkside of yesterday
To a time beyond tomorrow
From somewhere beyond infinity
But not as far as eternity
Can all creation be measured
In such an abstract way
If all those whomever existed spoke
And all spoken knowledge said
Would we then know everything
Or would it all be meaningless
Can we gather all the knowledge
To answer that question "Why"
Or should we just accept our place
Because "Why Not" is what we've got.

Trevor Bawdon

Potential

Potential is the promise
Of talent, yet to be
Which, if attained, must disappear
To become re-al-ity.

And yet we find potential
Is given pride of place.
Is used to ease a conscience
Or perhaps to save a face.

Elusive key to success door
'Tho' some may never find.
Better cleave it open,
With the axe, you have to grind.

For ability, is there to see
The promise has been met.
Potential, on the other hand
Is but a 'hunch' as yet.

Walter A. Ancliff

Perfect Day

The former self is blinded
by the light,
the dews of the morning
sing love,
a star in the sky
chased by the sun
and, burning, my heart
in its high.
You think of me,
I know.

Raluca Miu

The Path of Life

The strains of life,
So strong, so profound.
The ups and the downs
Only downs can be found.

Shall we go here,
Shall we go there.
Don't take a chance,
It's more than we dare.

The path of life,
Where do we go.
Is it uphill or down,
Does anyone know.

The grass is always greener,
Or so they do say.
They give it in one hand,
Then take it away.

Don't feel so bad,
Please show no hate.
Go, have a good life,
Before it's too late.

Lawrence John Weedon

Farewell to Winter

The sun is shining way up high,
The little birds are singing.
Across the meadow loud and clear,
Church bells are sweetly ringing.
Hedgerows now are turning green
And little lambs are prancing.
So open up
 heart to spring,
And on your way go dancing!

F. B. Turner

Return to the Hills

Take me to the hills
And do not talk to me
But let me stay and hear
The sounds I used to see;
And touch the grass and sense the deer
Move gently up the scree.
Let me feel, with foot and hand,
And if I fall do not comfort me.

An eagle sweeps with creaking wings
Before my sightless eyes
And golden plovers call,
But I have seen these lovely things
And know them all.

Is it hazy? Is it clear?
And can you see the sea?
Yes the sea is there and sky,
But boundless where they meet.
Rock and water round us lie;
The world is at your feet.
Come home

M. S. Palmer

With Hands

God gave me eyes to see with
God gave me ears to hear with
And hands for me to pray.

He gave me a mind to think with
He gave me a mouth to speak with
And hands for me to pray.

God gave His only son
And still I think of number one
With hands that do not pray.

If I could build wishes
On hopes and plans and kisses
I'd give them all to you.
You would do the same thing too
With hands that try to pray.

I cannot find a way now
To end this poem yet somehow
I'll do my very best
For God another test
With hands that always pray.

George Smith-Whittle

A Summer's Day

The misty haze of the last days
As sun brings bright fresh rays
Diamonds glitter on the grass
Lace lit up on trees and bushes
Stillness as morning awakens

Sun beats down, scorching
Sweat and work, unrelenting
In a box looking out repenting
As the world goes by
Under a shimmering sky

The last hot blaze of fire burns
As embers glow on darkening sky
Cool still shadows fall
As darkness breathes a fresh sigh

E. Downs

Daylight Breaks

Daylight breaks, another day
Just memories to live by
I try and hide this hurt inside
I laugh and smile and lie.
Daylight comes with much regret
I want to sleep forever
I try to wipe you from my mind
And forget our time together.
Nighttime falls, how glad I am
My tears will not be seen
No one will know my loneliness
Or the sadness I now feel.
Dreams, they never seem to be
The way that we once were
But as the daylight breaks once more
I'll forget today, I swear.

Evelyn McLeod

Jesus

Upon a cross our saviour died
I did it all for you He cried
The spotless lamb of God was slain
That full redemption we could gain.

His first abode a manger stall
The shepherds were the firsts to call
The eastern kings their homage paid
As Jesus on the straw was laid.

No kingly hall, no royal throne
No house that He could call His own
Yet He was rich beyond compare
That wealth with all He came to share.

He sits at God's right hand on high
To intercede for us—that's why
One day with him we will abide
If we believe for us He died.

The trumpet soon shall send its blast
Call all the ransomed home at last
Will you my friend stand at His feet
When he is on the judgement seat.

Maurice Reid

God Can Move Your Mountain

When things seem so impossible,
And life's so hard to bear,
God can move your mountain,
Before you reach despair.

He'll never leave you or forsake you,
Trust him all the way,
Be anxious then for nothing,
And never cease to pray.

So keep on climbing higher,
Be patient while you wait,
For God is never early,
And also never late.

Brian Webster

My Garden

I look into my garden
at the flowers all blooming there
And realize that blessings abound
from my tender loving care.

So sweet the scent of lilies
As they lift their eyes to the sun
And primulas and daffodils
All add to the Springtime fun.

What a joy there is in my garden
When I look with wide span eyes
At the marvels of God's creation,
A veritable paradise.

Margaret Ramsay

Memories

He started school,
I stood outside,
I felt a fool
Because I cried.

How could I ever
Let him go.
Will he be clever?
I love him so.

The time has come
The years have passed,
Where have they gone?
He's a man at last.

Happy days—all the way,
Lots of laughter—a few tears,
Now I'm old, I'm glad to say
Many memories of precious years.

E. Norris

England and Spring

England could be a great country,
The country that gave birth to
you and me, the green grass, and
the buttercups, spreading gold
in grassy glades. I'd like to
shout aloud and say, "Don't dig
away our heritage!"
The spring is a great joy to me,
the flowers, and the humming bee,
the birds' sweet song, when this
season appears, moistening our
gardens like (as if with tears).
But I will weep if I live
to see a child upon its
Mother's knee, crying "I've
no place to play"; all is concrete
here to-day, halt this progress
if you will it surely is a bitter pill.

Sheila K. A. Thompson

Death

He comes, a friend
To stop the laboured breath
Oh God, when my time comes
Be merciful to me
Let my end peaceful be
For I have suffered much
And long so for your gentle touch

M. Quantock

Listen

You took the rise
Telling me lies
Now you've gone bolder
As you've grown older

Time to reflect
Some thoughts to inject
The deeds you done
From father to son

It's never too late
To make amends
Give him support
New thoughts and new trends

He's cared and he's tried
To look up with pride
To have his own father
Right by his side

So look out and feel
The son that is real
Acknowledge the life
From you and your wife

Arthur Dominick

Father and Son

Why do our words not come easily
Are the barriers built so strong
Will the pain go on forever
It's already lasted so long

Perhaps it's the child within me
Tearing my soul apart
Am I asking for what can't be given
Two different views of the heart

For the heart is a fragile being
Based on desires and hopes and fears
Storing memories, loves and emotions
But supplying often sadness and tears

Who has the wisdom of Solomon
Who can balance the wrong and the right
Who can provide to these darkened minds
Some comfort, some peace, some light

I look at my son before me
And cherish his every hair
This feeling is surely eternal
Ours must be somewhere out there.

Joe Boyle

The Orphan

A little boy of five or six
Sits alone in a tiny room
Tears trickling down his face
As he hums a sad little tune

He knows that Christmas is coming
And dreads this time of year
He wants to be taken home
Not lonely left in here

He thinks of Sam, his friend
And how he jumped with joy
The day that someone told him
He'd be living with another boy

Hugging his teddy tightly
His tiny hands in prayer
"Hear my words dear God,
Please let someone care."

He reaches for a walking aid
Hobbles without a word
A hundred times he's prayed before,
But this time they'll be heard.

Annie Lane

Barren

Mother Nature's children sleep
Beneath the darkened sky.
Glittering winking diamonds keep
An ever watchful eye.

Hear the cries of birds in flight
Tremulous and free.
Soporific sounds at night.
A lonely buzzing bee.

Yet Mother Nature's eyes brim tears:
Blood in crimson pools,
Reflecting all her gruesome fears
Of war's voracious fools.

A butterfly's diaphanous wing,
Pastel petals bloom.
Myopic men in armies sing
The anthem of our doom.

Shattered peace brings silent sobs,
Reproachful daunting death.
Undulating harvest crops
No longer drawing breath . . .

Paulina Elizabeth Smith

To Dunblane

Sixteen pure white snowdrops,
One blossoming red rose,
Wiped out in just five minutes,
In a hail of bullet blows,

Who could have known the horror.
Inside that tragic place,
The fear, the hurt, the terror,
As death stared them in the face.

No one can give a reason,
No one can tell us why,
No one on earth can answer,
Why those babies had to die.

The loss, the want, the heartache,
Will never go away,
The pain, the hurt, the anger,
Will be there every day.

But earth's loss now is heaven's gain,
In peace they'll always play,
Eternal happiness is theirs,
Forever and a day.

Alison Anderson

Adultery

You say you are leaving,
Say you're not happy,
I just can't believe,
You went with that chappy.

You ask for forgiveness,
Never meant it you say,
But I just can't do that,
My love is away.

You say that you love me,
Say I am the one,
I'm starting to hate you,
Please leave me alone.

Now you have left me,
Gone far away,
You've left with another,
Hip hip hooray!

David Mitchell

Poems

No, and a second time no!
I tell you friend, I will not;
Sure, we learnt to crawl together,
Walked to school together,
Ate apple pies on Sundays
And on a Wednesday,
Stoned a Thief dead.
Now that you be buried,
Under a ton of pebbly earth,
No, my friend, I will not die for you.

Wagachima Kabucho Joseph

Peace

Trees in all their Autumn splendour,
Shades of orange, red and yellow.
Misty mornings, golden sunsets,
O what mellow
days to share.

Summer months are now behind me,
Too harsh and bright to bear;
Stormy days, restless nights,
They seemed to tear
my soul apart.

With the gentle morning skies
A fresh new hope is born.
Quiet times, peace of mind,
The time to welcome
a new dawn.

Jan Grimwood

Spring

O spring, sweet spring, when
dewdrops cling
To every flower newborn,
The birds take wing an' blithely sing
To greet the April morn!

Enchanting hours, 'mong the flowers,
Uplift this heart o' mine
The passing showers bedeck thy
bowers,
A' pleasures, great, divine!

The streamlets flow to proudly show
Cruel winter's surely past.
Sweet breezes blow, the sun's aglow,
Gay Spring is here at last!

Norrie Sinclair

Niente Problem—The I-Will-Not on the Streets

In doorways, on streets
The homeless sleep.
From litter bins and leftovers
The homeless eat.
While we're all warm
The homeless freeze.
While we waste food
The homeless starve.
Why don't we remember
Those who are poor,
Those who are so hungry
They eat of the floor.

Nikki-Ann Trow

Helping Mum

I got a pack of cornflakes
And dropped some on the floor,
I saw my doggy liked them
So I dropped some more.

I got a mop and bucket
To wash the floor clean,
Then I made lots of bubbles
The most I'd ever seen.

I knelt down on the floor
To rub the bubbles in,
Then I accidently
Knocked the rubbish bin.

All yesterday's rubbish
Was all across the floor,
So now I've decided
Not to help my Mum no more.

Catherine Thorp

March 1997

Too long, too cold, too gray,
This month of March.
No joy, no smile, no play,
No hope to catch.

Just heart and blood and brain
Feel spring around,
The sun is coming for certain
To revitalize the ground.

The sun will bring the red and pink
And purple will be another
Much blue and green we'll have I think
And yellow, the grains' colour.

Having all these, one could be happy,
One could be glad,
Could sing in words the mere beauty,
Could kiss the land.

Rodica Victoria Steriu

Shattered Thoughts

I like to sit on Graig-y-Llyn
Just looking at the view
I often think of childhood times
When I was young and grew

From the early age of eight
I always felt so frightened
It wasn't till I heard he died
That my life should have brightened

I can't erase those memories
In dreams and thoughts they're vivid
And now as I grow older
They only make me livid

She was there she must have known
She never said a word.
I think she was afraid of him
I knew him, that's not absurd.

It doesn't seem so fair to me
That now he's laid to rest
Even now she lies beside him
She still thinks he's the best.

F. M. Phillips

A Message from a Loved One

Don't weep for me by my gravestone
because I am not there.
Please don't shed your tears for me
and don't cry in despair.

Your heart is full of sadness,
I feel your grief and pain,
but I am all around you,
in the gentle falling rain.

You feel that space around you,
that empty void of time.
If only I could tell you,
I feel wonderful, I'm fine.

I whisper words of comfort,
I kiss your tearstained cheeks,
If only you could hear me,
before you fall asleep.

My loved one, please don't worry,
have faith in God above,
one day we'll be together,
in our Spirit home of love.

Margaret Sadler

My Guitar

Oh, how much I long for that day!
Oh, how I long for your touch!

When you feel sad,
take me in your arms.
Close to you I'll cheer you up.

When you are merry,
take me in your arms.
With you I'll share your happiness.

When you have troubles,
take me in your arms.
I'll help to find a solution.

Oh, how I long for the day
when your delicate fingers
softly touch my body,
made up of dumbly strings,
your caresses waiting,
to note and sing together
the sweet melody of our love.

Oh, how I long for your touch!
Oh, how much I long for that day!

Celia Franco Royo

Thirty-Two Feet, Per Second, Per Second
(Fourth View of a Tree)

Here I lie,
   gazing up, at a tree.
Cold am I,
   amidst dampened debris.

Where is this?
   Heaven? I see a pyre?
Hell? Would hiss,
   as angel tears quench fire.

In Limbo?
   the place of 'in-between'.
I lie low,
   am neither heard, nor seen.

Piercing voice;
   A friendly voice,—well known.
"Come; Rejoice;
   Survive the moment flown."

"Stepping-stone,
   to searching far beyond,
Your puny own.
   Hold fast this magic wand."

George Melmoth

All That Glitters

Hidden in a darkened room,
Filled with scents from cheap perfumes,
Lingering memories of kisses passed,
Fleeting kisses gone to fast.
Love was promised, never given
Now her head becomes her prison.

Sunbeams dance on creamy walls,
Inside her head, raindrops fall.
She was young, her heart sent reeling
Couldn't believe this newfound feeling.
All to soon, he loved and left her,
Reasons sent inside a letter.

All that glitters is not gold,
O wise words from days of old.
Why did she not heed their warning?
Save herself from days of mourning.
Hardened heart will trust no more,
Lest she sets new heights to fall.

Melissa Short

The Other Family Member

Some people try to ignore her
but that you cannot do
for as soon as you come in our door
she is there to welcome you

She is not like the rest of us
she can't even talk
but when you're feeling really sad
with you she'll take a walk

Sometimes when your heart is breaking
but she can't hold your hands
just look into her big brown eyes
and it seems she understands

And when she sits down next to you
she is trying to offer comfort
because she can't bear to see
a loved one feeling so hurt

Our family is like a set of wheels
in the centre is a cog
the other family member
is our loving, loyal Dog.

Lorraine Middleton

Moonlight

Where have you been O silvery moon,
Since last I saw you shine?
Since golden morn was ushered through,
To hasten your decline.

Where cast your mystic shadows round,
And silhouetted trees,
In pools reflection mirrored things,
And brightened shimmering seas.
The sun which bade you haste away
In turn, has disappeared,
And you return to take its place
And so, throughout the years.

Alice Mary Cule

Daggers

There was caring and sharing,
There was loving and trusting,
There was laughing and joking,
There was forgiveness,
There was friendship.

But deceit and pretence
Meant daggers were drawn,
Combat commenced
And the friendship was gone.

There is hatred and spite,
There is anger and hurt,
There is malice and scorn,
There is bitterness,
There are enemies.

Sharon Kemps

Springtime

Springtime is here,
Mother Nature has woken,
Do you agree,
it's a beautiful season?
Flowers bloom in pretty colours,
Falling from the trees,
pink scented blossom.
A bumble bee buzzes around my head,
and from the silence I listen to;
birds singing joyful tunes.
Tadpoles in the pond,
A baby lamb being born,
I wonder when I'll see a butterfly,
I really hope it's soon!
The sun shining down,
really lifts my spirits.
Yes, I do think you'll agree,
this is a wonderful season.

Janet Lane

The Sea

I love to watch the tide,
as it goes in and out.
White horses they are called,
as they dance about.

I love to watch the sun,
Shining on the sea.
The ripples look like stars glistening,
And very beautiful to me.

The sea is such an exotic blue,
it goes for miles around,
I love to sit by the sea,
and listen to the sound.

As the waves go in and out,
crashing in the sea,
I could sit here all day,
it's my favourite place to be.

Annette Carver

Love in a Shadow

Hidden by the dark,
in the night I see,
love in a shadow,
but dark is the fear,
so in words of emptiness,
to love I am unspoken.
To touch the shadow,
penetrate into the dark,
the heart is held,
as the body is caressed,
I want but to ask.
Smile of the angels,
sent of heaven,
gazing at the shadow,
the heart is empty,
dreams are unclenched
so holding on to myself,
love is but pain,
so if the heart be of love,
death to the heart.

Stephen Richard De Silva

Untitled

When I look into the mirror
It's not a face I see
But a landscape torn and ravaged
By my own crazed vanity;

By refusals to see clearly,
To look into the heart's store,
Discern the weak and selfish
And cleave to them no more.

But when last I looked in the mirror
I saw past the cratered mud
To the double helix glinting
In the caverns of the blood;

Beneath the pock-marked surface
Lurked the hooks of heredity
Snagging my good intentions,
Letting the warped work free.

So now when I scowl in the mirror
And catch that hard cruel look,
It's my father's eyes burn back at me—
And I know I'm off the hook!

Mark Cowley

Shoes

Shoes everywhere,
Shoes under the table.
Shoes under the chair.
Shoes everywhere.

Big ones, small ones,
High ones, low ones,
Shoes everywhere.

Black, and blue, white and brown ones,
shoes everywhere.

Shoes under the bed,
Shoes in the wardrobe,
Shoes everywhere,
All waiting to be filled by busy feet.

Elizabeth Wilkinson

Is Love

Is love what we all think it is?
Is love what makes us complete?
Is love the beginning of our lives?
Is love what makes us feel happy?
Is love what we live to look for?
Or do we live to be filled with
love inside ourselves.

Suzie McKeown

Grecian Goddess

Eyes azure-blue
contact mine from the sculptured
delicate and full face under
immaculate curls
that embrace dark Athenian virtue
loosely
softly projecting
understanding love
to all that intersect
that sector of her
art
her home
opened to Pegasus
who browses there
taking strength from her soft
suffusing
presence
of dark brows and smiling
oval opulent
eyes that
trap
my soul

Charles H. Muller

The World of Silent

Every day I feel alone
In the world of silent
For I cannot hear
Little children sing
And many other things.

I fell into the world of silent,
And I feel the pain
Because I used to hear
Sweet music in my ears
And many other things.

But I am not alone
There are people all over the world,
In the world of silent,
And we are not alone
For there is the world of Darkness
And many other things.

Michael Corcoran

The Tooth Fairy

When your tooth falls out
you panic and shout.
Your mum says wait till late tonight
when the tooth fairy is about,
but if you stay awake till late
I bet you'll see your mum slip in.
You ask her why she did come in,
she says to see that you are in.
So off to sleep you did go
to wake and find your tooth had gone
instead you find a big five pound.

Terri-Anne Williams

One May Afternoon Birdsong

As I walked along
Each little songster
Sang his song,
Each different yet
All blending in.
No sweeter sound
Will ever be heard
Than the orchestra
Of the birds.
Hear in each pure
Rounded note,
Coming from soft feathered throats,
Singing out with joy in May
Like Vespers at the close of day.

Peggy Oliver-Rayfield

Spring

The sun is shining all around.
Glorious rays are reaching down.
To the cool soft ground, gently
warming it as the day goes on.
Seeds and plants are being to sprout
reaching through the ground, finding
their way out.

Flowers gently unfold to reveal
the secrets of the colour that
they behold.

Birds are singing their own little
songs letting the world know that
spring has begun.

Animals awaken and come out
to play, all to enjoy this glorious
spring Day.

T. S. Pratt

That's Life

I'd like to be an actress
Because acting's very fine.
It must be great to watch and wait
And not too soon and not too late,
To take your cue in practiced state
And come in with your line.
In perfect period costume
I would strut upon the stage
A gesture here, perhaps a tear,
For tragedy or yet a leer
My voice the gallery would hear—
I would be quite the rage.

So dreams of fame pursue me
While I earn my daily bread.
An office stool's my drama school
A shorthand book my script. It's cruel
"There goes another stage-struck fool"
Yesterday someone said.

Winifred Robi

Untitled

When someone loses life so young
It's hard to comprehend
Especially when they're family
your wife your mum your friend
You sit there in the aftermath
and ask for reasons why
but the answer to that question
Is we know not who nor why
They say that time will ease your pain
this may not be a lie
but all you find at this stage now
Is time is passing by
Your pain is there still growing
eating at you day by day
Your loneliness and anger
taking over each new day
But please don't sit there stewing
because your pain is shared by all
I know it's not the same as yours
but please just make that call.

Julie Wilkins

Afternoon Sun

The scent of sun-lotion
Slides through the air
And reminds me
Of a moment in time . . .
When the sensual massage
Of lotion on my body,
By my mother,
Was proof of her love
Protecting my skin!

Michelle Ruse

Florets

When making love to marigold
Or consorting with sweet pea
Taking ivy off the wall while
  courting rosemary
Making eyes at myrtle, throwing
  a kiss at clover
Drinking from a buttercup
Having a wild-thyme lover
Forget me not, said Alison
And watch the ladies' tresses
Buy me a coral necklace
We'll feed on water-cresses
Well known for her 'honesty'
'Eye Bright' and 'Maiden pink'
She couldn't give a 'Fig wort'
What 'Hare-bell' and 'Herb-Robert'
  Think.

William Robinson

Bird of the Night

He renders his uninterrupted song
In the stillness of the night,
The little bird perches on the wall
The moon above shines bright.
No breeze to rustle in the trees
Or windswept leaves strewn about,
Just a lonely figure in his solitude
Feeling that love, has missed him out.
A silhouette against the evening sky
His song is of love unknown,
Oblivious that time is passing him by
Yearning for a miracle to come.
Then out of the shadows from beyond
Appears a tiny form, timid and shy,
He bobs up and down with sheer delight
So gently to his side she flys.
Now it's two silhouettes in the night
His song is ended, he is not alone,
They both lift and span their wings
Melt into the darkness and are gone.

Virginia J. Humphrey

I Love You

I've loved you since first we met
When you looked at me and smiled
My heart beat oh so fast
I felt I was on trial
T'was then you turned and kissed me
My head was in a whirl
You asked me oh so tenderly
If I would be your girl
With my heart all a flutter
I simply answered yes
Then I fell into your arms
And your warm caress
I long to tell you how I feel
But words fail me my dear
All I know is I love you so
And always want you near

Joyce Slowley

Grand-Daughter

Among the pastel sheets and frills
A tiny baby lay
So serene in dreamless sleep
She slept by night and day.
A darling little angel
Who one and all adored
Designed to dress in pink and white
With ribbons all adorned.

Alas, the dream of pink and white
Did not materialize.
This tom-boy who we love so well
Is an angel in disguise!

Marion Olley

The Mutiny

On a battered sailing ship
On a stormy sea,
There is a crew eagerly gazing
For any land that they might see.
The Captain said, "I'm bored of
Awful grog and salted meat
And frankly, I'm sick of
Sleeping on a wooden bed
And the ship beneath my feet."
The crew, who by now,
Were not such a merry band
Were nearly driven to mutiny
With weapons in their hands.
And then the Captain started a fight
And is now buried and dead.
The crew had shown a lack of respect
And grown an oak tree over his head.

Robert Old

Sunrise

I cannot take my Eyes off You
You are so Beautiful
Your magnificent yellow Light
Transforms the Water and the Sky
Into a stunning Sight
It bewitches my Mind
You are a gift from God
You are a Jewel of the purest
Gold

Peggy Dilks

Friends

Saying good-bye is as hard as hello,
For finding a true friend,
Is as hard as letting one go.

Kieta Papier

The Cave

Drip, drop
Dark, deceiving

Cavernous, creepy,
Clinging and cold

Looking and listening
Limestone, no light

Water a winding
Wet everywhere

Stalagmites, stalactites
Standing in shadow

Frightening, fantastic
Those underground falls.

Eunice Birch

To Hell and Back

I have been to hell and back
Lain on its barren shore
Wandered through its lonely hills
Heard its mighty roar
I have been to hell and back
Seen pain and suffering there
Climbed its lonely mountains
Seen its treasures rare
I have been to hell and back
For my heart's desire
Searching for it everywhere
Each long lonely hour
I have been to hell and back
In penance for my crime
Loving you too dearly
Once upon a time.

E. Hollis

Tears of Love

Tears of fear and pain,
The bruises do not count,
You hear your parents arguing,
All you want is out.

The pain stays inside,
No shoulder to cry on,
You hear your parents arguing,
Now he's beating mum.

He needs a drink,
He's in a mood,
You hear your parents arguing,
Now he's beating you.

The love you felt,
Turns fast to hate,
You hear your parents arguing,
The slamming of the gate.

You're all alone,
Your Mum has gone,
You cannot hear the arguing,
He knows that he has won.

Amanda Lord

My Wife

My darling wife I love you so
I'm sorry that I had to go
And every second we're apart
Tears into my breaking heart
If I could have my life again
The girl I'd marry would be the same
Through my darkest day and night
I saw your face then it was light
So smile the way I know you can
As I thank God that I'm your man
And when at last we're back together
I know that it will be forever.

Neal Garner

First Kiss

Softly sinking into.
Falling but never landing.
Held by the feathers surrounding you.
Inside comes tumbling down
as the outside fades.
Once strong feet
become unsteady as newborn.
Uncertain hands
develop confidence unknown.
Slip into the cooling seas,
holding the fire in your hands.

And you know you have arrived
to the place you always searched for
but had never known the search.
To the place you instantly belong.
Discovered in that first kiss.

Elizabeth Hall

Clouds

Wandering a path of tranquility
Such elegance, such grace
A spectator of the world
Embracing mankind with radiance
Caressing the atmosphere in movement
Constantly restless, yet still
To stare in enchanting
A visionary embellishment
Exhilarates a soul
So calm, so free
Exempt from fear
Unbounded in flight
A jubilant impression
Profound within itself.

Tracey Watts

Water

World within our world
Surrounding fish and plant life
In the oceans blue

Paul Christopher Holland

The Moment Is Now!

There is no past.
There is no future.
The moment is now.
The time is now!

Make your decision,
Act with precision.
Use not your mind,
But your intuition.

Do you feel it's right?
What does your heart tell you!
Act right now,
Create your future,
By your present moment.

Give yourself a new name!
You can do anything,
Be anybody
You are the creator,
And the creature,
Of your reality!

F. D. Kaye

Shona Holly

My daughter beloved,
Is waiting with joy,
What will it be,
A girl, or a boy.

Her husband so patient,
Waiting anxiously by,
Getting excited,
Now the time's almost nigh.

The miracle of birth,
Will be theirs to behold,
That treasured moment,
More precious than gold.

It's a girl! It's a girl!
Is the triumphant cry,
A baby so perfect,
We all breathe a sigh.

May God in his heaven,
Look down from above,
And touch this little baby,
With his wondrous love.

Cynthia A. Poole

Darkness

It's dark
It's very dark inside me
I can't see anything
even with my eyes wide-open

Why let myself be embraced
by this darkness
that torments and crushes me?
Yes . . . I know..
I let my life goes on and on
  without thinking
  not want to think . . .
It's easier . . . much easier
and here I am
not knowing where I really stand.

Now? . . . Now I can't see anything
even with my eyes wide-open

Till when?

Nuno M. Pereira

Holiday-Time Sea

As I ran towards the
wide open
holiday-time
sea,
children played
on the edge of
paradise
and the whole
of life was in
a grain of
sand.

Only the empty
shells
lay skeleton bare
in the
sun,
As I ran towards the
wide open
holiday-time
sea.

Josephine Thomas

Ghost

A disturbed soul cannot escape,
And is trapped in a dimension,
It's neither here, It's neither there,
can't seek its destination.

Melanie Hazzard

The Hand That Rocks the Cradle

A gentle hand, my mother's hand
A tender pair
Both pair of hands
Rocking me as a baby
Thrashing me as a child
Strengthening me to maturity.

My mother's hands
So firm and hard
Rebuking me when I am bad
Protecting me when I am lost
Providing for me when I am in need
My mother's hand
So free to give.

A faultless hand
That care for the child
A wonderful hand
To hold and feed me
The child so secure
In the palm of the hand
The mother's hand so strong and good.

Derin Aderemi

When I've Gone

Think of me with laughter
Think of me and smile
Think of all the funny things
We did all the while

The happy times at Christmas
The holidays we had
Remember what you meant to me
And how I loved your Dad

But if when I have left you
The tears begin to fall
Then please my loves I beg you
Don't think of me at all

For I hope I've left a legacy
Of love and hope and fun
And if I have succeeded
Then my work is truly done

Hazel Sturmey

Afraid of Dying

I'm afraid of dying.
Please don't let me die.
I can't help it, but I'm afraid.
I'm so so afraid.
Scared to leave my family.
Scared to leave my friends.
Scared to leave this world.
Scared to leave everything.
I'm scared.
Please don't let me die.
When I die
I don't want to die painfully,
Please don't let me die painfully.

Now I think of it,
When I die I'll be with God.
I'll be with the Angels.
Flying up above.
But still I'm afraid of dying.
I'm still afraid.

Nicola McBride

Black on Grey

A slow process
This metamorphosis
Lingering desire
As a cooling fire
Fights the slow death
Of the flame.
You became
Much more acceptable,
Far less susceptible
To young limbs
Velvet coated, glistening
In the evening rain,
Slim necks adorned with pearls

Poisoned peppermints of pain.

Gerardine Meany

Werewolf

He stands upon the moonrock,
In the darkness of the night.
As he looks with his mighty strength,
You'll see his snowy white fur glisten
In the moonlight.
Your heart will pound with fear,
To see his every moment,
Of lively life.
Sounds of his wolf pack will haunt you,
With a howl.
Don't get too near him,
Or he might start to growl.

Jenna Jones

Burning-Heart

I would rather die by
   the warmth of Satan,
Than to never had the
   chance of tasting thy love,
For on a tempest tossed sea
   the cruelty of the tides,
Could never ever stop,
   my hunger,
   my strength
      my love of thee.
Give'st thyself to mine arms
   lest we ne'er meet again,
No me're mortals cruelty
   or fire pained torture
      can'st,
Ever hurt my being
   my love is't
so-strong,
Burning-heart
   I love'st only thee.

Peter Keogh

The Drum

I have heard so many times, of late,
the beating of a drum,
That steady beat, that tells you,
of a battle, soon to come.

It is the drum of courage, that a
fighter knows so well,
The sound, that bids you to be brave,
when fortune turns away.

It makes your heart beat faster,
and the blood surge through your
veins,
Prepares you for the battle, the
suffering, and the pain.

The drum is beating faster, for the
time has come, you see,
To fight the battle of your life,
and end, in victory.

J. J. Clare

The Backstreets

Listen, no more silence,
A heartbeat in the night,
As I lay my body next to yours,
Our spirit shines a light,
For we are one, our secrets shared.
We touch, we love, we need,
Our love is based on friendship, trust,
Neither on take nor greed.
As I hold you close, I know
That we are stronger than we seem.
No more light can blind us,
Not one solitary beam.
Come, my lonely backstreet boy,
Warm your hands in mine,
Let me cradle you in my soul,
Let our love-lights shine.
Come with me to special place,
Where I know your heart will sing,
You maybe just a backstreet boy,
But to me, you're everything.

M. Southern

Betrayal

On the edge of my soul
you sit,
turning my rainbow dreams
into images of disbelief
at your betrayal.

Deep inside my consciousness
you enter,
putting into focus
my vision of you, committing
acts of deceit.

Playing with my reason
you suppose,
that while you celebrate
your new found love, I will survive
the break up.

Amna McCoska

My Dream

I turned to walk across the floor
Engulfed in work and plans of more,
And there she stood as in my dreams,
An angels face so pure, serene.
In my stride I stopped and faltered,
It was as always, nothing altered
A lonely vision all aglow.
Can she stay? She must not go!
I'll love her, dear God, all my life,
Please make us one, a man and wife.

William S. Winborn

Tiger

The tiger is a hunter,
He's a fire in the forest,
Which is the forest of the night—
Angry and alert,
Is this fire in the forest,
Its eyes burning so bright.

The tiger is a savage,
Golden eyes in the fire,
Sweet mammal flesh is what he craves—
Animals fleeing,
From this fire in the forest,
Some, engulfed by the flames.

The tiger is endangered,
By the man of the forest,
Stumbling, wounded, here about—
Dragged away,
Is the fire in the forest.
Fire will soon die out!

Katie Hawkins (Age 10)

Living with the Enemy

I wake up from my slumbers
I wonder oh! What's wrong
As usual it's the same thing
It just goes on and on
It runs throughout my spine
I start to cry oh no!
It travels up and travels down
How I pray that it will go
I say to myself ignore it
I hope I'll be that strong
But it keeps grinding out its message
It keeps howling out its song
This is my daily nightmare
It's my unnatural routine
How I wish that I will wake up
And it will all have been a dream
But for those who are oblivious
For those who do not know
It's pain, pure pain I live with
My enemy, my hell on earth below.

Patrick Brady

Winter Is Over

A young Robin has gone
He has been in my garden
Feeding from the lawn
I gave him crumbs
He chirrups something at me
I expect he said Cherrie
I will be back you'll see

E. R Allcock

Close My Eyes

Whatever comes into my mind
I shut it out and leave behind,
And start another day anew,
The trouble is I think of you,
The things I think,
The things I feel,
It doesn't matter my minds reels
I close my eyes and shut it out
Whatever is this day about!
The wind it blows,
The day is cold,
Somehow it makes me very old.
I'm like a leaf upon a tree,
But I can't drop and blow away,
How I wish the sun would shine,
But no! The wind it always whines,
Whatever is this day about,
I close my eyes and shut it out.

Carol Anne Stokes

A Peaceful Abiding Place

A Paradise God made the earth
A place where peace should dwell
But man has turned aside from God
   And from God's favour fell.
From Adam, down to men today.
Their own thing they must do
So when we look around this earth
It's not a pretty view.
Instead of peace, we have turmoil.
Not much love, but hate
Very soon God has a time
When he will put matters straight
Then everyone will live in peace
People of every race
When the earth becomes
A peaceful abiding place

Janet Belton

There Can Be No Other Mother

A smile touched upon her face
In that moment she was gone
A love I can never replace
Never again seeing another dawn
But death is not the end
Her love continues to live on
When I feel my heart will never mend
I feel her there keeping me strong
Wherever she may be
I can feel the warmth of her touch
Always here with me
I loved her so very much
The love she gave me from the start
Lives on always in my heart

Michelle McCusker

The Imitation

The curving of the bark
With each intimate detail inscribed
Continuous yet changing
With every second glance.

Branches sprouting,
Curling like a handicapped figure
Winding, rough to view
Yet elegant in every way.

And at the sorry end
Of each contorted arm
There is an old life rotting
And a new life starting.

The tree is an imitation
Tall, powerful, overwhelming,
Similar to the one we know
As the man above.

Orlagh Brogan

Peace

There once lived a gardener,
   a grower of roses,
A man with ambition,
   to a grow a fine rose.

War shattered the quietness,
   his country was ravaged,
His loved ones were scattered,
   his garden grew food.

But on one small patch,
   flourished embryo bushes,
And through the drear years,
   his project dreamed on.

At last the Great Day came,
   The horrors were over,
His hopes found fruition,
   The "Peace" rose was born.

Frances Mary Pelling

Thoughts

No bed have we to sleep in
No one to love or care
A doorway or a cardboard box
in the freezing cold night air

The shelters are full of people
Looking for a place to stay
It's raining and it's freezing
No room for us today

We are homeless this we know
We wish we had some place to go
Someone to love us
Someone to care
We hope there will be someone
Somewhere.

K. Longshaw

Absent Friends

If only you could see me,
As I go through each new day,
As through my tears I thank you,
For the love in life you gave.
If only you could hear me as I
Say a heartfelt prayer.
I feel that you are with me,
As though you're always there.
If only I could thank you for the
Lovely times we had, the memories
So wonderful, none of the times
Were bad. If only you could hold me,
As you did so long ago.
Throughout my years as a child,
You loved to watch me grow.
If only then time would stand still
And leave you here with me.
My love would be for you always,
Not just your memory.

Stephen John Griffths

Summer Rain

Placid as it falls
manna from above
raw, untouched
feeding Earth,
mother to child

Seeping to every
overlooked part
christening the first
early morning bud

Leaves bow as they
weep prisms of colour
from their jewelled tips
drop by drop by drop

Held in an uncontrollable cliche'
I stand high as
it purifies my mind
and soothes my soul
now I see through
clear eyes
the world at my feet

Lucy Protheroe

Spell It Out

Cute like a golden Labrador
Old like animals in the wild
Masculine as a heavyweight boxer
Puny like an underfed child
Underneath the soils of the earth
Tiny creatures live and crawl
Everything in this world is
   different
Remaining a land for all.

Mark Cole

Dogs

Dogs bite and growl and bark and snap,
They always like to have a nap,
But then again they're always there,
To give a hug and show they care.

Jemma May Finnie

The Car in the Mist

The sound was thumping
like drums in my ears,
"like drums, like drums".

The lights were coming
so close and so clear
"so close, so close".

The darkness was falling
so deep in the air,
"so deep, so deep".

Trying to run was so bare,
it was like the mist caught me,
holding me, "holding me",
waiting to wing me away, "away"

The brakes screeched like a flare,
"a flare",
nothing could be done though
I was left as a spare, "a spare".

Donna Calder

Searching

Upon the wall stood a mirror
With a crowd around it.
Each looked in and saw nothing

The last didn't need to look in
He already knew what he'd see—
A face, a heart, a soul

He didn't need a mirror to find this
He knew the others had seen
a pretty face and a cute smile
But they hadn't really looked.

Amy Archer

Infinite Love

Enticing, yearning power,
Cupid's almighty dart inflicts,
Piercing a solitary heart.
Buried deep in a soul,
An intimate bond,
No time nor distance will dare part,
The boiling blood of love, of hatred,
Seeking warmth in a lonely heart,
Passionate love,
A raging fire,
Smouldering embers,
Burning desire,
Infinite love,
Remains but a dream . . .

Rachel Neal

Untitled

There is nothing
When, I open my eyes,
Heaven has gone,
I cannot touch the skies.

And down our street,
An old lady cries
For the beautiful world,
In its shattered disguise.

Where is he now?
A saviour to put things right.
Someone who can save the human race?
Not quite.

Emily Marlow

Horse of My Dreams

Horse of my dreams
with mane and tail a golden brown,
Silken coat alight in the sun,
nose a-flaring, ears upright,
oh horse of my dreams
if only it were true!

I gallop the beach,
I ride the wind
Sea spray in my face,
it's heaven on earth.
She's my horse, my golden dream,
oh horse of my dream,
if only it were true!

Selena Kural

Life

It's time for me to wake from sleep
I rise and kiss her on the cheek
Monday morning weekend's over
It won't be long though for another

We eat and drink and talk and love
We hope and prey to God above
That dreams we have one day come true
Just one that's all for me and you
Until this fantasy arrives
We'll carry on with our everyday lives

Working shopping giving taking
Building on our future making
Running walking laughing crying
No one can ever stop us trying

Life's short and sweet until it's sour
It's precious like petals on a flower
Each petal represents a season
In our life and gives us reason
To carry on and appreciate
All that we've achieved to date

Michael Bodman

Memories of Christmas Past

Christmas, and our tree was bright
   with ornaments a glowing.
We sat beside the fire
   my Mother's memories overflowing.

She remembered all those years ago
   the little house with love in,
Mother, Father, Sisters too
   on Christmas Eve awaiting.
On Christmas morn she crept downstairs,
   Oh! The glory of it.
A Christmas tree with berries bright,
   A Holly crown upon it.
No ornaments adorned the tree,
   here and there were seen
A Chocolate Watch, a Sugar Mouse,
   amongst the leaves so green.
Many years have passed away,
   Still, I think on Christmas day
of that little girl in days gone by,
   And find a tear drop in my eye.

F. E. Todd

Untitled

Love is like a flower bud.
Day by day it grows.
A petal here a petal there.
Until the whole bloom shows.
Never cut the stem.
You will loose the gem.
The beauty can not come back again.
So treasure your love.
Just like a flower bud.

Sandra Frost

Out of Isolation

Slip gently,
Fall so deep
Into a safe and secure
Everlasting sleep.

To peace in a land
Where only flowers grow,
Now, to be there
You're much happier, we know.

Life's now no struggle
To your mind, there's no tease,
So rest gently now
Take things with ease.

Your presence is with us
So strong and kind,
The path that will rejoin us
Soon someday, we will find.

You will burn forever
In our hearts so dear,
Your spirits now within us,
That strength, we will always bear.
   A friend

Christopher Woodhouse

Conservation

What could exceed the charms of Earth
Where else is there such place
No heaven above could ere surpass
Nowhere in Outer Space

We sing of Heaven's Golden Gates
In hymns of yesteryear
Why go to Heaven—for golden gates
When we have them—right here

This Planet Earth must surely be—
A Paradise—a Haven
That man is seeking to destroy
What God to us has given

The beauty of the sea and sky
The flowers, the fields—the trees
What other place in Outer Space
Can offer all of these

God gave us time on earth to spend
Let's put it to good use
And preserve Nature—for all time
For others—after us

Frederick Boulton

Curiosity and the Modern Cat

Of all of heaven's spheres
It seems is made but one
To hold the cogitating part
Of all that God has done.

In equipoise depends
This thoughtful ball of deeds.
Can the starry space around
Absorb its noisy needs?

Understanding's window!
This lonely mirror made
To roll among the senseless orbs
Makes galaxies afraid.

Mankind's cerebellum
Sees no forbidden gates
Gainst surge of all his head reflects
Which tools to acts translate.

Will he live and prosper?
Or suffer like the cat
When all nine lives of science end
And the firmament fights back?

Crispin John Elliott

Love's Own Grace

O, I, Too, would like our
   world a safe and better
place by love's own grace.
O, I, Too, would like, Till,
   morn, Till night, hearts
filled with love and joy and
peace, to build a stairway
to the stars making each step
day by day, with faith love
and truth. Till reaching the
pure eternal light with marked
degree not forgetting humanity.
O, I, Too, would like to see
children playing in safety a
miracle done by wisdom from
a greater power putting things
to right, so we could all live
in happiness and peace letting
pain and poverty and battles
cease.

Lorna Penter

Hours

The clock which measures me
stopped at your hour.

The shout suffering from desert
breaks the stillness.

The silence
begins to speak.

Hourglass of tears
second over second.

I stop you at my hour
after I get over my wrinkle.

Mares Violeta-Mirela

Vade Mecum

For Caroline Carter,
written in a copy of Garden Poems

In a garden green and shining,
Among rich flowers, red and white,
Man began, the earliest gardener,
Who lived by still and deathless light.

On the lawn the dial's finger
Tells us that our days must run,
That we shadows never linger
Below the chariot of the sun.

Take this book upon your journey
Under the sun and through the showers,
And may it help, in dark and bright,
To bless your visionary hours!

Margaret J. Howell

The Magic of Daybreak

Have you seen the break of dawn,
When the sun-kissed dew, comes alive?
Each tiny, coloured jewel,
Seems to dance and thrive.

A myriad of sparkling lights,
Green or red or blue,
Crystals, spawned, in the night,
Born, as the sun shines through.

For timeless moments, they shimmer
On the grass, before my gaze,
Exquisite, in their purity.
In the early morning, haze,
But—as the sun grows stronger,
So, those dewdrops—dried.
The grass is stilled and green again,
Those twinkling lights, have died.

Evelyn Mary Eagle

Liverpool Child

I walked down to the Docks today
By way of Windsor Street.
With wary steps I made my way
My memories incomplete.
The Windsor Street I once knew well,
Not only changed but gone!
Meandering piles of rubble there
My past beneath the stone.
The Liver Buildings still stand there
The Mersey at their feet.
And echoes of the Beatles
Resound in every street
But, where now your magnificence
Oh, city of the Scouse?
No trace of any opulence
Where Deprivation grows.
Yet, someday, soon, Fair City,
Cathedral bells will ring
On new days filled with promise
And the Liver Birds will sing.

Patricia Winstanley

Star

Small, bright, silver light,
On a blanket of darkness,
Shining light of peace.

Claire M. Izon

Exams

Exam papers
Come in
Anxious, exciting
Turn out
To nothing
Only clock's hands
Keep moving

At last
Faces out
With satisfaction

Suddenly
Heavy rains
Down pouring
All feet
Return in
Glances exchanging
Another exam

Hong Zhou

Rock Bottom

There comes a time when all seems lost,
"Rock Bottom" hovers in sight,
But hold on fast until the last,
You may not lose the fight.

A joker hides in every pack
To bring a twist in fate,
Redundancy is now on track,
Another path to take.

"Rock Bottom" only means one thing,
A hard base stops one falling.
From there, just take a mighty spring
To find another calling.

"Rock Bottom" shows a side of life
Where one can learn to see
How others live amidst the strife,
And yet still hopeful be.

So take "Rock Bottom" in its stride,
Another day will dawn
In time to take some other ride
Across a greener lawn.

Russella Garner

The Snowman

S is for the snow that falls
No-one can ever hear
Out there children playing
Winter games are here
Many children gather
All the snow on the ground
Nice and fat, big and round
   a snowman they
   have found.

Roísin Hamill

Spring

One morning I awoke
And I became aware
Spring was in the air.
Catkins burst from pussey willow,
Crocuses in blue and yellow,
The first signs were there.

That morning with the dawn
Hope became reborn.
Singing birds in budding trees,
Baby chicks, busy bees,
Lambs newborn, growing corn,
Ponds awakening with frog spawn.

That morning I awoke
And thought of cowslips seen
In fields of lush May green.
Of bluebell woods and blackbirds cry
And rainbows circled in the sky.
Of life renewed, of hope reborn.
To me spring came that morn..

Joan Leach

Carpe Diem

Seize the moment,
Seize the day,
Sidetrack not,
Nor lose your way.

Strive for greatness
Do not rest,
Life's too short
For second best.

Squandered seconds
Don't return;
Live the passions
Let them burn.

Brave the heartache
Fight the tears,
You'll grow stronger
Through the years.

Search out truth
And do not lie,
One less minute
'Till we die

Naomi Faulkner

Why

You never said good-bye to me,
The day you went away,
I never knew it was good-bye,
The day you went away.
The sun still shines,
The rain still falls,
The clouds, they still roll by,
But I really never notice them
As I sit and wonder why.
Why did you go, so suddenly,
It's not for me to say,
But oh, my dear, I've missed you so,
Since the day you went away.

M. Pryor

"Friendship"

Friendship is a priceless gift,
That can't be bought or sold.
But its value is far greater.
Than a mountain made of gold.
For gold is cold and lifeless,
it can neither see nor hear.
And in times of trouble.
It is powerless to cheer.
It has no ears to listen,
No heart to understand.
It cannot bring you comfort,
or reach out a helping hand.
So when you ask God for a gift,
be thankful if he sends
No silver, gold or riches,
but the love of real, true friends!

Anthony Keith Ward

When I Was a Little Girl

When I was a little girl,
my age, I'd just turned four,
my mother said "goodbye" to me,
went out and shut the door.
I was staying with my Gran,
the rain was pouring down,
my mother caught the local bus,
and travelled into town.

Now I protested loudly,
I wanted Mother back,
I screamed and cried, then Gran came up
and gave my leg a smack!
"Oh Gran you've really broke my leg,
I'll have to tell my mother"
Gran said "if you don't shut up,
I'll come and break the other".

Jane Molloy

Underwater Love

I wish
I could take your soul
in my hands
to feel your sufferings,
to feel your smiles,
and then,
to tie you up
with endless grass strings,
to mould you in tears,
to hang them up
under my eyelids,
and side by side
we'll cry together
until the sea
will underwater us
forever.

Soica Veronica Alexandra

Passing Years

How much shall I remember
When I am tired and old
What threads of recollection
Will gleam like threads of gold
Upon life's faded fabric
The fabric of the years
Time wears away the colours
The pattern disappears
The things that brought great sorrow
Grow faint and fade away
The hopes the disappointments
The dreams of yesterday
The trails that now I follow
May vanish in the blue
But this will last forever
My memory of you

Doris Vera Howard

Trees in Winter

Twisted dark and bare
the sinister bark
roughens the air

Outstretched fingers claw
eye-sockets hollow
they shelter no more

Thrashed clean unstill
branches cut and thrust
Till winter winds have had their fill.

Martin S. Fox

Ject

Beauty fades,
But faded eyes are blind,
But where exists beauty
If not in the mind?
Classic poetry states
That all beauty is true,
But I have a soul-mate,
And the beauty is you.
Love and beauty.
Pleasure and pain,
Emotional emotions
What's in a name?
Everything changes
Never forget
In forty two years
The time that we met.

James Thorpe

Tortured Soul

He stands back from the crowd, refusing
to get too near, fear of touching his
tortured soul, he struggles alone with
his pain, pushing anyone away, who
tries to heal his pain.
If he comes too near, he fears, he will
be discarded, tortures of humiliation
and pain, so he tortured himself,
bringing his own pain, keeping it
at bay, but always feeding his soul
with pain. The laughter and the
tears he will not share, afraid to
get too near, blinded by fear. Afraid
to reach out and share his pain,
So day by day, month by month and
Year by year, he walks alone, blinded
by fear, afraid to get too near.

Caroline Hanley

Always Near

There is really nothing I can say
To ease the pain you feel today.
Although a new day starts tomorrow
This is going to be full of sorrow.
When we look death in the eye
We always ask the question why.
These is no answer we can find.
This can play tricks with your mind.
The wound we have goes so deep
All we want to do is weep.
We cry all night and then all day.
But this thing just won't go away.
They say in time we will heal.
We can not believe this is real.
But as the years roll on by
You will learn not to cry.
With the memories you hold so dear
You know they will always be near.
and you know it is so true
Their spirit lives on inside you

Paul Wilson

Cockney Sparrow

I am a Cockney Sparrow
And that I won't deny
When we talk to each other
I'll look you in the eye
We have no airs and graces
Honest and decent are we
We do not pronounce our H's
Or invite the vicar for tea.
Some move to a foreign island
That's not the place for me.
I'll stay in the east end of London
Co's that's where I want to be
When my life is done
And the good Lord calls to me
Come up my cockney sparrow
I need your company
Come up here and join us
My golden angels and me

Barbara Patten

A New Era of Hope

Tony Blair, you've been elected
Now you know what you must do
Rid our country of this sickness
We've put all our faith in you
We, your people, must have patience
Together we can see it through
And we'll find a better Britain
With God's help and hopes anew

M. Rodda

Being Different

Sometimes I wish
I wish I were different
Not who I am
And not who they think I am
But when night time comes
And I drift off to sleep
I realise I'm special
because I am different
Everyone is special
because everyone is different
so appreciate yourself
It's what you deserve.

Sarah Crawshaw

Finding Out the Truth

You hurt me like no other could
You took away my life
The sparkle lost in a veil of black
Entombed there for eternity

I thought I gave you all I had
I thought you felt the same
Instead I discover you're not destiny
You're part fantasy, part hope

Shattered hopes and dreams abound
Cascades of tear filled droplets
The sparkle lost in a veil of black
Entombed there for all eternity

Deborah Beazer

A Rose

In the beginning, little buds are seen
Surrounded, by leaves of green
Those prickly thorns, one can forgive
Because, they help the flower to live
They bloom, in colours, pale, or bright
Giving us all, so much delight
Its perfume so sweet and gentle
A token of love, so sentimental
Soon petals fall, this flower goes
Leaving us memories of a rose

Merril Morgan

Untitled

Time for bed, another night,
Tucked up comfortable,
Tucked up tight,

Pillow underneath my head,
Blanket all over me and ted.
Mummy comes and tucks me in
Turns out the light and says
Good night.

Then off to dreamland I will go
To dream of sweets and other things
And wonder what the morning brings.

Amanda Hampson

The Darkest Cloud

The volcano of life erupting
Colour, melting in a coition of flame
Petrified forms———revolting!
Cascading to a lunar plain.
Bubbles of breath bursting
Slaking, no blood to stain.
No echo———silence!
This earth the same.

Victor Tucker

Peace of God

I searched for peace in lonely wood,
  For peace in quiet field,
But nature gave no solitude
  To which my soul could yield

My footsteps turned to city streets
  Vibrant with people power,
Where solid, strong a grey church stood
  With rising, reaching tower

A tower with pointed spire that soared
  To pierce heaven's endless vault,
In that vast infinity to find,
  The eternal God men sought.

Beneath that Church's hallowed roof,
  In its stillness and its calm,
I felt an overwhelming love,
  My soul soothed by its balm.

Silently I knelt and knew
  That here my search would cease;
For all my doubts had disappeared,
  I'd found my God, my peace.

Irene Cullis

Remember

Remember when we walked together,
Late, so late last night.
Amongst a sea of mist and cloud,
And then you held me tight.

Remember when you kissed me,
Like stars that kiss the sky.
And then you spoke so lovingly,
While all I did was sigh.

Remember how I missed you,
When you went away.
Remember all the tears,
When I awoke next day.

Remember how I felt,
When I found it wasn't true.
That all our love was fantasy,
I'd never been with you.

Of course you don't remember,
That silent glistening stream,
For you were not there with me,
You were only in my dream.

Kirsty M. Stones

Forest

There I stood just 5 foot high
Beneath those noble trees
Feeling so insignificant
A need to kneel and cry
Here you've stood these many years
Known no sorrow, shed no tears
When mortals fight and fuss and strain
For wordily goods and other gains
You stand aloof and bathed in rain
Ignoring human grief and pain
And yet, you shelter bird and beast
Provide for them from large to least
And I have passed this way
And gazed in rapture at those tall
And lovely trees
And so feel grateful.

E. V. Ware

The Morning Sun

Let the morning sun
  kiss the dew from your petals
Satisfy my soul
  with your delicate scent
Awaken my thoughts with desire
  warming me up for love
Until the end of time
  you'll be there for me
Should God one day
  struck me blind
Your beauty I'll still see
Words are too weak to define
  just what you mean to me

D. Dallner

The Wilderness

There is a cat in me . . .
Soft fur . . .
Sharp teeth . . .
And a very loud purr . . .

There is a lion in me . . .
When I am angry . . .
I roar a big roar . . .
That's me . . .

There is a horse in me . . .
With the wind in my face . . .
Galloping free . . .
In this open space . . .

There is a bee in me . . .
I'm ready to bring . . .
The yummy honey . . .
But watch out, I sting . . .

Katherine Bradbury

Feeling

Sometimes it's joy,
A rush of happiness.
Sometimes it's pain,
When the world is cruel.
Sometimes it's regret.
When the wrong thing is done.
Sometimes it's passion,
A burning desire.
Sometimes it's spite,
If you've been wronged.
Sometimes it's excitement,
At the thought of something new.
Yet all the other times,
There's nothing,
The world has no thrills.
But always remember,
I feel too.

Ruth Mackie

What Is Love?

Love is a very precious gift,
Too often very rare.
Emotions will run deep,
If you show how much you care.
At times it really hurts you,
To show that life's unfair.
But given chance to work,
It's something all can share.
So when your partner's unhappy,
Has pressure too hard to bear,
Comfort, kiss, embrace them,
Show them you are there.

Brian Stevens

Realism

Love loses its sparkle
Flame its flicker
Heart stops beating
And blood runs cold

Oceans to cross
Horizons to see
Dead is the happiness
Which ran through me

Alone in the world
Thoughts nostalgic
Pick up the pieces
And open my eyes

Perhaps in the mist
Lies the turmoil of life
The day and the moment
You hear "be my wife"

Sparkle returns
And flicker too
Heart beats loudly
When he says "I love you"

Jane Kay

Someone Else to Love

They always had each other,
But always something was missed;
Something to complete their lives
And fill their aching hearts.
Now the waiting is over,
Their souls dance wildly on wings,
Plans that were dreams
  Can come true.
After waiting such a long time
Wanting this day so much,
Scared to admit to each other
The hoping suppressed.
Now they feel such emotions
Laughter ringing with tears of joy,
At last they can smile together
On the face of their new baby boy.

Hazel Scully

Coming Home

Coming home one evening
What should I chance to see?
Just one bright star all gleaming white
Shining down on me.
And as I gazed in wonder
Bathed in, its gentle light
My heart seemed to burst asunder
In the quiet of the night
Then turning quickly homeward
Now, on eager feet
Hurrying with happy heart
To the ones I long to greet
Fur turning round the corner
I knew that I should see
The lights of home, where all I love
Are waiting there for me.

Marjorie Romanis

Abandonment

Who is knocking at the door?
Here dwells only me,
Nobody else, so that I could imagine
Someone, except the wind,
Could possibly
Intend to enter.

So, who is knocking at the door?

I measured the distance in time.
What will change if I don't respond?
Even in my own hearing
Isn't my voice strange?

Theo Kalamboukas

Maggie

Baldness exposed her gentle mind.
I was closer to her emotions
When I kissed her head.
She smelt like a baby
Cradle-capped and delicious.

Thin white hair
Fought its way through.
A delicate protective layer
That didn't quite serve its purpose.
And the rays couldn't save her brain.

Shock turned into wonder
As I looked deeper into her eyes.
Ignoring swollen cheeks
And her motionless mouth,
I listened.

I heard and felt her weakness
But strength and bravery
Postponed it, until He,
Left her with no choice
But to sleep, deeper than a baby.

Helen Rosie

The Memory in Me

You're the star in the sky,
You're the face in my tears,
You're the fish in the river
You are the giver

You're the hope in my life,
the one that takes strife,
you're the one that sees all,
you are the one with the crystal ball.

You've the speed of the deers
which run like the wind

You're the memory in me
which will always be within.

Faye Thompson

Secret Wisdom

Yellow leaves of windy autumn
Take away the noisy spectrum
Make the dark shadow terminate
And allow this love to germinate

Loving Goddess of my life
Eternal light of the wise
Angelic host protect my wife
And let the secret on my side

Sailing hard through the sea
Yearning wisdom for you and me
Feeding the everlasting soul
Let the Old man achieve his goal

Moonlight shines through the night
Silent wolf on my right
Wise magician of the white light
Secret wisdom for the chosen one.

Juan Diego Chica

Memory

What should we remember
When a loved one is gone?
  First meetings?
   Past happiness?
  A fleeting smile?

When pain and shock,
Which numbed the senses,
Recede with passing hours,
and feeling comes creeping back.
What do we remember?
  A child going to school!
  A boy growing up!
  A man with a job to do!
  And then—
The cruel sea!

Catherine T. Edwards

Squeeze

Life is malignant
Love is benign,
I am legion
I am home.

Matthew Clemens

Tormented Love

We never kissed, we never held hands
but our eyes met and we knew
each time for a few seconds longer
our hearts knew

Years later I still remember
that love I cannot get over
though I do not know
where you are or where you could be
I love you

Tormenting my mind, that somehow
we will find each other again
would it ever happen, or if
you even think of me
for a second

The tears have slowed, but the
pain in my heart and worst in
my mind, tortures me
when will I be released
how I love you.

S. L. Stephenson

Summer's Choir

A majestic song of summer
Filters through the trees,
The songs of larks and nightingales
Whisper on the breeze.

A gentle tone of melody
Sung softly from above,
A sweet touch of harmony
Was the sound from a dove.

In all earth's many gardens
Woods and meadows too,
Our feathered friends are singing
To bring joy to me and you.

From the chirpy little sparrow
To the blackbird's symphony,
The sound of the feathered orchestra
Plays for you and me.

This enchanting little choir
This beautiful rhapsody,
Is heard throughout the land
Echoing peacefully.

M. Heathcote

Time and Pace

Time passes,
Like a mountain stream.
And rushing by,
Leaves little time to dream.

But caught at times,
in eddies 'neath the falls;
Peaceful; quiet,
Remembers all.

J. G. Flockhart

Spring

Is it Love's magic potion
that has made my heart
beat fast with inexplicable rhythms,
or is it Spring's amorous birds
that shed their angelic feathers
on my head and left me senseless?

What heavenly illusionist
caused the apparition
of a white-clad beauty
with golden swimming hair
and apple-juice tan
roam a fairy-tale dream
which I keep having?

Is it fertile imagination
or the wonder of Spring?

Natalino Attard

Sister across the Sea

My younger sister
Across the miles
Came to see me for a while
I enjoyed her company so much

But never mind I am
Sure I will find
Myself going over for a while

To enjoy the sand sea
And sun
Nothing quite like a
Holiday
Over the miles
To see a sister and
Have some fun.

I. J. Oates

Ode to a Friend Whose Birthday Had Been Forgotten

How sweet and precious is this day,
The sunshine and blue skies,
The gentle breeze the flowers sway,
As God's good world goes by.

From office window do I gaze
Upon grass so neat and green
And here's a robber in brown and gold,
As fine a coat as ever was seen.

The flowers bow at his gentle touch
And gladly give up their treasure
Their nectar sweet he loves to take
And pollen in good measure.

Over the wall the children play,
Released from lessons so hard
Girls with ropes are skipping about
And boys with yells besiege the yard.

This happy scene brings joy to me
But yet my heart is heavy
That I should forget a friend so true
And no birthday wishes send her.

F. J. Muranka

The Wilderness

There is a frog in me
a gribbit and a grunt.
The part that leaps to love,
lives on a lily in the valley,
The wilderness gave this to me,
and will not get torn away.

There is a butterfly in me . . .
The part that makes me flutter around,
lives on a bush in the park,
The wilderness gave this to me,
and I will keep it forever.

There is an owl in me . . . .
A tweet and a twoo,
shows I'm loving all the way through
lives in a barn way up high
The Wilderness gave this to me
And I will not let it go.

Louise Fletcher

Can You Replace a Life?

Can you replace a life?
The suddenly empty expanse,
No longer filled with strife.
His mind not there to dance.

He is not there to talk,
—A sudden vacuum of space.
No longer a partner to walk—
Only a memorized face.

An unwelcome word is death,
Yet the past is not the future.
Although he has no breath—
The thoughts of him mature.

D. S. Yanez

This and That

The war
Keeps knocking at our door,
It starts . . .
Like an argument,
And stops once more.

The murders
Are happening,
They can not be stopped.
A murderer is caught,
And the prison door locked.

The fox . . .
Keeps running,
From the dogs at his heels,
The dogs are on him,
And over he keels.

The babies,
Keep coming,
To those who are too young,
Lives are spoilt,
Because of one night of fun.

Emma O'Keeffe

Doll

I'm a doll
Bubbling and bright
With wide green eyes
Opening in delight
At the sight, sounds and
wonders
Of the passing night
Caught in the pensive
moon
Of the traveller's delight

Catherine Flood

Time and Space

The moon and the stars shine
  so bright tonight.
As I look to the heavens my
Heart feels so light.
My day has been dreary
And when I feel weary.
I look to the stars in their
  blanket of night
It's hard to believe the world
Is a troublesome place.
As I gaze with awe at time and space
And wonder when on earth
There will ever be peace.
As the moon and stars.
Whose wonders never cease.

B. M. Turvey

The Falling of a Dove

Warmth on a callous winter's night,
A hand to hold and squeeze tight.
Friendship to respect and ever share,
Someone there in an hour of despair.
When the world shuts you out blind,
A heart always there to find.
The brightness of the sparkling sky,
A feeling of the need to fly,
The sinking into a work of art,
A decision to never be apart.
Knowing that someone will always care,
Hoping that he will always be there,
The catching of a falling dove,
That's how I will always describe love.

Elizabeth Mortimer

Elizabeth II

This nation loved her as a child
and through her teenage years;
Wedding Bells-in Westminster
brought happiness and tears.

In '52 she left these shores
a happy smiling Princess;
Returning oh so suddenly
in mourning and distress.

We all felt deeply moved
that one so young and slight
be called to lead our country,
sifting wrong from right.

Years have passed—children grown;
with Phillip by her side,
Elizabeth has never failed
to do her job with pride.

So let us all rejoice,
sing and dance with glee;
Thank God that "Lillibet" our queen
has reached her Golden-Anniversary.

Enid E. Ross

A Visit to the Muir Redwood My Whitby

Getting ready to depart
To the place that stone my heart,
On the moors what kind of weather
Just to see the purple heather

The lambs agrazing on the way
Till you see the vast blue sky,
The glittering of the deep blue sea
Just makes a picture full of glee

The happy cries from afar
Tells you that the seagulls are,
Full of life so wild and free
Just to be at my whitby

Betty Turton

Straight Jacket Life

Trying to think of all the things
That I'd said, or I'd done wrong
Should I try and be ashamed
Because I could remember none

Do I try to protect myself
Simply as no-one else will
Can I really be to blame
Of being afraid to kill

Will I never give my all
Now I have been left tender
I must face this on my own
Every time my heart remembers

Gordon Downie

The Age of the Skate

With both feet I did dare
The looks I could not bare
At first I was slow
Then suddenly I would go
Up and down the road
My feet carried the load
How long could I keep this pace
I felt like the winner in the race
Passersby made me blush
My face felt quite flush
At last this was my dream
I was like the cat who got the cream
My skates were my new toy

Helen Nelson

Nevermore

Give me a field of poppies red
Beneath a sky of dazzling blue
Where I may relive my memories
Of those days I shared with you.

During that long hot summer
We loved and laughed and played
There was no future for us
We just lived from day to day.

Nevermore down leafy lanes
Nor through green fields will we roam
For you lie in a churchyard grave
And I am now all alone.

Lillian Rose

Re-Source

What's in a word, a sentence?
What's in a lifetime of goodbyes.

Words take all the power,
while silence hangs,
transpitory, in the air.

Dissipating into the eloquence
of your smile,
bidding farewell to every moment.

Holding still while, (in my memory)
a picture frames
scenes of the present,
as in the past.

Maybe we dream this life
inside our tombs.
The body like a mound, wearies
exposed to the elements,

air and wind, fire and water,
slowly fading into the earth,
no longer a stranger

and those who have come and gone,
will one day return.

Ruvina De-Alwis

A Child's View

A child needs guidance
with love and care,
a security of knowing
who they love,
will always be there.
A kiss and a cuddle
is all that it takes,
to make a child happy
Don't make mistakes!
Praise them and love them
in all that they do
And they'll always remember
your kindness,
when they think of you.

Ann Bradbury

My Very Own Best Friend

What shall I do without you
No more chatty chats
Laughing at everything we could
Anything—this and that.

You had so much love to give me
And received it in return
Not to have you near
Will be very hard to learn.

But you did not suffer at the end
And that's as it should be
For the dearest, kindest step-dad
And my very own best friend.

Margaret Cloke

To the Hale-Bopp Comet

As you glide through the sky
with your body of fire
and your tail of light

Do you ever think of those below
who stare at your beauty
and wish they were you

So that people could admire them
just for once in their short lives
then they too could disappear
and be just a memory

So oh mighty comet
grace this planet with your presence
so that we have the chance to gaze upon
your beauty and mystery

Before we do as you do
and disappear into infinity.

Terence Cussens

Snowdonia

Snowdonia, land of placid lakes
And slopes that sometimes kill
When bold and foolish folk do stray
Unheedingly at will,
In disregard of perils which
Abound on every hill.

Snowdonia, haunt of eagles once
Its snow-capped peaks arise
Through folds of clouds low-lying
And ever mournful cries
Of forlorn winds that lonely roam
'Neath ever-changing skies.

Snowdonia, your majesty
Reigns o'er my Welsh domain;
As long as Father Time permits
I'll come to you again,
For, in your bosom, when I'm gone
My soul will still remain.

J. Lewis Jones

The Memories

The silence of the wind
blows cold against my cheek
As I walk along the countryside
my eyes begin to weep.
There is no peace or harmony
no calm or thoughtful times.
The memories of happiness
are now destroyed in my mind.

The promises were broken
and then the prayers ignored
Those things were taken from me
things I could not afford
Yet sometimes in the sunlight
a vision comes to me.
To keep old memories warm and fresh
and set the new ones free.

Jacinta Houghton

A Plaint

With broken bones and broken hearts,
And flaws in all the vital parts,
The human lot is not so bright
With slow decay by day and night.
So, as I limp around the house,
I feel entitled to this grouse,
Why didn't He precaution take
To build us so we wouldn't break?

G. E. M. Broomhead

Elevation

The man is the mountain,
Mountain the man,
There is life on the mountain,
Life in the man.

The sides of the mountain
Life doth sustain,
The top of the mountain
Man's ultimate gain.

The gain of the summit,
Eve of the dawn.
Short pause on the summit,
Man's life out-drawn.

In the ether around,
Spirits "crescent",
Man's spirit flies outward,
The body doth bend.

Zechariah Moore

Blue Beneath

Come crashing waves
Upon the shore
And wash me out
To sea once more;
The raging tide,
The whispered foam,
The tranquil depths
That are my home . . .

Come, distant ships
Upon the sea;
Up anchor
And set sail for me.
The heart awaits the ocean's call,
Where being far away is all.

For freedom's sea
I can but yearn;
Come soon the day when I return.
The memories are filled with love
Of blue beneath
And blue above . . .

David Warner

Time-Lines

To future from past,
From first to last,
Not slow or fast:
Thus Time is cast.

Through night and day,
Goes just one way;
So we can say
Time does not stray!

The seconds run hot,
The eons do not;
But Time itself
Cares nary a jot!

Time can't be bent,
Nor ever be rent.
Who knows from whence
It first was sent?

Of us all is Time the seed
Whether we be flower or weed!
Time itself is its own lead
But pays us not the slightest heed!

Graham Shuter

The Storm

Before the storm came
I was lying in my bed
I had a terrible headache
And I could not get out of bed

When the storm came
I could see the lightening
and hear the thunder
It was very loud and noisy
So I hid under the bed covers

When the storm was over
All the roads were flooded
All the birds were sitting on the roof
And I was still in bed

Fiona Woods

Without You

My life fills with emptiness,
When you're not by my side.
My life fills with sadness,
When I can't look into your eyes.

A sense of loneliness from the start.
A feeling of coldness in my heart.

Michelle Norman

The Reluctant Scholar

Feminine flowery dresses
Floating through the hall
Hats with ribbons
And boaters and blazers
And laughter is the rule

Maytime for courting
And boating and dancing
Walking round the maze
Of countless encounters
Meeting momentarily,

Maytime for maidens
Dancing into your life
But exams are looming
No time to look for a wife,

Verily maidens are blooming,
But I am not ready
To look for a steady,
Books are the love of my life.

Fecundity in abundancy
But books must be the love of my life.

Valerie J. Barker

Joy

Crouched down low, a panther's stance,
Fat tyre's squat, on tarmac sat
In solitude, she lies in wait;
Pristine black and chromium plate.
Park discrete, avoid their gaze
But "take me now" her body says.
The joy of riding with me feel,
Burn my rubber, make me squeal.
He is the product of deprivation,
Resisting everything but temptation.
A flick of the wrist and he's inside,
Burning rubber, joy to ride.
This futile joy perceived in youth,
Through older eyes would see the truth.
If older they would ever be,
Aqua-plane, a bend, a tree.
There is no joy, your young life done,
A father's daughter, a mother's son.
There is no joy your life is lost—
forever is the final cost.
Mike Lyon

I Wish I Knew

So. Tell me what she's thinking
As she meditates in bed?
Tell me what's the answer
Going through her head.

She told me of her childhood
In London years ago,
When bread was tuppence Ha'penny
And trams went to and fro.

She told me of her Dad and Mum
Who tried to do their best,
And told me of the hard up times,
The struggles of the rest.

She told me how she married Dad,
And how a house they found.
She told me of the "Good Old Days"
Where love and joy abound.

But now I see Mum lying there
Unable to respond,
In pain and oh so tired.
I wish I had a wand.
Christopher C. Millard

The Mission

Life is a mission, a mission through
time; but time goes on and the
mission never ends; but the mission
gets easier as life gets older; but
man gets older, will he survive the
mission of time; but only time
will tell the outcome of his mission
through life itself.
D. McLeod

Singapore Bird

On the steps of jade Sentosa
I saw a very ordinary bird.
"No ordinary bird, I," said she,
"For I sit at the feet of the Merlion
Who commands the sea.
This figure you behold
Is a deceit
To hide the gold
Within."
So saying she sat
At the feet of her master
Bursting with pride song,
Whilst he,
With stone ground stare,
Remained absolute
In his silent kingdom.
Sandra Davies

Waiting

A need waiting to be needed,
A feeling waiting to be touched,
A hunger waiting to be fed,
A love waiting to be loved.

Need felt hunger's pain,
they cried out in despair.
Feeling heard the sighs
of the despairing cries.
Love shed a lonely tear,
for the fear that was near,
as they struggled in vain,
again and again, to attain the
right to come out into the light.

Like the bud of the rose,
that silently grows,
near the heart of her breast.
Awaits the embrace of the sun,
to blossom and bloom.
With the soul in control
and the whole being one.
Jenny H. Ewen

Untitled

As the rain falls down,
And the wind blows strong,
All the animals are sleeping,
And not a mouse is peeping.
The whistle in the treetops,
And the leaves holding on,
With the strength of the wind,
So the leaves flutter on.
The rain slows down,
And the wind steadies on,
The clouds weaken too,
And the sun peers through.
The trees give a greeting,
By the waving with their arms
The drops of water fall from things,
Like crystals formed by the sun.
Zoe Pope

Untitled

In darkness and in sleep.
  Unable to see.
My soul was lost unconsciously.

I travelled far in this unknown realm.
Floating free from earthly ties
It is a place where nothing dies.

In the depths of my mind
A being of light appears
Alive and living in this atmosphere.

You too were freed of earthly ties
  And together
We merged in Celestial skies.

The light enveloped us
As we became one.
Surrounding us like a morning Sun.
Allison McCabe

Suicide

She's sat in a corner
She's all alone
No one to turn to
Nowhere to go
All these problems trapped inside
All these feelings she hides
Only one way to face them
Only one way to go
Nobody could careless
Nobody will know
Terry Flavell

Reflections

A golden orb encircles the sky.
Withdrawing from its light
The moon and stars have taken flight.
Yet, in the shadows of the night
Return to fill the sky.

A velvet mantle cloaks the earth
Concealing light and giving birth
To the moon and stars in all their glow
Revealing life below.

The greater and the lesser lights
In all their splendour magnify
The earth, the sky, the hand unseen
Unfailing beauty in each thing.
A beauty held within each life—
A greater or a lesser light.
Glynnis Newboult

Death Is So Cruel

The lonely nights your empty chair
I call your name but you're not there
You left a void an empty space
The love you gave I can't replace
I close my eyes but in my dreams
I never see your face it seems
Your picture only soothes so much
I see your face but cannot touch
My life can never be the same
And so I'll quietly hide the pain
Audrey Robertson

Did I Miss You?

Did I miss you?
Did the sun rise in your east,
  and was it grey and cold in mine?

Was time empty, and was I
  hollow in its shell?

Did I starve for your smile,
  and the truth in your eyes?

Was I hungry for your touch,
  be it so slight?

Did I wonder where you were,
  and who with?

Was I lonely in your absence,
  and did I wander it alone?

Did I miss you?
Did I?
John M. Sunderland

The Season Is Winter

Now is the season to make
  Brand new friends.
Time to get together and
  Tie up severed ends.

Argument, enemies, they're
  All set aside.
Now is for feelings that
  Can't be denied.

Joy to the world,
  The child is born today!
The shepherds and the wise men,
  Came this way to pray.

Rich and poor, all around
  on Christmas day will sing.
The hopeful thoughts of the New Year
And wonderful times it will bring.
Andrena Lockley

The Moon

Shining beacon of the night,
Earth's stony satellite.
Catch us in your icy gaze,
Let fall on us thy silvery rays.

Your pale complexion cold and grey.
we see you not throughout the day.
When darkness falls we see you nigh,
Still and icy in the sky.

With the setting of the sun,
your nightly vigil hath begun.
'Til the light of day doth break
thy shall sleep and later wake.

Second always shalt you come
to the might of the fiery sun.
Still I love your whitish glow
as I worship you from far below.

Each night 'tis you I seek to find,
lest you wander from my mind.
Never shall I e'er forget
the way your rays thou doest project.

Deborah Lloyd

Adoption

Goodbye little girl
You're going to have a new life to lead
Away from the selfish whims
Of a Father's love for screams
They'll teach you to say thank you
They'll dress you up in pretty clothes
They'll take you to the seaside
Where all the seagulls go

And you'll never know
The likes of me
You'll never know we're here
And you won't recall the fighting
Or the stench of beer
And you won't remember sobbing
As I left you there
One dark night in a doorway
For someone else to care

Gill. Shaw

Untitled

Fear not, my love,
The dreaded solitude
   of dark corners,
Be like a desert rose,
Born from the sun,
Beaten by a storm,
And carried by the wind,
To share the incomparable
   freedom of a floating cloud

Roberta Jane Higgins

New Life My Son

Settle my Son
Your New Life has begun
Be happy and free
As you longed to be

Enjoy your New Life
No worries; no strife
Let the Lord be your guide
As you fly through the skies

Sail on the Clouds
Help paint a Rainbow
Dance with the Angels
A Fantasy Golden.

Play Golf with the Stars
At the close of each day
I will meet you tomorrow
By the way.

J. Ashcroft

Untitled

Way out in the land called Korea
The British Tommy fights
Fighting for his homeland
Against the communist's might

He's out there in the winter
And in the summer too
Through heat and snow he marches
With a heart that's always true

The English Scots the Irish
And Welshmen on the way
Will fight for the rights of freedom
With our blessings everyday

And when they return to Britain
With their colours flying high
The people will greet them in thousands
With a spirit that's never to die

Samuel Gilbert

You Look at Me, But . . .

You look at me,
Who is Me?
I am me.
You love me
I am me

Your eyes are on me
I laugh and grin.
I am popular.
What does that mean?
Who is popular?
Not me.

You don't see me.
Me is hiding
Me is scared
Me is alone
You don't see me
Me is a lie.

Rachel McIntosh

Sounds of the Ocean

Walking across a desolate beach
   Not a footprint of man,
life's out of reach
Just the sound of the sea
as it washes to meet the shore
Splashing, spraying, hear it roar.
   Taking each rock as its prey.
Capturing the sand with no delay
   leaving behind only a breeze
and in time, that too will cease.

Olinda Barr

My Dog

She sits by my side,
My noble hound.
She cares for nothing else,
When I am around.
She wags her tail,
And cocks her head.
And with a deep bark,
She circles my legs.
She would run for miles,
And then run some more.
She would sleep on my bed,
And not on the floor.
She barks at strangers,
And even the phone.
She barks at the door,
When no one is home.
She lies by my side,
Stretched out on the ground.
She cares for nothing else,
When I am around.

B. Thorn

Images

You shattered my identity
with the drop of a stone.
You cracked my physique
with your carelessness.
You stretched my appearance
with your pride and joy.
You distorted my face
with your copied angulared crystals.
You tried to clone me
with your smooth panes
but light was fading and
I escaped unharmed, for now.

Fiona Walsh

Dedicated to My Friend

Sometimes I sit and think,
   and my thoughts will turn to you,
Of all the things we've said and done,
   and all what we've been through.

No-one has ever been closer,
   or more dearer to my heart,
The friendship that we found,
   right from the very start.

As months turned into years,
   the closer we became,
And although we are so different,
   sometimes we're just the same.

I never could imagine,
   my life without you there,
Your thoughtful ways, and happy smile,
   just show how much you care.

And so my friend, I want to say,
   how much your friendship treasured,
You give me, so very much,
   it never could be measured.

E.

Honesty

If you, an honest Citizen
Should ever feel to stoop,
To do a low or cowardly act,
Stop first, think and look,
Lift up your eyes, to the skies,
Think you, of your Lord,
You will then, feel his comfort by
Holding, his shining sword,
Not one of vengeance
Or to use in strife,
But his to help you onwards
On the many paths, through life.

Margaret Muir Colligan

Dreams with Maiden Fair

Darkness comes I'm here at last
I've walked for miles along this path
Along this path people wait
They talk to me they don't stare
In this land I feel at home
I'm with friends I'm not alone
Then I see a maiden fair
With warm brown eyes and reddish hair
For many hours we stand and talk
I'm her equal she does not mock
I find true love she steals my heart
I'm so happy we'll never part
But daylight comes and she is gone
She disappears with the dawn
Then I realise it's just a dream
Life is not what it seems
For my life is full of fears
But in dreams there are no tears
Until tonight when I can share
All my dreams with maiden fair

Alexander William Todd

The Mask

Always smiling and laughing
and shows a heart of stone
Never giving way to emotion
of love that's past and gone

But alone the mask will slip
and reality shows behind
on a face that's always happy
the tears at last, freedom find

The sadness is never made public
the loneliness will never be proved
an exterior so obstinately moulded
the cover will never be moved

Melanie McDonagh

A Dedication to the Gallant Allied Troops

The gallant troops of England,
And other countries too,
Have earned the thanks and praises
Which they've received from you.

They fought for England bravely
When things were looking black,
But now they're fighting harder,
And driving Hitler back.

The famous "Eight" are fighting
To help to win the war,
And they are fighting better
Than any time before.

But Monty's now in England
To help the Second Front,
And when he lands in Europe
It's Hitler who he'll hunt.

And when this war is over
And victory is won,
We'll thank those gallant soldiers
We'll thank them, every one.

J. E. Funnell

The Smilely Poem

The writer of this poem
Is Skinny and tall
bouncy as a ball
light as a feather
more funny than a gorilla
tender as a Lilly
I got a best friend
she is very very silly
she has a dog his name is Billy
I am clever because I do a lot of study
I am never in any hurry
I can trick a pig
I am as smooth as an ice lolly
I am 1 in 5000?

Asha Ramchurn

The Pensioners' Lament

I pray that I won't go sick
On Saturdays and Sundays,
My brain must stay alive, not thick
To describe my ailment monday

My toes must not drop off at night
My bowels must work at all cost
I try to breathe with all my might
Appointment please, before all's lost.

You may be old but do it right
Let Peter at the gate wait
Keep your bits intact tonight
Come morning you will know your fate

Amy Frances Bourner

Suicide

You had it all planned
To the last detail.
On a cold Winter's Night
All alone, no one to stop you.
Stepping out onto the rails
Void of all feeling, empty.
Don't you know I love you.
I can't let you go like this.
Now lying on your hospital bed
I can see Hell resting within.
Hold on to life, don't let it go.
Step through the pain
Make it to the other side.
Time passes, a new life beckons
The light shines bright
And the darkness chased away.

Barbara J. Spencer

The Dying of the Light

As the candle reaches its lowest ebb
My time is almost done.
The flame flickers out in my heart
And I face my path alone.

My soul flies out like a timeless bird
Reaching high into the sky.
I turn around one last time
To say a last goodbye.

Farewell world for now I go
The dying of the light.
The air of tranquility, always there
That had made friends' lives so bright.

Off to a place darker than demons
A place which is darker than night,
This tunnel which leads to heaven,
For the dying of the light.

Melanie Loveland

Untitled

Silhouetted against the window,
 I saw you.
A vision of desire.
Moonlight shone brightly upon you.
Catching shadows of fire.
I drew breath deeply.
In anticipation of our meeting.
Advancing slowly towards me.
 Moments fleeting.
Smell, touch and taste
 combined.
Not a dream but final reunion.

Scott McDonald

Blue Moon

How the heart does quicken
When this beauteous thing appears.
The touch so soft, the gaze so pure
Enchanting as it nears.

But caution, as you reach out
Don't forget the sumptuous rose
Will stab you when you touch it
Draw your blood and then repose.

Soft bosom holds a stoney heart
Entrancing eyes hide stoney stare
Tempting lips are quick to chide
Of this beauty, please beware.

But, Blue Moon will entwine your heart
Should you touch the tender spot,
Love saved only for its vine
Will be given and ne'er forgot.

Christine Marshall

Untitled

We are no longer slaves
But does that mean we are free
We are no longer restrained
But does that mean we are happy

They say there's one human-race
But does that grant us equality
Or is this just another game
Another lie to sustain peace.

Mumbi Y. Kigwe

Africa's Bush

When the lion stalks his prey
The bush keeps still;
When the hippos go under water
Everything is startled,
When the zebra trots
All the stripes cover the bush.

When the spotted eagle flies
The song fills the air.
The hyena laughs
The other animals flee
When the moon shines
Brighter than the stars.

Diandra Glazer, 7 years old

Wonderment

O great and glorious thing,
It makes me feel so free,
As if I'm floating 'pon a wing,
The Earth at one with me.

To see the wide horizon,
The green and ancient tree,
To see the swirling river,
They're all at one with me.

The flowers in the meadow,
The sheep upon the scree,
The birds so high and soaring,
Are all at one with me.

The cause of all this splendour,
The things that set me free,
You know its name, my darling,
It's Love you've given to me.

P. A. Rushton

One Day

I was on my own, all alone.
When I saw a light, in the night.
The night was fading, dawn was breaking
And the sun came shining bright.

Claire Harris

'Spirit of Unity'

Tree!
All gnarled and lumpy,
Reaching to the heavens
In silent prayer.
How strong and wise
You seem to me.

I hear you softly call
Come! Lean on me,
And share the beauty
Of this hour—this day.

Then, together
we will leave this world behind,
Climb heaven's stairway,
And stand at heaven's gate
and smile—
Knowing in a little while
We'll share eternity.

Marjorie Quinn

Today and Tomorrow?

This culture that we live in,
Created by mankind.
Has subjected so many to torture,
In body, soul and mind.

We live in a sea of greed,
Where no man can pass or sail.
They swim in others' misery,
And dive as others fail.

With drugs as common as candy,
Used to arouse the brain.
Out comes all the decency,
And integrity they drain.

This passion we have for life,
As we would like it to be.
Discarding moral standards,
And living just for thee.

So look around this rich land,
See the faces so sad.
Watch as we lose touch,
With the English we once had.

Lesley Ann Swainston

Untitled

The heart moves with many
rhythms of beauty, yet
in between it rests, as it
sees reflection of self
in the mirror of love.
Pulsating a dance beyond rhythm.

Dawn Copley

Love Still Uncertain

My love still a germinating
Seed can suffer wither.
Dear tell me whether you love me.
Help me with your final words

About your thinking of me.
My love for you is still young, tender
And shallowly rooted.
Whether or not it will have long
Roots to be rooted deeper will

Depend on your thinking about me.
O' dear is it not time,
Know the content of your mind?
For how long can we live in
Silence and in doubts?

Esenezer Masi Binasila

Ashes to Ashes

He smokes all day, yet has no time
For me, his loyal wife.
I'll clean up all the ashes that fall,
As hoovering's my life.

He'll come to bed at two
With lighted cigarette, of course.
He'll kiss me with his 'Benson's breath
Lay down, show no remorse.

I'll wake up, smell of nicotine,
Then look round slowly to view
The old pack thrown onto the floor,
Then him, starting one new.

While he's inhaling, I look down
The carpet colour's grey,
The dirty man, he flicks the ash,
Then always misses the tray.

I'm sure of us two, he'll die first
I'll stay here, loyal wife,
His box'll fall off the mantelpiece,
I'll hoover up his life.

Vickie Howard

Spring

From valleys to hill tops
Sleep all the snow drops
On lease new life rises
Time for spring prizes

Early morning softly bright
With a golden sunlight
Birds that are singing
Spring—season for rejoicing.

Free from winter ransom
Will be able to blossom
On branches appear leaves green
For dormant everything has been.

Sprouting in every field
Wheat and daffodils
New musical spring flows
Amongst lambs white as snow.

Breeze by Spring angels wings
Mild and softly blowing
Bringing sweet nectar of blooms
Spring nature perfectly grooms.

Jean Marie Noel-Cephise

War

When countries have wars
People no-doubt die
Fighting for their country
or just passing by

Shooting a gun off everywhere
Not really caring who is out there
Bombs coming down, people screaming
Gas everywhere, people not breathing

After a while things calm down;
Then bang goes a gas bomb,
and people start to drown

Demelza Ruth Wells

To the Sea

Run little water run,
along your winding path,
to the sea, to the sea,
there to vent your wrath.
Innocent babbling brook,
flowing to the sea so vast,
those once gentle ripples,
now waves that shadows cast.
You friendly gift of nature,
distracting all the strife,
to the sea, you force of God,
you giver and taker of life.

R. T. Bourke

Why Did You Have to Die?

When you went away
I shed a tear,
Now I wish
that you were here,
all the time
we spent together,
now I have
happy memories to last forever,
why did you have to die?
When I think of you
I cry,
knowing things
will never be the same,
no one can replace you
no matter how they
try.

Emma Morris

Rain

Solitary listening to the rain
Pit a pat on widow pane
Wash and clean dust of past
Over God's garden a newness cast
Falls on flowers its beauty shake
Clean its face a difference make
Makes fine cobwebs in the grass
Glitter like diamonds when rain pass
Around the earth coloured rainbow cast
Clear blue sky appears at last
Gives us water, enough to drink
Fills each river, never lets it sink
Without the rain no plant live
Without the rain no beauty give
Hail the rain, will not complain
When you hit my window pane.

Pearl Powell

Dreamer

Head in the clouds
Thoughts up in the sky
Dreaming my dream
Time passing me by

Living like people
Dreaming of more
Wanting to know
What else is in store

Dreaming of angels
All sweetness and light
The darkness draws near
Cry into the night

I am like people
People are like me
Dreaming as mere mortals
Of what we wish to be

Lynsey Burt

Untitled

True love
　Comes from above
No one can sever
True love lasts forever
　Never dies
　It lives in the heart to stay
forever
Life goes on when the one we love
　goes to live above.
　We cherish the memories to
safely keep
From the day our great love fell
　asleep.
　Our marriage vows and till
　Dear do us part
But we always keep the wonderful
　Love is our heart.

Ethel E. Thorndike

The Last . . .

The last laugh
last dry
last noise
echoes the earth

Nothing to be seen
to be heard
to be touched

Now no last laugh
last cry
last noise
no last anything

The earth is not empty for the first
and last time!

Jennifer Morledge

The Shining Sea

So softly sang the shining sea
comforting all the thoughts in me.
Why, I cried, it hurts so much
to posses these feeling such,
Memories of past happiness
now my life is such a mess.
The water splashed and glistened still
be strong, it said, and then you will
Your life to live as it can be,
for such is the secret of the sea.

J. Phillips

I Miss You

I miss you
More than you can ever know
Your loss is like a death
Causing a shadow on my life
Like ink on blotting paper
The pain seeps through me
Like a thorn it digs in
The pain is not instant
Until it is unbearable and I weep
I weep for the loss of you
My loss—mine alone
My cross to bear
My yearning never relents
Like the sea you hold so dear
It is sometimes calm, sometimes deadly
But like the sea it is eternal
I will always love you
I am only yours
But you are not mine
So I am alone.

Alyson Thomas

An Apparition

Visions of the future
Hopes inside my heart
Fears inside my head
Visions of a perfect ending
That can never be

It may all begin
But will never end
With you and me

I try and try
The words are there
Yet trapped
They can shaped the future
But only if we try
Together.

Lucy Gray

Forgotten Dreams

Twisting, turning, sweating,
Running from a force,
Climbing rocks, higher, higher,
Waves are getting louder,
Smashing against the rocks,
AND THEN
Climb higher, higher from the sea,
Slipping, slipping,
Grips loosening,
Hands no longer strong,
Falling down and down,
And yet not getting wet.

Twisting, turning, sweating,
Eyes opening,
Eyes focusing,
A room, a bedroom,
A dream, perspiration,
A hazy recollection.
YET ANOTHER FORGOTTEN DREAM.

Teresa Kirwan

Is It Love?

Is it love? Or just devotion,
That causes me to say,
"He is what people made him.
He didn't choose to be that way."

Is it love? Or just emotion,
Makes it hard to say, "Good-bye,"
To say the things you want to,
To not break down and cry.

Is it love that makes me lonely?
Is it love's destructive way?
For you to go and leave me,
No matter what I say.

If it's love then you can have it!
If it's love I want no more!
If it's love then you can shove it!
If it's love show it the door!

If it's love don't bring it near me!
If it's love I'll shy away!
All love I know is painful,
And hurts you more each day.

A. D. Wheatley

"Lakeside"

A lonely figure
  By the lake,
    Reaching out
As the waters break.

Just a ripple
  A minor reflection,
    Awesome beauty
In the sun's reflection.

Words cannot express
  The peaceful scene,
    The lonely figure
Goes unseen.

A beautiful presence
  To joy and adore,
    Those precious "footprints"
Touched the shore.

A total serenity
  Enriches my eyes,
    My heart, my mind
Are in paradise.

William Cockfield

Autumn

Colours flying through the air
In the shape of leaves
Jumping, dancing in the air
Leave a memory.

Colours flying through the air
In the shape of leaves
Yellow, brown, green and red
Softly landing on my head.

Colours flying through the air
In the shape of leaves
Patterned and plain ones, none the same
But all original in their way.

Colours flying through the air
In the shape of leaves
Winter is coming, frost is here
Setting on the trees.

Colours flying through the air
In the shape of leaves
Trees are bare, where leaves once were
Silhouettes in the frosty air.

Fiona Stott

Jason

The thought of you sitting,
Wondering if I still care.
Makes me feel unhappy,
Knowing it's just not fair.

You mean the world to me,
I wish you could only see.
I never meant to hurt you,
I wish I only know.

Now I know how much you love me.
I wish I could of seen,
The pain, the hurt, the misery
That I put on you and me.

Angela Catt

Sorry Rhoda

I am sorry that I failed you tonight.
I am sorry because more than anything
I wanted to be the man I couldn't
I wanted to be the man that
You wanted me to be

I am sorry that I failed you tonight
I am sorry because more than anything
I wanted to be able to explain why
I couldn't be the man that
You wanted me to be

I am sorry that I failed you tonight
I am sorry because more than anything
I wanted to be everything for you but
I wasn't the man that
You wanted me to be.

Ewan Cameron

The Lady with the Cane

The night
had fallen.
NO ONE
was there
except the lady
with the red hair.

She carried
a cane
that was heavier
than pain.

NO ONE
to see
but me that watched.

As she moved closer
I could hear
the branches fall of
so near
as if once
her home
lay here

Suzanne Hind

The Softest Kiss

The softest kiss
Was mine for a moment
Then she was gone
And I was in torment

K. K. Dhatariya

My Poem

Distance
neither time nor space can bridge
love and feeling missing
succumbed to emotions
never trust feelings alone
only wise will choose
the lesser distance

Klaus Hanfler

The Bower

The seat is set beyond the flowers,
Permitting me some stolen hours
Seeking tranquility.
While bird song echoes through the trees,
Flower scents wafted on the breeze
induce reverie.

Only a rainbow can compare
with the brilliant colours that are there,
Abundant all around,
as the music of the waterfall
orchestrates harmony over all
of nature's soothing sound.

So loving are the hands that toil,
creating this garden from the soil
that gives such joy to me,
But I'm lost in daydreams, unaware
of how long I've been sitting there
until he calls out—"Tea?"

Pauline Launt

Contain the Pain

I cannot contain the pain that's twisting me up inside,
There's no way to relieve the hurt however hard I've tried.

Sometimes it's nothing but a pang that shudders through my heart,
Other times it rips and burns and tears my world apart.

Sometimes I will break down and cry and scream and shout,
Other times I just curl up to stop the pain from getting out.

I taste the salty tears that fall down my cold still face,
They're simply drops of bitterness that leave without a trace.

But above my world filled with anguish, hurt, and sorrow,
I somehow have a feeling I'll be stronger with tomorrow.

I can see an open pathway that will help me to cope,
So I can let the pain escape and make way for the hope.

Maxine Pickard

Silenced Sorrow

Another second, another minute just ticks away,
Yet nothing has changed.
The days are supposed to be longer than the nights
But sometimes my nights are endless.
The empty cradle besides me holds such significant memories,
But I cannot bear to look at it.
Now there is no noise, no sounds at all;
Just bereavement of whose movements once dominated the house;
Of whose small whisper would be the centre of attention.
As I embrace her clothes close to my face
I can still smell the very essence of her left in them.
Hot trickles of lonely tears fall loosely from eyes
That do not want to cry.
If I could only hold her once again,
Maybe that would soothe away the pain
That has since become my only companion.
How can time possibly heal a wound
That I will never recover from.

Ravinder Kaur

Pressure

Get up, get out, compete to win
Be strong, be right, climb up, go in
Don't slow, don't stop, don't ever cry
For if you fail, you're the reason why.

No time to think, to sleep or dream
No time to listen, to plan or scheme
Must do, must see, must test, must try
For if you fail, you're the reason why.

Be clever, be pretty, be young, be thin
Be wise, be witty, be always first in
Never grow old, grow fat or die
For if you fail, you're the reason why.

Mary O'Sullivan

Count Your Blessings

When you're feeling down and out,
Everything's wrong and you want to shout,
Just stop, look around, and think a while,
And never never loose that smile.
See the things that are given free,
Mountains, sun, trees, the sea.
The sea so deep, so cruel and cold,
Many a shipwreck its waters hold.
Mountains covered with snow look bleak,
Climbers mounting them, adventure seek.
The sun to the world brings warmth and light,
In a clear blue sky it shines so bright.
Trees in the breeze sway to and fro,
Birds make nests for their young to grow.
So when you're feeling down and out,
And you've sat and thought, and have no doubt
That life is full of wondrous things,
Just think of all the joy it brings.

A. Godly

A Walk in the Mountains

The moors are brown with heather and moss,
The clouds like wispy candy floss,
The mountains are hidden in soft white mist,
The tops of the trees are softly sun kissed,

My walking boots squelch in the mud,
My stick hits the ground with a comforting thud,
A startled bird shoots in the air,
From a nest, I don't remember seeing where.

A grass snake basking in the sun,
Does not wake as I pass and am gone,
I am at one with the birds and the sky,
For they all belong,
To the same world as I,
We respect and trust each other today,
I wish it could always be this way.

Alice Kershaw

Winter Address

Mongrel smells and swelling fat
cooked pungent in the tenement at night
to the dismay of strays.
Under his dark pan-tiled hat
the smiling electric crescent
peers into avenues
and through thickets of coal cloud.
Warm sheltered quarters lie asleep
as elsewhere the moon bleeds
onto sore, panged, dark-ageing folk
wrapped in blowing pages of newsworthy days.
Numb, gnawed pipes breathing virally acute,
through thawing sleet running streets
that flood and congest with ill banter.
Undiluted oaths slapping in the wind
which bends bowed backs, cracks fortune's palms
and conspires to put out their last rizla.

Simon Cox

Swans at Night

Silent white gondolas drifting aimlessly
Shimmering moons upon a calm sea
Eyes of onyx, feathers of silk
Belie the strength beholdent their ilk

Quest for life, endless searching
Food to seek, forever yearning
Established routes of generations past
Once and more, never the last

Appearing from nowhere, not a sound
Gliding slowly, glancing around
A moment passes, they appear as one
Into the night, the moons have gone

A. R. Freeman

What Is Love?

Do I know what love is? Have I touched
that star whose sparkle goes through each
fibre of your being to the end of each
finger and toe? My imagination had told me
this is how one feels when you've met that
one person who makes these feelings happen.

I stood beside a man once, whose electric
spark stirred my being. Like magic the
unseen charge crossed the space between us
Standing there talking of mundane things,
just to keep us there enjoying the vibrant,
unexpected pleasure we both felt.

But this was only a fleeting encounter.
This wasn't able to be. Circumstances told
us this could never progress. But had I
found the sparkle of love? Did I find and
silently touch the star, whose sparkle gave
my soul an unforgettable delight?

Jean Watson

The Message

Trees are brown with shades of green.
These are things that I've never seen.
Feeling around its crusty outer layer
I'm sure I felt a heartbeat there!
I know it's alive as it blossoms each year,
Yet I'm afraid; people, I'm full of fear.
The fear I feel is for you all
Wether you're black-white, tall or small.
Ancestral hatred must come to an end,
This is my poem and I have a message to send.
We live on earth for about one hundred years
And know of death-destruction - blood, sweat and tears.
This violence is too much, it causes too many pains,
Our world will be a better place, we'll have so many gains.
So let bygones be long gone, let your future be bright
For in my depth of darkness I can see the light,
So stop hurting with weapons and words of hate,
And for you who can't see unity, this message I dedicate.

Amanda R. Kelly

Whirlwinds

Yesterday I stepped backwards through my life.
It was like a great raging wind, stirring up the leaves
of a winter storm.

Through the mist of memories appeared an apparition
of what it was like before.

Did I really live those days and nights since,
am I destined to go on, remembering, questioning?
Am I the only one that can deal with this rationally,
coldly, or am I just pretending to myself?

You came in like a whirlwind
rustled up the leaves, stirred the mists,
shifted the clouds, then, wanted to leave.
Hoping that the things you left, would remain,
as they were before.

Judi Martin

Starstruck

One crazy night when stars shone bright
and witches cast their spells
you walked into my world and called my name
and led me to the darker side of heaven where
we sparked the fire and touched the burning flame.
Now passion's spent and life goes on
they say you're still with her
and my heart aches with anger, guilt, and pain
but still I pray that in another life
   where dreams come true
I'll feel your love surround me once again.

Violet Scott

O Shell

All is not well with thee O Shell.
For in the very midst of thee
You yearn for the sea
And in the very heart of me
I cry my God to thee
O Shell I take you to the sea for which you long,
for the waves to refresh you with their song,
O Shell no more to grieve,
Goodbye O Shell, all now is well.

Wendy J. Mansour

A Glimpse of Paradise

I'm feeling really tired, weary and worn.
I fall into bed, I toss and I turn.
I drift away to a blissful sleep,
after praying my Lord my soul to keep.
I open my eyes to a beautiful land,
of rolling green hills, and soft silver sands.
A mirror lake of azure blue—
too beauteous to describe to you.
A man that I know sits there on a stone.
I'm feeling really happy. At last I'm home.
A joy is bubbling up inside.
The man makes me smile and giggle like a child.
I feel his warmth and kindness and love. . .
. . . one day I'll return to my home up above.

Anne Hutchison

God Walks with Me

One day while out walking,
Just wandering on my own,
A sadness came upon me,
And I felt all alone.

Then into view, there came a house,
I know that's nothing odd,
But this place was very special,
It was the house of God.

I went inside, it was quiet and still,
A sense of peace I began to feel,
I sat in a pew, said a prayer,
Would God, I wondered, know I was there.

Then suddenly a bright light shone,
Enveloping me with its rays,
The feeling that it gave me,
Will be with me all my days.

Now when I go out walking,
I am never on my own,
For I know God walks with me,
And no more I walk alone.

Maud Eleanor Hobbs

Special I Want To . . .

You're so special, I want to hold you close to me
I want to wrap my arms around you,
and never let you go.
I can visualize us walking hand in hand,
walking along the beach,
our feet entwined with sand.
You're so special, in my life
If only you'd notice me,
I'm sure we are meant to be.
I want to run my hands through your
deep, dark brown hair.
If only you knew how much I really care
You are so charming, suave and debonair
we are a lot alike.
We'd definitely make a compatible pair
We both love romance, and candle-lit
dinners for two.
I just want you to know that . . .
I love you.

Sarah-Kelly Barron

Life

From birth to death, life is fleeting
Through suckling, weaning and family care.
To school, games and sexual fare,
Onwards, ever onwards.

Study, marriages, family, work,
Time is passing — age advances,
Retirement, illness, bereavement, death.
Life is but a moment.

I. F. M. Saint-Yves

The Challenge

The engines roar, propellers spin,
I wonder, who will finally win?
The foe is good, but so are we,
Will it be him, or will it be me?
The fight is on, he's coming fast,
Oh God, he's here, he looks aghast.
The guns spit fire, our eyes are fixed,
Our minds are one, our feelings mixed.
Will it be him, or will it be me?
When will it end, when will we be free?

The bullets reach their target
The fires begin to burn,
One by one the brave bale out
Now it is my turn.

I float to earth and try to see
If he has managed to get free,
Yes, there he is, we wave and smile
Our fight is over for a while.

What was it for, who wins in the end?
We land and we meet, I've made a new friend.

Jean Pannell

Labyrinth of the Spirits

Evil is as evil does,
and silence is our nightmare.
Chance is for the untouched fool,
and fate endures our misery.
Paranoia takes out all you've got,
and darkness thrills your senses.
The creepy murmur of the wind,
and the subtle, desperate moans.
The witching hour is close at hand,
and everywhere is silence.
Your guilty conscience gives in to madness,
as you know you'll be mine forever.
Sitting and waiting for time to end,
Screaming for freedom, for death!

Kathryn Arnot Drummond

Lost

I live here, but I have no home,
There are people near, yet I'm all alone.
They think I live, but I know I died.
Where did he go, when I cried?
Myself, just talks and works and walks
I eat, I drink, yet can no longer think.
I have lost my way in this dark empty lane
I'll be so afraid till I see him again.

Do I want to stay with this empty mind?
Do I want to leave the past behind?
But how can I, when a song, a laugh or voice is heard
It comes rushing back, and, oh the hurt.
So fierce is all the ache in my heart.
Then all in a second, I'm back being me
We're no longer apart, and I think, what would be

Have done, left all on his own?
Then, when my grief is a its worst
I am grateful to God for taking him first.

Bobby Butler

A Message from Mother

I am a sphere spinning in space,
I am host to a parasite, the human race.
They poison my veins and destroy my skin,
They burrow deep inside me to consume what's within.
Humans seem to thrive on greed and destruction,
Replacing my heart and lungs with steel and concrete construction,
Nature is there to be harvested and used.
She is a gift from your mother and must not be abused,
For I am mother earth, a jewel in space.
The host you consume can never be replaced.
So repair the damage whatever the cost,
You must, my children, before all is lost

Robert J. Schofield

No Work

Oh angry young man of today.
No, we didn't take all work away.
But there's been wars you see.
When buildings and lives were destroyed.
So we rebuilt the roads and new houses too.
And factories, where people could work.

Millions of lives were slain.
Yet thousands of minds still remain.
They remember the time, when hope of a future.
Drove them ever forward and onwards.
But that is all gone, all they have left
Are their memories.

Oh, youth of today, no don't look away.
Your time will come all too soon.
So don't reach for the moon, it's too far away.
It's not yours to have, be thankful for life.
It's not very long, cram in all you can.
For God and his great eternal plan.

Mary Coleman

My Son

I stood and watched you from afar
I wanted to heal each pain, each scar
But I knew that God in his wisdom and love
Would watch you more closely than I ever could

He knows my pain when my help is spurned
He knows my pain when love's not returned
He loves us all more than we'll ever know
And he knew my pain as I watched you go.

Olive Birkett

Faith in Your Parents

My mom and dad are wonderful,
They should be queen and king.
They've always loved and cared for
me, and given me everything.

I know that this is what parents are for,
But they deserve a rest,
To put their feet up and forget about me,
Oh, my parents are just the best.

Because I know for a fact that my parents
would not sit back and forget about me,
They care too much because they are
What decent parents should be.

No-one can ever replace them,
Of course there are no other
Who are as precious as my parents,
Like my wonderful father and mother.

If everyone did for their children,
Like my dear parents have done,
This world would be a better place
and be a lot more fun!

Sarah Cotson

Nowhere to Go

Bad weather on its way
That's what I hear them say
Hope there is somewhere to stay
Having nowhere to go haunts me every day
To have a good meal I hear my stomach say
The population of homeless
Grows every day,
Sometimes an overwhelming feeling
Hits me as I awake
Telling me to keep my eyes closed
And wish the day away,
Tell me there is another life
Beyond the one I live today.

Charlotte Dixon

Grandmother's Memories

Sweet are the memories in my mind
of a child I loved and knew
   But fate's been cruel instead of kind,
   it parted me and you.
I miss you gentle smiling face,
   your hearty laughter too,
And those simple words you'd whisper:
   "Nana I love you."
On cold winter mornings
   you'd climb upon my knee
And I'd wrap my Cardigan around you,
   and smug and warm we'd be.
So tonight before I go to sleep,
   in my prayers, of you I'll speak.
God keep him safe night and day
   and please reunite us one day.
   Nana

J. A. Jones

My Personal Loss

I ranted and raved inside at the start
At first a storm raged on in my heart,
Why did this awful thing happen to me?
It made no sense that I could see.

With this a period of numbness and shock
I seemed quite unable to sit and take stock,
Nothing I did seemed to make any sense
In fact at times I felt quite dense.

Then later I found time does not stand still
I was dragged along against my will,
Sometimes from the darkness and despair
I would find myself coming up for air.

As out of this mist and fog I groped
There was no peace, for which I had hoped,
And I knew by this time I had lost
The one on earth, that I loved the most.

Mechanically I go on from day to day
But the loneliness will not go away,
Somewhere there must be something to do
And God alone can help me through.

Margery K. Broad

Mummy

Mummy I love you a lot
You're like a pretty flower in a pot
I must tell you you're as pretty as a pearl
You keep me clean I treat you like a queen
Your love keeps us going
I hope you like this little poem
Roses are red, violets are blue
I really love you you are my mummy
You are special, you are like a pretty petal
You're my mummy you're my dear
You make my life so sincere.
Mummy

Gareth Hughes

Fairy Glen

In leafy glades, pale moonbeams fall
Fairies laughing, dancing call
Bewitching words, enchanting smiles
Beware their many, wicked guiles

For if you should stop, enraptured
Breath stilled, heart encaptured
Never again would you be seen
Forever prisoner of the fairy queen

So wandering through the woods at night
If you should see a beckoning light
Run away and don't turn around
Hurry back home, safe and sound

Alan Bills

Type Writer Mad

Fingers on the keys.
Producing a note for the milkman
A letter to Aunt Jessie or a
Masterpiece in hand.
It's as if it speaks to me
The way it plods along.
Turning out realms of data
To file away for reference later.
Its shabby appearance doesn't matter much.
I would not want to part with my old friend.
Although it's seen better days.
It helps me with conferences, lectures, and the like
We plod the streets of life
Together we are a team.
In good times and bad.
It sees me through.
A loyal friend it has become.
My old typewriter and me.

Jane Minter

Spring Time Sonnet

Snow like blossoms, on the trees
Blowing golden daffodils.
Gently glowing in the breeze.
On the green, green, O Vert fields
Trees covered in bud replacing leaves
Small flowers rendezvous again upon the hills
Gone at last the winter freeze
Birds sing, nests they build
Le bleu ciel, as blue as Mediterranean seas
Cocks crow! Hen's yield
Around the flowers buzz the bees
Balmy march winds, fill the air
Bright shiny glossy leaves.
Flowers on the window sill
Spring has now begun to tease
Winter wind no longer blows or shrills.
Brilliant hyacinths always please.
With high perfume the air is filled.
Magnificent colours, you can see
At last de soleil shining bright, glowing through the trees.

Josephine Ferguson

The Automobile

The automobile is a funny old thing,
it runs on air, and flies like the wind
It coughs and splutters on frosty morns,
when pushed or pressed it squeals from its horn,
It has a boot, a skirt and a bonnet.

To receive the music it has an aerial on it.
It gets well oiled, and smokes from a pipe,
and to allow it to see, it lights up at night.
It's got a head and doors at the side,
and springs underneath to give a smooth ride.

To be honest and truthful I can only say,
what would we do without them today.

C. Heard

Commitment

What a long word and with a whole lot of meaning.
Commitment you have to have a whole lot of feeling.
Commitment means forever or so we are told.
Commitment means having to be bold.

Commitment is too long a word for some.
Men in particular find it troublesome.
Commitment does not mean shackled or chained,
Commitment means understanding and tamed.

Commitment is the key to success,
Commitment means women's happiness.
Commitment means much to many.
Make that commitment Tommy, and marry!

Susan Brown

Laughing

It starts with a grin, that you can't keep within
Progresses to a chuckle
And then to a muffled
Sound that one just can't fathom
An atrocious uproar of the lung and guts
Your stomach is sore and it hurts very much!

Daniella Blechner

If Love Was All

If love was all, and all was love,
Then to eternity my soul would fly, more swiftly than the
speed of sound.

And in that vast eternity of space
My thoughts would reach into infinity,
As wordlessly as when time first began.

And there, within unnumbered years,
 I'd tell of joy more wonderful,
Of dreams that are as yet unborn,
And hopes that would unfold,
And in maturity a fusion of completeness gain.

And there, a joy as incandescent
As the stars from outer space,
Would wrap us closer than our beating hearts.

So take my hand, and come with me to those unchartered ways,
That other loves have known,
For at that moment I shall hear the echoes of your voice,
And drink from its deep mystery.

And as we wander in that strange and timeless world,
Where shadows are no more,
I then shall know for certainty,
That Love Is All.

Muriel G. Rabbitts

The Spectrum—Dreaming

Twisting, turning
Down the path of sleep.
It leads me by the hand
On to a far and distant place.

This place has no name, yet seems familiar
Faces around me are unrecognisable,
but, yet I see You.

You were there in the beginning,
You will, I know be there at the end
Despair . . . Hope . . . Shattered.
Before my helpless eyes.

Sometimes terrifying images
Sometimes a quiet remembrance
Of happier times.

Then, suddenly, it stops.
Consciousness; dazed; confused . . .
Slowly my life comes into hazy focus
You . . . smiling . . . life . . . sunshine . . .
I see . . .

Helen Bullen

The Undying Fate

If I die the sinner,
The righteous or saint,
It will not matter
That I was villain or martyr.

I will have no need
To obey a creed,
Nor possess the time
To rue a flawed deed.

I will not terror abhor,
Nor to the meek succumb,
Nor have any fear,
For the future or tomb.

I will not my plight ponder,
Nor with my neighbour's fate compare,
Nor contemplate in time dire,
The need to have a word with God.

I will with Him confer
(if He keeps the appointed hour),
As man can only be fairly judged at death,
I believe, hence, I will my case rest at death.

Eze Umezuruike

Beyond the Sunset

Just around the next corner
A place that's never reached, a dream never to be realized,
A hope that evaporates to join the mist.
When the sun shines to show the reality of the day,
The hope with the mist vanishes away.

A day that is real and concrete fear,
Another day to live through before the next sunset.
The dreams of the evening are not here today.
What good is hope if it cannot stay?
Yet looking on a sunset my hope rises again,
A place where all I dream will always remain.

In the bright light of morning, there is no place to hide my pain,
The evening will come with its shadows of relief,
A promise of tomorrow, of better things to come.
In my dreams hopes and fears join into one
Destroyed by the daylight with the rising sun.

Hiding in the darkness of the night
The gentleness of the moon comforts my fear.
Must hold on to my dream so I will wake each day
To live every moment, not running away
Something good around the corner, over the next stream,
Yet always beyond the sunset stays only a dream.

Hannah Sharples

Lost Love

It was a love so rare and intense,
    And as rich as the nectar of life.
We loved as if from afar
    Yet never two beings were ere so close.

We were as one in mind and body,
    Afraid to love for fear of fortune,
Desperately we would say adieu
    Yet never two beings were ere so close.

With dancing eyes all ink black rock
    What hope was there for one so young,
Ageless was the love we held
    And never two beings were ere so close.

He bade farewell through iron gates
    In the cold midst of desolate January
A tragic loss for two so near,
    And never two beings were ere so close.

A year past by with merest glances
    His return so unexpected and yet expected
So loved by thee but never meant to be
    And yet I fear never two beings were ere so close.

G. Dobbs

Ageism

'Do you like knitting', she said to me,
'Or perhaps a little sewing or music?'
'No I don't', I sighed,
'Heaven forbid!' I cried,
'I'm not an old dear who's nostalgic.'
'Well are you into anything quiet?
For instance, maybe a spot of croquet?'
'I like drugs and sex and loud rock and roll.
Why, what else is expected today?'
'Nothing, but for a lady of 92,
You seem to be exceedingly well.'
'92! Who said that! Well as a matter of fact,
I'm not half that,
And then times it by two!'

Heidi Mansell

The Flower Show

Blossoms rare with perfume so exquisite
    That one could only in his imagination
But pause, and ponder on such delicate a requisite
    Should vie, one with the other in such fine combination,
And all the petalled ballerinas give with generosity,
    That e'en the orchid with her fine upstanding splendour
Should Lord it with her haughty air and such pomposity
    To cherish thoughts that she was but the one contender.
The gentle rose with smiles, ignores all haughty airs,
    And softly chides the lily with her majestic stance.
Her scented charm infuses all to drive away all cares.
    All jealousies are gone amid such fine fragrance.
But who is this we find surrounding all in every way,
So coy, so shy, half hidden by extended shoots above,
Converging all in one, magnificent display?
    The bashful primula infusing all with love.
She is the jewelled frame enhancing all
    That mirrors, and reflects such beauteous array.
Succeeds in every way to each enthrall,
    And thus a magic madrigal that all portray.

H. G. Tupman

Childhood Memories

Childhood memories haunt me night and day,
Oh, how I wish these bad memories would go away!
The pain and suffering goes on and on,
My head feels like an exploding time bomb.
I want so much to forget the past
And get on with my life at last.
It's so hard to express my fears;
Every time I try, I end up in tears.
Maybe I don't want to remember the things he did!
After all I was only an innocent kid.
Why did he do those things to me?
It's so hard to express my fears
Of guilt and anger hidden inside for years and years.
The memories haunt me night and day;
Hatred and disgust, oh! when will they go away?
They all say I should have told.
But how could I? I was only 4 years old!!

W. J. Hurlow

Man's Sinful State

How wretched man is—so full of sin,
How can he ever hope for peace within,
When his thoughts and actions are full of hate,
And evil prevails—it's sad to relate

There is however no need to despair,
For our God is full of loving care,
And if we humbly turn to Him,
He will wash away our sin.

And if we then follow our Saviour,
He will help up to control our behaviour
And He will teach us how to love,
Which conquers all through God above.

Alicia Anne Griffiths

Why Me?

I lie awake at night and wonder "why me?" Then I think "why not?"
I lie awake at night and feel the pain, it cuts like a knife.
I lie awake at night and try to imagine a normal life, I can't.
I ask myself why no one protected me, was I so worthless?
I trusted him with my life, he abused me.
I loved him, he raped me.
I was abused for three years, yet I looked the same.
I hated my life, nothing changed.
I hated myself, no one knew.
Then I woke up from my nightmare, and everything changed.
I discovered people care.
I discovered I'm worth knowing.
I discovered life is worth living.
I'm glad I survived.

Agnes Adair

The Boomerang of Love

Love is to give away,
Not to look back, but ahead of the day.
Jump in, aim for pure gold,
Let the sun shine in, and drive out the cold.
There is no death while we remember,
Absence makes the heart grow fonder.
A new day, a new beginning,
Yesterday's mistakes have been forgiven.
Be dependant on our Father above,
From him we'll find our one true love.
Thank God for the care He's brought,
The wonderful things that He has wrought.
A new day is born, so silently pray,
Smile in the beginning and through the day.
Grab happiness by the scruff of the neck,
Each day is new so what the heck.
Regret not the things you've done,
Now you must act, then you've won,
Never give up, determine your thoughts,
Relax, be happy, not out of sorts.

Susan Whayman

Robin Red Breast

Little robin red breast sat upon a tree
Little robin red breast sang a song to me.

He sang about the winter.
With hardship by the score.

He sang about the spring time.
When he begs for crumbs on more.

He is now in the woodland.
All the summer long.

Keeping people happy.
With his merry song.

A. W. J. Knee

Halloween Night

Dark mists and mourning drifts
across the midnight streets.
Fires burn with evil fun
and spirit shadows meet.

Empty towns in rainstorms drown
in deadly silent fear.
Children cry in terror voice
as the midnight hour draws near.

Thunder rolls as lightning scores
its power in fearful wrath.
Lurking shadows cast their shade
to reveal their deadly mask.

Midnight lapses into dawn
to awake the ghost town streets.
And life begins to live again
as Halloween parts its grief.

Paula McGrath

Woodland Birdsong

A speckled thrush was singing; sound echoed through the trees.
Such a happy, lively little song, was carried on the breeze.
I had to stop, and listen, and as I stood quite still,
From every leafy hiding place, I heard a chirp and trill.

A harmony of sounds then came, from sparrow, finch and lark,
From blackbird, and from robin in this shady woodland park.
The floor was carpeted in blue, with moss and shrub between,
And the budding canopy above, was every shade of green.

The silent sunlight, through the trees, seemed to enhance the sound
Of the warbling, and the chirping, that came from all around.
When God surveyed creation, and saw that it was good,
I'm sure He too was listening to that birdsong in the wood.

Ena Parry

Harry

Harry is so charming,
Harry is so cute,
His little cry is so alarming.
His beautiful white suite.
Who is Harry? You may ask!
Well I've got for you a little task,
Read on my friend for more clues.
This person on certain days wear little blue shoes.
This person to me is very special
And sometimes he likes a little toy to wrestle.
If you've got a baby cousin you should have guessed
Because my baby cousin Harry is worth a million pounds
and not a penny less.

Amy Hilton

The Super Market

Today I'm not feeling very jolly;
Off to the super market, and there, wonky trolly.
This is the day I've come to dread.
So, first isle is fruit, salad and veg.
Round the corner are tins and packet soups.
Bumping into shoppers chatting in small groups.
Next stop, sauces, pickles, oil and jam.
Trying to stay calm, if I can.
Get a ticket for a queue and wait.
Because I have number eighty eight.
After that I'm on my knees,
I only wanted ham and cheese.
Off I go, to fish-fingers and meat.
This stupid trolly, I have to beat.
Now it's yogurt, fats and marge.
Do I want small, or shall I get large?
Mustn't forget the household goods!
I'd miss this trauma, oh if only one could!
At last I've finished, will I be quick getting through?
Have to find a check-out, with no queue.

Iris G. Timms

To All People Who Have Lost in Many Ways

Loneliness can suddenly swoop
It brings an aching void
Life stayed the same for all those years
A bomb went off and silence reigns.

Life jackknifed off in all directions,
Losing a mother, father, nephew, gaining an illness
Left us clutching to the daily rituals.

It scarred the living, smiles covering
the sadness, withdrawals of contact,
phone calls, easier to reach in not out.

Oh God, without you what will for life?
To trust you'll leave us with each other
and yet, in all the painful solitude,
The different life and different me,
A peace abounds so strong and new,
It must be Godly sent.

Janet B. Masters

I Stroll with You

When you think of me, remember that time we walked along the prom. So many days ago and I will think of you in a similar light.
Remember the rain forming puddles at our feet, expanding to a river far below the street. Like that river, so our dreams and lives will grow, hopefully together, but who really knows? (Though I do hope you care).
Think of me with a smile, as I do you, not frown or glare, just happy thoughts.
Like a child I rushed (your hand in mine) those puddles beneath our feet, like a child I dream of you.
You seem so many miles away, though it isn't very far!
But like the rain my dreams evaporate, the puddles go and back once more they are a memory, like you!

S. A. Jones

Seasons

Spring is here, snowdrops grow,
The sun is warmer, melts the snow.
Daffodils, in March winds sway,
Summer now is on the way.

Summertime brings long hot days,
Ice cream cornets, and holidays,
Fluffy clouds, and bright blue skies,
Birds and bees and dragonflies.

Autumn leaves turn gold, orange, and red,
Fall to the ground, a soft warm bed.
For hedgehogs, and maybe a field mouse
To help keep warm his little house.

The winter days are cold and dark
Jack Frost comes, leaves his mark,
Icicles, wind, sleet and snow,
The fire holds a welcoming, warming glow.

P. Thorley

Is It Really Over

Sometimes late at night
I lay awake and think of you.

Visions of you are still strong in my head
Silly little things that we are said.

You made me laugh, I made you cry,
I said hello and you said goodbye
I didn't mean to hurt you,
I never worked to see you cry,
And when said it's over, I just wanted to die.

So, I went home and laid in the floor,
With our song playing full blast,
Without you there was no future,
So I had to live in the past.

You know how much I still love you
and you should know that I still care

And like the shadow by your side,
you can guarantee I'll be there.

Acister James Ford

Pippy

A funny old pup, not everyone's choice
A will of his own so naughty, not nice
But after a while with love and affection
He soon became the dog of perfection

Life was so happy when Pip was around
A handsome hunk, adorable hound
Shadows were chased as they danced on the wall
A rough old game with his ring and a ball

Fourteen years these pleasures we had
When Pip said goodbye we were all very sad
He'll remain for ever in our memory
A faithful old dog was our 'Pippy'

Rose Biddulph

Through the Eyes of a Soldier

Houses are vacant and totally destroyed
Those who left here, were desperately annoyed.
There's food in the cupboard, on the table too
Leave quickly was what they had to do.

Children's toys, clothes and books too
Strewn on the floor, as children do.
But not 'cause of play from day to day
'Twas fear and hate as they ran away.

In gardens animals were left, tethered to die
Rotting away right where they lie.
Cats and dogs are now running wild
So full of fear, afraid like a child.

It's been four years, now families return
The stress remains, but now they learn.
Rebuild their lives, their families too
Turning the old back into new.

My time out here has come to an end
It's up to these people to make amend,
It's my turn now, I'm going home
I'm leaving the Bosnians, 'home alone' . . .

Terence L. Morgan

Merlin's Spell

Ye remember days of old, when men were fearless
And knights were bold.
A time of joy it doth bring,
The days of Arthur the King.
As boy and man he did reign
Uniting the land once again.
Protecting the poor from evil deed,
Camelot, his kingdom, would succeed.
As centuries have long gone by,
It doth bring a tear to my eye.
No grave, no sign, who can tell,
Did Merlin the Magician cast a spell.
No one knows, no one can say.
Would Arthur the King return some day.

Patrick Russell

Untitled

You mean so very much to me
My heart for you will always be
A thing called love that we do share
Is showing our feelings, showing we care
The things we do and the things we say
Can't make our true love go away.
Understanding each other can be hard to do
Forgetting our love we will never do.
Remember the promise we made to each other
That our love will last always and forever.

Deborah Rutter

Jemma Louise

We came over the water to see you
on that magical day you were born.
A thousand kisses inside us
o what a beautiful morn.

In absolute wonder we held you
our pride just ready to burst,
Just seeing our granddaughter perfect,
and you being our first.

So welcome our new little treasure
to a family who'll love you so much.
With arms now aching to hold you
and those small soft fingers to touch.

We hope that we see you quite often
so we can share your growing up years.
You have made us a proud gran and granddad
in fact you have moved us to tears.

Sheila Slaney

Nature's Masterpiece

New life beginning, what a joy to behold,
Springtime in the countryside, a wonder so I'm told,
Flowers bursting into bloom, dewdrops glistening in the morn,
Nature at its very best, little lambs will soon be born.

Strolling through a shaded wood, picnics by the sea.
Summer in the countryside, that's the place to be.
Lemonade and ice-cream, lazing in the sun,
Children racing home from school, the holidays begun.

Crunching through the fallen leaves, cocoa by the fire,
Autumn in the countryside a dream that I desire,
The lovely shades of brown and gold, a red and auburn hue,
A masterpiece of nature that I have to share with you.

Robins in the garden, lights on Christmas trees,
Winter in the countryside is always sure to please.
Building snowmen in the park, skating on the ice,
Hot dogs round the bonfire, it's all so very nice.

So if you get the chance to spend each season of the year.
Dwelling in the countryside. I'm sure I've made it clear.
Just keep your eyes wide open, look around and see.
That on your very doorstep, is God's own tapestry.

Julie Griffiths

Autumn of Inhumanity

When the woodland was stilled in the evening
And the gale from the north had blown out,
Amassed were the piles of brittle brown leaves.
So great was the fearsome assault
That it caused me to think of a time long ago,
Of a slaughter, that history re-run,
When night fell upon not brittle brown leaves,
But the heaped, bloodied corpses of men.

When the woodland was stilled in the evening
And calm had returned to the land,
The trees that had fallen now leant on their brethren.
Such was the constant demand;
That it caused me to think of a time long ago,
When the wounded cried out for a hand
And the agonized moans of men in death throes
Littered a scarlet land.

Colin Ayling

Dreams of You

Each broken dream I see your face
A face that is so honest and true
Yet one cannot help wondering
What thoughts are on your brow

Eyes that burn like embers in the night, fill with such soul
Igniting all the flames, which fills one with desire.
A desire that is so deep; one fear to tread for fear of
Falling in a sea of deep despair

A smile that lights up a thousand dreams
Say it's alright, you can wake up now

Dreams . . . one can only dream

Pauline Palmer

Memories Are Forever . . . . .

You lie in the green of a peaceful place
When I think of you—your beautiful face . . .
We had our time to love and play,
But your time had come to leave that day

Do you believe in fate? —Why does this happen?
We had a strong love—your leaving was sudden
I hope your peace prevails now you lie to rest,
Everything you gave—you gave no more than your best

I'll never forget you, in my memory so strong . . .
Who can say what is right or say what is wrong?
You were taken away, who can say why?
A smile when I remember and sometimes I'll cry . . .

Tracey King

Rain

As I peered to look down at your face;
I wished, that I could take your place.
So that you'd be alive, and I'd be dead,
And you'd be crying for me, instead.
And although I couldn't stand, to see you cry,
I'd prefer you crying, than to see you die.
And as I tried, to hold back my fears,
To hold back, the oceans and oceans of tears;
The heavens above, they couldn't stop,
Letting their millions of tears drop.
And the rain and tears, they were all for you,
Because you were so kind, and honest and true.
And it rained so much, that fateful day;
That day, that you went far away.
When you even made the heavens weep;
That day, when forever, you went to sleep.

Monir Akhtar

Mystery of a Dream

Behind the eye is where the dreams lie,
be it a picture or words on a page
sometimes on the screen, others on the stage,

The magic of your dream, is only for you!
Most dreams mean more than they seem.

Dreams are like diamonds
so pure and so strong.
They interpret the feelings
you've had all day long.

As pure as a sky of blue,
fluffy white clouds showing through,
Every dream is different
for me and for you . . .

Tracie Holland

My Invisible Friend

There are two men with whom I share my life,
but one has never been seen,
I know he is always there for me and on him
I can lean.
He is with me when I am happy and also when
I am sad,
Just knowing that he is always there makes
me feel so glad.
He helps me in so many ways and when life gets
hard to bear,
I know I only have to call his name and he is
always there.
It's Jesus of whom I speak and tell my troubles to,
For if he was not there I don't know what I would do.
So if you ever feel alone and have something to share,
Just take a quite moment and turn to him in prayer.

P. M. Brinn

Penicuik Woods

With the sun in the skies and the birds above
I sat there dreaming of those I love.
The trees around me reached up to the sky
Oh happy birds as they wheel and fly
All this beauty in my heart all day
Never dreaming it would die away
But life is love and love is duty
Oh I must see again the place where my heart clings
The memory of sweet half-forgotten things
New life is stirring all around
Young trees shooting from the ground
I told the birds, we sang together
As I sat with my feet in the purple heather.
Looking upward to the sky
The trees would soon be flying high.
And sighing winds would flick the leaves
Sending a whisper in the gentle breeze.
I'll hear that whisper as I go my way
Remembering beauty on a summer day.

Alexa Duncan

Life's Great Mystery

What is the purpose I wonder?
For our presence here on this land.
There must be a reason I'm sure
But the answer, is not at hand.

It may be a wonderful story
Which one day is bound to unfold.
And then the truth of the purpose,
Will no doubt, have to be told.
Are we here to impress some great being?
Or are we just passing through?
Are we fulfilling, great dreams and hopes?
And if so, why? And for whom.

There must be a reason for living,
But the mystery still remains
Why are we here?
And for what reason?
And where is the missing link in the chain

Bettie Gracia

Spring

Winter has almost gone
　A new spring has sprung,
Our feathered friends are daily visiting,
　The glorious colour of our flowers.
Hedgerows too are beginning to awake
　The rich yellow of the Daffodils the Snowdrops so serene
A little cluster of Primroses peeping as to say
　Spring is truly on the way.
Let's not think of the dark dull days
　Just keep on looking for each delightful bud to appear
And say this is a Violet to enjoy today.
　What next tomorrow, we shall see
The hedgerow has so much beauty for all of us to see
　The baby lambs are so much fun
Do stop a while and watch mother and child
　Each sharing such love and gentle caring.

Norma Pusey

Dying Love

Till death us do part and a dying love.
Wonderful memories cast aside
Feelings, once strong and glowing, now tarnished
Broken hearts hurting deep inside

A couple once happy, now desperately unhappy
Do they really wish to part?
Years of loving to be forgotten?
Not one last attempt to heal two lover's hearts?

Don't leave unsaid those lingering thoughts of love.
Try to revive that feeble, flickering flame
into a roaring, purifying fire from which ashes,
the Phoenix of a greater love will arise again

David Alderson

Seaview

When you walk, alongside a beach.
Close to the waves, you can almost reach.
Take a look, across the sea.
Where the sky, meets the water, a sight to be.

Hear the wave, rushing to land.
Spreading its mark, across the sand.
Take a breath, smell the ozone.
A peaceful place, to be alone.

You must return, again at night.
Imagine the scene, under moonlight.
A more romantic place, will never be found.
You'll fall in love, just with the sound.

Stars and moon, shining so bright.
Reflecting on water, a wonderful sight.
Once you have seen it, you're bound to come back.
If not in daylight, you will, in the dark.

Alan D. Flicker

Old Age

What is old age but a slow decline as the years pass by?
the world is out there but we know it not,
we have no family and our friends have died,
we have little money but we make ends meet,

The world is mad and cruel, but perhaps it always was?
so what awaits our closing years?
what can we hope for in this modern world?
a whiskery face, a dribbling mouth and a bib around our necks,
in high-backed chairs against a wall,
where no one ever comes to call?

E. M. Hayton

A Scottish Summer Saunter

Wandering through the golden valley,
On a carpet of flowers and leaves.
A swallow dances overhead.
On the warm summer breeze.
A cockroach climbs the lazy willow,
A dance upon its feet.
And a peregrine dives from the clear blue sky,
Upon its prey, which death will meet,

A mountain goat stands aloof,
On a rock above the trees.
And the salmon swim amongst the depths,
Of the locks and inland seas.
An old man rows his fishing boat,
To lay his nets and pots.
And the deer hunters stalk the ground,
To fire their well-aimed shots.

Oh buttercups beautiful yellow and green,
Oh daffodils of the same.
No more a wonderful sight can be seen,
In the light summer rain.

Barry David Dunne

With What Steep Steps

With what steep steps we lurch along the way,
Each step the tougher as the load grows more
And heavier yet, as each heart has its say
And pushes on to make itself more sore.
And yet we'd not be free, for that's our bug-
We hug our pain, enjoy the greater weight,
Talk with frail smiles of how we love to lug
Our dearest agony of wish and hate.
Yet, strangely, as we bend and shuffle on,
Each pace removes us further from the cause,
And what was unendurable is none
So heavy when we stand and stretch and pause.
Our load slips from us with no parting pain
As we walk on and leave it in the lane.

Philip Harries

Summer Time

Summer time is here again
Now we hope a bit less rain,
Carpets of daffodils colour of sun,
Children come out to play and run,
Out come the hustle and bustle of mowers,
And in go the seeds for flower growers,
The smoke is rising, barbeque I think,
People talking and laughing, some drink,
Don't forget the busy bees
Making honey for the family teas,
  The butterfly 'tis fluttering round,
  Very quiet, there is no sound.
  The lilows, the creams all around,
  Pink arms and faces to be found,
  Everyone loves the summer time,
  Drinking lots of lemon and lime,
  Ice cream and lollies melting away,
  Who cares, it's a beautiful day.

Brenda Locke

Untitled

The eighth of May was the blessed day,
I first set my eyes on my wife.
I thought she was nice and through trouble and strife
We're now together for life.

We awoke one morn' to find a child to be born,
To make our family complete.
A great gift from God to be honoured and awed,
Who we both could not wait to meet.

Our baby came as we thought she might,
Late in the hours of the night.
A bundle of joy, so small . . . like a toy.
She really is my pride and joy.

I can't describe what I felt inside.
Feelings that I could not hide.
Admiration for my wife adoration for my daughter
I could not believe that I was a father.

With tears in my eyes I held her close,
Counting ten fingers and ten toes.
The love that was forged for us that day.
Will last forever I'm glad to say.

Adrian Duke

Spring Neap at Benacre Broad—Suffolk

By Benacre Broad in the depth of the night,
A reflecting full moon as my guiding light,
Wandering with care along the cliff's edge,
Aware of myself and the fox in the sedge.

The roar of scouring shingle ebbing the beach,
Respect for nature, the sea is due to teach,
A rushing flight of wildfowl heading due south,
Answering calls of wild ducks from the broad mouth.

A ghostly white shape hunts the night air,
Two passing black shapes momentarily scared,
Moonlight on surf illumines the shore,
Scudding dark clouds shadow the bracken moor.

My motive was to witness a spring neap in flood,
North sea's surging force pounds over the mud,
The cliff's face shakes and trembles beneath,
Danger realized, nature's sword in sheath.

Crashes of falling cliff face, too near,
I stand and feel a deep inward fear,
Looking down at the surge, so close to the edge,
Time to go, leaving the fox in the sedge.

Stanley Gunn-Matthews

You Hate?

You created me and my ideology
You led me to believe in you
And now you torture with psychology
You warm to lies and hide from the truth.

You subjugated me and flourished
You seemed to catch me off my guard
And now You're tired but you are nourished
You're kind to all that's cruel and hard.

You hated all that's sacred or profane
You caused me to be confused
And now you follow me and the insane
You believe the lie but know the truth.

You debated with my strongest belief
You played on my vulnerable state
And now you'd like to take away all I see
You're unaware that all I see is hate.

You fated circumstance and blew out the flame
You made me sacrifice all I knew
And now you lift your head out of the shame
You fed the lies and you murdered the truth.

Elizabeth Thomas

Conflict

Conflict is the essence of all drama, so they say.
Two strong forces tearing one apart.
Dramatically, conflict is pulling me today
Tugging at my head and at my heart.

Shall I play the leader and use my head,
Marching out my problems from further battle?
Shall I play the woman, finding tears to shed,
Allowing storm to pass, as sleeping cattle?

I'm weak, I'm weak, I just don't want to fight.
I don't want unpleasantness or struggle any more.
No longer caring to be the leading light,
Or keep the snarling wolf from the door

Not liking to be weak, nor to be strong.
No longer knowing right, from knowing wrong.

Angela Brennan

My World

Everyone's world is their own private place,
the thought of this may put a smile on your face,
or a tear of sadness may run from your eyes,
for your world may be filled with nothing but lies
But I guess everyone's world is just a lie,
a lie to cover up the truth inside,
a truth that once hurt you so badly
and made you look upon life so sadly.
Take a look in the mirror, what do you see?
A face that's young and bright and happy?
I know my world's not a perfect place,
but my world's a world to put a smile on my face.
Hopefully one day that's what you'll see;
next time you look at a picture of me
and you'll remember the good times
we shared together.
I know my memories will stay alive forever.

Emma Hunter

The Cruel Waters of Time

Time seems to me a ferocious, rampaging flood,
Separating us.
Uncrossable,
The current too strong,
Plucking you from the bank,
And carrying you relentlessly away.
No boat,
No bridge,
No way of you ever returning.
Leaving us here looking back,
No heart to look forward,
Just looking back,
As silently, impotently, we watch you slip away.

Gemma Pett

The Polar Bear

The polar bear
Walks across the icy snow
Shining in the sun.
In the Arctic
There are no trees or butterflies,
No lions or play grounds.
He is alone with the seals, the fish
And the penguins maybe.
He hunts—anything will do.
He makes holes and puts his head in the water,
Looking for a juicy seal.
He grabs it, gets it out
and pulls off its tail.
A delicious lunch!
When he gets home
He goes to bed and has dreams
About monsters eating him.
He wakes up in a fright.
Jumps up and falls flat on the floor forever.

Natasha Michaelides

Safe

The sky is clear and beautiful tonight,
The moon shines a sordid yellow,
The light imprints its shape in my curious eye.

The landscape is empty,
Hidden under a veil of darkness.

The stars look like little dots of drowning hope
In a malevolent black sea.

Never before have I felt so alone,
But tonight, I am not afraid,
I want to lurk in the evenings unknown.

It is bewildering
I have never felt so safe.

Dee Oliver

Sunsets

Beautiful sunsets in the sky
Leaving reflections which catch the eye.
Slowly the shadows come into sight
As the last burst of colour is a delight.

As the sea flows over the sands anew
Watching the sun setting.
Reds, oranges, yellows and blue
Ending the day as the moon comes in view.

Along the road towards the coast
Over the sea which I love most
Was a glorious sunset drawing me
Heaven wards towards eternity.

Through my kitchen window I have a view
Always seeing something new.
What a glorious sight to behold the eye
As the sun setting colours the sky.

As the artist picks up his tools
One wonders how the sun rules.
What a wonderful picture to produce
On his canvas as he paints the truth.

Aves Swanson

New Awakenings

The air is soft as velvet against winter's weary skin,
The sun is gently warming all around and within,
The magic of spring time enters every waiting glade,
Dapples the earth in sunshine and soft deep velvety shade,
The birds are gaily singing now cold dark days are gone,
In celebration bringing the news to every one.

Get up you, primrose, daffodils, bluebells too,
It's time to show your beauty, to start your life anew,
Sweet pussy willows, fluff out your soft furry heads,
Flowers, flaunt your colours, soft golds, blues, and reds,
Creatures of the woodlands, your winter sleep must end,
Get up, start your mating, your messages of love now send.

What a lovely time this is for everyone and everything,
Promising new hope, new love, making you want to sing,
Get out and join the fun, start your life this day,
Man, maid, and everyone, come out, it's time to play.

Irene Webley

Ambered Spirals

When the dark skies slowly drift in and the moon mellows in gold
the geese will fly on dusky clouds and on the scent of the African lily.
Shallow waters run softly by the edge of the ambered marble—that sets in spirals.
Soft scented air slowly drifts across the plains and another enchantment has begun.
Yesterday's dust has settled and the moon is in full bloom. The long hot day is slowly fading and the warm coolness of the tropical night has just begun.

Vittoria Lucynda Vinchellii

Autumn

There came a day
   that caught the sun,
wrung its neck,
   plucked it and ate it.

"What shall I do with the bird,"
   the day said, "The birds I've
frightened, let fly. I'll hang out pork
   for the brave blue tits."

"What shall I do with the people?"
   the day said, "I'll stuff them with
blackberry and apple pie, they'll
   love me till the day I die."
Linda Harrison

E Is for Ecstasy

Ecstasy is the day of his birth.
His innocence, purity, the sunshine of our lives.

Ecstasy is his first day of school.
Absolute assurance that each tear was pure love.

Ecstasy is exam results day.
Delight replacing fear; "He's a smart wee lad!"

Ecstasy is his growth in High School.
Formals, prizes, dates and that photo in 'The Star'.

Ecstasy is yet ecstasy was
The sharp, cold end of his short life because

Ecstasy was the cause of his death.
His lifeless body in the morgue.

And, ecstasy is for us, now only
That photo in 'The Star'
The termination of our lives.
Corrina E. Allison

The Broken Pane

Your face is never far from my memory,
Your name rises readily to my lips,
And those moments we shared, so long ago,
Still hang in the misty past.
I hear you calling from the depths of the night,
Laughing and crying;
All the times we had have passed by,
The window has fogged up,
The moments live no more
As the wind blows and slams that door.
The window is a mirror now, reflecting only me,
As I hear you, see you,
Now drifting out of reach.
From the recesses of my mind
Gone are you
And I will be too, as I drift and fade,
Following you through the broken pane.
Caron L. Hunt

Forbidden Fruit

Dedicated and written for David Blades

Forbidden fruit that I cannot touch,
Even though I want him so much.
Someone else's orchard he lies in, not mine,
My orchard is empty, no fruits you'll find.
Temptation is hard,
The smell, the taste and the touch,
Why someone I can't have I want so much,
My instincts tell me to lay off
As the consequences will be so rough.
Bad mouthed and titled I would be
For trying to let the fruit go free,
Away from the orchard with walls so high.
My orchard no walls can confined
The greener grass that he will find
Is it greener on the other side??
Avril Thomson

Moon Child

Woman, I am
Moon, I am
Goddess, I am
as I look above and suckle on your milk
pouring through the fullness of my lips,
into the roundness of my breasts,
You nurture me, I am your child,
You cradle me in the curve of my own femininity.

My breasts rise and swell with the cycle of the moon,
pregnant with your seed that grows in me,
I sacrifice my menses in honour of the Goddess
that lives in The Temple of my own form,

Birthing Thy Moon Child inside of me,
I give my all,
my nakedness, my ghosts, my shadows, and my bones . . .
and lay them on your altar,

Praising you,
Raising you,
Bleeding you,
Being you.
Erika Brincat

One Regret

The rain has stopped, roof so quiet now.
Sleep to come?

Perhaps the curtained breeze will help to lift me past . . .
   last the days so troubled, first to cloudy nights
and cloudier dreams.

Dreams—that which keep life long and full; thoughts
ever thought times ever had.
   So maddening life can be but here, our salvation rests.
Lest we follow these self-same dreams, we drive
ourselves through a truly wasted world.

I've set so many dreams aside I cry to know these years
are through.
   But as the rain begun again so my dreams will come—
again to place me softly high and gently let me soar this night.
Timothy Upson

The Soul

Beneath your face of rough and tumble,
There lies a soul that can easily crumble,
This soul can crumble with hate or spite,
This soul is what gives you the will to fight.

Beneath your face of rough and tumble,
There lies a soul that can easily crumble,
This soul can crumble with death or fear,
This soul is what gives you the will to shed a tear.

So when you ask yourself "who am I?",
You are a body in which a soul does lie
Amie Kneale

Ode to Lars William Hansen
(13 Year Old Downs Syndrome)

My Dad is a fisherman with a yellow boat,
A Souwester Hat and a yellow coat.
He travels all around the coast.
To see if he can catch the most.
Some days he only gets a few,
But then again his nets are new.
Although I only am a boy,
I'd pull the winch and jump for joy,
To feel the sway and salty spray,
Help with the chores on a lovely day.
Lars William is the name of the Boat.
One day I shall have a yellow coat,
To help my Dad with Monk and Cod,
I'll take a fishing line and rod.
Who knows what life will have in store
With me on board, he may catch more.
C. E. Hansen

Bedtime Thought

Laying in my bed at night,
Curtains pulled together tight,
Snug and warm in my bed
With covers pulled up to my head.
I listen to the wind and rain,
Lashing against my window pane,
I wonder about the birds in the trees,
What do they do on nights like these?
Are they warm? Are they safe?
Does their mother take them to another place?
I think of all the creatures out there,
It seems to me, it's just not fair.
Laying in my bed at night,
Snug and warm and tucked in tight,
I close my eyes and say a prayer,
For all the animals out there.

Stefanie Radford

A Mother's Thoughts

No more diplomatic tact or premonition of impending doom,
No more guarded secrets hidden surreptitiously in each room.
No more frustrated tears as the fickleness of man
Invades a youthful mind and destroys a youthful plan.
No more frightened fears that there will be nought to give
To a world that seeks so much in order just to live.
No more fierce competition or security to be needed,
Words of advice have been carefully thought about and heeded.
The fears and tribulations that gradually receded when
My three little boys became three well adjusted men.

Pauline Ratcliffe

Weeping Willow

Weeping willow, you stand alone,
The things that you weep for are to some, unknown.
But I know why you're saddened and why you cry,
Why you don't stand tall and reach for the sky.

You weep for famine, you weep for war,
You weep for the fact that we'll always want more.
You don't understand why we fight and we kill,
And, to be honest, even we, never will.

You ask yourself 'Why, what's the point of it all?'
When the world is so special and is meant for us all.
You weep because you know that we'll always want our way,
And will plunder and kill until that day.

If only everyone knew why you cry,
Then maybe they'd stop and ask themselves 'Why?'
But they don't hear you, and I doubt they ever will,
They'll ignore you, weeping willow, as they continue to kill.

It makes me wonder, what's the point in war?
Why do we think that we'll always need more?
We have so many things, though we think we have none,
But we won't realize, until they're all gone.

Jennifer Ebrey

Memories

The open windows invite me to stay,
I feel I am taking part in a play,
And if I move, it will fade away,
I gaze at the scene as though in a trance,
A gentle breeze blows, the trees start their dance,
Tall grasses sway as the Ballet proceeds,
Then dark clouds gather at crazy speeds.
The movements increase to a noisy crescendo,
The sunlight fades and darkness replaces
The joy and excitement of the opening phases.
A threatening silence, a chilling fear, frightening.
A crash of thunder—a flash of lightning
The whole scene ruined by blinding rain,
Now there is nothing but a growing fear
That this moment of magic can ne'er reappear.

All this is just in my mind,
For, alas, I must tell you, I am blind.

Evelyn Fearnehough

More Than a Memory

You were there when I needed you—when I needed to cry,
You were there for me—when nearly died,
You were there in my sleep, my dreams.
You were my soul, as still it seems.

But when you needed me I turned a blind eye,
Your eyes filling with tears,
Yet I only sighed.
You prayed for me, I prayed for you,
But I were not there when you needed me too.

And when I realized that you were of a friend,
I'd lost you now to a different world.
Your soul remains a memory in its depth,
Your spirit form your body so cold.

I remember you as yourself,
Not as your cold dead body,
But as dancing spirit,
Free.

Sindy R. Martin

For Ben, Short Summer Days and Long Winter Nights

A smile that would melt an angel's wings,
Son you could have been so many things.
We misunderstood your mischievous ways,
How could we know how short the days.
Childish and beguiling looks,
Now just memories in photograph books.
Tiny, pale, and almost thin,
What a giant lived within.
Sweet memories of a little lad,
Mostly happy, sometimes sad.
Your life was short, how could we know,
We expected to be there, see you grow.
A boy that someday would make a lovely man,
A life almost over, before it began.
Grace, dignity, courage, never a grumble,
Ben you made us all feel humble.
Time can only ease, not heal,
The pain we left behind still feel.
One day we'll meet again in heaven son,
That's one promise you can count on

JR Hall

Innocence Lost

She lies in bed, she listens!
Listens to the sounds of the night
A dog barks, a car goes by,
The wind howls,
The rain beats upon the window pane,
A door clicks, a footfall sounds.
Please God; not again!
The cry in the night of a child in pain
who knows that life will never be the same again

Josephine Lane

Retirement

Since we retired, we've seen so much more
of this beautiful land than we ever did before.
We have time to travel, new friends to greet,
In caravan parks and out in the street.
We marvel at nature and stop to stare at lovely
trees and birds everywhere. We have time to
look at gardens and see the glorious colours, the
busy bee. As we leisurely shop we see different
faces from many countries and many races,
We have time to smile at each one and then,
maybe they will smile back again.
How did we find time to work each day?
Our days are so full, but we have time to play.
It's a wonderful world and we've learnt
how to care for this beautiful land
God gave us to share.

Audrey Shore

Out of Sight

What is hidden, but is so real?
It is Jesus Christ who is our keel.
He keeps us upright in the storms of life,
holds us steady through our trouble and strife.
No one sees the faith which is so strong,
or the Holy Spirit to whom we belong;
for both are out of sight where no one can see
but they are both essential to you and me.
Jesus said "Trust in me for I'm always there",
he keeps us safe by the Holy Spirit and his loving care.
On life's stormy seas we are certainly bound,
but by your faith you will be kept safe and sound,
by the power that surrounds you in God's armour;
on that you can depend and be forever sure.
So have trust and faith in what you cannot see,
that way you will be heaven-bound, definitely.
Now you know what is so real;
keep trusting Christ who's your unseen keel.

George W. Reed

She Doesn't Know

She doesn't know what she wants
So you don't know what to do.
She doesn't know what she wants
So you feel sad and blue.
She doesn't know what she wants
So we've been pushed aside.
She doesn't know what she wants
So do I swallow my pride?
She doesn't know what she wants
So you are waiting to see,
She doesn't know what she wants
So if she doesn't want you . . . you want me!

Beverley Willis

The Park

As I strolled through the park
I heard the singing of a lark.
A gentle breeze blew through the trees
Which made me sneeze.
Around the park, people laid on the grass with ease
With children playing, and feeling really pleased.
The bees and butterflies danced around
The sensitive flowers, which were planted in the ground.
Playful squirrels ran about
Without fear or doubt.
On the banks of the pound, ducks fed on bread
While grown-ups sat and read.
As I walked this way
I wished such a beautiful day, would stay

Deborah Ahmed

The Plum Crumble

Tinker, tailor, soldier, sailor . . .
The blue and white tale of China vanishes
beneath the rubble of plum stones.
The grown-ups spit them out and pass them,
still sticky, to me.
I wriggle around, longing to fly away with the turtle doves,
But Grandpa is still eating.
Free at last! I'm digging in the grass,
My fingernails black with earth.
I'm planting an orchard, not in rows,
but weeping willow shaped.
Twenty years hence fountain trees of white blossom
will shower this lawn.
Come autumn I will stand in their shade
with children of my own.
We'll gather up the falling fruit and carry it indoors
to make a crumble.
I'll serve it up on willow pattern plates,
They'll play tinker, tailor,
while I wonder where the doves have flown.

Georgie Sabin

Ode to Swampy

Human moles burrow deep,
in their tunnels eat and sleep.
The authorities scream "why the protest?"
As mankind fasts forwards the wheels of progress.
Poisoning air, plundering seas,
to fulfill man's growing needs.
Forests fall, fine trees so tall,
To supply the demands of Do It All.
A person dies, ten are born,
And so we carry on and on.
"The end is nigh!"
The nutters cry,
But no one hears above the noise
Of the industry that man employs.

Steve Harrison

I Need Your Love

I can't leave you alone, I am so in love with you,
no words can express, make me feel wanted and loved
as I am feeling for you.

I feel for you oh loved one,
I really do
I am so much in love with you, everyday make me feel
wanted and cherished. Make me yours tonight.

Girl, I try to make you understand that I want this love
to be real. What about us—I'm in need of your love—what
about us on and on we go.

Oh love me baby because I know just what I need,
I'm in need of your love and what about us making love
till the breaking of dawn.

Oh cherish my love, I want to love you, know and I always,
till the break of dawn I want to love you, I'm in need of
your love now and always.

You're in need of your love, as much I need your love.
Make me feel your tender mercy surrounding me always
I need you, you need me, make me yours tonight.

A. L. Wilkinson

A Collage

The lake faces me
With multiple of ripples canvassing its top.
The graceful pose of the swan, the heron,
Their eager looks penetrating for every sound.
The grassy verges surrounding this lake,
With hints of withered mosses,
Indeed catch glimpses of wild and unadorned beauty.
An almanac of wisdom,
Steeped in many histories
Known to learned people of this region.
Nighttime wonder of this view,
Beneath a galaxy of stars
Bring me closer
To a piece of Heaven upon earth.

Rita Cleary

Apathetic Junkie

Fed up with living, too scared to die
I escape this paradox by getting high
cocaine and heroin, life on the fringe
pure seratonin in a one mil syringe
tourniqued arm, bulbous vein
never mind the harm, just end the pain
chemical reactions in my bloodstream
unshackle my spirit, life becomes a dream
for a moment, I understand it all, don't feel so small
but the dream becomes a nightmare, I begin to fall
down, down, to the realm of despair
my beautiful dream beyond repair
back where I started, confused and heavy hearted
perhaps if I tried a little more,
I'd remember what I saw . . .

D. Mandary

An Evacuee

The noise was horrendous, I stood alone.
Mummy Mummy please, can I come home?
With my name on my coat, for all to see.
I was known as an Evacuee.

Herded like cattle on to a train.
Tears I was shedding were all in vain.
Mummy where are you? I need you now.
I cannot see your face in the crowd.

Land we covered from dawn to dusk.
Then we had a ride, on a bus.
In a hall we stood in a row.
One by one we had to go.

Once again I was all alone
Mummy O Mummy can I come home?
Behind a screen I heard them say.
We have no place for her to stay.

Tired and weary I fell asleep.
And than I woke and had a peep.
For I was cosy in my bed
Tears of happiness I shed, an Evacuee no more.

Mary East

I Love Thee Because

I love thee because thou art so gentle,
I love thee for being sentimental,
    Without you my life would have no meaning.

I love thee because thou are not mean.
I love thee because you always seem,
    To take me as I am and not expect a perfect mate.

I love thee for asking me to be your wife,
I love thee for giving me your life,
    To share with you till life is through.

I love thee because you are so strong,
I love thee for never doing me so wrong,
    You make the world a better place for me.

I love thee because you understand,
I love thee to take me by the hand,
    And feel your strength surge through my body.

I love thee because you always try to please.
I love thee because you try to ease,
    Life's burden for me when I am sad.

    I Love Thee

Iris Thompson

Spiders

Cradled moon
Within dense gossamer skies
Cries with tragic smile
The made lights
Spiders enjoy

Darkness in light
Cold in warmth

Noise! Beats boozey bars
Its music
Pings of tills
Mock screaming notes

Spiders, spiders spun and spent
Tighten quilts of cold eye darkened light

The moon cradles
Within its golden gondola
Not for slumber
But for equilibrium
Steadfastly to sail vast tides
Heralding day's end, the eternal truth
From which the spiders hide

Gail Harrison

Golden Chains (Inspired by Renoir's 'La Loge')

At the theatre, they both radiate
Riches which some can only ideate.
With lavish clothes and trinkets too,
Husband and wife—of the privileged few.

Their wealth holds them fast by a chain (of gold).
She plays the part that society, and its conventions,
Politely enforce.

At the theatre, but who are the actors?
Seemingly a spectator, the box becomes her stage.

Their distant nearness;
Joined at the shoulder, but spiritually worlds apart.

He, impassive in his corner, hiding behind the glass.
The binoculars, used to bring things closer,
Enable him to keep his distance.

She looks out and sees nothing. Her eyes, resigned,
Brimming with veiled tears.
And yet, she continues with the facade of concerts,
balls, and evenings at the theatre.

There is no better actor than that who lives the part,
And only a great painter brings life to his art.

Carla Calimani

Mouse Hunt

They chased me around the house all night,
That poor little lady almost died of fright,
As I dashed about this way and that,
It was worse than being chased by a cat.

They cornered me off to one small room,
The 'master' of the house carrying a broom,
All I could think of was doom and gloom,
Would he catch me, bash me or deliver me to my tomb.

Where should I hide—cupboard, draws or bed,
Oh! What a 'mouse hunt' I then led.
He's here! No he's not, could be—no!
Use your head little mouse and lay low.

Three hours later, I'm getting quite tired,
The engine not now so well fired,
So up I climb onto the bed,
What a merry dance I've led.

Not so funny now, this was all quite foul,
I think I will throw in the towel,
Here I am over here, I'll come quietly,
So out in the fields I go with glee—I'm so sorry!

Val Devonshire

The Belated Visit

Once in a lifetime possibly do people meet,
Such wonderful couples as I have met,
A meeting that created a twinkle in my eye,
Yet, coloured with a sense of loss that destiny had for us.

An awakening in the intensity of the recollection,
Of someone who was a mother to me, a sister to you,
Through whom I was made a part of you,
Yet unseen and unheard when her beloved's meet.

The dwelling where all her remembrances remain
Seems no longer a place for me to reside,
Having lost its beautician and rightful owner,
Appears to be a 'house' but no longer a 'home'.

Your standing near her and speaking in her manner,
Made her smile and say that you're too late
Which you couldn't hear since words were unable to express
The sisterly love for a brother as 'wonderful' as you.

The tears in our eyes were all for her,
Yet she seemed to be in a hurry and no longer wait,
To witness the cherished moment and feel
The warmth of the brotherly kiss meant for her.

Anindita Dey

The Ferrymen

Eight hundred years they plied their trade
O'wer the auld Queensferry passage
Baith North an Sooth their journey made
We' passengers and baggage

Life it was much simpler then
Time wisnae o' the essence
But life moves on, until when,
The word is Obsolescence

Ye'r boats ower wee! Can ye no' see?
They Canna tak' the load!
Whit ye need here, an' need it dear,
Is wan gigantic road.

An' sae across the forth they flung
Ae muckle massive brig
The queen she cam' its praises sang
Sae high, sae lang, sae, big!

Noo ower the forth the traffic flows
In never endin' streams,
While far allow the ferries go
But only in our dreams!

Robert M. Banks

Memories

The sun laughs from a sky
emphatically blue
I am searching through papers
heaped high on my desk but—
thinking of you.

We travelled across countries
our hearts full of joy.
We stopped in tranquil corners
where we were alone together
the car our new toy.

We climbed the mountains
we fished the sea.
We dined and wined everywhere
but always our happiness was complete
back at home for tea!

Then one Sunday night your heart
stopped suddenly—
no time to say good bye—
But ten years later memories
are still oh so comfortingly at my side.

Eva-Maria Callaghan

Where and When It All Began

One summer's day at the local church fete
July the 6th was the date
The day Paul met a Quarryman
Is where and when it all began.

They were introduced by a friend called Vaughan
And so the world's most successful group was born
Paul impressed the singer named John
Doing his impression of Eddie Cochran.

He knew all the words to Twenty Flight Rock
A song he'd listened to, down at the dock
John knew they needed this kid named Paul
If they were to be the greatest band of all.

George and Ringo both came along
Helping to keep The Beatles where they belong
Those four lads, epitomised those times
With songs like 'She Loves You' and 'I Feel Fine'.

They've left their mark in history
The greatest poets of the 20th century
Let's not forget where and when it all began
The day Paul met a Quarryman.

Adrian Hall

After the Rain

Like diamonds twinkling in the light;
Dewdrops gleaming in the sun;
From velvet flowers they softly fall,
Onto the rich, dark, moist earth below.
Filling our senses to the full,
Scent filling our twitching nostrils;
Touching of soft, silky smoothness;
The music pleasing to the ear,
Hearing the drip of tiny droplets,
Gently descending in quiet mood.
The sun shines forth upon the ground,
Sucking up moisture from the blooms,
Spreading their leaves with replenished feel,
Standing proud and erect
To reach to the skies with majestic respect.
The rising mist trailing upwards
Into the atmosphere retreats.
Reflections created thro' nature's glow,
Causing a wonderful sight;
A spectacular, iridescent rainbow!

Alice Stokes

Dream Land

Close your eyes, catch a ride
to dream land, it's up there in the sky.
Where the river flows of fizzy lemonade,
and ice cream flowers grow tall in chocolate rain.

Look at the sun, shinning down on Plasticine people,
lick it, taste it, it's made of toffee and treacle.

Count to three, make a wish,
see the jelly-green flying fish.
They'll take you home to your sleepy eyes,
until tomorrow's dream, and the yellow lemon lollipop surprise . . .

C. Leith

The Easter Parade

Said the Donkey to the Shire-Horse
"How did you fare, this day?
You posed so well throughout the course
I simply have to say.

You were Audacious in your baubles,
so cautions in your ways,
Your dauntless dawdle lingered on
Faultless they would say.

Your haughty naughty Jaunty sway,
had every one applauding,
and then you had to misbehave
their laughter leaves me maudling."

"Fret not, dear friend", the Shire-Horse claimed,
"had I been seen authentic,
this Night no doubt I might have been
A subject of Autopsy."

Thomas J. Kelly

Regrets

I wish that I could go back in time
And pick up the thread of our life as it used to be
My very soul was bound to yours and yours to mine
Our love was deep and endless like the flowing of the sea.

Doubts and fears and jealousy ate away my heart
Turning my love to hate and hurting you in many ways
Now we are many miles apart
And all I have are lonely nights and empty days

I walked away from you without a backward glance
But how I miss you and wish that I could have a second chance
Alas it is too late and I can only dream
The damage has been done—the loss is great
I mourn the passing of what could have been
And leave my future happiness to fate.

Mary Griggs

Identical Twins

How can one describe the joy one feels?
Two little girls, so sweet, so small,
So very dependant on you for all.
Sweet little faces, dear little mouths,
Hands opening and stretching, arms open wide,
Why are we waiting here on our sides?
Eyes that are open, we know we're alive.
We were safe in the womb, warm and cosy,
Oh why did we have to be born?
So very alike in every way.
"Love us and care for us please" they say,
"We didn't ask to be born."
"Precious babies," their mother replies,
"I'll love you more and more.
I'll try to make sure that your lives are good,
That you grow up strong and tall.
I'll try to protect you both from harm,
I'll feed you and keep you warm.
So that when you remember those first few weeks,
You will know you were meant to be born."

Ann M. Earley

Rainbows

Look at the rainbow high in the sky,
It's the only bow that you cannot tie.
All those colours, way up there,
It's so thin and fragile, it could easily tear.
You can never see the end of it, only in-between,
But you can still see all the colours, yellow red and green.
If you make a wish, when a rainbow is in the sky,
Don't take your time thinking,
Rainbows can go in the blink of an eye.

Nichola Ann Kennedy

24th November

She glides through my mind
Her voice a mere whisper
The fading warmth of her touch.
Where is she standing?
In front of a fountain?
Wanting to see me as much?
Her hand to a child
To wipe a falling tear
My Mother, are you still near?
Reach for the light
To fade the darkness
As I float away on a dream.
One flower I send you in Heaven
Sweet freesia of yellow so bold
Today is another birthday without you I'm told.
Each twenty-fourth of November
I gaze upon the evening star
I send you my love with a wish you are happy
Happy Birthday dear Mother,
Happy Birthday wherever you are.

Alison Dibb-Fuller

My Darling Baby

My innocent Angel
You smile but do not yet understand the meaning of it
I wonder if life will make you smile
Now as a tiny baby you have no worries
I look after and love you
I tend to your every need
Protecting you
You do not understand the joy you bring to me
Each time you look into my eyes and smile
You little angel, my heart feels so much love
I feel it could burst
Your tiny fingers grasp just one of mine
The warmth from your hand warms my heart
To my very soul
I kiss you as you fall asleep
I am the luckiest, happiest mother alive
Thanks to you, my own innocent angel

Trina Mayes

He Is

He is the One who was born as a babe
He is the One who in a manger was laid
He is the One in the temple who questioned and taught
He is the One whom all the crowd sought.

He is the One who died on Calvary's tree
He is the One whose blood was shed for you and me
He is the One who bore thorns on his head
He is the One who arose from the dead.

He is the One to whom we all pray
He is the Truth, the Life, the Way
He is the One who blots out our Sin
He is the One who gives us peace within.

He is the One who calms our fears
He is the One who wipes away all tears
He is the One who soothes our pain
He is the One who will return again.

He is the One who reigns on Heaven's Throne
He is the One who calls us his own
He is the One whose praises we sing
He is our "Saviour", "Redeemer", and "King".

Amy Gordon

Pretending Love

Can't you remember the love that we shared?
The fun and the laughter, the feeling that dared
Us to hold one another like husband holds wife
And the vow that you'd love me for the rest of my life.

Can't you remember our very last night?
The feeling of passion that we had to fight?
As I was wrong to love you as our love couldn't last
As she was your future and I was your past.

Can't you remember the tears that fell down my face
The hate that I'd felt as she'd taken my place?
My place in your heart, I wish was still there
But my place is hers now, for me you don't care.

But just you remember how much I need you
And if she ever leaves you as her love wasn't true
I'm here to turn to, to place back into your heart
To hold me tight within your arms and to say we'll never part.

And I won't remember that you really love her
I'll pretend that you care for me and when you whisper
That you love me, I'll pretend that you do
And I'll be your future, without love but with you.

Tracey Pearce

The Shamrock and the Rose

Sometimes, in the deep, dark, still of the night,
Down heaven's lofty stairway, starry and bright,
You travel to me—long dead—yet not dead,
And I shed gentle tears, at your fond words, unsaid.

Faces smiling, soft eyes shining
Journeying, again, roads, long and winding.
Two hundred years, our souls, dividing,
Enduring love, forever binding.

By lush green mountains, that sweep the sea
And mist-shrouded shore, where your hearts ever be.
I followed your footsteps, through wild Kerry's Ring
Such sad, haunting cries, to my heart, you all bring.

Now hush, be at peace, my ancestors dear,
My love for the shamrock, is crystal and clear
Because I be you, then you, also, be me
And we, through the barriers of time, have broken free.

So I'll wait with pride till you come for me,
Then we'll cradle each other, in eternity.
But from now, until then, and to what e'er will be.
God's love, will one day, our Ireland, set free.

Pamela Jackson

If Only

If only I'd been very clever
or studied and learnt more at school
I'd impress all I know with my knowledge
and never be seen as the fool.

If only I were more attractive
instead of being so plain
I'd dazzle the men with my beauty
not caring at all if I'm vain

If only I could have been perfect
then all would truly like me
I may even learn to like myself
when my perfect image I see

Yet I know I should be more accepting
and be thankful for that which I am
To follow my own true potential
doing the best that I can

We are all that little bit different
and there's purpose in every plan
"If only" we were more contented
there's a place here for every man

Jean Phillips

What Would . . . If It Could? . . .

I do sometimes wonder
what our world could look like,
if it were upside-down.
As we swam in the infinity of space
deep within the sky.

The world, the land, the contours
providing a lid to our curiosity.

Tree trunks would hang
like hairs from a dog's belly.
Buildings would jut forth
like limpets to the underside of rocks.
Rivers and lakes would truly defy gravity.
As if by suction, they could remain
embracing the ravines and valleys.
Leech-like
mountains could poke through the clouds
noseying their way down yonder.

The sun in its eternal playground
still skipping across the universe.

. . . But, what red faces we'd all have!

Rebecca Young

Mother's Memory

One Monday morning at five to seven
Our mother died and went to heaven
We did not see the angels come or go
As they carried off our mother's soul.

We knew she went, God only knows why
She lived her life, she had to die
We gathered, and we cried aloud
As her soul rose upon a cloud.

We know she went through the gates of heaven
That Monday morning at five to seven
That she was born to life anew
Up there beyond the sky of blue.

She had a temper, she had her charms
She is happy now in Jesus's arms
She died on earth, she lives in heaven
That is why the angels came at five to seven.

She lived on earth, suffered the strife
Now she lives her eternal life
Happy to be in heaven above
Sending down her lasting love.

David H. Venton

Lost

Only a few weeks, long ago,
I watched you from afar.
Did you even ever speak to me direct
Or I to you? I no longer remember,
Even that is gone.
All that is left is an impression
Of blond hair, a lopsided lameness
That only showed when you were tired,
But strong still, the burning integrity
That with one sentence defeated the whole group
Leaving the ringleader silenced.
And—for me alone
Dancing eyes above a smile.

Pauline Kontani

Summer Rose

I compare Thee to a summer rose
dressed to kill with an ivory nose
I guess deep down in my heart it was you I choose
Everyday has been and gone forever
I guess I'll never leave this place ever

Your touch is worth a thousand pounds
Your kiss is worth a lot more
I'm fast on my feet I can see the door
but I'll slip and hit the floor
I guess I'll wipe away your tears
but I have not seen you for years.

I compare Thee to my summer rose
dressed to kill with ten toes
everyday is coming to a close for me
it was too dark to see, did she love me?
I'll never know the reason to live
but when push comes to shove I'll give
My heart feels like it's torn on wire
cos in your eyes I can see the fire
summer rose, it was me, can't you see?

Peter Jay

Son

I hear the footsteps down the stairs, see your face shine round the door,
What response you're going to get you're never really sure.
Your glowing cheeks, your eyes of brown, that mouth that holds no shame,
When in doubt you shout it out 'I'm not the one to blame'.
You often fall and hurt yourself and every time I say
'Slow down and just go steady', but you carry on and play.
You cry, the game is at an end, my heart goes out to you
You're such a lovely little boy, I love you through and through.
That loving hug, that sloppy kiss, the one you've saved for me,
You're such a little character and so wise at only three.

Caryne Crane

Family Grocer

Family grocer, busy all day,
Working long hours for a small pay,
Slaughter-house floor, 'o what a sight',
Blow up a bladder and yell with delight,
Then hear the grind of the sausage machine,
Here comes the sausage, shining and clean.
Ernest the baker in floury mist,
Kneading the dough with a bang of his fist,
The counterman neat, all dressed in white,
Will slice some bacon and wrap it up tight,
Red polony and thick round black puddin',
Better hurry or you won't get a lookin',
Rows of deep drawers with shiny brown lacquer
Here comes a miner for a twist of tobacco,
The smell of spices, dried fruit and bran
Then into the shop strides the travelling man,
Who turns on the charm and winks a red eye,
And pulls from his coat a sample from Fry,
It's now getting late, we've done very nice,
Let's shut up the shop and catch a few mice.

Owen Davies

The River

Watch the winding river forever flowing on
Sometimes deadly silent, then bursting into song.
As it ripples over rocks and stones
and glides by mossy banks.
Not word of protest, not a word of thanks.
Oh bless you lovely river, for all your joy and grace,
You will flow along forever,
And none can take your place.

Mary Farr

Passing Time

Some men were born for great things, but fate was never sure.
Some men dance with feet of chance upon a golden floor.
Some men wait at fortune's gate and some are slaves to crime.
Though force of nature made me live, I'm just here passing time.

Through greater deeds of cruelty and hate that screams of love.
From orders pressed upon our hearts and judgement from above.
Who created anything, who fashioned yours and mine?
What is there left to care for? I'm just here passing time.

Mighty thoughts are given birth through history's telling tale.
Marvellous quests are fought and won, yet still more fighters fail.
Some set to forge a legend and yet they tow the line.
Even Queens and conquering heroes are just here passing time.

Great defenders of a faith and believers in a cause
are those that dream up every rule and those that make the laws.
And these who uphold our vanity and save us from ourselves
they dream up ways to kill us and then protect our health.
They are all our future as we follow every sign
in this life and the next, we are all just passing time.

Johnny Chappell

The Future

The nineteen nineties so they say
Will be the time to while away
To live in splendor and be gay
The happy sort not the (other way)

How can this be when everyday
Your time is ruled by bills to pay
The constant rush and endless hurry
All added to the constant worry

Gone are the days when time was yours
Now we are ruled by Hi-tech stores
The special offers, loans galore
All seen with camera's at the door

But times will change, just wait and see
When there are no natural things about
No native trees, or birds or bats
Just pack after pack of feral cats

The stinking brook, and stanching stream
All lost to-day in a hazy steam
Caused by pollution and decay
Surely there must be another way

T. Fazakerley

I Am Nothing

I have nothing, nothing but love for you
For you straight from my heart
I have nothing, but what else can I do
When we are apart I have nothing too
I have nothing but love holding you in the dark
Kissing you gently loving you hard
Nothing but love all the days of my life
Without you I have nothing
And I am nothing, nothing but an empty shell
Without your love life's a living hell
And nothing I do ever seems right
Without your love to guide me
and I have nothing
nothing without you nothing
I am nothing without your love.

Frank McNee

The Sea

The sea calls to me
For a while I'm free,
No one to laugh or frown
If I jump up and down,
Walk barefoot on the sand
Or do a hand stand.

The sun dances on the sea
Making it glisten and gleam,
Like some diamond merchant's dream.
With the wind in my hair,
Breathing in the salty air
I feel this moment is rare.

Skimming round flat stones
I watch them jump one, two, three
Before falling to the bottom of the sea.
A lonely gull cries "hello"
Reminding me I must go.
I have enjoyed this little time
The pleasure has been all mine.

Kathleen McDonnell

The Search

We move on in so many different ways
Our dreams and our ambitions take us to the unknown
To settle down will be such a strain
We seek to find, we try to unwind the ideas we have in mind.

We learn so much we meet so many different people
We make friends and then we part
With tears and laughter and memories that linger in our hearts.

Try as we may there are disappointments along the way
And success is a long, long way.
But press on, there will be luck someday
And this will be our big day
The sun will shine, as we celebrate that wonderful day.

Doreen Daley

A Human Defrosting

I hang in the shower,
Like a Christmas tree decoration,
Suspended on nothing.
I let the water splash my lips,
My eyelids and tongue.
My fingertips touch and brush.
A pale decoration,
I float,
Beneath a stream of water.
It runs over me,
And off me,
Covering every surface of my skin,
Like a film.
My hair clings to my face,
And whispers soft nothings to my earrings.
The heat thaws my toes,
Fills me with desire,
And stops.

Allys Williams

Disinterest

In this world of computers and technical might,
Where to survive is success in the boardroom fight,
Such arrogance is born of material strife,
And disinterest claims yet another poor life.

Tragic our world full of casual concern,
Where from History made there is failure to learn.
Conscience we please with the promise, next time,
And a thousand more children cry quietly and die.

They talk of equality these seekers of votes,
But are their motives as pure as their language and quotes?
The poor and the starving have no champions here,
For it's God we must trust, and these men we must fear.

R. J. Nelson

Mother Earth

We're Killing our home, Sinking the ship,
Our Own Mother Earth To You What's Her Worth?
Let me tell you people,
Just what We are All doing.
We must stop it now,
Thought it won't be soon.

Hair sprays, deodorants, fly-killers we spray,
Scientists they say it's Greenhouse Effect.
Now you know what it's called,
Earth's warming up, it's us She'll reject.

The Ozone's our protector it hates C.F.C's.
So no more spray cans,
The Sun is our Friend, or even a Foe,
Our future people is now in Your hands.

She floats on through space,
She's no Harbour or Moorings.
We can't let it end now,
With Pollution and Warring
We're Killing our home sinking the ship,
Our Own Mother Earth To You What's Her Worth????

Robert Cozens

Untitled

Have too many winters and summers gone by?
Will we smile like lost lovers
Or again will we cry?

Will I once again feel, safe in your arms
Or will too many winters
Have chilled all your charms?
Or will the lost summers
Bring their long forgotten heat?
Will I melt in your arms
The next time we meet?

Elizabeth Grey

Ode to Rabbie Burns

O' Rabbie Burns—a cruel fate has parted us
Holy Willie and the Kirk, about your way of life made such a fuss
Your the best poet your dear over Scotland even bore
And when they are recited we can hear the lion rampant roar.

But Rabbie let me say to your, none of us hold Holy willies view
You wrote about the lassies and it fairly made him spew.

O' Rabbie the lassies O' the day demand their equal rights
And are kent to cause trouble in Pubs which lead to many fights
You always portrayed the Lassies as gentle sweet and mild
But if you were here today you'd find some are really wild

I don't want to decry them or their past goodness mar
But now-a-day dear Rabbie they are first at the bar.
O' Rabbie you should see the dress wi jeans a'
ripped and torn, and laddies look like
Lassies, we' hair that's never shown.
Whatever some may think of you and your "snow flakes on the river"
We, here, will cherish your memory and hold you high forever.
You were born dear Rabbie in a cottage near auld ayr
and your poems, songs and sayings are pieces very rare.

J. Clarkson

The Painting

Take me to see the painting please.
The chair moves the light body with ease,
Eyes once so bright, now so dry
Gaze up at the painting of garden and sky.
The request is asked daily, the chair now so light,
Now confined to a bed, losing the fight.
The painting is bought—hangs by the bed
No more hospital walks—just a turn of the head,
The lights dim, the curtains are drawn.
Time for those tears, time to mourn.
In our memory corner—no more need of that ride.
The painting lives on—flowers either side.

N. I. A. Carpenter

Living in Wonder

Living in wonder is like living in hope,
things you're needing to know,
things you're wanting to know,
Just wondering everyday about the
same thing.
  Will I ever be able to stop all
  this wondering?
Maybe one day I'll meet up with my
wonder and then be the happiest
person alive, for the first time, but
some how I feel as though it's too
late to stop
  Wondering!

Emma Skinner

Untitled

The sky is dark, lights are going out,
People are heading for bed.
What do they think of lying there?
What comes into their head?

Fantasies, dreams, or places they've been,
Or things they have done in the past.
Friends, relations, and children too,
Or loves that did not last.

It's funny how things keep coming back,
Just when you're trying to sleep.
You close your eyes, and hope for the best,
But into your mind they creep.

Memories are all I have.
No fantasies for me.
So I'd better try to go to sleep.
I'll soon be seventy three.

S. Wallace

The Gift of Love

Love is caring, love is sharing,
Love is giving not counting the cost.
Love is forgetting, love is forgiving
When words and deeds tend to hurt us most.
Love is not having to say we're sorry,
Seeing another's point of view,
And taking the time to lend an ear,
It's surprising what love can do.
Love is giving a helping hand
To others worse off than you.
Love is trying to understand
As you travel life's journey through.
Perhaps you feel your love doesn't count
Against bigger things that are given,
But don't give up just let your love flow,
It's a gift that was made in Heaven.

K. A. Poulton

Killing of the Swan

Let me cry if I want to,
I don't feel ashamed,
I watch the swan, awesome in her beauty
White and graceful, drifting through my mind,
Like a pale, silent, prayer.

I watch the swan perform her water ballet,
In her quiet dignity
And my tears flow like rain,
At beauty tinged with pain,
The swan has lost her mate
A lifetime's friend,
She will never mate again!

In her swan song she dips her willing neck,
Ready to receive the executioner's blow,
Unable and unwilling to glide on
And I hear the poignant haunting cry,
Of the killing of the swan.

Tina Wardlaw

Alone

The sea by day is the same at night, it's all I see,
  it covers my sight.
I walk on my land, the land that I own, it must be mine
  because I am here all alone.
My new home, forced on me, after we sank, my home forever,
  who do I thank?
Here in paradise, or my own private hell, the worst thing of all,
  I have no one to tell.
Is this it . . . is this my fate?
  this is everything I have come to hate.
My memories are of love and of a happier time,
  these are the things which play on my mind.
There is no end, no end in sight,
  is it time to give up my fight?
The hand of death will soon be here,
  now it is not a thing that I fear.
I walk around my home's sandy floor,
  before I lay down to be no more.
I wonder who will find me, they'll wonder who I am
  Maybe I'll leave a note saying I was, the loneliest man.

   Andrew Gaskell

The River

The river runs dry
Where the old bridge stands
Mortar crumbles where the old man stands
There's still life in this bridge bay
So don't you be fooled
There's more to life than life boy
Live before you grow
The willows weep with the evergreens
Amongst leaves all gold and brown
Making way for a new life
That takes so much away
Whatever happened to the wild wood
Where we used to roam
Kicking up leaves in autumn time
Just before the snow
The old man's words they sail the sky
A tear wells in my eye but it's too
Late to cry
And the willows weep with the evergreen
Amongst leaves all gold and brown.

   Martin Crawley

The Death of a Loved One

Here I sit alone and think,
I'm not convinced that life doesn't stink.
First one thing and then another,
Have you ever lost your mother?
"Pick yourself up and solder on",
It's not so easy when faith has gone.
But carry on I suppose I must,
I really hope that cause is just.
So you'll see me on the road of life,
But please don't cause me to much strife.

   Stephen Stiles

Empty Saturday

I know I didn't need that piece of bread,
Extra, in the middle of the morning,
But, for a few dawdling moments, instead
Of empty nothingness there was something;
Neither needed I purchase yet more plants,
Yet putting them in was occupation,
And Wordsworth was right: Daffodils do dance,
Even with no cause for celebration.
I am resolved to look on the bright side,
Try, concentrate on yet another book,
Force myself to find something else beside
Just seeking more excuse to chop, stir, cook.
I shall survive; there is no other way.
But this Saturday I longed for Monday.

   Helen Penelope Little

Jamie

Liken to my Father, my husband, my son
All these people I have in you.
My Grandson, my baby, my joy
Born with love and devotion that's true.

I bless you my dearest beloved
My angel, my hero, my friend,
Joy, is the greatest endeavour
I ask for yourself to the end.

Please do not ever forget me
The woman who loved you so strong,
But the woman who born you with reverence
Is the one to whom you belong.

   Joyce Moody

Alone

In my dreams you are beside me, resplendent in your youth,
The ages of the years have gone, and yes, I know the truth.
I know how much you loved me, and I know how much you cared,
The depth of your devotion was more than I had dared.
But tho' our time together in this life has passed away,
Still in spirit you are here to guide me through each day.
Your strength I still rely on, your words still in my ears,
From all my special thoughts of you I can allay my fears.
And if I do get frightened, worried or upset,
I know the thoughts of you I have will help me to forget.
If in my dreams when you are there, I hold your hand so tightly,
It's just to help me through each day, to keep your love around me.
I close my eyes and think of you, I see you sitting there,
I know that in reality, your chair is empty, bare.
These are not some ramblings of a woman losing touch,
But of one, who once "belonged", and misses you so much.

   Nadine Gilbert

Baby Blues

Was it good news? Or was it bad?
Part of him was happy, part was sad,
Would all his toys still be his?
He really wasn't prepared for this.

He'd just look and try to keep his cool,
What would he tell his mates tomorrow at school!
Dad had just sat there, with a big grin on his face.
There was a thumping in his chest as his heart began to race.
Why did they tell him now? As alone he went to bed.
Wasn't he enough? Was it something that he'd said?

He'd tried so hard to be nice and oh so very good,
Saying 'Please and thank you' and all the things he should.
Things would never be the same,
He must have done something, he must be to blame.

He felt his eyes water, a tear dropped upon his cheek,
Everything now seemed so very bleak.
Then mummy came in, kissed him goodnight and he knew,
Everything would be alright, there was enough love for two.

   S. Hicks

Parasitic Heaven

'Tis a Parasitic Heaven,
To be a flea in Devon,
In the best houses,
Up skirts and down trousers,
That environmental pleasure,
Living somewhere a life of leisure,
Jumping on, jumping 'awf',
On the educated, of course,
In Totnes:
Oh what a life it is to be you,
A Devonian flea in a room with a view,
Where nothing disturbs your nightly labour,
Nibbling in Devon the next-door neighbour . . .
But just wait until I get my hands on you—
You Philosophical Sod!

   Donald Wagstaff

Images of Friendship

The flickering flame of candle-light
   Glows in darkness like stars at night.
So my friend, let's dance and sway,
   While sweeping hands pass time away.

As still waters gleam and glisten,
   To musical memories we will listen.
Black notes on parchment white
   Harmonize then fade from sight.

Mellow music, haunting sounds,
   Echo as the world turns round.
Melodies drift in mood of blue,
   And touch the heart of friendship true.

The dancing flame of candle-light
   Shines and glows with warm delight.
Fills the heart of friendship dear,
   With affection ever near.

So my friend, the time will pass,
   Reflected in the silvered glass.
Mirrored images of the time
   Love's emotions were sublime.

Valerie Lavers

Mother and Child

It begins in the womb.
From the first signs of life.
The mother cares
For the baby that is there.

Apprehensive about the birth.
Fears for not all being quite right.
The mother cares deeply—day and night

At last a child, perfect in every way.
Fed off the breast, kept warm and clean.
The mother cares, every hour of the day.

From baby to toddler, junior to teens.
When rebelling of pleasing.
The mother takes care of the scenes.

Nursed when sick, scolded at times.
Being directed and helped along.
The mother cares—right or wrong.

Whatever the time, never mind the age,
Good times, bad times, happy or sad times
The mother still cares.

Belinda Jayne Rea

Full Circle

The eyes look up, but know me not
He dribbles down his chin,
The frame that once so upright stood
Is feeble now, and thin.

The guileless stare, the toothless grin,
The innocence of a child,
No memory now of yesteryear,
Of youth, and strength and pride.

There was a time when he was God,
A mentor by my side,
Safe harbour from the storms of life,
My rock, my friend, my guide.

In his strong arms he carried me,
When I could go no more,
And now he needs my arms, my strength,
To walk across the floor.

I smile with him, hold back the tears,
And though my heart is sad,
For this old man, robbed of dignity,
I'm proud that he's my dad.

Irene Burton

Life Is a Cold War

To the person who accepts the
authenticity of our twisted lives
but life who takes one day by day
sufferance dwindles and minds are rectified.
Rectification of one's heart is a
damnation to a lyric sentiment.
Suffering is a sin to the believer
in pain but the endurance of
life is released into the optimists'
heart and yet they all suffer
the effects of the cold war.

Gemma Swindells

Wonder

Have you ever been in the midst of a wood
With its smell so musky and sweet.
A lush overgrowth of green tangled bush,
And bluebells at your feet.

Have you ever sat to meditate
In the heart of a cool, cool glade.
With sunshine filtering through the leaves
And birds, their nests all made

Have you ever sat to listen
To the tune of nature's sounds
The song of a bird, the hoot of an owl
The baying of a hound

The wind blowing through the trees
The crackle of creatures small
Have you never, stopped to wonder
At the beauty of it all.

Margery Edwards

Frost

The earth is held in its cast iron grip,
and crystals of ice bespatter the grass,
and the pond where the dragonflies danced on its lip
is now a dirty white sheet of ice.

The blue tits hang on their peanut net.
A plastic thing that swings from the line
where the washing once blew in the summer breeze
and the air was still in the hot sunshine.

The frozen earth will soften again
and the spring bulbs hoist their emerald spears
upwards to greet the morning light,
till the bulbs unfold, and the flower appears.

In its winter grip the earth must sleep,
till the breath of Spring caresses its face,
and life once more returns anew
to greet the new life born apace.

Mary Ward Hunt

The Bestest Friend

For Chris

He is always there,
When I need him most;
How he puts up with me I will never know.
I've said "will you go out with me?"
But he said "no! But friends forever we will be."
He's not like any boy you see,
Because he really cares about what happens to me.

He cheers me up when I am down,
He makes me laugh when I frown.
No lost of memory will intervene,
Because only you and I will know what our
love means.
But when we leave school you'll probably forget!
And get a new best friend and that will be that.
But my hopes and dreams will never forget,
What a great friendship we have to have yet.

Donna Bingham

"The Upturned Glass"

On the downhill slopes of later life,
We turn to words—away from strife,
Seeking beauty in the thought sublime,
Ere thoughts anneal within the glass of time.

Can faith be not crucible of thought?
Or is this fleeting life so dearly bought.
That man who sells his own immortal soul
Must ever hold the devils beggar bowl.

So brightly shine your shield of burnished youth,
with "torch" held high to light the way for truth,
Go staunchly, guard your "shining ideal's" hope!
Trade not—nor barter—even on the slope,
For he who in the morning mirror looks,
Should never face the one who cooked the books.

Next time you reach for solace from the hanging vine,
Or quaff the jug full with the barley wine,
Take heed from one who had the shakes
And was severely savaged by three-headed snakes,
Reflect! Reflect! How distorted life can be,
When through an emptying glass, in the only view you see!

Donald Morrison Thomas

Summer Days

Remember those long lazy summer days?
We'd sit in the meadow watching the butterflies dance
The sun was so warm and tender
It touched our skin and we were its rays
We had no cares as we listened to the birds compose their
    playful tunes
We made our daisy chains and lay in the grass
The sweet smell of the meadow filling our afternoons.
Our thoughts didn't ponder on the future
Our values and expectations were simple and clear
The summer would go on for ever and we'd drift along
Without cares or worries, without shedding a tear.

So when was it that summer turned to Autumn?
Then Autumn, in turn, to cold winter nights?
When did our carefree existence end
To be replaced by worry, fear and strife?
Did materialism, power and greed always surround us?
Were our simple pleasures immature and out of place?
Did the sun blind us from the truth 'til on its sinking
    it could blind us no more?
Oh! —How I long for those lost summer days.

Julie Stewart

Mothers

Of mothers, one of the best was mine!
From her, God's love did shine.
She taught us all, that was good and true.
She taught us to love you!
When tired, she comforted, held us tight,
Worked hard, with all her might.
When ill, or hurt, she came to our aid
We were not then afraid.
She showed us how to help others too,
Help them, for love of you!
She cooked, cleaned, sewed, often working late,
Laziness she did hate.
We were taken to parks, museums near,
Richmond, to see the deer!
Mother loved us all, and did her best,
Often put to the test
By our naughty trying ways,
But she loved us always.
Thank God for all mothers, good and true.
Loving us, loving you!

Lilian M. Loftus

The Bright Black Night Before

My life slumbers here;
Beneath the taboo woven sky.
I wander my weekly pilgrimage,
Offering sympathy to the outshone stars,
By my Voodoo Queen.
Leaving eclipsing clouds,
For the penumbra house,
A silhouette from the fire inside.
In your presence the veiled day loses its gloom,
Enhancement of the outshone.
How can such a lamentable colour,
symbolize evil, death and mourning,
When you reside within it?
The overcast, moonless dawn awakens,
I sepulchrally leave into obscurity.
Only now does my dusk begin,
Nightfall is upon me.
You make any shadowy opaqueness seem bright.
This is no dark elegy,
But the Bright Black Night Before.

Symon Poole

Where!

Where is there heaven, where is there hell,
How can we envisage, how can we tell,
Just ponder the problem, t'will not be in vain
For we all have been given a free thinking brain.

The first taste of heaven is here on this earth.
Beginning as always with the marvel of birth,
The cloud and the sunshine, the wind and the showers.
Animals around us, the colours, the flowers
These are a few things, we see, feel and hear
Hold and we cherish, so precious, so dear.

The first taste of hell is here on this earth
Created by evil of man, no matter his birth,
The shootings, the bombings, the killings, the slaughter
Of brother and sister, of parents and daughter
What of the turmoil, the anguish, the sorrow
We all have to live with, today and tomorrow

These are small samples of heaven and hell,
Now what to our brain did these then foretell
What was the message our brain did conceive
Surely just one thing, to trust and believe

A. S. Mankey

Voyages in Dreams

Ships berthed at the quay side, so quietly serene,
Please tell me the tales of the places you've been.
Now tall in the water, your holds wide and bare,
Tomorrow, perhaps laden, with cargoes to spare.
Then off, on the oceans, where? I only guess in my head . . .
Cold chills of the Baltic, warm ports of the Med?
Or some exotic island? A shore fringed with palms.
Through seas wild and stormy and quiet peaceful calms,
Days in the doldrums, under endless blue skies.
Over bright shining seas, how I wish it were I . . .
Above realms of the fishes, the dolphins, the whales.
Scorched brown in the tropics, suffer cold northern gales.
On the wings of the winds to places near and far flung.
See the bustle of quays, hear the jabbering tongues
of strange foreign faces, one thought on them all . . .
To unload and hasten us, to our next part of call.
Then sweet homeward journeys, my folks to enthral,
With stories and shanties and gifts, for them all.
But with always an eye, to once more on the main.
A seafarin' man! Away sailing again.

Derek Brown

Evacuee's Lament 1939–1945

Times were hard, wages small
Poland was about to fall
War was shouted around the streets
The men looked grim
While we chewed our sweets
Mother hid her tears from Bert
Waiting for the first alert
To Paddington to board that train
Will we see our mum again?

Down to Cornwall the engine flew
The cows, the trees, all were new
Arrived worn out, while tears abound
Please oh please let's turn around
Sweet ladies appear "yes I'll have that one"
The younger ones just suck their thumb
Trelawney's land looks so green
As Cockney kids had never seen.

In war you see, we all stand pain
Will we see our mum again?

Ron Brown

My Pressie—From Me

I treated myself to a small birthday pressie,
A soft, cute and cuddly—little puppy,
His parents were drinks—called "Whisky" and "Sherry"
So we called him "Brandy" and that made us merry.

We watched him from birth, so tiny and helpless,
He tiddled and pooped everywhere—what a mess!

But he couldn't help it, he had to be trained,
And when he was older, he had to be reigned.

We weaned him on puppy food,
    gave him his jabs,
Cost me a fortune—but was worth it—perhaps!

And as he got older, he went grey at the gills.
His hearing was going and he suffered from chills

I loved my dear puppy,
With me thirteen whole years,
Now he's gone—and I miss him,
    Here's to "Brandy"
        "Cheers!"

Liz Ryan

Remembrance Sunday—Enniskillen 1987

Daddy! Where's my daddy? Have you seen him anywhere?
He came to lay a poppy wreath, but now he isn't there.
I was standing right beside him, my hand was inside his,
But now it seems I've lost him—I don't know where he is.
We were standing by the Cenotaph remembering the dead—
"We have to show respect, my lad," was what my daddy said.
But then from out of nowhere an explosion ripped the air—
The sky fell in on top of us as we were standing there!
We all were blown forward, my head spun round and round
And then I lost all consciousness and fell down to the ground . . .
But someone's arms went round me and pulled me from the rubble,
Now I must tell daddy I am safe and not in any trouble.
Oh, there he is! I see him now—why does he lie so still?
Let me through! He needs me! I think he might be ill . . .
Daddy! Wake up, daddy, for the ground is cold and wet,
And mummy's waiting in the house—you don't want her to fret!
But he lies there, quite immobile, with his poppy on his breast
And now that self-same poppy-red has spread across his chest . . .

We were standing by the Cenotaph amidst the pouring rain.
They say the wars are over, but I still can feel the pain.

Sheila Elliott

The Black Swan

Here in a few lines is my swan song.
Not that I am saying farewell,
Rather, I am saying "Hello" - but,
A greeting from a swan that is sad.

Often I swim close to the river bank,
Sometimes there is some bread.
I look, listen, once I heard "Oh yes,
Swans are royal, special, quite grand.
They belong to the Queen you know".

More often, "Look-what a funny swan"
black, with a red beak." Is it fair?
I look at other swans, white, majestic.
Stately, beautiful, they look at me,
Then they look away - and swim on.

They see my feathers, but not my heart.
Sad, why of course, but not bad.
Am I beautiful? I have never heard so,
If I were beautiful, I should be happy.
I shall think beautiful thoughts, angels will know.

David Nicholson

Untitled

A pale vaporous light hits the room.
Suddenly there was thunder, it cracked through the air like a whip.
The boy turns quickly, he seems afraid, yet fascinated
with what's going on.
He's too young to understand.
He turns towards the window, his face a mask
unblemished, colourless, but, the boy's eyes were full of pain,
you can tell a lot from a person's eyes, you almost
know what they are thinking.
A voice of Authority was hurdled towards his bedroom
get out, the boy shuddered as the thunder cracked again
but this time it didn't stop, a bright light made its
way towards the window.
He heard a sound but it sounded so distant,
He opened his eyes to gaze up and see his father
Saying something, he couldn't understand because
the voice of authority which he had always known
was slowly fading away.
His floating thoughts are being drawn unwillingly
from his mind to a new world, a new place, a new home.

Jonathan Scott

The Mind

A waltzing, a gliding, a frolicking through,
Oh, sure 'tis of me and you know 'tis of you,
Sages come searching for soul in the stare,
Which delves to and fro, as it darts everywhere.

'Tis there, oh 'tis there, 'tis within, 'tis without,
Cognition and will with its logic and clout,
Emotions a-tumbling and ebbing to soar,
Away o'er the sky or within the heart's core.

And yet it can transit through all God's great things,
Or dwell in the willow or sit on silk wings,
Like four winds do scurry across seven seas,
Sometimes so in turmoil or sometimes in glees.

In all God's vast eternal plan,
To make a leaf, to make a man,
In all the wonders of the earth,
From conception through to living birth,
In all the mysteries that we see,
I look at you, you look at me,
What would we be but cloned of kind,
If Divine forgot to make the mind.

Bridget Briar Colleton

Untitled

I am the fruits of my Grandparents' children
Poisoned apples bitter to the taste
Nettle rash ascending stinging deep within my womb
And in my dreams, those dreams, sweet dreams
Honeysuckle and Marigolds bloom
Their seeds blowing in the breeze of the hot summer days
Sowing My fruits to blossom once again
No bitter taste of poisoned apples
Honeysuckle and Marigolds bloom.
   Vince S. Rankin

Beyond

Beyond human dimension or earthly comprehension
is the ocean of God's love to me—
Further than the outer stars or the planet Mars
is the impression or charity so free.
If we want to touch the unusual without any refusal
Then one must bend the knee.

Man is restless to explore, through the intellectual door
the values and wealth and eternal depths
of a human life given in sacrifice;
In the darkness over eastern land appears an outstretched hand
Pointing where we can be free
and that is only realised on bended knee.

The exploring mind of creatures endowed with many features
tries to unravel mysteries deep;
He delves with scientific skill
into realms that they try to fulfil;
But, let us remember, God holds the key
Which can only be obtained on bended knee.
   R. Brown

Roots

Autumn is my dear one's time
When the leaves are golden and russet brown.
She glowed, and made me feel quite blind
to see the light from her laughing eyes.
But God came and took her one sunshiny day.
When the leaves were still soft and coloured green
But her roots are my roots.
Sweet Mother mine.
Your birthday time draws nigh
For the woods and forests are glowing gold.
And the squirrels are gathering, and lining there
fold with sweet autumns feast.
Wonderful—glorious—season you.
To remind me, of my dear one's time.
   Rita Jean Blake

Hell in Japan

As the atom bomb left my plane,
I began to feel the peoples' pain.

All of a sudden came a blinding flash,
I bet the people had a bash?

The explosion formed to a mushroom cloud,
I began to smile and feel quite proud.

Hitler was dead we'd won the war,
It was all over now I'm very sure.

When I got home my house was gone,
Smashed like that because of a bomb.

It was just then I'd realized what I'd done.

I'd slaughtered people, nothing more,
I'm going to hell; there's no cure.

My wife was dead I'm so sad,
I've even lost my little lad.

This war, this war it makes me so mad.

Sorry Hiroshima, for what I've done,
I've made your country down to none
   Gareth O'Sullivan

And All Is Still

Sitting by my window wide,
Gazing at a swirl of mist
Slowly rising from the lawn
As the setting sun goes down
Behind the rain filled clouds;
And all is still.

In the closing hours of day,
The birds are hushed, their songs have ceased.
The flowers their gentle petals fold
As dew drops form upon their leaves.
Long shadows steal across the grass;
And all is still.

Low in the sky I look and see
As I close the window tight:
The evening star so bright and clear
Against the background of the night.
And timeless quiet prevails the passing hour;
and all is still.
   R. H. Dymond

To Have and to Not

You were in my fantasy
An escape from what is wrong with me
Not within my real life frame
But part of one illicit game

I care for you, of course I do
But never wanted much from you
So don't stand back, it does no harm
To have a neutral friendly arm

The pressures of life are all too great
So it's nice to have a no strings mate
If only sometimes, fine with me
'Cause that is what we did agree.

It would be nice to have some time
Away from your life and from mine
To escape into a life forbidden
From the world completely hidden

So ease the conflict, talk to me
Let's find a balance we can agree
I know the tension will subside
If we know what really is inside
   Toni Allen

Saturday Afternoon

Trains are very fast these days.
Slow.
Nowhere to go but they are sometimes late.
But who would hate the trains being late?
   Thomas Cullum

She

If beauty is only skin deep, you, my dear, are paper thin.
Fragile in your mortal frame,
A flash of that coveted grin
   Wins shallow hearts.
Cruel tongue hidden behind pearls that are sharp enough
To draw blood from innocents
   Who lay down that you may gain some height.
And yet through your narrow sight
You see only your reflection.
This too will splinter into shards that will scar.
The fools that laugh are not humoured by you,
They laugh in vain, for some reward at your soul,
For in this plash of being lies no wit,
   nor capacity of skill.
But the lambs flock around you still
For a glimpse of your summer face,
For seasons pass and years will end.
The trees shall be glad of you at last.
And then I shall laugh.
   Kirsty Scott

The Ever-Knowing Sea

I sat and watched the waves,
They roll in hard with such a crash,
Then soft, gently, gently,
Like the ups and downs of life.

But that sound I will never forget,
Firstly a silence that would almost deafen a person,
The resounding roar that diminishes to nothing,
As the next White Horse gallops in,
It is there again.

We have dwelled on this sphere but a twinkling in time,
But the deep she has been here a life time + 2,
She can be merciful, mild, like the most forgiving Saint,
But then she can be brutal, relentless, ruthlessly claiming her victims,
As for one who wants to undo a tangled mind,
There are few better places.
William. G. A. Lowe

Mankind

We all start the same, whenever we're conceived,
But when it is all over, what has been achieved,

Have we come out winning, or were we left behind,
That's all that seems, to matter to mankind,

Have we now completed, the tasks that were in hand,
Or are we still there, fighting for the land,

How much is destroyed, what has been created,
For all the loss of life, cannot be estimated,

It matters not what happens, events will never change,
For some do not think, the situation to be strange,

For someone, somewhere, wants to sacrifice,
The greatest gift of all, the gift of life.
Paul Foster

My Fairy

God made a young girl her name was Mary
He gave her wings and made her a fairy
A magical person with lots to share
The best little fairy that really did care
God took your wings and put you on Earth
He was with you then when you gave birth,
Two little boys and two girls to treasure
Who would love you most forever and ever
When we were sad and feeling blue
We'd call the fairy she knows what to do,
A sprinkle of dust and a magical word
The best little fairy you've ever heard
Memories come back when I saw this card
To remember the past isn't that hard
That fairy we had full of love and fun.
That fairy I love is you my Mum.
Kim Bunnett

Mary Rose

You sank to the sea bed a long time ago,
Four hundred and fifty-two years to be exact,
But then, once again you felt the wind blow
As they brought you up to the surface, amazingly intact.

Once King Henry VIII walked along your deck,
You were the pride of all his fleet;
Then tragedy struck and you became a mere wreck,
But now restored, you are almost complete.

Everyone worked very hard to bring you up from the deep,
Taking care not to damage your ancient timber;
They worked day and night, going without sleep,
To make sure things went right without any hinder.

All your crew drowned when you went down that day,
But you have survived all the years that have gone by;
Now inside a museum you have to stay,
So "Mary Rose" you are home and dry.
Margaret Crumpler

Questions/Answers

Where I'm going I have to go alone
No contact, visits or talking on the phone
I'm changing, growing, expanding my mind
Trying to find the questions/answers for the sake of my kind

A Saviour is sought
Battles to be fought
Hatred, envy and anger must be forgiven and forgot

Maybe the answers/questions are already spoken and written
Maybe all we need to do is really learn to listen

Our Love for all will take us there
To a place not too far from here
Free from pain, loss, tears and fear
And when you're ready, I'll meet you there.
Annette Smith

Spring's Rebirth

A new day starts the birds in song.
They're all at home where they belong.
All nature stirs life on its way.
This sure will be a lovely day.

The early dawn wakes you up so bright.
The lovely flowers - they add to the light.
Yes spring has come surely to the fore.
I've never seen it quite so bright before.

The snowdrops so pure, so white, so small,
The daffodil so sunshine yellow and so tall.
The crocus form a carpet of their own.
The rowan tree is very much at home.

Each season has its joys to share.
Spring time has a beauty oh, so rare.
A new life starts given from above.
So treat each other with tender love.
James H. Harvey

Look at Me Now

Bent, twisted and tortured by life
Memories of me, cut like a knife.

Very slowly I shuffle along
Oh God tell me, did I do wrong
To end up so bent and twisted by life
Memories of me, cut like a knife.

Sat by the window I watch people pass
I used to be happy, when I was a lass
I'll love to eternity the children I had
I saw to their needs through good times and bad
Now everyone's gone, the loves from my life
Memories of me, cut like a knife.

Bitter and twisted is all that's left now
Waiting for God, at his feet I will bow
So now I pray for the end of my life
Memories of me, cut like a knife.
Helen Barrington

A Discarded Temp

Outwardly calm I am seated at a table,
Surrounded by people who think I'm not able.
They're fully employed, but complain all the time.
That is why I'm composing this rhyme.

It's 1997 - I'm over the hill,
Of this life I've had my fill.
My contract has finished that I started with joy,
Now I am treated like a discarded toy.

They will give me an interview to show that it's fair,
But I might as well be a stuffed Teddy Bear.
I know future employment is all cut and dried,
On the other hand I know that I've tried.
Rosemary Jane Lasham

The Pardon of Eden

He rears his head, and calls your name,
Your guilty head bows in shame,
Twisting and turning through the grass,
Enjoy it now or your time will pass.
The hidden lies behind the blue,
The blue of undiscovered rue.
An innocent affair in a guilty state.
The wheel of fortune controls your fate.
Delilah out off Samson's hair,
You stumble into the serpent's snare,
And now emerging as a lustful cheater,
For the forbidden fruit is so much sweeter.

Caroline R. J. Busuttil

A Tale of Monotone Rainbows—New South Africa

What does home offer but disgust?
What do the evil and pain send but disgust?
I've seen the blood ebbing from ignorant cups and
I've felt no sincere sensation but disgust;
For the battered rainbow limps its tarnished colours
Across the sunshine - weeping.

Oh wretched burrows of time
He writhed with pain streaks
Daunting in splendor as the sun.
He turned; face adorned with golden locks,
Facing the light of solemn regret, for what they did,
What his people did?

Those evil cackling goats, horn spiked in the heart.
Hold back your minds from all the enemies,
Burning terror
Silent revenge
As if hatred devoured love's wand.
Our lonely grey rainbow rolls its sagging eyes.
How can he love?
When his world love's not itself.

Andrew Jorgensen

Petra

We each have our dream, and mine was Petra.
To walk to the Siq, no man led horse for me, within my dream.
Into the Siq. What size! What colour!
How small we felt in Nature's scheme,
Like ants trailing in the sand.
Suddenly, around a bend, there it stood—The Treasury.
No books, no words, had prepared us for this wonder.
Gleaming in the sun, a gentle monument to the ancient past.
Peace and serenity within this busy place,
The dignity and pride of a long lost race.
On we went, surrounded by glory,
The tombs and the rocks, all part of the story.
The noise and the bustle just passed us by, and
High above, the clouds in the sky linked the past with the present.
We each have our dream, and mine Is Petra.

Audrey Titley

The Gift of Self

The sun shone bright
on the shoe shop window.
The old lady with eyes of sight
looked down on her small bambino.

Her pension just she had drawn
dare she really chance.
A pair of tiny sandals colour fawn,
though old, the thought made her heart dance.

Come little bambino, she said,
into the shop to try.
They did but the child chose red,
a tear flowed from the old one's eye.

Love had won the day,
open purse, money sought.
Too late to worry, to self did say,
Happiness complete to have bought.

A. L. Cheetham

Innocence

I used to believe in Heaven I thought there was no hell,
And then you came into my life, you took my innocence away,
You said I was an evil child, a child born of sin,
That I made you do those things to me,
It was a fight I couldn't win,

You deprived me of my childhood, I couldn't laugh and play,
I was different than the others, it was my fault you'd say,
I couldn't tell a soul my life was full of pain,
My body being drained of love, They'd think I was insane.

You took my childhood, my innocence, my want and need to live,
You gave me fear, You gave me hate,

So please, when he returns in my thoughts and in my dreams,
For in my life he'll always play a part,
Please God don't let him take the music from my heart.

Natasha Watson

Junkie

If there is a God, can He not see,
The life I craved has deserted me.
I have no tears left to shed,
No pillow to place beneath my head.
These filthy pavements are hard and cold.
These squalid streets aren't paved with gold.
My wealth is in my empty hand,
Nothing has gone the way I planned.
My lover is smoke, on a silver tray.
But he comes to destroy, in his evil way.
I look at my servant, his eyes dark with greed,
For now I must pay for my desperate need.
The solace I seek from the needles each day,
Leave scars that will never go away.
But they aren't so deep as the scars in my mind,
As I ponder the life I can't leave behind.
And I think—while I can—of opulent slums,
As I sleep in Hell, 'til tomorrow comes.

Margaret Fink

For Joanne

I kneel and light a candle, for each day you're not
with me, I slowly strike a single match, and watch
it thoughtfully. It takes a lot of time and trust to
set the wick alight, but at last I have it burning,
this candle burning bright.

Dispelling thoughts of dark and gloom, this little
candle burns, through passages of right and
wrong, its tiny flame will turn. I look and see your
faith and love, that made this candle glow, that
picked me up from true despair, whenever I was low.

A time not being long enough, for us to watch and
see, my little light will slowly dim, as true as being me.
But I now know it only takes, a single match of love,
to light my life of candle
, for this, will be enough.

Claire Sweet

A Tribute to the NHS

Rosie went to the hospital she really had no choice
The locum on this Sunday said in clear calcutta voice
You have to go you surely do your legs are such a sight
We'll get you there by ambulance before the pain can bite
The men with chair and blankets came all done at super speed
And rushed her off with gentle care to meet that urgent need
They reached that lengthy corridor the one of TV fame
And there they parked as well they might
For just one hour and not all night,
Stretched out on her bed she fought her efforts made her tire
Her legs were hurting seeping red she thought they were on fire
But come the dawn and tender care with nurses to her aid
With doctors young and unsurpassed another cure was made.

Lionel Perry

Golden Boy

I saw a boy with golden hair
I looked again—he wasn't there.
I've searched the land—the sea—the air
In fact I've sought him everywhere.

I glimpsed him once in sunlight's glow
In mirrored pool—where I would go.
But when I offered eager hand
'Twas nothing there—but sea and sand.

Oh, golden boy—come back to me!
I've searched so long my soul to free
What is your secret—stripling fair—
Please show yourself to those who care.

I'll go on searching—through the years—
betwix my love and many tears,
Perhaps I've learned your secret charm
Your golden glow keeps us from harm.

You do not need our earthly pace,
You've had your time and run your race,
Oh Golden boy—your halos' bright—
Keep sending down your healing light.

Helen Woodford

Fifty Years On

Are these the chaps of yesteryear,
The strong young men who fought so well?
They may have felt it but showed no fear
And certainly gave the enemy Hell.

What has happened to that muscular frame,
The easy nonchalant way that they moved?
They look so different and yet still the same,
Quietly confident and so often proved.

Could that be Lightfoot the company runner?
Surely not! Why he can hardly walk!
He later won fame as a competent gunner;
Of his exploits we so often talk.

I didn't know he needed a walking stick!
But he had a stick to measure our pace—
Trained a drill squad to be very slick—
On any parade he would never lose face.

We are not much more than three score and ten
But old age I suppose is now the foe.
It seems so strange—we were all active men—
Now we get into our wheelchairs and go.

John Sharp

The Empty Chair

By the fireside there's an empty chair
but I still feel his presence there.
It's been that way six years or more.
A testament of time, that's gone before.

Childhood memories come to mind.
The ones that last, the precious kind.
For me no father could compare
to the one who should be sitting there.

Its occupant once was debonair.
Weather beaten face and raven hair.
A poetry book open on his knee,
its pleasures he would share with me.

With day's work done he'd take his place,
contentment written upon his face.
Recalling tales of long ago
of kindred I would never know.

The storyteller is long at rest,
his chair reserved for honoured guest.
But life goes on, comes what may.
In dreams he's sitting there today.

Catherine H. Harrower

"Joy"

They named me "Joy."
But before they could experience that joyful emotion
They had to experience both heartbreak and pain.

Their lives moved on,
And out of their sorrow a new younger child was born,
This time a birth that brought them joy.

But wherever I walk,
I still carry with me that initial sadness,
A shadow of the sorrow they lived through.

I still carry with me
That untold sorrow of time before me,
Hidden deep in the meaning of my name.

That unmentionable heartbreak
That haunts me now.
That touched them deeply.
Will it haunt me always?

Joy Skyrme

A Tale from a Harvest Mouse

What am I? I'm very small,
And climb high in grasses tall,
Scuttling here, scuttling there,
Is danger near or anywhere?

I build my nest in golden corn,
I cannot rest my young are born,
It's two weeks before they leave the nest,
They don't need me and that is best.

Four hours awake, four hours asleep,
A little grain is all I eat,
For I am indeed a harvest mouse,
And glad to be in field not house!

Endymion Beer

My First Pram Push in Emilia's Eyes

In your eyes, you saw the beauty of the world.
In my eyes you are the wonder of the world.
You fill my eyes with tears, of joy, of happiness of things to come,
of growing years and years, of people who you will grow to love,
and some, that you will never know,
they held you in your cradle days.
You are a breath of life, a chance anew,
their hopes and dreams they have for you.
    When you see the beauty of the flowers, birds, trees and sea.
One day I hope you'll think, of me.
The wind that whistles round your face, the sun, the sky, the stars
at night, the arms that hold you oh surely tight. Your eyes are
open wide and full look into theirs the life to come, for they will
hold you oh secure their love for you is more and more.
For the beauty of your smile—holds in their eyes the babe awhile.

Gillian Herbert

The Darkness

The room is dark, I'm dark
My hopes, my dreams
darkened and diminished
Darkness mumbles, words so hopeless
Black in colour
The dawn breaks—more darkness
as far as the eye can see
Stares of darkness—bleak and dreary
Soulless faces, weary.
Empty eyes weeping
Ears that can hear
only grey songs of mourning
Listening for the hollow sounds
of the darkness lifting
But no, the darkness stays—the darkness
Morbid thoughts, endless walls
Locking you in—captivity
holding the keys, no escape
from that place—the darkness . . .

Anne McGovern

The Remembrance of a Dream

Through Marsh land thicket in woodland deep across
the valley I carefully creep, over and under I give it a peep,
disturbing whatever's asleep, past and present swish the
breeze, haunting the hollows that wither and weep, a cough of
shiver sits on the stream
I look at a thrust as it cheerfully sings, boring its echo bounces and
springs, drowning the talk its wilderness breaths, but I, now closer
to catching its dreams, now dusk is ready to darken the greens luring
shadows prowl from the trees, and blinking eyes like glitter in
hedgerows hiding sneaks, brushing close together I hear their crispy
squeaks, then covering the mud the slithering tide floats the silt
oily grime, pushed by star time after time, reeling and casting its
whispering quest, lapping the shore massaging its chest, sighs in
relief its slack in its nest, but still confused by the storm on the
crest, breaking its heart weary for rest, now given a chance creatures
dash, cockle muscle crab, limpets unclasp, wriggling scuttle they
move in its path, hunted while danger runs round, two hundred years
the harbour is sound, then grabbed by the ocean the water like glass,
retrieved by the moon in the sky as it passed, yawning wide open the
bear on the land turning the tide without any hands.
Paul Maton

The Beginning

The big bang is why we're here,
Or so the scientists declare,
It spewed forth the universe,
A kind of cosmic, for better or worse.

Are we all to believe,
That's how it began,
The beginning of time,
The beginning of man.

If this was the great creation,
Then God is just imagination,
The big bang implies disorder and chaos,
Yet system and order,
Is the nature or the cosmos.
Wilf Allsopp

Drifting

Like ships on a raging ocean,
We drift together,
On a collision course.
Destined to meet,
Wind and rain lash our sails,
Wrestling control from our hands,
The destiny of our hearts,
Ruled by a greater force than we know,
And we collide,
One night in a sudden storm,
A storm of passion and feeling
That neither of us knew existed between us.
For a while we stay,
Locked together in the swirling torrents,
Safe in the knowledge we have each other.
In this void of emptiness and loneliness,
Yet now we drift apart,
Wrenched away by the storm's fury,
No longer safe in each other's love,
Exposed and alone, with little hope.
Robert Alexander

Silence

Silence, I sit and listen for its arrival.
The message friendly, it arrives heard, but unseen.
A large comforting form and a soothing hand
Confirms the arrival.
It spirals around me and I slip into its core.
Warmth, in the cool of the night and cool
In the heat of the day.
I lie, elevated, detached.
The mind empties, washed clean.
All that remains is silence and as an orchestra
Its crescendos about me.
J. Bishop

Ecstasy

I gave you life—
You gave me joy beyond measure.
A precious babe—
So many memories to treasure.
I watched you grow,
You skipped and laughed so freely,
A budding rose,
Your life marked out so clearly.

You came of age—
I filled with proud elation.
You kissed goodbye
And left with friends for celebration.
Such harmless fun—
That pill which pledged to heighten moments
But you were gone
And left no hope to ease my torments
Just darkness, despair and desolation.
"Who gave you death?" I cry.
A. McPartland

Memories

As a child the pattern of life
Falls into step and our thoughts though pure
Leave room for learning
The day to day changes that bring emotions
Of love hate and jealousy
Are all part of this growing concern
Which we call adulthood
Our emotions change as we learn the meaning of life
Suddenly our childhood is gone forever
Leaving only a memory
Let each memory be a part of the rest of your life
Because life is a miracle
Live it well, learn from each mistake
And always be proud of who you are
Elizabeth Cowan

See You When It's Too Late

To all in uniform—dead and lost—
french maidens experiencing one-night stands.
hot farm stock—new potatoes—
come join, join my humble page;
I'm the only one who listens,
when one of your family forgets your name.
you have numerous cousins,
every time I say the same,
every time I say the same.
There's time travellers in my world,
and I've been given this
to intervene in your road crash,
to control the new-mann falls;
Can you identify my body,
as it seems foreign to me,
shifting plate run over me,
articulate my post-sterile haze.
I can't tell you it's flying saucers,
tried the abominable snowman's card.
He was glad to deliver.
Anthoney Royles

A Contented Toothbrush

The all night vigil in my crystal clear surround
Nears its end, for night, dawn has found.
Soft pink light melts the shadows of my room
And cold, clean porcelain rises from the gloom.
Soon, mistress, eyes soft from pleasant sleep,
Will pluck me gently from my crystal keep
A wine glass really but to me a tidy home,
A place to savour tingling joys of minty foam.
Soon she'll hold me in her lips in sweet caress,
Too soon to end, this pleasure, but nevertheless,
I think my nightly vigil so worthwhile
When I behold her sweet and heavenly smile.
Geoff D. Parkin

Ode to Hale-Bopp

Last seen through the eyes of the Egyptians, on the
  edge of Cassiopeia,
Looking past tired morning dreams, I wondered
  would I see her?
A dragnet of ice filling the sky, such
  feast for emotions,
Brightest star, comet strength causing such
  commotions.

Orbiting around the celestial sky, a treat
  for any Arian,
North West the silver path by night, constant
  in its direction,
Andromeda, Cygnus, Perseus too, all will
  see in turn,
And he, caressed by Hale Bopp, tranquil
  in its sojourn.

Elaine Andrea Parker

Australia

Australia, with your brilliant skies
And golden beaches too,
Has made a home for many folk,
And uplifted them anew.

From the dreamtime to the present,
Man has travelled through this land.
Has also stood and wondered
How this country had been planned.

May everyone appreciate
The wonders that abound,
From its hills, and streams, and forests.
This great abundant land.

E. W. Farndell

Unfortunate World

I hear the rustle of the leaves,
And if you listen carefully sometimes just
sometimes you can hear violent gun fire the
sobs and grieves.
Accidents murders and suicides happen
every day.
We think we live safe lives, we don't, for
safety we must pray.
Committing crimes for stupid reasons,
Why can't people just let things be and others
live through all seasons.
For life they have encountered family and friends,
Of course everyone's life ends,
But does this way have to be,
it may not but maybe.

Therese Garvin

Hello Reader

My dearest reader, seconds, ago, before your
Decision to turn the page, there was nothing.
These very words were hidden away and thus
Unseen, to all intents did not exist:
Just like the beauty of the Jovian Moons
'Til "Voyager" beamed those pictures back to Earth.
For you have brought this page to life — yes you and only you!
You bring along a wealth of memories of your own,
Your feelings, thoughts, regrets and sorrows, joys
And fears, your hopes and fantasies.
You have the mountains of your mind:
Your personal rivers, clouds and suns: flowers and gasometers!
Landscapes, dreams and nightmares of your very own.
And me, as you sit reading this, I might be dead and buried,
Or with you right now, or maybe miles away.
To you I give the role of God: to breathe your life upon this page.
Take you away, dear reader, and there's nothing: formless void.
Yet now, together, you may join me, in a realm
Where Life, though challenged by evil,
Is warded by our love.

Paul Butters

Untitled

Why did I laugh last night? I hardly know.
So much has altered in the interval.
Now half a day seems half an age ago,
And laughter no more than the gutteral
And random sounds that imbeciles create
Who have no pain or pleasure to express
And otherwise might howl or ululate;
Inhuman, without mirth, and meaningless.

Why did I laugh? I neither guessed nor dreamt
That you were not the thing you claimed to be.
You never laughed with me, but with contempt.
I saw in you a friend. You saw in me
A prostitute you did not have to pay.
And knowing now, why should I laugh today?

Hilary Wade

A Summer Song

When the summer sun shines
The sea shimmers
Like a million frosted diamonds
The soaking seals bask on the shore
Sweet lilt of their song begs for more
Horse's heads stir and turn
But the crystal sea does not churn
Sweet caress and kisses of the breeze
Perfect summer sun puts me at ease
Take time to observe with me at will
That tranquil beauty and time exists still
Tiring wearing tearing of life is gone
My wish fulfilled I am at one

Paula Logan

Vision

A hazed view. A blurred vision.
Foliage green. Rushed
Images. Seventy miles per hour. Distorted faces. Nine-legged
animals and Stretched buildings.

The brain begins to falter. Non-communication.
Keine Kommunikation.
No comunicacion.

Mishapen, misforms of fluffy, multi-coloured
Clouds, racing. Quickly, Quicker.
The world is in turmoil.

The over-powering clatter of a
clapped-out car, Wooshing, hissing . . .
The crunching of Grinding Gears, The revving of
Rusting Rivets.

Slithering vehicles pass in silence.
The scintillating flashes
Spark an electrical
Impulse. I am Human.
The world is in turmoil.

Alison E. McLellan

The Last Goodbye

We said goodbye to our friend today
We knew she had to go away
A long, long journey she'll have to go
It may take a while for all we know
A journey unknown to a heaven above
A place that's filled with peace and love
A place where everyone's happy and free
Where there's peace and harmony for all to see
She's gone away to a different life
Where there's no aggravation, war or strife
Where there's no discomfort, fear or pain
Lots of sunshine and not much rain
We know we'll see her again some day
But when that'll be, who's to say
There's only one who can tell us when
It's the good Lord above, King of all men

M. Sutherland

Unspoken Words

We played away, we've played at home
We've been around the block

But father time hasn't been kind
He hasn't stopped the clock

For I stepped away for someone else to play
With affections I know I've lost

I'm a patient man which means one day
I'll have you but at what cost

Can we afford to be just you and me
But when I look at you what do you see

You never look me in the eye
I guess I know the reasons why

For what power there is in just one look
and in the unspoken word

For the words I write, I write for you
as you are the centre of my world.

Iain Hodgson

Sons and Mothers

He never left,
Just moved away,
He needed space to find himself.
A branch not severed,
But reaching out towards the light
And teased away by life's rich treasures.
Not lost,
His roots secure in love that never wavers
And in wisdom born from wrongly chaining slaves.
I watch and wait,
For in the letting go, we both find freedom
To go our separate ways, to grow
Unhindered by a sense of guilt or bound by duty.
The door is always open to come and go,
Not mine to own,
A son, a soul to love and cherish,
He will return,
He has returned,
He never really left,
Great teacher life our bond has strengthened.

Margaret R. Vessey

Reflections

If we had time to stop and stare
At nature's wonders we'd be aware
Of autumn's colours of gold and brown
Scattering of leaves as they tumble down.

The crispness of the snow so white
Sparkling in the evening light
The contrast of the berries so red
Against the ever-growing hedge.

The daffodils and tulips too
Yellow and red amid crocus blue
The blossom on the trees so pink
It really makes you stop and think.

The roses with their scented flowers
Give pleasure to many for hours and hours
The geraniums in their tubs so bright
A cherry welcome to all in sight.

From autumn days to winter nights
We revel in the glowing lights
Then spring comes forth with hope anew
As we charge our batteries all summer through.

A. F. Gibson

I Dream of You

"I dreamed I saw you
Standing on a sandy beach
So very close
But still out of reach.

I dreamed I saw you
Out at sea
And I honestly thought
You were calling to me.

I dreamed I saw you
In the night sky
I tried to reach you
But you were too high.

I dreamed I saw you
In the moonlight
But when I looked closely
My instincts were not right.

I dreamed I saw you, the other night
But I couldn't have done, you're way out of sight
I dream of you, dreaming of me
Dreaming of you.

Nichola-Louise Bent

Prisoners

Cemented desperate beings
With inescapable animal instincts
And stormy headaches,
Living in heartache cities
Nowhere to hide from a naked condition

Tied to making honey money
Inspiration and abilities instilled
In technology, a ketchup of wonderment;
Is there anything new about bones?
Conversation catching up on phones

Discourse about a house on a racecourse
Movement from one house to another
Houses can be prisons after thought;
Houses are just raisins and currents
Electricity charges a tax

Cold human beings cuddle
Come rain or sun beings will curdle
In an attempt to concentrate on sounds;
Playing with chains
And animal instinct trains.

Steven Ridley

What Is In a Name?

A name is a thing of which to be known,
That will be heard many times each day.
It will be shouted and whispered and screamed aloud.
A name is a thing of which to be proud.

A name is a thing that must be known,
To have a chat with friends.
Imagine if no one had a name,
We would certainly get confused.

Our identity is important to us,
Our name given by our parents.
We may not like it, it may not appeal,
We should not question it however we feel.

Our name is important,
It matters a lot.
Our parents gave it,
They must know a bit.

Our name wasn't given to us alone, so,
What is in a name?

Claire Vickers

Who Is There?

Who is it that breathes unspeaking at my door?
Would that I could touch you now, but unrevealed,
So cunningly illusive, as a breeze without a source,
Aimlessly you drift within and out of thoughts,
Too crowded with preoccupations of a lesser time,
Approaching unpredictably this solemn place of mine.

I know you're there!
So wait, I will in time arrive my frail approach
Withstanding to the last all counter forces which
In any common cause would render me such helpless prey
To every taunt and jibe of life, whose humour once
I knew, whose cackles haunt me so, but now I reach to see
And in that seeing will concede no less to sanity.

I feel your life,
Beating, urgent, somehow echoing my own,
As at last the dark dividing threshold chanced in hope
Halved with fear of meeting my inquisitor—I cross:
"Who is there?" I cried again—the door behind me closed.
A child appeared, whose face redeemed by light I almost knew,
Then, in that golden dawn revealed, we spoke as one—"it's you!"

Keith White

Past Memories

Think not back on your young life,
No love. Only sorrow and despair,
Accusations, arguments and drunken fights,
Little children hiding under the stairs.
"Hush now! Be still! Make not a sound!"
While mother is beaten and kicked to the ground.

Father next morning, now so tender,
Could not remember, full of remorse.
All will be well . . .until payday again,
Then more drink . . .and the same brutal force
"Wipe your tears Mother, please don't cry.
We will pray to Jesus, to make him die"!

The children wore clothes bestowed by neighbours
'For the poor and needy'. Boots issued free.
Such help and kindness, was their saviour;
Bringing warmth and respect to the family.
As adulthood arrived through those miserable years,
All flew the nest one by one.
Their torment, and fears are all in the past
And their parents are happy; together at last.

Violet Kirrage

Untitled

After all said and done, we are all flesh and bone,
A line of enquiry, a date in a diary,
A tombstone in gilt, some blood that is spilt,
A voice that cries out in pain, and in joy,
Sometimes a contribution and then perhaps not,
Plus and minus and a dot,
Abstract thoughts of abstract thoughts,
Plus and minus and a dot,
How to think and how to know,
How the wind attacks my skin,
And how the heat devours me so,
And ricocheted thoughts all end in nought,
With a dot in between,
That will never be seen,
By you, By me,
Created to be,
Forever,
Unseen.

David Charles Poupard

Stamina of Youth

To ride upon the stacks of hay
Of summertime we drew away,
Did eat the blackberries of overgrown lane,
And raced the engine in its pulling strain.

Summer gleamed as we sweat and toiled,
Never seemed there would be winter at all.
As barley ripped and bowed its head,
Again we rallied in young manly stead.

On railway hill we schemed huddled still;
For orchard lane we'd eat our fill.
Build great dams and swing on limbs,
Our daring feats and healthy wins.

We rallied, pranked, and fought till dark,
Shun'ed the hour we had to depart.
We'd lay in rest and await the dawn,
Sleepless ease seemed forever till morn.

Up she sparked and out we ran,
Heat of sun on burning tan,
Race and greet the toils of day,
The memory of youth I hold this way.

Thomas Crawford

Poverty

On the streets, it begs for your money;
   the children show their vulnerability.
And the adults dance in chaos,
   struggling to afford shelter and food.
Poverty,
   Society's nuisance.
Is there no place to send them?
   So as if to avoid what is so ugly.
But, to avoid poverty,
   give it strength
To prey elsewhere.
Reinvented in the unemployed, in single parents
   And, in the working poor,
Raping the victims of dignity and stability;
   leaving them isolated and confused.
Poverty,
   Taker of compassion,
And the giver of intolerance.

Helen Adams

Gone

I hear his laughter in my
head, I see a bright light
which was once his smile.
This man had charisma, plenty
of class and oozed style.

Though his life has slipped
away, I feel his force everyday.
From one world we little understand
to another we know nothing about,
my brother John has gone from this earth,
with all that once existed into God's turf.

Let's remember what we all shared
and what he gave, now he's at rest
in God's garden grave. Nothing
can harm him there, he's back where he started.
How I wished I'd seized the chance to say goodbye
before our lives were parted.

All we are left with, are pictures we
will find, of those fond memories
embedded in our mind.

Kevin McDermott

Goodnight

Like driftwood
we lie forgotten on the beach,
ignored by the stars,
as the sun bleeds into the sea.
Silence shrouds us;
we are lost in awe.
I raise my arm,
and trace the path of a satellite
sliding through the gap
between certain
and uncertain.
We think "Imagine
that somewhere people are looking back at us."

Candlelight flickers across the sand,
glinting off bottles and exposing the dozen bodies
that the beach cushions.
We are all friends here,
knowing each other's thoughts,
as the black unknown threatens its questions.
Ignored by the stars, we are drowned by their voices.

Robin Ashbrook

The Hapless Spectre

Evacuate your stormy stay
To a nearby dream with tinted breeze,
Experience the thunder fold . . .
Into a cast of wonderment.

Chased into the eerie corner of midnight
Its black arch fading beneath such splendour,
Following the lost trail northwards
In through a ploughing pastoral landscape
Into your ancestral cobweb
Where bodies wake with open arms
Fencing off the arrows flooding,
Witnessing how restless death is,
Destroying, the colour unmasking its flames.
What was once imposing now stands bare.
No thrilling gaze,
But emotions trapped in momentary haze
As bodies crumble into dust
And ashes re-enact a plague,
Recognize your chastised race
Your vessel afloat with a soul

P. A. T. Lehane

Untitled

Peter and Pat
have been married three years.

Peter hates to garden.
Pat compromises her love to a few pansies
on a sky-rise flat window ledge.

Pat hates to travel.
Peter compromises his love to town and back
every Wednesday afternoon (by rule)
and is back for tea.

Peter lost his dad to a heavy-goods truck
eight days before Pat gave birth. (A girl. 6 Lb.)

Jenny speaks no sense—yet.
Pat suffers obscure post-natal depression:
She speaks no sense—yet.
Peter cannot cope.

Pat smokes Lambert and Butlers.
Peter tends to drink a little more than he should.
Pat scares the postman.
Peter scares Pat.
Jenny howls.

Emily Berry

The Battle

The sounds of battle rage on ahead,
Upon this field all cloaked in red,
The lifeless bodies spread.
In crimson spangled dread,
Encrusted blades in flesh have wed.

The sounds of battle rage on ahead,
A steel forged creed, freed to breed,
The sin sheathed shrine on which to feed,
With weapons drawn, the mighty bleed,
So blind the deed, so foul the need.

The sounds of battle rage on ahead,
Will pity scorn the war-torn thorn,
So young to heed the warrior's throne,
The hand that lifts the shriven pawn,
In rivers of blood, to atone.

The sounds of battle rage on ahead,
The victor's reach with cooling dead,
To swear and preach on carmine steel.
This battle's won by death alone,
The sounds of battle rage no more.

A. D. Turnbull

Snoring

He lies, he sleeps, he snores,
Arms outstretched
Rhythmic rumbles as air is
Inspired . . ., expired.
Inspired . . ., expired.
Warm and long
Oblivious to my icy feet.
As I place them against his flank.

The snore has momentarily ceased.
Replaced in part by meaningful heave of chest
And now for . . .. Whale sounds.
Blowing . . . And sucking.
Blowing . . . And sucking.

Minus the garbled chatter of some evenings.
My entertainment is limited, save the reactions
to a well placed elbow to end my suffering
with the gesture of snuggled contentment
from him.
I sleep.

Suzanne Evans

Dazzled

What compels people to bare their grieved souls,
To heartless machines and conscienceless ghouls?
Cameras absorb, each detail recorded,
Journalists twist words, put quotes in your head,
Buying betrayal, intimate feelings,
Selling their papers, boost TV ratings,
Pride shrinking, inviolate secrets shed,
Running out of self-esteem, bone dry bled,
They'll mock you, being so eager to please,
They'll dig dirt, you'll sing like a canary,
Let a minor star stare down the length of his nose,
Flesh and blood just like you are before he arose,
Squeeze all the juice out, spit out the rest,
Privacy abandoned, play on your weakness,
Deadlines preventing them resting in peace,
Headlines must be found, they've fresh news to seek,
And you're left in a vacuum, picked cleanly out,
Brief flash of glory too minute to count,
Talk through your trauma, but not on TV,
Forget fleeting fame, it's friends that you need.

Ian Newman

The Mole

Spades and claws are my armour in the dark.
I, The Earth mover, tunnel below.
I see without eyes, feel through my fur.

Unafraid, I explore the underworld.
My solitary kingdom of tunnels,
Hidden treasures. It all belongs to me.

I read vibrations of food that slithers
As it goes down.
Worm killer I, Crunchier.

No boundaries apply to me.
I leave my refuse in your crops and disappear,
A velvet coated magician.

There are no seasons in the womb of the earth.
Winter's bitter fist touches not my fur,
Day and night pass in equal darkness.

You cling to the surface like ticks
I slumber, Mother Earth's favourite foetus.
Your cities rise, and fall.
Dawn King

Hope

Hope is the spirit that strives,
And penetrates the soul with joy within,
Until the shadows of nocturnal gloom,
Glides through the melancholy of the night.

Hope clings on to a slender thread,
When the hearts bowed down with sorrow and woe,
And sickness makes the body pine,
Within a world as false and vain as ours.

Hope is the spark of life that keeps on living,
Breathing the air of freedom rising,
Of mighty thoughts and deeds of daring,
The inner joys of the human heart.

Hope is the re-birth of better things to come,
Anticipating the times of mirth and joy,
Of influence that inspires the souls of gifted men,
To make this earth an Eden for all mankind.
Winifred Thompson

Election

If New Labour head the queue,
They couldn't do much worse,
With majority more than just a few
Those tories would curse.

Liberals will endeavour to win the day,
They say a change is as good as a rest,
Perhaps would be nice if they had their say,
Your votes put this to the test.

If Lib Labs got together,
To get us out of this mess,
I'd go hell for leather,
My vote, have a guess.

Mind you the tories, from inflation will recoil,
Put up tax at the drop of a hat,
They have frittered all the resources of oil,
Never mind, they can always increase VAT.

So in May, when you proceed to the poll,
Think very carefully before you vote,
God knows the way from out of this hole,
Consider a change, *take note*.
J. W. McCarthy

Seize the Day

In the darkness when your body is just a lifeless shell,
And your soul is in Purgatory, caught between Heaven and Hell,
You can forget the "if only's" and the "what if I had's",
Because your blood has ceased flowing, you will be dead.

So, while the Sun's rays warm your red rosy flesh,
And Life's spark burns inside you, the World looks so fresh,
Before you lie cold in mortal decay,
Hold Life in your grasp and then seize the day.

Turn Life upside down and shake it like a tree,
So Nature's fruits fall loose, and then you'll be free
To mark a place in history, where others can say you stood,
Don't be a forgotten memory when you can do some good.

If wishes remain wishes, nothing will be done,
Don't leave your dreams to the darkness, hidden from the Sun,
Let every experience fill you, your Mind can't throw it out,
There is so much to accomplish, so cast away the doubts.

Look at everybody, every single thing, from a different viewpoint,
From another plane, break the bonds of conformity,
There is more than just one way to live your life and die,
So rise up and seize the day.
Paul Nicholson-Taylor

Visionary Truths

She looked hopelessly through the window,
Through the square vision,
a barrier between her world
and the next.
But also her salvation,
a medium through which she looks
into the outside,
a real world
with real people free from the confines
of a four wheeled prison
Through this sheath
she is protected from the harsh realities
of life,
protected from the poisonous and venomous
insults,
the treacherous behaviour of those,
who are,
malicious through their own lack
of
knowledge.
Emma Louise Tinniswood

Opposite Succession

As we move along the river of life,
We meet its compassion and its strife,
For it is war and it is peace,
It starts the fights and calls the cease,
It is the right it is the wrong,
It is the music and the song,
It is the good and the bad,
It is the happy and the sad,
It is the young it is the old,
It is the sale and the sold,
It is despise and the glory,
It is the judge it is the jury,
It is the mad it is the sane,
It is the thunder and the rain,
It is the warm it is the cold,
It is the brave it is the bold,
It is the hate it is the love,
It's torn between satan and God above,
It's the drunken husband and battered wife,
The river is death the river is life.
Amy Hanson

To Versify

The poet's eloquence is not just words
But music penned in harmonious union
With all the sounds of ecstasy
A phrase, a glance, a chance to say
Those dreams those thoughts of every day
A magic moment that he will catch
A smell of fragrance so sweet
That hints romance

The lyric flames the inner soul
Its heart filled full of warming glow
A poem with Terpsichorean dance
Whose words a muse could not enhance
When time and nature join in one
The Poet sees the rising sun
As twilight slips into night
The poem recalls the everlasting light

Norman Scott Brittain

Beauty or Beast?

Animals sacrificed to satiate plebeian desires,
Perfumes, after shaves, mink and leather
Embellished to induce covetous gleam,

Alas, what eyes can see
The beauty on the body,
Do they see the "Graveyards" within?

A rabbit's agony in the luscious hair,
A Ewe's child in the soft fur hat,
A dead deer in the manly musk.

Is this all what beauty is about?

Barbarians and Sadists are souls, indeed
that for glamour and lust
bring all wildlife to dust.

Hanif Kanjer

Poverty

The young ones are ragged, feet are bare
Faces pinched and eyes that stare.
Mothers stand and wring their hands
As children die like grains of sand.
Eyes that weep for all to see
When will it end, this Poverty?

Lords in their mansions, Kings and Queens
Eat food the slums have never seen.
Chickens, hams, creams, and cake
Things that the poor never partake.
Women shout in anguished plea
When will it end, this Poverty?

Sam Thompson

Oliver Humphrey

Oliver Humphrey, he is a card
Likes punk music beat out hard
Oliver Humphrey, he doesn't care
For a life that's sweet and square
Oliver Humphrey, isn't a fool
And yet is just his parent's tool
Daddy's a lawyer, clever and smart
Success story from the start
Mummy is social, with it I'd say. never lets her hair grow grey
Brother and sister clever as well
Poor little Oliver struggles like hell
Worries his heart out trying to be just as smart as the family
Brother at Radley, sister assured
Oliver's gonna have to board just hope he makes it,
He will you'll see, even if it's misery,
Oliver Humphrey wants to be free, he wants time to climb a tree
Oliver Humphrey always says yes even if he doesn't agree
Could be that he's learning to be like the rest at last you see
He will vote Tory, just like his dad and become an undergrad
Oliver Humphrey, he was a card liked punk music beat out hard
Now he's a lawyer, just like his dad, Oliver Humphrey cannot be bad.

Peter Davis

Noontime

The day has no means now
To weigh infinity.
Within the light, no dial
Marks the stopped moment
Or tells where time and self
Their fusion seal.

Yet once on the noon-still lawn
Time lay embayed,
Trusting only a child's hand
To hold the mute presence
Tuned only to a child's ear
To know the crouched silence.

Midday had swelled to emptiness
When the arrow stayed the clock face,
But there in neglected warmth, he waited,
He saw when the stilled minute fell,
How past and future spilled then
And filled so strangely, his child's heart.

R. V. Melrose

Flat-mates

The alarm rings loudly, breaking my dream. "Oh no it's Monday Look at the time, get up rise and shine".

Race to the bathroom, "Got to beat her this time", or my job's on the line. Quick lock the door, while the water runs hot, fill that tub right up to the top, drop the towel and step in let the warm soapy water engulf me, and freshen my skin. My body floats, I drift and dream, as the room fills with steam.

Bang! Bang! At the door, "hurry up" she screams, as she paces the floor, outside the locked door. "Hurry I'm going to be late".
I couldn't help smiling, as that's usually my fate!

I guess my boss will faint, for once I won't be late, I'll be at my desk by half past eight. A pay rise maybe forthcoming at this rate.

Who do I have to thank, for keeping my job. My flat-mate, for getting up late!

B. J. Klosowski-Travis

Poetry and People

Poetry is like people.
A bunch, a crowd.
A Gathering of words, to read out aloud.
There are those you don't want to see again.
Others, maybe now and then.
Poems, like people can make you cry.
So I forget them and say "Goodbye".
Funny and happy prose,
Keep me content and free of woes.
Religious and political poems are not my scene.
Fit only for their party members, so keen.
Ancient poems from long passed,
Are like an old friendship, I want to last.
But the poetry of love and the special one in the crowd.
Makes me float on a cloud,
And is the one that is close to my heart.
Till death us do part.

P. E. MacPherson

Crossover

Through the darkness I do tread
Afraid until I reach the light ahead
Not knowing what lies before me
But the love that will set me free

My mind before like a battlefield
Now a golden glow, warm, still and healed
No pain, no worries, gone has the fear
Only thoughts of ones, once held dear

Sun shines down, an eternal light
Glorious colours, new to my sight
Loved ones forever gone, I thought to be
But alas we are as one, it's heavenly

Gerry Fagan

Midnight Battles

Flashbacks I need to forget,
Through silence are now met.
Leave my mind is my plea,
A minute of peace so I can be free.

Thoughts of today,
Thoughts of yesterday,
Thoughts of tomorrow,
Tend to follow.

Another day brings with it time,
Memories not yet defined,
With categories of head or heart,
New thoughts to make a start.

At last thoughts begin to fade,
Memories, visions all seem frayed,
Tired eyes full of sleep,
Memories of before will keep.

Enter the world of dreams,
As escapes so it seems,
Can't shake away unwanted thoughts,
In the realm of dreams the true battle is fought!

Surjit Gill

My Jewel Box

My life was full of pastel shades, pleasing but uninspiring
Then I met my love and the colours sprang to life
vibrant and full of brightness.
Time brought my sons and the colours became richer
so rich they gleamed and sparkled like jewels
Reds and yellows greens and blues, these hues,
The brightness of polished gems
Rubies, topaz, sapphires, emeralds.
My life was a box of bright jewels beyond price.
Tragedy my son was sick
A sickness that was beyond the cure of even the most
precious jewels
The jewel box turned to grey unpolished, dull, the brightness gone
A nothing colour, uncertain neither black nor white
without the courage of conviction.
I yearned for my life to be black or white, something definite
It came, death, black as jet, colours for him yes oh yes
In another jewel box as yet unopened by me
Colours of a brightness we can only guess
My jewel box remains full of stones lacking lustre, lacking sparkle
One gem has gone the colours drained. Close the lid, wait a while.

Christine A. Morris

The Horror of My Bikini

I had my first bikini, hand knitted by my Mum,
'Twas in wool and itchy, not a sexy one,
I put it on with trepidation and went to take a peek
In my bedroom mirror and tried not to screech!

I put my present in my bag and said thanks to my Mum,
Prayed my swimming lesson would be a happy one,
Off to the pool I went with my young handsome beau,
Of my handmade bikini I didn't want him to know.

All too soon I realised this secret he would know,
For once I was in the water my bikini began to grow,
I tried to hold it to me and also bravely smile,
As the pants stretched to my knees and the top dropped a mile.

Oh Lord, what a job I had to cover little me,
I could see my beau was in fits, his eyes full of glee,
Gone were my dreams of glamour, a real sexy dish,
Looking great in a bikini and swimming like a fish!

Doris Thordarson

The Road

The road ends here.
Purpose fading. Nothing left to pursue.
Only space.
Space desperate for feeling.
Memories twinkle, the rest is black.
Quivering on the brink of reality the girl stands,
feeling the compulsion to turn, run back down the road.
Run to love, run to security.
She's alone here, nothing forward but confusion.
No hope
but strangely no fear.
Tentatively she takes a step,
so small and insignificant, but it's a step.
The road becomes a chapter left behind,
although in her heart it goes with her.
Never can she shake the memories.
All the pain. All the joy.
But now she grows strong, the road is gone
She grasps what she can remember, and walks forward.
Towards her dreams, towards new roads.

Flo-Louise Hart

The Terrible Twos

You are two years old with eyes of light blue
and your temper, Grandson, is just showing through.
What a sweet little boy when first you met us
and of course, we Grandparents, made quite a fuss.
"He's lovely" "The Darling" and noises like that
as you lay, quietly smiling, upon the hearth mat.

So quickly you grew, Mum and Dad were so proud,
each time they visited they sang your praises out loud.
Soon your First Birthday—oh what a fuss!
Chocolate cake in your hair and jelly gulped in a rush:
Uncles and Nieces, Aunts and Nephews galore
Someone else here with presents knocking at the front door.

Your first year soon over, too soon you are two,
we ageing Grandparents are still fond of you.
Though you do tend to scream and are trying to bite
with those white little teeth that, Dad says, grew at night.
You can talk now a little—but you do tend to shout;
you throw things and have sulks, won't stay in, won't go out.

It's the Terrible Twos, Parents all come to know,
Yet through them all, Grandson, why do we love you so????

George A. Cooper

Fallen Tree

A tree lies fallen on the forest bed,
Not cut, but uprooted by a storm.
Helpless I look on, nothing can be done.
Like a whale washed upon on the shore,
Still living still breathing, still dying.

There is no way to return it to the sea.
Its eyes seem to weep
As does resin from the tree.
But it is not for themselves they are sad,
Cause their conscience is clear.
Clear as the waters in which they live,
Clear as the water drawn through their roots.
It is for man and his short-sighted ways.

Delusion creating pollution;
Amidst all this confusion
A tree throws itself to the ground
A protest to the mothers of invention
A protest to man, was the fallen tree's intention

The great whale, lying on the shore
In order that man will ignore . . . no more.

Martin Gibbons

Out of the Window

Out of the big, big window, I see the world go by—
Everyone living their lives; then having to die.

There's people all over Arguing; Soon they'll start a war,
It's all because of greed; because they want some more.

Next they lose their temper; Say words they do not mean.
By now it's all too late; The hatred has been seen.

So there's now no turning back; the fighting has begun.
Innocent people begin to get caught up, and all they can do is run.

But peace cannot be made; A way out cannot be found,
Too many people have been hurt; in a graveyard there's no sound.

I walk away from the window hearing every cry and yelp,
I wish that I could stop it all but in no way can I help.

The windows in my head; The fighting miles away,
And people never listen to what I do or say.
Natalie Robins

Baby Born

The day you're born, Mum's body torn,
   that's why they're called the newly born;
So new and sweet, those little hands and kicking feet;
   the first smile that makes the day complete.
The nine months wait for boy or girl,
so very pale and sometimes small, you never want to grow at all.

Just hold in your arms till bedtime calls
   then lay them down when night-time falls.
The first few steps and down to crawl;
   then to the chair and stand so tall
   and mother chasing down the hall, stands on rattles, dolls and ball
   baby looks back and takes that fall
The love and hug that's worth it all.
Malcolm H. Nobbs

The Addict

We're partying, a man is walking, he's nearing
We're realising, he's supplying, he's begging
He's cajoling, we're buying, he's smiling
He's leaving, we are giggling, it's so tempting
We're sneaking, and hiding, we are snorting
And smoking, injecting and popping
We're vomiting, we are waiting, we are now tripping!
This is amazing!
We are dancing, and laughing, and fornicating
and hallucinating—we are sadding and resting
and slowing and crying, we're going, I'm sleeping
and snoring and tossing and turning,
I'm waking and shaking and sweating and screaming
I'm needing and craving, I'm taking constantly
I'm regretting and wishing, I'm stealing and lying
I'm illing, I'm crying
Please help me—I'm dying.
Sarah Targett

Snow

So soft, so white, so pure,
It floats from heaven as a lure.
It makes one want to skip and play,
Be careful, there is ice underneath that layer.

Disguising poverty, ugliness and dirt,
It comes as a maiden—a flirt—
Like icing on a birthday cake,
It coats the branches at the gate.

Beautiful indeed if you're a connoisseur
An artist—with canvas the lure.
But who can paint that glorious sheen
Sent by God—a miracle to be seen.

Not long it stays unblemished, untouched,
As the sun goes down it appears to blush,
As though ashamed to acknowledge that on the morrow
All would be just black, downtrodden slush.
Stella Askew

Stepping Stones

Is this another day that all I do is work, with little time to do
the things that give me so much pleasure?
I stop and think, and realize that today is not like that,
Today is different, and is mine, all mine to use at leisure.

I now have time to use my hands to create and perhaps have fun
And let my mind relax and think on past and things to come.
Life will slow down, but be more full of things to do.
New friends will come, and old ones stay and the sky will still
stay blue.

All things around me that I saw and did not recognize,
I now have time to stop and look and really use my eyes.
The world is out there waiting for my quiet embrace.
My working days were stepping stones leading to this new place.

I do not need my slippers or pipe to be laid out.
I want to carry on my life with my family all about.
I hear a call from the room next door, perhaps it's tea and cake
But alas, no; it is a small request for me to mend the gate.
Joan M. Richmond

The Chair

Cold bars surround me as I sit inside this tiny cell
Nothing to do and nowhere to go, I wait for the bell,
Because when that damn bell rings, I'll have to go downstairs;
They're going to tie me down and lock me into the old electric chair.

As I sit alone and try to think of days that are long gone,
The clock is ticking and the hands of time are loudly moving on
And the priest comes in for a minute or two and tries to say a prayer,
But his blessing is wasted because I can't stop thinking about
the old electric chair.

I can hear the warden walking down the long dark corridor;
My mind goes blank and body numb as his keys rattle in the door
And he whispers in a cold, stiff voice, "it's time to go down there",
I don't know if he means to hell or the old electric chair

They strap me in, hands and feet, and then, they blindfold me,
I can feel the metal around my head and black is all I see.
I imagine the people looking sad as if they really care
But after all it's just going to be me and the old electric chair.

The minutes turn to seconds and my body starts to shake
I wish they'd get it over with, for God's and my own sake
I know the phone's not gonna ring, I know it wouldn't dare
Not after all they say I've done, to deserve the old electric chair
Aaron McVitty

A Dassia Sunrise

As darkness creeps upon us and light is devoured by the
hungry sky
I sit . . . and wait the predictable dawn
on a shingle screen, flat and parallel to the motionless ocean.
The gently rocking boats reflect the glow of the neon lit bars,
and the barely dressed trees
throw the moonlight on to the sunsoaked golden tresses of
the romantic couple,
who yearn the daybreak away.
But I covet the sunrise.
The first glimmer of radiance bestows the land.

The uncontrollable motion begins,
flourishing with an appetite for colour,
galvanizing the horizon into an array of rosiness.
The land thirsts the light and the heavens oblige.
Each new sunbeam dances across the surface, no obstacle too
great for it to conquer.
The shadows walking from their sleep wave the moon into
oblivion.
I greet a new day.

With the sun at its fullest potential and the once undecided
colours of the horizon,
a definite warm yellow,
through the privilege of the light
I see the world for the first time today.
J. Woolley

Untitled

Today I intend to be happy
To be happy come what may
And if negative thoughts dare to intrude
I'm determined to push them away.

Today I intend to be patient
As patient as patient can be
With family, friends and strangers I meet
Their outlook I will try to see.

I am determined today not to worry
Not to worry and bother and fret
Although I have problems—I'll push them aside
And just for today—I'll forget

Today I intend to be grateful
For the blessings and gifts that are mine
I usually take them for granted but today these treasures will shine.

Today I will take things more slowly I will live at a leisurely pace
Refusing to hurry like everyone else
With their energies running to waste.

With these good intentions before me today cannot fail to excel
And if I enjoy all these changes I'll repeat them tomorrow as well.

P. Martin

Freedom

I dreamed I was a blood-red dove flying on air of damp and must,
Circling to the shimmering earth and landing in an emerald dust.
Borne away by perspex hands—imprisoned in a world of jewels—
Celluloid faces stared through me in this world of faithless fools.

I smelled the breath of summers green, and yearned for fields of ripening corn.
I watched the stars, like diamonds, shine and disappear into the dawn.
And with the sun, I took my flight. I flew, far from this cruel, cold land,
With wings outstretched, until I tired and came to rest on moonlit sand.

The salt of freedom stung my breast. No jewels to fill my world had I;
No empty eyes; no vanity; no cage was mine in which to die.
When I awoke my room was full of jewels of a far richer kind.
The jewels of freedom I had gained, and peace at last within my mind.

Lianne Baily

Peace in the Early Morning

Have you ever risen early in the morning
And listened to the stillness all around
The peace of the day wells deep within your soul
And joy inside your being bursts abound

To hear the little birds in morning chorus When they greet the start of another day And the sun as it rises from the east in shining rays Lighting up the darkness in its way.

The world seems standing still in these moments And earthly things so very far away No honking horns or traffic passing noisily along If only this repose could always stay.

Life seems very insignificant on occasions such as this For there is another side to the great unknown If we have faith to accept the things that really count More consideration to others would be shown.

When in this world we look around at all we have for free The trees, the birds the flowers the ocean's waves How many of us appreciate that for these there is no cost We have them to enjoy until the grave.

Life was given for living and that is something we must do But it helps not to forget from whence we came And to remember that tomorrow will always come for some Accept the blessings and enjoy them just the same.

Kilbroney Lewis

Something Close to Me, I Wonder . . .

I don't know his name, but I know about him.
I remember my mum telling me about him when I was very small.
He was a builder, a good one too . . .
I can't boast that he was the greatest grandfather in the world
because I don't know him and probably never will,
unless it's in a far off distant place.
I remember my mum telling me about him when I was very small.
That my gran stayed with him while my Mum ran to the
telephone down the road with her sister and brother.
My mum phoned the doctors, but my grandfather died, a young man.
I remember my mum telling me about him when I was very small.
About the time just before Christmas when the snow began to fall.
How they watched it falling to the ground, softly, softly—no sound.
I know my mum blames herself for his death.
I know that she was very small when he died.
I don't know his name, but then again I've never asked . . .

Emily Dickinson

Innocents

It happened on that horrible day,
 where we all went to learn and play,
We were only five and six, we went to school happy to mix,
With our friends we played and played, never to realize we
 would be slayed,
By a man we never knew, how could he have done this to me
 and you?
School was fun where we met all our friends,
Never did we realize our precious lives would end,
We were young, no cares at all, we were innocents, our lives
 were a ball,
Until that second where he walked in, the loudness, the
 screams were such a din,
Terror, panic was the order of the day, why oh why did our
 lives end this way?
We were babies, our whole lives ahead, instead of our
 destinies now we are dead,
We will meet our maker in the sky, we will have some
 questions, first of all, why?
We will gaze at him with our innocent eyes, and say, dear God,
 didn't you hear our cries?
We have been taken from our mums and dads, we feel hurt,
 we were young, but now we are sad,
Our mums and dads are without their children now,
 how will they cope, answer me how?
We will gaze through the clouds only to see hurt,
 pain and misery
Until that day when we meet again, our hearts will always
 feel the pain,
So goodbye, God bless, we will always love you,
 and be by your side in everything you do.

Jacqueline A. Rennie

The Fisherman

Dawn has barely broken, and the sky's a crimson sea
The air is cool and still and silence waits expectantly.
The early mist is rolling over river, dale and meadow
And there, among the rustling reeds, the unmistakable shadow
Of the fisherman, who sits alone and ponders for a while
And then with such precision, casts with beauty, grace and style.
The gleaming silver bream becomes his sole preoccupation
His predatory mind immersed in total concentration.
His gaze, intent, is focused on the bobbing orange float
And life beyond the river seems so distant and remote.
A gentle breeze emits the rustic fragrance of the pine
As patiently he sits and waits for just the merest sign,
And then he strikes with awesome speed, thrusting masterfully.
The twisting, twirling, silver streak resists courageously
And instantly the fisherman adopts a rigid pose
In preparation for the fight, for all too well he knows
If he should err for just one moment, he may lose the bite
And thus with guile and steady hand, so expertly adroit
He manoeuvres her, affording her the greatest admiration
Until she finally succumbs to the fisherman's elation.

Martin Crossley

Five Items—No More

A pretty young girl dressed in uniform green stands alone in a
  supermarket store, her orders are plain, her directions quite clear
"Check out five items—no more"

Her long blond hair is tied back with a lace, her apron hangs down
to the knee, her painted red lips give a smile that's false
Her eyes cry out to be free

One day at a time a sea of faces rolls by
Some strange, some familiar, some new
The unemployed man whose lottery ticket she'll scan as he prays
  for those words: "It's you!"

The mother of two; the chain smoker who rasps and coughs
  with no shame
The man in a suit; some odious brute, foreign students
  who all look the same

So she dreams of romances and Friday night dances as
  laser-beams crisscross the dance floor
A house fit for sharing, a husband who's caring and
  rich so she's freed from this chore

But boredom she'll endure as the clock on the wall
  tells her the time's not yet four
Freedom she's yearning but to bolster her earnings
  she'll check out "Five items—no more."

Gary Young

Ode to Drink

I wait, I watch, I listen, no steps fall in the night,
No eerie wail to warn me, no sound to give me fright!!
But I know that it is out there crouching in the gloom
Gathering up its forces, which ere will be my doom!!!

A voice within me utters, a prayer to keep me sane,
It also keeps repeating life will never be the same,
If only I could alter time and start my life once more,
I'd tread a careful carpet and close the devilled door!!!

But fate has lead me to this place and fate is here to stay,
And nothing can deter my life nor outcome to delay,
I've trodden down the road to Hell and lost my footing there
And though I wish to leave this hole I've sunk into despair!

And so the demon drink has won and I cannot free its hold,
It wraps its fingers round my throat, it force's oh! So bold,
The golden liquor trickles down and I float and sing on high
A drunken heap for all to see, but my inner soul doth cry!!!

Diane Thomas

The Three Times-A-Day Ordeal

The distance between hand and mouth is far and the journey
is hazardous. I like food!
The process of eating, at twenty a natural pleasure, now at
eighty demands insurmountable effort that I am tempted not
to labour with.
"I know you can feed yourself if you try, I've cut up the meat,
there's no need to cry."
Her grip isn't weakened by arthritic blows, her arm doesn't
tremble like mine.
I'll use my fingers to pick up a piece of 'what's good for me'.
O, that appetite and joints had deteriorated to the same degree,
then I could sleep and ignore the 'Three times a day ordeal'.
She'll put a piece on the spoon quite soon and accuse me of
not trying.
She'll suggest that I'll never get well if I don't eat;
I'll acquiesce not to annoy her.
O, that the cure for old age was calorific and that protein could
repair the ravages of time upon human flesh.
The spoon enters my mouth under alien control, without
warning or my co-operation.
The taste is good! But another hurdle exists. Was chewing
always hard work? Did my dentures always move in equal but
opposite action to that intended?
She'll take the plate away soon and remind me that people are
hungry elsewhere.
If I had the strength and inclination I'd tell her that someone is
hungry right here.

Margaret Lewis

The House

The house was abandoned. It was like an old bird's nest in a
beach tree in Autumn; now the mother had reared her young
and deserted it.
The paint work peeled and discoloured, the eaves were
crumbling, leaves lodged in the water drain; tap, tap the
hanging basket hung there on a rusty chain, knocking against
the porch window. Its flowers once did flourish, now they
just drooped and withered in the wind. A cluster of silky
spiders webs lay dormant in the old stone fire place, no wisp
of smoke from this chimney stack; mucus trails meandering
from the larder, the stillness of the stagnant water in
the goldfish pond sent a stale odour into the air; in the cellar a
fox's lair. An old bird table lay on the ground, rotted by time
that made no sound. The pantry window was smashed, grim
slivers of broken glass looked threatening. Bees had buzzed
their way in and built a hive, bats took refuge in the attic, a
slate had slid, leaving a hole where a web hung thin, and
through it the ever changing faces of clouds floated by. In
the kitchen the weeds pushed their way up
between the cracks in the old floor tiles. The bright sun shone
dim through the dusty living room window, which sent rays of
dust dancing from the bare floorboards to the flaking ceiling;
the evergreen shrouded the garden shed, now green with
moss and crusted with frost. The rain trickled down the
windowpane resembling tears expressing pain in the darkness
of night its image like a vague dream was something mysterious that is hard to explain as if it had almost never been.

Michael John

The Evening Circus

Admiring a dress designed for the crowd,
Concealing the phantom within;
A shower of sequins fall, kissing the ground
With their galaxy of nonchalant stars.

Time-scarred rooms of waxworks, silhouettes, cameos;
Juggling magazine column conversations,
shop window observations.
The shadowed eyes reveal love lost in fear, life lost in hope,
But the parties are considered a sight to behold!

Must wander, keep occupied, look interested;
Decorations, ornaments, pictures—
  is this light entertainment enough?
The mind roams over past trivialities, misfortunate years,
To the symphony of wine and cocktail glasses.

Festivities finished, the pantomime is over!
Place the cameo back in her vainglorious box.
Regimental cars receive their marching orders,
Journeying to the safe haven of home.

The clock, soon our music in the still of night,
Our stars, the street lamp's distant halo.
Retire to our coffins, to where we are going,
And wake tomorrow; peaceful, yet full of unknowing.

Julie Gibson

Mother's Pride

I laid myself in your circumstance, to be what you desired of me,
I perceived myself through your eyes, to recognize what you
  wanted me to be,
Your pain I cannot take away, but I ached too
  whenever you felt them.
I anticipated all of your needs even before
  you knew you craved them.
I was your nurse and teacher, and I tried to be your friend.

I cried your tears when you were weeping,
I shared your laughter and smiles when you were smiling.
When you stumbled I held your hand,
When you were in doubt, I assisted you to understand.
Guiding and protecting you with everything I am.

Like a flower I watched you growing,
I provided you with a stem to lean on,
Watered you and made you strong.
It saddened me to watch you go, now that you've become a man.
You are my greatest achievement and I'm proud to be your Mum.

Dorine Walters

True Love

You are my whole existence,
You are the reason I open my eyes in the morning,
Why the birds singing seem beautiful . . .
My serenity is enhanced by our love,
You take my emotions to another dimension,
You are the reason I can laugh again.
Why a smile is back on my face,
I constantly worry about you, when we are apart . . .
I want to be by your side, to protect you,
If I could have one prayer answered
It would be to spend every passing moment with you,
Laughing, loving, helping each other . . .
We have but one day at a time,
Time was wasted until we met,
Now every second is precious,
Let's not spend a moment arguing, never let the honeymoon period end,
I truly adore you, I thank God above, that He has given me true love,
His will for me was you, I got lost along the way, searching for you,
He gently guided my footsteps and lead me
To the one and only girl on his earth for me.

Chris Perrins

My Enemy

I have an uninvited guest that's come to stay, you just crept in while my back was turned, thinking that I'd look the other way, because that's the kind of loathsome creature you are, people's worst enemy by far. I half expected you, because my life has been nothing but happiness for the past 34 years, and when I've listened to other people's troubles, I can only imagine the pain that's causing their tears.

It was such a shock when I was told of your arrival, for no one wants to be told that the visitor from hell is here, and all at once I was enveloped in a dark, foreboding fear.

But now that days have passed and many tears have been shed, I'm over being scared, now we know what were up against, we can get prepared.

My room is filled with cards and flowers, all sent with best wishes and kind words, of support, helping me find the courage I lack.
Knowing that so many people are on my side, gives me the strength to fight back.

So now I'm gaining strength again and can look forward, to the route that's planned, with courage to face my enemy, to say "Cancer from my body, you are banned!" You'll not be allowed to rest in my cells, you certainly don't have the right, for my future and my family. I must make sure I win this fight.

Carol Cierniak

Tomorrow's Hope

Ravenous with the will to consume and be consumed, there I was, a part of something not too alien, harbouring insecurities and secretly longing to be one of . . . 'them'. What an experience! More or less two fulfilled years and nineteen fresh faces, each blessed with their life time of 'something different'.

Perhaps preconceived ideas of dropouts (just like me), failures representative of class time misspent, pertained to our bonding—adhesive to the point of camaraderie. Yet by the second year, our alliances dwindle, we stood alone in our fight to the end.

We sacrificed a few of those faces along the way, casualties of obnoxious tendencies and misconceptions, they were quashed as infidels of our cause. How strange it is now that we forget their faces and the friendships formed so early on—perhaps indicative of life's perverse intentions (knowing that tomorrow is another day and yesterday is gone).

Parties and ceremonies facilitate dissemination; we (I) are now dexterous and fuelled with that ravenous appetite to consume the world and become its leaders. We are the future, we control the rise and fall, we have learnt and are a product of the knowledge. Possessed and possessing the urge to go forth and be, be known, just be, we go.

Jay M-L. Horton

To the New World

Standing by a harbour wall in 1493
He is wondering if the news he's heard is true:
Is the Earth a globe or just a disc? And is it wise to take the risk
Of setting sail in search of . . . something new?

It is said that Fortune smiles on those who venture, those who try:
Who can tell what might be his if he were bold!
Out beyond the far horizon where the ocean meets the sky
Are there continents where rivers run with gold?

He might come to unknown cities selling silver, silk and spice,
To a world of untold wealth beneath the ground!
He might find a blessed paradise, or a hell of darkness, fire and ice.
In stormy deeps he might be lost and drowned . . .

So we all stand at our quay sides and we all gaze out to sea
While a voice within keeps telling us "Set sail
To the new world that awaits you where your heart and mind are free!"
And another voice says "No! What if I fail?"

But the sun and tide are rising now, the wind is seaward-bound
And the inner voice has not yet ceased to call:
Perhaps the world is really round! There's so much more yet to be found
By someone waiting near a harbour wall . . .

David Monkcom

My Present to the Both of You

From the first day I found out that Mum had a date,
I thought "not bad", I thought "that's great".
She was no longer moping around, being a pain,
She actually started smiling and laughing again.

And when I saw him, I had such a shock.
He couldn't be more like her, even if he wore a frock.
They have so much in common, they make life such fun,
And when this day is over, their new life will have begun.

Still I'll have chores and work to do,
But I must admit it will be done mostly by you.
So much has happened within the past year,
The future now seems so crystal clear.

There'll be plenty of giving and laughter to share,
And I'm sure there'll be plenty of tender loving care.
You both are always with me, no matter what kind of day,
You are always both supportive in every kind of way.

You help me through life's little maze, I hope you both are happy today and always. I thought of a present—towels "hers and his"—and then I thought again—"no, tickets to the Nemasis", and then I thought again "what a lot of thinking I do! How about this poem? It's called "To The Both of You".

Carley Anne Stenson

King of Hearts

King of hearts, come down and dance, softly now, for minds entranced
With madness hear no music play. Through castle walls and empty halls,
Of candlelight, that flits and starts, await our Lord, the King of Hearts.

King of Hearts, come down and play, for bedlam fills the sky today,
And magic lingers in the air, and sweeps asunder those who stare,
And weep and wail in portals round, in tearful eye there is no sound.

King of Hearts, come down and sing, for loud does bell of steeple ring.
We wait in vain for summer moon, for halcyon days and nights too soon forgot,
By those who seek and choose, with deep delight, to suffer fools.

King of Hearts, come down and die, forgive our weakened deathbed cry,
The creatures of the night do scream and crave your audience.
Unseen by you the serpent at your throat, the ferryman has come to gloat,
And through your blindness now you see,
To never make a fool of me.

Carol Lawton

Maluna

I am thinking of going, going far from here
To a strange land where, I keep the freedoms that I lost.
Here only dark misery is brought to light, here cruel vengeance
Hatred's vile, a pain that ends nowhere. Beyond it another
  pain to come.

Oh blessed far off land where no one knows me
Where I can arrive with ordinary life, be left alone just to exist.
And I look through the glass to a sky of winter, grey.
To think of the friends I have lost, to think of my Maluna.

The one I love so much, like a youth, impetuous
When my dreams are lit by the clear sun of her love for me.
Sun to light up my dreams, happiness, vast unlimited
From a sky wide with hope, my wings are spread towards you.

And when in the end, with the tenderness which you gave me
In a grave covered by a grey sky, where there are no flowers
  that year
An absence of crosses, of roses, of lilies
Cover my tomb with cuts from a chisel, a verse from the Bible,
or a crown of thorns.

I lost a sun, my freedom, I gained a moon, my dream
I wake up to solitude to scream at the world my happiness.

Rolando Barrientos A.

Together Forever

It's no good waiting a lifetime for something that won't come,
Happiness and love for a lifetime only happen for some.
It doesn't matter if you are happy, it doesn't matter if you are young,
It won't come to you from cupid, with no arrow will you be stung,
Wanting it, waiting for it, hoping it'll happen to you,
If you desire it that much then to your heart be true.
Tell him you love him, tell him you care,
Tell him cold nights by the fire you hope to share.
If he loves you, if he cares he will want you back,
He will promise you the world and give you no flack.
But take heed and listen to all that I say,
Do you really trust him not to do it again someday.
Will he be faithful, loyal, honest and true?
Don't listen to his words, just listen to you.
Is his love true, is his love real?
Don't play his game, or do his deal.
If you both really care and love each other,
Then you'll find happiness and be together forever.
Love is wondrous, love is kind,
I hope that one day a true love you will find.

Paula Hawkins

Sweethearts

There are two sweethearts in my garden, who only stand and stare
I know not what they're thinking, so for me you will have to pardon,
Of course, it must be the love they share.

He's staring at her, but she's looking all coy
As she turns her back on him, this very shy boy.
He's gathered her skirt in his hand, to let her know he wants
her to stand with him forever more, as sweethearts do.

She's holding her chin as she looks down, a smile on her face,
or is it a frown,
Her apron is full of pretty flowers, gathered from the leafy bowers,
Before she met him in the morning dew.

Their thoughts are entwined as they share their love,
The sun is shining in the blue sky above.
They will stand there in sunshine and rain, in Winter, and Spring
and Summer again, and Autumn leaves will fall at their feet.

The two sweethearts in my garden, are in a creamy tone, as
they are only made of stone. But don't be sad if you see them
standing there,
As their love is all for us to share, the tender moments of
sweethearts in love.

In his hand he holds an apple for his queen, the prettiest girl that's
ever been, standing by this creamy throne, forever more immortal in
marble stone are the two sweethearts in my garden.

Marie Louise Sceats

Hole

As she swims into nowhere again,
She dives deep inside those somethings that are lost to find herself,
She dives, so very deep to breathe,
into a sea of dreams.

Charlotte Vassallo

A Day in the Life of the Wife

Who's up in the morning, bright and early, to face breakfast
T.V. and the hurly burly? Who puts on the kettle and butters
the toast, shakes out the frosties and picks up the post?
  The Wife!
Who opens the door to face a day's work, finds her bus has
just gone, she goes quite berserk, who shops in the hour that
should be her break and misses her lunch to buy hubby's
steak?
  The Wife!
Who comes home at five and starts washing the pots, making
the beds and emptying the slops? Who lays up the table with
everything clean, then does a mile sprint with her 'Mr.
Sheen'?
  The Wife!
Who cleans up the dishes, wipes and puts them away, then
does the ironing from yesterday? Who defrosts the fridge
then empties the bins, cleans out the loo and the bath's dirty
rims?
  The Wife!
Who puts out the empties and locks up the doors, airs off the
bed and mops up the floors? Who takes a quick bath then
jumps into bed, and when hubby gets close she's got a bad
head?
  The Wife!

Debra Hodgson

Michael

Tightened, gripping, shifted being, radiant beauty stands its ground
Boats on shimmering lake are racing melted peaks dwarf lands below;
Confused, emotions bruised and fractured, thinking, feeling
no longer whole.

Recent times a bird like spirit flew those magical mountains high,
Now plunges deep chaotic chasms, constant question why oh why?

Lessons to be learnt in life, alas I felt his change;
Connection barred between us; departures to arrange
Misguided, truths and sorrow, feelings unrequited.
Whispers still from deep in centre "seek within" afraid to enter?"
Such painful times in blighted hope, we often fail to hear.

It's in the fates!
How dare we, look straight, come face to face
Such purposes are guided our lives fall into place
Flames lit my soul, sweet sapphire eyes pierced deep within my heart
Such special love exists for him, I'd known it from the start!
Cool legal head blocked off that flow. He never took a chance
Then fate shows no relenting whilst reeling in life's dance.

Collective kindred spirits, cosmic love not lost
Deep my soul a place for him, forever at all costs.

Wendy Gregory

Love

Love is a very simple word but too seldom ever heard.
It's all around us!
Love is a powerful sentiment blessed by God and heaven sent
Shining all around us,
Love is in a baby's smile pure and treasured all the while,
Love is in a gentle touch from someone caring oh so much,
Love is a whisper on the breeze, like shimmering sunlight
through the trees.
Blessings showered around us!
Love is prayer at journey's end, as down memory lane we
slowly wend
Spreading joy around us,
Love is a gift we all share plenty for you and me to spare,
Love is a kiss and gentle touch sharing with you so very much,
Love is a very simple word listen it is often heard.
It's all around us!

Doreen Rudland

Grandad!

To my sadly missed grandad.
I guess I'm going to have to face the fact you've gone to a new world
A safer place were you can rest all day, a place I cannot go,
The place where I long to be, just to see you standing were you always used to be.

You've left us grieving, but we all know deep down
You are still with us in spirit,
so each time I look up at the stars, I remember you dreaming everything is new.

I guess I'll put it down to God saying "time is up".
I'm just going to have to accept it,
There's nothing I can do; not even my prayers can bring back you.

Every time I look at something, a bird, a tree, even a flower, it always reminds me of you,
Probably because you marked my whole life, even my heart.

We are all trying to look after Gran,
even though none of us can replace you.
Just you remember Grandad Popsy, it's so simple,
We All Love You!!!

Alexandra Payton

Untitled

Northern lady staring through, the colours that collide,
as she waits, she sees the sights, while family divides,
She hopes upon the moment when, all will become clear,
but now she knows, when this day comes, her heart will fill with fear,
think on ye woman of the night, your soul possessed by fright,
perhaps you'll be released, from the endless darkness we know only as night,
but if this day never arrives, will you ask for pity,
or could it be you are happy, in the eternal, forsaken, city.

Edward Cadenne

Thinking of You

I used to be an open hearted person with a warm and caring heart. The sun would always shine bright and warm, I did not want anymore from life but what I had at that moment in time. One person whom I loved dearly showed me love and warmth above all others, that one person did so much for me and spent time to do things with me, one day all the happiness that was spent over the years within seconds turned to despair and anxiety. The word cancer changes your life forever. The peaceful atmosphere turned to storm clouds and thunder, the rain lashed against the window. My throat felt tight and twisted, bitter tears came deep from my heart. All the comfort inside had gone; there was only despair. I visit the places we used to go too but that special feeling has gone. A part of me is missing inside and I cannot fulfil it. Something inside me broke and it has never repaired and it never will. I am much more solitary and quiet, my heart is cold and when I think of you I cry bitter tears. My face is devoid of smiles and any happiness or comfort.

Mark Anthony McKnight

One's Life Cycle

Oh to be young, and enjoying the pleasures of life!
One's born, lives and grows, goes through life's stages;
First kiss, first love, the joys and pleasures loving can bring.
The years go passing unnoticed, one's young, then one's not so young,
One's years begin to show, one's getting old.
One may try and fight it, most of us do, but it's futile;
Age respects no one, it will make its presence felt,
One should be thankful, one's been through the stages
And one has tasted the sweetness of life.
One's life cycle is high, one lives, one will die,
But one has been fortunate to have lived the good life,
And attain one's age.
Because until one's attained it, one's not sure to reach it, any age.
One should be proud of one's mature age, one lived one's life,
with few regrets.

Rudy Morgan

The Arrival of the Young Lady Debutantes in a Local Tavern on a ...

When the awaited suspenseful gorgeous girls arrive in the tavern on a longed for Saturday night, gloriously, like debutantes in a grand master painting by Renoir, there's a supercharged mood and feverish excitement grows among males. The scene is set to the classical composition theme, Arrival of the Queen of Sheba or Miami Vice. Girls make me feel wonderfully alright, soothed, comfortable Heavenly sweethearts, for you are like a/the soft, soft rain that falls at times when nothing else is on your side, and that's like a personified saviour, like Christ, of the oppressed, and the wronged wherever they may be hiding in fear, defenseless. May kindness prevail valuable.
Pacific surf with the violent grace and style of Fab Girls, aggressively attacks relentlessly and pounds US shores like dazzling white ice-like galaxies or a swarm of white tigers, angry. The girls' arrival is like a stylish Beatles' reunion but better. They reincarnate-time warp our ancestors to the present, all assembling in moving camaraderie. Just imagine for a breathtaking moment, the inventors of the wheel discussing ideas with Leonardo Da Vinci, Carl Sagan, Christ Plato, Kepler Neil Armstrong. The girls celebrate exploration of space and space shuttle liftoffs Girls mean wars end!. They're lovelier than the raging Pacific. When you know you've done so well like me for your English lecturer AC Rees What joy! What a great feeling it is! —a rich moral reward—beyond material value. Despite great achievements since the Neanderthals and neolithic times man hasn't been as perfect as he deserved to be. Girl's love could banish wars. My thanks to the bard tavern for boosting me like an H-bomb test in the Pacific Ocean.

J. G. Williams

Dialectics

As I travel along this lonely earth, still the same land, same skies,
The earth is brown, the grass is green, tears are always wet and salty.
Places are new, and people are different, but the world around us never changes.
Summer, autumn, winter, spring—the land is constant, only humans differ.

Cities rowdy, villages quiet, busy streets and lonely roads.
The poor, the rich, oppressor, innocent victim.
Hope, despair, neglect, compassion.
We change, though all around us remains still.

Catherine F. Conchar

I Did It My Way

With tearful eyes filled with glee,
I seek to quill my response to your eulogy,
Born as I have been poor indeed,
Shame I have none, for great has been my breed.

Dark alleys I have roamed, wandering alone
In search of bread crumbs to strength my feeble bones.
Friends, I had none to call my own, thank Heaven for same,
'Cause I would have gone insane.

In solitude I reaped wisdom of old from discarded books in attics cold
One fine morn in September 1939, corporal Hitler gave vent to his temper
Cities and countries he chose to conquer, but the sob never reckoned
He had me, a British sergeant to encounter.
The (bloody) war, with apologies I say, I won with praises unsung
But, I drank in the charms of a damsel fair and young.

Soon we were wed sans grandiose nor prelude,
Emphasis was placed on procreation.
And as years went by, our hearts in joyful bliss
Bambinos six were in creation.

I ask for nothing more but grandchildren by the score,
And ever lasting peace on God's trodden earth.

Maxime A. Jason

Life Bubble

Of all that passed beyond the glass, dreams were transported travelling first class.
All that had passed just a reflection.
Images changed by present thought and discoloured by amnesia, the looking glass with the dark, damp spots.
We try to remember to remember, like trying to breathe under water.
What we remember to write an ancient legend full of wishes and regrets.
We, somehow, want to burst the bubble and rush to the surface of the life glass we have been drinking,
And pop for the joy of making an impact, effervescent with the wonder of living.
Afraid to be the sediment, languishing and going nowhere,
Rather be bright and bubbly and pop before your glass is empty.
Quick, lively, sparkling, remembered, the one with the tickle that made someone laugh.
How little our lives all seem, watching the reflections of our dreams,
And the myths we drink in our wine glasses,
knowing there are worse things to be than bubbles.

A. Grundy

Let There Be Truth

The preacher on his pulpit raves,
Talks proudly of the soldiers' graves,
For God and country shouts the knight,
As he wiped blood off his sword, from a boy who died of fright;
May the rivers run red, for God, a Christian world.

When Oliver Cromwell came to power,
They then burnt women by the hour,
A cross was carved on a young girls throat,
For an insecure man's sexual gloat,
With her parents blessing, they killed this child,
She's better dead,
For God, a Christian world.

The path is stained, soaked in blood,
There was some help, even a flood,
The violence religions have portrayed,
This has now been turned into AIDS,
Along comes a time when the quest for power,
Will turn to the wonder in creating a flower,
When there's peace and there's harmony,
you will then be told, this beauty around you, is your creative soul.

Bill Bowen

Words

Words can say many things about how we feel each day
They can express our values and opinions of what our eyes portray.

Words can interpret our inner world of reason and personal feeling
Help us express our pleasant thoughts or our need for care and healing.

Words can give us comfort in the choice and tones expressed
They also provide a special warmth as a child at its mothers breast.

Words can be harmful and hurt us deep inside
And together with our inner feelings we may feel part of has us died.

Sometimes we find it difficult to find the words to say
Especially when emotional tenderness has a special part to play.

When we lose someone special that has touched a part of us inside
We often find it difficult to express the words that our heartache would provide.

Sad words seem to touch us all when mixed with our emotional past,
Because there are always thoughts of loved ones and the memories they have cast.

During our lives with family and friends, special bonds are made with each other
Bonds that are encapsulated with special words that provide a shell-like cover.

Barrie Sefton Guard

Prelude to Love

Lonely and desolate that's how I felt, heartbreak and anguish emerged from my soul,
Never to love and never to trust, to wander the road of sensual lust,
Bitter and twisted I tried not to be, feelings like these were alien to me,
Peace and contentment were all that I yearned, but life was too cruel was what I had learned,
Death and despair had tainted my heart, deceit and misfortune had torn me apart,
No one to hold me, no one to care, all of my feelings floating in the air,
Then into my life like a breeze of delight came love and affection so exquisite so right,
Tender and passionate, devoted and true, feelings awakened like snowdrops by dew,
Love in its splendour is now in my life, enchantment and wonder, I no longer feel strife,
Caresses and kisses that melt on my skin, how could this heaven be pondered as sin,
And now in my future I only see love, for angels have sent you to me from above,
A comet to comfort, to ease and to care, you are the someone I'll always want here.

Donna Penny

Sorrowless Blues

Over the edge he sent me with a wrought-iron harpoon in my hand.
A well-cherished vessel for valour.
Inviting no conquest to land.

The deep turquoise fruitlessly crashing the sides of an old London barge.
Pale turquoise of algae bedecked it and
nostalgic dreams were in charge.

Sun danced over the ripples.
We had left neon's splendour behind.
The light from the ultimate planet can nurture the urge of the sea.

Icing on a raisin cake with consumers needing no run.
The tinkering sheets of the cheekiest white.
With warm fluid breakers beneath.

We dived. We swam. We surfaced.
In effervescent hues.
Through flotsam and jetsam of wastage—and no packaged costumes as dues.

You can polish a clean reputation.
You can buy any choice you like
But you can't kill the bonds of the boundless in bizarre unconventional life.

Katrina Plumb

Verses on an Idea from Tolstoy

A little child, I was disgraced for sins I did not do;
A youth, I suffered punishment—accuser's words untrue.
And others who have suffered thus, or else by sland'rous talk
Are brothers to me in my mind with me seem to walk
Through life's long path where souls encounter countless loves and hates.
"God guide our souls, refine our hopes"—"God sees the Truth but Waits."

I lie upon my bed in pain, my death is drawing near;
The most consoling words of friends and others yet more dear
Cannot replace the words of truth, the words of God alone
But what will these be in the end, when life is truly gone?
I stand with diffidence, nay, fear, in front of heaven's gates;
A good man's words; a sinner's hope?—"God sees the Truth but Waits."

Postscript:
May God forgive the writer! To forget his only Son!
Christ died for lies and sins of ours, man's worst injustice done.
His Agony to save our souls will e're be understated,
But Christ will live for evermore—God saw the truth but waited.

Anthony C. E. Manville

Please Don't Cry

He's gone for good, we knew he would, so please don't cry.
The pain is plain, no need to explain, so please don't cry.
How could he be so cruel to you and steal your heart and then depart
His ploys and lies of whereabouts were quite untrue
without a doubt, so please don't cry.
The gifts he gave, the money he spent,
which he took back the day he went.
The pleasures you shared when he said he cared
how could you know it would end in tears, so please don't cry.
How ill you were when he departed,
he didn't know what he had started.
His loving words were but a con, he had his
way, then he was gone, so please don't cry.
How could he be such an unknown cad, and do so much to
make you sad.
Of trust and loyalty he knew not, of lame excuses he had the
lot, so please don't cry he married someone out of the blue, six
weeks later,
instead of you. Now you are left broken-hearted, life's not the
same since you have parted, please don't cry,may you be
given peace of mind, and leave all heartache far behind. The
day will dawn when 'Mr. Right' will come once more within
your sight, so please don't cry.

Sheila Saunders

Loneliness

Loneliness; when it's so quiet you can hear your heart
beating, or when there is noise and bustle, but you might just
as well be a ghost.

Some people grumble that they are always being bothered by
others, asking questions; wanting to know this and that. Just
think though, what it is like not to be asked, or not spoken to
at all, when your opinion doesn't matter to anyone!

Sitting, standing, lying, wondering how to waste your time
next, thinking, forever thinking of people you once knew and
what you would say to them if you could speak to them now.

Throwing yourself into work or a hobby, but finding yourself
just as bored and lonely. Taking walks, hoping to meet
someone to talk to; just to say "hello" or "nice weather." To
get into a crowd to feel normal, part of the community.

It is not just the old that are lonely, many young people are
too, they need to be spoken to; need to feel wanted; need to
have a reason for living.

I know!

Janet M. Norman

Lost Heritage

Steaming weary carcasses impaled in sunless concrete, monuments
To groaning stomachs that ache, as farmers' pockets are lined.
Countryside raped.

Bloodbaths of doctored offering, injected, coloured and battered,
To anaemic shadows and skin, packed into frozen supermarket
coffins.
Countryside raped.

Sprouting ears from seedless wastes, hardened under toxic hazes,
Pounded to whitest, tasteless bread, this grain of hope, too, is dead.
Countryside raped.

Bare brown ditches, bald of grass, hedgerows axed, trees uprooted,
Flora and fauna yield and die in the face of chemical war so vast.
Countryside raped.

Dust bowl prairies in lost horizons, where no hoof or claw has trod,
Beauty scarred, nature's law twisted by man, the monster and
machine.
Countryside raped.

God's countryside, his animals, and yet man's manipulating greed
Overfill our guts with tasteless food, of which we need less and less.
Countryside raped.

Oh sweet country greenery, is nothing sacred from this rape?
No beast, no leaf, even no weed, save but the sun and rain!
Countryside raped, forever.

Barbara Ann Carter

I'm Going to Be a Granny

I'm going to be Granny and I can hardly wait,
For that tiny little bundle, to be carried through my gate!
I sit and think about it, I'm really full of glee,
Thinking of all the things we'll do, dear little babe and me.
Penny's kept so well throughout it's been a lot of fun,
Each day we say "How's baby"? And fondly touch her tum.
We look in wide amazement, as it kicks around her bump,
You can really see it moving, it's going to be a lump!.
Penny says she will not waddle waddle she will not!
But have to say, as from today, she's waddling quite a lot!
We're waiting here in limbo now, with just three weeks to go!
Wish the days would hurry by, time's going really slow!

The day will dawn, and she'll be off, with a smile on her lovely face
Will it be a boy or a girl—you'll have to watch this space!

P.S.
Oh what Joy! It was a boy!
His name is Owen John Hughes.
Blond hair, blue eyes, the cutest smile,
Thought you'd like to hear the news!

Fay Evans

The Burial

A swarm of black ravens flapped and flocked into the church
with plumes of white handkerchiefs, wiping eyes and blowing nose.
The progeny sauntered by, heading the progression,
  maintaining a pose.
Then came the corpse, plucked reverently from the hearse.
The coffin in varnished teak and cranks and gold, resplendent
  with rose.

The oratory was cold as the organ played, sniffles, coughs
  and cries of woe.
The guest of honour, motionless laid, ashen and inert,
  sepulchre await
Moans depart, a look, a pray, and belated tears from the faces
  left to fight.
Another soul defeated by life.
Who cried longest, who screamed the most? the issue, the
  spouse or the holy ghost?

Uncles, Aunts, cousins, friends and their friends too,
  came to see the facade, the soul depart, the body the lender.
Ashes to ashes the flesh render, the soul surrender,
  to kingdom come, beyond the sky of cerulean blue,
Spades poised to full the hole, the soil reversed as good as new.

Abandoned hearts depart to heal, to dance, to eat, to grief,
  to feel renewed.
Red eyes scolding and wondering why,
while the world goes on turning, smiling, passing them by.
No one to see the pain within, behind black veils, blue hearts bled.
Why the ordeal? Why cry? Why wail? It's only life, another
man dead

Dorine Walters

Easter Morn

Gentle spring, reach out to me, intercept me,
look beyond today, intensify your promise and
then soon I shall ponder on previous demise.

Dear tomorrow, shower me with your expectancy of wonder,
the wonder of life, life of living, real living,
help me to examine myself more
critically.

Open as it were to the windowed air a future
upon which to draw new vitality, to be young
again, unscarred, uncluttered, to be with a
young voice and with the sound of wonder.
Oh new life, fill me with a new resolve.

But youth I envy you not, I look instead
to erase your follyful days like a phoenix
feather is revived through its ashes and
left to rest on tomorrow's wing,
there too may I rest my new intent.

Alban L. Pinkney

The Advent of Spring

New hope comes with the advent of spring
When the cold, bleak winter dies.
And the earth begins to soften.
Where green fields now gently lie.
A new creation dawning
When birds begin to sing.
And soon we'll see new life unfold
Bringing with it, a reminder of spring.

As daffodils begin to blossom
Revealing their golden hue.
Sweet violets burst into life again
Portraying fresh colours anew.
Earth is alive with a radiant joy
And is clothing herself for spring.
New life can come to all mankind
Through Jesus Christ our king.

Then from his cross he beckons you
New life he offers thee.
He paid the price for everyone that from sin, we might be free.
It was for the world that Jesus died on calvary's rugged hill.
And we now can experience new life again by surrendering to his will.

Albert L. Pike

Over All These Years

We've been through thick and thin,
And we've been through everything,
over all these years, and still we're together,
I've cherished every moment that I've spent with you,
you make my whole all brand new,
over, over all these years.

Over all these years, since we've been together,
you help me through all kind of stormy weather,
you gave me so much hope, when I was down,
you help me to keep my feet on the ground,
over, over all these years.

Sometimes we thought, it was finally over,
sometimes we thought it wouldn't last forever,
but our love was so strong
and it made us both stronger,
and now I know that it will last forever
over over all these years
being with you was one of
the best thing that has ever happen to me
over over all these years.

Carmen Stevens

To Dad

Dear Dad forgive me for not being there
When your life came to an end, it just wasn't fair.
All the hours before, I sat at your side
The words you could not speak but your love you did not hide.

Oh Dad, when you left this world my heart went too
And all my love I have will only be for you
Thank you Dad for saying you love me
I'm so pleased now all your pain is free
The kiss you gave me I will never forget
Not being there is my only regret.

My heart is broken without you Dad
Thank you for the wonderful life I've had.
Rest now Dad, you'll soon be well again
My love for you will always remain.

In Heaven I'm sure your own garden you'll grow,
Because your garden at home you love, I know,
We will be together Dad again one day
The words I feel, I just can't say.
You are the only one who's ever loved me Dad
Thank you for the life I've had.

You will be in my thoughts every minute of the day.
In Heaven you'll have peace, I will pray.
Goodnight Dad until we are together once more.
A Dad you're the best that's for sure. I Love you—Sue.

Susan Styles

Friendship

To Barbara

What is it? A connection here or there
which blossoms on a common thread.
It needs only to be nourished by affection over time
to grow into a permanence,
which even lack of hours together cannot break.
But one whole week of hours—to talk,
to reminisce in quiet relaxation!
It was a gift to treasure
and a time when friendship deepened.

Eunice McLeod

I Know You

We met before but once, briefly,
'twas then the spark ignited.

This time I knew you, hands grasped in greeting
eyes met in recognition. Words came, facile, inane,
your eyes held me merciless, unrelenting,
insisting that I acknowledge, yes, I know you.

Oh yes I know you, from when time began,
the taste of you, the smell, every contour.
From the deep fathoms of my memory
echoes a soundless scream of joy, remembered ecstasy.

I pull away, any excuse, "Have to rejoin friends," "Happy New Year,"
you say, "The same to you, so nice to meet again," and
"No more patronizing mutual appreciation" you mouth.
Shell shocked, I can't respond, except with another platitude.

Realization only came later, our time is not now.
It will come sometime, in the endless aeons of future.
Our time, next time we shall be reunited.
Oh yes, I know you.

Margaret Honey

Another Spring

Daffodils dancing in the breeze, black birds singing in the trees
Butterflies fluttering on silent wing new life's beginning again
it's spring
The cuckoo's calling with its distinctive sound,
primrose and bluebell carpet the ground
Raindrops are falling gently to earth,
nourishing the season of rebirth
Crocus and snowdrop the hum of the bee I'll frame them all in
my memory
One last stroll down a leafy lane for I'll not pass this way again
My life is fading and no more will I see this glorious land
but don't weep for me
For there's a rainbow of colours across the sky
and no I'm not afraid to die
But oh to live for another year oh to see and feel and hear
The sights and sounds of everything that will come again with
another spring.

Carol Humby

Mother

We were as one before we came
Closer then, but all the same
You sheltered us with love and care
In our lightness that love we share

All those years without a grumble
Only now, we feel so humble
You gave to us, as any other
Love, we mean, dearest mother

Now the angels have kissed your hand
We are now, on our own to stand
In our lightness you have gone away
In our hearts you will always stay

You are lost in life, but to a better place go
Believe us mother, because we know
Where you are is a better place
You look upon it with your grace.

Roger Williams

Untitled

I'd like to write a little story
It's time to vote, but don't vote tory
The tories they have had their day
So vote for labour on the first of May
Tony Blair and his merry men
Will soon be running number ten
As for Major and his crew
Send them all to Timbucktu
That is where they all belong
Maybe there they won't go wrong
With Tony Blair at number ten
Maybe we can be great again
Lower crime and plenty of work
When we get rid of that dozy berk
To let the tories win once more
The British lion will lose its roar
So on the first let's vote for Blair
And give old England a breath of fresh air

M. G. Thomas

Singed Wings

I heard the turning of the lock at the front door,
The faintest whisper of footsteps on the hall floor.
A stair step creaking as it bore someone's weight,
This was the end of my daughter's first big date.

My bedside clock showed it was late into the night,
Soon would appear the first glimpse of the morning light.
She begged to go to this late night disco in the city,
Not to let her spread her wings would have been a pity.

How does one warn about the dangers of the bright lights,
What does one say about having too many late nights?
About being careful of the drinks with the crowd at the bar,
Putting into his place the smart guy who thinks he's a star?

She has entered the period of glitter, laughter and fun,
Finding that at midnight the party has only just begun.
Shall I tell her about the moth and the lighted candle,
The one that found the searing flame too hot to handle?

F. W. Hirst

Untitled

This world so full of hate
Is now clinging to her fate,
Why is there no more love?

The spoken word is kind no more
Our families are facing war,
Why is there no more love?

Our Mother Earth's veins are so filled
With poison so She's slowly killed,
Why is there no more love?

The animals have right to fear
That they soon may not be here,
Why is there no more love?

For without love there is no life
And our world will cease to turn
So let's open our eyes and our hearts
To know it's through love that we must learn.

Vhari Annette Powney

Spring Joy

A feeling of elation enters my heart
On a spring day fresh and bright
The joy of sweet flowers, the greenness of grass
The blue of the sky where white clouds pass
The riotous colour invades my sight

The heady perfumes, the wonderful scents
The lightness, the brightness now winter is spent
The promise of summer with birds on the wing
Oh beautiful day! Oh glorious spring

Lynn Barnard

To Have and to Hold

Like me, discarded, my wedding dress and veil,
Now lifeless and colourless they hold a hidden tale.

They symbolize my shattered dreams,
Torn and faded, jagged seams.

My wedding day role as a bride,
My awaited new life thrown aside.

He knew in his own heart the day would not come,
When husband and wife we would become.

Was it a look in his eyes, or in silence a glance,
When I knew we wouldn't dance the first dance.

Never to say the words "To have and to hold",
Joyful hopes smothered in each careful fold.

Wrapped up and boxed never to be worn,
My dress, my veil, my future, torn.

Lilian Cuggy

An Ode to Winter

The darkest day has yet to come,
I gaze upon the barren trees
A filter of sunlight, beautiful to see
And shadows cast the lonely path to home.

I walk along with silent thoughts
A carpet of mold of years gone by
The beauty serene, and bliss is nought
Even though the darkest day is nigh.

A ripple of a stream, a muffled call
Of a bird, a winter's scene I sigh
Light is fading sun shines no more
Yeah, the darkest day is nigh.

But sigh no more, darkness, turns to light
The hope of better things to come,
The dawn brings beauty sheltered by night
Our thoughts of winter chills soon be gone.

E. Mayor

A Puff for the Trainspotter

Anoraked at the end of the platform
I watch the steam loco go by
While I tackle a vague plastic sandwich
And a cost-ineffective pork pie.

And I pity the chattering classes
Who deride me for wasting my time
When I'm lost among mystical gasses
And sweet love-songs that clank down the line.

John Killeen

A Slave to the Pen

Help me, help me!
I'm drowning in a whirlpool of thoughts.
Caught in the endless flow of ideas,
I'm a slave to my pen
Pouring out my thoughts.

Unable to control the pen,
just writing, forever a slave.
This pen is moving across the page
with words I do not know.

Is it me in control of my pen
or is it the instrument of my soul?
Unable to stop, I fight with myself,
Only at ease when lost in its flow.

a forest I could fill
With leaves of my words
Falling down on me from a power within.

How many pages I will write I do not know,
As long as my heart beats,
My pen will flow.

Dymphna Griffiths

Graduation

This is one of the best days of your life
A milestone has been reached.
The Derry Journal your picture to be seen.
You looked so like your Dad. It made me feel so glad.

Alas it's Sunday night again, to Milford you must go.
When you came through the door.
Your uniform cleaned and pressed by Josie.
Happily may she rest.

Exams and tantrums. Teenage years.
Ballet, singing, dancing, speech and drama.
I also modelled with you too, and to the feishes I did run
And to see you win was so much fun.
Then learning how to drive and for promotion in your job.
You certainly did strive.
The rows and laughter, smiles and tears, sure it was so much fun.

But where have all the years gone to.
How quickly time has flown.
The little babe that I once knew. Into a girl has grown.
I had to let you go Gita an adult to become.
For you to see the world at sea. I know there is a God above.

Philomena D. Nic Lochlainn

Vicissitudes

If that day was about anything, it was about birth.
After all, gathering for a census had little worth
For the poor people of an imprisoned nation.
No cause for them to feel a frisson of elation.
And yet the shepherds knew, and the kings,
That something changed that night, that things
Could never be the same again.

Let this day be about if anything, a re-birth
For we, who in the wasted years, had little worth.
Our star has drifted, yet has taken station
To grant us soon a wondrous re-creation.
For love, the message of that babe, that King,
Has come to us by fortune's swing
And things can never be the same again.

F. Peter Lee

Hope

A pale moon beamed in a velvety sky
As darkness cloaked the earth.
Stars twinkled as they blinked their eye,
And the world slept,
As night creatures crept.
Daybreak at last, woken by the dawn,
The sun was shining—and a new day was born.

Sylvia Hutton

In the Next Room

Death is nothing at all.
I have only slipped away into the next room I am I, you are you.
Whatever we were to each other, that we are still.
Call me by my old familiar name
Speak to me in the easy way which you always used
Put no difference in your tone.
Wear no forced air of solemnity or sorrow
Laugh as we always laughed at the little jokes we enjoyed together.
Play, smile, think of me, pray for me.
Let my name be the household word that it always was.
Let it be spoken without effort, without the ghost of a shadow in it.
Life means, all that it ever meant.
It is the same as it always was.
There is absolutely unbroken continuity
What is death but a negotiable accident
Why should I be out of your mind because I am out of sight?
I am waiting for an internal . . . I am here, very near
Just around the corner all is well
Nothing is past . . . nothing is lost
One brief moment and all will be as it was before.

Kirsty Dziennik

Machines

I watch machines, their dar, unblinking eyes
Their tireless hands, unreasonably clean.
I should be Lord but, say what have I been
Amid these tungsten legs and copper thighs?

They have deceived, they have denied me joy
And all my worth is cogs and wheels and springs,
I cast away the joy that caring brings
I burn my strength to dust in their employ.

I serve a robot master who restores
The pain and guilt and laughter I desire
And of the lust and passion I require
My need is filled by subtle, metal whores.

And there is one, with bronze hips, tinted green
Whom I adore and whom I'm loath to share.
Each day I breathe my steel and stainless prayer
Why can I too not be reborn machine?

Albert Oxford

Morn Mourning Dawn

Mourning: you and I;
At morning, no joyous eyes;
Yearning, for years gone by;
Burning in frustration, I'm . . .

Mourning, for your lively face;
Mourning, for those years were great!
Forlorning, your physical gait.
At morning for your voice I'd wait . . .

Mourning, for my own lost years;
Mourning, with such bitter tears!
Afore morning I would sleep in fear;
A forewarning would have helped me steer well clear . . .

Now the morn takes my mourning, as forewarning,
Of my tears, and my fears;
Until dawn.

Donna Marie Crawford

Domestic Bliss

You have to cook marrow in water don't you?
Yeah
Don't shout at me like that
Sorry
Do you have to take the skin off?
What, on marrow?
Yeah
Yeah and the middle
It doesn't leave you with a lot does it?
No.

Jill Carter

Love

I was there at the moment of conception,
Young blood floating in a sea of ecstasy.
I was there at the moment of your birth
The moment long awaited to change us into three.
I was there when they laid my Lovely down,
Throat tightened by a grip vice-like.
I rubbed my cheek against your golden crown
To give you life she made the greatest sacrifice.
I was there to heal your broken knees.
To run with puppies in the summer breeze.
I was there the silken dresses to admire—
Stand in the background whilst you played with fire.
I was there to walk you down the aisle.
The strains of Handel still bring on a tear.
Not ours to know the change in your lifestyle,
Alas left on your own within the year.
I was there to try and mend your heart.
Not quite as easy as to dry your childhood eyes
And now as you this weary world depart
Yes I'm still here your little one and I.

Noeline Murray

A Day in Venice

We stepped on to the waterbus that was going to Venice
The high waves lashing past were really quite a menace
We stopped at the pier just at St Mark's Square
We really were delighted to be finally there
We went to the Doges' Palace where Napoleon once stayed
But the Venetians exposed him and sent him away
We went on to St Mark's and went up the stairs
Right to the Basilica and then said some prayers
We saw the Mosaic all glittering with gold
So very beautiful and colourful and priceless we're told
We went down a side street to The Bridge of Sighs
The last stop for prisoners to say their goodbyes
We then stopped for a picnic in a small park
Right opposite the pigeons who eat at St Mark's
Then it was nightfall and the Venetians don masks
Where they are going nobody dare asks
The Gondoliers take them they dart in and out
And as they all pass them they give them a shout
We then went for the waterbus to take us away
It was all so exciting and Oh What A Day

Moira Gerrie

Alone

Voices swirl, collect, disperse.
Laughter echoes, screams, reverberates.
No one shivers out of sight;
No one darkens the warm light.

Alone, yet accompanied.
Alive, yet dead.
One person shivers, in the shadow border.
One person's light can't beat the darkness.
One person's war has just begun.

So life's battles claim one more victim;
Maybe never to return.
Hope extinguished, hope forgotten;
Memories of light, put out.

Linda Chambers

My Ted

I have a very special friend—
My Ted.

My Ted loves to snuggle up to my shoulder;
Listens to all I have to say;
And knows just when to give a hug or two.

My Ted, yes he's a very special Teddy Bear;
Listens to all I have to say and
Can bring a cheer to my day.

Ah my Ted, what would life be without you?
I hate to think. You're my buddy and pal;
Guess I'll never grow old 'cause you're my best friend.
My Ted.

Helen Smith

Mystic Night

My eyes behold a magical sight,
A glistening fountain of delight.
The moonlit sky is calm and still
As snowflakes gently fall at will.

A carpet of splendour covers the ground.
With a path of bold footprints homeward bound,
A majestic church steeple plays host to the sky
In a gown of pure crystals enchanting the eye.

Branches laden, glistening white,
Silence haunts the mystic night.
Fields of stars display their charms
As heaven holds them in its arms.

These precious moments will fade too soon
As my gaze is drawn to the silvery moon,
A glowing disc, an eternal light
Of beauty embracing a picturesque night.

Phyllis R. Harvey

The Hopeful Golfer

I am a golfer born and bred,
Who would rather play than lie in bed.
I swing my club, aim at the ball,
And if I hit the ball at all
The boys will say, "a good shot!"
Whether I hit the ball or not.

They say it's in the swing you see,
The back, the hand, just bend the knee,
And when you think of all this lot
The ball doesn't fly to the right spot.
But when you reach the blooming green
The boys will ask, "Where have you been?"

Then out comes Putter from my bag.
From there in four, another snag
But I will have a lovely day,
If I can win the match today.

George J. Ford

Eniasin

Turn to the sun, blind yourself Eniasin
So you shall not see me cry, so you shall not see these tears
falling from my eyes
That my tear may raise rocks, set mountains
Boundaries between lovers, like you and I, shall never cease to be
If I cannot have my beloved, then let no one else have another
If I cannot have you by my side, then I sow in eternity,
boundaries between lovers
Cupid has not heard the last of me
He gave me a rose and then pilfered my nasals
Mine Eniasin is the pain and the restless turn, mine the heart
popped in sorrowed corn, to break, to tear, to bleed words of
muffled laments
Mine Eniasin is the hope, mine the wish
Mine the dream of the river, split 7 tributaries
hoped that one would reach the sea
Turn Eniasin Eniasin Turn
I bleed my glands for Cupid thirst

Olufemi Akinyemi

Looking Back

Last week, I stood looking into a park,
with tears in my eyes, I broke my heart.
My building had gone, and my childhood with it,
a horrible feeling, just for a minute.
They'd come with tractors and diggers clearing
the ground, with no thought for people
like me, nowhere to bring my grandchildren to see.
I'd lived there from cradle, to youth, to maturity,
and men sitting at desks decided
to erase my past and leave nothing to posterity.
But life must go on, and it's
good to know it takes more than bricks
to be remembered.
If we love and are loved, that's all that matters.
For what is a building? Just bricks and mortar.

Margaret Smith

David at Three

David at three, oh goodness me, there's such a lot to say;
He makes us feel a child again, when he asks us out to play.
The sandpit and the bicycle, the barrow and the ball,
There's just no way to get out of it, he wants us to try them all.

What an imagination, when sand becomes ice-cream,
Without his Kwik-Fit Fitter's suit we just couldn't keep him clean;
He's outgrown Thomas the Tank Engine, and even Fireman Sam,
Now it's Turtles, Rugrats and Power Rangers he watches
when he can.

He knows exactly what he wants and lets us know quite clearly,
We all jump to his commands, because we love him dearly;
Granny is his sparring partner, and what battles he has won,
She makes sure David always wins, he thinks it's so much fun.

Margaret Bell

Missing You

Silently you slipped away to that fair place
You always said "a wonderful adventure we have ahead".
Now you live in this wondrous place
Far from, yet so near, to us who love you more, not less.

Your garden still as it always will be
Roses, pansies, yellow poppies we see,
All of which you tended with care—
Dearest David, how we miss your smile.

But we know His face that you gaze upon now
Is as the flowers you so tenderly grew—
Which you always knew.
We miss you, we miss you.

Betty A. Creedon

The Mansion House

Resplendent in riches
Nothing surpasses the landed classes
Brandy glasses and port
And blood sport.

Silverware everywhere
Portraits of people who once were
Inexorable life path
Seated on the chesterfield of the mansion house

Landscaped vistas
The views from the mansion house
The butler so well mannered
It is all that matters.
Betrayal in the hands of the experts
Their well considered plans in hand
I am not selling you any lies
I am an ordinary man whom you despise.

The mansion house set in symmetrical grounds
How beautiful the thoughts of money sounds.

Patrick Brett

Pictures of My Heart

Everything I do with you in mind,
Every day I take the time to find,
Little things you tend to leave behind,
Like these pieces of my heart,

Though it's not the art you've come to know,
When you study Michelangelo,
Or even purchase classic Picasso,
They're just
 Pictures Of My Heart,
Smile awhile, you're supreme;
Others try but they just dream,
When you speak and when you sing,
You are the best at everything,

Sometimes words are not enough to call,
This love I'm feeling for you great or small,
So I just let my music say it all, with these
 Pictures Of My Heart

Edward Boyle

Ode to the Company

We love the Company,
Oh yes we do.

They are so good to us,
you know it's true.

The Chairman gets a Million plus,
but he don't give any to us.

They put the coffee up to make a penny,
then they stopped our breaks, don't give us any.

They cut the overtime,
then "kick" us out.

We love the Company, there is no "Doubt".

S. E. Mitchell

Poem to a New Baby

Springtime clouds scud fast across the sky,
The warm springtime wind has Winter's clothes to dry.
Birds from nest to ground flit by,
The seagull shrills his eerie scream
 Don't' die!
 Don't die!
New spring grass glitters green,
Paints the back cloth to Spring's new scene.
Warmth, brightness, freshness and hope.
All is well in new spring's cry.

Ewen Grimes

Evacuation

Walking around in the smoky atmosphere,
Seeing people waving goodbye.

Hearing the churning train wheels draw forward,
Listening to all the children cry.

Tasting the musty air in the stream train,
Eating your food out of packets or bowls.

Smelling the stench of the old train engine,
Inhaling the smothering flickers of coals.

Feeling the roughness of the gas masks around your neck,
The tags make you feel like something to buy.

Wondering where you'll end up and where you're going,
Wondering why? Why? Why?

Evacuation is frightening and exciting,
Evacuation is an adventure but fearful too.

Parading round like you're in the army,
Parading round like you're a creature in the zoo.

Aimi Gauld

My Best Friend Is a Psychopath

Backs propped against the groyne that day
We sought out all the smoothest pebbles
The ones that were good to fondle
While you spoke of Ros and future plans.
Invigorated by ozone, your bony fingers twitched
And closed around the throat of your old adversary.
Brooding clouds of anger, bloodlust and her popping eyeballs
Spurred you on towards
A murder rap! Life in Lewes jail!
In Lewes jail life means life
Beady-eyed demented warders jangle keys and swear
"No one has ever escaped from 'ere!"

Oh, how good it is to have the sea so close at hand
At Hove, where the ozone clears the head;
Somewhere to be sane at last.

Mike Millard

In Loving Memory

Cold lips, aching heart
Deep down inside we'll never part
Ups and downs were part of life
Lots of fun, lots of strife
As friends we laughed, sometimes we cried
That empty feeling since you died.

Maybe one day our paths will cross
Help ease this pain of such a loss
Your face, your smile, your scent I smell
Each day goes by, my living hell
You suffered, you hurt, you gave your best
Your pain inside was laid to rest.

Often I cry, fond memories stay
My one true love has gone away
You gave much love, your love so pure
That special feeling, that missing cure
Life goes on, my hands are tied
That empty feeling, since you died.

Craig James Fiddler

Thoughts

Have you ever stopped to wonder
What other people think,
Their secret thoughts, their secret dreams,
Their hidden pasts and future schemes?
How each one born in any land
Has this great gift placed in their hands?

Not one day passes, nor even one hour
From child to man we use this power.
It starts in childhood and day by day
we use it more in work and play.

Some thoughts are good and others bad,
They can be happy, they can be sad,
Deep thought can help a troubled mind
And the answer to a problem find.

God gave this gift for man to use,
So treasure always, never abuse,
So think your thoughts, but make them good.
It was intended that you should
Margaret Motion

Love Is . . .

Love is a poem in a book, when it opens you are filled with joy.

Love is a blow of warmth on a cold winters day. The scent of you brings me near.

Love is two bodies locked together forever. A booming sound inside me when you are near.

Love is a cuddle when you need one, It shows how much you care.

Love is a sweet friendship of two hearts, a friendship that never dies.
Fiona Hooker

Life at Sea

Life at sea was cold and grey
As my Grandad would say
The cold, green waves splash up and down
and it makes him frown
As I think of my Grandad on the boat
it makes me shiver and curl-up in my coat
Just imagine a day at sea
thinking about having a nice cup of tea
but all he gets is sandwiches and cake
not enough to keep him awake
as catching fish makes him tired
he will be glad when he has retired
Catherine Maughan

Everlasting Life

Throughout time and toll life will prevail
exhausted and stressed, frightened to fail
as each day passes a new life starts
farewell to the old as it gently departs.

The meaning of life is the question to ask
the daily routine, the ever growing task
before our eyes the changes unfold
we welcome the new and banish the old.

The sunshine, the glow, is abundant to see
everlasting dreams that could possibly be
for seeing the future, praying to last
clinging to hope, the nightmares past

A new beginning that heralds the dawn
great expectations so fresh and unworn
filled with desire, the future secure
moment of wonder that's worth living for.

We dare not look back to dwell what has been
the past years vacated so torrid, so mean
go forward, advance, seek ultimate pleasure
the miracle of life awaits at our leisure.
Phillip Carroll

The Attic Room

The walls so pale but not so square
And skylight windows that give fresh air
The creaking when the wind begins to blow
And the birds are the only ones who seem to know
The roof beams give their firm protection
Like loyal angels without objection
So high up and so quiet at night
The moon and stars being the only light
But those who walk on floors on the ground
Oblivious to its lonely sound
They never venture far above the noise and disorder they
Seem to love
So here it stands above the rest
Inhabited by the odd bird's nest
And some old toys and nursery rhymes
And photographs of happy times.
Anne Jamieson

Song of the Memphis Belle

Memphis Belle, Plane's name, Pilot's Broad.
Picture on crafts side, all by plane,
When King and Queen inspected it.

Awake when briefed, many raids.
At ten thou, need oxygen masks.
Gloves needed at 2,5, thou feet.

Hitler's guard drawn, so all fly east,
Hero banks south, rest still go east,
Some anon, to the north banked.

Intercom, Ack Ack, Fighter planes.
Flying Fortresses, bomb Sub. Pens:
One plane burns, goes low, is shot down.

Out of control, spun a warplane.
Another sliced in half one.
At base, they wait return of planes.

One's Screws stop, bank to port, crashed.
Medics, Firemen, free injured.
Last raid, back to States, teach recruits.
Gordon Linc

A New Awakening

Never have I opened my eyes to such a beautiful morn
The sun so bright and all so calm,
Yesterday's election fever's in the past,
Could be an 'Omen' of peaceful times ahead,
First news to greet me this morning was labour to victory:
Everything of significance must be
Recorded, especially world events.
I refer of course to the millennium,
The coming of our 21st century
too great for us to comprehend,
Worldwide leaders, astrologists
planners, throughout the world
prepare for celebrating,
Great thinkers of our time
recording history,
I wish for peace, "Love one another"
Maybe if we wish hard enough it
could be so, above all else, thank God for everything.
Lilian Veal

Pressure

I sit at my window it's quarter to three
I dream of my island in my jewelled sea
Palm trees and sand dunes, dolphins at play
Sea birds that come on the crest of a wave.

This is my island where I feel free
My visits are frequent away from the pressures so constant me
My piece of heaven made just for me
My refuge, my haven, my sanity,
Away from all dread, it's so ironic, it's all in my head!
Jane Cullen

The Doll

Your beautiful eyes so peaceful and nice!
Are you a fairy or rather a dream?
Your long wavy hair so shining and fair!
Shall I call you Alice or Irene?

Your beauty instantly attracted me,
Just as my glance met your sight.
Behind the shop window you were standing;
So peaceful, attractive and bright.

Time cannot touch your beauty,
eternal will be your fascination.
Fragile you maybe but I'll care for you.
The subject you'll be of my admiration.

Like a princess or a fairy;
wonderful, long haired, serene.
A lifeless thing? But you can talk to my soul,
you can revive my childhood's dreams.

How you remind me of my mother!
So certainly I'll call you Irene.
With light blue eyes and golden hair
you are my shining warm sunbeam.

Stella Charalambous

Innocence

A sweet and soft bundle of innocent youth
Laying peacefully and silently asleep,
No concerns about anything that's not in their world
No thoughts that could ever be classed as deep.

The world of a child is so pure and clear
With an innocence that can't be explained,
Every little thing they do is new to them
They've an openness that cannot be trained.

They look at the world with different eyes
It's like one great adventure to them,
They don't see what the world is truly like
They don't see the evil side of men.

But a child should be nurtured and cared for and loved
They should always be protected at all costs,
So they may grow up and mature in their own way
And find happiness without ever getting lost.

For they are the most precious gift we can receive
Something special sent to us from up above,
Not only a child but a part of ourselves
And for eternity will deserve all our love.

P. A. Heighton

Hear Me

Give me a sign that you are there
When I feel lost and in despair

Let me feel your gentle touch only you can do so much
To ease my troubled world alone
I turn to you for you have known

With each life that you have spared
Shown us all how much you cared

It's only faith which drives us through
Our days and nights our whole life too

Without your image in our mind
Love would die in all mankind

I've seen the sign that I asked for as I opened wide my door
And for this wondrous moment
Felt your love and golden sunshine
Bringing such comfort and warmth as never before

I pray that all who dwell on earth
Will also feel strengthened
And know your worth if only these moments
Of utter peace will overcome
Pain and wars and all turmoil cease

M. V. Golledge

And I Will Love You

I want to walk in the countryside, away from other's gaze.
I want to walk with you—away from everyone.
I want to hold you, in a summer's evening haze
And love you in the grass, in dappled sun.

I want to stroll, hand in hand, through woods
through Autumn leaves, along a babbling brook
and join ourselves, and love you midst the trees
where only mother nature steals a look.

I want to wander, along a lonely beach
where wild and crashing seas meet placid land,
where life seems sparse—there's just we two,
and I can love you in the sand.

Sid Thomason

Mind Warriors

The only thing that binds people is their minds.
Inspiration comes through freedom, the freedom to achieve, to hope,
To reach out to dare to grasp.
We all can be great, can be giants in this world, but we
Are shackled by ourselves,
Our limitations, our lack of imagination.
Pioneers are all a proud people.
We are distinguished because we aspire,
Aspire to achieve, to achieve immortality through our deeds.
There is a glimmer of hope within us all,
A feint whisper of pride imprinted in our spirits.
A cry to break from the shackles that are so thick
And so strong, yet so thin and so weak.
Not content to exist but to live

Garry Thomas

Poor but Blessed in the Good Old Days

We met and we married a long time ago,
We worked long hours when wages were low,
No TV, no wireless, no baths, times were hard.
Just a cold water tap and a walk down the yard.

No holidays abroad, no carpets on floors,
We had coal fires and we didn't lock doors,
Our children arrived, no pill in those days!
And we brought them up without my state and

They were safe going out to play in the park,
And our old folks were safe going out in the dark
No valium, no drugs, no LSD.
We cured all our ills with a good cup of tea.
No vandals, no muggings, there was nothing to rob.
We felt well off with a couple of bob.

People were happier in mose far off days
Kinder and carry in so many ways.
Milk men and paper boys would whistle and sing.
A night out at the pictures was our weekly fling

We all had our share of muscle and strife
We just had to face it, not pattern of life.

Karen Foote

Father

Father we thank you for everything
The creation of the world
to the bread in our mouths
We thank you for being there when
We need you most
for never leaving our side
and for opening our eyes

We pray for the day when you will return
and take us away from the suffering
and pain
We understand the reason why we have
to wait
Although we can't take much more
of this hate.

Melissa Hollowell

England's Football Skills

Our English teams we toast in every bar
For Ravanelli's skills give us a glow,
What would we do without a Cantona,
But hope that we can sign Tor Andre Flo.

Our goals secure, Miklosko holds the line,
At other end Srnicek does the same,
For Man United Schmeichel's doing fine
And they all add to England's football fame.

Now, Wenger fields Vierra in his team
With Berghamp in, Desailly yet to come?
To win the league, that is all Arsenals dream,
Moussa Saib could help to get that done.

Can Gullit with the cup in Chelsea's name?
Will Zola or Vialli raise the score?
Can't we remember that it's just a game,
Not only English skills come through the door.

How we applaud the footwork of Asprilla,
Porborsky and Ginola, much the same,
How we admire Juninho's great endeavour,
We English must be masters at this game.
  R. Todd

Arach-no-phobia?

A very hairy spider was sitting in my bath
I screamed and ran away from him, but all he did was laugh

His legs were long and twiddly . . . .they took up all the room
I dashed off to the kitchen to find a deadly broom

I tiptoed in that place again to squash him in the plughole—
The sneaky thing had vanished, to thank me for my trouble

I heard him trundle down the hall; he sounded like a lorry
I crept up on him broom and all—yes, I would make him sorry

He turned around and looked at me and scrunched into a ball
His eyes shone with a dewy plea—I couldn't do it after all

So he and I, we are now friends, I will not kill another—
And hoping I can make amends, I treat him like a brother
  Deborah Banks

The Nunk-Man

O what is this that shines and gleams
Among the oily olive-leaves?
'Tis the phosphorous bones of a Nunk-man
A jingling and a jangling
Like fairy-bells on a Christmas-tree
The little girl gazed at him in adoration
And he handed her a toad speckled lollipop
"Be quick!" he shrieked,
"Or you will miss your bus
Too late! There it goes! There it goes
Over the steeple and under the sea
What now? But Hark!
Hark and eat bark
Here's a go!
What's a penny?"
  Lionel Downing

My Dad Was a Builder

He built the house in which we played.
He fought in the war when just a boy.
He built the house in which we danced.
Four little girls and a beautiful mother.
He built the house in which we slept.
He made us laugh at silly jokes.
He built the house in which we sang.
He had big rough hands and soft wavy hair.
He built the house from where we married.
Brave and kind and full of laughter.
He built a life, and we lived in it.
  Norma Rabaiotti

Yes My Love

Yes my love,
There's only you in my mind,
It's you that makes it right,
yes my love,
I think of you each and every night,
It's you that makes my life bright.

Yes my love,
we're listening to our song,
You try to sing it, but get the words all wrong,
yes my love,
You cheer me up when I am down,
I am glad that you're always around.

Yes my love,
I love you in every way,
I think of you each and every day,
Yes my love,
I'll always keep you in my heart,
Hoping that we will never ever part.
  Karen McCormick

Past Reflections

Upon reflection of the past, how strange it all now seems,
Our aspirations long ago, when we were in our teens,
Of friendships forged and lost through life. It was so long ago,
That happiness was shared by all, but little did we know
How cruel and wicked ways of fate dealt mortal blows to some.
For those who planned and worked so hard for better things to come,
Were left alone with shattered dreams and very little hope.
Though difficult and lonesome times, we really had to cope,
But through the joy and sadness, we made amends and met
Some more new friends and partners. This time, we aim to beat
Such pitfalls, troubles and the like, with tolerance we bear.
As now we know what to expect and even more to share
Our love, devotion, trust to all, so everyone can see,
Great happiness it gives to all, especially you and me.
  Roy T. Gough

Ode to an Imprisoned Goldfish

Two eyes behold another world in vain:
The only look reflected is their own
For Sadness is the king of their domain
and silence is the august silver throne

So smooth, so light, so splendid are his curves;
With Psyche's deepest yearning he is one
For only pure sincerity deserves
a dance with threads of humble sunlight spun

Be dancing in the shimmer of that ray!
Until, at length, another day breaks free
When you will see the cloudscape float away
to once again be swimming in the sea
  Anders Lindqvist

Dancing Up to Heaven

Dad was a wannabe actor,
He collapsed and died on stage,
Mum died soon from a broken heart,
Kathy was ten years of age.
But through all her pain she carried on,
Her home was the clothes she wore,
Begging survival out in the town,
Still begging when her blisters were raw.
She danced to the tune of the buskers,
Danced with a tear in each eye,
Tears of pain and determination,
To earn pennies to help her get by.
The snowflakes began their annual show,
The dark nights were soon closing in,
But Kathy danced on when the buskers were gone,
Until she was too fragile and thin.
Now Kathy slept under the moonlight,
Her tear stained face had turned blue,
They found her next day as she peacefully lay,
And to her parents cried "She's dancing with you."
  Jane L. Howick

Dreams

I woke up this morning full of fright
now what was I dreaming of last night?
But no it was nothing bad
and just remembering made me glad
for I was once more with the girl I had
met and loved.
Together we faced the trials of life
and as you may guess I mean my wife.
In my dream we once more walked the lanes of Kent
and our lives seemed heaven sent.
We saw the world through glasses rose tinted
with love in our hearts serenely minted.
If all our dreams could be so sweet
there's so many loved ones I want to meet.

Joe W. Simpson

Untitled

What is this thing that is called light?
It's just a word to me,
For I am one that they call blind.
I am one who cannot see.
They talk about the colours, the blues, the greens, the white,
But black is the only colour,
To us who have no sight.
They talk about a baby's smile,
The sky above, the sea;
To me, they are just part of darkness,
The things I cannot see.
I can smell the scent of flowers,
I can hear the birds that sing,
But I cannot see these beautiful things,
Of this world that I live in.
I cannot see my mother's face, I cannot see her smile;
But I have often heard her laughter, and also heard her cry.
To me in all my darkness, to me who cannot see,
The greatest feeling within my heart
Is my mother's love for me.

Desmond Hurley

An Irishman's Loss of Faith

I slept contented.
Now I'm demented.
To call me adorable
Was deplorable:
To take my purse
Was even worse.

I gave my trust. You slaked your lust,
Then stole from me. Me heart is bust.
You were the man I pinned some hope on.
Henceforth I'll sleep with one eye open.
How dare you have your cake and eat it!
I'm in despair 'cause doubly cheated.

Clive Murphy

Woods by Night

As the night starts to fall,
I hear the animals start to call,
I hear them howling through the night,
In the woods out of sight.

Smaller animals creep and crawl,
Trying not to make a sound at all,
Walking silently along their way,
Not wanting to be another animal's prey

But as the moonlight lingers on,
I hear the birds singing their sweet song,
The song that tells me morning has come,
The Moon's gone to bed and out comes the Sun.

As the Sun comes beaming down,
I suddenly feel myself start to frown,
Because of the animals that walk the night,
Are afraid to be seen in daylight.

Karen Marshall

Sweet Prince

For my sweet prince who invades all my senses,
Disturbs the peace to break down my defences,
Whose milky and honeyed tongue does never lie
And my stone cold resolve does so defy.
If this is living, then please let me die.
My life is now wrought back and forth with madness,
Not seeing him could only bring me sadness,
Could fate have dealt such an ugly blow?
Should my affections on him I bestow?
This then could only bring me brutal sorrow,
There never could be any bright tomorrow.
But brave the heart that faces life's long battle
And never fears the sound of sabres' rattle.
Bestow upon me strength to meet the foe.

Ellen Hillary-Fawcett

Our Home

This is our home product of nature and man at their best
A symbol of progress to bring peace and rest
It keeps us safe from the cold and the snow
From the rain and winds that blow.
We have colour and beauty, precious light
Trees and flowers, nature's delight
Home is our friend right to the end
Whatever troubles life may send
Our home has cradled our young from birth
Filling our lives with happiness and mirth.
Our home is our faith in the way of life
Together always man and his wife.
Our home is to treasure the rest of our days
Our anchor—our haven now and always.

Jean Anderson Davies

Another Boy from Nazareth

I went so school with a boy called Jesus,
Briefly—no irreverence—some kid;
And all that the elders ever tried to teach us
We guessed he would know it all—and he did!

I served my time with that lad named Jesus,
For his Daddy, called Joseph, was now my boss;
Heads down all the time, no need to beseech us;
Firm, fair and generous can guarantee no loss.
The next time we met, there was something about him,
We all stood aghast—"Changing water to wine?"
At that wedding in Cana—you might think I'm going dim;
I couldn't be more certain, for that wedding was MINE!
And so to the Big City, starting out on my own;
The tales of his stories and deeds reached my ears
On everyone's lips we were hearing HIS name alone;
But at the back of it all, I was wrestling with my fears.

We were caught up in this crowd, so fierce and so thick
To three victims suffering on dark Calvary
The centre one I'd made; for I knew by my own nick,
But He'd made the Cross for all the World—and for Me!

Norman G. Connell

Perry My Son

To-day I would like to pay respect in every way
To my son who makes me proud, standing out in a crowd.
As a family man he always included his nan.
Now alas she has passed on,
Leaving fond memories of days gone,
The bond they shared gave him his start,
His strength and soft heart.
The love he showers on his own,
Gives him a special home.
His wife and girls he does adore,
Giving them his all, and more.
He works away must of the day,
Continuing on life's way.
His motto being not to give in
As less than your best is surely a sin.

Eve Young

Broken Wing

Eternity, why do you wait?
Yet I'm young but I'm broken, and locked in this kingdom of white
How pitiless this lonely end
How piteous these crippled bones
But, noble I will remain
So I'll lift my head one last time, although
My feathers are no match for this bitter wind
That wraps its steely fingers around my heart
And shrieks and moans around my ears,
Mocking.
Arrows of ice pierce my eyes
Arrows of fire burn my side
While all the while, visions stab at my brain
Of far away friends bathed in pale winter sunshine,
Oblivious.
Strange, I feel no fear
Only deep peace and a longing for sleep
So eternity, why do you wait?
Come, bring me your darkness now, cover my soul
Eternity, open the gate.
Patrick Mayer

A Baby Boy

A new little person was born today.
He is so perfect in every way,
Ten little fingers, ten little toes,
A cute little mouth, a little button nose,
Two little blue eyes can't focus clear,
Two little ears with which he can hear.
A little son so precious and dear,
He'll bring you much joy now that he's here.
Cherish the moments you all spend together,
He'll not be a baby for ever and ever.
Be there for his anger, his laughter, his tears,
Give him your love and support through the years,
Try not to spoil him, give what you can,
And he should grow into a happy young man.
Avril Thompson

Morris

They say that a dog is man's best friend.
   That's probably very true.
But to all who knew Morris from beginning to end,
   he was one of the family too.

He grew up with Hannah and Abbi, Olly and Joe.
   They never knew life without him,
never even dreamed he would ever have to go,
   or that he wouldn't be there when they shouted at him.

Now he'll never show off with his tricks any more,
   Like catching his biscuits or giving his paw.
He's gone off to peace now, away from the pain;
   but it's so sad for us, we won't see him again.

But we won't forget Morris—no one will.
   Not the children, Aunts, Uncles, Grandparents,
   or Jeffrey and Jill.
Frank Sutheran

The Emigrant

I have witnessed their scurrilous cries
Cries of "Death to this damnable land!"
And the fore bearers who've etched their lives
While to the four winds I saw them disband.
Bound for pastures fresh and green
Embracing the hopes of the pioneer.
Shirking attempts to intervene,
From those who once were held so dear.
And I have seen on distant shores.
The shattered dreams of the young,
In the eyes of he who implores.
To hear the songs of his childhood being sung.
In that loving, lilting air of his mother
On that soil, soil he once believed would smother.
Deirdre Curley

In Praise of Athol

Take me back to the sweet Vale of Athol,
Take me back to the mountains I love,
Let me lie on the slopes o' Ben Vrackie,
And watch the sweet heaven above.

When the summer is warm in sweet Athol,
When the heather takes on its fine hue,
I rejoice in the beauty around me,
And the friendship I've come to renew.

O'er the wide world I have wandered,
O'er the sand of the desert I've strayed,
But each hour when away from my country,
I dreamt of the glens where I played.

Where else would you find such a picture,
The mountains, the forest, the Glen,
From the far lonely shores of Loch Rannoch,
Right up to Creag Dhubh's rocky Ben.

And now let me rest in sweet Athol,
By the Tummel, the Garry, the Tay,
By the echoes of Auld Killiecrankie,
Let me dream till the end of my day.
Jack Smith

Clinical Depression

My world is one of gaudy technicolour.
Me? I am a grey lifeless clown, a mass of bland sombriety
My hopes and ambitions are fading
I am drowning in a murky black ocean of hopelessness
Although I try to swim through my synthetic abyss
my limbs are weary from the strain of treading water
for so long.

I am tangled in an intricate web of hurt and upset—
a colourless kaleidoscope of a million inadequacies
with no conceivable remedy—
an infinity of problematic matter with no visible solution.
Just a spirit-crushing plateau of frustration and anguish.

My witty banter has become hollow and devoid of sincerity—
merely a cloak for the macabre discontent
and harrowing inhibitions that I harbour.

Unfathomable unhappiness, diminished hope and sparce solitude
follow me through every waking hour,
enforcing the chemical imbalance that makes me so destitute.

My life is owned by daily drudgery and hourly heartbreak.
Emma Teale

Growing Old—Joie de Vivre

But yesterday we were children
And ran with dancing feet
But now it seems the years have won
We hobble up the street.

With face unlined and radiant
Each smiled upon her lover.
But now with dentures nicely cleaned
It's simply too much bother.

The years so quickly took their toll
We soon were middle-aged.
We worked and worried round the house
We felt that we were caged.

The children grew up fast and left
And sometimes husbands too
The workload seemed to slacken off
We had much less to do.

And some are left as widows our stories have been told
We really can't believe it that we are getting old.

The chores we once took in our stride have now become too weighty
Yesterday we were twenty-two. Good gracious—we are eighty.
Katie Stewart

Go East Go West but First Find the Best

I went east and I thought I will be lost
At last I returned west where I was at first
   All I wanted was the best
   Who will handle me like a nest
And make me forget the past
Where I changed men like breakfast
   But I decided to take blood test
   And it seems I need a rest
I was late and I am lost
Only what I do is pray for Christ
   No more days remain I will be the ghost
   After going east and west, I never found the best.

Prudencia Paul Kimiti

Autumn

The trees are wearing cloth of gold,
They stand there shivering in the cold,
It seems they really have no shame,
They have started stripping.

They shake their heads beautifully,
Make room for next year's leaves, dutifully,
We raise our eyes and see their limbs,
Very nearly stripped.

We walk through the wood,
Crackling, crunching leaves underfoot,
The tangy smells invade our nostrils,
The trees are stripped.

A few will keep their clothes on,
This wood's not quite abandoned,
They stand there, chaste, as if to say,
We will not! be stripping.

Joyce Purbrick

God Is Love

When there's love in your heart you have everything,
Look forward each day to what new life it brings,
The wind and the rain, the joy and the pain,
It makes your heart cry, it makes your heart sing,
With love in your heart you have everything.

When there's love in your heart
what strength it can bring,
Where does it come from, why do I sing?
It comes from our Lord so far up above,
Let's share with each other that gift that he gave,
From the moment of birth, until still, in his grave,
Yet far beyond that, it's eternally ours,
So open your heart, and let it come in,
For with love in your heart, you have everything.

Anna Murray

Forever and a Day

The very first time I stood close to you,
I knew then it was love at first sight.
The warmth of your Aura, Karen,
The emotions I felt were just right.

I knew you felt the same about me,
I could see the want in your eyes,
You gave me Christopher and Sarah, my love,
My life's most wonderful prize.

We're bound to have dark times,
And though I hate us being apart,
Our love will always shine through,
I can say that with hand on my heart.

You've always stood right beside me,
We've promised our love 'til the end,
You are everything that I have asked for,
My lover, my wife and my friend.

When we're all back together again,
In peace and love, then I pray,
That we'll be together forever,
Forever and a day.

Nigel Wood

The Whale's Song

When a whale sings,
He sounds like a king.
The sweetness of his call
Brings rocks to a fall
And enchants all those who listen,
That's why so many people listen in unison,
To this wonderful sound
That echoes around.
For this beautiful tune is the song of
the whale.

Jenny Westwood

Our Heroes

You're in the desert some miles away,
   And fighting for our cause.
It only takes a power greedy man,
   To start these bloody wars.

But we have faith in all our boys,
   And know you'll do us right.
Saddam will crack, turn himself in,
   So we will win this fight.

He is no man nor human too,
   But a blood-seeking hypocrite.
He kills the young and innocent,
   Remorse—felt not a bit.

So why can't someone end this war,
   As quickly as they can,
So Saddam's gone and his forces too,
   And we have back our man.

And when that happens, they'll all come home,
   With their triumph and their pride.
But never forget the brave young men,
   Who for our country—died.

Juliett Arnold

To Those I Leave Behind

When I close my eyes, one last time,
Knowing I've done my best.
When my body tires of living,
And my soul is laid to rest.
I will still be with you, in every breath you take.
I'll shine in every sunrise, each morning when you wake.
I am the salt in every tear you may ever come to taste.
The tenderness in every kiss to ever touch your face.
I am the warmth in every smile to ever come your way.
I am the strength within your heart to help you through your day.
I am the love of open arms to ever hold you tight.
I am in every star to shine on you each night.

Catherine Jane Sullivan

Proof

One thousand steps up a mountain,
A stone's throw away from the moon;
One furlong from the end of the National,
Two months in a comfortable cocoon.

Eight months into a pregnancy,
One day from Christmas Eve;
Two pages till the end of Mark's Gospel,
Six years from when I first believed.

A sand castle away from the desert's end,
One metre away from the Pole;
A king away from a full deck of cards,
A reindeer away from the gold.

A cheque book closer to nothing,
A shopping trolley nearer still;
A passport photo to take me there,
The bucket being carried by Jill.

All these are the workings of You,
All show that You are alive;
The clown, the trees and the sky scrapers,
The joy when the heavens arrive.

John McDermott

An Awakening

Throughout the winter months, frequently frozen,
The garden pool—yet life still abounds in its depths.
Early February saw the first contribution
Of frogspawn—soon followed by many more batches.
Later the sound of frogs—not the usual croaking
But a contented cadence resembling
The blissful purr of a contented cat.
Each evening, and in addition to that joyful sound
Frogs' heads appear, each one so still and unmoving.
Finally the masses of frogspawn become
Large heaps of twiddling, wriggling tadpoles
Remaining in their clumps for several days.
The final achievement comes when those tadpoles separate
And swim here and there to explore their strange surroundings.
Much later legs will appear; tails will disappear.
Then one fine day tiny, wee froggies will depart
Leaving their safe haven to venture further afield
And explore the unknown regions of the garden.
Hopefully they will survive to repeat this yearly procedure.

Ada M. Witheridge

Our New Baby

Our new baby so precious and sweet
With her skin all roses and cream
And as we peep beneath the sheets
To reveal the cutest hands and feet
Her hair so blonde and silky
A tiny little nose so pert and shapely
And as she opens up her eyes
The deepest blue of sunny skies
her ears against her shapely head
all pearly and pink like shells from seabed
and as she's lifted to be fed,
a mouth so lovely a rose bud of red,
our new baby's a little girl a gift of God
we shall do all we can to please her
we've proudly named her Ruth Louisa.

Thora Melling

First Love

The torrential rain beats heavy on my window
Resembling my heart when I think of you.
I see us together on the verge of my mind, hand in hand with
The aroma of the perfumed daffodils sweeping by us in the
Moderate breeze of the spring season.
Our love, I thought, would not cease, but when it ended,
My life also declined. My heart shattered when you uttered
those two intense, momentous words 'so long.'
Everything went frightfully secluded in those few seconds of
Heartbreaking horror. Time stood still, all I could hear were
Those words being repeated inside my bewildered and
confused mind.
For days I sat alone, tears of hurt and fear building up,
I had to let go, but to no avail.
Nobody understood what my heart suffered for you.
And to this day, the pain grows deep inside but I try to
Conceal the emotions I still have for my first love.

Emmaline Tuff

A Precious Friend

I want to say thank you more than anything else.
For being a friend like nobody else.
The world could I search but none would I find
to compare with you so true and so kind.
I hope that I can be to others
the friend you are to me
and may the happiness you've shown be there
for all to see.
There're relations we have and parents we love
but a friend like you a blessing from above
—more special than a flower growing in the desert
is a friend amid our foes. And just like a flower
given time and friend snip grows.
Thank you for the secrets that never will you tell.
Thank you for being there and for being a friend as well.

Fiona MacDonald

Where My Linda Walks

Awake sweet morning, cast cold dreams to flight,
Where all but eyes of stars, dared hush the night.
For lo, when silent sun her place retires,
Quiet footsteps of the West, enfold soft light

And dreaming here beneath sweet Even's sky,
A voice did breathe, and through my soul didst sigh.
Awake fast, my little ones arise,
Before these fleeting streams of life be dry.

Let all our words be fragranced by the rose,
Where Lynda walks in whispers, no one knows,
And lo, as to the nightingales she cries,
Oh find the reeds, whereby the water blows.

Hold fast my love, upon the arms of spring,
As to the bitter earth thy sorrows fling,
I give to you eternity, and then . . .
Your tears shall fly, as birds upon the wing.

Oh sister wait not long, for we shall meet,
before time's shadow slips beneath our feet.
Our yesterdays are gone, and where's tomorrow,
Grieve not for them, if our today is sweet.

Annemarie Dickinson

Rain

Gently falls the rain from above
To the parched land below.
Merciful rain, how welcome you are!
Brightly shines the sun
Dries up the rain,
The Arid Land is parched again.
Come back rain, to bring back the green,
To feed the land unseen
That will bring forth
New growth that will
Feed those that hunger and thirst.

Glenys M. Lipscombe

The Crucifixion of Jesus

A cross stands stark, high on a hill,
In the hope for mankind, there would be no ill.
Poor Jesus died in agony,
Just so that all on Earth will be free.

He said "Forgive them they know not what they do".
But still said prayers in His heart for you.
They placed thorns in a crown, upon His head,
And He suffered until He was actually dead.

Lord Jesus died, doing his part,
It's time to take Him, into your heart.
On the third day from, the grave He was risen,
He died that others may be forgiven.

John Thorn

The Iceman

In the high valley among summer trees
Turning to Autumn,
Stooped the hunter.
Three thousand years before Christ,
He made his knife, his bow, his axe,
With weathered hands.

Soon he would leave his mountain home,
The comforts of those dwellings,
To seek the food for winter life,
Tread the amazing Alps,
Stalk and surely kill
Before the snow and ice encompassed all.

When forced by driving winds to shelter,
Pinned fatally between the rocks,
What were his thoughts
Of home, of others, of his world,
As he lay down to die,
Five thousand years ago.

Rowland Ablett

Zulu Madonna

When hunger cries wring swollen breasts to yield
Nomusa drops her hoe
and uninhibited calls across the field
to have the infant brought: 'Nothando!'

Ousted from her back, to heel, Felokwakhe
follows his nurse girl sister; she
croons a lullaby and drums the beat
upon the footpath with calloused feet.

Kneeling, as before a shrine, in fascination,
they watch the small impostor appease his need;
the eager nuzzle, the panting plucks
as he begins to feed
on salty, sweated nipple—sweat which soon sucks
off as no more than a peerless lamination.

Gratified, the clinging lips of silk
reward Nomusa with a cornered smile
which channels a momentary leak
of lush libation from a pulsing phial
and milk, immaculate as the Madonna's milk
trickles white over the dusky infant cheek.

Helena Barnard Rich

The Last Farewell to Dad

The time has come, my darling, when we must say goodbye.
But do not weep, my darling, for we'll hold you in our hearts.
A heart that's full of joys and pleasure, sunshine, snow and rain.
Holidays and laughter that shielded us from pain,
We trod life's path together, from beginning to the end.
In you, my dearest darling, I found my greatest friend,
A friend in need, a friend indeed, three bonny children too.
How proud they are, though one's afar, to have a dad like you,
We'll keep you in our memories and smile with secret pleasure.
We loved you, Dad, and always will, eternally, forever.
God bless you, Dad from your family.

H. M. Morgan

Piggy's Weekend Break

Two little pigs needed some time on their own,
A romantic place without a phone,
Then Robbie the pig had an idea in his brain,
Let's go to France, we'll take the train.

Champs-Elysées, Eiffel Tower,
We'll be there within the hour,
Euro Disney the place to be,
I only hope that you'll agree.

Three whole days "oh, what bliss!"
To laugh and talk and hug and kiss,
The day arrives, and here we are,
I know not how, we got in the car,
With luggage, presents, cards and a cake,
It was from her mum, one she did not bake.

And so with my little pig,
I will sing and dance and do a jig,
because I am so happy to be,
In your very fine Piggy Company.

D. Lelliott

Years Apart

Why today, has wrong become right?
Has the meek taken over that once was the might?
This does not show when the battles begin,
The strength of the heroes that's born within.
So why when it's calm,
Do we smile and return home,
To the drums and the bugles,
That left others alone?
We have thought of our loved ones,
"The fields" what a wonderful sight.
But we come down to earth
When we witness wrong has become right.

Francis Kenneth Ruston

Ode to the Survivors

I have nothing to live for, my family's all gone,
I just don't see the point in carrying on.
He has destroyed my life, burnt my home,
Taken away my loved ones, left me on my own.
He took away my dignity and my will to live
Now I'm left here by myself with nothing left to give.
What reasons did he have for doing this to me?
How evil and heartless can one man be?
Why didn't I die with them? Why leave me here instead?
Without my family I am already dead.

Rhianydd Lewis

Untitled

As I sit upon the deck
I look out to the sea, full of sun fleck
The yacht slowly rocks, bobs and sways
Breezing along eloping the day
I chime my glass to the love next to me
And the rays soak our skin so delightfully
I drop my hand to the life below
And graze my tips through the sparkling flow
Gliding in further so I'm silky in blue
A rainbow of birds fan over you
Powder dusts our feet as we explore white sand
Our teeth start to chatter like maracas in a band
Entwining each other—our closest yet
The grains bind our bodies as the sunsets

V-J R. Duffy

Someone like Me

Someone like me can love you.
Someone like me can share your dreams.
Someone like me can fill your heart.
Someone like me that you can trust.
Someone like me you can depend upon.
Someone like me when times are tough.
Someone like me to come home to.
Someone like me to open up the door.
Someone like me to be right at your side
Someone like me just wants your love.
Someone like me will hold you till tomorrow
Someone like me to be your guide.
Someone like me to show you the way.
Someone like me right at your side.
Someone like me to love and kiss you.
Someone like me to cry your tears.
Someone like me in joy and sadness.
Someone like me to comfort and joy.
Someone like me just to be there,
Today and forever more.

Patricia T. Thompson-Massey

Revelations

The city is sleeping
In buildings quiet and still as air.
In Markeaton Park
The leaves are moving on the water,
Going somewhere.

In the darkness
The eye-sockets of the stony bridge,
Are black as currents,
And the breeze fabulous as the God,
But whispering.

Here there is something
On the other side. If you stand with your
Back to the eyes,
You will see where the white gushes
Between the bars,

A wheel is turning,
Beating the night and rushing at the moon.
Touch the glitter
Of frost on a railing, and birds sing
In the dewy dark.

James Manlow

Sheffield Steelers

The season of hockey has come to an end,
The Nottingham Panthers home we send,
The Sheffield Steelers proved their name,
By winning the final, the very big game.

The puck drops, then there's action,
We can't loosen up, not even a fraction,
In fifty six seconds there was Bobyck's score,
That made Greco determined to shut the door.

The fans were screaming for their own hero,
The Panthers tried but nothing passed Piero,
Ron Shudra got it in Robbin's net,
It was a tight game that no one could forget.

The Nottingham Panthers wanted more,
But Kovacs and Lafreniere built up the score,
After sixty minutes the final whistle blew,
The Steelers fans sang, "Whoosh it's behind you!"

Priestlay and Plommer held up the prize,
The trophy meant everything in the supporters' eyes,
The players were thinking the same thing too,
They looked up and said to us, "We owe it to you!"

Sarah Colley

The Executive Male

There he stands in all his splendour
Looking quite the man
From his well groomed hair and trendy suit
Posing, if he can

The briefcase, belt, don't forget the shoes
Shining in their glory
The shirt he wears, his tie and socks
They all tell a story

He stands up straight and walks with pride
His head is elevated
From top to toe he's dressed in style
Nothing he wears is dated

A well polished desk, a padded chair
Everything with taste
He holds his pen with such a grip
There's no time to waste

The Executive male, a law to himself
A well presented image
Approved by all, regarded well
Peacock of his lineage.

Nicolette F. Walsh

The Seeds of Love

Two men were given some seeds one day
To plant in their own inimitable way
We are not gardeners is what they said
But they took the seeds and went ahead

So they looked and searched till they finally found
What they thought was arable ground
But a piece of advice they were given too
Remember the seeds and what they do

So they planted the seeds, till all was sown
Watered and fed them, then left them alone
One went away, never took no more heed,
They will grow by themselves, they are only seeds

But the other he stayed, worked hard all day
Raking and weeding, digging the clay
He nurtured and cherished them, with his own hand
For at last he had come to understand

Than an uncaring heart, wherever it's found
Is like planting seeds on stony ground
But a heart that is true, and kind indeed
Will flourish and grow like the tiny seed

Sarah Shoulin

The Last Showing

You are there in abundance, pink pastel against green,
soon you'll diminish, leaving fruits to be seen.
I've waited so long for last season to end,
now you've blossomed again, pink pastel, dear friend.
You have tapped on my window as you've rocked to and fro,
while the wind bends your boughs, soft petals do blow.
Supple and green, your partner is dancing,
dark pink over pastel, your dress entrancing.
Layers of pastel petals blow,
like the Ballet, when the dresses flow.
How I remember my first steps,
the entr'acte and my pirouettes.
Today the strongest winds are blowing,
so I really must hurry, to see the last showing.

Shirley Ann Berrows

Earth, Sea, Air, Fire

The autumn's orchestra blows red and ochre:
Trees' brass and flashing sounds, though sparse, I hear
With pipes and woody instruments bassoon—
Curling and sprinkling notes of citrus gold.

    The oily olive sea,
Its feathers ruffled as a wing-fledged sky
With herons flocked heavily flickers, is netted
In open locks of trellised shade's translucence,
Lit through with every tint of green and grey,
Labours towards the roped-in tinkling boats
On waves made wayward and, buoyant, wades over
What knocks and ruckling stones to seaweed shores
And rugged contest with the knuckled cliffs
And maws of misers' caves.

Air,
Philosopher's material.
Accordion, it cadences our lungs.

Fire, liar, unsteady,
Maroon and white as blown magnolia buds,
Your flames are all about.

David Hendtlass

The Journey

Life-destiny written for both you and me,
journey road to the unknown,
Living for day to day hour to hour minute to minute,
Bodies rushing, minds working, brain thinking,
Vocal cords singing, laughing, joking,
Routine schedules timed appointments,
Business propositions working 9-5
Bills red alert flashing
We're dashing panicking
Need heat light for sight,
Babies screaming gurgling,
Siblings fighting population multiplying,
Lonely hearts crying,
Death sadness surrounding,
Wedding bells chiming harmoniously
Unity thanks-giving,
Apartheid deleted,
Black and white hand shaking,
Life-world creation don't stop for hesitation
Goal delayed destination!

Aisha Sohni

Remembering You My Friend

It's been a while since I've thought of you,
But suddenly you are near—in my heart.
I find myself smiling, remembering the good times,
The childish laughter and the quiet moments we shared.
Thinking of you has cheered my day,
And reminded me that I will never be alone with you in my heart.
Remembering you with love,
My friend.

S. Rumsam

Diminuendo

Do you listen when my thoughts give voice
or scatter my words like ashes
blown on a breeze, soon lost?
At times you seem to move
beyond my comprehension
into a world of strange slogans,
confusing rituals.
Look over your shoulder once in a while
as you rush into your future.
You may see me waving
as I retreat into your history.
Elizabeth Farnham

The Elfin Chase

The day was bright and the sun was shining,
The sky was blue and the clouds had a silver lining
And down on the branch of a sycamore tree
Sat a nightingale next to a hive full of bees.
The elf was collecting his food for the cold winter coming
Little did he know he soon would be running
He bathed in the heat of the high midday sun
Unknowing of the dark eyes watching, waiting to end his fun.
The elf was sleeping, the sun shining bright,
The time was now, it was all so right.
He made his move, he appeared quick and nimble,
But the elf was faster and hearing him was simple
Up he jumped and ran into the wood
The other followed as fast as he could.
They continued speeding through the trees
Then the elf saw his abode under the hive full of bees
The elf worked his magic and his home disappeared.
The other annoyed and confused, then he heard
The nightingale singing his old cheery song
And he thought to himself next time it won't go wrong . . .
Victoria Buckley

Your Poem

When I look at you, I see your strength,
It shines through like the sun shines through the rain.

When I look at you, I see your beauty,
It radiates your heart, but fails to ease the pain.

When I look at you, I see your love,
It rescues my soul without questioning why.

When I look at you, I see your warmth,
It burns inside of you and will never, ever die.

Then I look at you, and I see your sadness,
It hides behind your smile, tortured by violence.

And I look at you, and I see your desperation,
It screams out loud, but can never break the silence.

I look at you, and I see your pain,
It hurts me too, reducing me to tears.

But then I look at you and I see you,
The one I live for, who can cure my fears.
Jemma Levy

Untitled

The angels smile from heaven,
As they all look down to you.
Their eyes, they shine like diamonds,
As they think they're being good to you.
Giving us a world that's full of flowers,
The beauty of the wide bright sky,
The loveliness of the green green grass,
And no one seems to sigh.

Then all of a sudden everything's changed,
The moon with the darkness, things rearranged,
The smile becomes twisted,
Your heart fills with pain,
As you look in the coffin to see the remains.
Margaret Daly

Scorpions of Suspicion

Stung by several scorpions of suspicion,
Sometimes my mind is splendidly swinging
Betwixt and between tweedledee and tweedledum
In transparent betweenity ringing.

'Tis misery of misunderstanding,
Miasma of mutual mistrust sure
Which can respect or auspicate nothing
Except the expectance of things e'er dour.

Doesn't this defile atmosphere of mind?
Instead of entertaining gleeful thoughts
If we continually think of things unkind
Will it not offend the canonical hours

Horae canonicae? These two rival
Proverbial musicians tweedledum tweedledee,
Unable to break cord umbilical,
Will make brusque the countenance of lea.

But when the wished—for moment arrives,
A simple piece of paper, a telegram
Changes cosmos of consciousness and vies
With celestial commingling, the noble van.
M. Wadikar

A Friend in Need

When I looked to the west at the sunset,
  heard the swell of a grand organ note,
heard the bells as they peeled, I felt sad; yet
  I tried hard to hide tightness of throat.

How I longed for a friend, and a soul mate,
  the comfort from someone, who cared
to bring joy, in exchange for my sad state;
  but to find such a one I despaired.

And the tears that I shed were in sorrow,
  as I, silently, breathed out my prayer
for release, "Let there be no tomorrow;
  let me die, for there's no one to care."

Then, I almost decided to end it,
  and I wondered what people might say,
"Oh, poor creature; her soul; God defends it
  safe from hell, in His merciful way."

But I found the dear friend I'd been seeking;
  now, if ever my feelings are low,
she can cheer me up, fast, without speaking
  for she loves me, her bark tells me so.
Grace Mills

Lonely Highland Bay

Golden sands that sparkle, a secluded highland bay,
Pulling at the heart strings, draws me there today,
Where nature carves her beauty free for all to see,
Amid majestic splendour is where I long to be.

Craggy rocks stretch upwards reaching for the sky,
Sea birds circle freely breaking silence with their cry,
Back drop of towering mountains, barren, bare and high,
And quiet of timeless wonder is broken with a sigh.

Breakers rolling softly whisper on the shore,
Scenes of precious beauty stay for ever more,
Walk in peace and splendour in this haven of delight,
As daylight turns to twilight in tranquility of night.

I have seen the sands that sparkle on a lonely highland bay,
As I walk alone in silence on a northern summer's day,
No footprints mar the shoreline, all is pure and bright,
And waves of the Atlantic here disguise their might.

Empty glens stand silent, memories of the past,
In splendid isolation eternally they last,
Strands of mist caressing distant rocky Ben,
Deserted now my country, bereft of life and men.
Alister H. Thomson

A Parent's Plea

The day you were born brought us great joy.
We did not mind if you were a girl or boy.

We were so proud as we watched you grow
It's just as well we were not to know

That on your way to school that day
Your life would be suddenly taken away.

As you crossed the road, a speeding car
Struck you down and threw you far.

Your poor broken body gave up the fight
In my arms you died that night.

Please God, let this broken heart of mine
Forgive the one who caused this crime.

Who took my child so young from me
Through driving their car so recklessly.

They say time heals the endless pain
And one day, I'll learn to live again.

No punishment given out for this
Can ever bring back my happiness.

To anyone who drives, I plead,
PLEASE DRIVE WITH CARE AND DO NOT SPEED.

Sybil Smith

What Can I Say?

What can I say? What can I do?
I am so deep down in love with you.
What I want can never be mine.
All I want is to be thine.
If you want me, I would come,
Without a second thought.
I need to be with you, thou' you know I
Shouldn't ought,
Take me away on wings of gold,
Love me till I am ever so old,
Far away lands I do not care,
as long as you and I are there.
The tears I cry are just for me,
Since I know all this will never be,
I want so much,
to feel your touch—as one to be forever.
I wish you would say,
a yes or a nay, how you feel for me,
Is it wrong to feel this way?
Can "we" ever be?

Sarah Victoria Stratford-Wight

For My Mother—Alone

When I came into the world
The blow was hushed by loving arms.
A strength and warmth yet unsurpassed
The beauty of maternal calm.

Then from the crawl to tiny steps
The arms secure still there,
A union new and yet so close
My mother dark and I so fair.

And as years progressed, my awareness grew
Of sacrifices made.
That I might live a life complete
And not feel pushed into the shade.

And when pain and hurt and men's deceit
Encroached themselves upon her,
She managed still to comfort me
With ferocious love and honour.

And when times are hard—when life is cruel,
When brother may turn against brother,
I shall feel forever strengthened by
My love for you, dear Mother.

Claire Meaden

Rare Colours of the Sky

The sky over the sea looks beautiful tonight with its
colours so rare. It looks like a battle between the
elements, colours clashing with colours, over the sea and
land. In the distance I see a ripple of red and orange
like a sunset on the water's surface, so beautiful in the
light. As the night gets closer the rare colours have
nearly gone, only the blue and green is seen now in the
distance as the gray clouds push it away. As the
sky moves, the battle moves too, fading into the
distance with gray clouds looking over my head.
Darkness is coming, pushing the rare but beautiful
colours farther away from me. It's time for me to
fade away in the safe, but warm surroundings of home
and family.

Susan M. Drakley

Rain

Here it comes again—at last!
Beating heavily, thick and fast!
It trickles down the windowpanes,
Filling all the roads and drains.
Rain, is like manna sent to us from
Out of the skies, without a fuss.
Especially when the sun has shone
Every day and all day long.
To hear the sound of rushing rain
Is exciting when you hear it again—and again!
The leaves in the trees drip and droop,
The birds are halted in their swoop,
They beat their wings, the rain runs off,
The old man in his bed gives out a cough.
He shuts the window and sighs once more,
"Oh dear, here is another downpour".

Shane V. Simons

Life

We are born to live, we are born to die and
Life's long toll goes rolling by,
We laugh, we cry, we work, we play,
We do our duty in God's way,
Life's ups and downs, grief and sorrow, happiness
And joy bring forth tomorrow,
Our life span is but three score years and ten
Yet God only knows of where and when,
So all you kind folk take extra care as
Life and love is ours to share,
As well we know before we die that God is
Watching from on high,
And in the evening of our day, before
We sleep we all must pray,
Make the most of life as time goes by, as
In the end we must say goodbye.

Audrey Margaret Helena Brooks

Surgeon Hope

I had an operation, I met the surgeon's knife,
Then after anaesthesia, I'd another view of life.
I could not go on as I was, I wanted to do more,
So I tried to change my work which was becoming such a bore.
Yet though I got positions they were all of the same kind.
The underpaid monotony almost destroyed my mind.
Though in a nervous breakdown, I continued in my work,
Then became ejected from it into gloomy jobless murk.
I couldn't get another job, so spent some time in college,
Then on to the University to gain some skills and knowledge.
I wore a gown and mortar and went upon a stage.
I hoped a B.SC. would help me earn a living wage.
I thought I'd find a worthwhile job, but put too much reliance
On being better qualified, a Bachelor of Science.
But this proved not to be the case, I found no true profession,
And consequently plummeted into a long depression,
Which then gave me the motive to leave this mortal coil,
Thus giving little purpose to the kindly surgeon's toil.

Christopher Toyne

Hidden Heart

There is a softness that you rarely dare to show,
There is a warmth beneath, that clutches to your soul,
A caring that you hide, with a strong soldier's stand,
A depth of knowledge that you pretend not to understand,
There is a road of emotion through every vein to your heart,
There is a vulnerability that can be crushed and wrenched apart,
A flow of your will, strong—pulling as the tide . . .
Lays beneath its seas, secrets hushed and pushed aside.

Angie Duarte

Death Defined

Lightning strikes and thunder rolls
To destiny I've paid my toll
Enslaved unto the book of time
He plays out people like a rhyme

The rain pours down, the thunder thrashing
And somewhere near, two wills are clashing
The wind whistles as if in song
And I know now it won't be long
The sky lights up, I feel him near
And in a heartbeat all is clear

A breath of wind, I know he's waiting
I turn my head, his touch so tainting
His hand extends, a finger beckoning
Now it's him with whom I'm reckoning

I take a step, the time is near
No longer scared, my path is here
The thunder rolls, it seems so long
But in a heartbeat I am gone

Joanna Wilson

You Look at Me

You look at me
You choose not to see me

Your eyes
Once filled with love
Are filled with anger

My heart is heavy with love for you
My body aches for your touch

Your arms strong and safe
Do not reach for me
As they once did

Your smile has faded
I no longer bring it to your lips.

My heart beats hard in my chest
My hands shake
My lips will not speak what my heart screams

Could you ever love me
The way I love you.

Laura Grindon

Night Walker

With a smooth, sleek body encased in black fur,
And a long, white tail that twitches when he purrs,
With emerald eyes that shine so bright
And light up his face in the darkness of night,
He swiftly creeps upon the ground
Like a cool, soft wind not making a sound.
Through every neighbourhood he can be seen
By the light of the moon and the street light's gleam.
Free from the clasping arms of the pound,
Never an owner for him has been found.
No welcoming arms are held out to him
And no one fixes his injured limb
Because he's not a normal family pet.
For on one night through the streets he crept
On the cold, wet pavements he padded along,
But a car came by and his life was gone.
But he still walks there, that cat of ours
Who walks through walls and under cars.

Leanne Watson

Rainbow's End

Have you stood at the end of a rainbow,
With the trees glistening after the storm,
The unearthly feeling that grips you,
When the moving clouds start to perform?

You imagine the world all around you,
The memories! Some happy, some sad,
The sad ones you push far behind you,
The happy ones make you so glad.

You hold out your hand, but catch nothing,
The colours you never forget,
Your life flashes by, in the blink of an eye.
But who knows what's to come yet?

You're rooted to the ground you see;
Your limbs refuse to move,
The earth is so near, there's nothing to fear,
But there's so many memories to prove.

There's gold at the end of the rainbow,
A saying so "True", or "Pretend",
So, if ever you're lucky enough to be there,
Let's hope you're at the right end.

D. E. Bullard

Why?

Why? Have we not learned from agonies past.
The wars, and hatreds, we've amassed.
Why? Not all live as human beings,
With thoughts of peace, and love that lasts.

Whatever your colour, whatever your creed.
Surely, we are all God's seeds.
Let's all blossom, as humans should.
Banish all evil, think kindly, think good.

Why? With our knowledge and brains of today
Can we not rationalize and say:
"I do not want this way of life,"
"I have a family, a loving wife."

That's all we need in our lives today.
Anything more, let's give away.

Vanish all thoughts of war and greed
Let the people choose, what the people need

Leslie Rushbury

You Are the Sun, I the Sky

Something strange just happened to me.
I truly believe I met my destiny.
Two spirits of old,
He'll wonder away, but always return,
His touch, like never before,
The feel of water gently swallowing the shore,
Renew a time, we could never know before
I wonder?
You are the sun, I the sky.
I feel the warmth of you where ever
I am.
The moments we live are gone so quickly,
They should always be taken,
They may only last a minute,
but the memory may last forever.

Michelle Tanfield

Daffodils in Spring

Seas of glorious passionate yellows.
Every hue and shade.
Melodious, harmonious, just wonderful.
Splendid, merry and bright.
A joy to behold.
Outrageous, bubbly and spontaneous.
Green stems and happy faces.
A refreshing perfume, a rainbow of memorable delight.
A choir of beautiful rapturous spring flowers.

K. A. Davis

Despair

There is a woman, an old woman
Who shuffles along with a bag
And a pint of beer.
Almost oblivious, seeking oblivion.
Her hair in metal curlers
Under an old tweed cap.
Her face is the face of someone drowned.
She has never been young
And her mind is numb.
She only floats to the surface
Now and then, from a sea of misery.
And I, who lower my eyes as I hurry by
Am ashamed, as I wonder why despair
Troubles to curl her hair
   Daphne Ritchings

The River

Just flowing, splashing
Gently, quiet, noisy, clean
Peaceful dark light, frothy merry little scene
Making its way to the sea, gurgling and dancing.
The dazzling thing bubbles away
Over the rocks and pebbles and the still sands goes the wild
rapid gushing current.

Winter comes, the swollen stream is not gushing now,
lying cold it will be.
The frothy little scene
will not until another summer be
Dangerous, peaceful.

Lying cold, pebbles stuck.
Sand hard, and still.
Not for another year
Will we see
the frothing, dancing, dazzling sea.
   Catherine Morrison

Autumn

All the leaves are falling,
Red, brown and gold,
They twist and turn and dance around,
In winds that feel so cold.

The ground outside is carpeted,
with leaves all crisp and dry,
The trees all stand like skeletons,
thin and bare but high.

All the squirrels search for nuts,
To store away somewhere,
But family cats are comfortable,
Their food is always there.

People get ready for winter,
Buying new clothes and things,
Jeans, jumpers and trousers,
Never sure that the weather might bring.
   Verity McGivern

Soul Destiny

Listen to the feelings deep down within your heart
The gentle sound of breathing and the joys about to start

Take time to reflect upon the emotions of the day
A lesson to be learned in every single way

Take refuge in your soul when you feel a little low
The magic is inside us all, some already know

Keep your spirits high and challenge doubtful ways
Don't be led by others when you feel a little stray

Be true to yourself and your path will unfold

The soul is very special and can lead us all the way
A powerful source of energy, in a very mysterious way

Nurture it with kindness and it will show you the way
Share it with another soul, you know then you've found your way!
   Katie Naylor

Insight to Happiness

While travelling home upon the bus, my baby on my knee,
A little man alighted, his face was full of glee.
He smelled of gin and whiskey, and he danced along the aisle,
He called to everyone he passed, and tried to make them smile.
But they, (With stony silence) pretended not to see,
Except my baby daughter, who laughed out happily,
The old man turned, and touched her cheek,
And then he swore and cussed
At all the icy glares he got, so filled with low disgust.
And then he held my daughter's hand, and so she gazed and smiled,
And in his eyes, a gratefulness, for trust from this small child.
And then he said (So All Could Hear) you're the only one to see
That "someone" in this world must smile, it might as well be me!
A happy drunken little man, whose only "crime" it seems,
Was wanting every other one to share his happy dreams.
He did no harm, he sang and danced, but as he went away,
He said, 'Your Eyes Are Beautiful', you 'See' far more than they,
You like me don't you little girl? And you don't seem to mind.
How could I disillusion him,
And tell him, She Was Blind!
   M. G. Shakespeare

Food—For Thought

A glut of guns, growling greedily
Platters of men—collops devoured by death,
Poppy pools—gravy, a shroud, for meat
starved by the sycophants sugary lies
Barbarous battalions banquet on breath,
belching blatantly.

Hearts—raw with despair.
Etched indelibly with the intimacies of invasion.
Minds ravaged by futility,
Hungry for tranquillity,
Forage for some meagre morsel to feed
their floundering faith.
Peace. Just an anorexic hope.
   Mary Simpson

The Jewel in the Void

Beyond destruction lies this beautiful sphere.
Through virgin eyes I see this spangled miracle of innocence.
Man in his mindless world of greed and
degradation will not afford himself
this vision. So sad.
Will it be too late to save such a
precious heavenly creation.
No more to be held in the bosoms
of our minds nor yet to be entered
upon for eternity. Lost forever to the void.
This beautiful spectrum of paradise
   Pamela Hollis

The Art of Living

Life in high quality print, in unpolluted pastel shades
denotes the art of living.
Easel standing tall, stooping slightly,
Nicotine stains on the curled edges—artistic?
Brush past the smoke and the primary colours, to a plump,
juicy cherry
—oh the calories in that oil pastel.
Artistic amputation.
A sketch of an ear, deafened by rave streaked with
Gangrene gold and hoarded silver hangs in the gallery. But
Triple bypass to computerised drawings
of the city—how pretty in their polluted gluttony.
A hazy streak of peach schnapps the malibu sunset, marring
The bounty of the future
As the salt and the stress of the heartfelt red,
Colour the low cost paper of the demented, charcoal covered,
A life oblivious as the inspiration dies in the English class.
Wasted crayon scribbles pitter out at the edge and a
Wavery line of pencil stops.
This is the art of the living (the death of the future).
   Kathryn K. Stevens

What Is Love?

Is it that feeling in the pit of your stomach,
When you feel like you're spinning inside?
When you feel so light, and your cares have gone,
And all you have left are your feelings inside?
Is that what love is?

Or is it when you think about him day and night,
When he's constantly on your mind?
When your legs go weak when he talks to you,
And the words to say you just cannot find?
Is that what love is?

Or is love when your eyes meet and they stay that way,
for what seems like hours on end?
And he smiles at you, in a certain way,
That tells you he's more than just a friend?
Is that what love is?

Love can be one, or all of these things,
When you're in love you'll find out.
These feelings, desires, that tremble inside,
They all mean love, without a doubt.
Tessa Plimley

It's Just a Dream

I see him in my dream again
He smiles and slowly fades away
I reach out my hand, I shout his name
I try to run his way

I try but I can't move
He does not hear my voice
I lose him slowly in the dark
Wake up . . . I have no choice

I can't stay longer in my dream
And see him go away
Oh, please, come back! I beg you, please!
"It's just a dream", they say
Ksenia Belaya

Seasons

Hello to spring, let's all sing
the daffodils are out, I want to shout.

Summer is here, the sky is clear
lollypops and ice creams are eaten every year.

The sky is dark around the Park,
the leaves are falling, Autumn is calling,
the wind is blowing, the Cock is crowing.

Winter will appear at the end of the year,
the cold has come, it's just begun,
the snow will fall, Happy Christmas to you all.
Lewis Merry

The Ice Bridge

Across the plateaus of time
At the end of this universe,
And before the spiritual domain above
Lies a bridge suspended in space.

A vertebrae of meteorites curving into white light
Built of pure diamond ice, spanning worlds
Hewn out of quarries cut by comets' teeth.

A white hammock draped round the toes of sleeping angels,
Their outstretched arms weighted by harps of stalactites
Anchored at the shoulders by giant beads of frost,
Threaded by the breath of ghosts.

Wrapped round their waists, flutes of parchment silk
Call the shadows of prophets from the gantry of cosmic dust.
Slowly, the angels breathe, their eyes flicker and sweep the bridge.

Leaping shafts of dancing colours vibrate,
Tuning, expanding the blue ice rivets.
A thousand saints sigh, a muted bell tolls

And all disappear into the spiritual light of pure thought.
Sandra Peacock

The Story of Life:

If you don't like your life you can rewrite the script
The storyline changed, the fuzziness clipped
New plots can be set and plans can be made
To create once again the part you'd have played

On the screen of the mind you can picture anew
All the roles that you'd play, all the things that you'd do
Sort them and test them and try them for fit
But choose with the heart the one that's a hit

For the mind is a tool that can easily fail
The illusions of glamour have a sting in their tale
Inside our heart is wisdom untold
If only we let its insight unfold

So rewrite your story as best as you can
And keep your mind set on achieving your plan
And never forget, if it doesn't go right
Return to the plot, don't give up the fight

Some stories become myth and ever endure
And touch people's hearts, perhaps open a door
Whatever you do, don't let go of your chance
To help one and all in life's rich romance
Noel E. Raine

Nature's Trespass

Picture now, the tranquil morn,
Rabbits emerging, of course, by pairs
Sniff the air with long-eared hare.
Dormouse stiffly climbs the corn
To catch the rays of sun's first warmth.

But life stood still, with the huntsman's call
Save one who knew, that to tarry, spelt that death was due.
The hounds come now in full cry!
Close by, the huntsman, vested red,
In hot pursuit of quarry that swiftly fled.

Like an arrow from a bow it went . . . fleet of eye!
One might just catch a glimpse of brown within the grass.
The urgency given by fox as he fled,
Gave a swift return of movement to world
Momentarily shed.

Back they return, more leisurely paced
Still scarlet-breast, though more red-faced.
Sweat-soaked flanks and lolling tongues abound,
Hounds, first passed at bay, now hang back.
Wily old fox, gone to ground . . . breathes life to run another day!
Jack Grainger

This Crazy World

I read the papers and I watch the news,
of family crisis connected with booze.
Battered wives and molested kids,
this is the world we have in our midst.

Children with guns and so high on drugs,
I ask myself—who are the mugs.
Is it really their fault for the lives that they lead?
it's prison they get when it's loving they need.

Where they're held, I'll never go back
I've kept in line and stayed on track
to be acknowledged as a player in a society lost
like the Big Issue vendors who trade in the frost.

But lying there as they do in their solitary detention
hoping and praying for God's intervention,
To take them away from her majesty's regime,
and lay them to rest in a field, in a dream.

How hard they pray and likewise they hope,
too many years of booze and dope
they failed themselves and toughened with pain
with nothing to lose and nothing to gain.
Anton Dempsey

The Sunflower

Beneath the light of the golden sun
The sunflower grows
In peace and gentle breezes
The young child blows
Smiling in the spotlight
Growing safe and strong
Spreading its roots in the soil of knowledge
Tasting right and wrong
Living through the wind and rain
Shining in the cold
Dancing in the garden of life
Standing wise and old
But time does kiss the face of youth
Weary golden eyes
The gardener comes to take his prize
And the sunflower dies.
Neil McCarthy

The Search

Am I a warrior? There's no fear in me—I am man!
But who Am I? I can't hide from my God's plan
My soul cringed within me to shut out the sight
Of myself, standing bowed, at the end of the fight.
I hate to kill! I hate to maim!
My name's not endorsed on war's hall of fame!

I'm one of thousands who stand looking on
Appalled at the loss of each mother's son.
For Christ is crucified time and again
He lies on the field with everyone slain.

My soul cries again, what man am I?
Tell me dear God before I die.
I yearn to do much but I've little to give
So show me the way for I want to live.
To learn, from your eternal design
The warp or the weft, which one is mine?

The message came quickly, from God above
Just love everyone—For I am love
You're in my family and there you'll be
One among millions—But special to me!
Frank Robins

Vultures

Greedy eyes watch the suffering
Like birds of prey tearing at what they see
A terrifying scene becomes a feast
They become fat and obese—
Morsels of information digested inside.

Later, they'll caw to friends
Details regurgitated one by one
Picking at scraps, adding flesh
To their grisly tale.
Long after the bones have gone.
Helen Prescott

The Inner Light

Behind closed eyes, doors open in expectation.
A kaleidoscope of perspectives incessantly intrude,
　to juxtapose the periphery of imagination.
Destinies sighted never to conclude.
Private lives free from life's complication.
Limits are forgotten and non-existent.
Intimate crimes are committed by the existentialist ego,
　as the wandering mind becomes omnipotent.
Swirling mists on mountainous landscapes billow.
As the storyteller's fight for supremacy remains persistent.

The face changes with the wearer.
The mask revolves around the Ferris Wheel,
　once more around the world wayfarer.
There will come an end as must to every deal.
Whereby a new beginning will last forever.
Gavin G. McIntosh

Memories

As I sit in my chair in the evening shade,
I reflect of days gone by, of the love and joy we
all did share, those precious days of yesteryear.
But now the birds have flown the nest, my
Dearest love, I have lain to rest. Now all I
Have is loneliness, you taught me to be strong,
Now I am alone, the ache in my heart, I have
To hide, as I look deep into the eyes
Of our daughter's child, thank you my
Darling for those wonderful years.
With peace in my heart as I climb the
stairs, I whisper "Good Night" my love
　Not goodbye, just God bless!
Edna Carter Sr.

My Secret Love

I'm in love with a man, so near, but yet so far,
Sometimes he so distant, sometimes he's so close,
But yet he should know, I love him most,
His mind is in a tangle, his heart is in a mess,
but I know, he doesn't love me best,
I've cried so many tears, when I've been alone,
How I wish he come and make this his home,
He's a caring and loving man, that I can tell
I'd do anything to bring him out of his shell.

He doesn't tell me he loves me, only that he cares,
And this is the burden I have to bear,
We've had a laugh, we're had a cry,
But this man I will love until the day I die,
I would move heaven and earth, if we could be together,
Then life could be like floating on a feather,
No matter what happens in life,
How and if we grow apart, this man will always,
Hold a special place in my heart.
C. Benn

Deborah

She made me confident,
She inspired my performance,
Like a true fighter I battled my fears;
She came like an angel,
When I needed some help,
She taught me to be brave and she wiped away my tears.
She made me believe,
She taught me to win,
Her lessons will stay forever in my heart;
She urged me to succeed,
She made it worthwhile,
Without her I wouldn't have known where to start.
I was like an injured soldier,
But she mended my wounds,
She was there for me, right by my side;
She took me to success,
She made me smile,
Now I believe in myself deep inside.
Thanks to her I am happy,
Thanks to her I've got confidence,
And now I just want her to know;
That I admire her a lot,
And I love her very much,
Thanks to her I'm the star of the show.
Debs.
Victoria Gearing

The Bird and the Tree

I am the tree, lonely in the field,
You are the bird who lightens the way
for knowledge and understanding each and every day.
But if I were the bird and you were the tree,
would I be able to teach you all that you've taught me?
All I know is always to be strong,
and if I ever need you I only need to pray that you'll
be watching over me every step of the way.
Samantha Smith

Peace

Peace walks alone through the streets of Northern Ireland
It is forever stalked by terrorism and fear,
The riots caused by religion year after year
Bring home the deepest, darkest fear,
That in this land of hope and fun
Smoke from bombs will cloud the sun,
And in the darkest hour of night
Our homes and neighbourhoods be set alight,
Blazing fires, burnt out cars
Policemen armed with metal bars,
The distant sounds of drums and flutes
Frenzied cries as people loot,
Business' and shops no longer there
Still they go on
Still they don't care,
When will it end
No one knows
But if will all unite, friends and foes,
We can create peace and make it last
Then fighting and killing will be a thing of the past.

Kathleen Dougherty

Pilgrim's End

I was the parched pilgrim who had traversed
the earth a thousand times. The weary traveller
who, having given up all hope of reaching home,
found it suddenly before me.
You were the light shining through the stained
window of our forgotten shrine. Your arms,
the branches of the willow that embraced me
as I stepped through your eyes. Your voice,
the gate that led me to your door.
How many times had I been there before?
Breathless, I watched it softly swing,
in the tired sleep of Autumn's dream.
But the winter wind watched too,
its whisper harsh with icy jeers.
With bitter breath it blew it closed,
and threw me back a thousand years . . .

Dorreya Wood

Happiness

Happiness is yellow,
It tastes like fresh bread,
and smells like a field of flowers.
It looks like a child playing by the sea,
and sounds like wind blowing through your hair.
Happiness feels like holding a newborn baby.

Natasha Cousins

What Is Flight?

What is flight?
Man's millinery dream, come true,
The crop of a field, after it grew
The life of an ill child, saved
A photo of this entire world so great.

What is flight?
Space and time defined,
Flying much faster than the sound,
Controlling the burning of fuel in a torch
The symphony of energies turning into force.

What is flight?
The fight of two pilots high, above the ground,
Thousands people dying quickly, if a war breaks out
Man rushing for miles in the air, when he feels the need,
Man travelling among the planets at high speed.

What is flight?
Only a step for the men of our times,
The joining in ecstasy of all sciences,
A human's gentle floating in the stratosphere,
The proof of him being the master of Earth, space and atmosphere.

Ioan Lehoczki

The Widower's Crime of Passion

Mind filled with anger, head shrouded in pain,
He batters the wall with his fists once again,
"Why was it you love?" He sobs—and cries—
"I should have been the one to have died."

Uncontrollable moaning from the depth of his heart,
For gone is the love of which he was a part,
With hands swiftly shaking, eyes streaming tears,
Memory takes him through beautiful years.

Leadened with anguish, the soul sadly burning,
Depressed, twisted mind, flickers infinite yearning,
In God and compassion, there is no belief,
There's no silver lining, in dark clouds of grief.

For weeks and months, living cold and alone,
Weight loss increased, from a pound to a stone,
When nerve finally broke, losing all pride,
A reflection of death, pushes life—to one side.

Lonely and hurt, pain turns to panic,
Actions are wild, somewhat satanic,
With a trembling smile, he draws back the knife,
For re-union in heaven, he takes his own life.

Christine Rooth

Garden of Love

Think of your heart my darling as like a garden fair
For I have planted lots of seeds of love and caring there.
I know within that garden there's been many storms and showers,
As I too in my garden have had my lonely hours.
But if within that garden you can find a quiet part
And feel the seeds of love I've sown grow within your heart,
Then surely as the sunshine that must come after rain,
Will help the love within your heart to learn to live again.
And then my darling we'll forget the darkness and the showers
Within the gardens of our hearts and share the sunny hours.
Then the seeds of love I've sown in that garden fair
Will surely grow to lovely flowers, two lonely
hearts can share.

Elizabeth Horsley

Don't Do It

Please don't interfere with my D.N.A.
The way I am, is the way I want to stay.
Don't plan for me a blue-eyed baby
Or take away my "if's" or "maybe's".

Don't tell me what to think or feel
I don't want the world to be virtually unreal
Don't force my brain to accelerate
While my physical body vegetates.

Stop the information technology
And data machine
Before they stop me from living
As a Human being.

Audrey Young

The Chindit

A seventy-one-year old man stands reminiscing at the cenotaph
Watching him move so slowly and often has a cry,
Wondering the reason why,
So many people had to die.

Standing proudly with medals galore,
This is what we show for war,

Where once he killed with his bare hands,
Now knuckles deformed with arthritic bands.

So have a thought for the old soldier,
Who put his life at risk
To give us our freedom,
So please put away your fist,
Let us all come together and say a little prayer,
(God Bless all you old soldiers everywhere).

Michele T. Scott

Wild and Free

Jet black stallion, hooves a stomping,
Upon the ground, as hard as flints,
The long mane flowing, nostrils snorting,
Whilst in its eyes, defiance glints.

Mother nature looks on fondly,
Upon this creature, wild and free,
No one's his master, that's for certain,
He stands there strong for all to see.

Then suddenly, from out of nowhere,
A neighing sound is gently heard;
A warming Whinney from out the darkness,
She has arrived, he's had the word.

Her breathing's soft, her coat is downy,
A jet black foal stands by her side,
She feels content and he is happy,
In mare and foal he shows great pride.

They walk away, whilst in the distance,
The sunshine glistens on the sea,
The stallion, mare and foal together,
The perfect union, wild and free.

Ricky Herridge

Jo, When You Smile

Captured by your eyes, spellbound in a trance,
Moments so few, yet taken by chance.
A brief encounter when you stop for a while
And the gentle innocence of a child when you smile.

My thoughts are lost, no sense of direction,
Angelic profusion, so soft your complexion.
In this world we live, where rainbows are rare
In your face bright colours for others to share.

A woman, yet a child, so vulnerable, yet strong,
In the stillness and beauty of a nightingale's song.
When the carousel of life seems to stop for a while
And the gentle innocence of Jo when you smile.

Imagine the warmth of the sun breaking through
Where dark clouds uncover an ocean of blue.
If only you could see what I can see,
If only you could feel the peace within me.

A lullaby of memories, each one freely given,
Wrapped as a gift in a silk coloured ribbon.
These things I see when you stop for a while,
These things I remember, Jo, when you smile.

Gerard Jones

Moving On

Tears dripping down my face,
Sitting on my bed base,
Empty room, moving soon,
How would I cope?

Knock at the door,
My heart hit the floor,
Who would it be, someone for me,
How would I cope?

He went silent,
My heart went violent,
Like a dove, my first love,
How would I cope?

He said goodbye,
I wanted to die,
He walked out the door, I fell to the floor,
How would I cope?

Get in the car,
Shouted my Pa,
Weston goodbye,
Devon hello.

Helen Burn

Why Her?

There she lies in the bed of death,
The girl that I once knew.
She seems so happy and full of life,
Until he said we're through.
I remember it like yesterday,
The blood upon the gleaming knife,
Plunged through her warm, soft, tender flesh,
Her lips now pale blue.
For four days she's been lying there,
and that's where she will stay,
No-one knew her like myself,
She said no-one else cared that way.
But I did, for I was her best friend,
and the pain I did share.
The mother bares no sorrow
for not even she did care.
But I'll always love her
from the start,
and from that day
she's been in my heart.

Alexandra Lewis

Random Thoughts

Amid the bustle of the world today,
No peace is the price we have to pay.
No time to notice the beauty of a tree,
With sprouting leaves, like golden filigree.
No time to linger to watch a tiny bird,
Trilling away melodiously, golden notes so seldom heard.
Just stop and watch a butterfly, when it comes to rest on a flower.
A beautiful thing, when you look at its wing
Lovely shape, jewel colours, full of power.

We can travel each day to every part of the earth
Get on the Internet too,
Jetting and surfing we haven't got time,
There is always so much to do.
But when all's said and done at the end of the day,
Most people I am sure will agree,
The best things in life, as they always have been,
Are generally utterly free.

Ruth Standbridge

Beauty Was There

The fist was about to strike.
A butterfly chose that wrist for a two seconds' home.
The hand opened in wonder to welcome the guest
Like a tiny god of the palm in a tender day
of a tender world.

Simina Danciu

Remembering (1914–45)

I sit in a warm room drinking German Lager
Made with spring water tasting clean and fresh
My mind dwelling on things I would rather
That we all appreciated and felt blessed
For many a man did his best.

Not so long ago under foreign skies
The sound of the bugle, midges and flies
Echoed and taunted the half living men
Who raised from the dead would fight again
And many a man would do his best.

Now I hear the groans of many who think that
They are under pressure, what from? Well wait!
The essay's deadline, "the showers broke", the bus was late,
The toaster's smoke, the rainy weather, the sagging breast
Oh but they do their best!

Next time you feel a little weak do not fret
Just think of the past but do not regret
Their lives they knew were given to save
Us from a dark unknown cave
Remember they did their best.

T. Palmer

Untitled

The candle flickers,
Casting its shadows upon the wall,
Mysterious, enchanting.
The girl watches,
Lost in a world of her own,
A world no-one seems to understand,
And nobody seems to care,

As she watches the shadows dance,
She thinks about her life,
A life of misery, and a life of regrets.
She's out of touch, out of reach,
She cries for help,
But no-one reaches a hand for her to hold.

Life is too much for her,
Too painful, too lonely,
But she's past caring,
She sees a light ahead,
Then it is gone,
And eventually as her candle fades,
So does she.

Sarah Bannister

In Silent Cry

As tumult abates—in silence profound—
Unmoving bodies litter the ground,
Grotesquely left for time to rot,
Their flames extinguished by musket shot.
In sightless stare at sun filled sky,
No tears to wet both drying eye,
Nor shudders none for biting fly,
Mouth's agape in silent cry.
To lie there a still—a frozen picture upon that grassy hill,
The shear insanity, the inhumanity, man's necessity to kill.

Mervyn Lewis

The Reaper

In the mist of eventide he rides,
His mount soaked with sweat,
Its mouth gaping wide,
Its eyes are ablaze with terror,
For its journey is to the end of never,
Across the abyss of time,
Looking for souls, maybe yours, maybe mine,
The rider grim a reaper is,
And gathering souls, the task of his,
Neath his visor is a hollow smile,
A wherewithal, his charges to beguile,
To some his coming is a welcome sight,
For others he comes like a thief in the night,
His coming heralds an end to pain,
Soft and sweet as a gentle most rain,
Peace at last in our last deep sleep,
No more tasks, or trysts to keep.

J. W. Clark

Marching to War

Young men march to war, their souls and spirits glowing,
Remembering things they saw, believing but not knowing,
Their families watch and wave 'goodbye' they try to hide their fear
The soldiers smile and say 'don't cry'
The day of war draws near.
Now sad and lonely, full of hate they think of things to come.
Quietly they sit and wait, their spirits are now numb
At last the wait is at an end, the soldiers start to fight,
Pleasant England they defend, through the day and night.
All is silent, non can tell, their souls are now at rest.
No one knows just where they fell, nor how they did their best.
Their bodies lie on ruined land, their blood, a deep, dark red,
A gun rests by their outstretched hand,
No memories in their head.
Now as the darkness falls the young men cry 'no more'
But no one hears their calls,
And still, men march to war.

Kathleen Hefferon

Retirement

I am here, I am aware
At last I have time to stand and stare
My working years are at an end
No rush, no bustle, take your time
A new world unfolds before my eyes
I stand at my window breathing in
The beauty of nature, how much to learn
I must make up for the time I missed
When to me a garden was a piece of land
Grass to cut, seeds to sow, it was a duty
I did not know, my garden was a living thing,
I was too busy to see, God was working miracles,
But now I know, He is there
In everything in every way
Buds bursting, flowers unfolding, beauty all around
Sparrows, blue tits, starlings, wrens
Filling the air with sound
Each day is now filled with the rarest pleasure
How thankful I am to be able to be
Away from the struggle and striving
Peace is now in my heart O, Lord let it last.

Rhoda Brown

Twins

"Go away" I'd scream, she was always there,
My twin sister always had to share.
We had to go to the same places,
People would stare at our identical faces.

We'd have to wear the same clothes, hair and things,
Same bracelets, badges even the same rings.
Our school marks had to be the same,
She was intelligent, I wasn't,
And as always, I was to blame.

So you can imagine her being centre of attention,
People would treat me like "the dull cup on the shelf";
But now I'm thirteen I've found out,
What sisters are all about.

Louise Wride

Growing Up

Growing up is such a drag,
Following the trend is being sad.
Having many things to do;
Be it at home or at school.
Parents shouting all the time,
Sometimes you want to willow and die.
Getting heartache from everyone,
Not knowing when there will be none.
Having trouble at school,
Not knowing what to do.
Crying yourself to sleep at nights,
No one cares, no one's in sight.
Having to hold onto memories,
That may never ever be . . .
Seeing yourself old and grey,
Is growing up all it's cracked up to be?

Ozlem Yikici

The Forest Is Dead

I remember a sweet time
A gone time,
A time before
Woodcutters strode into the forest
Brandishing their axes.
They started hacking away at the trees
Until they cried out with pain.
Then they fell, never to stand again.
The goats came eating the trees' bark
Until they were bare.
Then, one by one, the trees gave in and fell.
The monsoon came
And pushed the soil away
With its iron strength.
The forest was dying.

Daniel Francis Vaughan Howell

My Son

It is not to hurt
that I correct you

And not to control
that I guide you

It is not to curb
that I discipline you

And not to possess
that I protect you.

I know the world and I am anxious

As your mother and friend
I wish no ill upon you

I have experienced the struggle to survive
each moment—a test of my endurance

As I watch you develop and blossom
as I behold again life's miracles

I try to instill a sense of balance
so you may avoid the pitfalls of the extreme

Son, I have naught to give but these humble tools
with the dearest wish that you can build a future

... Better for yourself and better for the rest.
Shobha Sud. Banerji

Magical Moments

When we first meet.
You touched my face with just sweet, tenderness:
You looked into my eyes
and I looked back into yours
and my heart skipped a beat the one moment, I was yours.
Two very different cultures one coming from the East.
And the other from sunny south
But what does it matter
Mother Nature, did her best
Two hearts that beat together
Two skins that aren't the same
But love that found each other.
Now only to decay:
Spring time and old cherry blossom
gently drifting into the wind
and old church bells swiftly
ringing for all the world to see

And beautiful magical moments,
When you placed the gold wedding band on me.
Our, love would last forever and will always be.
W. Joy

Impression

Thinking of what's happening around me
the lives of old and new
what impression is this massacre leaving on me and you

The playground behind our house was a join of every nation,
a child would never sit alone ever in desolation,
and let the colour of his skin reflect off his crystal tears.
Joined together we stand
and refuse to in—a—vengeance hide our
deepest darkest fears.

A shudder shook the land that day
as the explosion once again took place
Every child's expression dissolved no more
Soft, radiant and full of grace.

The playground where I used to play has faded
silently drifted away.

Why couldn't we all just turn back time
to unravel, expose who really committed this brutal crime

This savage dispassionate analysis is becoming increasingly
true the real answer is the balance of cruelty can often rest
with me and you.
Joanne Doudican

Genicide

Night hits with a thick darkness
Shivering sheep scattered across the mountain side,
Hear the red wolves's howls rise and subside,
Suddenly flock and pack collide—
confused sheep run but few find to hide
Bloody tide coming in across the mountain side.

So easy for the wolves it's a game like—
winning a race against the lame:
Sheep's frantic crying slowly dying into silence.
Red wolves march on glad of their violence
Bloody tide running down the mountain side.

New sun shines to reveal the field—
decorated with empty twisted bodies
smeared with blood and paw marks.
Their eyes wide open still searching
for their shepherd.
A frail lamb in a corner licks his dead mother
already rotting into the soil,
Bloody tide seeping into the mountain side.
Elaine Woolmington

My Dad

My Dad was special and I miss him every day
He died when we still had so much to say
He was my friend, my confidant and always on my side
He was someone in whom I knew I could confide.
He lived to be eighty, so I shouldn't complain
But that doesn't always take away the pain
I sometimes feel that I've lost part of me
There's this big empty space that no one can see.
But then I remember the good times and smile
Even laugh out loud, every once in a while
You could rely on his wisdom, his endearing ways
He could make the sun shine on dreary days.
I hope my children will look back some day
And remember me in the same loving way
So I'll try to be a bit more like my Dad
And hope I can give them as much as I had.
E. Cameron

Change

I hate it, I detest it like the spider,
Its silvery web engulfs me, smothers, chokes me.
Closing in, ever tighter and I am defenseless.
I see it from day to day,
In a face once young and tender,
Flowers in bloom, trees in seed.
I too am changing, I notice it too often,
Not really for the better, but because it is expected.
Yet I tell myself, life would not be without it,
Everything would cease to exist,
I would have no dreams, no future,
And my past would be the day to come.
So although it saddens and upsets me,
I must sit and watch until the day I die.
Caro Cooke

The Things I Cannot Say

I used to be glad, but now I'm sad,
My life began like an open book,
But now I take a second look.
I've made mistakes, haven't we all?
But now I feel like the biggest fool.
You say that one day we'll be fine,
I wan to know, what happened to that life of mine?
Is it the end? Or just the start?
All I know is the pain in my heart.
I have my children and I love them so.
But what are you? Friend or foe?
This question I've asked time and again
But still my heart is filled with pain . . .
So tell my now, what can I do?
When all I've ever known is you.
Joanne Graham

Human Emotions

People smile and laugh
To express pleasure and amusement,
The instinctive elements of emotion.

We are a social species,
Nobody invented laughing or crying,
No more than walking or sleeping.

Humans are aware of themselves,
Comprehend the past and future,
Feel pain, sadness and confusion.

Laughter and tears are defence mechanisms,
As are happiness, joy and contentment,
And relieve the brain's emotions.

These feelings when shared are the strength,
Creating a social bond between individuals,
Receiving and giving help and comfort.

Babies cry and laugh to themselves,
Soon win a loving response from their parents.
All these basic emotions are part of our human heritage.
Milly Saunders

Save Nature

Save the beauty of nature;
Because it's our treasure,
Which is helpful for our future;
Don't destroy living things pleasures

Look at the sandy deserts of heat,
where the temperature is hot on your body and feet;
place where no one can meet;
and nature is left to heat.

Save the world's environment;
where Sun, rain and Moon are entertainment,
for our Earth's contentment.

By keeping our Earth clean;
and beautiful when seen;
where we'll love to live and dream;
also keep our minds from ruin.

So save our Mother Earth;
Don't you think it's worth?
Understand this poetry;
and save Nature from misery.
Mohamed Fazloon

Hommage to Nature

The sweet magnolia,
A goblet of white wine,
Of the purest colours,
Of foliage quite divine.

With heavenly stretching arms
To capture the golden sun.
Oh, come let me caress you,
And eternally praise your springtime beauty.

A set of graceful swans
Swimming on the breeze.
How angelic and voluptuous,
How pretty are these.

From lime green pegs holding washing,
To full grown curvaceous tightrope walkers,
Bring them out from behind the evergreen,
Set them off against the beach,
Let the sun reflect their pale innocence,
The carefree, the individual, the dignity of each.

A luminous virgin crowd, a full branch, and a full tree
A flutter, a sighting such beauty to you and me.
Rachel Russell

A Child's Gift

A child can be so very thoughtful
Bringing small gifts for you
Brightening up your darkest hour
In the things they say and do.

Giving a painting from the classroom
That was especially done for you
Rembrandt, he could not paint better
This picture means the world to you.

To make in school your special cards
Mother's day and Christmas too
It's made so careful and given with love
A child so proud, it's just for you.

A child loves to gather flowers
A daisy chain to make for you
To pick a posy of wild flowers
All these things say "I love you"

If you're feeling sad and lonely
Then a child lights up your day
With these small gifts so freely given
I'm now so happy, I love you too.
C. H. Molton

Filipina Smile

Filipina girl is everywhere, and for me,
A superabundance of breathtaking beauty.
But still, I have the time to observe;
Black hair cascading down one girl's chic figure,
The gentle breeze captures a flowing lock
And flies onto her face, as she turns.
So pretty, as she thoughtlessly smiles and brushes
The glossy sable over her shoulder in a familiar gesture.

The warmth remains in her deep brown eyes and curving lips
When she notice me, walking toward her.
And truly, I cannot help but beam my greeting
Indeed, I would want to do nothing less for this enchantress.

With felicity she greets this handsome foreigner, and it's
A kind of special magic, the very essence of Asia,
The most beautiful reason for being alive
To receive all the warmth of her soul
And gaze upon such lovely gorgeousness,
Aglow with true friendliness, just and only for me.
A smile to light my heart, so natural, so free
As we offer so much to each other, with our shared affection.
Leigh Billett

The Giver and the Taker

Two children were born on the very same day
But to a different path, each went his own way:
One grew up, and acquired great riches,
The other made his living by digging ditches;
One was mean and under hand,
This man was so hard to understand.
The other was kind, compassionate too
Loving and giving, to give him his due.
One took all, and gave nothing back,
The virtues of life, he did sadly lack.
The other was happy to share all he had
For his nature was giving, which made his heart glad.
So he said to the "Lord" look into my heart
Whatever you need, I'll be glad to impart".
So the Lord inspired his wealth ten-fold
For this man's heart was as pure as gold.
To the other, he said, "you will never know gain
For into this life, you brought nothing but pain.
For this is my law, and I am your Maker
For we reap what we sow, be it giver or taker".
Dana Shovlin

Who'd Be a Mum?

Who'd be a mum,
do you need to ask?
Everyday there is some new task
cooking and cleaning, ironing too.
There are so many things
that you have to do.

Can I have this mum,
Can I have that,
Can I do this
Can I do that?
You help with their homework,
just like at school.
Now don't you think, that's really cruel.

But with each new day, you carry on
trying to teach them right from wrong,
but when they say they love you,
and give you a great big smile,
it's then you know, that being a mum
Is all worthwhile.

Gina Holzherr

Hale-Bopp, April 1997

Stood in the garden, looking at the sky,
We watched entranced as in a robe of light
A shining visitor crossed the golden galaxy
Shedding its splendour on a warm spring night.

We know it has a name of all its own,
An orbit, and a history and a fate;
Its contents have been detailedly described
And we've been told its last, and next, appointment date.

Its last, four thousand years at least, they say
People who watched that robe of golden rain
Couldn't have dreamed of how their world would change
Before the starry guest would come again

Neither can we, in our own ignorance
Guess what four millennia will give birth,
Some say New Eden, demi-Paradise,
Others foresee a grim polluted earth

I like to think, whatever may befall
That someone looking on that bright-tailed star
Will see it, like the rainbow in the clouds
A messenger of hope come from afar.

Elsie Karbacs

The Maypole Dance

Reds orange pinks and blue
Greens yellow and purple too
Round and round off we go
Weaving in and out to and fro

Singing dancing so! Much fun
Now the dance of the maypole has begun
Oh! What a tangled weave we've spun

Laughing-singing-dancing so much fun
Bumping into every one
Dropping ribbons one by one
Now the dance of the maypole has begun

Thinking how! Can we ever get this right
Looking up—it's a terrible sight
We are told "it will come right in the end"
"Persevere" wow! It's driving us all round the bend

Oops! Wait a minute—it is taking place
The plaits looking lovely—with a smile on my face
It is! Coming together—at last it looks good
Well—it's only ribbon at the end of that wood

Mary Shaw-Taylor

Enchantment

Cold grey rain falls on the cold grey city
and cold grey people hurry home
seeking the light of fire and hearth
for shelter from the storm.
Some in this ancient hall
have crept from the storms of life
from the hurry, rage and strife that make our day.
Now, soft notes of music hang in the air
and resolve into harmonies rich and rare, and spread before us,
is a new creation, born of wondrous imagination.
A world of summer sun, of golden day and starlit night
fills the room with radiant light.
Fountains toss their sparkling drops
into the blue of summer skies
and shafts of gold stream over valley, rock and hill.
Restless waves lap gently on the golden shore
of this enchanted faery land
conjured from a great magician's hand.
And this magician, who is he?
Debussy.

M. F. Law

Passing Memories

As I glanced at a picture from the past,
Emotions came rushing back.
Songs and music triggered memories,
Back came those thoughts that I had banished as enemies.
On a tide of love they came and went,
Reminding me of the time that we had spent.
Lying in each other's arms,
Knowing that we could come to no harm.
Running fingers through soft glowing hair,
Loving in the knowledge you would always be there.
Why did it end? It still isn't clear.

I can't recall saying that I would take my love away,
I can still feel you in my mind every night and every day.
I never believed in soul mates and "it was meant to be's",
To me they were just fanciful dreams.
Thought up by those who couldn't handle reality.

We were so right, nothing was wrong.
Love and lust made us so strong.
As the old saying goes, all that is good must end.
But I still need your love, even if you give it as a friend.

A. A. Jones

Wake

The fading sunlight threw long shadows
On the hillside
And a hint of evening mist
Crept in among the hollows.
Radiant white cliffs
Dotted with small coves
And hidden beaches
washed by a blue and infinite sea
Beckoned to me.

Feeling listless in that special way
Particular to wet afternoons
Spent in plush surroundings;
I stand for a long time gazing out to sea.

I wonder how I am to fill
Such an expanse of empty time;
A moment of quiet panic
At finding myself alone at the top of the earth
Gives way
To the sense of
Being a long way from you.

Zahra Homeira Laidler

The Filey Brigg

It was in 1937
That I used to drive my little Ford 8
Across the Pennines in foul weather and fine
To go to Filey to see my heart's desire
Who lovest me.

And quite often we would take a walk
Hand in hand across the sand to see
The Filey Brigg—that rocky headland
Stretching out into the sea. And when the
Tide turned huge waves came bounding in
Bounding in relentlessly with such force and power
It was hard to see and to bear. But eventually
The tide did turn and there on the rocks were
Various sea shells and bunches of seaweed too.

But that was before we were
Married. How times change! Now love and
Marriage are as dated as the horse and
Carriage.

David Robertson

Big Black Ball

One morning I arose, looked through my window,
Stared in amazement at the newly cut lawn.
It was not the lawn that occasioned surprise
But what was on it: a big black ball.
Black as the ace of spades—even blacker.
I thought instantly of my neighbour's child:
Had he thrown the ball and left it there?
Imagine my surprise—the big black ball
Turned sideways, and appeared to my eye
A blackbird—which promptly spread wings.
And flew off . . . !

Ken Round

Patience

I sit miserably at my breakfast table
Impatiently, awaiting to be fed,
I subconsciously glance out through my window,
And spy a bird with a breast of red.
A little Robin is perched upon my fence
Cheerfully, chirping its happy song,
Obviously waiting to see a worm or grub,
Hoping his wait will not be too long.
But this little red breast has patience,
And will chirp for as long as it takes,
Until, in the garden, it spots a worm,
Of which a good meal it makes.
With feathers fluffed against the strong wind,
As no fire it has to keep warm,
It will perch for hours for one good fill,
In frost, or in snow, or in storm.
Why can't I be tolerant like this little bird,
And wait patiently for my food,
Sit happily at my table, whistle a tune,
Instead of starting each day in a mood.

P. Spencer

The Bread of Life

Bring to your old mother the bread of life
Good son that you are
Bring with your own two hands what it represents
Good son that you are
For only a mother's heart does know
The sweetness of the gesture
She has at all no need for words
Nor wild extravagances
She treasures not as you would think
Those trinkets that you give
All her heart sees without a doubt
Of this you can be sure
Is just your presence, your own sweet self
To her,
The bread of life.

Evelynne Goldberg

Silent Fear

I do not care to walk the streets at night,
more honestly, I fear too;
every passerby I furtively eye,
for fear stalks silently,
causing me to hurry
my stumbling feet.

How have we come to this sad state?
When no one feels safe anywhere.
Old people murdered in their beds,
children robbed by mindless yobs.
Destitutes, homeless, sleeping rough,
no families to care, no justice there.

The night is cold, but I am warm
with apprehension deep inside:
I feel so vulnerable and lone,
how I long to be safely home,
doors locked and windows barred
by my warm secure fireside.

Ruth Barclay Brook

Wet Revenge

I sat upon the garden stone
To draw and colour on my own
But she would not leave me alone
She swore and spat by the fence
This of course did not make sense
I sat there twiddling my thumbs
Wondering what have I done.
I thought . . . And I thought again
I have done nothing . . . Nothing to her
Well that's it, I've had enough
Of that idiot acting tough
Now it's my turn to get rough
I've got the jug of water
Which is sure to sort her
Now she's wet
And looks like my pet
As for me I had the last laugh
Yes sir-ree

Tracie Thyer

Hilsborough

Disasters happen, but not like this.
The worst in football history,
I guarantee this.
Flowers now are laid, and tears are still shed.
Over Hilsborough many, many, dead.
Mistakes have been made,
and lessons now are taught.
Is it then too much to ask, for a minute's
thought?

Mark Lee

Mining Memories

I remember phantom figures in the gallery's dust filled gloom
And the dark forbidding underworld where miners' cap-lamps loom
I remember the coal conveyors down roadways dim and dank
And the banter in the cage when miners were coming to bank
I remember the blue scared colliers at a spitting fossil face
And the fear of firedamp igniting in that subterranean place

I recall the towering stacks belching noxious smoke and grime
The shapeless seething canopy that was a symptom of the time
I recall the railway sidings and tang of wet steam coal
The rusty iron footbridge beneath which wagons used to roll
I recall the terraced houses along a hillside dark and bleak
The choirs and the brass bands formed of a culture quite unique

I recollect that time of turmoil when strikes were all the rage
When pickets barracked in unison for the right to a better wage
I recollect the sight of cloth-caps like cobblestones on a square
When news about the closure was more than most could bear
I recollect that melancholic morning when a mining tradition died
When pit-head wheels stopped turning and hard-bitten miners cried

Kenneth Charles Francis

Untitled

I never knew a new dawn could bring sadness.
I never knew the stars would cease to shine.
But he is no longer living;
And the fault is mine.

I stay in my room and I cry and I pray,
And I say that I'm sorry, all the time.
But he is no longer here to hear it;
And the fault is mine.

I'll never hear his voice again,
Or the doorbell merrily chime
His arrival; he's dead;
And the fault is mine.

I drove him to do it, I know this;
And I wish I could take back my words.
But he can't be reached, he's gone on;
And it hurts.

Margot Stanislas Marie-Fleur Rowland

Blindman

Blindman, lead me from this restless soul
   that lies beneath thy wake,
take me from the demon, which the devils
   slaves shall make.
Show me where the beauty lies and
   love surrenders all,
guide me from the heart of which my
   spirits slowly fall.
The world I see is complex, the vision
   hath hold will stay,
yet the path of truth is dark and
   obscured,
Blindman, forsake your eyes of courage
   and help me find the way.

Kerith Pepperdine

Home Views

As I survey the skyline o'er,
I see the Hill of Dinedor.
On the horizon and graced by the slope,
Is the church of Bullinghope.
Looking to the West, when I desire,
Peeping through is St. Martin's Church Spire;
Partly shrouded by trees in full leaf,
This scenery is sometimes beyond belief.
Much nearer to home, and at its height,
The River Wye comes into sight;
Flowing briskly, and with such charm,
Through the green fields of Bartonsham Farm.
Looking North, I can admire
St. James' Church and St. Peter's Spire.
So when I regularly look around,
I realise where such beauty is found.
Now as I examine this poem with care,
And think of the joy from these landmarks I share,
I sincerely hope that they will remain,
As I shall not pass this way again.

Trevor Vaughan

Time to Sleep?

When the sun goes down and it's time to sleep
When it all goes dark and my memories creep
When I hear you breathing deep and sound
When there is nothing to see I look around
Into the shadows of my mind and heart
When I realize we're together never to part
To be with each other 'til our lives are spent
When suddenly it's not just a dream I've dreamt
I cuddle you just to have you near
To remove all despair and any fear
Of losing you—now I know it's not true
To have you close 'cus I love you

Sally Burtenshaw

Polluted Life

A river flows down a valley.
Over a mountain until it reaches
The huge open sea.
A tear flows down the lonely cheek
From the lonely eye, of a lonely mother.
Tears creep for hours on end.
A symbol of sorrow; of love,
And of mourning.
Rivers crawl ever lasting
A symbol of life of freedom,
of movement.
But now we realize
in the darkness of death,
in the horror of murder,
that the river is murky
It's dark, jet black.
The river is polluted,
like all the people.
The river is polluted,
A symbol of their death.

Elizabeth Phipps

True Love

True love means many different things
The instant love and bonding one feels for a child.
Love and passion for your man that almost drives you wild
A deep and lasting love which continues
until you both grow old.
A trust between the two of you
A silent look—a dream come true
To share the good times and the bad
and laugh at all the fun you've had!
To share grief and pain but still
smile together again
This is true love a commitment to each other.

Annette Childs

Friends

Friends are special and unique beings
that embrace warm care when hidden
deep feelings need to share, without
despair that lingers in the atmosphere.
Yet yearns for a trust and reinforcement
that the other partner is just and faithful
that is not painful.
Joy is like a musical instrument that
rhythms and synchronises in tune.

Love is the greatest unique gift that is
forever true, sent by God which is especially
for you.

Francisca Adedoyin

The Prophet

The prophet came in a ragged Barbour
and I heard what he had to harbour.
Leaning on a gnarled old staff
he mocked the world with grunted laugh.
Gazing at the foam flecked stream
he spoke his lines as if in dream.
With Monte Cassino's ears and dodgy heart
he read his lines and played his part.
For him the world was full of laddies
and things were run by weak chinned baddies.
"They couldnae raise an army noo,
the future's bleak that much is true."
The world was washed up, our country bled
and he well knew his creed was dead.
His autumn gone his twilight near
he'd meet the end with scornful sneer.
As he left, his smile was wry
I think he knew he'd burst the lie,
the naive dreamings in my head
and placed his bitter gloom instead.

Bruce F. Downie

My Rocking Chair

You're always there to comfort me, at the end of a tiring day,
You bring me happy memories, and take all the sad away.
You soothe away my troubles, and ease away the fear.
And gently rock them all away, until they are no longer there.
And when tomorrow comes, and the day is near its end,
I know you'll be there waiting, my dear and faithful friend.

Jane E. Watson

Timing

When I was young there was a park
with a big green roundabout.
It had four long handlebars
evenly spaced for holding onto.
The older kids didn't need to hold on,
they could jump on and off with ease.
When they made it go fast I would cry
and beg to be let off.
They called me "baby."

The greatest trick of all was to run and jump
onto the spinning roundabout.
Timing was the key.
You had to pinpoint your spot, get your speed just right,
find your opening and run.
It all seemed so dangerous to me.
What if I should fall, or miss my spot, or collide
with someone already on?
And so I never tried.
I just skirted around the edges
of the spinning green roundabout.

Bernadette McFadden

Time after Time

I lie close beside you, I feel your soft skin
I hear your heart beating so true
In Rhythm with mine
The warmth of our love comes through
Time after time

You stroke my face, my neck and my back
I love the feel of your fingers
Entwined with mine
Your love for me lingers
Time after time

We walk hand in hand, talking and laughing
Our eyes meet and stare deeply
I know you are really mine
We kiss lovingly and gently
Time after time

Our love is so strong, a bond for life
We were born for each other
Together our love will shine
You are my best friend and lover
Time and time

Ruth S. Foster

Ben

The colour of watered jade reflected off the ground.
A shuttlecock glided past the sun.
A lonely figure under the apple tree
Shadowed by sadness, twisted by sorrow,
Eyes like rock pools, harbouring thoughts,
Yearning to play.
Friends have been lost by this figure
Scared of the truth.
Crying out in silence, but no signs of emotion
Invisible to the naked eye.
Wasting the life that wasn't to be.
Trapped in a world of eternal loneliness.
Tortured by an overhanging cloud of darkness
Floating in waves of diluted memories just out of reach.
Looking at a world within a mirror of dreams
Only to be shattered by reality.
Dry tears burnt his face
Against the mild summer sun.

Rebecca Houghton

Sunset

In the evening, as day was ending,
As sky and horizon were blending
Both together, it did seem
As though I were seeing a dream.

The sun was the colour of burnished gold
With clouds that seemed themselves to mould
Into shapes beyond compare,
With colours that I'll try to share.

Several different shades of blue,
Pink, yellow and orange too.
Light grey, dark grey, even jade.
So bright they surely could never fade.

I hope that I've made you aware
Of all the beauty that was there.
The loveliness up in the sky,
The day my beloved wife did die.

Frederick J. Hollingsworth

An Ode to the Old

We spent our youth during World War Two,
Blood, sweat and tears were nothing new.
Now it seems we were born too soon,
Perhaps they'll send us to the moon!

In the Battle for Britain thank God for the few,
Brave young pilots, day and night they flew.
In every family lives were lost,
We're here today because of the cost.

In those days we had to be bold,
Don't write us off just because we're old!

Maud Fletcher

The Wounds of War

He marched down the roads of hell,
He stepped on bloodstained rocks,
He was only a boy, but he was a soldier,
Who had seen the wounds of war!

He had seen the living nightmares of hell,
The grasping coldness, the devouring hunger.
He had seen the cruelty of man against man,
The decimated bodies of the dead,
He had known the wounds of war!

He had felt the sadness that had swept the land
And felt bitter anger, the overpowering hate,
He had wanted revenge with a madness that conquers all.
He had felt the wounds of war!

As he marched down the roads of hell
Tears dripped from his hardened face,
There was the crack of a gun, a trickle of blood,
And the boy suffered no more
The wounds of war!

Audrey Kearney

Dreamland

I am the dream that never never dies
I am the dream that embodies the mind
I am the dream that lives for tomorrow
I am the dream that lives for today
I am the dream that lives for now
I am the dream that needs to be fulfilled
I am the dream that needs to be satisfied
I am the dream that is made of desires
I am the dream that the soul beholds
I am the dream that needs to be beholder
I am the dreams that yearns for life
I am the dream that needs to be lived
I am the dream of love's passions
I am the dream of joys and wonders
Because I am the dream, the dream is me
The dreamer of them all.

Tehseen A. Khan

Sorrow (A Painful Memory)

And the power ebbs away . . .
. . . like a child dying in a mother's womb . . .
As the blood turns bad
And the world grows sad
I cry . . .

As the sun melts away . . .
. . . like cool ice on a sunny day . . .
As the frost bites
In the cold nights
I cry . . .

Snow storm blows wild . . .
. . . like a windswept hair-do . . .
As the stars disperse
As I change a verse
I cry . . .

Shadows dance before eternal flames . . .
. . . like a loved one's bad memories . . .
As I once thought they filled my heart with song
They now fill my heart with woe
I was wrong

Kelvin Mayes

Christmas Day

It only seemed like yesterday,
When we saw the stockings hanging.
Running down the corridor and down the steep stairs,
Though the hall and past the door,
A Christmas tree against the wall.
Eyes wide,
Faces surprised,
Turn the paper, open the box,
A football, a doll, no a jewellery box.
Surprise, surprise,
What a day.
But now it's gone gone, gone away.

Jennifer D. Jones

A Mother's Heartache

Every time I look at your photograph my heart aches so much
I long for your presence, I long for your touch
I think about how you'd look, and the things you'd say
If only, oh if only, you were here with me today

I imagine myself reading to you and singing you to sleep
The ache in my heart goes so very deep
I think of the time that we spent together
I thought then that it would last forever

Sometimes I feel angry, why did you leave me?
But then it wasn't your fault, you were only a baby
You were so small and fragile and yet so brave
And how great was the happiness and the joy that you gave

Time is a great healer, or so they say
The pain will slowly but surely fade away
But how long must I wait to know that it's true?
When will I be able to smile at the memory of you?

C. A. Perkins

Feelings I Have

I dream of no bracelet, or a gold or diamond ring,
I dream of no money, which near love, costs nothing.
I dream of a small, silent house only for two,
Where you can only love and there's nothing else to do.
Everything I want, my love, is to be yours and mine,
I care about nothing else even if the sun doesn't shine.
I know we could die, but since we're together,
To me, death means life for now and forever.
As since we're two hearts acting as one,
There's nothing ever that can't be done.
Even if it comes to picking a star from up high.
I would do it, I'll be so brave, but never shy.
Because, my love, I only do it for you,
As I know when I need love, of course I'll turn to you.

Deena Mohamed Sherine El Attar

Depression Lifts

Hardship and troubles lay deep in her mind,
Worries and problems weighed heavy.
Laughter and happiness both far behind,
She wondered why she paid the levy.

But strength of her character made her fight back
From sinking to depths of despair,
Although in her life, of good luck there was lack,
She knew of a friend who was there.

So she looked at the leaves on the trees and the sky,
Both beautiful, green and blue splendour,
And emotion brought more than one tear to her eye,
As nature had come to befriend her.

Sometimes despair hovers round us so much,
It's unfair, some get more than their share.
Until warmth and love put us right back in touch
With the things for which we strongly care.

Joan Crutchfield

Life

Life has loveliness to sell—
All beautiful and magnificent things.
Blue wave whitened on a cliff sways, and sings.
And children's faces looking up
Holding wonder like a cup.
And for your spirit's still delight,
Holy thoughts that star the night; for one hour of peace
Counts many a year on strife well lost,
But it and never counts the cost; what does this mean?

Freedom is cheap or again
As a garment is so costly, men pay their lives
Rather than not have it.
Life has loveliness to see—
Music like a curve of gold,
Scent of pine trees in the rain,
Arms that hold,
And for a breath of ecstasy
Give all you have been or could be.

Claudia Secrieru

Millennium

There was a ghostly frost
Covering the earth.
It matched the paling faces
Of all who waited.

The air was humming with anticipation.
The moon and stars were cold and bright.
The dark sky was a menacing cloak
Concealing the future that night.

The clocks began to chime the hour.
The world stood silently still
Stricken with fear of what God would will
On the eve of the year 2000.

Gabrielle E. Roberts

Memories

You asked me about my life?
The answer: They're working days five,
There's a big coffee in a quiet morning,
With a cigarette, if I'm smoking.
I'm talking sometimes with friends,
About things which never end,
They're plans but they'll never happened,
And a reality that seems always a battle.

If you're curious I'll show you,
The difference between your past and this morning,
And you'll teach me how to hide my emotions
Behind a curtain that offers me
The feeling of false security.
But what you really want is to make me
To recognize that you conquered me.

Peli Margareta

Me and You

Down, into my deeply heart,
With shadows and screams into the night
I see the face, I see the light,
I see in you, in your heart
The crying blood.

   I feel again the love, inside,
   Inside your brain, inside your heart.
   I look at you, with tears in eyes,
   I suffer for the dirty smiles,
   I cry.

But everything is blue and black,
I live into the smog, into the dark,
Is like the baby loose the precious Mom
Is like my heart became a rock into the mount
My eyes are now with your face, with your lips,
   with your smile,
I die.
   But I loved you, with all my heart.

Nina Muresan

The Star That Shines So Bright

Don't cry a precious tear,
From behind that cloud a smile will appear,
Keep that smile upon that precious face,
Them stars will come out in eyes,
To find the happiness that lies in the skies above,
So never feel down, you will always be here in my heart,
Please stay strong, someday we'll meet again,
Up above the stars that shine so bright,
No-more hurt, no-more pain
You're safe now, so rest in peace,
So please keep shining like the star that you are.

Kirsty Jane Berryman

Feelings

I'd like to know how a person felt,
What they really felt inside
What their hearts were saying but their lips were not,
The feelings they were trying to hide.

I'd like to be able to read their minds,
See what thoughts were really going on,
Inside the whirlpools of their mind's eye,
Thoughts there for a second—then quickly gone.

I'd like to know if they felt the same way as me,
What life seems like to them.
See if they feel as I do,
And get confused now and again.

If just for once in the rush of living,
They stand still for a second and think,
What other people must be feeling;
If they stand on realities brink.

Jennifer Cooley

Peace and Harmony

Freedom to the people of every creed,
Power to those who say "Live and Let Be"
Music is the language everyone understands,
So stand up and clap your hands.

We don't need your aggression,
We hate your oppression.
We don't want your war,
So why you crucify our laws.
Music is love, music is live,
So listen to this sound advice.

The lyrics are water that always flow,
So listen to the words and feel their soul.
The world is in chaos, we live in a haze,
If we get it wrong the world will be ablaze
So let's all live in Peace and Harmony

Jeffrey Michael Church

My True Feelings

It comes hard for me to say
   how I take for granted the beauty of this world we live in
every day.
The sun that shines so bright and warm
   these gifts for free when we are born.

The flowers and trees; animals too
   joy of life for me and you.
My eyes to see, a scent to smell
   flowers and rain, grass as well.

All free to roam the countryside
   or on a park where children slide
   with merry-go-rounds to take a ride
   or on the swings and climb so high.

The air around we breath inside
   our Church, our faith we mustn't hide.
I thank our Lord for my life on earth and that I share
   with love and feelings in my prayer.

Malcolm Nobbs

Love

Love swept over me like waves on a shore
My feelings for you I am definitely sure
it caught me by a big surprise
So quick, as quick as sunrise

You don't feel the same
I know this as well as I know your name
You don't care for me at all
You never have and I know you never will

I can't fall out of love with you
I can't forget you, there's no button stop
Besides it's set on start
I'll die if we're kept apart.

Sarah Huntington

You Went Away

The days seem long
Nights so cold
My love for you I now unfold

You are gone away, just for a while
I miss you darling, your warm sweet smile
Our land and sea, you will come to me.
I'll wait for you each night, and day
And when you return, you will hear me say
Darling I love you with all my heart
Stay by my side, never let us part.

I look round the room, the empty bed,
The dent in the pillow where you rested your head.

Yes I dream a while, of our love and bliss
The tears in your eyes, at our farewell kiss

Oliver O'Hanlon

Sundown

Enshrouded in the aureate glow of eve,
As the Sun's final rays, arc, spiralling skyward to the stars,
Beyond the horizon a wonderful rainbow of opportunities
appear then disappear,
Falling as a tree shedding leaves.

Transparent Moon's pallid hue,
Like Onyx cut wafer thin, quivering in the hot night sky,
Surrounded by uncut Diamonds, flashing with brilliance then
fading to die,
As Cloud obscures my view.

Flash of lightning, peal of thunder;
The sky again illuminates, as sheet steel, machine pressed,
rolls, reverberating across the ether,
The caterwauling of forgotten souls, bemoaning their fate,
berating one another,
Captivated, entranced, I gaze in wonder.

C. Watkins

Untitled

Do you remember the ones who died,
In world war one and two?
I also think of those who survived.
The question is, do you?

We say prayers and have a bid bay,
For the men who died fighting for us.
Yet when it comes to those who survived,
We don't seem to make a big fuss.

These are the men who have nightmares.
The ones who lost all their youth.
Shouldn't they be honoured more often,
Isn't it time for the truth?

The young don't care for the old.
And the old may look down on the young.
Some people don't care at all,
If these men's bravery goes unsung.

Therese Breen

Beach Sunset

The sun goes down through a deep red sky,
The waves crash and the seagulls fly.
The sands are coloured golden-brown,
The cliffs are faced with a rocky frown.
The sun is covered by wondrous clouds
In little bundles of fluffy mounds.
Isn't it a wonder the sea never dies,
Isn't it a wonder the sands always fly?
As the seagulls fly back home,
The sea grumbles with a little moan
The beach begins to realize it is alone.
As the night is drawing near
The blue-green sea is very clear,
With a glimpse of sparkle from the sun,
There is a sand-castle where children have been having fun.
There are a lot of questions that we ask,
Will the seas and sands always last?
Will the cliffs always frown?
Will the sands last as golden-brown?
These are the questions we will always ask.

Charlotte Read

Thoughtless Games

Scuffling noise and uncertain sound
Of Colonels hovering over artificial ground,
Plotting a battle for a war that won't end.
Killing off soldiers that they cannot amend.
Without all this confusion it wouldn't be fun,
The troops on the front line would not be over-run.
The radio goes and they tell you to move.
What are these murdering bastards gonna prove?
When will they realize it's not just a game.
That Colonels, soldiers and enemy are the same?
Man kills Man like Ape killed Ape,
It's not evolution, it's a total disgrace.
One day we'll all unite into one,
Only then can the Generals and Colonels call it fun.

Mark A. Maddock

Dad

It has been a long time since I held your hand.
When lonely and sad, you would understand.
The reality of losing you shattered my life,
Although a grown woman, mother, and wife.
Your pain, your suffering that lingered on
broke our family which I thought was strong.

Kindness, gentleness, calm and quiet
Peace and loving eternally bright.
All these things remind me of you.
Thoughtful, caring and never blue.

Your family has grown now and life has gone on
but I've lost a father, a very special friend,
thoughtful and caring right to the end.

Iris Thomas

Once Again It's True

Even though the sun declines each day.
Bidding and exacting that all fade away.
But in my inward eye eternal memories.
That are bounded for all the victories
The touching love of yours
Your kindness overflows
The tender look dissolves the pain.
My pensive nights didn't go in vain.
You set my mind and my soul free.
You made life mirth and glee
I am glad that memories are once again true.
I am glad I am back with you
And alone again I'll never be
Because a gift from God has been given to me.

Perryhan Mohamed Fat-hey

Maelstrom!

A new day brings new experiences, ideas, thoughts that add
to the maelstrom in my mind,
A maelstrom of swirling, churning emotions engulfing
everything in its path.
Through the mind's minute and intricate network of channels, I find
It following me, at every twist and turn, curve, and bend of life
It can soothe me like a balm, but can also cut like a knife!
It can make my spirits soar, make me light with ecstasy;
Or plummet me in the doldrums of despondency!
I wonder if I could ever break free,
From this vortex that shackles me,
That entangles me in its web of
Pain, passion, lies and ire
It never seems to die,
But burns like the
glowing embers
of a
Fire!

Phalguni Parikh

Ghosts in the Night

Ghostly bodies float around over villages into town,
Wispy hair and long white flowing gown,
Haunting places late at night giving folk an awful fright,
Spooks and ghouls make eerie sounds all around,
Clanking chains in dungeons heard, black as night the raven bird,
The bloody tower it is said you see the body then the head,
Piercing eyes and haunting shriek outside my window dare I peak,
Halloween comes but once a year time again for us to fear,
Seek the churchyard hallowed ground nothing bad can then abound,
My shadow follows me at night from lamps above through
misty light,
Watch the candles gently flicker makes the movement even quicker,
Creaking stairs and lightly tread rush the footsteps into bed,
Jumping into bed at night covers over head in fright,
Never venture out at night blankets over head held tight.

Jennifer Gymer

Peace

What is peace
Peace is when a crying baby goes at last to sleep
When a calf is born to a bellowing cow.
When a man storms out to go to the pub
After a family row
Peace is the calm one finds in a park
or a garden, the sent of flowers after dark
Peace is the joy at the end of a war
When lights go on and there's food in a store
A missing piece from a jigsaw purple
or the warmth of a dog when it gives you a nuzzle
Peace is the calm at the end of the day
When toils of life are put away
To put one's head on a soft clean bed
and clear off the place where loved ones meet
sure the greatest peace for man was given
by the Lord himself of a place in Heaven
a peace for the world in our prayers are asked
each nights as we fall asleep at last.

Margaret Vinell-Barnett

Days End

I was there
There in the wild
Where time was open and the music played
For the soul to enjoy as the rattle swayed

The rattle was wise, quite full of charm
So peaceful yet angry, as the day passed along

This rattle I respect
So elegant and wired
To the tune of time
So graceful entire

I stand here alone, not a passage of words
As the rattle now plays a song with new chords
I know not what to say or feel
The rattle of old had a charming appeal

For I must venture to places of new
Whilst the rattle now follows a more regular tune
Such parting sorrow and fear of release
As the rattle grows further a distance
A distance never to meet

Karl Neville

Alone

There's nobody left to turn too
Since my Nana passed away
She was the only one who loved me
And with her I wanted to stay.
The day she died I lost a friend
and failed to find another
For somehow nobody saw me
In the same way as my Nana.

My lonely life is like a tree
Who has lost all its leaves of trust and forgiveness
When I look back over the years that have passed us
And my dreams that will last always and forever
Breathing for my Nana in heaven
And hoping that someday soon we will be together.

I wish I were a bird so I could fly far, far away.
Away from my broken heart
And the problems that follow me everyday.
And everyday I hope and I pray
That the pain will go away
And that sometime soon love will find its way.

Rachel Leanne Watts

Colours

Sometimes when I wake in the morning
The colour outsides is Grey
And there are times when I wonder
How I will get through the day

Another day the sky will be Blue
With sunshine all Yellow and bright
So I go around with a smile on my face
And my footsteps are easy and light

I go to the shops and buy some food
Tomatoes so Red and cabbage all Green
I may even buy a flower or two
The prettiest Pinks that ever were seen

Oranges, Plums and a carton of Cream
A piece of White cheese and some ham
And to put on my Brown bread when I get home
My favourite Black current jam

My pet Ginger cat is a purring
His huge Amber eyes gaze at me
And I feel that I know what he's thinking
"Is there Rainbow trout for my tea?"

Kath Rogers

Bunty the Bully

Bunty was a bully at home and in the street,
His parents thought him clever and met his every need;
They showered him with play-things and pocket money too, but
Bunty was not happy, always wanting something new.

Bunty was a meek lamb the day he started school.
He smiled up at the teacher and thought—this one will do.
I'll get my way with teacher, the kids I'll manage too.
So I'll not need to worry, I'll battle my way through.

He whispered in the classroom a silly joke or two,
He flicked some balls of paper across to teacher's shoes,
Teacher looked at Jimmy—no play for you today lad!
Bunty smiled and lowered his head, the ugly little cad.

Out from school at luncheon time, the pupils skipped and ran,
And up and down the playground they teamed up into gangs.
From marble groups to ball groups, to skipping groups and all,
But no one wanted Bunty, he tried to rule them all.

From day to day, from week to week, the lesson Bunty learned,
That rules of good behaviour beget you many friends;
That sporting lads like Jimmy will surface to the fore,
While cheats, liars and weaklings will always walk alone.

Elizabeth O'Mahony

A Dark Walk

I walk on alone
On a dark stormy night,
Where the thunder and lightning cackle.
The clouds are now coming to
Alter the light,
And a blanket of black surrounds me.

The woods shield my light
Like armed knight on horseback
Trying to save me,
But the trees and bushes try to enfold me
And the leaves on the trees try to smother me,
And the branches that try to hold me are
Like the arms of a starved child.

The bats flying high
Like changing jumbo jets.
As a flash of traffic passes by,
Like a comet I have never seen,
It lightens my way,
My fear is at bay and I can walk safely home.

Dawn Evans

Peace

As a young soldier in the Second World War
And a Granddad now at seventy two,
Remembering the sacrifices made by the many,
And not forgetting those made by "The Few."

With some exceptions in fifty years,
Our world has largely enjoyed peace
Bought for us all, in the two world wars;
The price was great, for they gave their all.

The wars in the Falklands, and in the Gulf,
No less important in sacrifice made;
To maintain peace throughout the world,
The ultimate price by many was paid.

Let us never forget the debt we all owe them,
All those who paid that terrible price,
To keep us all free, to enjoy the peace.
May many happy years of peace increase.

It is now up to our countries' leaders
To keep this peace so dearly bought;
Our prayers we make to aid their guidance,
To you, our Lord, the Prince of Peace.

Bill Speake

The Climb

Eternity waits. Gaping there.
Nothing between us but sweet clean air.
Triumphant feeling as I cling
with aching fingers and sinews stretched
to their utmost, before the next step upwards.
Gently, slowly, unwind the rope
that holds each safe, or so we hope
and each on each depend our lives
until the end is reached.
Closely knit, minds, bodies, move as one.
Man trusting man 'til the great climb is done
and we stand now like Gods above slow moving plough.
Exultant feeling as I stand,
breathless, tired and aching
seeing with new eyes
the patchwork land.
And I feel big as the mountain
which we have conquered.
A giant looking down upon little people
and Lilliputian town.
Helen M. Colthorpe-Parker

Sunrise

The wind sears its icy path
across the bleak raw land;
screams in the tree tops;
scrapes the fields, all cold, wet and dead,
of crops devoid,
stark, stripped as far as eye can see of life,
except where the black rook horde drops,
or where a wandering gull wheels lazily
and the ragged scarecrow flaps arms crazily,
as if to warm his ancient wooden props.

A dead dreary scene as far as eye can see.

WAIT, what rose-flushed wonder paints the hill
What delicate shades and shadows gently spill
over the valley and then outward fan,
lighting the horizon's once gloomy sill
with rainbow shafts that shift and span
the hilltops with a dance of joy for man,
whose heart can break asunder if he will
behold the fire in the sky—the fire of life,
and, lost in wonder, so forget his strife.
Frank Allen

The Souvenir

Rolling betwixt, I catch a tear
And drink to taste its tiny breath
She knew I dreamt about her peer
She smelt it on me—wished me death.

Ah, but an autumn sunset soldier!
Whose pursed lips are soft and twee.
She slowly throws the hands that hold her
The woman simply walks from me—

(!a dream of red reamed cord!
to fray, the morning after yesterday)

She's left her jacket with me
The tide will soon be coming in
To stroke it out, to wash it free
Of rocks remaining in soiled skin.

I'm glad, you see, and curl upon
The still-warm flesh of clothing
And wonder at the running gone
And vow I smell

   Of nothing.
James McNulty

Don't Pass Me By

You look at me, wrinkled and old,
but with a lot of history yet to be told,
I had a life, once like you,
you'd find it hard to believe it's true!

I was young,
and had a great life,
but it was not without
its trouble and strife.

I met a man,
fell in love,
thought he was sent
from the Lord above.

We had four children,
now all flown the coop,
And I'm here alone,
with a tremor and stoop.

I know I'm old,
and maybe regressed,
but please talk to me,
you may be impressed.
Mairead O'Connell

Here Are My Moans

I'm on the way out. I suffer from everything except perhaps, gout.
Life is so precious when one is young and feeling well.
When one can hear birds singing and church bells ringing.
We cherish the things that come our way.
We take joy in events that occur each day.
So unaware of tragedies held at bay.
Life ahead is so quite vague and exciting
But it takes so long to become enlightening
Sudden tales emerge when one is old and frail.
Memory fails one, and one forgets what to say.
Faces remain families, the names we know no more.
We remember childhood, but forget the day before.
Our bones start creaking our knees become bent,
Oh, our faces, there is a new duet.
I feel like a robot with many new parts.
I've a hearing aid to hear and strong glasses to see!
I've an implant in my eye, a new pin in my knee
I now wear a wig—I'm almost bald with no hair
I lost all my assets there's nothing left there
Living to this age is not at all fun.
I'd like to fly away, alas, I cannot even run.
Sadie Williams

Have You Ever?

Have you ever been to Mars,
Flew past the faraway stars,
On a high, wishing could lie down and die,
In a World of fear,
You wish you could shed a tear,
On a boat trying to mellow out,
But all you can do is scream and shout.
Sitting in an empty room,
Sitting in a World of never ending doom,
You try to improve it with all your might.
But you realize you're slowly losing the fight,
With no-one to turn to,
You think of your life.
Nothing but endless strife,
You think of how it would be,
Well, try, but your mind can't reach that far.
You look at a distant star,
Thinking of your everlasting scar,
There's nothing you can do to heal it now,
You've ruined your life . . .
Victoria Louise Taylor

Sheltered Innocence

Raindrops like tears, softly falling from the sky,
You are so far away, I only wish I knew why?
I closed the door to innocence and walked into a world so bad,
Full of cruelty and despair, I never even knew that I had,
I was so young I thought that life was just one big game,
Now all I have left is a cold grey stone engraved with your name,

I put on a brave face every day,
Hoping all my troubles will fade away,
But soon the pain comes back from the dead,
I am haunted by every word that was ever said,
The faded memories are never completely dissolved,
The anger and frustration is never entirely resolved.

There is not much in my life I regret,
Except that once I began to forget,
I forgot the love you gave when I woke,
I forgot your smile when I told a joke,

Now sweet smelling flowers are a symbol of death,
Each one a reminder of the day you left.
There is nothing here to take my pain away,
Because never again will you brighten my day.

Theresa-Anne Squire

Let's Free the White Doves

Don't destroy my dreams,
My hopes and my future.
Let's free the white doves
For everyone's sake.

We want peace,
And — we want it now.
But without your help
The question is how?

Filled with dread,
Filled with sorrow.
Please make it stop,
Please now—not tomorrow.

Peace is what we want,
Why can't they see?
Don't they want it too?
Why can't it be?

"Peace in our time," was once what was said.
They thought it divine let's not be mislead.

**Let's free the white doves
For everyone's sake.**

Sarah Boyles

An Axe to Grind

A land that lives within the head,
the name of which has not been said,
where cradled from the sweeter seed,
the sparked and chiselled plans of need.

To mammoth lakes come warmer days,
our shackles forged to better plays,
and buried deep beneath the soil
the blood that flowed around our toil.

With common winds that torch and turn,
we'll watch the F.T. index burn,
and from all points beneath the sun
we'll blast the blarney spider spun.

Then rise like fury spreading wings,
to where the mountain rivers spring.
And where we high and mighty go
upon the springtime torrent's flow.

Teifion Paul Hughes

Memories

White frothy fingers ripple along the seashore,
inviting enticing offering much more
excitement and pleasure in clear blue water,
now remembering young son and daughter.

Cheeks kissed with sunshine and cornsilk hair,
sparkling eyes of these children with no care.
Bright coloured kites, buckets and spade,
sand castles and moats our children had made.

Shrieks of joy, giggles of delight
recoil in my mind when life seemed so right.
Piggy backs, donkey rides, games we would play,
like pillow fights, cartwheels and daisy chains in May.

Oh far off days seem so long ago
children have grown and had to go,
alone on the shore now white horses at sea
almost entice and beckon me,
but life goes on, there is much more
as white frothy fingers ripple along the seashore.

Elizabeth Squire

A Time and a Place

There is a time there is a time for everything
there is a certain time for a bird to sing.

There's peace on earth love in the air
and the joy we all share

There are people good and people bad
there are people happy and people sad.

There's a time for pain a time for sorrow.
Hope it will just be for that moment and not tomorrow

We see happiness we see life,
we see our children our husband and wife

A time for romance to be together
to love each other forever and ever

There's laughter from the children singing in the rain.
Going on the buses going on the train.

There's a time for always, we must give a little time to someone
who needs us to share their problems and to start having fun

There's a time for prayer
because people do care,

Time is all we have don't let us be enemies lets all be friends
Forever to eternity that means to the end

Janice Bond

A Forest Full of Trees

Was there ever a forest full of strong and
healthy trees I wonder?

When the first seeds were planted they
met with such resistance, it was
surprising that any survived, and yet some did.

They had the strength to grow because
they were resilient from disease around them.

They became firmly rooted in the good soil.

The sun shone on their branches and the
rain watered their roots.

The light breathed life into their veins
and they found nourishment.

And as they grew they shed some fertile
seed to keep the earth from becoming a
desert, and the wind scattered them widely.

B. Leamon

Through Granny's Eyes

The park lit up with summer sunshine
And nature's colours everywhere
I watch with pleasure, children playing
Youthful, happy, not a care

But these are someone else's children
So why should I feel they are mine
Something from the past shines through them
Turning back the sands of time

A sideway look, a smile, a gesture
Each familiar, every one
The little ways of one before them
They call him daddy — he is my son

In the years that are to follow
Others will do the same as me
Standing looking, thinking backwards
Remembering how it used to be

Little children, young and innocent,
Each a very special star
Why can't we stop life's camera rolling
And keep them just the way they are

Catherine McMullan

My Boy Soldiers

For Dean and Brett from Mum

Little boy soldiers wave at the gate
Uniforms smart, you must not be late
Boots highly polished, berets just so,
You wave again fondly and march as you go.

Paint on your faces, guns in your hands
I thank God it's not real, your fight for this land,
I pray in your lifetime you never will know
the horror of real war and fighting of foe.

Many brave souls were lost on the way
to bring us this peace we live in today.
We must never forget the suffering and pain
In the fight for this land that wasn't a game.

That we can be safe in our beds through the night,
So you won't leave me to go to the fight
And so my boy soldiers whom I love so dear,
Live your lives in true peace and never in fear.

Jackie Wickers

Assignation!

Within the semi darkness of murky waters
The prehistoric mineral, extracting its electromagnetic
beams of complexion,
Lay desperately waving on the outer limits
of existence,

The divine unexplained small native
Diving swiftly with the composed characteristics
of a swooping falcon hungrily seeking its prey.

I vibrated with Awe, as the solicitude,
Interspersed itself within my hemisphere
of respiration,

Emerging submissively, secured inwardly,
He held the jewel, my possessive casing of eternal
facility, constitution had become adjacent.

Silently, beyond defect, He ceased to exist,
with the realization, I consequently held the key.
Permitting me access toward the perception
of Interpreting the system and signals of communication.
I had become the assignee.

E. Preston

The Passionate Flames of Death

A dispassionate afterbirth of order in mankind
Of favouring males only is demeaning and crude,
It disturbs my soul and sickens the mind;
A barbaric choice shielded behind the Bamboo Curtain,
All because of an indoctrinated and sad tradition.

This wholly defies the convention rules of Geneva
Thus amorally strips all dignity from humanity—
By detachment of mother and child from one another,
So all mother virtues are systematically violated
For life can be cruel, but let not this be tolerated.

Once the male fish meets an egg, it blossoms with life,
Then one's own gender is laid down by Mother Nature:
Via procreation between the husband and his wife,
As total freedom does not exist without responsibility
In the light to appreciate reality more clearly . . .

Yet this culture defines that boys are best reared,
That reflects from the ancient pond of eugenic:
but eliminates the biology that cannot foster a beard.
So too, is it not viewed as a form of mass genocide
To allow the sacrifice of girl offsprings to die!

Casey Wan

Distant Places

Distant places, many strange faces
Street signs you can't comprehend
The people hustle, so much bustle
Under the shadows of the tall hotels
The screaming traffic, the cars' noises
frantic
The sound of their horns at you yells
Sounds unfamiliar can't fall to thrill you
The columns of vehicles never ends
be careful as you step on the
Pedestrian crossing
you take your life in your hands
They drive on the right side, not
The left side
In these faraway foreign lands
This novel experience will always be with you
It is said travel broadens the mind
We all want to eat, drink, and make love,
and live to be ninety two
We're all the same just like me and you.

M. Lyons

The R.A.F. Flying Instructor

"What did you do in the war Daddie?" "Taught people to fly Laddie"
"Like a Teacher in the class?" "No! In a tiger on the grass"
A Tiger Moth, a little plane, trainer plus—of wartime fame.
As tough as nails and rugged too. Let's fly away into the Blue.
Take off now and then we climb. Then straight and level for a time,
Turns, rate one, both left and right, Thro' a cloud, no sense of
height,
Stalls and spins and then recover. Loops the loop and then another.
Time now then to go back home. Where? Oh where's the
aerodrome?
Instructor knows, it's soon in sight. Left on circuit, never right.
Downwind leg now, level flight. Left hand turn to Crosswind leg,
Now throttle back and into glide. Engine quiet—oh, what a ride!
Gliding turn now—not too fast. Boundary hedges we soon pass.
All clear ahead, stick gently back. Ground rushes by—we're
on the grass!
So now we're down and yet no fight. We've done it. Yes.
Your fine first flight
Later on, day's more tuition. First solo flight your full fruition.
"What did you do in the war Daddy?" "Taught people to fly Laddie
We turned up trumps—Spins and Stalls and "Circuits and Bumps"

W. E. Crook

Nature's Love

In a flaming red-gold sunset, which sets the sky on fire and
  stirs the warmth in our hearts
In the burning, melting, barren heat which gives us raging thirst
  that we may find blessed relief in quenching it
In a shaded leafy glade which soothes, heals and at the same
  time stimulates our senses
In the sudden flash of lightening strike which bolts us
  out of our dreary complacency
In the music of the cool, refreshing wind which cleanses
  our cluttered minds and sends them soaring
In a raging hurricane which tears away all our possessions
  in nature's passion,
Reminding us that our greatest possession is the nature-being
  within us,
In the azure blue ocean swell which comforts us
  as our mother's womb
In the gasping, choking, drowning fury of the tumultuous sea
  which claims our bodies as nourishment for the earth
  and releases our spirits to communion with our nature-being
  who never betrays us.

Pamela Hampton

The Sky

It's everywhere, always there, above us;
Do we ever see it, really look at it's beauty
As we go on life's journey, doing our daily duty?
It's a painting, ever changing, it's God's canvas on high.
Imagine a storm, the darkness and the noise,
The lightning, the thunder, or is it a voice?
Some really love it, whilst others may cower;
Yet it's just "Mother Nature" showing her power.
Suddenly, the rain will cease, the sun will shine
What is that? High in the sky, it's a rainbow.
It's green, blue, violet and pink and indigo.
The colours are gorgeous, they're brilliant, God's own.
Just a promise of Heaven, to us he's shown.
The vivid blue of a summer's sky, fluffy clouds of grey or white,
Followed at dusk by a glorious sunset, all shades of pink.
We stand and marvel as we gaze, afraid to blink,
And is there not a more wondrous sight?
As a midnight sky, with the moon and stars so bright.
This was all created by God's gentle hand
As a protective cover, for his land.

Diana D. Hawkins

Untitled

You've gone and left me. Without a good bye.
All I can do is sit down and cry.
All my tomorrows will be without end.
No letters to write, no message to send
But I shall go on loving you until
Life's through.
Until we meet at the door you went through.

Alfreda Ward

What Is Freedom?

Is it when you get released from Jail?
Or when you run out like a fox being set free?
Or is it when your parents go out?
When you phone all your mates and
eat all the food in the house?
Freedom is like being a bird, flying high in
the sky.
With nothing on your mind, just your sights set high.
When the bell rings at three you can
relax and go home,
Stop thinking about teachers who never
leave you alone.
Freedom is about being alone with no-one
around you,
But most of all freedom is about making choices,
Using your own mind instead of
someone else's.

Adele Payton

Destiny

Who are you? Who are you looking for?
I hear a voice, I hear you call.
But if there's you who doesn't care,
You'll know I'm here, you'll know I'm there.

You are what you are,
I am, what you want me to be,
You've got your rules, your everything
I've got nothing, but you!

You are the voice of my conscience,
The voice of my soul,
You are the reason for my acts
The reason for my entire existence.

I live through you, you live through me;
I belong to you because you've chosen me.
You rule me, but I rule nothing,
Because you own, even my nothingness!

I'd live in darkness without you,
I don't know how, but I know why . . .
I'm sometimes desperate because of you,
But you don't mind, because you know, I need you!

Raluca Grada

A Tree at Woburn

You stand defying all around,
Your branches bare, still strong and proud.
Through summer heat and cruel weather,
Lasting endless years in leisure.

Did laughing children climb your arms,
Exploring youthful leaf-filled charms?
How many birds entrusted you
To watch their young, as off they flew?

And did the weary traveller find
Your bursting branches cool and kind?
Alas! Those days are far behind.

If you could hear, what would I say
To comfort creeping age away?
If I were you I'd be content to know
Not all my leaves were spent.
That passing birds still paused to rest
To give your lasting years some zest.

But wait! I've just begin to see
Your years might still outnumber me.

So mourn I'll not the passing years
But smile and hide my foolish tears.

Dorothy Bentley

Elemore Epitaph

This colliery, it is no more
Tubs so filled each to a score,
Twin towers so high, razed to the floor,
So sad the fate of Elemore.

The voices gone, the miners, all
Have disappeared to Thatcher's call,
She placed our backs against a wall
Coal now entombed, with no re-call.

Few local shops and streets a mess,
The people buying less and less,
Shops not selling, more distress,
Our village now, so characterless.

No sun to see although it shone,
A thousand feet down, dark and forlorn,
So many faces now have gone
Transferred, leaving, passing on.

And so I look at this green land,
Where our proud colliery used to stand,
Used only now by the golfer's hand
And Elemore bunkers, now of sand!.

William Saint

Her Parting

It was my day long obsession, my joy, my torment,
To such an extent indeed that one day,
I found myself at her death bed,
I caught myself
With eyes focused on her tragic temples;
In the act of shock I searched for life
Among the coloured gradients,
   death was imposing on her motionless face,
Blue, yellow and grey tones.

Nothing is more natural than a person parting from this life,
I was profoundly attached,
In spite of myself
I was being involved by my reflexes,
In an unconscious process,
In which I was resuming the course of daily life.
   Caroline Walker

Deep within the Heart and Soul

The heart and soul went out to play
Got struck by evil and lost on the way
So the gut and the brain took over the reign
While the spirit, cradled the hurt and the pain
It was soon to be clear that to keep what is dear
They must stand together to fight against fear
That's not very easy when you're falling apart
And the sharp shooting rays, strike deep at your heart
Rescued from aching and placed in a shell
It's a shame that people can't always tell
The tears feel like swelling, but are fought back inside
For it's no good letting them rip out your pride
If only they knew what torment they do
Would they still go on batting, hard against you
You really feel sleepy, tired and weak
So lay your head down to the peace that you seek
   Angie House

So Dark

It's so dark outside
And so dark in my soul
And I'm so alone and so blue
My eyes are so sad and so cold
And I'm so weak
And the spring's so far away
'Cause now it's dark, so dark outside
And so dark in my soul
When I see your fear
I hide in myself,
But everything that's closed is close to me
It's dark
And my dreams are dying one by one
And I bury them in my soul
And I'm dying with every little dream I bury
But I go forever
And I come back forever
That's just me
'Cause it's so dark outside
And so dark in my soul.
   Alina Chivari

Time Heals

Time heals, so the saying goes
But like every lonely person knows
It takes a very long time, in fact
Quite a feat to get through intact
The need to be needed, to have someone near
To be loved and cherished, it's all so clear
The endless hours, the constant thought
What I shouldn't have done and what I ought
In your smug little world, you have no idea
You hear but don't listen, when I tell you my fear
Of being alone, of being surplus
I've made my bed, lie on it, no fuss.
   Sue Collier

More Than a Toy

My dearest Teddy Bear
As we draw to the end of our days
With a stitched arm and ruffled hair
My mind recalls and peers through the haze.

You were always by my side
Through times happy, and some sad
Alone, and yet together we would hide
Just clutching your paw made my heart glad.

Think of all the places we have been
Thrills and spills, scraps and scars
The great excitement we have seen
And the night we forgot you under the stars.

Those long walks in the rain
Summer sun and lapping shores
And pleading moments spent in vain
With fluffy friends in toy stores.

But through it all, together we stand
At a different time, a different place
With attire just a touch more grand
Yet, every step a pleasure to retrace.
   John Wynn

Tea and Toast for Two

I was awakened one hot May morning by
the sunlight coming into my bedroom
Looking out of my opened window I saw
a stranger wearing a coat of red, much to my amazement I saw a
Robin sitting on the arm of my best garden chair.
A Robin, I said, I do declare
I like to partake of my tea and toast in the garden
weather permitting of course, going outside to my garden chair I
expected the Robin would fly away, but no, she still sat there.
I didn't get much to eat, for the Robin had other ideas.
She ate my food and decided to stay in the garden.
Going to the front garden gate I pasted a notice saying,
9 a.m. serving tea and toast for two.
A gentleman stopped to read the notice
and brought his dog in, too.
This went on day after day and the
Robin was really angry and appeared to say,
I was here first, you had better go.
This went on, day after day and she decided it was time to go.
Dear God, pray for our beautiful
feathered friends, as we ourselves must do.
   Connie Nicholson

Covering Up (For My Mother, Mina)

I stood looking in the mirror wanting to see your reflection
And when it did not appear I painted it on.

As you had no more need for those mysteries in that bag
That coloured everything yet hid nothing, I put them to use.

With quivering hand who was I trying to be
Powdering my eyes blue and a soft blush upon my cheeks.
I glanced over to the sleeping woman, then back to the child.
There has no in-between as I brushed deep red onto my lips.

I did not see you stir even though you were over my shoulder
When you awoke calling my name I was startled
Reaching to wipe away the evidence before I faced you.

But as in a mirror image you saw exactly what I do when I look closely
My attempt to cover up was as feeble as yours had once been.
Nothing can be hidden.

In the time that followed my tears washed away the blue
But that blood red kiss of reassurance was a lie—
As you knew then and I know now.
It remained even after it had long faded but the colour was not
needed.
How could it be when your blood quickens constantly through me,
For just as you are me—I am you.
   Donna Ellen Wilson

A Prayer for Every Day

Thank you Lord for giving us this brand new day,
Thank you Lord that we can talk and pray,
To you we give our hearts and minds, so you can give us all your signs.
To pray to you in faith anew, and keep us from being blue.
You are our saviour and our friend, and we will worship you till the end.
It is our great ambition, to follow you and listen,
For your word is a gift to us all, for us to pray and hear you call.
To pray to you, till the end of time, to sing to you with love sublime.
And pray to you all the time, our love for you is love so true.
For what you do for us each day, and we will walk with you all the way.
You look down on us with loving care, and protect us from the Devil's snare.
You are our God and we are glad, that you make us happy and not sad.
You are the one we all do praise, all the nights and all the days.
You gave us life, when we were dust, you made all things anew for us.
Thank you Lord, thank you Lord, thank you Lord, Amen.

R. T. Whiston

Short Lives

Today clouds are not lonely in the sky,
(As tears never fall singularly from an eye).
They are en-mass, an angry brooding crowd,
Covering the sky completely in a dark blanketing shroud.

Yesterday, the soft breeze that kissed the daffodils,
Touched my cheek, with the sweet promise spring, would fulfil.
Today the shrieking gale, rattles windows, and throws hail on the sill.
Battering the flowers, tearing at their yellow frills.

Tomorrow, the supple stems will stand tall,
Crowned, with the golden flowers, that did not fall.
Fallen ones have had their day, a short life prematurely whisked away.
A year long preparation to stand in perfection, for one short day.

Our lives stand fragile, when the strong winds blow,
Whether we stand or fall tomorrow, it is better we do not know.
Generations come and go, like a field full of poppies,
Like a garden full of snow.

Thousands of people, all different, each unique,
Lives interwoven, each with a special time to peak.
Nature's, recycling, recreation.
A reason for everything, but not always an explanation.

Valerie Lillie

My Solitude

Yesterday I was with you, now I have gone, don't concern yourselves because I have left you.
I have taken nothing from you, and not anything to sustain me in my flight away from the chaos of this world.
I have found my inherent gift that has been waiting for me that was born with me, a gift that had been squeezed into the finer recesses of my soul.
Through my mental wanderings and my search for peace I came across this gift in desperation.
Now I will expose it and let it reveal itself to me,
let it take me by the hand and lead me through the paths of the universe, my gift of solitude.

In its gift of silence it does not instruct me, neither in the secrets of the past, nor of the present, and not of the future.
It can not alarm me because of its very nature of tranquility,
it comes to me as a soft light that envelopes and warms and only lets me see myself when I choose it to do so.
So my friends, do not search for me, for whilst I am in solitude you will not see me. I move faster than the speed of light.
I can encompass all the stars known to me in less time than the blink of your eye.
You cannot touch me for I become something of the air that surrounds you, you will not hear me,
even though I can clear a valley of strewn boulders and place them in the hills from whence they came.
In my solitude I am all things that I choose to be.

Brian Hunter

In the Woods

The cackle of a witch chanting in her cranky house, the chirping of a bird I think it's a louse.
The snapping of the branches as I stand upon their middle, it feels as if the trees are having a quick giggle.
I can see some smoke lifting in the air, but no one is here to see me so they don't really care.
Whimpering and dirty but cold as cold could be, if only I could be so someone would see me.
The shouts of people helping is ringing in my ears, sounds of footsteps pounding and people close to tears.
I hear a voice close by, it's God but he's way up high
It's going to be alright as I hear the sounds of night.
Another voice is coming, it's really close to me
I can see it's my mum and she's come to find me.

Joanne Kitchen

To Find Me

Listen and you will find me
Where the breeze rustles through newly grown leaves.
Soft to the touch on the bough.
Listen and you will find me
Where birds sing their new songs, joyful in spring.

Feel me to find me on a warm summer's day
With the sun to caress, you'll find a way.
Feel me to find me when you walk along the shore
I'll be there once more.

Find me in autumn when leaves change colours
Look around, remember our golden hours,
When we walked through paths of red, gold and brown.
Find me in nature's gown.

Touch and you will find me
When winter shows its hand with clouds
That bring snow to cover the land,
Touch the softness as it floats in the air
For this will be me, I'll be there.

V. Hales-Owen

Sad

As we stood there almost touching, only my passion in the air.
I spoke to you with an open heart, but you had lost that passionate stare.
My lust would be forever, how it had always been, your lustful door was closing,
I had lost the key.
My life is flashing past, I don't know what to say, these three words are in my head,
Stay Another Day.

Hayley Barrett

Father

I never knew you
Like I should
It wasn't easy to talk we never really could

It's sad to realise
when it is too late
but we'll have our opportunity
when you meet me at the pearly gate.

Every day I think of you
I suffer the same pain
But to think of happy times keeps me insane.

There's things I want to say to you
But have to resort to prayer
and to know you now listen makes it easy to share.

I hope in time I'll except your death
and look back with no regrets
at the moment I still feel lonely
cause you haven't left me yet.

Be happy where you are
I hope you have found release
your death eased your pain and gave you eternal peace.

Ashleen Henry

Keats
26, Piazza di Spagna, February 1821

The fountain's voice, outside,
When the square falls asleep:
Rome's permanence. Water-echoes.
Sabrina, nymph of the Severn,
Lost now, abandoned, —ah,
A posthumous life. The laudanum
Has been removed. No prayers.
His mail unopened. Joseph, sent out,
Returns from the pyramid: sheep
Among the tombs, early daisies
And violets. Then, tersely, directions:
No public notice. The epitaph
. . . writ in water. And silence.
In his hands continually
The large cornelian,
He holds it fast, a gift
From Fanny Brawne.

Alfred Behrmann

The Eagle and the Dove

She is the dove, her soft white feathers white as snow,
Her gentle brown eyes intent on feeding from the grassy green slope.
Peace is her emblem, as she pecks sustenance under the sun's warm glow
And she lives her life in her own quiet aura of hope.

He is the eagle, striking metallic feathers cover his frame,
His glittering yellow eyes miss nothing on the grassy, green slope,
He spots the peace lover, sharp talons quivering, eager to maim,
Then the wings spread, and he glides towards her as if joined
   by an invisible rope.

Contact is made, in a flurry of red blood and white feathers,
The peace lover dies a horrible death in humiliation and pain,
The mistake of the dove, always hopeful trying to live together
With the predator, who allows no bird or beast to share his domain.

Shirley Rashid

Rose

Behind her, a giant red house
A busy street, my new home.
The noise of bleating sheep, so new to me
The rich smell of farms.
She was smiling, standing on the doorstep
Tea towel in hand,
Waiting for my approach.
The sun beat down from a cloudless sky,
Painting a beautiful picture.
I felt warm and changed
Making a new start.
Why was my stomach fluttering
With a million butterflies?
Her friendly, cheerful smile
Took my sadness away.
A warm loving mist filled my heart
And in her company I felt safe.

Laura Young

The Traveller

Please stay oh, weary traveller and with me share my bread,
then I will find a cosy room for you to rest your head.
For you have travelled far and wide across this rugged countryside,
but I would now have you abide with me a while.

Then on the 'morrow traveller, if you must say farewell,
to persevere in journeying through leafy glade and dell.
I will bid you fond adieu and watch until you fade from view,
but always will remember you and your sweet smile.

Should you return, dear traveller please do not pass me by,
for I would make you welcome until the day you die.
When all your travelling will be done through wind and rain
and shining sun, and need of shelter you'll have none mile
after mile.

June M. Liggins

My Life?

My life is empty, my life is void, teased by past expectations
and taunted by future hope and dreams.

Giving life would validate my life, I would be remembered when I am
gone. There is one thing I want, one thing I know I would be good
at, the only thing that is really important—a good Mother.

A little arm wrapped round my neck, a little hand in my hand, an
exchanged glance between mother and child, a loving gaze, the
laughter, the loving, the bond.

What do I have now? Nothing. A life empty, but full of longing
and pain, a constant pain.

There is always something there to remind me about what I
haven't got—a child's cry in the supermarket
—a "baby on board" sign - I'd love one of those
—"families welcome" signs, how I'd love to be a family, a unit of
   People, not a singular lonely figure, battling my way through
   every sad day.

Estranged from "normal life", on the outside of everything,
looking in like a friendless child who looks longingly at other
children, their toys, their lives.

Nothing else matters, everything else pales into insignificance,
the want is so huge, so overbearing, so engulfing.

What will I do? What will fulfil me? How will I ever feel true
happiness? Why am I here if not to be a Mother?

Jane Eleanor Bennett

Khouniatonou in the Mosque of Sultan Hussan

"The long lamp chimney shaped like the stem
Of a slender palm, stood but a day;" Yeats

An aquamarine bottle, resting on a balcony,
Watches the sheer white bazaar, pointed doorways
Awash with harlequins, the elaborate square.
Bold in its flashes of the triangles,
Reminiscent of the deep tombed cliffs it stares ahead.

"I have trespassed among the Mughal tents:
Has Allah really felled every warrior every robber?
And then does the essence of liberation lie
in flags, baskets and heaps of turban cotton . . . "

A slice of fruit cake crumbles at the banquet for ten thousand; the
Arabic wedding has disappeared into phantasmagoric dust, among the
alleyways gartered with old fountain and daggers; every discolouration
of this canopic jar. A cockerel in Muslim Assisi.

" . . . Or in lotus capitals and the gods of shards, or even Spain
lost and won, memories of chameleon hypostyle overrun by
archaeologists?"

The lime green bottle turns towards a ram-headed sphinx,
Whose tail is pent against curly chinks of mane,
Waiting for the grandfather clock to chime.

Peter Fane-Saunders

A Precious Gift

   Whilst gazing from my window into deep and sunny skies,
watching birds in flight searching for wayward flies, I saw clouds
leisurely drifting, patterns from my imagination in them constantly shifting. A thought then entered my mind. What if I
were blind?
   Would the fragrance of flowers become something to treasure,
for their stimulation of the sense's pleasures? Would I feel their
petals and thrill to the touch and appreciate more, the breezes
and such? This thought then entered my mind. How sad to be blind!
   For could fragrance replace seeing the dance of a child, or of
woodland and valley rugged and wild, or seeing the joy in two lovers
meeting, or the outstretched hands of friends offered in greeting.
   Such thoughts took over my mind. How awful to be blind! For
though my senses might be more acute to the beauty of other
things, such as the frantic beat of a fledgling's flapping wings,
or of the rustle of leaves on the trees that stand outside. They
surely could not quite replace, the sight of rushing tide.
   This thought then overwhelmed my mind: Thank God I Am Not Blind.

S. M. Wiffen

Just Take a Chance

Life is meant to be an adventure,
Don't allow to become common place,
No sitting around and bemoaning,
While the world goes on at its pace.

Get up and get going my hearties,
There's more than at first meets the eye.
Try making a new acquaintance,
Whenever one catches the eye.
They may be very beguiling,
You'll never know if you don't take a chance.
They may be the one for whom you are searching
Or maybe they'll lead you a dance.
Just take a chance.

We can't all sail the high seas
To visit far away distant lands
Adventure is around every corner
If only you'll just take a chance.

M. J. Sheard

From the Outside

Thoughts for you who absorb so much knowledge inside your head about art.
You who know so well the history of art.
Every painting, sculpture and artist locked inside your mind,
You who can only see from the outside,
If you could only see art from the inside, the painting and sculpture,
Feel every brush stroke and shape that's formed by the artist's hand and mind.
Then you would know and understand art.

Lynn Neild

Loneliness

My entity, like the limitations of the solar realm,
Is one tiny matter in the conscience of beings.
I'm detached, misconceived;
My mind is warped with thoughts, passions, luring me to insanity.
The ride of delusion grows stronger
But thirst for meditated impressions lifts my neglected spirits.
A desire for inner maturity is expressed when
The confusion of time brings understanding.
We, as mere spirits, just learn to drift through life
And the waves of intellect and telepathy
Caress our feeble, twisted senses.
The nature of this solitude is fading my creative sparks
That seek to find some reason for my existence.
Feeling isolated it numbs my fibres, twists and tears,
Straining strength, pushing fears into the corners of darkness.
Wondering through a chasm of lyrics my manuscript matures.
Dreams are for comfort, my mind swims amongst the bric-a-brac.
Not a dramatic dream but in worlds where beauty lives.
Throbbing no longer beats but time joins hands bringing peace.
To live light, to love light, to live life: is joy.

Anna-Louise Eden

My Daughter

Daughter is epitome of everlasting love
from a girl to a lady, daily, changing
continually in high flight, like a dove
the eternal feeling of life staging

In this world of perpetual change
Honesty, integrity, love and fidelity
must keep single and yet complete range
escaping and rising above all, especially mediocrity

Playing the piano for happy memories
Knowing the father without trying
Remembering well few bedtime stories
And the times when both were, joyfully, playing

A diamond, almost polished, she is now
Wishing and hoping to hold the world without bars
To the young becoming lady all should bow
Expecting future with the purest stars

Jefta Lakovic

Journey into My Dreams

Fly me away, so far, far away to never never land.
Take me to your distant home,
Where the oceans are blue,
And the skies are clear.
Where the bees are busy, and honeysuckle a plenty.
Take me to a land afar,
Where the flowers have been painted with the rainbow,
Their sweet scent is carried along with the wind.
Take me to the land of dreams,
Where the mountains carry the echoes of laughter.
Somewhere to rejoice as the sun kisses the morning sky,
And the moon lights the midnight sky.
Where the stars gleam a bright and dance in the festival of the night.
Let me chase a shooting star.
Let me run free.
Let me wish for all I have ever wanted.
Make my dreams reality.
As I wipe away my tears, I know that there is no land of dreams.
Never never land, you are just another abandoned dream.

Kahlda Kusar

My Mother, My Garden

Did the Daffodils bloom last springtime, half hidden Primrose too
And Tulips raise their stately heads,
    all coloured glorious yellow and red,
Anemones and Crocus, Bluebells 'neath budding trees,
The lovely Apple Blossom? I must have missed them if they did.

In Summer did the Roses scatter petals everywhere
On Pansy faces all aglow and Sweet Peas of brilliant hue?
Did Honeysuckle sweetly smell, late in the evening sun,
The Thrush and Skylark sing all day long and Cuckoos call 'Beware'?

Then Autumn came with all its shades of brown and gold and russet,
The leaves were falling in the wind, the berries glowed and bonfires crackled
Bare branches showed on trees and shrubs where life had been but now at rest,
My mother died last Springtime, that's why, last year, I've lost.

But she would not want us mourning long, her happy soul's not gone,
So we scattered all her ashes where we knew she'd love to be
Amongst the Rhododendrons, in their splendour on the hill,
Dark days are here, but all will come alive again in Spring.

The Winter's flowering Jasmine with its yellow blossom shines
And the faces of my Grandsons are great comfort to my heart.
We're born, we grow, we live, we die, that's how it has to be,
So in my garden, peaceful now, new flowers soon will come.

Beryle Overy

A Birthday Poem

What lies hidden in the washing up bowl
    like the bicycle in its canal?

In the fridge, behind the fresh and fit, do you detect
    A whiff of neglect? Don't resurrect

With tender heat the mortal soup, don't contrive
    To keep half alive what won't revive.

Cast your eyes upon the shelves, the grisly plots
    Of mysteries in pots, and there are lots!

Or worse—the surreal disputes of the football pitch,
    The scratchcard itch of the nearly rich,

The angry clash of the broadsheet's pages,
    The columnists, the sages, the obscene wages.

Today let the highlights flash and finish,
    The huge stadia diminish to a distant hush.

Let the green baize wither and the TV cool,
    Unplug the TV fool, let tranquility rule.

On your birthday I wish you peace and health,
    And anything else just for yourself.

M. McAuliffe

When the Comet Comes

The shepherd stirs, his senses gear to the firmament high above him;
Through reeds of papyrus green his fear-struck eyes take in the stellar scene.
Giza glows, its towering pyramids sprayed with the radiance of some strange celestial soul;
Who art thou? Good or evil? The comet answereth not, then in ire swings its awesome tail of fire and swiftly streaks to threaten earth;
Where the mighty pharaoh of all Egypt takes birth
Anew in the mastaba of his own creation.

Memphis mourns, a kingdom passes into the pages of oblivion.
Sans warning then it comes again

At the dusk of another millennium;
Far removed from the flax fields of an ancient day.

Is your long impending visit some dark presage? The grey-haired gazer hails for a message.

No reply he hears. His straw-drawn eyes turn wearily away; to the telly screen and the thunder of a legion war-drums seen.

The portent seems clear.
Is Doomsday indeed very near?
Russell J. Foulds

Too Late

Cold, grey winding gear rising like a dinosaur between towering heaps of jet black coal,
Reminder of a time now gone, a way of life now just a memory.
A playful breeze plays round the yards, whisking dust into the autumn air,
Only to sprinkle it like pepper onto lines of once-clean washing.

Gone are the days when there was work, though hard and grimy toil,
When fathers, sons and brothers worked side by side in dark, damp seams of coal.
Gone are the days when families stayed together from the cradle to the grave,
Always there for one another, in times of crisis and of joy.

Now slowly creeps the tide of change, to wash the valley clean,
A green, but artificial, landscape shrouds the land which once stood black and bare.
Embryonic factories huddle together; cheap, prefabricated, not built to last.
New red brick dwellings spring up to house outsiders who will come to take the jobs.
Too late, the change, to save our town, our sons and daughters all have flown.
Too late, for us, for what is left when youth and heart are gone.
Too late.
Judith M. Dickinson

In Honour of Rumi and Rilke

Dear friends,
Some of whom I've met
And many I have not,
When you wrote, did you know that I would cry with relief to read your words?
Did you know that I would resonate with wonder,
That your hand would reach across time and touch a heart that is made of your own being?

And when I am lonely
I remember you and sit
At peace, safe in Mother's arms,
Reading letters from friends dear and loved
Whose humanity reaches out from the page, vibrant
With every sadness of the human heart
And glorious with that paradox of resolution.

And I ask, as friends do in that intimacy,

Is there a part in the play for me
And will my part make you cry too?
Kiaran Maria Lawton

Alexander

Earth's glorious, laurelled mortal, whom the Gods of heaven revered, now lies within his sepulchre, so silent, pale and cold, and yet this conqueror so fair, so young to bind the earth in chains was stricken as a bud unopened, with no flourishing bloom of age to grant the promise and the hope of ripening from a wondrous dream the gleaming marble cities and nations drawn within the chaste and Godly grasp, of Alexander, king of kings, beloved hero born of mortal woman's womb.

His lonely, tortured spirit wandering the desert regions of the earth. Sought, but could not find the sacred crystal waters of divine becoming, succour from that pure fountain which would bestow the gift of life eternal and confound the Gods above by whom his destiny was written. Thus, he raged in torment, raping cities, laying barren paths of desolation to great empires and kings, bloody, hellish in his fevered search to find those vital, precious mortal years to dwell as God of humankind.

He cried to Amon-Ra for life, but this great God with vapid sapphire eyes looked silently beyond the temple wall and whispered, 'Babylon', Thy destiny is Babylon, my verdant city of the Babel tower', then turned away with cold white lips which moved no more. But within this city's walls, Alexander found no sacred succour, no quenching of fate's thirst, but only death's soft touch upon his brow, the prophecy fulfilled, his life to pay on fair youth's funeral pyre.
Beverley Ann Fairfoull

A Millennium Wish

It's Christmas Eve the lamps are lit
The snow is glistening on the ground
The Robins are looking for every little bit
Any morsel of food left lying around.

For some there will be no Christmas Day
It will be just another day of sorrow
It is especially sad when children have to pay
For some there will be no today and no tomorrow.

But for most it will be a joyous season
They will be spending time with the ones they love
A baby boy born in Bethlehem is the reason
And who now looks down on us from above.

Let's hope in time things will improve
When ones' awful inhumanity to man will cease
Which tyrant leader will make the first move
Towards a united world and Christmas peace.
Theresa Josephine Llobet

Tonight at 7:30

Summoned by bells of innumerable alarm clocks.
Kick-started by caffeine.
The files of memory snap open from blank passivity of sleep.
Faces marshalled into significant expressions limber up for the day;
And minds pick up the weight of awareness,
And 'In trays' loom with things ' undone'.
Day begins.

For: Foreign diplomacy, bathing the baby,
Life giving surgery, unblocking drains.

Continues with: Demands made by other people, and dishonest replies.
Situations to be got out of. Situations to be applied for.

And agendas for: The busy, the bored, the rich,
And even the thoroughly wicked. And all conditions of men.

Summoned by bells from crush bar and foyer, tonight at 7:30
In theatre, studio, concert hall, opera house,
Some of these people will go in, and sit down,
Begin to forget, be passive again.
And their faces will be quiet and limpid,
Ready to reflect whatever the performance gives them.

Rows of little moons.
Charlotte Howden

The General

There was a general whom I knew, who rode into battle with
Only a few. Now in battle, they stand side by side and they
will fight until they die. The union flag is held aloft,
The going is hard and not for the soft. The battle is fought
All day long, with no one singing the victory song,
Oh, those men in all their glory, who will tell about this, their story?

I lay on the ground crying out in pain, among my friends,
Comrades who had been slain, my tears run freely from my eyes
And mingle with their's from the skies. The general and his men
forever will lay, in trenches of thousands they will stay. Men
will fight to protect their land, the price is high like grains of sand.
Oh, those men in all their glory, I am left to tell this, their story.

Michael James

One Day You'll Rise Again

I can hear the wind rushing past my ears,
I realise time has passed with the falling of my tears;
The sea rolls gently towards the open shore,
Is this forever? Is there no more?

I have often dreamt of places such as this,
Places where you'd give me just one last kiss;
I dream of you reaching out to hold my hand,
And then I realise you've slipped through like grains of sand.

The air is warm, yet somehow, I feel only cold,
It's all just a part of life, or so I'm told;
Somewhere deep inside, there's still a ray of hope,
But for now, I'm finding it difficult to cope.

I see you dancing on the horizon, so far away,
As I see you in my dreams each night and day;
While I have never felt such sorrow, such pain,
I know, though you have gone, one day, you'll rise again . . .

Sultana Ara

What Is Life?

What is life? What's it for?
Everyone ends up wanting more.
Life's for living; life's for love,
Is it complete when you have enough?
Life's for happiness; life's for joy,
Life's there for you, you mustn't destroy,
What you have; what you take,
This is life; it's what you make.
So live your life, do what you can,
Live it well, maybe have a plan.
But be open-minded; don't shut away,
And make your love always stay.
Life is precious; Life's not long,
And remember this: We all belong.
Treat everyone equal, 'cause that's what we are,
Black or white, near or far.

Sarah Freeman

Satan's Horns

I cannot sleep, I cannot rest,
All I can do is try my best.
My mind's functions will not cease
When all I really want is peace:
Instead hot irons, glowing red,
The thoughts of life inside my head,
Burn earnestly toward my soul,
Help mind and heart remain a whole.
And conscience shows its sternest face
To try and save the human race
From its evil, greed and hate,
To lead us to a better fate:
But man still laughs when conscience scorns
And drinks instead from Satan's horns.
So now the world is full of corruption,
The one thing left is utter destruction:
The Lord looks to our evil disgrace,
And He'll wipe the smile off the whole damn race.

Richard Bates

Christmas

Another Christmas over, another year almost past,
I hope the presents, I had chosen with very great thought, will last.

Kids of today want Electronic games, Computers and such like,
When I was a child, and things were simple, I hoped for a doll
and longed for a bike.

Kids and Adults of today alike forget the true meaning of Christmas,
It's when we celebrate the birth of our Lord Jesus Christ.

Sue Barratt

Challenge

Yellow fields of corn uneasily swept by wind,
Sunflowers spewing seeds,
Beheaded in a vase in a sparsely denuded room,
Wrinkled faced men toiling in the departing day,
And peasants huddled together eating over a dim flame,
Scorned and yet confident;

Like a flame in the dark,
Like a lark in the morning
Like a scream in the calm,
Like a dwindling candle flame,
Like a ripple in the water,
The stone slowly turns to reveal creatures and sights hidden:

Eyes flickering bring to life,
The unseen marsh and woods,
The unplumbed depths of human emotions,
This is the precious moment,
Hold it even though madness:
The imagination severed—remember its warmth
A jewel in the brain!

Henry King

Mother

Mother is weak, she's not strong.
She won't stay with us for long.
I wonder when did it first go wrong.

Smoke from factories drew a face
It'll kill her and destroy her grace
Unless we leave forests in place.

Rockets destroy the atmosphere,
Then we look at each other in fear.
Now I see a vision that's clear.

We'll all die with her, no doubt in that.
Mother kept warning us from the fact
That life without her shall never last.

Sorry Mother Earth, for we caused you pain.
We promise you, we'll never do it again.
Just stay! You have to win that game . . . Mother Earth.

Magda Mohamed Ismail

Untitled

These people, they drown my lungs with smoke,
They drown under their sorrows,
They push me beneath their collar,
Beneath their ashtrays full of death, and take away my respect,
As a full time night watcher,
That watches through the night.
All night I watch the clouded sky with stars of bright,
I always shed a light when a passerby becomes alone in their
thoughts of a world like ours.
Ours is a world of thoughts alone,
That needs a metal brain to work its needed hearts.
I've been drifting,
Drifting from this place of back gardens, washing lines,
squashed ears and socked feet,
That walk along the bare minds of unwanted souls of games
and golf clubs,
Looking at the stubbled chins of freshly sprouted men,
I push away the whitened stick, that burns, as the razor is
scraped along the fresh sprouts of
the scrambled noses pegged, along the washing line of despair.

Saydi-Anne Drake

"My War-Time Bride I Left Behind"

She was so lovely my war-time bride I left behind
For she knew she would always be on my mind
Her hair is fair her eyes a lovely deep blue
For I knew that my darling would always be true.

As I was looking at her lovely soft lips
When I held her tight in my strong grips
For she trembled a while, then gave me a wee smile
She was thinking of the miles I would be away for a while.

There were tears in her eyes that were concealing no lies
For broken was her heart on that cloudy day we had to part
For I knew that she would be lonely my lovely sweet dove
That her heart was aching for she required my love.

Don't worry my darling I will write you a letter
To help you along it will make you feel much better
I will send you a kiss that I am sure you have missed
For the sun will shine after the rain then I will be home with you again.

She was a nurse and very helpful for what she knew
All the children loved her and all the patients too
She always had a smile any time of the day
For patience was her kindness and that was her way.
Frederick G. Brown

My Little Rosebud

I lay you down to go to sleep, your breathing hard, your body weak,
Those trusting eyes as still you lie, look into mine as you wait to die.
Your eyelids close as sleep comes on, I stand and watch and fear you've gone.
No words are spoken but we all know, it'll soon be time for you to go.
We all try hard as life goes on, but what will we do when Kriss is gone?
If there's a God and he lives in Heaven, what sort of life has Kriss been given?
A life full of illness and days of pain, like a Rosebud dying from unending rain?
My little Rosebud so still you lie, it's hard to believe you're going to die.
I cover you up and stroke your hair, a beautiful child, so loving and fair.
I sit and wait for each new day, to hold you tight and laugh and play,
But my little Rosebud grows weaker each day, too tired for laughter, too weary to play.
A little Rosebud in a gilded cage, dying unopened never from age.
Margaret Leeson

A Living Memory

At night she cries herself to sleep wanting darkness to surround,
To take away the constant pain that always comes around.

She opens up her blurry eyes and turns over in her bed,
Smiling—feeling good until the thoughts inside her head
Tell her how it used to be, show her why she is upset,
For in her blissful silent sleep, she had forgotten her regrets.

She looks upon herself, recognizes her own state
She moves her hand across what's left, her tiny unborn babe.
Her glimmer of glee fills her with guilt as she remembers what he said
"This is the seal of our true love, so never be afraid".

She walks across the landing, looks at the other doors
Behind the one in front of her are things to upset her more.
The room they did just for the babe, but that was just before . .

More tears fall upon her cheeks, more tears, then some more.

All throughout the labour she never felt alone
And when the babe was finally born,
 she knew she was not on her own.
She'd had one love torn from her, that she had found too hard
But now she and her newborn babe would go home and restart.

She thought about the babe she held,
 young Charlie awoke and smiled
How could she tell her baby son how Charlie senior had died.
Joanne Robbins

I Am

I am, yet What I am no one knows . . . Why care?
An empty husk of love I am 'tis a veil I wear
All is hidden, all a sham 'neath the mask I share.
As I study, try to cram, is there someone there?

The fruit has all ripened, the small birds have flown
So why be so frightened? Why feel so alone?
He . . . has taken all I had, sucked me dry, and then
Wondered off upon a fad on a younger yen

Called me boring, called me old . . . Said the bed was growing old . . .

Time to wake and face the day.
Time to see what made him say.
Could it be . . . we grew away?

I will succeed, I must do well, along the road come many more,
And each a different tale to tell who enters through the 'open' door.
Christine Sherman

Erotica, Erotica

I feel the beat of your blood
your heart drawn taut under its cargo of passion
power strung like a hammer crashing onto white hot light

I flash through tricks of time to be with you
I watch in awe your metamorphosis as you rise above me
pulsating within the boundaries that vanish and darken
as you shape yourself around my soul
until catching my rapture as easy as falling leaves
you gather me in your quivering column of light
hold me shimmering in your towering gold ecstasy as only you know how
in the mysterious eclipse of total surrender
light crackling behind my eyes
your name a prayer
and sweeter than the sound of angels
the triumphant cry of your homecoming
releases me skywards in splintering arcs
a sparkling rainbow arched in ecstasy over the glorious Eden
that is forever
You my Beethoven
Christine Louise Baker

Untitled

I thought I'd go rustic, live in a tent. Glorious outlooks and minimum rent.
Fresh milk and eggs from down on the farm, living like that would do me no harm.
Long country walks in the lovely fresh air, lambs and small rabbits with never a care.
Hedgerows and blossom unlimited view, given the choice, wouldn't you like it too?
No traffic jams on the road every day, fighting the hustle and bustle away,
queuing at checkouts in each grocery store, pushing and shoving, need I say more?
Leave it behind to the ones that can cope, I'll be well away from the dirt and the smoke.
Retire with the sunset and get up at dawn, admiring the daisies and dew on my 'lawn' I would grow calm and gentle, settle down and relax.
No more alarm clocks, no income tax.
Well I tried it. I tell you it's not all it seems, all of that stuff that you want in your dreams.
There's no running water, well, just in the brook. No table lamp for reading your book.
If you fancy a pizza there's no take away, unless you drive off for half of a day!
You can't chat with aunty by lifting the phone, and you can't pet the dog, or find him a bone.
And I missed all the reruns without a TV, and the only one there to agree with, was me.
It was healthy and pretty and oh, very cheap, but there's no one to talk to, just cows and those sheep!
Sheila Greening

Ageing

I know I'm getting older, my hair is going grey
And it seems there's more appearing each and every day.
Where did all these lines come from that are showing on my face?
Is it from the stress and strain of living in this rat race?

I seem to bag, sag and wrinkle where I never did before
And to keep old age at bay is becoming quite a chore.
It doesn't make much difference what potions or creams I use,
It's an uphill and endless battle that's determined I'm going to lose.

There are suitcases under my eyes now, they used to be just bags
And to find a remedy for these, I've poured over glossy mags.
I know I'll never be a super model but one has to do one's best,
So I decided the local beauty salon would have their ultimate test.

I thought of starting gently, but heck that's not my way!
So the anti-wrinkle treatment was booked to save to the day.
I decided next on a massage to relax and tone the body,
I never thought this beauty lark would be such an expensive hobby.

Now I've had all the treatments and dyed over all the grey,
I bet you're all wondering did this indulgence really pay?
Well, stealing a glance in the looking glass I'd never pass for nineteen
But at least all this palaver has saved me from being an old has-been.
Mhari Emslie

The Heavens Can Wait

Earth, Sea and Sky, this is our world,
Minute in the flow of time but, it a glorious world, a generous earth
that provides to the human race.
Still, "We look to the Heavens for new worlds to conquer.
So "to all Astronauts and Scientists" I say,
"bide your time" your price is to high.
First, put our world in order.
People cannot wait, "poverty's around every corner.
Look to the Earth it will provide.
Then look at the Seas "they'll too supply."
Then look at yourselves "Earth needs you".
And, for each and every man "create the chance to work", to
be useful.
For he, too has pride. He, too has ambition.
And when Earth's destiny's been fulfilled
The Astronaut's ambition can resume at will, "to study
the mystery of that endless space"
For, a Virgin World, an El Dorado place.
Yet it's only dreamers "Who can fantasia" on the horizons
beyond the skies or dreamers who will—will debate on
creative beings, that God has made.
Mollie Clarke

Grandad

I remember—His brown rimmed glasses that slid down his thin
  nose every time he spoke.
His slightly grey hair, that fell over his wrinkled forehead.
The small dimples at the side of his mouth, which showed
  when he smiled.
His blue eyes which shone in the daylight.

I remember—the strong cigarette he smokes, the tobacco and
  papers that formed them,
The loud boxing matches, which he used to swear at, huffing
  and puffing.

I remember—The happy holidays we used to have, down in
  Cormwall and in Wales.
The coloured candy and sweets he used to buy.

I remember—The depressing hospital and the single bed were he lay.
The big operation, the sadness I felt.
The illness that was terminal.

I remember—The bitter grief,
The hysterical sobs that came from my throat,
The emptiness I felt inside as if someone had taken a part of me.

I remember—The wooden casket where he lay,
The smell of sweet white roses,
The dismal grave with no headstone,
And the warm, mixed memories which are all I have left of my
Grandad.
Rebecca Popejoy

The Quiet Fight

If this is the big C, I shall fight with all my will. I don't think
it will be a fight of strength, but one of determination.

He is the old enemy of our family, and will not kill us all.

I will not fight with strong words and loud voice, but with
quiet assurance and resolution.

I am not frightened of this enemy: Our fight is an old one,
planned before I was born.

He can stand before me like a dragon, with fire and thunder
around him, or he can slink in like the lowest snake.

Who is this enemy with the taste for life, yet cannot contain it?

Even when he is the Victor, in his victory he is empty and worthless,
of no value or worth no matter how many times the winner.

Even the lowest of us are greater than him.
So come, show your great power.

I will show my great protection of this body. Should I die, your
victory would be hollow, a worthless thing of no substance,
as you surely are.

To live you need me.
So who is the winner in the end?
Doreen Hagger

Behold

Behold the fishermen:
onto the blazing beach of sun-tanned torsi
do rivers crawl, do hungry algae crawl, and the silence, and
the tempest,
and the churches within the armpit of the Leviathan.
Behold the fishermen:
to this day still their trawls are filled with
the eyeballs of lost carmen, and their muteness,
and two fish and five loaves of bread
while mobs of unknown strangers darken the shore
with their number, with their hunger, oh, such frightening hesitation.
Behold the fishermen:
bruised-kneed apostles sipping the ambrose of the gods;
under their feet flourishes the foot-trodden surf of sweet wet salt,
it's under their feet that crash and plunge so many sunsets . . .
all else is hallucination, there is only the seas, the sacrificial
burnings,
and immortality, half saint, half pagan.
The boats of the fishermen are the only bearers of that knowledge
for they alone know, crossing the evening sky like flashing spears,
they alone understand that it's for them alone
that bleeds the night.
Andreea Sepi

Let Our Souls Be

What about the blind, who can't explore your creativity,
What about the deaf and dumb, who can't expose your words,
What about the weak and venerable, who aren't witnessing
your love?

Let our souls be, in seeking to find thee,
Let our souls be, in setting them free,
For our souls are to be a living sacrifice to thee.

What about the sick and dying, who are far off your salvation,
What about the homeless and poor, who are desolate to seek
the aspiration, what about the famines and hunger, which are
costing innocent lives?

What about the wars and crimes, which are destroying our world,
What about the guiltiness and selfishness, which is pulling
our world apart,
What about the love and sorrow, which I feel deep within my heart?

What about your love and mercy,
Taking our souls as one,
What about declaring your power,
So, we shall live as one,
What about your coming now,
As we are depending on thee, when we declare our love to thee?
Austin Satz

I'm Glad That I'm Alive

I'm glad that I'm alive,
to smell the flowers and hear the birds,
and see the greenery of trees,
all swaying and dancing in the breeze.

I'm glad that I'm alive,
to see the new born lambs,
the crocus shoots pushing through snow topped grass,
and hear the first cuckoo telling us it's spring.

I'm glad that I'm alive,
to see and feel refreshing rain,
feel the sunshine and watch the rainbow arc across the sky,
and listen to the autumn leaves, their reddish browns rustling beneath my feet.

I'm glad that I'm alive,
to hear the children laughing, playing,
touch their soft skin and see their happy smiles,
While joining in with them the games that we as children played.

I'm glad that I'm alive,
to smell, to hear, to see, to feel,
all that shows us, this life is real.

Bettina Lees

Your Waves and My Wind . . . A Poem

"My lady: You carried inside your eyes the migration sign, your eyes have the same smile, how can it stay ever smiling? My lady when I couldn't carry my pains alone, when I felt the separation will be my "last shore" I came to you without knowing anything about your underworld. I came to die between your arms, die under your breast.
My lady: this is my hand. I give it to you like a last chance, I give it to reach your moonlight. My lady: I walked one step, than I felt in the middle of the distance, I fell in a deep ditch, I fell on an old heavy boat, push it many wounded men without guide.
—She answered: I waited for many years to meet your love, and collecting for you my remembrance, my disappointments, my poems and tones. I made a magic wine only for your lips. I watered your love in my heart, I was following your angelic steps.
—She answered, "my last hero, the moon is our hope, it can never go away, only if you left me alone and to a far point went". My lady: I fell alone in the ditch, then I ascended again by your light, step by step. Till I met your face.
My lady: look "there were many people and nations here, look "it was a clear world there, it was built then destroyed".. And they put all the past over my shoulder and ordered me to walk alone! "How I can understand the bird's language again"?
—She answered. "My last angel, come to Uproot all the seeds"! I asked her. "Why the heavy boat can run easily on the stagnant river"?
—She answered, "Because your light wind go to my ardent breast, and my exciting waves go to your warm chest . . . !"

Saad Farouk

Like God—9243

Like a flower in the field,
Like the rain in the forest,
Like the wind that whispers through the trees,
Like the stars that shine,
Like the cool still waters,
Like the fresh air that we breathe,
Like our God with peace.

Like a hot blazing sun,
Like the rage of the sea,
Like a tornado or whirlwind ripping, tearing, destroying,
Like the moon so far or mountain so high,
Like the thunder and lightning,
Like the powers unseen,
Like our God when He judges.

Like the law He gave,
Like the law without grace,
Like a God without a son,
Like our life without Christ . . .

Jacob D. Abraham

A Walk with God

As I walk along the pathway in the dappled woodland sun,
I sense that God is with me and a journey has begun.

He tells me as I walk with Him to open up my eyes,
To look and see the wondrous things, the birds, the butterflies . . .

I see a tiny cluster of sweet violet flowers,
Their dainty heads a-dancing, leaves moist from morning showers.

The scent of honeysuckle fills the tranquil air,
God shows me deep into their flowers and I watch a bee sit there!

He leads me then to riverbank where I see otters swim.
They move so swiftly through the reeds, undisturbed by me or Him.

We sit a while and watch these things, enjoy the quiet peace.
It makes me realize this life is precious and unique.

God asks me if I want to stay, or go home and learn more?
How could I ever leave this place, the Father I adore?

He smiles and takes my hand in His, and says to me, "My child,
As you walk the path of life, I will never leave your side!"

So I agree to now return to the world that I once knew,
To learn the lessons I must learn 'til I return to You.

Joanne Burrows

Reflections on Reality

I sit on the back-step and watch the sun go down,
A mug of tea in my hand but loneliness in my soul.
Even with loving people all around me I still feel lonely,
For I am trapped in my own head
And there are some secrets that can never be told.
As dusk begins to settle and my tea cools enough to drink,
I look up into the sky and sense my isolation and unimportance
Yet at the same time I feel part of the universe,
Even one so insignificant as I is part of a living breathing world.
One that I both help to create and destroy.
One that never fails to astound me with its beauty, power and finesse.
Even after all my failings and misadventures,
All the lonely times and stressful times,
I still manage to look to the stars
With hope in my heart and ambitions in my head.
I do not know the answers to everything.
I know my conceptions will change with time,
But I also know that in the end,
Most of the things that seem to be so important
Really do not matter at all.

Heidi May

Death of the Pits

Boldly withstanding elements of passed decadent years,
Where men have braved the onslaught of the deep without fear,
Their fate and fortune awaiting, but their lives went slipping by,
Digging for those 'black diamonds', with each new dawn they die,
For no braver men will inherit the earth,
Nor follow the imprints they leave behind,
Coal dust running through their veins, imprisoned in the mind.
The rancour of stale air and sweat inhaled
in heaving congested lungs
No key could unlock the door of mystic strength,
no better valour sung,
Defiant and with dignity headstocks stand
in columns of anchored steel,
A landmark of the valley reaching out of its blood of life congealed.
The heart pulse that once beat within its veins forever still and cold,
And dormant wheels on axles rest, death seals and an eerie hold,
Creeping vines of nature spread their arms in endless quietude,
This air of silence floats o'er the hills, embraced in lonely solitude.
As forgotten men with stalwart hearts and faces that hide the pain,
See their landmark rusting with the wheels that will ne'er turn again.

Alfred Bough

My Dream

I had a dream all about me,
I was a mermaid in the sea.
Beauty holding everything as well as me,
As I looked over the land and sea.
Then the sea washed me to the side,
Nearer and nearer comes the tide.
I looked around in an intelligent way,
I saw the islands far away.

A group of dolphins swam up close,
They chattered and smiled and nibbled my toes.
"Climb aboard", one cried aloud,
And there I sat amongst the crowd.
We were diving and splashing all around,
Excitement and happiness I had found.
All of a sudden I fell in a pool,
I was awake and it was time for school.

Lauren Seager

Untitled

A mirrored image to the centre of pain
an indigoes aura—dancing, swaying, too close to the flame
of madness, the result of loneliness, the evidence of grief
A haunting refrain, fluttering overhead, forever spinning
in a leather padded cell, a lacklustre beauty in a living hell
Long fingernails, cracked and bent
hours, days in her madness spent
clawing at reality, searching for a way outside
lucid moments bringing tears, as a river wide
Unable to bridge the crumbling illusion to the hidden dream
left only with the sounds of terror—a Scream
Pulling at the tatters of life's seams, spun in ephemeral purple
wisps fraying at the edges of misty longing
. . . . . . and in a corner,
the ashes smoulder, holding the fading cognitive glow
a drifting orb, floating in the glassy pool of despair.

J. C. Thompson

Envy

Many of us will admit
we envy others quite a bit.
Those who complain with woe
wishing they were so and so.

Famous people have their problems
don't think their lives are always high.
A smile can often hide a heartache
disappointment gossip lies.

Envy shadows your achievements
relationships that you enjoy.
Why let your life be full of longing
casting doubt on your belonging.

Better work towards contentment
a challenge to improve your life
or you may find regret your partner
a life unfulfilled forever after.

Diane L. Towner

Woodlands

Wander through the woodland, see through nature's eye,
Sun filtering downwards, its rays descending from the sky.
A small river winding, as on an unending journey, to where,
Birds, dragonflies, insects drinking from the water, unafraid,
  no care.
Beneath the trees, the delicate yellow of the primrose in bloom,
They brighten the woods bringing colour, here there is no gloom.
Soon now more buds will open—creating a carpet of blue
As the bluebells bring alive the ground, with their own distinct hue.
The woods are full of music, a gentle breeze rustles fallen leaves,
And bird-song fills the air, their young fledglings waiting in trees
For food, to make them strong enough, and then also soon to fly,
Tentatively at first, then with confidence soaring upwards to the sky.
The birds, trees, flowers and insects they make the woods come alive,
For without this combination, the woodlands could never survive.

Irene J. Mooney

The First New Moon

It was the first new moon of year,
The sky so bright and crystal clear,
Stars were aglow like fairy lights,
As I gaze up at these beautiful sights,
Everything seemed oh! So serene,
The air so fresh and very clean,
I took a breath of this fresh air,
Whilst I looked around with a fixed stare,
Never before had I seen it so clear,
On the first new moon of the year,
So clean and crisp was this night,
As I gazed around with such delight,
No noise to hear except my breath,
As I gasped with joy and clasped my chest,
In memory of this wonderful sight,
I've locked the picture of delight,
In my brain this will always be clear,
On the first new moon of the year.

George Brett

Life after Death

Is it because I can't stay?
Is it because I'm going away?
Maria, Maria, don't shed your tears,
I have something to calm your fears.
Even though I'll leave you one day,
A piece of me will stay,
My spirit will never go away,
Remember me this way.

You know I'll never leave,
Right beside you I'll stay,
Just as long as you believe,
And you'll always believe,
You'll never forget me, that much I know,
Because you're the best friend I've found!
I'll stay with you everyday.

I know I can't stay, now I must go away,
I'm everywhere, If you need someone I'll be there,
You'll never be alone,
You'll always have a friend in me,
In your heart I'll stay for forever and a day.

Erin Saxton

Unusual Senses

If only I could touch the wind that whistles in the trees.
And catch the blue tit's song and put it in a jar with the breeze.
If only I could feel the snowflake's heart beat with delight.
And smell my eyes that are golden brown and light.
I'd like to taste a bumblebee that shines so yellow and black.
I'd like to smell the sky that stays so blue by day.

Rachel Miller

Hooked

Little bird up there in the sky
It's just not fair that he can't fly
He sits by the window day after day
Dreaming and thinking he must find a way
  You're so free and clear from any harm
He's falling slowly where no one will find
'Cause it's locked up there within his mind
To watch your glide is such a charm.
  To look at him, he's such a mess
His basement clothes, his hollow face
He doesn't like the way I stress
I think his life is a big disgrace.
I feel as though he's floating round
His head and feet won't come to ground
Just another spike and his life is vowed
And very soon he's going to reach that cloud
This is how he got his kicks
Now it's become a regular fix
I wish there was a way
To say he just can't play with "Life"

C. Fynes

To End It All

Oh, how easy it would be to end it all,
to leave all the pain and suffering behind,
to let my troubles become someone else's,
to close my eyes for the last time.
What is there to live for anymore?
My wife? My children? My money?
They've all gone long ago.
My wife is miles away, with her man,
My children are children no more,
And as for money, it's scraps of paper,
Only good for one thing.
It buys me alcohol, the only cure for my troubles,
Temporary of course, I need a permanent job now.
Pill after pill after pill, each one easing my pain,
I'm known as a nobody, yet nobody knows me,
I'm a man without a name.
One last drink, I'll say I'll have,
for the good old times, years ago, I never did get to finish it though.

Edel McCaul

Farewell to a Friend

There's a little corner in my heart that you have made your home,
and special thoughts are in my mind, that belong to you alone.
We've shared a special bond, that has meant so very much,
a precious kind of friendship that no one else could touch.
And so, if you must slip away, please leave the door ajar,
so that for everyone who loves you, you'll never be too far.

Christine Koukos

My Paradise

The tall palm trees and the buzzing bees,
The golden sand and the great steel band,
The turquoise sea all around me,
The blazing sun and I'm having fun.

The sweet smell of fruit, the birds are going to toot.
The lovely smell of flowers, I could be here for hours.
The smell of salty sea, I need a cup of tea.
The smell of sun tan lotion, hey that gives me a notion!

The palm trees' bark is rough and really tough,
Oranges and apples, their skin as smooth as can be.
The sea is all around as far as I can see,
mangoes smooth and sweet I don't want to move
   from this spot today.

The oranges are sweet, the sand under my feet is hot as hot can be.
The mangoes are fat and I need my hat or my head will start to burn.

The birds are singing and I will start bringing some food for
   tomorrow today.
I want to come back but one thing it lacked is another person
   with me!

David Smellie

Time after Time

The Sun is rising
Bright as the furious fire furnace
Lighting up the whole world with its light
The dawn of another day
The times roll by
Time and tide waits for no man

The Moon is shining,
The stars are out and in their places
All lighting up the black dark sky.
Another day is gone past
Never to be seen again
Be upright, up and doing
Make hay while the sun shines

Day after day, year after year, time after time
procrastination is the thief of time
Never put off till tomorrow what you can do today
Yesterday is gone forever
And tomorrow may never come
Now is the acceptable time

Bamidele Esudia

The Living Years

Sunshine as the Hearse rolls up,
Inside, the weak strengthless body of an old woman,
No she was old, but somehow seemed young,
Young in her thoughts, her care, and her love.

Her love hasn't changed,
Her care was warm,
And her thoughts were good,
for she had died,
But somehow still lived,
And will always live,
In my mind, my strength and my tender love of which
I tried to show her in the living years.

But those years are now gone,
Except the hope of new life which is anticipated
in each new day.

But I shall not be afraid,
In the hope of again meeting her,
In a new life, with new thoughts,
But that same love of which I shared with my nan,
In the living years.

Stuart Reynolds

Untitled

I never thought he would really go,
After all the years we had shared.

I couldn't believe it when he said, that
in truth he no longer cared.

He had met someone else, a friend of
mine, he wanted her for the rest of his life.

And that I should forget him, and start
a new life—stop feeling I was still his wife.

If only I could, I have tried, though
in vain, to live through this valley of pain.

But I love him still now, as I loved
him then—I will never be whole again.

Marie Carroll

Shades of Grey

Standing ridged, at the palm of my doom,
I stare at the anguish I am soon to lose.
Far below, people are waving,
A sign—Departure awaits me.
The Death Bell strikes,
My time is over.
Sentenced am I, to a world far kinder,
I jump towards my sweet destiny.

Nita Desai

Religious War

Oh, Irish fellowship,
Open your heart!
And listen to the Lord
Give your hand to your brother
And if you're the better Christ,
You do the first step.

Rivers of blood mixed up
With the salted tears of mothers and kids,
Poisoning the whole land
Getting the cows crazy.
Don't wait until this river
Reaches the ocean around you
If you don't want to eat crazy fish.

Rivers of blood in your baby's milk
It it can need of the apple tree to be
In competition with the pear tree
If you're an apple tree, be a good one
If you're a pear tree, be a good one
The difference is just in the fruits you give.

Sven Asian Jungbauer

I'd Like the Whole Not to Be Parts No More

I want your pure and undevoted soul,
Too much travel in the sinworld.
I want your fire-hot heart,
To bring me eternal love and luck.

I'd like the whole not to be parts no more,
As in life geography, we are two maps;
To be the same white light again,
Worshipping the Love that will come.

I'd like the destiny to follow slowly,
As a river in the plains, as a peaceful wind;
But you are the river in the mountains, with rapid waves,
You are the wind announcing unexpected storms.

When the target is close, to hurry you must do;
Without a ladder, you can't get to the highest branch.
When the lifetime trail ends up in Light,
The sky opens its eternal peace.

Vartosu Ioana

Sunset over Key West

The bay is all but deserted. The dusk is drawing in,
The dark shadows are growing taller. As the sun sets ever near.
The warm night breeze is softly blowing, gently swaying the
outstretched palms.
Rippling waves creep up to the shore. Covering footsteps
that are there no more.
Sailing boats drift in to view to watch the
spectacular sight
People gather in the square to sit and wonder, not a
sound or a whisper could be heard.
The sun is slowly setting with the hissing of the sea.
Like a ball of fire it disappears. Ever to be free.
The pink satin clouds are fading, floating out of sight.
Carried away by the gentle breeze deep into the night,
Another day will soon be here. Bringing up the sun.
To shine upon the bay once more.
A new day has begun.

Kim Hayes

Untitled

The pain goes deep within my heart.
I didn't think we'd ever be apart.
Life seems painful without you here.
My heart just bleeds, it's like a spear.
It goes deep within my heart.
It goes so deep it leaves a scar
It bleeds and bleeds and never stops.
I wish I were dead then there would only be a drop.

Andrew Rochell

The Man from Galilee

They say he was the Son of God,
That man from Galilee.
They say he came to earth
and died for such as me.

They say he was the Saviour,
That man from Galilee,
But many turned their backs on him,
His love they could not see.

And so upon a cross he hung,
That man from Galilee,
Two bad men hung beside him,
One other was set free.

As he hung there in the heat,
That man from Galilee,
He cried 'I thirst'; a sponge with wine was raised,
He drank, forgave and died for all humanity.

I know he came to save me,
That man from Galilee,
Oh how I wish I could deserve such love,
Such pain, suffered to set me free!

Patricia Browne

Night Magic

The dew has fallen; like tears of a child
they droop from each blade of grass.
The sun has gone, to bring morning and light
to yet another land.
A soft breeze blows. It knocks the fragile petals
to the soft green carpet below.
All is still, all is quiet.
The little hovering flies are the only inhabitants of the sky.
She is coming. She is coming.
I see her standing in the sky as she spreads her cloak.
And within the wink of an eye—
The fading blue is drowning in her magic.
All is dark. All is dull.
Then bursting through her evil cloth
comes one lone star, shining, shimmering.
Then comes another and yet another.
Looking all around I see
A Nation of stars.
All is calm. All is beautiful.

Ciara Payne

A Cat

Those bright green eyes bewitching me, body stiff and sleek,
poised ready to pounce sharp and alert, listening keenly, waiting
For a tasty morsel that he mighty sample,
Hidden by the green ferns and leaves, he is unnoticed.

His coat is ebony black, silky smooth, his senses are sharp,
he is any owners' pride but he is not a belonging,
he is his own person free and immensely proud to be so
But now . . . he sees something:

He is now erect, smoothly and silently, he moves
Towards a brown mouse sniffing about gaining, then, sensing her
predator, she runs scurrying away, small and frightened
Aware of the majestic animal behind.

He swipes, a blood curdling cry rings out and as he removes his
paw delicately, all that is left, is a mess of mouse flesh,
the eyes glazed and dull surrounded by a pool of blood
And he, the murderer, gobbles it up with relish.

His sufficient meal devoured, he begins to groom himself
Licking his lips, his fur and blood streaked paw; then he moves on,
gently lolloping away to hunt some other poor defenseless animal
But that's nature to him and me.

Bethan Stephens

The Child Remembers . . .

The child remembers her parent's smell,
The adult remembers a life that was better,
You never knew who I was,
You never heard me knock,
I love you now,
I loved you then,
You never knew of my love,
Someday soon you will,
My love,
I am the one who,
Is closest to you now.

Amy Leech

Untitled

The hum of nature catches my eye.
The honey buzzing sound of bees near by.
Near by? Good God. Run for your life.
How could I get into so much strife?
Squish it. Squish it.
  Get It Away.
No. Not near the cakes for Tilly's birthday.
Look out. Look out. It's near your shirt.
No. Don't touch it, for the sting really hurts.
Don't laugh at me I can't help what I feel,
  I Hate Them.
They are hairy, scary, bug-eyed bees from Hell.

Clare Topp

Oh to Be a God

Oh to be a God and have their wisdom and have their immortal lives be blessed.
A wondrous thing and in all grace be adorned with golden crown and sceptre.
To be the brightest star surrounded by a multitude of shining diamonds
Glittering in adoration lighting up with angelic glows suspended in ore above the earth.
To have eternal flight to stir such wings too sore above the darkened skies,
and set the day alight transforming all things into colour, the beauty of the sight.
To play with such perfection music upon a golden lyre
and send it down on angels wings such pleasures to the ear.
That dawn attending in her veil can cover with her precious pearls.
The jewel in God's own golden crown and with this blossom's life.
To see with eyes' all seeing these wonders on display.
Her tear's will fall like gentle streams' of love and quench all thirst below.
Oh to be a God and know all there is to know.

J. M. Hall

Ten Commandments

To worship me is what I ask, and worship me alone
And make yourself no idols, from wood or glass or stone.

Take not my name upon your lip, in dire contempt or vain
And I will walk with you this trip, and send the needed rain

Remember too the Sabbath day, and on this day to rest.
And don't forget that I'm your God, so put me not to test.

Honour your father and your mother, that you may know long life
And do no wrong to one another, be faithful to your wife.

Love your neighbour as yourself, that you may know my will
And do no harm to fellow man, nor anybody kill.

Put away all evil deeds, your lying and your stealing
Love and serve the Lord your God, that you may know your healing.

Covet not your neighbours ox, his donkey or his house
Speak not a word that isn't true, and covet not his spouse.

So look at me, the Lord your God, and let me hold your hand
And do all that I ask of you, 'til you reach the Promised Land.

Frank Mulrooney

Good Bye

As the days and weeks have past us by
I have always thought how I would say "Goodbye."
I remember those days when we were kids
The things that made us laugh with what you did.
A day has not gone by this year when I have not shed a tear.
I remember at the end of a long day
How you would always come to my bed at night and sit beside me.
We would talk about everything and anything
From my school to my friends.
Now I wish those times had never come to an end.
I know life in our house was not always what you liked
But you had a beautiful wife and seven great kids
With number seven a bit of a tike.
I'm sorry that I was not there when you left us that day,
But I know in your heart you knew I was on my way.
I know I might have not always done what you wanted or asked me to be
But I always tried so hard for you to be proud of me.
Saying "Goodbye" to someone you love can be hard to do,
But always remember Dad I will always love and miss you.

John Routt

My Birthplace

Like a Phoenix from the ashes
In a place where no famous man
Is lying in the churchyard
There was born a poet
Whose every word would in latter days
Be praised by learned men
And women, pricing locks from his head
Would make him bald before his time.

The squalid slimy back street terrace
His birthplace will become a shrine
Where tradesmen will peddle tasteless tawdry tea-towels
Promulgating words from Ollerenshaw's hands.

Students will be told to put away their Shakespeare
Like the growing child was told to put away his toys
And his former English teacher will rummage through his files
To find valuable remnants of his work
And feel foolish at the marks he gave him
And perhaps
A little humble.

Ian Ollerenshaw

She Said, I Said

"I don't want to talk about it." She said
　"OK." I said
"I'm glad you understand that." She said
　"It's cool." I said
"Because you know if I had to talk about it, I'd have to remember." She said
　"I understand." I said
I'd have to think about the pain, the anger, hurt, the self recrimination, the horror, the guilt, the dirtiness inside." She cried
　"Maybe." I said
"I can't do that. I can't put myself through it again." She sobbed
　"I guess not." I said
"I would feel his hands tearing, pulling, scratching, hitting, hurting, pounding, robbing all over again." She moaned
　"Probably." I said
"I would feel his body clawing, gnawing, whoring, scoring." She whispered
　"Possibly." I said
"You Bitch. I said I didn't want to talk about it." She screamed
　"I know." I replied.
"But you had to."

Jo Bicanic

Society Today

What's happened to society today?
We're all stuck up in our money grubbing ways
Though it shouldn't really matter whether you're rich, poor or gay
What's happened to society today?

The world should be perfect some say,
Everyone rich, everyone perfect every day.
Although it might not happen quite this way
There will always be the rich, the poor and the gay.

Some think in your country you should stay
and not leave unless you're on a holiday.
People black or white are all the same within
It doesn't matter about the colour of the skin.
For it's the skin that covers the heart, and that my friend, is the most important part.

Don't judge people by the way they look or if they are rich or poor

For the heart my friend is the most important part.

Charlene De Jesus

She Left without Hope

Opened eyes reach the dark,
Blindmen get through it on a spark,
Pain and pleasure melt together,
Hearts are devoured forever;
For life's core's bright
Giving birth to a shallowing light.

Worms fly,
People crawl, fish cry,
Hearing light's soul lie;
And suddenly you decide:
"I'm gonna make things right,
I'll deny it, I won't be sucked into the meal,
This squelching crowd from which I want out;
I'll scream, I'll shout and think aloud
Before I touch the cold ground,
Where on a surface spread around
Blobs of my blood will form a vein,
Which I suppose will be in vain."

Soica Alin

The Spider

She wraps her silken web of longing
Around your soul. You lie in her midst,
Tangled in reminiscence. Waiting, doomed,
For your past to consume you completely.
Her sticky fingers reach out and reinforce
Her hold on your heart, and you give up the struggle
to live.

Z. Scowen

Why God?

Why him, why now, why us,
Why so young, so sudden, so what if he caused a fuss,
What harm did he ever do you, what stupid rule did he break,
That you could justify such punishment? His life you had to take.

We knew him rather personally, and he wasn't all that bad,
He made us laugh, he made us cry, he even made us mad,
That cheeky, saucy, devilish face, en route from trouble, soon disclosed.
He wasn't the guilty party, just a big lamb in small wolves clothes.

His mother misses him, indeed she's often said it,
His big sisters miss him, maybe I'm intruding, but quietly I've read it.
Little Tara misses him, no rows, no games, no laughter,
The boys silently miss him, they've no one to look after.

So God, the next time you need to fill a space,
pick a life that's nearly run.
Not one that's needed here on earth and barely just begun.

Right God! I see your point, if you fill
heaven with crocks and sick and lame
You need an odd good character, or you too would go insane.

Tadhg Murphy

The Zen Followers

Far from the surprising Zen followers,
Illuminated figures of the Father flicker,
Glow maybe on the faces of the church goers,
Hiding the famished fangs of the slickers.

The thousands of fanes are feckless
In their fight to fictionalise the unseen,
Nobody can bring down the fearless,
Glacial demon that flourishes in the sheen.

Denial, this is the failure of mankind, the fact.
Reaching towards further dimensions
After centuries of civilization, in fact
Gives humans another comprehension.

Ought we search more answers?
Nobody knows.
Sometime, maybe, some answers
Will come from the surprising Zen followers.

Adina-Maria Unguras

Return to Nature

Up here, where spring springs into life again,
That which has lain dormant
During the long, cold, dark days of winter.
The first white blossoms blooming forth:
Pretty yellow flowering shrubs
Dotted on the hillside.

Rarely seen, seldom heard.
Creatures come to life again;
Following blindly and instinctively
The way nature has dictated.

Our lives, so much more complex and diverse.
Struggling to survive each day against the odds
We have created for ourselves.

Beyond this mortal existence
Do we regenerate ourselves
Perhaps in some other guise
Or do we simply die?

Jane Jones

From Poems of Grief

I burn a torch inside my grief,
to carve a window in this night
and watch again your days with me
recede, to disappear from time.

Our yesterdays hold pride of place
for gardens rich with summer flowers
responding to your springtime joy,
to complement the loveliness
your presence made, with grace and charm
while love's enchantment spanned your years.

My torches shine on yesterdays
alone, cast shadows on all else,
console a thousand days of grief
and light me to my waiting hour.

Too blindly as my sight grows dim,
I see you waiting on the path
that pines away through love-lorn flowers;
and by my window wait my turn,
to watch the willow bow her head
and weep awhile, for me as well

Rol P. Price

We Sat by the Fishpond

We sat by the fishpond, my grandson and I,
Watching the clouds floating by in the sky.
It was such a perfect summer's day.
At least it was to me in every way.
Occasionally a fish popped up for some air
And bees seemed to be busy—everywhere.
The trees were fanned by a gentle breeze
And butterflies went to and fro as they pleased.
We talked awhile of many things,
The problems and pleasures that this world brings.
Age was no barrier, our souls were as one
That wonderful day in the summer sun.
Magical moments—still as fresh today.
I do not think they will ever fade away.
Yes, we sat by the fishpond, my grandson and I.
I shall treasure those moments until the day that I die.

Beatrice Smithies

Nature

The stars are bright for tonight,
So spare a thought for the dead tonight.
Your life is crumbling before your eyes,
Just like a building in the sky.

A child is born every day,
Spare a thought for the dead today.
What nature gives you take away,
not to see another day.

Kevin Peart

Tumult

On stormy night when howling wind sings deep lament
To blackened skies and rain soaks every stone and blade of grass,
The traveller braces shoulder 'gainst the wind,
And curses life for such a plague as this.
With hands outstretched he seeks to gain a hold
On thrashing thorny branches near his eye,
But earth is soft and fluid underfoot,
The way is dim and angry as the thundering heavens,
Rent by lightning, split the sky in silver forks
Of heavenly rage, sparked from cruel talons of an angry god.
As earth's breath shrieks round every hill and vale
And drives all living things to shelter from its icy blast,
The gasping traveller tumbles to his door and with freezing fingers
Lifts the latch, to be embraced by gentle golden light and warmth,
A welcome mortal haven from Gaia's torrid, shrieking song.

Beverley Ann Fairfoull

To See Purity

You, me, two angels lie between us
On beautiful clouds
They fly although their feet do not yet carry them
Showing us what we once saw
As angels
But now fail to remember
It is nature's clever law
I am elated
Kind to us, the privilege to see purity
Something that has always been lost
That is why you saw me and I saw you
Now two angels lie between us.

Kirsten Moffat

Lining Up the World

England's heart is sound enough
There lies the world full of wonder
With wistfulness strange hidden stream
Under high-arching cliffs
Trembles like shifting water
On a huge cave full of skylight.

Recognitions, greetings of half-acquainted things
As the clouds of blue distance blunders horizon
Here in the swelling fresh the great activity working
As year's fall, fades in the wood
Are remembered by the closing distance
Catching the scent and colour of the coming features.

The perfect practice glisten with sunlight
Passing through round into the next corner
Beating the throne of honest desires.
Under which unshaken cloud holds the world
Brings sharply back something of flowing memory.

Heather Aspinall

Africa 1994

Racism, religion, pacifism, patriotism, you have it all
I don't look right I am white.
My mind is with you, my spirit, my soul lives your pain
Suffers your resentment, suffers your patriotism,
That has made you what you are.
Taken our dignity, taken our identity.
We know why we are here, to take what is ours.
Our freedom.
A freedom that you feel is only yours.
Only when your freedom is found, will ours be total.
Land of dreams, land of hypocrisy.
In this small world, will you find your serenity?
It is there and I need its touch.
The sadness and pain you feel, feel in your soul.
Spoils of war that cost so much.
So much in lives and land.
Land and honour, honour amongst men.
Men of strength, strength of culture, strength of courage.
Courage to meet you and be with you forever.

Neil Chase

The Beach

When I am by the deep blue sea
I look around at people like me,
Children laughing and playing in the sand
Just metres away from where I stand,
Ice-creams melting in the sun
Everyone happy, having fun.
The tide washes down a newly built castle
But making a new one is no big hassle,
Out at sea are children swimming
With little faces that are just brimming
Full of excitement and full of joy
They like this more than their favourite toy,
Buckets and spades and lollies each
That's what I see when I go to the beach.

Gillian Grace

Cross on the Wall

I'm looking at the cross on the wall
prayers can't help the ones who always want it all.
I'm listening to advice for the first time
wondering why I can't make up my own mind.
Please don't be surprised at my short smile
you only get a laugh when you make it worth my while.
Train to be the best that is all you can do
don't need a firm hand to guide me through.
Don't swear on holy bible to tell the truth
if you have no faith don't offer God as your proof.
Just looking at the statue, piercing my eyes
with thorns round the head and blood for the cries
fighting for a cause you hear the gospel preach
what can the church learn if it only wants to teach
convents of nuns filled with peace, no crying
but outside our world. Open your eyes we're dying
there's no food for the hungry or money for the poor
no ozone for the earth, no healing for the sore.
So many things come to mind, does it for us all?
Just through one simple thing the cross on the wall.

Terena T. J. Wilds

A Few Words for Our Dad, Who Died of His Burns

What fate decreed that you should end like this,
Your independent life abruptly gone.
I tried to find an unmarked place to kiss,
So glad the flames had left your lips alone.
How bravely you endured that tiny bed,
Although you whispered "Wish I could go home".
And looking at your poor old blackened head
I would have loved to say to you, "then come."
To end your days within the place you loved,
To gaze out at the hills that soar so high.
I'm sorry dad you just could not be moved,
So unfamiliar faces watched you die.
But we were close at hand I'm sure you knew,
Before you sank into that final sleep.
The things you asked seemed reasonable to you
and promises I made I'll try to keep.
But things don't always work out as they should
And sometimes other things can cause distress.
I know I will have done the best I could
Rest well, love, and for now, God Bless.

M. E. Campbell

Friends

Friends are a must,
People you can really trust.
Friends are people you can tell your problems to,
They're also usually very loyal to you.
Friends are kind and caring.
And very good at sharing.
Friends can always be relied upon,
Plus they'll always be there if you ever need a shoulder to cry on.
Friends tell all their secrets and more.
With friends you'll never really be poor.

Samantha Williams

Golf Crazy

Golf is not an easy game
The average man will not find fame,
You stand and hit a little ball
Then listen for the fatal call.
If fore is called, then do look out
Someone's received a nasty clout.

You stand for hours perfecting your grip,
Try hitting the ball, but nothing moves it
You jump up and down in a fit of rage
While passersby shout "Hey mate act your age!"
To the clubhouse you make a hasty retreat
For a pint and a chat and something to eat.

Home to the wife with a tale so tall,
Of how perfectly well, you've been hitting the ball
When deep down inside, you know darn well
It's a ruse to be out with the boys for a spell

Dawn Maggs

Reflections on Thought.

Think black.
Think it above and below and all around.
Not a pitch black, but just a velvet darkness.
Sink into its softness,
It is mystical, eerie, other worldly.
Think white.
Think it above and below and all around.
Not a pure white, but just a silky brightness.
Float upon its radiance,
It is magical, strange, ethereal.
Think sound.
Think it above and below and all around.
Not a symphonic sound, but just a musical lightness.
Rise above its resonance,
It is heavenly, vibrant, spiritual.
Think silence.
Think it above and below and all around.
Not a profound silence, but just an aural nothingness.
Drift upon its serenity,
It is inscrutable, calm, spectral.

Audrey Young

Holiday Time

Corfu Corfu here I come
14 days in your beautiful sun
Slip on grit broken leg.
First nine days Corfu hospital bed

Daughter Jill travelling far
Sometimes bus but mostly taxi car
No sandy beaches no laying in the sun
Just waiting for my daughter Jill to come
Bringing some food that I can eat
The big tomato is really a treat

July it all started I still limp about
One wrong move and I give a shout
Not for much longer I really do hope
Then we will sit back and think it's all been a joke

June Christensen

Desire's Night

Shine stars on the sky like glowworms in the night
And the moon surrounds us in his light cloak
A peaceful night without the end,
Like an old story from ancient time.
The solitude what presses you hard, and
The time who passes flying
A moment to can stop it,
To exist an eternity in this night
To turn into one of the stars who falls down
To be a ray from the cloak of the moon
is all what you can wish in this night
Without beginning and without end.

Alina Duciuc

Decline . . .

A thought goes back and reaches our genesis,
one might recall, through clouds of nepenthes and mists,
Jehovah, when inspiring clay with sacred breath . . .
Since then, we, wretched creatures, seemed very loath . . . ,
loath to keep ourselves celestial and,
therefore, among tempestuous seas of days of yore,
existence carved within our hearts and reason,
with rows of hieroglyphs . . . with feelings—the entire human nature.
Perhaps these are the ones to take the blame
For man's departure from his noble origin . . .
Yet, above them all, his vanity remains the one because of
which the most expensive debt was paid by our world,
and thus, so many, were the victims of discord, vice or even fame . . .
And that is why we've seen the temples of our future wrecked—
the smile on every youth's face, slowly fading way
just like the divine whisper of a poesy . . .

Marius Ivascu

The Wonder of England's Beauty

Tall waving hedgerows enveloped us,
Entwined with wild-scented honeysuckle.
And foxgloves bowed their bell-like heads
To buttercups dancing in the breeze,
Whilst spiky thistles with purple crowns
Hid tiny golden celandines.

Then, the lane climbed high to the vista beyond,
A spectacular patchwork quilt
Of patterns and tints from this wonderful world,
Where cascading conifers rolled down the hills,
To meet us in the valley below,
Oh the wonder of England's beauty . . . .

Pauline Wienholt

Fire Bug

The crackle of newspaper, excites your red eyes.
The taste of ash, brings saliva to your tongue.
The air breathe ignites your black heart.
The dark shadow smother his last lung.

Torch his strata, flesh to blood and bone.
His eyes sting, the veiled flickering flame.
As he tries to extinguish, you see
the smouldering beauty, too wild to tame.

Overcome with a thick blanket of crimson,
you rock and breathe that blackened air.
he burns and begins to asphyxiate,
his cremation, a result of your unstable dare.

Torridity and inferno stimulate your brain.
Fire-fly and fire-bugs cling to double-sided tape
Believing you're incombustible, you worship that fuel.
Intimidated by the hydrant, gasoline in hand, the next ritual.

Tristan Reed

Being Alive

All too soon the frost of death had come,
Another flower had withered too soon.
The blanket of glistening frost had won,
Pools of dead water with ice are strewn.
Man stopped short in his tracks reflecting,
Wooden his gaze on death, detecting.

Barren was Winter, unfruitful ways,
Interaction 'twixt man and seasons,
One in his prime, and ending of days,
Bleak winter's sleep, it is the reason.
The fire is dead, no longer burning,
Of death and life, man has been learning

Man has to depart to be reborn
Nature had her way, the earth is sleeping,
A soul of fifty winters had worn.
Trees bare of leaves, fruit and flowers keeping.
Rebirth, hallmark of creator, king
Perennial miracle in spring.

Ann Easton

The Urchin

A little boy with tattered coat,
A dirty scarf wrapped round his throat,
An urchin from the slums of hell,
Who couldn't read, write or spell.

But he could whistle, sing and laugh,
As he wiped his face on his dirty scarf,
Making his way down through the trees,
His golden hair blowing in the morning breeze.

He had a small rough dog on a string-made lead
A lively fellow from an unknown breed,
The boy was kicking an empty tin,
The dog was barking, the boy would sing.

The October air was crisp and clean,
As more boys gathered on the patch of green,
Goal posts made from coats and hats,
As they picked sides for a football match.

The boy who couldn't read write or spell,
The urchin from the slums of hell,
Enjoying the pleasures not the strife,
Exploring the treasures what a wonderful life.
Johnnie N. Mills

A Glimpse of Nature

Out to the mountains I did cast my eye
To catch just a glimpse of a bird fly bye.
This creature so wonderful and yet so small
Is very seldom noticed by a stranger at all.
Its wings did move in a rhythm so grand,
But what I was wondering was where it would land,
And now this bird I can no longer see,
Its beauty and splendor will be remembered by
  Me!
Siobhan Rice

A Mother and Father's Love

A mother and father's love is a daughter's prayer
In loving arms and tender care.
A mother and father's love should depend
For their daughter to be their friend.
A daughter is there to love and comfort her
father and mother,
To share thoughts and secrets in times of trouble.
A mother and father's love shouldn't be hard to find,
Like a breath of pure flowers they should combine
Their love should be measured not in years
but in moments that they share.
In every smile and word and touch
Which should show how much they care
for moments of togetherness.
In laughter, joy and sorrow
Adds strength and beauty to their love with
an every new tomorrow.
Leanne Sheerin

Desire

A desire so strong
That burns inside,
A need to complete,
And a will to survive.

Some people disbelieve,
Laugh at my dream,
But the dream will become real,
Someday I'll be part of that team.

No matter how long or hard,
I must feed this ambition,
And quench this fire,
Only when the elite is achieved,
Will this burning need,
Again become a seed,
And give way to another dream or reality?
Abigail Penne-Stuart

Commuter April, 1997

I wish I could write a poem,
To while the slow minutes away,
I wish that the words would just tumble . . .
Ulu Ululu Ululay.
Apple, alpine, altitude,
Pepper, pomp and pulchritude,
Uxorious unctuous unguent,
Zeolite, zebra and zest.
An alpinist Zebra on zeolite crest
Ate an apple with pomp and zest,
Lord of the world at this altitude,
Uxorious, sniffing the pulchritude
Of his herd, peppered over the plain . . .
A crooked hyena, unctuous,
Bent a leg at his Court,
Offered him unguents, spices and wine,
Doubloons, ducats and dollars galore;
Tyrian purple. Gossamer fine
Lace cuffs and collars. Rugs from Lahore.
And a damned season seat on a Privatised Line!
Frances Searle

Lost at Sea

O come into my parlour, come in and look around
Where timely recollections from all the world abound.

Trinkets from the Orient, a Prayer from Katmandu
Set within a scarlet frame from one I loved so true.

Woven silken roses, a shawl of lace so fine
So often did encumber those bonny babes of mine.

A faded Persian Carpet lies worn beneath my feet,
It carried forth a magic, it made our life complete.

A dusty Book of Poems so often did inspire
A wealth of rosy images all gathered by the fire.

A host of faded memories all carried by the Sea
It came into my Parlour and took them all from me.
Greta Bayliss

The Comet

Travelling around the heavens, millions of miles and more . . .
See the power of the Almighty as we peek through Heaven's door.

Older than the sands of time, brighter than any Sun,
One wonders 'where Comet do you go' and from whence you come?

Racing across the heavens, through the never ending sky . . .
Are you from Mercury, messenger of the Gods, or Zeus, from
  His throne on high?

How swiftly, mighty Comet, you travel on your way . . .
On through, distant endless space as you leave our Milky way.

How many Solar Systems will you see, and so pass by . . .
How many distant Suns like ours—illuminate your sky?

You are living energy, straight from the Source of Power
You do not measure distance—as we do, by the hour.

How great is the Almighty—if you, as a sample came,
Dare we hope, to be a part—of that 'Eternal Flame'.
Rose Marie Lister

Spirit

A relentless desire to take charge and stand,
no jeers disconnected will fade my command.
I fear to breathe, as this simply speeds up my time.
To torment emotion unless trapped and caged
dismember, deprive, destroy the remains.
A world at my feet, so how do I sleep,
in pain of my failure.
Damned by foes and by friends,
By the gallows I still condescend.
Sweetness scurries slowly as I taste success;
Shallow a heart that hinders progress.
I confess I confess I confess.
Michael McGinty

Life?

Why do I feel love, why do I feel hate?
Why do things happen, is it all fate?
Why are some things good and others bad?
Why do things make me miserable and sometimes sad?
Where did I come from, where have I been?
I often wonder—what does life mean?

Is there a purpose in me being here?
Why does hurt provoke me a tear?
Who am I really? I need to know,
After I'm dead, where will I go?
What have I experienced, what have I seen?
I often wonder—what does life mean?

Joanna Hastings

Children at Heart

The waves from the north sea seem to greet me,
The huge sky at night fills me with delight.
The comet star has appeared and I know that next time it
    will I shall not be here.
Down by the sea-front on our mountain bikes we go,
My love and I,
Feeling like children in our late years.
We watch the sleepy town wake up in the morning,
As we sit in the Victorian Garden eating our cakes for breakfast.

We laugh and kiss.
The sea air from which nothing can compare,
Lifts us on a magic carpet.
The shiny pebbles on the beach, are like precious jewels for
    us to reach.
Red and white sails in the horizon,
Complete the picture all around.
It is a wonderful day to be by the sea . . . .
Maybe because the love of my life is with me.
As we gather our mountain bikes,
We say to each other,
'It's a great day to be alive.'

Anna Tolley

Observatory Station, Cape Town

With their thin, cracked voices
And their thin, cracked faces
The old man and the old woman
Sat waiting for their train
She said
Surely you are not going into town all alone?
He said
No, oh no, I am going on my own,
They spoke louder than anyone else on the platform
And they wore their jerseys in the heat.

Katherine Moon

A Walk on the Wild Side

Ramblers are a crazy breed
They walk in wind and rain and sleet
Pack on back and hat on heed
In heavy boots to protect their feet

Through the field and over the stile
The snake-like procession goes back for miles
The sheep and the cows all stand bemused
As these two legged humans take a comfort stop
In the field that they use

Ramblers are a happy bunch
At one o'clock they stop for lunch
Then it's dine by the river, or is it a lake
A voice from the back, is heard to say
How much time did we take

Ramblers are a motley crew
At the end of a walk there's always time for a brew
Or a pint . . . or a short . . . core . . . that's the life
Then it's on to the bus and home to the wife

Mary Smith

Save Their Future

Laughing, playing in the sun,
Two young children having fun.
Across the dusty yellow sand,
They're running, jumping hand in hand.

Swimming, splashing in the sea,
Great big smiles a pleasure to see.
The future for them when they are grown,
Is a worrying thought of complete unknown.

The earth is deteriorating day by day,
It's us that are making it happen they say.
Polluted air and acid rain,
CFC's and gases that maim.

What can we do to make it right?
And know that it will shed some light.
This planet we must try to save,
And return the goodness it so gave.

We must make a future for them,
Not give up hope and leave to condemn.
We need to protest and forward our case,
To give our offspring a good future to face.

D. M. Davidson

Rejection

Why cans't thee not hearest me, is my voice so dumb?
Thy face doth turn into the wall and the wall too dense.
Thy is lost to the senses and senses render not to thee
Cans't thee not look beyond and in the looking wilt thou not come?

Wherest hath faded fine thoughts and wishes of love?
Once thee would stand before us and we all love prove,
Now thee stands aloft—I am bereft of thee,
Now why the longest path and the widest sea?

Cans't there not be a glimmer to catch before all is lost and away?
Cans't thee not turn thy head and speed like the wind to my side?
Would thou have me beg my soul for thee to friendly be?
Cans't thee not find one kind word in thy memory?

Thy intent is clear now thee must make haste, now go
I wish not to blame or claim a heart that is not mine own
The door is ajar soon it will wide open be,
Thou hast spoken thy silence with mouth moved not for me.

Pauline Nash

The Enchanted Forest

We enter, walk, talk, stop, listen to the
stillness and then the rustling of the trees.
We walk, stop and listen to the singing of the
birds in the leafy boughs.
We walk, talk and look at the beauty of the
trees in all their splendour standing high and
low with the blue sky peeping through.
We walk, then stop to look at the beauty of
the woodland flowers, red, blue, purple and
white, in colours arrayed, what a beautiful sight!
We walk, talk, stop, look and listen to the
wonders all around; knowing this is where
peace, happiness and beauty are found.

Isobel Pillar

The Sporting Dogs

Going into the country today,
To visit the greyhounds; Hurrah;
Oh, what Fun to see them run
Up the hills and down again.
Round and round they go,
Twisting this way and that.
Imagine them on the track,
There's Punch and Essick and Teddy too;
They're real beauties, that's very true,
So wait and wait,
Until they are full grown;
And onto the track to come into their own.

M. Hunt

Thoughts in Time

Tick, Tock, Tick, Tock that clock sings me that song,
to soothe my mind to ponder on my thoughts.
My mind is full of dreams though happy they may seem
they rush swiftly in a race to keep with its ticking pace
Ah! I forgot what they call this song.
They say thoughts take time, that keeps moving on.

I travel miles afar I meet people I not yet know
the person I want to be, the places I want to see
my heart thumps with glowing glee
I glimpse a world of ecstasy
Ah but listen! Tick, Tock, Tick, Tock,
that beat of monotony forces me to reality.
That didn't last for long.
Ah! I forgot what they call this song.
They say thoughts take time, that keeps moving on.

Sheena Marie Lawlor

Hail Solitariness

O Solitariness! Glory glory to thee;
For sweeter than honey presence thine.
Hail solitariness, ever ever thy kingdom;
Lo, battles no more and peace friend thine.

Adorned with lilies chariot thine thither;
Behold! On her couch conception inside.
And soft fingers her veil a slide and slide;
Beckons poet, thou go enjoy and mind fill.

And wild wild land thou wander yon poet;
O mind fill and fill with love her wine sweet.
Happy happy faded flowers and fallen leaves;
And ye gain tinct and life again forever.

No lark, nor a sweet song of nightingale;
Yet what unheard melody in soul repeats.
Sweet and bitter tingling, a tale in soul;
O poet, all forget and sing on lilies and dead leaves.

M. J. Gabrial

Man Alone

Inward outward stuck on a street,
A man alone, impure indiscreet,
Burning inside . . . yet a cold fish to see,
Spitting his slime at the powers that be.
A man alone . . . who won't shed a tear?
A martyr to his kind . . . he's forgotten
His own fear.
Time is the Devil . . . and he can't grasp the
Plot, and immune from his fall . . . are you
Certain you're not?
Know—man alone, your company's good—
We all stand alone . . .
We are all of your blood.

Jim Thompson

The Pain Inside

Here I stand as a year before,
My lonely retreat upon the moor;
It's strange now that alone I stand,
No-one left to hold my hand.
The peace and tranquility wash through me,
The soft glow of evening colours in the sky entrances me.
A fine mist is rising off the land
And at every calm, deep breath I take,
I feel my body is going to break
And smash like a mirror into a thousand pieces;
But I am numb to the pain.
I feel my body screaming, my heart cries out
"I love you, please come back to me, I need you."
But my pleas are unanswered; and it will never be
That he'll stand here again with me.
So I stand all alone, gazing into the distant orange sun,
Knowing that his race is run.
I never want to leave this place;
This lonely, solitary, comforting place,
Where we once stood. Where I can grieve.

Laura Trowbridge

Nurses

Nurses are a special breed, they do all the things we need,
Help the rich and the poor. and the stubborn and the dour,
Of the filthy jobs they do, bring healing to me and you.
All their days they do strive, every day to save lives.

It is no job of glamour.
As our T.V. screens do clamour,
They watch us constantly through the night,
And during the day, they keep us right.
They give us relief when in pain, their work is not in vain.

They are both loving and kind, in this world, so hard to find,
We see the angels God has made, that is the mark of their trade.
So, M.P.'s remember the nurses,
And give them larger and fuller purses.

A grateful nation should be proud.
And shout praise long and loud.
To those gallant girls in white,
Administering angels of the night
So thanks to them from all of us,
Who do a great job without a fuss.

Sandy Lowrie

The Storm!

In a storm the wind whistles the thunder,
howls and everything is frightening, roaring lightning
flashing angrily, the rain pitter pattering and
everyone singing drip-drop, drip-drop, hoping that
it will soon go away, the moon running away
and a horse galloping far away.

Razwana Alyas

The Clown

A lonely figure sits surrounded by a crowd,
His heart is sad, but his laughter is loud,
The tears roll down his painted cheeks
as he performs his act every night of the week.

The show must go on, or so the saying goes,
But the sad old clown with the big red nose
has a secret which he tries hard to hide,
and through the laughter and jokes, his heart
is breaking inside.

The little daughter he adored with long golden curls
who delighted the people with tumbles and twirls
had been stricken down with an illness so grave
that the Doctor had said she could not be saved.

The light had gone out of the old clown's life
He had already lost his beautiful young wife
but he carried on smiling and making the children cheer
and hoping that God his prayers would hear
To help him get through the heartache and pain
Until his broken heart was mended again.

Beryl Lowe

Image of Man

Hate to hate, let's fight, let's fight
Makes for long dark days,
and darker nights.
Arab and Jew can't equate, too late, too late.
Their promised land given to them by their God's right hand.
Wailing walls and minarets,
Won't let man forget, forget.
A relative the monkey maybe,
But it's the son of man who's up the tree.

The ills of the world,
The pollution of Earth, Sea and Space,
Are all the work of the human race.
The answer, simple though it may be,
Is for man to come down from his tree.
To use the gold of knowledge freely given,
To make planet earth another heaven.

G. R. Leslie

Revenge

The naked bloody bodies lie entangled in the pit
The putrid smell of death that the corpses emit
The nudity of people made even more obscene
By bones protruding wickedly from bodies starved so lean.
All worldly goods were plundered by their butchers long before
Stained with blood and mucus, fragments of the gore
Like cattle branded orderly the numbers all in view
To show their masters' mark by the ink of a tattoo.
But does the motherland recall and do they ever rue
When they'd persecute a man just because he was a jew
Did this holocaust occur by men thought now deranged
Or did some spiritual incitement initiate God's revenge!

S. McFauld

Impotence

He looked, he trapped, salvaging her body
She submitted, crying, pleading for deliverance
The epitome of her joy played
He strangled, pleaded, his mute calls unheard
She danced as girls in a line before his gaze,
Diaphanous, beyond his vision,
His pain tangible above his sigh.
She sequestered his thoughts for future mastication,
He bled her, expostulating his thick bile,
All the time, she strummed a nameless tune
A tattoo for the living.
He devoured, he ate, ruminating like a scholar
of some unspoken law,
He fought, submitted, clamored, nails raised in
supplication to blank skies,
Her mind an eddy, a maelstrom of modern fixation.
He died, exhaled lugubriously the last whim of a fanatic,
Her laughter echoed mirthlessly as that of a child deserted.

Louise Griffin

Hi Life, How You're Doing?

Hi life, how you're doing?
I see you're dying.
Or are you 're-borning'?
Hi, what's the point—
Don't you know
You will bleed again?
Well, if you live with me!

But I ain't gonna hold
Your hand again.
You asshole,
Think
Think
Think
Where do you think
you will be going?

Bikash Das

Our Children's Children

A tempest crashed through a brilliant blue sky
causing havoc with a capital H.
duck you suckers, here I come!
Chaos on every street corner throughout this precious land of ours,
the world's oceans whipped up a violent rage,
giant waves engulfed the once unique Manhattan skyline,
the shores littered with sorrow,
the sun blacked out by a dead sky just hanging there above
the muffled horizon, all our worst fears now reality, all our prayers unanswered.
Too late now, too late to help, to intervene or is this what you wanted? To rid your supreme creation of darkness.
Back to the old drawing board eh!
But surely not, not all this pain, we never wanted this, we don't deserve this, there must be something you can do, surely we can work something out. Just turn back the clock for a while and rectify the damage, they'll listen then, our leaders, they'll listen, we'll make the bastards listen and save our children's children.

Martin King

John Lennon

Forget about the Quarrymen, the Beatles
The Cavern too,
John Lennon is a legend, quite different
from me and you.
Born in 1940, this man who changed the world,
His heart was full of peace and love
and honesty was his word.
He fought against the establishment, to
show his love for mankind,
but they all "ragged him", "bagged him"
"shagged him" to face, from above and from behind.
Why do we treat these good people in
this callous and uncaring way.
Man's inhumanity to man, is definitely
the norm of today
love, peace, happiness, that has the
message from John, but fate has
twistered cruelly again,
and now John Lennon has gone.

Hugh Jon Dillon

Palm Tree, Juhu

Pregnant fruit
fake veils conceal.

Dark pendulous testicles
are heavy
with bearing.

Anahite Contractor

Moule in Your Eye!

Chocolate body paint was meant to be
An erotic experience on Valentine's night.
Is it over hyped?
The thought is terribly titillating
But the reality a turn off.
In unappealing it
With a good appetite
And needing calories
Misstating over the erotic zones
Caressingly we spread and moulded
Always with a wary thought for
The Egyptian cotton sheets
Enough.
Tongues tentatively licked
Over sickly sweet coverings
We persisted but nausea came
Vigorously we massaged
Then suddenly stopping
Headed for the flannel and bathroom sink
To restore our former cleanliness.
With relief we agreed we hated food in bed.

M. Rooney

Coquette

He spies a young girl with dyed blonde hair,
She fixes a stare, smiles, he doesn't really care.
He can see beyond her face another face,
As for her other face, he hasn't the time or the place.

"Are we beneath her?" she seems to think,
He turns away and buys another drink,
He can recall the time they both became one,
what he had said and wished he had done.

Again in conversation she tries her luck,
All he wants is a beer and a fuck.
Coquette indeed she is, everybody knows,
and so easy to talk her out of her clothes.

His body is old. Immature is her mind.
A poem so true, even though it's unkind.

Antony Leadbitter

Stevie's Dogs

Rocky is a lovely dog; his coat is black and gold
He's never bitten anyone, unless of course he's told.

He's never bitten the postman and he's never bitten the vet
But Gloria had better watch herself 'cause she's collecting debt.

He's never bitten a doctor and he's never bitten a nurse
But that didn't save the window man who had a chunk taken from his a**.

Rocky is a lovely dog; he doesn't mind the cold
He's never bitten anyone, unless of course he's told.

He has a furry jacket; it's very long and thick
But it doesn't slow him down when he's running for a stick.

He's always causing havoc and won't leave Kong alone
The only time he's quiet is when he's chewing on a bone.

Rocky is a lovely dog; he's very big and bold
He's never assaulted anyone, unless of course he's told.

Rocky pleaded not guilty to carrying out the attack
He tried to pin the blame on Kong for assaulting Davie Black.

So both denied the incident and swore a hundred fold
"We wouldn't attack auld David, unless of course we're told!"

Stevie O'Hara

Not Elephant Men

I'm still a white n**ger, nothing has changed.
My people are sick, our politicians deranged.
I've got no job, no life, no hope.
Perceived as Catholic, worshipping the Pope.

I practise contraception, I don't want kids.
Why suffer little children, persecuted like Yids?
I'm bitter, but British, of that there's no doubt.
Could life have been worse, if we'd lost to the Kraut?

We're human beings, not elephant men.
South Africa has changed, but oh Ireland, when?
I'll never forget, but am prepared to forgive.
God, give us peace, let all your Christians live.

Oh saints and scholars, you must turn in your graves.
To see gunmen as masters, your people as slaves.
There'll always be fighting, while there's orange and green.
A nation divided by 'God Save The Queen.'

It's time to stop marching and beating the drums.
Time to bury the hatchet and not some mother's sons,
I've said it before, I'll say it again:
We're human beings, not elephant men.

Michael Foy

That's All

Hail, Rasta! Time's gone by since last we loved.
And sighed for all that might have been.
Now, here we are but, what has changed? I still am not your "Queen."

Emotions break my heart in myriad fragments.
Each one a taunt, a doubt, a hope. What can I do?
I'd hushed your words, said: "please don't promise.
You know that what I feel for you is with me 'til I die."

There's so much more I need to know of you, your hopes and dreams.
But, someone stops me learning more.
Your "Rose" has thorns, it seems.
Don't be alarmed, feel trapped, or blue — I'm one of life's survivors.
Provided all the things you said were true, not lies.
I'll wait for you.

I love your smile and wicked laugh, your locks, your shyness too.
And offer up a sanctuary from all that troubles you.
A haven, safe from life's harsh winds which try to sink your ships.
My heart, my love, my lips. I've nothing else to tempt you with.
I'm at your beck and call. If that's a burden in your life
Tough s***. I'm here. That's all.

Wendy Gaynair

Ghost Town

Social stagnation
biological perpetuation
Sub-race, the main race
emotion free embrace
leads to this situation.

Call this a life?
Temporary pleasures
like the sharpest knife
Carve the world around you
into shapes you know and understand
Dick is just a weapon
That easily comes to hand.

5 lives 2 rooms
Acid clothes to make me look
but to look is not to understand
Too much acid makes me blind
to the bare survival
That is your life
in these prosperous times.

Eleanor Stella Jorgensen

Slaughter

No leather shoes upon my feet,
No animals to kill for meat,
No pigskin wallets,
No rats full of drugs,
Only for human vanity,
For it's we who are the thugs.
No baby seals slaughtered to make a b**** a coat,
Could you put a blade to a human's throat?

Carla McBride

Star-Laden Sky!

...So...Climb the Ladder!

The way to see the Father,
We have to climb Jacob's Ladder
Like Daniel who was in the Lion's den,
Only He can put us back together again,
Like Job who walked the way, upright,
The good Lord did not let Him out of sight,
David who faced that giant Goliath
How brave He was as the good Lord saith,
No man on Earth can come between me,
So dim your lights and let me be,
Like the devil who tried to strangle Her
That ground God cursed because of His Anger
That Adam and Eve created—and—
Because of that then came hatred—
    Then came the Garden of Eden!

Yvette Avonda Wiggins

Now, If Only

Great golden goose up in the sky.
Please look at me kindly with your eye,
That I may indulge in a life of pleasure,
Surrounded by bits and bobs of treasure;
That I may be rid of this pestilent wife,
Whose nagging I've suffered for half of my life!

Of men in such misery there are surely few!
Who have to endure such a wretch of a shrew;
'More money' she shouts, 'work harder' she says,
Whilst lying in bed, surrounded by trays
Of chocolate and food, and bottles of wine,
But nary a thought for the troubles of mine.

And so, great goosey, out of that gleaming golden bill,
My prayers please to answer,
If now only you will;
Of this dear lady, to whom I'm so steadfast wed,
You'll drop a bloody great cheque book,
To land right on her head.

Alistair McLean

Heartsease

Refreshment for the heart is found
In the dew of little things;
A dear child's face; a rose of grace
And beauty whence it springs.

A kindly deed done by a friend;
A cheerful word that p'rhaps will end
A day of loneliness and fear,
When spirits droop and eye sheds tear.

A meal enjoyed in company;
A prayer that soothes eternally;
The balm of sleep and well-earned rest;
The knowledge that we're truly blest
By gift of God, who bears our leaning.
Thus does the heart find its real meaning.
Anne H. Sanderson

Tia

Tia was the name of our cat,
a sparkling black and white coat
so soft and smooth to touch.
A small Jellicle Cat.

A member of our family for eleven years;
physically gone but remembering her . . .

Love and dog-like devotion;
appearing at a window, waiting to be let in;
prowling through the garden in search of food and adventure;
pushing her head under a hand, asking to be petted;
curled up on a knee or on top of the gas fire;
purring in happiness;
talking, saying good morning or demanding attention

. . . keeps her alive for ever.
Peter T. Swan

The Legend

1990 what a year,
A brand new band got into gear,
5 young lads joined the game,
Searching for a little fame.

Mark, Gary, Howard, Rob and Jay,
Their songs were the highlight of the day.
They revolutionised what we knew as pop
Then they made their way to the top.

94 the new image came,
But we loved them all the same,
95 oh what a hit,
That's when Robbie Williams quit.

96 They made us cry
promises they made were such a lie,
The truth is out we can't pretend
We must accept this is the end.

Our love for them will live forever,
their dream will be forgotten never,
And although for now they are gone
But take that: Legend will live on!
Claire Murray

Concorde

On a fine, June day,
The Queen's Birthday,
Over the Trafalgar Square,
Almost making Nelson sway,
Flew the Giant Concorde there
In its grand majestic flight,
Sweeping the surrounding skies,
Off all the pigeons, in great fright
As off they flew in one black cloud above,
As this 'Great Bird' came into sight,
For them, this was no dove.
I. M. Klein

Why Do the Living Suffer

As time passes by, and hearts are broken,
People ask why, but no answer is spoken,
Babies for no reason, suddenly die,
Heartbroken parents want to know why,

Kids loose their dads and mums,
Parents lose daughters and sons,
Some children just vanish,
How do the parents begin to manage,
It's one question I often ask,
How does one cope with such a task,
No-one can say if the dead really feel,
But why for the living, don't the scars ever heal,

Living with pain till its their turn to die,
Remembering loved ones they sit and cry,
You give us love, that we forced to let go,
Is there a God, that's what I'd like to know,
Debbie Craggs

Day Dreams

Each day as I sit by your place of rest,
In sunshine bright, and with flowers blessed,
I feel your presence, Oh! So near,
If only your voice just once I could hear.

They have seen my tears, they have heard me say,
As unashamed each day I pray,
And say, "thank you Lord for the happy life",
We were privileged to share, as Hubby and Wife.

I can see your eyes and your smiling face,
your chair in the dining room, and the vacant place,
I miss you so much Dear, I cannot express
The feeling of loneliness, pain and distress.

Why did you leave me? The questions oft asked,
In the days and the months that have long since passed,
You are deep in my memory, and there you will stay,
Until God calls me Home on that very last day.
V. V. Wright

Hospitals Everywhere

Bless our hospitals oh Lord we pray,
Keep them safe by night and day.
Bless the patients when sick and low,
Stay close beside them a light to glow.

Keep the staff happy, loyal and true,
In doing so continue their love of you.
Let all our hospitals always aid,
Our faith in them never fade.
Remembering their matrons gone and past,
Like mothers to us all
A roll of honour to last.
Ruby Hughes

The Bushman

There's life on the plains with the bushman—
Beneath that burning, blazing, hot, hot sun.
With the sun on his back he hunts in the heat;
He must keep going, he must find meat.

Through that burning, blazing desert of sand,
Over that smouldering, flaring African land—
With its strange and unknown traps and snares,
With its wild and untamed creatures to beware.

There're beetles and bugs that sting like wasps,
If the bushmen aren't careful their lives will be lost.
There're creatures that bite, there're creatures that sting,
There're creatures that stalk, there're creatures that spring.

At night as the sun goes over the hill—
The bushman is there, waiting to kill.
There's life on the plains with the bushman—
Beneath that burning, blazing, hot, hot sun.
Holly Manuel

Time Again

Running here, running there;
  never any time to spare.

The world spins around;
  our lives do the same.

Maybe, reborn in the future we'll
  do it all again.

History repeats itself but
  we never really learn.

We must stop, look and listen
  before making the next turn.

Still, keep still—look! The trees
  have lost their leaves.

Calm down, lie back;
  hear the birds and the gentle breeze.

We'll keep searching and forever trying,
  But time will keep ahead of us and always be flying.
    Janette Hyatt

Do You or Will You

We wake up in the morning and hear the sweet birds' call
tucked up in our beds where we can not fall.
But do we know what it's like to live out on
the streets on our own,
with no one to return to, no family, no home.
We can help, you and I, but when you
say you want to help, is that just a lie?
To give up just a little money, to help or save someone else's life.
Will that really cause you any pain, or any strife?
To them this is a world of coldness and hate,
To you are they just a fuss, just another gate?
A gate that can be pushed aside, another obstacle in the way.
Or will you help them, so they will no longer have
to live their way.
    Cara Mortimer

Untitled

Roses spell the wonder of colour
Of Reds and Pinks, Vermilions and Ochre,
From the bare thorns of winter, spring
exudes the depth of foliage,
to be followed by summer's kaleidoscopic rainbow,
velvet the sense of touch betrays the petals,
and aroma dwarfs coffee-time,
Shades subdue the spectacle of portraits
whilst bees burst forth in complete opulence,
Yes, its seasonal interlude
and creative aliveness spawn the land
whilst the inner stirrings prompt new life
old shadows retreat to the darkest recess of winter's solstice
Wake up—wake up—wake up
Lenten period is here—rejoice for
temporary abstinence seek avowed
prodigiousness, rejoice the sun, seek
absolution from its eclipsed performance,
rejoice, the warmth of the sensual rose
is soon to grant us its benediction.
    Robert G. E. Manning

Plea from the Heart

Let my heart be lightened of this pain
My senses and spirit be lifted to the highest plain
Let the light from the sun the moon and the stars
be mine to ever walk in.

Never then again, the heavy rain
of tears from my very being,
The tornado of emotion that has frozen my very soul
Let me thaw in the warmth of
love, and treasure the glow of
perpetual joy and peace.
    Kathleen Ireland

Not Alone

Look back upon the last twelve months,
Look back, and you will see
That someone walked beside you
Through your grief and misery

Who was it that walked beside you
Each step, yes every mile,
Who wiped your many tears away
And replaced them with a smile?

How often have you sat alone wondering what to do,
When through the door someone has walked, a friend to
comfort you?

Many times have you wondered how these friends
knew when to call,
Did someone whisper in their ear
"Go and call on Mrs. Ball"?

Do you ever get the feeling that you are not alone?
You quickly glance to right and left to be sure you're on your own.

Who is it that walks beside you then, each step of every mile,
Who is it that wipes those tears away
And lights your face with a smile?

The unseen form of Jesus is there. He walks at your right side.
He's been with you now for quite a while and forever He'll abide.
    William Yale

My Dreams

I get ready for bed with a very sleepy head
and I look through the window and think,
what shall I dream of this fine winter's night
and then off under the covers I sink.

I drift away without a thought
and a castle appears in my sight,
The turrets are high, all the way in the sky
and a dog cries into the night.

And here this fine night in the pale moonlight
is a girl all alone with a key,
I tell her my name, she whispers the same
and that's when I realize it's me.

I look in my hands, I'm holding a key
I wonder what it is for,
then near the castle I can just about see
what seems to be some kind of door.

I walk over to it with the key in my hand
and place it into the door,
it turns with ease and I walk in the mist
and wake on my bedroom floor.
    Lorna Baines

The Love of my Life

You are the love of my life.
You help me in times of need,
Through all the trouble and strife.

When all things seem to go wrong,
And life seems to be one big storm,
You are always by my side to help me along.

We were made to be together,
Through all our lives,
To calm the stormy weather.

Times are good and bad,
We stand together through it all,
It makes me very glad.

As the years go on and our love grows,
The more time we spend together
The more the passion flows.

As we grow old,
We become more frail and slow,
We will still have each other to hold.
    Rebecca Simmonds

Dancing Feet

Dancing feet without shoes
Shuffling, Kicking, Spinning
Balance you do not lose
Your rhythmic cuts and slices
Fluid strokes and glides
Blends with music like spices

Dancing feet without shoes
Stomping into the ground
Raising dust clouds to amuse the expectant crowd
Wildly cheering your gyrating spin in the midnight air

Dancing feet without shoes
Magically moving to the drummer's beat
Twisting, stretching like elastic
Must dance until your tired body comes to rest
Amidst the radiance of ecstatic guests

Dancing feet without shoes
Though weary, stands ready to dance again
Any time, any place, to shine the torch of happiness
Upon every expectant face.
Anthony Jules

Time Is Passing Me By

Time is passing me by, and what do I do?
I laugh and play and forget all day
That what I am will end one day
And what I will be depends on me
On me alone and nobody else
Just me.
On me now, how I live now, my life now.
For every day I say:
"Tomorrow I'll start again
For tomorrow is another day."
But . . .
Tomorrow never comes . . .
And my today will soon be yesterday,
And my tomorrow, today.
For . . . time is passing me by . . .
And though today is still young, tomorrow is nigh.

And I still laugh and play and forget all day
That time is passing me by.
Helga J. Zahra

Thinking of You

I'm thinking of you, why can't you see,
You mean everything in the world to me.
I just can't find the words I want you to hear,
inside I'm shaking with fear,
The fear of rejection, the fear of pain,
I'm praying that you feel the same.
Nobody loves you more than I do,
I'll always be here for you.
I truly understand the meaning,
of "I can't explain this feeling".
Always thinking of you, why can't you see,
You mean everything in the world to me.
Sarah Shaw

Autumn Years

We have come to the Autumn of our years
Not without shedding many tears.
We have come to pay homage to friends that have passed
And share with each other friendships that will last.

The child in us lives, though the years have flown;
Many have families now fully grown,
No more to endure the anguish of youth.
We have serenity, patience, tactfulness, and truth.

We have time now to sit and enjoy one another
Remembering each one of you now is my brother.
We each share one thing to the end of our days
It's the loved one who left us, to walk in God's ways.
Mary O. Farrell

Memories of Yesterday

I try to think about tomorrow but
yesterday seems to fall in my way.
Thoughts of today castaways for my
knowledge of yesterday.
Captured sailing down the river of my
memories I'll set my feelings free.

Scenes of my past close in before my eyes,
I remember the events of before which
have pleasured my life.
These make me smile for a while
until the shadow of tomorrow
pulsates through my mind.

The doors of my future have opened
once more,
where the path is lit for my
tomorrow.
Louise Ince

Ben

Life enhancing
wet nose, soft paw, silken ear,
eyes brimming with an overwhelming love for me
a requited love

Precious memory
laughter, sparkle, sheer joy,
united in a bond incomprehensible
an eternal bond

Such emptiness
aching, sadness, silence,
the warmth of you no longer in my reach remains
an endless warmth

In my heart.
C. Cheetham

Loss

Where so e'er I stood upon the perimeter
The sky hung with wonders
Of life, of love, of her,
Even though we're miles asunder.

A vision of her beauty none can quite compare
With a faultless nature, plenty,
And a voice as tranquil bare.
My beloved stole my heart
And wore it right away

She left me cold and desolate, so, so cold.
So cold, alone and bare.
O life, O love, O God,
How can I abide in this abyss of despair
And not forget that scandalous beauty?
Soon, immaculate oblivion upon the perimeter.
Martin O'Mahoney

Invisible Divide

In that very first moment, between awakening and awareness,
My thoughts go drifting aimlessly, till suddenly I find,
Images of you start appearing with sureness,
And once again reality starts filling my mind.

You are no longer here, to share joy and laughter,
No words will be spoken between us again,
Memories are all I am left with hereafter,
Until I am with you, they'll hold me till then.

Love held us together with a vow never broken,
Best friends and lovers, never apart,
Your wedding ring I'll keep as a token,
Just as I keep your love safe in my heart.

The pain of remembrance brings me deepest sorrow,
And I know one day surely I'll see you again,
But how will I greet you on that wondrous tomorrow,
When there is no divide, and love wasn't in vain.
Mary McGhie

Fire

Fiercely flaming in the midst of the field,
Stands the great wild beast in need of no shield,
Huffing and puffing waiting to pounce,
On all that rubbish every ounce,
There it stands flickering its flames,
Like five ferocious lions shaking their manes,
I can feel its hot breath sweeping my back,
Hot, damp, and dark a cruel midnight black,
Red, orange, and yellow flames jigger,
Crackling and blazing its magnificent figure,
Dazzles fade and down creep the flashes,
And all that remains is a pile full of ashes.

Laura Simcox

2 in 1

Two teenage girls, sitting on one stool
One is at home, the other is at school

One girl is bold, the other is too shy
One's always laughing, but all she does is cry

One always shouts, the other only mutters
One is so sure, but she just sits and stutters

One's so relaxed, the other is too tense
One takes things lightly, the other takes offence

One takes the lead, the other's like a mat
One has good looks, the other thinks she's fat

One's a success, the other only fails
One's always bright, the other sits and wails

One's always high, the other's always low
One thinks of hope, the other things of woe

One's jokes are funny, the other isn't witty
One is respected, the other just gets pity.

Eleanor Clifton

The Seasons

Winter dawns both cold and clear,
Both at the start and end of the year,
Frost glistens bright, like diamonds on the ground,
When hedgehogs and badgers, asleep may be found.

Next comes springtime, life bursting anew,
Green shoots and buds, grass wet with dew,
New lambs are gambolling, birds singing bright,
Days seem to be longer, evenings are bright.

Now is the summer, long, hot sunny days,
Children are laughing and playing in all different ways,
A riot of colours and noise, in gardens and parks,
Flowers in full bloom, and the songs of the larks.

Then comes the autumn, with its carpet of gold,
The mornings are darker, the evenings grow cold,
The animals are foraging, building their store,
For the long winter sleep to enter once more.

Susan Jones

Real

What will you know when you know too much?
A race for reason, taste, and touch.
Finding the truth, see, and hear,
trip over the edge with nothing to fear.
What will you see when you've seen it all?
repetitive turn on a spinning ball.
Twisting with wind, sweat under the Sun,
hail and snow are loading a gun.
From a rolling stream can you pluck your dream?
I think this is real or so it would seem,
there may be interference on the satellite screen.
From a bloodshot eye can you see an age
of no blood to spill or wars to wage?
I think this is real at least at this stage,
the satellite blinks when the winds rage.

Geoffrey David Williams

The Longing

Always happy when I hold your hands,

Your longing becomes an ember in me,
If you are far away.

I am completely enthusiastic with your love,
Like the joy of children.

If my eyes are tearful while turning a corner,

If my heart is aching,
Remembering you with every beat,

If my hands are shaking in the mid-day heat,
I don't even then regret that I am affected by you.

This melancholia attaches you to me day by day,

Your languid eyelashes come to my mind in every sunset,

I read you like the book, that is next to me,

Where ever I am I think of you,

Take my word—believe in me.

Snleyman Yozgat

Vaughan

I was sat in the darkness
with nothing to do.
Staring at a candle thinking of you.
Your eyes are like the stars up above.
Your smile is like the tail of a dove.
I look out of the window I saw your face.
You are pale.
You are thin.
I am wondering where have you been.
You're fading away I start to
cry all I want to say is
 Goodbye!

Emma Miles

Wishes for a Daughter

May happiness just come to you,
And laughter fill your days.
May the love you give come back to you,
In a million different ways.

May you have ribbons in your hair,
And flowers at your feet,
May friendship come to you my love
From everyone you meet.

May fortune smile upon your face,
And brush away your tears,
May children warm in your embrace
And brighten up your years.

May joys be yours to have and hold
Life's wonders may you see,
May your days be filled with love untold,
Like the love you brought to me.

Jean Ecob

Home Truly Missed

The wind gently playing with her hair
Eyes filled with tears—memories everywhere
soft and warm
running down her face
In harmony with all creations beauty and grace
how wonderful it is here
but soon comes the good bye
she'd love to always be there
but lives mountains are high
she will leave—filled with sadness
Blossoms in her hair
her tears swallowed by gladness
she thanks God
he made her there

Pia England

The Hope of Northern Ireland

The Newsreader speaks of another sectarian murder,
The power of Bomb and Bullet
Words heard too often in this divided land
The lack of surprise the listeners feel
fails to ease the sense of despair.

Among many, the passion for revenge is paramount
Dealing a further savage blow to hopes for peace
Their politics, tradition, history, their pride
must not be weakened by the 'other side.'

Centuries of hatred, fear and mistrust
cast a bitter shadow over this beautiful land
But a light also shines, brilliant and strong
from the people, joining together, who ache for peace.

After twenty five years, people felt the promise of peace
A warmth that many had never tasted
This was cruelly snatched away
But never before has there been a greater will to fight for it back.

Solutions will not be found immediately, there has been too
    much sorrow,
Bridges cannot be easily built to unite a segregated people
But we must continue to aspire to the time when
the flame of peace is stronger
than the breath which fights to extinguish it.

Caroline Newell

Remembrances of a Friend

She came to bring me unwanted pain
and in naive beginnings, I stood alone,
a frailty of life itself;
sentenced to her child-like execution.
And though inside I knew so well that it was
wrong, my early death, my skeletal shape,
could not change my fate, so I stood alone;
always, and knew nothing of escape.
She conquered my breathing form and pushed,
and crushed the spiritual me and though I grew
in a physical sense, inside I crumbled;
mistreated and weak. She swelled
her pride with her ignorance of myself and
won her throne as Queen of the dead,
she smiled, threw her words like stones
and lost to her, I never felt
but sadness that she could not forgive
my difference in her world of games,
that she could not smile for me a smile
that spoke of sorry in all its simpleness

Aileen Lee

Looking Well!

You're looking well! Too blind to see I'm living in hell
just smile and say thank you and accept it as a compliment to
filling up with shock horror, cringing deep within.
Look beyond this healthy glow and maybe you'll see I'm full of woe
If only they saw the constant battleground, see
I'm fighting to win closing the lid of this rubbish bin,
Been too close to waving the white flag.

You're looking better! But the rain's pouring harder and I'm
getting wetter it's a constant struggle and fight;
I hope to fly free like a kite, easy it won't be;
I'm the only one who holds the key, with the acceptance of support
and tender loving care I'm determined to make it there.
Things won't always be so black and white,
It's the middle ground that I've got in sight
No expectation of the grass to be so green
on the other side of the fence, remains to be seen.

A change I'm so desperate to make, I'm giving it my all,
not a piece of cake. My best friend, time, is on my side?
A brand new beginning to find and when I do . . .
Compliments will be accepted too and the real me will shine through
and I will mean and say thank you, because I will feel well!

Julia Raymond

The Party

Glasses clang;
    The party has began!
The music starts,
    And so does the dancing.
Short skirts fly up,
    Hair goes flying.
Laughs and whistles fly through the air,
    Chatter mingles in the crowds.
It all has a bad side;
    We know it too well
Of drunkenness and hangovers,
    But worst still:
A fatal tablet,
    A little murmur.
Hand over the money:
    You have bought the ticket to Hell!

Harriet Whittaker, Age 13

Creation

The flower of life embodies all creation
From atom, molecule to species man
Herein you find the Universal secret
Undreamt alike by science and profane,
Whose eyes as yet have not been widely opened
To see the truth in all its majesty.
All previous races held this enigma
In esoteric circles ruled by priests.
But now a new Renaissance dawns for all
Who seek release from Karmic bonds on Earth.
The One Creator God has thus decreed
The new Millennium precedes transformation
As pole shifts bring to us increased vibrations
And cosmic forces focus on the Earth.
Awaken Man! Adapt the breath of life
To power mankind into the Fifth Dimension.

Ian N. Bowerman

Spanish Eyes

Spanish eyes, too deep in my heart to
ever let go.

Spanish eyes, sweetly smiling, so beguiling
softer than the petals of a rose.

Spanish eyes, that can say with a glance
what a chance for a big romance, before
they close.

    I could swim the Atlantic,
be Titanic, be forever, eternally
romantic; for Spanish eyes, too deep
in my heart to ever let go.

B. J. Dalton

As the End Begins

Come, shine on me, the blazing sun
Once more, I beg of you
To give me your energy
Before I leave and start anew

I often wondered of the time I'll go
Now it's before me and my yesterdays seem not long ago
And for the last time I yearn
For the nature's breeze
And the flower's bloom in the summer fields

How sad it is to leave you behind
But there's another place where I must be
And though, our times together were short
The fond memories will always be with me

I hear the call, so now I must go
Somewhere far and for a very long time,
But cry you should not as the time will come
Once again to reunite us
And so until then, to you . . . goodbye.

Marjorie V. Young

Man or Spirit?

Where does he go as he wanders so far?
Why does he walk? Why not just use the car?
Why does he move in such silence unheard?
No sound in the air, like the wings of a bird.

Morning dew freezes as he walks just past,
The Sun's on his back but no shadow he casts.
No sound of his footsteps are heard as he walks,
It seems like he's thinking but I'm sure there's no thoughts.

He moves like a mist and he blows with the wind,
His mind's in such worry like he has been pinned.
Maybe he's grieving the pain of lost love.
His heart is not here now, it's floating above.

But now I see through him, I see fields and trees,
He trips on a stone and he falls to his knees.
He just disappears, it's weird isn't it?
Then I just realised, he was a spirit.

Hayley Foran

I Do Understand

I have to sell these Magazines to people in the City.
It's full of interesting things and called "Big Issue"
Few people apologies for not buying this from me,
Pensioners find it pricey, do not wish to appear mean
Because there's more sense in paying bills and taxes,
So they too, do not join my scene, but how do they manage?
These folk, I do not know, their homes they struggle to keep
Their clothes they need to wear, their food, drink and heat.
What most receive in pensions, unless of course topped up,
Private one's to add to states stingy one.

They know how I feel, I stand here day in day out
Too cold, too weary, too tired to shout "Come buy this Magazine
Would love to go home to eat and cosy warm bed
To feel soft covers over head, keeping out reality, I dread
I live on streets, no fault of own, unless earn't keep tonight
No known relatives to call my own, in care, now turned out
Unfortunately I grew up, too old for roof overhead
Too young for help, no address, so no work? No one needs me.
So please if no money to spare, don't cross over
Just say few words, I'm lonely too, and I do understand.

B. L. Fenn

The Never-Ending Journey

From Jordanhill, Thornwood and Dumbarton, we came,
to travel and visit, the places so named.
By car and ferry, we had gone,
to Argyll and the Isles, and those further on.
From Loch Fyne, Inverary and Taynuilt,
to Oban and others, were the result.

Alongside, the lochs, and over the 'Rest',
to reach those places, we did our best.
In all types of weather, throughout the year,
in hail, rain and snow, we did appear.
To arrive, at all those destinations,
at all those geographical locations.

From Oban harbour, the boat did leave,
through the Sound of Mull, it did cleave.
To Craignure, Tobermory and Tiree,
passing the Isle of Coll, far out to sea.
A visitation, not to be missed,
to the land of barley, at times sun-kissed.

So, we follow that route with many bends,
hoping, to reach, where that journey ends.

David. N. Inglis

Windsurfer

Skimming across the rippled water
Fuelled by the wind and a bright pink sail
Mountain backdrop and hard bright light
The ebullient scene distills for us
The essence of summer for winter nights.

Mary Hewat

Ode Tae a Wid Tink

A lorry's for life,
As he said tae his wife,
This man 'o the forest
They crie the Wid Tink.

As he cranks up his crane,
Wie nae heed tae the wane,
Gobblin' up a puckle o' wid,
Aye makin' sure o' a couple o' quid.

Come rain or shine, sna', glaur or grief,
Yon Wid Tink battles on,
Fir a' us in need o' some wid,
We're glad and full o' glee.

Grabbed and secure,
And altho' sometimes,
A bit dour,
We a' love this Tink o' the Wids.

And to keep him sweet,
A' thru' the year
The odd bottle o' yon yellow nectar,
Keeps oor Wid Tink aye in guid cheer!

Fiona Melville

Dunblane

To Nanny Wyn who passed away the 17th of July 1997

All the woe and pain from the town of Dunblane,
Is because of the dear little children that will never be seen again.
Asleep in their tiny coffins never to be woken,
The spell of their life has now been broken.
All you can hear from the parents are cries,
So much that it will bring tears to your eyes.
Remember at Christmas to pay your respect,
To the brave little children that you must not forget.

Danielle Martine Estlea

Gold Sandals

I came, like I promised,
Came at the time you said,
And knocked at your door.
I'd put on the best I had—
My wide gold belt, and the white
Swinging skirt, and a super
Shirt, ruby colour—you know,
Warm, with a glow to it,
Not hard like scarlet,
Real heart's blood red—
And little gold sandals—new, they were,
The sort you like,
And those big earrings you bought for me, remember?
That day we went to the sea.
I put on the best I had
And came, like you told me,
And knocked at your door.
The door of an empty room
It was. I waited, don't know how long,
Just waited. And no one came.

Katharine Vivian

Finding Paradise

The stream flowed steadily.
The warm sun penetrated its beams of
light on the surface, as if there was
tiny crystal beads in the water.
Old willow trees let their branches
fall into the lapping stream,
almost as though they were too worn out
to hold them up any longer.
Everywhere was filled with a soft golden light.
The tranquility was immense.
I looked at my reflection and it looked
back, smiling.
I had finally found paradise.

Brenda Stephens

Present Past

At first,
Child noises,
Bewildered merriment in playland,
Adult wonder at their actions and sounds.

First universal child talk,
Lost in language,
Contacts,
Reaching out to colour and
Holding breaths instinctively under water,
Rude awakening for some to be grown up,
Adult return to bliss time,
Sometimes called senile,
Just smile and let them play awhile.

Return can lead to anger;
Frustration at their state perhaps?

Kids are nice.

No hate, envy, jealousy or prejudice.

The still of birth like death,
Similar photographs of time.

A. Ohene-Djan

Oh Death

Oh, death, why are you watching me?
Do you not know, that I am not ready for you yet?
I see you there, waiting for me, and calling
My name, but do you not know, that I am not ready for you yet?

Oh, death, turn away your eyes, and leave me
In peace, for do you not know, that I am not ready for you yet?

Oh, death, why do you take my loved ones,
And leave me here alone, but do you not
Know that I am not ready for you yet?

Oh, death, I hear you calling me, and
Telling me, it is time, but do you not
Know, that I am not ready for you yet?

James Finlay

Untitled

How full of hope, is the quiet new dawn,
And how sweet, the bird's first call,
Our hearts must know,
It was God who set,
Such beauty over all,
How full of gifts, the harvest is,
With the fruits, and golden grains,
We must recall,
It was God who planned
The fall of gentle rains,
And so, the days will pass, and
Each day, the sun still shine,
And we will know, it was God who gave
These days, to be yours and mine.

Elizabeth O. Wright

Clock Radio

An eclipse of inky blackness
shadowy sea crashing in white noise
around dim corners of consciousness
obscure rock speaks hour: minute in red glow
digit by digit
song by song
music never heard before
never heard again
create destroy as lights play
moment last's breath lasts lifetime
DJ whispers softly, feminine
urging sleep but not:
break a thousand insomniac hearts
the glow shifts
new minute new sound
blackness draws further . . .

Stephen McGreal

Nowhere

The relentless fear goes on and on
All hope for a better life, long since gone.
This world is such a cruel place
With heartache and misery in every space.
No wonder hope has been and gone.

Who chooses whom to feel the pain
If fate and destiny are pre ordained.
In this harsh world we all are not equal
When few are happy and many are fearful.
So how do the lucky ones get to be named.

Is there a better life over the rainbow
Where does it start, which way does the wind blow.
Can I hitch a lift, or walk or run there
Will someone or something help me to somewhere.
Or an I destined to stay here, in nowhere.

Sandy Sanderson-Key

Treasured

Is it true that you are going, beyond civilization once longed for
And the lemon scented air, will be alone with I?

Is it true that you are crying, for those innocent lost at war?
Many Evil, Devils, and Satan will say it's one up and their score

Is it true that you are fading on and out of my being
And it will be on spiritual ways, not seeing?

Is it true that you are climbing on to a new path with dream-like landscape?
But it is truth, is it the want or is this image all fake?

Is it true that you are dying, on this fresh like hopeful day?
Will you fly free, like those of birds
Or will you slowly decay?
When you're gone and relighted, like those sons of God
Then birds shall fly freely on and to worlds beyond

Louise Hale

Animals and Creatures

We humans should take lessons from animals and creatures,
No doubt about it, they're easily the best teachers.
If we were as wise as the owl, we'd make less mistakes,
Method and concentration is all it would take.

We are judged by the company we all keep,
So don't be blind followers like the gullible sheep,
Though the ewes with their lambs, I must confess,
Look after them with loving care, and tenderness.

Be independent, learn to relax like the cat,
Just watch how it lies sleeping on the mat.
Be like the dog, ever faithful and true,
Friends we will have in plenty, enemies few.

Yes, animals and creatures can teach us quite a lot,
Uncaring and stupid, they certainly are not.
Sufficient to say we should treat them with respect,
Never to be cruel to them, and never neglect.

Jane Osborne Clachrie

Spaced Out

Did you see those funny beings from the Planet Earth to-day
They move about in bodies, heaven knows how much they weigh
Their development is roughly at the embryonic stage
With so many silly habits, it's impossible to gauge
I laughed to see them stuffing food into those little holes
Munching, chomping, slurping, like some prehistoric trolls
But what about the games they play, they really make you smile,
Metal sticks, and small round balls, they think can go a mile
And then those crowds all screaming as their heroes fight it out,
Their boxing game's no better, as they knock each other out.
But what about the mating thing, to have babies so they say,
And some get fatal viruses, and yet they say they're gay,
Now I like the religions bit, where they all pray to God
Then try to kill each other, each one a silly sod.
Well we're off, back into space again, it really has been fun,
Perhaps they'll get it right some day, and live like us as one.

John Haggerty

Aaahh Zzz

Isn't it great on a Sunday to lie in bed until late?
Isn't it great on a Sunday to lie in bed late with your mate?
Isn't it great on a Sunday to doze away minutes and hours,
To hear other folk working, other folk using their mowers?

Isn't it great on Sunday to lie in bed comfy and snug?
To forget other days—working,
Of other days being a mug.
Oh! If every day was a Sunday!
And I could lie in bed comfy and snug.
Next time I'll come back a bed bug,
Then I won't have to work like a mug
   R. T. Dennis

The Grandfather Clocks

Down in our hall
The grandfather clock stood
Tall and made of mahogany wood.
And all he can say is
tick, tock, tick, tock
till round comes the hour and he sounds
out his chimes.
I bet he can tell a queer tale or two,
cause he's being standing there since 1872,
I guess some would be funny
and some would be sad.
But dear old grandfather seems quite glad,
to just stand there with his tick, tock, tick, tock
Many people admire him and say
what a wonderful clock
I guess he is smiling although
he just says tick, tock, tick, tock.
   D. Sewell

Birthday Wishes to My Husband

My birthday wish to you today
Is so very true and sincere
You're the one I love and always will
And I'll always want you near

Life without you I cannot imagine
As both our hearts beat as one
All through the day from early dawn
Right through to the setting sun
Our life together has been happy and sweet
And everything in it is so complete
So on this special day of days
I wish you all you deserve
For the kindness and love you gave since we met
I never ever shall forget

So today it is your birthday I wish you a lovely day
And thinking back all through the years
I'd have it no other way
Happy Birthday darling
   Mary Warnock

The World We All Abuse

Who do we think we are, who put us in charge?
We spoil the air we breath
We take trees and hedges with ease.
The land we all abuse.
Who do we think we are, who out us in charge?
They're starving we don't care
if disabled we stop and stare.
They're not the same as us.
Who do we think we are, who put us in charge?
The animals we kill to feed.
When we hunt ivory and skins for greed,
The rest we just disregard.
Who do we think we are, who put us in charge?
We fish the seas until they're dry.
There's a hole in the ozone in the sky
The world we all abuse
Who do we think we are, who put us in charge?
   Sheree Russ

The Summer House

At the summer house by the lake,
Are sweet moments spent there
Still awake; when the breeze
Ruffles the water sensuously,
Does dead love return
Ever so fleetingly?

Do our love words yet whisper
Through the reeds somewhere,
Yesterday's kisses scent flower and air;
Are our tears still staining weed and willow
Where tenderness laid us a pillow;
And the promises we made to break,
Are they revealed in paint work cracked and flaked,
At the summer house by the lake?
   Mike Monaghan

Assassin

Among the sides of old lands' end,
with the wind blowing through my hair,
and at that time you just might spend
that time in the field with the rabbit and the hare.
But something's edging away in my mind,
perhaps it's whether to be cruel or kind,
Or maybe it's about an old lost friend,
or just the thought of a friendship to mend.
But no, something's not right,
the moon doesn't seem to shine so bright,
what could it be,
Something inside of me or something I can see,
It's a field of dreams to get so far,
but I'm still here trying so hard
to find out what's inside my head,
and to live a peaceful life instead,
I'm all mixed up inside,
and really, I want to hide,
but it's time to come out and face the fact,
is it time for me to kill and act.
   Serena Marie Claire Harrison

It Is Going to Get Better

Straining against that veil of tears,
Pushing onwards to the top,
Having someone to share your fears,
And the strength to sometimes stop.
The road of life is a lonely one.
Share that load through love's fickle ways,
On the beach, on the setting sun,
Under gannet's Eire,
Where speckled light plays.
To affirm our love, our being,
To show the world unseeing
  Forever onward.
   Alan Lo-Giacco-Smith

The Unseen Hand

She sits and thinks of bygone days
of roads she travelled on life's highway
was the path she trod already planned
a master stroke by an unseen hand.

Her teenage years she does recall
ambition fulfilled she walked so tall
self-centred she thought she knew it all
was it pride or fate that caused her fall.

She tries to forget the years in-between
the heartache and pain when war intervened
the hopeless struggle when life was lean
and she sits and thinks of the might-have-been.

She sits alone in her twilight years
her eyes awash with unshed tears
she reason perhaps it was all planned
and she was but a pawn in an unseen hand.
   Bella McMillan

Writing Home (Thoughts of a Soldier Writing Home During 1914–1918 . . .)

My page is a field
Of freshly mown hay
Cowslips in the breeze gently sway
My page is a hedgerow
Of soft yellow primroses, violets too
Woods paved with bluebells in the soft dew.

My page is a sound not forgotten,
The quiet in the cowshed as milking is done,
Cocks crowing in the silent morn
My page is the touch
Of newly laid eggs, soft and warm
Of woolly lambs, not yet shorn.

My page is a memory,
Of meandering streams and the green dell
Of drawing spring water from the old well.
My page is full,
My face and future, so unsure
Oh, to be at mountain's gate, your every open door.

Gillian Harries

Winter at Cardiff Dok, Pier Head

To John Favas

How many seagulls had to die,
Whose feathers now as snowflakes fly, to paint the ships all white?
How many birds scraped bare their back,
Their feathers now touching the waters black,
Who put them in this plight?

How many ships have had to sail,
Amongst the winter's snow and hail, upon the raging foam?
How many ships have sailed away
From the coal-slimed waters where they used to lay, never to come home?

Why do the cranes swing up aloft,
Touched by each snowflake, white and soft, and triangulate the sky?
Why should the men go out in boats?
Why should the women pray it floats?
Why should the sailors die?

So as each ship comes into dock,
It passes through the narrow lock and sails within the land.
The seagulls give their tortured cry,
For the bodies of their spirits lie locked in the drifting sand.

Mark Turner

Friendship

At five it was who you played hopscotch or hit with,
But there was never a major fuss,
So now at fourteen, are you surprised we're confused,
'Cause now it's all loyalty and trust.
But that doesn't matter as long as you're happy,
And your friends are true to you,
If you can smile through the good and laugh at the bad,
There's nothing else you can do,
As time goes on your friendship's still there,
So let's propose a toast,
Even if you rest and relax a little too hard,
You'll have much more fun that most,
So remember to be grateful for what you've got,
A friendship for which most would kill,
So just pray that the fun and games will stay,
And I'll bet my last penny they will.

Chloe Burke

The Destroyed Library of Alexandria

For all the books that have been lost here,
for all the books that have been purposely destroyed,
Over their graves I weep as were they my children:
Ghosts haunt here,
also, also weeping

J. R. A. Bailey

A Memorandum of Love

My life passes by me, so quick and short,
my dreams are pictures in its scrapbook.
My tears are glue to hold them down,
my blood engraves the message beneath it.
My family and friends are the cast of a play
that will never be seen,
My heart is the cover of it all,
Will someone ever read it?

Denise Jennings

Falklands

Peaks covered in snow, cold and barren
Full of wild life, from seals and penguins, and many others,
A picturesque place for all to see.

Greed of man fought over this Island.

A haunting place of war and cries,
and blackness that filled the skies,
A bloody battle was there once fought,
Where honour and love was lost, not to count the cost.

Lots of lives and loved ones, gone forever

Flak and burning, scars and vivid memories . . . left
Of the brave who fought and died.

For they gave so much that we might be
Free to see that love conquers all,
So each one of us live in harmony,
Without the guns of battle.

So let all of us pray, to live and love,
From now in peace and the rest of our days.

Aline McInnes Ross

Response o' the Loch Ness Prankster

Through these tranquil waters ah love tae swim
Along the great Loch Ness
Appear tae unsuspectin' fawk an' watch them scream, nae less
In shock sae fast awa' they run, when oot the Loch ah pop
"Och aye the noo, howzitgaun?" but their screamin' disnae stop
A' their goods are left behind, their hooch an' picnic lunch
So wi' a gallant sniff an wander o'er an' ha'e masel' a munch
Then soon comes a' the cameras, reporters an' their boats
Afore lang the news is broadcast fae land end tae John 'O' groats
Ye see, ah find it awfy funny at the lengths ye humans go
Wi' yer boats, harpoons an' nets ah jist love it, whit a show
For ahim jist a harmless beastie, aye Nessie is ma name
An' every time the waters stir ah always get the blame
Well fowks, ah've had ma wee bit furn noo
So atill swim back tae the deep
Sink the whisky you nice fowks left
An' ha'e a guid nights sleep
But if e'er ye come tae the Loch an' a sightin' ye should see
Dinnae worry if ye've brought along a dram or two for me.

Vince MacFarlane

Remembering . . .

How gently you took my cold dead heart
And breathed it back to life.
How you dispelled the emptiness,
The turmoil, the discord, the grief.

How patiently you shouldered my weaknesses
Provided strength when I was down.
How you lifted me out of dark despair
Made a smile replace my frown.

How tenderly you taught me to love once more
Allayed all my hidden fears.
How you took me, moulded me and made me
A special someone—for too few years.

How silently you slipped from me
No goodbye, no tears, no pain.
How gently you took my cold dead heart
And killed it once again.

Mary G. Mitchell

Sea Breeze

It was beckoning to me
so very pliant
Almost urgent
The wind was intense as if it had cognition
Of what was to prevail

My soul drifted into a lapse of trepidation
the aura had a way of encircling
receptive of the perpetual radiance

I inhaled the aroma
and let nature vivify my adjournment
For this, I knew, was my glorification.

Lisa Chambers

Summer

The summer is beautiful in every way,
The sunshine is nice, I love every 'day'.
You wake in the morning, and it's lovely and light,
You look in the garden, the flowers are so bright,
And out in the country, it's so lush and green,
Fields full of contented cows are now to be seen.
The trees are laden with blossom, sometimes with fruit;
Children play in the park, and they are so cute,
Then there's cricket, tennis, bowls and much more.
We have a holiday, and day trips to the sea by the score,
And the lovely light clothes that we all wear,
With such pretty colours for this time of year.
We can have windows open for fresh air,
We can have a barbecue and lounge in a chair.

Emily Turton

My Mum Doesn't Live Here Anymore

Mum doesn't live here anymore,
She did 'till I was three or four,
But then one day I found her gone.
There's been Aunty Sue and now it's Kay,
I'm not bothered really either way.

Mum doesn't live here any more,
I saw her once in Market Street,
I didn't know if we should meet,
So I walked on by, then I glanced behind;
She hadn't seen me and I did mind.

Mum doesn't live here anymore,
When I'm grown up I'll find her, then
I'll say "Look Mum, I'm like the other men!"
And she'll gaze at me and be really proud.
I hope she will, but she might be sore.
She might say out loud,
"I'm not your mother anymore!"
Better keep it as it is, wondering why
And how and who I am because
Mum doesn't live here anymore.

Norman Burslem

Pennyless

Sheltered from the rain
Lonesome and feeling pain.
Once had a life full of glory

Sleeping any place on cold pavements
Reaching out my arms to you
Asking for money begging for food
Can you help a young man

I haven't a home to go to
Warm welcoming and full of love
This is my bed blanket and one cardboard box
I share the street with the rats
Each day is a hopeless helpless one
People look but don't see
Quickly pass by another embarrassment to feed.
Give us a couple of pence
Something hot not a lot
Just for today until tomorrow.

Sue Fisher

A Lust for Blood

From the dark side of me
There's no turning back.
You see the hate that burns my soul,
The Devil incarnate in me,
A lust for blood, a rage unbound.
I won't rest, I won't cease
Until I've tasted the richness of your lips,
Your infernal kiss.

Have I not given of myself,
What more do you require,
Have you not drunk your fill of me?
I've nothing left to give,
My soul is empty.
A former shadow of myself,
I wield life no more,
I lie before you unchained.

I've seen enough of hatred,
I've seen enough of pain.
The things that have passed these eyes
Have torn this soul apart.

James Leung

Freedom

The feeble heart that beat within her chest,
has ceased, her pulse is still.
Her eyes once gazed unseeing,
now the lids have drawn their veil.
Her tiny frame; her vehicle, so broken, so forlorn,
has given up her spirit, borne so long within this form.

But, oh, the smile upon her lips,
what did she glimpse as she flew free?
Her freedom knows no boundaries now,
the treasured prize she sees.
She planted deep her roots of love,
The plant now flowers, way, way above.

Juliette Blencowe

The Ocean

I fly by the ocean,
I hear dolphins crying.
I see whales dying,
Fish a man throwing rubbish into the ocean,
Polluting the world,
I stop at the beach
I see dolphins, fish and whales wash
Up by the shore,
I try to push them back in but it was too
late; their lives were finished,
And so was mine.

Gemma Savory

Reality Hurts

I can't believe that after 3 years,
And after all those pain-felt tears,
My affection for you is still so strong,
My feelings for you have gone on this long,
I guess at first it was just a dream.
Just a wonderful ongoing dream,
I don't know how it happened but we became friends.
Reality crept in, my dream came to an end,
But reality wasn't like my dream.
Reality was so cruel, so harsh, so mean,
It picked me up, then let me go,
What was going on, I didn't know.
Then she was back, back from the past,
Right there before me, moving in so fast.
Now between my dream and reality she stood,
It hurt, so I cried but it did no good.
Just as I gave up, you gave me new hope,
With this new hope I thought I could cope.
For a wonderful moment I thought we had something
Until I realised it was just a stupid fling.

Gemma Addison

Abortion

I thought it was a good idea,
I thought it all felt right
to sleep with him, unprotected
alone throughout the night.
I should have taken precautions
and bought a pack of three,
Instead I've got a baby that's
growing inside of me.
I didn't stop and think for a moment
I didn't ask myself why,
I had to have an abortion
And let my baby die.
now I finally realize it's a heartless thing to do,
to end the life of a child that's growing inside you
there maybe some good reasons like religion, rape, incest,
But think of that poor child and do what you
think is best.

Lindsay Wilkins

The Mighty Aphrodite

Oh 'Mighty Aphrodite'—she has fallen,
Rapt—in clouds of time—she lies sullen.
Bathed in tender memories—she rejoices!   And she mourns,
The touch—of nubile bodies—in the haze of lovers' dawn.

Sweet girl, she is a woman now, with all the 'added' charms,
Though time has altered certainty—in lovers' open arms.
Her innocence past, she feels lost, feels ravaged by the drive—
Yet still begs Aphrodite's zest, when a lover does arrive.

Cries, "where are you now my taut little temptress—
When women need you most?"
Cannot deny her fraught distress—
If she finds her Nymph a 'Ghost'.

But soon she'll shine—and soon she'll share—in times she'll
   feel are meant.
Her all consuming quest endures—until her love is spent.
Then once again—'she must be sure'—she'll savour the amour
And hope that it will prove the pure perfection she'll implore.

Caroline Borg

Growing Old

Time doesn't wait nor does it pass you by,
I can't do like I used to do, no matter how I try.

Old folks that once I loved and knew,
One by one they disappear from view,
And as I move up to take their place
The road to eternity gathers pace.

The fire within me once burned bright,
Now hard of hearing and failing sight.
That flame is now but a flicker,
And as one grows old the time goes quicker.

So little time to fulfil my dreams,
I've resigned myself to fate it seems.

I watch the children as they play,
But their laughter only mock,
For all too well I know,
I can't turn back the clock.

Richard Walter Burrell

Riverside

Two maintain the silted sand-face.
Each prickly gorse
Leans out to wrap and, entwining, races
With hushing silken waters. Scarred shells
Flick away the wind's embrace.

In other arms the two remember
Finger at ebb, flint, the folded core
Of chalks; but not the brushed river,
The cool, insistent wind's embrace.

Mary Arnold

Dreams

Comets destined to dart across the sky
A young resilient star waiting to die
A blazing fire to soon burn out
Veracity to erase the doubt

Aurora shines light against dainty walls
A giant spoken shadow slowly falls
Secret truths told of, whispered and said
An array of stars have been misled

Pieces of the puzzle come together
To avoid that road I shall endeavour
Jig-saw finished by a guiding light
Sunlight hidden by the blackest night

Thor spoke yet they swore that the sun shone bright
Me against failure a hard constant fight
Living dreams that were stolen from her
Robbed by a cold repugnant rifler

A dream is like an unwritten story
Believe to make it a reality
The crisp white paper touched by black ink
The chain weakened by a missing link

Umah Kathirgamathamby

Untitled

Memories of my School Days. My walk to school.
When I was just a tiny child. I used to walk three
lonely miles to school through woods and lanes and
fields with shoes that were sometimes down at heel.
The gypsies used to stop and camp and rest their
horses' legs and then they would sit around
their fine making clothes line pegs, we didn't think
a lot about their gaily painted vans, but years have
passed and times have changed just like their caravans.

Folks will travel for miles to see their vans to-day
and to spend a holiday in one they don't care what they pay
I wandered on through lanes and banks on which wild
strawberries
grew and then on past the old time films which sounds in true

Then there was the apple tree with apples rosy red sometimes if I
was lucky I'd find one in the hedge through a farmyard
with a pool and up a stoney road finally I reach my school
I was glad to sit and rest even at the old school desk
when I look back on those days and children of to-day
What a lovely memory of my nature walk each day
To-day they travel by car and bus and everyone is in a rush.

Ruby Roberts

The White Knuckle Ride from a Boy to a Man

No! Please! No! Now! I said no!
Yeh and I said now, give it to me!

Everyday argument! Don't guarantee,
Please God stop him screaming at me.
What have I done to deserve this pain?
What has turned my son insane?
He screams, he shouts he yells and roars,
Please get me out, lock all the doors.

Nothing at all can make you prepared,
For what explodes from inside of his head.
He's turning my family into one full of rage,
I'm told, "It's common for kids of his age!"
People don't live with him, people don't know
To all you outsiders it just doesn't show.
My friends never falter, they never fall,
Throughout this crisis they've helped me stand tall.

How long do I have to live in distress?
When will he cease the need to impress?
"Someday we'll get there we always decide,"
But I want to be off of this white-knuckle ride.

Kirstie Taylor

Taid

As I watch the car draw in,
I know what has happened,
I wait as it glides into the drive
Anxiety takes over.

I walk to the house.
A gentle breeze passes over me.
I dread what's to come.
I haul open the door.

The house is dark and bleak,
No furniture is present.
There stands a man
All forlorn.

The worst has arrived,
My heart begins to break
I wait, it has arisen
As the qualm approaches.

I break down; as my life comes to a halt.
It's not fair,
Why, my close friend has gone.
Come back Taid.

Kate Evans

My Last Thoughts

As the transport glided around the corner of an empty street,
My mind turned to the fact that like now,
I would spend my life looking out of windows,
I will never be free.

My attention is drawn to a couple of foolish girls,
giggling innuendos about where they were last night,
but then I realize it was me.

I watch the life outside pass me by,
smiling insipidly at people I thought I knew
but living inside my head,
I continue to stare at other lives with glazed eyes.

The transport jerks.
A thousand shards of glass shred my body,
A thousand needles caress my head,
I will spend the rest of my life looking through windows.

Hayley Kemp

Autumn Leaves

Dirt-brown and sullied
By a summer breeze.
—and into beds, long tempted by absence,
they fell—
Only to find winter's cold embrace.

Lesley-Anne Jefferies

The Gambler

It's another Saturday evening and
   his worst dream is born;
Pockets that are empty, which way should he turn?
He's heading for the snooker club, his
   head is low, and step is slow,
His mind is numb after another self-inflicted blow.

Inside the club a mate gets him a tea and snack,
"Having a game?" he asks, and a reply of "no" comes back.
the gambler says, "I've done the lot,
It's one hell of a life I've got."

He sits there for a few hours
While his mind goes on its usual tours.
He says a few quiet hello's and slips off home
Promising once again it's the last
   blasted money he's blown.

The following day he draws up new plans,
Next week his wages have different demands
In principal it's sounds great,
Though, next Saturday evening, can you guess his fate.

John Bosco Egan

Happy and Sad Poem

Happy is my name, I am so lucky,
A day I was born I was so loveable,
Pretty is so nice I could be so glad,
Yesterday I was so lively not loveable,
Pretty polly is a name so I am excited,
Lonely is a name so I am sad.
Yesterday I was so poorly and very miserable,
Nutty is Paul and drives me mad,
Edward is so depressed and sad,
Lonely is an old name I need my old
friends back.
I am so moody and bored,
chocolates are exciting I like them,
I am very loveable when my nan cuddles me.
When it rains it is so sad,
I was depressed when my budgie
and my grandad died,
I am excited when I go on holiday.

Kim Lyon

First Encounter

Is there a higher Heaven than the touch
New to an unsuspecting hand or lip,
Which, through a quick pulsating heart, can tip
The equilibrium of life too much?
Yes? Then why must I tenderly retouch
Both cheek and arm, yet even knee or hip,
Losing a dozen consciences, to sip
The sweet improbability of such
A loving? In your life's September
My Summer flowers bloom wildly, could it be
The scent intoxicates, and you remember
Forgotten shades of love's inconstancy?
Yet lost in this affection, madly I
Would reap but half the kisses that you sigh.

Judith Clarke

Mental Hospitals

Your hands are sweaty,
Your heart is pounding,
And all you want to do is scream,
If you do, nothing will happen,
no-one will come.
Bad images run through your mind,
Legs paralyzed, arms strapped to the bed,
   "I'm not crazy", you shout, "do you hear me? I'm not crazy!"

It's just like a prison cell,
Trapped and depressing thoughts surround you,
It's as if your sanity was being put on auction, and sold to the
   (highest bidder).
You dream that you are running in an unknown place,
"I'm free", you tell yourself, "I'm free!"
When you awake, you realize that you are not in that wonderful
   (place where dreams come true),
But instead in that cramped, solitude room, where no-one can hear
   (you scream).

Gemma Smith

Enigma

For me, the whole world is an enigma
From the mirage in the desert
To the dawning of the sun
Why does the stream flow in its own course
And the flower bloom in its own time?
Why is the ocean a mirror of
—the heavenly sky?

Like the dunes in the sand
Like the hues of autumn
Everything has its story
Everything is a clandestine
Behold in my ignorance, beauty is seen
And through creation, wisdom is gained

Geoanne Tadeja

Butterfly Gypsy

Come watch with me,
the motionless sea.

On shimmering gold sand,
arm in arm we both shall stand.

Wind is the moving air,
that lifts and carries your hair.

I see the colours with which you dare,
I try so very hard not to stare.

For, if away you should fly,
my heart would then surely die.

While you will always take life as a dance,
to me your love is my only chance.

So may your heart be good and true,
for I do so very much love you.

Lucy Insley

How Green Is Your Home?

How green is your home the place where you live?
How clean is the air that you breathe?
How friendly's the food you buy from the store?
The starch you put on your sleeve?
How clear are the waters, the lakes, and the ponds?
Are fish still happy and bright?
How conscious are you of the damage you do
From morning to night?
And what of the children who'll be left with the
World that we damage each day?
How green is the grass their children will play on?
Will the parks have been taken away?
How green are the contents of cupboards and shelves?
How much is recycled? And where?
How green is your home the place where you live?
How much do we all really care?

Mike Robinson

The Arrow

An arrow is drawn from the bowman's quiver,
He squints and frowns to perfect his eye,
He shoots at his target, no matter how far
And listens hard for that wounded cry!

The arrow is strong, is the craftsman's treasure,
Crafted in hope that the shaft will fly,
He sets another arrow to best his first,
His fingers clench though his mouth runs dry.

A baby is born to the watchful mother,
With her perfect boy she laughs and cries,
She dreams his future though the distance be close,
His fingers clench to her heartbeat's sigh.

The moon at night is like the earthly mother,
Keeping watch over the wayward sky,
She circles his lifetime, shimmering she glows,
She'll shine there still when his heartbeats die.

Keith M. Rowland

Testing Times

"These pregnancy testing kits you sell,
How much are they? Do they work very well?
Oh, not for me, for a friend you see."
(The shop assistant thought that most unlikely!)
She paid for the package and with minimum fuss
She walked down the hill to wait for the bus —
Once home, she read the instructions through,
You're pregnant if both of the boxes turn blue.
She completed the test then sat back and waited.
If she was, would he leave his wife whom he hated?
Or would he think she was being extremely unfair
To make him pay for her not taking adequate care.
Well, with him or without him, one way or the other
The blue boxes declare she's becoming a mother.

Yvonne Garman

My Invisible Friend

Oh wonderful wind blowing around,
Are you sending me messages here on the ground?
With hair blowing wild as our hats fly away,
One would think you are asking me come out to play?
I hear you in chimney, and slamming of doors
As I try to get on with my daily chores.
The flowers at your command lower their heads
As you fly gently over their garden beds.
Your gusts are so strong, yet your breeze is so gentle
That when you have blown yourself out and you settle,
I miss you, and long for another day's prattle.

Sylvia R. Jones

At Your Bedside

Your eyes have died tonight.
Night is drawing near for you
I hope it is painless.

The touch of your hand has gone cold
or so it feels in my vice grip,
your face paler than the white sheets.

I half-close the blinds,
a cage of light and shadow
dances on your body.

How can you fail like this when you're in my care?
If you hear my words, do you hear my prayer?
"Don't shed no tears"—easy for you to say,
I'm helpless here watching you slip away.

Silence fills the air,
Like a fist around my heart
getting tighter.

At your bedside as the banshee calls.
Waves touch the shore everyday.
At your bedside willing night to fall.
Can't stop time slip away.

John Lee Marshall

Blue Whale

Blue whale,
Blue whale,
I can hear your cry in the sea,
calling out for other whales
deep down in the sea,
where are you, brother and sister,
mum and dad?
Soon you will realise that they are dead.
Soon you will be the same as them,
So if you can hear my cry,
Blue whale,
Blue whale,
Get out before you die.

Sarah Crowther

A Step into the Green World

There I was, swiftly striding
Within the depths of a shadowy wood.
I spotted squirrels, the minority were hiding,
Scampering, scurrying like mad, they could.

I gazed around, standing on a green floor;
Many things I detected, a rabbit tightly curled.
As I pensively looked up at poplars galore
I perceived I was standing in an endless green world.

I cut through the trees; what a wide scenery!
The mountains afar, misty meadows in near sight.
The summer sun, glimmering over the greenery;
The radiance of sunshine, so vivid and bright.

I discerned from high on a prospect, so grand
And saw flowers upon flowers, like a giant festoon.
This dazzling green world is a celestial land,
But hence down to earth, I must proceed quite soon.

Christina Berardi

Absent Friends

Listening to the sound of Big Ben
Thinking back to the times when
Friends and family were all together
Having fun in the winter weather.

Times have changed, now we're getting old
But memories are as precious as gold
Times move on and so do friends
But love remains and never ends.

Wishing my friends from far and near
"A very happy and glad New Year".
Tess Whitlock

My Friend

My friend is getting very old,
Her nose today is very cold.
She sleeps more now than she's ever done,
But even now she's full of fun.

She's my best friend I have to say.
I wish she could forever stay.
But one day soon she'll go back home.
Unfortunately God's not on the phone.

I love my friend now even more.
I feel so safe she guards the
Door. Who is this friend? you want
To know. That gives your heart a certain glow.
Now here's a clue, now here's a lead.
A tail, a paw, a bark, a feed,

My friend's a dog.
"A dog" you say!
A chum, a pal, a mate, a stray!
Laura I. Gordon

The Embarrassment of Youth

There's my mom and my brother, and don't forget my dad
and they're the worst family that a girl could ever have.
I get shown up in public and so I go bright red,
and when I'm a little angel mom pats me on the head.
My friends all think it's funny but I really don't agree
that I should get picked on by him, him, and she.
As for my brother, I can't really tell.
All I know is when he dies he's going straight to hell.
That only leaves one person, and dad's got to be the best,
apart from the orange, green and purple vest.
Well that's my family for you and I think you will agree
that I'm the most patient girl there could ever ever be.
Jacqueline Bayliss

Memories

When I grow up show me this poem.
I'm writing it now at just eleven years old.
I want to know what all my memories are,
I want to know all the lessons I've been taught and told.

If I'm old and withered, and useless,
Just show me this poem and you'll see,
I'm sure my face will light up,
As I remember the memories of me.

I want to remember my birthdays, my holidays, and years to come.
And if this cut ever stopped hurting—the one I have on my thumb.
I can see myself in this poem, the time and the years that
have passed.
I'm sure I'm going to grow up, ever-so, ever-so fast;

That's why I'm writing this poem,
So I remember the good not the bad;
I want to read this when I grow old.
Yes let it cheer me up when I'm sad.

Come round, sit down and talk to me!
I'll be listening, I'll tell you that now,
Although I may seem far away,
I'm remembering! Understand that somehow!
Sarah Pittaway

Gemini Shadow

Crying,
dry tears on lost walls—
pondering your invite
of keeping us together.
My childhood of lost innocence,
Grateful love
my chances are stealing.

In an unconscious wish
I dream to follow my Gemini Shadow
through the misty field, into the calm garden—
where everything is wet.

What would you say,
if I asked you to take me?
Something Sacred? I'm longing to go with you.

Would we be kept?, does Iscariot marry
Angel
I'm too tired to sleep,
'Grateful Love.'
Steven Victor Martin

When Time Stood Still

When first we met and time stood still,
I did not know his name was "Bill",

We walked beside a little stream
Where we used to sit and dream.

In Summer when the sun was high,
We wandered through the woods close by.

Now married fifty years and two.
We still had lots of things to do.

He has gone now, I love him still.
And I know I always will.

Today I sit alone and dream
Of all the things that "might have been".
Betty Mason

Memories

Come—walk with me down the lane.
So we can remember once again
The walks we have taken over the years,
The laughter, the heartaches, and the tears.
Come—take my hand and let us go.
To the hills above and the valley below
To see the flowers that bloom each spring,
and we can listen to the birds that sing.
Come—let us go in harmony.
To where the gentle wind blows free;
And let us look to those above,
And fill our hearts with heavenly love.
S. D. Clark

Blue Lavender

Of yesterday,
When she asked why do you smile
I answered thoughts—thoughts that formulate
She knows a lot about me and remains silent
Her silence is of blue lavender
She is impartial—and I'm glad
Blue Lavender how sweet the blue lavender.

Today,
I'm as the condor flying free
Free from coventry
I soar and smile the more
How little—they—know of me—
I'm a Jack Russell among adversaries
I am as the bone breaker
They write plaudits unto themselves
I have closed the eyes of the dead
I drop lollipops
Blue lavender how sweet the blue lavender
I sip the fragrance.
Gilbert

Sisterly Love

Sisterly love, needs not to be spoken
It weaves a spell, that cannot be broken
We use it, with guidance from above
A gift to you, my sisterly love

Jane May

Life

The voices inside my head
Scream; they're getting louder
I want to run, I want to escape from it all
I want to die
Is it any wonder?

The pain, the fear
Will it ever leave?
Or will it stay forever inside?
Never to leave me
In peace, alone to grieve.

The thing I fear is life, not death;
Of never being free, alone to live the life of hell
That's developed inside me.
But I know somehow I will survive
I know this because, I'm still alive.

I breathe, I think I will survive
I have so much to give
I breathe, I know I will survive
I'll find the will to live.

Carolyn M. Lack

Untitled

No longer do tall ships with cargoes squeezed tight,
Face tempest, and storm, and all nature's might,
Great horses no longer pull cart loads of jute,
Encouraged by carters, in tackety boots,
Steel shod blinkered workers, coats drenched in cold sweat,
Obedient tired Clydesdales, peching, droothy, and wet,
No more do they woa to drink long at a trough,
Quenching a thirst that would empty a loch,
Gone are their slow plodding clip-clopping motions,
No longer admired, their majestic proportions,
Silenced the din, from shuttles, and levers,
All gone with the spinners cop winders, and weavers,
No more does the odour from jute taint the hair,
Of mothers, and sisters, and sweethearts so fair,
The clarion of bummers, like the Piped Piper's flute,
Dundee's Piper of Hamlin, now silent and mute,
Gray sinister mills, massive structures of stone,
With tall reeky chimneys, like the dodo all gone,
Jute from Calcutta, it no longer holds sway,
Over life in that city on the banks of the Tay.

Michael McGlinn

Ode to July's Babe

I ask no more of life than that I see
Why I am me?
Why am I not April's child?
For then I might rise bright as a lark
That wakens with dawn to greet the morn.
I am my mother's child,
My mother bore me ill, and yes, I chide
Her still for this her cruel mistake.
Why was I not the child of May?
I would be fair and sing a joyful air.
Oh pity me, for I did not come forth
As June's pink blushing rose.
My mother bore me, mistaken so it seems,
To bring me forth one damp December day
When all around was cold and grey.
And cold I am this very night,
Much colder still by day.
Oh child of mine, rest easy at this breast,
For you, dear one, are sweetly blessed.
Warm cheerful child of brightest July sun.

Pauline Gutteridge

Love with You

I can use the word love so freely.
How can I not when I love you so dearly
When I wake, I see your face so clearly
When I see you, I see that you are so true to my
very thought

I say your name just before I open my eyes.
I open them to the lingering scent that covers your chest
I dream of your white open shirt looking down on me,
Your strong tender hands awakening me,
Your intense green eyes kissing my forehead and shaking me,
Your gorgeous smile on a face so beautiful.

I can use the word love so freely.
My love for you is such that I cannot express.
No charming lyric can depict the feelings that
I have for you.
My sincerity overwhelms me.
My beautiful boy I need you with me,
I love you so, and so I can use the word love so freely.

J. Neil

Tears

Tears of worry I silently weep
As the rest of the world is fast asleep
What will become of you, who will care
Who will look after you when I'm not there?

Tears of mourning I have also cried
Although you live, the old you died
Selfish tears, laced with guilt and grief
sometimes must be cried to give relief

Tears of anger flow readily too
Can't help you at all, nothing I can do
God tell me, what purpose does this serve?
I'm sure it's not what you deserve

Tears of self pity are easiest to cry
As I ask again, Lord why oh why?
I ask these questions, no answers come
It's hard for me because I'm your Mum

But the tears that hurt me most of all
Are the tears that from your sad eyes fall,
Tears of frustration, confusion and pain
When you ask, will I ever be well again?

Moira Angus

Stranger

Where do you come from my young man
Did you cross the sea of Japan
Or some other ocean, soft and deep
Or do you dwell here in my sleep
A sleep that my mind cannot control
For I am half, and never will be
Once again complete
Or is this word I seek whole
Such a complex thing am I
Do I sleep beneath the same sky
No in a dungeon dark and deep
So cold, that I cannot sleep
My mind still I think, in control
For as I said, I am still half
And never will be completely whole
Think not bad of me, when I ask you
What was that sea you came from
That lies north of the islands of Hong Kong

Eddie Barrass

Magic Mia

Magic mia gets out of bed and puts on her cloak.
She pours all the nit-eggs in her hair into a bowl.
Then she pours milk on them and eats them.
So if you pass Mia's house and hear a crunch-crunching
you can be sure that it's nit-eggs she's eating.

Katie Weeks

Autumn Field in Dovaston

Trees stand like sentinels against the sky
When day is nearly done
And at their feet a million soldiers gleam
Like emeralds in the evening sun.

With spikes held aloft
Like the cohorts of old
The dance and they play
In their green and their gold.

And the bowmen stand undaunted
The challenge the blue of the sky
Their arrows pointing upwards
As the swallows go homing by.

If I could stay forever
It would not be too long
To listen to their music
And the poetry of their song.

But when my life is finished
And death has taken hold
I'll be marching with my soldiers
In their glorious green and gold.

Doris Ginsberg

One Frosty Day

Crystal forms so clear and bright,
Twinkling in the morning light.
Shapes unfold from their disguise,
As silhouettes against the crimson skies.

In the midst a far off cry
Echoes through the trees so high.
All around, the earth is still,
Covered by a frosty chill.

A lonely Robin hops around,
In search for food on the hardened ground.
In vain she turns and flies away,
As the sun awakens to another day.

Barbara Nicholson

War or Peace?

War is a cold and frightful word.
One that should never ever be heard,
It puts a sad look on children's faces,
Different ages, different cultures, different races.

War is a punishment to the Earth,
All the sorrow, pain and unhappiness is not worth
Owning a country or winning a bet,
It makes thousands of people ill and upset.

Peace is something everyone needs,
Especially children of any creed.
Peace should be in our schedule of life,
No more gunshots or any knives.

War or peace that's your choice,
Go ahead and let your voice
Be heard. As long as you choose the right one,
You can make the world a lot more fun.

Natalie Jones

Springtime

Flowers growing in the sun,
  Pretty colours, one by one.

Sun is shining, lovely day,
  Girls and boys shout out "let's play".

Skipping and jumping, playing kiss and chase,
  Dancing on the new grass, the world's a wonderful place.

New buds bursting all around,
  Birds are tweeting, it's a lovely sound.

Little lambs they frisk and run,
  Blossoms waving in the sun.

Louise Jones

A Guardian Angel

Why weren't you there in my childhood,
When demons invaded my sleep,
When I'd run without moving, through walls of white water,
My screams of fear lost in the deep.

Why weren't you there when my hands felt so tiny,
My body so frail and so slight,
When great walls of white water, forever engulfed me,
Why didn't you know of my plight.

And yet as exhaustion brought my submission,
And I dropped to my knees in the sand,
You stood there before me, face gilded with sunlight,
You smiled, and you held out your hand.

You lifted me up from the walls of white water,
And we flew as if we had wings,
To blue skies, and flowers, and trees filled with blossom,
To where night ends, and morning begins.

You were there in the dreams of my childhood,
And I know you are with me to-day,
When I'm down, and the walls of white water surround me,
You lift me, and show me the way.

M. Hall

To Care for the Old

Once they were like you and like me,
So full of pride and quiet dignity.
Holding down jobs, children to raise,
Fighting in wars through the dark days.
Asking for nothing, sharing their last,
Grieving for loved ones they'd lost in the past.
Independent, relying on none,
One day youth has suddenly gone.
Now those same people who were once so free,
Sit there just waiting so helplessly.
You have to wash them and dress them and comb their hair,
Feed them and tend them with such loving care.
So may God bless all those who care patiently,
For the people who once, were like you and like me.

Sheila Mannion

Cat's Eyes

Its pupils streaked chatoyancy,
Charms away sorcery,
A cure for sores and a protection of children,
A bringer of wealth and a sense of good humour,
An image of the great divine,
With a parallel pattern crystalline,
Pools of quarts, beaming and glowing,
A sacred, golden jewel, blinking,
The scarce cat's eye Alexandrite,
Green in the daylight, red in the fake light,
It reflects light passionately,
The lens gleams antiquity,
A trinket against psychosomatic illness,
Or a talisman to ward off evil spirits,
The story of cat's eye is a legend in itself,
Disillusion people in its beauty's wealth.

Rachel MacLean

Three Old Women Waiting for a Bus

The first wears a white coat speckled with damp.
Her Alzheimer's stare trails across the street,
But she only sees the soldiers who beat
Her mother as she cried in the death camp.

An ugly brooch made from shells crouches on
The second's lapel. Arthritic arms sag
With shopping and a brown leather handbag
Full of sweets and photos of friends long gone.

Phrenological nightmares lurk under
The thin, blue rinsed hair of the third lady.
She's not quite sane after a large brandy,
She can hear the voice of God in thunder.

Paul Kester

Serenade of Equality

Just as roses need the rain,
when our fate is carried by angels,
only when the lost loves are found,
and faith shines over sarcasm,
if the lies finally believe truth,
because souls have forgotten their pride,
then life will overcome death,
since day following night will remember,
that when the wrong overshadowed the right,
our freedom once hung in chains.

Charlotte Dewson

Thou Haunting Muse

Elude me not, evanescence sublime
Nor let my knees, bend vainly at your shrine
While heav'n wards soar my thoughts, transcending time
Pray, let your golden rays, on my verse shine!

Through fleeting mists, betimes, you haunt me still
While silken wisps, your graceful form unveil
Such mystic sight, you poor bard's pen to thrill
That but one glimpse, should over all prevail!

On wintry nights, when tall trees bend and sigh
With lashing winds, that land and seas deform
I seem to hear your call, o'er waves blown high;
T'is then I feel you take my mind, by storm!

And when the languid waves the shores caress
Or gentle breezes whisper through the brush,
I hear you still and my good fortune bless
That I can sense your presence o'er the hush!

Walter Mallia

Anxiety, Panic and Fear

Anxiety, panic and fear;
why do they appear?
From where or why, I really don't know.
But one thing I do know, I want them to go.
Not today, not tomorrow, but yesterday,
I realize now that's not the way.
With a little help and a little encouragement,
This anxiety, panic and fear can be sent,
Far, far away, never again to be found,
So I can carry on with my life and stand my ground.
I want to be free, like a bird on a breeze,
Instead of panicking which makes me wheeze.
For this I have to be strong and brave, I know,
For all of these feelings to eventually go.
If you ever feel this, please live in hope,
You may not think it, but deep down, you know you can cope.

Angela Broome

Elegy to an Old Soldier

The poppies drop on the great congregation
Who quietly and reverently mourn for a nation
Remembering the life of each brave lad
But some came back and we were glad.

You were one of those who lived through that hour.
Somehow you survived that terrible war.
You lost your family from a bomb.
Later you lost your wife and son
But, Alec, you lived on.

When you went into hospital
We feared it was the end.
But "Old soldiers never die" I wrote
And you came home again.

But now, in a moment, you have gone
Your merry twinkle no more shall be
We pray, dear Lord, you will keep him safe
On that unknown, uncharted sea.
We pray we will see our Alec again
When our time comes and we go to Thee.

Sheila Brown

Whitemail

Before we came to their dreams,
hatched in the Cauldrons of Hate,
we did not know
There could be such Deception,
Such Depravity in the Mind of Man.

Before we came to their visions
born in the Nightmares of time,
We could not realize
that there could be such Hate
Such Deformity in the Soul of Man.

But the shimmer of their Midnight
Befuddled us, bewitched us,
Bedazzled us.

And we crept into their Shrines
onto their altars,
Forgetting, that We Too have Shrines, and
Leaving behind us in the Limbo
Our hallelujahs of sorrow
And the magma cries of the Lost Generation

Kris Atta Pappoe

Sweet Memories

A glance across a crowded room
will but for a moment release
a fragrant memory. Encapsulated
in its purest form.
Has time stood still? Or am I
just dreaming of those bygone days
when in my mind I saw all things tangible.

Christine Marshall

Resilience

You didn't cry, just stood your ground,
like some wild creature stamping its dignity
on an African sky.
We'll get by.
Jelly stained and high as a kite,
you were the only one without a dad
to bring you home from the party,
but you didn't cry.
You got by.
Prizes, and certificates came and went.
The growing up, the secrets and the agonies.
Just the two of us.
We managed.
And when I howled my loss to the predatory sky,
you soared above it all to high-blown clouds,
like a condor.

Eileen Hudson

Little Girl Dancing

In the dim church, beneath whose hallowed ground
The dead their final resting place had found,
Curious and faithful walked with decorous tread
Or knelt in prayer with bowed and reverent head:
Suddenly out of the clouds the sun broke through;
The great rose window glowed with light anew,
Emerald, ruby, sapphire, all ablaze,
Topaz and amethyst, their shimmering rays
In liquid light were spilled upon the stones
Carved with grim symbols, awesome skulls and bones;
Amazed by this sweet gift of magic light
A small girl stood and gazed in mute delight,
Caught in a coloured dream, enticed, entranced.
The playful lights bewitched her, and she danced;
An iridescent sprite she skipped, she twirled,
She danced alone in her own secret world;
Heedless of many a disapproving frown
She danced; but surely God Himself looked down
On all the solemn piety—and smiled—
And blessed the innocent joy of a dancing child.

Esther Latham

Love

What is love between two souls.
It starts with their eyes sparkling
And their faces lighting up.
The holding of hands, the lingering kiss,
Their exultant feelings for each other.
So they come together,
With a loving relationship,
That knows no bounds.
Together they stand in an embrace,
That shows their feelings for each other,
A hug that pulls them together.
Unmindful of who is watching,
Lost in a love for each other.
C. Reisdorf

Bedrock of Sour

Oh Monster! Oh frown!!
The gloomy spirit that reflects
Speaking the mind's thoughts, and
saying the mind's feelings

On the red it alerts
Set to dispel all looks
And host well no face
Therein resides the heart-beater

Oh frown, bedrock of sour
That trail the move of a walking life
So is it parley the doom? And
surely it's happiness drowning ocean

Onward be the world of smile
Sidney that treads upon doom
As the happy life nightingale,
That is good smile across face, radiating.
Hamid Mutiu Abiola

Loneliness

No one knows what loneliness is
Until you're on your own.
No one knows what it is like
To sit and eat alone.
No one knows what it is to climb
The stars last thing at night.
To get into bed with love, no one there
To cuddle and kiss goodnight.
No one calls to see if everything's alright
Family, friends, and neighbours they don't
really understand.
But one day that too will be all alone.
They they will know and understand
Just what loneliness is all about.
So if you have at least two good friends,
Hold on to them tight
Because they're the ones who make
Everything seem all right.
M. Moakes

The Untouchable Child

A lonely mother, gazes out of her window
At the daughter
That she will never be able to touch
The child looks up
And for a moment their eyes meet.
In her face, a sign of recognition shows,
But then she turns away
Unable to understand the few memories she has of her.
Who is she? She wonders, who?
The mother seems to read the child's mind
She puts out her hand, and touches the cool glass
'One day you will understand everything', she whispers
Then she closes her eyes and falls onto the chair.
Out of her hand flutters a photograph
Of the child she will never be able to touch.
Joanne Louise Dimond

Untitled

We've detained our sober senses?
Despite humanity gone.
Murder.
An outcried brute of our knifes and of our guns.
Carnage in the day,
Night,
And ritual decease of sun.
Have we reached a returnless point,
Or have we just begun?

Disfigurements of our star,
The vaunt of a self-proclaimed authoritativeness.
An earthy existent,
A percentage would leave headless.
Red bricked armies,
I squint for a wilderness.
Earthquake shrugs, bomb,
Our star is becoming restless.
Danny Graham

Time

'Time' is the Universe, the Sun, and the Stars.
The regular turn of the Earth as it turns on its Axis.
Never to speed or falter.
'Time' is the next million years and another million after that,
'Time' does not exist, yet it is still there.
It cannot be altered, broken, or destroyed.
'Time' is the river that flows down to the Sea.
Only to return and start again.
The once proud oak that stood the test of centuries,
Now twisted and bent by winds and snows of many winters.
The wrinkles on the old man's face.
The Foetus in its Mother's womb, from child to manhood,
To the Grave. The flesh rotting on the bones
To take up life in some other form.
'Time' heals, 'Time' destroys, gives pleasure and sadness,
It has no destiny, 'Time' is never final.
Thomas Nicklin

Atwig

Our family life does shape the mind,
As tree is bent the trees inclined,
If other house had shaped my will,
Would I be straight, or more bent still.

If other minds can shape me so,
Which part is me, I'd like to know.
Is my life geared to other's will,
They write the order, I pay the bill.

How to rid those burnt-in phrases
'Tis hard to change, to rid the traces,
It's lots of fag, all bother and all,
Climb will cost, I'm sure to fall.

While time to think, I must learn other,
Not meander, with songs from mother,
Whate'er do blossom on my shoots,
Inherits from those early roots.
H. Cotterill

Those Peaceful Days

How tranquil down a country lane,
Through an avenue of trees
With the sweetest warbling of our birds
Upon a summer breeze.

A sudden scent of new mown hay,
As we come to turn the bend
And in our view, earth's fairest flowers,
With the fragrance that they sent.

These are the moments in our life
When we do not need to pray,
For we are so much nearer God
Than on any after day.
Marion W. Cooke

More Than a House

A house is made of bricks and mortar
for husband and wife, sons and daughters
when they live there, it becomes a home
until the children leave to roam

Upon this earth where their fancy takes
but they still come home for the parent's sakes
for it's their home, a welcome abode
and a place to go by the nearest road

A home maybe smart with lots of staff
elegant furniture and more than one bath
or perhaps it's small and very humble
just two rooms and walls that crumble

No matter what, it's still called home
they all say that, wherever they roam
so speak of your home with a certain pride
whether rich or poor, it's a place to bide

You know you're welcome when you get there
it's more than a house, it's home, and you care
a place for memories you know so well
of childhood stories remembered to tell.

Patricia Thompson

'Tis Over

You asked me what was wrong
But I could not answer
I didn't know what to say
And when you said you where leaving
I didn't ask you to stay

It's not because I don't love you
And I cannot pretend I don't care
Although I tell my friends
I'm glad you're not there

So now you've found someone new
And believe me I'm happy for the both of you
Because deep down I know
The love between you both will never be
As strong as the love you shared with me.

D. Thornton

Autumn

A golden mattress lies upon the ground.
The rustling leaves are falling down.
Different fruits hang from each tree.
A shiver travels down my spine.
Swallows with a direction, fly across the darkened sky.

Death's odour fogs the air.
A fire crackles, making faces in the night.
The sweet perfume of turnips is familiar.
The whistling wind, trying hard to get in.
In your bed, watching hard,
The clouds begin their midnight carnival.

Eimear Caher

Mam Tor: 1000 BC

Stark, silent statues stand,
Black against a satanic sky.
They scan the wolf-haunted valley below,
Shrouded now in an early morning mist.
Beyond, the bronze tinged land stretches
Breathing,
Scratched blood of their struggle.
In an arched malevolent smile
The forest clutches at the cleared land,
Which shimmers in the dewy half-light.
With deliberate ease the dark figures turn
And pace towards rounded hearths
Seeking warmth from the chill dawn,
A solitary hilltop oasis.
Safety in a land
Pregnant with capricious primeval forces.

Lesley Court

Who Cares?

The death of a homeless one
who was so brave and bold,
To sleep outside in desperation
In the bitter cold,
usually prompts the phrase of exasperation
From the well-off majority,
It's not our fault!

The stories we hear
Of some far away lands
Bogged down in poverty, hunger and disease,
And the resulting starvation and death
Usually induce few words of sympathy
And the usual phrase,
It's not our fault!

If every single one of us
Adopted this selfish, self-centred attitude,
Forgetting to show some spiritual gratitude
For not being in the same situation
Who would in turn care for us
When our own lives suddenly go wrong?

Elizabeth Lartey

Grandfather

Like a child's tear on endless fear,
for your sun has faded, dipped into dark.
Hair perfection, hands never undone at the crack.
I know I must let go, go, go, but believe me I loved you so.

Your car was white like the purest of souls,
Your heart was made out of pure, solid gold.
Arms as long as the whole wide world,
Warm at the touch of a button

I'm sorry I didn't cry, I'm sorry I forgot,
But still you lie still, solid, rotting in the ground;
She didn't want it, we didn't want it, breaking down.

So now this prayer must end at last
And I'll never forget you as fast.
The black shiny stone, the vicious moon,
Did you ever know how I felt?
Goodbye my love, sleep tight, sleep tight,
Don't forget me, my gracious might.

Kerry Tuck

The Damaged Bud

Eyes dim,
moments stretch out into eternity,
but in earthly reality,
less than a few dozen heartbeats,
as life dissolves within a damaged bud.
A gentle forgiving kiss now spans the gulf,
between the living and heavenly call,
then, as a deep comforting sleep
numbs and innocent mind,
a journey begins to a better place.

Hasim Jeneck

Goodnight, Godbless

Close your eyes now, it's time to go.
People you loved and lost are waiting to say hello.
I can see you're tired, this has got to be.
Your journey now will be pain free.
The sun is shining, the sky is so blue.
It's as if heaven is opening just for you.

Your journey's begun now, I can tell by your face.
Gone is the pain
There's a smile in its place
As I kiss your cheek, and stroke your hair
Wondering why life's so unfair
But realizing I'm not the only one
To lose a very special mum
And when it's time for me to go
I know you'll be there to say hello.

Gina Holzherr

Away from It All

As a city dweller I love to roam
The countryside—not far from home.
In North Kent hamlets are tucked away,
So little changed from yesterday.
Who would think so near to town
Trees so fresh, the earth so brown.
I forget my troubles as I trudge along
And chat to my friends until we long
For the lunch break, always a pub,
Tucked away from the hub—of the City.

Renewed we set off—well fed—
Averting our eyes from steep hills ahead,
But panting, we finally reach the top
For views that leave us all agog.
Of Kentish churches, strong and true,
Who could wish for a better view.
So down we go, our breath regained,
Over stiles, through woods, over muddy terrain,
Over streams, till we reach our train—back to the city.

Elizabeth Webbe-Wood

Souls Set Free

Speech is insulting when they do not understand,
No words can describe the pain you feel.
Grief numbs the mind, and bitters the heart,
And these tragic events make life seem unreal.

I won't pretend to know how you feel,
Or pretend to understand why
You have to suffer this horrifying evil,
Or why your children had to die.

All I can do is try and console you,
With a few thoughts and heart-felt words.
To remind you where your children are now,
Their souls as free as birds.

Remind yourself that your children left us,
Without realizing the sin and cruelty of our time
They all left us as sweet innocents,
Thinking life was one long fairy rhyme.

There is no greater love than between mother and her child,
A bond no one can break
Not even the swift, heartless hand of death,
From you that sweet love can take.

P. M. Joseph

I Hear His Cry

In the dark I hear him cry,
In pain in pain, sorry he'll die.
One more poor soul that's what he is,
Just one more man on a remembrance list,
But deep in my mind as morning mists,
I hear his cry he still exists.
How lucky he is the cold didn't bite,
God must have seen him, took pity on sight,
But as we go to haul him in, the cry's,
They stop, he's given in.

Robert Mitchell

A Search for the Hero

The voice pushed him on,
And cries carried him forward.
Though his escapade was long,
Still he struggled onward.

He was sure he'd had enough,
For the gloom to him was haunting.
But with the smooth he took the rough,
Until all became less daunting.

What was it he needed?
Something else in his life's role?
Soon the message came clear and pleaded:
"Don't escape what's in your soul."

Charlotte Dewson

Poems . . . from within Inspired by Michael Jackson

Past . . . Present . . . and the Future
The sky—The only thing we share
Full of inspiration and hope.
Let your eyes talk
. . . your mind drift

Destiny—something that prediction can not fulfill.

Temptation is very high
Peace is caving in
What can we do now, where will we go . . . ?

The sky—The only thing we share.
Black and dullness surround us now
Chalky tastes gulp in our mouth . . .
. . . and our eyes unlit like the future.

Medina Harrison

My Man

I sit and stare at his silhouette
thinking back to when we first met,
remembering good times, remembering bad,
our years together, some happy, some sad.

Recalling our children when they were babies,
decisions we made, shall we or shan't we,
move to a new house, buy a new car,
start some new venture or stay as we are.

Reliving memories down through the years,
the joys that we shared, oh yes, and the fears,
the tears that we've shed at some sad time
and the comfort he gave me, this man of mine.

I wonder what time we have left together,
wishing that it might be forever,
and I wonder if I'm able to remain strong
if he's not at my side where he's been all along,
if I'm left on my own, the one left behind,
without the love of this man of mine.

Valerie Copley

Flowers of the Earth

The beauty of the bluebell flowers,
The glow of the golden rose,
The floating of the pearl white clouds.
Over banks where the river flows.

The cherry, and the blossom trees,
The waving meadow flowers,
The fire of the stately poppies,
As they silently live each hour.

There's a secret place of the world of flowers,
Where green hills glow with joyfulness,
Honey suckle close their horns,
As the fading day is blessed.

H. M. J. Cole

On the Shore

Oh to be down by the sea again
With the call of the running tide,
Where you swing and toss in little boats
As on wave's crests you ride.
Hear the breakers thundering in
And crashing on the shore.
Hear the Seagull's plaintive cry
As they wheel around once more.
See the spray glint in the sun
As it spills back down the rocks.
Over in the harbour a fishing trawler docks
Bringing back a catch of fish,
Or maybe lobster pots.
Where you feel the bite of the wind
Get the tang of the salt sea air,
So many of nature's wonders
Are waiting for you there.

Audrey A. Allocca

One of Nature's Gentlemen

One of nature's gentlemen,
Black tie, top hat, and tails,
No socks, odd boots upon his feet,
But Oh, so dapper and so neat,
Always a flower, always a smile,
As he walks the street mile after mile.
Everyone knows him, from granddad to babe,
One of nature's gentlemen, born, not made.
He once was a rich man, lived in a grand street,
Now he's a poor man, odd boots on his feet,
Eats from the dustbin, sits in the shade,
One of nature's gentlemen, born, not made.

D. M. Huddlestone

Betrayal

My mother's grave is on a hillside,
overlooking the ugly side of town.
A large sprawling cemetery
of rectangular headstones, dead flowers.

It should have been otherwise.

A small country churchyard,
Old tombstones. Tall trees.
White roses and some fuchsia.
A natural outlook.

As it is, the Celtic Cross
of Cornish stone and Latin inscription
is out of place.
An elevated, lonely incongruity.

I am reminded my mother died
among strangers.
As now she lies
in awkward proximity,

It should have been otherwise.

Margaret White

Joy

Is it because it's Spring my heart feels free, and wants to sing
to all the birds on high?
Is it the look of budding primrose shoots pushing up their
heads in my secret nook, unknown to passers-by—
that makes my heart beat faster with a new found joy?
Or is it the memory of your touch that warms my heart and
helps me carry on?
The answer could be in any of these things, but it is not—
The reason for my joy is your love for me,
and your promise to be true, eternally.
I do not mind if life deals out a hand of sorrow,
If days are filled with doubts and nameless fears,
If plans made for tomorrow tremble on the brink then disappear.
As long as I have you I have all.
Your love for me shines like a soft warm light,
As long as I have you, then all in life is happy,
I am at peace, and all the world is right.

Dolores Maloney

The End of an Affair

Don't think that I'll forget you
I loved you for too long
We shared so many years together
When we knew that it was wrong
I miss your smell, your touch, your feel
The days are long, the ache is real
And if I see you with another.
I'll pretend that I don't care
The pain will fade as time goes on
And you'll be out of my hair
I know we parted suddenly
A clean cut is the best
Soon the memory of you will die
And you'll be off my chest
Broken-hearted you must be joking
I've finally given upon smoking.

Patricia Murray

Realize

You and I are equal. I know I'm not wrong; skin
deep is what I mean so why fuss and fight over
things that should belong to you and me? Naturally it's
hard to see reality when a smoke screen is blocking
our sight, our vision of life around us. What
you don't see is poverty, the people on the streets.
Know I've been there, in poverty with restless nights,
Wondering how I'm gonna get from one night to
the next. As one man said, "you don't need eyes
to see, you need vision." How can you see when
the smoke screen is blocking your path? So light you
flare and get out your flags because they don't hear
your calls. So show the signs most things in life.
the land and sea are for everybody, but wars go on
for the land and sea, so only back to basics we could
go. So many lives would live. So realize! Get wise
and see the eyes that cry in poverty and see it's not
only you and me in poverty! Others are too! But
if you are rich, understand and see! Realize the pain amongst
people in the 90's! It's not just poverty.

Ramona L. Seddon

Life Today

I think I'll take a walk on Oak Tree hill
Oh; but I have to pay the phone bill.
Life today
is nothing like yesterday
Rape, murdering, stealing.
To crooks it's soooooooo appealing.

Emma Louise Ginn

Living on the Fen

The landscape's bleak, the trees are few,
They uprooted all the hedgerows too.
The land they borrowed from the sea
To spread the corn and grow the seed.
The farmers they are robust men,
Living and toiling on the fen.

The wind it howls and rushes through,
With wide open space it roars on anew.
The dykes and streams with water fill
And down to the sea the rivers spill.
Elements are harsh for kith and kin,
Living and working on the fen.

Stock farms, you only see a few
Horses, there are one or two.
The mighty shires, serenely grazing,
With foals at foot, in paddocks lazing.
No longer working alongside the men,
Just lazily grazing on the fen.

A. Sheppard

New Home

Liverpool eight
Welfare state
Red light, blue light waiting to clash
sex for sale, if you've got the cash
Streets of decay and dilapidation
child born with no expectation
Pot, crack fed to the streets
10-year-old addicts, hard to beat
start them young, feed the need
Thatcher's orphans are starting to breed
Our winter of discontent is 15 years long
destroy this country, and receive your gong
Community spirit torn and tattered
city after city the tories have battered
Crime is up, dole queues increase
will the nightmare ever cease?
Poor get thin, rich are fatter
now I'm a number do I really matter?
The boys in blue follow the men in grey
do as you're told, so as they say!

Tim Snelling

I Always Wished . . .

I always wished to be a ballerina,
and wear a pink, silk dress,
dance and twirl, with little pink shoes,
but I always looked a mess.

I always wanted to fly to the moon,
In a great, big, silver rocket,
but all I got on my 7th birthday,
was a toy I could fit in my pocket.

I always dreamed of being a bird,
that flew so high in the sky,
sing beautiful songs all day long,
When I couldn't, I wanted to cry.

I guess sometimes it's better that,
you are just what you are,
but still I haven't stopped dreaming,
of the day I become a film star.

Tamsin Andrews

Pops!!!

My ideal Man I can never find
Someone who's loving, Caring and Kind

A man who is strong and full of fun
When problems arise, you'll never see Him run!!

He'd laugh at the jokes I would tell
Mother me, when I'm unwell

Where can you find a person so true?
Married to my mum—Yes Pops!

   IT'S YOU!!!

Elaine Youden

On Bleasdale Fells

My sweet dark hills, stained against the sky,
The light around them streaming as through glass,
How many memories are pressed against their slopes,
Held in their pools, and in their treasured ways?
   Taken memories that we can never lose,
   Kept like pictures pasted in a book.

They fade a little but yet are clear enough,
To show us the charms that ever drew us there,
The streams still sliding round remembered stones,
The larks still springing from the sun-swept grass,
   In the place we loved to sit,
   And, silently happy, watch them soar.

The fells will stay, the memories too,
As long as we are here to know,
They will go with us down into the dark,
But there will be others always in their place:
   Youth will forever find the hills,
   And know the joys that once we knew.

Dorothy Millington

You Were Mine

When I first met you,
I knew you were mine.
You made me feel special
All of the time.
Nobody could take you away from me,
Because you were mine.
In your arms I felt safe. Safe from the world.
Nobody could take that away from me,
Because you were mine.
Then one day something happened. Something terrible
You were gone.
You no longer made me feel special.
You no longer protected me from the world.
But I knew you were still here,
Because you were mine.
We would never part,
Because you will always
Be in my heart.

Shalita Radia

Good Bye

Good bye my first love
I will miss you forever
For it's hard to admit but from this day on
We no longer belong to each other.

We promised to treasure our memories together
No one could take it away from us
For this is the only piece we left to one another
When we decided to part.

It was really hard to say the word 'good bye'
But it had to be done
I saw the tears rolling from your eyes
I tried to hide my feelings
But I could not help it, I just had to let it out.

Now we're gone our separate ways
I wish you good luck and happiness
I hope you and I will find our love someday
So both our hearts will be glad once again.

Carmela Hullana Gapuz

A Politician

A politician only wants to know me when
He or she wants my vote
They don't care how the country run
And they do not listen when I tell
There's something very very wrong

But these politicians know how to give
Themselves pay raises of 26 per cent
While the working man is given only 3
Percent and they ask me to vote for
Them, not me

We put them in parliament to do what
We want them to do and all they do is
Howl at one and another so please politician
Put your act together if you want my vote
And tell other countries stop telling
Us what to do and stop dictating
To us we don't want them to run
This country of ours, then I will vote for one of you.

M. W. Lowe

The Way with Music

Save me from the evil.
   Save me from the dark.
      Light my path with music straining from the harp.
         Send me sounds of saxophone,
            Or sweet soft melody.
               As music means so much to me.

Ailie Corke

Picasso's Figure Seated on a Rocking Chair

He sits in lonely grandeur on his tree throne
His face turned right, the pristine profile calm.
Twin serpents glide up and round the seated figure
Forming a resting-place for his arms.

But no bird sings, no animals adore, he holds no flute.

The throne is of wood, a tree imprisoned in the room.
The carved serpents, dumb and motionless,
Can neither kill nor protect their Lord,
Who slow but sure sinks back into the tree,
His blood, its sap, sucked down by the thick trunk.
Resisting hands clutch feverishly the sides,
The white half-face masks nothing but a void,
For the head, striving to escape, to hide, has dropped
And stares out from the lower bowel.
One piercing eye glares,
The gaping, rang-rimmed mouth
Emits a soundless scream of dread and hatred
The great final shock of emotion before inevitable petrifaction.

Here there is no guitar, no speaking, singing wood.

Angela Kilbride

A Father's Son

I sit and brush away my father's tear
Holding his hand calmly nothing to fear

Helping him pass from life to life
Waiting for him is my mother his wife

He whispers son I can see the pearly gates
Always remember life is guided by fate

Be strong and hold your head high
For there is life beyond the sky

A father so proud he has a son
To pass his name on in years to come

Another man's daughter will become my wife
Together creating the precious gift of life

From a love so strong was born a son
A tiny heart beating a new life begun

As I cradle our baby I look up at the sun
Whispering father meet your grandson my son

Vivien Wallis

Connemara You're Beautiful

Scenic panoramic, oh so beautiful, that's you Connemara,
your mountains, rivers, lakes, all grand,
even the corral strand, glistening by sunlight and by moonlight.

Flowers wild and tame, I don't even know your names,
but you are all pretty ever so pretty,
through wind and rain, I do hope you're not in pain.

Beautiful lakes, large and small,
scattered about this colourful paradise,
so vast, so lovely, Connemara you are the garden of Eden.

Connemara you are indeed beautiful,
wild and wonderful raw nature tempered by the elements.
How old are you? God only knows

John Dunne

Internal Harassment

Love has the secret to create and undo
The strength to control and submit.
Love has the magic to give birth and to kill
The reason to hurt and protect.
Love has the notion to trust and deceive
The power to honour and hate.
Love has the knowledge to be right and wrong
The wisdom to give and to take.
Love has the fire to energize and destroy
The air to breathe and suffocate.
Love has the water to quench and to drown
The earth to grow and decay.
Love has the choice, one or the other
The decision to fall or deny.
Love has the question, now or forever
The answer, to never ask why.

Jenni Lynn

The Awakening of the Underworld

The black desolated ocean shimmers
so innocently in the glowing moonlight.
A crash of thunder and the gales pick up.
The wind howls and screams and squeals terrifyingly
whilst swiftly circling high
over the ghostly waters.
The sea rises violently and abruptly, defying all laws,
reaching higher and higher.
It's swirling now. Around and around and around.
Unearthly noises ring out in this unearthly world.
Haunting howls bellow out of the sepulchral darkness,
whilst ferocious explosions pervade the sky.
They have awoken.
It has awoken.
Only eternal terror, morose and massacre
is to follow.

Natalie Cooke

Goodbye World

Goodbye world, I've only myself to blame,
I tried to fulfil but only brought shame,
To the ones who care, to the ones who've card,
Paths, cross-roads, ambitions, goals,
Interference's you meet when life's full of holes.
A hand lent a person befriended,
Till patients run out then you've offended.
Am I sorry, hurt, do I give a damn.
The room is so big from where I am.
Sitting knees up, head down, I'm already dead, there's not a sound,
except the cry from my inner-self,
my own conscience trying to help.
Telling me try again what ever the cost,
Find that light, that shoulder, that prayer, all's not lost.
Now I'm juggling with life, it's time to decide
The gun is loaded, the dagger sharpened, the pills are beside.
My face is broadening, I'm starting to smile,
I'm feeling confident, my tears have run dry.
My hands are loosing, from the strands of hair on my head,
Death has lost this time, but only by a thread.

Dan Barry

Feelings

Deep in my bones I feel
That life is like one long meal.
Through each day I walk,
People watching me like a hawk.
I sleep, I eat,
Nobody I meet.
Feeling like this I wander through each day,
Wondering my way.

Then one day the sun does shine,
And then I think why not keep it, it's now mine.
Gradually my spirits rise at which I cheer,
The sounds of sweet bliss I do hear.
The pain I used to feel is no more,
I think of it more as feeling of bore.
What I should have now is a feeling of sadness left,
But I am much too deft!

Catherine Payne

The End

Eight years we've been together
If you'd have asked how long it would last
I would have said forever.
Now you've said there's not a hope . . . no!
Never!
This is it.
I know it's the end
I think we could only now be friends
We both know what we want
We've both done our bit
We've tried and tried to get it together
But it just so happened the pieces wouldn't fit
It's so hard to face when you love the one you're with
But you also know one of you has to give
My heart is breaking but as they say———
Time heals!

Beverley E. Bozzoni

The Glory of War

Staring numbly the boy remembers,
Confused by his subconscious imagery
Crying! Screaming! Yelling! "Stop Stop Stop"!
Who possessed such unjustified evil?
It was I.

Yes, you are the enemy who killed me, my friend
That bullet tore apart my heart as it did yours
As my blood exploded, choking my lungs
I realised
that you did not pull the trigger
blood spilt not for you but for my country
Ha! What hypocrites portray such lies?
The hypocrites of war, my comrade.

Claire Cooper

My Greatest Love

My greatest love in life of course is not a
man but is a horse.

Its flaxen mane its shining tail stays the
same through rain and hail.

It does not change except to grow even
through the wind and snow.

Its hoof beating on the turf, its head held
high, its eyes a glow.

Its ears aloof to the noise around,
'Oh my' how his qualities abound.

It hears the trumpet and the howl of the
hounds the huntsman and of course the horse.

It dreams of pastures far away in travelling
through night or day.

He knows not that there is many other horses
that are treated without care.

But in his heart of hearts he well knows he
is better off than all of those.

Yes my greatest love in life of course is not
a man but my horse.

Lisa Carter

Backstep

Dreams Dead, Worries Waver
Am I on the right road home?
I don't know, as I'm not sure what's home and what's sacred

Head hurts, stomach stumbles
Will I get it right this time?
Will I settle, will I reason?
Oh! God help me to free my soul

Pastures Green are left behind
Returning to that barren land
The land where I could neither blossom
Or find some air to help me grow

Decisions made, now pride must suffer
Humiliation, Defeat will "Roar"
Or maybe life will stretch her hand out
Lead me through the tangled path
Tell me I'm as good as another, tell me I can go and laugh

Is this world a great illusion
One that appears in different traits?
Will I sigh and close my eyes?
Open up and all is right.

Arlene Scanlon

Golden Autumn

Autumn's aura on the moors and fells,
Casts upon us countless spells
As we gaze upon her golden tints,
A sight worth more than those precious mints.

Russet heather shimmers in the breeze.
Copper leaves dance around stately trees.
Green whin berries shake with scarlet lips.
Shining ferns twist their fine blonded tips.

As her bewitching beauty we behold,
Our hearts are gathered in love's fold.
To this precious endearing autumn
We sigh, entranced, in sheer devotion.

Bronzed autumn with her feathery fan.
Dreamily she shows her healthy tan.
Waiting for King Winter's cold soft kiss.
Enchants us with this mystic warm bliss.

Autumn's face is wrapped in joyous glints.
Wondrous are her beauteous prints.
In England's fair country so fresh.
Such splendour in her September dress.

Mary Freeborn

Silent Sea Gulls

They killed the children of Scotland last week
God's heart was the first to break, they say
And Ailsa Craig stood lone and bleak
Weeping into the sea that day

They cut down the flower of Scotland last week
In a lovely wee village on Mother's Day
Don't tell us to turn the other cheek
Let us grieve, let us mourn, in our own Highland way

Auld Nick did his worst in Scotland last week
Bonnie bright-eyed bairns were made to pay
Schiehallion and Nevis knelt bowed and meek
As the sea gulls glided silently for a minute today

Please leave us alone in Scotland next week
The earth will not waken this springtime, they say
In the glens and the forests, by burns and by creek
For the souls of the children, our children, we pray

Craig McK. Duncan

Crowning Glory

Your hair,
a little bit of Heaven showing.
Alight, golden, dancing, glowing.
Given by a loving, lavish Hand,
strong and invincible today
but fragile, fleeting,
remembered soon as in a childhood dream,
but still, a promise, of perfection
Everlasting.

Roy Millman

Wishing We Could Be Together

As I pass you by in the street
My heart falls to my feet
Feelings of guilt and hurt well up inside
Everything's rushing towards me
I feel a need to just run and hide
I picture us together that one last time
Memories of you and me run through my mind
The times when I was all yours
And you were all mine
Me standing close to you
Gazing deeply and lovingly into your eyes
I lusted for you till the end of time
Just to feel the sensation of holding you again
Wishing things were still the same
Just to see the passion in your eyes one last time
I know the flame has gone
But what a dream it would be
So sensational and divine
Just to be with you one last time

Jane Stanton

Sweetness to Weakness

From chuckles and giggles and cute little freckles
To pain you have caused that stings like a nettle
A web of lies a circle of deceit
Drugs are your food you have no urge to eat
I know it's not you it's the way it must be
Addictions gripped tight like the roots of a tree
You lied and robbed us but took more than possessions
Why has life sent us such painful lessons
I know it's not you and you've just lost your way
But Russian Roulette is the game you play
To see you so thin so grey and in pain
My tears just won't stop, keep falling like rain
I've tried to help you but my strength has gone
A heroin addict takes care of number one
It's funny, I still search for someone to blame
That someone is you brother but we can't break the chain
Although you have hurt us all deep inside
All we want is to speak of you with love and with pride
But we cannot believe you or trust you no more!
Umm! So different now than when you were just four

Sharon Wilkinson

Alive

Magic shall gleam in booming waves
And sunshine glisten on the leaping froth;
Wild winds will gust from daylight's dawn
Instilling energy anew,
And from the dews first damp on grasses
Washing the world to Eden's boll.
The freshness clear to life's beginning,
Seen like the crack of lightning blasting,
Heard in the depths vibrating louder,
Felt to the heart and in the blood it stirs.

S. A. Vincent

The Fairground

The fairground is an exciting place
And is packed with shocks and frights
It's hard to resist the smell and the noise
With the vast array of lights

The waltzers and the dodgems
Will surely make you feel
Ready to tackle anything
Including the big wheel

And those who wish to remain on the ground
A little kinder on their hearts
Can enjoy the many sidestalls
From hook the prize—to darts

If you're looking for a bite to eat
The fairground's full of treats
There's hot-dogs, burgers and candyfloss
Or you can stuff yourself with sweets

It caters for the young as well
With rides that go nice and slow
And when the money's running out
It's nearly time to go.

Julian Arnold

"In This World"

In this world, there is war and starvation
Families learning to cope with devastation
In this world, there are muggers, killers and rapists
I look through the newspapers and read the latest
Good things and sad things that happen each day
Is it fair for our children to grow up this way.

In this world, there are good people and bad.
Happy times that happen along with the sad.
In this world, there is love and hate.
Can't we live in peace before it's too late?

But wouldn't it be good if the whole world could
Hold each other's hand, and be peaceful like we should
If we all stopped the anger, the hatred, and fighting
So the goodness of this world could go on surviving.

P. Freeman

Music and Sounds that Mirror Your Senses

If music be the sounds that mirror your emotions,
What is the type that reveals your devotions,
Are you addicted to a certain type of music or song,
What is the mixture that drives you along,
What shapes the face you show to everyone.

That sweet Irish lilt will not let you wilt,
It will spur you on and add skirl to the kilt,
The drone of the pipes, the beat of the drum,
Talk of great deeds both to be and already done.

There's a tunesmith working, all night through,
Just to reach, those inner feelings that govern you,
For in the very depth of your soul and being,
There's a tune and a song to reach you even into your dreaming.

For without the love of music and its making,
We are nothing, but an empty emotionless being,
Our ears unfeeling, not being able to realize our potential,
To bring out all those feelings so fundamental.

Malcolm Ross

Chance

He wealthy, successful, has a lonely soul
   seeks money and power as his goal.
She a warm-hearted Leo, eyes navy blue
   incurably romantic, sensual, but true.

To her lonely heart's advert he replied
feeling once again a teenager inside
sharing intimate secrets over the phone
with much in common—both alone.

The time has come for them to meet
he thinks she's attractive, and oh, so sweet
she senses a man of strength and power
yet he holds her tenderly like a flower.

His fingers gently touch her breast
she lays her head upon his chest
her heart's pounding, can it be true
when he softly whispers I love you.

Sadly alas, love comes to an end
he no longer wants her, not even a friend
for although he says they are worlds apart
she has what he craves—a loving heart.

Rita Keeping

Why Does She Shed Tears?

Why does she shed tears?
Why does she cry herself to sleep at night?
It's all because of a broken heart that she has to fight.
The boy who said he loved her
Has fallen for someone else.

She loves him so much
And anyone can tell
All her dreams and hopes are shattered
Because of another girl.

Why does she shed tears?
Why does she cry herself to sleep at night?
It's all because of a broken heart that she has to fight.

Kerry Turvey

My Love

In my garden so beautiful
Where trees and flowers grow
Sit a while and look around.
The beauty your eyes to see
Buttercups and bluebells
Twinkling in the sun,
Daffodils and tulips upon my window sill.
The grass is green, the sky so blue,
Feel healed my love and weep no more
For tomorrow will bring another dawn
With bright blue sky and golden sun.
Please sit with me and feel the beauty
With me, my love.

Iris J. Klein

Forgotten Patience

   If I was the ocean, I would let your soul dance, dance
in my waters to be free from its pain, pain in the soaking,
sky so thick, like rain, that we could cry.

   If I was strength, I would build a strong wall, wall around
your heart, around your soul, and nothing could hurt you,
hurt your heart, make it bleed, make it weak or make it starve.

   If I was belief, you could believe in me. I'd walk in
front of you, day and night, and no one and nothing could let you
down, let you fall to the ground.

   If I was love, I would protect you. I'd embrace you, with
all my warmth. I'd recreate your burning soul with my light
and with my patience.

   I am a promise, with open arms, my door is always open for you.
I am your friend, in your darkest light.
I am here for you.

Zoë Morello

At Peace

I am sitting here quietly, I am all alone,
The peace seeps into me, to ease every bone,
A bird sings a song high in the tree,
Almost as though it knows the peace within me,
A squirrel flits by, I stay very still,
He stops, compelled by some kind of will,
He hops closer, so cautious is he,
Every nerve so alert, ready to flee.
Alas! There is no food I can give.
I rustle no bag, to help him to live,
Oh! What is it that's startled him so?
No one is here—only he can know.
The things in life that I have for free,
Are the pleasures each day that are here for me,
For how very content I find I can be,
Just to sit, and linger, and look, and see.

Beatrice Newman

Tigress Tigress

She lies on the ground, silent as night.
Pouncing her prey. She gives it a fright
Tigress Tigress
Don't become extinct.
Tigress Tigress
What do you think?
When a hunter comes along. What do you think?

She looks at her cubs. Clear as day.
She feels proud, keeps her head up high
Tigress Tigress
Don't become extinct.
Tigress Tigress
What do you think?
When a hunter comes along. What do you think?

She closes her eyes. Feels someone watching
Ready for an attack. She carries her cubs to safety.
Tigress tigress. Don't become extinct
Tigress tigress, what do you think?
When a hunter comes along. What do you think?

Catherine Hall

Unexpectedly

You were in my thoughts for quite sometime
out of concern I dropped you a line
you can imagine my delight
when a letter you did write
my heart gave a leap and skipped a beat
your letter my dear was quite sweet
soon the ink began to flow as my heart was all aglow
you were straight right from the start,
so I knew what was in your heart out of
 world you came and into mine
bringing love and laughter all the time
a life once filled with despair
is alive with loving tender care
quite unexpectedly you came melting away
hurt and pain
setting me free to love again and all
quite unexpectedly.

J. Gardiner

Seaweed, Sand and Sea

When I go into the sea,
All the seaweed tickles me,
It tickles my fingers,
It tickles my toes,
It tickles my tummy,
It tickles my nose,
Then Mum shouts,
"It's time for tea"
I have sand in my sandwiches,
And sand on me.
After tea I go back in the sea,
And a great big wave falls on top of me.

Justine Hayter

Winter Nights

A dim cold night falls upon this day,
away from the cold I want to stay.
I don't like the way lightening roars like a lion,
when it bolts through the sky like a fist of iron.
The thunder beats and down pours the rain,
as the lightening strikes like a teacher's cane.
The fog—a white sheet—wraps around my skin,
tonight in the cold I feel frail and thin.
A spine tickling wind brushes up my back,
as the wind rushes forward to make an attack.
The lights getting dim and the sound fades away,
I just dread for the time it comes another day.

Hannah Mitchell

Untitled

I know you'll be safe
in God's world up above.
But, I won't be able to express to you
my undying love.

You'll be gone from this earth
from hearing and from sight.
I won't see you again
in the winter's moon,
or the summer's night.

So it's goodbye I suppose,
This is the end.
But, maybe in heaven we will meet again.

Goodbye Aunt, Godmother and Friend,
I wish your life did not have to end.
I wish your death to be as peaceful
as a dove's flight, and as warm as a Caribbean summer's night.

I don't know where you'll go,
I don't know what you'll do,
but whatever happens remember
that I'll always love you.

Louise Brandreth

Human Ants

Busy, busy, busy, that's what we all are.
Human ants, rushing here and there,
No time to stand and stare,
No time to spare for other folk.
They may be lonely, desperate and in
despair, want someone to listen to them.
What's that? You want to talk?
Sorry I must take my dog for a walk!
Busy, busy, busy, just like ants
Running here and there and we get nowhere.
That's modern life I fear.
Where will it all end? I ask.
Oh well, I must go.
I've my washing to do, you know!
Busy, busy, busy. Human ants
That's what we all are.

Ena Stanmore

Hope

Forget all your sorrow anger and pain,
There is always tomorrow
When you can be happy again.
There is no justice in this sad cruel world
But you carry the fight right to the end.
Remember at the end of the tunnel there is always light
With beauty around you and friends who care
They are there when you need them
You are never alone
So dismiss all your anger the frustration you feel
Trust in God do not despair
And in time you will see that you will heal
The future is bright just wait you will see.
Phoenix flies high out of the mist
Enchanted no longer your demons depart
The battle is over at last you are free.

K. Morgan-Jones

Boxed In

Pushed on through each dreary day,
Locked behind the door of the classroom.
Lost in this world,
Unsure where to go,
Our lives planned out
Before we have begun to grow.
Our confidence destroyed as we try to build it;
Children's dreams smashed as they are blooming.
Young people's minds destroyed as they are
Creating, by the twisted minds of the world.

Joanne Murray

Doomed Loved

I love you darling, can't you see
Tearing me apart, what are you doing to me
You tug at my heart with all of my might
Forever in my mind but never in my sight
Future plans, all, but none
We had so many, where have they gone

I lie her basking in the midday sun
You and I cloud have had so much fun
I watch a butterfly in the flower
Thinking this could be our final hour
Together, forever, it felt so right
We took each other to a great height

Marriage was always on our list
But we couldn't see our luck because of the mist
Like not seeing the woods because of the trees
Sometimes you were on bent knees But
What has doomed is our Love
You flew away just like a Dove

Tina Scammell

Winter

Lofty trees stand straight and bare,
Stark boughs a tracery weaving,
Dark silhouettes 'gainst winter's sky,
Moving, twisting and heaving.

Your garment cast upon the ground,
Now crisp, now soft and moulding,
A shroud to rot and nurture the sod,
Recycling, fresh nutrients holding.

Brown furrows stretch in symmetrical form,
Awaiting the seed of the sower,
Grass besmirched by icy blast,
Halt then the blade of the mower.

Disturb not nature in her sleep,
So brief her winter slumber,
Tread softly, ere her treasures fade,
Heed not the woodman's blunder.

Soundlessly falling to blanket the earth,
Heedlessly drift into mountainous heaps,
Relentless the force of the gale which drives,
The whiteness of snow, when all earth sleeps

Isabel Ellis

Find the Key to My Heart

My heart is empty and surrounded by pain.
So much vexation and misery.
The key to unlock the empty heart lies so near.
It only takes one person to unlock it, to free it, and
fill it full of exaltation.
All would then blossom once again in my heart.
The day will finally come when you unlock the gate,
to emancipate my soul, which I will devote to you.
I will love you for evermore and we will be together
for eternity.
Several others tried the wrong key and only freed
a small part of me.
You will free everything which I will give to you;
All in time.

Karen Young

Lost and Back Again

When I think of home
I think of love, family and known surroundings.
I feel like I'm in a dome.
Because now something is missing.

I don't know what this something could be
Right now I feel lost,
Everywhere seems isolated, only me,
I seem alone in the streets, just a phantom ghost.

Love has a meaning
Mostly friends and family
It's so strange, I've started winning,
I'm not alone, there are people out there who love me.

What I have lost is now back again,
All these thoughts for nothing,
It's always sunny, never rain,
But I still don't know what was that missing something.

Elsie Okorafor

The Perfect World

In the perfect world there would be no wars,
everyone would be ideal, nobody locked behind bars,
No-one would be homeless, everyone would have a home,
no-one would lose loved ones, no-one would be alone,
When we got older, we wouldn't grow old,
there would be no animals left out in the cold,
Everyone would be equal, no rich no poor,
for good or bad, everyone would have an open door,
We all know this could never betide,
the human race could not abide,
This is something we all have to face,
there could never be a perfect world, there's no such place.

Nilpa Khistria

Memories of Edinburgh and No. 13
A Dear Old Family Home

Beautiful home—why did I let you go?
I love you so!
Treasured memories! Thoughts all a glow!
Life's richest experiences
   Were lived out there
Births and deaths and loving care
There, most of my life was spent,
   Going to school,
Then on to work and a life so full.
Marriage, a husband to love,
   Our children to sweet
Familiar faces down our street
All gone but life must go on.
No one seems to care or understand
Then leave things now in God's good hands!

Janet Wallace Wight

The Fox

We live in the country where we run wild and free,
And live in deep holes under hedges and trees.
We're fast and we're crafty, and some call us sly,
But we all have to eat if we don't want to die,
We go near humans when food gets too short,
But they chase us with horses, and dogs for the sport.
We're not really fussy about our eating habits,
But the food we like best are those furry young rabbits.
They live just like us in long holes in the ground,
And breed all the year so there's plenty around.
We stalk them and chase them for the juicy red meat,
And don't kill for sport, but we all have to eat.
We chase them through hedgerows, and grasses, and shrubs,
For we need lots of food to feed our young cubs.
The winters are hard but we still have to eat,
To stop us from starving we need that red meat,
The food's a bit scarce like mice, and small voles,
That we catch in the woods when they leave their warm holes,
Then in the spring when the ground starts to thaw,
We're chasing the chickens and rabbits once more.

Graham Hancox

Sometimes

In the spring days children are playing in the sun
Enjoying themselves and others who are looking at them
The sun shines more in the sky
Seeing the happiness in everyone's face
The birds too are singing in the trees
And the whole nature is very happy.

In the summer nights the young are walking on the streets
Admiring the world with all its beauties
And breathing the air at the moon shine.

In the autumn the old men are thinking of God,
Of all the goods he gave us.
And when the trees get down their clothes
A great peace comes from nowhere to spend its holidays.

In the winter days and nights I wish thinking of you
Of our little time together.
And then, among these happy remembrance
The snow seems more white
The stars are among myself
And I'm thinking of you because
Sometimes, I think you're thinking of us.
  Palade Nedioara

World Tour

If I were a child
I would take you by the hand
and tell you how much I like you
while we were strolling around the world.
  Karen Larsen

Legacy of Thought

It was the 14th day of February, Valentine's Day!
A day, full of love and happiness . . . "so they say",

But, not this day . . . A Tuesday,I recall, outside, icy and frail
Snow thick on the ground, sterile and pale.
Just like my heart, when I learned the details . . .
'Stale', and in 'limbo' when my brother lost his fight

A fight, I'll remember for the rest of my life.
An abyss, remaining, in the depths of my soul.
A vivid impression, in colour, not fading!
His presence, remaining.
A brief exclusion, in this "relative-time".
In my sub-conscious mind.
In your face, 'etched-in-time'.
I embrace the nightfall, to gain brief solace.
For there, is the only place.
Where I can look upon your face.
Where dreams, are reality, for a moment in time.
A 'cerebral-link'; only contact remaining.
My incomplete being, without solace or place
Waiting for the sun, to hide its face . . .
  Gina Butler

Live vs. Death

"It's pointless really", I heard death say
while sitting off my shoulder he chatted away.
Life, on the other hand said it was fun,
"there's so much to do and so much to be done."
The comment had come from my right hand side
where life decided to join in the ride,
Death seemed so evil and so sarcastic
where life on the other hand was extremely fantastic.
The debate went on hour after hour,
the tension was mounting, much more than before,
I was nearly asleep, because it was boring,
but as I looked up it was life who was snoring.
I suppose life was tired with the stories Death told,
Now we all know life isn't easily sold.
Eventually death gave up all hope
of beating life, he couldn't cope,
Life conquered death, so the golden rule
is not to be scared to live life to the full.
  Stephanie Reynolds

Sounds

Remembered sounds and the times they recall
Some gay some sad
But with love in them all
Like the sound of your heart
Just like a drum in my ear
Sounding like surf
On a far away shore
I think I will hear this evermore
The good times bad times
Fights and the rows
Only good times remembered
The rest are just sounds
The years have passed and at the last curtain I call
The sound of your voice
Will be the last sound of all
  Edith Mary Adams

Memory's Friendship

If I never more hold you close to me,
Or feel your warm arms thrill me once again;
Never more kiss your lips, if this has to be,
But instead feel the smart of parting pain;
If I should no more gaze into your eyes,
Or see the wonder of your lovely smile;
If the time must come when our sweet friendship's ties
Be broken; still our friendship was worthwhile.
For finding you I've found a friend so rare;
Not all are given to find. Staunch and true.
And the parting would be easier to bear,
For in my heart I have a place for you,
And you have given me a memory;
A memory which makes my heart to glow.
Memory of a friendship beautiful to me,
Undying friendship that few mortals know.
  Wilf Farries

Missing You

As each hour goes by, I think about you
I miss you more and more everyday
It's like something inside me is missing

When we are together I am happy
My love for you just keeps on growing
My life feels complete when I am with you

When we are apart I feel sad
But my love for you keeps me going
I miss you like crazy

When I am in your arms, I know it's where I belong
And that's where I want to stay
My darling I love you now and forever.
  C. Creighton

Victims of Greed

Our ancestors all roamed the land
And scratched for worms, their life was grand.
But we are caged up here all day
With nought to do but lay and lay
The eggs the farmer wants to sell;
He cares not if our life is Hell.

When we were chicks we ran and played
At chasing flies. We were dismayed
The day our freedom was outraged
And I and my playmates were caged;
No more we could the wheat fields glean,
Each one became an egg machine.

Now our slave-master has great wealth
But all we have is ruined health;
Pellet and water is our feed,
They think that's all a bird should need.
Now we are old, we've got to die
To make room for more slaves to cry.
  Mervyn S. Whale

A Rebel's View of Freedom

What is this bright elusive flame
That burns eternal in the souls of men
And like the whispering wind in the trees
It calls and runs and calls again?

For oft when in the midst of toil
We stop and dream of far-off lands,
Of living free beneath a different sky
And lazy days on foreign sands.

Then we return to hearth and home
And all those things that steal our time away,
Till all too soon we find our day is done
And life is but a shell of vanity.

Freedom is for those who take it,
Take the cup of life and break it
And cast it to the winds and sea.

The taken not the taker,
The broken not the breaker,
Must there be a compromise with man
   half-slave half-free?
Doris Ginsberg

Spring

Spring is the best time of year
when the clouds are clear
the children are singing
when the bells are ringing
I hear the singing from the Sunday school
when the boys and girls
are in the swimming pool
when the lambs are born
the bull gets his horn
the spring months are
March April and May
Oh today, today is a wonderful day!
Emily Bentley-Leek

Sticks and Stones

In the playground stands Mary-Jane, Mary-Jane "super brain".
Ginger pigtails pulled too tight, today invisible in their sights,
left alone Porky George, whose 'truffle shuffle', they do applaud.
Tired eyes on one so young, stayed awake, hoping morning
won't come.
Stomach-ache it is to Dad, confronting Monday feels so bad,
satchel tag says Mary-Jane, but the contents just aren't worth the
pain. Bell rings for time to play, nowhere to run, to hide away,
one O'clock relief sets in, back to class with Mrs Flynn.
Good at all the work that's set, "No I'm not a teachers pet!"
Whispering and giggling from behind, passing notes that are so
unkind, "I'm not so different" thinks Mary-Jane, "why then do
I feel such shame".
Harmless kids people say, but they don't have to live this way,
Should I tell my story fully? I just can't live amongst these
bullies. Smiling again stands Mary-Jane who shared her pain.
Joanna Chalmers

Yesterday

Fond memories of mine
Are when I lived by a railway line.
It was always a joy to see
Those locomotives going up and down, our valley.
The passengers waving as they pass,
Green engines with red bands and shining brass,
The stoker, piling on the coal and coke,
Providing power and constant trail of smoke.
Soon they will become museum pieces,
As lines are closed and service ceases.
Maybe one day someone will restore
And bring back these locomotives, once more.
Lots of people love to go
To an old steam engine show,
Now to see those things from yesterday,
Quite a lot of money one has to pay.
So be careful before you cast away
Those loved things from yesterday.
Hilda A. Ralphs

Holidays

Who loves holidays, who loves a change?
Who loves going away where everything is strange?
Every day is different, so many things to try,
Things we would never do, although we wonder why.

Who loves a holiday, it's nice to get away.
We wear all sorts of clothes and don't care what folks say.
No-one knows us in a foreign land
We can feel so very free,
Mixing with folks we do not know
And folks who don't know me.
Mary Campbell-Bridgman

Love Poem

The long and lonely years so cruel and bleak
Have suddenly gained meaning in one week
Of learning how to love and how to care
So deeply that your love is always there
When you're alone, when you're awake and when you sleep
your every thought, your every dream becomes so deep
so full of pain and yet of perfect joy.
A feeling that no one can ever destroy.
Abigail Osborne

My Five Furry Friends

The trees at the bottom of my garden
Have branches with leaves bright and green
Encumber a family of five squirrels
The tamest that I've ever seen

They sit below my kitchen window
Looking up to see if they're in luck
I throw them down a handful of nuts
The ones with a shell and a shuck

Along branches and down tree trunks
They run with such great speed
Scampering across the lawns each day
To collect their daily feed

How do they know just what's inside
And know so very well
Turning them around inside their jaws
So as to crack the shell

Now Christmas is on top of us
As another year like the rest ends
And a cold and bitter winter threatens
I feel sorrow for my five furry friends
S. Arrowsmith

The Duck Pond

Jim and his three children called for me,
They were on their way to town,
And took me to accompany them,
For have come to spend weekend.

I filled two bags with bread scraps,
To go out to visit the ducks,
'Twas lovely at Loch Faskally,
And the children loved it so much.

Ours was the only car in car park,
And the ducks came quacking by,
As we got out among the throng,
Then the picnic they did enjoy.

The children broke their scraps small,
As lots of coloured ducks soon came,
Much to the delight of all of us,
For they all seemed very tame.

I love this visit to see the ducks,
Have not been here for some time,
Jim took snaps of all of us,
The children, me, and quackies tame.
May Scott

What I Want in a Wife

Most importantly
I want a wife who is nice to me
But hopefully who doesn't act too uxoriously
Pretty? Most certainly
She'll be as clever as I want to be
Outgoing—not too gregariously
And we would talk about things neverendingly
Whilst regarding each other respectfully
I would devote myself tirelessly
To make our relationship work magnificently
And if we were to argue pugilistically
I would be on my knees immediately
Remarkable as it may seem to me
My life revolves around her constantly
Regardless of the fact that she remains totally imaginary
Her perfume fills my nostrils—so sweetly
My life seems so very empty—just totally
Yet very soon, hopefully, she will join me
The vote would go unanimously
That someone like that would be perfect for me!

Ketan Dhatariya

Daffodils

As I walked in the garden one morning
And saw the cracked open sod,
My mind, like an arrow shot heavenwards,
And I thought on the power of my God,

A few days later when I strolled again,
To view that favourite spot,
Clusters of green stems greeted me,
Like Churches reaching their spires to God.

And while I gazed on this wondrous sight,
A breeze played on the tender stems,
Criss-Cross they bent before my eyes,
Like the beams on Calvary hill.

A moment later the beams were gone,
And in their place stood praying hands,
Which seemed to reach up with a plea—
Perhaps a prayer for you and me.

But oh! the last visit to my garden plot—
Has filled my brain with fever,
For behold I saw a chalice gold,
Awaiting the blood of my saviour.

Emily Hanney

Spring

What a wonderful thing
Is the coming of Spring,
The warm sun and gentle rain
Bring plants and trees to life again,
The scent of blossom and buzz of bees
A gentle breeze caressing the trees.

Oh! What a sight to see
Spring flowers in their glory
A never ending joy to me
If they could tell a story
Only the birds sing
When they open their bills
to the violets, primroses and daffodils.

When the clouds shed their tears
Who tells the flowers
There's going to be showers?
Do the birds or the bees
Say it to tease
Or do the trees
Whisper through their leaves?

M. R. Warne

Farmer's Wife

Life is arranged by parents in a most amazing way
Lucky was I to be the daughter of a farmer
Whose life was quite hard not easy
As in the modern world today.

No regrets to meet a farmer
To marry and parents be
Life is still hard but enjoyable
As it becomes a way of life you see
To feed to care and love the extended family.

During our lives there cannot be
Anything closer to real earthly wonderment
Than to see the newborn animals
Striving for their first breath of life
With the continued help of the farmer
   And his ever-loving wife

Jean Chapman

"A Passage in Time"

The sun burst through the day you came
My life was never quite the same.
Your smile, your wit, your eyes so blue,
I'll never quite get over you.

The day we parted came so soon.
Without a word you left that day
I cried and cried and wondered why
I had to lose a love so true.

Now all have is memory of days I shared with you

I must go on, and let you go
Knowing that you'll never know
How precious was that passage in time
And knowing that you'll never pass this way again.

So farewell my love to days with you
Next time perhaps who knows,
Another world, another time,
We may be blest with a passage in time.

Janet Rosen Stripp

The Silent Visitor

What is this that alights so silent and majestic
Throughout the night?
Next morning has all God's children
Screaming with delight,
As their elders, frowning, scurrying to and fro
With their man-made havoc,
Blaming everyone in their way.
Never hesitating to enjoy the splendour
As it casts its beautiful veil
Over hills and dales;
Never ceasing
Until it adorns the tallest tree
To the smallest hedgerow.

Deliberate in its silence:
That the children's laughter can be heard at play
With their little faces all aglow
As they enjoy this splendid visitor;
One will never know
Why their elders call this
An ordinary blanket-of-snow

Ann Muirhead

A Blind Man's Message

You have your sight, yet fail to see
Your learning, knowledge could set us free,
If you see with your heart the gift of each day
All greed and corruption will soon pass away.
Open your eyes, what is there to gain
From power, wars, destruction and pain?
Let peace be your strength to banish all sorrows,
With kindness and love for all our tomorrows.

Annette Hayes

To Feel Nature

The Sun sets over the trees to west,
As a cold wind shivers
And a mist of night, takes a hold,
Like a perpetual pendulum.
The forces of nature continue.
Such an eerie rime is the transformation,
from A.M. to P.M.
Anti maritime, post maridium,
such small words, for such repeat change
yet always there.
The days are full of life and happening
But the nights in all her starry glory
Are so mellow and quiet.
The last twittering sounds, of song—
Birds fade,
And a stillness one feels like cold—
Steel to the bone.
Good-night my lonely world,
Pray God give me one more awakening,
   H. J. Dillon

Dream Island

Once as a child, as children do, I dreamed of an Island and
   skies of blue
With miles and miles of golden sand, happiness spreading all
   over the land.
I became a woman, a wife, and a Gran and I knew it
   was time, I started to plan,
To search for my Island, my dreams all came true
I found my Island and happiness too.

Mountains of Pine, birds on the wing,
Almond Blossom in early spring,
Joy in the hearts of everyone,
Oranges, kissed by the morning sun.
Rising each day to a Rose-coloured dawn,
Church bells ringing on Sunday morn,
All the people warm-hearted and kind,
Lovely Majoror,
   It's the happiest Island you'll ever find.
   Iris Gulliver

Stored Memory

A few drops of rain fall gently from the sky
and from my front room window a rare sight caught my eye,
For the rain had formed a puddle from which a Robin took much glee
In having, wash and brush up, right there in front of me.
He stayed there, after washing to drink water cool and clear
He fluffed his feathers, sang a song
Which was music to my ear.
It made me think how often we miss the special things to see
and that the real best things in life are
absolutely free.
Now the sun is shining
and the puddles gone away
I'll store this special memory
To recall another day.
   T. J. Smith

My Afternoon Rest

I lie on the bed and think and think,
I'm sure I haven't slept a wink.
I left my favourite book downstairs
Carelessly—in my special chair.

What can I do to pass the time?
Think of lots of words that rhyme,
And then of a subject to use them for,
When I suddenly hear a knock on the door,

Hooray "Come in!" I shout with glee
Someone is bringing a cup of tea,
I get up to drink it, I've a letter to write
In time to take to the post tonight,

I really think to write a letter,
Rather than verse, is something better
When taking a rest, for passing the time
Than to have to struggle to make words rhyme.
   Ethel Holloway

Never Forever

In the evening shadows, of the evening sun,
Home she goes, now her job's done.
Down, down, down, to the rippling cool water,
Now she's flying further and further.

It happened so quick, it happened so fast,
What has just happened is now in the past.
What has just happened? What was it?
Was it because of that little blue tit?

They're on this earth for the daylight's reason,
But did it have to happen to that poor, little beacon?
That's why the worms squirm so low,
Like a mammal in a tide, it goes with the flow.

Her soft white fur was pure and clear,
She didn't even sense that danger or fear.
Like a horse would off, in his rear,
Even if dangers not all that near.
   Katrina Williams

The Hero

He shuffles unseen, weary and worn,
through crowds of colour and course,
veiled by his age and his pain and decay,
drained by a haunting remorse.

He struggles alone, wasted and weak,
aching and fragile he fights,
heir to his life by his fate and his force,
tortured and torn by his plight.

He's yearning November's remission,
grasping small comforts from pain,
glad that its poppies all scarlet like blood,
are seen by the people again.

And he marches that Sunday each year,
with comrades, glory and pride,
displaying his medals, proving his worth,
but wishing he too could have died.
   Angela Rogerson

The Glastonbury Alphabet

A for Abbey known nation-wide.
B for Barn, the museum inside.
C for Chalice, the hill and well.
D for Druids, their mystery to tell.
E for Energy, radiates from tor.
F for Freedom, the town's core.
G for Glastonbury, glory and place.
H for Healing, and here it takes grace.
I for Island, now Glastonbury land.
J for Jerusalem hymn song of its stands.
K for Knights, who rode here of told.
L for Legends, there are many here old.
M for Mystery, spiritual you find.
N for Norman, their building so fine
O for Ozone, blowing over the tor.
P for Pilgrims who come even more
Q for Quantock, lovely hill mark.
R for Ruins in the beautiful park.
S for Somerset, county of this town.
T for Tor, where magic abound.
U for Universe, isle of Avalon's place.
V for Visitors, all creeds and race
W for Well, in chalice garden blooms.
X for Xmas, when the holy thorn looms.
Y for Yore, books on those times.
Z for Zodiac, around lie the signs.
   Margaret Hurd

Four Months

Four months together
a time of passion and strife
never before did I feel the tether
of a love so strong, I'd give my life

Four months together, now there's none
as in your fear you severed our future's head
and put me through hell; as my head spun
me you abandoned, it hurt so bad

Four months now we've been apart
slowly, slowly myself I find
with another I've made a new start
in many ways, you're two of a kind

Four months together
he I try, but cannot trust
is it because I'm afraid that tether
will again be broken and apart I'll bust?

Four months more and it will be a year
since our four months together first began
on that day, we'll be very near
a completed circle in the four-month span.

Atheana Rowe

A Day in the Life of Betty

I am a loving person if life just gave me a chance.

Sitting in my memory rotten room,
As thoughts run round my mind like shooting stars.

Slowly I reached up to the shelf to get my wedding ring,
the last thing to remind me of my lost joy.

I look around, I see my family everywhere in the cheap
tacky but loved figures brought every christmas.

The feeling of abandonment always dwells on me
like a shadow.

The pound on the shelf enough to buy my dinner
but too weak to collect my pension.

I'm like a creased shirt forgotten in its drawer.
I have been through the stages of life I remember
war and sickness, I have loved.

I remember death, it never leaves me alone, but I can wait.

Claire Williams

Elliot

I have a little brother with a serious disease.
It is much worse than a cough or a sneeze.
Neuroblastoma is what it's called,
Because of the treatment now he is bald.

Cancer . . . . is its name,
Oh no! What a shame.

I don't like to think this but I don't know why,
Elliot might unfortunately die.

People say that it must be hard to cope.
But me and my family, we just live in hope.

On the 22nd of April Elliot died.
He did his best, he tried and tried
to keep us happy and try to be strong.
We thought he'd be OK but we were wrong.

I love and miss him so very much.
If only I could feel his tender touch.
Now I'm in such a muddle,
I just wish I could give him a kiss and a cuddle,

An only child again am I.
Why did this have to happen,
OH WHY OH WHY?

Lara Parsons

Rhythms of Life

Here are some written thoughts—thinking of Tom.
Now it may be so that some will go where I'm coming from.
Many people come and go, each at a different pace,
Reflections of the crazy flow that makes the Human Race.
My life—lived with vitality, along the parallels of reality,
Partners in the play of life—states of consciousness and time,
Worlds perceived via state of mind.
Each moment holds unique perfection
Maybe a measure of our affection—for life, perhaps . . .
Perhaps a reflection—Mirror of our actions.
All our thoughts or spoken words—all are sent
Thus all are heard. Thoughts . . .
Don't think—Feel
Is this reality real?
Reveal, revelation, life is an open invitation
To live, to give a cycle of love and creation.
I have many thoughts, they were but a few.
Where you are from—is where you are going to . . .

Tom Ramwell '97

Parting

For parting is such sweet
a sorrow.
And parting must we
Happy to leave
and sad to part
For, when I escape a
bee's sting,
I also lose its
sweet honey.
Mountains don't meet
because they've never
But we've ever
So we will!

Harrison Wahome

A Housewife's Dilemma

My mind is in a turmoil, I don't know what to do.
Shall I wash the dishes, or shall I clean the loo.
Shall I pick up all the things that litter all the floors,
Or shall I clean the dirty marks that cover all the doors.
Shall I clean the bedrooms, and put away the toys.
Or shall I wait 'til after school, and clear up with the boys.
Shall I do the washing, and peg out all the clothes.
Or shall I do the ironing, and stay again indoors.
Shall I bath the baby to make him nice and clean.
Or shall I just change his nappy, and sit down and watch Mr. Bean.
Shall I go out in the garden, and feel the sun so bright.
Or shall I go back in, and clean all day and night.

Ruth Elizabeth Westhoff

In Retrospect

Why could I not believe when you were here
What I know now so well that you are gone.
I did not think you modest all those years
And yet kept from me so much
That you accomplished, what went wrong?

That we could not communicate and I not know
When I felt you unfeeling, you were spent
On energies for people in your work,
Needing encouragement and guidance to perform
Their duties to the utmost, to ensure
Success, advancement in their chosen tasks.

I could have understood had you but shared
The knowledge that my lonely hours had been
To the purpose put for those who followed in your path,
Who say their thanks to me for what you did
And send condolences on my sad loss.

Evelyn May Berrisford

Untitled

Who dares to read the reading of the Mind? Which hunts as
deep inside. As the heart hails in sight. Who dares to see the
letters behind the words. Which have great tails beside
them in every corner of the mind. Who Dares? Who
dares? To enter the story that started but never ended
Speak now or be silent forever in the story which ended
but never started! I do says a voice not too loud nor
quiet but right. I am not scared of words or letters just of
myself who knows what I can say or do to you? For
I'm not scared of what people say or do to you!
For the meaning means another day to me of
thunder and lighting which only strike once! My chance will
go so will you. For who cares what they say or do to you?
My mother always said you never can trust yourself
alone where no man has ever been. Which
shows how strong you are like the cry of emotions
which carry on generations and generations. Could
I stay forever with you or am I just like you? I wish
I had the clue to all of you.
Suzanne Hind

We Tried and Kept on Trying

When all around is sorrow, darkness and despair,
we only have to ask Him and He'll show us how he cares.
He lets us follow our freewill, till we find it's not enough,
so we seek to find the reason, our life's pathway is so rough.
Without His Love and Blessing, our way through life is dark,
but all we need is inside us, that all redeeming spark.
We need not ask His forgiveness, He never lays the blame,
whatever we may do or say, He loves us just the same.
What's needed? What's the answer? We must look within,
our minds, our hearts must open, to be cleansed of every sin.
only we can give forgiveness, for every thought and deed,
that we know keeps us from heaven, then we can be freed.
If we forgive ourselves our mistakes, go and err no more,
live out our lives in Love and Peace, our spirits they will soar.
If we bless all those around us, everyone within our sight,
we will see the greatest difference in the world so bright.
Then when that time comes, we all know must surely come,
for Him to call us to Him, and He welcomes us back home.
Then we can say, when asked, what have we done through life?
We tried, and kept on trying, to help others through the strife.
Irene Ashton

Eulogy to the Niger

To you my magic wand.
Blissful, beautiful, bounty, my Niger!
You so long and beautiful, surrounded by evergreen Savannah.
You my Niger! Shiny and Crystal clear;
Shimmering! Glistening! And Glittering, my blossom Niger.

You my magic wand!
Sweet and tasty petals of love!
My beautiful Niger. My strong ever sweet river of love!
You so deep and strong, my Niger!
You my magic wand!

Oh my Niger! When I look at you,
I look at you with pride.
I see your beautiful proud face in my mind's eyes.
My Niger, My Niger, Oh! My beautiful blustering Niger
of the Eastern Winds.

You my Niger of the evergreen Savannah.
Amazon, conqueror of the mightiest.
You my beautiful Niger! Bounty-beauty of Africa!
My Niger, giver of life, my Niger!
My Niger! My beautiful Niger! Are you the mightiest?
Patricia Okoro

Young Love

He held her hand, she looked at him.
They walked along the woodland lane.
Their hearts were fresh as sun and wind
with not a thought but each a friend.
The sun rose high beyond the white clouds
like a golden ball standing strong and proud.
Hand in hand, oh what a thrill they walked toward that
moorland hill.
A secret glance he caught her eye and quickly
turned with nervous sigh.
Her hand sought his and squeezed it tight
as if to say that's just alright.
At last they reached the moorland hill with grassy
knoll and heather fill.
For miles and miles and far beyond, those heather
filled moors went on and on.
They stopped, looked but did not see the magic
of this moorland scene.
A love so strong held gaze are long.
Blind to all but one another tells the age old
story of young lovers.
Clarence Gascoigne

God's Little Child

I remember the way you smiled,
  the special name only you would call me
Those small remembered things that can bring you such pain
Your silent, empty chair, the photos on the wall
The toys that remain exactly as they were
But with the pain comes the joy.
I think of you and believe that somewhere
You are watching me now, writing this to you.
I believe that never again will you feel hurt or pain.
You can walk freely, see freely,
I imagine you running, talking, laughing,
Making up for all those lost years, all the pain you suffered.
There will never be a day when I don't stop thinking about you.
To wish you were back with me,
  to reach out and hold you just one more time.
To tell you those things that I never got to say.
But, as long as I keep all those images of you—
  laughing, talking, running about,
I can convince myself that this was the way it was meant to be
That your life was not in vain.
You were God's little child, sent to bring us so much joy.
Nicky C

Harvest

As harvest time is getting near,
The yellowing corn, of rain in fear,
Great combines thundering day and night,
Till work is done, and all seems right,

No more the gently swaying stems,
Where children often made their dens,
Now it lies pre'packed and bound,
Upon a course and stubbly ground,

The fires start, and all looks black,
While bales form into awkward stacks,
From these our winter cattle fed,
The rest kept back, to make your bread,

The fields look desolate and in despair,
Only a field mouse scurrying, here and there
But there isn't a sad ending to this story,
It'll be there next year in all its glory.
Brigitta Logan

Running of Life

A muffled yell from the beautiful blonde assistant
"It's the bomb alarm for the precinct we've got to get out."
There was only me and my girls, my sister and niece left in the shop.
There was nobody else there; nobody else was about.

Half eaten snacks and hot cups of tea adorned the tables of the cafe.
And an eerie silence filled the air as my throat filled with burning bile.
It reminded me of a story about a lighthouse, but the flashing lights were real.
We all held hands and ran together, medalists for the two minute mile.

Then a woman appeared in a flashy fluorescent tabard, radio in hand
Directing us like a pleasantly plump policemen directs traffic on Sunday.
"Your nearest exit is that way." Why are we the last ones in here
And why is every shop fronted with glass from top to bottom anyway.

My sister was painfully pale, terror and tears in her eyes as were in mine.
Two old dears carefully picking their steps followed by a young mother
"Get out of the way," she yelled, "this ain't a bloody Sunday stroll y' know."
Out on the street hearts savagely pumping we held each other.

Reality dawned, it had only taken thirty seconds to visit hell.
How easily and thoughtlessly can life be stolen without goodbye,
I kissed my lovely daughters what a privilege to be alive and to see,
I'll never take them for granted I promised myself in a silent soliloquy.
Dawn Owen Thomas

Biographies of Poets

ABIOLA, HAMID M.
[pen.] pace; [b.] 26 March 1973; Ibadan; [p.] Mr. and Mrs. Y. O. Hamid; [ed.] Communication and Language Arts Department, University of Ibadan; [occ.] student; [memb.] All-Nigeria United Nations Students and Youths' Associations (ANUNSA), The Journalists' Club; Kuti Hall Press Organisations (KHPO), University of Ibadan; [hon.] Grand member of Kuti Hall Press (GMKHP), 11 January 1997; [oth. writ.] several poems published in magazines, articles published in National Dailies, and creative works yet to be published; [pers.] Knowledge is the power of the pen, and not the fluid; [a.] Ibadan, Nigeria

ABRAHAM, JACOB D.
[pen.] The Elder; [b.] 19 July 1955, India; [p.] Keith Abraham and Dawn Abraham; [m.] Jacqueline Abraham, 12 July 1980; [ch.] Timothy, Tracy and Darren; [ed.] Aston College; [occ.] Minister of Sacred Africa Church; [oth. writ.] Several poems published in church magazines articles also published in church magazines.; [pers.] I try to reflect God in every part of my life. "If God is not in all our thoughts, then what is?"; [a.] Birmingham, Warwickshire, UK, B20 1EE

ABRAHAMS, MARK
[b.] 25 May 1952, Botesdale; [m.] Barbara; [ch.] Kate, Victoria; [occ.] Chartered Surveyor and 'Architect'-working for N.H.S.; [memb.] Associate of the Royal Institution of Chartered Surveyors and Member of the Association of Planning Supervisors; [hon.] Architectural Design Awards; [oth. writ.] My work is extensive, including poetry, music, songs, books and plays which are gradually being edited for publication.; [pers.] Spanning all subjects for all ages, my writing delves into the deeper meaning of existence but maintains a light-heartedness enabling difficult subjects to be more easily interpreted. Influenced by those I love and my experiences, my work is the essence of life.; [a.] Norwich, Norfolk

ADAM, TRICIA
[b.] 16 August 1960, Scotland; [p.] Margaret and Francis; [m.] Divorced; [ch.] Scott—10, Holly—8; [ed.] State Comprehensive, Hertfordshire; [occ.] Therapist and Counsellor (Independent); [memb.] Int. Inst. of Health and Holistic Therapist, Int. Council of Holistic Therapist; [oth. writ.] No other published works.; [pers.] Self-expression in its many and varied forms is as necessary to a human being as food or air. It feeds 'The Self' and nourishes others. Without this, part of our being becomes 'Hollow'.; [a.] Cheadle, Cheshire, UK, SK8 5DR

ADAMS, JAMES M.
[pen.] J. M. Adams; [b.] 28 January 1908, Ballymena; [p.] Samuel and Margaret—Deceased; [m.] Patricia Leith Adams, 3 June 1946; [ch.] Four; [ed.] Reading by light of a candle on the knob of bed. When brothers were sleeping I was crossing the Alps with Hannibal.; [occ.] Retired Art Dealer; [memb.] Associate Member Belfast Art Society, Caster Royal Ulster Academy; [oth. writ.] West African Review, 140 page book of poetry published, some reporting printed in local paper.; [pers.] The work of the Creator has amazed me, as viewed in British Isles, Africa and America.; [a.] Belfast, Antrim, UK, BT16 0AT

AINDOW, BRIAN HENRY
[pen.] Brian H. Aindow; [b.] 9 August 1942, Huyton, Liverpool; [p.] James Henry, Lilly; [m.] Christine Hall (Divorced), 12 March 1979; [ch.] Michelle, Rachel, Elaine, Francess; [ed.] St. Lukes Jr, Holy Trinity Jr, Formby County Secondary, Liverpool Collage of Building; [occ.] Medically Retired; [hon.] City and guilds; [pers.] I spend my lonely hours relieving memories of my happiest past I have made mistakes but I believe the have made me into who I am now, no regrets.; [a.] Liverpool, Merseyside, UK, L21 2PE

AKINYEMI, OLUFEMI
[b.] 1 October 1971, Nigeria; [p.] Prince N. O. A. Akinyemi and Mrs. Aderonke Akinyemi; [ed.] Maryhill Convent School, Loyola College, University of Ibadan, Pushkin Institute of Russian Language; [occ.] Student; [memb.] University of Ibadan Poetry Club; [hon.] Okigbo Memorial Poetry Award (1991); [oth. writ.] Several poems written.; [pers.] The mind is home to all things, big and small, the judge and jury of all truth and sincerity.; [a.] Ibadan, Oyo

ALDERSON, DAVID A.
[b.] Wolviston, Co. Durham; [p.] Frank and Evelyn Alderson; [m.] Sylvia; [ch.] Michelle and Liesl; [ed.] Various GCE Passes; [occ.] Civil Servant; [oth. writ.] A dozen poems written over a number of years when some personal experiences created an impact words have come to mind easily under these sort of circumstances; [pers.] "Dying Love" was written with deep sadness, when the marriage of close friends of mine failed but offered hope for a reconciliation; [a.] Farsley, West Yorks, UK, LS28 5DA

ALLEN, LYNN
[b.] 29 October 1948, Oxford; [ch.] Four children; [ed.] Comprehensive; [occ.] H/W; [oth. writ.] Poetry, Song; [a.] Oxford, Oxfordshire, UK

ALLERSTON, DOUGLAS JOHN
[pen.] Jack Allerston; [b.] 10 July 1918, Hull; [p.] John Henry and Eva Allerston; [m.] Gladys (Deceased 1979), 5 April 1947; [ch.] Jean Allerston, Mone Jainroy; [ed.] Local Elementary; [occ.] Retired 1981, Author/Historian; [memb.] University of Third Age, Veterans, Fight Army Veterans, New Writers Group, Society; [hon.] Royal British Legion, Writers, publications Local History Publications, General Day Society; [oth. writ.] Poems about local history, various writing local publications on separate list.; [pers.] Age 79, 1983 started writing, none able to resume unfinish work at home.; [a.] Hull, E. Yorkshire, UK, HU5 5DA

ALOKWE, MISS ELIZABETH OSAS
[pen.] Elsie O'Freddie; [b.] 21 September 1979; Bristol; [p.] Dr. Sylvester and Mrs. Helen Alokwe; [ed.] Our Lady's High School, Nigeria, Auntie Rose Secondary School, Nigeria; [occ.] Student; [memb.] 1.) The Writing School (Redhill, RH1 6BR) 2.) The United Kingdom Taekwon Do Association. 3.) Kensington Temple Video Ministry; [oth. writ.] Unpublished novels, short stories and poems. Published articles in School news bulletin (I am the Editor); [pers.] Grasp life by the neck and choke it. Believe in writing what pleases you and live life to the full without regretting past actions; [a.] London

ALYAS, RAZWANA
[b.] 11 January 1983, Wakefield; [p.] Mohammed Alyas and Azra Alyas; [ed.] (yr. 9) Wakefield City High School; [occ.] Student (At W.C.H.S); [pers.] I think I would like to pursue a career in science, but I will also carry on writing poetry in my spare time.; [a.] Wakefield, West Yorkshire, UK, WF1 4EA

ANCLIFF, WALTER A.
[b.] 30 May 1914, Plumstead; [p.] Walter H. and Elizabeth; [m.] Joan Veronica Chenery, 26 October 1941; [ch.] Sharon Lorraine and Melanie Jane; [ed.] London County Council Elementary School Polytechnic Regent St; [occ.] Retired; [hon.] L.C.C. Trade Scholarship 1928, Hooper Scholarship and IB Cam Silver Medal 1930, Harland Silver Medal 1930; [oth. writ.] Several unpublished poems a nearly completed autobiography.; [a.] Upminster, Essex, UK, RM14 3QJ

ANGELL, GRANVILLE
[pen.] Lord of Cannock; [b.] 13 November 1932, Cannock; [ed.] Severly disrupted because of world war (1939-45) latent development, left school with no qualification; [occ.] Teacher and Royal Navy Retired; [memb.] 46 holder of title Lord of The Manor of Cannock Knight Templar; [hon.] London University B. Sc (Economics) 1971. M.Ed. Birmingham University 1981 open University BA 1981; [oth. writ.] "It's Good to talk" in between a laugh and a tear poems used for children's hospices. Poems For Fund Raising Animal Welfare Rescue.; [pers.] First non-commissioned officer in the history of the Royal Navy to get degree entirely by Correspondence courses.; [a.] Cannock, Staffordshire, UK, WS11 1AA

APAKAMA, IKENNA
[pen.] Paxo; [b.] 4 September 1977; Onitsha;[p.] Japhet Apakama, Patricia Apakama; [ed.] Second year undergraduate student of the department of pharmacy, University of Nigeria, Nsukka; [occ.] Student; [memb.] Editorial Board, Pharmaceutical Association of Nigerian Students, University of Nigeria, Nsukka; [hon.] Best student in economics, Federal Government College Okigwe, Nigeria, 1993/94 session; [oth. writ.] Poems and articles on topical issues published in various national dailies; [pers.] I derive great joy and satisfaction from writing and reading poetry, especially as a means of sharing one's ideas with a teeming audience; [a] Amazand, Njaba local government area

ARNOLD, JULIAN R.
[b.] 7 December 1971, Brighton, Sussex; [p.] Richard Arnold (Deceased), Pamela Arnold; [ed.] Ralph Thoresby High School Leeds, Hereward Further Education College Coventry; [memb.] Social Member Headingley Golf Club Fern Christian Fellowship; [hon.] G.C.S.E. Eleven subjects a level, Law; [oth. writ.] Several poems published for Golf Club Magazine; [pers.] My poetry reflects things from a normal physical perspective, which must, sadly be contrasted with today's more blinkered images from the wheelchair, which I tend to ignore, allowing my formative memories and views to override these images and form the structure for my poetical works.; [a.] Bingley, W. Yorks, UK, BD16 1AT

ARNOLD, MISS JULIETT
[b.] 15 August 1970, High Wycombe; [p.] Brian and Margaret Arnold; [ed.] Hatterslane Secondary School; [occ.] Nanny; [oth. writ.] A bag full of poems that I've never done anything with.; [pers.] I dedicate this poem to my mother. Without her persuasion I would never have sent it off. I hope to do more in the future.; [a.] High Wycombe, Bucks, UK, HP13 7JF

ASHCROFT, MRS. D. M.
[pen.] Dawn Ashcroft; [b.] 14 May 1947, Stockport; [p.] Roderick Little and Mary Little; [m.] John Ashcroft, 22 June 1968; [ch.] David John and Tina Diane; [ed.] Saint Thomas Primary Belmont Secondary Modern; [occ.] School Secretary Pear Tree County Primary School; [memb.] The Elliot Singers Choir; [oth. writ.] Two poems published with "Poetry Now", Edited by Andrew Head; [pers.] Following the tragic death of my 23 year old son David on 9th August 1996. I was miraculously inspired to speak and write poetry. I have never even read or composed poetry before and yet words poured from my pen. I know my heart was linked with David's as he discovered the joys of heaven. I felt his intense excitement, happiness and joy as he discovered his new life. "New Life, My Son" was written especially for him and I was able to read the poem at his funeral. Poetry has entered my life in a wonderful way because of a mother's love for her son.; [a.] Gt. Haywood, Staffordshire, UK, ST18 0RN

ASPINALL, HEATHER L.
[b.] 31 October 1945, Bolton; [p.] Mr. A. R. Aspinall; [ed.] Private School in Bolton then went to boarding school in Southport. Went to two finishing schools, Shropshire and Bucks.; [occ.] Retired as a company director.; [memb.] Salopian Poetry Society, Oris Magazines, Envoi

Mag, Town Women's Guild; [hon.] None, have done lots and lots of competitions haven't won any awards.; [oth. writ.] Haven't done further writings poetry has been my first subject. More recently I have been giving some thoughts into trying article writing.; [pers.] I was a director of a lady's gown shop, Burnley and Rawtenstall, as well as writing poetry. I do a lot of tapestry pictures if there's time. I like to play on the keyboard.; [a.] Bolton, Lancashire, UK, BL1 5AS

ASTON, VIVIAN PAULETLE
[pen.] Poupee; [b.] 14 August 1939, Paris, France; [p.] Eta and Max Aston; [ed.] Brussels Belguim followed in Montreal Canada and boarding school in England, Royal Academy of Music Megiu, University and Trinity College of Music; [occ.] Music and Poetry; [memb.] Royal Academy of Music Club and a friend of U.S. British Federation of festivals for music dance and speech; [hon.] Medals and trophies in piano and medals in poetry a medal for essay awards, certificates for piano music composition, poetry and essay; [oth. writ.] Poems for festival competitions.; [pers.] I get a lot of pleasure from doing competitions. I strive to be a good poet.; [a.] London, UK, NW2

ATTARD, NATALINO
[b.] 29 December 1959, Pieta, Malta; [p.] Cataldo and Dolores Attard; [m.] Marvic Attard Gialanze, 20 July 1985; [ch.] Sarah (8), Martha (4); [ed.] The Lyceum Secondary, University of Malta; [occ.] Civil Servant/Solicitor Manager, Legal Section; [memb.] Chamber of Solicitors (Malta), Henley Alumni, Marsascala Residents Association; [hon.] 1st Prize Poetry Competition (Local) 1979, Masters (European Law); [oth. writ.] 'Misrepresentation in the Contract of Insurance', 'The Role of Local Authorities within the Framework of the E.U. Institutions,' 'Structure and Operation of Local and Regional Democracy—1996', 'Rabat - A Town for All Seasons,' several articles/poems published in local magazines.; [pers.] I always look at the bright side of things, and also believe that there is a good trait in every person. My poems reflect the sensitive and colourful aspects of human kind. I greatly admire poets Wallace Gulia (Local) and Thom Gunn and Ted Hughes.; [a.] Marsaskala, Malta, ZBR 10

AUSTIN, JENIFER ELLEN
[b.] 29 March 1965, Sproxton; [oth. writ.] My very first poem in 1990 "Dear Lord and Father" was unpublished due to illnesses of my own. It won an editor's choice award and a place in the Hall of Fame. "Compassions" won both awards in 96.; [pers.] Our souls have destiny of their own! A powerful force greater then ourselves! Travelling around the universe, connecting with spirits of their own!; [a.] N. Yorkshire, UK, YO6 5EG

BARLOW, SUSAN EVELYN
[pen.] Eve Henderson; [b.] 4 May 1944, Prestbury Cheshire; [p.] Douglas and Eve Henderson; [m.] John Barry Barlow, 30 March 1963; [ch.] John Rowan and Victoria Jane; [ed.] Leigh Girls School. Cheshire.; [occ.] Factory Owner. Textiles; [memb.] Craftsmen's Potters Ass.; [a.] Hyde, Cheshire, UK, SK14 5HH

BARNARD, TARA
[b.] 16 October 1941, Dublin; [p.] Mae and Kevin McMenamin (Deceased); [m.] Robert Barnard, 31 January 1987; [ch.] Maggie, Tom and Kevin; [ed.] St. Louis Convent, Carrick Macross, Co. Monaghan, Ireland; [occ.] Registered General Nurse; [memb.] Boundary Players Drama Society, Rowledge, Surrey, A Lice Holt W.I. Rowledge, Surrey; [hon.] "Progress Prize" 1960 Moorfields Eye Hospital City Road, London; [oth. writ.] None so far, lots of material in my head.; [pers.] I hope that by the time I die the people of this world will have opened their eyes—

it is the main suffering that they are causing each other, the animal world, and the planet itself.; [a.] Farnham, Surrey, UK, GU10 4RT

BARRASS, EDDIE EDWARD
[pen.] Marcus Quintus; [b.] 20 July 1938, Ryhope; [p.] William and Lily Grace; [m.] Margaret, 17 March 1959; [ch.] Two boys, one girl; [ed.] Modern School; [occ.] Retired Miner; [memb.] Chairman Founder Member "Northguard" Roman Research Society VIth Legion "Pia Fidelis"; [oth. writ.] Poetry "Friend", "Feelings", "Thoughts" etc.; [pers.] I enjoy writing poetry. When I have time away from teaching Roman History and dressing as a Roman, writing relaxes my mind. Favourite poets: "Masefield," "Byrone."; [a.] Sunderland, Co. Durham, UK, SR2 0DH

BARRATT, SUE
[b.] 29 February 1952, Leicester; [p.] Norman and Irene Barratt; [ed.] Moat Girls Intermediate University of Life; [occ.] None due to disability with multiple sclerosis; [memb.] M.S. Society. Creative writing course for people with disabilities St. Chad's Church; [hon.] 1993 Overall Winner at Boughton House for carriage driving; [oth. writ.] Another poem is hopefully going to be published about the writing course.; [pers.] Due to the loss of both my parents, and leaving me with time on my hands, I joined a writing course and I haven't looked back since. Work is a great healer; [a.] Wigston, Leicester, Leics, UK, LE18 4YE

BARRETT, HAYLEY
[b.] 3 December 1979, Mile End Hosp.; [p.] Susan Barrett and John Barrett; [ed.] Raines Foundation School and Raines 6th form; [occ.] Student; [memb.] Air Training Corps, Duke of Edinburgh's Award; [hon.] I've had many awards with the air training corps. And the Duke of Edinburgh award, I also won a GNUQ and took part in a 6th form production and got a certificate for comic relief; [oth. writ.] I have written many other poems one of which was read at the memorial of my head teacher from Raines Foundation.; [pers.] 1st World War poetry influenced me first when I started to write poems at the end of last year. I've now started to write more love poetry.; [a.] Bethnal Green, UK, E2 9JG

BARROWES, SAVITA
[b.] 17 November 1982, Kingston, Jamaica; [p.] Hyacinth Sarju and Michael Barrowes; [pers.] Live every day to the fullest and aim for the top. The sky is the limit.

BARRY, NOEL
[pen.] Dan Barry; [b.] 24 December 1969, Tipperary; [p.] Vourneen and Joe Barry; [a.] Templemore, Tipperary, Eire

BATEMAN, MILDRED
[b.] 8 October 1921, Tipton; [p.] Richard Harper and Mildred Harper (Both Deceased); [m.] John Dudley Bateman, 10 April 1943; [ch.] Lesley Jane, Mark Dudley, Andrew John; [ed.] Kings Norton Grammar Wednesbury Commercial College; [occ.] Freelance Journalist, poet and playwright; [memb.] Brierley Hill Choral Society, Chair, West Midlands, Writers Circle Officer of Christian Church. Present: Royal Agricultural Soc., National Trust, R.S.P.B., Int. Library of Poetry; [oth. writ.] Poetry Collections play, TV and Radio, Chiefly, non-fiction on the law and order, of English precedence, i.e. the British Constitution; [pers.] As Pacifist, Republican, Humanist, I am scientifically opposed to the existing British Constitution.; [a.] Kings Wimford, West Midlands, UK, DY6 9RD

BAXTER, REG B.
[b.] 13 September 1918, Hoxne; [p.] Harry and Eliza Baxter; [m.] Mary, 26 July 1947; [ch.] Clive; [ed.] Hoxne Primary School; [occ.] Retired Journalist; [memb.] Royal British Legion Dunkirk Veterans Association; [oth. writ.] Local Press 50 years; [a.] Eye, Suffolk, UK, IP21 5AS

BAYLISS, JACQUELINE
[b.] 15 February 1986, Worcester; [p.] Julie and John Bayliss; [ed.] Currently at Westacre Middle School, Droitwich; [occ.] School Girl; [memb.] Droitwich Library; [hon.] Represent School in rounders and cross country.; [oth. writ.] "Changes", "Dreams" and the "Nearing of Winter" are some of the other titles I have written, but have not yet been published.; [pers.] I have been inspired by the atmosphere around me and shall continue to write poetry to the best of my ability.; [a.] Droitwich, Worcestershire, UK, WR9 9ES

BEAUMONT, BERNARD HERBERT
[pen.] Ben H. Brumel; [b.] 9 December 1939, Halifax; [p.] John Beaumont and Cecilia McLarnon; [m.] Divorced— Eleanor Harris, 1 July 1980; [ed.] Rastrick Common Secondary Modern Brighouse Yorkshire and Huddersfield Tech.; [occ.] struggling author; [hon.] GSM Active Service Medal for Fighting in Malaya; [oth. writ.] A Diary of Rhyme which, has now gone to press, "A Crushed Toad Apart" —biography, which I hope to have published soon.; [pers.] I take life as it comes, with all its ups and downs, and always have a smile, for other people's frowns. I let the sun shine in, and meet life with a grin.; [a.] Gillingham, Kent, UK, ME7 4DG

BEAZER, DEBORAH
[b.] 30 July 1967, Chipping, Sodbury; [p.] Alan Beazer and Carol Beazer; [ed.] Mildenhall Upper School; [occ.] Psychiatric Nurse; [hon.] Registered General Nurse 1989, Registered Psychiatric Nurse 1991; [pers.] A traumatic event in my life inspired me to write this. Something good emerged from all the hurt and pain I felt.; [a.] Littleport, Cambs, UK, CB6 1PX

BECK, CLIFFORD HERBERT
[pen.] Herbert Ford; [b.] 27 January 1954, Melton; [p.] Eileen Beck, Kenneth Beck; [m.] Mary E. Barker; [ch.] Daniel John Adam Kenneth; [ed.] Framlingham Secondary Modern; [occ.] Flour Miller; [oth. writ.] First attempt as only been writing poems since 1996.; [pers.] I was inspired by the beautiful places on this earth, and my concern for their survival.; [a.] Felixstowe, Suffolk, UK, IP11 8AH

BENACS, MRS. PHILIPPA CATHERINE
[b.] 7 May 1944, Birkenhead; [p.] William George and Ethel Townson; [m.] George Benacs, 14 June 1986; [ch.] Mark Edward and Kathryn Jane; [ed.] Secondary School and Carley Park College of Further Education; [occ.] Rest Home Proprietress, Bunkers Bounty Rest Home; [oth. writ.] Several poems published by the International Library of Poetry and the Poetry Guild; [pers.] Writing poetry is an extension of oneself which can be a release of encaptured feelings. When shared with others such poetry, whether serious, mysterious or amusing, usually proves to be rather interesting and entertaining.; [a.] Blackpool, Lancashire, UK, FY6 9AN

BENOY, KENNETH
[b.] 5 April 1920, Plymouth; [p.] Lieut W. J. Benoy RN, MBE and Russian born Katie; [m.] Rosemary Benoy, 4 June 1954; [ed.] Southern Polytechnic Portsmouth School of Architecture; [occ.] Chartered Architect (Retired); [memb.] ARIBA (Resigned '87); [oth. writ.] Poems published in 20 different Anthologies.; [pers.] Influenced by my artist Russian mother, my life has been dominated by the arts. I try to paint in words and endeavour to relate to the complex emotions of the human scene both past and present.; [a.] Solihull, W. Midlands, UK, B93 8DW

BENZAQUEN, DINAH
[pen.] Dee De La Roca; [b.] 3 February 1975; Gibraltar; [p.] Esther and Sam Benzaquen; [ed.] B55 Seminary, Manchester, Bury College, Manchester (A levels), University of London (King's College); [occ.] Undergraduate student,

reading French and Hispanic studies; [memb.] University of London debating society, King's College French and Spanish society; [hon.] Nominated for the poet of the year award, awarded outstanding achievement in poetry; [oth. writ.] My ultimate ambition would be to publish a book of Anglo-Hispanic poetry; [pers.] My poetry consists of an interesting mix of both Hispanic and English literary styles; [a.] Gibraltar

BERROWS, SHIRLEY ANN
[b.] 2 May 1937, Sussex; [p.] Lilian Ellens, Ralph Ellens; [m.] Raymond Berrows, 12 January 1962; [ch.] Two daughters, three sons; [ed.] Secondary Modern; [occ.] Product Commercial Designer Inventor; [oth. writ.] Penned winning lyrics to royal wedding song for the wedding of Prince Andrew and Fergie in a competition run by 'That's Life'. Article in VQ on Battery Hens Poetry published in small anthologies.; [pers.] Nature's wonders are my inspiration, they are my friends with whom I wish to talk and laugh.; [a.] Wordsley, West Mids, UK, DY8 5HW

BINGLEY, GARY
[pen.] Gary Bingley; [b.] 17 May 1955, Shipley; [p.] Arthur Bingley, Joan Bingley; [m.] Lorraine, 5 July 1980; [ch.] Gavin David, Christopher John; [ed.] Bradford Boys Grammar School; [occ.] Civil Servant (H.M. Inspector of Taxes); [memb.] British MENSA since 1989; [oth. writ.] Other poems in 'Jewels of the Imagination', and 'A Lasting Calm', for the International Library of Poetry, and 'Images' for Abbey books.; [pers.] Many thanks to my parents and to Lorraine and the boys for their love over the years.; [a.] Shipley, West Yorkshire, UK, BD18 3BZ

BLACKHALL, SARA
[b.] 20 April 1987, Chelmsford, Essex; [p.] Suzanne and Frederick; [ed.] Howbridge Junior School Witham, Essex; [memb.] St. Nicolas Church Choir Philips School of Dancing; [a.] Witham, Essex, UK, CM8 1ET

BLANCHFIELD, MRS. KATHLEEN
[p.] Catherine and John Glendon (Deceased); [m.] Michael Blanchfield, 14 August 1969; [ch.] Denise, Marie, Caroline and Michelle; [ed.] Primary, Bonnettstown National School, Secondary Education Kilkenny, City Vocational School; [occ.] Housewife and mother writing short stories and poetry in my spare time; [hon.] Two achievements for National Letter, short story writing from "An Post", 1995-1996 and received book with letters published each year, at a special awards ceremony in Dublin's Writers Museum; [oth. writ.] Writing some short stories and poetry in my spare time. One poem published in the anthology "Between a Laugh and a Tear" in 1996; [pers.] I appreciate the blessings of each day, and thank God for a healthy husband and family. I love writing, and my inspiration comes from my own feelings within, as I study the wonder of life itself.; [a.] Acragar, Ballyragget, Co. Kilkenny, Eire

BLANEY, MR. T. P.
[pen.] Scotchtommy; [b.] 15 September 1929, Coatbridge, Scotland; [p.] Deceased; [m.] Wife Beryl Blaney, 27 March 1954; [ch.] Two sons; [occ.] O.A.P.; [oth. writ.] A big sale, a sorry tale, one of the many unknown soldier's, the taxpayers know it's not fair nearly all our MP's end up millionaires.; [pers.] 3 R's at school very, very bad. I learned 4 R's from my loving dad—R.I.P. At school—writing, reading, 'rithmatic from dad—right wrong, respect, responsibility.; [a.] Coatbridge, Scotland

BLENCOWE, JULIETTE
[pen.] Juliette Somerton; [b.] 29 March 1946, Sulgrave; [p.] Frank and Ida Somerton; [m.] Herb Blencowe, 26 September 1964; [ch.] Kim Susan and Andrew Peter; [ed.] Secondary Modern, then North Oxon College Further Education; [occ.] Physiotherapy Assistant, Administrator; [memb.] Local History Society, Diocesan Guild Bellringers, Local Amenity Society (Sec:); [hon.] English GCSE 1992, ACCESS to Higher Education 1993; [oth. writ.] Article Ringing World, Newsletters, Church Magazine, Short Stories (as yet not published).; [pers.] My poetry is reactive, instinctive, a source of expressing my emotions. Short story writing is challenging, yet very relaxing and a source of great satisfaction. Whether poetry, an article or a story, I'm eternally grateful for the source of energy that flows from head to hand and paper.; [a.] Brackley, Northants, UK, NN13 6EQ

BLESI, LINDA
[b.] 8 October 1951, London; [p.] Joyce Allin; [m.] Divorced; [ed.] Tottenham County Grammar School, then B.A. in German and French (Lon. Ext.) (70-73), then M.A. in English and German at Zurich University (80-84); [occ.] Teacher of English at grammar school in Switzerland; [memb.] Zurich Comedy Club; [oth. writ.] Three novels and two collections of short stories as yet unpublished. I've only recently started writing poetry.; [a.] Walchwil, Zug, Switzerland, 6318

BOSWORTH, JAMES ALFRED
[pen.] J. A. Bosworth; [b.] 16 February 1936, Hastings, Sussex; [m.] December 1960; [ch.] 5 Sons; [ed.] Bruton Grammar School, Open University (BA); [occ.] Poet, Literary Critic/Theorist; [memb.] Poetry Society, Open University Poets, Founder, New Traditionist Movements; [hon.] IBC 'Man of the Year 1996' (for service to Poetry and the Arts), Nominee for IBC 'Man of the Decade 1990's' (for service to Poetry and the Arts); [oth. writ.] Neknus and other poems, Clouds of Glory and other poems, Natural Memories and other poems. In preparations: Prefaces (Arts Theory), Helvetian Harmonies and other poems.; [pers.] Prefaces postulates that all the fine arts are interlinked through common principles, to create an holistic corpus of activities which unite individual and universal experiences of existence and enhance the quality of human lives.; [a.] Cugyford, Switzerland

BOULTON, JANET M.
[b.] 21 March 1949, Bognor Regis; [p.] Olive Boulton, Frederick Boulton; [ed.] Villa Maria, Bognor Regis; [occ.] Police Officer; [memb.] British Horse Society; [oth. writ.] A few poems published by small printers.; [pers.] Money and possessions are not everything they can help, but happiness comes from within.; [a.] Billinghurst, Sussex, UK, RH14 9UQ

BOURNER, MRS. AMY F.
[b.] 22 May 1918, Southend; [p.] Mr. and Mrs. Whitbread; [m.] Sidney Coleman Bourner (Deceased), 23 August 1945; [ed.] Elementary; [occ.] Retired; [a.] UK

BOYLE, FINNAN
[b.] 1 October 1960, London; [p.] Patrick and Therese Boyle; [ed.] Maths School Rochester, Dominican College Portstewart, Manchester University, Magee College, University of Ulster; [occ.] Artist; [memb.] Roe Valley Art Soc. Limavady Coleraine Art Society N.J.; [hon.] Hon. degree Town Planning, Dip. in Community Development; [oth. writ.] Several poems published by Anchor Books and local magazines. Prize winner in International Poetry Competition 1997.; [pers.] I like to highlight social issues. I have been influenced by the social writers of the Victorian Era.; [a.] Limavady, Londonderry, UK, BT4 9AT

BOZZONI, BEVERLEY E.
[b.] 13 February 1957, Leicestershire; [p.] John Smith and Dorothy Smith; [m.] Mark Bozzoni, 16 January 1995; [ch.] Sadie, Lindsey, Craig, Shaun, Marc-Ross; [ed.] Lutterworth Grammar; [occ.] Housewife; [pers.] I find that I can express my feelings in my poetry of issues that are close to my heart.; [a.] Sapcote, Leicestershire, UK, LE9 4JL

BRADY, MARY
[b.] 30 May 1937, Armagh; [p.] David Brady, Edith Brady; [ed.] Mount St. Catherine's Convent Armagh, Armagh College of further Education; [occ.] (Retired) Assistant Manager of Armagh Credit Union Limited; [oth. writ.] One poem published in last year's anthology "Awaken to a Dream"; [pers.] From early childhood I have loved poetry and it was always my ambition to have at least one poem of my own printed.; [a.] Armagh, Armagh, UK, BT61 7QU

BRANDON, MARIE ANTONETTE DIAZ
[b.] 13 August 1942, Guyana, South America; [p.] Edward and Catherine Diaz; [m.] Anthony Peter Brandon, 14 January 1966; [ch.] Samantha and Anthony; [occ.] Nursing—Retired; [hon.] Being a mother to Samantha and Anthony; [pers.] My poem is dedicated to my first granddaughter Rebecca Marie Blackey, still born 23 April 1992. Too beautiful for this world.; [a.] Victoria, Australia, 3084

BRANDRETH, LOUISE VICTORIA
[b.] 17 October 1982, Poole, Dorset; [p.] Thomas Brandreth; [m.] Frances Brandreth, 28 September 1974; [ch.] Camilla and Louise; [ed.] Brightlingsea Junior School —Colne Community School, Brightlingsea; [occ.] Student; [pers.] I wrote the poem because my aunt was dying and I wanted to say goodbye to her. She struggled with cancer for seven years died peacefully at home.; [a.] Brightlingsea, Essex, UK, CO7 0NB

BRETT, PATRICK
[b.] 5 May 1960, Liverpool; [p.] Carole Ann; [ed.] Reading Franz Kafka; [memb.] Member of the Human Race.; [hon.] I hope I get my reward in heaven.; [oth. writ.] The Druids, Josef K., The Great Hunger; [pers.] When I was younger, my dad told me all about the great hunger, about a nation that reaped a whirlwind and a potato blight that was darker than any night, a death-camp country that had the effrontery not to cope.

BROBBEY, CAPT. DR. JACOB ASARE
[b.] 2 November 1955, Kumasi; [p.] Dinah Arkeifie; [m.] Mrs. Otilia Mariana Brobbey, 29 October 1988; [ch.] Nerissa Adela Isabella; [ed.] Mfantsipim Sec School, Cape Coast, Presec Legon, Accra, Ghana. Faculty of General Medicine, Bucharest, Romania. Ghana Military Academy, Accra; [occ.] Medical Officer. Post graduate study in Cardiology. Poet, Dramatist; [memb.] Church Warden of Anglican Church of the Resurrection Bucharest, Romania.; [hon.] 9 'O' Levels, 4 'A' Levels, M.D. for General Medicine. Military cane for best Officer Cadet. Editor's Choice Award for the Poem 'Fair Spring'. Military Medals—Unifil, Unamir, Ecomog; [oth. writ.] Plays: Memories Of Love, Woman on the Moor Part 1 and 2, Truth Seekers, Murder by Lovers. Poems: 'Fair Spring' published. Others published in local papers in Ghana several articles and short stories.; [pers.] I combine my talents in poetry, drama and scientific background to create works of art. Poetry, drama, religion and science are a source of inspiration.; [a.] Accra, Ghana

BROOKS, AUDREY MARGARET HELENA
[b.] 2 August 1928, Wallsend-on-Tyne; [p.] John Andrew and Edith Hall; [m.] Richard William Brooks, 18 September 1948; [ch.] Pauline, Hazel, Loraine, Shirley, Colette; [ed.] Primary School, Western Girls, Wallsend-on-Tyne; [occ.] Retired, Housewife; [oth. writ.] Valentine's Day poems, which won a prize at the Ritz Cinema, Wallsend which is now a bingo hall.; [pers.] My poems come from inside me, through heart, mind, body and soul and the spirit within. I get an urge to write poetry at once, which I greatly love to do.! I left school at 14 yrs. old, and I still got in an "Estate Agents Office".; [a.] Newcastle-on-Tyne, Tyne and Wear, UK, NE6 4PB

BROTHERTON, ANNETTE
[b.] 24 October 1937, Bromford; [p.] Eric and Winifred; [m.] Brotherton; [ed.] Saint Agnes's Convent and Saint Joseph's Convent. Kenilworth Warwcks and Birmingham; [occ.] Road Sutton Coldfield, U.D.U. Operator and Punch Tape and Short-hand Typist, Filing Clerk and General Office Duties; [hon.] Certificate Short-hand and Typing, 100 wpm and intermediate; [oth. writ.] I like writing. It releases tension—putting words on paper. I would like to write more and become well-known to people.; [pers.] Poetry brings my thoughts to mind as I write. This is one of the hobbies I enjoy. I hope you like reading my work in verse.; [a.] Birmingham, UK, B35 7HS

BROWN, MR. FREDERICK GEORGE
[b.] 1 September 1918, Brampton, Abbotts; [p.] Kate and Charles Brown; [m.] Dorothy, 27 October 1945; [ch.] Two; [ed.] Junior, Secondary Schools, Brampton, Abbotts; [occ.] Retired; [hon.] School Attendance for 8 yrs., never late, 6 miles to walk to school, one medal for 3 years and additional for next, 5 years long service and good conduct; [oth. writ.] Medal 25 years. Staff Car, Driver for Central Mediterrean H.Q. Italy (after war).; [pers.] Admire: William Wordsworth; [a.] Austerfield, Doncaster, South Yorkshire, UK, DN10 6QR

BROWN, PAMELA
[pen.] Libra; [b.] 26 September 1928, Gillingham, Kent, UK; [p.] Charles Henry and Florence Mary Weston; [m.] Frederick Thomas Brown, 22 December 1951; [ch.] Kevin John, Gary Richard, Jillian Carol; [ed.] Elementary; [occ.] Retired; [memb.] A.A.W. (Association Anglican Women) Guild, Senior Kiwi, Greypower, Historical Society, Geneological Society Craft Group; [oth. writ.] Occasional poems in local newspaper, Editor's Choice in Quiet Moments and due to be two poems in The Light of the World.; [pers.] I aim to leave the world's resources protected so other generations may benefit and enjoy them. I write of happenings as I see them usually with humour.; [a.] Blenheim, Marlborough, New Zealand, 7301

BROWN, STEPHANIE
[b.] 5 February 1980, Birmingham; [p.] Sharon Smith and Karl Brown; [ed.] GCSE's at Hodge Hill Girls's Secondary School, Joseph Chamberlain VIth Form College (Currently) for A-Levels.; [occ.] Student; [oth. writ.] Other poems have been written, but none have been published; [pers.] I feel that the best poems are those that have a different meaning each time they are read, this is why my favourite poems are by Wilfred Owen and Shakespeare.; [a.] Birmingham, West Midlands, UK

BROWN, SUSAN
[b.] 18 January 1962, Bishopstorford; [p.] Anne Brown, Peter Brown; [ed.] Earnock High; [occ.] Revenue Officer; [oth. writ.] None so far, but hoping for the future to write.; [pers.] Dreams can come true. My dream was to have my written word published thank you International Library of Poetry.; [a.] East Kilbride, Glasgow, UK, G75 8AP

BROWNE, PATRICIA
[pen.] Patricia Browne; [b.] 21 June 1937, Plaistow; [p.] William Harry and Doris Beardall; [m.] Alan Browne, 31 August 1957; [ch.] Paul David and Andrew Mark; [ed.] Secondary, followed by Commercial College and then Nurse Training College; [occ.] Nurse; [hon.] Various mostly English and Literature; [oth. writ.] I belong to a drama group and write scripts etc. and latterly pantomimes—all of which are performed for charity.; [pers.] I believe very firmly in the great value of close family relationships and attribute all I am today to the great love of my parents and in particular the example set by my father.; [a.] Romford, Essex, UK, RM7 0HA

BRYNIN, LEONI HADASSA
[b.] 3 March 1980; [p.] Rachelle Sacks, Robert Brynin; [ed.] Brighton and Hove High School, Hasmonean High School (Girls); [memb.] KJY; [oth. writ.] No previous published work.; [pers.] Some of my writing is true, some isn't, but it all comes from my heart, to yours.; [a.] Wembley, Middlesex, UK, HA9 9RY

BUCKLE, GLENYS C.
[b.] 28 August 1943, Newport, Gwent; [p.] Arthur and Lilian Williams; [m.] Anthony Buckle Obe, 4 August 1967; [ch.] Christopher, Kevin, Timothy; [ed.] Newport High School, Manchester University; [occ.] Teacher, Hawthorn High School, Pontypridd; [memb.] Cwmbran Tennis Club; [hon.] Hons Degree in French; [pers.] Interested in the depth and complexity of human emotions.; [a.] Cwmbran, Gwent, UK, NP44 1VD

BUDGE, ELIZABETH MARGARET
[b.] 1933, London; [m.] Derek John, 24 September 1960; [ch.] Two Sons; [ed.] Ordinary; [occ.] Receptionist; [oth. writ.] Nearly 300 Written to Date, 1 book published end of the year 2 others published in anthologies, 1 in a magazine; [pers.] Started last year, never had any inclination before then, but once started it just flowed. Anything but mostly about life around me; [a.] Hemel Hempstead, Herts, UK, HP3 8HB

BURCH, MRS. PEARL
[p.] Harold and Emily Read; [m.] Douglas Harry Burch; [ch.] Two; [occ.] Housewife; [hon.] Certificate of appreciation from Royal British Legion poppy appeal, Certificate in nursing; [oth. writ.] Several poems and one story.; [a.] Colne, Huntingdon, Cambs, UK, PE14 3LY

BUTLER, BOBBY
[b.] 11 September 1914, Portsmouth; [m.] Albert Joseph Butler, 9 May 1936; [ch.] Brian and Andrew; [ed.] Ordinary Junior and Senior Schools in Brighton, Leaving at 14 years of age; [occ.] Retired; [oth. writ.] A few other poems in contemporary poetry anthology—several years ago; [pers.] Poems written about deep personal experiences, mainly through very unhappy childhood and later life, after the death of husband.; [a.] Weymouth, Dorset, UK, DT4 8JD

BUTTERS, PAUL
[pen.] Paul Summers; [b.] 27 May 1952, Leeds; [p.] Pete (Deceased) and Louisa; [ed.] Upper Wortley Infants and Primary, Cow Close County Secondary, Farnley, Leeds, West Leeds Boys' High, Huddersfield Polytechnic, Leeds University, Trent Polytechnic (Nottingham); [occ.] Senior Careers Adviser (Humberside Careers and Guidance Services); [memb.] U.N.I.S.O.N., Former member of N.A.S.E.N.; [hon.] B. Ed. Degree (English), Dip. C.G.; [oth. writ.] "Game of Never' in "Voices on the Wind" (1996-"The International Society of Poets"), and eight other poems accepted for publication in various anthologies.; [pers.] Compulsive writer. Besides poetry, I also like to write stories and the odd play. Am interested in religious matters, cosmology, science fiction, and sport.; [a.] Cleethorpes Humberside, NE Lincolnshire, UK, DN35 8EN

BUTTON, MR. GREGORY LEIGHTON
[b.] 2 April 1972; [p.] Mr. Sam Button and Mrs. Joy Button; [ed.] Methwold High School at Downham Market Sixth Form Centre; [occ.] Nursery Worker; [oth. writ.] 'Aspirations of the Enigmatic Son,' poem published in "Quiet Moments." Many of my works have been published in local magazine.; [pers.] Within all my works I aim to express my deepest emotions, which are intended to inspire the observers intrigue and curiosity.; [a.] Gooderstone, Kilynn, Norfolk, UK, PE33 9BX

BYRNE, MICHEAL
[pen.] Paul White; [b.] 9 February 1951, Ireland; [p.] Micheal and Mary (Deceased); [ed.] Sec Grammar; [occ.] Retired (Army); [memb.] C.B.S.I.; [hon.] UN Peace Keeping Medal of Merit Scouts, Semi Finalist in the National Library of Poetry. Published in Portraits of Life (Spirit in the Sky); [oth. writ.] 10 Short stories for children plus about 40 poems awaiting on publishing.; [pers.] I write as I feel this poem I wrote when I was feeling very low and my life seemed lovely. I have since found the love I was looking for, and I have written a poem (called Touched By Love).; [a.] Limerick, Clare, Ireland

BYRON-RASMUSSEN, BARBARA
[pen.] "Barbara-Anna" (Music name); [b.] 1 March 1944, Lewes; [ch.] Diana, Denise, Debbie, Karl; [ed.] Mountfield Road Secondary School, Lewis, Sussex; [occ.] Early retired voluntary worker; [memb.] W.R.V.S., Red Cross, Age Concern; [oth. writ.] 400 more poems—odes, 50 songs, 3 prayer books, life story in poetic form, available for publication.; [pers.] Inspired to write by a big life, home and abroad—and the people I have met from many nationalities. I did not choose to be a writer. I just am, uninfluenced by other poets. Coming from the heart!; [a.] Brighton, Sussex

CALDER, DONNA
[b.] 4 July 1980, Kircaldy; [p.] Keith and Anne Calder; [ed.] Waid Academy School/Pittenweem Primary; [occ.] Assistant Baker; [a.] Pittenweem, Fife, Scotland, KV10 2NB

CALLENDER, MR. DUDLEY HAYNES
[pen.] Charlie; [b.] 19 January 1929, Barbados; [p.] Lavinia and Cornelius; [m.] Madge Marion, 21 March 1959; [ch.] Six— five sons, one girl; [ed.] Elementary, Army —Police—Civil Defence Medical Rescue Officer —Biet Engineer, Psychology. Cabinet Maker; [occ.] Retired; [memb.] Ex-service Legionneer British Legion. UK. London and Barbados. And Commonwealth Clubs. Ex-reader digest "Credits"; [hon.] Army AI Professional. America Inventors Corp. UK Invention, payment fees. Engineering Electrical and Mechanical; [oth. writ.] "The Poetry Guild". Marlborough Wilts. SN8 2HP UK. Millennium and will be in three books of poems.; [pers.] I am a book worm. Never stop reading. A Bible, Cherisher, never seems to understand, the books of love, and wars, to the end. I am nothing without my teachers. Who teach me. My praise to, them all. "Amen".; [a.] Leicester, Leicestershire, UK, LE3 1ES

CARLIN, ANTHONY
[b.] 11 February 1939, Coatbridge; [p.] John and May; [ed.] St. Augustine's R.C Smyllum Park School, St. Ninnian's House of Falkland Fife, Scotland; [occ.] Self Employed; [oth. writ.] Several poems in anthologies, one of which was published in America poem published in local news paper.; [pers.] I love to write about things I see about me, when I am working or visiting, I love the wildlife and open spaces of the countryside.; [a.] Nottingham, UK, NG9 5NE

CARTER, BARBARA ANN
[b.] 6 December 1947, Suffolk; [p.] Thomas and Kay Hignett; [m.] James V. Harbord, 3 July 1991; [ch.] Jonathan, Matthew Carter; [ed.] Claydon High School, Suffolk Ipswich School of Art, Suffolk; [occ.] Housewife, Voluntary Country Rep. for CCHF, London; [hon.] Certificate by CCHF for Completion of Training Course in Child Protection and Recruitment and Assessment of Host Families; [oth. writ.] Several Poems written but so far unpublished; [pers.] My interest are: Environmental Issues, Natural History, Archaeology, the Supernatural and my work with socially deprived children from London. And these concerns are reflected in some of my poems.; [a.] Alnwick, Northumberland, UK, NE66 3NQ

CASSON, IRIS
[b.] 24 April 1929, Enfield, England; [p.] William Peaper and Lilian Peaper; [m.] George Casson, 1 August 1953; [ch.] Ainslie George and Jacqueline Clare; [ed.] Wartime Technical School for City and Guilds. Court Dressmaker; [occ.] Retired Dress Maker; [memb.] "War Research Society"; [pers.] In my retirement, I have travelled on many Battlefield Tours WW1 and WW2. They are very moving and very personal. I just had to put my pen to paper for my dad".; [a.] Hertford, Hertfordshire, UK, SG14 2HX

CASTLE, MR. JOHN THOMAS
[pen.] 'Jacko'; [b.] 15 July 1942, Romsey, Hants; [p.] Mr. Liberty Castle and Mrs. Dorethy Amelia Castle; [m.] Pauleen Castle, 6 February 1965; [ch.] Maria, Angela, Barbara, Brenda, John, Desmond and Nicholas; [ed.] Secondary Modern School, Alton—Hants, Salisbury Tech.; [occ.] Head Gardner and Groundsman; [pers.] I was inspired to write this poem due to the love, hard work, and dedication my wife has given to myself and seven children over the last thirty two years.; [a.] Gillingham, Dorset, UK, SP8 5SD

CHAPPELL, JOHNNY
[b.] 15 April 1966; [p.] David John Chappell and Elizabeth Anne Chappell; [ed.] University of Life; [occ.] Deep Sea Diver, Britain and Overseas; [oth. writ.] Various obscene limericks on toilet walls throughout Britain and indeed the world.; [pers.] If only I could find a word that rhymed with 'Orange' I would probably be the greatest poet that ever lived.; [a.] Biggar, Lanarkshire, UK, ML12 6LU

CHARALAMBOUS, STELLA
[b.] 19 January 1957, Mykonos; [p.] Spiros Irene (Poet); [ch.] Basilios Kalogridis; [ed.] English Literature; [occ.] Private Lessons; [memb.] Group of Amateur Artists and Stained Glass Artists; [hon.] Editor's Choice Award for my poem lovely melody printed in "Jewels of the Imagination" last year; [oth. writ.] Poetry in Greek and in English. Most unpublished for the moment.; [pers.] Love each day, come what may.; [a.] New Heraklion, Athens, Greece, 14122

CHARNOCK, MR. CHARLES
[b.] 24 April 1907, Bolton, Lancs; [p.] Charles and Mary Elizabeth; [m.] Margaret Charnock, 16 January 1932; [ed.] Elementary St Edmunds RC Bolton; [occ.] Retired; [oth. writ.] "Soldier on the Move" ISBN 095232404 from author poem "Related Valentine" published in last anthology. Won cup for descriptive story of family trade of "Horn Cumb Manufacturing" now in Museum Archives.; [pers.] I can't understand why people don't seek able to think straight possibly due to political interference in Educational Curriculum in past war years; [a.] Darwen, Lancashire, UK, BB3 2LZ

CHASE, NEIL
[b.] 12 August 1959, N Shields; [ch.] Jane Philip Kyla; [ed.] Rojubury Primary School Morpeth Comprehensive; [occ.] Prison Officer; [a.] Newport, E. Yorks, UK, UU15 2PW

CHATTERTON, DOROTHY
[pen.] Gray Chatterton; [b.] 15 March 1939, Edinburgh; [m.] Jack, 21 March 1988; [ch.] Three all adults, three grandchildren; [ed.] Secondary Modern; [occ.] Accounting Clerk, Special Needs Tutor; [hon.] City and Guilds; [oth. writ.] Other poetry. One other submitted to the International Library of Poetry; [pers.] Writing is easy—getting others to read it is hard.; [a.] Stockport, Cheshire, UK, SK3 8TN

CHEETHAM, ALICE LYONS
[b.] 19 March 1916, Salford; [p.] Deceased; [m.] Deceased, 2 October 1939; [ch.] Two; [a.] Thornton Cleveleys, Lancashire, UK, FY5 1PU

CHRISTIAN, ROMA CADWGAN
[pen.] Roma Cadwgan Christian; [b.] 10 July 1914, Blaengarw, South Wales; [p.] Henry William and Hilda Winifred Thomas; [m.] Albert James Christian (Deceased), November 1947; [ed.] Garw Gammi School State Registered Nurse; [occ.] Retired; [memb.] Ledbury Baptist Church; [oth. writ.] Poems various; [pers.] The wonder of God's handiwork and the many things man does to spoil it.; [a.] Ledbury, Herefordshire, UK, HR8 2HN

CLARK, STELLA DOREEN
[b.] 12 November 1924, Tillingham, Essex; [p.] Rose and Alfred Saward; [m.] Harry Clark (Deceased), 8 August 1945; [ch.] John Allen Clark and Evelyn Rosie Head; [ed.] St. Nicholas Elementary C of E School, Tillingham, Essex; [occ.] Retired; [oth. writ.] None published as yet, but one poem may be so shortly by The Poetry Guild (Witts) which I entered into last May 1997. This poem is not the same as the other one.; [pers.] I started writing poems in my childhood days, but it was only during my 3 years 1942-45 in the A.T.S. (Army) and after my marriage, that I wrote more seriously. All my poems are based on fact. About my family and friends.; [a.] Tillingham, Essex, UK, CM0 7SA

CLARK, WILLIAM JAMES
[pen.] William James Clark; [b.] 26 February 1987; Harlow, Essex; [p.] Roger and Freda Clark; [ed.] Hoo St. Werburgh County Primary School; [occ.] school boy; [a] Rochester, Kent

CLARKE, CHRISTINA MARIA
[b.] 18 January 1944, Birmingham; [p.] Gwendoline and Donald Lomax; [m.] Michael; [ch.] Lewis and Gary, and grandsons Lewis and Adam; [ed.] Secondary School—Birmingham Swindon College—English-Sociology Cirencester College—Management and Admin; [occ.] Assistant Manager "Oxfam" West Market place Cirencester; [memb.] Cirencester Operatic Society.; [hon.] Awarded a prize by Penhaligan Page LTD "Editor's Choice Award", The International Library of Poetry.; [oth. writ.] Several Poems published in various anthologies with arrival press and poetry today Penhaligan Page LTD.; [pers.] I seek to fathom life and its mysteries those inner feelings that we all feel but sometimes cannot express, bringing comfort and reassurance to the reader as only the written word can.; [a.] Cirencester, Gloucestershire, UK, GL7 1TB

CLARKE, SIMON
[b.] 5 September 1926, Paddington, England; [p.] Ralph Clarke and Rebekah Clarke; [m.] Widow, 21 October 1952; [ch.] Christopher, Caroline, Alison, Eton; [occ.] Landowner in Sussex; [memb.] The Travellers Club, Pall Mall, London, The Bluebell Railway, Preservation Society, Sheffield Park, Sussex; [pers.] I admire the works of Rudyard Kipling; [a.] Isle of Wight, UK, PO30 3HH

CLEMENS, MATTHEW
[b.] 28 November 1970, Truro; [p.] Graham Clemens and Leola Clemens; [m.] Nicola Barnes; [pers.] The art does not redeem the artist.; [a.] Hayle, Cornwall, UK, TR27 4EJ

COLE, SPENCER
[b.] 27 November 1969, Corringham; [p.] Sylvia Deeprose; [ed.] Hassenbrook Comprehensive School, Stanford-Le-Hope; [occ.] Estimator, Ford Direct, Tilbury Docks.; [oth. writ.] This is my first attempt at getting any of my poems published, and I am honoured that it has been chosen. To be published in your anthology; [pers.] I draw my inspiration from things that happen around the world, and also from personal feelings. I have many poems and hope one day I can have a book published of my own.; [a.] Corringham, Essex, UK, SS17 7HP

COLLETON, BRIDGET
[pen.] Bridget Briar Colleton; [b.] 15 March 1945, Republic of Ireland; [p.] Michael and Mary Colleton (Deceased); [ed.] Primary, Intermediate and Leaving Certificate. Registered, General Nurse and State Certified Midwife; [occ.] Nursing; [memb.] The Irish Nurses Organization; [hon.] Won "The Childrens National Art Competition" in the 1950's (In the Mich Nineteen Fifty Years). Won cups and trophies for poetry and art in the early 1960's; [oth. writ.] The Folling titles were published—"Shannondene", "Orla" and "Why Damien Oh Why" (The above are mystery thrillers) "The Collected Works of Bridget Briar", "The Second Collected Works of Bridget Briar", "Scarlet Ribbons" by Bridget Briar Colleton (The above three titles are poetry books); [pers.] I believe there is a reason for all things under heaven.; [a.] Bray, Co Wicklow, Republic of Ireland

COLLIGAN, MARGARET MUIR
[pen.] Tammy; [b.] 31 March 1920, Saline Fife, Edinburgh; [p.] Thomas Lawrie Colligan, Mary Cunningham Colligan (Deceased); [m.] Deceased, 4 October 1940; [ch.] Four—3 boys, 1 girl; [ed.] I left school at age 14. Considered bright and different.; [occ.] Housewife before shop assistant, managers (2); [memb.] Was in a few writers' groups.; [oth. writ.] Children's poems (Animals and Fairies), few stories. Adult love poems, etc. autobiography. New Festival Theatre Edinburgh "Lived" opposite stage door 1924-44 written my memories.; [pers.] Honest and true, from early childhood onwards ambition to be famous and my family successful in life. Have always put my trust in God. Would like to inspire others through my writings and thoughts.; [a.] Edinburgh, UK, EH17 8PR

COLLINS, KEVIN P.
[b.] 4 November 1945, High-a-Walton, Nr. Preston, Lancs; [p.] Peter and Catherine Collins; [m.] Eileen Collins, 12 November 1994; [ch.] one daughter, step-daughter, one stepson, 6 grandchildren; [ed.] St. Mary's Sec, Modern Bamber Bridge, Nr. Preston, Lancs; [occ.] Security Officer; [memb.] Distinguished Member. International Society of Poets (UK).; [hon.] Editor's Awards (1996), (1997), (1997) International Society of Poets, Romantic Poet of the year "Anchor Books Peterborough".; [oth. writ.] Several poems published by Triumph House—Peterborough, Anchor Books Anthologies, "Poetry Today", "Poetry Guild '97") "Poetry Guild '97", "International Library of Poets", " Arrival Press", "Anchor Books"; [pers.] My poems are a reflection of life which consists of pain, sorrow, love, and happiness which we all experience.; [a.] Melbourne, Hertfordshire, UK, SG8 6HX

COLLINS, LILIAN
[b.] 2 August 1957, Cardiff; [p.] James and Sheila Gauci; [m.] Michael Collins, 22 July 1978; [ch.] Matthew, Diane and Monique; [ed.] Willows High School; [occ.] Housewife; [memb.] Metropolitan Health Club; [pers.] I dedicate this poem to my sister Maria. For being the beautiful, caring person that she was. The courage and tenderness she showed throughout her illness, will remain with me forever, is will her smile. To Mum, thank you for loving us, all unconditionally. I love you Lilian; [a.] Cardiff, Wales, UK, CF2 2SX

COLLINS, MARIE BRUCE
[pen.] Bruce Collins; [b.] 20 October 1963, Edinburgh; [p.] Ann Bruce Collins; [ch.] Bonny Bruce Collins; [ed.] Theiseis, 'O' Level, City and Guilds; [occ.] Out of work actor; [memb.] Equity; [oth. writ.] Plenty but have not been established, (Med!); [pers.] I think that exhalation, is the only way, to exalt, your metaphysical, points, of view.; [a.] Cambridge, Cambridgeshire, UK, CB9 9JQ

CONCHAR, CATHERINE FULTON
[b.] 19 November 1971; Irvine, Scotland; [p.] John Conchar, Isobel Conchar; [ed.] Cumnock Academy, University of Aberdeen, University of Nottingham; [occ.] personnel assistant, Nottinghamshire County Council; [hon.] MA (hons) History of Art/History, MA Mediaeval History, Advanced Diploma in Adult Education; [pers.] Unless we dare to be useless and unimaginative we will never succeed; [a.] Nottingham, Nottinghamshire

CONNOLLY, HELEN
[b.] 13 February 1953, Glasgow; [p.] James Duncan, Mary Duncan; [m.] Joseph Connolly, 5 March 1970; [ch.] Susan Jane, Julie Ann; [occ.] Administrative Manager; [oth. writ.] Short stories—unpublished; [pers.] Writings inspired by the "Thistle".; [a.] Invergordon, Ross-Shire, UK, IV18 0NG

CONTRACTOR, ANAHITE
[b.] 14 September 1962, Bombay, India; [p.] Amy and Jamshyd Contractor; [ed.] M.A. (1985) English Literature, M.A. (1989) Art Criticism registered for PhD. (Sylvia Plath) Maharaja Sayajirao University, Baroda, India; [occ.] Writer, Art Critic; [oth. writ.] Essay in a recent anthology on Indian Art, about 500 articles on Art and Architecture published in Indian newspapers, catalogues, scripts for videos on art, Art Consultant for film on art produced by the Indian Ministry, Foreign Affairs, Avante Garde forms and writing for children.; [pers.] Life reveals to me, a dazzling complexity, and I mean to cull the occasional miracle from it.; [a.] Baroda, India, 390 002

COOPER, CLAIRE
[b.] 4 December 1981, Dundonald Hospital, Northern Ireland; [ed.] I attend Movilla High School and I am currently on my last year. My subjects include both English and English Literature.; [pers.] In war, it is my belief that the soldiers are the victims. I have been greatly influenced by Wilfred Owen, I would like to say a big thank you to my history teacher, Mr. McMullan, for 'widening my horizons' on warfare. Also to my English teacher, Mr. Hawthorne, who has helped me lot and encouraged me greatly.; [a.] Newtownards, UK, BT23 3YN

COOPER, NORA KATHLEEN
[b.] 14 August 1934, Glossop, Derbyshire; [p.] Edgar Hallam, Ellen Hallam; [m.] George Ernest Cooper, 11 July 1953; [ch.] Norman, Leslie, Derek, Joy, Diane, Roger; [ed.] Whitfield School, Glossop, Derbyshire, West End School, Glossop, Derbyshire; [occ.] Farmer's Wife; [oth. writ.] Several poems.; [pers.] I think I am very lucky to have my poetry published, I hope whoever reads my poem will enjoy it.; [a.] New Mills, Derbyshire, UK, SK22 4QN

COOPER, PETER S. A.
[b.] 16 March 1915; [p.] H. Charles Cooper (of Manchester) and Louise Florence Cooper (nee Smith) (of Plymouth); [m.] Angela Cooper (Nee Stranzl of Austria, Deceased); [ed.] St. Christopher's School, Letchworth; [occ.] Freelance Translator, Chief Translator at General Electric Co. (1948-1963); [memb.] English-Speaking Union, Institute of Linguists, Publicity Club of London, Anglo-Austrian Society, Trollope Society, Georgian Group, Irish Georgian Society; [oth. writ.] "Irmgard und Ian" (Munich, 1961) German translation of "Lake Isle of Innisfree" (W.B. Yeats) in "The Linguist" (1990). Since 1994: 8 poems published in anthologies by Poetry Now (and Anchor Books) Peterborough and 1 by Beyond the Cloister Publications, of Brighton.; [pers.] Flo, the subject of all my poems, hails from the Emerald Isle, lives on the Sussex coast and has most wonderfully transformed my life.

COSTELLO, EDWARD
[b.] 19-9-1926; Waterford,Eire; [p.] Edward and Sara;[m.] Catherine; 1949; [ch.] Jacqueline and Catherine; [ed.] Taught by nuns for six years in convent, four and a half years in Monastery School by Christian Brothers; [occ.] retired; racing carriage builder; [hon.] Editor's Choice Award as author of "Dunblane" in Quiet Moments; [oth.writ.] "Dunblane" published and many others unpublished—not yet submitted; [pers.] My greatest pleasure apart from writing my poems is the pleasure I'm told others get in reading them. I have to thank the nuns for teaching me to write poetry and God for the gift of inspiration. I wrote many poems for servicemen to send home during World War II; [a.] Bushey, Hertfordshire.

COULSTON, LINDA
[b.] 12 February 1954, Merseyside; [m.] George Coulston; [ch.] Graham, Helen; [occ.] Housewife; [pers.] Words are priceless and for all to share.; [a.] Warrington, Cheshire, UK, WA4 3BD

COUNIHAN, RUTH
[pen.] Rue; [b.] 29 September 1972, UK; [p.] James and Catherine Counihan; [ed.] St. Teresa's Convent, Effingham, UK and Convent of Mercy, Kilrush, Co. Clare Ireland; [occ.] Office Manager, Acromil, Shannon, Co, Clare, Ireland; [memb.] Kilrush Western Yacht Club; [hon.] Diploma in Business studies and currently enrolled for 2 year IC Accountants course; [pers.] I try to be as modest as I can. Influenced greatly by Shelley and Poe; [a.] Kilrush, Co Clare, UK

COWDELL, ALISON
[b.] 4 January 1979, Dudley; [p.] Rosemary Cowdell and Ivan Cowdell; [ed.] Ellowes Hall AM School, and 6th form, Roehampton University; [occ.] Student and P/T chef; [memb.] Marilyn Harris School of dancing, Ellowes Hall Scuba Club; [hon.] Advanced Royal Academy ballet, Advanced I.S.T.D tap and modern.; [oth. writ.] Fictional short stories, collection of poems (not published); [pers.] I try to imagine ways in which life arrived on this planet, and how it has developed into this complicated mass of emotional humans. I seek to make sense of this world in which we live, we must, while we're here.; [a.] Dudley, West Midlands, UK, DY3 2RR

COYLE, EVELYN
[pen.] Eva Ceeye; [b.] 30 December 1946, Foxpoint; [p.] Deceased; [m.] Separated, 12 April 1969; [ch.] Three; [ed.] Primary and Vocational School; [occ.] Housewife, Secretary; [oth. writ.] Short Story Comp.—Harvest Morning Visitor, Poetry Comp.—Waves of Peace; [pers.] Live a quiet simple life. Being free of stress one's mind has room to think.; [a.] Ballina, Mayo, Ireland

COZENS, ROBERT JOHN
[pen.] Cozen Robbie; [b.] 1 May 1950, The Villa, Brinton; [p.] Dick and Iris Cozens; [ed.] Brinton C.P. School, Melton Constable Sec. Mod. Kingslynn Tech.', evening classes, Plymouth Marine College, Life in the Royal Airforce Marine Sqdn.; [occ.] Agency employee, Cox in Seaman, RYA Costal Skipper; [memb.] The Ocean Youth Club, The Air Sea Rescue Marine Craft Section's Club, (A.S.R.M.C.S.C.), The Vampire Club (Blood Doner); [hon.] R.Y.A. Costal Skipper's Certificate. Being thanked by 4 of my friends and their families for saving their lives over the years this is a real honour; [oth. writ.] Short stories, one currently in a competition with the B.B.C. more poetry, stories about my village 1,950-2,000 in progress. Articles to 'Yachting Monthly' (not yet accepted?) also to 'Sailing Today', letters in newspapers.; [pers.] "Mother Earth", Our Planet Home, this beautiful globe is out in rough sea. I see her as a ship in desire's sending out a "May Day". We must help her, the crew don't care but we must. If we pollute our home, she some how will go on not us.; [a.] Brinton, Norfolk, UK, NR24 2QQ

CRACKNELL, MARIA
[b.] 9 October 1975, Welwyn Gen City; [p.] Dick and Sue Cracknell; [ed.] Presdales Secondary; [occ.] Assistant Manager all days in Ware; [oth. writ.] Twelve other poems published up to now in various books.; [pers.] I want to thank my family: Dick, Sue and Eve Cracknell, Lee, Hannan, Emmie and Davey. Also my close friends, Dean for the inspiration of this poem. To Ross Livermore, my friend I told you! To Ricky Archer, thanks for being a great friend.; [a.] Ware, Herts, UK, SG12 7HN

CRAWFORD, MISS DONNA-MARIE
[b.] 30 September 1972; [p.] Peter Vincent Crawford (D), Winifred Crawford; [ed.] University of Plymouth—BSc (Hons) Sociology/Psychology-graduated 6/96. Previously—Cornwall College of further Higher Education, Pool, Redruth, Cornwall.; [occ.] Student of the Institute of Traditional Herbal Medicine and Aromathery.; [memb.] Mensa Membership Pending. I have exhibited paintings in both watercolours and oils throughout Cornwall.; [hon.] Kernow Award for Poetry; [oth. writ.] Poetry published in Crowan Parish Local Magazine in Cornwall.; [pers.] The journey of life can feel a lonely one. Through the words of poetry one may find a soulmate, to tread each road along side.; [a.] Basingstoke, Hampshire, UK, RG23 8AQ

CROWTHER, NANCIE
[b.] 23 October 1931, Portsmouth; [p.] Ronald and Eva Wells; [m.] Frank; [ch.] Three; [ed.] Worthing High School; [occ.] Retired; [hon.] School Cert and Matric Exemption; [oth. writ.] Unpublished poems; [pers.] Reading is one of life's greatest pleasures.; [a.] Worthing, W. Sussex, UK

CUNNINGHAM, KAREN
[pen.] Karen Cunningham; [b.] 4 May 1983, Castlebar; [p.] Noel and Noreen Cunningham; [ed.] St. Angela's National School and still attending St. Joseph's Secondary School; [occ.] Student; [memb.] Order of Malta, Shotokhan Karate Club; [pers.] I try to examine the forces of life and death in my writings.; [a.] Castlebar, Mayo, Ireland

CURTIS, RICHARD A.
[b.] 10 August 1942, City of Bath; [p.] Wm. A. Curtis, Muriel M. Curtis; [m.] Susan, 5 September 1992; [ch.] Jane, Severine, Justine; [ed.] Oldfield Boys Secondary Modern, Bath, Alexandra Park Secondary Modern, Bristol; [occ.] Heavy Good Vehicle Driver; [oth. writ.] Several poems entitled 'Poppies' (1st World War), 'The Black Stuff' (Coal Mining), 'The Fly Fisher', none published to date.; [pers.] The larger part of my working life, was working in agriculture (30 yrs). I have always had a deep love of the countryside and animals. I adore fly-fishing and visit the Outer Hebrides every year with my wife and dog.; [a.] Frampton Cotterell, South Glos, UK, BS17 2AV

DAVIDSON, MRS. DEBBIE MARIA
[b.] 28 February 1968, Guildford; [p.] Mr. B. Gray; [m.] Gene Paul Davidson; [ch.] Chantelle—10, Leanne—5; [ed.] Broadwater Secondary School, Farncombe, Surrey; [occ.] Sales Assistant for Corop.; [memb.] Langstone Harbour Fishermans Association; [oth. writ.] I have written many poem on many subjects as presents for friends and family. But I have never taken it any further because I was insure until now.; [pers.] I have enjoyed writing poetry for many years and after many years of pushing from the family I decided to enter a competition and am glad I did.; [a.] Portsmouth, Hampshire, UK, PO4 8LP

DAVIES, DENNIS N.
[b.] 20 February 1937, West Bromwich; [p.] William and Edith Davies; [m.] Marie, 16 June 1962; [ch.] Jason; [ed.] Church of England; [occ.] Production Operative; [oth. writ.] Assorted poems for forward press—International Library of

Poetry, Poetry Today.; [pers.] I have found a great way to express people and different times in my life served in British Army as a driver in R.S.C. Eyapt, Tripoli.; [a.] Telford, Shropshire, UK, TF2 6RA

DAVIES, MRS. J. A.
[pen.] Jean Anderson Davies; [b.] 2 July 1921, Durham; [p.] Mr. and Mrs. J. Lock; [m.] Stanley Charles Davies, October 1942; [ch.] 1 daughter, twin sons; [ed.] Modern Secondary; [occ.] Housewife; [hon.] The Editor's Choice Award from previous Competition; [oth. writ.] "Too Young" published in "Jewels of the Imagination"; [pers.] I am still writing poetry and enjoy the happiness I seem to give its family and friends with my thoughts of them. A whole new world is open to us with precious words.; [a.] Crawley, Sussex, UK, RH10 4JN

DAVIES, PATRICIA
[b.] 20 October 1938, Cambridge; [p.] Alice Tomlinson (now 83); [m.] Trevor Davies, 2 April 1960; [ch.] Phillip Davies, Stephen Davies; [ed.] Croft and Yarpole Village School then from 11 years old Leominster Grammar School; [occ.] A receptionist at 'Hergest Croft Gardens'; [memb.] 'The Kilvert Society'; [oth. writ.] 'When', a poem about the tragedy and destruction of nuclear war; [pers.] I am very aware of the beauty of this world we live in, and the creatures who share this earth with us, I try to reflect this in my poems.; [a.] Kington, Herefordshire, UK, HR5 3AA

DAVIS, PETER
[b.] 8 November 1937, Birkenhead; [p.] Ada-Mary and Frank; [m.] Ann Elizabeth, 17 October 1957; [ch.] One— Jason; [ed.] Degree (Honours) Fine Art; [occ.] Sculptor and Designer; [oth. writ.] Poems and short stories.; [pers.] 'Observing life, is almost like living it.'; [a.] Longstanton, Cambridge, UK, CB4 5BZ

DE BOER, ROGER FREDERIC
[pen.] Penregor (v. occ.); [b.] 4 April 1946, Moseley, Birmingham; [p.] Henri A. and Winifred A. De Boer; [ed.] St. Laurence C of E, Northfield (1950-57), Kings Norton Grammar School (1957-1965); [occ.] Civil Servant; [memb.] Society of Civil Service Authors (Incl. Poetry Workshop), Battery Vehicle Society (B.V.S.), Coventry Diecast Model Club (C.D.M.C.), Historic Commercial Vehicle Club (H.C.V.C.), Model Bus Federation (M.B.F.), Council Vehicle Society (C.V.S.), Mechanical Horse Club—(Abb. to Misc. Transport Societies); [hon.] Highly commended in 1996 poet of the year competition (Hilton House Publishers) for "Chinese Landscape" poem (1987); [oth. writ.] "Birmingham's Electric Dustcarts" (1990), Poetry Collections: "A Birmingham Collection" (1991 and 1997), "Mainly Russia of Other Lands" (1993) (Self-published), contributions in "Focus" (AW/SCSA), "Purple Patch" (Poems), "Wheelspin" (House Magazine of C.D.M.C.) (Prose Articles); [pers.] Always strive to be interesting favourite people of history—artists Soc. Matthew Arnold, Georges Bizet and Vincent Van Gogh (Works).; [a.] Northfield, Birmingham, UK, B31 2QW

DE-ALWIS, RUVINA
[pen.] Ruvina De-Alwis; [b.] 4 October 1972, Maradana, Ceylon; [p.] Mithra De-Alwis and Champa De-Alwis; [ed.] School, College, University (BSC Environmental Science)—never completing the third. Mostly self-taught, or self-educated with an instinctive love of philosophy and poetry.; [occ.] (Unofficial) studying or training with Tibetan Buddhist Master. (Sifu Simon Wong); [memb.] Member of Yellow Dragon Centre, (Ancient Chinese Arts and Philosophy). Member of True Buddha School (Jen Wai Tong) Tibetan Buddhism.; [oth. writ.] The poem "Re-Source" is actually part of a series of poems, from my manuscript, entitled "A Prayer for the Dye-Ing", which I am trying to publish, at present. (It touches on the stages of visionary experience.);

[pers.] There are many forms, types, levels and even realms of knowledge, but ultimately only wisdom arises, from emptiness.

DELAMORE, NOELEEN
[b.] 29 June 1957; Old St. Helen's Hosp., Ponsonby, Auckland N.Z.; [p.] Barry and Beryl Delamore; [m.] Lawrence V. Pitman (deceased 10 May 1991 in a car accident); 22 October 1988; [ch.] Jeremy, 20 years, Barry-Len, 15 years, and Elizabeth, 11 years; [ed.] Being rebellious, I was expelled from High School at 14 years of age. As an adult, I studied and qualified as Enrolled Nurse, Print Journalist, Television and Video Production Journalism Course, Advanced Secretarial Studies, Introduction to Community Work and Teaching; [occ.] At present, I am on a widow pension and write from home; [memb.] I sang in a local Whangazei Band for many years, wrote my first song when I was ten years old. I studied the piano, ballet, and marching as a child; [hon.] The honours in my life have been the birth of my awesome children and my marriage to my precious deceased husband; [oth. writ.] Seven books of poetry unpublished to this date—"Grieving Sibling," "Grieving Woman," "Grieving Widow," "Grieving No-more," "Grieving Mother," "Grieving Girlfriend," "Grieving Friend." I have also completely finished a book on widowhood from a biblical perspective. I am now writing my ninth book, discussing the times we live in P.T.O.; [pers.] My aim is to help bring spiritual and emotional healing to those suffering through the loss of a loved one through my writings. I admire the writings of Helen Steiner Rice; [a.] Whangazei, Hikurangi, Northland, New Zealand

DENNING, CLAIRE REBBECCA
[b.] 23 August 1980, Bradford; [p.] Susan Denning and Stuart Denning; [ed.] Rhodesway School; [occ.] Student at Rhodesway School; [hon.] I achieved a Business Diploma; [oth. writ.] Several other poems, "Tears", "The Lonely Dove", "Forever I Sleep", "Great Fields", and "The See-Through Girl". Many more are on their way.; [pers.] I was inspired by other poets and the enthusiasm from a past teacher and present friend, Mr. Phil Stead helped me to achieve my potential.; [a.] Bradford, West Yorkshire, UK, BD15 9JA

DEVLIN, MISS HELEN
[b.] 17 February 1970, Chatham; [p.] Angela Devlin; [ed.] Rainham School for girls; [occ.] Photographer; [pers.] I feel poetry provides a window on the inner soul and I hope this poem touches the reader in the way that poetry I've read has touched me. Poetry to me is very special and will always hold a part of my being.; [a.] Rainham, Kent

DICKINSON, DENNIS
[pen.] Dennis Dickinson; [b.] 24 February 1945, Hull; [p.] Lilly and George Dickinson; [m.] Joan Davey, 1 May 1992; [ch.] Victoria Dickinson; [ed.] Secondary Modern; [occ.] Builder; [oth. writ.] Various poems; [pers.] Having had a tear-away lifestyle and a moderate education. I wanted to have done or said one thing in my life for my own satisfaction.; [a.] Woodhall Spa, Lincolnshire, UK, LN10 6UU

DIMOND, JOANNE
[pen.] Jessie Mallone; [b.] 20 September 1982, Caerphilly; [p.] Elaine Dimond and Roger Dimond; [ed.] Coed-y-Brain, Infants/Juniors. Lewis Girls Comprehensive School; [occ.] School Girl, Lewis Girls Comprehensive School; [pers.] In my poetry I reflect other people's sadness and try and understand what they go through. I am inspired by music and the books I read.; [a.] Caerphilly, Caerphilly, UK, CF83 3NA

DOBBS, GILLIAN
[b.] London; [ed.] BA Degree (Open University); [hon.] Diploma European Humanities

DODDS, GODFREY
[b.] 17 April 1926, Newcastle upon Tyne; [oth. writ.] A collection entitled 'A Piece of Blue' is available from the Pentland Press Ltd 1 Hutton Close, South Church, Bishop Auckland, Durham, England also at Raleigh, North Carolina, USA. A poem included in each of the collections 'Quiet Moments' and 'A Passage in Time'.; [pers.] A seventy year old Northumbrian whose poetry is an expression of feelings and philosophy covering a wide range of ideas.; [a.] Croydon, Surrey, UK, CR0 1HQ

DRURY, MONICA EILEEN
[b.] 2 June 1920, Manchester; [p.] Sydney Jennings and Emily Jennings; [m.] James Drury, 26 August 1939; [ch.] Michael, Shaun Thomas, Gaynor Mary; [ed.] Elementary; [occ.] Retired; [memb.] C 3 A (College of 3rd Age); [hon.] Open College Federation Adult Education Credit one at levels one and two.; [oth. writ.] Poems and short stories published. Book of self work of poems. Published, local writers group.; [pers.] I strive to write with a woman's inner feelings. Influenced mainly by inspirational poets.; [a.] Manchester, Lancs, UK, M9 8PB

DUARTE, ANGIE
[b.] 4 November 1953, London, UK; [p.] Chris, Rene Constandinou; [m.] Eusebio Duarte, 21 July 1993; [ch.] Andrew Graeme, Christopher George, Leana Marie; [ed.] Weir Hall Comprehensive, Paris Academy of Fashion (Oxford St); [occ.] Housewife; [pers.] I have been writing for myself since the age of 14 and my dream has always been to share it. If it helps to ease . . . then I've succeeded. "I write what I feel and I feel what I see. My pen and paper have always understood and comforted me".; [a.] New Southgate, London, UK, N11 2RJ

DUFFTY, VICKIE-JEAN
[b.] 9 June 1976; [oth. writ.] poetry collection entitled "Passion" being currently published by Paper Doll Publishers September 1997; [pers.] Poetry reminds us who we are; there are no limitations and poetry takes us further; [a.] Bracknell, Berkshire

DUNCAN, CRAIG MCK
[b.] 28 January 1949, Airdrie, Scotland; [p.] William Duncan, Elizabeth Baxter; [m.] Paulette Eichperger, 22 May 1975; [ch.] Christopher, Douglas; [ed.] University of Glasgow, University of Boston; [occ.] Marketing Director; [a.] Brussels, Belgium, 1200

DUNCAN, REBECCA
[b.] 15 August 1968; Denver, Colorado; [p.] Gypsie and Phread Duncan; [ch.] Jamie, Josephine, Catherine, Matthew; [ed.] Methwold high School; [occ.] Fulltime mother and housewife; [oth. writ.] Many poems for my personal enjoyment, family and friends; [pers.] The thing is that many good poems are triggered by personal tragedy, but also by great happiness, never by anything in the middle of life; [a] Wisbech, Cambs

DUNNE, BARRY DAVID KEVIN
[b.] 10 December 1968, Fleetwood, Milton Lodge; [p.] David Sharples, Margaret Doyle; [ch.] Liam Sharples; [ed.] Lime House School, North Lakes, Cumbria, 3 Eng, Hist, Maths, Geog, Quals. Economics; [occ.] Fisherman; [memb.] Fell Running Association; [hon.] Music prize, offshore fire-fighting and survival cert., farming, cert, building cert.; [oth. writ.] Children's stories, short stories, poems and songs, none published just a hobby.; [pers.] Educated at Lime House Boarding School in the Lake District I enjoyed English and Music. I have written children's stories and enjoy anything to do with the outdoors and how people used to love.; [a.] Fleetwood, Lancashire, UK, FY7 7HG

DYER, BARBARA
[b.] 9 July 1926, Portsmouth; [p.] Leslie and Lilian Slade; [m.] Archie Dyer, 28 March 1959; [ch.] Lesley Jane, Anthony and Sara; [ed.] Army Education School; [occ.] Retired; [oth. writ.] 1 poem published in "Doors 9" in 1981 (A Dorset poetry magazine), 50 unpublished. Selection of children's stories as yet unpublished.; [pers.] In writing poetry, I find I can write in words my feelings which often I am unable to express in speech.; [a.] Warminster, Wiltchire, UK, BA12 8EQ

EAGLE, EVELYN MARY
[b.] 15 February 1926, London; [m.] Douglas Eagle (Deceased), 22 March 1947; [ch.] David, Terry, Mandy and Pipe and 10 Grandchildren; [occ.] Retired Housewife; [memb.] International Society of Poets.; [oth. writ.] Poetry children's books and tapes for my grandchildren.; [pers.] My writing reflects, the way I see life, an expression of my soul, and a never-ceasing amazement of the wonders of our world.; [a.] Malvern, Worcs, UK, WR14 1BD

EARLEY, ANN MARGARET
[b.] 31 July 1928, Hull; [p.] Hubert and Marjorie Rafferty; [m.] Dennis Ronald Earley, 4 January 1955; [ch.] Brendan Damian, Fiona Justin, Willstan, Mary-Anne and Aidan; [ed.] St. Mary's Priory, Princethorpe, Holy Child Convent Harrogate, Athol Crescent, Edinburgh (Domestic Science) Villa Beata, Fribourg, Switzerland, London College of Secretaries, Queensgate; [occ.] Semi-retired/Carer of the elderly, children and babies; [memb.] Member of several drama and operatic societies, over the years, but not currently; [hon.] Nothing specific just school certificate, Domestic Science Certificate and Secretarial Certificate and colours and cups for games and gymnasium at school; [oth. writ.] Only one other poem published in local newspaper, and one letter in a national newspaper.; [pers.] It sadness me to know that everything that was once considered bad is now quite acceptable, and I'm sure that, if there is a God, He must be weeping for the world He created.; [a.] Holme upon Spalding Moor, York, UK, Y04 4HT

EASTON, ANN
[b.] 30 November 1940, Garvery, NJ; [p.] Richard Benson, Violet Benson; [m.] Alexander Easton, 16 November 1959; [ch.] Christopher, Lorraine and Alexander; [ed.] Alexandra College, Dublin; [occ.] Housewife, Bank Officials; [hon.] Music Piano Forte; [oth. writ.] Poetry published by the Poetry Guild and Poetry Today; [pers.] I consider poetry to be one of the purest forms of writing. Yates and Wordsworth have been my greatest inspiration.; [a.] Bangor Down, UK, BT20 4UA

EL ATTAR, DEENA
[pen.] Tracey; [b.] 7 September 1983, Pittsburgh, PA, USA; [p.] Dr. M. S. Elattar, Mrs. Nermine Raslan; [occ.] High School Student; [pers.] Sister's name: Hania; [a.] Alexandria, Egypt

ELFORD, JOHN BERNARD
[pen.] Gilgalad The Gallant; [b.] 18 May 1967, Mackay, Queensland, Australia; [p.] Shirley Anne and Trevor John Elford; [m.] Wendy Christine Elford, 15 May 1993; [ch.] Jessica Anne Elford; [ed.] Year 12 Aldridge State High School, Maryborough Qld. Australia; [occ.] Carpenter; [oth. writ.] Two other published poems "My Love a Butterfly", and "Springtime of My Heart". I also have a variety of unpublished poems.; [pers.] In Australia writing romantic poetry is hardly an acceptable pastime for a young bloke. If by chance any of my mates happen to see or hear some of my work I'll bluff my way through with a detrimental comment like "The women like that sort of thing." Often times I wonder of the society that shapes such a response. However in reality I'm not a closet poet and such a reaction is more of a running joke that anything else. In a country that tends to bury its feelings I enjoy prospecting for the essence of emotion. I love poetry and will always be a true blue romantic at heart.; [a.] Kingaroy, Queensland, Australia, 4610

ELLIOTT, CRISPIN JOHN
[pen.] C. J. Jonnie; [b.] 15 February 1962, Windsor; [p.] Adrian Elliott, Barbara Elliott; [ed.] St. Edwards School, Oxford, St. Peters College, Oxford University; [occ.] Solicitor; [memb.] Datchet Players Amateur Dramatics Society, Datchet Conference St. Vincent De Paul Society; [hon.] Scholarship Modern History—St Peter's College, Oxford. First Class Honours - Modern History; [oth. writ.] 'Songs From The Slump'—unpublished collection of light verse. 'The Disturbed'—Novel—comedy thriller about noisy neighbours and airports.; [pers.] I try to aim for the 'Bigger Picture'. My fascinations range from the book of job and the psalms (for me, mind bending in their poetic power) to the verses of Albert Einstein.; [a.] Ascot, Berkshire, UK, SL5 9EB

ELLIOTT, SHEILA
[b.] 30 October 1961, Coleraine, N. Ireland; [p.] William Henry Chambers, Jean Chambers; [m.] William Elliott, 9 August 1991; [ch.] Richard-4; [ed.] Portrush Primary School, Bushmills Grammar School (Later to be known as Dunluce School), University of Ulster Coleraine; [occ.] Primary School Teacher at Portrush Primary (my old school!); [hon.] B.A. (Hons) in Education with English literature and language as secondary subjects (graduated July 1984); [oth. writ.] Scripts for school concerts. Also from time to time I've had the urge to write poems, short pieces of prose inspired by anything from humorous family happenings to tragic National events. Never submitted any for publication before.; [pers.] The poem 'Remembrance Sunday—Enniskillen 1987" was written on a scrap of paper as I travelled in my father's car with news of the bombing just being broadcast on the car radio.; [a.] Portrush, Co Antrim, UK, BT56 8HB

ELLIS, ISABEL E.
[pen.] "Berlewen", Old Cornish Meaning Morning Star; [b.] 1 April 1932, Cornwall; [p.] Violel James and Glen James; [m.] Derek Ellis, 2 June 1951; [ch.] Angela Christine Ellis; [ed.] St. Erme County Primary, Plus "The School Of Life"; [occ.] Retired; [memb.] Local Garden Club, Ramblers Association, R.S.P.B. Local Ladies Choir; [oth. writ.] One article published in Canadian Bruce Trail Mag and poem "My Cornwall" currently with Vancouver Cornish Association, once in local Mag. Plus other poems.; [pers.] My inspiration comes mainly from nature itself, in particular all aspects of plant life. Wildlife too especially our feathered friends. Plus all things Cornish of which I am extremely proud.; [a.] Newquay, Cornwall, UK, TR7 2HJ

ELSEY, KATHERINE S.
[b.] 30 September 1981, Abergavenny; [p.] Alyn Elsey and Ruth Elsey; [ed.] Oakdale Comprehensive School; [occ.] Pupil (year 11); [memb.] North Gwent Youth Orchestra, Oakdale Youth Choir; [hon.] Associated Board Grade 5 Violin, Grade 3 Piano; [pers.] A poem is written by the poet to enable the reader to sense the same things as the writer. In 'The Somme' the senses are used to reveal the true horrors of war, the inhumanity of man against man and the ability of mankind to view these horrors with indifference provided the horrors have no affect on them.; [a.] Aberbeeg, Gwent, UK, NP3 2DA

EMMINS, MARTIN VICTOR
[pen.] Martin Victor Emmins; [b.] 22 October 1960, Taplow Berks; [p.] Jean Emmins and Thomas Charles Emmins; [ed.] Holland Park Comprehensive London two A-Levels for Art and Design and Science; [occ.] Was a specialist driver working for the Royal Parks in London; [hon.] Have won seven trophies for photography; [oth. writ.] Has written seventeen poems of which four have been published, and also wrote a science fiction book containing 94,000 words.; [pers.] I am sending in this poem in memory of our son who died suddenly on 9 November 1996 before he could see any of his work published.; [a.] Great Yarmouth, Norfolk, UK, NR30 4NF

ENTICKNAPP, DANIEL
[b.] 10 January 1959, Hove; [occ.] Caretaker Cardinal Newman School; [pers.] I try to show love affection, and understanding in all of my poems.; [a.] Hove, Sussex, UK, BN3 5LB

ESTIEN, VEDA E.
[pen.] Eve Estien; [b.] 17 May, St. Mary, Jamaica; [p.] Deceased; [ed.] Jamaica, Primary Hillside School, Crandall High School; [oth. writ.] Unpublished (and others) Letter to Mother/The Voice of the Sea Beyond the Sea, Lady of Rosehall, Grandfather's Song at Twilight. Sound of Summer/Story in the Dark; [pers.] I thanked my mother for keeping the exercise book with some of my poems from school, until her death. It's given me pleasure in writing to please myself, and hope that listener/readers will enjoy what they hear.

ESUOLA, BAMIDELE ALAKE
[b.] 2 September 1969, London; [p.] Mr. and Mrs. Daramola Esuola; [ed.] Opebi Grammar School, Lagos Nigeria, Methodist Girls High School Lagos, Nigeria, Obafemi (Pharmacy) Awolowo University Ile-Ife, Nigeria (but course not completed); [occ.] Catering, I intend to be a pharmacist; [hon.] First Prizes in English Literature, General Science and Yoruba; [oth. writ.] Son and Daughter, I Have a Priority, Strangest Passion; [pers.] How high you go depends on how hard you try.; [a.] London, Middlesex, UK, N1 9AT

ETRIDGE, MISS KELLY
[b.] Dulwich; [p.] Linda and Doug Etridge; [ed.] Student at Kingsdale School Alleyn Park, Dulwich; [memb.] Dulwich Youth Orchestra Southwark Concert Band, Kingsdale Jazz Band and Percussion Ensemble; [oth. writ.] My poem "Exams" was published in Awaken to a Dream.; [pers.] I am not influenced by other writers. I have a style of my own very individual. I want to stay that way.; [a.] East Dulwich, London, UK, SE22 8RW

EVANS, CYRIL C.
[b.] 4 August 1904, Ebbwvale, S. Kent; [occ.] Long retired; [oth. writ.] Local poems.; [pers.] Long retired local government servant

EVANS, DAWN KIRSTY
[b.] 10 June 1986, Wrexham; [p.] Steven Evans and Glenys Evans; [ed.] Black Lane C.P. School Pentre Broughton; [occ.] Still at school; [pers.] I would like to thank Mrs. Lloyd for introducing me to poetry and my Mum and Dad for all their encouragement.; [a.] Wrexham, Wrexhamborough, UK, LL11 6AG

EVANS, JACQUELINE
[b.] 28 April 1970, Keighley, W Yorks; [p.] Michael and Mary Evans; [ed.] The Holy Family School, Keighley, St Mary's University College, Middlesex; [occ.] Actress; [hon.] B.A. (Hons) Drama, English Literature; [pers.] My writing is a vehicle for self-preservation, exploration and fulfilment. My influences lie with authors Brian Patten and parodist Wendy Cope.; [a.] Keighley, West Yorkshire, UK, BD21 1BN

EVANS, KATE
[b.] 23 October 1980, Pen-Coed, M-Glam; [p.] Ann Ward and Phillip Evans; [a.] Neath, W. Glamorgan, UK, SA11 3YL

EWEN, JENNY H.
[b.] 5 January 1946, Rosehearty, Aberdeenshire; [p.] Alexander and Helen Ritchie; [m.] John Ewen, 29 May 1965; [ch.] Helen, Isobel, Jennifer, Emma; [occ.] Housewife; [a.] Macduff, Aberdeenshire, Scotland, AB44 1XT

EWUOSHO, LARA
[b.] 15 June 1965, Lagos, Nigeria; [p.] Mr. S Ewuosho, Mrs. S. Ewuosho; [ed.] Archbishop Aggey Memorial Secondary School, University of Lagos, Radio Nigeria Training School. (All in Lagos, Nigeria W. Africa); [occ.] Free Lance Broadcast Journalist; [memb.] Nigeria Union of Journalists (NUJ). Member, Cork Women's Poetry Circle Ireland; [hon.] B. A. French, National Winner, "International Year of the Child" (IYC) Essay Competition. (1979) Nomination, National Youth Service Corps State Awards, Katsina Nigeria; [oth. writ.] Reports on women's Health, such as the scourge of 'Vesico Vaginal Fistulae' for T.V. as a specialist reporter, Katsina, Nigeria. Produced and presented many scripts of 'Soul Lift' for voice of Nigeria. Poems and more poems.; [pers.] I aim to weave words that portray the power of the essence of man, regardless of the odds. I have been intrigued and influenced by modern African poets: Wole Soyinka, Ben Okri, and Irish, Patrick Savanagh.; [a.] Cork City, Cork, Ireland

FAZAKERLEY, MR. T.
[b.] 25 March 1947, Mawdesley; [p.] Thomas Fazakerley, Elizabeth Fazakerley; [m.] Sheila Fazakerley, 26 November 1966; [ch.] Mark (Deceased), Ian, Lisa; [ed.] St Mary's Secondary Modern; [occ.] Working Supervisor Environment Agency; [pers.] To see everything no matter how small. To get great joy from the wonder of nature.; [a.] Ormskirk, Lancashire, UK, L40 2QS

FEARNEHOUGH, EVELYN
[b.] 30 September 1910, Milton, Stoke-on-Trent; [m.] Harold Wilson Fearnehough, 27 December 1937; [ch.] 1 daughter, and 1 son; [ed.] Certificated Teacher trained at Southlands College, Wimbledon 1929-1931; [occ.] Retired Headmistress; [memb.] NAHT (Pre Retirement); [oth. writ.] 3 Novels written, but not accepted for publication. Award for original embroidery at School of Art, Chesterfield 1942.; [pers.] Music is my only inspiration for writing, and occasionally, painting. Without it, life would not be worth living.; [a.] Derby, Derbyshire, UK, DE22 2UT

FENSOM, PAUL T.
[b.] 18 May 1954, Gomersal; [p.] George, Jenny; [ed.] Birkenshaw Secondary; [occ.] C.N.C. Machine Operative; [oth. writ.] A book of poems accepted but awaiting publication. "The Reluctant Bachelor."; [pers.] There are no limits to anyone, only the limits they put on themselves! So draw eyes, break hearts, steal souls but be yourself.; [a.] Gomersal, West Yorks, UK, BD19 4QJ

FEREK, MARGARETA
[b.] 20 December 1982, Zagreb; [p.] Bozidar and Ivancica; [occ.] Pupil of XVIII. Gymnasium in Zagreb; [hon.] Editor's Choice Award presented by The International Library of Poetry, 1997; [oth. writ.] I write poems and lyrics in English being my second language. A poem published in the anthology "Jewels of the Imagination". One poem will be published in the anthology "Treasures", 1997.; [pers.] Life is an extensive question with many different answers, but only poetry could give us the right one.; [a.] Zagreb, Croatia, 10000

FINCH, KERRY ELLEN
[b.] 24 November 1976, Germany; [p.] John and Joan Finch; [ed.] Thomas Magnus Upper School, Newark, Nottinghamshire; [occ.] Supervisor/Catering Manageress; [pers.] You cannot hurt time, without hurting eternity.; [a.] Newark, Nottinghamshire, UK, NG24 2EZ

FINLAY, MR. JAMES R.
[pen.] James Sherwood; [b.] 26 September 1944, Bath; [p.] Mr. James Finlay and Mrs. Evelyn Selina Finlay; [ch.] James; [ed.] St. Johns Roman Catholic School, Bath, Somerset; [occ.] Gardener; [pers.] I was inspired to write this poem, "Oh Death" by the loss of two very good friends of mine, who died much too early in their lives.; [a.] Corsham, Wiltshire, UK, SN13 8LR

FINNIE, JEMMA
[pen.] Jade Gerrard; [b.] 19 September 1984, Peterhead; [p.] Brenda and Duncan Finnie; [ed.] Mintlaw Academy; [occ.] Budding Poet; [hon.] Many, quiet previously; [oth. writ.] Sun, and others not been replied to.; [pers.] When I am writing a poem I tell the truth. I don't just make it all up. I like to express my feelings; [a.] Mintlaw, Scotland, AB42 5BT

FISHER, SUE
[pen.] Sue; [b.] 6 April 1951, Barnes, London; [p.] Mr. and Mrs. R. N. Kerry; [m.] David Fisher, 27 August 1969; [ch.] Jason Fisher, Bruce, Gemma; [ed.] Went to school in London, educated at local schools in Barnes. Art is one of my favourite subjects and English which I passed exams on.; [occ.] Care Assistant in Residential Home in Sawtry; [hon.] I haven't any honors or awards maybe one day it will happen. I am still trying.; [oth. writ.] Written words for song about Vietnam in the seventies (Boats without a Hope). Poem published "In Poetry Now" local publication called "Gone"; [pers.] I have many poems written but not published. Would love to write short stories for children now I have a lot more time. My next idea for a poem will have to be about my work with the elderly—that could be interesting.; [a.] Sawtry, Cambs, UK, PE17 5SH

FLAMSON, BARBARA
[pen.] Barbara Frances; [b.] 17 September 1935, Whitwick, Leics; [p.] Mary Agnes and Thomas Wainwright; [m.] Denis; [ch.] Stephen, Jacqueline, Michael and Simon; [occ.] Housewife; [memb.] ISA song writing Asso. Ireland, Limerick City; [hon.] One award for poem; [oth. writ.] Book published, children's story; [pers.] I love my writing it gives me peace of mind, I also write songs and stories.; [a.] Ashby-de-la-Zonck, UK, LE65 1EG

FLOOD, CATHERINE
[b.] 9 December 1946, Dublin, Republic of Ireland; [p.] Catherine Smyth, John Flood; [m.] Professed Religious; [ed.] Mercy Secondary School, Inchicore Dublin, Carysfort Teacher Training College, Dublin; [occ.] Primary School Teacher; [memb.] I.N.T.O. (Irish National Teacher's Organization); [oth. writ.] Newsletter (Mercy Provincial); [pers.] In my writings try to reflect local issues, raise awareness to people's search for meaning in life. Influenced by Old and New Testament, and for the sheer joy of writing.; [a.] Dublin, Republic of Ireland

FORD, GEORGE JOHN
[b.] 3 July 1931, Edinburgh; [p.] Percival Hendry Ford, Christina Wilson Gold; [m.] Celia Reaburh Jones (Ford), 6 July 1971; [ch.] Kathryn, Jane Ford, Alan George Ford; [ed.] Abbey Hill Primary, Bellevue Secondary, Bellevue Night School; [occ.] Micro and Film Operator National Utility Services; [memb.] 1963 to present date 1997 Secretary—Treasure Forth 66 golf club Duddingston golf, club 1980-1997. Former member Edinburgh Ski Club, Former member Royal Edinburgh Photographic Society; [oth. writ.] Two poems published approx 1960, The Edinburgh Ski Club Magazines. Poems published.by The International Library of Poetry, "Awaken to a Dream"; [pers.] They say my grandfather wrote a poem or two and if my poems give pleasure to just one or two then it is a pleasure to write them for you. Grandfather's name: John Gold.; [a.] Edinburgh, Midlothian, UK, EH7 5PJ

FORREST, HAZEL
[b.] 7 September 1950, Wallsend-on-Tyne; [p.] Audrey, Margaret, Helena & Richard, William Brooks; [m.] David Forrest, 12 December 1970; [ch.] Paul David Forrest; [occ.] Sales Distributor; [oth. writ.] poems published in local newspaper. Also in anthology 'Quiet Moments' poem 'Existence' recorded on tape 'The Sound of Poetry', 1996; [pers.] The spiritual preparation for writing a poem is influenced by life itself. As long as there is life, I shall endeavour to write poetry.; [a.] Whitley Bay, Tyne & Wear

FORTUNE, MISS JACQUI D. P.
[pen.] Donna Starr; [b.] 31 January 1954, Hastings; [p.] Arthur Fortune, Margaret Fortune; [occ.] Care Assistant; [memb.] National Trust; [oth. writ.] I have written a few, but this is my first to be published.; [pers.] My inspiration for writing my poetry comes from everyday life, and the beautiful county that I live in Sussex, I wrote this poem for my partner Alan, Cheese Man.; [a.] Eastbourne, Sussex, UK, BN21 2LW

FRANCIS, KENNETH CHARLES
[b.] 21 March 1938, Swansea; [p.] Marjory and Charles Francis; [m.] Gwynneth Francis, 3 March 1963; [ch.] Wayne and Jane Francis; [ed.] Oxford Sts and Swansea College of Art; [occ.] University Technician (Ret); [memb.] Monkstone Cruising and Sailing Club; [hon.] Schools Scholarship Swansea College of Art; [oth. writ.] Several poems in Anthologies.; [pers.] My aim is to enrich the lives of others through my poetry and paintings.; [a.] Swansea, W. Glamorgan, UK, SA1 6XP

FRASER, LORRAINE DIANA
[pen.] Lorraine Diana Fraser; [b.] 19 May 1963, Montevideo—Uruguay, British Nationality; [p.] Charles Duncan Fraser, Ana Maria Fraser; [ch.] Jonathan Fernando, Malaga Fraser; [ed.] Universidad da Republica Del Uruguay/Theather Teacher, Escuela Technica—Ipsiproda—Peru Informatic Technique; [occ.] Material Manager; [oth. writ.] Several poems, beginning at 9 years old, never published them. This is the first time.; [pers.] I think that writing is the best way to express our deep feelings, and help us to reflect on what we really felt. Also we can help other people, showing that even if this world is getting cold, we can still have our heart warmth and sentimental.; [a.] Estoril, Portugal

FRATTALI, ALEXANDRA
[b.] 21 October 1976, London; [p.] Marcella Venturi, Rito Frattali; [ed.] St James Choir School—Grimsby and King Edward VI Grammar School Louth; [occ.] Student; [hon.] Having a poem published in "Awaken to a Dream"; [oth. writ.] "Youth" which was published by the International Library of Poetry and others which have only been seen by friends.; [pers.] I'd like to thank my family for believing in me and my friends who encouraged and helped me in the last 5 years. Thank you very much I hope I've made you proud.; [a.] Downe, Kent, UK, BR6 7JD

FREEBORN, MRS. G. M.
[pen.] Trudy; [b.] 11 May 1913, Sherburn-in-Elmet; [p.] James Rainbow, Gertrude Rainbow; [m.] Harold Freeborn (Farmer), 4 April 1942; [ed.] Selby Girls High School, Pitmans College, York, Pitmans College Leeds; [occ.] Retired (Widow); [memb.] Barwick-in-Elmet, Historical Society. Horticultural Society. Conservative Society. All Saints Church Barwick-in-Elmet.; [hon.] Bookkeeping Shorthand Typing, Drawing Elementary, Musical Piano 1st Grade.; [oth. writ.] Poem—"Trees" Historical Society, "Down on the Farm" "Farewells and Farm Sales", "Memories of Canon Grey", "The Maypole Stayed Up"; [pers.] "Nature's Beauty is the great Healer."; [a.] Leeds, Yor9kshire, UK, LS15 4HN

GABOKGATLHE, BOLETILEMANG PSYCHO
[b.] 20 August 1964, Xhomo, Botswana; [p.] Mr. Umangwa and Mrs. Lebiditswe Gabokgatlhe; [ed.] B.A. in Politics and Administrative Studies from University of Botswana. To complete MSC in Human Resource Management in September at Sheffield Hallam University; [occ.] Civil Servant in Ministry of Education in Botswana; [oth.

writ.] Few poems and short stories published in various newspapers and magazines; [pers.] I strive to be accessible to a cross section of people in my writing. Poetry need to be enjoyed by everybody.; [a.] Sheffield, S. Yorkshire, UK, S2 3QE

GALLAGHER, PAUL
[b.] 9 March 1964, London, England; [p.] Patrick and Susan Kelly; [m.] Deirdre Cahill, 1 July 1994; [ch.] Eoin Paul; [ed.] St. Bernadette's N.S. Perth W.A, St. Fergals B.N.S. Finglas, Dublin, Coolmine Community School, Clonsilla Dublin, Bolton St. College, Dublin City; [occ.] Maintenance Fitter; [a.] Swords, Dublin, Ireland

GARCIA, MRS. EDITH
[b.] 30 June 1925, Denton, M/C; [p.] Fred and Edith Barlow; [m.] Leonard Garcia (Deceased), 4 August 1970; [ed.] Denton St. Lawrence Cole, Manchester Conservatoire of Music and Drama; [occ.] Retired; [memb.] International Society of Poets; [hon.] Diploma and Merit, Voice Production and Solo Singing Diploma and Merit Guitar and Musical Theory, Editor's Choice Award 1996 'The Other Side of the Mirror', Editor's Choice Award 1997 'Jewels of the Imagination'; [oth. writ.] Numerous. I have five poems in print and hope to have many more.; [pers.] The observance of my surroundings, and the beauty of nature, together with my vivid imagination and love of make believe, are my source of inspiration.; [a.] Blackpool, Lancashire, UK, FY4 1HE

GARDNER, MELISSA TELERI
[b.] 14 January 1976, Carmarthen; [p.] Ian and Sue Gardner; [ed.] Bacon's City Technology College, Cambeth College; [occ.] Toy Analyst, Central Scientific Laboratories; [oth. writ.] A request for peace published in "Jewels of the Imagination"; [pers.] I would like to dedicate this poem to Daniel Hawkins, a friend who has and will always be there for me. Thank you.; [a.] Peckham, London, UK, SE15 4HX

GARTON, A.
[pen.] Jordan Mylan Garton; [b.] Grantham; [p.] Lincolnshire Fens People have been 3 right ones; [ed.] Junior, Secondary student; [occ.] Art of Living; [memb.] Some; [hon.] Some; [oth. writ.] Adventures in understanding being theme of works; [pers.] Don't let anyone tell you what you're feeling isn't so. And never been towards horrified or horrify. Do not shock yourselves, accept the way of things. Use your self pocket.; [a.] Walcott, Lincolnshire, UK, LN4 3JB

GAUNT, HOWARD TREVOR
[b.] 5 October 1931, Weybridge, Surrey, UK; [p.] Deceased; [m.] Anne Gaunt (Separated), 10 September 1955; [ed.] Working Grammar School for Boys and Kingston University; [occ.] Retired Chartered Architect; [hon.] National Service Medal 1950-53 (Army Infantry Intelligence); [pers.] Now a retired Chartered Architect, 65 years young, he is actively fighting lung and heart failure. Diagnosed a cancer patient two years ago he was given six months to live. He has a wager with his medical consultants that he will still be alive in another seven years time (until 9th March AD 2003) and beyond (?) He illustrates his poems in pen and ink and water colour. Separated from and by his wife after 42 years of marriage, he started to write again in hospital - something he hadn't done since grammar school. Howard (He) survived a fourth heart attack just before Christmas 1996.; [a.] Reading, Berkshire, UK, RG8 8NT

GIBSON, ANGELA FAY
[pen.] Fay Coleman; [b.] 13 July 1937, London; [p.] Phyllis Johnson and Edward O. Johnson; [m.] Tony Gibson, 30 September 1961; [ch.] Richard and Antony; [ed.] Southgate County Grammar; [occ.] Retired—Area Sales Manager Branch Leader—Herb and Spice Company; [oth. writ.] Composed Farewell Odes for Staff Personnel Leaving Presentations. Insertions in Company Bulletins.; [pers.] My aspirations is to compose poetry for others to enjoy.; [a.] Winchmore Hill, Middx, UK, N21 3JY

GILES, DR. RSA. ANNE P.
[b.] 14 August 1941, Argentina; [p.] Hugh M. Dennis, Esq., B.A. Hons (Oxon) and Rita N. Dennis; [m.] Stephen P. Giles, 14 August 1989; [ed.] Northlands School, Argentina (Public), Brighton Polytechnic; [occ.] Language Teacher at Adult Education Institute, Tele-Sales (Daytime) for Charity for Disabled (Radar); [memb.] Association for Language Learning, Anglo-Argentine Society, RSPCA; [hon.] RSA Diploma in Teaching Foreign Languages to Adults; [oth. writ.] Letters in "The Guardian", "The Telegraph", (Quoted In " Class—Where Do You Stand" Book) Local Press, "Folk Roots", articles in "Spare Rib"; [pers.] I feel very strongly about all animals.; [a.] South Croydon, Surrey, UK, CR2 8TB

GILL, SURJIT
[pen.] Nicky; [b.] 12 November 1971, Birmingham; [p.] Lashkar Gill, Raj Gill; [pers.] Putting pen to paper gives me a chance to express my feelings and ideas. Life brings with it confusion and many ups and downs, my writing helps me understand myself better. This is dedicated to my 'best friend' Asha Chauhan.; [a.] Ilford, Essex, UK

GILLMAN, DULCIE BEATRICE
[b.] 21 October 1922, Plumstead; [p.] Mr. and Mrs. Arthur Hill; [m.] William S. L. Gillman, 29 July 1944; [ch.] Maureen and Richard; [ed.] Welling Central School, Kent; [occ.] Housewife, Artist, and an interest in Pottery; [oth. writ.] 'Granny's Lace' published 'Jewels of the Imagination' other poems awaiting publication.; [pers.] I enjoyed writing this poem for my husband Bill, a hardworking man all his life, now retired to enjoy his leisure. We have five grandchildren. I write poetry for pleasure.; [a.] Abbey Wood, London, UK, SE2 0BN

GLAZER, MICHELE
[b.] 28 January 1958, Sandrow, South Africa; [p.] Bernard and Etty Glazer; [m.] Divorced; [ch.] Diandra; [ed.] Bachelor of Arts, Majors English and French, A-levels in England (Was too young to complete them); [occ.] Poet, landscape gardener, also manage a building; [hon.] Have been published in seventeen hard-back anthologies. 13 poems have been published. (Some of them three times) was head girl of my school and was awarded first prize every year at school); [oth. writ.] A book is being published or mine called "A Wishing Well of Words" I was invited by the publishers to be published. T. S. Eliot has influenced me passionately.; [pers.] Any creative process is a spiritual gift and cannot be flaunted for the benefit of one's ego. Artists/Poets are the shafts of light through which esoteric wisdom descends.; [a.] Sandrow, South Africa

GOLLEDGE, M. V.
[pen.] Maud Victoria; [b.] 2 February 1916, London N.; [p.] Mother and Father Woolls; [m.] Husband—W. L. A. Golledge, 9 December 1939; [ch.] Two sons born 1943, 1947; [ed.] Council Schools, very satisfying education; [occ.] Retired now and a widow; [memb.] I used to belong to a manuscript club (through the post which was very interesting.); [hon.] Have had poem published by and edited by Helen McNally, Ancore Books 1993 on the box. On David Jason Actor.; [oth. writ.] I have many poems that I have written over the many years—on a very varied type and have been highly commended for them.; [pers.] I like to include Beauty, Nature, and places that impress me when travelling. To me, poetry is a personal way of sharing what has given me pleasure. I have also written many poems for children.; [a.] Reading, Berkshire, UK, RG4 5EY

GORDON, LAURA ISABELLA
[b.] 23 July 1959, "Newport" Scotland; [p.] Janet and James Robertson; [m.] Louis J. Gordon, 24 September 1982; [ch.] Jonathan and Jenna; [occ.] Housewife; [oth. writ.] Several poems; [pers.] My poem "My Friend" is about my dog, Pepper, who is now 14 years old. And I feel she will live on through my poem forever. We all love her dearly.; [a.] Rhyl, Denbighshire, UK, LL18 1HU

GOUGH, ROY TERENCE
[b.] 16 May 1942, Edgbaston, Birmingham; [p.] Victor and Kathleen; [m.] Margaret Joan, September 1973; [ch.] Five; [ed.] Summer Lane Secondary Modern, Birmingham England; [occ.] Purchasing, stores supervisor; [memb.] Lucas and Birmingham Settlement Chess Club; [oth. writ.] A Paupers Lament (Voices In The Heart); [pers.] Dedicated to, my dearest wife, Margaret Joan.; [a.] Birmingham, UK, B27 7PH

GRADA, RALUCA
[b.] 26 August 1982, Timisoara; [p.] Florentina Grada and Mihai Grada; [occ.] Student - X (10th Grade, W. Shakespeare High School); [oth. writ.] Poems and Philosophical ideas; [pers.] There are things that are known, there are things that are unknown— in-between there are doors.; [a.] Timisoara, Romania, 1900

GRAHAM, DANNY
[b.] 25 April 1978, Norwich; [p.] Brian and Julie Graham; [ed.] GCSE's just finished A-levels in Music, English and Biology, results unknown, hopefully soon to go to Uni.; [occ.] Student; [hon.] Hopefully I'm soon to attend Greenwich University for Natural Resource Management to help try to help third world countries; [oth. writ.] Very many, but not published, hopefully this competition and publication shall give me the confidence I need.; [pers.] Take an elephant or mouse, black man or white, all grand or small and give them a brain. They feel pain, cry, suffer and die a language known by one, all, and everything.; [a.] Norwich, Norfolk, UK, NR7 8NQ

GRAHAM, THERESA ADELA BELL
[pen.] Adela Graham; [b.] 19 June 1938, Wigton, Cumbria; [p.] Rosalind and Richard Turnbull; [m.] William Edward Graham, 22 August 1969; [ch.] James Edward B.Sc, Christina Adela; [ed.] The Red Gables School, Carlisle Underwood Secretarial College, The Cumbria Training Co. Ltd.; [occ.] Housewife; [memb.] City Library; [hon.] Music, Art, Botany Shorthand, RSA advanced typing (LCC) NCVQ Business Administration; [oth. writ.] Various poems: Crofton, Thursby, Peterborough and Marlborough; [pers.] Poetry is: Relaxing to read, stimulating to create, encouraging if published and rewarding to capture the imagination of an audience.; [a.] Carlisle, Cumbria, UK, CA2 5QS

GRANT, STUART
[b.] 24 February 1962, Ballymena; [p.] Derek Grant, Mildred Stewart; [m.] Mary Grant, 22 April 1994; [ch.] James and Katherine; [ed.] Ballymena Academy, Queens University Belfast; [occ.] Chemical Engineer; [oth. writ.] Several poems published in different anthologies. Several scientific publications in international journals.; [pers.] Often I do not know why I write poetry. I only know that when I do I feel good.; [a.] Eglinton, Londonderry, UK, BT47 3XJ

GRAVES, SUSAN
[pen.] Susan Pickard; [b.] 3 June 1962, Dilston; [p.] Nora Pickard and John Pickard; [m.] Mr. Martin Graves, 19 February 1982; [ch.] Kyle Martin Graves and Aaron John Graves; [ed.] English Lang CSE, English Lit CSE, English Northern Counties; [occ.] Retail Assistant; [pers.] I have been greatly influenced by growing up in Northumberland, the countryside and especially my grandfather who was a wonderful dreamer, and refined my imagination even as a child. Allowing me, to write the things I feel and see.; [a.] Southgate, UK

GRICE, ANNE M. C.
[pen.] Anne Campbell-Ashwell; [b.] 19 November 1948, London; [a.] East Sheen, London, UK, SW14 8NJ

GRIFFITHS, ALICIA ANNE
[b.] 18 September 1946, Colwyn Bay; [p.] Alice Griffiths, George Griffiths B.E.M; [ed.] Secondary Modern School, Colwyn Bay Technical College; [occ.] None due to illness; [memb.] Distinguished member of the International Society of Poets; [hon.] Grade 8 (final), Royal Schools of Music Piano Forte Playing; [oth. writ.] Poetry (Approx 65) published in 14 other anthologies, since 1972.; [pers.] I am a born-again Christian and wish to share the gospel in verse. The Lord has transformed my life and I praise His name. And wish to glide others to Him.; [a.] Llanrust, Conwy, UK, LL26 0LS

GRIGGS, MARY
[pen.] Mary Griggs; [b.] 9 June 1938, Walthamstow; [p.] David Thomas and Kathleen Thomas; [m.] Richard Griggs, 11 November 1956; [ch.] Stephen, Karen, Paula, Samantha; [ed.] Walthamstow Technical College; [occ.] Retired Nurse and Care Attendant; [memb.] M. I. Hummel Club (1 Collect Fine Porcelain Figures). Bexley Library; [hon.] 'A' Level in English Literature at the age of 56; [oth. writ.] Several poems for my own and my family's pleasure. (None published); [pers.] With a Welsh heritage which includes a great uncle T. E. Nicholas who has had many books published and was known as 'The People's Champion'. I have grown up with a love for poetry and classic literature. My favourite poet is Wordsworth.; [a.] Sidcup, Kent, UK, DA14 4EY

GUARD, BARRIE SEFTON
[b.] 30 April 1947, Swansea; [p.] Olga Maria Guard and Edward Janes Guard; [m.] Roberta Ann Guard, 3 August 1968; [ch.] Martin Sefton and Peter Michael; [ed.] Diploma in Counselling; [occ.] "Cruse" Bereavement Counsellor; [a.] Swansea, W. Glamorgan, UK, SA4 3EE

GULLIVER, IRIS
[b.] 30 April 1916, Leamington Spa, Warwickshire; [p.] Major Owen Underhill O.B.E., Mary Ann Corbett; [m.] Peter John Gulliver, 17 November 1937; [ch.] John, Byron (Deceased), 3 grandsons—Paul, Jason, Richard, 3 great-grandsons—David, Adrian, Martin and 1 great-granddaughter—Melanie, all living in Mallorca both Paul and Richard having married Mallorcian girls.; [occ.] Retired; [oth. writ.] "Paradise Found" published in "Jewels of the Imagination" The International Library of Poetry 1997.; [pers.] My latest entry "Dream Island" was written when I lived in Mallorca many years ago, when we owned "Casa Florentina" we loved the Mallorcians with hearts of gold they will always be our best friends and they are still our family in Mancol del Valle.; [a.] Duras, France, 47120

GUNN-MATTHEWS, STANLEY
[b.] 23 June 1937, Tottenham, North London; [p.] Stanley Ernest Matthews, May Matthews; [m.] Margaret W. Sennett, 31 July 1958; [ch.] Stephen Stanley, Angela Margaret, Colin Roy; [ed.] Tottenham Grammar School, Tottenham Technical College; [occ.] Retired; [memb.] Kessingland Writer's Group, Performing Arts and Theatrical Drama; [hon.] English Language (University of London, 1953, Ordinary Level). English Literature, Social Science, Geography G.C.S.E. 'O' Level, 1953; [oth. writ.] Poems published in Calendar production. Story articles concerning the natural environment and aspects of nature's wildlife. Essays on general subjects.; [pers.] After witnessing Divine Revelation in the sky, I know that all creation and material substance (on this planet contain spirit life existence once lived.); [a.] Kessingland, Suffolk, UK, NR33 7SQ

HALES-OWEN, VI M.
[b.] 28 March 1939; [m.] Robert, 14 July 1962; [ch.] Three girls and two boys; [occ.] Housewife; [pers.] I just write according to situations and feelings.; [a.] Bracknell, Berks, UK

HALL, CATHERINE ANNE
[pen.] Catherine Anne Hall; [b.] 12 August 1984, Bellshill; [p.] William and Helen Hall; [ed.] Currently at Hawick High; [memb.] SSPCA; [hon.] 8 June '95, Highly Commended, 1514 Club Art Competition generously supporting, help the aged, March '93 TSB Thistle Award (Bronze) Athletics 1 July '96, Young Writers 1997 Anthology, Calypso Books; [oth. writ.] Fireworks; [pers.] I hope this poem has made you realise the danger tigers are in (i.e. the Baltnese tiger was extinct in 1959) and many more will become extinct if we don't stop and think. I'd like to dedicate this to my family for helping me and pushing me this far.; [a.] Hawick, Roxburghshire, UK, TD9 8BT

HALL, JEANNINE
[pen.] Jeannine Anderson Hall; [b.] Lancaster; [p.] Margaret and Percival Anderson; [m.] George Hall; [ch.] Valerie, Linda, David and Sheralyn; [pers.] Poem from a selection not yet published entitled "The Flowers of Heaven" in cherished memory of our darling youngest child Sheralyn—20 July 1951-21 March 1973. And for those who suffer "The Seeming Loss" of a loved one. Life is not ended—but renewed.; [a.] Blackpool, Lancashire, UK, FY4 1PZ

HAMILTON, DUNCAN
[b.] 7 April 1970, Glasgow; [p.] John Hamilton and Helen Hamilton; [m.] Catherine Hamilton, 10 September 1994; [ch.] Andrew and Louise; [ed.] Cumbernauld High School; [oth. writ.] Several poems and short stories as yet unpublished.; [pers.] I would like to dedicate my poem, "Father to Son", to the memory of my dad. John Hamilton—Love never dies.; [a.] Cumbernauld, N. Lanarkshire, UK, G67 2SJ

HAMILTON-SNEATH, JENNY
[b.] 20 October 1930, Tain, Ross and Cromarty; [p.] Isobel and George Hamilton; [m.] Divorced; [ch.] Fiona Bailward and Jonathan Hamilton; [ed.] Tain Royal Academy, St. Andrews University; [occ.] Retired Area Manager, Kingston Adult Education Service; [memb.] Studying International Affairs and Music, University of Surrey; [hon.] M.A. Hons Modern Languages F.I.L. (Fellow of Institute of Linguists) P.G.C.E.; [oth. writ.] Erlebtes Deutschland, A Glimpse of Old England, Surrey by the Tillingbourne, Poems published in Anthologies; [pers.] I wrote 'Adult Education' at the time of my retirement in 1994. After thirty happy years in AE, I was sad at recent trends in the organisation of a service which means so much to every community.; [a.] Leatherhead, Surrey, UK, KT22 7BU

HAMPSON, JOHN D.
[b.] 1 December 1951, Chatham, Kent; [p.] Donald Hampson, Winifred Hampson (nee Watson); [m.] Janet Hampson (nee Perkins), 11 September 1971; [ch.] Adele, Nicola, Alan; [ed.] Pontefract Secondary Modern; [occ.] Unemployed, Disabled Ex-miner; [hon.] Several trophies for snooker; [oth. writ.] Many—lots about life in coal, love, and some funny. Had several poems published in local papers, Yorkshire Miner also for Welsh Miners Christmas, 1984 main influence is life.; [pers.] Live your life with a smile.; [a.] Pontefract, Yorkshire, UK, WF8 2EJ

HANDS, HAZEL
[pen.] Hazel Hands; [b.] 2 February 1928, Leigh-on-Sea, Essex; [p.] Agnes Mason, Ian Edwards (Deceased); [m.] Thomas Edwards (Deceased), 4 March 1925; [ch.] 2 daughters (one deceased); [ed.] Convent School: Left at 16 to train in Secretarial Abilities; [occ.] Retired (and enjoying it!); [memb.] Church of Christ the King, The Parkinson's Disease Society, Readers' Digest, ARP Over 50's; [oth. writ.] None published (lots waiting for somewhere to say it's worth coming out and shaking off their cobwebs!); [pers.] Looking back over my life, I can see the patterns woven 'round the "good" and "bad" points. I've been very fortunate in the jobs I've had. Nothing can beat retirement!; [a.] Hope, E. Sussex, UK, BN3 1LU

HANSEN, CONSTANCE ELLEN
[b.] 1 January 1914, Sharpness, Gloucester; [p.] Florence Ellen Smith, Swimbourne Charles Smith; [m.] Leslie William Hansen, 11 April 1936; [ch.] Leslie Charles Hansen; [ed.] Small School in Sharpness, left at 14 to work; [occ.] Widow and pensioner for 21 years; [memb.] When my husband was alive we belonged to several clubs, I haven't been since.; [hon.] In November 1993, the Welsh Industrial and Maritime Museum, Bute St. Cardiff. Published a hard back book on my husband and my work of ships at Cardiff. I was overjoyed when I was presented with mine. It's the greatest treasure in the Museum.; [oth. writ.] A few small ones nothing published at any time. My sister did have a poem published years ago.; [pers.] I made the poem up about Lars as I sat and watched him, looking at football on the television. He is so full of life. "Shipping at Cardiff" can be had from the Welsh Museum or book shops.; [a.] Devon, Bideford, UK, EX39 1NZ

HARRISON, MRS. DAPHNE MARY EMILY
[b.] 5 May 1936, Wallington, Surrey; [p.] Mary and Albert Tegg; [m.] William Harrison, 29 March 1958; [ch.] Jane Mary Harrison, Richard John Harrison; [ed.] Secondary Modern School, High View, Wallington, Surrey; [occ.] Housewife; [oth. writ.] Several more poems.; [pers.] My inspiration for writing poems comes from my love of nature, and the wonderful world we live in and that God created. "The Best of time is now."; [a.] Whitehaven, Cumbria, UK

HARRISON, LINDA
[b.] 30 November 1960, Watford; [p.] Mr. and Mrs. Peacock; [ch.] Two boys; [ed.] Southall All Girls School, Russell Lane Whestone London; [occ.] Single Mother; [hon.] City and Guilds Communication Skills (Word Power) Stage one. Adult Learners Award for central region, poetry, creative writing; [oth. writ.] Creative writing, more poems; [pers.] I have always liked reading and writing poetry. I enjoy writing what I see and do, everyday, at all seasons.; [a.] Wolverhampton, West Midlands, UK, WV10 9LZ

HARRISON, SERENA MARIE CLAIRE
[b.] 21 December 1983, Newcastle-upon-Lyme; [p.] Mr. Ian and Mrs. Christine Harrison; [hon.] Sport: Won the sports sheild three times in a row. First in cross country out of ninety. Also ran at Stafford for Newcastle county. Work: Written letter from the Headmaster for excellent work.; [oth. writ.] I had wrote several pieces of poetry and my father who believed in my talent, encouraged me to enter the poetry competition which he read about in the local tabloid.; [pers.] I enjoy writing poetry. It inspires my imagination and wildest thoughts.; [a.] Newcastle, Staffordshire, UK, ST5 4AW

HARROWER, CATHERINE HELEN
[b.] 4 June 1955, Inverness; [p.] Thomas Stewart, Margaret Stewart; [m.] John Harrower, 26 August 1972; [ch.] Tracy and Helen; [ed.] Fort Agustus J.S. School; [occ.] Former Social Care Worker/Housewife; [oth. writ.] Published Local Press.; [pers.] Poetry gives me the opportunity to express my feelings on everyday life. I especially enjoy writing poems for friends and family.; [a.] Genrothes, Fife, UK, KY7 4EQ

HARTLAND, JOAN
[b.] 9 September 1931, Sunderland; [p.] Robert and Margaret Mackel; [m.] John William Hartland, 24 September 1977; [ed.] Secondary

School; [occ.] Retired; [memb.] HF Cha Hiking Club, RSPB, International Fund for Animal Welfare, Ramblers Ass; [oth. writ.] My Shangri-La, Seasons of My Life. Anguish Longing. Missing You. Divorce the World Today. So Lonely A Barmaids Reverie. Far Away Countries. If Another Parting; [pers.] When things went wrong I could never understand why me, now I don't question it I just put it down in poetry and some day I will know the answer and then, sadly, there maybe no more poetry in me; [a.] Doncaster, S. Yorkshire, UK, DN4 0UB

HARVEY, JENNI-LYNN
[pen.] Emerald O'Lea; [b.] 6 January 1976; Crewe, Cheshire; [p.] Eris Harvey, Hilary Harvey; [ed.] Ruskin County High School, Crewe; [occ.] Unemployed; [memb.] Various Animal Rights Grounds; [oth. writ.] One poem published in last year's book 'Voices on the Wind'; [pers.] My poetry is the only way I can express my innermost thoughts and feelings without the barriers that everyday life puts up; [a.] Crewe, Cheshire

HARVEY, JOYCE SUSAN
[b.] 4 May 1954, Southend-on-Sea; [p.] Kitty Tanner and Albert Tanner; [m.] Michael Dennis Harvey, 1 September 1972; [ch.] Paul Michael and Claire Susan; [ed.] Porters Grange, St Mary's Cofe School Westborough High for Girls; [occ.] Housewife who used to be a children's nanny; [memb.] I.F.A.W. Pet Rescue; [hon.] Awarded "The Editor's Choice Award" for outstanding achievement in poetry, from The International Library of Poetry 1997; [oth. writ.] Previously published poem entitled "China Blue".; [pers.] I first became interested in poetry, at the tender age of eleven, when I had a poem entitled "God" put up on the classroom wall. Since then, I have enjoyed writing poems, on a variety of subjects, and my ambition is to have a collection of poems published, one day.; [a.] Southend-on-Sea, Essex, UK, SS0 0NL

HAWES, DAVE
[pen.] Davina James; [b.] 20 January 1957, Newcastle-upon-Tyne; [m.] Susan Helen Hawes, 25 November 1989; [ch.] Joanne and Derek; [occ.] Civil Servant; [oth. writ.] With Mother; [pers.] Dum Vero Spero; [a.] Rochester, Kent, UK, ME2 2XE

HAYES, KIM ELIZABETH
[pen.] Ladee Bassett; [b.] 20 February 1957; Braintree, Essex; [p.] Ann Hayes, nee Polley, William Allen Hayes; [ed.] Zweibrücken High School Germany, University of Maryland; [occ.] Computer Programmer; [memb.] Basset Hound Club, Canine Concern; [hon.] B.Sc. Computer Science, Sustained Superior Performance Award from Ministry of Defense; [oth. writ.] Children's book entitled "Sherlock Visits Seal Island" due for publication by Minerva Press shortly, Recording contract offered in 1987 by CRS Records for 3 sets of lyrics recorded by "Talent-led Rosen," Lyrics self-recorded; [pers.] When my soul departs and I'm physically gone, the words I have written shall linger on and on. I have been greatly influenced by all those near and dear to me, especially my grandparents Eric and Eileen Polley, my late mother, and late dog Miss Bessie. In light of our nation's current tragedy may my poem serve as a poetic tribute to the memory of Diana, Princess of Wales, 1961-1997. My poem was read on several radio stations during our nation's week of mourning as it suited the moment; [a.] Weeling, Suffolk

HAYES, KIM ELIZABETH
[pen.] Ladee Bassett; [b.] 20 February 1947; Braintree, Essex; [p.] Ann Hayes and William Allen Hayes; [ed.] Zweibrucken High School, Germany, University of Maryland; [occ.] Computer Programmer; [memb.] Basset Hound Club, Canine Care Concern; [hon.] BSc. Computer Science, Sustained Superior Performance from Ministry of Defense; [oth. writ.] Children's book entitled "Sherlock Visits Seal Island" due for publication by Minerva Press shortly. Recording contract offered by CRS Records in 1987 for 3 sets of Lyrics. Lyrics self recorded in studio. Lyrics recorded by "Talent—Ted Rosen"; [pers.] When my soul departs and I'm physically gone the words I have written shall linger on and on. I have been greatly influenced by all those near and dear to me, especially my grandparents Eric and Eileen Polley, my late mother and late dog Miss Bessie.; [a.] Weeting, Suffolk, UK, IP27 0QT

HAYWARD, MR. LEE
[b.] 6 October 1957, Rochford, Essex; [p.] Mr. and Mrs. Hayward; [ed.] King John's School, Thundersley, Essex, England; [occ.] Personal Care Assistant; [memb.] International Society of Poets; [oth. writ.] I have written over two hundred poems on all sorts of themes and personal feelings and moods and experiences.; [pers.] I love all life, human and animal, and vegetable. Although I am not formally religious, I firmly believe in the sanctity of all forms of life and of nature. I detest war and all forms of killing. I hate racial and sexual and all other forms of discrimination, but take no part in political movements. I am not learned, but have practical abilities and love friendship and toleration.; [a.] Southend-on-Sea, Essex, UK, SS1 2TZ

HAZZARD, MISS MELANIE
[pen.] Melanie Hazzard; [b.] 3 March 1977, Weston-s-Mare; [p.] Geoffrey and Pauline Hazzard; [m.] Nicholas Charles Wilson, (Engaged); [ed.] Broadoak Secondary School, Weston-s-Mare College, (want to go on to Bristol University to study to be a midwife); [occ.] Care Assistant and Part-time student; [hon.] N.N.E.B Certificate in Nursery Nursing, 3 Cross Award in First Aid, Food Safety Certificate, G.C.S.E.'s in English, Psychology, Biology, Technology; [oth. writ.] One poem published in school magazine, and a poem being published in a book called 'Whispering Winds' by Poetry Today.; [pers.] When I write, I lose my mind in a forest of thoughts, opening doors already there, drifting from the norm into escapism. When I write, I seek answers.; [a.] Weston-s-Mare, N. Somerset, UK, BS23 4AE

HEARD, COLIN
[pen.] Col; [b.] 13 October 1941, Tiverton; [p.] Father Deceased, E. M. Heard; [m.] Doreen Margaret Heard, 5 November 1977; [ch.] Four; [ed.] Secondary Modern Schools; [occ.] Welder; [memb.] AEELL; [oth. writ.] None published, but many more poems in draft form.; [pers.] I have been greatly influenced by English poets. And aim to reflect in my poems times gone by in England and her counties.; [a.] Taunton, Somerset, UK, TA1 5DU

HEDLEY, MARJORIE
[pen.] M. Hedley; [b.] 30 November 1920, Manchester; [p.] William and Elizabeth Tracey; [m.] Robert Hedley, 18 March 1939; [ch.] 3 Children; [ed.] Manchester Training College; [occ.] Retired Lecturer; [oth. writ.] Selected poems. 1956 verse play 'Not Proven' Long poem "Experiment In Space"; [a.] Colchester, Essex, UK

HEFFERON, KATHLEEN
[b.] 23 October 1976, Liverpool; [p.] Joan and Michael Hefferon; [m.] Paul Barker; [ed.] Rossall Boarding School 1983-92; [occ.] Dental Nurse/Receptionist Forshaw, Dickinson Dental Practice; [hon.] English Literature/Language; [oth. writ.] Other poems, short stories (unpublished); [pers.] I have been greatly influenced by my family especially my father whose stories of war encouraged me to write this poem.; [a.] Dalton, Lancashire, UK, WN8 7RJ

HELMAN, MRS. E. V.
[b.] 29 June 1940, Eastbourne, Sx; [occ.] Housewife now, I do tapestry and poems; [memb.] Save Our Wildlife Fund, Oxfam and Cancer Fund; [pers.] Most of the poetry I have written is about true life today so that our children of the future can get an insight of how it was in our time and strive to make the world a better place. Give me love, peace and beauty of nature and I am content.; [a.] St. Annes, Lancashire, UK

HENDERSON, MISS ANGELA
[b.] 13 May 1961, Edinburgh; [p.] Stella and Edward Henderson; [ed.] Firrhill High School, Edinburgh; [occ.] Sales Assistant Shoe Fitter; [memb.] I.S. Poets, Hall of Fame; [hon.] Nomination for Poet of the Year 1997; [oth. writ.] Ten poems confirmed publication in 1997, a few more still awaiting a decision, included in the ten are "The Massacre" (Book-Moods and Reflections) "The Scotland" (Boo—A Major Change) "Passing Years" (Book—Among the Roses); [pers.] I hope my poems will encourage thoughts and feelings of our time and will go on to do so in the future.; [a.] Edinburgh, Midlothian, UK, EH13 0HU

HILTON, MANDY
[b.] 27 August 1963, Anglesey, Gwynedd; [p.] William and Elizabeth; [m.] Stuart, 3 May 1987; [ch.] Clair—5, Christopher—3; [ed.] Ysgol Gyfun David Hughes, Gwynedd Technical College, Ysbyty Glan Clwyd, gained R.GN. qualification in 1985; [occ.] Company Secretary, Director; [memb.] National Trust, The Red House Book Club, in the hope of encouraging the enjoyment of reading in my children.; [hon.] Won 'Editor's Choice' with just ever poem. 'When the Evening Comes'.; [oth. writ.] 'When the Evening Comes' published in 'Jewels of the Imagination'.; [pers.] This poem is dedicated to my son Christopher who was diagnosed as having autism in Jan. '97.; [a.] Truro, Cornwall, UK, TR3 6DT

HOLDER, RITA VIOLET
[pen.] R. V. Holder; [b.] 22 April 1919, Birmingham; [p.] Elsie and Edward Morris; [m.] John Holder (Deceased 1979), 14 December 1940; [ch.] Anita, John, Keith, Nicholas; [ed.] Birmingham Schools and College Bromsgrove City and Guilds (London) for flower arranging. 4 years W.I. Dewter Craft and Teaching Demonstration; [occ.] Housewife, Hobbies—Handicrafts, Gardening, Floristry; [memb.] Many years in Women's Institute, Stone Kidderminster Worcestershire, Art Club as above. Not now, I don't drive.; [hon.] Won first prize out of 10,000 artists, International newspaper, year 1970. Chosen Holiday 2 weeks in Italy for my love of arts painting and poetry alike.; [oth. writ.] Two stories one adult, one children's poem about daffodils in N.A.F.F.A.S. magazine which was published.; [pers.] I am so happy doing all arts and crafts writing verse. Gardening passing on skills when possible. Not enough hours in each day. ; [a.] Kidderminster, Worcestershire, UK, DY11 6NX

HOLLAND, PAUL
[b.] 4 February 1986, Blackpool; [p.] Brett and Caron; [ed.] Hambleton County Primary and St. Aidan's Church of England School; [hon.] Boys Brigade, currently yellow belt, green tag at Taekwondo; [pers.] After learning about haiku at school it became my favourite style of poetry. I like to reflect on nature in my work.; [a.] Hambleton, Lancs, UK, FY6 9ES

HOLLIS, MRS. ELSIE
[b.] 25 July 1937, Tideswell; [p.] Ella Wragg and Benjamin Walter Wragg; [m.] John Hollis, 9 February 1957; [ch.] Elizabeth Oulsnam; [ed.] Bishop Pursglove School, Tideswell, Derbyshire; [occ.] Resident Manager of a sheltered housing complex; [memb.] Member of International Society of Poetry, Member of International Library of Poetry. Member of Poets Guild; [hon.] A distinguished member of Society of Poetry; [oth. writ.] Several poems published in Library of Poetry today, also Poets Guild and

350

Poetry Today.; [pers.] I try to keep a sense of humour, it helps through many awkward situations. I dedicate this poem to Anthony George Luckings, "My Golden Boy".; [a.] Tideswell, Derbyshire, UK, SK17 8PX

HOLLOWELL, MELISSA KATHLEEN
[pen.] Mel; [b.] 24 May 1982, Northampton; [p.] Debra, Dawson; [ed.] Stanton Middle Stantonbury Campus. Secondary Milton Keynes; [occ.] Student; [oth. writ.] Just enjoy writing poetry.; [pers.] I am a very shy person, and writing is my way of expressing the issues that are important to me. I hope it helps other people who read it.; [a.] Milton Keynes, Buckinghamshire, UK, MK13 7BY

HOLMES, JO-ANNE
[pen.] Jo-Anne Stoker/Holmes; [b.] 27 February 1960, Sedgefield; [p.] Kathleen and Thomas Gouldsborough; [m.] Derek Holmes, 29 March 1980; [ch.] Gemma and Christopher; [ed.] St. Johns R.C. Comp Bishop Auckland, Night School Don Valley High Scawthorpe Doncaster; [occ.] Domestic Assistant at Furniture Factors, Doncaster; [memb.] Line Dancing Club, Homestart Volunteer; [hon.] Merits for Embroidery Pictures; [pers.] I like to think that everyone I touch, I can make them smile and remember me always I'm a hopeless romantic. My husband and my family are the most important people in my life.; [a.] Doncaster, S. Yorks, UK, DN5 9JU

HOLNESS, A.
[b.] 20 August 1962, London; [ed.] Catford County Girls School, Woolwich College; [occ.] Rehousing Assistant Local Government; [oth. writ.] Couple of poems published.; [pers.] Sometimes good can happen when you least expect it. With a bit of luck hope springs eternal.; [a.] Sydenham, London, UK, SE26

HOOPER, MRS. HAZEL JUNE
[pen.] Avaline Lyle; [b.] 8 June 1928, Newton, Abbot; [p.] Isabel and George Lyle; [m.] Don (Deceased), 26 July 1958; [ch.] Karen Lesley; [occ.] Retired previously eight years in the Woman's Royal Air Force as telephonist; [oth. writ.] Reflections of life books 1 and 2: Poppies of the Field, A Time for Dreams.; [pers.] To count our blessings and reach for the stars.; [a.] Bournemount, Dorset, UK, BH1 3DV

HORNE, LOUIS A.
[b.] 28 August 1967, Rochford, Essex; [p.] Carol-Ann and Stephen Lawford; [m.] Samantha Sian, 2 July 1994; [ch.] Sophie Georgia and Olivia Rose; [occ.] Builder; [memb.] MENSA; [hon.] Only sporting; [oth. writ.] Sophie Georgia, Worthy Down!, I Never Felt So . . . (only published poems); [pers.] Personal opinion life without children was so simple—but so meaningless.; [a.] Winchester, Hants, UK, SO23 0NP

HORROBIN, NITA
[pen.] Nita Walker and "Niz"; [b.] 25 August 1942, Leicester; [p.] Ivy Walker and Frank Walker; [m.] George, 29 July 1995; [ch.] Andrea, Samantha, Russell; [ed.] Thomas Rawlins Grammar School, Quorn, Leics; [occ.] Semi-Retired; [oth. writ.] Several topical letters published in National Newspapers and Magazines.; [pers.] I enjoy words, they can express so much in different ways.; [a.] Alfreton, Derbys, UK, DE55 1BZ

HOWARD, VICKIE
[pen.] Vickie Liz, Vicks, Vick-H.; [b.] 3 May 1979, Bassetlaw; [p.] Sue Howard, Chris Howard; [ed.] Dinnington Comprehensive School 1991-1995; [occ.] PA/Secretary to Sales Manager and Sales Executives, at Llanrad Distribution PK; [hon.] 'Trainee of the Year' Award in 1996 (October); [oth. writ.] Publication of 'Yorkshire's Child' in 1995. Received royalties. Wrote stories and poems for BBC (Unaccepted yet received positive advice for future).; [pers.] I enjoy writing poetry and I will continue to do so in the future. I hope, one day to have a book published with all my work in it. I have been writing poetry since I was seven years old. I find it easy to express my thoughts in poetry.; [a.] North Anston, Sheffield, UK, S25 4GJ

HOWDEN, CHARLOTTE
[b.] 6 August 1981, Wimbledon; [p.] Alan Howden and Judith Howden; [ed.] Wimbledon High School; [occ.] Studying for A-levels; [oth. writ.] Published by Roald Dahl Foundation poetry competition and poetry now young writer's competition.; [pers.] I am very pleased to be published in this anthology as I was only 14 when I wrote this poem.; [a.] Wimbledon, London, UK, SW19 4NG

HOWE, DEREK
[b.] 29 July 1967, Leamington Spa; [p.] Beverley Howe; [m.] Lucu Maxwell (Long term partner); [ed.] Myton High School, Midwarwickshire College; [occ.] Warehouse Operative; [hon.] Having this poem publish.; [oth. writ.] A personally binded book of poems which have not been looked at for publishing.; [pers.] In my writing, I want to widen narrow minds and show people the grass is not always greener.; [a.] Leamington, Warwickshire, UK, CV31 3BX

HOWELL, MARGARET J.
[b.] Exeter, Devon; [ed.] Egerton Park School, Exeter, Stover School for Girls, Newton Abbot, Indiana University (Bloomington); [occ.] English Teacher at Crofton House School for girls, Vancouver, British Columbia; [memb.] The Society of Authors, The Byron Society, The Jane Austen Society, The Angelican Catholic Church of Canada (TAC) British Columbia College of Teachers; [oth. writ.] Byron Tonight (Springwood Books, 1982) The House of Byron (Quiller Press 1988) Miscellaneous articles and reviews.; [pers.] Man must restore his soul by recovering the past and the power of imagination. Books provide a very present help in the trouble and chaos of these evil days.; [a.] Vancouver, British Columbia, Canada

HUBBARD, EVELYN
[b.] 4 February 1980, County Cork, Ireland; [p.] John and Eileen Hubbard; [ed.] I received my primary education at Ballyvongane N.S in County Cork and my second level education at Coachford College, Cork; [occ.] A student awaiting third level education; [memb.] I am a member of 'The Cork Women's Poetry Circle' in Cork City; [hon.] I have been 'highly commended' in local radio competitions. My poems have been published in local and national magazines as well as school magazines; [oth. writ.] I have a collection of 70 poems on all aspects of life, also short stories.; [pers.] For me, poetry is something to look forward to and look back on. Writing poetry plays a big part in my life. I have been greatly influenced by Brendan Kennelly—a great Irish poet. I believe the desire to write poetry has been handed down to me by my mother—Eileen and other relations.; [a.] Cork, Ireland

HUDSON, EILEEN
[b.] 17 April 1944, Rochdale; [p.] George and Joan Stott; [m.] John Hudson (Deceased), 4 September 1971; [ch.] One; [ed.] Rochdale Grammar School, Leeds University; [occ.] Director and owner of Microught A/C Manuf.; [memb.] Popular Flying Association, British Microlight A/Craft Association; [hon.] BA Hons English and Philosophy; [oth. writ.] Occasional articles and poems in magazines.; [pers.] I write poetry about anything that moves me at the time. No particular influences.; [a.] Rochdale, Lancs, UK, OL11 4BD

HUGHES, RUBY HUTCHIESON
[pen.] Nony; [b.] 19 January 1936, Dennistoun; [p.] Tom Easton, Ruby Easton; [m.] Harry Hughes, 8 November 1954; [ch.] Carol, Harry, Steven, Dorothy, Richard and Craig; [ed.] Whitehill Senior Secondary Dennistoun Glasgow; [occ.] Retired Aux. Nurse; [hon.] Honour being loved by Harry, awards seeing our children and grandchildren grow to be decent loving "Folks" what more can I say?; [oth. writ.] Competitions in Glasgow evening times; [pers.] Inspired by the love I feel towards the sick in our society and my wonderful colleagues who still nurse them.; [a.] Glasgow, Scotland, G42 7AW

HUNT, ELLEN JOAN
[b.] 30 September 1924, Kennington, London; [p.] Herbert Atkins and Mabel Monk; [m.] Mr. Alfred Saunders (Deceased), Mr. George J. Hunt (Deceased), 1st Marriage 31 March 1945, 2nd Marriage 29 December 1992; [ch.] Five—1 son and 4 daughters; [ed.] Secondary Modern, Central Girls School, Sidcup Kent, then Bluecoat Girls School Point Hill Greenwich, (Trade Training) War Interrupted Studies; [occ.] Retired/worked for container firms invoicing and printing; [memb.] R.A.F.A. 1107 Basildon. Royal Air Force Association started by myself and half a dozen others. I was Wings Officer for first 2 years. At 17 1/2 was a W.A.A.F. in 2 World War - 3 1/2 yrs. a M.T. Driver; [hon.] One from yourselves for my first poem in 1996 entitled "The Driving Test To Jossie" if this is an award, George's dying words were "I Love You— you were the best thing that happened in my life and I worry at leaving you all alone."; [oth. writ.] None/except for the second poem 1997 entitled "Ode to George"; [pers.] I learned to paint from my brother in Australia (Who is a wonderful artist and stained glass worker) yet I cannot draw a straight line. It's all done with brushes in oils. I am quite proud of my pictures. As we were all abandoned as young children—I was eight years old put in an orphanage—always had to fend for myself.; [a.] Basildon, Essex, UK, SS13 3HS

HUNTER, ALISON JENNIFER
[pen.] A. J. Hunter; [b.] 5 April 1972, Belfast; [p.] Hilary Hunter, Michael Hunter; [ed.] Victoria College, Belfast University of Strathclyde, Glasgow; [occ.] Travel Consultant, British Airways; [memb.] Interests include Literature, Art, Theatre, Skiing, Swimming and Charity Work; [hon.] BA joint honours degree in Marketing with Hospitality Management; [oth. writ.] No other work sent for publication; [pers.] Poetry, for me, is expressing emotion on paper—permitting myself to feel pain as well as happiness in a society that promotes an "I'm Fine" facade.; [a.] Belfast, Co Antrim, UK, BT9 6TH

HUSSAIN, SADIA
[b.] 1 October 1977, Manchester; [p.] Mohammad Hussain, Hamida Hussain; [ed.] St. Margaret Primary School, Whalley Range High School for Girls, Loreto College (presently attended); [occ.] Student at Loreto College, studying GNVQ H and SC level 3; [oth. writ.] I have had a poem published in 'Jewels of the Imagination' and it was called 'Hurt'.; [pers.] I was inspired to write poems after reading others and by events that have taken place in my life. Writing poems help relieve me from emotional stress.; [a.] Chorlton, Manchester Lancs, UK, M21 0YH

IRONSIDE, PHIL
[b.] 6 December 1963, Wolverhampton; [ed.] Dyson Perrins, Malvern, Worcester Technical College; [occ.] Nurseryman, Bransford Gardens Plants; [memb.] Welsh Clay Target Shooting Association; [oth. writ.] A large number of poems and prose unpublished.; [pers.] I am interested in the struggle between the human condition and the spirit. I have been painting since I was 13 and had an exhibition in Dec. 1993.; [a.] Malvern, Worcs, UK, WR14 1SS

JACKSON, HUGH DAVID
[b.] 26 August 1948, Ards Hospital; [p.] Mary Jackson, William Jackson; [m.] Divorced; [ch.] Carol Jackson, Paula Jackson; [ed.] Primary School, High School, left at 15 yrs.; [occ.] Self Employed Plasterer; [oth. writ.] "Free Beer—

Tomorrow", "U.S.A.", "Raymond's Philosophy", "Tommy Day Rice, A Soldier", "Time Waster", "Titanic Struggle"; [pers.] $ Money, money's no problem, I don't have any.; [a.] Ballygowan, Down, BT23 6LS

JAMIESON, ANNE
[b.] 6 June 1956, Paisley, Scotland; [p.] James and Margaret; [ed.] Barrhead High School (Glasgow); [occ.] Finance Assistant; [oth. writ.] Several poems published in local newspaper when I was just 18, also several in books in 1970's.; [pers.] A good poem can come from or touch the very depth of your soul. That's what I aim for and know I have a long way to go.; [a.] Hounslow, Middlesex, UK, TW3 3DD

JEFFREY, MRS. BETTY DOROTHY
[b.] 30 January 1930, Yan Yean, Victoria, Australia; [p.] George and Clara Walts (nee Cannings); [m.] John Raymond Jeffrey, 30 August 1952; [ch.] Meredith, Lester and Fraser, Grandchildren Michelle and Stacey Jeffrey; [ed.] Yan Yean Primary School No. 697, University High School Melbourne, Stott's Business College Melbourne; [occ.] Farmer and Housekeeper; [memb.] Central Victorian Gospel Radio, Religious Education in Schools Salvation Army; [pers.] I write because I find it difficult to obtain Australian poems to suit the things I am teaching and I write to the Glory of God.; [a.] Glenburn, Victoria, Australia, 3717

JENKINS, SHEILA ANN
[pen.] Sheila Ann Jenkins; [b.] 30 August 1940, England; [p.] Mrs. E. Peason; [m.] Divorced, 3 August 1997; [ch.] Four; [ed.] Secondary Modern; [occ.] Housewife; [oth. writ.] Lots but I've never entered any competitions before, I'm a bit of a softy I like Patience Strong. She seems to write poems that most people can relate to.; [pers.] I wrote "The Face at the Window" for a friend I used to look after. His name was Gerry. He had a stroke at the age of 45 yrs. He lived on the 12th floor of a high-rise block and spent a lot of time looking out of the window.; [a.] Liverpool, Lancs, UK, L27 7BN

JENNINGS, DENISE
[pen.] Denise Jennings; [b.] 20 September 1980, St. Finbarrs, Cork; [p.] Cornelius and Mary Jennings; [ed.] St. Joesephs Primary School, Clonakilty, Co. Cork. (Currently At) Sacred Heart, Secondary School, Clonakilty, Co. Cork; [occ.] Student; [memb.] Carbery Pony Club; [pers.] Live life as if tomorrow was your last.; [a.] Clonakilty, Co. Cork, Ireland

JENNINGS, SHARON
[b.] 19 June 1976, Bristol; [p.] Philip Jennings, Marlene Jennings; [m.] Kit Rhodes (My partner, living together), 15 May 1996; [ed.] Brislington School, Brunel College; [occ.] Sales Administrator, Certex, UK (Part-time writer); [memb.] Out of this World Society; [oth. writ.] I have been writing stories and poems since I was 6 yrs. old. Just recently I have decided to look through them, re-write and send them off in hope of publication.; [pers.] Writing is my therapy. It's like falling asleep. Going through the day in my mind and then switching over to my imaginative world—where only I can decide what is going to happen next.; [a.] Bristol, UK, BS6 5QX

JENNINGS, VALERIE J. A.
[b.] 27 September 1947, Slough; [m.] Donald Jennings, December 28, 1978; [ch.] Helene Jane, Victoria Joanne, Robert James; [ed.] Slough High School for girls Roehampton Institute, London University; [occ.] Mature student conservation and restoration BA (hons); [hon.] BA (open), PG.CE, Ad dip Ed (Technology); [oth. writ.] Previously published poetry.; [pers.] Poetry is a release for the emotions both for the reader and the author and it is much cheaper than a counsellor.; [a.] Gosberton Spalding, Lincs, UK, PE11 4NL

JEYARAJ, PRAVIN
[b.] 11 July 1977, Harrow; [p.] Ponnampalam and Kaushalya; [ed.] Wilson's School, (Wallington), University of Surrey (Guildford); [occ.] Student (Maths); [memb.] Poetry Society; [hon.] Grade Four violin and piano; [oth. writ.] Several unpublished poems. Two published already "Ode to Food", "Loss"; [pers.] Death is nothing to be afraid off. It never goes where it is not allowed to. We must embrace it with the same love we have for life.; [a.] Sutton, Surrey, UK, SM2 6JU

JOHNBOSCO, HAMAD ILKUL
[b.] 2 May 1976, Korr, Kenya; [p.] Galsaracho Ilkul, Bichowlo Ilkul; [ed.] Korr Pry, Chuka High School, Moi Univ. currently 3rd year, Medicine and Surgery (Undergraduate); [occ.] Student; [hon.] Okoth K-B Play Writing Awards (National Award).; [oth. writ.] Two plays: Victory, In favour of two; [pers.] Write poems as my hobby. Men should not unnecessarily associate with societies of those who by their acts would weaken the purpose to do right. Time is the worst enemy to lovers. Men complicate what God simplifies.; [a.] Eldoret, U. G. Municipality, UK

JOHNS, WENDIE ROSEMARY
[pen.] Wendie Johns; [b.] 3 May 1942, Swansea, S. Wales; [p.] Oswald and Rowena Thomas; [m.] Allan Johns, 11 June 1960; [ch.] Kevin Lawrence; [ed.] "Llwyn-y-Bryn" Grammar; [occ.] Retired Social Worker; [memb.] Member of a Christian Church; [oth. writ.] My only writing has been for personal achievement and self-satisfaction.; [pers.] My love of poetry as a means of expression was influenced by my father. He was taught English Literature by Dylan Thomas. Talented Father Dylan went to the same grammar school as my father and we were born in the same town.; [a.] Swansea, Glamorgan, UK, SA4 6SX

JOHNSON, ELWYN
"Ashamed of attempting to ease my wife's hands from my shoulders during a heart attack (rasping for breath makes any pressure unbearable) "Viva Septuagenaria" is an apology and heartfelt thank you for all those hands have done for me/us along our furrows of time."

JOHNSON, KAREN
[b.] 17 September 1972, Harrogate; [p.] June Rose Hudson, John Michael Hudson; [m.] Matthew Johnson, 20 July 1991; [ch.] Elliott George and Niamh Catherine; [ed.] Rossett High School, Harrogate; [occ.] Housewife and Mother; [a.] Ripon, North Yorkshire, UK, HG4 1LJ

JONES, JANE
[b.] 6 November 1957, Herts; [ed.] Mainly residential special schools due to developing optic atrophy at an early age O-A level Eng. Lang/Lit/ Drama-Arts; [occ.] Housewife; [oth. writ.] Nothing else submitted as yet; [pers.] Inspired by the miracles of nature.; [a.] Sudbury, Suffolk, UK, CO10 0LA

JONES, JEAN
[b.] 14 November 1955, Barry; [p.] Mary and Trevor Newton; [m.] David Jones, 29 November 1975; [ch.] Melissa and Heather Jones; [ed.] Holton Rd, Secondary Barry College of Further Education; [occ.] Receptionist/Co-ordinator P/T Typewriting and I-T Teacher; [memb.] Founder Member of Service Social Ladies Guild Sports and Social Club; [oth. writ.] Various short stories and poems not published mainly written for pleasure.; [pers.] I enjoy writing for pleasure and I am pleased to be given the opportunity to share this with others.; [a.] Barry, Vale of Glam, UK, CF62 7EJ

JONES, JEAN ANN
[b.] 5 December 1949, Stoke-on-Trent, Staffordshire; [p.] Violet Coller, Harry Coller; [m.] Raymond Jones, 6 December 1969; [ch.] Terence Clint Adrian Gareth Tracy; [ed.] Norton Primary School Ballgreen Secondary School Staffordshire; [occ.] Housewife; [pers.] My writing helps me to express the way I'm feeling when I am sad or happy inside, and this helps me with the day to day pressures of life. I feel better and closer to God and want to help mankind.; [a.] Newcastle, Stafford, UK, ST5 9HJ

JONES, JOHN LEWIS
[b.] 6 December 1913, Bala, Merionethshire; [ch.] Two; [ed.] Primary, Grammar College, Secondary School Teacher. Head of Business Studies in England and Wales; [occ.] Retired; [hon.] All other writings; [oth. writ.] Dozens of poems many many prizes won in Welsh Eistedaludan (competition festivals throughout Wales) Book Welsh poems published several in magazine.; [pers.] This is my first attempt at English poetry although I have read widely in English. Am fascinated by the works of Wordsworth, Aklat's especially. Fascinated by the sound of words.; [a.] Mold, Flint, UK, CH7 4AB

JONES, LEWIS
[pen.] Lewis Jones; [b.] 22 October 1947, Aberystwyth; [p.] Rhys Tom and Jane Jones; [m.] Divorced, July 1972; [ch.] Patricia Ann, Mark Illtyd, David Andrew; [ed.] Tregaron Secondary Modern Home Studies and Tech Training; [occ.] Gas, Electrical and Heating Engineer; [memb.] Institute of patentees; [oth. writ.] Several Welsh poems published in local papers.; [pers.] Like a picture to an artist my poetry presents a compassionate short story on the subjects I write in a somehow artistic and romantic fashion. I wrote "God's Little People" through the understanding of a very loving Down's Brother.; [a.] Tregaron, Ceredigion-Wales, UK, SY25 6RR

JONES, MRS. VIOLET
[pen.] Vee Jay; [b.] 9 March 1940, London; [p.] Mr. and Mrs. Springett; [ch.] Trevor, Martin and Darron; [ed.] Keeble High School, Amberley Road, London; [occ.] Unable to work now, due to bad health; [hon.] I have had an Editors Choice Award Certificate; [oth. writ.] Poem Published last year, by the International Library of Poetry, it is called "In Memory Of My Dog Lady; [pers.] I was looking back on the past years after coming out of hospital, then I was inspired by my thoughts, and wrote this poem for my sons, Trevor Martin and Darron.; [a.] Norton, North Yorkshire, UK, YO17 9DE

JORGENSEN, ANDREW
[b.] 18 April 1974, Durban, South Africa; [ed.] Matric Exemption Hilton College Hotel and Catering Management Higher Diploma, and ML. Sultan Technikon, Durban South Africa; [occ.] Self Employed; [oth. writ.] Collection of short stories and poems.; [pers.] My poetry takes the form of a personal diary reflecting my loves, hates, fears of dreams. I have been influenced by life itself and the manner in which I perceive it. "Never stop dreaming boy cause when you do it's time to die".; [a.] Pietermaritzburg, South Africa, 3206

JULES, ANTHONY
[b.] 5 July 1952, Grenada; [p.] John and Veronica Jules; [ch.] Taj Jules; [ed.] Bloomfield Boys Secondary School, SE London College, SW London College; [occ.] Local Government Officer; [memb.] Oware Society and Africa Collective; [oth. writ.] Articles for Journal Newspaper in 1980's. Plus various magazines. Currently engaged in the process of having a compilation of works published.; [pers.] Be guided by the spirit which is all powerful and seeks always to manifest the very best in us.; [a.] London, UK, SE13 7XG

JUNGBAUER, SVEN
[pen] Jungbauer; [b.] 20 October 1978; Almeria; [p.] Gustavo and Christel; [ed.] Military School; [occ.] Military service, Canary Islands; [memb.]

Culture Center Charismatic Group; [hon.] Student Military; [oth. writ.] Several literary works in German and Spanish of different kinds, still not published; [pers.] I tried to write songs to better the reputation of hard core music in The Canary Islands because it was possible with rock music, giving it a more positive image; [a.] Los Cristians, Spain

KALAMBOUKAS, THEO
[b.] 3 February 1946; Thessaloniki, Greece; [p.] Markos and Smaro Kalamboukas; [m.] Doreen Ansell, 9 January 1980; [ch.] Markos; [ed.] State Grammar School, State Theatre of Northern Greece Drama School, State Odeou Drama School, "K. Charatsaris" Drama School; [occ.] Director of Theatre; [memb.] Writer's Union of Northern Greece; [oth. writ.] "Perhaps You Believe That...", "Alcohol," plays, short stories, essays and magazine articles published in local art magazines; [pers.] We live and legend. Everyone creates a personal myth, constantly changing, that filters reality. Fortunately, because we would experience life as "naked numbers" without our myth, losing the beauty of variety, the spiritual sense, arts and happiness; [a.] Thessaloniki, Greece

KALANTZIS, BEVERLEY
[b.] 13 November 1940; India; [p.] Joan and Ken Beaumont; [m.] Spiros Kalantzis, 13 November 1969, (Spiro died, 1989); [ch.] Natushka; [ed.] Queen Margarets School Yorkshire, Evendine Court Domestic Science College flew as an Air Hostess for B.U.A. and Laker Airlines; [memb.] Corfu Tennis Club, IFAW; [pers.] My motto in life is positive thinking and a sense of humour; [a.] Corfu, Greece

KATHIRGAMATHAMBY, UMAH
[b.] 1 February 1982; Essex; [p.] Balasubramuniam Kathirgamathamby, Sakuntala Kathirgamathamby; [ed.] Royds Hall High School; [occ.] High School student; [pers.] An unfulfilled dream is a lifelong regret; [a.] Huddersfield, West Yorkshire

KAUR, RAVINDER
[b.] 1 October 1974; Manchester; [p.] Kher Singh Landa, Kuldeep Kaur Landa; [m.] Divorced; [ch.] Mica-Sheela Singh; [ed.] Whalley Range High School; [occ.] Administrator; [oth. writ.] Currently writing a book on the Sikh Wedding; [pers.] I wrote my poem for my daughter Mica, hoping she will be thinking of me wherever she may be; [a.] Manchester, Lancs

KAZER, EMMA JAYNE
[b.] 12 January 1979; Chorley; [p.] John Kazer, Janet Kazer; [ed.] Balshaws High School, Leyland, Runshaw College, Leyland; [occ.] Student; [hon.] GNVQ Advanced Art and Design; [pers.] I enjoy reading and writing poetry and try to express my feelings and experiences in my writing for the enjoyment of others; [a.] Leyland, Lancs

KEELEY, MARY A. T.
[pen.] Mary A. T. Keeley; [b.] 12 June 1924; Forno Vecchio, Naples, Italy; [p.] Percival Reginald Nesling and Alexandra Jeanette Nesling (Both Deceased); [m.] Widowed three times; [ch.] Michael Jensen and Tracy Adlam; [ed.] Simon Langton Girls School, Canterbury, Kent, Clough's College Canterbury, Kent; [occ.] Retired, ex Civil Servant, Keyboard Typesetting for Unwin Bros Printers Woking Surrey; [memb.] Canterbury Operative Society about 1956; [oth. writ.] Poems published in five Anthologies since 1972. Poems published in Works Magazines. Birthday, Xmas and Get Well Cards I personalize with my own poems and am well known for this with working colleagues and friends; [pers.] Poems inspired by love of nature and animals. People and events taking place can trigger up verses very easily to me. Because I am strong and healthy it gives me a lot of pleasure to work and help those unable to help themselves and a purpose in life; [a.] Woking, Surrey

KEMBLE, MISS CHARLEY
[b.] 18 July; Northampton; [ed.] Bedford High School, I am studying 3 A-Levels at the moment; [occ.] Student; [oth. writ.] Articles published in 'The Surrey Advertiser'; [pers.] Our words will be those of the future and in this world of madness we need a sanctuary; [a.] Bucks

KILLEEN, JOHN
[b.] Leeds; [ed.] St. Michael's College, Leeds, University of Leeds, University of London; [occ.] Antiquarian Bookseller; [memb.] Provincial Booksellers Fairs Association (PBFA); [hon.] M.A. (Leeds); [oth. writ.] Occasional Freelance Articles for New Statesman, Punch, Yorkshire Post, etc., Antiques Page in Profile (Harrogate and District 'Glossy'), An as yet Unpublished Novel called Ryan's Riding; [pers.] My imaginative writings usually attempt an ironic focus on the complacency which lurks behind much majority opinion. Among writers I respect are Pope, Hopkins and James Joyce; [a.] Ingleton, North Yorkshire

KING, MARTIN BRENTON
[b.] 11 September 1973; Hull; [occ.] Student (Journalism); [pers.] I am concerned with the post modern condition, space, time, identity, Technology. The flip side to capitalism in the 20th Century. I try to mix such concepts with a kind of romantic theme. Even a stopped clock tells me time twice a day; [a.] Hull, Yorkshire

KLAUS, HANFLER
[b.] 11 August 1966; Ahlen, Germany; [ed.] FH Bochum, Germany; [occ.] Account Manager; [a.] 61350 Bad Homburg, Germany

KLOSOWSKI-TRAVIS, B. J.
[pen.] Tara Travis; [b.] 5 January 1953; Bebbington; [p.] Victor and Frances Klosowski; [m.] Fergus Carlo Dougal Adam Travis; 10 January 1992; [ch.] Carmen Natasha Klosowski Travis; [ed.] Little Shutton High School for Girls, Wirral Stanley Night School, Nr Chester Studied Art and Design; [occ.] Homemaker and mother; [oth. writ.] Troubled Waters, Friend or Foe, To Meet You Again, A Friend of Mine, Passing of Time "Well Hello," Dear Mother, and many others, mostly for friends, family, greetings cards. I will be designing and writing my own cards; [pers.] Every person is gifted, some see the world, in bright colours and paint it, others sing. But we all have a love story, to read for pleasure!; [a.] Chester, Cheshire

KNEALE, AMIE
[b.] 17 December 1987; Sutton Coldfield; [p.] Ray Kneale, Gail Kneale; [ed.] Perton Middle School, Wolverhampton; [occ.] Student; [memb.] Orchestra first act of centre stage drama groups. Founder member of animal carer kids; [hon.] Taking grade 3 in Flute.; [oth. writ.] Several poems performed at local events and festivals. As I walk, the Schoolchild, love conquers death, what are we all?; [pers.] I oppose any forms of cruelty. I am an animal lover and I strive to help and support animal charities; [a.] Wolverhampton, Staffordshire

KNEDLIK, SHANON
[b.] 20 June 1982; Banff, AB, Canada; [p.] Vaclav and Alicia Knedlik; [ed.] Entering Gr. 10; [occ.] Student; [hon.] Piano, Handball, Swimming; [oth. writ.] This is my first.; [pers.] I love poetry and was inspired by the poems of Edgar Allen Poe; [a.] Calgary, AB, Canada

KUSAR, KHALDA
[b.] 26 March 1972; Birmingham; [p.] Saleema Kusar and Mohammed Ashraf; [ed.] Handsworth Wood Girls Secondary School; [occ.] English Student; [oth. writ.] Several poems have been written for my own pleasure; [pers.] The world may seem a corrupt place to be, where beings indulge in inflicting harm to fellows, and nature, life itself and existence one the greatest mentors of all. I hope to express the goodness that many cease to forget through my writing; [a.] Handsworth, Birmingham

LACK, CAROLYN MARGARET
[pen.] Carolyn M. Lack; [b.] 18 September 1978; Edinburgh; [p.] Richard and Margaret Lack; [ed.] Musselburgh Grammar School, Musselburgh. Currently studying Psychology through "Oxford Open Learning"; [occ.] Customer Service Advisor — British Telecom; [pers.] "Life" is based on a personal experience of mine. I wrote it, as it was the only way I could express how I felt at the time. It is dedicated to all of those who at some stage have felt the same. Believe in life, not death. Don't give up; [a.] Musselburgh, Midlothian

LAIRD, ANNE CHRISTINE
[pen.] Anne Laird; [b.] 30 June 1955; Melbourne, Australia; [p.] Richard Noel Laird, Valda Laird; [ch.] Bodhi Richard, Shanti Bianca Waite; [ed.] Certificate in Business Studies. Williamstown Primary School, and Girls High School. Mornington Senior High Sch. Port Hedland Junior High School, Geraldton Senior High School.; [pers.] I hope that people find some pleasure in reading my poetry. I am a great fan of Agatha Christie's, Mervyn Peake's and Pam Ayres's writings; [a.] Perth, Western Australia

LAIRD, PETER
[pen.] Peter; [b.] 25 November 1940; Edinburgh; [p.] Foster Elizabeth (Bell), Thomson Stonehaven; [m.] Dorothy Laird, 4 August 1962; [ch.] Sandra and Joanne Laird; [ed.] Dunnotter School, Stonehaven, Kincardineshire Castle Hill Primary, Edinburgh, Southbridge, Edinburgh and James Clark Secondary Edinburgh and Royal Air Force; [occ.] Council Employee, Public Services City of Glasgow; [memb.] Royal Air Force Association, Church Wishaw, distinguished member of I. L. of Poetry, R.A.F. and Defence Fire Services Association; [hon.] Editors Choice Award, The International Library of Poetry; [oth. writ.] Entry published in 'Awaken To A Dream' called an "Ode To A Caladonian Belle" and some Scottish and Canadian poems (not yet published) and also about Andalucia, Spain; [pers.] Ambition to see Vancouver Island and see mighty trees, 1,000 years old forests. The Grand Canyon, USA, and listen to Indian communities in USA and Canada sing their scenery. Great regard for Red Indian philosophy to the land and nature: Robert Burns's, John Buchan and Sir Walter Scotts's works: The Amer. Author; [a.] Wishaw, Lanarkshire

LAKOVIC, JEFTA
[b.] 6 June 1948; Belgrade, Yugoslavia; [p.] Mrs. Olivera Lakovic, Colonel Konstantin Lakovic; [m.] Divorced over a decade, 24 July 1971; [ch.] Aleksandar, Nikolai, Natasha; [ed.] Belgrade University, Meca. Eng., Birmingham University, Mech. Eng., Imperial College, London, Mech. Eng.; [occ.] Food Industry Executive and Chartered Engineer; [memb.] Institutions of Mechanical, Electrical and Manufacturing Engineering, European Engineer, Institute of Management, full Professional Membership of all; [hon.] Grant from British Scholarship Trust for Yugoslavs, 1968, Sandifer Memorial Prize for Design, 1971, Tesla prizes for machine elements and design, for Manufacturing Technology, 1966.; [oth. writ.] None published yet; [pers.] In this world of change, honour, valour, honesty and integrity are everlasting values. Know these values and live by them; [a.] Maidenhead, Berkshire

LANGFORD, KAI A.
[b.] 18 December 1954; London; [p.] R. R. Langford (Father), A. G. Stevens (Mother); [ch.] Tama P. S. and Simeon C. J.; [ed.] Comp - London, Grammar-Sussex; [occ.] Writer, Poet, Visionary, Mother; [oth. writ.] Mostly poetry and prose, several articles, children's verse and stories; [pers.] Where real communication wears thin in our world, I believe poetry offers a link and connection that techno-hype cannot: A finer form of interaction, immortalized; [a.] Bristol, Avon

LANGRIDGE, JENNY
[b.] 3 December 1943; Cheltenham; [p.] Ronald and Kathleen Green; [m.] John Harold Langridge, 15 February 1975; [ch.] Gary and Claire; [ed.] Tenkesbury High School For Girls; [occ.] Technical Illustrator; [memb.] Charlton Kings Choral Society; [pers.] Using words and watercolours, I love to portray the way in which the wonders of nature continually inspire me; [a.] Cheltenham, Gloucestershire

LARKIN, WENDY
[pen.] Lynden; [b.] 23 May 1943; Ripley, Surrey; [p.] Alan and Jean Rickman; [m.] Keith Larkin, 12 October 1968; [ch.] Mark Owen, Robyn Davies and Christopher Keith; [ed.] Aylwin Grammar (London), Cripplegate Secretarial College; [occ.] Self-employed Administrator; [memb.] None currently as I have recently returned from Hong Kong after 14 years; [oth. writ.] Book in progress including other poems; [pers.] Poetry reflects the soul's release of spiritual emotion, I have been influenced by classical poets of the victorian era; [a.] Chippenham, Wilts

LASHAM, ROSEMARY
[b.] 5 November 1941; Bridport, Dorset; [p.] Bernard House and Phylis House; [m.] Richard Lasham, 16 April 1960; [ch.] John Lasham, Amanda Creasey, Hayley Lasham; [ed.] Ware Grammer, Ware College; [occ.] Residential Social Worker/Young people; [memb.] Ware Riding Club; [oth. writ.] Just for friends/relations; [pers.] I tend to write about events that promote a great depth of feelings; [a.] Welwyn, Herts

LAVERS, VALERIE
[pen.] Valerie Lavers; [b.] 30 June 1943; Luton, Beds; [p.] Ronald George and Vera Beatrice Willis; [m.] Gordon Roy Lavers (Deceased), 30 July 1966; [ch.] Michele, Andrew, Kevin; [ed.] Priory Secondary Modern School, Britain; [occ.] Welfare Assistant Ashtree JMI School, Stevenage, Herts; [memb.] Stevenage Bowls Club in Art and Pottery attend classes; [oth. writ.] This is my first; [pers.] This poem began as a few words on a gift tag to accompany gifts for a friends special birthday. It then developed into the poem "Images of Friendship"; [a.] Stevenage, Herts

LEE, AILEEN
[pen.] Aileen Lee; [b.] 30 May 1981; Co. Cork; [p.] Patrick and Johanna Lee; [ed.] Scoil Mhuire National School, St. Aloysius Secondary School; [occ.] Slave to the empire that is our educational system; [memb.] I am currently a member of the elite society group that is the human race; [hon.] My one true honour is that I am alive; [pers.] 'Life is the dream that comes into the light, where angels dare to tread, where all around you magic drifts, and fills your days with peace of mind'; [a.] Ballincollig, Cork, Ireland

LEE, FELIX PETER
[pen.] Peter Lee; [b.] 26 August 1930; Ilford, Essex; [p.] Dr. J. I. and Mrs. P. Lee; [m.] Kate L. Soragna, 29 May 1997; [ch.] Simon, Andrew and Sarah-Jane; [ed.] Parkside Prep School, The Perse School, Cambridge, University of Western Australia; [occ.] Retired/Writer; [oth. writ.] "A History of the U.S.A.", "The Night Watch" — 240 short horror stories for radio. Journalism; [pers.] I write what I feel compelled to write; [a.] Malpas, Cheshire

LEECH, AMY
[b.] 24 July 1978; Gt Yarmouth, Northgate Hosp.; [p.] Frances and Neville Leech; [ed.] The Denes High School Lowestoft; [occ.] Photographic Lab. Assistant; [hon.] 5 GCSE's one B in English Literature; [oth. writ.] Have been writing since I was nine, although previously unpublished; [pers.] I'd like to acknowledge my family, especially my Nan, June Jennings, who told me to hold onto dreams because they will come true; [a.] Lowestoft, Suffolk

LEIGH-TURNER, CORINNA
[b.] 19 May 1951; Oxford; [p.] Dr. David and Mrs. Rosemary Leigh; [m.] Col Keith Turner, 29 August 1992; [ed.] Westonbirt School, Gloucs. and St. Clares, Oxford; [occ.] Owns and runs a stud and rehab centre for physically and mentally unwell horses; [oth. writ.] Too numerous to mention but only for my own comfort and indulgence. Never attempted publication; [pers.] Mine is a deep and abiding passion for the natural world — its preservation and recognition; [a.] Wincanton, Somerset

LELLIOTT, DEBORAH
[b.] 15 April 1950; Surrey; [p.] William Mould, Doris Mould; [m.] John Lelliott; [ch.] Chantelle, Belinda, and Ben; [ed.] Comprehensive; [occ.] Myself and my husband own a small carpentry and Doubie glazing business; [oth. writ.] My most recent poem "The Trial," being in my opinion, my best yet; [pers.] I try in these tedious times to inject humour into my work; [a.] Haywards Heath, W. Sussex

LEWIS, MRS. MARGARET
[b.] 15 February 1942; Wales; [p.] Amy and Islwyn Harris; [m.] Melville Lewis, 3 September 1960; [ch.] Two daughter, one son; [ed.] Lewis School for girls Hengoed, Reg General Nurse, Diploma in Community Health Studies (College of Medicine Univ. Hosp. of Wales Cardiff); [occ.] Health Visitor; [memb.] Local Amateur Dramatic Group; [oth. writ.] 'The Pre-Natal Class,' 'Mam,' 'Dad' and 'The Rest Of Us,' 'And Why', short sketches for use in youth groups pantomime script. Humpty Dumpty (unfinished); [pers.] My work with families throughout the life cycle has most influenced my writing. My childhood is the Welsh Valleys as part of a large family with a father who worked in the mines has also influenced my view of life and my writing; [a.] Blackwood, Gwent

LEWIS, RHIANYDD
[b.] 21 March 1983; Carlisle; [p.] Jeremy and Jayne Lewis; [ed.] Parkstone Grammar School; [occ.] School pupil; [oth. writ.] Several poems published in anthologies; [pers.] I feel, therefore I write!; [a.] Poole, Dorset

LEWIS, SHANI
[b.] 31 July 1979; Camden, London; [p.] Ann and Fraser Lewis; [ed.] Hertford Junior School, Brighton Varndean High School, Brighton then Varndean Sixth Form College, Brighton where I studied A' Levels in Chemistry, physics and Biology; [occ.] Student and I work part-time as a Pharmacy Counter Assistant; [pers.] I am hearing impaired and I find it easier to express my thoughts and feelings on paper. This is where my inspiration comes from, through past experiences and events; [a.] Brighton, East Sussex

LIDDELL, THOMAS A.
[b.] 29 November 1933; York; [p.] Thomas and Eileen Liddell; [m.] Divorced; [ed.] Nunthorpe Grammar School York; [occ.] Retired Instrument Maker; [memb.] Ex member of York Chess Club, Ex member of York Railway Institute (Boxing Section). Ex member of Prescot and Knotty Ash Chess Club. Liverpool. Ex member of York Boy's Club; [hon.] Two awards won at Chess 1973 Kirkby open York school boy boxing champion at my weight, Member of York Youth Boxing Team 1950, Played football for four local teams; [oth. writ.] Won Editor's Choice Award for poem published in "The Other Side of the Mirror" and entitled "The Steam Express 1946," won Editor's Choice Award for poem published in "A Lasting Calm" and entitled "Away, At The Sea-side"; [pers.] Assisted a good motor Company (Halewood) with their apprentice training scheme (Engineering) for seven years full time. Such was their enthusiasm, if any of them read my poetry they will become poet by the next day; [a.] York, Yorkshire

LIGGINS, JUNE M. B.
[b.] 12 June 1943; Leicester; [p.] Horace Jeffs, Kathleen Jeffs; [m.] Geoffrey B. Liggins, 2 August 1969; [ch.] Joanne Kathryn, Fiona Dawn, Debra Gayle; [ed.] Gateway Girls' Grammar, Leicester; [occ.] Housewife; [oth. writ.] None other than a further poem written recently; [a.] Narborough, Leicester, Leicestershire

LINDROTH, KATARINA
[b.] 25 August 1978; Sweden; [p.] Rosalind Lindroth, Mats Lindroth; [m.] Sophie Lindroth; [ed.] Christ's Hospital Boarding School, Horsham, West Sussex and now study Russian/ Arabic Lang. at Leeds University; [occ.] Student of English (Lang. and Lit.), French and Russian A-levels; [memb.] 2 Choirs and 2 Orchestras at school, RAF section of combined cadets force, Dramatic Society (Shakespeare) and Dance; [pers.] My philosophy — there are no limits to your dreams but there is every reason to try and fulfill them; [a.] Reading, Berkshire

LINDSAY, ROBERT
[b.] 10 May 1944; Belfast; [p.] James William and Lilian Lindsay; [m.] Thelma Edward, 1 April 1967; [ch.] James Israel, Joel and Helina; [ed.] Former Special Education Teacher now living on a farm outside Belfast; [a.] Carryduff Down

LINNEY, MISS B. A.
[pen.] Barbara Ann Linney; [b.] 29 August 1937; Surrey; [p.] Deceased; [ch.] David Falcon, Susan Pernice and Angela Kerkup; [ed.] G.C.E.S. A level in Art and Design Kidderminster College and R.S.A. in computing; [occ.] Lecturer and Model; [memb.] Kidderminster Libraries Labour Party take a break Letters Bookers; [hon.] 3 Awards from the Editor of the International Library of Poetry; [oth. writ.] Life story of my life; [pers.] Where there's life there's hope; [a.] Kidderminster, Worcs

LINNEY, SYLVIA MAUDE
[b.] 28 July 1921; Steyning, Sussex; [p.] Adeline Maud Camps, P. A. Harry Camps; [m.] H. John Linney, 7 July 1951; [ch.] Vanessa, Anthony; [ed.] Aldrington and Hove High School, Glebe Villas Hove, Sx. Miss Bollans Boarding School, Deal Kent; [occ.] Active interest occupying several hours weekly involving well being of elderly folk. By that I mean older than myself!; [memb.] Brighton and Hove Albion Football Team supporter, (Member) 69 years of loyal support, sadly after nearly 100 years, the ground has been sold. No home to go to!; [hon.] Brought up in a musical environment and sport of equal importance. School medals for many sports events, two brothers and parents all sporty and musical; [oth. writ.] For personal pleasure only stories and poems; [pers.] Life proves in part to be a journey of personal injuries. "Do as you would be done by" would lessen the bruising, bloodshed, and heartache — en route; [a.] Hove, Sussex

LIPSCOMBE, GLENYS MAY
[pen.] Glesnig-Mai; [b.] 18 May 1927; Swansea; [p.] W. P. and W. J. Davies; [m.] Archibald Singleton Lipscombe, 7 January 1950; [ed.] St. Helen's School for Girls National School's Swansea Brynmill Senior School for Girls; [occ.] Retired; [memb.] M.U.; [oth. writ.] One poem in Words on the Wind also one poem in Christian Messenger (this year); [pers.] I have always loved poetry and to me the written word conveys beauty and so many more emotions, such a joy, sadness, love and so much more besides, an everlasting tree; [a.] Swansea, West Glam

LITTLE, HELEN PENELOPE
[b.] 25 December 1942; Surrey; [ed.] Colston's Girls', Bristol, University of Kent, Canterbury; [occ.] English Teacher, Aufbaugymnasium, Essen; [oth. writ.] Occasional magazine articles; [pers.] Have very recently discovered that poetry gives me a private "English" garden in a very public "German" landscape of life; [a.] Essen, Germany

LLOYD, MR. WAYNE
[pen.] William Arthur Pen Dragon; [b.] 18 December 1958; Mountain Ash; [p.] David Islwyn and Audrey; [m.] Georgina Lloyd, 23 July 1977; [ch.] Jason and Steven; [ed.] Mountain Ash Comprehensive; [occ.] Unemployed; [hon.] 1 Award; [oth. writ.] "Wings of an Angel," "Fame and Glory," "Metal Heroes," "Scarlet Heroes," "Country Side," "Sir George and The Dragon," "By The Light of the Moon," "World Reunite"; [pers.] I am inspired by the 24th of foot regiment S. Wales borderers Brecon Museum

LONG, BRUCE M.
[b.] 11 October 1963; Bridgewater; [p.] Gordon and Judith Long; [ed.] Heles School Exeter, HMS Ralieoh, HMS Daedalus, HMS Heron, HMS Drake, Somerset College of Arts and Technology, Southwest College of Health studies, Plymouth University; [occ.] Nurse; [memb.] British Legion Chapletown, S. Yorks, White Ensign Naval Club, Exeter, Winners Circle, Mensa; [hon.] South Atlantic Medal; [oth. writ.] Poem, "An Ode To The Falkland Islands" published last year in the International Library of Poetry Book, "Awaken To a Dream"; [pers.] Now that I have had 2 of my poems published one at each end of my portfolio, both different in their writing, I am in the process of getting my book published, "Poems from inspiration," 30 poems on a wide spectrum; [a.] Sheffield, S. Yorks

LONG, SUSAN
[pen.] Susan Long; [b.] 1 September 1947; Marlborough; [p.] Mary Watts, Lancelot Watts; [m.] Peter Long, 5 March 1966; [ch.] Samantha Jayne, Victoria; [ed.] Marlborough Secondary Modern; [occ.] Office Administrator; [oth. writ.] A few personal poems relating to experiences; [pers.] I like to write to overcome stress and my ambition is to write my life story in the form of poetry; [a.] Fareham, Hampshire

LONGYEAR, SUE
[pen.] Suzie; [b.] 21 January 1950; Portsmouth; [p.] Alfred Longyear, Esther Longyear; [ch.] Sara Louise Longyear; [occ.] Make my own Ceramics, Mould, Paint, Fire; [oth. writ.] A poem about my cat, who died after being with me for 14 years, enclosed a copy for you to read!; [pers.] I love writing poems, I keep all the pieces of paper that I write, and often get them out to read to be able to express to yourself that your mind is wonderful

LORD, AMANDA CATHERINE
[pen.] Amanda C. Lord; [b.] 9 May 1983; Liverpool; [p.] Diane Lord and Richard Lord; [ed.] Ballakermeen High School, Douglas Isle of Man; [memb.] Manx Youth Choir; [pers.] "My poem is a poem that came straight from my heart." I would like to add a special thank you to my mum and gran for everything; [a.] Onchan, Isle of Man

LOWE, MARY WINEFRED
[b.] 21 March 1924, St Mary Hospital; London; [p.] Both Deceased; [m.] 5 December 1959; [ed.] Very good Education; [occ.] Kennel Maid; [oth. writ.] I write about every thing, the earth and what we are doing to it, the politicians, the mess they get us into, and animals and how we treat them, I do not eat meat as I know what the pain they are in; [pers.] I look at this world and see what man is doing to it and I write these poems just hoping that man will stop and look around and just see what he is doing to this earth of ours; [a.] Canvey Island, Essex

LOWRIE, ELIZABETH
[pen.] Lizelle Mack; [b.] 2 March 1946; Paisley; [p.] John and Isabella McIntyre; [m.] David Lowrie, 30 September 1972; [ch.] Heather, Alyson, Gordon; [ed.] Ferguslie Prim. School Abercorn Junior Secondary School — both in Paisley; [occ.] Housewife, Ex-Local Govt. Officer; [memb.] Distinguished I.S.P, Lladro Collectors Society Thimble Guild of Scotland Brownie Guider since 1983; [hon.] Editor's Choice Award ISP 1996, for entry submitted and published in "Voices on The Wind"; [oth. writ.] In U.S.A. mid 1970's, In Barnardo's Charity Book 1996, In "Voices On The Wind" I.S.P. 1996, others offered publication by same in Britain and U.S.A., plus "Internet Coverage" offered; [pers.] Live and enjoy your life the best you can, doing what you like best; [a.] Glasgow, Strathclyde

LOWRIE, SANDY
[b.] 1 May 1908; Kirkcaldy; [p.] Helen and Alex Lowrie; [m.] Helen Cusick Lowrie, 27 May 1941; [ch.] Son; [ed.] West Public School, Kirkcaldy; [occ.] Retired Engineer; [memb.] In RAF from 1939-1945 — Engine fitter; [hon.] War Medals; [oth. writ.] Regular Anecdotes in local paper on a variety of topics. Response from H. M. Queen to his poem "Nurses"; [pers.] My poems reflect the reality of everyday life and the importance of man's charity to mankind; [a.] Kirkcaldy, Fife

LOWY, JACKIE
[b.] 3 May 1957; Canterbury; [p.] Philip E. High, Pamela C. J. Baker; [m.] Matthew, 20 November 1993; [ed.] Frank Hooker Secondary Modern, Leicester University, Loughborough University; [occ.] Optical Advisor; [memb.] RCN (Royal College of Nursing), BAC (British Association of Counselling), Richard III Society, various Babylon S Fan Clubs; [hon.] Hons-History of Art; [oth. writ.] Several poems published in various magazines and periodicals. Reviews of conventions for fan magazines. Articles for Opera Society about opera; [pers.] I am on a journey, discovering my 'real', my 'true' self. I use my poetry to explore my feelings and psyche if I can discover ways to grow and renew my life then I know I can aid others in the same task; [a.] Benson, Wallingfort, Oxfordshire

LUBY, PATRICIA
[b.] 3 November 1979; Birmingham; [p.] Alo Luby, Ann Luby; [ed.] Attending Ballyhaunis Community School, last year in school, about to do leaving cert; [oth. writ.] I have written several other poems that have not seen the light of day. Let alone be published and had it not been for a nosy but persistant friend, neither would this one; [pers.] People should be true to themselves and stop always trying to meet other people's expectations

MACARTHUR, MRS. NORMA ANNE
[pen.] Norma Anne; [b.] 8 March 1940; Edinburgh; [p.] Both parents deceased; [m.] Divorced in Canada, 16 July 1974, 20 March 1963 in Scotland; [ed.] Higher Leaving Certificate, McLaren High School, Callendar Perthshire; [occ.] Registered General Nurse (Night Sister); [memb.] Church of Scotland; [hon.] Several Nursing Prizes won during training at the Royal Infirmary Edinburgh and Princess Margaret Rose Hospital Edinburgh; [oth. writ.] "A School Boy's Prayer," "Hurray Scurray Up The Stairs," "Railways Echoes," "In The Park," "Autumns Aura," "The Expert," (amongst others); [pers.] I became poetic when my marriage was dissolved some time ago over the years it has become a creative expressive outlet for my deepest joys and sorrows I regard it as a gift from God; [a.] Edinburgh, Midlothian

MACDONALD, FIONA
[b.] 23 January 1978; Irvine, Ayrshire; [p.] Jean Ann and Alistair MacDonald; [ed.] I left high school and never had any further education, well I didn't go to college anyway.; [occ.] Self employed, Buy and Sell Stuff; [oth. writ.] I have other unpublished material inc. "The Way Things Are," "Love Bird," "You Can't Do Magic" and others unpublished also and unknown.; [pers.] Treat everyone like family and you'll be welcomed in many homes. That's my get along scene; [a.] Kinlochleven, Argyll

MACHALE, MICHAEL PHILIP
[b.] 13 December 1939; Dublin, Ireland; [p.] Thomas MacHale, Eileen MacHale; [m.] Maureen Wright, 25 August 1964; [ch.] Laurence, Michael, Hilary, Helena; [ed.] Chris Brothers College, Jesuit College Ind. Relations (Dip) Family Law University College Dublin, Chinese Civilization Univ. College Dublin; [occ.] Working on Novel plus Poetry; [memb.] Leophrastown Horse, Racing Club; [hon.] 1996 "Editors Choice Awards" for Outstanding Achievement in poetry. From your Society Int. Library of Poetry. Invited to Membership Int. Society of Poets U.S.A, which I will take up. Applic. form sent 22 July 97 U.S.A.; [oth. writ.] Poem dedicated to memory of Murdered Journalist Veronica Guerin, Poem dedicated to my grandson Evan and poetry that reflects changing Irish Society in all its aspects; [pers.] I try to reflect modern life in my poetry and writing; [a.] Dun Laoghaire, Co Dublin, Ireland

MACPHEE, ILONA ROWENA
[b.] 29 November 1941; Poulton-le-Fylde; [p.] Edward Dodgson, Florence Dodgson; [m.] Gordon Charles MacPhee, 30 March 1963; [ch.] The late Gordon Norman, Stuart Edward; [ed.] Fleetwood Grammar, The University of Lancashire, St. Martin's College, Lancaster; [occ.] Retired English Teacher; [hon.] B.A. Hons — English/Ed Studies P.G.C.E. Teaching Qualification; [pers.] I endeavour to empathise with human experience and the depth of human emotion; [a.] Poulton-le-Fylde, Lancashire

MAHER, JESSICA
[b.] 13 February 1968; High Wycombe; [p.] Joe Maher, Mathleen Maher; [ch.] Shannon, Ronan; [ed.] Tullow Community School; [occ.] Housewife and Mother; [pers.] I dedicate this poem to my daughter Shannon and family and friends; [a.] Tullow, Carlow

MALLIA, WALTER
[pen.] Walter Mallia; [b.] 30 June 1935; Msida, Malta; [p.] Emmanuel / Elizabeth (Both Deceased); [m.] Doris Ne' Bugeja, 12 April 1964; [ch.] Hilda, Fiona, Jonathan; [ed.] The Lyceum, Malta; [occ.] Night Manager/Day Controller; [memb.] Former Member, Dragonara Cultural Group, Malta Science-Fiction Society; [hon.] 1st. prize in Maltese Poetry Competition in Gozo. 2nd Prize Poetry, in Local Competition. Prize in Art, Dragonara Cultural Grp; [oth. writ.] Poem Published in England. Currently publishing poems in different languages, in various local newspapers and magazines, usually with own illustrations; [pers.] Greatly influenced by English, Maltese, Italian Literature in General and Art; [a.] St. Julians, Malta

MALONE, TOM
[b.] 22 September 1976; Hartlepool; [p.] Ken and Margaret; [ed.] High Tunstall comprehensive moving to Hartlepool College of further Education studying Electrical Engineering and Physics; [occ.] P/T Delicatessen; [oth. writ.] None published; [pers.] The fool, the fool folds his hands and ruins himself, better one handful with tranquillity, than two hand fulls of toil, and chasing after the wind; [a.] Hartlepool

MALTBY-BAKER, ZOE
[b.] 15 July 1980; Redhill; [p.] Mr. G. Maltby-Baker, Mrs. G. Weston; [ed.] Buxton Community School 6 GCSE; [occ.] Studio Junior; [memb.] Macclesfield Library; [hon.] Achievement in Mathematics Nolage of the order (St. Johns); [oth. writ.] None of which have been published; [pers.] Dedicated to my two Nephews Carl Lewis Thorpe and Jamie Niel Thorpe; [a.] Macclesfield, Cheshire

MANNING, ROBERT G. E.
[b.] 21 August 1960; Watford; [p.] Anne and Frank Manning; [ed.] Merchant Taylors' Cardiff, Warwick, Exeter, Universities; [occ.] Promulgator of the Healing Arts; [pers.] Attuning to our ancestral inheritance via the teachings of the illumined ones leads to accessing their sense of cyclical, harmonious, joyful living. Manifesting this eternally is the source of inspiration; [a.] London

MANUEL, HOLLY
[b.] 3 January 1984; Nakuru; [p.] George and Janet; [ed.] Pemboroke House School and Peponi School; [occ.] School girl; [memb.] Nakuru Players Theatre, Wild Life Clubs of Kenya, East African Wild Life Society; [oth. writ.] One poem published "Pirates," but many poems still unpublished waiting for their publishing; [pers.] I am interested in poems which tell a story or are exciting or ghostly; [a.] Njoro, Kenya

MARAIS, ELIZABETH M.
[pen.] Elizabeth Farnham; [b.] 5 June 1923; London; [p.] Leonora and Frank Farnham; [m.] Michael Marais (Deceased), 23 December 1960; [ch.] Angela and Marilyn; [ed.] Independent School, Norwich City College; [occ.] Retired Head Teacher, Special School — children with learning difficulties; [memb.] National Assoc, Head Teachers, MEBCAP, RSPB, RSPCA, Norwich Writer's Circle, National Trust; [hon.] MBE; [oth. writ.] Book — 'Lives Worth Living' short stories, articles and poems in a variety of magazines and newspapers, also broadcasts; [pers.] Every person regardless of mental ability has equal rights and must be accepted and enabled to achieve their potential. This has been my life commitment; [a.] Norwich, Norfolk

MARLOW, EMILY J.
[b.] 19 September 1982; Northampton; [p.] Marianne and Jeff Marlow; [ed.] Student at Secondary School - (The West Somerset Community College); [memb.] Minehead Tae Kwon-do Club; [hon.] Two bronze trophies for Sparring in Tae Kwon-do Tornaments; [pers.] I wish to thank my family and friends but most of all my Grandad who inspired, encouraged and loved everything I did; [a.] Dulverton, Somerset

MARR, MRS. LESLEY
[b.] 2 March 1958; Bebington; [p.] Andre and Angela Lawrence; [m.] Stephen Patrick Marr, 8 September 1984; [ch.] Vicky; [ed.] Wirral County Grammar School for Girls and University of Manchester; [occ.] Homemaker; [memb.] Ivy Cottage Evangelical Church; [hon.] First Class Honours in Spanish Studies B.A.; [oth. writ.] Christian Songs; [pers.] As a Born-Again Christian I seek to give God the glory for my life and all the good things He has done for me; [a.] Manchester, Lancs

MARSH, JANET
[pen.] Rose Lee; [b.] 5 February 1959; Poplar; [p.] Jessie and Herbert Marsh; [ed.] St. Pauls Way School Bow E3; [occ.] Unemployed; [memb.] Int. Society of Poets Distinguished Member; [hon.] The 96 and 97 Editors Choice Award; [oth. writ.] Several poems published in the Int. Library of Poetry and Christian Anthologies; [pers.] All my poetry is written from hidden depths of my heart about 'Robert' who I've secretly loved without his knowledge throughout my life; [a.] Bow, London

MARSHALL, KAREN
[b.] 16 March 1980; Sunderland; [p.] Paul and Anne Marshall; [ed.] St. Anthonys Grammer School, Monkwearmouth Collage; [occ.] Student; [oth. writ.] Several poems but none published; [pers.] I find poetry an inspiration and a joy to read and write; [a.] Sunderland, Tyne and Wear

MARTIN, JUDITH ANNE
[pen.] Judi Martin; [b.] 2 March 1945; Auckland, New Zealand; [ch.] Jason Martin; [occ.] Office Supervisor; [memb.] Manukau Performing Arts; [pers.] I enjoy expressing my feelings through my writing; [a.] Mangere, Auckland, New Zealand

MARTIN, MRS. SUSAN MARGARET
[pen.] Sue; [b.] 26 October 1950; Chingford, Essex; [p.] Mr. and Mrs. J. B. I. Bampton (Deceased); [m.] Mr. Christopher John Martin, 2 September 1972; [ch.] Ann Michelle and Claire Louise Martin; [ed.] St Joseph's Convent, Canvey Island, St Gregory's (R.C.) School Ealing, St Thomas Moore's (R.C.) School Colchester, St Benedict's (R.C.) College Colchester, Colchester Institute, Colchester; [occ.] Housewife; [memb.] Member of the Chiropractic Patients' Association, supporter of International Fund for Animal Welfare; [hon.] RSA Shorthand 4 RSA's Typing Teeline shorthand with Distinction; [oth. writ.] My first poem ever seriously written is being published by the International Library of Poetry in Autumn 1997; [pers.] A wonderful experience to have my poetry accepted to be published in this anthology with our daughter Claire. Writing feelings and everyday life experiences has been a wonderful way of expressing deep emotions, which open your heart to share with others. The most precious gift is the value of family unity and unconditional love, quality of life, and freedom, this we cannot buy; [a.] Colchester, Essex

MARTIN, STEVEN VICTOR
[b.] 31 May 1977; Canvey; [p.] Maureen and Robert Martin; [ed.] Cornelius Vermuyden School, South East Essex College, Kent Institute of Art and Design; [occ.] Graphic Student; [memb.] Lead Singer and Bassist in a band called 'Single Entity' (c); [hon.] English Literature and Mathematics; [oth. writ.] I compose lyrics for my band; [pers.] I hate it when the pen stops flowing and thoughts dry, like the mudbanks when the tide ebbs. Slowly drained of fluids and dehydrated; [a.] Canvey Island, Essex

MASAND, MISS BINA
[b.] 5 August 1977; London, UK; [p.] Mr. W. L. Masand and Mrs. Anita Masand; [ed.] 9 GCSE's: 5A* 3A 1B, 3 a levels, Maths (B) Spanish (D) Economics (C) Studying Maths and Management Degree at King's College London; [occ.] Student; [memb.] Indian Dancing at Dudden Hill Community Centre, Part of Sindhi Association; [pers.] Although very young in age, at the time of the Zeebrugge disaster, I was very moved by the tragic occurrence, having acknowledged the courage evidently shown by the survivors. I was able to write this poem while empathizing with them; [a.] Willesden, London

MASKILL, RITA
[b.] 27 August1955; Chesterfield; [p.] Gertrude Jones, Clifford Jones; [m.] Peter Maskill, 28 May 1982; [ch.] Barry, Steven, Anthony, Allan, Wayne, Tammy; [ed.] Moorfield Comprehensive School, Bolsouer, Chesterfield; [occ.] Housewife; [memb.] International Society of Poets; [hon.] Editor's Choice Award; [oth. writ.] Several poems published in books; [pers.] I dedicate this poem ("Survival") to my parents, without them today would not have been possible; [a.] Tredegar, Gwent

MAYES, TRINA
[b.] 2 April 1957; Ipswich, Suffolk; [p.] Val and Violet Goodall; [m.] Alan Mayes, 20 August 1995; [ch.] Tania Gavin and Jake; [occ.] Mother and housewife at present; [oth. writ.] In the process of writing children's stories which I would like to publish — with any luck!; [pers.] "Feelings from the heart should be captured forever on paper"; [a.] Lawford, Essex

MCARTHUR, FRANK
[b.] 16 May 1938; N Ireland; [p.] Sam and Martha; [m.] Sybil, 5 November 1960; [ch.] Ian and Michael (Grandchildren — Megan, Katie, Christopher); [ed.] Eyemouth High School, B.H.S. Duns; [occ.] Self Employed Gardener; [memb.] W. Barns Bowling Club, Meadowmill Bowling Club; [hon.] High School Sports Champion, East Lothian Bowling Champion of Champions etc.; [oth. writ.] "Autumn" "Yet So Free" etc.; [pers.] I never cease to admire country, nature, wildlife. If all countries were not armed our world would be more charming; [a.] Dunbar, E. Lothian

MCCANN, KEVIN
[b.] 18 October 1950; Lough Gall; [p.] Terence, Kathleen (Deceased); [ed.] Late Developer, Good Grammar School Education, no qualifications, self-taught in poetic style of expressing thought process; [occ.] Carer, looking after John who is exceptional; [hon.] Editor's Choice Award for "Maggie's Place" (Outstanding Achievement in Poetry), 1997; [oth. writ.] "Maggie's Place" in anthology, `Jewels of the imagination' — am awaiting other publications of poems in forth coming anthologies — also am preparing poems for a publisher to read with a view to having my work in book format; [pers.] I strive to portray the actual area where I live, the natural environment, times past and present, experiences of interest to both myself and those close to me (family, friends and others touched by my writings); [a.] Lough Gall, Armagh

MCCARTHY, NEIL
[pen.] James Douglas; [b.] 27 June 1979; Birmingham; [p.] Michael McCarthy, Lee McCarthy; [ed.] Rawlett High School, Staffordshire England, St. Fachtna's De La Salle, Skibbereen, Ireland; [occ.] Student, Chef; [oth. writ.] Yet to be published; [pers.] To me life is not about winning or losing — it's about both. Some people are born to lose — others live to win; [a.] Skibbereen, Cork, Ireland

MCCASKA, AMNA
[oth. writ.] "Nile Wedding," "It is over," "Passion," "Consider Last week," "Answerphone"; [pers.] "My poems speak for me, I do not seek control over their destiny they belong to you, and you and you"; [a.] UK

MCCORMACK, SUZANNE
[b.] 18 May 1974; N. Ireland; [p.] Terry and Rosemary; [ed.] Co. Tyrone, N. Ireland; [occ.] Clerical Ass.; [hon.] Editor's Choice Award — "Pomeroy"; [oth. writ.] "Pomeroy"; [pers.] It is a great honor to see my work published; [a.] Cheltenham, Glos

MCDERMOTT, KEVIN
[b.] 30 December 1958; Salford; [p.] John and Margaret; [m.] Andrea Lee Strickland; [ch.] Elliott; [ed.] Hope High Secondary; [occ.] Transport Operations; [memb.] Neil Sedaka Fan Club, Britannia Music; [hon.] Certificate of Merit; [oth. writ.] "Seeking a miracle".; [pers.] In the two poems I have written, I have found peace of mind in coming to terms with the loss of my brother. I now hope to write about the joys of life; [a.] Salford, Lancashire

MCGHIE, MARY
[b.] 26 October 1940; Coatbridge; [p.] Anne and David Jeffrey; [m.] Walter McGhie, 2 December 1961; [ch.] One, Paul David; [ed.] St Patricks High Coatbridge; [occ.] Northern Regional Credid Controller; [memb.] Member of the Woman's Royal Voluntary Association; [oth. writ.] Personalized Greetings Cards; [pers.] Words are a heritage to be shared and enjoyed by everyone.; [a.] Coatbridge, Scotland

MCGLINN, MICHAEL
[b.] 26 December 1935; Dundee; [m.] Divorced; [ch.] Michael, Michael Stuart; [ed.] Left school at 15 years, returned to adult Education some time ago, and I am at present doing an H-N D works in fine Art and learning Spanish; [occ.] Bricklayer/Student PT; [oth. writ.] Poems and one Novel nothing published as yet.; [a.] Dundee, Glos

MCGOVERN, ANNE
[b.] 9 February 1962; Galway, Ireland; [p.] Mary and Joseph Gorham; [m.] Andrew McGovern, 6 July 1991; [ch.] Aine and Andrew; [ed.] Leaving cert in 9 subjects in Ireland; [occ.] Housewife and Mother; [oth. writ.] A handful of poems scribbled on a pad; [pers.] Poetry is the therapeutic voice of the soul spilling fine words onto paper and so becoming our great art; [a.] Kilburn, London

MCGRATH, PAULA SUSAN
[b.] 12 October 1979; Derry, N. Ireland; [p.] Patrick McGrath, Carmel McGrath; [ed.] Sion Mills Primary, Our Lady of Mercy High, Strabane, Co Tyrone, N. Ireland; [occ.] Production Operative; [pers.] Many authors and poets have influenced me through their works, but the top most on my list would have to be W. B. Yeats. Though I could never equal his infallible talent, I would like to eventually publish my own book, dedicating it to Yeats and my family, especially my parents; [a.] Braunstone, Leicester

MCKENZIE, ERROL
[b.] 16 May 1948; West Indies; [p.] James Augustus McKenzie, Miriam McKenzie; [m.] Lurline McKenzie, December 16, 1967; [ch.] Sean, Tanya, Alistair & Leon; [ed.] Hillcroft School, London; Open University, Milton Keynes; [occ.] Petro-Chemical Engineer, Freelance Consultant; [memb.] The Writers Bureau, Manchester, The Writers Guild of America-East, The Institute of Chemical Engineers; [hon.] Bachelor of Arts Degree (Chemistry Bias); [oth. writ.] First novel being finalised for publication in 1997. Numerous unpublished poems and short stories; [pers.] To be a beacon of inspiration to my fellow men and women of this earth, and to utilize the gift of writing to make a difference in the lives of those less fortunate than myself; [a.] Sanderstead, Surrey

MCKNIGHT, MARK ANTHONY
[b.] 14 July 1979; Barnstaple; [p.] Foster Care; [ed.] Excluded from Aberaeron comprehensive secondary school. Have been to college since and just finished Cardigan C.S. School; [occ.] Student; [memb.] Air Training Corps at Aberporth, Pony Club and BHS Member; [hon.] Duke of Edinburgh Award; [pers.] I want to show thoughts can be expressed in writing and not just spoken as so many do; [a.] Plump, Ceredigion

MCLELLAN, ALISON ELIZABETH
[b.] 29 November 1977; Paisley; [p.] Douglas and Janet McLellan; [ed.] Attended Houston Primary then went to Gryffe High, due to father's job, moved to Girvan and attended Carrick Academy and then Strathclyde University; [occ.] Student; [memb.] 'Poetry Now' magazine Student Association, English Literature Society, History Society; [hon.] Turnberry Cup for Business Management, Young Poet of the year 1995 in Ayrshire Regional winner in a Business Management competition for the Chartered Institute of Management Accountants; [oth. writ.] Several poems published in 'Poetry Now' magazine, poem published last year in a book called 'Rapture'. Dissertation on Seamus Heaney; [pers.] My poetry reflects day to day issues which I feel is important to us all. My aim is to write poems which are not fully understood the first time, but each time it is read, one gains another meaning; [a.] Girvan, Ayrshire

MCMILLAN, BELLA
[pers.] Having become housebound with arthritis for the last five years until her death in March 1997 started writing poetry as a hobby. This poem is an example of her work and is a reflection of her own life; [a.] Campbelltown, Argyll

MCTAGGART, DONNA MARIE
[pen.] Don/Nonny; [b.] 17 June 1978, Donegal Eire; [p.] Lena and Gerard McTaggart; [ed.] St. Conal's National School, Kilclooney, Co. Donegal; St. Columbas Comprehensive Gienties; [occ.] student; [memb.] 'Lifelines Ireland' (penpals on death row in U.S. or Caribbean); [hon.] Raphoe Diocesan Projects competition award in appreciation of work done. Swimming certificates.; [oth. writ.] "Inner and Outer Beauty"—a short story in which I received third prize (Kenny Naughton Short Story Competition) "From Pier to Strand to Heaven", published in local magazine.; [pers.] Never question happiness, because it makes you think that you're really not happy. Live for the moment, not the moment that's past. I believe that "every sound has a voice."; [a.] Donegal

MCVITTY, AARON
[b.] 9 January 1978; Belfast; [p.] Mary McVitty and Aaron McVitty; [ed.] St. Malachy's College, The Belfast Institute; [occ.] Photography Student; [memb.] The Institute of Amateur Cinematographers (I.A.C.), and Renegade Productions (Film Company); [hon.] Three Blue Seals — Movie '95, One Bronze Seal — Movie '96, One Silver Seal — Movie '97; [oth. writ.] Several short stories, numerous poems and songs, and three film scripts; [pers.] 'For Charlie'—my inspiration—"Carpe Diem" (Seize The Day); [a.] Belfast, Northern Ireland

MEGSON, JENNIFER
[b.] 26 January 1985; Paisley; [p.] Brian Megson and Liza Megson; [ed.] 2nd Year Park Mains High Erskine; [memb.] David Lloyd—Sports and leisure Centre—Poetry New Club; [hon.] Robert Burns Certificate of Merit, 2nd Best Girl in Girls Brigade; [oth. writ.] 3 other published poems; [a.] Bishopton, Renfrewshire, Scotland

MELMOTH, GEORGE FREDERICK
[b.] 1 November 1923; Plymouth; [p.] George Leonard and Lillian Angeline; [m.] Audrey, 10 December 1947; [ch.] Christopher George, David Charles, Daniel, Stephen Eric, Jonathan Mark; [ed.] St. Boniface, Plymouth, St. Vincents, Torquay, South Devon Technical College, Air Training Corps, RAF, Wartime Service; [occ.] Chiropractor, Physiotherapist; [memb.] MB Ch Ass. Diploma of Phyl, sometime member of Paignton Chess Club, Society of Genealogists; [hon.] Distinguished Member of The International Society of Poets; [oth. writ.] 'The Melmoth Story Through The Years'—Privately published, 6 yrs. of research, Co-author, brother, John, 'The Rose', 'Voices on the Wind', (International Soc' of Poets), 'Rhythmic Woodpecker' accepted also, 'Thirty-two Feet, Per Sec, Per Second.; [pers.] "To see life from a new angle, with humour. To constantly seek for truth, however unpleasant it may sometimes be"; [a.] Ponders, Enfield

MELROSE, RACHEL
[pen.] R. V.; [b.] York; [occ.] Retired; [oth. writ.] Others poems of different types—and style; [a.] Edinburgh, Midlothian

MELVILLE, FIONA
[b.] 13 March 1963; Dumpehline, Fife; [m.] Alan Melville, 19 June 1993; [ch.] Baby due on 27th August 1997!; [occ.] Forester; [pers.] 'Ode Tae A Wid Tink' was inspired by my dear husband Alan and describes that rare breed of Woodham, the timber Haulier—in this case a man called Sandy to whom Sawhills across the country are eternally grateful!!; [a.] Crossgates, Fife

MICHAELIDES, NATASHA MELISSA
[b.] 20 October 1987; Portland Hospital, London; [p.] Jane and Andreas Michaelides; [ed.] Heath Mount School Watton-at-Stone Hertfordshire; [occ.] Natasha attends the above school and will be entering form III in September; [memb.] Headmaster: The Reud. H. J. Matthews; [oth. writ.] Natasha is a keen writer but has not yet entered anything else for publication; [pers.] Natasha has attended Heath Mount School from the age of 6. She has always been an imaginative writer and wrote the 'Polar Bear' when she was 8 yrs. old. Her teacher assured us that "Natasha has exceptional talent and will one day become a famous author"; [a.] Cuffley, Herts

MILLICAN, JONATHAN
[b.] Worcestershire; [m.] Patricia, 1972 (Met 1970); [pers.] Born in Worcestershire I have returned after years abroad in the Bahamas, Hong Kong, I was a lawyer. It is my great love for my wife that inspired me to write poetry, I've never stopped since 1970! Rodmckuem is my favorite poet his poems have moved and influenced me tremendously; [a.] Worcester, Worcestershire

MILLMAN, KEITH ROY JOHN
[pen.] Roy Millman; [m.] Pamela Brierley; [ch.] David Millman, Vicky Williams, Peter Brierley Millman; [pers.] Enjoy the sun, enjoy the rain this day will never come again!; [a.] Wellington, New Zealand

MITCHELL, HANNAH-MARIE
[b.] 5 April 1983; St. Albans; [occ.] Student at Sandringham School; [hon.] Distinction in R.S.A Computer skills; [oth. writ.] "Inside-Out World," "The tear Drop," "Wonders of The unknown"; [pers.] Dedicated to my parents, nan and granddad, my brother Stephen, my Nephew Dominic and Michelle Rankin; [a.] Hatfield, Hertfordshire

MITCHELL, P. E.
[pen.] Steve Mitchell; [b.] 10 February 1950; Burton upon Trent; [p.] George and Peggy Mitchell; [m.] Maria Del Carmen, 16 November 1974; [ed.] Patcham-Fawcett, Brighton; [occ.] Security/Safety Specialist; [memb.] International Institute Risk and Safety Management, International Professional Security Association; [hon.] Dip SM.; [oth. writ.] Various poems as yet unpublished; [pers.] Inspired by my father who wrote his own verses for greeting cards and love poems; [a.] Horsham, West Sussex

MITCHELL, THOMAS
[pen.] TJJ; [b.] 18 December 1949; Greenock; [p.] Thomas Mitchell, Elizabeth M.; [m.] Margaret Ann, 24 July 1981; [ch.] Scott Thomas, Stuart Ian; [ed.] City and Guilds Adv, City Guilds Blessed William Howard School, IBICC, FTC; [occ.] Joiner, self employed; [pers.] We are surrounded by words and thoughts, they just need writing down; [a.] Stafford, Staffordshire

MOMEN, S. I.
[pen.] Shumon; [b.] 20 December 1979; London, UK; [p.] (Father) M. A. Momen, (Mother) Nilufar Ibn Momen; [ed.] Ilford County High School (Grammar); [oth. writ.] Shumon Momen Poetry '95 Posthumously book published. "Sparkling Lake" published in Awaken To A Dream.; [a.] UK

MONK, BEATE
[pen.] Beate Monk; [b.] 13 January 1965; Willich, Germany; [p.] Anita and Josef Himmel; [m.] Stuart James Monk, 4 January 1986; [ch.] Sean Karl (25 May 1987) Halley Marie Louise (17 February 1990); [ed.] Kindergarten teacher went to school in Germany. I brought up my children first; [occ.] I started as an assistant in a day care center and nursery and now have my own little business; [oth. writ.] None published "My Favorite Time Of Year" was the first ever poem that I had the bottle to enter into a competition in my entire life, and I can't believe it's a semi finalist; [pers.] I write about my life as a mother, housewife, private person, the pain and the joy. There's always something to be learned "If" we're humble enough. I found myself constantly worrying and rushing. I made myself stop and write things down and started to find beauty where I never expected to find any before; [a.] Lower Quinton, Warwickshire

MONKCOM, DAVID
[b.] 30 August 1950; Winchester; [p.] Cecil and Doris Monkcom; [m.] Catherine Rousseau; [ch.] Emily and Sarah; [ed.] Peter Symond's School, Winchester, St. Edmund Hall, Oxford; [occ.] Translator, European Commission (Brussels); [memb.] The Brussels Choral Society, other choirs and music groups; [oth. writ.] Poems, songs, essays, translations of song lyrics. So far I have submitted very few for publication; [pers.] At its deepest level life should, I feel, be a striving after truth, beauty and goodness, in this, music, poetry and art go hand in hand with philosophy and the inner spiritual life. It's a voyage of discovery; [a.] Tervuren, Belgium

MOON, KATHERINE
[b.] 5 August 1964; Bulawayo, Zimbabwe; [p.] Mr. David Moon and Mrs. Margarett Moon; [ed.] Townsend School, Bulawayo - O and A Levels University of Cape Town, R.S.A, B.A., major in English and History, advanced diploma of Remedial Music, Librarianship Diploma; [occ.] Librarian and Part-time Singer; [memb.] Cape Town Science- Fiction and Fantasy Society, belong to group of women who perform original songs, poems, drama; [oth. writ.] 3 Poems published in local women's anthology "Siren Songs"; [pers.] Influenced by the huge mix of cultures, myths, strife and beauty that has surrounded my growing up and living in Southern Africa; [a.] Cape Town, Green Point, South Africa

MOONEY, IRENE J.
[b.] 10 April 1938; London, Edmonton; [p.] Alfred George and Elsie May Maw; [m.] Martin Brian Mooney, 20 October 1962; [ch.] Steven Martin and Paul James; [ed.] Higher grade selective central London; [occ.] Registered General Nurse and Marie Curie Nurse; [memb.] National Trust and Derriford Leisure Centre and Ladies Dart Team; [hon.] Dowbiggan award in Editor's Choice Award 1994 and 1996 by the National Library of Poetry; [oth. writ.] Poems published by Triumph House, poetry now, arrival press, National Library of Poets, International Soc of Poets, Poetry Guild.; [pers.] My poems reflect the real me, personal experiences, my innermost thoughts and feelings and continue to be influenced by the beauty of nature and friends that express themselves through me; [a.] Plymouth, Devon

MOORE, ARTHUR STANLEY
[b.] 5 May 1917; Poplar; [p.] Deceased; [m.] Deceased, August 1958; [occ.] Disabled O.A.P.; [memb.] Ex Master Builder London Met J. Division, Ex Police Constable, Special, Med 25 yrs., Ex Army 1940-1946. London Irish Rifles (1st Batt.) Nat. Health Hosp. Service 20 yrs. Qualification 1st Class, PN, Tech IV; [hon.] Charge Department, 1st Diploma, ever presented, by Chief Pathology of Melbourne Australia, Ex Br. Sec of Coshe Union, Chairman of Guild Mary Technisions, Passed driving test at 69 yrs. old, after 6 private lessons, Life Sav-Cert at the age of 12 yrs; [pers.] I've always gained knowledge where possible. I've always spent my life trying to be a Human Being, the way my dearest parents taught me; [a.] Ashford, Kent

MOORE, DORIS
[b.] 11 May 1947; Aberdeen; [p.] Mrs. Flora Goa; [m.] Ronald Peter Moore, 5 August 1983; [ch.] Two; [ed.] Leaving Certificate only; [occ.] P/T. Carer, Nursing Home Animal Welfare Carer; [oth. writ.] "Late At Nights," "Anchor," "Books," "Dear Father" "My Haven," "The Beagle," "Our Changing World," "A Dog Is For Life," "Who Is The Beast," "I Called Her Lass," " A Dog Is For Life Not X-mas Or Birthdays," etc.; [pers.] Thank you for writing and accepting my poem, "Then The Moments Gone"; [a.] By Insch, Aberdeenshire

MOORE, KATHLEEN
[pen.] Kathleen Moore; [b.] 1 December 1942; Batley, Yorkshire; [p.] Jack Soodall and Mary Soodall; [m.] Divorced; [ch.] Gary and Peter Jason; [ed.] Princess Royal School, for Girls (comprehensive); [occ.] Work self employed in my snack bar (Fast Food Take-Away); [memb.] 'Cobwood Trophies' Netball Club. Linthwaite Badminton Club; [hon.] 'Still Living in Hopes'; [oth. writ.] "That's Hi Dad" (Broad Yorkshire), "Sons," "Looking Back," "Last Summer"; [pers.] If my verse can bring a little comfort, joy, a ray of hope, and yes laughter, then in some small way I have achieved something. (For the ones we love—don't give up on life, or love, and so for your dreams); [a.] Huddersfield, Yorkshire

MORELLO, ZOE
[b.] 30 December 1969; Gothenburg, Sweden; [p.] Isabella Morello and Giuseppe Morello; [m.] Nicholas Perkins, 9 August 1997; [ch.] Pregnant with our first child; [ed.] Equivalent to British 'O' levels in Gothenburg, Ester Masessons Hotel and Restaurant College, 2 years City and Guilds Photography (Credit); [occ.] Proof Reader, Translation Co-ordinator; [oth. writ.] "Angel," "True Love," "The Best Gift Ever," "Mr. Right," all above (incl. "Forgotten Patience") have been turned from poems into songs; [pers.] I am a Christian and my will is to reflect a higher love, the one of God; [a.] Henley-on-Thames, Oxfordshire

MORGAN, FRANCES
[b.] 5 October 1946, Newry, N. Ireland; [p.] John and Ellen McIvor; [m.] H. A. Morgan, 10 February 1964; [ch.] James Anthony Morgan and Caroline Jane Smith; [ed.] Our Lady's Grammar School Newry; [occ.] Community Tutor in Adult Education and Aroma/Therapist; [memb.] I.S.P.A., B.A.S.C.A; [oth. writ.] Songs published Aroma Therapy workbook, published; [pers.] Writing for me is great therapy and relaxes.; [a.] Newry, Co. Down, UK, BT36 2PE

MORGAN, MISS JULIE-ANNE
[b.] 30 August 1972, Aylesbury; [p.] Ian Petworth, Christine Petworth; [ch.] Michael James, Sinead Francesca; [ed.] Quarrendon Secondary; [occ.] Market Trader; [pers.] There is no greater feeling than love and I try to reflect this in my writing. My greatest influence is life.; [a.] Aylesbury, Bucks, UK, HP21 8QY

MORGAN, MERRIL
[b.] 29 September 1940, Hereford; [p.] Welsh; [m.] Derek, 19 November 1960; [ch.] 2 sons, 1 granddaughter; [ed.] What was then known as secondary modern; [occ.] Housewife unable to work become disabled; [oth. writ.] So in all but I have all copy rights as many not given any or only as little as 1 pounds per poem, or in local newspaper to please local readers.

MULLER, DR. CHARLES H.
[b.] 11 August 1942, Ladybrand, South Africa; [p.] Aubrey and Winnie Muller; [m.] Carolyn Joanne Muller, 6 January 1979; [ch.] Winifred, Valerie, Carol, Angus, Bruce; [ed.] B.A. (Natal), B.A. Hons (OFS), MA (Wales), Ph.D. (London), D. Litt. (OFS), D. Ed. (S.A.); [occ.] Hotel Owner/ Novelist Ex-professor of english (UNISA and UNIN, RSA); [oth. writ.] Dynamic English (Juta), Practical English Handbook (McGraw-Hill) Wheel of Destiny (Diadem Books), Fiction Studies (McGraw-Hill), Explorations in the Novel (MacMillan), Workbook of Practical Criticism (OUP), Study Guide for English skills (MacMillan); [pers.] Novels and poetry grapple with the dilemma of the conscious mind in a sometimes bewildering world. The Wheel Of Destiny is a first novel that explores a love relationship in a thriller format with international settings, and has strong psychological and erotic action with understated religious and novelistic themes.; [a.] Jedburgh, Roxburghshire, UK, TD8 6JJ

MULROONEY, FRANK
[b.] 23 November 1955, Burnley, Lancashire; [p.] John and Mary Mulrooney; [ed.] St Theodores R/C School Burnley obtained 6 O' levels; [occ.] Assistant Church Administration P/T Sales; [memb.] Bethel Christian Centre, Drama Group-Dnoylsden Manchester; [hon.] S.E.N. (State Enrolled Nurse, Gen); [oth. writ.] Published in Church Magazine "In His Image", "Noah", "Jonah"; [pers.] An ex alcoholic changed by the power of God. I became a Christian at 32 after abusing alcohol and drugs for many years. As a born-again Christian I take pleasure now in glorifying God as much as possible in my life and have been lead by God in writing this and other poems.; [a.] Ashton-u-Lyne, Tameside, UK, OL7 9DR

MUNDAY, MRS. JILL
[pen.] Jill Munday; [b.] 15 August 1949, Hertfordshire; [p.] William Tarlton, Ivy Tarlton; [m.] Barry Munday, 26 June 1971; [ch.] Son - Barry Joseph; [ed.] St Pauls County Secondary School, Addlestone Surrey; [occ.] State Enrolled Nurse at present housewife; [memb.] The Presbyterian Church of Wales; [hon.] City and Guild's Coach and Assessor for Care Workers; [oth. writ.] Poems published in church magazines and Christian collections of poems each in different books. Everyday poetry published as well.; [pers.] As I read God's Word, He teaches me to see life as it really is from all different points of view. Then I put it into poetry with His help. Truly a gift from God.; [a.] Llanelli, Carmarthenshire, UK, SA15 5NH

MURPHY, TADHG
[pen.] Justin Seine; [b.] 7 February 1963; Cavan, Ireland; [ed.] St. Bricins College, Cavan; [occ.] Dairy Farmer; [oth. writ.] National Farming Press The "Irish Farmers Journal" published "The Lunatics Are Running The Asylum" My Satirical Look At The E.U.; [pers.] I just wish to dedicate "Why God" to the memories and families of Adrian's everywhere; [a.] Ballyconnell, Cavan, Ireland

MURRAY, ANDREW DAVID
[b.] 18 December 1969; Larne Moyle Hosp; [p.] Andrew and Jean Murray; [m.] Christine Murray, 29 July 1995; [ed.] Larne High School, University of Ulster, Jordanstown; [occ.] Quantity Surveyor; [memb.] RICS, The Royal Institution of Chartered Surveyors, Britannia Music Club; [hon.] Bsc (Hons) in Quantity Surveying, Rics (Headquarters) Prize 1994/95; [oth. writ.] Lyrics for songs written for family band. Poems and personal art given to friends and family as presents. Calligraphy in wedding albums, bibles etc.; [pers.] My literary work usually reflects events which have occurred in my life and include people who mean the most to me. However some lyrics have been influenced by societal problems such as drink, drugs, violence and promiscuity; [a.] Larne, Antrim

MURRAY, FREIDA
[b.] 8 May 1948; Dublin; [p.] Lawrence and Theresa Greig; [m.] Ian Murray, 26 May 1988; [ch.] Fraser, Steven, Lisa; [ed.] Lawside Academy Dundee, Lauder College, Dunfermline; [occ.] Housewife; [a.] Breakish, Isle of Skye

MURRAY, JOANNE
[pen.] Joanne Murray; [b.] 10 August 1979; Ireland; [p.] James and Bridget Murray; [ed.] I have completed both my junior and leaving Certificates at St. Columbus College, Stranorlar, Co Donegal; [occ.] Student; [hon.] I have received certificates for visiting the elderly in a local community hospital; [oth. writ.] I was a runner-up in the beat the blues short story competition run by aware and my story "Depression" was published in one of their monthly magazines. "Boxed in" has also been published in the book 'Echoes of the Mind'; [pers.] I feel that writing is a beautiful way of expressing inner feelings and thoughts; [a.] Ballybofey, Donegal

MURRAY, NOELINE
[b.] 22 December 1937; Postnoo Co, Donegal, Eire; [p.] John and Anne Boyle; [m.] Peter Murray, 3 September 1960; [ch.] Caroline (Byrne) Ian, Helen (Blunden), Clodagh (Cockroft), Peter and Joanne; [ed.] St. Dallan Forgaell's N. S. Rikboney Co Donegal, St. Louis Girl's Secondary Convent, Carrickmacross Co Monaghan; [occ.] Homemaker; [memb.] St. Laurence's Church Choir where she is a soloist.; [hon.] Poem published at 12 yrs of age, award for an essay on family matters, a competition held in connection with the year of the family; [oth. writ.] "Christmas" written at 12 yrs. "Jenny's Blue Ribbon," a family story both published, lots of poems inspired by my insomnia and the various

happenings in my life. One poem "Friend or Foe" was inspired by the accidental deaths of my twin brother in N. Zealand and the birth of my first grandchild Amy; [pers.] I love letter-writing and feel if a letter isn't enjoyable to the writer, it cannot be enjoyed by the recipient. I love animals, flowers and enjoy Wordsworth's poems. Christmas is my favorite time of the year (my birthday and I enjoy giving and seeing the delight on my seven grandchildren's faces!); [a.] Dublin 14, Ireland

MWENESI, CLIVE
[b.] 15 January 1978; Munoywa Village; [p.] Mr. Alfas Mwange and Mrs. Brenice Mwange; [ed.] O-level (means grade B-) preparing to go to the University; [occ.] Unemployed (student); [memb.] Kibaala P.A.G Assembly United Youth for Progress (U.Y.F.P); [hon.] Certificate of recognition by world bible course, 3rd prize Islamic Library contest, Certificate of participation (National Science Congress for Lubinu Sec. School); [oth. writ.] 30 poems, 3 short stories entitled "Smooth All The Way" and "Encounter with God" a Religious Satire, and "The Paradise" about street children. A novel 'Getting Rich' about corruption; [pers.] Life is living, so live wisely; [a.] Mbale, Kenya

NAIDOO, JOHN
[pen.] John Naidoo; [b.] 1 November 1933; Durban, South Africa; [p.] Narappa Naidoo; [m.] Jagathambal (Deceased), 27 September 1957; [ch.] One son and one daughter; [ed.] Sastri College, South Africa and Natal University South Africa, British Rail Examination Distinction—1st and 2nd year; [occ.] Retired; [memb.] At present engaged in voluntary work at British Red Cross, Benson Primary School, Croydon, John Ruskin College, Croydon; [oth. writ.] Wrote about 25 poems as an hobby; [pers.] I try to bring to the notice of the world starvation among children in the third world and "unnecessary" wars; [a.] Croydon, Surrey

NEILD, LYNN
[b.] 6 July 1948; Dagenham, Essex, England; [m.] Ron Neild, 18 March 1967; [ch.] Angela, 28, Michelle, 27; [ed.] Secondary Modern in Australia and England, 'O' and 'A' levels in sculpture and ceramics, majored in Art; [occ.] Housewife and artist although qualified in teaching; [hon.] Awarded 10 years of exhibitions of paintings by the havering arts council, two per year in the local queens theatre and the main exhibition rooms, Romford Library; [oth. writ.] Various works written, currently under review for evaluation; [pers.] I write as I paint, purely from my reflections on life and feelings within; [a.] Hornchurch, Essex

NELSON, ROBERT JOHN
[b.] 25 June 1950; Essex; [p.] Robert Gilmour Rodcar Nelson, Alice Nelson; [m.] Angela Pauline Nelson, 7 July 1973; [ch.] Stuart James, Samantha Louise; [ed.] The Royal Liberty School Gidea Park; [occ.] Civil Servant; [oth. writ.] Several unpublished poems; [pers.] My poetry tends to reflect the reality of modern living. I have been greatly inspired by the writings of Tennyson, Coleridge and Oscar Wilde; [a.] Harpole, Northamptonshire

NEVILLE, KARL
[pen.] Klaus Kinder; [b.] 24 May 1974; Newmarket; [p.] Marilyn and Alan; [ed.] Samuel Ward Upper, and University College Suffolk; [occ.] Student of Nursing, West Suffolk Hospital; [memb.] St. Wendred Masonic Lodge, Newmarket; [pers.] To live in life is an illusion, to explore life is reality itself; [a.] Bury St. Edmunds, Suffolk

NICHOLSON, DAVID
[pers.] The Black Swan—The Black Swan is symbolic, Black and White Swans were chosen for diametric contrast also—Thematically to remind that the Black Swan represents many who feel disadvantaged, wishing. For various reasons that they were different actually—Black Swans are really beautiful. The Black Swan in the poem feels isolated lonely and sad because it is not accepted by its companions: And longs for its idea of beauty. So the B.S. seeks a compensatory factor, thinking beautiful thoughts, turning inward. So arises the internal and external. The poem's theme is that beauty is within. "Blessed are the pure in heart" as the stars look down that is what the angels see. Thinking on this the B.S. feels less sad just as a river has patches of shimmering light and shadow, likewise the river of life flowing ever on. We both project and reflect if we have a fine nature, this will radiate. The graceful movement of the swans gliding on the water suggests this. Shelly was right "Beauty is Truth" influences. Wordsworth, the lake poets. John Clare, The Romantics. Other writing, on art, especially constable; [a.] Weybridge

NICHOLSON, JOHN A.
[b.] 7 July 1934; Coatbridge; [p.] Florence and Thomas Nicholson; [ed.] Clifton High School Coatbridge Glasgow School of Art; [occ.] Town Artist, Sculptor East Kilbride Dev. Corporation; [memb.] I am a member of a recently formed concert party performing solely for charity; [hon.] Commended certificates and medal in Glasgow Art Gallery Drawing competition. Diploma in Graphic Design Glasgow School of Art; [oth. writ.] Include: "May" a romantic poem, and "Divine Dedication," a tribute to a retiring minister both of which I was delighted to have published by the I.L.P. Hitherto, I had written mainly for personal satisfaction; [pers.] Being a romantic at heart in expressing the gentler side of human emotion—I strive to attain a rhythmic, lyrical quality; [a.] Coatbridge, Lanarkshire

NICHOLSON, MRS. CONNIE
[b.] 31 July 1908; Newark, Notts; [p.] Deceased; [m.] Lloyd Nicholson, 12 November 1936; [ch.] Two; [ed.] Left School at 14 years of age. Too poor to accept a free scholarship; [oth. writ.] I have a few articles written but used them; [pers.] I am a flower arranger and garden winner; [a.] Newark, Notts

NICHOLSON, PATRICIA BARBARA
[b.] 14 October 1955; Penrith, Cumbria; [p.] Tony and Barbara Simonini; [m.] Jan Nicholson, 12 February 1983; [ch.] Hollie, Rebecca and Steven; [occ.] Housewife; [oth. writ.] None at present I am doing a home study course in writing books for children; [pers.] My second child Mark Ryan sadly died at Christmas time 1986 aged 71/2 months. My poem is dedicated to him; [a.] Penrith, Cumbria

OATES, INGRID JANETTE
[b.] 27 December 1943; Stretford, Nr M/C; [p.] Father, (Mum Deceased); [m.] Deceased; [ch.] Two grown up people over 21 yrs; [ed.] Open Air School then Secondary Modern; [occ.] Home Carer for the Social Services; [memb.] Currently doing a writing course. Enjoy the Piano; [hon.] Been Lucky enough to have two other poems printed; [oth. writ.] In the process of writing children's stories also hoping to put down on paper about my childhood; [pers.] My talent must be a gift from God, not long really realising I loved the art of words, poetry to me is wonderful, putting the ordinary sometimes every day experiences into words, (It's a Joy); [a.] Bury, Lancs

OGBUAGU, KECHI UCHENNA
[pen.] Kechi; [b.] 9 February 1981; Worcester, UK; [p.] Dr. and Mrs. B. O. Ogbuagu; [ed.] All Saints Primary School, Onitsha, Nigeria, Federal Gov't Girl's College, Owerri, Imo State, Nigeria; [occ.] Student; [memb.] Press Club, Literary Club, Red Cross Society; [a.] Onitsha, North L.G.A., Nigeria

OHENE-DJAN, MR. ANTHONY
[b.] 5 October 1961; London; [p.] Dr. and Mrs. I. L. Ohene-Djan; [ed.] 'O' Level 9, A Level 3, BA in Law, attempted Solicitor Course Chester College of Law; [occ.] Disable - Writer; [hon.] B.A. in Law; [oth. writ.] Short Stories, Poems; [a.] London

OLIVER-RAYFIELD, PEGGY
[pen.] Margaret Cunningham; [b.] London; [p.] Dr. and Mrs. Oliver (both Deceased); [m.] Edgar Rayfield (Deceased), 1948; [ch.] Four; [ed.] Convent Education; [occ.] To find time for all my poems now; [memb.] Twelve years in the Seaford Bonfire and Carnival Society of Great Britain; [oth. writ.] Small written piece called "Nightmare Road," published in monthly magazine called 'Prediction.' Poem coming out in the autumn in the poetry guild anthology . . . ; [pers.] To help family, friends and pets when needed, also hope my poems give a little pleasure to some people. Some poets I like Emily Bronte, Wilfred Owen, T. Hardy . . . ; [a.] Seaford, E. Sussex

OLLEY, MARION
[b.] Walthamstow; [m.] Ray Olley; [ed.] West Bridgford Grammar School Nottingham. Anglia Polytechnic University. English Learning Centre, London; [occ.] Teacher of English to Foreign Students; [hon.] B.A. Combined study degree english and history. T.E.F.L. Certificate - English Learning Centre. London; [oth. writ.] Poem "Grandson" published in 'Awaken To A Dream'; [pers.] My writing influenced by and dedicated to my family and grandchildren; [a.] Elmstead, Nr. Colchester, Essex

OLUSEYE, IGBAROOLA SAMUEL
[pen.] Samuel Barools; [b.] 4 April 1963; [p.] Timothy Ayodele and Janet Mopelola; [ed.] i. Ibadan Grammar School, Ibadan ii. The Polytechnic, Ibadan iii. Yaba College of Technology, Yaba Lagos; [occ.] Freelance Writer and Artist; [oth. writ.] (i) "A Hunter in the Forest," ii. "The Tortoise And The Elephant," iii." Why The Tortoise Is Bald," children's stories, (Ibadan, on Ibonoje publishers, 1995 in addition to other books on poetry, fiction and drama); [pers.] I strive to appreciate the kindness, goodness and supremacy of God in my writings. I also teach good virtues. By God's special grace, it is my very humble desire to become a poetry super star in the nearest future; [a.] Ibadan, Nigeria

OLUWOLEAYODELE, JOSHUA
[pen.] WoleJoshua, Woljosh; [b.] 26 August 1966, Lagos, Nigeria; [p.] Mr. and Mrs. Olusola, Joshua Pelinah M. Joshua; [ed.] C.M.S. Grammar School Lagos Federal School of Arts and Science, Lagos, Obafemi Awolowo University, Ile-Ife, Nigeria; [occ.] Literature Teacher, Holy Martyrs of Uganda Seminary Effurun, Delta-State; [memb.] Man O' War Club, Nigeria, Dramatic Arts Students Association, (DASA) IFE, Association of Nigeria Authors (ANA), C.R.M. Theatre, Lagos; [hon.] English Literature, Poetry and Film titled "The Zumma Queen" as a writer and director.; [oth. writ.] Poems, short stories, articles, published in local magazines, short story, "The Joker," read on B.B.C. Published a play titled "Double Six and Six", written several film scripts, poetry, and stage scripts awaiting publication and sponsorship.; [pers.] The goal of my writing is to make people know and come closer to God, through the arts as I feel the sciences have disappointed Him.

ONG, MARLENA
[b.] 7 August 1983; Selangor, Malaysia; [p.] Dr. B. Shah (Mother); [ed.] Currently a student attending an Independant School situated in Chislehurst called "Babington House School"; [occ.] Pupil/Student—I wish to eventually gain a law degree and practice as a Queens Counsellor; [memb.] Member of R.S.P.C.A, opera Club and Karate Club; [hon.] Special prize in a poetry; [oth. writ.] competitions in an Indian newspa-

per—poem titled "Love" (Newspaper called "Gurui Gujarat"). Titled a Book for the Teenage author Ian Strachan called "Which Way Is Home"; [pers.] I enjoy writing and reading poetry, to me poetry is an art which enables me to express with a passion issues which are close to my heart

OSBORN, DORIS
[b.] 7 July 1942; Lincolnshire; [p.] Albert Ernest Flower and Florence Mary; [m.] Frank Osborn, 23 March 1963; [ch.] Simon, Mandy, Maria; [occ.] Home Carer, Housewife; [memb.] Local Residents Council Group and Friendship Club for the Elderly; [oth. writ.] I have had one of my poems published by the International Society of Poetry in a book titled "Quite Moments." Also I have sent my poetry to various magazines; [pers.] I have enjoyed writing poetry for many years since I was a young girl. Although now when I am at home and have some spare time on my hands, I love writing poetry. I enjoy writing about many different things. Depending on the way I feel and the mood I'm in; [a.] Milton Keynes, Buckinghamshire

OSBORNE, JOHN
[b.] 11 October 1930; Lansdown Grange Bath; [p.] Gerald and Kathleen Osborne; [m.] Rosemary, 19 October 1957; [ch.] Philip and Michael; [ed.] Bath Technical College; [occ.] Farmer; [memb.] Church National Farmers Union Chairman, Parish Council; [hon.] Hedging, Thatching, Cattle Judging, Singing; [oth. writ.] Volumes 1,2 and 3 of "Poems Of A Farmer" and "Flowers In Life's Garden"; [pers.] John Osborne. My poems are my Philosophy of life. Working all my life with nature as a farmer I've had the opportunity to think a great deal about life and have tried to write with simplicity and sincerity. Sometimes serious sometimes humorous; [a.] Bath, Somerset

OWERS, JESSICA
[b.] 6 December 1980; Cork, Ireland; [p.] James and Katherine Owers; [ed.] Presently a fifth year student in Loreto Secondary, Fermoy, and I hope to study BSC Environmental studies in University, to venture into environmental journalism.; [memb.] I am a sponsor of the horses in Redwings Horse Sancuary, Norwich, as well as regular sponsor of the save the tiger campaign with "Care For The Wind"; [oth. writ.] I have written 89 other works of poetry, several published in my local paper, and articles on environmental issues; [pers.] I find the most inspiration I get is from simple, and largely overlooked sources, like the sky. They have so many stories to tell, yet so few listen; [a.] Fermoy, Co. Corks, Ireland

PAPIER, KIETA SUZANNE
[b.] 24 December 1983; Kalulushi, Zambia; [p.] Henri and Linda Papier; [ed.] Lechwe Education Trust, Kitwe, Zambia; [occ.] Student; [hon.] Scholarship book award for creative writing 1994 and 1996. Award of Merit, English Literature 1996, International Library of Poetry Editor's Choice Award, 1996; [oth. writ.] "Imagination Sensation" published in International Library of Poetry anthology "Quiet Moments," 1996; [pers.] Vivimus Vivamus; [a.] Kitwe, Zambia

PARASKEVOPOULOS, KLEANTHIS
[b.] 11 March 1970; Nicosia, Cyprus; [p.] Nicos and Antigone Paraskevopoulos; [ed.] Pancyprian Lyceum (High School), University of Athens, Greece (Bachelor in Pharmacy); [occ.] Pharmacist, Editor of Fuse Magazine on "Alternative" music and arts; [memb.] PRS (Performing Rights Society) with some recorded songs under the pseudonym "Svetlana Brainwash" in the field of alternative rock; [oth. writ.] Poems in English and Greek, Articles and fiction in Greek for my magazine, poem called "Nothing" published in That Dangerous Supplement magazine (University of Norwich, Dept. of English Literature) June '95; [pers.] Plan to devote myself to music (play the Bass guitar and maybe singing), love the Beatniks, love surrealism in any form, "Urban Creaturescape" is part of a larger poem I wrote with the same title; [a.] Nicosia, Cyprus

PARNWELL, JOY DOREEN
[pen.] Joy Doreen Parnwell; [b.] 23 January 1926; Kingswood, Surrey; [p.] Nellie and Alfred Barrett (Deceased); [ch.] Robert, Richard, Ronald Garner; [pers.] I was born in 1926 in Kingswood, Surrey. I now live in Camberley, Surrey I have three boys age 35, 36, 40 years I have written and have never had any pleasure and have never had any published. I love ballroom dancing and go every week to London; [a.] Camberley, Surrey

PATRICK, WENDY LANA
[b.] 16 December 1939; Fareham, Hampshire; [p.] Deceased; [m.] Harry David, 16 August 1983; [ch.] Three; [ed.] Secondary Modern; [occ.] Housewife; [oth. writ.] Also three previous poems published; [pers.] My greatest wish, peace for all mankind kindness to all animals and only wish, all hunting sports, to be banned. Not to spoil our beautiful country side; [a.] Fareham, Hampshire

PATTEN, BARBARA
[b.] 26 December 1937; Bow, London; [p.] Harriat and William Denham; [m.] George Patten, 29 March 1958; [ch.] Antony Sharon and Terry; [ed.] Secondary Modern; [occ.] Stettlements Clerk London Stock Exchange; [pers.] I write my poems I have written fourteen to date about things that happened to me as a child most of them are true; [a.] London

PAXTON, DAVID NICHOLAS
[b.] 12 September 1942; Leicester; [p.] Grace Weightman, Ronald Wake Paxton; [m.] Valerie Paxton, 12 June 1965; [ch.] Sharon Caroline Paxton, David Ian Paxton; [ed.] Durham School, Houghall and Seale-Hayne Agricultural Colleges; [occ.] Farmer; [oth. writ.] First poem published at 13 "Thoughts" in Light of the World, 1997, written poems on and off all of my life; [pers.] Interests include: Philosophy, Russian, History, Art, and Architecture, Russian Language, Russian Poets. Peace and Harmony throughout the World; [a.] Northallerton, North Yorkshire

PEARCE, MARK
[pen.] Mark Pearce; [b.] 25 April 1967; Sudbury Suffolk; [p.] Barry Pearce and Jean Anne Adams; [ch.] Rachael, Martin, Josh; [ed.] Sir George Monoux High School for boys and University of Life; [occ.] Computer Operator; [hon.] English Speaking Board; [oth. writ.] Many poems; [pers.] I strive to illuminate in words the strength of human emotions to which we are all slaves; [a.] Harlow, Essex

PEARCEY, JENNY
[b.] 3 December 1959; Exeter Devon; [ed.] O Levels only!; [occ.] Course ware Designer Training Company; [memb.] Chairman of Local Social Group for Professionals in their 30's; [oth. writ.] Write for my own pleasure and love past and present, first poem to be published; [pers.] I have a heart and feelings with love to share; [a.] Southampton, Hampshire

PENFOLD, RUTH
[pen.] Ruth Pinnow; [b.] 12 July 1979; Dorchester; [p.] Alec Penfold and Rita Penfold; [ed.] Dorchester Thomas Hardye School going on to study English Literature at University; [occ.] Student; [memb.] Bournmouth Sinfonietta Choir Thomas Hardye Chapel Choir; [hon.] A prize winner of poetry today, J. Coffin Award for classical civilisation.; [oth. writ.] Articles, features and reviews for local and county newspapers; [pers.] I attempt to portray the experience of emotional triumph and suffering in my poetry. I have been greatly influenced by Shakespeare and more contemporary poets such as T. S. Eliot and Sylvia Plath; [a.] Dorchester, Dorset

PENNE-STUART, ABIGAIL
[pen.] Penne, Stuart; [b.] 20 June 1981, Oxford; [p.] Yvonne and Julian (Pennestuart); [ed.] Cheltenham Ladies College; [occ.] Student; [oth. writ.] Only personal poems, nothing published; [pers.] All my poems are about personal reflection and inner feelings, which I hope other people can relate to, I find relief in poetry and I would like to think others can; [a.] Brackley, N. Hants

PENNY, MS. DONNA
[b.] 18 September 1958; Banbridge; [p.] Mary McIlroy, John McIlroy; [ch.] Leanne, Stephen, Lynsey; [ed.] Dromore High School North Down Group School of Nursing; [occ.] Unit Manager Day Care Services for Adults with Learning Disability; [memb.] R.C.N, U.K.C.C; [hon.] State Enrolled Nurse; [oth. writ.] None published; [pers.] I have gained immense satisfaction and fulfillment from my writing of poetry which has mainly been inspired by the many experiences I have encountered throughout my life; [a.] Lisburn, Antrim

PENTER, LORNA
[oth. writ.] I've written two children's books, and one adult; [pers.] I love writing about the 20th century; [a.] Redcar, Cleveland

PETERS, BERNADETTE
[pen.] Bernadette Peters; [b.] 3 April 1969; Woolwich; [p.] Jillian Phyllis Groves-Cooper and Alfred Cooper; [m.] Mark Peters, 19 December 1992; [ed.] Picardy School; [occ.] Communications Officer, Metropolitan Police; [memb.] Cats Protection League; [oth. writ.] Several poems published in other anthologies; [pers.] Introduced to poetry as a child by my grandmother CA Great undiscovered poet. We share the same style, sometimes quirky, sometimes not—but always from the heart and soul; [a.] Welling, Kent

PITTAWAY, SARAH
[b.] 26 June 1981; Swindon; [p.] Ruth and Stephen Pittaway; [ed.] I have recently completed my GCSE's and aim to gain further levels in History, English Language, Biology and one A/S in Psychology; [pers.] I'd like to thank my grandfather—Edgar Saunders—for encouraging me to express myself through poetry since an early age; [a.] Cirencester, Gloucestershire

PLUMB, MISS KATRINA
[pen.] Katrina Plumb; [b.] 25 September 1967; London; [p.] Mr. and Mrs. R. L. Plumb; [ed.] Varied and incomplete as well as incompletable; [occ.] Student and Writer; [memb.] N.O.J. Quaestors Theatre the recruitment Society women in Journalism open University Psychological Society; [hon.] Photographic display at the South Bank Centre to be accepted as an incomplete idiot by many; [oth. writ.] Too much too unappreciated too young headlines in verse—famine the west in her eye: Society word of mouth: Cat's life six phases of feline; [pers.] The ideal man is not a Hypothesis. It costs just keeping his dream afloat. Destination Le Harure, the prize freedom to provide him a twenty four house service; [a.] London

POLLINGTON, ANNIE
[b.] 29 August 1918; Leeds, England; [p.] Patrick Joseph, Ethel Lyons; [m.] Peter Fredrick Pollington (Deceased), 2 June 1976; [ch.] One daughter; [ed.] Stanhope St. Convent, Dublin, Eira; [occ.] Retired; [oth. writ.] Loads of Poems, written after my darling husband passed away, 1994; [pers.] Though I am paraplegic of House bound. I find happiness in everything I see. The clouds in the sky the birds flying by. The trees that grow so high. No matter where I look I see beauty. I am very lucky; [a.] Ealing, London

POPEJOY, REBECCA
[b.] 12 September 1981; Burton-on-Trent; [p.] Ian Popejoy and Rosemary Popejoy; [ed.]

Overseal County Primary School, William Allitt School, Newhall; [occ.] G.C.S.E. Student; [pers.] I am dedicating this to my late granddad, Arthur John Micklin, who inspired me to write this poem when he died on the 25th of July 1990, at the age of 58 after a long battle against cancer; [a.] Swadlincote, Derbyshire

POTTICARY, JAMES
[b.] 7 October 1964; Southampton; [m.] Julie Anne Potticary, 2 January 1993; [ch.] Matthew James Potticary; [ed.] Hambue Comprehensive Barton Peveril College; [occ.] Refrigeration Design Engineer; [memb.] Hampshire Refrigeration Society (HRS); [hon.] Pirelli Prize For Design and Technology, Pirelli Prize for Engineering Drawing, HRS-Apprentice of Year Award; [oth. writ.] This is the first piece of poetry I have written for someone—my wife; [pers.] This poem was written as a wedding gift for my wife—a true inspiration!; [a.] Southampton, Hants

POUPARD, DAVID
[b.] 28 May 1962; Hammersmith, London; [p.] Ann Poupard, John Poupard (Deceased, 1978); [m.] Linda Poupard, 29 April 1995; [ed.] Secondary education and life itself; [occ.] National Trust Warden; [oth. writ.] No other published work; [pers.] To move or inspire another person is a great thing, but to find the highest love and to have it returned is the highest thing of all, for my wife Linda; [a.] Wendover, Buckinghamshire

PRATT, KENNETH
[pen.] Aze; [b.] 8 MArch 1969; London; [p.] Chrispin and Jasmin Pratt; [m.] Joanne Shand; [ed.] Colchester Boy's High School, Colchester Gilberd Grammar, Colchester Institute, London Guildhall Universtiy; [occ.] Freelance computer graphic designer; [memb.] Book Club Associates, Writer's Society, Musician's Union, Equity; [hon.] Associate of London College of Music, diploma in music, Duke of Edimburgh Gold Award, St. Johns Ambulance First Aid Certificate, 7th Keup (Brown Belt) tae Kwon Do; [oth. writ.] "Post-its", a collection of inspirational thoughts and quotations, "Poetical Symphonies", several poems ranging from politics to romanticism; [pers.] By absorbing infinite streams of concerns and awareness, we can saturate beings with idiosyncratic portraits of the ingredients of self—thus embracing the illuminating theme of Peace, Love, and Harmony in one's odyssey. Life seeks to transmitus to a quintessential level of appreciation; [a.] West green, London

PRESTON, MR. HAZEL
[pen.] "Serph" & "Democrat"; [b.] 4 November 1904; Barwick-in-Elmet, Leeds; [p.] Herbert Preston, Charlotte Annie Hazel; [m.] Mrs. Annie Preston, 14 May 1932; [ch.] Haldane Bertram, Gordon Stuart; [ed.] Council School, Normanton Grammar School, Electrical & Wireless School, R.A.E. Mettulah Outpost, Palestine, RAF.; [occ.] Retired Civil Servant; [memb.] Labour Party Civil Service Association; [hon.] 4 War-time medals, proud to have sorted out signals "Enigma" machine, & helped train "Churchill's Few!" as F/SGT RAF; [oth. writ.] Publication in verse, my autobiography: "My 'Hello' Gram!" by "Serph". (After "Myelogram" Operation for "Spastic Paraplegia" lower legs); [pers.] From birth on, through life, effects of S.P. gradually increased. At 60, was member of D.D.M.C. later, as now, in wheel-chair, using "Home-Help" each day for bed help. Jobs: Street Hawker-Dye works—Motor Mechanic Clerk P.O. & RAPC—Wireless OP. RAF (Peace & War); [a.] Prestatyn, Denbighshire

PRESTON, MRS. ELIZABETH
[pen.] People say I walk Cissy Spaceship Around with head in clouds; [b.] 19 February 1961, Newton Abbot, Devon; [p.] Mr. and Mrs. Rose and Ron Stickland; [m.] Divorced; [ch.] Emma Sarah Spry; [ed.] Knowles Hill School, C.S.E. English Maths; [occ.] Unemployed; [memb.] I am a member of the International Library of Poets; [hon.] Editors Certificate for my poem printed in between a laugh and a tear; [oth. writ.] I also enjoy writing short stories, and eventually would like to have an autobiography of my own printed. I am also working on writing a spiritual book; [pers.] I strongly believe mankind has been the result of killing Mother Earth and her creatures within, if we do not accept the help we are offered the destruction of this planet will be sooner than we think; [a.] Newton Abbot, Devon

PRICE, MRS. PATRICIA ENA
[b.] Hereford; [p.] Albert and Margaret Bowkett; [m.] Reginald Clifford Price, 26 December 1973; [ed.] G.C.E. Ordinary level, Professional Qualifications in Hospital Operating Theatre Technique; [occ.] Hospital Operating Department Practitioner; [memb.] Medical Defence Union, British Assoc of Operating Department Assistants, Memb Church of England; [hon.] 'Editor's Choice Award' International Society of Poets 1996, Editor's Choice Award', International Library of poets 1997; [oth. writ.] Two other poems published.; [pers.] Ability is nothing without opportunity; [a.] Hereford, Herefordshire

PRICE, ROLAND POWEL
[b.] 27 December 1917; Seven Sisters; [p.] Rhys and Annie Powel Price; [m.] Lily (Deceased), 21 September 1946; [ch.] Rosalyn Sian, Granddaughters Tiffany Jane, Jade Alexandra and Harriet Victoria; [ed.] Brecon Grammar School and St David's College Lampeter; [occ.] Retired Schoolmaster, one-time Head of Classics King Edward VI Grammar School Stratford-upon-Avon; [hon.] Mentioned in Dispatches; [oth. writ.] Fun verses for children, based on their own experiences; [pers.] My primary influence has been the romantic poets, but I have drawn also from The Aeneid and Eclogues of Vergil. My poetic muse took a dramatic impetus when I met my wife-to-be in the winter of 1940, love at first sight, vitally sustained throughout our life together. The poetry that emerged has been a loving and compulsive exercise. My intention was always, not to seek publication, but to present, first to the muse herself, and latterly, to our girls, an insight into the enchantment of this remarkable woman, in the medium best suited to that purpose—a collection of verse based on truth. It was at the insistence of our girls, that I entered this competition. Other activities include portraiture in watercolour and oils; [a.] Stratford-upon-Avon, Warwickshire

PRICE, WILLIAM GRAHAM
[pen.] Cudmore; [b.] 13 January 1933; South Wales; [p.] George and Gladys Price; [m.] Pamela Yvonne, 7 April 1958; [ch.] Lawton; [ed.] Cowbridge Grammar School, Swansea University, London School of Economics and Political Science; [occ.] Managing Director of Cudmore Associates; [memb.] Cardiff County Club, Cardiff Rugby Football Club, Welsh Academicals; [hon.] BSC (Econ) 'Cum Laude', Post Graduate Diploma Business Studies, Ford Trust Scholar, University Colours, Boxing; [oth. writ.] Co Author Superfit for Business. Computopia in Across the Universe. Compusense in Jewels of the Imagination. Sleep in Silence of Yesterday; [pers.] I carefully study the impact of computers and telecommunications on social mores; [a.] Ross-on-Wye, Herefordshire

QUIGLEY, MR. TIMOTHY
[b.] 21 March 1962; Nottingham; [m.] Catherine Norma, 24 October 1987; [ed.] Markland Comprehensive School, Creswell, Nr Worksop Notts; [pers.] Living near ocean country side, I learnt to love nature and gardening and this gave me the inspiration to write about the poem: The Seasons; [a.] Belph· Nr. Worksop, Notts

QUINN, AMANDA ROSS
[b.] 3 July 1986; Bellshill; [p.] Helen Ross, Felix Quinn; [ed.] Hamilton College where recently completed primary education; [occ.] Pupil at Hamilton College; [a.] Mothernell, Lanarkshire

RAMADAN, MISS KONCE
[b.] 25 February 1978; London; [p.] Mr. Ibrahim Ramadan, Mrs. Nazif Ramadan; [ed.] Currently studying Psychology at King Alfred's College, Winchester, Winchmore Secondary School; [occ.] Student at King Alfred's College of Higher Education; [memb.] The Writing Club; [oth. writ.] Several poems published in anthologies and newspaper, both English and Turkish writings.; [pers.] My poetry is born from experience. The heart is the art and the mind is the tool of expression.; [a.] Winchester, Hampshire, UK, SO23 2BN

REA, MRS. R.
[pen.] Rita Rose; [b.] 16 March 1931; Redditch; [p.] Mr. and Mrs. N. Smith; [m.] Mr. S. Rea; 28 October 1950; [ch.] Pamela, 44 and Susan, 42; [ed.] St. Stephens Girls School, Day Course Art; [occ.] retired; [oth. writ.] "No Time No Time" and in 'Awaken to a Dream'; [a.] Bromsquare, Worcs

REED, GEORGE
[b.] 21 May 1941, Fleetwood; Lancashire; [p.] Annie Reed, Father deceased; [m.] Divorced; [ch.] Keith Graham, Adrian Peter, Simon Paul; [ed.] Duckmanton Junior School, Bolsover Secondary Modern School; [occ.] Nil. (On Invalidity, because of Chronic Obstructive Airways Disease.); [oth. writ.] The fear of dying, Published in Inspirations from the Midlands. Also several poems in the church notices/ magazines.; [pers.] I am a redundant mine worker, and a born again Christian 10 years, and I write mostly Christian poetry, I get inspiration from books and sometimes television programs.; [a.] Chesterfield, Derbyshire, UK, S44 5EP

REEVE, TREVOR
[b.] 7 July 1947, Cambridge; [p.] Claude Reeve and Miriam Reeve; [m.] Christine Reeve, 16 October 1971; [ch.] Karen, Paul and Claire; [ed.] Keysoe Secondary Modern; [occ.] Sales/Purchasing Clerk; [oth. writ.] Several poems published by the International Library of Poetry.; [pers.] Better to be five minutes late in this life than five minutes early in the next.; [a.] Kempston, Bedfordshire, UK, MK42 8NT

REID, HELEN M.
[pen.] Aunt Nellie; [b.] 28 March 1911, Ayr; [p.] Helen Dickson and George Muir; [m.] Alexander Reid, 25 November 1933; [ed.] Ayr Grammer School 1916-1931, Hendon Technical College 29/6 Ct - 28 July 1953; [occ.] Housewife; [hon.] County Certificate in Crafts Botany pass 17th June 1960

RENDALL, MR. J. H. E.
[pen.] The Bard of Umbarleigh; [b.] 10 May 1922, Twickenham, Middx; [ed.] Hampton Grammar School, Kingston Technical College; [occ.] Retired; [oth. writ.] "The Muses Retire", "The Collected Rhymes of the Band of Umberleigh"; [pers.] Most of my poem are narrative poems and are therefore longer than the twenty lines required for publication.; [a.] Umberleigh, Devon, UK, EX37 9AR

RENNIE, JACQUELINE
[p.] Coral Rend; [b.] 25 September 1968; Salford; [p.] Peter and Pauline Rennie; [ch.] Chelsey Jade Rennie; [ed.] Buile Hill high school, Sitec college; [occ.] Receptionist in a medical centre; [oth.writ.] Poems published in magazines and paper; [pers.] My innermost feelings are reflected in my poems. "Innocents" was inspired by the terrible tragedy at Dunblane; [a.] Salford, Lancashire

RENNIE, JACQUELINE A.
[pen.] Coral Rees; [b.] 25 September 1968, England; [p.] Mr. Peter and Mrs. Pauline Rennie; [ch.] Chelsey Rennie; [ed.] Buile HilL High School; [occ.] Receptionist Health Centre; [memb.] I am a member of Manchester County Netball Society; [oth. writ.] Poem to be published in...; [pers.] I have always kept my feelings deep inside. The poetry I write reflects my inner most feelings, whether it affects me or other people. "Innocents" was inspired by the Dunblane tragedy.; [a.] Salford, Lancashire, UK, M6 5QA

REYNOLDS, STUART
[pen.] Stuart Reynolds; [b.] 29 November 1976, Basildon; [p.] Terence and Sheila Reynolds; [ed.] Bromfords Comprehensive School, Wickford, Essex; [occ.] Runner on Life; [pers.] Vera May Reynolds was a strong and loving influence on my life in her living years and I dedicate this poem to her.; [a.] Wickford, Essex, UK, SS12 0HH

RICHARDS, GEOFF T.
[b.] 8 July 1977, Chesterfield; [p.] Maurice Richards, June Richards; [m.] Louise Richards, 3 August 1996; [ed.] G.C.S.E.'s at Netherthorpe, Comprehensive School; [occ.] Quality Control Manager at Hamilton Cables Ltd; [oth. writ.] Several, but none published as of yet. I hope to publish some more work soon.; [pers.] Too many people hold themselves back because they have no faith in their own ability. Have faith and succeed.; [a.] Chesterfield, Derbyshire, UK, S43 3UY

RISSO, NADINE
[b.] 21 April 1978; Gibraltar; [p.] Henry and Margaret Risso; [ed.] Loreto convent, Westside comprehensive, University of Bristol; [occ.] Student of chemistry; [pers.] Writing poetry is the most complete form of emotional release for me: the rush of thoughts condenses into form and brings me peace; [a.] Bristol

RIVETT, LYNN
[b.] 20 September 1967, Dryburn Hospital, Durham; [p.] Patricia and Leslie Rivett; [m.] David Lonsdale (live-in partner); [ch.] Michael S. Joseph Rivett, Katie Lonsdale; [ed.] Hermitage Comprehensive School; [occ.] Sale Assistant at Woolworths, Chester-le-Street; [oth. writ.] Only other poems I have written but have never tried to get published; [a.] Chester-le-Street, Durham, UK, DH3 4HX

ROBBINS, JOANNE
[b.] 16 October 1978, Cirencester; [p.] Lesley Robbins (Deceased) and Dennis Robbins; [ed.] Cirencester Deer Park School and currently Stroud College; [occ.] Student; [pers.] I would like to dedicate this poem to my Mum - whom I will miss forever.; [a.] Oakridge, Gloucestershire, UK, GL6 7NZ

ROBERTS, GABRIELLE E.
[b.] Wirksworth; [p.] D. W. and B. G. Roberts; [m.] Affianced; [occ.] Administrative Assistant; [memb.] Derby Choral Union and Mensa; [hon.] BA (Hons) Business Administration, Economics and Literature - Derby University Grade 8 in Piano and Singing; [pers.] I believe in the musicality of Poetry.; [a.] Derbyshire, UK

ROBERTS, SUSAN JACQUELINE
[b.] 25 December 1951, Borehamwood, Herts; [p.] Caradoc and Elizabeth Roberts; [m.] Andres Rigo Rigo, 21 January 1979; [ch.] David Agustin (16); [ed.] Holmshill Comprehensive School, Borehamwood. The British Language Centre Palma, De Mallorca; [occ.] Teacher of English as a foreign language; [hon.] 'A' Level German plus fluent in Spanish and Catalan, course in journalism; [pers.] I have been very much influenced in my writing by the beautiful Mediterranean Island where I have spent the past 25 years.; [a.] Llucmajor, Majorca, 07620

ROBERTSON, MS. SUSAN MARY
[pen.] Susan Mary Robertson; [b.] 1 October 1952, Cardiff, UK; [p.] Mr. and Mrs. Robert Robertson; [ed.] Birkbeck College London 1995-97 certificate and diploma in Media Practice King's College London B.Sc; (Hons.) Biochemistry B.T.E.C Management Studies; [occ.] Library Assistant; [memb.] A.I.M.L.S. (1978) British Labour Party (1980-1997); [hon.] Nominated International Poet of The year 1997; [oth. writ.] "Blood, Sweat And Tears" in "Awaken To A Dream" 1996 "Working Holidays" 1995 "Choosing a Package Deal" 1996, "Health For Humanity" 1982, "Dawn of Space Age" 1994.; [pers.] My interest include books, music, art, theatre, films, travel, environment and politics.; [a.] London, Middlesex, UK, W14 9XT

ROBINSON, GUY PHILLIP GRAHAM
[pen.] Breusac; [b.] 3 July 1940, British India; [p.] Frederick and Beatrice Robinson; [m.] Mary Jaqueline Robinson, 20 February 1971; [ch.] Alex and Jeremy; [ed.] 49-56 Portora Royal School, 57/58 Welbeck College, 59/60 Royal Military Academy, Sandhurst; [occ.] Retired from British and (Latterly) Oman Forces. Now part time Historical Analyst and also various business interest; [memb.] Institution of Royal Engineers, Royal Geographical Society, Institution of British Management, Royal Engineer Yacht Club Anglo-Omani Society; [hon.] Royal Geographical Society Cuthbert Peek Award 1965; [oth. writ.] A few articles and poems in club and service magazines and journals.; [pers.] I find that loyalty, integrity, duty and courage, tempered with humour and kindness, evoke trust and fellowship from people of all types and background. Give of your best and you usually find the best; [a.] Andover, Hampshire, UK, SP11 7SB

ROBINSON, MIKE
[pen.] Mike Lazerus; [b.] 22 December 1963, South East, London; [p.] Samuel Robinson, Patricia Robinson; [m.] Gillian Robinson, 6 August 1988; [ch.] Lara Elise Robinson, Madison Louise Robinson; [ed.] B.A. Hons Drama/Theatre Roehampton Institute, MBA Greenwich University (to be completed in 1999); [occ.] Part-time Teacher full time Career; [memb.] Musical director of Theatre Valisse, guild of song writers and composers; [hon.] Nathaniel Memorial Scholarship from the London Mime Centre; [oth. writ.] Songs for Theatre including original works for the British Arts Council.; [pers.] It is better to have lived life with a dream than to have lived and died with no dream at all!; [a.] New Cross, London, UK, SE14 6DN

ROBINSON, WILLIAM G.
[pen.] William George; [b.] 11 September 1939, Sutton, Coldfield; [ed.] Nominal Secondary Modern and further education, Electrical and Electronics and B.K. Accounting, (N.E.C. Report Writing, including "Astronomy" etc via - (WEA), "Scriptural" - gained: "A.T.T.C.": (Emmaus B/S); [occ.] Varied - or semi skilled; [memb.] R.A.F.A. - Life member also Blood Donor Ambassador to N.B.T.S., in short - I'm a "Long Term" Blood Donor, For the Good of Other's Life in Life; [pers.] I write poetry as personal developing, may others develop via their reading. Reading to write, is writing to read.; [a.] Birmingham, West Midlands, UK, B23 5UP

ROCHELL, MR. ANDREW
[b.] 11 August 1949, Dewsbury; [p.] Mrs. Olive Pickles and Mr. G. Lewis Pickles; [m.] I had a girlfriend Susan who died 5 October 1996; [ed.] Thornhill Secondary High, Dewsbury; [oth. writ.] Short story The Lost Years Of My Life, printed by Womans Own, I think it was June 8th 1974.; [pers.] I write my poetry with deep honest emotions with no embarrassment of showing the rawness of pain, by doing this I hope people who feel the same, pain, but felt they were the only ones who do, will feel, they are sharing their hurt with me, surely that is what any kind of writing is about.; [a.] Batley, W. Yorkshire, UK, WF17 5LF

RODDA, M.
[b.] 15 December 1912, Scotland; [p.] Deceased; [m.] Deceased; [ch.] two; [ed.] Higher Standard; [occ.] Retired; [hon.] The only award I can recall was for general excellence in English and Writing at school.; [oth. writ.] Book (novel) being published, early 1998. In process of another book (early stages); [pers.] "Think Well On" and write what you feel, such matters as give interest. What is the use of writing if you can't try and share your thoughts on paper.; [a.] London, N6 5RW

ROMANIS, MARJORIE
[pen.] Marjorie Romanis; [b.] 31 March 1918, Bulwell; [p.] Loisa and John Crane; [m.] James W. G. Romanis, 8 June 1940; [ed.] After Exams sent to "Cottesmore School" Nottingham, (Very Modern); [occ.] Seaside Hotelier also Professional Singer; [memb.] Hoteliers Ass. Skegness Lincs now retired and my husband is deceased; [hon.] Two silver statuettes of Jolly Fisherman, given for special services to the town; [oth. writ.] Pantomine each exam. All in rhyme performed by friends and family.; [pers.] After so busy a life, being retired has given me time at last, to enjoy my love of words and the joy writing poetry gives me.; [a.] Skegness, Lincs, UK, PE25 2TA

RONALD, MRS. JILL MURIEL
[pen.] Jill M. Ronald; [b.] 11 May 1933, Guildford, Surrey; [p.] Herbert Ford and Hilda Jenkins; [m.] Colonel Francis John Ronald (Deceased), 6 June 1970; [ch.] Two stepsons; [ed.] Upper Chine School, Shanklin, Isle of Wight, Queen's Secretarial College, London; [occ.] Charity Fundraiser; [memb.] Royal British Legion - Haywards Heath Branch, University of the Third Age - Haywards Heath; [hon.] Royal British Legion Poppy Appeal Certificate of Appreciation; [oth. writ.] A number of poems published during the last three years.; [pers.] I have suffered from M. E. for the last ten years and since overcoming the worst of the disease, have found writing poetry both relaxing and therapeutic. With the opportunities for publication that have presented themselves during this time, it has proved to be very satisfying and rewarding as well.; [a.] Haywards Heath, West Sussex, UK, RH16 3NZ

ROONEY, MS. MARIE K.
[b.] 22 September 1982, Inverness, Scotland; [ed.] Educated to MA level in Fine Arts and Film and T.V. studies at the Royal College of Art, also trained as a lecturer; [occ.] Freelance poet, Media Artist and secretary; [memb.] British Film Institute, Museum of Moving Image; [hon.] Awarded Arts Council Grant to make a short, aesthetic film has a body of film work in The National Film Archive; [oth. writ.] Several poetry today and poetry now anthologies carry my poems, also published in Psycho Poetic, poetry monthly and fingertips magazines.; [pers.] In my creative work I emphasise the meditative aspect of the everyday. I enjoy friendships and creativity in life.; [a.] West Norwood, London, UK, SE27 0AY

ROSIE, HELEN
[b.] 13 November 1978, Frimley; [p.] Peter Rosie and Kate Rosie; [ed.] St. Nicholas School Farnborough Sixth Form; [occ.] Student; [hon.] 11 GCSE's 4 a levels; [oth. writ.] A selection of poems.; [pers.] Presently, my poetry focuses on the personal experience of losing my auntie, who suffered terribly with cancer. I write not only for myself but in remembrance of her.; [a.] Fleet, Hampshire, UK, GU13 8TA

ROSS, MRS. ENID E.
[b.] Skelton-on-Ure, North Yorks; [p.] Sydney and Elizabeth A. Wright; [m.] Lewis Henry Neil Ross; [ch.] Four; [ed.] Skelton Newby Hall School, Boroughbridge Modern School at 11 years of age;

[occ.] Retired, Ex Civil Servant; [hon.] English Language B Pass 1975; [oth. writ.] 2 articles Yorkshire evening press, 1 article in popular magazine.; [pers.] As a child of 7 years I had a picture of the then Princess Elizabeth beside my bed and have since taken a great interest in her life and family. I felt now is the time to show my respect and admiration for her majesty.; [a.] Boroughbridge, North Yorks, UK, YO5 9DQ

ROSS, MALCOLM
[pen.] Ditto; [b.] 11 July 1937, Nottingham; [m.] Georgina, 2 September 1967; [ch.] Four - 3 girls and one boy; [ed.] Sir Jess Boot College; [occ.] Retired; [memb.] Solihull Federation of Residents Associations (Chairman), Fordbridge Area Residents Association (Chairman), Local Councilor, School Governor; [oth. writ.] The Choice (Aimed at peace in Ireland.) Home is were the heart is.; [pers.] Grateful to be alive. Try to express innermost thoughts.; [a.] Solihull, West Midlands, UK, B37 5BN

ROWE, APRIL
[b.] 14 February 1961, Newcastle; [pers.] Please dedicate my poem as follows. Dedicated to Mark my perfect love and the beautiful child we lost. Who'll never be forgotten.; [a.] Newcastle, UK, NE2 1UY

ROWLAND, MARGOT
[b.] 3 March 1982, Ely; [p.] Richard Rowland, Margaret Rowland; [ed.] Ursuline Convent/College, (Kent); [occ.] Student; [memb.] Mensa, Duke of Edinburgh's Award Scheme, British Sub-Aqua Club; [hon.] Bronze and Silver D.O.E. Awards, Snorkel Diver Qualification.; [a.] Cambridge, Cambridgeshire, UK, CB4 1FP

ROZYCKI, JAN
[b.] 13 November 1986, London; [p.] Jan Rozycki, Margaret Rozycki; [ed.] St. Mary's R.C. School Chiswick; [hon.] Certificated Polish Literature, The Literary Guild writing a verse competition, Father's Day Poem Competition; [oth. writ.] Several poems published in "Polish Daily" at Soldier's Daily.; [pers.] I wish the whole world was an ark, that kept all animals in content and peace, away from the palms of hunters. Let the hands of peace grasp the world and shine its rays down on the people.; [a.] London, Hammersmith, UK, W6 0XA

RUHRMUND, HARRY
[b.] 22 August 1922, Pretoria, South Africa; [ed.] Tolcarne Elementary School, Newlyn; [occ.] Retired; [memb.] The Cornwall County Scouts Council, The Royal British Legion; [hon.] M.B.E., For Service to the Scout Movement, the 1939-45 Star, The Burma Star With Pacific Clasp, The Defence Medal And War Service Medal For Service to Great Britain; [oth. writ.] Poems and Essays not yet published. Write a column for the quarterly "Cornish Scouter" regularly.; [pers.] I have always enjoyed good poetry and prose, and hope in a small way to make my contribution.; [a.] Newlyn, Penzance, Cornwall, UK, TR18 5NL

RUPINDER, MISS KALSI
[b.] 31 July 1984, W-ton, England; [p.] Harjinder (Father) and Amarjit Kalsi (Mother); [ed.] 2nd year at High Arcal Secondary Sedgley England; [occ.] Student; [hon.] Been guest of honour at Bramford Primary School got 20 merit awards from school, plus a star in several subjects. Got BBCI Blue Peter's Honoured Badge.; [oth. writ.] Written 30 poems hoping to write enough poems to publish a book.; [pers.] Got natural talent in writing poems. Wrote first poem at the age of 11. I would like to become an English teacher.; [a.] Coseley, W. Midlands, UK, WV14 9UD

RUSE, MICHELLE
[pen.] Michelle Grace; [b.] 21 July 1964, Plaistow; [p.] Carole Cowdrey and Leslie Lee; [m.] Richard Ruse, 21 June 1996; [ch.] One on the way; [ed.] Leyton Senior High School, Walcham Forest College, Middlesex University; [occ.] Grooming Advisor/Counter Manager for 'Aramis'; [hon.] B.A. (Hons) Social Science; [pers.] My poetry is inspired by my childhood experiences... My parents had an explosive marriage and divorce; this has been a catalyst for me in that I value the feelings of children the world over!; [a.] St. John's Wood, London, UK, NW8 9XT

RUSHBURY, MR. LESLIE
[b.] 23 May 1921, Birmingham; [p.] Amy May, Charles Henry; [m.] Dorothy May, 19 December 1941; [ch.] Ian Paul, Leslie Frederick; [ed.] Grammar School; [occ.] Retired, Ex warehouse and Transport Manager; [hon.] Service Medals only for armed forces service during 1939-1945 War; [pers.] This is my first attempt at poetry competitions. To me, it has been, and always will be a wonderful way to relax in my reclining years.; [a.] Birmingham, UK, B32 2JX

RUSSELL, DAVID A.
[pen.] Braxton Sherman; [b.] 27 May 1969, Stourbridge; [ed.] King Edward College; [hon.] English Literature; [oth. writ.] Poems published in city limits magazine, six feature length motion picture screen plays, currently being marketed. Poem published 'Awaken to a Dream' anthology.; [pers.] I endeavour to interpret the world in an original, creative way. I am influenced by the epic and romantic poets.; [a.] Hackney, London, UK, E8 1LG

RUSSELL, JAYNE E.
[b.] 17 January 1977, Falkirk; [p.] Robert and Sandra Russell; [ed.] BSC (Hons) Applied Human Nutrition.; [occ.] Student 4th year Queen Margaret College (Edinburgh); [memb.] Aerobics, Box-A-Case; [oth. writ.] None as yet published, although have a built collection of a similar standard.; [pers.] "What ever will be, will be". (Que Serg Serg); [a.] Folkirk, Stirlingshire, UK, FK5 4US

RYAN, VALERIE
[b.] 18 November 1958; St Helier's Hospital, Carshalton, Surrey; [p.] Eddie and Margaret Norman (ancestors of Grace Darling); [m.] Louis Ryan, 22 May 1993; [ed.] Cheam High School, Chatworth Road, Cheam, Surrey; [occ.] Children's nanny; [memb.] Downs and Weald Rambling Group, Cheam Social Club; [oth. writ.] Stars in Heaven, In our Garden, (The Kiss of the Sun), (Home Counties Poets); [pers.] I like to recall my childhood and other people's; [a.] Cheam, Surrey, UK

SABIN, GEORGIE
[b.] 10 January 1965, Cuckfield; [ed.] Hertford College, Oxford, Courtauld Institute, London; [occ.] History of Art Tutor, Surrey University; [hon.] Finalist "Writers' Weekly" poetry competition BBC Radio.; [a.] Lingfield, Surrey, UK, RH7 6BG

SAMPSON, MARK
[b.] 16 November 1964, Burham, Kent; [p.] Peter Sampson and Iris Sampson; [ed.] Burham Primary Schools, Ditchling Primary School, Lewes Priory; [occ.] Civil Servant and History Student; [memb.] PTC Union, Harvey Hopper, Romney Hythe and Dymchurch Railway Association; [oth. writ.] Poems published by South Street Bonfire Society in Lewes, and by Fanzines run by Brighton and Hove Albion Supporters. 'Early Friday Evening' published in 'Jewels of the Imagination'.; [pers.] I try to write poems that are a true reflection of the world I see around me.; [a.] Lewes, East Sussex, UK, BN7 1XN

SANDERSON-KEY, V. L.
[pen.] Sandy; [b.] Sheffield; [p.] Jack Sanderson, Irene Proctor; [m.] Divorced; [ch.] Dominic G. Sanderson-Key; [ed.] Owner Lane Intermediate, Hinde House Comp.; [occ.] Personnel Administrator, The Royal Mail; [memb.] I.P.D.; [oth. writ.] Unpublished poems.; [pers.] Life goes on.; [a.] Sheffield, S. Yorkshire, UK, S9 1SA

SANDERSON-SMITH, WENDY
[b.] 19 December 1970, South Africa; [p.] Peter and Maria Sanderson-Smith; [occ.] Landscape Designer; [oth. writ.] Two poems published in poetry today's 'Life' and 'Nothing Left Unsaid.'; [pers.] In dedication. My work speaks of earth and skin, chilling and scorch. And too much terrible love.; [a.] Cape Town, South Africa

SAUNDERS, MRS. LJUDMILLA
[pen.] Milly; [ed.] An Arts Graduate; [occ.] Retired Teacher; [memb.] She was an active member of the former Tresillian Women's Institute, whose remaining members still meet socially each week and for Christmas Lunch. She is a bookkeeper, and treasurer of Carrick/Kerrier Bookkeeping Group. She is also treasurer of Tresillian Senior Citizen's Club and of the Village Magazine. She thus still leads an active life, accompanied by her loyal friend and champion, a Staffordshire Bull Terrier, Benny.; [hon.] Earlier this year she was awarded the Editor's Choice Award for "Outstanding Achievement in Poetry" by the International Library of Poetry, for her twenty line poem "Tranquil Thoughts" which was published in their anthology "Jewels of the Imagination". She was also nominated by the International Society of Poets as "Poet of the Year for 1997" and invited to attend the induction in Washington on 8th August this year during the seventh Annual International Society of Poets Convention and Symposium, and to present a 40 line poem specially written for the occasion.; [a.] Truro, Cornwall, UK, TR2 4BW

SAVAGE, SHAUN
[b.] 25 June 1963, Norwich; [p.] Bryan Savage and Patricia Savage; [ed.] Hewett School, Norwich City College; [occ.] Printer/Technician, Hewett School, Norwich; [oth. writ.] Other poems appear in A Passage In Time, and Awaken To A Dream.; [pers.] I was depressed when I wrote this poem, and it was an attempt to describe the blackness that had descended upon me. This occurs when the areas of the brain shut down, and in the darkness the identity is born.; [a.] Norwich, Norfolk, UK, NR1 2JD

SCOTT, KATIE SHEILA
[b.] 29 August 1981, Bury, Lancashire; [p.] Hugh Scott, Sheila Scott; [ed.] Hopwood Hall College, Rochdale. Rochdale IDL Centre (for Dylexics); [occ.] Student; [hon.] Certificate of Achievement in recognition of distinguished achievement in reading and spelling skills. Contribution to the community award; [pers.] I have always been a keen story and poetry writer despite my dyslexia. Through special tuition I am able to achieve my goals. I was greatly influenced by Wilfred Owen's poetry.; [a.] Heywood, Lancashire, UK, OL10 4TA

SCOTT, MICHELE
[b.] 16 February 1960, Liverpool; [p.] R. J. Scott, and V. E. Scott; [m.] Divorced, 23 September 1979; [ch.] R. J. Scott - 11, Scott Saifer - 5; [ed.] Educated up to C.S.E. Standards (taken 8); [occ.] Residential Care Officer; [memb.] Groaver World Spiritualist, Scientology Church (Clairvoyant Medium); [pers.] I was inspired by my father, who was a brave man, a 'Chindit' in 2nd world war. (When was very strong and as he got older, I noticed how feeble he had become, he passed away on 18. 11. 96 war wards); [a.] Douglas, Isle of Man, UK, IM2 6LS

SCREEN, DAVID ROBERT
[b.] 28 January 1934, Nottingham; [p.] The Late Arthur and Ethel Hilda Screen; [ed.] Trent Bridge, Secondary School Nott'm; [occ.] Warehouseman; [oth. writ.] "An April Shower", "Averting The Elements", "The Ultimate", "The Choice Was Mine" plus a personal album of my own work. Co-produced by Int Library of Poetry.; [pers.] By keeping your eyes and ears open and keen observation you can amass so many thoughts which are inspirational. People can be very inspirational too. One such person is a dear friend John Paul Leonard, a very talented young man.

SCRIVENER, BARBARA A.
[pen.] Barbaranne; [b.] St. Mary's; [p.] Dora and John Horridge; [m.] James; [ch.] Pamela Susan and James John; [ed.] Yew Tree School, Northenden Cheshire, Secretarial College M/C; [memb.] Northenden Operatic Society, Photographic Society, Local Art Club; [hon.] Secretarial skills word processor, etc.; [oth. writ.] Several poems, short stories, medical articles, etc. unpublished.; [pers.] I am an incurable dreamer and romantic and am interested and influenced by all the great artists in all fields.; [a.] Warrington, Cheshire, UK, WA4 2JE

SEARLE, MISS F. M.
[b.] 2 March 1940, Helston; [p.] Clara Winifred and Edward Searle (Deceased); [ed.] Helston Grammar School; [occ.] Retired; [memb.] Helston Old Cornwall Society, Helston Camera Club, Friends of Helston Folk Museum; [hon.] 16 Awards Since 1976 in Poetry competitions including 4 1st Prizes/Trophy cups of Gorseth Kernow (Cornish Gorsedd); [oth. writ.] Published in 6 Anthologies by triumph house, anthology by King designs, and poetry today, also this England, in 1977 published my own Anthology 'A Bridge For Crossing' by outpost publications.; [pers.] I am always seeking to create the perfect poem that projects the inner heart.; [a.] Helston, Cornwall, UK, TR13 8UN

SEDDON, RAMONA
[b.] 10 October 1982, Nottingham; [p.] Janice and Kevin; [ed.] I am currently in full time School. I attend the William Crane. Comprehensive School Aspley. Nottingham.; [oth. writ.] I get my own inspiration from situations that have happened in my own personal life, and things that I have been through; [pers.] I write poems to free my mind of thoughts.; [a.] Nottingham, UK, NG8 3PA

SELVESTER, ELLA-DEE
[pen.] Ella-Dee; [b.] 21 October 1980, Flintshire; [p.] Maxine Jones and David Selvester; [ed.] Ysgol Croes Atti - Primary Ysgol Marsgarmon - Secondary; [occ.] Student; [memb.] YRDD Gobaith Cynru, Local Youth Club - Member of all Sporting Teams; [hon.] Winners in Flintshire in Girls Football, Badminton, Pool and Netball; [oth. writ.] None published but have many poems written privately retained in a file at home.; [pers.] I enjoy, writing poems as I can switch off to the world and relax completely.; [a.] Northop, Flintshire, UK, CH7 6DB

SENIOR, SUSAN ELIZABETH
[b.] 9 September 1962, St Mary's, Leeds; [p.] Mr. Sidney Daniel Lawton and Mrs. Renee Lawton; [ch.] Micheal - 14, Maria - 11, Amanda - 9 and Gemma - 5; [ed.] Hunslet Church of England Middle School and William Gasgoinge Girls High; [memb.] Midlands Rock 'n' Roll Club, Heeds United Supporters Club, and Choices Women's Circle.; [hon.] Was presented the Editor's Choice Award in 1996 by The International Society of Poets; [oth. writ.] 'All Alone' am I published by Poetry Now Spring 1995 'Please Take Me Home' published 1996 by International Society of Poets. "In Memory of Steven" Autumn 1996 by Poetry Today "Dad You Won't Be There" also by Poetry Today Spring 97.; [pers.] I mainly write poetry to express my feelings for someone or if I find it difficult to tell a person face to face how I feel about them. It also pleases me to know that other people get pleasure out of reading my work.; [a.] Leeds, West Yorkshire, UK, LS9 7UA

SETIAWAN, AGATHA
[pen.] Janis Casparindina; [b.] 31 March 1980, Kediri; [p.] Johanes Wahyudi and Chandra Rahayu; [ed.] School of Hotel and Tourism at Prisma Professional Surabaya; [oth. writ.] Several novels and poets for personal collection.; [pers.] Don't run away from your fear, because there is courage in it, and when you feel very sad, on the moment you're feeling the greatest happiness, too inside your heart.; [a.] Kediri, Jawa Timur, 64126

SETON, LILIAN
[pen.] Timotay, Shadow and Jude; [b.] 24 February 1936, Seahouses, Northumberland; [p.] J. E. Scott, Retired Rabbit Trapper; [m.] Deceased; [ch.] Michael, Robert, Steven; [ed.] Saint Josephs Primary School for Girls, Plus Chathill Northumberland Jnr School; [occ.] Retired and Psychiatric Nurse; [hon.] One award, others are being submitted, at Kent, who wish one a month for twelve month, I have put my thoughts I own on paper since I was 14 yrs., never thought to submit any till now.; [oth. writ.] Counting our blessings, our heritage, our world, The Tall Ship, In Ages Past, Time Forgot, Timeless Love; [pers.] If anyone is thinking, or wanting, to hurt someone, make sure it's yourself you hurt not others. I was born at Chapel Row Seahouses, my father was a trapper in the war, on the Duke of Northern Ireland Estate. He died on the beaches, Dunkirk, with two of my uncles.

SHARP, JOHN H.
[b.] 15 March 1925, London; [m.] Ivy, 2 June 1951; [ch.] David John, Kim Andrew; [ed.] School of Engineering and Navigation, London but terminated on 3rd September 1939; [occ.] Happily retired; [memb.] 7/9th Royal Scots Asso., The Royal British Legion, Burnham Hillside Bowls Club; [hon.] Only the mundane type of medals issued to anyone who served in Civil Defence and H.M. army during the 1939-45 period.; [oth. writ.] "A Royal Sessenach" (Unpublished") Memories of earlier years as a Child Stockbrokers' Clerk and Salesman. Many rhymes about family, politics and life generally. (None submitted); [pers.] Life is too short so live and let live.; [a.] Burnham-on-Crouch, Essex, UK, CM0 8RA

SHAW, GILL
[b.] 18 April 1958; [ed.] Manchester Central High School for Girls, Manchester University; [occ.] Counsellor, National and International Master Practitioner in Neuro Linguisrie Programming; [oth. writ.] "The Child's Prayer" Re and Gallery of Artistry, The Poetry Guild. "The Auction Room, Uncertainly Right, I Wish I Could Write A Poem, England 1936 Re "Expressions" Abbey Books.; [pers.] I appreciate The Hell of Childhood, Confusion of Adolescence, Unrequitted Love, Humour, Embarrassment and the general stumbling through life which feeds my writing.; [a.] Upton Priory, Macclesfield, UK, SK10 3RZ

SHAW, SARAH
[b.] 13 March 1983, Darlington; [p.] Anne Shaw and Derrick Shaw; [ed.] Alderman Leach Infant and Junior School, Branksome Comprehensive School, Darlington; [occ.] School Girl; [hon.] Ballroom Dancing Medals up to 1st Gold Bar Standard - I.D.T.A.; [oth. writ.] English course work at school.; [pers.] Keep your chin up and you'll never fall, even if you're short, always walk tall.; [a.] Darlington, Co Durham, UK, DL3 0DX

SHAW-TAYLOR, MARY
[pen.] Donna-Marie; [b.] 16 September 1938, Bradford, W. Yorks; [p.] David and Ada Bottomley; [m.] Divorced; [ch.] Pamela Eva-Karen, Holden-Kenneth Taylor and Anne Taylor; [ed.] Secondary Modern School; [occ.] Retired; [memb.] The North Operatic Society, The Bradford Players, The International Library of Poetry, Editor's Choice Award to receive medal, also been made an honorable member received V.I.P. Badge and a Distinguished Member plaque; [hon.] Nomination for Poet of the Year award Washington, DC, 1997; [oth. writ.] 'All is Not Lost' poem published in 'Awaken to a Dream' Book accepted into another book of Memories and Day Dreams' from the 'Poetry Guild' poem called 'Diet' short stories in magazines many years ago now write Music also and short stories.; [pers.] To be a well known and professional writer of poetry short stories - music and plays. I was influenced from mother and father's music, (Romantic Words) Robby Burns's poetry also. I admire, 'Pam Ayres'.; [a.] Bradford, West Yorkshire, UK, BD4 8PA

SHELABARGER, DALE
[b.] 29 February 1976, S Wales; [p.] Wayne Shelabarger (Deceased) and Elaine Shelabarger; [ed.] Dyffryn School, Port Talbot, Afan College, Port Talbot, Brunel University, London; [occ.] Student; [pers.] I try to express my personal view of life through my writing. I find inspiration through my own experiences.; [a.] Twickenham, Middlesex, UK, TW7 7DZ

SHELDON, HARRIET OLMAN
[b.] 26 April 1948, Amsterdam; [p.] Lo Olman, Renee Olman-Roos; [m.] Martin John Sheldon, 23 March 1984; [ed.] Breitner College, Amsterdam, Schoevers Secretarial School, Amsterdam; [occ.] Housewife, Translator; [oth. writ.] Poems published in Dutch National Newspapers.; [pers.] Universal love is omnipotent.; [a.] Cuckfield, West Sussex, UK, RH17 5LA

SHEPHERD, LINDA
[b.] 5 May 1935, Glasgow; [p.] Thomas and Mary Shepherd; [ed.] St. Gerard's Sec. School Glasgow London University; [occ.] Retired (from teaching); [hon.] B.A. Honours Degree (London); [pers.] I am profoundly moved by beauty, of people, of places. I have been mainly influenced by T. S. Eliot and by Garcia Lorca.; [a.] Prestatyn, Denbighshire, UK, LL19 7PR

SINGH, MR. AMARJIT
[b.] 28 February 1969, Coventry, UK; [p.] Mr. Darshan Singh and Mrs. Rattan Kaur; [ed.] President Kennedy Com. School; [hon.] Poem published in Awaken to a Dream; [oth. writ.] I've written hundreds of poems on every kind of subject. I can also write songs. I intend to write songs for Cliff Richard who will analyze some songs that I've written for him and hopefully some records will be released in the future.; [pers.] I've an ultimate ambition to become the greatest poet of all time, which is only possible with God's blessings who inspires me to write fabulous poetry. I thank God for blessing me with so much poetic talent.; [a.] Coventry, West Midlands, UK, CV6 5TE

SLYM, WINIFRED M.
[pen.] Wyn Slym; [b.] 23 January 1925, Derby; [p.] Annie Huffer, John Huffer; [m.] David Slym (Deceased), 11 September 1948; [ch.] Kevin Slym, Karl Slym, Grandson Oliver Slym; [ed.] Local Schools only (Hardwick) and Normanton; [occ.] Now Retired but previously care assistant for elderly; [memb.] Hobby - Indoor Bowling Sunny Hill Club Derby; [hon.] Some poems accepted by magazines over the years.; [oth. writ.] One previously published by International Poet's Society and some to local mags.; [pers.] My inspiration for "Turn The Page" was a special friend I had for eight years, generally I take my ideas from observing people, I like romantic poets.; [a.] Derby, Derbyshire, UK, DE23 7JZ

SMELLIE, DAVID
[pen.] Smellie; [b.] 24 February 1985, Wandsworth, London; [p.] Norma S. and Douglas S.; [ed.] Wilson Grammar School Wallington, Surrey; [occ.] School Boy; [memb.] 13th Croydon Boys Brigade; [hon.] Honours Board Winterbourne Junior boys school, Thornton Heath Surrey; [pers.] I strive for excellence.; [a.] UK

SMITH, BARBARA
[pen.] Elizabeth Wooliscroft; [b.] 9 January 1944, Ashbourne; [p.] Alice (Deceased); [m.] Live with Jack Lover's best friend; [ed.] Uttoxeter Sec Med girls, Derby Tech, C. F. Mott College, Edgerhill certificate slow learning children; [occ.] Stopped teaching 83 because of MS, now attempting French; [memb.] Liverpool writers group gave me much support now attend the Inklings; [oth. writ.] Poems for magazines some poems in anthologies.; [pers.] Once my poor eyesight made me slow down to observe carefully the minor miracles, kindness of life, and this I continue to do.; [a.] Liverpool, Merseyside, UK, L17 7AJ

SMITH, JACK SAMUEL
[b.] 25 March 1990, Stafford; [p.] Stuart and Karen Smith; [ed.] Wolvey Primary School, Wolvey Nr. Hinckley; [hon.] School Wolvey - Class 'Endeavor Award' 1997., Awarded several 'Achievement Awards' throughout school life.; [pers.] Enjoy reading and writing poetry. Only 6 years old when poem was written.; [a.] Coventry, UK, CV7 9JP

SMITH, JOAN O.
[pen.] Lara; [b.] Birmingham; [p.] Walter and Margaret Snape; [m.] Leslie Smith (Deceased); [ch.] Pamela, Michael and Sandy; [ed.] Kings Norton Grammar School; [occ.] Housewife; [oth. writ.] "Dream Lover" A poem published in Jewels of the Imagination.; [pers.] I have written so many poems over the last 3 years, mostly expressing my emotional feelings and dreams. "Sweet Bliss" and many, many more were written for Colin, a very special person, who became part of my life for just a short while. He was my inspiration and always will be.; [a.] Teignmouth, Devon, UK, TQ14 8RU

SMITH, JOHN
[pen.] Jack Smith; [b.] 15 August 1930, Longniddry; [p.] Helen and William Smith (Both Deceased); [m.] Elspeth B. MacRobert-Smith, 4 June 1955; [ch.] Fionna Helen Smith; [ed.] Longniddry Public School, Preston Lodge, Benneth College, Army Police; [occ.] Retired Police Officer; [memb.] International Police Association. Scots Guards Association. Order of St. John of Jerusalem. Elder of The Church of Scotland. Member of West Lothan Twinning Association. Kirk Magazine Editor; [hon.] O. St. J. Dip. Eng.; [oth. writ.] I have written a number of poems over a number of years. The only poems published have been in local magazines. This poem is the first I have submitted for a competition. I have had a book on local history published.; [pers.] There is no more pleasing exercise of the mind than being able to express oneself in verse. The satisfaction and reward are in the gratification of producing on paper those thoughts which one finds pleasing to the mind but most of all, are a product of the heart.; [a.] Torphichen, West Lothian, UK, EH48 4NB

SMITH, MATTHEW
[b.] 22 July 1976, Sheffield; [p.] David Smith and Carol Smith; [ed.] Wales High School; [occ.] Labourer; [pers.] Please allow each verse to romance your soul, and may poetry take you to wherever you may dream. I have been influenced and taken to many places by early romantic poets, especially Thomas Hardy.; [a.] Kiveton Park, Yorkshire, UK, S26 6NU

SMITH, TRACY LEE
[b.] 21 December 1976, Dublin, Ireland; [memb.] Distinguished member of the International Society of Poets; [hon.] Editor's Choice Award for poem "Heartbeat Fast"; [oth. writ.] 'Heartbeat Fast' printed in Jewels of the Imagination; [pers.] The poem, "Long Black Hall" was the first poem I ever wrote and I started writing January 1995 and I have not stopped writing since then.; [a.] Dublin 8, Ireland

SMITH-WHITTLE, GEORGE
[pen.] George Smith-Whittle; [b.] 18 September 1948, Tyldesley; [p.] Thomas and Bertha Smith-Whittle; [m.] Jill Robinson-Dale, 17 February 1996; [ch.] Katie, Robin and Sally; [ed.] Secondary Modern Heskfth Flethire School; [occ.] Retired; [oth. writ.] North West Words; [pers.] He that sings forgets and he that listens remembers.; [a.] Leigh, Lancs, Lancashire, UK, WN7 5QT

SOMJEE, MISS SHEHNAZ
[pen.] Shehnaz Somjee; [b.] Karachi, Pakistan; [p.] Rahim Somjee and Khairunissa Somjee; [ed.] MBBS, DLO, FRCS (England) also studying Law part-time; [occ.] Otolaryngologist, Head and neck surgeon; [memb.] Numerous Medical Bodies and Committees, International Society of Poetry; [hon.] Winner of International Poet of Merit Award 1997, Nominated for International Poet of the Year 1997, Gold Medalist in Medical College, Winner of numerous prizes and trophies for music, debating, quizzes, flower arranging; [oth. writ.] 'Sometime Somewhere', a collection published in Karachi, 'Destiny' published in 'Quiet Moments'. Several medical papers and articles - invented the 'Somjee-Crabtree Temporal Bone support Clamp!; [pers.] My poems reflect my surgical experience, my travels and philosophies - I write as a natural gift since the age of 9 years. A poem just enters my head and is penned down.; [a.] Melling, Merseyside, UK, L31 1DJ

STEBBINGS, PAMELA
[b.] 24 July 1928, Penarth, S Wales; [p.] Mr. and Mrs. Hookway (Deceased); [m.] George Ernest Stebbings, 22 September 1956; [ch.] One son; [ed.] Left school at fourteen; [occ.] Housewife; [pers.] Poetry is my way of seeing beauty everywhere.; [a.] UK, OX3 8QW

STENSON, CARLEY ANNE
[b.] 22 September 1982, England; [p.] Christine Evans, Eric Stenson; [ed.] St. Peters RC H School Orrell; [pers.] It came as a great surprise to hear what happened to my poem. My beloved mother had failed to tell me what she had done with it. Thinking it had been shoved in the cupboard with the rest of the papers, I am happy now to think that people appreciate and admire perhaps something that I wrote for people whom I appecriate and admire myself. I don't write poetry that often and when I do, it has got to be about something that means something to me, as it should to every body, for what else is there to write about?; [a.] Freshfield, Merseyside, UK, L37 7HL

STEVENS, MRS. DOROTHY
[b.] 27 December 1927; Normandy, Surrey; [p.] James Crooke, Eleanor Crooke; [m.] Geoffrey Stevens, 28 May 1949; [ch.] James Paul, Charles John; [ed.] Church of England, Secondary School; [occ.] Retired Civil Servant; [memb.] Arthritis Club, Western Line Dancing; [oth. writ.] One poem published. It is the only one I have submitted for publication; [pers.] I love people and my poems often reflect their comical side of nature; [a.] Farnborough, Hants

STEVENSON, ELIZABETH
[b.] 28 March 1960, Kirby-Cross, Essex; [ed.] Boston High School, Trent Polytechnic University of Nottingham; [hon.] BA (Hons) Humanities, BA (Hons) Psychology; [pers.] Writing poetry has enabled me to express and examine painful feelings. It has allowed me to make sense out of chaos.; [a.] Nottingham, UK

STEVENSON, ROSALYN
[pen.] Rosalyn C. Ellis; [b.] 28 November 1916, Beckenham, Kent; [p.] Mr. and Mrs. A. E. Virgo; [m.] Arther Noel Stevenson, 19 August 1963; [ed.] Howard Secondary unable to learn, as I suffer from Dislexia, self-taught; [occ.] Retired; [memb.] The International Library of Poetry; [hon.] I won a small prize for art, age eight yrs. Later, I had an oil painting accepted for hanging in gallery, for a while. Have good references.; [oth. writ.] 38 poems, and two prayers. Letters to politicians and royalty. Writing a book. But held up for the time being.; [pers.] I was a dunce at school but have taught myself. So am a late starter. I still have trouble with the dislexia I suffer from. I have a good ear for music.; [a.] Seaford, E. Sussex

STOCK, BARBARA
[pen.] Christine Payne; [b.] 14 October 1946, Wales; [ch.] Two grown up daughters; [ed.] Secondary modern, left school at 15; [oth. writ.] Short stories, lots of poems. I love writing for personal pleasure and have never attempted to get published before.; [a.] Newport, Gwent, UK, NP9 0RU

STOKES, ALICE
[pen.] Alice Kendall; [b.] 10 October 1934, London; [p.] Louisa and Frederick Kendall; [m.] Albert Alexander Stokes, 9 March 1957; [ch.] Gary, Kevin, Craig and Jamie; [ed.] Glyn Rd., M.S, Clapton E.5. and further Education Studies at Harlow Tech. College. (Later); [occ.] Caring for the elderly; [memb.] 'Harlequin' Entertainment Group of Harlow; [hon.] English Literature; [oth. writ.] Writings for pleasure Inc. 'A Childhood' (My Childhood During 2nd World War) plus other poems.; [pers.] My love of writing enables me to express how I truly feel and likens to the unlocking of 'A Secret Chamber'.; [a.] Harlow, Essex, UK, CM18 7SF

STOKES, CAROL
[pen.] Carol Stokes; [b.] 5 June 1949, Exeter; [m.] Bernard Stokes, 27 April 1968; [ch.] Lisa Marie and Neill Andrew; [ed.] Secondary Education; [occ.] Nursing Auxiliary Operating Theatre; [hon.] G.C.S.E. O Level English; [oth. writ.] Stories only for my children's pleasure.; [pers.] Scottish History has been a big influence on me. I try to make my writings interesting and to take the reader wherever the setting is.; [a.] Exeter, Devon, UK, EX2 8UF

STONE, JOAN E.
[b.] 6 May 1939, Croston, Lancs; [p.] Elizabeth and Thomas; [m.] John; [ch.] Gary and Joanne; [ed.] Ormskirk Grammar School; [oth. writ.] Several poems.; [pers.] Observing life happening to my friends and family brings words to my heart and mind.; [a.] Torquay, Devon, UK, TQ1 3LA

STONEMAN, BRIAN
[b.] 4 May 1965, Walthamstow; [p.] Alan Stoneman, Gwen Stoneman; [m.] Kelly Stoneman, 12 March 1993; [ed.] Erkenwald Comprehensive School Dagenham Essex; [occ.] Mini cab driver; [pers.] This poem is dedicated to my mom and dad, for all the support and encouragement they have given me. I hope seeing my name in print will make them proud of their eldest son.; [a.] Romford, Essex, UK

STONES, KIRSTY MARIE
[pen.] Kirst; [b.] 20 June 1984, Wythenshaw; [p.] Karen Stones; [ed.] Currently attending secondary school.; [occ.] Student; [hon.] MENSA, Swimming, Horse Riding, Cheer Leading Trophy; [pers.] I have been influenced by my grandfather's poems and would like to emulate him.; [a.] Altrincham, Cheshire, UK, WA15 7EP

STRONG, RICHARD S.
[b.] 16 March 1963, South Shields; [p.] Bob and Audrey Strong; [m.] Veronica Muckble; [ed.] Whitburn and Boldon Comprehensive's Life - 34 years; [occ.] Storeman - Onwa UK; [memb.] Sergeant - Territorial Army, 101 Regiment Royal Artillery; [hon.] I.S.P. Certificate of Merit - for "White Coated Sadists"; [oth. writ.] 'White Coated Sadists' - Jewels of the Imagination, and a large collection of as yet unpublished material.; [pers.] No matter how difficult the task, or how heavy the burden, remember, that even the smallest stream will eventually carry the mountain to the sea.; [a.] South Shields, Tyne and Wear, UK, NE34 8TE

STURMEY, HAZEL D.
[b.] 22 November 1932, Beare Green; [p.] Doris and Harry Way; [m.] John Sturmey, 6 March 1954; [ch.] Two sons, one daughter; [ed.] Secondary School; [occ.] Retired; [oth. writ.] Various other poems some serious, some humorous.; [pers.] I am 64 1/2 years of age and now retired after a lifetime of all aspects of accounts work and secretarial work. I also ran the local boys club for a number of years.; [a.] Dorking, Surrey, UK, RH5 4JA

SUTCLIFFE, HELEN ELIZABETH
[b.] 19 October 1978, Halifax; [p.] Mr. and Mrs. R. C. Sutcliffe; [ed.] Bradford Girls Grammar School, Greenhead College, Huddersfield; [occ.] Student; [pers.] Live life to the max!; [a.] Halifax, West Yorkshire, UK, HX3 8SY

SWANSON, AVES
[b.] 19 December 1933, Sturminster, Newton, Dorset; [p.] May and Hugh Spicer; [m.] David Henry Swanson, 9 February 1963; [ch.] Louise Turnbull and Stuart Swanson; [ed.] Higher School, Sturminster Newton, Dorset; [occ.] Care attendant at a residential home; [memb.] RSPCA, RSBP, IFAW, Blue Cross; [oth. writ.] 7 anthologies I am having my own book of poetry published.; [pers.] I write poetry as I am inspired to promote natures natural beauty in things I see and hear around me the mystic things in life.; [a.] Sheringham, Norfolk, UK, NR26 8XR

TAYLOR, MR. LACHLAN
[pen.] Lachlan Taylor; [b.] 26 June 1922, Falkirk; [p.] William and Margaret Taylor (Deceased); [m.] Anne McFarlane Henry (Deceased), 3 March 1967; [ed.] Comprehensive Left at Fourteen Years with Day School Lower Certificate; [occ.] Retired Pensioner; [memb.] Church, British Legion; [hon.] War Medals 1939/1945; [oth. writ.] Now have fifty three poems in anthology and four in magazines. Have been writing poetry for seven years but it was only four years ago that I sent them to publishers.; [pers.] I have always loved poetry. My favourite poets loved poetry my favourite poets being, Wordsworth, Shakespeare, Shelley, Burns and Scott.; [a.] Falkirk, Stirling

THOMAS, IRIS
[b.] 22 January 1952, Bow, London; [p.] Esther Stannard and Harry Stannard; [m.] David Thomas, 6 January 1979; [ch.] Claire Louise and Marie Lisa; [ed.] St. Paul's Way Secondary School; [occ.] Housewife; [a.] Dagenham, Essex, UK, RM9 5AG

THOMASON, SID
[b.] 3 November 1944, Paisley, Scotland; [p.] Sid Thomason, Jessie Thomason; [ed.] North Salford Secondary Modern Boys School; [occ.] Senior Prison Officer; [memb.] Radio Society of Great Britain; [oth. writ.] This is my first published work and was done as a gift to my loving life-partner and future wife - Christine.; [pers.] The gift of reading and writing is to be treasured and, if one can communicate with another person because of it, then that is another gift.; [a.] Chorley, Lancashire, UK, PR6 8TR

THOMPSON, MRS. PAULINE
[b.] 29 September 1940, Blackpool; [m.] G Rodney Thompson, 11 May 1974; [ch.] Two; [occ.] Housewife; [memb.] RSPB Local Towns Women's Guild.; [oth. writ.] Soon to be published in poetry today., "The Flowing River".; [pers.] A love of nature and cruelness by man upsets me.; [a.] Crumpsall, Greater Manchester, UK, M8 5AU

THOMPSON, MR. SAMUEL
[b.] 28 May 1936, Arbroath; [p.] Theresa and Thomas; [m.] Andreoina, 17 December 1955; [ch.] Seven; [ed.] State School; [occ.] Early Retired; [memb.] Member of Baxter Park, Bowling Club (Private); [oth. writ.] Poverty is one of a number of poems I have written. I had one published in a local paper a few years ago.; [pers.] I wrote the poem "poverty" after watching a news broadcast on wars in the Middle East; some of scenes were horrific.; [a.] Dundee, Tayside, UK, DD4 8QG

THOMPSON, SKA
[pen.] Was Kathy; [b.] 8 June 1931, Feltham, Midx; [p.] Elizabeth Jane Thompson, Bert Thompson; [m.] Ex, 19 April 1958; [ch.] Jacqueline Martin Nigel; [ed.] Secondary Sunday School; [occ.] Retired Dressmaker; [memb.] N.L. Girl Guides; [hon.] Pride of my parents self Employed respect; [oth. writ.] Motherhood, the Ass, Questions, Emily Pank Hurst, now is the time "Dad" "Mum", Happiness, Give And Take Listen And Watch, Dawn, God's, Emily Pank Hurst "Dawn" "God's"; [pers.] No regrets, ambition earn respect from all.; [a.] Scunthorpe, North Lincs, UK, DN17 1UD

THOMSON, AVRIL
[b.] 19 April 1970, Irving; [pers.] "Forbidden fruit" written about and dedicated for David Blades. My poems are all about true feelings and emotions.; [a.] Ardrossan, Ayrshire, UK, KA22 7DW

THORNDIKE, ETHEL ELIZABETH
[pen.] Ciss; [b.] 24 November 1904, Highbury; [p.] Albert G. Hilder, Edith E. Hilder; [m.] Ernest James Thorndike (Deceased), 1990; [ch.] David, Keith; [ed.] Elementary 1 left school December 1923, David December 1948, Keith Easter 1955; [occ.] Retired I have been on holiday cause of delay.

TIMMS, IRIS E.
[b.] 11 September 1939, Plaistow, E13; [p.] Harry, Ethel Freeman; [m.] James Timms, 28 March 1959; [ch.] Peter, Heather, Carol, Gwen, Kay; [ed.] Secondary Modern; [occ.] Housewife; [memb.] Dancing and Church Club; [hon.] Medals and Certificates for Dancing and poems; [oth. writ.] Poems in magazines. Also in one hard back.; [pers.] I love my grandchildren dearly. Colleen and Chantel, Carrington, April and Lewis, Sherlock.; [a.] Leigh-on-Sea, Essex, UK, SS9 5YE

TIPPETT, RICHARD
[b.] 6 January 1966, Newquay; [p.] Leslie and Fillomena; [ed.] Treviglas Secondary School and life; [occ.] Chef; [memb.] Born Free Foundation; [oth. writ.] Merely for my own pleasure.; [pers.] Paper is the poets canvas the words upon which are his paints, close your eyes and a picture is formed, no frame here to restrict your view.; [a.] Redruth, Cornwall, UK, TR15 2HT

TOMBE, ISOBEL
[pen.] Kilbroney Lewis; [b.] 8 February 1941, Ballyclare; [m.] Brian, 12 April 1985; [ch.] Eleanor, Samuel, stepchildren: Michele and Siobhan; [occ.] Retired Civil Servant; [memb.] Gracehill Golf Club, near Stranocum; [oth. writ.] My Childhood Days, The Failing Crop, published by the poetry guild and poetry now. Press reports for my local golf club and poem Gracehill near Stranocum in local press (about golf course).; [pers.] I wrote poetry as a child and have only recently took it up again inspired by the beauty and peace of the parkland course where I play with my husband. I also have more time to do different things since I took early retirement.; [a.] Ballymoney, Antrim, UK, BT53 6RP

TOVELL, JANET
[b.] 14 January 1939, Bradwell, Gt Yarmouth; [p.] Deceased; [m.] David, 1 March 1958; [ch.] Neil and Sally; [ed.] Gorleston High; [occ.] Home Carer for Norfolk County Council 21 years; [hon.] Editors Choice Award 1997 from the International Library of Poetry; [oth. writ.] Three poems published by Anchor Books, Peterborough and one by the International Library of Poetry; [pers.] I enjoy writing poems of everyday life on the Humourous side; all my love and thanks to my family and friends for always being there for me.; [a.] Gt Yarmouth, Norfolk, UK, NR31 7LY

TOWNER, LILLIE DIANA
[b.] 18 January 1925, East London; [p.] Russian Birth; [m.] Widow, 20 September 1947; [ch.] Two; [ed.] Secondary and College; [occ.] Retired; [memb.] Evening Classes; [hon.] 2 Certificates of Dist. Curtain Theatre Festival of spoken arts also London College of music, First class oral Communication Grade 4; [pers.] Have always been interested in speech and Drama and dancing - only as amateur. Wrote poetry in moments of inspiration. Enjoy this pleasure now. Very satisfying.; [a.] Wandsworth, London, UK, 9SJ

TRAVERS, EDWARD
[b.] 7 November 1947, Dublin; [p.] Thomas, Mary; [m.] Antoinette, 19 March 1973; [ch.] Julie Ann, Louise, Jillian; [ed.] De La Salle School, Ballyfermot, Dublin; [occ.] Taxi Driver; [memb.] The Planetary Society Pasadena, Astronomy Ireland Dublin; [hon.] Editor's Choice Award by The International Library of Poetry 1997; [oth. writ.] Several poems published by International Library of Poetry.; [pers.] I wish to dedicate the poem in this book to my daughter Jillian.; [a.] Dublin, Ireland

TUCKER, VICTOR
[pen.] Pentone; [b.] 17 November 1913, Wellington, Somerset; [p.] Alice and George Tucker; [m.] Florence Ann, 9 August 1937; [ch.] Rosemarie; [ed.] Wellington School Somerset; [occ.] Retired; [memb.] Chairman West Somerset Writer's Group, Black Down Association; [oth. writ.] Echoes In the Spiral Of Time - There - An Aria To The Black downs - Sunset O'er Exmoor; [pers.] Art is created by the Brush the supreme art is painted with the pen.; [a.] Taunton, Somerset, UK, TA1 3EQ

TURNER, FREDA BERYL
[b.] 9 July 1922, Tillingham; [p.] Rose and Alf Saward; [m.] Cyril T. Turner (Deceased), 25 December 1944; [ch.] Meryl and Megan (Deceased); [ed.] Elementary at Tillingham Church of England School; [occ.] Retired; [pers.] Served in ATS 2nd World War on gun sites. For 41 1/4 years, I spent several hours awake during the night, that's when I write poems.; [a.] Tillingham, Essex, UK, CM0 7SA

TURNER, KIM LOUISE
[pen.] Kim Louise Turner; [b.] 5 May 1968, London; [p.] Peter Turner, Patricia Fletcher; [m.] Phil Langdon, 2 August 1997; [ed.] Edge Hill College of ME B.Ed (Hons); [occ.] Primary Teacher; [memb.] Thistles Musical Theatre Company; [pers.] I have always written poems about life and its effect on us since a very young age. There is an inexhaustible inspiration therein.; [a.] Theudon Bois, Essex, UK, CM16 7JR

TURNER, MARK
[pen.] Tarka or Topsy; [b.] 9 February 1954, Cardiff; [p.] Roy and Thelma Turner; [ch.] Naomi and Rachel; [ed.] Howardian Boys Grammar, Cardiff, Nonington College of Physical Education/Joint Services School of Physiotherapy; [occ.] Studying History and English, Demontfort University, Bedford; [memb.] London Division Royal Naval Reserve, Island Cruising Club, Salcombe, Royal Naval Sailing Association, Chartered Society of Physiotherapy, British Association of Bobath Trained Therapists; [hon.] MCSP, Grad Dip Phys, Cert Ed, Certificate in Neuro-Developmental Therapy.; [oth. writ.] Numerous poems and song "Beyond The Distant Hills".; [pers.] Have worked for various voluntary agencies in Nigeria, Israel and Romania. Recently changed career from Physiotherapist following injury in road traffic accident. "Too much worrying about the 'what ifs' of the present leads to a future regretting the 'if onlys' of the past".; [a.] Bedford, Bedfordshire, UK, MK45 3PY

TURVEY, B. M.
[pen.] Beryl Turvey; [b.] 23 October 1930, Stourport-on-Severn; [p.] Caroline Glaze, Arthur Glaze; [m.] Eric Turvey, 6 June 1953; [ch.] Two; [ed.] Harry Cheshire Girls School; [occ.] Housewife; [pers.] Thank you for your time, and the opportunity for my poem to be published.; [a.] Kidderminster, Worcs, UK, DY11 7AQ

TWIDALE, MARK AUSTIN
[pen.] Austin Satz; [b.] 14 February 1970, Wirral; [p.] Elizabeth and George Twidale; [ed.] Ashworth Further, Education Centre; [occ.] Graphic Designer; [hon.] Poetry Guild - Acclaimed letter of acknowledgement x 4 with 2 poems published - certificate and awarded 30 pounds for coming between 1st and 3rd in Koestler Competition.; [oth. writ.] 'Cause Thou Hast Loved Me, I Just Can't Stop Thinking About My Saviour, Let Her Soul Be Love and Power in memory of a dear cousin suffering from anorexia, You Loved Us

For a Reason, Twelve Months On in memory of all who suffered in Dunblane these and others were published by Triumph House and in Peterborough.; [pers.] I endeavour to touch the creative consciousness of others and to inspire hope.; [a.] Wirral, Merseyside, UK, L49 4PP

UDAYAMALEE, IRESHA
[b.] 29 January 1984, Colombo; [p.] J. P. Nimalsiri, Pushpa Ranasuriya; [ed.] Musaeus College, Colombo 07; [hon.] English; [pers.] My feelings influence most of my writings. They play a main role in my writings.

UNGURAS, ADINA-MARINA
[b.] 8 May 1981, Timisoara, Romania; [p.] Cleopatra and Petru Unguras; [ed.] "William Shakespeare" Secondary School and High School - 10th grade 3rd year student American University By Mail-International University, Rector-American Academy for Youth; [occ.] Student; [memb.] Debates Club "William Shakespeare", Radio Timisoara co-working stuff; [hon.] Several artistic performance awards, yearly awards for results at school, Best Speaker in the Regional Debate Contest 1997, awards for poetry in Romanian - F.I.T.T. Independent Foundation for Youth - 1996; [oth. writ.] Articles and poems in English published in the school magazine.; [pers.] The art of living requires skills. I try to make writing my chief skill. It is the most beautiful way to keep one's spirit and others alive.; [a.] Timisoara, Romania, 1900

UZELE, JENNIFER W. WAYIO
[pen.] June, Junipher, Jenny; [b.] 12 July 1957, Nairobi; [p.] James and Josephine M. Kabiru; [m.] Lamech Wayio Uzele, 1st February 1986; [ch.] One Son - Uvon J. Uzele; [ed.] High School graduate, Bible School graduate, 1 year Institution Correspondence - Cookery, Music, Art; [occ.] Musician, Teacher in Counselling; [memb.] Christian Union Club, Aerobics, Swimming; [hon.] Certificates Bible Honour Music, Hall of Fame from Poetry Library International, Hollywood Honour, Election of recording my songs; [oth. writ.] Spiritual Songs, Gospel Songs, Jingles, Chereography set-up, Plays; [pers.] In the beginning God.... when all goes wrong... God. There is nothing that has been so challenging, demanding like breakthrough, meeting dreams like doing it in Africa perseverance. Backbone pluck and gut stubborn discipline and cosmic power has been the key.; [a.] Machakos, Kenya

VALENTINE., ALEX JR.
[b.] 22 February 1956, Dumbarton; [occ.] Civil Servant; [oth. writ.] 'Return To Edinburgh' published in 'Awaken To A Dream' anthology.; [pers.] In my poetry, as in my life, I try to be totally honest, to share truth and valuable experiences, and to be pleasing to my maker. We are each responsible for writing the poem that is our life.; [a.] Alexandria, Dunbartonshire, UK, G83 9LY

VEAL, LILIAN
[pen.] Dremer: Family pet name; [b.] South Wales; [m.] Roache (Deceased, 1986), 29 June 1937; [ch.] Daughter; [ed.] Good Local School. Loves Reading, anything interested in politics family interests also; [occ.] OAP - Home, was lady's companion help; [oth. writ.] Enclosed new poem God's Beautiful Garden, I write and speak from the heart: Hope you like the enclosed poetry - Lilian Veal.; [pers.] Private I am not financially secure. At the home, C.L. Pension goes towards my keep - so cannot commit myself to ordering star laden sky yet.; [a.] St. Ives, Cornwall, UK, TR26 2BZ

VEAL, LILIAN
[b.] December 1908, South Wales, Valley Mid-Glam; [m.] Roache; [a.] St. Ives, Cornwall, UK, TR26 2BZ

VELLA, THERESA
[b.] 30 September 1957, Malta; [p.] Liberata Vella and Late Anthony; [ed.] Secondary Education at Maria Regina Grammar School and Sixth Form, Old University, Valletta B. Educ (Hons.) at University of Malta; [occ.] Teacher of Geography and French in a Girl's Junior Lyceum; [hon.] Editor's Choice Award from the International Society of Poets; [oth. writ.] Several poems published in local newsletters and magazines. Several short stories written for B.B.C. short story competition and Commonwealth short story competition.; [pers.] Hesitancy through life's journey is like sowing the seed for an unknown harvest. Whatever life brings forward in terms of joys and anxieties serves as water and nutrition to each young plant. A poem signposts greenhouses or seed - stalls. For me and for whoever hesitates to sow.; [a.] Manikata, Malta, SPB07

VENTON, DAVID
[b.] 28 March 1944, Moretonhampstead, Devon; [p.] Olive (Deceased) and Charles Henry; [m.] Jennifer Anne Venton, 5 October 1968; [ch.] Christopher and Andrew; [ed.] Secondary Modern Schooling; [hon.] Awarded the General Service Medal for the Borneo and N. Ireland campaigns whilst serving 22 years in the army.; [oth. writ.] I have written several poems, but I have never tried to have them published before. Also I have never entered any competitions before this one; [pers.] I strive to put my emotions into my poems and reflections of my moods at the time.; [a.] Rotherham, S. Yorkshire, UK, S60 5HF

VERNON, JOHN
[pen.] George F. James; [b.] 9 September 1946, Goole, Yorks; [p.] George and Lena Vernon; [m.] Janice Deeley, 1 February 1969; [ch.] Kathryn Elaine, Laura Elizabeth; [ed.] Thorne Grammar; [occ.] Tax Manager; [oth. writ.] Several poems, travel articles; [pers.] My writing gives me pleasure, and I hope to please others. I am greatly influenced by all around me.; [a.] Saint Peter, Jersey, UK, JE3 7AS

VESSEY, MARGARET ROSE
[pen.] Frances Allen; [b.] 17 July 1938, Bolton, Lancashire; [p.] William Bate and Alice Bate; [m.] Michael A. Vessey; [ch.] John, Andrew, Philip Popplewell; [ed.] Whitecroft Road Secondary Modern School Bolton, Lancashire; [occ.] Receptionist Student Hall of residence, Manchester University; [oth. writ.] Poems unpublished.; [pers.] My first husband, father of my sons, died in 1975. Friends bought me the anthology "Darkness to Light" by Victor Gollanez. It has been a great source of comfort and inspiration. I have always enjoyed reading poetry and I am interested in books and writings concerning the inner-life.; [a.] Didsbury, Manchester, UK, M20 6EG

VINNALL-BURNETT, MARGARET
[b.] 3 October 1913, Haslemore Sry; [p.] Arthur Frances Benneyworth; [m.] Albert Vinall, Robert Burnett (Deceased), 1940, 1945; [ch.] Naney, Jim, Carolina, Rosalind, Bill Dorothey, Jeffrey Kenneth; [ed.] Cross in Hand Village School, Sussex; [occ.] Retired; [memb.] Disabled Association, Sussex Across, International Library of Poets; [oth. writ.] Magazines, Anchor Books, Pibi Deven something to say poetry now, Sussex poems.; [a.] Eastbourne, Sussex, UK, BN22 7DE

WAGHORN, TANIA
[b.] 1 July 1972, Surrey; [p.] Vivian and Philip Waghorn; [ed.] St. Teresa's School, Surrey, Middlesex University, Sussex University; [occ.] Editorial Assistant of Agenda Magazine and Publications, Accommodation and Welfare Officer at the International Language Academy; [hon.] Scholarship into College, BA (Hons) English Lit Studies. Middx Uni RSA Cambridge Cert Tefla. Post-grad Diploma in Creative Writing and Personal Development (Sussex Uni) Poems published in other magazines and reviews.; [oth. writ.] Article 'My Earliest Memory' to be included in PHD Thesis on 'Autobiography and the Self', Celia Hurt, Director of Creative Writing Programmes, (Sussex Uni). Review to be published in Agenda Magazine and Publication.; [pers.] Simple honesty eloquently put is the mark of a good poem. What I would like to convey is the passion I feel for things I see as true.; [a.] London, UK, SN17 8RL

WAHOME, HARRISON
[b.] 1 June 1975, Karatina; [p.] David Wahome and Susan Wahome; [occ.] Starting a little business; [hon.] (Informal) poet of the year 1994, Kagumo High School; [oth. writ.] One poem published in a local magazine. Other poems yet to be published.; [pers.] Like a ball, the world is small, we can always meet. I am greatly influenced by William Shakespeare and all romantic poets.; [a.] Karatina, Kenya

WALL, MABEL
[b.] 18 September 1921, Chesterfield; [oth. writ.] Poetry in anthology publications. Arrival press (midlands) 1994, Poetry Guild (Spring) 1997, International Library of Poetry also Editor's Choice Award (Spring) 1997; [pers.] When writing, I'm engrossed in a magical deep thinking world of meaningful detailed phrasing.; [a.] Chesterfield, Derbyshire, UK, S42 5XD

WALLACE, MR. ALAN
[pen.] Alan Wallace; [b.] 4 September 1959, Mansfield, Notts; [p.] Ray Wallace and Kathleen Wallace; [m.] Laura Timmons, 2 May 1981; [ch.] Danny Wallace; [ed.] Joseph Whittaker Comprehensive, Mans. West Notts College, Mansfield; [occ.] Retired Electrical Engineer and Health and Safety Officer due to ill health; [memb.] Institution of Occupational Safety and Health. Committee Member of the Stuart Strange Trust for Wegeners Granulomatosis Disease. St. Lawrences Church, Mansfield; [oth. writ.] Write poems for the Stuart Strange Trust, quarterly magazine; [pers.] I was influenced by putting a different prospective on life after being diagnosed with an incurable disease in October 1996 and write. Poetry regarding life, loneliness and appreciation of life in general.; [a.] Mansfield, Notts, UK, NG18 3BQ

WALLIS, MRS. VIVIEN
[b.] 24 July 1947, Slough Berks; [p.] Mary Summersby and Idris Lewis; [m.] Martin Wallis, 14 September 1996; [ch.] Michael, Tony, Donna Sheridan; [ed.] Secondary Modern, Bayliss Court, Slough Berks; [occ.] Housewife; [memb.] Husband and Wife (Joint Social Clubs) and Royal Navy Ass. South Harrow; [oth. writ.] 'The Empty Rocking Chair' and numerous others written for different occasions.; [pers.] The first poem I wrote was for my Granddaughter's first day at school a few yrs ago. I have verses and poems 'A Father's Son' is the only one sent for a competition at present.; [a.] South Ruislip, Middx, UK, HA4 0HX

WALSH, NICOLETTE F.
[pen.] Nicolette F. Walsh; [b.] 18 October 1956, Manchester, GB; [p.] Rita and Denis Taylor; [m.] Paul S. Walsh, 3 May 1980; [ch.] Dean-Paul (16); [ed.] St. Joseph Convent, Ashton College; [occ.] Housewife; [memb.] W.CC. Marsh Health Club, Minneapolis Athletic Club; [oth. writ.] Various articles (some published) other poetry and short stories.; [pers.] My work tries to reflect the subject in hand. Family and friends are a wealth of subject matter.; [a.] Wayzata, Hennepin, MN, 55391

WARD, ALFREDA KATHLEEN
[pen.] Freda; [b.] 2 December 1933, Bethoral, Green; [p.] Katie and Alfred Morgan; [m.] Leonard Ward, 16 February 1952; [ch.] 1 Daughter, 1 Son; [ed.] Secondary School, always wanted to be a writer. But never pursued it.; [occ.] Housewife, Widower; [oth. writ.] I have always read Pabronce Strong. Helen Styner Rice works. Have written quite a few poem. But this is the first I have sent

in.; [pers.] I have quite a lot of poems. I have written, I'm afraid they seem rather sad, but it must be how I was feeling. But I do enjoy writing them. They give me great feeling.; [a.] Hackney, London, UK, E9 6HJ

WARD, T. F.
[pen.] Terry; [b.] 7 February 1922, London, E. H.; [m.] Mrs. Margaret Ward, 5 January 1946; [ch.] Two; [ed.] Secondary Sch.; [occ.] Retired - Ex Reg. Army, 39-46. Coach Driver, Retired; [oth. writ.] Short Stories (6) Local Paper "Echo" HH (Now De Funct.) Consolation Prize.; [pers.] Wrote letters and poems for many friends and sent home - (Army) love to paint in oils and water colorsl. Writing just a hobby. At 75th - just an interest.; [a.] H. Hempstead, Herts, UK, HP3 8JN

WARDLE, NIK
[b.] 11 December 1976, Edmonton; [p.] Peter Wardle, Sally Pirkhoffer; [ed.] Thornden Secondary, Eastleigh College; [occ.] Health Insurance, Norwich Union Health Care; [memb.] Tottenham Hotspur Football Club; [hon.] County Honours in football and athletics; [oth. writ.] None published; [pers.] I live and will die by the statement 'Manners and Morals Maketh Man'.; [a.] Chandlers Ford, Hampshire, UK, SO53 2NH

WARE, MRS. D. V.
[b.] 19 March 1916, Bude Cornwall; [p.] Mr. and Mrs. J. L. Andrews-Maidment; [m.] Fredrick G. Ware, 19 December 1941; [ch.] Barry James, Deryn Janet; [ed.] Local Council Schools; [occ.] Retired Nurse; [oth. writ.] I have had several poems in competitions and magazines. Have written a great deal over the years from school days.; [pers.] I have always loved the old poets particularly the Scottish ones. And could recite many of them - in fact I still can.; [a.] Plymouth, Devon, UK, PL5 3SZ

WARNER, DAVID
[b.] 7 April 1965, Camberley, Surrey; [p.] June and Robin Warner; [ed.] St. Marks Comprehensive, Harlow, Essex; [occ.] Storeman, Flexible Lamps, Harlow, Essex; [oth. writ.] "The Purpose of Dreams" from the anthology "Days and Dreams Gone By".; [pers.] My inspirations for writing come from the experiences and observations of my life, their realisation in poetry comes from my ability to elaborate on them.; [a.] Epping, Essex, UK, CM16 6PZ

WATKINS, JADE
[b.] 1 December 1952, New Port, Gwent; [p.] Lilian Pope, Trevor Pope (Deceased); [m.] Daniel Keith Watkins, 24 December 1994, second merriage; [ch.] Christopher Pave, Lucy and Grace Catley; [ed.] Abersychan Secondary Modern School and Blandare College of Further Education; [occ.] Poet/Writer; [memb.] Pontypool and District Writers Group, Brynteg, Abersychan; [hon.] English Literature, Typing and music (Piano) Editor's Choice Award for Poem published in "Awaken to a Dream" poem: "Let's Pretend" published by The International Library of Poetry. March 1997; [oth. writ.] Several Anthologies Inc. "Heart And Soul", "Poets in Wales", "Lovers and Others", "In My Thoughts", "Special Occasions", "Expressions Of Love", plus others anthologies. Magazine "My Weekly", and: Pontypool Market, Centenary.; [pers.] I write purely for the love of writing, and the pleasure it gives to me, and I hope to others who read my work. I would like to mention my 18 yr. old daughter Lucy Catley who has her first poem published in this Anthology, I'd like to wish her every success. I would also like to mention a very dear friend John Morgan, who inspired me to write many of my early poems, and lots of love and kisses to my husband Keith.; [a.] Abergavenny, Monmouthshire, UK, NP7 6AJ

WATTS, MRS. RUTH
[b.] 22 August 1958; [p.] Janet and Frank Huntbach; [m.] 21 July 1977; [ch.] Stella, Aaron, James, Tina; [ed.] Hazelwich School Crawley; [occ.] Airport Clean Gatwick Switched from broom pushing to pen pushing; [memb.] Crawley Cage Bird Society, British Rabbit Council; [hon.] Best Foreign 2 years running; [oth. writ.] Four poems published by The International Library of poems also select publications and Tree Spirits. Only started writing poetry in Sept. 96, A Lasting Calm, Light of the World. The Star-Laden Sky, (Pause for Thought select. pub.); [pers.] Writing poems is like a match, river and the sea strike the pen and in motion, the poems flow, they flow continuously one after the other, like a river flows on until it reaches the sea. For them the sea becomes the book.; [a.] Crawley, Sussex, UK, RH10 7BT

WAWMAN, YVONNE
[b.] 14 December 1936, Luton, Beds; [p.] Kenneth Bloomfield and Irene Bloomfield; [m.] John Wawman, 28 October 1961; [ch.] Roxana, George and Stephen; [ed.] St Dominics Convent School Harpenden Herts; [occ.] Housewife; [memb.] The National Trust; [hon.] The British Federation of Music Festivals Diploma for verse speaking with honours St. Albans competitive Music Festival. Certificate of Merit for Elocution. The Royal Drawing Society Group III stage 1, 2 honours standard stage III honours; [pers.] I was inspired to write poetry while on my travels abroad to describe the many wonders that I saw.; [a.] Norwich, Norfolk, UK, NR10 5HG

WEST, MR. ALAN CHARLES
[b.] 19 February 1961, London; [p.] James West and Sylvia West; [ed.] Willesden High School (Comprehensive); [occ.] Clerical Officer for a local health authority; [oth. writ.] A collection of song lyrics and poems which I began writing in 1978. One poem published in "Jewels of the Imagination". Two of my songs have been performed in public.; [pers.] I dedicate "those who die tomorrow" to all those who have died of A.I.D.S. Life is a minefield, obey your instincts and you won't' go far wrong!; [a.] Chiswick, London, UK, W4 2QY

WEST, MAC
[pen.] The G Man; [b.] 24 November 1955, Valletta, Malta; [p.] Mr. and Mrs. West; [m.] Dawn Julie Cole, living in sin; [ch.] Petra Ann West, Phillip West, Malcolm West, Micheal West, Sadie Cole, Johnny Cole and one more to come; [ed.] Life's Rich School; [occ.] Artist's, Poet, Writer, Madman; [memb.] Human Race, The Kartu; [hon.] I am honoured to have such a lovely woman as my partner Dawn in my life.; [oth. writ.] Various poems and philosophical writings, short stories, and many pictorial statements with a paint brush.; [pers.] To challenge injustice and then I am better than your attitude. We all come into this world the same way, and we leave the same way. Who says, who is better than who?; [a.] Portsmouth, Hampshire, UK, PO1 5AY

WESTWOOD, RICHARD
[b.] 28 December 1976, Birmingham; [p.] Clive Bayliss, Denise Bayliss; [ed.] Washwood Heath Comprehensive, Washwood Heath Sixth Form, University of Wolverhampton; [occ.] Studying for BA (Hons) English and Media Studies and Philosophy; [a.] Birmingham, West Midlands, UK

WHALE, MERVYN SHEPHERD
[pen.] Mervyn S. Whale; [b.] 1 July 1927, Bath; [p.] William John Whale and Edith Whale; [m.] JoAnne Whale, 12 May 1979; [ed.] Keighley Boys Grammar School (Terminated Early for Health Reasons); [occ.] Pensioner; [memb.] Horsforth Art Society; [oth. writ.] Poems in various and anthologies and one magazine "Happy Gardening". Paper back book to help amateurs to enjoy their property. Still Available.; [pers.] My old age is enjoyed in writing, painting and my garden. Days in the country sketching and walking help my health.; [a.] Leeds, W. Yorkshire, UK, LS16 7BA

WHITE, SARAH J.
[b.] 13 November 1973, Winchester; [p.] Grace White, Peter Turner; [oth. writ.] Poems, Prose, Short Stories - Contemporary Songs/Music.; [pers.] Love, - in whatever form it comes, is the power of everything: From the moon to the heart, it is the true inspiration as it is life.; [a.] Bournemouth, Dorset, UK, BH4 8HP

WILCOX, ENID KATHLEEN GRACE
[pen.] Enid Wilcox; [b.] 7 October 1919, Monmouth; [p.] Oliver and Martha Young; [ch.] Revd. Colin John Wilcox; [ed.] Mitchel Troy School; [occ.] Retired; [oth. writ.] Two poems published with the International Library of Poetry, 'Along The Lanes', 'The Wye Valley', 'The Park At Dawlish'; [pers.] I strive to write, what I see.; [a.] Monmouth, Gwent, UK, NP5 4DZ

WILD, TONY
[b.] 11 March 1964, Darwen, Lancashire; [p.] William and Edith Wild; [ed.] Darwen Moorland High School, English Language 'O' Level, English Literature 'O' Level, Religious Education 'O' Level, Economic History 'O' Level; [occ.] Plastic Recycling; [pers.] Poetry is a way of expressing the inner feelings you can't say out loud.; [a.] Darwen, Lancashire, UK, BB3 3AJ

WILDS, TERENA T. J.
[pen.] Tracy Wilds; [b.] 8 August 1973, Manchester; [p.] James and Mary Wilds; [ed.] Our Ladies R/C High School and Moston College; [occ.] Student of Psychology at Moston College; [oth. writ.] I have books of my poems from my teenage years up to present day.; [pers.] Life throws us different situations, which tell a different story. These stories inspires my poetry. My family and friends have also influenced my writing. I love them all.; [a.] Manchester, Lancashire, UK, M9 5SW

WILLIAMS, GEOFFREY DAVID
[b.] 25 March 1969, Liverpool; [p.] Margaret Anne; [m.] Julie Dee England (Engaged), 17 March 1996; [ch.] Ellena England; [ed.] West Derby Comprehensive; [occ.] Unemployed Chef; [oth. writ.] Several unpublished poems written over the last four years.; [pers.] If I can write honestly then I can learn from my work, as well as appreciate lyrical art.; [a.] Bolton, Lancashire, UK, BL5 3QQ

WILLIAMS, LESLEY
[b.] 9 August 1966, Ormskirk; [p.] Marion and Brian Daniels; [m.] Carl Williams, 21 June 1996; [ch.] Tasha Danielle Williams age 4 3/4; [ed.] Old Hall High School, Maghull; [occ.] Housewife and Mother; [pers.] 'Write from the heart'.; [a.] Maghull, Merseyside, UK, L31 5NZ

WILLIAMS, PETER VAUGHAN
[pen.] Vaughan, Theo Vaughan, Dragonfly; [b.] 7 June 1944, Bolton; [p.] Anne Williams; [m.] Frances Elfreda (Lean) Williams, 28 February 1966; [ch.] Gareth Andrew, Theo Jason; [ed.] Smithills Moor Grammar, Bolton College of Art (NDD) Leeds University A.T.D. Lancaster University B.Ed (Hons) Psychology and Sociology; [occ.] Retired head of year Smithills Comprehensive School; [memb.] British Academy of Song Writers Composers and Authors (B.A.S.C.A.), member of Society of Industrial Artists and Designers (M.S.I.A.D.); [hon.] Co. Director of Octagon Youth Theatre (1972-78) several prestigious Art Exhibitions, Bachelor of Education (Hons), National Diploma in Design (Specialised Illustration) N.D.D. Art Teaching Degree A.T.D. (Leeds Univer.) represented Great Britain for Painting & Drawing 1963; [oth. writ.] Soon to be published 'Star-Laden Sky', Editor's Choice Award 1996-1997, International Library of Poetry 'Voices of the Wind' and Awaken to a Dream offered most distinguished membership short stories - 6 L.P.S. Theo Vaughan Records R.V. scripts, music and lyrics for over 800 original songs. Published novels: "Point", soon to be

published: "When A Child".; [pers.] Whether painting, writing or creating music, at all times I attempt to pursue truth which is an elusive element of life and hopefully the empathy of others.; [a.] Bolton, Lancashire, UK, BL1 6NE

WILSON, ELIZABETH
[b.] 10 March 1954, Liverpool; [p.] Robert Wilson and Elizabeth Muriel Wilson; [ed.] Cuddington County Primary School, Hartford Girls' School, The Cheshire School Of Art; [occ.] Portrait Artist; [memb.] Political Animal Lobby Honorary Member; [hon.] MENSA Certificate of Merit; [oth. writ.] Poem published in the following anthologies, The British Poetry Review '95, Mind's Eye, Between a Laugh and a Tear, Jewels of the Imagination, The Power of Words.; [pers.] My poems are written in a variety of styles on various themes from Nature and Romance to Political Affairs and Animal Welfare. The latter is a concern closest to my heart, and for which I use my talents in both art and poetry to express my feelings.; [a.] Chester, Cheshire, UK

WILSON, MRS. JULIA
[pen.] Ellen Hillary-Fawcett; [b.] 9 November 1947, Buddle House Farm, Richmond, N. Yorkshire; [p.] Thomas and Eva Jane Fawcett (Deceased); [m.] William Wilson, 15 January 1973; [ch.] Esther Jane and Hannah Lucy (Twins); [ed.] Marske (Swaledale) C.E., Junior School, Richmond (N. Yorkshire), County Modern, Scarborough College of Technology; [occ.] Process Operator for 'Glaxo Well Come' Barnard Castle; [oth. writ.] 1 previous poem published by the International Library of Poetry.; [pers.] Many people feel. Very few express.; [a.] Barnard Castle, Durham, UK, DL12 9AS

WISE, THERESA JOSEPHINE LLOBET
[b.] 9 February 1940; Perivale; [p.] Mr. and Mrs. L. A. Wise; [m.] Jaume Llobet, 11 October 1968; [ch.] Four; [ed.] St. Anne's Convent, High School for Girls, Little Ealing Lane, Ealing. W.4; [occ.] Housewife of Author (as yet unpublished until now); [oth. writ.] "Lilac in Spring," "A Cry in the Wilderness," Editor for Georgina age 5 years, "Christmas Remembrance," "FebruaryThoughts in Spain," "Lost Souls in the Night," "The Eclipse of the Moon," "The Traumas of War," Poems: Books The Wonder of the Christmas Eve Star, Two Children and the Mermaid's and many more; [pers.] For children I write fiction. For adults things which appear into real life past or present. I would like to think my writing has some depth and purpose. Also that anything I pen is enjoyable, meaningful and uplifting; [a.] Blanes, Els Pins, Gerona

WOOD, JAMES JOHN WILLIAM
[b.] 18 June 1981, Malton; [p.] Maxine and Neil Wood; [ed.] Just Finished GCSE and Awaiting Results. Educated at Wolfreton School Anlaby-Hull.; [a.] Hull, E. Yorkshire, UK, HU10 6HE

WOOD, NIGEL PATRICK
[b.] 24 July 1959, Halifax; [p.] Dennis Wood, Eunice Wood; [m.] Karen Wood, 26 October 1985; [ch.] Christopher James Wood, Sarah Louise Wood; [ed.] JH Whitley, Sec. Mod. Halifax; [occ.] Property Developer; [pers.] Being a prisoner and serving time for a crime I did not commit, brings out many talents. This is one of them.; [a.] Halifax, West Yorkshire, UK, HX1 2EN

WOODS, MISS FIONA
[b.] 27 November 1970, Stamford; [p.] Mr. Icenneth Woods, Mrs. Anne Woods; [ed.] St. Augustines Roman Catholic School Fane School; [occ.] Production Operator Arnold Wills and Co. LTD Uppingham; [hon.] Won a writing competition when I was in secondary school; [pers.] I was inspired to write poetry by Walter De Lamare.; [a.] Stamford, Lincolnshire, UK, PE9 1JQ

WOOLMINGTON, ELAINE
[pen.] Lion; [b.] 12 August 1979, Kilkenny; [p.] Margaret and Jimmy; [ed.] 5th yr. student in Wilsons Hosp. School Westmeath; [occ.] Student; [hon.] Silver President's Award; [oth. writ.] 2 other poems published in school magazine.; [pers.] Look to see, listen to hear, fear to feel. I'm influenced by various rock/alternative bands, modern poetry and life.; [a.] Arklow, Wicklow, UK

WRAY, JAMES TINLEY
[b.] 3 July 1938, Kensington; [p.] James and Mary; [m.] Kathleen, 10 September 1962; [ch.] Jim and John; [ed.] Caledon National Primary, Dungannon Technical Institute; [occ.] Early Retirement due to ill health; [memb.] House member to Armagh City Golf Club, Dungannon Golf Club; [hon.] The International Library of Poets Hall of Fame, The International Library of Poetry Distinguished Member; [oth. writ.] The Clinging Mists, Sweet Tyrone, Let's, Thanking God, My Wife Is My Life, Reminder To The Human Race, The Gift Of Peace, The Hat "all published".; [pers.] Poetry is my way of expressing myself, I am able to give entertainment, and keep to the fire many things that have vanished for future generations. Gives me lots of pleasure.; [a.] Caledon, Tyrone, UK, BT68 4UX

WRIDE, LOUISE
[b.] 30 September 1983, Neath; [ed.] Llandovery Ysgol Rhys Prichard, currently at Ysgol Gyfun Pantycelyn Llandovery; [memb.] British Diabetic Association (BDA); [oth. writ.] First ever poem.; [pers.] As I am a twin myself I feel other twins can relate to this poem.; [a.] Llandovery, Carms, UK, SA20 0YE

WRIGHT, MS. BEVERLEY
[pen.] Beverley Wright, Beverley Belding; [b.] 3 April 1958, Westcluff-on-Sea, Essex; [p.] Thomas and Ann Wright; [ch.] Serena Jane Ann Wright; [ed.] Comprehensive and Girls High School, Private, Vocational and Community Colleges; [occ.] Single mother and student; [memb.] U.S. Trotting Association Studio Players, East Essex Players Salle Volte Fencing Club, Rospa and Southend Advanced Driving Associations; [hon.] In 1997, English Literature, Drama and Theatre, Mathematics and Poetry, most notably 'In A Child's Face'.; [oth. writ.] 'In A Child's Face' published in the anthology 'Awaken To A Dream'. Numerous other poems, short stories and magazine articles.; [pers.] I am so proud to appear in the same anthology as my talented. Grandfather R.B. whose heartfelt creativity amazes and inspires me. I love my family, and to my daughter Serena, I love you.; [a.] Southend-on-Sea, Essex, UK, SS1 2EY

WYNTER, TRICIA
[b.] 13 April 1972, London; [p.] Mable Harper - guardian; [ed.] Wembley High School East Lane - HAO, G.C.S.E. English, Art, Music, Science and Child-Development; [occ.] Catering Assistant; [memb.] I will be a member very shortly to The Writers Club, P.O. Box 269 - Redhill RH1 6BR; [hon.] R.S.A. - National Vocational Qualification Computer Course Level (2) (Information Technology); [oth. writ.] I have done a lot of poems, which are of my inner feelings. I haven't got anything published yet, but I am working on it!; [pers.] My writing is directed towards reality experiences, that occur in everyday life. Not of just my own experiences, but also of my surroundings.; [a.] London, UK

YATES, GARRY MARK
[b.] 20 September 1967, Bolton; [p.] Kathleen and Graham Yates; [ed.] Little Lever School, Salford College of Technology; [occ.] Disabled; [memb.] International Song Writers Association; [hon.] Royal School of Music grades in Piano, Clarinet and Theory; [oth. writ.] Had poems published in anthologies (3), won slogan writing, competitions at National Level (Consumer Competitions).; [pers.] God moves within and without. His spirit moves through your soul.; [a.] Bolton, Lancs, UK, Bl2 3LS

YATES, HELEN MARY
[pen.] Mary Yates; [b.] 19 January 1917, Wallsend-on-Tyne; [p.] John and Sarah Richardson; [m.] John Yates (Deceased), 30 August 1941; [ch.] Sarah, Elizabeth, Katherine; [ed.] Southend High School Southampton University; [occ.] Retired Teacher; [hon.] B.A. (London University); [a.] Brackley, Northants, UK, NN13 7AG

YOUNG, JENNIFER
[pen.] Mary Leutchford; [b.] 11 July 1944, Glasgow; [p.] Joyce Asgill; [m.] James Young; [ch.] Joanna, Stepchildren: Andrew, Diana, Caroline; [ed.] St. Joan of Arc Convent School, Rickmansworth, Hertfordshire, Harrow Technical College; [memb.] Friends of the Arvon Foundation Edinburgh Antiques and Fine Arts Society The National Trust for Scotland Dalmeny Golf Club; [hon.] Open University Arts Degree 1992; [oth. writ.] Novel (just completed) and various in most genres (unpublished), wrote for newspapers, magazines in my youth as reporter, features writer.; [pers.] Keep going no matter what!; [a.] Edinburgh, Midlothian, UK, EH12 6BQ

Index of Poets

A

Abangwu, C. George 63
Abbott, Isabel 32
Abiola, Hamid Mutiu 319
Ablett, Rowland 255
Abraham, Jacob D. 289
Abrahams, Mark 127
Abrahamson, Joan 36
Abram, Aubrey 171
Abrey, Nancie J. 141
Abul-Wafa, Reham 166
Abussaud, Hanan 116
Adair, Agnes 205
Adam, Tricia 176
Adams, Edith Mary 329
Adams, Helen 231
Adams, James M. 176
Addison, Ann 178
Addison, Gemma 311
Adedoyin, Francisca 271
Aderemi, Derin 186
Adlan, M. A. 12
Adlington, Joyce 12
Aduwa-Ero, A. 115
Agolini, Lucie 89
Ahmed, Aisha Isa 75
Ahmed, Deborah 213
Aindow, Brian H. 80
Akhtar, Monir 208
Akinyemi, Olufemi 247
Al Muls, Karina 114
Alder, Frances 132
Alderson, David 208
Alderson, Maureen 140
Aldridge, Joan 179
Alexander, Ken 107
Alexander, Robert 228
Alexandra, Soica Veronica 190
Ali, Shah Abdul Karim 152
Alin, Soica 294
Allan, Jacqui 112
Allcock, E. R. 187
Allen, David 143
Allen, Frank 277
Allen, Kim 119
Allen, Lynn 18
Allen, Steven 157
Allen, Toni 224
Allerston, Jack 89
Allison, Corrina E. 211
Allocca, Audrey A. 321
Allsopp, Wilf 228
Alyas, Razwana 299
Ambrose, Kathleen 106
Ancliff, Walter A. 180
Anderson, Alison 182
Anderson, Denise 92
Anderson, Elizabeth 157
Andrews, Alethea 26
Andrews, Alethea 125
Andrews, Fleur 86
Andrews, Jacqueline A. 104
Andrews, Jacqueline A. 28
Andrews, M. 114
Andrews, Tamsin 323
Angell, Granville 35
Angus, Moira 316
Ansah-Eshon, James 155
Anthony, A. 153
Antoniou, Chris 60
Apakama, Ikenna 43
Aphra, Pat 158
Ara, Sultana 286
Archer, Amy 188
Archer, Lisa Anne 112
Arnold, Julian 326
Arnold, Juliett 254
Arnold, Mary 312
Arrowsmith, S. 330
Arter, Elainea 96
Arthur, C. A. 61
Ash-Smith, Christine 47
Ashbrook, Robin 232
Ashcroft, J. 196
Ashley, John 175
Ashman, Margaret 177
Ashton, Irene 334
Ashworth, Eileen 68
Askew, Stella 236
Aspinall, Heather 295
Asquith, Graeme 103
Aston, Vivian Paulette 151
Atkinson, David 167
Atkinson, Eileen K. 99
Atkinson, Michael Major 149
Attard, Natalino 192
Aukett, Kay 72
Austin, Jenifer Ellen 11
Axon, Kaye 94
Ayling, Colin 207
Aze 165

B

Baggott, Julie 118
Baguley, Joan 22
Bailey, J. R. A. 310
Baily, Lianne 237
Bainbridge, Keith 152
Baines, Jean 19
Baines, Lorna 303
Baird, R. J. 27
Baird, T. Henry 165
Baker, Christine Louise 287
Baker, Colin 26
Baker, Gemma 156
Baker, Jay 12
Baker, Steven 160
Baldwin, Florence 27
Ball, Mischelle 84
Banerji, Shobha Sud. 267
Banks, Deborah 251
Banks, Robert M. 215
Bannister, Michelle 102
Bannister, Sarah 266
Bannon, Stephanie 39
Barber, Maureen 145
Barber, Paul 105
Barker, Elsie 59
Barker, Valerie J. 194
Barley, Angela 169
Barlow, Susan 62
Barnard, Lynn 245
Barnard, Tara 48
Barnes, Amy 123
Barnes, James 55
Barnes, Julie 176
Barnett, Eunice 12
Barnett, Rodney 104
Barr, Olinda 196
Barrass, Eddie 316
Barratt, Sue 286
Barrett, Hayley 282
Barrett, Saoirse 146
Barrientos, Rolando A. 240
Barrington, Helen 225
Barron, Sarah-Kelly 201
Barrow, Sarah 63
Barrowes, Savita 123
Barry, Dan 324
Barton, Ivy 117
Bassett, Ladee 126
Bateman, Mildred 65
Bates, Richard 286
Bawdon, Trevor 180
Baxter, G. M. 90
Baxter, Reg 81
Baxter, Ted 119
Bayliss, Greta 297
Bayliss, Jacqueline 315
Beal, Corina 162
Bearman, Deborah 24
Beazer, Deborah 190
Beck, C. H. 89
Beddard, Penny 10
Bedford, Olive 157
Beer, Endymion 227
Beer, Pauline E. 155
Begum, Sahara 167
Behrmann, Alfred 283
Belaya, Ksenia 262
Bell, Agnes 43
Bell, Jonathan 85
Bell, Margaret 247
Bell, Thomas 135
Belton, Janet 187
Benacs, Philippa C. 19
Benn, C. 263
Bennett, D. 100
Bennett, David J. 123
Bennett, Diane 17
Bennett, Jane Eleanor 283
Bennett, P. A. 55
Benoy, Kenneth 145
Bent, Nichola-Louise 230
Bentley, Dorothy 280
Bentley, J. 59
Bentley-Leek, Emily 330
Benzaquen, Dina 39
Berardi, Christina 314
Berezai, Nicky 73
Berrisford, Evelyn May 333
Berrows, Shirley Ann 257
Berry, Deborah Jayne 69
Berry, Deborah Jayne 70
Berry, Emily 232
Berryman, Kirsty Jane 274
Betts, Jaime 138
Bevins, Carrie 52
Bevins, Pauline B. 161
Bhasi, M. K. 146
Bhattacharji, Anjali 177
Bhogal, H. S. 135
Bicanic, Jo 293
Biddulph, Rose 206
Biggin, Susan 134
Biggs, Susan 42
Bigley, Imelda 83
Billett, Leigh 268
Bills, Alan 203
Binasila, Esenezer Masi 198
Bingham, Donna 221
Bingley, Gary 28
Birch, Eunice 185
Birch, Eunice M. 147
Bird, Adrianne 144
Birkett, Olive 202
Bishop, J. 228
Bjornsdottir, Helena 176
Black, Tania 101
Blackhall, Sara 139
Blackman, Stacey 49
Blair, Ann Christine 145
Blake, Rita Jean 224
Blanchfield, Kathleen 151
Blaney, T. 29
Blechner, Daniella 204
Blencowe, Juliette 311
Blesi, Linda 167
Bloomfield, June 25
Blundell, Stephen 149
Boast, Joyce 4
Bodman, Michael 188
Boey, Suie Yim 135
Bonaventura, Okolo 151
Bond, Janice 278
Boosey, Sandra 21
Booth, Rachel 124
Borg, Caroline 312
Bormond, Jacqueline 139
Bosworth, J. A. 93
Bough, Alfred 289
Boulton, Frederick 188
Boulton, Janet 25
Bourke, R. T. 198
Bourner, Amy Frances 197
Bourton, Samantha 121
Bowden, Colin 148
Bowen, Bill 242
Bowen, Frances 179
Bowerman, Ian N. 306
Bowers, Robert 94
Boyce, Caroline 67
Boyle, Edward 248
Boyle, Finnan 39
Boyle, Joe 181
Boyles, Sarah 278
Bozzoni, Beverley E. 324
Brace, Pat 68
Bradbury, Ann 194
Bradbury, Katherine 191
Bradford, Mary 91
Bradshaw, S. M. 158
Brady, Kitsy 60
Brady, Mary 142
Brady, Patrick 187
Brandon, Marie 173
Brandreth, Louise 327
Breen, Therese 275
Brennan, Angela 210
Brett, George 290
Brett, Patrick 248
Briar, Bridget Colleton 223
Bridgewater, David 32
Brightwell, Estelle 115
Brighty, Andy 119
Brincat, Erika 211
Brinn, P. M. 208
Brittain, Norman Scott 234
Broad, Margery K. 203
Brobbey, Jacob Asare 120
Brogan, Orlagh 187
Brook, Ruth Barclay 270
Brooke, S. 33
Brooks, Audrey Margaret 259
Broom, Anna 162
Broome, Angela 318
Broomhead, G. E. M. 194
Brotherton, Annette 87
Brown, D. 5
Brown, Derek 222
Brown, Diane L. 16
Brown, Doris 91
Brown, Frederick G. 287
Brown, Gladys Mary 101
Brown, Lavinia 11
Brown, Lucy 161
Brown, Michelle 160
Brown, Pam 63
Brown, R. 224
Brown, Rhoda 266
Brown, Ron 223
Brown, Sheila 318
Brown, Stephanie 45
Brown, Stephanie 154

Brown, Susan 204
Browne, Patricia 292
Bruce, Marie Collins 127
Brumel, Ben Herbert 101
Brunell, Gladys Eileen 58
Bryan, D. V. 129
Bryans, Nicholas 24
Bryans, Nicholas 31
Bryce, Alexander 73
Brynin, Leoni 175
Buchanan, E. H. 100
Buckingham, Molly 174
Buckle, Glenys 160
Buckley, Victoria 258
Budd, Sandra 157
Budge, E. M. 64
Bullard, D. E. 260
Bullen, Helen 204
Bullen, Patricia 102
Bullingham, S. I. 92
Bunnett, Kim 225
Burch, Pearl 171
Burditt, Kenneth C. 151
Burgess, Antonia 102
Burke, Chloe 310
Burn, Helen 265
Burness, Sarah 75
Burnett, Josephine 30
Burnett, Moyra Teresa 13
Burnham, P. A. 163
Burns, V. L. 162
Burrell, Richard Walter 312
Burrows, Joanne 289
Burslem, Norman 311
Burt, Donald 55
Burt, Lynsey 198
Burtenshaw, Sally 271
Burton, Emma 153
Burton, Irene 221
Burton, Jennifer 86
Burton, Sally Elizabeth 143
Burwell, Della B. 108
Busuttil, Caroline R. J. 226
Butler, Bobby 202
Butler, Gina 329
Butters, Paul 229
Button, Gregory 66
Byrne, Micheal 137
Byrne, Rhonda 64
Byron-Rasmussen, B. D. 126
Byron-Rasmussen, Barbara 20

C

C, Nicky 334
C., Peggy 18
C., T. 70
Caddie, I. S. 30
Cadenne, Edward 241
Caher, Eimear 320
Calder, Donna 188
Calderwood, Matthew T. 13
Caldwell, James 83
Calimani, Carla 214
Callaghan, Eva-Maria 215
Callender, Dudley H. 43
Cameron, Denise 46
Cameron, E. 267
Cameron, Ewan 199
Cameron, James Stephen 33
Cameron, June 81
Campbell, Alexandra 116
Campbell, Bill 169
Campbell, Jeffrey 49
Campbell, M. E. 295
Campbell-Ashwell, Anne 177
Campbell-Bridgman, Mary 8

Campbell-Bridgman, Mary 330
Campbell-Sturgess, Christine 122
Caplin, Henry 17
Carlin, Anthony V. 117
Carlin, Jim 71
Carlton, Edward 5
Carpenter, N. I. A. 219
Carr, Barbara J. 138
Carroll, Marie 291
Carroll, Phillip 249
Carter, Barbara Ann 243
Carter, Deborah 163
Carter, Jill 246
Carter, Lisa 325
Carter, Michael 52
Carter Sr., Edna 263
Carver, Annette 183
Cassar, Mariella 3
Casson, Iris 102
Castle, J. T. 105
Catley, Lucy 172
Catt, Angela 199
Cave, Natalie 51
Cawley, Linda 177
Cenizo, Sheron 131
Challis, Tim 5
Chalmers, Joanna 330
Chamberlain, C. J. 153
Chambers, Linda 247
Chambers, Lisa 311
Chapman, Jean 331
Chappell, Johnny 218
Chapple, Tara 138
Charalambous, Stella 250
Charbit, Annabelle 31
Charles, Kelly 102
Charlton, Lynne 151
Charnock, Charles 10
Chase, Neil 295
Cheetham, A. L. 226
Cheetham, C. 304
Chica, Juan Diego 192
Childs, Annette 271
Childs, Graham Peter 66
Chivari, Alina 281
Chowdhury, Saleha 175
Christensen, June 296
Christian, R. C. 62
Chrystal, Linda 160
Church, Jeffrey Michael 274
Churchill, Dale 107
Cierniak, Carol 239
Clachrie, Jane Osborne 308
Clare, J. J. 186
Clark, Beryl 147
Clark, Dian 115
Clark, H. 139
Clark, J. W. 266
Clark, Linda 122
Clark, Mary K. 35
Clark, S. D. 315
Clark, Wayne M. 141
Clark, William J. 99
Clarke, Anna 106
Clarke, Christina M. 30
Clarke, Judith 313
Clarke, Mollie 288
Clarke, Simon 74
Clarke, William 34
Clarkson, J. 219
Clay, Pauline 143
Clear, June 159
Cleary, Rita 213
Clemens, Matthew 192
Clements, Judith 32
Clements, Laszlo 11

Clifton, Eleanor 305
Cloke, Margaret 194
Clydesdale, Alison 167
Cockfield, William 199
Codd, Trevor 44
Cole, H. M. J. 321
Cole, Mark 187
Cole, Spencer 103
Coleman, Mary 202
Coles, Mary 118
Collard, H. W. F. 62
Colley, Sarah 257
Collier, Sue 281
Colligan, Margaret Muir 196
Collingbourn-Beevers, Margot 145
Collins, Kevin P. 72
Collins, Lilian 106
Collins, Vera Margaret 31
Collocott, Bruce 155
Colman, A. L. 124
Colthorpe-Parker, Helen M. 277
Conboy, Linda 137
Conchar, Catherine F. 241
Condron, Elizabeth Ann 154
Connell, Norman G. 252
Connelly, E. J. 166
Connolly, Helen 174
Connolly, James J. 47
Connolly, James J. 125
Connors, Aoife 98
Contractor, Anahite 300
Conway, Pauline 19
Cooke, Caro 267
Cooke, Constance Joyce 57
Cooke, Jennifer 94
Cooke, Marion W. 319
Cooke, Natalie 324
Cooksley, Sarah 139
Cooley, Jennifer 274
Cooper, Claire 324
Cooper, George A. 235
Cooper, K. J. 171
Cooper, M. D. 111
Cooper, Nora Kathleen 147
Cooper, Peter S. A. 6
Cooper, Vincent 76
Cope, Nadine 30
Copland, Ann 21
Copley, Dawn 198
Copley, Valerie 321
Copper, John David 74
Corbett, William 142
Corcoran, Michael 184
Corke, Ailie 323
Costello, Edward J. 151
Cotson, Sarah 202
Cotter, Nora 130
Cotterill, H. 319
Cotton, L. 5
Coulston, Linda 110
Counihan, Ruth 92
Court, Lesley 320
Cousins, Don 12
Cousins, Natasha 264
Couzens, Leah 162
Cowan, Elizabeth 228
Cowdell, Alison 174
Cowell, C. 161
Cowley, Mark 183
Cox, Gillian G. 51
Cox, Simon 200
Coyle, Evelyn 115
Cozens, Robert 219
Cracknell, Francine 70
Cracknell, Maria 24
Craddock, Sally 140

Craddock, Stephen J. 14
Craggs, Debbie 302
Craig, Jennifer 155
Craigmile, Clive 16
Crane, Caryne 217
Crawford, Donna Marie 246
Crawford, Janette 41
Crawford, Thomas 231
Crawford-Ward, Alison 176
Crawley, Martin 220
Crawshaw, Sarah 190
Creedon, Betty A. 248
Creighton, C. 329
Crisp, Gordon Jack 53
Croall, Kathleen 6
Crook, W. E. 279
Crosby, Edward Lee 179
Crossley, Martin 237
Crowe, Sylvia 76
Crowther, Nancie 165
Crowther, Sarah 314
Cruickslanks, Doreen 129
Crumpler, Margaret 225
Crutchfield, Joan 273
Cubitt, Ann 47
Cuggy, Lilian 245
Cule, Alice Mary 183
Cullen, Jane 249
Cullis, Irene 191
Cullum, Thomas 224
Cundall, Dorothy Ann 115
Cunningham, Carolyn R. 14
Cunningham, Dawn 136
Cunningham, Karen 137
Curley, Deirdre 253
Curtis, R. A. 84
Cussens, Terence 194
Cutts, Noeline 46

D

Dabrowski-Oakland, Stanislaw 65
Dale, Kathleen Heyden 50
Daley, Doreen 218
Dallner, D. 191
Dalton, B. J. 306
Daly, Margaret 258
Danciu, Simina 265
Daniels, Valerie 102
Darke, Nyx 38
Das, Bikash 300
David, Russell Gill 21
Davidson, D. M. 298
Davidson, Marjory 130
Davies, Dennis N. 23
Davies, Jean Anderson 252
Davies, Owen 217
Davies, Patricia A. 165
Davies, Patrick 48
Davies, Sandra 195
Davis, K. A. 260
Davis, Leonard 161
Davis, Paul 153
Davis, Peter 234
Davis, Sally 144
Davison, Brian J. 147
Davison, Ruth J. 147
Dawson, Jean 163
Dawson, Marjorie 57
Dawtry, Rhoda 164
Day, Elaine 162
Deall, Avril C. 167
De-Alwis, Ruvina 193
Deans, Alaina 65
De Boer, Roger Frederic 91
De Gruchy, Ruby 155
Dehavilland, Rhonda 100

De Jesus, Charlene 293
Delamore, Noeleen 169
Deliens, Tonia 52
Dempsey, Anton 262
Denning, Claire 161
Dennis, R. T. 309
Denyer, M. 123
Deol, Sarwan S. 143
Desai, Nita 291
De Silva, Stephen Richard 183
de Souza, Marion 170
Deutsch, Barbara 24
Devaney, T. M. 4
Devine, Donna 42
Devlin, Helen 34
Devlin, Helen 151
Devonshire, Val 214
Dewey, Elizabeth A. 18
Dewson, Charlotte 318
Dewson, Charlotte 321
Dey, Anindita 214
Dhamani, Zahra 17
Dharmpaul, Helga I. 144
Dhatariya, K. K. 199
Dhatariya, Ketan 331
Dhillon, Bal 97
Dibb-Fuller, Alison 216
Dickins, Bobby 173
Dickinson, Annemarie 255
Dickinson, D. W. 171
Dickinson, Emily 237
Dickinson, Judith M. 285
Dickson, E. M. 17
Diggory, June 164
Dilks, Peggy 185
Dillon, H. J. 332
Dillon, Hugh Jon 300
Dilloway, V. K. 121
Dimond, Joanne Louise 319
Dingwall, Gwen 140
Dinnal-Allen, Kiri 63
Dinning, Jean 125
Dixon, Charlotte 203
Dobbs, G. 204
Docherty, Elizabeth 148
Docker, S. 79
Dodds, Godfrey 166
Doherty, Rosemarie 167
Dominick, Arthur 181
Donnelly, Patrick 42
Doonan, Janice 79
Doudican, Joanne 267
Dougherty, Kathleen 264
Douglas, Gwen 87
Douglas, Sandra Hughes 126
Downie, Bruce F. 271
Downie, Gordon 193
Downing, Lionel 251
Downs, E. 180
Downs, Rita 109
Drake, Claire Francine 99
Drake, Saydi-Anne 286
Drakley, Susan M. 259
Draper, Adele 77
Drummond, Kathryn Arnot 202
Drummond, Sally 138
Drury, Monica 152
Duarte, Angie 260
Ducharme, Audrey 128
Duciuc, Alina 296
Dudgeon, E. R. 146
Duffy, V-J R. 256
Duke, Adrian 209
Duley, Pamela 35
Duncan, Alexa 208
Duncan, Craig McK. 325

Duncan, Rebecca 103
Dunker, Douglas 24
Dunne, Barry David 209
Dunne, John 324
Dyer, Barbara 125
Dyer, Sandra 54
Dymond, R. H. 224
Dyson, Yvonne P. 20
Dzanado, Emmanuel Kwabla 69
Dziecielewski, M. E. 89
Dziennik, Kirsty 246

E

E. 196
Eagle, Evelyn Mary 189
Eaglesham, Iver 71
Earley, Ann M. 216
East, Mary 214
Easton, Ann 296
Ebrey, Jennifer 212
Ecclestone, G. 148
Ecob, Jean 305
Ede, Elaine 15
Eden, Anna-Louise 284
Eden, John 135
Edmonds, Eve 79
Edwards, Angela 114
Edwards, Catherine T. 192
Edwards, Claire 49
Edwards, Laura 22
Edwards, Margery 221
Edwards, Susan 164
Egan, John Bosco 313
Ekong, Anne 73
El Arabi, Soraya 164
El Attar, Deena Mohamed 273
Elapata, Nalini 21
Elford, John Bernard 48
Ellerton, M. J. 131
Elliott, Crispin John 188
Elliott, S. 36
Elliott, Sheila 223
Ellis, Isabel 328
Ellis, Rosalyn C. 64
Ellner, E. F. 123
Elloway, Terry 39
Elphick, Amanda 99
Elphick, Amanda 162
Elsey, Katherine 79
Elsworthy, Kerry 15
Emmett, George R. 62
Emmins, Martin Victor 54
Emslie, Mhari 288
Endlar, Toby S. 53
England, Pia 305
Enticknapp, Daniel 59
Enticknapp, Daniel 74
Epie, Humphrey A. 92
Estien, Veda 75
Estlea, Danielle Martine 307
Esudia, Bamidele 291
Etridge, Kelly 9
Evans, Cyril C. 164
Evans, Dawn 276
Evans, Fay 243
Evans, Jacqueline 174
Evans, Kate 313
Evans, Sharon 168
Evans, Suzanne 232
Ewart, Beatrice Mary 160
Ewen, Jenny H. 195
Ewuosho, Lara 92
Eyre, Bridget 140

F

Fagan, Gerry 234
Fairfoull, Beverley Ann 285
Fairfoull, Beverley Ann 295
Fairweather, David J. 57
Fall, Patricia M. R. 19
Fane-Saunders, Peter 283
Farina, Marco 159
Farley, Mark 58
Farndell, E. W. 229
Farnham, Elizabeth 258
Farouk, Saad 289
Farr, Mary 218
Farrell, Mary O. 304
Farries, Wilf 329
Fat-hey, Perryhan Mohamed 275
Faulkner, Karen 152
Faulkner, Naomi 189
Fazakerley, T. 218
Fazloon, Mohamed 268
Fearnehough, Evelyn 212
Felix, Inez 160
Fellingham, R. B. 35
Fenn, B. L. 307
Fensom, Paul T. 120
Ferek, Margareta 48
Ferguson, Josephine 203
Ferguson, Violetta J. 142
Ferguson, W. A. N. 154
Fiddler, Craig James 248
Field, Alice 148
Finch, Kerry 178
Findlay, Mary 171
Fink, Margaret 226
Finlay, A. M. 174
Finlay, James 308
Finnie, Jemma May 188
Fish, George Henry 9
Fishburn, Glenys 5
Fisher, E. 46
Fisher, E. 51
Fisher, Liz 14
Fisher, Sue 311
Fishwick, Sue 153
Flamson, Barbara 53
Flavell, Terry 195
Flavin, Pamela 9
Fletcher, Louise 193
Fletcher, Maud 272
Fletcher, Nicholas 51
Flicker, Alan D. 208
Flockhart, J. G. 192
Flood, Catherine 193
Flynn's, Henry Mum 288
Foote, Karen 250
Foran, Hayley 307
Ford, Acister James 206
Ford, George J. 247
Ford, J. V. 143
Fordham, K. W. 173
Foreman, Kevin 38
Forrest, Hazel 150
Fortune, J. 176
Foster, J. S. 50
Foster, Paul 225
Foster, Ruth S. 272
Foulds, Russell J. 285
Fowler, Donna-Marie. 95
Fox, Kitty 79
Fox, Martin S. 190
Foy, Michael 301
Francis, Connie L. 133
Francis, Kenneth Charles 270
Francis, R. H. G. 146
Francis, Sue 107
Frankish, Phyllis 177

Fraser, Lorraine Diana 152
Frattali, Alexandra 8
Freeborn, Mary 325
Freeman, A. R. 200
Freeman, P. 326
Freeman, Sarah 286
Fretin, Christine 109
Friery, Christine 68
Frost, Mark 154
Frost, Sandra 188
Fuller, John 76
Funnell, J. E. 197
Fynes, C. 290

G

Gabokgatlhe, B. P. 90
Gabrial, M. J. 299
Gabriela, Greatwood 48
Gallagher, Paul 6
Gallery, Sharon 169
Gambles, Stephen 34
Gannon, M. 109
Gapuz, Carmela Hullana 323
Garcia, Edith 38
Gardiner, J. 327
Gardner, Gemma 85
Gardner, Melissa 145
Garman, Yvonne 314
Garner, Neal 185
Garner, Russella 189
Garrard, Mary 100
Garriock, Jolene 114
Garton, A. 10
Garvey, Alan 82
Garvey, Andrea 133
Garvin, Therese 229
Gascoigne, Clarence 334
Gaskell, Andrew 220
Gaskin, Rosson 116
Gauld, Aimi 248
Gaunt, Howard Trevor 67
Gaynair, Wendy 301
Gearing, Victoria 263
Gench, G. G. 143
Gentle, Joan 13
Georgiades-Mitchell, Hebe 8
Gerrie, Moira 247
Gess, Mabel 146
Gibbons, Hilda 159
Gibbons, Martin 235
Gibson, A. F. 230
Gibson, Julie 238
Gilbert 315
Gilbert, Nadine 220
Gilbert, Samuel 196
Giles, Anne P. 91
Gilhooly, Sarah L. 51
Gill, Surjit 235
Gillanders, Florence J. 49
Gillion, Kenneth 75
Gillman, Dulcie Beatrice 22
Ginsberg, Doris 317
Ginsberg, Doris 330
Girasole, Natasha 83
Glazer, Diandra 197
Glazer, Michele 161
Glen, Jim 15
Goddin, Heather 118
Godding, Lena 173
Godly, A. 200
Goldberg, Evelynne 270
Goliger, Jean 23
Golledge, M. V. 250
Gomez, Rosanne 140
Gonsalves, S. M. 125
Goodchild, Christine 43

Gordon, Amy 216
Gordon, Laura I. 315
Gorman, Maree O. 178
Gough, Paul David 132
Gough, Roy T. 251
Grace, Gillian 295
Gracia, Bettie 208
Grada, Raluca 280
Graham, Adela 111
Graham, Danny 319
Graham, Joanne 267
Graham-Gordon, W. 128
Grainger, Brenda J. 175
Grainger, Gillian 27
Grainger, Jack 262
Grant, Stuart 161
Graves, Susan 73
Gray Chatterton, Dorothy 140
Gray, Elizabeth N. S. 12
Gray, Kathryn 82
Gray, Lucy 199
Green, Dorothea 143
Green, Jacqueline 16
Green, Rema A. 3
Greenall, Irene 18
Greenfiell-Goodman, Amy 40
Greening, Sheila 287
Gregory, Wendy 240
Grey, Elizabeth 219
Griff 88
Griffin, Louise 300
Griffiths, Alicia Anne 205
Griffiths, D. 93
Griffiths, Dymphna 245
Griffiths, Eileen 147
Griffiths, Geraldine 158
Griffiths, Julie 207
Griffths, Stephen John 187
Griggs, Mary 215
Grimes, Ewen 248
Grimes, Norman E. 133
Grimwood, Jan 182
Grindon, Laura 260
Grounds, Patricia Evelyn 80
Grundy, A. 242
Guard, Barrie Sefton 242
Gubbins, Linda May 121
Guignard, Joan 147
Gulliver, Iris 332
Gumush, Suzan 9
Gunn-Matthews, Stanley 209
Gutteridge, Pauline 316
Guy, R. 16
Gymer, Jennifer 275

H

Hafiz-Alam, Robina 75
Hagger, Doreen 288
Haggerty, John 308
Hale, Louise 308
Hales-Owen, V. 282
Hall, Adrian 215
Hall, Catherine 327
Hall, Elizabeth 185
Hall, Frank 21
Hall, Jeannine Anderson 168
Hall, J. M. 293
Hall, J. R. 212
Hall, M. 317
Hamer, Abi 99
Hamill, Louise 163
Hamill, Roísin 189
Hamilton, Duncan 178
Hamilton-Sneath, Jenny 175
Hammond, C. 163
Hampson, Amanda 191

Hampson, John 138
Hampton, Pamela 280
Hancox, Graham 328
Hands, Hazel 120
Hanfler, Klaus 199
Hanley, Caroline 190
Hanlon, Christine 121
Hannaford, Loraine Elizabeth 89
Hanney, Emily 331
Hansen, C. E. 211
Hansen, Henrik Rivera 154
Hanson, Amy 233
Hanson, David 124
Harcus, A. R. 4
Hardie, Sally-Anne 110
Harding, Evelyn M. 11
Harding, J. 14
Hardy, Tamzin 150
Harland, Louise 77
Harries, Gillian 310
Harries, Philip 209
Harris, Beth Amanda 65
Harris, Claire 197
Harris, Megan 64
Harris, Ralph L. 6
Harrison, Alan 141
Harrison, D. M. E. 45
Harrison, Gail 214
Harrison, Linda 211
Harrison, Medina 321
Harrison, Pat 162
Harrison, Serena Marie 309
Harrison, Steve 213
Harrison, Suzanne 137
Harrower, Catherine H. 227
Hart, Flo-Louise 235
Hart, Lillian G. 110
Hart, Stuart 21
Hartland, Joan 5
Hartwell, Jacquline 94
Harvey, Gill 105
Harvey, James H. 225
Harvey, Joyce Susan 46
Harvey, Phyllis R. 247
Hastings, Joanna 298
Haswell, Margaret 84
Hawes, David 178
Hawkins, Katie 187
Hawkins, Diana D. 280
Hawkins, Paula 240
Hay, Betty 70
Hay, Jeannie 29
Hayes, Annette 331
Hayes, Kim 292
Hayter, Justine 327
Hayton, E. M. 209
Hayward, Lee 151
Hazzard, Melanie 186
Healy-Moore, Niamh 97
Heard, C. 203
Heath, Donna 172
Heathcote, M. 192
Heckler, Frances 140
Hedley, Marjorie 15
Hefferon, Kathleen 266
Heighton, P. A. 250
Helman, E. V. 56
Helman, E. V. 153
Hemmant, Maurice 135
Hemmant, Vivienne 19
Hemming, N. 94
Henderson, A. 155
Henderson, A. 160
Henderson, Angela 28
Henderson, Eve 77
Henderson, Lade 127

Hendtlass, David 257
Henry, Ashleen 282
Herbert, Gillian 227
Herbert, Margaret 179
Heritage, A. C. 167
Herridge, Ricky 265
Herring, H. 144
Herwald, Emanuel 87
Hewat, Mary 307
Hicks, S. 220
Hicks, Samantha 152
Higgins, Julie 46
Higgins, Roberta Jane 196
Higginson, J. H. 80
Higgs, Roger D. 62
Highley, Lucinda 6
Hill, Katie 70
Hillary-Fawcett, Ellen 252
Hiller, Roland 143
Hilton, Amy 206
Hilton, Mandy 145
Hind, Suzanne 199
Hind, Suzanne 334
Hinds, Steven 98
Hines, Emma 152
Hirons, K. R. 155
Hirst, F. W. 245
Hiscocks, A. F. 50
Hislop, Stephen 159
Hoare, Gordon 70
Hobbs, Kate 37
Hobbs, Maud Eleanor 201
Hodgson, Debra 240
Hodgson, Iain 230
Hoffman, Jennifer 61
Hoffman, Jennifer 69
Hogan, Doris 44
Hogg, Wilma 75
Holder, Rita Violet 71
Holding, Robert 28
Holford, Pauline 39
Holland, Doris 37
Holland, Paul Christopher 185
Holland, Tracie 208
Holliday, Marilyn 113
Hollingsworth, Frederick J. 272
Hollis, E. 185
Hollis, Pamela 261
Holloway, Ethel 332
Holloway, Gertrude 72
Holloway, J. 132
Hollowell, Melissa 250
Holmes, Stuart M. 122
Holness, A. 16
Holohan, D. H. 169
Holzherr, Gina 269
Holzherr, Gina 320
Honess, Brenda 105
Honey, Margaret 244
Hooker, Fiona 249
Hooper, Hazel June 116
Hopson, Barbara 172
Horne, Judy 165
Horne, Louis J. A. 162
Horrobin, Nita 166
Horsley, Elizabeth 264
Horton, Jay M-L. 239
Houghton, Jacinta 194
Houghton, Rebecca 272
Hoult, Pam 111
Hounsell, F. H. 33
House, Angie 281
Howard, Doris Vera 190
Howard, Evelyn 66
Howard, I. T. 84
Howard, V. B. 81

Howard, Vickie 198
Howden, Charlotte 285
Howe, D. H. 89
Howeld, Keir 173
Howell, Daniel Francis 266
Howell, Georgina 78
Howell, Margaret J. 189
Howens, Margaret 15
Howick, Jane L. 251
Howsam, Stephen 108
Hubbard, Evelyn B. 88
Huddlestone, D. M. 322
Hudson, Chris 22
Hudson, Eileen 318
Hughes, Chirene 96
Hughes, Gareth 203
Hughes, Ruby 302
Hughes, Teifion Paul 278
Hulme, F. G. 179
Humby, Carol 244
Humphrey, Virginia J. 184
Humphries, Natalie 109
Hunt, Ann 52
Hunt, Caron L. 211
Hunt, Ellen J. 41
Hunt, Emma 16
Hunt, Emma 174
Hunt, M. 298
Hunt, Mary Ward 221
Hunter, Alison J. 109
Hunter, Brian 282
Hunter, Emma 210
Hunter, P. A. 79
Hunter, Paul J. C. 151
Hunter, Rachael 111
Huntington, Sarah 274
Hurd, Margaret 332
Hurley, Desmond 252
Hurlow, W. J. 205
Hush, Rose Anne 113
Hussain, Sadia 87
Huswait, Irene 37
Hutchison, Anne 201
Hutton, Sylvia 246
Hyam, Maureen 142
Hyatt, Janette 303
Hyer, Carole 134
Hyland, Rachel A. 136

I

Ilkul, Hamad JB 126
Ince, Louise 304
Inglis, David. N. 307
Insley, Lucy 314
Ioana, Vartosu 292
Iqani, Mehita 165
Ireland, Kathleen 303
Ironside, Phil 100
Irving, Margaret 172
Ismail, Magda Mohamed 286
Ivascu, Marius 296
Iwamoto, Tokiko 143
Izon, Claire M. 189

J

J., Sarah 81
Jackson, Hugh 60
Jackson, J. Fred 124
Jackson, M. 54
Jackson, Margaret 147
Jackson, Pamela 216
Jackson, Sidney 115
Jacobs, Nadine 137
James, Fred O. 122
James, Michael 286

Jamieson, Anne 249
Jarvis, Joan 3
Jasiek, Joan 21
Jason, Maxime A. 241
Jay, Peter 217
Jayne, Samantha Webb 166
Jeanes, Harry James 76
Jefferies, Lesley-Anne 313
Jeffrey, Betty 176
Jeffrey, Eric Johnson 136
Jeneck, Hasim 320
Jenkins, S. A. 75
Jennings, Denise 310
Jennings, Sharon 83
Jennings, Valerie 71
Jeyaraj, Pravin 22
John, Michael 238
Johns, Wendie Rosemary 88
Johnson, Elwyn 158
Johnson, Karen 113
Johnson, Olga 7
Jones, A. A. 269
Jones, Ada Forrest 148
Jones, Donna 148
Jones, Gay 58
Jones, Gerard 265
Jones, J. A. 203
Jones, J. Lewis 194
Jones, Jane 294
Jones, Janet 142
Jones, Jean 133
Jones, Jenna 186
Jones, Jennifer D. 273
Jones, Lewis 108
Jones, Louise 317
Jones, Mary 22
Jones, Natalie 317
Jones, Olive 122
Jones, Pat 141
Jones, S. A. 206
Jones, Susan 305
Jones, Sylvia R. 314
Jones, T. R. 172
Jones, Vie 112
Jorgensen, Andrew 226
Jorgensen, Eleanor Stella 301
Joseph, P. M. 321
Joseph, Wagachima Kabucho 182
Joshua, Wole 17
Joshua, Wole 30
Joy, W. 267
Jules, Anthony 304
Jungbauer, Sven Asian 291
Junor, Anna 53

K

Kalamboukas, Theo 192
Kalantzis, Beverley 179
Kane, Mary G. 29
Kanjer, Hanif 234
Kankaanpaa, Louise 101
Kaplan, T. 116
Karbacs, Elsie 269
Kathirgamathamby, Umah 312
Kaur, Karmjeet 162
Kaur, Ravinder 200
Kay, Jane 191
Kay, May 156
Kaye, F. D. 185
Kazer, Emma Jayne 85
Kazmi, R. 95
Kearney, Audrey 272
Keeley, Mary A. T. 34
Keeping, Rita 326
Kellow, Edith N. 10
Kelly, Amanda R. 201

Kelly, Irene Patricia 158
Kelly, Shyrell 118
Kelly, Thomas J. 215
Kemble, Charley 105
Kemp, Hayley 313
Kemps, Sharon 183
Kennedy, M. 41
Kennedy, Nichola Ann 216
Kennedy, S. P. 59
Kennedy, Sara 163
Kent, Katie 36
Keogh, Peter 5
Keogh, Peter 186
Kerfoot, B. 104
Kerrison, Sidney A. 157
Kershaw, Alice 200
Kershaw, D. C. 3
Kester, Paul 317
Khan, Saira 144
Khan, Tehseen A. 272
Khistria, Nilpa 328
Khullar, Roochi 143
Kiener, Melanie 97
Kigwe, Mumbi Y. 197
Kilbride, Angela 323
Killeen, John 245
Kimiti, Prudencia Paul 254
Kind, Sarah 14
King, Barbara 117
King, Carol 172
King, Cicely M. Hart 112
King, Dawn 233
King, Henry 286
King, Martin 300
King, Tracey 207
Kirkham, John 156
Kirkwood, Susan 155
Kirrage, Violet 231
Kirwan, Teresa 199
Kitchen, Joanne 282
Klein, I. M. 302
Klein, Iris J. 326
Klosowski-Travis, B. J. 234
Kneale, Amie 211
Knedlik, Shanon 40
Knee, A. W. J. 205
Knight, Audrey 179
Knight, Claude A. 8
Kontani, Pauline 217
Kopel, Harold 12
Kops, J. 7
Koukos, Christine 291
Kousar, Shabana & Rehana 81
Kural, Selena 188
Kusar, Kahlda 284

L

Lack, Carolyn M. 316
Lacy, Marilyn 150
Laidlaw, Nicola 33
Laidler, Zahra Homeira 269
Laing, Moira 142
Laird, Anne 179
Laird, Peter 9
Lakovic, Jefta 284
Lander, A. 111
Lane, Ada 152
Lane, Annie 181
Lane, Janet 183
Lane, Josephine 212
Langford, Kai A. 46
Langford, Richard 49
Langridge, Jenny 70
Langwith, Kevin 32
Lara 149
Larcombe, Jacki 153

Larmer, Colin L. 76
Larsen, Karen 329
Lartey, Elizabeth 320
Lasham, Rosemary Jane 225
Latham, Esther 318
Launt, Pauline 200
Lavers, Valerie 221
Law, M. F. 269
Lawlor, Sheena Marie 299
Lawton, Carol 239
Lawton, Kiaran Maria 285
Layland, Mabel 149
Le Jeune, Caroline 47
Lea, Ruth 157
Leach, Joan 189
Leadbetter, J. 173
Leadbitter, Antony 300
Leamon, B. 278
Ledgerton, Selena 40
Lee, Adam James 86
Lee, Aileen 306
Lee, F. Peter 246
Lee, Mandy 175
Lee, Marion A. 66
Lee, Mark 270
Lee, Samantha 149
Lee, Stephen 168
Lee, Zoë 138
Leech, Amy 292
Lees, Bettina 289
Leeson, Margaret 287
Legender, Walter 65
Lehane, P. A. T. 232
Lehoczki, Ioan 264
Leigh-Turner, Corinna 98
Leight, Mary 61
Leith, C. 215
Lelliott, D. 256
Leslie, G. R. 299
Letts, Joan 106
Leung, James 311
Levy, Jemma 258
Lewis, A. M. G. 81
Lewis, Alexandra 265
Lewis, Kerry. 178
Lewis, Kilbroney 237
Lewis, Margaret 238
Lewis, Mervyn 266
Lewis, Rhianydd 256
Lewis, S. 91
Lewis, Shani A. 156
Liddel, Thomas Anthony 59
Liddle, Carol 68
Liepins, K. W. 36
Liggins, June M. 283
Lillie, Valerie 282
Linc, Gordon 249
Lindqvist, Anders 251
Lindroth, Katarina 51
Lindsay, Robert 150
Linney, B. A. 149
Linney, Barbara Ann 20
Linney, Sylvia M. 126
Lipscombe, Glenys M. 255
Lister, Rose Marie 297
Little, Dolly 3
Little, Helen Penelope 220
Little, P. 52
Llewellyn, Anne 71
Llobet, Theresa Josephine 285
Lloyd, Deborah 196
Lloyd, Wayne 63
Lo-Giacco-Smith, Alan 309
Locke, Brenda 209
Lockley, Andrena 195
Loftus, Lilian M. 222

Logan, Brigitta 334
Logan, Paula 229
Logan, Victoria 92
Long, Bruce M. 4i
Long, Emma 141
Long, Helen 145
Long, Mildred Florencia 29
Long, S. J. 85
Longman, Suzelle 159
Longshaw, K. 187
Longyear, Sue 165
Lord, Amanda 185
Lord, Sue 168
Louise, Emma Ginn 322
Loveland, Melanie 197
Lovell, Helen 71
Lowe, Beryl 299
Lowe, M. W. 323
Lowe, William. G. A. 225
Lowrie, E. I. 144
Lowrie, Sandy 299
Lowy, Jackie 23
Luby, Patricia 41
Lucas, A. 50
Lucas, Manley L. 100
Luckhurst, Audrey 27
Lyall, Kiran 71
Lynch, Suzanne P. 32
Lynden 162
Lynn, Jenni 324
Lyon, Kim 313
Lyon, Mike 195
Lyon, Richard Kenneth 150
Lyons, Isobel 124
Lyons, M. 279
Lyons, P. M. 99

M

Macarthur, Norma Anne 141
MacDonald, Anna 144
MacDonald, Fiona 255
MacDonald, Jim 111
Macdonald, Stuart 288
MacFarlane, Vince 310
Machale, Michael 78
Mackie, Ruth 191
Mackness, Noele 7
MacLean, Rachel 317
MacNicol, Duncan M. 142
MacPhee, Ilona Rowena 128
MacPherson, P. E. 234
Maddock, Mark A. 275
Maggs, Dawn 296
Maguire, Jacqueline A. 20
Maguire, Julie 154
Maher, Jessica 97
Mahony, Maureen 169
Mallia, Walter 318
Malone, Tom 167
Maloney, Dolores 322
Maltby-Baker, Zoe 117
Mandary, D. 213
Mankey, A. S. 222
Manlow, James 256
Manning, Robert G. E. 303
Mannion, Sheila 317
Mansell, Heidi 205
Manson-Herrod, Pettr 166
Mansour, Wendy J. 201
Manuel, Holly 302
Manville, Anthony C. E. 242
Marchant, Tracey-Jane 170
Margareta, Peli 273
Markham, Pauline R. 147
Marlow, Emily 188
Marquis, Sarah 148

Marr, Lesley 160
Marsh, J. R. 149
Marsh, J. R. 150
Marshall, A. J. 150
Marshall, Christine 197
Marshall, Christine 318
Marshall, John Lee 314
Marshall, Karen 252
Marshall, Vicki 142
Martin, Adrian 65
Martin, Claire M. 139
Martin, Fiona 135
Martin, J. 96
Martin, Judi 201
Martin, Lynda 98
Martin, Margaret 177
Martin, Mark T. 170
Martin, P. 237
Martin, Sindy R. 212
Martin, Steven Victor 315
Martin, Susan 76
Maryan, Joan Ester 17
Maryan, Joan Ester 18
Masand, Bina 84
Maskill, R. 55
Mason, Betty 315
Mason, Hilda 142
Massey, Keith G. 113
Masters, Janet B. 206
Matheson, R. J. 168
Maton, Paul 29
Maton, Paul 228
Maubec, Patricia 103
Maughan, Catherine 249
Mawer, Deborah 86
Maxwell, Helen 145
May, Heidi 289
May, Jane 316
Mayer, Patrick 253
Mayes, Kelvin 273
Mayes, Trina 216
Mayor, E. 245
McAlpine, Andrew & Renee 133
McArthur, Frank 153
McAuley, Brenda 47
McAuliffe, M. 284
McAvoy, Joan 44
McBride, Carla 301
McBride, Nicola 186
McCabe, Allison 195
McCann, Jane Elizabeth 78
McCann, Kevin 34
McCarthy, J. W. 233
McCarthy, Neil 263
McCaul, Edel 291
McCormack, Suzanne 146
McCormick, Karen 251
McCoska, Amna 186
McCusker, Michelle 187
McDermott, John 254
McDermott, Kevin 231
McDonagh, Melanie 197
McDonald, Cindy 179
McDonald, Jean 102
McDonald, Scott 197
McDonnell, Kathleen 218
McFadden, Bernadette 272
McFarland, Iris 56
McFarland, R. J. 122
McFauld, S. 300
McGhie, Mary 304
McGinty, Michael 297
McGivern, Verity 261
McGlinn, Michael 316
McGovern, Anne 227
McGrath, Eamonn James 146

McGrath, Paula 205
McGreal, Stephen 308
McGuinness, Damian 178
McGuinness, Lesley-Anne 173
McHugh, Margaret 15
McIntosh, Gavin G. 263
McIntosh, Rachel 196
McKay, Kerry 38
McKay, Mia Jo 103
McKell, Lisa Marie 19
McKenzie, Errol C. 59
McKeown, Suzie 183
McKnight, Mark Anthony 241
McLaughlin, Ellen 85
McLean, Alistair 301
McLellan, Alison E. 229
McLeod, D. 195
McLeod, Eunice 244
McLeod, Evelyn 181
McMillan, Bella 309
McMillan, Sheila E. 155
McMullan, Catherine 279
McNee, Frank 218
McNulty, James 1
McOwen, T. J. 36
McPartland, A. 228
McTaggart, Donna 92
McVitty, Aaron 236
Meaden, Claire 259
Meadows, Margaret 97
Meadows, R. 173
Meany, Gerardine 186
Meazza, Dean F. 65
Megson, Jennifer 95
Meister, Vera 87
Meldrum, Catherine Janet 95
Melling, Thora 255
Mellor, Marjorie 4
Melmoth, George 183
Melrose, R. V. 234
Melville, Fiona 307
Membury, Nigel 104
Menday, Pamela 94
Merry, Lewis 262
Mevor, T. 156
Meyer, Dagmar W. 51
Michael, Keszeg C. 169
Michaelides, Natasha 210
Michaels, Joseph 72
Micklethwaite, Anne 140
Middlebrook, E. W. 121
Middleton, Lorraine 183
Midwinter, A. E. 47
Miers, Jennifer 115
Miles, Emma 305
Millard, Christopher C. 195
Millard, Mike 248
Miller, D. E. 17
Miller, Lisamaria 138
Miller, Rachel 290
Millican, Jonathan 78
Millington, Dorothy 323
Millman, Roy 325
Mills, Grace 258
Mills, Johnnie N. 297
Millson, Louise 58
Milne, Iain P. 101
Minter, Jane 203
Mistry, Reena 119
Mitchell, David 182
Mitchell, Hannah 327
Mitchell, Mary G. 310
Mitchell, Robert 321
Mitchell, S. E. 248
Mitchell, Thomas 86
Miu, Raluca 180

Moakes, M. 319
Mobberley, David 146
Moffat, Kirsten 295
Molloy, Jane 190
Molloy, Rachel 165
Moloney, Pamela 180
Molton, C. H. 268
Momen, Sarafat Ibn 125
Monaghan, Mike 309
Monk, Beate 54
Monkcom, David 239
Moody, Joyce 220
Moody, Liz 123
Moody, Mechelle 173
Moon, Katherine 298
Mooney, Irene J. 290
Moore, A. S. 154
Moore, Alan 113
Moore, C. 85
Moore, Daniel 155
Moore, Doris 171
Moore, Kathleen 173
Moore, Maggie 48
Moore, V. M. 148
Moore Suffolk, V. M. 156
Moore, W. Haisley 74
Moore, Zechariah 194
Morello, Zoë 326
Morgan, B. 176
Morgan, Claire 34
Morgan, Debbie 110
Morgan, Frances 134
Morgan, H. M. 256
Morgan, Julie 180
Morgan, Merril 190
Morgan, Peter 131
Morgan, Rudy 241
Morgan, Terence L. 207
Morgan, Tracy Ann 62
Morgan-Jones, K. 327
Morledge, Jennifer 198
Morris, Christine A. 235
Morris, Emma 198
Morrison, Catherine 261
Morrison, Stuart 139
Mortimer, Cara 303
Mortimer, Elizabeth 193
Motion, Margaret 249
Mountney, C. 124
Mowlah, Sally 40
Muchmore, Janet 40
Mugford, E. 34
Muir-Ward, Isabella 69
Muir-ward, Isabella 45
Muirhead, Ann 331
Muirhead, Joan 113
Muirhead, M. 33
Mulholland, Maria 136
Mullan, Pauline N. 148
Muller, Charles H. 184
Mulrooney, Frank 293
Munday, Jill 82
Munns, Kenneth Roy 149
Munro, Margaret 149
Muranka, F. J. 192
Muresan, Nina 274
Murphy, Clive 252
Murphy, John Burns 132
Murphy, Philip P. 157
Murphy, Tadhg 294
Murray, Andrew 177
Murray, Anna 254
Murray, Claire 302
Murray, Freida 136
Murray, Gary 148
Murray, Joanne 328

Murray, Noeline 246
Murray, Patricia 322
Murrell, Natasha Maria 169
Mwenesi, Clive 161

N

Naidoo, John 61
Nash, Pauline 298
Naughton, Blanche 119
Naylor, Katie 261
Neal, Rachel 188
Nedioara, Palade 329
Neil, J. 316
Neild, Lynn 284
Nelder, Dee 56
Nelson, Helen 193
Nelson, R. J. 218
Netcott, Peggy 35
Neville, Gail Leanne 77
Neville, Karl 276
Newboult, Glynnis 195
Newell, Caroline 306
Newell, Peggy G. 131
Newman, Beatrice 327
Newman, Ian 232
Newman, Joyce T. 8
Newton, David 28
Nic Lochlainn, Philomena 246
Nicholls, Jennifer 172
Nicholson, Barbara 317
Nicholson, C. 170
Nicholson, Connie 281
Nicholson, David 223
Nicholson, John 48
Nicholson-Taylor, Paul 233
Nicklin, Thomas 319
Nicolaou, Anthea 119
Nineham, Vivien 108
Njuguna, Kamau Wa 120
Nobbs, Malcolm 274
Nobbs, Malcolm H. 236
Noden, Maglan 165
Noel-Cephise, Jean Marie 198
Nono, Charles 168
Norman, Janet M. 243
Norman, Michelle 194
Norris, E. 181
Nowak, Elizabeth 106
Nyman, Emma 87

O

Oates, I. J. 192
Oboh, Kenneth 105
O'Brien, Margaret R. 55
O'Callaghan, Anne-Marie 101
O'Connell, Mairead 277
Oddie, Anne 13
Odger, Ann 134
O'Donovan, Sheila 104
O'Dwyer, Martin 112
O'Flaherty, Michelle 126
O'Freddie, Elsie 95
O'Gara, Rossline 141
Ogbuagu, Kechi Uche 54
O'Gorman, Katherine 159
Ogunnaike, R. J. 93
O'Hanlon, Oliver 274
O'Hara, Stevie 301
Ohene-Djan, A. 308
O'Keeffe, Emma 193
O'Keeffe, Laura Jayne 57
O'Kelly, Pauline 100
Okorafor, Elsie 328
Okoro, Patricia 334
Old, Robert 185

O'Leary, Maureen 160
Oliver, Dee 210
Oliver, Nicola 67
Oliver-Rayfield, Peggy 184
Ollerenshaw, Ian 293
Olley, Marion 184
Olley, Natalie 149
Oluseye, Igbaroola Samuel 165
O'Mahoney, Martin 304
O'Mahony, Elizabeth 276
O'Mahony, Elizabeth G. 117
O'Malley, A. A. 50
O'Neil, Miss Helen 84
O'Neill, Denis 179
O'Neill, Jack 75
Ong, Marlena 117
Openshaw, Katherine Ruth 163
O'Regan, Siobhan 180
O'Reilly, Bernadette 147
O'Reilly, Laurence M. 156
O Riordan, Katherine 110
Osborn, Doris 88
Osborne, Abigail 25
Osborne, Abigail 330
Osborne, Cynthia 149
Osborne, John 32
Osborne, Wendy 158
Osoba, Margaret M. 50
O'Sullivan, Gareth 224
O'Sullivan, Ken 60
O'Sullivan, Mary 200
Overy, Beryle 284
Ovington, Karen 98
Owers, Jessica 178
Oxford, Albert 246

P

Page, Ann Marie 147
Page, Sarah 137
Paget-Brown, Dudley 67
Pallicaros, Stephanos 134
Palmer, M. S. 180
Palmer, Pauline 207
Palmer, Susan Margaret 4
Palmer, T. 265
Pannell, Jean 202
Papier, Kieta 185
Pappoe, Kris Atta 318
Paraskevopoulos, Kleanthis 131
Parikh, Phalguni 275
Parish, Daniel J. 36
Parker, D. A. 170
Parker, Elaine Andrea 229
Parker, Jean 98
Parker, Melanie 169
Parker, Sheila Margaret 116
Parker, Shirley Ann 103
Parkes, Dennis 51
Parkin, Geoff D. 228
Parley, Douglas 27
Parnwell, Joy 67
Parry, Ena 206
Parsons, Lara 333
Patel, Priti 110
Paton, Hazel Mary 106
Patrick, Margery J. 61
Patrick, Wendy L. 6
Patten, Barbara 190
Paul, John E. 136
Paxton, D. N. 67
Payn Le Sueur, Dorothea R. 128
Payne, Catherine 324
Payne, Christine 163
Payne, Ciara 292
Payne, Helen 96
Payne, Iris 7

Payton, Adele 280
Payton, Alexandra 241
Peacock, Sandra 262
Pearce, Mark 110
Pearce, Tracey 216
Pearcey, Jenny 120
Pearse, Angela 128
Peart, Kevin 294
Pease, P. 55
Peck, Jean 64
Pelling, Frances Mary 187
Pelling, Naomi 58
Pemberton, Carolie 179
Penfold, Ruth 98
Penne-Stuart, Abigail 297
Penney, Mary E. 121
Penny, Donna 242
Penter, Lorna 189
Pepperdine, Kerith 271
Pereira, Nuno M. 185
Perkins, C. A. 273
Perkins, Caroline 97
Perrins, Chris 239
Perry, Lionel 226
Peters, Bernadette 176
Peters, Christina 96
Pett, Gemma 210
Phillips, F. M. 182
Phillips, G. 109
Phillips, Helen 45
Phillips, J. 199
Phillips, Jean 217
Phillips, Margaretta 156
Philp, Michael Charles 4
Philp, Michaela 99
Phipps, Elizabeth 271
Pickard, Maxine 200
Pickering, Trudy 173
Pickett, Edward Jellicoe 158
Pickles, Susie 83
Pigg, Sylvia 63
Pike, Albert L. 244
Pillar, Isobel 298
Pinkney, Alban L. 243
Pinnock, Bernadette 154
Pittaway, Sarah 315
Piwowarski, Claire 130
Plimley, Tessa 262
Plumb, Katrina 242
Plume, V. I. 165
Poku-Awuah, Abena 132
Polledri, Jennifer 25
Pollington, Annie 28
Pomm, Elaine 89
Ponder, Margaret 168
Poole, Cynthia A. 185
Poole, Symon 222
Pooley, David 10
Pope, Zoe 195
Popejoy, Rebecca 288
Porter, P. J. T. 7
Potter, Charlene 166
Potter, Ida 53
Potticary, James E. 99
Poulton, K. A. 219
Poupard, David Charles 231
Pow, Alan 144
Powell, Geoff 57
Powell, Pearl 198
Powell, V. I. 175
Powles, Olive A. 64
Powney, Vhari Annette 245
Pratt, Mary 114
Pratt, T. S. 184
Prescott, Helen 263
Preston, E. 279

Preston, H. 69
Preston, J. M. 93
Price, Annie L. 118
Price, Patricia E. 152
Price, Rol P. 294
Price, W. Graham 146
Protheroe, Lucy 187
Proud, Margaret 178
Prouse, Margaret 147
Pryor, M. 189
Purbrick, Joyce 254
Purnell, A. R. 167
Pursey, Peter 73
Pusey, Norma 208
Pym, Mary 163

Q

Quantock, M. 181
Quigley, Timothy 123
Quinn, Amanda Ross 91
Quinn, Elizabeth 3
Quinn, Marjorie 197
Quinn, Shirley Ann 133

R

Rabaiotti, Norma 251
Rabbitts, Muriel G. 204
Radford, Diana 157
Radford, Stefanie 212
Radia, Shalita 323
Raine, Lena Maureen 55
Raine, Noel E. 262
Ralphs, Hilda A. 330
Ramadan, Konce 80
Ramchurn, Asha 197
Ramsay, Margaret 181
Ramsden, F. 53
Ramsden, J. 64
Ramwell, Tom 97 333
Randall, R. A. 86
Randall, Sarah 23
Rands, Christine 157
Range, Donna-May 93
Rankin, Naomi Turner 144
Rankin, Vince S. 224
Rashid, Shirley 283
Rass, Norman 37
Ratcliffe, Pauline 212
Rathbone, Enid 141
Rawlings, Maureen 41
Rayers, C. L. 69
Raymond, Julia 306
Rayner, Julie 112
Rea, Belinda Jayne 221
Rea, Rita 11
Read, Charlotte 275
Read, J. T. 110
Reck, Brian 90
Reddish, David Ashley 88
Reece, Helen K. 152
Reed, George W. 213
Reed, Tristan 296
Reeve, Trevor 24
Reevell, Katie 170
Reeves, Sheila 45
Reid, Helen 56
Reid, James 127
Reid, Maurice 181
Reilly, Eileen 13
Reilly, Jennifer 123
Reilly, Sonia 168
Reisdorf, C. 319
Relator, Harry Ventura 49
Rendall, John H. E. 166
Rennie, Jacqueline A. 237

Reynolds, Stephanie 329
Reynolds, Stuart 291
Rhodes, K. D. 162
Rice, Siobhan 297
Rich, Helena Barnard 256
Richards, Christopher 15
Richards, Geoff 121
Richardson, A. 6
Richardson, Diana 3
Richardson, Phyllis 93
Richardson, Sarah 161
Richmond, Joan M. 236
Rickhuss, Lucy 56
Ridgley, Carol 14
Ridley, Steven 230
Ring, Irene 25
Ripley, Laura Ann 171
Risso, Nadine Pilar 103
Ritchie, June 159
Ritchings, Daphne 261
Rivett, Lynn 112
Robbins, Joanne 287
Roberts, Carol 42
Roberts, Gabrielle E. 273
Roberts, Helen 129
Roberts, Linda 30
Roberts, Maisie 63
Roberts, Ruby 312
Roberts, Susan J. 109
Robertson, Audrey 195
Robertson, David 270
Robertson, Elizabeth 170
Robertson, Lisa 7
Robertson, Louise 37
Robertson, Susan Mary 107
Robi, Winifred 184
Robins, Frank 263
Robins, Natalie 236
Robinson, A. 101
Robinson, C. 160
Robinson, Christopher 97
Robinson, G. Phillip G. 120
Robinson, J. R. 43
Robinson, Mike 314
Robinson, Rosalind Mary 46
Robinson, William 184
Rochell, Andrew 292
Rodda, M. 190
Rogan, Edmund 132
Rogers, David H. 72
Rogers, Kath 276
Rogerson, Angela 332
Rolls, Steven 161
Roman, Danielle 177
Romanis, Marjorie 191
Ronald, Jill M. 82
Rooney, M. 300
Rooth, Christine 264
Rose, Lillian 193
Rosewell, Margaretta 74
Rosie, Helen 192
Ross, Aline McInnes 310
Ross, Enid E. 193
Ross, Jean 58
Ross, Malcolm 326
Rothery, Christopher 127
Round, Ken 270
Routt, John 293
Rowe, April 159
Rowe, Atheana 333
Rowland, Keith M. 314
Rowland, Margot Stanislas 271
Rowntree, Shirley P. 138
Royles, Anthony 228
Royles, Melanie 60
Royo, Celia Franco 182

Roysons, Mike 94
Rozycki, Jan 63
Rudland, Doreen 240
Ruhrmund, Harry 90
Rumsam, S. 257
Rupinder, Kalsi 176
Ruse, Michelle 184
Rushbury, Leslie 260
Rushton, P. A. 197
Russ, Sheree 309
Russell, Christina 149
Russell, David A. 35
Russell, Jayne E. 178
Russell, Pat 56
Russell, Patrick 207
Russell, Rachel 268
Russell, Sharon 66
Ruston, Francis Kenneth 256
Rutherford, Iris M. 119
Rutter, Deborah 207
Ryan, Liz 223
Ryan, Valerie 59
Ryder, Alan 45
Ryemarsh, Thomas C. 172

S

Sabin, Georgie 213
Sackett, Shirley 13
Sadler, Margaret 182
Saggers, Clare 154
Saint, William 280
Saint-Yves, I. F. M. 202
Sampson, Mark 31
Sanderson, Anne H. 302
Sanderson-Key, Sandy 308
Sanderson-Smith, Wendy 168
Sandford, Peter 134
Sandhu, Satveer 30
Sandie, Katherine 167
Sandover, Mary Elizabeth 141
Sands, Davina 43
Sani, Pat 68
Sargent, Nadine 141
Satz, Austin 288
Saunders, Ann 95
Saunders, Gemma 166
Saunders, Maurice J. 129
Saunders, Milly 268
Saunders, Sheila 243
Savage, Audrey 29
Savage, S. 13
Saveker, Cathryn 131
Savory, Gemma 311
Saxton, Erin 290
Scammell, Tina 328
Scanlon, Arlene 325
Scaplehorn, Eileen 158
Sceats, Marie Louise 240
Schofield, Robert J. 202
Schroder, Piffa 145
Scott, F. 128
Scott, Jonathan 223
Scott, Katie Sheila 180
Scott, Kirsty 224
Scott, May 330
Scott, Michele T. 264
Scott, Violet 201
Scowen, Z. 294
Screen, David Robert 131
Scrivener, Barbara Anne 173
Scully, Hazel 191
Seager, Lauren 290
Searle, Frances 297
Searle, Frances M. 17
Secrieru, Claudia 273
Seddon, Ramona L. 322

Seddon, Stefan 21
Seifert, Anna 19
Selfe, A. E. J. 54
Selvester, Ella-Dee 160
Semark, Donna 146
Sembhi, Ninder 108
Senior, Chris 24
Senior, Susan Elisabeth 38
Sepi, Andreea 288
Seren-Dat, Rene 85
Setiawan, Agatha 9
Seton, Lilian S. 15
Sewell, D. 309
Sexton, John W. 159
Shaill, Brynne 96
Shakespeare, M. G. 261
Shallard, R. M. 8
Shand, Ginny 159
Shankland, Ruth 163
Shanley, Suzy 81
Sharp, John 227
Sharpe, Anja 177
Sharples, Hannah 204
Shaughnessy, Kathryn 95
Shaw, Andrew 171
Shaw, Gill. 196
Shaw, Michaela 119
Shaw, Sarah 304
Shaw, Sheila 175
Shaw-Taylor, Mary 269
Sheard, M. J. 284
Sheerin, Leanne 297
Sheffield, Lisa M. 125
Shelabarger, John Dale 82
Sheldon, Harriet 175
Shelton, Louise 42
Shelton, Martine L. 132
Shepherd, E. R. 155
Shepherd, Linda 84
Shepherd, Morfydd 127
Sheppard, A. 322
Sheppard, Dawn 68
Shergold, Bettina 23
Sherman, Christine 287
Shiels, G. M. 28
Shires, Colette 62
Shore, Audrey 212
Shorrocks, L. 42
Short, Melissa 183
Shoulin, Sarah 257
Shovlin, Dana 268
Shovlin, Sarah 39
Shram, Sandra Margaret 177
Shuckburgh, Rachel 57
Shuter, Graham 194
Simcox, Laura 305
Simmonds, Rebecca 303
Simms, John Young 9
Simons, Shane V. 259
Simpson, Joe W. 252
Simpson, Leonora 157
Simpson, Mary 261
Sinclair, Norrie 182
Singh, Amarjit 143
Singh, John 164
Sinkinson, Glyn 37
Skeaping, Dave 29
Skidmore, Tony 117
Skinner, Emma 219
Skinner, I. K. 4
Skyrme, Joy 227
Slaney, Sheila 207
Slatter, Mary Evelyn 107
Slowley, Joyce 184
Slym, W. 71
Smellie, David 291

Smith, Alan Brett 121
Smith, Annette 225
Smith, Charlie Boy 50
Smith, Christine E. 20
Smith, Claire 83
Smith, E. F. 31
Smith, Gemma 313
Smith, Graham 7
Smith, Helen 247
Smith, Irene A. R. 130
Smith, Jack 169
Smith, Jack 253
Smith, Joan 61
Smith, Margaret 247
Smith, Mary 39
Smith, Mary 298
Smith, Matthew Lee 174
Smith, Paulina Elizabeth 181
Smith, Rachel 7
Smith, Samantha 263
Smith, Sybil 259
Smith, T. D. M. 159
Smith, T. J. 332
Smith, Teresa J. 26
Smith, Tracy Lee 52
Smith, Yvonne 157
Smith-Whittle, George 180
Smithies, Beatrice 294
Snaith, Rita 155
Snee, Clair C. 44
Snelling, Tim 322
Snow, D. 104
Sohni, Aisha 257
Somjee, Shehnaz 156
Southern, M. 186
Southey, Eileen 68
Sowter, Peter 150
Spain, A. 114
Sparrow, Doris 96
Speake, Bill 276
Spencer, Barbara J. 197
Spencer, I. 105
Spencer, P. 270
Sperring, Emma 10
Spooner, Phyllis M. 25
Squire, Elizabeth 278
Squire, Theresa-Anne 278
Squires, Geraldine 5
Stafford, Dawn 174
Staley, K. W. 44
Standbridge, Ruth 265
Stanley, Charlene 97
Stanley-Smith, Mary 31
Stanmore, Ena 327
Stansbie, Kirsty 175
Stansfield, Tony 162
Stanton, Jane 325
Stanton, Natalie 90
Steadman, Katherine 139
Stebbings, Pamela 166
Steedman, John A. 129
Steenson, Suzanne Low 61
Steer, Adam 88
Stemp, Linda 81
Stenson, Carley Anne 239
Stephens, Bethan 292
Stephens, Brenda 307
Stephenson, S. L. 192
Stephenson-Ellams, M. 118
Steriu, Rodica Victoria 182
Stevens, Brian 191
Stevens, Carmen 244
Stevens, Dorothy 26
Stevens, Kathryn K. 261
Stevens, Tim 74
Stevenson, Elizabeth 161

Stewart, Julie 222
Stewart, Katie 253
Stewart, Paula 172
Stiles, Stephen 220
Stoker Holmes, Jo-Anne 44
Stokes, Alice 215
Stokes, Carol Anne 187
Stone, Joan E. 164
Stoneman, Brian 49
Stones, Kirsty M. 191
Storton, J. E. 50
Stott, Fiona 199
Stratford-Wight, Sarah 259
Street, Dorothy M. 107
Stripp, Janet Rosen 331
Strong, Joyce 95
Strong, R. S. 27
Stuart, David Campbell 133
Stuart, Ron 150
Stubbs, Christine 40
Sturmey, Hazel 186
Styles, Susan 244
Sullivan, Catherine Jane 254
Sumner, A. 170
Sunderland, John M. 195
Supan, Josipa 151
Sutcliffe, Helen E. 177
Sutheran, Frank 253
Sutherland, M. 229
Sutherland, Morag 85
Sutton, Poet 9
Swainston, Lesley Ann 198
Swan, Peter T. 302
Swanson, Aves 210
Sweeney, Gerard K. 33
Sweet, Claire 226
Swindells, Gemma 221
Sykes, Gemma 170
Szeremeta, Anna 130

T

Tadeja, Geoanne 313
Tanfield, Michelle 260
Targett, Sarah 236
Tattersall, Barbara Winifred 98
Tattersall, P. A. W. 108
Taylor, Alison 130
Taylor, Barry 137
Taylor, Jean 130
Taylor, Kirstie 312
Taylor, Lachlan 44
Taylor, Michelle 109
Taylor, Paul Scott 3
Taylor, Victoria Louise 277
Teale, Emma 253
Teasdale, Valda 38
Tennent, Iris 31
Terris, Theresa 153
Tester-Ellis, Freda 116
Tetlow, Sophie 61
Tew, Margaret 102
Thackway, Emma Jayne 36
Thomas, Alyson 199
Thomas, C. A. 88
Thomas, Dawn Owen 335
Thomas, Diane 238
Thomas, Donald Morrison 222
Thomas, Elizabeth 209
Thomas, Garry 250
Thomas, Iris 275
Thomas, John M. 54
Thomas, Josephine 186
Thomas, M. G. 245
Thomas, Mark A. 83
Thomas, Mary C. 144
Thomas, Pauline K. 108

Thomason, Sid 250
Thompson, Avril 253
Thompson, Faye 192
Thompson, Helen 140
Thompson, Iris 214
Thompson, J. C. 290
Thompson, Jim 299
Thompson, Patricia 148
Thompson, Patricia 320
Thompson, Pauline 82
Thompson, Sam 234
Thompson, Samantha 179
Thompson, Sheila K. A. 181
Thompson, Winifred 233
Thompson-Massey, Patricia 256
Thomson, Alister H. 258
Thomson, Avril 211
Thomson, Diane 18
Thordarson, Doris 235
Thorley, P. 206
Thorn, B. 196
Thorn, Evelyn 118
Thorn, John 255
Thorndike, Ethel E. 198
Thorne, B. P. D. 66
Thornton, D. 320
Thorp, Catherine 182
Thorp, Sarah 174
Thorpe, James 190
Thyer, Tracie 270
Tickle, Mary 169
Tidball, Kirsty 77
Tighe, O. A. 4
Timbers, Racheal 23
Timbers, Racheal 143
Timms, Iris G. 206
Tinniswood, Emma Louise 233
Tippett, Richard 104
Titley, Audrey 226
Todd, Alexander William 196
Todd, F. E. 188
Todd, R. 251
Tolley, Anna 298
Tolley, W. M. 74
Tolly, Helen 114
Tomaras, Alexander 174
Took, David M. 150
Topp, Clare 292
Tourle, K. J. 169
Tovell, Ian James 119
Tovell, J. M. 168
Towner, Diane L. 290
Townsend, Ann 148
Townsend, Roy 164
Toyne, Christopher 259
Travers, Edward 27
Trikomitis, Deborah 105
Trow, Nikki-Ann 182
Trowbridge, Laura 299
Trump, Philippa 25
Tuck, Kerry 320
Tucker, Denise L. 154
Tucker, Victor 191
Tuff, Emmaline 255
Tupman, H. G. 205
Turnbill, Alexander 170
Turnbull, A. D. 232
Turner, F. B. 180
Turner, Heather 163
Turner, Josephine 175
Turner, Kim Louise 165
Turner, Mark 310
Turton, Betty 193
Turton, Emily 311
Turvey, B. M. 193
Turvey, Kerry 326

Tweed, Lydia 106
Tyson, Jessica 170

U

Udayamalee, Iresha 82
Umezuruike, Eze 204
Unguras, Adina-Maria 294
Upson, Timothy 211
Uzele, Jennifer W. K. 77

V

Valentine, Alex Jr. 11
Vanhoven, June 94
Vargeson, Hayley 77
Vassallo, Charlotte 240
Vaughan, Trevor 271
Veal, Lilian 249
Vella, Theresa 66
Venton, David H. 217
Ventris, Dorothy 129
Ventris, Dorothy 145
Verity, Virginia 167
Vernon, Joe 80
Vernon, John 175
Vessey, Margaret R. 230
Vickers, Claire 230
Vickers, John 107
Vinall-Burnett, Margaret 31
Vincent, Joan 16
Vincent, S. A. 326
Vinchellii, Vittoria Lucynda 210
Vinell-Barnett, Margaret 275
Violeta-Mirela, Mares 189
Violo, Giovanna 57
Vivian, Katharine 307

W

Wade, Hilary 229
Wadikar, M. 258
Waghorn, Tania 80
Wagstaff, Donald 220
Wahome, Harrison 333
Waite, Ken 56
Waldock, Paul 11
Walker, Caroline 281
Walker, Mark 112
Walker, Patricia Elizabeth 60
Walker, Sheila 89
Wall, Mabel 113
Wallace, Alan 163
Wallace, J. M. 174
Wallace, S. 219
Wallis, Vivien 324
Walsh, Fiona 196
Walsh, Michael 28
Walsh, Nicolette F. 257
Walsh, P. 171
Walsh, Sarah 16
Walsh, V. H. 100
Walters, Dorine 238
Walters, Dorine 243
Wan, Casey 279
Wander, Debbie 19
Wandscher, Paula 171
Ward, Alfreda 280
Ward, Anthony Keith 190
Ward, E. 136
Ward, Joy Playford 154
Ward, Terry F. 10
Wardlaw, Tina 219
Wardle, Nik 176
Ware, E. V. 191
Warman, Ronald J. 77
Warne, M. R. 331
Warner, David 194

Warnock, Mary 309
Warren, Lynn 80
Watkin, Wendy 8
Watkins, C. 274
Watkirs, Jade 166
Watkins, Lynsey 145
Watson, Jane E. 272
Watson, Jean 201
Watson, Leanne 159
Watson, Leanne 260
Watson, Margaret 151
Watson, Natasha 226
Watt, Joyce 114
Watt, William D. 57
Watts, R. 68
Watts, Rachel Leanne 276
Watts, Ruth 153
Watts, Tracey 185
Wawman, Yvonne I. 116
Weaver, T. C. 111
Webb, Barbara 152
Webbe-Wood, Elizabeth 321
Webley, Irene 210
Webster, Brian 181
Webster, Leiann 164
Weedon, Lawrence John 180
Weeks, Katie 316
Weight, Hazel 168
Welch, A. J. V. 124
Weller, Amelia 58
Wells, Ashley 20
Wells, Demelza Ruth 198
Wells, Florence M. 18
Welsh, Clare 69
Wenn, R. A. 11
Wesley 88
West, Alan Charles 14
West, Mal 168
Westhoff, Ruth Elizabeth 333
Westmore, Susan 178
Westwood, Jenny 254
Westwood, Richard 70
Whale, Mervyn S. 329
Whayman, Susan 205
Wheatley, A. D. 199
Whelan, Charlene 150
Whiston, R. T. 282
White, Dorothy F. 136
White, Elizabeth 55
White, Keith 231
White, Margaret 322
White, Sarah J. 80
White, Sharon 174
White, Stephanie 172
Whitlock, Tess 315
Whitney-Holmes, Millie 158
Whittaker, Harriet 306
Whittaker, Jackie 144
Wickers, Jackie 279
Wienholt, Pauline 296
Wiffen, S. M. 283
Wiggins, Yvette Avonda 301
Wight, Janet Wallace 328
Wilcox, Enid 158
Wild, Tony 139
Wilds, Terena T. J. 295
Wileman, J. G. 20
Wilkes, Tracey 37
Wilkins, Julie 184
Wilkins, Lindsay 312
Wilkinson, A. L. 213
Wilkinson, Elizabeth 183
Wilkinson, Nicola Gabrielle 151
Wilkinson, Philip 58
Wilkinson, Sharon 325
Willetts, Beryl 6

William, Frederick Westley 56
Williams, Allys 218
Williams, Claire 333
Williams, D. 78
Williams, Geoffrey David 305
Williams, Gill 30
Williams, J. G. 241
Williams, Katrina 332
Williams, Lesley 178
Williams, Pearl 45
Williams, Peter Vaughan 153
Williams, Philip Trenor 142
Williams, Roger 244
Williams, Sadie 277
Williams, Samantha 295
Williams, Terri-Anne 184
Williamson, Anne 26
Williamson, D. M. 23
Williamson, Jessie 72
Willis, Beverley 213
Wilson, A. 104
Wilson, Christopher 26
Wilson, Donna Ellen 281
Wilson, Elaine Marie 158
Wilson, Elizabeth 140
Wilson, Emma 145
Wilson, Ethel 73
Wilson, G. 146
Wilson, Joanna 260
Wilson, Paul 190
Winborn, William S. 186
Winch, Sarah Louise 120
Winfield, Eric 93
Winkley, Dorothy 164
Winskill, Joy 74
Winstanley, Patricia 189
Winter, Robert 111
Winterburn, Mae 156
Wise, Sharron 106
Witheridge, Ada M. 255
Wolfenden, Janis 167
Womack, Dianne 69
Wong, Heiderose 25
Wood, Colin 92
Wood, Dorreya 264
Wood, James 122
Wood, M. 166
Wood, Margaret 141
Wood, Mary 60
Wood, Nigel 254
Woodcock, Amanda 60
Woodford, Helen 227
Woodhouse, Christopher 188
Woodley, Patricia 10
Woodrow, Sylvia 140
Woods, Fiona 194
Woods, Victoria 45
Woodward, G. 171
Woodway, Layne 78
Wooliscroft, Elizabeth 157
Woolley, J. 236
Woolmington, Elaine 267
Worthington, Julie 160
Wray, James T. 140
Wray, Louise 156
Wren, Elizabeth 26
Wride, Louise 266
Wright, Beverley J. 20
Wright, Christopher 146
Wright, Elizabeth O. 308
Wright, Joanne 47
Wright, Myrtle 86
Wright, Teresa 90
Wright, V. V. 302
Wyatt, Lisa 171
Wylson, Viola 172

Wynn, John 281
Wynter, Tricia 153

Y

Yale, William 303
Yanez, D. S. 193
Yates, Betty 159
Yates, Garry Mark 76
Yates, Gladys E. 172
Yates, Mary 93
Yikici, Ozlem 266
Youden, Craig 84
Youden, Elaine 323
Young, Audrey 264
Young, Audrey 296
Young, Eve 252
Young, Gary 238
Young, Jennifer 156
Young, Karen 328
Young, Laura 283
Young, Marjorie V. 306
Young, Rebecca 217
Yozgat, Snleyman 305
Yuill, Jacqueline 177
Yule, Struan 62

Z

Zahra, Helga J. 304
Zhi-Jun, Wang 22
Zhou, Hong 189